ANNALS OF THE

NEW YORK STAGE

VOLUME XI

[1879–1882]

ROSE COGHLAN IN FORGET ME NOT
From a Photograph by J. M. Mora

ANNALS OF THE NEW YORK STAGE

BY

GEORGE C. D. ODELL

VOLUME XI
[1879–1882]

AMS PRESS
New York

Reprinted with permission from the edition of 1939, New York
First AMS EDITION published 1970
Manufactured in the United States of America

International Standard Book Number:
Complete Set: 0-404-07830-3
Volume 11: 0-404-07841-9

Library of Congress Card Catalog Number: 77-116018

AMS PRESS, INC.
NEW YORK, N. Y. 10003

TO
MY SISTER, CLARA ODELL
WITH WHOM I SAW
VERY MANY FINE PLAYS AND PLAYERS

CONTENTS

VOLUME XI

BOOK EIGHTEEN. A CHANGING THEATRE, 1879–1882

I. Wallack's, Union Square, Daly's, Madison Square, Booth's, Fifth Avenue, Lyceum, Park Theatre, Standard, Grand Opera House, Niblo's, 1879–1880 1

II. The Olympic, Broadway (Bijou) Opera House, Windsor Theatre, German Theatres, Academy of Music (New York), Theatre Comique, Variety Theatres, Minstrelsy, Circus, Miscellany, Concerts, 1879–1880 61

III. Brooklyn, Williamsburgh, Queensborough, Staten Island, 1879–1880 167

IV. Wallack's, Union Square, Daly's, Madison Square, Booth's, Fifth Avenue, Haverly's (Lyceum), Park, Standard, Bijou Opera House, Niblo's, 1880–1881 218

V. Grand Opera House, Windsor Theatre, German Theatres, Academy of Music (New York), Theatre Comique, Variety Theatres, Minstrelsy, Circus, Miscellany, Concerts, 1880–1881 . 273

VI. Brooklyn, Williamsburgh, Greenpoint, Queens County, Staten Island, 1880–1881 383

VII. Wallack's New Theatre, The Union Square, Daly's, Madison Square, Booth's, Fifth Avenue, Haverly's Fourteenth Street Theatre, Park, Standard, Bijou Opera House, Niblo's, 1881–1882 431

VIII. Grand Opera House, Windsor Theatre, German Theatres, Academy of Music (New York), Theatre Comique, Variety Theatres, Minstrelsy, Circus, Miscellany, Concerts, 1881–1882 . 486

IX. Brooklyn, Williamsburgh, Greenpoint, Queens County, Staten Island, 1881–1882 604

Index 653

CONTENTS

VOLUME XI

ILLUSTRATIONS

VOLUME XI

Rose Coghlan as Stéphanie, in Forget Me Not . . . . . . *Frontispiece*

FACING PAGE

W. J. Leonard 2
Kate Bartlett 2
Kate Forsyth and J. T. Raymond in Wolfert's Roost 2
Emma Loraine 2
Ada Dyas 2
Rose Wood 2
Maurice Barrymore 2
Harry Edwards 2
Gerald Eyre 2
J. B. Polk 6
Walden Ramsay 6
Harry Courtaine 6
C. R. Thorne, Jr., in The Two Orphans 6
Maud Harrison 6
Ellie Wilton in The False Friend 6
Sarah Cowell 6
Mrs. E. J. Phillips 6
Frederick Paulding 6
John Drew 12
Isabelle Evesson and Estelle Clayton 12
Harry Lacy 12
Ada Rehan in The Royal Middy 12
Catherine Lewis in The Royal Middy 12
Hart Conway in The Royal Middy 12
Regina Dace 12
Mabel Jordan 12
Helen Blythe 12
Annie Ellsler 16
Eben Plympton 16

[ix]

ILLUSTRATIONS

FACING PAGE

Gabrielle du Sauld 16

C. W. Couldock as Dunstan Kirke 16

Effie Ellsler 16

Dominick Murray and Joseph Frankau in Hazel Kirke 16

Cecile Rush 16

J. Steele MacKaye 16

Georgia Cayvan 16

"Dot" Boucicault 28

John Clayton 28

Edward Compton 28

Blanche Davenport (Bianca La Blanche) 28

Adelaide Neilson as Isabella, in Measure for Measure 28

Mrs. D. P. Bowers 28

Mlle. Angèle and Victor Capoul in La Fille de Mme. Angot . . . 28

Jessie Bond and J. H. Ryley in H. M. S. Pinafore 28

Paola Marié and Victor Capoul in La Périchole 28

Mora's Photographs from The Pirates of Penzance 32
  Blanche Roosevelt; Rosina Brandram; Jessie Bond; Signor Brocolini;
   J. H. Ryley; Fred Clifton; Hugh Talbot; Furneaux Cook; Alice Barnett

G. W. Stoddart as Elder Sniffles, in Widow Bedott 40

Neil Burgess as Widow Bedott 40

W. A. Mestayer in The Tourists in a Pullman Palace Car 40

Maude Granger 40

Frank Evans 40

Emily Rigl in The Galley Slave 40

De Wolf Hopper 40

Adele Belgarde 40

Gustavus Levick 40

Henry E. Dixey 44

J. E. McDonough 44

Leonora Braham 44

E. A. Sothern as The Crushed Tragedian 44

J. K. Emmet as Fritz 44

Lotta in The Little Detective 44

D. E. Bandmann 44

Annie Pixley as M'liss 44

Mrs. D. E. Bandmann 44

ILLUSTRATIONS

FACING PAGE

Jennie Yeamans	60
Olympic Theatre (624 Broadway)	60
Amy Lee	60
Dollie Pike as Henriette, in The Two Orphans	64
Gussie De Forrest	64
Signora Majeroni in The Galley Slave	64
Windsor Theatre (Interior)	64
Gustav Adolfi	72
Magda Irschick	72
Bernhard Rank	72
Max Lube	72
Mathilde Cottrelly	72
Marie Marimon	92
Anna de Belocca as Carmen	92
Emilie Ambre	92
Alwina Valleria as Margherita, in Faust	92
Annie Louise Cary as Nancy, in Martha	92
McIntyre and Heath	108
Lina Tettenborn	108
The Whitings	108
Charles Dockstader	108
Lena Aberle	108
Lew Dockstader	108
Bennie Grinnell	108
Harriet (Hattie) Grinnell	108
Alice Daily	108
Frank McNish and the Leland Sisters	124
Willis Pickert	124
Harry McAvoy and Emma Rogers	124
Alice Montague	124
Russell Brothers (John and James)	124
Little Todd	124
Fayette Welch	124
Fostelle	124
Paddy Murphy	124
William (Billy) Birch	140
Dave Wambold	140

ILLUSTRATIONS

FACING PAGE

Charles Backus 140
San Francisco Minstrels (Views of) 140
Emma Lake 144
Weston, the Walker 144
Elise Dockrill 144
Rowell, the Walker 144
A. P. Burbank 144
Sidney Woollett 144
Belle Cole 144
Henrietta Markstein 144
Anna Granger Dow 144
Carlotta Patti and De Munck 152
Hattie Louise Simms 152
Amy Sherwin 152
Franz Rummel 152
Rafael Joseffy 152
Max Pinner 152
Annie E. Beeré 152
Adolphe Fischer 152
Marie Louise Swift (Mlle. Dotti) 152
Agnes Elliott 224
Marion Booth 224
Adelaide Detchon 224
Osmond Tearle as Charles Surface 224
Rose Coghlan as Rosalind 224
Stella Boniface in The Guv'nor 224
Gerald Eyre as The MacToddy, in The Guv'nor 224
William Elton 224
Harry M. Pitt 224
James Lewis in Cinderella at School 232
Mrs. G. H. Gilbert in Cinderella at School 232
Ada Rehan in Cinderella at School 232
May Fielding in Cinderella at School 232
Rose Eytinge in Felicia 232
Frederic de Belleville 232
Bessie Sansone 232
John E. Brand 232

ILLUSTRATIONS

FACING PAGE

Laura Joyce 232

Sydney Cowell as Dolly Dutton, in Hazel Kirke 236

William H. Gillette 236

W. B. Cahill as Barney O'Flynn, in Hazel Kirke 236

Madison Square Theatre, with stage set for Hazel Kirke 236

Tom Karl as Ralph Rackstraw 240

George Frothingham as Dick Deadeye 240

H. C. Barnabee as Sir Joseph Porter 240

Mathilde Phillipps 240

Marie Stone in Fra Diavolo 240

Adelaide Phillipps 240

Myron W. Whitney 240

W. H. Macdonald 240

Mary Beebe 240

Sarah Bernhardt as Phèdre 248

Sarah Bernhardt as Marguerite Gautier (Camille) 248

Tommaso Salvini 248

Emma Abbott in Faust 248

Genevieve Ward as Stéphanie, in Forget Me Not 248

Selina Dolaro 252

Ostava Torriani 252

Kate Forsyth 252

Lillian Spencer 252

Catherine Lewis as Olivette 252

Topsy Venn 252

Jennie Weathersby 252

M. B. Curtis as Sam'l of Posen 252

Robert Downing 252

Charles Plunkett in Yorick's Love 256

F. C. Mosley in Yorick's Love 256

Ben G. Rogers in Yorick's Love 256

J. T. Raymond and Lizzie Creese in Fresh, the American 256

Lawrence Barrett in Yorick's Love 256

Laura Don in Fresh, the American 256

Sol Smith Russell 256

Samuel W. Piercy 256

James T. Powers 256

[xiii]

ILLUSTRATIONS

FACING PAGE

Tauffenberger in La Fille du Tambour-Major 264

Duplan in La Fille du Tambour-Major 264

Mauras in Carmen 264

Paola Marié as Carmen 264

Cécile Grégoire 264

Kate Claxton in The Snow Flower 264

Alfred Cellier 264

Jacques Kruger in Dreams 264

Fanny Wentworth 264

Franco Novara as Mephistopheles 300
Ravelli as Edgardo, in Lucia di Lammermoor 300

Carl Sontag 300

Alwina Valleria as Aïda 300

Marie Geistinger 300

Dan Collyer 316

William Henry Rice 316

Barney McNulty 316

Lillian Russell 316

May Ten Broeck 316

Dollie Thornton 316

John E. Henshaw 316

Flora and May Irwin 316

F. F. Levantine (F. F. Proctor) 316

Lizzie Mulvey and Barney Fagan 364

Amy Stone 364

Goss and Fox 364

Tom Sayers 364

St. Felix Sisters 364

George W. Monroe 364

George Shannon (of Murphy and Shannon) 364

Charles T. Ellis 364

John Murphy (of Murphy and Mack) 364

Isidora Martinez 380

Mr. and Mrs. George Henschel 380

Emma Howe 380

Imogene Brown 380

Mme. Chatterton-Bohrer 380

ILLUSTRATIONS

FACING PAGE

Ella Earle 380

Max Heinrich 380

Isabel Stone 380

Theodore Thomas 380

Katie Baker 384

Katie Gilbert 384

Lillie Glover 384

Carrie Wyatt 384

Edwin F. Thorne 384

Mrs. Edwin F. Thorne 384

Lawrence Barrett as Hamlet 384

Dora Wiley 384

Minnie Monk as Mrs. Candour 384

Meta Bartlett 392

Tony Denier 392

Sara Lascelles 392

Marion P. Clifton 392

Geraldine Ulmar 392

Mrs. Charles Walcot, the younger 392

William Gill 392

Owen Fawcett 392

Joseph E. Whiting 392

Interior of Wallack's New Theatre 428

Wallack's at Thirteenth Street (Exterior) 428

Sarony's Photographs of Youth at Wallack's 432

      Wilmot Eyre; Osmond Tearle (2); Gerald Eyre; Alma Stuart Stanley;
      Harry Edwards; C. E. Edwin; John Gilbert; William Elton

Sarony's Photographs of The Rivals 440

      Mrs. John Drew; Joseph Jefferson (2); Thomas Jefferson

Eugenia Paul 440

Eugenie Legrand 440

Maud Harrison as Shakespeare Jarvis, in The Lights o' London . . . 440

Sara Jewett 440

Eleanor Carey as Hetty Preene, in The Lights o' London 440

James Lewis and Mrs. G. H. Gilbert in The Passing Regiment . . . 444

Helen Bancroft 444

Ada Rehan and John Drew in The Passing Regiment 444

[xv]

ILLUSTRATIONS

FACING PAGE

Hélène Stoepel (Bijou Heron) 444

Henry Miller 444

Agnes Leonard 444

Charles Leclercq 444

May Sylvie 444

William Gilbert 444

Anderson's Photographs from Esmeralda 448

    Leslie Allen and Annie Russell; Eben Plympton; Thomas Whiffen and
    Agnes Booth; May Gallagher; Agnes Booth; Kate Denin Wilson; John
    E. Owens; Davenport Bebus; E. A. McDowell

Mlle. Rhea as Adrienne Lecouvreur 456

Henri Laurent as Ralph Rackstraw 456

Eugene Clarke as Grosvenor 456

Robert Pateman 456

Ernesto Rossi as Hamlet 456

Bella Pateman 456

George Riddle as Œdipus 456

Mary Anderson as Galatea 456

Georgia Cayvan as Jocasta 456

The Hanlons 476

Carrie Burton 476

Minnie Maddern in Fogg's Ferry 476

Digby Bell as Grosvenor 476

Adelaide Randall 476

J. H. Ryley as Bunthorne 476

W. T. Carleton as Bunthorne 476

Harry Hawk 476

James G. Peakes as Captain Corcoran 476

O. H. Barr 492

Corinne 492

Elma Delaro 492

Augusta Roche as Ruth, in The Pirates of Penzance 492

Lillian Russell as Patience 492

John Howson as Bunthorne, made up as Oscar Wilde 492

Blanche Chapman 492

Jesse Williams 492

Alonzo Hatch 492

ILLUSTRATIONS

FACING PAGE

Käthi Schratt 508

F. Haase as Hamlet 508

Franziska Ellmenreich 508

Minnie Hauk in L'Africaine 508

Emma Juch as Margherita, in Faust 508

Antonio Galassi in L'Africaine 508

Mme. Galassi as Amneris, in Aïda 508

William Rignold 508

Paolina Rossini as Aïda 508

Mora's Photographs from The Major 524
    Edward Harrigan and Tony Hart; Annie Mack and Tony Hart; John
    Wild; Edward Harrigan and Annie Yeamans; John Queen and Harry
    Fisher

Kate Monroe 540

Signor de Novellis 540

Montegriffo 540

Pauline Hall 540

Rudolf Bial 540

Annie Theresa Berger 540

Patti Rosa 540

Marie König 540

Marie Vanoni 540

Eddie Girard 556

Cool Burgess 556

William Girard 556

Tom Daly 556

Charles McCarthy 556

Bill Daly 556

Billy West 556

Press Eldridge 556

John Sparks 556

Louise Montague 572

The Lorellas 572

Kitty Allyne 572

Sanford (of Sanford and Wilson) 572

Edward M. Favor 572

Viola Clifton 572

ILLUSTRATIONS

FACING PAGE

Flora Moore 572
John B. Wills 572
Clara Moore 572
Italian Theatre in East Forty-second Street 588
Chickering Hall (Interior) 588
Locke Richardson 592
Oscar Wilde 592
Jennie Dickerson 592
Robert J. Burdette 592
Linda Da Acosta 592
Constantine Sternberg 592
E. Aline Osgood 592
Letitia Fritsch 592
D. Kennedy 592
Nicolini 600
Teresa Carreño 600
Amalia Friedrich-Materna 600
Etelka Gerster 600
Adelina Patti 600
George Sweet 604
Wallace Macreery 604
Maggie Mitchell and Julian Mitchell in The Pearl of Savoy 604
Nate Salsbury, Nellie McHenry, John Webster 604
John Sleeper Clarke 604
Mr. and Mrs. McKee Rankin in '49 604
Fanny Davenport as Camille 604
Ray Samuels 604
Marie Jansen 604
Millie Christine 620
Harper Brothers (one-legged dancers) 620
Admiral Dot 620
Karoly Ordey 620
Chang, Chinese giant 620
Augusta Ordey 620
Susie Russell 620
Enid Hart 620
Maggie Cline 620

BOOK EIGHTEEN

A CHANGING THEATRE, 1879–1882

CHAPTER I

WALLACK'S, UNION SQUARE, DALY'S, MADISON SQUARE, BOOTH'S, FIFTH AVENUE, LYCEUM, PARK THEATRE, STANDARD, GRAND OPERA HOUSE, NIBLO'S, 1879–1880

WALLACK'S famous playhouse, still the best in the country, opened on August 18, 1879, for a preliminary season, carried through by John T. Raymond, in George Fawcett Rowe's adaptation (in part) from Washington Irving — Wolfert's Roost, or, a Legend of Sleepy Hollow. In this Raymond, whose odd personality would seem exactly to have fitted the character, played Ichabod Crane, with F. Hardenberg as Brom Van Brunt, J. W. Shannon as Baltus Van Tassell, Henry Lee as Dolf Haverstraw, of Wolfert's Roost, E. M.Holland as Coroner John Tappan, P. A. Anderson as the Ghost of Wolfert, C. E. Edwin as the negro, Jake, H. Pearson and F. Lull as the villagers, Ploos and Amstel, Kate Forsythe (*sic*) as Katrina Van Tassell, Mme. Ponisi as Dame Haverstraw, Courtney Barnes (Mrs. Raymond) as Emma, her daughter, Connie Thompson as Phebe, a mulatto girl, Josie Myers as the lively Widow Perkins and Little Allie Dorrington as Katie Van Schaick — certainly a good cast. George Heister painted the scene of Act I, "Van Tassell's Farm House and Orchard — Early Autumn, with Distant View of Wolfert's Roost," and also the last scene of Act IV, "The Farm and Orchard — Early Winter." Other scenes, by J. Clare, represented "Ichabod's School and Old Dutch Church at Sleepy Hollow," and the "Interior" and "Exterior of Van Tassell's Farm." A Hallowe'en Frolic figured in the proceedings. The whole thing sounded attractive, and it remained at Wallack's up to and including September 27th. Allston Brown has, unfortunately, stated that Maurice Grau's fine opéra-bouffe company opened here on September 15th; it really began on that date at the Fifth Avenue Theatre.

REGULAR SEASON, 1879–1880

Wallack's actors might change in part from season to season, but Wallack's was always Wallack's. When the regular season opened, on October 4th, the house had been thoroughly renovated, redecorated, carpeted and upholstered, under the supervision of Wallack, and was found to be richly effective in tones of red and gold. The first audiences were much impressed. Rose and Charles Coghlan were not in the company, but Ada Dyas returned, and Maurice Barrymore tried, not with complete success, to replace the finished artist, Coghlan. Barrymore was handsome, popular and in many respects admirable as an actor, but Charles Coghlan was, I believe, unique. The opening play was Contempt of Court, "constructed from two French comedies, by Dion Boucicault"— almost playwright in ordinary to this theatre:

Clicquot	Harry Beckett	Colonel Lucenay	C. Rockwell
Fanny	Ada Dyas	Giraud	J. H. Gilmour
Dr. Delacour	Frank Hardenberg	Mazas	J. W. Shannon
Louise	Rose Wood	Mariolle	Miss E. Blaisdell
Clairville	W. R. Floyd	Leopold	W. J. Leonard
Lalouette	E. M. Holland	Baptiste	C. E. Edwin

No matter how often I write a cast for the Wallack's of those days — those dear, mellow days — I am conscious of a thrill of delight; there was our "Old Drury," there our Théâtre Français, with the same actors (only a few excepted) appearing year after year and by co-operation producing a finished result in comedy, impossible in any other of our theatres. The Union Square company was incomparable in melodrama, and Daly's company had been excellent in his plays "of contemporaneous human interest," but, for delicate or high comedy, there was no Wallack's but Wallack's. In reading the cast just cited, one observes the inclusion in it of Frank Hardenberg, so long at Daly's, and of J. H. Gilmour, new to our record, but often to be met with hereafter. One also notes the beginning of the latter-day custom of printing the names of men and women actors in one mingled congregation, rather than in separate groups as heretofore. I may say that Joseph Clare still remained as chief scenic artist, with Thomas Baker in charge of the music, T. J. Kelly in charge of mechanism, and F. Dorrington of furniture and appointments. John Gilbert (at this time very ill) was stage manager, J. S. Wright prompter, and Theodore Moss treasurer.

The last performance of the new play fell on November 5th. On the 6th, Wallack staged Our Girls, a new comedy by Henry J. Byron, author of Our Boys. In this appeared for the first time at Wallack's Maurice Barrymore, Henry (or Harry) Edwards and Emma Loraine, and in it Stella Boniface and Mme. Ponisi made their entrance for the regular season. Harry Edwards, a first-rate comedian, came to us by way of San Francisco (he had played in September, in My Partner, at the Union Square), and he remained with the Wallack company until it disbanded in 1888. In the cast of Our Girls he played Josiah Clench, with J. H. Gilmour as Lord Aspland, Harry Beckett as Plantagenet G. Potter ("something in the city"), Maurice Barrymore as Tony Judson ("a young sculptor"), C. E. Edwin as Thomas, W. J. Leonard

W. J. LEONARD
(OF WALLACK'S)

KATE BARTLETT

KATE FORSYTH-RAYMOND
IN WOLFERT'S ROOST

EMMA LORAINE

ADA DYAS

ROSE WOOD

MAURICE BARRYMORE

HARRY EDWARDS

GERALD EYRE

as Mr. Mallet ("a tent furnisher"), Mme. Ponisi as Mrs. Clench, Stella
Boniface as Clara Merton (Mrs. Clench's daughter), Rose Wood as Mabel
Clench, and Emma Loraine (*sic*) as Jane (a servant).   As in the case of Our
Boys, Our Girls failed to achieve here the success that might have been ex-
pected.   It was acted for the last time on the evening of December 5th.
Omitting the usual matinée on Saturday, the 6th, Wallack brought out on
Saturday evening, Estelle, or, False and True, partially founded, by Albert
Lancaster, on Victor Cherbuliez's novel, Samuel Brohl and Company.   The
company of the theatre revealed, this year, its strength slowly but surely; in
Gabrielle, Frederic Robinson returned, Effie Germon made her first appearance for the season, and Gerald Eyre, an excellent actor, acted for the first
time with the company which afterward he adorned for some years:

Count Petrovsky	Gerald Eyre	Dr. Millington	G. C. Sherman
Arthur Morton	F. Robinson	Nicolo	T. Morgan
Horace Chantry	Harry Edwards	Giacomo	H. Pearson
Barkwood Beech	Harry Beckett	Estelle	Ada Dyas
Mr. Blair	E. M. Holland	Princess Koronoff	Rose Wood
Lord Milroy	J. H. Gilmour	Mrs. Blair	Effie Germon
Levi Rosenthal	C. E. Edwin	Miss Percival	Miss E. Blaisdell
Mr. Moncrieff	W. J. Leonard		

The scenery, by Clare and J. Johnson, represented various situations in
Rome, and, as usual at this house, was, for its day, of the best.   But the
play was not a success, and, after the performance on December 23rd, went
to the limbo of lost hopes.

JOHN GILBERT AND LESTER WALLACK

And now began that for which Wallack's will always be famed — a series
of old comedies presented beautifully.   The first, on December 24th, brought
a highly appreciated Christmas gift in the return of John Gilbert, who had
long been dangerously ill and was now restored to his devoted following.
He emerged as Jesse Rural (one of his finest characters, in which I still see
him), the other parts in Old Heads and Young Hearts falling to Charles
Rockwell (the Earl of Pompion), J. H. Gilmour (Lord Charles), Gerald
Eyre (Tom Coke), Barrymore (Littleton), Harry Edwards (Colonel
Rocket), Harry Beckett (Bob), Ada Dyas (Lady Alice), Mme. Ponisi (the
Countess), and Rose Wood (Kate).   That cast is remarkable — almost too
good to be true.
      On Monday, December 29th, Wallack took the centre of his own stage,
as (I fear) a mature and rather stout, but (I know) light-mannered Charles
Marlow (always a favourite part with him and his audiences).   Gilbert
and Mme. Ponisi as ever, pillars of support as Mr. and Mrs. Hardcastle, and
Miss Dyas as Kate, Miss Boniface as Constance, Beckett as Tony and
Holland as Diggory were well-known and oft-approved interpreters of those

rôles. The important novelty was the Hastings of Maurice Barrymore, a part which I believe would have interested him but slightly. Con T. Murphy was Jeremy. Wallack's second week (January 5th-10th) was devoted to A Scrap of Paper, Ada Dyas now succeeding Rose Coghlan as the brilliant Suzanne, and, according to the Herald of January 6th, labouring under the disadvantage of comparison with that actress, "whose great success in Suzanne was of so recent a date as to live in the memory of the public. That she read the lines intelligently can be said with truth, but that she succeeded in effacing the impression made by her predecessor cannot be conceded, and it must be said that her costume was a marvel of incongruity of color." "Tom" Jefferson (son of Joseph Jefferson) played the youthful Anatole, and, according to the Herald, was warmly received. Emma Loraine was Pauline; John Gilbert, Rockwell, C. E. Edwin, Miss Germon, Miss Boniface and Kate Bartlett resumed their former rôles. A brilliant London Assurance began on January 12th:

Dazzle	Lester Wallack	Dolly Spanker	W. R. Floyd
Sir Harcourt	John Gilbert	Cool	E. M. Holland
Max Harkaway	Harry Edwards	Lady Gay Spanker	Ada Dyas
Charles	Maurice Barrymore	Grace	Stella Boniface
Mark Meddle	Harry Beckett	Pert	Effie Germon

I have always thought the Lady Gay of Ada Dyas among her most brilliant performances; it sparkled in light, airy speech and in exquisite appreciation of the situations in which the character is involved. Miss Dyas could not weep in the theatre, but she could rise to elegant comedy. She Stoops to Conquer had another week (January 19th-24th), and, on the 26th, Wallack again played Adonis Evergreen, in My Awful Dad, with Beckett once more as the perturbed Dick, with George F. De Vere (another Daly-ite turned Wallackian) as Humphrey Lovekin, and with Shannon, Edwin, Leonard and Rose Wood, in their original parts. Mme. Ponisi succeeded Mrs. John Sefton as Mrs. Biggs, and Kate Bartlett was Emma (vice Josephine Baker). Wallack's last evenings, for the present, were devoted to My Awful Dad (January 28th), London Assurance (29th and matinée 31st), She Stoops to Conquer (30th), and My Awful Dad (31st).

BOUCICAULT; THE SHAUGHRAUN; THE COLLEEN BAWN

It is always a delight to write of Wallack's; but especially pleasing are the recurrences of that great specialty of the house — The Shaughraun. Boucicault, fresh from failure in attempt to manage Booth's, came back, on February 2nd, in his incomparable rôle of Conn, and with him were still several members of the original cast. The beloved Harry Montague doubtless was greatly missed, though Barrymore was a handsome, if less chivalrous

Captain; but Miss Dyas, Mme. Ponisi, Gilbert and Beckett cheered the hearts of old admirers in their famous original parts:

Captain Molineux	M. Barrymore	Sullivan	C. E. Edwin
Robert Ffolliott	J. H. Gilmour	Doyle	R. Warren
Father Dolan	John Gilbert	Donovan	Degez
Corry Kinchela	Gerald Eyre	Claire Ffolliott	Ada Dyas
Harvey Duff	Harry Beckett	Arte O'Neale	Rose Wood
Conn	Dion Boucicault	Mrs. O'Kelly	Mme. Ponisi
Sergeant Jones	W. J. Leonard	Moya	Stella Boniface
Mangan	E. T. Morton	Bridget	Miss E. Blaisdell
Reilly	C. T. Murphy	Nancy Malone	Minnie Vining

On the 11th, Gilmour played Molineux (*vice* Barrymore, ill); Kennedy was Ffolliott. The Shaughraun was played for the last time, at present, on February 23rd; on the 24th, The Colleen Bawn had its first performance by Wallack's regular company:

Myles-na-Coppaleen	Mr. Boucicault	Corporal	R. Warren
Father Tom	John Gilbert	Servant	H. Pearson, Jr.
Danny Mann	Harry Beckett	Eily O'Connor	Stella Boniface
Hardress Cregan	C. Rockwell	Anne Chute	Ada Dyas
Kyrle Daly	J. H. Gilmour	Mrs. Cregan	Mme. Ponisi
Corrigan	Gerald Eyre	Shelah	Miss E. Blaisdell
Bertie O'More	W. J. Leonard	Ducie	Minnie Vining
Hyland Creagh	C. E. Edwin	Kathleen	Jennie Boyd

Much as I admire Wallack's actors, I am forced to admit that this cast seems less brilliant than that great aggregation at Laura Keene's Theatre which originally produced The Colleen Bawn. Boucicault and Mme. Ponisi were still in the rôles they then created, but Stella Boniface was no Agnes Robertson, even if Ada Dyas might have been a fair successor to Laura Keene. This play ran until March 4th, when The Shaughraun came back; with the first and second acts of the last-named piece, on the 5th and 6th, Boucicault played Kerry, assisted by Maurice Barrymore as Gerald Desmond, Charles Rockwell as Colonel Coldham, W. J. Leonard as Dr. Mellish, Miss Dyas as Blanche Desmond, and Miss Boniface as Kate.

On March 8th, Wallack returned, after his very successful month at the Grand Opera House, soon to be described; he elected to re-appear in Charles Mathews's two-act version of Foote's old comedy, The Liar, in which, of course, he, no longer young or *svelt*, played the irresponsible, unveracious rattle-brained Wilding, and in which, equally of course, John Gilbert was Old Wilding and Harry Beckett Papillion. Barrymore essayed Sir James Elliott, Ada Dyas Miss Grantham and Mme. Ponisi Miss Godfrey. Wallack physically was mature and heavy for the mendacious hero, but he carried the part with reckless spirit, grace and glib enjoyment of his lies, even when they landed him in extreme comic predicament. Gilbert and the brilliant Miss Dyas lent admirable support in rôles exactly fitted to their best abilities. And the costumes were of a period appropriate to the period

[5]

of the original, Le Menteur. The Liar carried, as afterpiece, My Wife's
Dentist, with Henry (still constantly so printed) Edwards as Sir John
Beauville, J. W. Shannon as General Squadron, Gerald Eyre as Richard
Hazard, Edwin as David, Miss Boniface as Lady Letitia Beauville, Emma
Loraine as Cecily, and Effie Germon as Rhoda.

LESTER WALLACK AND DION BOUCICAULT

This double bill endured for six nights, and, on March 15th, the patrons
of the house, a loyal band, were treated to a sensation, the joint appearance
of Wallack and Boucicault in the latter's comedy, How She Loves Him —
"being the only occasion these artists have ever acted together in this
theatre." Wallack advertised the cast as "unprecedented"; if not that, it
was, at least, remarkable:

Tom Vacil	Lester Wallack	Dr. Sparks	C. E. Edwin
Sir Richard Hotspur	John Gilbert	Mrs. Vacil	Rose Wood
Dick Hartley	Maurice Barrymore	Atalanta Cruiser	Stella Boniface
Captain Yawley	J. H. Gilmour	Lady Selina Raffleticket	Mme. Ponisi
Diogenes	Dion Boucicault	Mrs. Tucker	Annie Myrtell
Dr. Maximum	W. J. Leonard	Tippet	Minnie Vining
Dr. Minimum	Harry Edwards	Miss Dilwyn	Jennie Boyd
Dr. Skwertz	J. W. Shannon		

The reader observes that Wallack and Gilbert assumed once more the parts
they originally played in 1864; in the Wallack cast of that year Floyd was
Captain Yawley, Charles Fisher Dick Hartley, Norton Diogenes, Mary
Gannon Atalanta, Madeline Henriques Mrs. Vacil, and Fanny Morant
Lady Selina. Perhaps we should not be wrong in believing that the earlier
assignment was the stronger in women and that of 1880 the more brilliant
in men, though as to this latter conjecture I am, on the whole, rather
doubtful.

On St. Patrick's Day, March 17th, an extra matinée was given in almost
every New York playhouse for the Herald Fund for the starving poor in
Ireland; Wallack's, for that charity, offered How She Loves Him. The
play ran for two weeks (it had not been a success in 1864), and yielded the
stage, on Easter Monday, March 29th, to Old Heads and Young Hearts,
cast as in December. On April 5th, Wallack unearthed another forgotten
thing — Mrs. Inchbald's To Marry or Not to Marry — and in it played
Sir Oswin Mortland, with Gilbert as Lord Danberry, Beckett as Willowear,
Effie Germon as Lady Susan, Stella Boniface as Hester, and Mme. Ponisi as
Mrs. Mortland. The concluding farce was To Oblige Benson, always a
favourite with Harry Beckett as Trotter Southdown; Shannon played Benson, Gilmour John Meredith, Kate Bartlett Mrs. Benson, and Effie Germon
Mrs. Southdown. This bill lasted for two weeks, She Stoops to Conquer
returning on April 19th and 20th.

J. B. POLK

WALDEN RAMSAY

HARRY COURTAINE

C. R. THORNE, JR.
IN THE TWO ORPHANS

MAUD HARRISON

ELLIE WILTON
IN THE FALSE FRIEND

SARAH COWELL

MRS. E. J. PHILLIPS

FREDERICK PAULDING

The last novelty of this interesting season came on April 21st — George Hoey's adaptation from the French, entitled A Child of the State. It has been observable that, during the last few years Wallack had called in outside help for his casts — perhaps an early indication of the breakdown of the old stock system which sometimes entailed the fitting of round pegs in square holes. Maude Granger, we remember, had been specially engaged for Diplomacy, and now Emily Rigl enters Wallack's, for the first and only time, in A Child of the State; Marion Booth and Rosa Rand also were new in this company. Of course, Wallack's was an aggregation trained in high comedy; if stronger, more emotional acting was required, Ada Dyas could not qualify, though Rose Coghlan could. In any case, the cast of A Child of the State is extremely interesting, not to say extraordinary:

Count de Lancy.........Maurice Barrymore	Hans Verner....................C. E. Edwin
Christian.......................Gerald Eyre	Carl............................H. Pearson
Von Helmich..................John Gilbert	Gertrande......................Emily Rigl
Heinrich....................Harry Edwards	Louise von Helmich.............Rosa Rand
Gros René..................Lester Wallack	Marie........................Marion Booth
Fritz.......................W. J. Leonard	Carline....................Stella Boniface
Bidoche.....................George Ulmer	

With such a group of actors, and with fine new scenes by Clare and Johnson, A Child of the State ran until May 22nd. For the last week of the season, Wallack reverted to previous comedy successes, a week of revelry by night to lovers of great comedy acting. On May 24th and 28th he gave My Awful Dad; on the 25th and 29th (evenings) She Stoops to Conquer; on the 26th, The Liar and To Oblige Benson; on the 27th, London Assurance; and at the matinée, on the 29th, Old Heads and Young Hearts. No other theatre in the city could so finely have staged and acted these classics and pseudo-classics.

W. R. FLOYD; F. S. CHANFRAU

On Monday evening, May 31st, a benefit was tendered to W. R. Floyd, who had been absent for a great part of the season. The programme was superb, beginning with To Oblige Benson (cast as before); proceeding to the third act of Othello, with Booth (Iago), John McCullough (Othello), Charles Rockwell (Cassio), Marion Booth (Desdemona), and Genevieve Reynolds; continuing with Wallack and Ada Dyas, in A Morning Call; presenting thereafter the third and fourth acts of London Assurance, with Gilbert, John T. Raymond (Mark Meddle), Frederic Robinson (Dazzle), Barrymore (Charles), Harry Edwards (Max), Floyd (Dolly), Con T. Murphy (Cool), Rose Coghlan (Lady Gay), and Stella Boniface (Grace); and ending with The Irish Lion:

[7]

Tom Moore..................W. J. Florence	Mr. Wadd......................R. Warren
Mr. Squabbs....................T. J. Hind	Ginger..........................C. E. Edwin
Mr. Puffy....................W. J. Leonard	Mrs. Fitzgig...................Ellie Wilton
Captain Dixon...............J. H. Gilmour	Mrs. Crummy............Miss E. Blaisdell
Mr. Mackenzie.............C. T. Murphy	Miss Echo.................Emma Loraine
John Long.................H. Pearson, Jr.	

This is one of the most remarkable bills in our history; the inclusion in it of Booth, McCullough, Wallack, Raymond and Florence would make it such, without the aid of so many fine stock actors, chiefly of Wallack's, past and present. Rose Coghlan's presence in it apprises us of the fact that next season she was to bring back to Wallack's her fresh beauty, her exuberant comedy and her deeper emotional charm. And her glorious voice! With the end of 1879–80, then, Ada Dyas departed finally from the Wallack force; and Maurice Barrymore, who never, I feel, quite fitted into this theatre, was to be succeeded in the autumn of 1880 by Osmond Tearle, who grew to fit perfectly and to become one of the most popular of leading men. Rose Coghlan and Osmond Tearle — what memories those names awaken! And Harry Beckett finally left Wallack's with a benefit on June 1, 1880, at which were given The Household Fairy, and acts of She Stoops to Conquer, Married Life, and The Lady of Lyons. Wallack's, without Beckett, was not quite what it had been.

A supplementary season began, on June 5th, with Frank S. Chanfrau in his long-established success, Kit, the Arkansas Traveller, employing, as usual with actors, in summer seasons at Wallack's, some of the regular members of the theatre:

Kit Redding..................F. S. Chanfrau	Major Squiggs...............H. A. Weaver
Manuel Bond............R. Fulton Russell	Bart.........................R. L. Tayleure
Wash Stubbs ....S. H. Verney	Jerry Sleepers.................C. E. Edwin
Mary Redding ⎱ ....Stella Boniface	J. Cæsar Smith...............G. Woodward
Alice Redding ⎰	Captain Wheeler.............W. J. Leonard
Little Allie...................Carrie Elberts	Sid Parker..............W. V. Ranous
Jeff..............................G. Sherman	Mrs. Stubbs.................Marion Booth
Lord Fitzfolie.................J. H. Gilmour	Mrs. Temple.............Victoria Cameron
James Temple...............B. F. Horning	Frau Pedders.................J. McDonald
Judge Suggs...................Leslie Allen	

There was no killing of Kit, Colonel Sellers, Bardwell Slote or any other of those essentially American types in poor plays; Kit, therefore, remained at Wallack's until June 25th, when the theater closed for a few weeks, over the heated term.

UNION SQUARE THEATRE, 1879–1880

The ever-popular Union Square re-opened, on September 16, 1879, for a preliminary season, with what proved to be an outstanding success of the next few years — Bartley Campbell's play of My Partner, which utilised much of the Western material made familiar by Bret Harte and Mark Twain, and especially (for playgoers) in Joaquin Miller's extremely successful The Danites.   In The Danites Louis Aldrich and Charles T. Parsloe had latterly met, and they now came forth in parts not dissimilar to those they had lately acted together in that play.   The cast of My Partner:

Joe Saunders	Louis Aldrich	Josiah Scraggs	J. W. Hague
Ned Singleton	Henry Crisp	Sam Bowler	J. H. Burnett
Wing Lee	C. T. Parsloe	Jim Johnson	John Dailey
Major H. Clay Britt	Frank Mordaunt	Mary Brandon	Maude Granger
Matthew Brandon	Harry Edwards	Grace Brandon	Minnie Palmer
Wellington Widgery	Charles Webster	Posie Pentland	Alice Grey

We here first meet Harry Edwards, that excellent actor, later in the season enrolled, as we found, at Wallack's.   My Partner dealt with the debonair Ned Singleton's "seduction" of Mary Brandon, honest Joe Saunders's angry remonstrance with his carefree partner, the murder of Ned, the trial of Joe, falsely accused, and the clearing up of the mystery by the comic Chinese "help" in the hotel.   All this sounds old-fashioned, but the audiences of that time loved it; the reader is not soon to be freed from the spell of My Partner. Allston Brown says that Campbell wrote the play for Aldrich, receiving therefor $12,000 in royalties, and, after five years, selling his author's rights to Aldrich for $3,000.   For a success like My Partner this sum seems pitiable indeed.   At first, Parsloe had a financial interest in the piece.

It was liked immensely, at this, its first season in New York, and could have run much longer had not the return of the regular Union Square actors forced its withdrawal on October 18th.   The famous company re-appeared, on October 21st, in French Flats, a farce wholly different from the kind of play heretofore identified with them.   I have always wondered why Palmer selected this piece for that company — a group known to be excellent in emotional plays of intense interest.   Of course French flats were then becoming interesting to New Yorkers, hitherto chiefly house-dwellers; and, besides, the farce so named was very hilarious, a wild helter-skelter of pursuit from flat to flat and hiding of various characters in room after room or closet after closet, poor M. Blondeau, owner of the flats, looking in vain for that quiet, the very thought of which had induced him to invest in the flats. The jealous tenor and the impressionable baroness were, so to speak, "all over the place."   J. H. Stoddart (Recollections of a Player) says, "contrary to our expectations, the piece was received with much favor."   His "broken-up" scene, in which, after a supposed encounter with the jealous opera-singer, he came on "in a most disheveled condition . . . caused the longest continuous laughter I ever heard."   J. B. Polk scored a great hit as the singer aforesaid, and, as the temperamental baroness, Ellie Wilton (replacing Linda Dietz, then started on her long London career) made her first appearance with the company:

[9]

M. Blondeau	John Parselle	Painter	W. H. Wilder
Bonay	J. H. Stoddart	Upholsterer	W. S. Quigley
Ernest Vallay	W. J. LeMoyne	Brisquet	Hattie Anderson
Signor Rifflardini	J. B. Polk	Mme. Blondeau	Sara Jewett
Marquis	Harry Courtaine	Anna Blondeau	Maud Harrison
Billardo	Walden Ramsay	Baroness de St. Amaranthe	Ellie Wilton
Tancredi	H. F. Daly	Mme. Bonay	Ida Vernon
Martin	M. V. Lingham	Bianca	Sarah Cowell
Old Pluchard	T. E. Morris	Mariette	Roberta Norwood
Gustave	Edwin Morris	Frozine	Courtney Barnes

Courtney Barnes (daughter of Rose Eytinge and second wife of John T. Raymond) had not previously played with the company, nor had Harry Courtaine, rather prominent here during this season, and only this.

French Flats ended its stay on January 20th, achieving a run of almost, if not quite, a hundred nights. It was followed, on the 21st, by a serious play by Edgar Fawcett — The False Friend, founded, in part, on the famous Tichborne case. Lucien Gleyre, the hero, is, so to speak, a male Mercy Merrick; believing Cuthbert Fielding to be dead, he returns to England, impersonates him successfully, until confounded by the return of the real Fielding. This genuine heir is assumed to be an impostor, is imprisoned, and is finally freed through the cleverness of his sister, who, by leading on the love-sick Gleyre, wrings from him a confession of his guilt. If the play had a weakness it was in making the offender a very sympathetic character; C. R. Thorne, Jr., who had been out of French Flats, made a great success of the part. Mrs. E. J. Phillips, also returning, and J. H. Stoddart were highly successful as, respectively, old Lady Ogden and Andrew, a retainer of the house:

Lucien Gleyre	C. R. Thorne, Jr.	Bailiff	H. F. Daly
Cuthbert Fielding	H. Courtaine	Gamekeeper	Alfred Becks
Cyril Garland	Walden Ramsay	Edith Fielding	Sara Jewett
Andrew	J. H. Stoddart	Lady Ogden	Mrs. E. J. Phillips
General Santley	John Parselle	Rebecca Santley	Ellie Wilton
Abercrombie Courtwell	J. B. Polk	Eugenia Maitland	Ida Vernon
Farmer Meadows	L. Thompson	Margaretta Maitland	Marie Wilkins
Farmer Bayard	T. E. Morris	Mrs. Chauncey	Sarah Cowell

This second play of the season ended its run on March 20th; during some of the last nights, Miss Wilton, ill, was succeeded, as Rebecca, by Maud Harrison, then one of the most popular members of the company. The benefit, on March 17th, for the Herald Irish Relief Fund, offered an extra matinée of The False Friend.

Palmer brought his season to an early close (the company was going to Boston) with a three-weeks revival of The Two Orphans, that great specialty of his theatre, now cast (March 22nd) as follows:

[10]

Chevalier de Vaudrey	C. R. Thorne, Jr.	Officer of the Guard	Frank Losee
Jacques Frochard	H. Courtaine	Footman	S. P. Du Bois
Pierre	Walden Ramsay	Louise	Sara Jewett
Count de Linières	John Parselle	Henriette	Maud Harrison
Marquis de Presles	H. F. Daly	Countess	Mrs. E. J. Phillips
Doctor	T. E. Morris	La Frochard	Mrs. Marie Wilkins
Picard	J. B. Polk	Marianne	Ellie Wilton
M. de Mailly	Alfred Becks	Sister Geneviève	Ida Vernon
M. d'Estrées	Jacob Graff	Julie	Annie Levian
Martin	Lysander Thompson	Florette	Florence White
Antoine	W. S. Quigley	Cora	Mabel Miller
Lafleur	A. H. Stuart	Sister Thérèse	Mrs. De Forrest
Chief Clerk	W. H. Wilder	Victorine	Netta Guion

Auditors who had seen the first two productions of this play at the Union Square may have reflected sadly, in reading that cast, on the transitoriness even of the stock-company system. Here were Thorne, Parselle, Morris, Lysander Thompson, Marie Wilkins and Ida Vernon in their original rôles; but where were Rose Eytinge, Kate Claxton, Fanny Morant, F. F. Mackay, James O'Neill, Stuart Robson, Claude Burroughs, Kitty Blanchard, Maude Granger? Well, this is life in the theatre. Sara Jewett and Maud Harrison, two charming actresses, had played the rôles now assigned them, in the final nights of the second run of the play at the Union Square in 1876; and I have no doubt that a general high excellence was still maintained in 1880. In the last of the run, Ellie Wilton was appearing with Booth, at Booth's Theatre; her place as Marianne was supplied at the Union Square by Sarah Cowell. E. H. Gouge's benefit matinée, on April 8th, offered J. T. Raymond and Laura Don in A Conjugal Lesson, Harrigan and Hart in The Mulligan Guards' Surprise, and three acts of The Two Orphans.

It will be seen that Palmer had gone through this season, as he had gone through the preceding one, with only three plays. The Two Orphans departed on April 10th, and, on the 12th, back came My Partner, with a less pleasing cast; A. D. Billings, Walter Lennox, Jr., Dora Goldthwaite, Laura Thorpe and Josephine Laurens succeeded, respectively, Harry Edwards, J. H. Burnett, Maude Granger, Minnie Palmer and Alice Grey — a decline, so far as the ladies were concerned, in the important item of pulchritude. The popular play continued through May 15th; on the 17th, Suppé's delightful opera, Boccaccio, was first heard by New York in English (it had recently been done in German at the Thalia Theater). Mahn's English Opera Company produced the work at the Union Square, with the clever Jeannie Winston in the title-rôle:

Boccaccio	Jeannie Winston	Lotteringhi	Fred Dixon
Fiametta	Alice Hosmer	Isabella	Marie Somerville
Pietro	W. A. Morgan	The Unknown	W. A. Hudson
Scalza	Vincent Hogan	Leonetto	Bertha Foy
Beatrice	Hattie Richardson	Tofano	Annie Winner
Lambertuccio	A. H. Bell	Chichibio	Clara Douglas
Petronella	Fanny Prestige	Guido	Mary Winner

One reason for assuming that this cast was not flawless lies in the fact that the names of nearly all have been swallowed in oblivion; actually, the recruits from "Variety," Bertha Foy and the Winners, are the only ones, except Miss Winston and Miss Hosmer, with which the reader is familiar. Boccaccio, one believes, should have run all summer; as a matter of fact, it remained but four weeks, and was succeeded, on June 14th, by The Love of His Life, Frank Rogers's new play, in which Frederick Paulding made another attempt to become a star. He engaged a good company, including the wandering Emily Rigl, recently at Wallack's:

Paul Danglars	F. Paulding	De Lancy	Alfred Becks
Harnot	Frank Mordaunt	Hortense de Merville	Emily Rigl
Count de Lancy	B. T. Ringgold	Adrienne	Louise Muldener
Duc de Beaulieu	Lysander Thompson	Mme. Lavernie	Mrs. Carrie Jamieson
De Beauvais	G. C. Jordan	Cécile	Carrie McHenry
De Massin	John Matthews		

I regret to say that The Love of His Life lasted but two weeks; it faded out, on June 26th, and behind it closed the doors of the Union Square for the season — a term interesting, if not in any way great.

DALY'S THEATRE, 1879–1880

The important event of this season was the return of the intrepid Augustin Daly, and the opening of the new Daly's Theatre, which was in time to supplant the long-established Wallack's and become one of the most distinguished theatres in the history of the American stage. Daly's retirement in 1877 had been a great sorrow to many; he had produced so many excellent plays in various kinds, had introduced and trained so many actors and actresses of later fame, that his name had become synonymous with a kind of wizardry of potent charm. And, without warning, he had dropped the reins, in seeming defeat. But one cannot defeat a Daly, and here, in 1879, he was doing exactly what he had done in 1869; he was taking a seemingly unlucky house (the Broadway) and installing in it a company of players the majority of whom were absolutely unknown to playgoers. But that was Daly's way; his fertile brain was teeming with ideas of new things and new kinds of things that he wished to do, and only young actors, malleable, pliant and willing, could be moulded into the sort of interpreters he wanted.

The old Broadway Theatre, once Wood's Museum, at Broadway and 30th Street (southwest corner or nearly), he entirely remodelled, redecorated and refurbished, until it became really a drawing-room home of the drama. Many remember fondly the long, richly furnished entrance (once the exhibition room of freaks and museum-pieces) which, by broad steps led to the luxurious lounge which Daly ultimately made an art-gallery of things per-

JOHN DREW

ISABELLE EVESSON
AND ESTELLE CLAYTON

HARRY LACY

ADA REHAN IN
THE ROYAL MIDDY

CATHERINE LEWIS
(THE ROYAL MIDDY)

HART CONWAY IN
THE ROYAL MIDDY

REGINA DACE

MABEL JORDAN

HELEN BLYTHE

taining to the stage.   Daly encouraged his patrons to arrive early, in order to inspect the treasures of art therein exhibited.   How charming it all was! And do you remember the Chinese boy in Oriental dress who, in the later years of the theatre, used to hand you your programme, as you went up the richly carpeted steps?   Ah, Daly's, love of our hearts, when comes there such another theatre?

Or such a company?   Yet, as I have said, when Daly began, in 1879, many of his people were unknown, and playgoers who might reasonably have expected to find in his new force most of the old and well-liked Fifth Avenue company were surprised and disappointed to discover in the roster the names of only such favourites as Charles Fisher, William Davidge, John Drew, George Parkes and Charles Leclercq; not a woman of the old guard had been engaged!   Only philosophical oldsters, as they looked back to a similar feeling in 1869, could have consoled themselves with the reflection that, if Catherine Lewis, Ada Rehan and Helen Blythe were in 1879 unknown to fame, so, ten years before, were Agnes Ethel, Fanny Davenport, Clara Morris, Kate Claxton and Sara Jewett, actresses whom from 1869 to 1872 Daly had started on the road to fame.

Judge Joseph Francis Daly (The Life of Augustin Daly) supplies interesting details in the engagement of the new company.   John Drew wrote (June 29th) that he hoped his terms of forty dollars a week would not seem an "iniquitous" demand; he felt that he had improved in at least one point — "my manner of speaking, which, as you are aware, frequently rendered what I had to say in a degree unintelligible by reason of bad enunciation and rapidity."   Later, Drew wrote to accept Daly's offer of "thirty *or* thirty-five dollars per week," strongly hoping it would be in Daly's power to make it the latter.   Ada Rehan (later America's most talented comedienne) finally accepted $35 a week, "with the understanding that you will increase it as you promised should I be worth more to you — which I sincerely trust will be the case."   She made it plain that what she was most "anxious for is to play good business, as I am refusing a positive leading position & higher salary to accept the engagement with you."   Fisher demanded $100 per week, and Davidge and Leclercq each accepted $50.   George Parkes's letter of July 3rd opens amusingly: "Shades of Cesar *Napoleon* — never!   Well, hardly ever.   Star in Dundreary one season, and offered $35 the next! 'Après moi le déluge!'"   He would "descend from Mount Blanc (the heighth I had placed the salary) to $40," and was "Yours in melancholia," G. Parkes.   Judge Daly gives the weekly budget for the first season: "Weekly salaries for seventeen ladies and fourteen gentlemen were $1077, and for twenty-three chorus, $248; the mechanics' or stage hands' wages were $236; the scenic artist's $60; the ushers', doorkeepers', etc., $88; the gas bill, $80; and advertising in sixteen papers, $300."   E. R. Mollenhauer furnished an orchestra of sixteen and himself as conductor for $280 per week.

These figures, as Judge Daly says, "strike us to-day as marvellous. They show what the people of the stage were willing to do for Mr. Daly and for art; and that they knew that his economies put no money in his own pocket at the expense of others."

The venture began on September 17, 1879 (not the 18th, as Judge Daly says), and according to his recollection, "the spectators deemed the transformation of the old Broadway Theatre a miracle of ingenuity and taste." We may obtain an idea of the new company by examining the casts of the two plays joined in the opening bill. The first was a one-act piece entitled Love's Young Dream, in which Charles Fisher appeared as Jotham Dibble, Harry Lacy (a handsome young man, afterward a star) as Fred Schermerhorn, George Parkes as Jack Beers, E. P. Wilks (an amusing little man) as Nap, May Fielding (her first appearance on any stage, and recommended to Daly by Agnes Ethel) as Florence, and Ada Rehan (later to be the great light of Daly's) as Nelly Beers. Following this trifle came a musical piece by Olive Logan Sykes, which staggered under the unpleasing title of Newport, or, the Swimmer, the Singer and the Cypher. Daly had become possessed of the idea of putting on musical pieces — whence he derived the idea, I know not — but fortunately after a season or two his success in other kinds led him to abandon this notion. For such purposes he had engaged a large singing force, headed by Catherine Lewis (sister of Jeffreys Lewis), and I print the cast of Newport, to apprise the reader of the personnel of what proved to be the minor singing aggregation. Curiously enough, most of the pretty young women involved became, if not well-known, at least worthy of record; their names are still familiar to students of our stage history, though but few of my readers could recount their actual performances on the stage:

Hon. Peter Porter	Charles Leclercq	Thompson	E. Sterling
Hon. U. B. Blode	William Davidge	Officer	P. Hunting
Ben Boulgate	Hart Conway	Midget	Laura Thorpe
Captain Chickering	George Parkes	Hon. Mrs. Porter	Catherine Lewis
Tom Sanderson	John Drew	Widow Warboys	Mrs. Charles Poole
Captain Blackwell	F. Iredale	Belle Blode	Georgine Flagg
Crutch Reynolds	Walter Edmunds	Cosette	Annie Wakeman
Undo	Frank Bennett	Miss Byrdde	Estelle Clayton
Toggs	Maggie Barnes	Miss Fysshe	May Bowers
Ginger	E. P. Wilks	Miss Cattelle	Blanche Weaver

The studious reader knows the after history of those talented young women, Catherine Lewis, Ada Rehan and Estelle Clayton; possibly even that of Blanche Weaver, whose first stage appearance this was.

That opening bill was a disastrous failure; Newport was just about as bad as such a thing could be. The Herald was very outspoken in condemnation. I looked anxiously for a criticism of Ada Rehan, but found, in the Herald, only the statement that Love's Young Dream was "well acted" by

Fisher, Lacy, Parkes, Miss Fielding and Miss Rehan — all lumped in a very general modicum of praise. The account books of Daly's Theatre, now in the Brander Matthews Dramatic Museum, Columbia University, show how badly the new venture was starting in the box-office. Opening, on the 17th, to gross receipts of $778.20, the double bill sank steadily in financial returns to $209.90 (18th); $142.50 (19th); $45.15 (matinée, 20th); and $188.50 (evening, 20th) — a wretched total of $1,364.25. On the debit side of the ledger, we find for "Saturday Saleries" (*sic*), $400.69; "saleries" of actors, $992.92; salaries of orchestra, $200.00; bills for advertising, $152.81; gas bills, etc., $53.90 — in all, $1,800.32. The loss on those opening performances, then, was $436.07 — a staggering disappointment, in view of "preliminary expenses" listed as $20,024.

On September 30th, Daly revived his still possible play, Divorce, with what he advertised as "this very important cast":

Alfred Adrianse	Harry Lacy	Guinea	Watson
Captain Lynde	George Parkes	Mrs. Ten Eyck	Mrs. Charles Poole
Rev. Harry Duncan	John Drew	Lu Ten Eyck	Ada Rehan
De Wolf De Witt	W. Davidge	Fanny Ten Eyck	Helen Blythe
Templeton Jitt	Charles Leclercq	Mrs. Kemp	Sydney Nelson
Mr. Burritt	Charles Fisher	Grace	Margaret Lanner
Judge Kemp	John Moore	Flora Penfield	Regina Dace
Dr. Lang	J. F. Brien	Molly	Maggie Harrold
Jim	Frank Bennett	Kitty Crosby	May Bowers
Richard	E. M. Smith	Alfred	Little Belle Wharton
Christmas	E. P. Wilks		

Of course old-timers set their tongues wagging on the glories of the original cast of this play, especially of the ladies, but the Herald, of October 1st, was rather pleased:

Mr. Harry Lacy "did admirably, giving the part a manly, gentlemanly interpretation, which gave the author's intention a thorough translation." Davidge, of course, had his old part, and Fisher repeated the detective, playing "with richness peculiar to himself" and "without the least vulgarity." Leclercq "was not alone good, but . . . he was original and borrowed none of his points from Mr. Lewis' famous 'business.'" Mrs. Poole was "as good a substitute for Miss Morant as could have been had. Fanny Davenport's beauty, Clara Morris' talent and Linda Dietz's pleasant presence were not there last night to enrich the cast, but Miss Rehan and Miss Blythe and Miss Lanner — notably Miss Blythe — are a trio which, under Mr. Daly's schooling and direction, will, we predict, be of great value to him. Much is wanting as yet to make them as serviceable as they will yet be found to be, but they improved so steadily throughout the performance, and gave such promise of future development, that we can well afford to wait a little for the result. As the company now stands it is strong in its men and, as a whole, weak in its women."

[15]

A bad failure in novelty and a merely nominal success with a revival did not look very promising for Daly's venture; nevertheless he kept on with Divorce, and worked hard in preparation of his third bill — Wives, Bronson Howard's amalgamation of L'École des Femmes and L'École des Maris, thus produced on Saturday, October 18th:

Marquis de Fontenoy	Charles Fisher	Captain Ballander	W. Edmunds
Sganarelle la Marre	W. Davidge	Commissary	Mr. Hunting
Vicomte Ariste	George Morton	Notary	Mr. Sterling
Chrisalde	John Drew	Agnes	Catherine Lewis
Horace de Chateauroux	Harry Lacy	Isabelle	Ada Rehan
Captain Fiermonte	George Parkes	Leonora	Margaret Lanner
Dorval	Hart Conway	Lisette	Maggie Harrold
Alain	Charles Leclercq	Georgette	Sydney Nelson
Jean Jacques	F. Bennett		

Judge Daly prints an amusing letter from Bronson Howard, then in London, expressing humorously his distress when he heard that his version of Molière was to be tricked out with a chorus, etc. Miss Lewis sang a song, I'm Such a Little Fool, and behold, there is, on the programme, a chorus of Musketeers, "by the ladies of the chorus," among whose names some, to this day, awaken a sweet pang of remembrance — Sara Lascelles, Ellie Stewart, Gussie Lang, Mlle. Malvina (the ballet mistress), Emma Turner, Blanche Weaver, Isabelle Evesson (sister of Estelle Clayton, and later well known), Fanny McNeill, Dora Knowlton, Ella Remetze, Grace Logan, Emma Hinckley (long at Daly's), and Miss Maxwell. There was also listed a group of men as Men of the Night Watch, but I will ask the reader to take my word for it that they remain to this day, more than half a century later, still absolutely unknown. According to the Herald, Catherine Lewis made the hit of the evening; but "Miss Rehan was fair as Isabelle."

Wives was something of a success, playing forty-eight times. "Had it been presented," grieves Judge Daly, "as the opening bill, it would have made a difference in the fortunes of the season." Yet the budget did not balance. The week of November 10th–15th grossed receipts for eight performances, including a Wednesday matinée of a revived Fernande, of only $2,713.55 to offset weekly expenditures of $2,983.32 — a loss of $269.77, not to mention a gradually increasing debt since the opening night of the season. The rent of the theatre was $275 weekly, the salary of actors, $1,443.50 per week, and that for the orchestra, $320. Advertising and printing had risen to $359.82. Daly had the good idea of varying his bills, and to that end, at the mid-week matinée, on October 29th, he revived Fernande, with Lacy as Marquis André, Parkes as Philip Pomerol, Leclercq as the Commandeur, George Morton as Ronqueville, John Drew as Bracassin, May Fielding as Fernande, Helen Blythe as Clothilde, Ada Rehan as Georgette, Mrs. Poole as Mme. Seneschal, Estelle Clayton as Mme. de la Brienne, Ellie Stewart as

ANNIE ELLSLER

EBEN PLYMPTON

GABRIELLE DU SAULD

C. W. COULDOCK
AS DUNSTAN KIRKE

EFFIE ELLSLER

DOMINICK MURRAY
AND J. FRANKAU

CECILE RUSH

STEELE MACKAYE

GEORGIA CAYVAN

HAZEL KIRKE (MADISON SQUARE THEATRE, 1880)

the Baroness, Sara Lascelles as Gibraltar, Blanche Weaver as Peachbloom, and Georgine Flagg as Thérèse.   As I read the names of those pretty young actresses whom Daly was quite obviously trying out, in his search for another Clara Morris or Agnes Ethel or Fanny Davenport, I am touched by the equal chance he gave to all and by the fact that only one — Ada Rehan — ever reached the height of the earlier actresses at the Fifth Avenue Theatres. The Herald, on October 30th, speaks of "the admirable delineation of Miss Ada Rehan," who "repeated her former artistic successes."   This genius was even then forging ahead.   Fernande was repeated at the Wednesday matinées, on November 5th and 12th, its three performances netting, respectively, $175.00, $112.50 and $117.

On November 29th (Saturday being then a rather favourite first night with Daly) came the first real success of the season, another of Daly's adaptations from the German.   This time von Moser's Haroun al Raschid was the source of Daly's new piece — An Arabian Night, or, Haroun al Raschid and His Mother-in-Law.   In this John Drew played Alexander Sprinkle, a devoted young husband, whose fatal passion for The Arabian Nights got him into deep trouble, especially with his mother-in-law; Harry Lacy was Herbert Rumbrent, artist in pursuit of the ideal; Davidge had his usual rôle as Uncle Major, "a dear old soul to confide in"; Parkes was Lafayette Moodie, "not such a fool as he looks for, in the matrimonial market"; Leclercq had a part perfectly fitted to his comic ability in "Signor" Hercules Burrown, "premier cannon ball tosser, and first heavy weight in Boom's Greatest Show on the Planet"; Bennett was John, the Butler; Hunting was Peter, the waiter at Mrs. Portley's; Margaret Lanner the perfect wife, Louise Sprinkle; Ada Rehan Kate Sprinkle, "brought up abroad, and astonished at the ways at home"; Mrs. Poole was the dread mother-in-law, Mrs. Weebles (Daly always had a knack at getting delightful comic names); Sydney Nelson was Mrs. Portley, who kept the summer hotel on the Boulevard; Georgine Flagg was Susan, chambermaid at Sprinkle's; and, above all, Catherine Lewis (who made a great hit) was Rosa Maybloom, of the circus, "with a fleeting vision of the 'Corsair's Bride,' and a brief revelation of the 'Great Indian Act.'"   This was very good fun, indeed, and pointed the way to Daly's ultimate success in adaptations from German farces. The receipts for January 5th–10th were $4,262.55, rising on the 15th (evening) to $983.65.   During the run of An Arabian Night, the manager put on Man and Wife for a Wednesday matinée or so (it had actually been given on November 26th, to a receipt of $86.50!) with Miss Blythe as Anne, Mabel Jordan (daughter of George Jordan and Emily Thorne) as Blanche, Mrs. Poole as Hester Dethridge, Morton as Geoffrey, Drew as Arnold, Leclercq as Sir Patrick, and Davidge (the only member of Daly's original cast) as Bishopriggs.

In December, says Judge Daly, Mrs. Gilbert, on her way through New

York with Abbey's company, called on Daly; it was "a great meeting and outpouring of souls," and Mrs. Gilbert — finest of "old ladies" — engaged for 1880–81 at the to us absurd salary of $70 a week. She told Daly that she was resolved to bring James Lewis back into the fold, and, thanks to her resolve, an engagement with the sensitive comedian was effected for the next season.

On January 28th, Daly gratified his desire to bring out a musical offering, and produced The Royal Middy, adapted from Der Seekadet of Genée and Zell by Edward Mollenhauer (Daly's *chef d'orchestre*) and Fred Williams. It was a very great success and in it Catherine Lewis as the gipsy girl turned "middy" made one of the two great hits of her career. For reasons previously cited, I give the complete cast:

Don Lamberto	Alonzo Hatch	Julio	May Bowers
Don Januario	Hart Conway	Giovanni	Blanche Weaver
Don Domingo	Charles Leclercq	Paulo	Isabelle Evesson
Captain Norberto	Charles Fisher	Enrico	Nellie Howard
Francesco	Walter Edmunds	Carlo	Sara Lascelles
Joaquino	E. M. Smith	Jago	Lillie Vinton
Mungo	Frank Bennett	Queen of Portugal	May Fielding
Rodriguez	Mr. Sterling	Fanchette	Catherine Lewis
Diego	Estelle Clayton	Donna Antonina	Ada Rehan
Sebastino	Georgine Flagg		

The Herald thought Catherine Lewis too vivacious and lively for the girl who wandered in search of her lover, but Daly managed, by beautiful scenery and costumes, and by the aid of his clever young players and pretty girls, to win a run of more than eighty nights for the production. Compared with the sickening losses of the first weeks of the season, there is something heartening about the returns, in January and February, for the new piece: $887.05 (January 28th); $1,039.95 (29th); $1,127.60 (30th); $628.00 (matinée, 31st); $1,356.35 (evening, 31st); $933.50 (February 2nd); $723.00 (3rd); another — An Arabian Night, $121.00 — not so encouraging (4th, matinée); $880.70 (4th, evening with The Royal Middy again); $790.90 (5th); $918.45 (6th); $695.00 (matinée, 7th); and $1,289.40 (evening, 7th). There were lawsuits incident to the success; Operti, the leader of orchestras, for instance, was ejected from the theatre, on one occasion, under suspicion of taking notes of Daly's version for rival companies, and, of course, promptly sued Daly. There was much pother about this in the Herald (see that paper under date of March 25th), many persons rushing in to express opinions, generally adverse to Daly's procedure. During the week of February 16th, Catherine Lewis fell ill, and, for a short time, Mabel Jordan played her rôle in The Royal Middy. In that week, the Park Theatre, Brooklyn, was giving Wives, and a part of Daly's company, John Drew, Harry Lacy, Annie Wakeman, Mrs. Poole, Mabel Jordan and Margaret Lanner were to give An Arabian Night, soon, in the same sister city.

On February 18th, Daly, ever restless, staged Charity, for the Wednesday matinée; Fisher was Dr. Athelney, George Morton Ted, Leclercq Jonas Smailey, Hart Conway Fred, Ada Rehan Ruth (she was rapidly arriving), Helen Blythe Mrs. Van Brugh, Regina Dace Eve, and Blanche Weaver Charlotte. It was repeated at the two subsequent Wednesday matinées. During the entr'actes in early March, either Frank Gilder or A. H. Pease played on a piano in the handsome lounge of the theatre — a pleasing innovation. The Royal Middy, in mid-March and later, was attraction at the Wednesday and Saturday matinées. Daly's gave a matinée on the 17th for the Herald Irish Relief Fund. In late March, Catherine Lewis was again ill, and Maggie Harrold (sic) took her place as Fanchette.

Again Daly used Saturday evening (this time April 10th) for production of a novelty. On that occasion he offered The Way We Live, adapted from Die wohlthätige Frauen of L'Arronge. "In it," says Judge Daly, "Mr. Drew and Miss Rehan were cast for the first time in comedy parts of the kind they afterwards made famous." The play dealt with society women who engage in charity for worldly reasons, to the neglect of their own duties, and a great number of women were apparently needed to drive home whatever satire the play possessed:

Major Lincoln	Charles Fisher	Harriet Langley	May Fielding
Clyde Monograme	John Drew	Fanny Martin	Georgine Flagg
Frederick Van Schaick	Harry Lacy	Maria	Blanche Weaver
Rutherford De Peck	Georges Parkes	Jeanette	Kitty Maxwell
Bryan O'Dodd	Charles Leclercq	Belle Remmerson	Margaret Lanner
Little Georgie	Lillie Waters	Alpha De Jones	Isabelle Evesson
Governor Rensler	J. F. Brien	Mrs. Stuttervent	Regina Dace
Colonel Remmerson	P. Hunting	Miss Hurd	Lillie Vinton
Commissioner Schatz	W. Edmunds	Miss Beevoort	Sallie Williams
Judge Stuttervent	J. Watson	Miss Rensler	Miss Knowlton
Hon. Mr. Beevoort	E. M. Smith	Mrs. Shatz	Sara Lascelles
Jack Sprint	E. Sterling	Miss Curd	Miss Howard
Cherry Monograme	Ada Rehan	Mrs. Schimmer	Miss Hinckley
Mrs. Van Schaick	Mrs. Charles Poole	Mrs. De Smythe	Miss Remetze
Jackie O'Dodd	Maggie Harrold		

So immense a cast might have carried a poorer play, but The Way We Live achieved only twenty-one performances. The last week of the season, like the last at Wallack's, brought repetitions of previous successes: The Way We Live (on April 26th and matinée, 28th); The Royal Middy (April 27th, 28th, and 29th, and matinée on May 1st, John E. Brand now joining the cast; An Arabian Night (April 30th and May 1st — evening). Thus all the actors had a chance to say farewell, and Daly could close with the comforting assurance that he had won through a hard year and firmly established his theatre. But, alas! as Judge Daly ruefully admits, in spite of three decided successes, the balance of expenditures and receipts was on the wrong side, and Daly departed, full of worry. He divided his company, sending out the musical part in The Royal Middy, and the comedy part in An Arabian Night. But a very hot summer gave the box-office a frosty outlook. To us, so many years later, it is a joy to read once more of the founding of Daly's famous playhouse.

The theatre was rented for a supplementary season by Salsbury's Troubadours, who began on May 3rd in their very successful trifle, The Brook, which flowed peacefully on till May 29th, when Daly's closed for the summer. The visitors, with The Brook, gave Cross Purposes.

MADISON SQUARE THEATRE, 1879–1880

Second in importance to the beginning of Daly's Theatre was the inauguration of the famous Madison Square Theatre, a house which for a few years was better known than any other in America. We attended Steele MacKaye's revival there, in the preceding spring, of his play, Won at Last, and were rather dubious when we learned that the money of the reverend brothers Mallory, editors of The Churchman, was to back MacKaye's efforts to remodel, refurnish and re-establish the theatre as the most beautiful known up to that time in the country. MacKaye's inventive genius had been busy in devising many important innovations in stage and audience room, and many postponements had whetted curiosity in regard to the new house (for new it really was). At last the theatre was ready, and the opening performance occurred on February 4, 1880.

The most notable novelty was the double stage which, lifting up and down by the mere touch of accustomed fingers, allowed change of scene, if desired, in two seconds, and which permitted the beginning of the play at the then incredibly late hour of eight-thirty. Other mechanical features were 364 tubes in the basement, which carried warmth or ventilation, as required, to the seats; also the admission of air into the auditorium through fine wire gauze. Great tubes, larger than a man's body, assisted in the ventilation. All these things were controlled by the mere touch of a finger. Gaslight was not permitted to vitiate the air, the burners being enclosed, and connected with orifices through which the heat found vent. The orchestra played in a room or balcony over the stage, on a line with the gallery, and a beautifully embroidered drop curtain by the Louis Tiffany studios added to the charm of the house. Many will remember the exquisite interior, in which no colour seemed to prevail at the expense of others, but which gave an effect of rich, simple elegance hitherto unknown in New York theatres. The seating capacity was about seven hundred.

The opening play was Steele MacKaye's own serious drama, Hazel Kirke, which he had formerly acted in other places (we saw it in Brooklyn) as An Iron Will, and which he had reworked considerably for the present occasion, even writing in a new character for Joseph Frankau. The decade of the

[20]

'80s is upon us, and new players are treading hard on the heels of departing celebrities of the '70s. Hazel Kirke introduced Effie Ellsler, charming actress and daughter of John A. Ellsler, well-known as theatrical manager and actor in Cleveland; Mr. and Mrs. Thomas Whiffen (Blanche Galton) also became leading favourites of the Madison Square company. The first cast of the play here included Miss Ellsler as Hazel, the sweet girl who had been promised in marriage by her iron-willed father, Dunstan Kirke (C. W. Couldock), to Aaron Rodney (Dominick Murray), for financial help Rodney had given him. Of course Hazel loved Arthur Carringford, Lord Travers (Eben Plympton) and agreed to elope with him; to the surprise of all, Rodney yielded his claims, joined the hands of the lovers, and begged for the forgiveness of Dunstan, who cast out Hazel, "adrift forever from thy feyther's love." Well, the marriage on Scotch soil causes question of its validity, and poor Hazel, like Camille, gives up her love, all at the request of Lady Travers, her Arthur's mother (Mrs. Cecile Rush). Mingled with these afflicting scenes is much humour provided by the eccentric Pittacus Green (Thomas Whiffen) and the miller's niece, Dolly Dutton (Gabrielle du Sauld). I hurry through the sad events of Act III, Hazel's return, in the storm, to the old mill house, her overhearing the continued obduracy of her stern parent, now blind, and her attempted suicide in the mill-pond. And the curtain speech, or cry, of Dunstan when he learns of her danger: "In my blindness, I cast her out, and now that I would save her, I cannot see!" Well, Act IV attends to all that, and sends home a happy audience. Remaining parts in the play were performed by Mrs. Whiffen as Mercy Kirke, the miller's wife, Annie Ellsler as Clara, the maid, Joseph Frankau as Met Miggins, Edward Coleman as Barney O'Flynn, F. P. Barton as Joe, George Gray as Dan, and Henry Jones as Thomas. Says the Herald of February 5th of the theatre and the performance: "As a theatrical interior, it is a revelation to New York as absolute as was [sic] the rich stage settings first accorded to the society drama in New York years ago, under the management of Mr. Daly. . . . Mr. Daly years ago showed what might be done behind the footlights, Mr. Mackaye last night showed . . . what could be done before the curtain, in arranging and [sic] auditorium, the like of which New York has never dreamed of for comfort and elegance . . . and for the grace of its decoration. . . . It [the double stage] worked to a charm." Furthermore, at the end of the play, its working was shown to the audience. The paper does not highly praise the play, but Couldock's Dunstan was "a powerful piece of character and emotional acting, especially in the conclusion of the third act"; Miss Ellsler "made a strong point in the second act, and always did well, if she was not great in her part." Miss du Sauld and Whiffen lightened the piece by their good acting.

The new play did not go well at first. Rose Coghlan was a member of the company and, for her, Masks and Faces was put in rehearsal. Then, suddenly, Hazel Kirke took a joyful rise, and, business steadily improving, it began its run, unprecedented up to that time, of four hundred and eighty-six performances. According to Allston Brown, Rose Coghlan drew $8,000 in salary, without making a single appearance. A professional matinée was given on March 4th, to which actors and actresses and theatrical people only were invited. On February 26th a fire, just before the time of performance, completely destroyed the beautiful Tiffany drop-curtain, but proved the efficacy of MacKaye's fire-extinguishing apparatus. The play was given, as usual, the audience gathering while the stage-hands were cleaning up the wreckage. A beautiful new curtain of silk and satin was displayed on May 3rd. Account of all these proceedings may be gleaned from Percy MacKaye's Epoch — his life of his father. The fiftieth performance of Hazel Kirke fell on March 22nd, the hundredth on May 11th; on that occasion, the pretty new entrance to the theatre was first opened to the public.

Meantime, on the afternoon of April 1st, some of Mapleson's best artists appeared here in concert — Campanini, Galassi, Mlle. Marimon, Emilie Ambre and Anna de Belocca, with A. H. Pease to accompany. The prices ranged from $1.50 to $3 — rather high for that time. Percy MacKaye (Epoch) gives an amusing picture of Campanini sinking down, with the frightened Belocca, on the double stage, and, as he disappeared, shaking his hand blandly at the audience. That boyish escapade sounds exactly like his successor of so many years later — the great Caruso. At the concert on April 8th, Emma Thursby appeared, with the contralto, Julia Christin (first appearance in New York), Lencioni, Signor Angele Torriani (baritone), Christian Fritsch, Bernhard Mollenhauer, A. H. Pease and G. W. Colby. On the afternoon of June 28th, occurred a benefit for the fund to erect a statue of Poe, in Central Park. A host of volunteers included Clara Morris (sleep-walking scene from Macbeth), Edwin Booth, Effie Ellsler, Thomas Whiffen, Murry Woods and Louisa Eldridge (in Katharine and Petruchio), George Clarke, George A. Conly, Maud Morgan, Bianca La Blanche (Blanche Davenport), F. C. Bangs, Harry Edwards, the Swedish Ladies' Quartet, and Bernhard Mollenhauer. Steele MacKaye recited The Raven, and Percy MacKaye (Epoch), stating that Booth sat in a box with his daughter, then a girl of eighteen, cites a letter from the daughter (Mrs. Edwina Booth Grossman) in which she says that her father remarked on this recitation, "How strongly Steele MacKaye resembles Edgar Poe! He is undoubtedly the greatest dramatic reader of this generation. His genius, as such, is unspoiled by theatricalisms."

Meantime, Hazel Kirke still ran on, but with summer changes in the cast. This theatre was the first and perhaps the last (unless one remembers Daniel Frohman's Lyceum) to give out very pretty programmes, on good stiff paper and with excellent printing. How we prized them! Unfortunately, since they were printed probably in great quantities, they bore no date. Hence it is impossible for me to date such a programme now before me which bears merely the legend "Summer Season of 1880." Effie Ellsler, Mrs. Rush, Mrs. Whiffen, Annie Ellsler, Couldock, Whiffen, Frankau, Coleman, George Gray and Jones are still in their original rôles, but Henry Aveling is now Aaron Rodney, Gustavus Levick Arthur Carringford, and Georgia Cayvan (a recruit from Boston, and soon to be Hazel Kirke and a leading lady of renown for years thereafter) was down for the pretty part of Dolly Dutton. The Madison Square under the Mallorys was constantly changing casts in the home theatre, and sending travelling companies far and near in the country at large, many members of which were scattered fragments of the original cast of any play at the home theatre. That policy had not yet begun, but soon Hazel Kirke companies would carry the glad tidings to even remote theatrical communities. Hence my statement, earlier, that the Madison Square became perhaps the best known theatre from one part of the country to another, east, west, north, south — to say nothing of Canada. The staff of the theatre, set down in the programme from which I have just quoted, includes Steele MacKaye, as manager, Daniel Frohman (his first appearance in our story, and very welcome) as business manager; Aaron Appleton as treasurer; Bernard [sic] Mollenhauer as musical director; Hughson Hawley as scene-painter; Nelson Waldron as stage machinist; Fred B. Barton as prompter; Frank Goodwin, in charge of properties; E. O. Cutter as chief usher; James Barnes as engineer, ventilating department; and John McGowan, gas machinist. A large staff for so small a theatre! On June 30th, Hazel Kirke reached its hundred and fiftieth showing, the two hundredth making glad the evening of August 19th, when (for that occasion only) Steele MacKaye appeared as Aaron Rodney.

Booth's Theatre, 1879–1880

Booth's, that hope, in earlier days, of the finer drama, had retired, in 1879, to the rearward of importance; it seems to me of less importance than the four "stock" institutions I have just commemorated. I therefore make no apology for placing it, in this new section of our work, in a position somewhat lower than that to which I formerly assigned it. Dion Boucicault, who had not achieved, since The Shaughraun, anything like his earlier successes in the drama, became lessee of Booth's, and re-opened it, on September 4th, with another of those frequent new plays of his, seemingly foredoomed to failure. He had thoroughly renovated and altered the auditorium, especially installing in the place formerly occupied by the first two rows of orchestra seats, large, comfortable folding chairs, which sold at the then unprecedented high price of two dollars each.

He also engaged a good company, inducing the brilliant Rose Coghlan and the veteran John Brougham to leave the snug haven of Wallack's to embark on the uncertain seas of his venture. His new play bore the sentimental title of Rescued, or, a Girl's Romance, and this cast tried unsuccessfully to make it a success:

Earl of Mount Audley	A. D. Billings	Jane Garside	Marie Prescott
Lady Sibyl Ferrers	Rose Coghlan	Maggie	Lizzie Kelsey
Ruskov	George Clarke	Jennie	Miss A. Barnicoat
John Weatherby	John Clayton	Dan	Pearl Eytinge
Jerry Tarbox	Dominick Murray	Mme. Aurélie	Nellie Mortimer
Dr. Manifold	George F. DeVere	Coaley	Virginia Clary
Dicksie	Ada Gilman	Buster	Agnes Elliott
Phœnix O'Reilly	John Brougham	O'Leary	Maud Stuart
Blind Biddy	Mrs. Cecile Rush	Checkers	Nellie Ransom
Servant	W. G. Mordaunt	Widdicoff	W. Herbert

Even as I write the names of those actors, I feel a glow; many were celebrated, or became so, in their time. One unexplained mystery lies in the fact that certain of the players appeared at the opening of the Madison Square Theatre or were at least members of the company kept out of the bills by the success of Hazel Kirke — Miss Coghlan, Dominick Murray, Ada Gilman, Cecile Rush; even George Clarke soon joined MacKaye's forces there. I follow my suspicions in saying that Rescued was not a success, yet Boucicault kept it afloat for about six weeks; perhaps I have grown to gauge success in terms of the run of The Shaughraun.

Townsend Walsh, in his The Career of Dion Boucicault, states that the actor-author-manager took Booth's in this autumn of 1879 "with two cherished objects in view: one was to introduce to the public his son, Darley George ('Dot'); the other was to gratify his own ambition to appear as Louis XI." This latter desire seems at first inexplicable, until one remembers Boucicault's work as a character actor and his face, somehow suggestive of that of the French monarch. The production of Louis XI, in Boucicault's own version of Casimir Delavigne's play, fell on Saturday evening, October 11th:

Louis XI	Mr. Boucicault	Tristan l'Hermite	W. B. Cahill
Nemours	John Clayton	De Lude	Alice Barnicoat
Marie de Comines	Rose Coghlan	Jarnac	Virginia Clary
Coitier	John Brougham	Beaujeu	Miss Chase
François de Paul	G. F. DeVere	De Rohan	Nellie Ransom
Philippe de Comines	A. D. Billings	Rosette	Miss Stockton
Marcel	Dominick Murray	Reine	Agnes Elliott
Marthe	Nellie Mortimer	Dauphin	Dion G. Boucicault
Olivier le Daim	W. Herbert		

Well, in this exploit Boucicault gratified both desires attributed to him by Townsend Walsh; he emerged as Louis XI, and presented his son Dion G. (so advertised) as the frightened Dauphin.

Walsh recounts the story of the first evening as told to him by George Clarke, a member of the company, but without a part in Louis XI. Clarke found Boucicault in his dressing room, in the theatre, "nervous almost to prostration," and unable to make up as the wily French monarch.   He was "slapping on the grease-paint," until "he looked more like a Sioux or a Kickapoo in full war-paint" than Louis XI.   Clarke helped him, and practically made him up for his part.   And Boucicault went on.   "Never," says Clarke, "did monarch receive less grave and reverent treatment.   Boucicault's brogue came out thick and strong . . . a French king with a Dublin brogue was too excruciating," and the audience at first tittered, then roared.   "To make matters worse," Brougham, Dominick Murray and Cahill, Irishmen all, spoke a fine Irish-English, and as the play went on, Brougham, "who loved a good joke better than anything else in the world, began to exaggerate the unctuousness of his own fine, natural brogue.   Next John Clayton, an Englishman and the son-in-law of Boucicault, felt in duty bound to fall in line, and he too assumed a broad brogue.   The rest of the company, either out of deviltry or catching the infection, became Gaelic instead of Gallic, and before the play was half over the French tragedy had degenerated into an orgy of Hibernian dialects."   I cannot but believe this story to have been slightly exaggerated by time in Clarke's memory; but we know John Brougham was capable of anything to carry out a joke. The brief review in the Herald of October 12th conveys no note of this Hibernian revelry.

I go back reluctantly for Sunday concerts, which, in my understanding of ethics, have no right in a theatre.   But Booth's, like the Grand Opera House, had become committed to the nuisance (reader, forgive my music-loving pen that inadvertently slipped into such a word!).   On Sunday, October 12th, Booth's stage was occupied by Carlotta Patti and the company that had recently supported her at Chickering Hall — Ketten, de Munck, Ciampi-Cellaj, Phelps, and Marzo; she sang the showy air from Dinorah, an Ave Maria by Lucantoni, and in concerted music with members of her troupe.   The same aggregation appeared on the 19th.

Boucicault, sensitive to ridicule, soon withdrew his Louis XI into the vale of disappointed hopes, and restored (October 17) Rescued to the bills. He closed his season on October 25th, and, on that night, the veteran Brougham made his last appearance on the stage; he died in New York on June 7, 1880.

Booth's re-opened on November 24th, for three weeks of Maurice Grau's French Opera Company, which had recently finished a successful term at the Fifth Avenue Theatre.   On November 24th, 25th and 27th (matinée) Paola Marié appeared as Serpolette, in Les Cloches de Corneville; on November 26th, 27th (evening), 28th and 29th (matinée and evening), the same charming performer was La Belle Hélène, with Angèle as Orestes and Capoul as Paris.   On December 1st, 2nd, 4th and 6th (matinée), Mignon (first time here out of grand opera) enlisted Paola Marié as the heroine,

Angèle as Frédéric, Mlle. Leroux-Bouvard (new) as a rather thin-voiced Philine, Capoul in his original character of Wilhelm Meister (which he had sung here in Italian with Christine Nilsson), Juteau as Laerte, and Jouard as Lothario. This first performance of the work in French was successful, and was heard from time to time in 1879–80. Revivals of December included La Fille de Mme. Angot (3rd), Giroflé-Girofla (5th) and Les Cloches de Corneville (6th). Capoul's benefit, on the 8th, provided the second act of La Fille de Mme. Angot, the third of Mignon, and the third of Faust ("first time in America in French") with Mlle. Leroux-Bouvard, Gregoire (Siebel), Delorme, Jouard and Capoul. Those bits of Mignon and Faust, along with Act I of La Vie Parisienne, made threefold joy on the 10th. Mignon, on the 9th; La Grande Duchesse, on the 11th; La Belle Hélène on the 12th; Les Cloches de Corneville, on the 13th (matinée); and Mignon on the evening of the same day, carried the French successfully from the friendly haven of Booth's Theatre. They were becoming fixtures, almost, of a busy season. La Camargo, a new operetta by Lecocq, had been announced for December 11th, but was not given till the company came back to New York, later in the winter. I need hardly say that, during this present tenancy of Booth's, they could not resist giving Sunday concerts.

An unnecessary season of Italian opera, far from first-rate, began on January 19, 1880. Max Strakosch had promised for that date a performance of Aïda, with a new soprano, Teresina Singer, about whom a fog of puffery had been raised; unfortunately, she was ill, and Lucia, substituted, presented a very uninteresting cast, including Marie Litta, Miss Cervi, Petrovich, Storti (a fairly good baritone), Ferrario, Barberis (Arturo), and Lafontaine (Normanno). One can imagine the result. On the next evening came La Traviata, with Bianca La Blanche (daughter of E. L. Davenport), Miss Lancaster (Flora), Mlle. Arcone (Annina), Lazzarini (Alfredo), Storti, Lafontaine, and Ferrario. Of course we are interested in Blanche Davenport, and read, eagerly, in the Herald of the 21st that "her voice is fairly good, and its quality sweet; she phrases well and she has strong dramatic instincts. . . . Her upper register is the best, and at times is powerful and telling, though occasionally she allows a tremolo to affect the beauty of some of her high notes. . . . Her execution is deficient in brilliancy." What did the reader expect? Wednesday, January 21st, brought Faust, with Marie Litta, Bertha Ricci (Siebel), Mlle. Arcone, Lazzarini, L. Gottschalk (Mephisto), Lafontaine (Valentine), &c. Litta took the place of Miss La Blanche, indisposed. At last, on the 22nd, came Aïda, with the début of Teresina Singer, who proved to be a heavy songstress, with a tremolo and uncertain intonation. Anna de Belocca (toward whom the Herald had considerably cooled) was Amneris, Petrovich Radames, Storti Amonasro, Castelmary (a much heralded and disappointing basso) Ramfis, and Lafontaine the King. Why Strakosch, in view of Mapleson's recent great success

with this opera, should have expected to satisfy with such a cast it is difficult to surmise.   Well, he didn't please.   Mlle. Singer was to have tried
Norma, on the 23rd, but the upsetting of all Strakosch's plans forced, instead, Mignon, with La Blanche, Litta (Filina), Bertha Ricci, Lazzarini,
Gottschalk and Lafontaine.   The matinée, on the 24th, presented Belocca as
a pretty, ineffective Carmen, with Baldanza as Don Jose, and with Ida Valerga, Bertha Ricci, Lafontaine, and Miss Lancaster (Micaela) in other
rôles.   A miserably disappointing week!

I Puritani, on the 26th, brought into requisition La Blanche (or La-
blanche), Valerga, Lazzarini, Storti and Castelmary; Carmen lured again
on the 27th.   A big cast of The Huguenots, on the 28th, was wrecked by the
continued illness of Singer, and, instead, La Favorita (so great a success at
the Academy with Miss Cary and Campanini) had at Booth's interpretation
by Belocca, Petrovich, Storti and Castelmary.   La Blanche, Lazzarini,
Gottschalk and Tagliapietra (Alessio) did La Sonnambula, on the 29th,
and Faust, on the 30th, enlisted Litta, Ricci, Petrovich, Castelmary and
Gottschalk.   Mignon, at the matinée on the 31st, closed the losing venture;
in view of Mapleson's season at the Academy, assuredly a needless expenditure of energy.   But managers must at least try to live.

HENRY E. ABBEY

Henry E. Abbey, developing into the great impresario he was to become,
leased Booth's Theatre, and brought life into the dying body.   He opened
on February 3rd (Brown says 4th) with George H. Tyler as business manager, J. S. Maffitt as stage director, John L. Vincent as stage manager, Henry
Wannemacher as musical director, and J. Cheever Goodwin as treasurer.
His first attraction was Humpty Dumpty, a special feature of which was a
band of Spanish Students, with mandolins, guitars and other sentimentally
tinkling or twanging instruments balanced against a single violin.   Needless
to say, they became the rage in this, our crazy town.   Otherwise, the leading
performers were James S. Maffitt (or Maffit) as Humpty Dumpty Sr.,
Robert Fraser as Humpty Dumpty, Jr., W. H. Bartholomew as Old One-
Two, N. D. Jones as Old Three-Four, Robert Butler as Reddy, a policeman,
A. S. Matthews as Grouty-Gritz, Frank Crane as Kwill Pen, J. F. Raymond
as Tommy Tucker, Mlle. Elizabeth Menzelli (sic) as Bobby Shaftoe, Pauline Barretta as Goody Twoshoes, Thomas Johnson as Hamlet, Kate Francis
as Little Miss Muffet and Stalacta, A. Carpenter as Korn Shock, &c.   A
host of supernumeraries figured in the cast as characters from nursery
rhymes, stage plays, etc.   Specialists engaged were the Brothers Valjean
(jugglers), Fred Levantine (equilibrist), the Snow Brothers (acrobats), and,
of course, the Spanish Students.   Bonfanti, Menzelli, Barretta and Elise
Scott led the ballet.   Apparently, this was a success; at any rate, it ran for

eight weeks, closing on March 27th. The Spanish Students gave a concert on February 8th, along with Amy Sherwin (her first appearance in New York), Levy, Carreño, Tagliapietra, Charles Pratt, and Wannemacher's orchestra. During the week of March 1st, Abbey advertised other performers for Humpty Dumpty — Hattie O'Neil, Marie Langley, Henriette Raymond, Little Belle Wharton (in whom, since the run of Pique, we have had interest), Mrs. Ellen Wharton, Henry Flohr, and Charles Thorne. The Rajade Troupe of Prince Awata Katsnoshin was then doing its best for us. Of course Humpty Dumpty was given for the customary Herald Irish Fund; February 20th was the day.

On March 29th, the Spanish Students offered a grand farewell at Booth's as a tribute to Cervantes, and in aid of the fund for raising a statue to him in the Park. Dr. Marti read a poem in Castilian; a play, Un Español en Boston, enlisted P. Olive, E. Molino, M. Delgado, L. Cusachs, E. Godinez, Misses A. Sydney and Rosalba Beecher; Miss Beecher and the Spanish Students then appeared; a farce, A Soup Tureen without a Cover, continued the fun; Mrs. George Vandenhoff read; and Olive, Delgado, Molino, and Miss Sydney gave the farce, La Cara del Campo. A big feature was a tableau of The Crowning of Cervantes by the Muses, posed while Mrs. Vandenhoff read a poem by Mrs. E. T. Porter Beach.

Edwin Booth; Farewell to Adelaide Neilson

Abbey's management winged higher flights. On Tuesday, March 30th, Edwin Booth entered the theatre he had once owned, in an elaborate revival of Macbeth, assisted by the excellent Mrs. D. P. Bowers as Lady Macbeth, and by Mrs. Bowers's husband, J. C. McCollum (or McCollom) as Macduff. The other actors were not very distinguished, including O. H. Barr as Malcolm, M. Rainford as Duncan, M. V. Lingham as Banquo, W. F. Owen, E. C. McCall and Louisa Eldridge as the Witches, &c. One notes with profound interest that Otis Skinner was the Wounded Officer, and Master Harry Woodruff (a popular actor of later years) was Fleance. The younger generation is upon us; the actors of the '80s are not, by any means, the actors of the '70s. On April 1st, Booth changed to Richelieu, with McCollum (or McCollom) as de Mauprat, James M. Hardie as de Baradas, Harry Pierson as Louis XIII, John Dailey as De Beringhen, Otis Skinner as François, Belle Flohr as Marion, and Ellie Wilton (who had given up her rôle of Marianne, in The Two Orphans, at the Union-Square) as Julie de Mortemar. The Herald, next day, says the cast was "unequal to the task imposed on them," but "Miss Wilton and Mr. Skinner were rather the best of them all." At the matinée, on April 3rd, Booth and Mrs. Bowers acted Benedick and Beatrice — neither, I suspect, very sprightly or exhilarating.

On April 5th, 6th and 7th, Booth appeared as Richard III (in William

[28]

"DOT" BOUCICAULT   JOHN CLAYTON   EDWARD COMPTON

BLANCHE DAVENPORT   MISS NEILSON
AS ISABELLA   MRS. D. P. BOWERS

ANGELE AND CAPOUL
(FILLE DE MME. ANGOT)   JESSIE BOND — J. H. RYLEY
(H.M.S. PINAFORE)   PAOLA MARIÉ — CAPOUL
(LA PÉRICHOLE)

Winter's version), with Mrs. Bowers as Queen Margaret, McCollom as Richmond, Ellie Wilton as Lady Anne, Kate Meek as Queen Elizabeth, Louisa Eldridge as the Duchess of York, Hardie as Clarence, Walter C. Kelly as Edward IV, O. H. Barr as Buckingham, Harry Pierson as Hastings, Otis Skinner as Catesby, Belle Flohr as the Prince of Wales, Master Harry Woodruff as the Duke of York, W. F. Owen as the Lord Mayor, Milton Rainford as Stanley, &c. On April 8th, Booth was Othello, and McCollom Iago; on the 10th (matinée), the parts were reversed. Mrs. Bowers played Emilia, and Miss Wilton Desdemona. In The Fool's Revenge, on April 9th and 10th, Ellie Wilton played Fiordilisa, with Kate Meek as Francesca, to Booth's magnificent Bertuccio.

Hamlet waited for performance till April 12th, 13th, 14th, 15th and 17th (matinée), with Ellie Wilton as Ophelia, Kate Meek as the Queen, McCollom as the Ghost, Rainford as Polonius, Hardie as the King, Barr as Laertes, Owen as Gravedigger, and Skinner as First Actor; on the 16th, Macbeth returned, and, on the 17th (evening), Booth gave both The Merchant of Venice (with Mrs. Bowers as Portia) and The Taming of the Shrew (so announced). During his last week, Booth was seen, progressively, as Richelieu, Iago, Macbeth, Bertuccio, and Ruy Blas (this last at a matinée on the 24th). This engagement interests me, from the participation in it of so many well-known actors.

Adelaide Neilson, after an absence of three years, began her last engagement in New York, immediately following Booth. It was announced as her farewell to the New York stage, but some persons, used to broken farewells, might have taken this warning rather lightly. Alas! it was farewell forever to one whom the advertisements not without reason called "the greatest living representative of classic heroines." Miss Neilson was tired and ill, and was anticipating a life of well-merited rest.

She began, on April 26th, in one of her loveliest characters, Imogen, supported by a company that a mere glance shows to have been quite unworthy of her and of the occasion. Edward Compton was a handsome young actor, announced later as husband of the actress, and he may have been tolerable in certain parts, but the others certainly formed the poorest aggregation that ever supported this fine actress. Look at the cast of Cymbeline, and perpend:

Imogen	Miss Neilson	Iachimo	J. B. Studley
Posthumus	Edward Compton	Caius Lucius	M. Leffingwell
Cymbeline	H. A. Weaver, Jr.	Pisanio	L. F. Rand
Cloten	C. H. Bradshaw	Cornelius	Mr. Lickfold
Belarius	H. A. Weaver, Sr.	Philario	Mr. Leffingwell
Guiderius	W. A. Eytinge	Varus	Mr. Smith
Arviragus	J. H. Miller	Lewis	Mr. Burnham
Madan	G. R. Sprague	Helen	Katie Baker
Locrine	F. Currier	Queen	Kate Meek

Cymbeline was given on Monday, Wednesday and Friday, April 26th, 28th and 30th and May 1st (evening); on the 27th, 29th and May 1st (matinée), the actress restored to our public her exquisite Viola, in Twelfth Night, her support including Compton as Malvolio, F. W. Sanger as Orsino, Edwin Cleary as Sebastian, L. F. Rand as Antonio, young Weaver as the Friar, H. A. Weaver Sr. as Sir Toby, Leffingwell as the Clown, Bradshaw as Sir Andrew, Josephine C. Bailey as Olivia and Lizzie Goode as Maria. Next day the Herald is outspoken in critical judgment of these actors. New York "has taste, experience and critical judgment . . . and it is supreme folly for a management to foist a lot of insignificant people on the public." Miss Neilson carried the entire play on her shoulders.

The second week presented Miss Neilson (May 3rd, 5th, 7th and 8th) in the character still identified with her fame — Juliet, with Compton as a handsome and not unsatisfactory Romeo; As You Like It was promised for the 4th and 6th, and Twelfth Night for the matinée on the 8th. The Herald was very hard on the support, especially in As You Like It. The lovely actress was scheduled, on the 10th, for Julia, in The Hunchback; illness prevented her appearance. She played the part on the 12th and 15th, with Ellen Cummins as Helen; Twelfth Night on the 11th and 13th, The Lady of Lyons on the 14th, and As You Like It at the matinée on the 15th made a week to be fondly remembered in days to come. On Sunday, May 16th, Robert G. Ingersoll lectured on What Shall We Do to be Saved? The last week of the Neilson engagement repeated Juliet (May 17th and 22nd), Viola (18th and matinée on the 22nd), The Lady of Lyons (19th), As You Like It (20th), and Cymbeline (21st). For her Juliet, on the 22nd, the exterior of the theatre was illuminated. That was the last of this most admired and beloved of actresses, except for a remarkable benefit and farewell, on Monday, May 24th. In this she offered, in order, selections from the second and fourth acts of Twelfth Night, the balcony scene from Romeo and Juliet, the fifth act of Cymbeline, and the second and third acts of Measure for Measure, which she had never played in New York, though London had greatly admired her Isabella. In this bit from Shakespeare's gloomy play her Isabella had the support of Compton as Claudio, the elder Weaver as the Duke, F. W. Sanger as Angelo, L. F. Rand as Escalus, Walter Eytinge as Lucio, Edwin Cleary as Elbow, Bradshaw as Pompey, J. H. Miller as Froth, young Weaver as the Provost, and Louis F. Massen as Thomas. In the scene with Angelo, the Herald asserted that the actress "rose to positive grandeur."

In her farewell speech, on that memorable evening, Miss Neilson said, "It seems to me that I am leaving not only friends, but happiness itself; that the skies can never again be as bright as they have been to me here, nor flowers bloom, nor music sound any more. . . . Take, then, the assurance that I feel deeply your unvarying warmth and appreciation, and let me bid you goodby with the thought that as I shall never forget you, so shall you keep a small place in your memories for me." That place they surely kept, and she has her place in the hall of fame. She went, immediately after the New York engagement for five weeks at Baldwin's Theatre, San Francisco; there, on July 17, 1880, she made her last appearance on the stage, acting the balcony scene from Romeo and Juliet and Amy Robsart. She returned to New York, and sailed for Europe on July 28th. "In eighteen days," as Allston Brown succinctly says, "she was dead." She died of acute indigestion, on August 15th, in Paris. A gloom fell on all who had ever seen or known of her; it seemed impossible that that radiant personality could have been darkened in death. We simply could not believe it. Ellen Terry, Modjeska and Mary Anderson, in different ways, carried on the tradition in the '80s, but Adelaide Neilson's place was never filled by any one of these.

On May 23rd, Ingersoll lectured, this time on The Gods. Booth's reopened, on May 25th, for an Irish play, The Croothawn, written for W. B. Cahill; T. F. Meagher was set down as manager. In this new piece Cahill was Pauge Pender, and Rose Lisle Maureen Lacy. The other actors included H. S. Duffield, J. F. Peters, John Matthews, George S. Robinson and Florence Robinson. It lasted three nights, the last night drawing $25 to the treasury. On June 2nd, says Allston Brown, a charity performance presented Booth as Iago, Frederic Robinson as Othello, Ellen Cummens (*sic*) as Desdemona, and Miss Atkinson (first appearance in America) as Emilia. I found no trace of this. On the 3rd, a testimonial to John T. Raymond, about to sail for Europe, offered A Regular Fix, with Sothern, Blakeley, W. L. Dennis, E. Dee Sothern (our E. H. Sothern), A. Manning, Louisa Eldridge, Ada Trimble, Alice Mansfield and Libbie Noxon; John McCullough and Alexander Fitzgerald then gave the dagger scene from The Wife; John Gilbert and Rose Coghlan acted the quarrel scene from The School for Scandal; Raymond appeared in the fifth act of Colonel Sellers; Harry Edwards recited A Showman's Story; Nat Goodwin, Eliza Weathersby, and C. W. Bowser showed a bit of Hobbies; and W. J. Florence, Raymond, W. C. Kelly, Kate Meek (an actress much in evidence in 1879–80) and Agnes Elliott ended the bill in The Returned Volunteer. Surely the audience had its money's worth!

FIFTH AVENUE THEATRE, 1879–1880

The reader and I can never overcome our astonishment at the long-continued vogue in America of that peculiarly Gallic manifestation, opéra-bouffe. Tostée, Irma, Aimée — how lasting the empire they had founded! Maurice Grau took the Fifth Avenue Theatre for a lengthy season of the reigning form, and began, on September 1st, with the well-known Aimée, in

Le Petit Duc, assisted by the usual Mlles. Beaudet and Raphael, and MM. Duplan and Jouard. Mlle. Delorme made her début as Lucrezia. As always, changes came thick and fast into the bills — Les Cloches de Corneville (September 2nd, with the star as Serpolette, Mlle. Gregoire as Germaine, Mezières as Gaspard, Jouard as Henri, Juteau as Grenicheux and Duplan as the Bailiff), La Petite Mariée (3rd, with Aimée as Graziella and Mlle. Delorme as Lucrezia), Mme. Favart (4th), La Marjolaine (5th), La Boulangère a des Écus (6th), La Jolie Parfumeuse (8th), Les Brigands (9th), Le Petit Duc (10th), Mme. Favart (11th), Les Cloches de Corneville (12th), Les Brigands (13th, matinée), and (13th, evening) Aimée's farewell benefit, with Le Petit Duc (Act II), La Grande Duchesse (Act II), and La Vie Parisienne (Act III). There, in a nutshell, is opéra-bouffe breathlessly packed tight for our edification.

And now, in 1879–80, comes flashing into our ken, another queen of the Offenbachian realm — Paola Marié, sister of Irma, once our favourite, and sister, also, of Galli-Marié, actually the original Carmen in Bizet's beloved opera. There is a trio of sisters, a sorority to be envied of all college maidens of these, our later years.

I have felt, during Aimée's last seasons here, that something of the bloom was off her voice and her performances; but Paola Marié was fresh and lovely, on September 15, 1879, when she made, at the Fifth Avenue, her first bow to an American audience. According to the Herald, next day, she was a "revelation." Pretty, piquant and Gallic, she won immediate success, and New York gladly attended, in that season, many of her charming performances. She came out as Clairette, "her original character," in the undying La Fille de Mme. Angot. Maurice Grau had engaged an unusually fine company, including the stately Mlle. Angèle, who appeared on the opening night as Mlle. Lange, and Victor Capoul, who had sung here previously with Christine Nilsson, and was now cast as Ange Pitou. This trio became the rage. Angèle was not acclaimed immediately, but appreciation of her art grew from character to character; indeed the Herald of the 16th found Capoul unsatisfactory till, in Act III, he introduced a romanza written especially for him "by the author." Old friends, otherwise, in the cast of La Fille de Mme. Angot were Mlle. Delorme (Amaranthe), Juteau (Pomponnet), Jouard (Larvandière), Duplan (Louchard) and Vilano (Trenitz). On September 24th, Paola Marié sang that former success of Irma, her sister, and indeed of Aimée — La Périchole, her chief assistants including Mmes. Gregoire, Raphael and Beaudet, and MM. Jouard, Duplan, Mezières, Vilano, Poyard, and Capoul. One has a feeling of assurance in reading these names of interpreters tried and true; in fact one can hardly imagine an opéra-bouffe season without Jouard, Juteau, Duplan and Mezières. La Périchole sang her songs on September 26th to 30th, inclusive, La Fille de Mme. Angot being the bill for October 1st. On October 2nd, 3rd and 4th, the reigning

BLANCHE ROOSEVELT

ROSINA BRANDRAM

JESSIE BOND

SIGNOR BROCOLINI

J. H. RYLEY

FRED CLIFTON

HUGH TALBOT

FURNEAUX COOK

ALICE BARNETT

MORA'S PHOTOGRAPHS FROM THE PIRATES OF PENZANCE

Paola Marié showed what she could do with Giroflé-Girofla, with Angèle as Pedro, Capoul as Marasquin, Mlle. Delorme (set down as "the original representative") as Aurore, Mlle. Beaudet as Paquita, Jouard as Mourzouk, and Duplan as Bolero. All three of these successful revivals were heard (Giroflé-Girofla most frequently) in the week of October 6th — 11th. On October 13th, Paola Marié sang Boulotte, in Barbe Bleue, with Capoul in the title-rôle; others in the cast were Mmes. Gregoire, Delorme and Armand, and MM. Jouard, Mezières, Duplan and Poyard. This offering ran a week. On the 20th, 21st and 22nd, Le Petit Faust enlisted Paola Marié ("first time") as Marguerite, Mlle. Beaudet as Lisette, Juteau as Faust, Vilano as Valentin, Mlle. Angèle as Mephisto, and Duplan as the Coachman. For her benefit, on October 23rd, Paola Marié presented herself as La Grande Duchesse, with Angèle as Wanda and Capoul as Fritz (first time). This was repeated on the 24th and 25th, and, on the 26th (Sunday), Paola Marié, Angèle, Capoul and others of the company appeared in a concert ("sacred," of course); Henrietta Markstein assisted.

La Grande Duchesse reigned on the evenings of October 27th, 28th and 29th, and, on the 30th and 31st, and November 1st (matinée and evening), Les Brigands held the passes, with Paola Marié as Fiorella, Angèle as Fragoletto, and Capoul as Falsacappa. All this, except for new interpreters, sounds very familiar; I wonder how many times most of the auditors in this season had heard each of those long-popular operas? The "first and only" concert having succeeded, a "second and last," fell on November 2nd, with the three French stars, Levy and Henrietta Markstein. The last week of the welcome French invasion was very busy: La Périchole (November 3rd); Giroflé-Girofla (4th and matinée, 8th); Barbe Bleue (5th); for the benefit of Angèle (6th), the second and third acts of La Fille de Mme. Angot and the third act of La Vie Parisienne (with Paola Marié as Gabrielle and Angèle as Pauline); La Grande Duchesse (7th); and Les Brigands (8th). I need hardly say that another "last" concert enlisted the favourite singers (also Miss Markstein) on November 9th. And then, temporarily, the triumphant company departed, perhaps the most successful exemplars of opéra-bouffe recently seen in a city that could not, apparently, tire of that form of entertainment.

On November 10th a curious and unnecessary performance occurred. Ion Perdicaris had painted a colossal picture, and about it he built a play, which he produced under title of The Picture:

Rudolph	Joseph Wheelock	Grand Duke	Charles Loveday
Mauritz	Master Harry Woodruff	Von Biesen	Lester Victor
Ludwig	Philip Beck	Jailer	Mr. Pardy
Franz	J. R. Anderson	Baroness	Mrs. Post
Carl	Mr. Robertson	Netta	Charlotte Adams
Count Witgenstein	Harry Colton	Elsa	Annie Mitchell
Heltzke	L. S. Outram	Caterina	Marie Prescott
Schwindler	Lawrence Denham	Irma	Nard Almayne

The "Picture" at basis of the play was The Triumph of Immortality, in which the hero, Isorg, "who occupies the centre of the canvas, turns from temptation, overcomes Materialism, typified by a lion, and is invited by Justice and Charity to accompany them upon their mystic barge to the farther shore, upon which stands the Temple of Immortality." One tries to imagine the play. Another offering of the same evening was La Sociétaire, an "absurdity," joint production of Perdicaris and Townsend Percy, acting manager of the theatre, under Maurice Grau, still set down as "lessee and manager." This piece was "to present in its proper light the present absurd style of claptrap theatrical advertising, and the theme is the much-talked of American engagement of Mlle. Sara Bernhardt." The cast of La Sociétaire included Nard Almayne as "Sara" Bernhardt, Mme. Sontag as Louise, her companion, Harry Colton as Mr. Sergeant-Major, "the great American manager, with a mania for scarf pins," Philip Beck as George Clairin, an artist, Cyril Bowen as Lord Fitz Maurice, D. Robertson as Compte de Luneville, J. R. Anderson as Prince Bellagio, and Lawrence Denham as Rotomago. There was evidently an attempt, in these pieces, to magnify Nard Almayne (a pretty name and a pretty woman), the playbill containing many applauding notices of her three previous appearances in America, all as Ophelia (New York, Boston and Providence). Alas! all failed, and on November 18th, came another failure, Self-Conquest, founded on Wilkie Collins's The Frozen Deep:

Lieutenant Wardour	Joseph Wheelock	Dr. Graham	Mr. Hartshorn
Captain Helding	L. S. Outram	Bateson	Mr. McNair
Lieutenant Crayford	Harry Colton	Mrs. Crayford	Ida Jeffreys
Lieutenant Aldersley	Philip Beck	Mary	Miss Richmond
Lieutenant Stevenson	J. R. Anderson	Clara Burnham	Nard Almayne
John Want	W. B. Cahill		

On November 24th, Dame Trot, or, the Wonderful Cat, began a single week, with James Maffitt and W. H. Bartholomew, and with specialists in the persons of Charles Dashway ("great athlete"), Williams and Sullivan ("musical comiques"), Carrie and Lizzie Farwell, Louise Fox, and Elizabeth Menzelli (sic).

GILBERT AND SULLIVAN; H.M.S. PINAFORE; THE PIRATES OF PENZANCE

All these last three weeks of failure had filled in time prior to the great night of December 1st, when Gilbert and Sullivan, triumphant masters of the new form of operetta, came out at the Fifth Avenue, in their own version of Pinafore, with a company specially brought from England, and with R. D'Oyly Carte, so long connected with their fame, as manager and director. It was indeed a noteworthy occasion, lending lustre to our stage. As we know, to our shame, these eminent men, author and composer of Pinafore, had received from this country no remuneration for their vastly popular work; lack of international copyright had brought about that deplorable result.   To forestall any such injustice in connection with their new opera, they had decided to bring it out first in America, thereby availing themselves of the advantage of copyright in this country.   To this fact we are indebted for the proud distinction of enjoying the initial performances of The Pirates of Penzance, which except for a performance or two, privately, in England, merely for copyright purposes, first faced the lights at the Fifth Avenue Theatre, on December 31, 1879.

Before that proud event, however, Pinafore, as I have said, was staged at the Fifth Avenue, under the supervision of Gilbert and Sullivan, and with Sullivan directing the orchestra.   I have heard it stated that Gilbert, in sailor garb, moved about among the chorus.   The cast, largely imported for the occasion, included J. H. Ryley, a richly humorous comedian, as Sir Joseph, Signor Brocolini (really John Clark, who assumed his Italian name from his native Brooklyn) as Captain Corcoran, Hugh Talbot as Ralph, Furneaux Cook as Dick Deadeye, Fred Clifton as Bill Bobstay, Cuthbert as Bob Becket, Blanche Roosevelt (an American girl) as Josephine, Alice Barnett as Buttercup, and Jessie Bond as Hebe.   J. H. Ryley made a great hit and remained in the country; we came to depend on him for the patter rôles of the later Gilbert and Sullivan operas.   Alice Barnett and Jessie Bond became features of London representations of the Savoy operas; Miss Bond, particularly, became a Savoyard *par excellence,* and has left a book of remembrances of the dear old days at the Savoy Theatre.   The Herald, of December 2nd, thought the performance of Pinafore, thus sanctioned by its librettist and composer, but little better than some of the best of the preceding season; but the stage-management brought new life into the show. After the opening, Alfred Cellier conducted.   Pinafore lasted for a month, and, on December 31st, came the first public performance on any stage of The Pirates of Penzance:

Richard	Signor Brocolini	Mabel	Blanche Roosevelt
Samuel	Furneaux Cook	Kate	Rosina Brandram
Frederic	Hugh Talbot	Edith	Jessie Bond
Major-General Stanley	J. H. Ryley	Isabel	Miss Barlow
Sergeant of Police	Fred Clifton	Ruth	Alice Barnett

Sullivan conducted and Gilbert directed the first performance; subsequently Alfred Cellier (well-known English composer) led the orchestra.   If Alice Barnett was a Savoyard, Rosina Brandram became one pre-eminently.   She later succeeded Alice Barnett in the comic contralto rôles, and will long be remembered as the original London representative of Katisha, the Duchess of Plaza Toro and susceptible Dame Carruthers.   The Herald, on the 2nd, declared The Pirates "a great improvement on 'Pinafore' . . . it is brighter, prettier and more artistic." The Sun described it as "sparkling with humorous dialogue, refined in suggestion, pure in style, admirable in dramatic situation and embellished with music at the same time musicianly and popular." And, asserted the World, "compared with 'Pinafore' it is infinitely superior in music, plot, language and humor, while musically there can be no comparison. . . . The text is exceedingly funny."

All of this I thoroughly believe, yet, in view of the last-season craze for Pinafore, The Pirates of Penzance did not achieve a triumph; it did not then have anything like the run one might have expected, nor has it ever equalled in popularity either Pinafore or The Mikado. I find this difficult to account for. A mildly interesting note in the Herald of January 11th lets us know that Jessie Bond had been ill and Miss Lennox had taken her place "very well, though she has never appeared in an opera before." And the Herald of February 21st informs us that Blanche Roosevelt, ill, had been succeeded as Mabel by Marie Conron, but would return on that evening. The Pirates plied their trade until March 6th, the last nights flurried by a little quarrel between Hugh Talbot and no less a person than W. S. Gilbert; naturally, Talbot retired, and, when he wished to return, was informed by D'Oyly Carte that the part of Frederic had been given to another. All this I learn from the Herald, and also that, just before the company left, peace had been declared, and Talbot would rejoin his colleagues in Boston. In Brooklyn, on March 8th, Pfau sang Frederic.

And back to the Fifth Avenue, on March 8th, came Maurice Grau's victorious French company, in La Fille de Mme. Angot. On the 9th, we had Mignon; on the 10th, Les Cloches de Corneville; on the 11th, La Belle Hélène; on the 12th, La Grande Duchesse; on the 13th, Giroflé-Girofla (matinée) and La Périchole (evening) — practically all the cornucopia, so to speak, in a nut-shell. Paola Marié, Angèle, Mlle. Leroux-Bouvard and Capoul were still the magnets. A concert, on Sunday, the 14th, was Gallic to the core. Mme. Favart began the second glad week, on the 15th, and came again on the 18th; for the benefit of A. Durand, treasurer, Le Pré aux Clercs presented, on the 16th, Capoul as Mergy, Bouvard as Comminge, Jouard as Girot, Mme. (or Mlle.) Leroux-Bouvard as Isabelle, Angèle as Marguerite, and Mme. Gregoire as Nicette; this was set down as the first performance of the work in our city. It was repeated on the 19th. On the 17th and 20th (evening) Paola Marié assumed the favourite rôle of Aimée's, in La Marjolaine; Mignon sang and dreamed on the afternoon of the 20th. Paola Marié appeared "for the first times," on March 22nd and 23rd, as Le Petit Duc, assisted by Mlle. Raphael, Mme. Gregoire, Jouard and Duplan. And a novelty, beginning on the 24th, finished the week — La Petite Muette, by Serpette; in this, Paola Marié was Mercedes, Angèle was Casilda, Capoul Don Rafael, Juteau Don Henrique, Duplan Don Jose, Mezières Camonillas, and Poyard Pedrillo. To the strains of this new thing, the company again bowed farewell, on the 27th — except for a customary concert, on Sunday, the 28th.   One observes that in certain operas Paola-Marié was sole star of eve.

Some theatres of New York changed managers as frequently as ladies changed the fashion of their hats.   Edward E. Rice and Jacob Nunnemacher now opened the Fifth Avenue, on March 29th, with the first appearance in New York for many years of James A. Herne, known later as a very fine dramatist and an excellent actor in his own plays.   He now presented Hearts of Oak, derived from Henry J. Leslie's English drama, The Mariner's Compass, but in itself a rewriting by David Belasco and Herne of a play, Chums, submitted to Herne, in its first shape, by Belasco, and reworked by both men into Hearts of Oak.   Professor A. H. Quinn, in his History of the American Drama, points out the improvements put into Hearts of Oak by Herne.   In this piece, Mrs. Herne (Katharine Corcoran) made her first appearance in New York, playing Chrystal, who sacrificed her love for Ruby Darrell, because she felt she must repay the love for her of her foster-father, the self-sacrificing Terry Dennison.   The cast was not strong in well-known names:

Terry Dennison	J. A. Herne	Chrystal	Katharine Corcoran
Ruby Darrell	H. Mainhall	Aunt Betsey	Henrietta B. Osborne
Uncle Davy	W. H. Crompton	Little Chrystal	Alice Hamilton
Mr. Ellingham	J. W. Dean	Tawdrey	Dollie Hamilton
Owen Garraway	H. M. Brown	Mr. Parker	Mr. Harvey
Foreman of the Mill	J. S. Andrews	Tom	J. Sherman
Clerk of the Mill	W. Lawrence	Sleuthe	T. Crossman
Will Barton	Lillie Hamilton	The Baby	Herself

Does the reader perceive that by the passing of the old stock system he is called on to become acquainted, in every new combination of players, with people whom, many of them, he never heard of before and may never hear of again?   Does he realise how much of friendly feeling goes, for him, out of the theatre under these new conditions? how much of delight in watching the progress of familiar actors and actresses?   Four stock companies remain, in 1880, but, by the end of the century, or a little beyond, the stock system will have broken down and "combinations" will rule the day.   Hearts of Oak lasted up to and including April 24th; but, on April 8th, Paola Marié and Grau's company gave a matinée of Le Pré aux Clercs, and, on Sunday evening, April 11th, the same popular lady, with Henrietta Markstein, Angèle, Capoul and Mlle. Leroux-Bouvard appeared in concert.   And, on April 15th was held a matinée benefit for Charles White, the aged minstrel, at which were to appear Frank Hart, "champion pedestrian of the world," Josh Hart, A. C. Moreland and John Wild.   J. B. Polk came in, as star, on the 27th, in a part (Christopher Columbus Gall) in George H. Jessup's A Gentleman from Nevada, that seems to suggest his George Washington

Phipps, in The Banker's Daughter. In this new play he had a supporting company which, like Herne's, makes one again regret the passing of the stock system:

Gall	J. B. Polk	Captain Vereker	Charles Harkinson
Alfred	W. F. Edwards	Rogers	George Mordaunt
John Castle	Harry Dalton	Conductor	Frank Johnson
Ah Tye	Harry Pratt	Lady Alice	Emma Pierce
Mr. Sellers	D. H. Chase	Countess	Minnie Monk
Hank Curtis	Frank Losee	Lady Edith	Emily Bigelow
Pete	Jerry Lant	Johnson	Alice Hastings

This piece ended on May 15th, and, on the 17th, The Pirates of Penzance again gaily sang their lays on the home-stage. Hugh Talbot and Blanche Roosevelt were replaced by Wallace McCreery and Sallie Reber, but otherwise the fine company was unchanged. The hundred and fiftieth night of the D'Oyly Carte company was listed for June 2nd, and the engagement closed on the 5th.

The last important event of the season was the production, on June 7th, for the first time in English, of the extremely popular operetta, The Sea Cadet, or, the Very Merry Mariner, a piece which had had an extraordinary success at the Thalia Theater, with Mathilde Cottrelly, and which, of course, had supplied Augustin Daly with the basis of his very successful The Royal Middy. The cast of almost two dozen not very noted performers I reluctantly put in, merely for completeness of record:

Fanchette	Blanche Chapman	Sebastino	Clotilda Operti
Donna Antonia	Marion Bernard	Giovanino	Emma Santley
Dom Lamberto	Eugene Clarke	Paolo	Florence Burton
Dom Januario	H. R. Archer	Enrico	Maud Waldemere
Dom Domingos	Matthew Holmes	Carlo	Gracie Sherwood
Captain Norberto	W. L. Van Dorn	Iago	Lottie Deretta
Donna Carlina	Fannie Howe	Claudio	Madeline Andorci
Donna Louisa	Clara Howe	Brabantio	Emily Lascelles
Marie	Henrietta Sennach	Julio	Fanny Miller
Mungo	A. Van Houten	Francesco	Edward Burton
Jacquino	W. H. Newborough	Antonio	Blanche Andorci
Roderigos	Clinton Stevens	Cassio	Louisa Maurel
Diego	Rose Regenti		

Am I wrong in printing those names, many of which we shall probably never meet again? I suppose it depends on how the reader feels about such matters; some may wish to know all. The Sea Cadet lasted here till June 12th. On July 19th, Minnie Cummings appeared in a play written by herself — Suspected:

Agnes Vanderpool	Miss Cummings	Cynthia	Jennie Yeamans
Henry Boutwell	Leslie Edmonds	Alice Vanderpool	Connie Thompson
Jerome Yorke	J. H. Brown	Mrs. Templeton	Adelaide Thornton
Commodore Nelson	Sid Hicks	Mrs. Boutwell	Henrietta Irving

Others were L. H. Haywood, G. H. Griffiths, Master Harry Woodruff, Donald Robertson, Genevieve Mills, Dora St. Clair, Bessie Byrne, and Lottie Adams.   The piece and the "star" failed; the Herald next day asserted that Jennie Yeamans as a negro girl and Connie Thompson as the maniac wife made the hits of the evening, in a play that needed much revision.   Suspected dragged on for a few nights.   Minnie Cummings promised to speak, on July 28th, on "the recent attempt to crush her."   And she was to act Leah, for her benefit, on the 30th.   Alas! before that speech and that benefit the theatre closed tight, and Miss Cummings for the present faded away.

HAVERLY'S LYCEUM THEATRE, 1879–1880

A brief season, beginning on August 18, 1879, introduced Adele Belgarde, an actress destined to a slight success in the American theatre.   She began as Rosalind, in As You Like It, which Ada Cavendish had played but a few weeks earlier at Wallack's.   Miss Belgarde engaged a fairly good company:

Rosalind	Adele Belgarde	Sylvius	George Reed
Orlando	Gustavus Levick	Amiens	Tom Macpherson
Jaques	W. E. Sheridan	Corin	John Matthews
Touchstone	Ben Maginley	Charles	T. H. Davids
Banished Duke	J. R. Grismer	William	C. W. Allison
Adam	T. E. Morris	Celia	Helen Tracy
Duke Frederick	J. Swinburne	Audrey	Mrs. Emma Skerrett
Jaques du Bois	E. Tannehill	Phebe	Mamie Sheridan
Le Beau	Clarence Merighi		

After the unknown names in casts just recorded for the Fifth Avenue Theatre, it is a pleasure to come on the familiar people with Miss Belgarde. Emma Skerrett, we remember, first appeared in New York at the old Park Theatre, in 1844!

On August 20th and 21st, Miss Belgarde essayed Julia, in The Hunchback, and on the 22nd, and at the matinée on the 23rd, she was Parthenia. After this taste of the "legitimate," Haverly's Theatre brought out, on August 25th, The Magic Slipper, an operatic extravaganza, presented by Samuel Colville's company:

Cinderella de Boulevard	Eme Roseau	Miss Harebell	Annie Deacon
Prince Popetti	Alice Hastings	Miss Honeydew	Alice Wright
Hightoni	Ella Chapman	Daffydowndilla	Susie Winner
Penotype	Ada Lee	Primrosa	Bessie Temple
Swagger	Carrie McHenry	Violetta	Elsie Dean
Baron de Boulevard	Ed Chapman	Daisyana	Louisa Loring
Seraph	Roland Reed	Cloverina	Mary Winner
Clorinda	R. E. Graham	Sweetcornia	Laura Adams
Thisbe	Fannie Wright	Wheatina	Nita Gerald
Petitoe	A. W. Maflin	Heartseasa	Annie Winner
Elfina the First	Rose Leighton	Roseleafa	Theresa Lamborn

Again I apologise for burdening the page with long-forgotten names.   The Magic Slipper was alleged to be decked out with "charming scenery," "excellent acting and singing," "exquisite fun and delicious foolery." It danced a merry round of nights, under the musical direction of Jesse Williams, until September 15th, when the Criterion Comedy Company, managed by F. F. Mackay (not recently seen in New York) and J. Gosche, came in with a new play entitled Our Daughters:

Jacob Van Dale	F. F. Mackay	Rose	Louise Sylvester
William Knabe	DeWolf Hopper	Emily	Emma Fellman
Alfred Herman	T. F. Egbert	Fanny	Helen Gardner
Edward Galen	W. A. Whitecar	Ann Eliza	Mary Davenport
Peter Kline	J. Ogden	Margaret Kline	Mattie Earle
Philip Hartman	A. H. Canby	Katrina	Virginia Newbold

Well, if Emma Skerrett belonged to a remote past, De Wolf Hopper and Mattie Earle are unquestionably of the '80s — the new generation knocking at the door. Our Daughters lasted three weeks, one week for each daughter (pardon the frivolity!), and gave way, on October 6th, to Nat C. Goodwin's Froliques, in Hobbies, the cast including Eliza and Jennie Weathersby and Venie Clancy; Goodwin gave imitations of Booth, Sothern, Barrett, Jefferson, Raymond, Stuart Robson, Fechter and Frank Mayo. In addition, we had the farce, Romance under Difficulties. The group, in their frivolity, or "farrago," carried through for four weeks, and yielded the stage, on November 3rd, to a similar organisation — The Tourists in a Pullman Palace Car, with W. A. Mestayer (always funny) as T. Henry Slum, James Barton as Sir Henry, Augustus Bruno as the Conductor, Will H. Bray as the Porter, J. N. Long as the French Valet, Ethel Lynton as Isabella, Rosa Cooke as Miss Baby, Jennie Reiffarth as Pamela and May Livingston as Marie. This was a very popular thing, and, though its present run was but for a brief two weeks, it came into New York frequently thereafter. Such combinations of song, vaudeville, thin plot and constant clowning grew constantly during the '80s, and developed a number of richly unctuous comedians — Goodwin, Mestayer, Dixey, Roland Reed, Louis Harrison, and many others.

The visits of Goodwin and Mestayer make us wonder at the next guest at Haverly's Lyceum (November 17th) — nothing less antiquated than The Octoroon, with J. Newton Gotthold as Salem Scudder, Frank Losee as the villainous McClosky, L. R. Stockwell as Uncle Pete, H. S. Duffield as Wah-no-tee, Madge Butler as Paul, Charles Mason as George Peyton, J. E. Kirkwood as Sunnyside, Rena Maeder as Dora, Mrs. Sarah Baker as Mrs. Peyton and Florence Elmore as the doomed Zoe, certainly a weak aggregation compared with earlier casts, especially the original, with Boucicault, Agnes Robertson and Jefferson.

The ever-productive Bartley Campbell came forward, on December 1st, with another success (previously seen at Haverly's Brooklyn Theatre and elsewhere). This piece, The Galley Slave, had a fine cast:

G. W. STODDART
AS ELDER SNIFFLES

NEIL BURGESS
AS WIDOW BEDOTT

W. A. MESTAYER
(THE TOURISTS)

MAUDE GRANGER
(1879-1880)

FRANK EVANS

EMILY RIGL
IN THE GALLEY SLAVE

DE WOLF HOPPER

ADELE BELGARDE

GUSTAVUS LEVICK

Cicely Blaine............Maude Granger	Baron le Bois............J. J. Sullivan
Francesca Brabant..........Emily Rigl	Franklin Pitts............T. H. Burns
Psyche Gay............Estelle Mortimer	Oliphant............C. A. McManus
Mrs. Phebe Gay............Rose Graham	Napier............G. A. Henderson
Nichette............Charlotte Neville	Carot............Charles Webster
Dolores............Little Georgie	Philippe............H. W. Montgomery
Sidney Norcott............Frank Evans	Sentinel............L. Denny

According to the Herald, Emily Rigl as the sadly distressed Italian girl made the hit of the play; Miss Granger hardly had a chance to be more than pretty and pleasing and beautifully dressed. The Galley Slave ran for five weeks, and retired merely because of previous arrangements at Haverly's; the play was transferred to Niblo's, with Signora Majeroni in the rôle so skilfully treated by Miss Rigl. Signora Majeroni, in fact, first played the part, on December 22nd, at Haverly's.

The Tourists in a Pullman Palace Car now came back (January 5, 1880), and revelled in a comforting run of six weeks. On January 29th, a benefit for the family of Henry C. Mount, a fireman killed at the fire of the Eighth Avenue car stables, enlisted the actors involved in acts from The Galley Slave, The Tourists and Fairfax (then current at the Park Theatre); a benefit for that same charity occurred on the same afternoon at the Grand Opera House. The Tourists moved out on February 7th; on the 9th, John A. Stevens, with Lottie Church, entered, for two weeks, in Unknown. The cast included W. H. Bailey as Jack Salt, A. H. Stuart as Albert Stormking, Ralph Delmore as Dr. Richard Brinckton, George Sprague as Arnold Tyson, George F. Ketchum as Jimmy, Lottie Church as Bessie, and Angie Griffiths as Louise. On the 23rd, Salsbury's Troubadours came in, in The Brook, or, a Jolly Day at the Picnic, with Nate Salsbury as Tracy Thornton, John Gourlay as Festus, John Webster as Percy, Helen Dingeon as Blanche, and Nellie McHenry as Rose. Cross Purposes preceded this trifle in the bills. The Brook flowed very pleasantly in several theatres at that time, and now lasted at Haverly's till March 13th. In the spring it was at Daly's. On March 7th, a Sunday concert brought in Gilmore's Band, Isabel Stone, Lanzer, Reynolds, and, of course, a performance of the mooted Columbia.

And now, on March 15th, came another typical thing of the '80s, a long-enduring joy to rural communities and not unpleasing to larger centres. This was Locke's (Petroleum V. Nasby's) dramatic version of the famous Widow Bedott Papers (previously seen at Haverly's Brooklyn Theatre), which was acted under the name of Widow Bedott:

Widow Bedott............Neil Burgess	Mr. Harriman............W. H. Meeker
Elder Sniffles............George W. Stoddart	Melissa Bedott............Mrs. G. W. Stoddart
Tim Crane............Harry Rich	Dotty Sniffles............May Taylor
Fred Harriman............Charles S. Dickson	Widow Jenkins............Nellie Peck
Tom Follet............E. D. Tannehill	Mrs. Harriman............Mrs. Mary Hill

This really was good fun, with nothing in it of the complexes and psycho-analytic states of plays of fifty years later. Neil Burgess, we remember, had served in "Vaudeville" as the impersonator of American spinsters, and here, in Widow Bedott, he found the very vehicle to carry him until he arrived at his later success in Vim and The County Fair. I still see him as Widow Bedott in the kitchen, making pies, straightening out the affairs of the neighbourhood, and personifying, in spite of his sex, the attributes of a managing woman. He was not the least bit effeminate, not at all like the usual female impersonator of minstrelsy or of variety, and yet he was Widow Bedott to the life, and with little suggestion of burlesque. The play ran now for seven weeks. The '80s loved the rural drama — Joshua Whitcomb, Uncle Dan'l (of Jarvis Section), Widow Bedott; in later years of the decade or perhaps beyond, The Old Homestead, The County Fair, Shore Acres. We were simple-minded and happy. George W. Stoddart we remember in the '60s as brother of J. H. Stoddart; let us now hail him as father-in-law of Neil Burgess.

Widow Bedott abdicated on May 1st, proud and happy, I am sure, at her metropolitan success. On May 3rd, entered, on wings of magic, Herrmann, famed prestidigitateur, announcing as part of his show the Onofri Brothers (Achille, Charles, Fortune and Oreste) in grotesque dances, as well as Val Vose, ventriloquist, and the Lorellas. Unfortunately, the Onofris did not arrive in time for the opening (their steamer getting in very late); they finally appeared on the 5th. Specialties of Herrmann advertised on May 17th were the Arabian Dream, or, Suspension in Mid-Air of Mlle. Addie, and Le Cabinet du Diable. His last *séance* fell on the evening of June 2nd; on the 3rd, the Jolly Mariners, so-called, with Angie Schott, appeared in Trifles. They closed on the 12th. I again call attention to the new type of show then developing — Salsbury's Troubadours in The Brook, the Goodwin and Weathersby Froliques in Hobbies, the Tourists in a Pullman Palace Car, The Jolly Mariners, in Trifles; how likes the reader the frivolity of such offerings?

On June 14th came to Haverly's (straight from Haverly's in Brooklyn, where it had been the week before) another such band, Mitchell's Pleasure Party, in William Gill's piece, Our Goblins, or, Fun on the Rhine; in this Gill played Benjamin Franklin Cobb (of Chicago), Francis Wilson, late of the minstrel team of Mackin and Wilson, and soon to be the great Cadeaux of Erminie, played Alfred Comstock Silvermine (of Leadville), Augustus J. Bruno was Octavius Longfellow Warbler (of Boston), Elinor Deering was Mrs. Cobb, and Amy Gordon was Tillie St. Aubyn. This trifle had only a four-weeks run, but it amused; the Herald of June 15th asserts that "Mr. Wilson's Baron was simply immense." In his Life of Himself Francis Wilson states that because of this hit, his salary was raised to one hundred dollars a week — a great remuneration this would have seemed to John Drew and Ada Rehan, who started this same season at Daly's on so miserable a pittance.

[42]

A company headed by Elma Delaro was to open at Haverly's on July 12th, in The "Bells" of Normandy; alas! circumstances over which neither Mr. Haverly nor the artists had control forced abandonment of the scheme. On the 26th, the Stewarts, a family from Australia, appeared in Rainbow-Revels, one of those curious mixtures of a type then raging, on the heels, so to speak, of our last craze, Pinafore. In this newest specimen of the protean form, Docy, Maggie and Nellie Stewart, and Richard Stewart, father of the three girls, assumed various characters, and kept Haverly's open for two weeks of a very hot summer. The doors closed, with apparent reluctance, on August 7th, thereby ending the season of 1879-80; and they gladly re-opened two nights later, for the season of 1880-81.

PARK THEATRE, 1879-1880

On August 25, 1879, Marion Darcy, a new actress, and known thereafter, if known at all, as Marie Acosta, rented the Park Theatre for one week and presented herself in a play called The Living Statue:

Naomi Keller	Marion Darcy	Mr. Victor	W. G. Regnier
Count Paul	Joseph Wheelock	Erminie	Stella Congdon
Lucian David	Harry Dalton	Prassed	Meroe Charles
Marquis Tourbulu	T. J. Hind	Susanne	Eva Garrick
Pelagio Adriani	B. T. Ringgold	Eugenie	Josie Wilmere
Father Anselmo	L. F. Rand	Lucy	Eleanor Reed
Mr. Silvester	W. A. Whitecar		

Miss Darcy did not win everlasting renown, but we can at least thank her for giving us a company most of whom we know; this is a blessed relief after some of the casts of strangers recently recorded at the Fifth Avenue. And whoever expected to see again the veteran T. J. Hind, relic of a former age?

SOTHERN; EMMET; BARTLEY CAMPBELL

E. A. Sothern (the elder Sothern) returned, on September 8th, and in his company was his son, Edward H. Sothern, the "younger Sothern" of our later times. The star came out in Dundreary's Brother Sam, his support including several fresh importations of English players, the exquisitely comic W. Blakeley being the best:

Hon. Sam Slingsby	E. A. Sothern	Man Servant	H. Faulkner
Mr. Trimbush	Percy Compton	Telegraph Boy	The Genuine Article
Jonathan Rumbellow	W. Blakeley	Alice	Julia Stewart
Peters	George Jones	Mrs. Trimbush	Ida Lewis
Cab Driver	A. Manning	Marie	Ada Whitman

The representative of the Cab Driver in the production was Edward H. Sothern, who tells, in his The Melancholy Tale of "Me," of his stage-fright, his forgetting the one and only line of his part, and his spoiling his father's scene. Perhaps memory heightened the calamity in the younger actor's mind. After his début with his father, young Sothern played for a time at the Boston Museum. We shall soon be eagerly watching his progress.

On September 22nd, the older Sothern reverted to The Crushed Tragedian, his support including Blakeley (Frank Bristowe), W. Bragginton (Sir Michael), R. S. Hill (Ernest), Ed Lamb (Captain Rackett), Percy Compton (Mandeville), Harry Harwood (long thereafter a favourite — Gadsby), Julia Stewart (Florence), Ida Lewis (Mrs. Mountcashel), Laura Le Claire (Mrs. Gulpin) and Lillie Boole (Maid). Two weeks of this but paved the way for the inevitable — Our American Cousin, on October 6th, with Ed Lamb as Asa Trenchard, Harry Harwood as Sir Edward, Bragginton as Abel Murcot, Blakeley as Binney, Charles Harkinson as Lieutenant Vernon, W. H. Young as Coyle, Ida Lewis as Florence, Julia Stewart as Mary, Laura Le Claire as Mrs. Mountchessington, Elsie Moore as Georgina, and Blanche Vaughan as Augusta. Our American Cousin passed out of the bills on October 18th. And equally in demand was Sothern's incomparable David Garrick, seen on October 20th, with Blakeley as Ingot, Ed Lamb as Chivvy, Bragginton as Smith, Harwood as Brown, Percy Compton as Jones, Laura Le Claire as Mrs. Smith, Julia Stewart as Ada, and Ida Lewis as Araminta Brown; with this, Sothern also acted Hugh de Brass, in A Regular Fix, except for his benefit, on the 31st, when he combined Sam and Dundreary Married and Settled. Those who think of Sothern only as Lord Dundreary, should examine the varied bills of this, his last important engagement in New York; the engagement closed on November 1st.

He was succeeded, on November 3rd, by that entertainer of charm and great personality, Joseph K. Emmet, who came in with his usual popular impersonation, in Fritz in Ireland, or, the Bellringer of the Rhine, and the Love of the Shamrock:

Fritz Schultz	J. K. Emmet	Goldfinger	J. H. Ryan
Lawyer Priggins	John Mackay	Master Herbert }	
Baron Hertford	J. H. Rennie	Lena Schultz }	Little Annie Rennie
Captain O'Doud	W. Carleton	Louisa Herbert	Emily Baker
Splodger	J. H. Rennie	Lady Amelia	Lenore Bigelow
Lord Seaton	W. Christie Miller	Mme. Schultz	Mrs. Louisa Watson
Charles Seaton	Oliver Doud	Judy	Tillie McHenry
Patrick Blackeye	J. O. Burk		

The harmless sentiment of this piece and Emmet's sweet singing of his songs carried Fritz for eight weeks, always a comforting run for my busy pen. He departed on December 27th, leaving in fond hearts memories of his new songs — The Bells Are Ringing, The Swell, the Cuckoo Song, Love of the Shamrock, Lullaby, etc.

On December 29th, Bartley Campbell, in heyday of his success, brought out one of his best plays — Fairfax, or, Life in the Sunny South, with a very

HENRY E. DIXEY

J. E. McDONOUGH

LEONORA BRAHAM

E. A. SOTHERN
(THE CRUSHED TRAGEDIAN)

J. K. EMMET
(FRITZ'S LULLABY)

LOTTA
(THE LITTLE DETECTIVE)

D. E. BANDMANN

ANNIE PIXLEY
AS M'LISS

MRS. BANDMANN

fine cast (the Park still had a stock company, though it often was away from home):

Edwin Fairfax	J. E. Whiting	Sheriff	F. E. Bond
Dr. Guy Gaylord	Frederic Robinson	Mrs. Marigold	Agnes Booth
James Marigold	Louis F. Barrett	Diana Dorsie	Sydney Cowell
Webster Winne	W. J. Ferguson	Mrs. Dorsie	Mrs. G. H. Gilbert
Uncle Ben	W. F. Owen	Tibbetts	Marie Chester
Willie Wagstaff	Alfred Selwyn	Virgie	Little Effie Barrett
Moses	W. Cullington		

In this play Agnes Booth made a hit as the much wronged woman, who tried to live down the past with a brutal husband, only to find herself, when happily married to another, in danger of being tried for the murder of her first wretched mate; but it was the "sunny south" and threatening clouds passed away.

I called Fairfax a success, yet it lived here only till January 31st, when was staged W. S. Gilbert's play, The Wedding March, founded on Labiche's well-known farce, Un Chapeau de Paille d'Italie, involving, as the reader knows, the distresses of a bridegroom on his wedding day; he thinks it necessary to replace a lady's panama hat, which his horse has destroyed, and he cannot find a new hat, hunt as he may. The cast included James Lewis (his first appearance this season) as Poppytop, a market gardener; W. F. Burroughs as Woodpecker Tapping, the bridegroom; W. F. Owen as Uncle Bopoddy; W. J. Ferguson as the emotional Duke of Turniptopshire; James Dunn as Major-General Bunthunder, a knight of the Bath; J. H. Hazelton as Captain Bapp, William Cullington as Cripps, a milliner's book-keeper; Land as Wilkinson, a policeman; Alfred Selwyn as Cousin Foodle; Rachel Sanger (her first appearance in New York) as the Marchioness of Market Harborough, an emotional noblewoman; Marie Chester as Anna Maria Poppytop, the bride; Marion Booth as Sophie Crackthorpe, a milliner; Agnes Elliott as Leonora Bunthunder; Miss A. Mowbray as Lady Popton; and Florence Roberts as Patty. The play, it was said, was produced under the direct supervision of Gilbert himself, then here for The Pirates of Penzance. One could secure seats for this theatre by the aid of Bell's telephone; think of it! The Wedding March was preceded, appropriately enough as to titles, by Sweethearts, in which W. F. Burroughs and Rachel Sanger played the leading rôles, with Cullington as Wilcox, and Florence Roberts as Ruth. The bill lasted but two weeks, and was followed, on February 16th, by another play with a title very suitable to that of the two pieces just mentioned — Engaged, with Lewis, Whiting, Owen, Agnes Booth, Mrs. Gilbert, Marie Chester, Sydney Cowell and the original cast, except Minnie Palmer and Grattan Riggs, whose places were now occupied by Agnes Elliott and W. J. Ferguson.

[45]

On February 24th came H. J. Byron's comedy, "Chawles," or, a Fool and His Money, which eked out nearly four weeks, with James Lewis as "Chawles" Liquorpound, W. J. Ferguson as Brabazon Vandaleur, J. G. Saville as Percival Ransome, W. F. Owen as Mr. Pentland, W. Cullington as Milligan, Rachel Sanger as Kate Vandeleur, Ada Gilman as Mary Draper, Marie Chester as Jane, and Lily George as Mrs. Ramsay — a compact and interesting cast. Champagne and Oysters was revived on March 19th, for eight nights and two matinées. I am not sure that the Park was drawing much money to its coffers by its offerings, since Fairfax.

LOTTA; DENMAN THOMPSON

Lotta, buoyant, vivacious, irresistible, came to the Park on March 29th, in The Little Detective, a piece with no pretence to serious consideration, but offering the star a great chance for protean changes and for indulgence in the tricks and whimsies that — let the critics carp as they might — so delighted the loyal subjects of the little lady. In this play, it was her duty to assume various disguises, track the villain to his lair and bring down a happy curtain. She played Florence Langton, disguised, successively, as Grizzle Guttridge, as Mrs. Gamage, as Harry Racket, as Barney O'Brien and Gaunze-a-sh-Joseph. Her supporting cast included Julia Hanchett (formerly with Ada Cavendish) as Stella, Lulu Jordan as Una, Mrs. George Boniface as Mme. Ritzdorf, Ed Marble as Ludovic Stuyvesant, Clement Bainbridge as Barry Mallison (the robber), P. A. Anderson as Roderick Tracy, W. H. Wallis as Sir Gervais Langton, Fred Percy as Phoebus Rockaway, H. B. Bradley as Stephen Radcliffe, C. W. Parker as Captain Gustave, P. Cooke and G. White as Dozer and Nab, watchmen, another interesting cast. On April 3rd and 10th, Lotta acted Musette, at the matinées. On the 12th, she began a week of Zip; her last week provided Musette throughout, except that, for her benefit, on the 23rd, she reverted to Zip, and for the matinée, on the 24th, to The Little Detective. As Musette, one of her very best parts, she said goodbye, on April 24th. Lotta was not a great actress; she was simply, as I have so often said, one of the funniest and most likeable entertainers of her time. Few could resist her charms (or shall I say?) her alluring ways. Lotta was Lotta; that satisfied her admirers, and later generations cannot but agree.

Something of the same sort may be said of Denman Thompson, who succeeded her at the Park, on April 26th, except that, of course, within the narrow, self-imposed limits of his art, he was a finished actor. He came back, now, in that universally popular rural drama, Joshua Whitcomb, with Julia Wilson, of course, as Tot, and with fine new scenery to embellish the simple yarn. Perhaps, in view of these dignified surroundings, I had better print the cast:

[46]

Joshua Whitcomb	Denman Thompson	Sam Foster	D. Nourse
Roundy	Ignacio Martinetti	Tot	Julia Wilson
John Martin	E. O. Jepson	Nellie Primrose	Isabelle Coe
Frederick Dolby	Walter Gale	Susan Martin	Virginia Bray
Cy Prime	George Beane	Mrs. Johnson	Edna Weedon
Bill Johnson	R. Benson	Aunt Matilda	Mrs. D. Nourse
Reuben Whitcomb	Charles Peters	Amantha	Blanche Vaughan
Mr. Burroughs	G. Adams	Aunt Martha	Miss E. Rogers

How many striking personalities of the '80s this season had brought forward, mostly in small parts! Well, here is Walter Gale, the happy tramp of The Old Homestead, and here also is Isabelle Coe, leading lady of a few years later. It becomes exciting. Joshua Whitcomb remained at the Park through June 12th, and with Thompson's departure the season closed. Interesting from the engagements of Sothern, Lotta and Thompson, and from the performance by Agnes Booth and the regular company in Fairfax, it was not, on the whole, a memorable year or one for which the historical muse can sing an ode or dance a stately measure.

Standard Theatre, 1879–1880

The new season at the Standard Theatre (William Henderson still manager) began on September 10, 1879, with Mr. and Mrs. Daniel E. Bandmann (Millicent Palmer) in an elaborate revival of his favourite play, Narcisse. In this, of course, Bandmann had the title-rôle and Mrs. Bandmann was Doris Quinault. Gerald Eyre (then new to us) was Choiseul, Henry Aveling Du Barri, Lawrence Denham De Grammont, E. S. Gofton Baron de Hohlbach, Percy Lyndal (also new to us, but to become familiar in years to follow) Silhouette, and Bella Murdoch Mme. Pompadour. Among numerous supporters in minor rôles were L. S. Outram, Harry Barfoot, Marguerite Bennison (or Benoison), Miss A. Myrtelle (or Myrtell), &c. In the same bill was a short piece by Bandmann, The Radical Cure, acted by E. S. Gofton, Philip Beck, Denham and Miss Benoison.

By natural or artificial stimulus Narcisse was kept alive for an astonishing number of nights; it gave way, however, on September 29th, to Hamlet, with the Bandmanns as Hamlet and Ophelia, Gerald Eyre as Laertes, Wilmot Eyre as Rosencrantz, Percy Lyndal as Horatio, Mr. Ionides as the Ghost, Henry Aveling as Claudius, Barfoot and Denham as the Gravediggers and Elinor Aicken as the Queen. Hamlet also lasted longer (considering these interpreters) than might have been expected; it departed, on October 8th, for The Merchant of Venice (Shylock having ever been Bandmann's most acceptable Shakespearian rôle), but came back on the 9th and again, on the 11th, yielded the stage to Narcisse. On October 17th, Mrs. Bandmann made her last appearance as Ophelia, for Saturday, the 18th, she had "graciously resigned" the part, "for that occasion," to Nard Almayne, who thus made

[47]

that single New York appearance as Ophelia, about which we heard, when she filled her regular engagement at the Fifth Avenue. The matinée offering on the 18th, was The Lady of Lyons.

Well, I for one am surprised that Bandmann could have kept going so long in 1879; he was both old-fashioned and foreign. H. M. S. Pinafore sailed gaily into the Standard, its first New York haven, on October 20th, with Thomas Whiffen (by permission of Steele MacKaye), Wallace Macreery (Captain Corcoran), Alonzo Hatch (Ralph), Miss Mills and Vernona Jarbeau in familiar rôles; F. A. Parmental was Dick Deadeye (*vice* Davidge, now at Daly's), Alfred Holland was Bill Bobstay, and Estelle Mortimer Buttercup. Trial by Jury, as part of the bill, enlisted Vernona Jarbeau, W. A. Paul, Wallace Macreery (now *sic*) and Holland (so, at least, says the Herald advertisement). In late October W. A. Paul had Whiffen's rôle of Sir Joseph, in Pinafore. The good ship Pinafore remained in Standard harbourage until November 15th, when it scored its two hundred and twelfth performance there. It will be seen that it sailed away just about two weeks before Gilbert and Sullivan's Pinafore entered the Fifth Avenue Theatre.

Fatinitza, revived on November 17th, presented Vernona Jarbeau in the title-rôle, with Frederika Rokohl as Lydia, A. Van Houten as Izzet Pacha, George S. Weeks as Julian, A. Franosch as Count Timofey, L. N. Guyon as Wasili, Clinton Stevens as Osip, and with a host of minor celebrities (?) in other rôles; among them I am pleased to note as Beseika, the name of May Sylvie, for so many years a "utility" at Daly's. The last of Fatinitza came on December 10th; the theatre closed on the 11th and 12th, for rehearsals of Princess Toto (by W. S. Gilbert — everything was Gilbert in those days — and Frederic Clay). This was produced on December 13th, Leonora Braham making her American début:

Princess Toto	Leonora Braham	Prince Doro	H. C. Campbell
Jelly	Vernona Jarbeau	Prince Caramel	O. W. Wren
Follette	Miss Lawrence	Count Floss	Alfred Holland
Divine	Miss Shandley	Baron Jacquier	H. R. Humphries
King Portico	H. W. Montgomery	Prisoner	J. A. Oliver
Jamilek	W. A. Paul	Zapeter	W. Hamilton

Neither Fatinitza nor Princess Toto realised the hopes of the Standard. Princess Toto bowed her way out, on January 3rd, and, on the 5th, E. E. Rice's Evangeline and the dancing heifer once more held sway. Vernona Jarbeau, become a fixture at the Standard, was Evangeline, Louise Searle was Gabriel, the fat and funny George K. Fortescue was still Catherine, Rose Dana was Eulalie, Edwin S. Tarr Basil, Richard Golden (once the hind legs of the heifer) was now Le Blanc, Harry Hunter still the Lone Fisherman, and Charles Rosene (or Rosine) Captain Dietrich.

The old joy remained with us for two weeks, and, on January 19th, Richmond and von Boyle, graduates from "Variety," came in, in Our Candidate;

the leading parts fell to Harry G. Richmond, Ackland (or Acland) von Boyle, Alfred McDowell, I. N. Drew, Bob Harrison, Florence Stover and Mrs. von Boyle — an aggregation that leaves me cold and dark. New York stood the strain for two weeks, and relaxed, on February 2nd, with Rice's Surprise Party, in the familiar Horrors; the company included Alice Atherton, Marion Singer, Lina Merville, Marion Elmore, Florence Baker, Pauline Hall, Nellie Beaumont, Emma Burgess, Jean Delmar, Jennie and Jessie Calef, Lizzie Dana, Edith Smith, Rose Wilson, Ida Glover, Carrie Perkins, Emma Duchateau, Carrie Vinal, Willie Edouin, Louis Harrison, Henry E. Dixey, George W. Howard, Donald Harold, D. P. Steele, Edward Morse, W. Josephs, E. H. Aiken, R. H. Nicholas and J. P. Cooke — many of them top-notch entertainers in the years immediately following. I can only repeat that it is great fun to come upon the modest beginnings of people like Pauline Hall, Louis Harrison, Alice Atherton and Henry E. Dixey. Horrors lasted for three weeks, and gave place, on February 21st, to Hiawatha:

Hiawatha	Alice Atherton	Honey Dew	Pauline Hall
William Penn Brown	Willie Edouin	Hazel Dell	Nellie Beaumont
Remus Brown	Louis Harrison	Afraid-of-His-Whisky	D. P. Steele
Romulus Smith	H. E. Dixey	Scar-Face William	E. H. Aiken
Mr. Lo	George W. Howard	Minnehaha	Marion Singer
Yenadizzi	Lina Merville	Mrs. Lo	Marion Elmore
Telegraph Boy	Jennie Calef	Sally Bohee	Florence Baker

If Evangeline, why not Hiawatha? both by Longfellow and both by Rice. Well, the thing cannot be done twice over; Evangeline succeeded, and Hiawatha failed — failed, that is, by standards of Evangeline. It ran, now, for two weeks, and gave way, on March 8th, to the popular Robinson Crusoe, with Lina Merville (replacing Alice Atherton, ill) and Willie Edouin in the leading rôles; I wonder if Lydia Thompson, clever, handsome and shapely (see her photographs by Mora, as Crusoe) was missed? But there was Edouin still as Friday. The last week of the Surprise Party gave us Robinson Crusoe (March 15th and 16th, and matinée, 17th); Hiawatha (17th and 18th), and Horrors (19th and 20th). On Sundays, March 21st and 28th, "Professor" H. Cooke, and Miss Selome Crawford, rather conspicuous at this time, attempted to expose Spiritualism; May Leyton assisted on the 28th.

And now we are ready to welcome Annie Pixley, long by legal procedure kept from our eager eyes, in her famous rôle of M'liss. Freed from such entanglements, she came, on March 22nd, as the living personification (except in the matter of extreme youth) of Bret Harte's heroine:

M'liss	Annie Pixley	Judge Beeswinger	Ben G. Rogers
Yuba Bill	J. E. McDonough	Templeton Fake	Murry Woods
Juan Walters	Robert Fulford	Jude Thompson	Thomas Coleman
George Smith	W. T. Johnson	Harry Ringwalt	Rob Hays
John Gray	Frank Kilday	Clytie	Miss Marion
Sam Carson	Harry Murphy	Mrs. Smith	Alice Grey

[49]

According to Allston Brown, "Miss Marion" was the daughter of J. E. McDonough; but Annie Pixley was a daughter of success, and kept M'liss on the stage for years. She remained at the Standard for five weeks; during the first nights in April, I am interested to note that she, Lotta and Maggie Mitchell, actresses in a way of the same type, representatives of very young girls, were playing in New York at the same time — a great opportunity for analytical students of acting!

On April 26th, the Weathersby-Goodwin Froliques returned in Hobbies, finishing the regular season of the Standard on May 22nd. In May Salsbury's Troubadours, we remember, were at Daly's, and Evangeline was at Niblo's, with Our Goblins soon to begin at Haverly's; again I stress the popularity of happy parties — Troubadours, Froliques, Rice's Surprise Party, Tourists — in light entertainment of such character. I wonder if the '80s were just a wee bit frivolous in choice of theatrical fare? Slavin's Uncle Tom's Cabin, at any rate, should have been serious enough, when, on May 24th, it began a summer season at the Standard, with all the then customary adjuncts of plantation scenes, jubilee singing, etc. I fear it was too serious; or perhaps it was the heat of early summer. At any rate, this show soon took its way to vaguer regions of chance, and the Standard on June 20th was advertising, nightly, Cooke, Crawford and Miss Kingsland, in Tricks of Mediums. They did not tarry long. Allston Brown says the theatre was sold in foreclosure, on June 28th, for what would seem an astonishingly low sum of $29,000.

GRAND OPERA HOUSE, 1879–1880

The Grand Opera House offered first-rate attraction in 1879–80; the prices were low (75 cents for orchestra chairs), but the entertainment was prevailingly high. I honestly believe that a regular patron of that house in the season now under review saw more good acting and more notable stars and more established plays than did the patron of any other theatre in New York. This was, in fact, a banner season for Poole and Donnelly's theatre.

The term began on August 25, 1879, with Joseph Murphy, in his established success, The Kerry Gow, in which, as Dan O'Hara, he was supported by Emmie Wilmot as Norah Drew, Belle Dickson as Boy Bill, Walter Bronson as Captain Sidney, Luke Martin as O'Drive, Charline Weidman as Alice Doyle, John S. Murphy as Dennis Doyle, A. A. Armstrong as Patrick Drew, H. Rees Davis as Major Gruff, and J. Winston Murray as Valentine Hay. The Grand Opera House now had no company of its own, and "stars" brought in their own "combinations." The house had not yet begun its policy of a week for each visiting company; hence this season provided lengthy stays for several attractions. Murphy remained two weeks, and, on September 8th, Emma Abbott, never long resident in any of our theatres, though very popular in what we today call the hinterland of the American stage, entered with her opera company in Paul and Virginia (never heard here):

Paul	William Castle	Margaret	Emily Gilbert
Virginia	Emma Abbott	St. Croix	A. E. Stoddard
Meala	Zelda Seguin	Domingo	Ellis Ryse
Mme. de la Tour	Pauline Maurel	Negro Boy	E. Archer

It will be seen that the company was good; at the matinées, on the 10th and 13th, Marie Stone sang Virginia, and in some performances of the week Tom Karl was Paul. On the 15th, other members appeared in The Bohemian Girl — Tom Karl as Thaddeus, Wallace Temple as Florestan, and Edward Seguin as Devilshoof, of course with Miss Abbott as Arline, Mrs. Seguin as the Gipsy Queen, and Miss Gilbert as Buda. Matinée lure on the 17th was The Chimes of Normandy, with Marie Stone, Mrs. Seguin, Ellis Ryse and Castle. On the 19th and 20th, Faust assembled Tom Karl, Stoddard, W. H. Macdonald, A. W. Tams, Miss Abbott, Mrs. Seguin and Pauline Maurel (Martha). During this second and last week of the operatic force (September 15th–20th), The Bohemian Girl chiefly held sway, with Paul and Virginia (Castle and Marie Stone) sweetly loving on the 17th. Some may regard as a drop in the artistic scale the visitors of the week of September 22nd — Tony Pastor with a host of variety performers — John T. Kelly, Alicia Jourdan, Georgie Kaine, T. J. Ryan, John Morris, John F. Sheridan, William Hoey, Fred Bryant, Flo and May Irwin, Lena and Minnie French, John Sheehan, James Niles and Charles E. Evans, Frank Girard, &c. Charles Evans and William Hoey — gentlemen, observe!

FLORENCE; JEFFERSON; FANNY DAVENPORT; BOOTH

And now follows a progression of the greatest stars of the American stage — one after another, to the glory of the Grand Opera House and the edification of its patrons. I wonder if this theatre ever, before or after, had so distinguished a succession of stars? Mr. and Mrs. Florence began the glad story, on September 29th, with, of course, The Mighty Dollar:

Hon. Bardwell Slote	W. J. Florence	Hon. George Smith	T. L. Coleman
Mrs. Gilflory	Mrs. Florence	G. W. Skidmore	Oliver Jenkins
Charley Brood	F. E. Lamb	Clara Dart	Florence Noble
Roland Vance	Frank G. Cotter	Blanche	Helen Just
Arthur Lemaitre	Davenport Bebus	Libby Ray	Mollie Maeder Steele
Cairngorm	Julian Young	Laura Seabright	Miss Grant
Colonel Dart	M. C. Daly		

Two weeks of this delightful familiar fare carried us to something even more familiar — Joseph Jefferson's Rip Van Winkle, which began two weeks on October 13th, with a company including Charles Waverly, James Galloway, William Burton, Henrietta Vaders, Little Maggie Gonzales, Eugenia

Paul, &c. October 27th brought Fanny Davenport's almost classic impersonation of Mabel Renfrew, in Pique, her support furnished by E. K. Collier, Edwin Price, J. F. Dean, Harry Hawk, W. F. Edwards, Emma Pierce, Minnie Monk, Fanny Montcastle, Emma Maddern, Josie Smith, &c. — surely the weakest aggregation we have yet discovered for Daly's popular play. Observe what the passing of the stock system has done for us! For her second week Miss Davenport attempted higher flights; on November 3rd and 4th, she was Rosalind, in As You Like It (and with such a company!); at the matinée, on the 5th, and on the evening of that day, and the 6th, she tried Divorce; and on the 7th (her benefit) and 8th, she gave London Assurance and Oliver Twist. The last matinée (on the 8th) was devoted to Pique. One likes to think of the beautiful Fanny Davenport of those years.

The Grand Opera House was in that time committed to Sunday concerts. On November 9th, Gilmore's Band, Ethel Howe (soprano), Haydon Tilla, Liberati, the Saxophone Quartet (Lefebre, Walrabe, Steckelberg and Schultz), with A. H. Pease, called mightily to music-lovers of a certain type. These weekly allurements would, if we permitted, terribly impede our journey. Abbie Carrington, Charlotte Hutchings, Pease, Liberati, Carl Lanzer (violin) and F. N. Innis (trombone) were Gilmore's helpers on the 16th, and, with Ethel Howe, Levy, Liberati and De Leauhodny (zither), on the 23rd, appeared Marie E. Gibson (mezzo). Stella Botsford and Bertha Monis (sopranos) did as they might, on the 30th. And now I may go back to the evening of November 10th, when no less a great one than Edwin Booth came to the Grand Opera House in his most famous characterisation — Hamlet, with a support including Gustavus Levick, John A. Ellsler, L. M. McCormack, Charles Harkinson, George Morris, Louis Barrett, Kate Meek, Louise Muldener, and Kate Williams. This is epochal — the greatest of American tragedians in one of the cheaper playhouses! I pause in my excitement to record the fact that, since Booth did not play at the Wednesday matinées, Kate Meek, on the afternoon of the 12th, acted Miss Multon, with Louise Muldener as Mathilde, Mrs. Fred Williams as Arabella, Sally (sic) and Master Fritz Williams (our Fritz so beloved in later years!) as the children, Mrs. W. Scallan as Kitty, G. Levick as Maurice, William Scallan as Dr. Osborne, and McCormack as Belin. Since, also, Booth would not play two heavy rôles in one day, he acted Hamlet, at the matinée, on the 15th, and Ruy Blas and Katharine and Petruchio, in the evening. Hamlet, Miss Multon (Wednesday matinée) and Ruy Blas (Saturday matinée) carried through a second week of this remarkable engagement, all to the credit of the West Side. On the 24th, 26th, 28th and afternoon of the 29th, Booth played Iago to the Othello of Frederic Robinson; on the 25th, 27th and 29th (evening) the actors reversed those parts. For the Wednesday matinée, the company gave Camille, and, on Thanksgiving afternoon

(November 27th), Booth enacted Don Cæsar de Bazan. One feels almost as if the Booth's Theatre of Booth's day of management had moved two blocks down 23rd Street, westward from Sixth Avenue to Eighth Avenue. An extraordinary engagement!

Richelieu began the fourth week, on December 1st and 2nd, with The Merchant of Venice, and Katharine and Petruchio, on the 3rd, 4th and 6th (matinée), and The Fool's Revenge (evenings of the 5th and 6th). Camille filled the afternoon of the 3rd with sickly scent and sentiment. In Katharine and Petruchio, Marion Booth, advertised as "niece of Mr. Edwin Booth," made her début here as Katharine. On December 5th and 6th, she was Fiordelisa, in The Fool's Revenge; in this play, I am surprised to find Irene Worrell listed for the small part of Ginevra. Booth's engagement closed on December 6th. Later in the season, he appeared, as we know, at Booth's. The Sunday concert, next evening, presented C. Fritsch, Franz Kaltenborn (the "marvellous young violinist"), Stella Botsford, B. C. and A. Bent, Pease, and Gilmore's Band. The artists on the 14th included Nellie Campbell (contralto), Miss Markstein, Kaltenborn, the Bents, and the Saxophone Quartet previously mentioned.

SOTHERN; FRANK MAYO; MR. AND MRS. McKEE RANKIN; ADA CAVENDISH; WALLACK

There was no end to the glorious procession of stars. Sothern came, on December 8th, in Our American Cousin, supported, practically, as at the Park; on the 15th, 16th and 17th, the West Side laughed with The Crushed Tragedian, and, on the 18th, 19th and 20th, sympathised with David Garrick. Dundreary's Brother Sam and Dundreary Married and Settled formed the double bill of December 22nd. For his benefit, on the 26th, Sothern joined David Garrick, A Regular Fix and Dundreary Married and Settled, repeating that bill at the matinée on the 27th. He said good-bye on the evening of the 27th with The Crushed Tragedian and A Regular Fix. Howard Reynolds, Henrietta Markstein and Bernard Mollenhauer supplied part of the concert fare of December 28th; Gilmore was no longer leading the musical hosts, but, on January 4th, we had notable performers in Mme. Chatterton-Bohrer, Mollenhauer, Reynolds, Agnes Wallace, Mrs. E. Watson Doty (soprano), and Luigi Lencioni (baritone). Meantime, the week of December 29th had been filled by the excellent Frank Mayo in The Streets of New York, with H. S. Duffield as Bloodgood, J. V. Melton as Adam and Paul Fairweather, Mason Mitchell as Livingstone, Fred Kent as Puffy, H. Victor as Dan, Master Fritz Williams as Bob, Estelle Mortimer as Lucy, Marion Booth as Alida, Mrs. Fred Williams as Mrs. Fairweather, Fanny Denham as Mrs. Puffy, &c. On January 5th, Mr. and Mrs. McKee Rankin entered the house with the Western excitement of The Danites, their support, seemingly good, including W. E. Sheridan (as the "Parson"), Alexander Fitzgerald, Ben Maginley, Lin Harris, Frank Budworth, George B. Waldron, W. B. Murray, J. F. Stevens, Cora Tanner, Isabel Waldron, Emma Marble (daughter of Dan Marble) and Little Belle. The Rankins remained for two weeks.

The artists at the Sunday concert (January 18th) were H. L. Cornell (a basso from Boston), Mme. Chatterton-Bohrer, the Saxophone Quartet, and others previously heard in these functions. The play of the week, beginning on January 19th, was Mercy Merrick, with Ada Cavendish (never, seemingly, quite able to establish herself in New York) as the heroine, S. W. Piercy as Julian Grey, Archie Cowper as Horace Holmcroft, E. A. Eberle as Ignatius Wetzel, Adelaide Cherie as Grace, and Mrs. Eberle as Lady Janet. A benefit on the afternoon of January 22nd was for the starving women and children in Ireland. Ladies only appeared on the stage. The managers were Celia Logan and Mrs. Cynthia Leonard (mother of Lillian Russell), and a "dramatic committee" consisted of Mme. Ponisi, Mrs. G. H. Gilbert, Louisa Eldridge, Mme. Michaels, Mrs. E. L. Davenport, and Emma Skerrett. As ushers, those entering the house might identify Lillie Eldridge, Courtney Barnes, Saidee Cole, Helen Tracy, Nellie Sanford, Mabel Jordan, Elsie Moore, &c. The programme was to include Marie Le Baron, Ella Hersey, Marie Dausz, Henrietta Markstein, Agnes Booth and Marie Chester (these two in the tart scene from Engaged), Sydney Cowell in a ballad, Maude Granger (in the potion scene from Romeo and Juliet), Clara Brinckerhoff, Belle Cole, Marion Lamar and Mrs. George Vandenhoff. On January 26th, Miss Cavendish put on Tom Taylor's striking play, Lady Clancarty:

Lady Clancarty	Ada Cavendish	Sir George Barclay	L. Eddinger
Lord Clancarty	S. W. Piercy	Cardell	J. Matthew
William III	E. A. Eberle	Lady Betty Noel	Adelaide Cherie
Lord Charles Spencer	J. F. Hagan	Mother Hunt	Mrs. E. A. Eberle
Earl Portland	J. L. Carhart	Suzanne	Ellen Sedgwick
Lord Woodstock	Archie Cowper	Princess Anne	Miss Gerry

At a matinée (January 29th) for the benefit of the family of Henry C. Mount (the fireman for whose family a matinée was given on the same day at Haverly's), Miss Cavendish played Beatrice, in a scene from Much Ado about Nothing, and Tony Pastor, Howard Reynolds, George S. Weeks and others volunteered. On the 30th, for her benefit, Miss Cavendish essayed Juliet, stressing the comedy elements possible in the earlier scenes. At the matinée on the 31st, she and Piercy repeated Romeo and Juliet, and in the evening of that day they said good-bye in The Lady of Lyons. Ada Cavendish lacked just that something indefinable (it was not wholly charm) that made Adelaide Neilson, Mary Anderson and Ellen Terry so pre-eminently acceptable in the style of part she strove to play; perhaps it was too much melodramatic outburst required for Mercy Merrick that caused her (not failure, but) lack of whole-hearted acceptance in Shakespearian rôles.

After faithfully recording the Sunday concert of February 1st, with the Young Apollo Club, of twenty-five singers, Reynolds, Agnes Florence, Bessie Louise King (ballad singer), Weeks, Mollenhauer, Letsch, and G. Morosini (one of these, saith the Herald reviewer, did not appear), I can proceed to Lester Wallack, who, on the 2nd, began a five-weeks engagement, opening, I need not say, in Rosedale. One wonders that he would thus appear in opposition to the offerings of his own theatre. He was supported by J. W. Shannon as Myles McKenna, W. H. Lytell as Bunbury Kobb, Harry Dalton as Matthew Leigh, Charles Rockwell as Colonel May, George F. Browne as Farmer Green, Louise Muldener as Lady Florence, Virginia Buchanan as Lady Adela Grey, Kate Bartlett as Rosa Leigh, Mrs. Fred Williams as Sarah Sykes, Mrs. D. Vanderen (or Van Deren) as Tabitha Stork, and Little Carrie Elberts as the stolen child — a much better cast than many recorded thus far in support of stars this season, at the Grand Opera House. The last performances of Rosedale were given on the afternoon and evening of the holiday (Monday, February 23rd); on the 24th, Wallack appeared in My Awful Dad, which he continued for the rest of the week. A Scrap of Paper filled Wallack's last week (March 1st-6th), his Prosper Couramont being associated with the Suzanne of Kate Meek (a bit heavy?), the Louise of Miss Muldener, the Mathilde of Kate Bartlett, the Anatole of N. S. Wood (specially engaged), the Brisemouche of W. H. Lytell, and the Baron de la Glacière of Shannon. If Booth, earlier, had seemed, almost, to have moved Booth's bodily westward to the Grand Opera House, Wallack now might be said to have transported Wallack's to the same western abode. But, of course, in neither case was the supporting company quite so good.

J. K. EMMET; MAGGIE MITCHELL; JOHN T. RAYMOND

Let us not neglect the Sunday concert on March 7th, with Belle Cole, Angele Torriani, Jr. (baritone), Frank Gilder, George S. Weeks and C. E. Pratt. On March 8th, J. K. Emmet began a four-weeks engagement, in Fritz in Ireland. The Sunday night performance on the 14th was to have proffered Professor Cooke and Selome Crawford, in Spiritualism Exposed, but a certain amount of police interference prevented Cooke's performing his tricks openly on a Sunday stage; the exposé, therefore, was decidedly flat. On the 17th, the Opera House, like every other theatre in New York, gave a benefit for the Herald Irish Relief Fund. At the Wednesday matinée (March 24th), the company acted Charles Reade's dramatisation of Tennyson's Dora. The Sunday concerts were now advertised as for 25 cents; for that sum, on March 28th, one could have heard Ethel Howe, George S. Weeks, Fred Specht (tenor), Arbuckle and Frank Gilder; possibly 25 cents was all it was worth. Emmet's engagement closed on April 3rd, and on the 4th, the usual concert brought (I hope) an outpouring of quarter-dollars.

On the 5th, Maggie Mitchell, perhaps no longer the fairy-like sylph of the '60s, came to the Grand Opera House as (of course) Fanchon, with William Harris as Landry. Others in her company were R. F. McClannin, Julian Mitchell (her son), A. G. Enos, Annie Mortimer and Marie Henley. Ethel Howe, Kate Mitchell (soprano), Esther Du Bois (contralto), Carlos Florentine (baritone) and others were offered, on April 11th, in exchange for twenty-five-cent pieces. Then, this weighty business finished, Maggie Mitchell, on the 12th, could dance her lightsome way, as Fanchon. On the 14th, she gave Little Barefoot; on the 16th, she played, for her benefit, Jane Eyre, Lettie Allen, Marion P. Clifton and those mentioned above assisting. This she repeated on the 17th. The Grand Opera House still presented stars; John T. Raymond followed Miss Mitchell, on April 19th, in his recent success — Wolfert's Roost, his company including George Holland, M. B. Snyder, George C. Boniface, Jr., J. J. Holland (have we met him before?), F. Wise, Affie Weaver, Laura Bascomb (daughter of Emma Skerrett), Mrs. J. H. Rowe, Gracie Hall, Nellie Dickson and Little Dora. For his second and last week, beginning on April 26th, Raymond reverted to Colonel Sellers, the part in which he was indelibly stamped on the public mind. On April 25th (Sunday), the German Heinebund gave a concert there, presenting Fanny Pollak, "Charles" Fritsch, L. Dingeldey (piano — and a fitting name for a pianist), F. Bergner, &c., &c.

With Raymond, the year's procession of stars ceased. On May 3rd, the Colville Opera Burlesque Company brought in The Magic Slipper, which we remember as an autumn gift at Haverly's, several months before. The cast still boasted of Eme Roseau, Ella Chapman, Kate Everleigh, Rose Leighton, Emma Carson, Carrie Elberts, Roland Reed, R. E. Graham, A. W. Maflin and Ed Chapman. On May 10th, this merry group gave us "Byron's best burlesque," Ill Treated Il Trovatore, with Eme Roseau as Manrico. Tony Pastor, again on his travels, came in, on May 17th, accompanied by the Kernells, Flora Moore, Lina Tettenborn, Fred Bryant and William Hoey, Bonnie Runnells, the St. Felix Sisters, Frank Girard, the French Twin Sisters, Fannie Beane and Charles Gilday, &c. The extravanganza was that recent success of his home theatre — Go West! On May 24th, James A. Herne was seen in Hearts of Oak, which lasted for two weeks. On May 31st (afternoon), a benefit for William McCoy, treasurer of the house, brought a host of volunteers, including Kate Meek, Mrs. Fred Williams, Fanny Denham, Constance Hamblin, Emma Carson, Alexander Fitzgerald, Brookhouse Bowler, Ben Maginley, &c., in The Sailor of France, The Days of the Commune, The Rough Diamond, and other dainty delights. The house technically closed its season on June 5th, but Pat Rooney had a week here, beginning on June 21st. The reader agrees with me, I am sure, in thinking that patrons of this theatre had had, this year, a wonderful succession of stars; of course none of the plays had been new.

NIBLO'S GARDEN THEATRE, 1879–1880

Niblo's Garden, fallen from its high estate in the early '6os, re-opened on September 4, 1879, with a new Kirafly spectacle, Enchantment, in which a ballet host was led by Mlles. Cassati, Cornalba, Carnis, Zattei and Ortori, with Rosa Lee (from Covent Garden), Jessie Greville (from the London Alhambra), and Eugenia Nicholson (from the Crystal Palace, Sydenham). C. J. Campbell, a tenor from London, and an orchestra of one hundred, led by Charles Puerner, added to the joys of the show.   The mere actors were J. B. Studley as Arbra, Young America as the Ape, Amy Lee as Madelon, Otis A. Skinner as Maclow, Matthew Holmes as Casmagon, C. J. Campbell as Andre, S. A. Hemple as the King, George R. Edeson as the Duke, and William Davidge, Jr. as Peter.   In its review, on September 5th, the Herald declares that the elevated railroad has restored Niblo's to its old position!

And Enchantment seems to have restored it to its earlier career of success. On September 28th the Herald advertisement offers the additional delight of the Davene Family of French gymnasts; Fantoches Valotte (*sic*) had been for a time back features of the spectacle.   On October 6th, Elise Conly was the Good Fairy.   In late October, Studley was out of the cast, while he was acting Uncle Tom at the Olympic.   The hundredth performance of Enchantment was celebrated on November 25th, and the run terminated on December 13th — a comfortable run indeed.   And it introduced to New York the excellent Otis Skinner.

Entirely different in style was the offering of December 15th, an Irish play entitled Hearts of Steel, produced with an enormous cast, heavy enough in bulk to sink any venture:

Terry	George Clarke	Peter Kelly	Mr. Barron
Dermid	C. Wheatleigh	Blind McGee	Andy Sheehan
Shane-na-Shrad	Gustavus Levick	Paddy Grogan	J. J. O'Brien
Lieutenant Burke	D. E. Ralton	Phil Milligan	Frank Norris
Duke of Sheffield	F. S. Hartshorn	Johnny O'Reilly	Samuel Hart
Sir Francis Mowbray	Otis A. Skinner	Ould Nan	William Cronin
Phelim	W. B. Cahill	Lady Alice	Lillian Cleves Clark
Father Fitzpatrick	J. A. Kennedy	Lady Pauline	Annie D. Ware
Captain Reinhardt	J. P. Winter	Ellie	Alice Hastings
Sergeant Funkenhausen	C. A. Gardner	Judy Riley	Francis Brown
Derby	Thomas F. Kerrigan	Mary O'Kelly	Rose Slate
Red Donohue	James Cooke	Kitty McNamara	Tessie Naylor
Lord Walter	Andrew Jacques	Ann Mulcahy	Rose Stark
General Sarsfield	E. Kearney	Peggy Duffy	Jessie Lee
Adolphe	Harry Hogan	Jenny Boyle	Kitty Brennan

Depended on to lure the public was Red Donohue's "terrific leap over the chasm of the broken bridge," a feat to be performed by the celebrated equestrian, James Cooke. Harrison Millard sang "Oh, for the Swords of Former Days," and a chorus nobly sustained the actors. But something failed to lure the public, and, on January 3rd, Hearts of Steel broke to adverse fate, and retired.

The Galley Slave, forced from its success at Haverly's Fourteenth Street Theatre, transferred, on January 5th, to Niblo's, the cast including most of the original performers — Maude Granger, Signora Majeroni (replacing Emily Rigl), Estelle Mortimer, Mrs. M. B. Snyder, Charlotte Neville, Little Georgie, Frank Evans, J. J. Sullivan, T. H. Burns (as Franklin Fitts), C. A. McManus, Graham Henderson, Charles Webster and Eugene Elberts. On January 22nd, this group having departed for Chicago, an entirely new cast came to The Galley Slave at Niblo's; Emily Rigl resumed as Francesca, and Lillie (or Lily) Glover, Joseph Wheelock and Owen Fawcett took other prominent rôles. February 14th was the last for the present of this popular play; the night before was listed as its hundredth metropolitan performance. For two weeks only The Black Crook came back (February 16th) to its original home, with Mlles. de Rosa, Cornalba, Cassati, Cappelini, and Zallio (*sic*), and Arnold Kiralfy, fleet-footed leaders of the dance, and with, as "specialties," les Fantoches Parisiennes, the Herbert Brothers, Carling, the boy caricaturist, and the Ulm Sisters. The cast included C. G. Craig (Hertzog), N. Roberts (Rudolph), Walter Page (Wolfenstein), I. Davidson (Greppo), John Dunn (Puffengruntz), Sadie Bigelow (Amina), Mrs. J. W. Brutone (Dame Barbara), Laura Dempsey (Carline), Nellie Larkelle (Stalacta), Arnold Kiralfy (Dragonfin), and John Atwell (Zamiel). The old spectacle could not die.

The Boston Ideal Opera Company, cast as before, presented, on March 1st, the ever-desired Pinafore, which stayed at Niblo's till March 20th, always comfortable, always gay. On the 22nd, blithely came to Niblo's An Arabian Night, fresh from Daly's, where the musical success of The Royal Middy allowed the mere actors of the company to go on tour for whatever profits might accrue to the anxious manager. The cast for An Arabian Night included John Drew, Harry Lacy, George Parkes, William Davidge, Jr., J. F. Brien, Maggie Harrold, Annie Wakeman, Mrs. Poole, Sydney Nelson and Blanche Weaver, doubtless all good and many of them in parts they had played at the home theatre; but Catherine Lewis and Ada Rehan must have been missed.

Niblo's was announced on March 29th as under the management of J. H. Haverly, then in charge of the old Lyceum and of the new Haverly's in Brooklyn; in 1880-81 the Fifth Avenue was to be part of his chain of houses. E. G. Gilmore was now set down as associate manager of Niblo's. To open his period of control in a truly big way, the new proprietor and manager brought in Haverly's Mastodon Minstrels, a huge aggregation in which Billy Emerson, Billy Rice, Sam Devere and Harry Kennedy were chief stars; but surrounding their radiant humours were (I will spare the reader and my overcrowded index not a single name) Billy Welch, Frank Cushman, Harry Parker, Pete Mack, Johnny Rice, Tom Sadler, John Stiles, Barry Maxwell, Dan Thompson, James Adams, John Lee, Frank Casey, Paul Vernon, James, John and George Gorman, W. A. Huntley, Harry Roe, J. K. Buckley, Charles Turner, Dan Emerson, E. M. Kayne, Horace Bushby, T. B. Dixon, Otis H. Carter, Will K. Lavake, Chauncey Alcott (Chauncey Olcott!), George Lawrence, Fred Walsh, Harry King, Fred White, C. F. Shattuck, W. S. Belknap, G. W. Harley, Frank West, George Wood, Bob Hooley, William Barbour, Lem Wiley, Charles Freeman, George Frankum, Harry Miller, George Barbour, Eddie Quinn, Melville Wilson, George Lennox, E. Brooks, James Morrissey, William Goldie, Charles Burns, Thomas Ford, Fred Bruce, Don Ferreyra, W. Chatterton, E. K. Marshall and Harry Shirley. Reader, forgive me! It is just conceivable that there may be, somewhere 'neath the glimpses of the moon, some solitary soul who may be interested in that catalogue as a whole, and some few who may thrill at the sight of one or more of the names, individually. Thus ever in hope, I pursue my way along the occasional sandy stretches of our journey. Nevertheless, I wonder what George Christy or Dan Bryant would have thought of this mastodonic host of minstrelsy? or what, indeed, Birch and Backus may have thought of it in their little nest at Broadway and 29th Street. Could they have felt that this newer mighty kind of minstrelsy was going to snuff out such cosy little bands as theirs? Verily, the old order changeth. Two features of the Mastodons may have been amusing — Spanish Stujents and Four Claws Cirkuss. And what was the homely intimate feeling between the minstrels and their patrons that led to the Charley and Billy and Tom and Dick of the minstrels' given names? One might speak of "Joe" Jefferson and "Billy" Florence, but the playbills kept them to the austerities of Joseph and William. I have even heard his most cherished friends speak of "Ned" Booth; but fancy a playbill announcing "Ned" Booth or, worse still, "Eddie" Booth, as Hamlet or Richelieu! The imagination shrinks, appalled. All of which means, I suppose, that the masses took minstrelsy and minstrels to their heart o' hearts. Thanks to this kindly instinct, Haverly's Mastodon Minstrels occupied Haverly's Niblo's Garden Theatre till May 8th — a goodly occupancy for the massive show. These Mastodon Minstrels soon thereafter departed for England.

On May 10th, Joseph Murphy entered Niblo's in The Kerry Gow:

Dan O'Hara	Joseph Murphy	Mr. O'Drive	Luke Martin
Major Gruff	J. H. Rowe	Dennis Doyle	John S. Murphy
Patrick Drew	W. H. Seymour	Boy Bill	Belle Dickson
Raymond Drew	Frank Roberts	Officer	A. J. Brook
Captain Sydney	Hugh Fuller	Norah Drew	Helen Tracy
Sergeant Bull	C. B. Hawkins	Alice Doyle	Charline Weidman
Valentine Hay	J. Winston Murray		

Perhaps "Mr. Reed" played Sergeant Bull; both names occur in Herald casts. This play ran for two weeks, and, on May 24th, in came Evangeline, also for two weeks, Vernona Jarbeau heading the cast. The Child Stealer, on June 7th, presented Annie Ward Tiffany, Frank Mordaunt, Charles S. Rogers and Mattie Vickers — the last two engaged for the specialties in the Cremorne Gardens scene. Our Boarding House opened at Niblo's on June 21st.

Even the most casual reader would know that, granted Haverly as proprietor and manager, these recently recorded events were but preliminary to something "big" already hatching in the managerial brain. And the reader conjectures aright; June 28th brought the expected "massive" thing — Haverly's Minstrel Carnival of Genuine Coloured Minstrels. This again caught idle fancy, and lasted through the summer; on July 18th the Herald advertises as among the performers Kersands, Green, Holden, Devonear, Bland, Bowen, Otter, Anderson, McIntosh, Hawkins, Mack, Grace, Ousley, Reynolds, Burton and Simms. The last appearance of these entertainers fell on August 14th. On the 16th, Milton Nobles acted The Phœnix, "as played by him over twelve hundred times." He remained at Niblo's for two weeks, adding so much to the already excessive score. Here I leave Niblo's for the season, casting back a rather dubious glance at the outstanding features of the term — Enchantment, The Galley Slave, Haverly's Mastodon Minstrels and Haverly's Coloured Minstrels. Who will say, however, that the merriment of the minstrels was to be despised?

Francis Wilson, in his Life of Himself, speaks glowingly of Billy Emerson, as "an exceedingly gifted player" with "a genius for comedy." His hungry Jake, in a sketch of that name, was "imbued with an earnestness and drollery not exceeded by any player in the legitimate drama. It was of a piece with the superb character acting of Luke Schoolcraft in 'Mrs. Dittymus' Party,' or with the equally intense playing of Ben Cotton in similar negro sketches." Emerson also "had a singing voice of unusual range," and "danced with skill and in perfect rhythm." In such "melodious songs as 'The Big Sunflower' and 'Nicodemus Johnson,' he was captivating." To this day, the fast-thinning bands of minstrel admirers speak lovingly of Billy Emerson, in 1880 a star of Haverly's Mastodon Minstrels.

AMY LEE

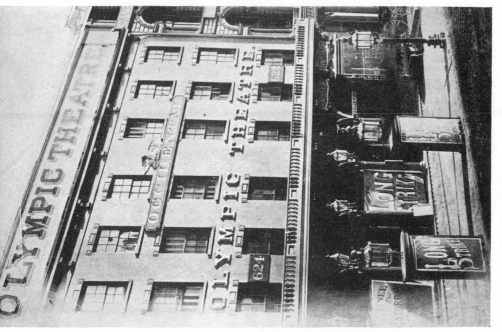

OLYMPIC THEATRE, BROADWAY

JENNIE YEAMANS

CHAPTER II

THE OLYMPIC, BROADWAY (BIJOU) OPERA HOUSE, WINDSOR THEATRE, GERMAN THEATRES, ACADEMY OF MUSIC (NEW YORK), THEATRE COMIQUE, VARIETY THEATRES, MINSTRELSY, CIRCUS, MIS-CELLANY, CONCERTS, 1879–1880

THE Olympic, seat of Laura Keene's glory, of Jefferson's and of Sothern's, not to mention George L. Fox, died this year of complete inanition. Re-opening, on September 8, 1879, as Hofele's Olympic, it tendered a choice morsel called Mitt (Life in California), with Jennie Yeamans, J. W. Summers, Edwin Brink, W. Murdock, Charles Foster, Walter Fessler, Louis Mestayer, Helene Adell (*sic*), and our old friend, Mrs. W. G. Jones. This offering lasted for two weeks, possibly under the impression that it might equal The Danites, M'liss and other theatro-veracious tales of Western life. On September 22nd, Isidore Davidson came in as Grif, in Benighted, his associates being F. A. Tannehill as Richard Handfield, George O. Morris as the Tender-hearted Oysterman (an affecting idea), Johnny Walsh as Old Flick, L. J. Mestayer as Nicholas, Ethel Allen as Alice Handfield, Helene Adell as Milly, Mrs. W. G. Jones as Mrs. Nuttall, Frances Kemble as Marian, and Charles Foster as Nuttall. The company, one sees, was good, with a distinct Bowery or late Niblo flavour. Jennie Hughes, striving to escape from "Variety," was the star of the week of September 29th; her ancient vehicle was The French Spy, extra inducement being Mlle. Paglieri and a *corps de ballet*. For the week of October 6th-11th, Miss Hughes acted not only as the French Spy, but as Lizette, in Why Don't She Marry? Many stars of "Variety" assisted on the night of her benefit — October 10th.

The attraction for the week beginning October 13th was Across the Atlantic, with John W. Ransone as Horace Durand, a young actor, as a coloured servant, as a German guide and an Irish coachman, and with Mrs. Ransone as a Bavarian girl and a waiting maid. This, then, was another of those things so popular in 1879–80, and so similar, call them what you will — Fun on the Bristol, Hobbies, or what not. Assisting performers in this Olympic revel were Tannehill, Walter Fessler, Charles Foster, De Los King, Helene Adell and Mrs. Jones. What is a failing house without its Uncle Tom's Cabin? Prepare, therefore, for the "entirely new" Uncle Tom's Cabin of Robert Johnston, brought out at the Olympic on October 20th with this cast:

Uncle Tom	J. B. Studley	Mr. Wilson	John Walsh
Topsy	Jennie Yeamans	Tom Loker	Edwin Brink
Eva	Little Eva French	Master George Shelby	Louisa Fox
Haley	Frank Whittaker	Shelby	Fred Lloyd
Legree	F. A. Tannehill	Eliza	Ethel Allen
Marks	L. J. Mestayer	Cassy	Helene Adell
Senator Bird	Charles Foster	Aunt Ophelia	Mrs. W. G. Jones
George Harris	De Los King	Mrs. St. Clair	Carrie Livingston
Phineas Fletcher	J. R. Lewis	Mrs. Bird	Frances Kemble
St. Clair	Walter Fessler		

We have met far worse casts of this "classic"; and Mrs. W. G. Jones, Aunt Ophelia now, was the original Eliza, at the National, in 1853, and later Mrs. Bird, in a revised version in 1854. All this in the Aiken version; in 1852, she had in Taylor's unsuccessful adaptation, enacted Crazy Meg of the Glen! Turn backward in thy flight, O Time! and let us count the number of her parts in this play.

Uncle Tom's Cabin now provided but two weeks of hope for Hofele. On November 3rd Angie Schott appeared in Firebrand, and, on the 10th, Fatinitza filled the stage with comedy and music; but not, I fear, the auditorium with auditors! Reca Murelli had the title-rôle, but otherwise the cast was practically that seen later at the Standard Theatre. On November 24th, the Herald advertises the once proud theatre "to let." On January 17th, two performances of The Colleen Bawn were for the benefit of the sufferers from the Irish famine. W. B. Cahill (as Myles), F. A. Tannehill, D. Ralton, Emily Delmar, Effie Vaughan, Mrs. Van Deren and Mrs. Mary Barker were in the cast.

FRANK MAYO; LAURA DON

The last running of the once rich Olympic vintage began on January 31st, with Frank Mayo as manager, and as Davy Crockett, in the play most closely identified with his fame; his support included Edwin Varrey, Edwin Frank, Harry Colton and Laura Don. This sturdy craft he kept afloat for over three weeks, and, on February 23rd, reverted to his other popular impersonation, Badger, in The Streets of New York, with Laura Don as Alida, Edwin Varrey as Bloodgood, Blanche Mortimer as Lucy, Fritz Williams as Bob, the Bootblack, Edwin Frank as Paul, and Colton as Mark Livingstone. This also carried on for three weeks, and yielded, on March 8th, to Man and Wife, with Mayo and Miss Don as Geoffrey and Anne. On the 15th, The Ticket of Leave Man presented Mayo as Bob and Miss Don as May, with Frank Tannehill as Hawkshaw, W. H. Lytell as Melter Moss, Charles Harkinson as George Dalton, Edwin Varrey as Gibson, Blanche Mortimer as Sam, Isabella Preston as Mrs. Willoughby, &c. This always thrilling drama sufficed for two weeks. A more novel play, on March 29th, was Cadet la Perle, or, the Beggars of Pontarme, with Mayo as Henri d'Arcourt and Cadet la Perle, Harry Colton as Maurice, Varrey as St. Amaut, W. Scallan as Paret, Blanche Mortimer as Charlotte, and Laura Don as Hilda. No one could deny that Mayo snuffed out the candle in style. On April 5th, 6th and 7th, he and Miss Don were Charles de Moor and Amelia, in The Robbers; on the 8th, 9th and 10th, they were Ingomar and Parthenia. The last week of the famous Olympic Theatre was devoted to Davy Crockett (April 12th, 13th, 14th, 15th, and matinée, 14th) to Hamlet (16th and matinée, 17th), and to Richard III (evening of the 17th, for the benefit of Mayo). In the last-named play, besides Mayo as Richard, we had Frank A. Tannehill as Richmond, Harry Colton as Buckingham, John Swinburne as Catesby, Oscar Wolf as the Lord Mayor, Laura Don as Anne, Mary Bryer as Elizabeth, Ray Alexander as the Duchess, Genevieve Mills as the Prince of Wales, Edwin Mayo as Norfolk, and F. Chippendale as King Henry VI. And that was the end. It seems incredible that hereafter the Olympic will be missing from our chronicle. Soon after Richard called for a horse on the evening of the 17th, the theatre was torn down (New York's way) and business houses rose on the site. If the reader has a tear, let him shed it now.

WOOD'S BROADWAY THEATRE (BROADWAY OPERA HOUSE, BIJOU OPERA HOUSE), 1879–1880

The house opened in 1878 as the Brighton Theatre was to have, in 1879–80, three distinct names, by one of which it is still remembered. As Wood's Broadway Theatre it began, on September 29, 1879, with Padgett and Bassett's nondescript entertainment of a style so popular at that time —a mere medley of songs, dances, fantastic scenes and characters. Many such have been recorded in the preceding chapter. This one, under the appropriate title of Bric-a-Brac, lasted until October 18th; the company of four consisted of J. C. Padgett, Bassett, Miss B. Norton and Cora Daniels. Perhaps the Vokes Family started the fashion of such things. A New York Juvenile Opera Company followed, on October 20th, in Pinafore, with Miss Ennis as Ralph, Lillian C. Reynolds as Josephine, Inez de Leon as Hebe, Maud Elmendorf as Buttercup, Irene Perry (later in real, adult opera) as Sir Joseph, and Master Jerry Cammeyer as the Captain. One week sufficed for this childish piping of Gilbert's wit and Sullivan's melodies, and Wood ceased to be manager of the house.

As the Broadway Opera House, the theatre re-entered the lists on November 10th, "re-modelled, redecorated," etc., with J. C. Fryer as manager, and with last season's very successful Gorman's Philadelphia Church Choir Company, in the inescapable Pinafore, then likely to appear on any stage; Louis de Lange, A. N. Palmer, Emma Henry and Miss A. V. Rutherford were in the company. On November 29th, this craft sailed for other waters, and, on December 1st, Clinton Hall's The Strategists began a run, with Hall and T. J. Hind as Jack and Arthur Rutledge, Sol Smith as Major Abijah Howard, J. F. Herne as Reverend John Mildman, W. A. Rouse (at least on December 8th) as Capsicum Pepper, Sam E. Ryan as Terence O'Flam, L. F. Howard as Sergeant Gumbleton, Ada Monk as Nellie Howard, Mrs. Sol Smith as Mrs. Howard, and Lizzie Newell as Araminta. All things considered, I am surprised to learn that this venture kept afloat till January 3rd. January 5th introduced J. S. Crossey's American Comic Opera Company, in Crossey's military opera, First Life Guards at Brighton; the performers included Florence Ellis, Laura Joyce, Elma Delaro, Mrs. M. A. Sainger (*sic*), Hattie Arnold, Maria Brewster, Lucy Somers, Eugene Clarke, Edward Connell, W. Howard Seymour, Charles F. Lang, Charles Foster, Harry Allen and Jerry Taylor. On January 19th, the same people appeared in Mme. Angot's Daughter, hardly a novelty at that time; Eugene Clarke was Ange Pitou, Florence Ellis Clairette, and Laura Joyce Mlle. Lange. Those three singers were good, and Mme. Angot's Daughter kept on for two weeks. Next (February 2nd) came in Caverly's English Folly Company, in Princess Carpillona, or, the Kings of the Golden Valley; in the cast were May Ten Broeck, Nita Gerald, Emily Maynard, Alice Montague, Capitola Forrest, Louise Dempsey, the Richmond Sisters, Cecile Romaine, Ida Morris, J. H. Stuart, John E. Henshaw, the Three Brazziers, Blanche Raymond, Carrie Fuller and James A. Sturges — certainly a list of names — mostly from "Variety"— that posterity has not unduly cherished. According to Allston Brown, the show lasted only four nights. On March 1st, Uncle Tom's Cabin and the South Carolina Jubilee Singers came in for two weeks.

And at last the theatre entered on its real career. John A. McCaull, a Baltimore lawyer, and Charles E. Ford took the place, thoroughly altered and refurnished it, and re-opened it on March 31st, as the Bijou Opera House, a name under which it is still pleasantly remembered. It began its new career, on the 31st, with Opera di Camera, presenting two little musical pieces — Ages Ago, by W. S. Gilbert and Frederic Clay, and Charity Begins at Home, by Bolton Rowe and Alfred Cellier. The performers were Marie Nellini, Marie Beauman, Carrie Burton (she had just graduated from the chorus of the Boston Ideals), William Courtney, Digby V. Bell, William Herbert, Frank Pearson, and Alfred Cellier (conductor). This trifling but pleasing entertainment carried through, surprisingly, to May 15th. The Spectre Night was joined (May 17th-22nd) with Charity Begins at Home. This was the last week of the season.

WINDSOR THEATRE, 1880

The second Stadt-Theater, long devoted to German plays, had in 1878–79, we saw, been rechristened the Windsor Theatre, and opened as a

DOLLIE PIKE IN
THE TWO ORPHANS

GUSSIE DE FORREST

SIGNORA MAJERONI
IN THE GALLEY SLAVE

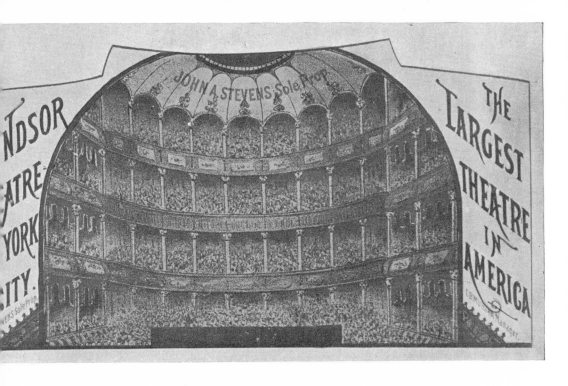

home of "Variety." In the Herald of March 7, 1880, it is again marked as open, with John A. Stevens as lessee, and Frank B. Murtha as manager. Beginning on Monday, March 1st, Buffalo Bill appeared in Knight of the Plains, changing on the 8th to Buffalo Bill at Bay, or, the Pearl of the Prairie, a band of genuine Indians and the boy chief of the Pawnees being part of the show. The company included L. R. Willard, Alfred Beverly, Nellie Jones and J. J. Louden. The week of March 15th brought Mrs. G. C. Howard, in Uncle Tom's Cabin, to a public that had not recently seen this Topsy as often as in former years. The Windsor settled at once into a week-stand for plays of somewhat ancient lustre. On the 22nd, Frank I. Frayne was here in Si Slocum, and, on the 29th, came Joseph Proctor, in that hoary antiquity, Nick of the Woods. The Windsor, one sees, took, in some degree, the place of the old Bowery, recently become a German playhouse.

One week of A Celebrated Case (April 5th–10th) led to Tony Denier's Humpty Dumpty Troupe and Standard Company, which entered the Windsor on the 12th, with G. H. Adams as Grimaldi. Oliver Doud Byron, in Across the Continent (April 19th), and in 10,000 Miles Away (April 26th), with Joe H. Banks, John Pendy and Charles Gardner, in specialties in both pieces, gets us comfortably to May 3rd, when John A. Stevens entered his own portals, in Unknown. On Sunday evening, May 9th, the Everett Family displayed The Wonders of Spiritualism. Advertising itself as "the largest theatre in the United States," the Windsor offered, on May 10th, Maude Forrester, with her horse, Lightning, in Mazeppa. She rode that Lightning steed for a second week, beginning on the 17th, and then it was announced that Lottie Church had been specially engaged. Harry G. Richmond and von Boyle, on May 24th, put up Our Candidate; George C. Boniface came, on the 31st, in his familiar offering, The Soldier's Trust.

Sprague's Original Coloured Georgia Minstrels filled the week of June 7th, and James A. Herne, in Hearts of Oak, that of the 14th. J. F. Peters, in Inshavogue, carried the record through June 21st–26th, his support including R. E. Jewett, Harry Vaughan, O. W. Blake, Frank Turner, John Redding, Julia Blake and Josie Rathbun. W. H. Leake, on the 28th, revived the ever-popular The Three Guardsmen; for his benefit, on July 2nd, he proffered Oliver Twist (he playing Bill Sykes), in addition to The Three Guardsmen. It is rather unexpected to find Kate Claxton and Charles A. Stevenson here in the heat of July; on the 5th, 6th and 7th, they gave The Double Marriage, falling back, on the 8th, 9th and 10th, on the ever-dependable, The Two Orphans. With them were Gussie De Forrest, Dollie Pike, Mrs. Brutone, E. K. Collier and H. B. Phillips. Terrible heat, according to the Herald of July 10th, was raging in the city — a fact that may have lessened sympathy for Miss Claxton's Louise, supposed to be shivering in the snow. Norcross's "Celebrated" Fifth Avenue Opera Company, with Lisetta Ellani and Haydon Tilla, filled the week of July 12th–17th, with, of course, Trial by Jury and H. M. S. Pinafore; during the week of the 19th their lure (if their plans did not miscarry, as I fear they may have done) was The Chimes of Normandy. N. S. Wood, on the 26th, began in Jack Sheppard; Maggie Weston also entertained. This was all for the present in a theatre become merely a "combination" house, as opposed to the old Bowery, which long was famous for its stock company. But the Windsor, with such changed conditions, was to be for years a Mecca for East-side playgoers seeking performances in English. We cannot afford to overlook its importance in the amusement-life of the city.

Germania Theater, 1879–1880

Adolf Neuendorff began his new season on Tuesday, September 16, 1879, opposed by a powerful company that had only a few nights earlier started a new *régime* at the former Bowery Theatre. This was the first time that two good German companies had, for a protracted season, carried on side by side in our city. The opening play at the Germania was Die Frau ohne Geist, a comedy by Hugo Bürger; in it, as the reader observes, several newcomers appeared:

Julius Westerburg	Herr Reinau	Richard Werner	Herr Sauer
Hedwig	Frl. Bensberg	Felix Bogenau	Herr Lichtenthal
August Kopsch	Herr Raberg	Anton	Herr Kummer
Stephana	Frl. Necker	Lorenz	Herr Fortner
Bella Palmer	Frl. Setti	Fanny	Frl. Umlauf
Oswald Lutz	Herr Meery	Ein Treiber	Herr Kästner
Adrienne	Frl. Wagner		

It was pleasant, doubtless, to greet old favourites who returned after absence. The new piece was repeated on the 17th and 18th. Luftschlösser, on the 19th, introduced Herr Feuchter as Pinneberg, Frl. Schmitz (always a hit) as Minona, Frl. Wagner as Elise, Frl. Bagab (new) in the Cottrelly part of Frau Josephine Grillhofer, Rank as Wirkholzer, Meery as Hagedorn, and Frl. Heller as Paula. Saturday, September 20th, brought forward another novelty, a Conversationstück by Bauernfeld, entitled Aus der Gesellschaft. The cast included Reinau (whom we are pleased to find again in the fold), Kessler, Bojock, Frl. Schmitz, Lichtenthal, Frl. Necker, Frl. Wagner, Frl. Bensberg, Frl. Stange, Frl. Behringer (*sic*), Kummer, Hecker, and Frl. Romanus. Certainly, despite new arrivals and departures of some of last year's players, we recognise many familiar well-liked performers in that aggregation. Perhaps to Kleindeutschland the Germania actors were as beloved as were to Broadway the members of the stock companies at Wallack's or the Union Square.

After Luftschlösser on September 22nd, we essayed, on the 23rd and 24th,

Karl Wartenburg's comedy, Die Schauspieler des Kaisers, for "the first times in America," with Kessler as von Caulaincourt, Marschall von Frankreich; Bojock as Gaspard Didier, Regisseur am Theater français; Reinau as Maurice Bernard, Fortner as Anatole Malpré, Lichtenthal as François Bourdin, Meery as Urbain Sansnom, Schauspieler des Theater français; Frl. Setti as Manon Ballier, Schauspielerin; Kummer as Thibaud; and with Heinemann, Kästner and Hecker in minor rôles.   On the 25th, a mass meeting in Tammany Hall prevented the play in the Germania; but on the 26th and 27th, the actors, with Adolph Feuchter as Regisseur, put on a Volkstück mit Gesang — Die Probir-Mamsell; in it disported Bojock as Baron von Schmerling, Frl. Heller as his wife, Rank as Müller (Souffleur), Feuchter as Federweizz (Friseur), Kessler as Grünwald (Musiklehrer), Frl. Pagay (new) as Fanny (seine Tochter), Frl. Schmitz as Frau Putzig, Frl. Umlauf as Frau Zwicker, Frl. Romanus as Frau Siebenfüss, Lichtenthal as Morgenroth, Pinow as Schwerdtfeger, and, in minor rôles, Hecker, Heinemann, Fortner, Frl. Strüvy, Hopf and Kummer.

This piece came again on September 29th and 30th, and, on October 1st, Die Herren Eltern (the German version of Byron's well-known Our Boys) cast Raberg as Bardenstein (Gutsbesitzer), Meery as Bruno (sein Sohn), Frl. Schmitz as Clarissa von Bardenstein, Feuchter as Schliemann (Rentier), Sauer as Theodor (sein Sohn), Frl. Bensberg as Hedwig von Winterberg (eine reiche Erbin), Frl. Necker as Julie (deren Cousine), Frl. Wagner as Lena (ein Dienstmädchen), Kummer as Johann, Fortner as Puffert (Factotum) and Frl. Umlauf as Rose (Köchin).   I reproduce these tags of character description that the reader may glance backward in the history to see what rôles were played in 1875 at Daly's Fifth Avenue Theatre by James Lewis, Fisher, Barrymore, Fanny Davenport, Jeffreys Lewis, Sydney Cowell, &c.   He can then gauge the métier of the various actors at the Germania. Die Herren Eltern ran continuously to October 7th, and yielded the stage, on the 8th, to another Volkstück (by Görlitz) entitled Gross Feuer:

Wohlmann	Herr Feuchter	Lotte	Frl. Pagay
Edouard	Herr Meery	Bianka	Frl. Bensberg
Marie	Frl. Necker	Riese	Herr Bojock
Jonathan	Herr Raberg	Walter	Herr Kästner
Dorothea	Frl. Heller	Merz	Herr Fortner
Urban	Herr Rank	Anton	Herr Pinow
Hermann	Herr Lichtenthal	Louis	Herr Kummer

Though this piece was acted "for the first time in America," it achieved but four performances.

On October 13th, the Germania presented "for the first time in America," the newest "Schwank" of G. von Moser, Harun al Raschid, a merry farce which Augustin Daly presented most successfully, later in the season, under the title of An Arabian Night. At the Germania, the cast included Bojock as Pierre Duval, Sauer as Arthur Duval (his nephew), Frl. Setti as Louise Duval, Frl. Schmitz as Louise's mother, so delightfully played in later years by both Mrs. G. H. Gilbert and Mrs. John Drew, the elder, Meery as Henri Morel, Frl. Necker as Adele Duval, Lichtenthal as Charles Gaudier, Frl. Bensberg as Rosa Ducombier (Catherine Lewis's great hit at Daly's), Raberg as Lefort, Frl. Heller as Mme. Schneider, Wirthin, Kummer as Jean, and Frl. Umlauf as Suzette.

The Germania was feeling the opposition of the Thalia Theater, which was from the very first a popular success. The Thalia announced Schönthan's play, Sodom and Gomorrha, and Neuendorff stole a march, giving it at the Germania one night before his rivals were ready to stage it. He produced it on October 15th, with Sauer, Frl. Bensberg, Meery, Frl. Setti, Reinau, Raberg, Frl. Schmitz, Frl. Necker, Bojock, Frl. Wagner, &c. And the play, despite this flurry, apparently failed at both houses; it was given again at the Germania on the 16th, but, on the 17th, Harun al Raschid, really a success, was restored, and ran uninterruptedly to and through October 28th. The performance on the 27th was for the benefit of Julius Witt, then ill in San Francisco. And still the rivalry raged between the two German theatres. The great size of the former Bowery Theatre allowed the Thalia company to play at a top price of a dollar; on October 28th, the Germania, small as it was, dropped from its former schedule of $1.50 top price, to a dollar — all to meet opposition on its own ground. The Thalia, on October 27th, brought out a highly successful musical play, Genée's Der Seecadet; the Germania, not to be outdone, announced for the 31st Der Marine-Cadet, obviously a trumped up version of the original. The management closed the house on the 30th, for preparation; but the law stepped in and prevented the production. In any case, New York suffered, that season, no dearth of Seecadets and Royal Middies.

On the 31st and on November 1st, therefore, the Germania presented a farce by Malchow and Elsner — Wenn man im Dunkeln Küsst, with Raberg, Frl. Schmitz, Frl. Bensberg, Frl. Necker, Frl. Setti, Sauer, Meery, Bojock, Frl. Wagner, Frl. Umlauf and Kästner. Before the play Frl. Necker, Frl. Bensberg, Sauer and Rank gave Ein Toilettengeheimniss (by F. A. Sauer). Die Herren Eltern returned on November 3rd, and the theatre was dark on the 4th. "For the first time in America" came, on November 5th, Wohlthätige Frauen (by L'Arronge), with (I must give those long-rolling German tags) Reinau as Major Rudolf von Rodeck, Frl. Heller as Verwittwette Geheimräthin Clementine von Pross (I love that one), Meery as Emil von Pross, Frl. Schmitz as Generalin Weissling, Bojock as Stadtrath· Riesel, Lichtenthal as Rentier Süssholz, Kummer as Kirchenvorsteher Wurm, Sauer as Friedrich Mopsel, Lederhändler, Frl. Bensberg as seine Frau Ottilie, Julie Heller as the child Julius, Frl. Setti as Martha Stein, Rank as Hans Werner,

Frl. Behringer (*sic*) as Frau von Sänger, Feuchter as Hubert, &c. This, fortunately for all concerned, ran through November 15th. Daly's adaptation of this piece, The Way We Live, came at his theatre, on April 10th.

Magda Irschick

Magda Irschick, the famous actress from Vienna, who had finished an engagement at the Thalia Theater, in which she had relied heavily on tragic rôles, now transferred her allegiance to the Germania, and appeared there on November 17th in Friedrich Halm's play, Griseldis, with Bojock as König Artur, Reinau as Percival, Sauer as Lancelot vom See, Kessler as Tristan der Weise, Meery as Gavin, Lichtenthal as Kenneth vom Schottland, Frl. Heller as Genevra, Frau Irschick as Griseldis, Raberg as Cedric, Frl. Bensberg as Oriane, Frl. Necker as Mercia, Frl. Schmitz as Ellinor, Feuchter as Ronald, &c. For Frau Irschick's performances prices were again raised, with $1.50 as highest figure. Der Postillon von Müncheberg came on November 18th and 22nd, and Wohlthätige Frauen on the 20th, both, of course, with the regular company. On the 19th, Irschick appeared as Brunhild, in Emanuel Geibel's play of that name, supported by Meery as Gunther, Reinau as Siegfried, Frl. Bensberg as Chrimhild, Lichtenthal as Gieselher, Raberg as Hagen, Bojock as Volker, Frl. Heller as Sigrun, Frl. Wagner as Gerda, and Kummer as Hunold. Irschick's third night, November 21st, presented her as Donna Diana, with Frl. Bensberg as Laura, Reinau as Don Cäsar, and Meery as Don Luis.

Griseldis (November 24th), Wohlthätige Frauen (25th), Irschick as Maria Stuart (26th, with Reinau as Leicester, Meery as Mortimer, and Frl. Setti as Elizabeth), Der Postillon von Müncheberg (27th), lead us, on the 28th to Graf Essex with Irschick, of course, as Elisabeth, Reinau as Essex, Raberg as Raleigh, Frl. Bensberg as Gräfin Rutland, and Meery as Southampton. On the 29th, the star repeated Donna Diana. On December 1st came our first touch of Shakespeare — Viel Lärm um Nichts:

Don Pedro	Herr Raberg	Margarethe	Frl. Necker
Don Juan	Herr Lichtenthal	Ursula	Frl. Wagner
Claudio	Herr Meery	Borachio	Herr Kummer
Benedikt	Herr Reinau	Conrad	Herr Dieckmann
Leonato	Herr Bojock	Ambrosius	Herr Feuchter
Antonio	Herr Fortner	Cyprian	Herr Rank
Hero	Frl. Bensberg	Bruder Franziskus	Herr Kessler
Beatrice	Frau Irschick		

Der Postillon von Müncheberg and Wohlthätige Frauen still figured on evenings when Irschick did not play. On December 3rd she essayed Die Waise von Lowood, and, on the 5th, 6th and 8th, appeared in Die Erzählungen der Königin von Navarra:

[69]

Karl V........................Herr Raberg   Eleanore ....Frl. Bensberg
Franz I........................Herr Reinau   Guattinara....................Herr Bojock
Isabella........................Frl. Necker   D'Albret........................Herr Meery
Margarethe....................Frau Irschick   Babieça........................Herr Sauer

On December 9th and 11th, Frl. Pagay played the ever-popular Therese Krones. And, on the 12th and 13th, Irschick actually descended to Marie-Anne, ein Weib aus dem Volke. This last drop rather surprises me. On December 10th, Irschick appeared at the Brooklyn Academy of Music, for the benefit of the Frauen-Verein of that city, her medium being Die Erzählungen der Königin von Navarra. And on December 18th, for the benefit of the German Hospital and Dispensary, the Germania players acted Der Fechter von Ravenna, at the New York Academy of Music, with Irschick as Thusnelda, Raberg as Caligula, Frl. Setti as Cäsonia, Lichtenthal as Cassius Chärea, &c. On that evening, there was no performance at the Germania.

Otherwise the evenings sped by, thus equipped: Irschick in Graf Essex (15th); Wenn man im Dunkeln Küsst and Ein Toilettengeheimniss (16th); Donna Diana, with Irschick (17th); Der Sohn der Wildniss (19th and 20th), with Irschick as Parthenia, Kessler as the Timarch, Raberg as Polydor, and Reinau as Ignomar; Harun al Raschid (22nd). On the 23rd, 24th and 25th, the Posse by Dr. Schweitzer (with music by Michaelis), Der Nichte des Millionärs, enlisted Frl. Heller, Frl. Bensberg, Frl. Schmitz, Kessler, Feuchter, Rank, Frl. Pagay, Frl. Wagner, Bojock, Lichtenthal, &c. On the 26th, Irschick played Deborah, and, on the 27th, for her last appearance acted Goethe's Iphigenie auf Tauris, assisted by Raberg as Thoas, Reinau as Orest, Meery as Pylades, and Kessler as Arkas.

Tragedy in purple robe having stalked out, Neuendorff, on December 29th, 30th and 31st, invited his patrons with Die Nichte des Millionärs, and, on January 1st, "for the first time in America," staged Dr. Klapp's comedy, Rosenkranz und Güldenstern, with Bojock as Fürst Albert von Liebenstein, Meery as Graf Ernst, Sauer as Baron Rosenkranz, Frl. Heller as Gräfin Kienborn, Frl. Necker as Clarisse, Raberg as Obersanitätsrath von Düring, Frl. Bensberg as Vilma, Kessler as Baron Schallenberg, Rank as Schmählich, Feuchter as Anton Sanftleben, Lichtenthal as Ernst, &c. This trifle ran up to and including January 10th. On Sunday, the 11th, came a Plattdeutsche Reuter-Vorlesung by F. Gressmann. Heinrich Laube's Germanisation from Octave Feuillet, Eine vornehme Ehe, had, on January 12th and 13th, a cast including Reinau, Frl. Setti, Frl. Necker, Frl. Heller, Frl. Schmitz, Sauer, Meery, Bojock, Lichtenthal, Frl. Wagner, &c. For the benefit of Regisseur Adolf Feuchter, on January 14th, we were offered no less an antique than Lumpaci Vagabundus, which was repeated on the 15th, 16th, 17th, 19th, and 20th. Reinau's benefit, on the 21st, gave him as Faust, Raberg as Mephisto, Frl. Bensberg as Margarethe, Meery as Valentin, Frl. Schmitz as Martha, Bojock as Wagner, Rank as Brander, and Feuchter as Siebel. This classic was repeated on the 22nd, and, on the 23rd, "for the first time in America," came a Schwank by Oscar Justinus — Eine stille Familie. It had been announced for production on the 16th, but was postponed. It now had but two performances, and Lumpaci Vagabundus again rushed into the breach, on the 26th and 27th. Bertha Necker's benefit, on the 28th of January revived Anna-Lise (sic), which was repeated on the 29th, 30th and 31st.

It would seem that the Germania was in straits. Its new productions had failed to make lasting impressions, whereas the Thalia was running its Seecadet for (it alleged) a hundred times or more, and enjoying repetitions of several jolly farces or operettas. February, at the Germania, certainly rolled up a record for ancient joys renewed: Faust (February 2nd); Eine stille Familie (3rd); Das Versprechen hinter'm Heerd, Das Fest der Handwerker and Zehn Mädchen und kein Mann (4th, 5th, 6th, 7th); Zehn Mädchen und kein Mann, and Wenn man im Dunkeln küsst (9th and 10th). The benefit of Hans Meery, on the 11th, once more brought forth Don Carlos, with Meery in the title-rôle, Raberg as Philipp II, Frl. Bensberg as Elisabeth, Reinau as Posa, Frl. Setti as Eboli, and Frl. Schmitz as Herzogin von Olivarez. Repeated on the 12th, Don Carlos gave the stage, on the 13th, to Julius Rosen's play, Starke Mittel, then seen "for the first times in America." Bojock appeared as Kanzler-Direktor Mohrmann, Frl. Schmitz as Babette, seine Frau, Meery and Frl. Necker as their children, Frl. Keller as Olga Kratzer, Frl. Bensberg as Louise Grüner, Sauer as Dr. Storm, Raberg as the Registrator, Frl. Umlauf as Caroline, and Frl. Strüvy as Anna. This piece ran through February 21st, except that, on the 18th, Henriette Wagner had a benefit with Hasemann's Töchter, repeated on the 19th, 23rd and 24th. Helene Bensberg, for her benefit, on the 25th, appeared as Der Vicomte de Létorières, and repeated the part on the 26th, 27th and 28th.

Repetitions marked the first week of March, with Hasemann's Töchter (March 1st), Starke Mittel (2nd), and, for the benefit of Josephine Pagay (March 3rd) and subsequently to the 9th, Ein Blitzmädel (by Costa, with music by Millöcker). In this Frl. Pagay played four parts and Rank four; others were Feuchter as Baron Juhasz, Meery as Casimir, Bojock as Theobald, Frl. Schmitz as Laurentine, Frl. Setti as Marie, and Lichtenthal as Rudolf Kern. And now, on March 10th, was played "for the first time in America," von Moser's farce, Der Bibliothekar, a piece which, as The Private Secretary, was to be one of the great successes in 1884–85 of the English-speaking stage in New York. The cast at the Germania:

Marsland	Herr Bojock	Sarah Gildern	Frl. Schmitz
Edith	Frl. Necker	Leon Armadale	Herr Lichtenthal
Harry Marsland	Herr Reinau	Patrick Woodford	Herr Dieckmann
Macdonald	Herr Raberg	Gibson	Herr Rank
Lothair Macdonald	Herr F. A. Sauer	Der Bibliothekar	Herr Meery
Eva Webster	Frl. Bensberg	John	Herr Kummer

This was repeated only a few times, a fact surprising in view of the subsequent history of the play; it ceased on the 16th. But benefits, with their assumed need for novelty, rushed one new thing after another across the distracted vision of the regular patrons. The benefit of Eugenie Schmitz, for instance, on March 17th, gave us for the "first time in America," Die beiden Reichenmüller (by Paul Lindau), with Kessler as Reichenmüller, Fabrikbesitzer, Frl. Schmitz as "seine Frau," Sauer as Willy, "beider Sohn," Raberg as Blaamer, "aus Amsterdam," Frl. Pagay as Lisbeth, "dessen Tochter," Feuchter as August Knoche, Frl. Umlauf as "dessen Frau," Frl. Bensberg as Elise, "deren Tochter," Rank as Balthasar, Lichtenthal as Eduard Bucher, Bojock as Lunger, &c. After six performances of this, Auguste Setti must get up, for her benefit, on the 24th, another piece by Lindau, also for "the first time in America." I hope the reader notes the quotation marks I so carefully put, every time, about that slogan of "first" performance; I merely tell the reader what the purveyors said. The Lindau play for Frl. Setti's night was Gräfin Lea, with the beneficiary in the title-rôle, with Frl. Bensberg as Comtesse Paula, stepdaughter of Lea, Bojock as Erich, Graf Fregge, Paula's Oheim, Frl. Heller as Freifrau von Leeson, "dessen Schwester," Reinau as Freiherr von Deckers, Sauer as Dr. Brückner, Kessler as der Vorsitzende des Gerichtshof, Raberg as Lörtsch, Meery as ein Dandy, Rank as ein Reporter, &c. This had four performances, Ein Blitzmädel returning on the 29th and 30th. Only a German student could properly appraise these varied offerings.

Fanny Heller's night, on March 31st, put on Operationen ("first time in America"), by Oscar Blumenthal and Carl Hartmann-Plön, the cast including Raberg, Frl. Bensberg, Meery, Frl. Heller, Frl. Necker, Frl. Setti, Bojock, Sauer, Feuchter, Frl. Pagay, Frl. Wagner and the excellent Rank. This was played also on April 1st, 2nd and 3rd. April progressed stalely toward the close of the season: Lumpaci Vagabundus (5th); Wohlthätige Frauen (6th, for the benefit of the Herald Irish Relief Fund); Die Karlsschüler, at the Academy of Music (8th), for the benefit of the German-American Seminary; Der Bibliothekar (8th, in the home theatre); Ein Blitzmädel (9th); Ein geadelter Kaufmann (10th, 12th and 13th). On the 14th, Neuendorff brought out Onkel Knusperich, oder eine Nacht in New York, another of those farces of local import, with songs, which he could so cleverly put together. This one was after an old idea of H. Raberg and H. Haliener, and Neuendorff arranged and composed the music. The cast included Feuchter as Knusperich, "grocer aus Pittsburgh"; Sauer as Gustav Wieland, Fabrikant; Frl. Bensberg as Amalie, dessen Frau, Knusperich's Nichte; Meery as William Thompson, Wieland's Partner; Hermann Raberg as Alexander Flott; Reinau as von Patzki, genannt Mitrailleusenspritze; Rank as Fritz Lerche aus Meissen; Frl. Pagay as Lori Zerbst, aus Wien, Nächterin, seine Verlobte; Frl. Schmitz as Malvine Sheppard, Kummer as

GUSTAV ADOLFI
(Photograph by
Naegeli)

MAGDA IRSCHICK
(Photograph by
Sarony)

MAX LUBE
From a Photograph by Falk

MATHILDE COTTRELLY
From a Photograph by Naegeli

BERNHARD RANK

August, ihr Bruder; Frau Raberg as Cäsarine; Lichtenthal as Stockelius; Dieckmann as Carambolini, tenor, &c.   So there is a kind of German Harrigan and Hart sketch to be added to the history of American drama; it ran up to and including April 20th.   For the benefit of Adolph Feuchter, on the 21st, we had Inspector Bräsig, and, for that of Reinau, on the 24th, Die Räuber, with Reinau as Karl, Raberg as Franz, Frl. Setti as Amalia, Kessler as Graf von Moor, and Rank as Spiegelberg.   I have an idea that Reinau was a good actor. If so, he had but slight opportunity, that season, to show the more serious side of his talent.

Ein geadelter Kaufmann (April 26th), and Die Karlsschüler (27th), bring us to Sport, "neuester Schwank in 5 Akten," by J. Rosen, which, for the benefit of Albert Kessler, began a brief run, on April 28th, with Kessler, Frl. Heller, Meery, Frl. Bensberg, Sauer, Frl. Schmitz, Frl. Necker, Raberg, Lichtenthal, Frl. Strüvy, &c.   This ended a comfortable sequence of showings on May 6th, allowing Josephine Pagay, for her benefit, on the 7th, to revive Mein Leopold, with Rank as Gottlieb Weigelt, Frl. Pagay as Emma, Frl. Necker as Marie, Frl. Wagner as Anna, Frl. Bensberg as Clara, Sauer as Leopold, Kessler as Zernikow, Reinau as Rudolph Starke, and Meery as Fritz Mehlmeyer.   And here we are, safely and thankfully, at the last week of the season (May 10th-15th), with repetitions of Mein Leopold (10th), Die Grille, with Frl. Necker as Fanchon (11th and 12th), and (for the 13th, 14th, and 15th) for the "first times in America," Ein grosser Redner, by Schrieber; the cast of the last-named included Kessler, Frl. Necker, Frl. Schmitz, Sauer, Frl. Heller, Frl. Bensberg, Rank, Raberg, Frl. Umlauf and Hopf.   This really was the end of a term that offered little but froth and fun, except, of course, for the heavier bills of Magda Irschick and of Reinau and a few others for benefit occasions.   The German stage at that time was assuredly amusing and clever, if not profound; and New York imported its novelties almost as soon as they were produced.

THALIA THEATER, 1879-1880

The old Bowery, home of English plays since 1826, became in the season of 1879–80 a fastness of German art.   The first season, thanks to a preponderance in the offerings of operetta, then becoming the rage the world over, would seem to have been unusually successful.   And the new venture certainly bore hard on Neuendorff further uptown.   The Thalia opened on September 11th, with Wilhelm Kramer as Eigenthümer, Mathilde Cottrelly, sadly missed of late, as Directrice, Gustav Amberg as Geschäfts-Agent, and Heinrich Conried as Regisseur of plays, a formidable opposition for the Germania, and employing two of the strongest former props of the Germania — Cottrelly and Conried.   The first bill was of classic flavour — Kabale und Liebe:

[73]

Präsident von Walter.....Herr Dombrowsky	Miller........................Herr Conried
Ferdinand..................Herr Schönfeld	Frau Miller.....................Frau Horn
Hofmarschall von Kalb...........Herr Puls	Luise.........................Frl. Krafft
Lady Milford..........Frl. von Trautmann	Sophie...........................Frl. Ahl
Wurm.......................Herr Hauser	Kammerdiener...............Herr Wagner

Mathilde Cottrelly opened the proceedings with a prologue, and doubtless all was felt to be well. Somehow, with the exception of Conried, the players on the first night impress one with a certain sense of flatness, but we may grow to regard them highly.

On September 12th, the Thalia, having eased its artistic conscience with that initial application of Schiller, got into the swing of its intended winter course by producing (with Lube as Regisseur) Die Lachtaube, "Posse mit Gesang" by Jacobson, with music by Michaelis, which ran steadily up to and including September 18th:

Ernst Warnaw...................Herr Puls	Clarissa........................Frau Lube
Richard Temme............Herr Schönfeld	Adelheid........................Frl. Kelly
Herr von Klamm........Herr Dombrowsky	Kipperling..................Herr Schnelle
Lehmkühl......................Herr Lube	Lohmeyer....................Herr Hauser
Pauline.....................Frl. Cottrelly	Bertha..........................Frl. Ahl
Hedwig.......................Frl. Krafft	Johann....................Herr Rohbeck
Fritz Rämig.................Herr Schmitz	

Two important newcomers were Frl. Emma Fiebach and Gustav Adolfi (an excellent comic fellow), who made their début on September 19th. In Quecksilber, by Leon Treptow, Dumbrowsky (sic) appeared at Dr. Zornbock, Frau Horn as his wife, Puls and Frl. Fiebach as her children, Lube as Dr. Gottfried Knops, Frl. Kelly as Ella Rosen, Schönfeld as Bruno Toller, Schmitz as Franz, Frl. Ahl as Nettchen, Frau Lube as Pompeja, &c. The performance ended with Suppé's one-act comic opera, Flotte Bursche, with Frl. Fiebach as Lieschen, Adolfi as Fleck, Cottrelly as Frinke, and Frl. Schlag (once of the Germania) as Gerhard. Others were Herr and Frau Lube, Frau Telle, Frl. Camara, Frl. Spitzner, and the young ladies Weiss, Grothusen, Barre, Bischoff, Ahl and Arnold as students, Loë as Anton, and Wagner as Der Wirth. This double bill ran, somewhat irregularly, up to and including the 25th, with the matinée on the 27th (the Thalia was giving matinées regularly on Saturdays); Die Lachtaube came in again on the 23rd and the 26th, with a matinée on the 20th. Dr. Klaus, on the evening of the 27th, allowed Conried to renew his hit of last year, with Adolfi assisting as Leopold, Frl. von Trautmann as Julie, Schönfeld as Max, Frau Lube as Marie Klaus, Frl. Fiebach as Emma, and Puls as Paul Gerstel. It was repeated on the evenings of the 29th and 30th, and October 1st, and on the afternoon of October 4th; on the 2nd, 3rd and 4th (evenings), Conried appeared in Der Pfarrer von Kirchfeld, as Der Wurzelzepp, with Dumbrowsky (sic) as Graf von Finsterberg, Hauser as Lux, Schönfeld as Hell, Frau Horn as Brigitte,

Lube as Vetter, Frl. von Trautmann as Anna, Adolfi as Berndorfer, Rohbeck as Thalmüller, Puls as Hausel, &c.   On the 6th, 7th and 8th, Ehrliche Arbeit introduced Carl Fritze, "from the Victoria-Theater in Berlin," as Max Wohlmuth, with Lube as Schultze, Frl. von Trautmann as Lydia, Cottrelly as Margarethe, &c.

Thus we are fairly started on the fine month of October, hoping for equally fine things at the Thalia.   Ehrliche Arbeit was the old friend of October 11th (afternoon).   Unser Zigeuner (by Oscar Justinus), seen once last season at Terrace Garden, began a brief career on October 9th, with Conried as Commerzienrath Klugemann, Fabrikherr, with Frl. Kelly as his daughter, Erna, with Cottrelly as Ottilie, Dombrowsky as Wilfert, Hauser as Baron von Meermann, Puls as Adolar, Schönfeld as Otto Kobbe, and Fritze as Ernst Fessler.   Repetitions of works already seen carry us to October 16th, when, one evening after the *coup* of its anticipatory production at the Germania, the Thalia staged Sodom und Gomorrha, with Dombrowsky (*sic*) as the Baron, Frl. Kelly as Ludmilla, Schönfeld as Richard Christen, Frl. Krafft as Elsa, Puls as Paul, Adolfi as Weinmüller, Frl. von Trautmann as Gustel, Frl. Fiebach as Fränzchen, Schmitz as Blasius, Frl. Ahl as Hanne, Weinacht as Seppel, and Schneider as Ein Führer.   Here, also, the piece failed.

The Thalia for this and the next two seasons or so was to become famed as the home of operetta.   It showed its bent on October 18th, when it produced Die Fledermaus (its first performance here), with Schnelle as Gabriel von Eisenstein, Mathilde Cottrelly as Rosalinde, Lube as Frank, Frl. Ahl as Prinz Orlofsky, Lenoir as Alfred, Fritze as Dr. Falke, Rohbeck as Dr. Blind, Frl. Fiebach as Adèle, Frl. Krafft as Ida, Wagner as Ramison, Adolfi as Frosch, and Schneider as Ali Bey.   It ran through the matinée on October 25th.   On the evening of that day, the Schauspiel of Verlorene Ehre (by Bohrmann-Riegen) had a cast including Dombrowsky, Frl. von Trautmann, Frl. Krafft, Rohbeck, Schmitz, Fritze, and Conried (as Baranski).

DER SEECADET; MAGDA IRSCHICK

And now, on October 27th, the Thalia brought out that which made its season a glittering success and shaped the future policy of the management. Comic opera was to become, as we shall see, the raging, the devouring element of the theatrical history of the '80s.   Pinafore had started the epidemic, and now, just a few months later, came the first of the great German successes, in shape of Genée's Der Seecadet, a piece which Augustin Daly, a few months later, fashioned into his captivating The Royal Middy.   At the Thalia the array of officers and Seecadeten was printed in one long bill; I will follow, in order that the reader may see who contributed to the triumph of the show:

Marie Franziska	Frl. Fiebach	Dom Lu	Herr Menges
Don Domingos	Herr Lube	Diego	Frl. Ahl
Donna Antonia	Frau Lube	Antonio	Frl. Schlag
Lambert	Herr Schnelle	José	Frl. Spitzner
Fanchette	Frl. Cottrelly	Frederigo	Frl. Camara
Dom Januario	Herr Adolfi	Agosto	Frl. Grothusen
Rodriguez	Herr Puls	Bernardino	Frl. Bischoff
Franzesco	Herr Loë	Henriques	Frl. Barre
Joaquino	Herr Rohbeck	Sebastiano	Frl. Weiss
Norberto	Herr Wagner	Gomez	Frl. Grünewald
Cesario	Herr Weinacht	Carlos	Frau Dombi
Ricardo	Herr Schliemann	Gonzales	Frau Arnold
Dom Silvio	Herr Lenoir	Bonifacio	Frau Telle
Dom Contreras	Herr Kreutzberg	Mungo	Herr Schmitz
Dom Ruiz	Herr Pege	Pages	{ Frl. Petri / Frl. Libussa
Arthuro	Herr Rothschild		
Dom Philippo	Herr Herz	Heralds	{ Herr Markovitz / Herr Seidl
Umberto	Herr Wilke		

Of course the reader, when I tell him that all the rôles from Franzesco to Dom Lu were Officiere, and all those from Diego to Bonifacio were See-cadeten, will at once perceive that he is dealing with, practically, the chorus, dignified by inclusion in the cast; doubtless the best of them, as in similar cases today, had a few lines to speak, or even to sing.

Der Seecadet (always so printed in the Staats-Zeitung advertisements) could have run uninterruptedly, had the management not made arrangements for a star engagement of Magda Irschick. She came in, on November 3rd, in Grillparzer's Medea, with Dombrowsky as Kreon, Frl. Krafft as Kreusa, Schönfeld as Jason, Frau Lube as Gora, Conried as ein Herold der Amphiktyonen, and Wagner as ein Landmann. On the 6th and 8th, she played Maria Stuart, supported by Fritze as Leicester, Frl. von Trautmann as Elizabeth, Dombrowsky as Shrewsbury, Conried as Burleigh, Puls as Davison, and Schönfeld as Mortimer. On the remaining evenings of the week (4th, 5th and 7th), Der Seecadet made merry; the matinée, on the 8th, gave a triple bill, Gringoire (of course with Conried), Ein bengalischer Tiger, and Die Verlobung bei der Laterne. On the 10th, Irschick played Deborah, with Dombrowsky (who acted parts as heavy as his name) as Lorenz, Schönfeld as Joseph, Conried as der Schulmeister, Frl. Schlag as Röschen, and Fritze as Ruben. On the 12th Maria Stuart, and on the 14th Deborah finished this brief engagement of Irschick. Next week, as we know, she went to the Germania; Mr. E. H. Zeydel (The German Theater in New York City) states that she moved from the Thalia because the leading tragic actor there was inadequate, whereas at the Germania the man in similar position was very much better. All this I can well believe. Der Seecadet filled every bill, except those in which Irschick appeared, and except that for the Saturday matinée, November 15th, when Die Fledermaus once more fluttered gaily in. Der Seecadet ran all of the week of November 17th–22nd, except for Die Eine weint, die Andere (sic) lacht, on the 18th, in union with Die Verlobung bei der Laterne, and Die Räuber, on the evening of the 22nd. On November 23rd (Sunday) a concert for the sick Julius Witt enlisted Magda Irschick (who declaimed), Schönfeld, Lenoir, &c.

Variety marked Thanksgiving week: Die Lachtaube (24th and matinée, 27th), Die Räuber (25th), with Schönfeld as Karl, Conried as Franz, Dombrowsky as Graf von Moor, and Frl. Krafft as Amalia; Der Seecadet (26th and 27th); Einer von uns're Leut' (28th and 29th); Der Seecadet (matinée, 29th). There, I maintain, is a pretty week's offering and a pretty week's work. Der Seecadet and Einer von uns're Leut' divided the week of December 1st–6th. On December 9th, Der Mann der Debutantin (by Meilhac and Halévy) presented Cottrelly as Mina Brunet, Frau Horn as Frau Capitaine, Lube as Lamberthier, Adolfi as Graf Escarbonnier, Conried as Marasquin, Frl. Kelly, Frl. von Trautmann, Frl. Krafft and Frl. Ahl as his daughters — Bertha, Pauline, Amalie and Marguerite, respectively, Dombrowsky as Mondesix, Theater-Direktor, Schnelle as Vicomte de Champdazur, Fritze as Biscara, &c. This ran continuously till December 18th, except for a matinée of Der Seecadet, on the 13th. The management advertised for December 19th the hundredth performance of Der Seecadet; it certainly could not have had half that number of showings. The evening of December 20th gave the first rendering of Der verkaufte Schlaf, by Jacobson and Girndt, with music by the yard. This was set down as "Romantisch-komische Zauber-Posse mit Gesang und Tanz, neu bearbeitet." The cast included Frau Lube as die Nacht, Frl. Kelly as der Schlaf, Frl. Meta as der Traum, Frl. Krafft as die Furcht, Frl. von Trautmann as die Reue, Conried as Kraps, Gutsbesitzer, Puls as Engelbert, Maler, Frl. Schlag as Clara, Mathilde Cottrelly as Frl. Mutzel, Lube as Eichelkraut, Frl. Ahl as Gretchen, Adolfi as Zappel, and Lenoir as Schwalbe. This ran all the next week except on Christmas eve, when there was no performance, with matinées on the 25th and 27th; it also re-appeared on December 29th, 30th and 31st, and on January 1st and 2nd. There was no matinée on Saturday, January 3rd, the theatre being closed because of preparations for Fatinitza, produced on the evening of that day, with Adolfi as Kantschutoff, Frl. Meta as Lydia, Lube as Izzet Pacha, Dombrowsky as Wasil, Fritze as Osipp, Frau Telle as Iwan, Schnelle as Julian, Frl. Cottrelly as Wladimir, and, of course, with many others in minor rôles. On Sunday evening, January 4th, a concert gave us Carl Kaltenborn's Young Philharmonic Orchestra, Johanna Meta, Cottrelly, Schönfeld, and others. Fatinitza ran every evening to January 16th; on the 17th, for the benefit of Conried, Narciss had a cast including the beneficiary in the title-rôle, Frl. Kelly as the Pompadour, Dombrowsky as Choiseul, Frl. von Trautmann as Doris Quinault, &c. For the matinées on January 10th and 17th, children acted Ein Stündchen in der Schule, with, on the 10th, the adult regulars in Die Eine weint, die Andre (sic) lacht, and, on the 17th, in Aus Liebe zur Kunst. On Sunday,

[77]

January 18th, a benefit concert for the poor of Silesia employed the Young Philharmonic Orchestra, Cottrelly, Conried, Adolfi, von Trautmann, Meta, Schnelle and Schönfeld.

The week of January 19th-24th also offered varied pleasures: Fatinitza (19th and 21st); Narciss (20th); a new piece by August Förster, from the French of Sardou, and entitled Flattersucht (January 22nd, 23rd, and matinée, 24th), with Schönfeld as Champignac, Frl. Krafft as Constance, Frl. Trautmann as Camille, Puls as Fridolin, Dombrowsky as Niverol, and Wagner as Josselin. For the benefit of Max Lube, on the 24th, Robert und Bertram emerged, and continued through the five succeeding evenings, and the afternoon of the 31st. On the evening of the 31st, Frl. Charlotte Kelly took her benefit, with Der Verschwender, she playing the Fee Cheristane, with Fritze as Azur, Schönfeld as Julius, Dombrowsky as Chevalier Dumont, Frl. Krafft as Amalie, Adolfi as Valentin, and with Margarethe Raspe and Caroline Schrötter to lead in the dances. Robert und Bertram was seen on February 2nd and 3rd, and Der Verschwender on the 4th (for the benefit of Carl Schönfeld), 5th, 6th and 7th. Children, on the afternoons of the 7th and 14th, acted Königin Tausendschön und Prinzessin Hässlich. On February 1st, at the concert, had appeared the Young Philharmonic (forty players), Arbuckle and Lanzer. The week of February 9th-14th was even more interesting. The return of Emma Fiebach gave us, on February 9th and 10th, Spielt nicht mit dem Feuer, the cast including Fritze, Frl. von Trautmann, Schönfeld, Dombrowsky, Frau Horn, Frl. Fiebach, Frl. Kelly and Rohbeck; in the same bill, Die Sonntagsjäger enlisted Schmitz, Lube, Frau Lube, Schnelle, Lenoir, Schneider and Loë. Fatinitza returned on the 11th and 13th, and Robert und Bertram on the 12th. Ida von Trautmann, for her benefit on the 14th, revived Käthchen von Heilbronn, as reworked by Holbein, herself acting Käthchen, with Conried as der Kaiser, Hauser as Graf Otto, and Schönfeld as Friedrich. The week of February 16th-21st was also varied and attractive in offerings: Käthchen von Heilbronn (16th) Fatinitza (17th and 19th), Preciosa (18th and 20th), Robert und Bertram (matinée, 21st), and, for the benefit of Gustav Adolfi, Der Seecadet (evening, 21st). In Preciosa, given on the 18th, for the benefit of Marie Krafft, the beneficiary played the heroine, with Puls as Don Franzisco, Schönfeld as Don Alonzo, Hauser as Don Fernando, Frau Lube as Clara, Fritze as Eugenio, and Adolfi as Don Contreras.

And now Magda Irschick returned, presenting, on February 23rd, 25th and 27th, Die Jungfrau von Orleans:

Johanna	Frau Irschick	Margot	Frl. Kelly
Carl VII	Herr Schönfeld	Louison	Frl. Schlag
Königin Isabeau	Frau Lube	Talbot	Herr Conried
Agnes Sorel	Frl. Krafft	Raoul	Herr Lube
Philipp der Gute	Herr Dombrowsky	Lionel	Herr Fritze
Graf Dunois	Herr Meyer	Fastolf	Herr Puls

On the 24th and 26th, Der Seecadet again conquered the fair, and, on the 28th, for the benefit of Adolf Dombrowsky, we had Christ und Jude, along with Zwanzig Mädchen und kein Mann.   In the former piece, Dombrowsky acted Adreas Eichhorn and Frl. Cottrelly Rebecca; in the latter, Cottrelly was Sidonie, Wirthschafterin.   Repetitions of this bill on March 1st and 3rd, of Die Jungfrau von Orleans on the 2nd and 4th, and of Der Seecadet on the 5th, with a matinée on the 6th of Fatinitza, brought a Shakespearian item on the evening of the 6th — no less a thing than Romeo und Julie, which, after all, does not to English ears sound quite like Shakespeare:

Julie	Frau Irschick	Mercutio	Herr Meyer
Escalus	Herr Conried	Tybalt	Herr Fritze
Paris	Herr Schnelle	Bruder Lorenzo	Herr Dombrowsky
Montague	Herr Hauser	Die Amme	Frau Horn
Capulet	Herr Lube	Gräfin Capulet	Frau Lube
Romeo	Herr Schönfeld	Benvolio	Herr Rohbeck

A "sacred" concert, on March 7th, congregated Conried (in reading), the Arion Society of Williamsburgh, Magda Irschick (in recitations), Johanna Meta, Lube and Letitia Fritsch — assuredly an interesting group.   The engagement of Irschick progressed with Romeo und Julie (March 8th), Die Jungfrau von Orleans (9th and 11th), and Deborah (12th), with a stray Seecadet on the 10th.   Children, on the afternoon of the 13th, acted Aschenbrödel; the evening of March 13th staged, for the benefit of Heinrich Griener, Kapellmeister, a revival of Offenbach's delightful Orpheus in der Unterwelt:

Aristeus } Pluto }	Herr Schnelle	Morpheus	Herr Jürgens
		Eurydice	Frl. Cottrelly
Jupiter	Herr Adolfi	Diana	Frl. Meta
Orpheus	Herr Schmitz	Die offentliche Meinung	Frau Lube
Hans Styx	Herr Lube	Juno	Frau Horn
Mercur	Herr Puls	Venus	Frl. Krafft
Bacchus	Herr Wagner	Cupido	Frl. Ahl
Mars	Herr Fritze	Minerva	Frl. Camara
Neptun	Herr Weinacht	Ceres	Frau Dombi
Æsculap	Herr Lenoir		

Naturally this had some repetitions.   On March 17th, Irschick (for the last time this season) acted Maria Stuart; on the 19th, she appeared as Katharina von Medici, in Albert Lindner's tragedy, Die Bluthochzeit, oder die Bartholomäusnacht.   Others in the cast were Conried as Carl IX, Schönfeld as Heinrich von Navarra, Rohbeck as Anjou, Puls as Alençon, Meyer as Guise, Hauser as Cardinal von Lothringen, Dombrowsky as Coligni, Frank as Poltrot, Fritze as von Rioux, Frl. Krafft as Marquise de Fontanges, and Frl. von Trautmann as Margarethe von Valois.   Repetitions of this offering, of Orpheus, Christ und Jude, Der Seecadet, and Dr. Klaus, led to Magda Irschick's benefit and farewell (March 31st), with a repetition of

Medea, cast as at her début on November 3rd. This serious business concluded, Thalia audiences could settle down, in early April (benefit of Frau Auguste Horn) to Im Rausch, a Volkstück mit Gesang, by L. Herrmann and R. Hahn, with music by Michaelis, with Mathilde Cottrelly as Käthe, Fritze as Otto Holzdorf, Adolfi as Spargel, and, in other rôles, Frl. Krafft (Anna), Schmitz, Frau Horn, Dombrowsky, Lube, Frl. Ahl, Puls, Rohbeck, and many others. Fatinitza (April 6th), Käthchen von Heilbronn (7th, and matinée, 10th), Hasemann's Töchter (8th, 9th and 10th) all sound like old friends; the concert, on April 11th, was for the benefit of the orchestra of the house, and enlisted Levy, Cottrelly, Sohst, Adolfi, J. Lefebre (saxophone), Meta, Lube and Schnelle.

The season had but a month more before it died. Johanna Meta, for her benefit on the 12th, sang Leonore, in Stradella, with Joseph Weinlich as Bassi, Jacob Graff as Stradella, Max Schnelle as Barbarino, and Fritz Lafontaine as Malvolio; the opera was repeated on the 13th. Kabale und Liebe re-emerged on the 14th, and at the matinée on the 17th. Fanny Witt began a Gastspiel, on the 16th and 17th (evening) in Mutter und Sohn, of course playing die Generälin von Mansfelt. For her benefit and "last" appearance, on the 22nd, and also at the matinée on the 24th, Frau Witt played the Countess, in Die Danischeffs, with Meyer as Wladimir, Fritze as Paul, Dombrowsky as Prinz Walanoff, Frl. Kelly as Prinzessin Lydia, Schönfeld as Roger de Taldé (perhaps to show his versatility), Frl. Krafft as Baroness Dozene, Conried as Osip, and Frl. von Trautmann as Anna. This sounds like an interesting cast.

On Sunday, the 18th, Maurice Grau gave a concert with Paola Marié, Angèle and Capoul. Die Fledermaus was heard on April 19th, 20th and 21st; on the evening of the 23rd came the first performance of the thenceforth raging success, von Suppé's Boccaccio, with Frl. Cottrelly in the dashing title-rôle; with Schnelle as Prinz von Palermo; Schmitz as Scalza, Barbier; Frl. Meta as Beatrice, sein Weib; Lube as Lotteringhi, Fassbinder; Frau Lube as Isabella, sein Weib; Adolfi as Lambertuccio, Gewürzkräner; Frau Horn as Petronella, sein Weib; Frl. Ahl as Fiametta, beider Tochter; Lenoir as Leonetto, Student; and with many, many others in minor rôles, constituting, if truth must out, the chorus of the merry operetta. May 1st brought the benefit and farewell of Conried, who departed in the character — Gringoire — which had served for his début at the Germania, in September, 1878; his farewell bill also included Boccaccio. On the afternoon of Saturday, May 1st, Magda Irschick gave an extra performance of Deborah, and said farewell, on the evening of the 3rd, in Die Jungfrau von Orleans. Except for this, Boccaccio filled evenings up to and including May 10th; with it, on May 8th, Max Lube, for his benefit, joined Dr. Peschke. On the afternoon of the 8th, Fatinitza once more held the stage, with Emma Kuster featured in the cast. What was announced as the "last" week of the season

(May 10th–15th) provided a procession of Boccaccio (10th), Die Fledermaus (11th), Der Pariser Taugenichts and Die schöne Galathée (for the farewell of Emma Kuster, 12th), Fatinitza (13th), Einer von uns're Leut' (14th), and Die Lachtaube (15th).   But threats, like promises, sometimes mislead. Extra-Vorstellungen gave us Boccaccio (17th); Die schöne Helena (19th), with Emma Kuster as Helena, Schnelle as Paris, Adolfi as Menelaus, Frank as Agamemnon, Frl. Ahl as Orestes, Frl. Camara as Pylades, Schmitz as Calchas, Rohbeck as Achilles, Lenoir as Ajax I, and Puls as Ajax II.   And Der Seecadet figured in Cottrelly's benefit, on the 21st.   That really was the last of the regular season.

And, on May 28th, began an "Ensemble-Gastspiel" of Ottilie Genée, friend of former years, and a "Gesellschaft aus San Francisco."   They gave Emma's Roman, oder Blaustrümpfe, a Schwank by Kneisel.   The company included Ottilie Genée, Bertha Fiebach, Eugenie Lindemann, F. Urban, Heinrich Kadelburg, Herr and Frau Lube, Bojock, and others.   The performance began with a humorous prologue, Californier auf Reisen, delivered by Frl. Genée.   On the 29th, these strollers moved to Terrace Garden. Well, the season at the Thalia had certainly provided much enjoyment to lovers of lighter fare, with high-class operetta, and to devotees of the classics the "legitimate" (to use an English connotation) repertoire of Magda Irschick.   The Thalia was launched for a prosperous career of several years to follow.

OTHER GERMAN PLAYS, 1879–1880

On October 25th, a benefit at Turnhalle for Julius Bledong, "blind and lame," presented Der Sängernarrisch (by Köllner) and Mein Schifflein treibt (by Beschnitt).   On December 11th, the Apollo Dramatic Association and the Yorkville Männerchor united for an evening of Meg's Diversion and The Little Rebel, the Lexington Avenue Opera House housing their ambitious attempts.   The Turn-Verein, on December 14th, gave O! diese Männer, and, on January 17th, at the Germania Assembly Rooms, the Dramatic Verein "Wir" played Er ist Baron.   On May 25th, at Germania Assembly Rooms, Ein rettender Engel was to have enlisted Adolfi, Marie Krafft, Elise Römer, Otto Meyer, Carl Fritze, Frank, and Max Loë.   I do not know the inspiring cause of this professional visit; in any case, it seems to have been postponed.

The Concordia, on September 27, 1879, was presenting as concluding piece. So bezahlt man seine Schulden; on October 6th, Ein alter Junggesellen; on October 25th, Görner's Die Mitgift.   Abgeblitzt finished the evening, during the week of December 1st–6th.   The closing play, on December 22nd, was Seine Dritte, oder Amerika und London.   Bleib bei Mir was the appeal (January 17th); Im Zauber-Salon called on February 9th; Der Kesselflicker

[81]

closed the bills (February 14th), and Die Folgen einer Zeitungs-Annonce (March 13th).

At Terrace Garden (or should I write Garten?), on October 25, 1879, the Verein Frohsinn, with the aid of the Thalia Theater company and Mathilde Cottrelly, presented Edison's 500ste Erfindung and Verlobung bei der Laterne, some of the interpreters being Puls, Schnelle, Schliemann, Frl. Ahl. and Frl. Fiebach. A benefit, on October 29th, was for the Hebrew Sheltering Guardian Society. On December 7th, occurred a concert and ball for the widow and orphans of Andreas Meyger. The Harmonia ("früher Maimonides Coterie") was here, on December 28th, with a show and a ball, the former enlisting Bertha Necker, Max Schnelle, Fanny Pollak, Adolf Sohst, Mathilde Cottrelly, and an amateur Philharmonic Quintette. On January 17th, the Eichenkranz had here its Erste Carneval-Sitzung. The second Abend-Unterhaltung and ball of Harmonia provided Max Lube, Gustav Adolfi, Agnes Florence, Kate Nuffer, Emil Senger (bass), and J. Salinger ('cello), the evening of January 25th being the date. The maskball of the Männerchor came on February 10th. On February 29th, a performance of Der Seecadet was stopped by the police as an infringement of Sunday laws. On March 3rd, the Eichenkranz Mask Ball ran gaily through. The Harmonia returned on April 25th, with a notable array, including Emma Juch, Ida von Trautmann, Heinrich Conried, Adolph Sohst, Henriette Honigmann (declamation), and D. Krakauer (violinist, and, let us hope, master of a sweeter tone than that inherent in his name).

On May 30th, Frl. Angela Drucker appeared in concert, with Liberati, Ida von Trautmann, Tagliapietra, Max Schnelle and Max Drucker. Meantime, Ottilie Genée, after a single performance at the Thalia Theater, transferred here (May 29th), her performance of Emma's Roman; her farewell occurred on June 3rd, in In Marmor ausgehauen, oder die Büste (by F. Zell) and Ein alter Postillon, oder die letzte Fahrt. The New Yorker Männerchor concert, on June 10th, presented Frl. C. Schulte, Frl. J. Ackermann, Jacob Graff, and Leiboldt's orchestra. On the 12th, the Arion Society held here a Sommernachtsfest, with a concert in the garden, the operette (by Carl Hopfner) of Der Ring des Nibelung (sic) in the hall, and a ball to close the function. The Liederkranz functioned here on June 19th. August 1st brought to Terrace Garden the Schleswig-Holsteinischer Verein for the usual Germanic idea of a good time by day and by evening's starry glow; and, on the 9th, the Mainzer Carneval-Verein came, with a farce, Die Maskerade in der Dachstube, and Nein (a Lustspiel in one act by Benedix). Frau Granget and Max Schnelle helped. The record for 1879–80 shows a thinning-out of interest in Terrace Garden.

OTHER GERMAN ACTIVITIES, 1879–1880

The reader by this time knows accurately the sources of German amusements. Therefore, without any desire to provide an exhaustive list for
1879–80, I will cite some of the more interesting events. On September
21st, at Jones Wood Colosseum, came to pass a Sänger-Anzahl von Tausend
Stimmen zum Besten der New Yorker Volks-Zeitung, to which contributed
Frl. Helene Weingarten, Frohsinn of Long Island City, the Marschner
Männerchor, and Wilhelm Flugrath. On the 27th, the Arion Society ten-
dered its first Musikalisch-Dramatische Abend-Unterhaltung; at this time
Künstler Halle, 214 Sixth Street, gave every evening a concert, with Luigi
Ander, lyric tenor "aus Wien," and Eduard Lux, pianist. The Eichenkranz
held its first Abend-Unterhaltung, on the 28th, at Turnhalle, and, in its
own "Lokal," the Liederkranz, on the 30th, had a "Geselliger Abend."
Opening balls of the season were advertised at Dramatic Hall, the Concordia
Assembly Rooms, the Teutonia Assembly Rooms and at Wendel's Assembly
Rooms (334-344 West 44th Street). At the Germania Assembly Rooms,
another benefit to Adolf Schmidt, violinist, held the night of October 19th,
the assistants being Helene Weingarten, Georg Peters (bass), Liberati, Frl.
Lorsch, and an orchestra. A concert, on October 25th, at Tyroler-Halle,
385 Bowery, stressed an Alpine Sänger-Gesellschaft, with three men and
two women. At Künstler Hall, at about the same time, appeared Miss
Meyers (soprano), Pfannenschmidt (violin), Charles Krumm (guitar), and
Karl Kaiser (flute). At Turnhalle, on October 25th, a benefit for Julius
Bledong (blind and lame, poor man) brought, as we saw, a performance of
plays.

The first concert of the Arion Society, held at its rooms in St. Mark's
Place, presented (November 2nd) Anna Drasdil, Ida Mollenhauer, Jacob
Graff (*sic*), the ever-faithful, Charles Belfort (violin), and Henry Mollenhauer ('cello); on the same evening came at Turnhalle the tenth annual
Stiftungsfest of the Eichenkranz, and at Tyroler-Halle (385 Bowery) Professor Rutini and the Tyrolean singers aforesaid. The Gesäng-Verein
Schillerbund was at Turnhalle, on November 9th, with Frau J. Poggenburg
(soprano), Carl Fuchs (baritone) and Griffin (cornet). On the 9th, also,
the Gesang-Verein Arminia was at the Vereins-Lokal, 71 West Fourth Street,
and the Orden Germania had a Stiftungsfest and ball in the hall of the
Beethoven Männerchor. On November 10th, the Arminia Loge, No. 256,
met at Turn-Halle. About November 10th, at K. Bolz's Concert Hall, 98
Allen Street, might have been attended the début of the Hamburger Sänger-
Gesellschaft, including Frau Ehrenfried, Frl. Constancia, Frl. Ellis, C. Ehren-
fried, Du Barry and Keller. On the 9th, the Mozart Männerchor, at the
Germania Assembly Rooms, was assisted by Frl. Meta, Frl. Langer (piano),
F. G. Händel (tenor), and G. Peters (bass). In the "overhall" of the same

rooms, on the 15th, met the Sängerrunde. On the 16th (Sunday), the Harugari Liederkranz was at Walhalla; the Marschner Männerchor sang in the Concordia Rooms; the Mozart-Verein had a concert, banquet and ball, in celebration of its twenty-fifth jubilee, at the Germania Assembly Rooms, its concert offering Marta Schenck and Luise Klugelmann (sopranos), Carl Alves and others even less notable. The Turn-Verein also, on the 16th, had a concert and Kränzchen, in its hall; the Liederkranz concert, at the Vereinslokal, introduced Fanny Pollak, Fritz Steins and Ludwig Dingeldey (piano); and the Gesang-Verein Oesterreich held Beethoven Hall. At Künstler-Halle were H. Arthur (zither), Ander (tenor from Vienna), and Mme. Giessel (concert-singer from Chicago). Sunday, the 23rd, likewise burbled away in musical terms: the Beethoven Mannerchor held a concert and ball, with Misses M. and E. M. Conron, H. Bersin, H. Prehn, Biedermann, and C. Träger; the Jefferson Verein der deutschen Arbeiter was at Kern's Hall, 101 Avenue A; the Heinebund went to Lyric Hall, with Fanny Pollak, C. Steinbuch and a large orchestra; the Gesang-Verein Wormatia was in the Concordia Rooms.

On November 24th, the Bismarck Quartett Club was at the Germania Assembly Rooms; on the 27th, the Mainzer Carneval-Verein began their season, in Turn-Halle (usually then so printed), the Gesang-Verein Sängerlust was at E. Zobel's Beethoven Hall, 431 Sixth Street, and the Schwäbischer Sängerbund celebrated Thanksgiving in the Concordia Rooms. And, on November 30th, the Kreutzer Denkmal concert and ball, at the Germania Assembly Rooms, joined to its purpose the Arion Quartett Club, the Kreutzer Quartett Club, the Franz Abt Schüler, the New Yorker Liedertafel, the Theodor Körner Liedertafel, the Yorkville Männerchor, the Mozart-Verein, and members of the Philharmonic Society — surely a significant evening! On December 6th came another Musikalische Abend-Unterhaltung (*sic*) of the Liederkranz, and, on the 7th, at the hall of the Beethoven Männerchor, one might have heard the Beethoven Quartett; on the 7th, also, at the Germania Assembly Rooms, the Sängerrunde held sway, along with Johanna Meta, Katie Nuffer, Carl Alves, Carl Steinbuch and Emil Senger; the Haydn Amateur Musical Society held Lyric Hall on the 8th. On the 10th, Friedrich Bodenstedt read at Liederkranz Hall; the Arion Society, at Steinway Hall, on December 13th, had, for aids to its concert, Leopold Damrosch, Anna Bock, Letitia Fritsch, Jacob Graff, Franz Remmertz, A. Dehnhoff (tenor), and E. Urchs (bass). In mid-December balls galore! including those of the Teutonia Club, the Knickerbocker-Verein, and the lightly and delicately named Frauen-Verein Victoria, Kronprinzessin des deutschen Reichs.

The "last" appearance of Magda Irschick, who made several, was for the benefit of the German-American Institute and Kindergarten (East 82nd Street); it came, on December 29th, at Parepa Hall, Third Avenue and 86th

Street.   On that same date, the concert of the Frauen-Verein proffered, at Steinway Hall, Anna Drasdil, Letitia Fritsch, Adolphe Fischer, Hermann Rietzel, F. Steins, and F. Dulcken.   I have under other captions referred to the Liederkranz Mask Ball, on February 5th, at the Academy of Music, and that of the Arion Society, on February 19th, at Madison Square Garden.

Meantime, on February 1st, the Gesang-Verein (*sic*) Schillerbund went to Steinway Hall for a concert, Antonia Henne, Graff and Fuchs (baritone) assisting.   On February 13th, at the Teutonia Assembly Rooms, assembled the Aschenbrödel-Verein, the Heinebund having wended its way two nights earlier to Wendel's Assembly Rooms, West 44th Street.   On the 14th, the Rheinischer Sängerbund was at Zobel's Beethoven Halle; on the 15th, the Mainzer Carneval-Verein at the hall of the Beethoven Männerchor; and, on the 16th, the Bloomingdale Turn-Verein at Wendel's.   On the 22nd, the Liederkranz, at their hall, sang H. Hoffman's cantata, Cinderella.   For March 7th, the Beethoven Männerchor arranged its third Carneval-Sitzung; on the 9th, the Liederkranz opened its house for another geselliger Abend. A vocal and instrumental concert of Wilhelm Groschl, on the 21st, brought to the Teutonia Assembly Rooms the helping and possibly saving grace of Frl. Weingarten and Fritz Steins.   On the 14th, the Sangerrunde held, at the Germania Rooms, an Abend-Unterhaltung.   The 15th brought to the Beethoven Männerchor-Halle, the Mainzer Carneval-Verein, all for a ball in masks.   And the Marschner Männerchor functioned in a concert, in the Concordia Rooms, as did the Loreley Männerchor in Carl Diem's Loewen-Halle.   March 28th gave us two events: the Allemania Quartett Club had a Stiftungsfest, concert and ball, at the Turtle Bay Assembly Rooms (45th Street, between First and Second Avenues); and the Beethoven Männerchor, at their hall in Fifth Street, arranged a big concert, at which were to appear S. B. Mills, Emma Juch, Prehn and Trost (bassos), Riedel and Althaus (tenors), G. Dreyer (flute), Herren Juch and Biedermann (accompanists). On the same evening, the Gesang-Verein Germania was at the Germania Assembly Rooms.   On March 30th, the Hudson Männerchor were at Beethoven Hall.   The Hungarian Verein, on April 3rd, acted and danced in the Germania Rooms.   March 30th saw the opening of the fair of the Turn-Verein, with the Liederkranz singing to assist.   On April 4th Mathilde Cottrelly, Max Lube and the Thalia Orchestra lent brilliancy to the occasion. And so we pass to balmy spring.

Serious must have been the evening of April 7th, at Liederkranz Hall, with the Vortrag von Herrn Robert von Schlagintweit, who held forth on the "thema," Das Leben und die gesellschaftlichen Verhältnisse der Europäer in Ostindien.   The third Arion concert, on April 11th, brought to the Vereinslokal Nannie Louisa Hart (soprano), Florence Copleston (pianist), Emilie Urchs (alto), Graff, Remmertz and Richard Arnold.   The 11th witnessed also the Gemüthlige Abend-Unterhaltung and Tanz-Kränzchen of the

Gesang-Verein Harmonia "im neuen Vereinshalle," 62 Ost Vierte Strasse. The Arion Quartett Club Concert, at the Germania Assembly Rooms, on that same 11th, availed itself of the aid of A. Gerling (tenor) and Frl. S. Göggelmann (soprano). On the 18th, the Gesang-Verein Schillerbund closed its season; on the same evening, at the Germania Assembly Rooms, the Sängerrunde concert had, as soloists, Johanna Meta, Frau Marie Dausz (soprano), Graff, Jerome Lenoir, A. Liberati, F. Krämer (piano), and A. Neuendorff (director); the 18th also provided the concert of the Mainzer Carneval-Verein, held at Beethoven Männerchor-Halle, with Emma Juch, O. Schmittbauer (violin), and M. König ('cello). And Adolf Schmidt's musical soirée at Freimaurer Tempel (East 15th Street between Second and Third Avenues) was another joy of the 18th, as was a zither concert (with William Hain) at Krisch's Weinhandlung (6 Rivington Street). Verily, a distracting Sunday! whither should we flee for the biggest artistic bargain? April 19th found single in the field the concert for Joseph Harrison, held at the Germania Rooms, with Frederika Rokohl, Gustav Adolfi, Schnelle, Puls, and S. A. Walker (baritone). Three events hold us on April 25th: the New York Zither-Verein, at Teutonia Assembly Rooms, with Fred Krämer (pianist), Otto Schuster (tenor), the Wallfisch Quartett, and L. Philipp Koch, directing; the concert and ball of the Mozart Männerchor, at the Germania Assembly Rooms; and the third Liederkranz concert. And bigger still — the concert of the Heinebund, at the Grand Opera House, with Fanny Pollak, Dingeldey, F. Bergner, &c.

Again the spring, merging into early summer, called afield; on May 2nd, Löwen-Park gave its first concert of the season. On Pfingst-Sonntag and Montag, May 16th and 17th, came a Picnic der drei vereinigten Vereine — the Turn-Verein, the Germania and the South Brooklyn Turn-Verein — all in Wendel's Elm Park. The Turn-Verein, on May 17th, went to Jones Wood Colosseum and the Söhne der Freiheit were at Harlem River Park. June, as usual, inaugurated the run of summernight festivals. The H. Herrmann-Verein, on June 2nd, journeyed to Sulzer's Harlem River Park, and, on June 3rd, the Aschenbrödel-Verein celebrated at Bender's Schützen-Park. On the 5th and 6th, however, the Turn-Verein gave in its own hall its thirtieth annual Stiftungsfest. Jones Wood and Washington Park were called, on June 9th, in requisition by the Amt Osterholzer K. U. Verein, and, on the 10th, the Stoteler Gesellschaft went to Held's Hamilton Park. The Free Order of Red Men were in this last-named pleasance, on June 12th. The Sängerrunde, on the 6th, flitted to Clifton, Staten Island, and Euphonia fled to Hartung's Park, East 134th Street. Sacred concerts graced Sunday, June 13th, at Turtle Bay Park (43rd Street and First Avenue) and Wendel's Elm Park; at the latter place appeared Louise Linden (saxophone), Fred W. Bent (cornet) and Justus W. Koch (pianist). Mozart Lodge, 38, K. P., held, on June 14th, the spaces of Jones Wood Colosseum. The Jahres-Fest der deutschen Patrioten von 1848 und 49 took place, on June 21st, at Bender's Schützen-Park, 63rd Street and First Avenue.

And the papers bristled with advertisements of excursions (not wholly German these) to Coney Island, Manhattan Beach, Fort Lee Park, West Brighton Beach, Long Beach, Glen Island, Rockaway Beach, Bridgeport and the Fishing Banks. The Haydn Männerchor and the Mozart Männerchor jointly held Ridgewood Park, on June 20th. On the 20th also came the Ausflug of the Theodor Körner Liedertafel to Martin Euler's Broadway Park, Williamsburgh. On the 27th, the Beethoven Männerchor Wasserfahrted, so to speak, to Oscawana Island; on the 28th, the Sommernachtsfest of the Veteran Gesang-Verein thrilled through Sulzer's Harlem River Park. I suppose the participants really enjoyed these things, especially with beer to drown the finer critical sense.

I hurry to the end of the season. On July 5th, the Bloomingdale Turn-Verein went to Löwen-Park, and, on the 12th, the twenty-fifth Jubiläum des Concordia Männerchor held Turtle Bay Park, along with the Allemania Quartett Club, the Quartett-Club Frohsinn, the Harlem Männerchor, and the Sozial-Reformer Gesang-Verein. The Heinebund, on the 11th, flitted to Linden Grove, Staten Island, all for an outing fair. On the 18th and 19th of July, the fifth Schweizerisches National-Fest der Vereinigten Schweizer-Vereine filled Jones Wood Colosseum and Washington Park with its syllables and its glee. The Danish Veteran Society breaks into our narrative, on July 22nd, with its sixth annual Picnic and Sommernachtsfest, at Held's Hamilton Park. On the same date, the Arion Society had its seafunction at West Brighton Beach. The Fidelia and Uhland-Bund joined picnics on July 26th, at Turtle Bay Park. On Sunday, the 25th, Wendel's Elm Park announced the engagement of the Tyrolean Alpen-Sänger Gesellschaft. Ferdinand Göbel's Sommergarten, 57th Street and East River, had, at this time, a "grand" concert, and I dare say beer, every evening; the Beethoven Sommergarten, connected with the Beethoven Männerchor-Halle stressed "beer" as its chief attraction.

On August 8th, the Badischer Männerchor indulged in a Wasserfahrt to Excelsior Grove, and the Eichenkranz boldly adventured to Cold Spring Grove, Long Island. The German Masonic Temple Association, on August 10th, possessed Jones Wood Colosseum, gracefully yielding it for the two following days to the New York Central Schützen-Corps. A pyrotechnic display, on August 20th, may have drawn Germans and Americans to Long Beach, especially as music by the orchestra of Kleophas Schreiner, with solos by Theo. Hoch, was part of the inducement. On the 21st, the New York Turn-Verein were at Sulzer's Harlem River Park, and the Liederkranz ventured up the Hudson to Iona Island. August 23rd took to Wendel's Elm Park Hudson Lodge No. 17, Orden Germania. On the 25th, at Turtle Bay Park, the Beethoven Männerchor had an Italian night, all by the light o' the moon (if there was one); on the 30th, the Allemania Quartett Club was at Turtle Bay Park, and the Social Reformer did their duty at Jones Wood Colosseum. At Sulzer's Harlem River Park, on August 30th and 31st and September 1st was scheduled the Bayerisches Volksfest (*sic*), and, on September 6th, 7th, 8th and 9th, at Hartung's Park, 133rd Street, near Harlem Bridge, the Plattdeutsches Volks-Fest (*sic*). Thankfully I leave this subject for 1879–80. Ladies and gentlemen, this German festival is just about all my pen can endure; the details are hard in research and very, very dry in after feasting.

FRENCH MISCELLANY; ITALIANS, 1879–1880

Nothing could be more in keeping than to open the French record with Paul Juignet; this inheritance, this institution, this undying obligation had his annual concert and ball, on October 12th, in Tammany Hall; he promised Cécile Gregoire, Sara Raphael, Louise Beaudet, Emile Jouard, E. P. Boyard, Vilano, Josephine Estèphe, Paul Alhaiza, Célestin Tangoy and Max Schwab — all familiar to followers of the French stage in New York. On November 16th, at Irving Hall, the "Grand Fête Extraordinaire" of the choral society, L'Espérance, was to profit by the assistance of Mlles. Buzetti and Estèphe and MM. Seiffert, Tangav (*sic*) and Max Schwab. And, on November 27th (Thanksgiving Day) the concert and ball of the Cercle Musical et Philanthropique de l'Orphéon Français promised the co-operation of Mlle. Buzetti, Zélie de Lussan, J. G. Brigiotti, Lencioni, Gavaut, F. Groux (*directeur musical*) and Max Schwab (*chef d'orchestre*). La Gaieté Française (Réunion de Famille) presented on December 20th, at Irving Hall, its *grand bal paré et masqué;* on the 21st, the Gardes Lafayette, in the same place, held a concert and ball.

Now on with the dance! the Union Fraternelle Française, with its *bal paré et masqué,* on January 10th, in Irving Hall; the similar function, on January 12th, in the spacious Academy of Music, of the Cercle Musical et Philanthropique de l'Orphéon Français; another of the same kind, held, on January 19th, in Irving Hall, by the Société Française l'Amitié; and still another, also on the 19th, and in the Academy of Music, arranged by the Cercle Français de l'Harmonie, with Max Schwab and Grafulla concerned with the music. January 31st also fluttered out with double wings: the *bal paré et masqué de la Société Culinaire Cosmopolite,* held in Ferrero's Rooms, and another festivity of the same kind provided at Irving Hall by Huron Tribe, No. 35. On February 3rd, the eighth bal des Cuisiniers — la Société Culinaire Philanthropique — occupied both the big Academy of Music and Nilsson Hall; February 21st allowed La Concorde to dance in costume and in masks at the Germania Assembly Rooms.

March provided, on the 6th, in those same Germania quarters, the ball of L'Union Alsacienne and La Société Chorale L'Espérance; and the same rooms opened, on March 20th, for the ninth anniversary of the Revolution of March 18, 1871, given by the refugees of the Commune, with "concours de plusieurs sociétés révolutionnaires de New York." Much less inflammable was the ball of the Société Fraternelle Cosmopolite, held, on March 27th, at Beethoven Hall, Fifth Street, near the Bowery. Irving Hall, once more called into requisition, admitted, on April 11th, the concert and ball of the Cercle Musical et Philanthropique de l'Orphéon Français. L'Espérance, I hope, was successful with its concert and ball, on May 1st, at Dramatic Hall, East Houston Street; at Lyric Hall, on May 2nd, the director of the Orphéon Français gave a benefit concert and ball; and, on May 2nd and 9th, Soirées Chantantes, at 148 Bleecker Street, were listed as Cercle de Famille. And, in this spring season, La Gaieté Française, at 364 Sixth Avenue, advertised a Réunion de famille, with a "grande tombola pour les dames." Lyric Hall, 21 South Fifth Avenue, summoned, on May 16th, for a concert and ball given by A. Fornairon.

Let us bask in the balmy breezes of summer. The united French societies of New York celebrated July 14th with a concert, a ball, a "pique-nique" and games; the fête nationale suisse held Jones Wood Colosseum and Washington Park, on July 18th and 19th, with games and various divertissements. The Cercle Français de l'Harmonie held its summer-night festival, on August 12th, at the Iron Pier, Coney Island; for the benefit of the French Benevolent Society, the Gardes Lafayette celebrated, on September 6th, the anniversary of Lafayette, Lion Park sheltering their patriotic loyalty. L'Amitié functioned, on September 16th, in a "grande fête de nuit," at Hamilton Park; and, on September 19th and 20th, at Washington Park and Jones Wood Colosseum, the fiftieth anniversary of the independence of Belgium was celebrated with a concert, illuminations, a ball and a *fête de nuit*.

The Italian scrip, as usual, supplies but little of value. On November 30, 1879, the Società Corale Italiana Palestrina celebrated, in Tammany Hall, the first anniversary of its founding. December 15th allowed Professor A. Rosse and *suoi allievi* to give a concert in Lyric Hall. Having thus cleared the docket of concerts, we may recur to December 8th for the fifth annual ball of the Società Firenze, bravely held in the Teutonia Assembly Rooms. At the Liceo Italiano in Leonard Street, a concert directed, on January 12th, by Maestro Moderati, enlisted Miss Townsend, Oudin and Mrs. Lowerre; and, on the 21st, in the Teutonia Assembly Rooms, the Società di Unione e Fratellanza Italiana held its fourteenth annual ball. The double gift of February comprised the fourteenth annual ball of the Associazione Italiana de Tiro al Bersaglio — Guardia Colombo — held, on the 3rd, at the Teutonia Assembly Rooms, and the tenth annual ball of the Società Ticinese de Mutuo Soccorso, on the 14th, in the same place. Tammany Hall, on March 19th, housed the sixth annual ball of the Società

[89]

Legione Garibaldi, and the Teutonia Assembly Rooms, on March 31st, opened for the annual ball of the Circolo Italiano. All this leads us to June 7th and Bender's Schützen Park, for the fourteenth celebration dello Statuto, under the auspices of the Tiro al Bersaglio (Guardia Colombo). In that same park, on June 19th, the Società Operaia Italiana held its sixth annual *festa campestre.* The Società di San Antonio di Padova ferried, on Monday, July 5th, to Dittmar's Bellevue Park, West Hoboken, for its third celebration of American Independence. And here, on June 26th, in Jones Wood, we find the annual *festa campestre* of the Società Spagnuola di Beneficenza, La Nacional — this rare item recovered from the Eco d'Italia.

The annual excursion of the Associazione Firenze, on Sunday, July 18th, bravely journeyed to Linden Grove, Staten Island; I could not discover where the Festa Nazionale Italiana di Beneficenza held, on August 3rd, its *festa campestre.* The Garibaldi Association, on September 7th, celebrated, in Jones Wood, the entrance of Garibaldi into Naples; and the United Italian Societies, on September 19th and 20th, commemorated, in Benders' Park, the ceding of Rome to Italy, the festivities taking the form of dance, games, and *tiro al bersaglio.*

ACADEMY OF MUSIC, 1879–1880

Our first opportunity to enter (for 1879–80) the dignified portals of the Academy of Music, was vouchsafed on September 25th, when Max Maretzek conducted his own opera of Sleepy Hollow (words by Charles Gayler), in which appeared Annis Montague as Katrina Van Tassell, Florence Rice Knox as Frau Van Spuyten, Ada Whitman as Frau Van Tassell, Charles Turner as Brom Bones, Charles Collins as Van Tassell, H. Gardier as Rip Van Riper, W. C. Gardion as Ichabod Crane, and J. Fink as Van Ness. It is odd that John T. Raymond, at this very time, was acting Ichabod Crane, at Wallack's. Maretzek's visit was brief. The last performance of his opera was announced for the afternoon of October 4th. The Two Peters (Czaar und Zimmermann) was advertised for October 6th, and H. M. S. Pinafore for the 7th; a note from Maretzek in the Herald of the 6th declares his abandonment of the season, in accordance with "the unanimous opinion of the press and public that the Academy of Music is not the proper place to risk English or American opera. Under the circumstances the management feels justified in discontinuing the performances for the present." Allston Brown states that, on October 1st, Bianca La Blanche (Blanche Davenport) made her American début in opera at the New York Academy of Music; a glance at the New York Herald for October 2nd will show my reader that it was in the Philadelphia Academy of Music that Mlle. La Blanche, on that night, faced an audience of her fellow countrymen, in the difficult rôle of Violetta, in La Traviata.

[90]

Mapleson, on October 20th, began with that same opera, La Traviata, which, with Minnie Hauk, Frapolli and Galassi, had started his American career in 1878.   Now the cast included Emilie Ambre as Violetta, Runcio as Alfredo, Galassi (fortunately returned) as Germont, Monti as Il Medico, Rinaldini as Gastone, Grazzi as Il Marchese, and Mlle. Robiati as Annina. I regret to say that the new soprano and the new tenor did not succeed to the height of desire.   Next day the Herald stated that Mme. Ambre sang flat, and was very uneven in accomplishment; she failed in the *brindisi,* and greatly exaggerated *Ah! fors e lui.*   And another failure came on October 22nd, in the basso, David, whom Mapleson had injudiciously extolled.   His Mephistopheles, at his début, was not liked, and the public lamented his substitution for last season's Mephisto, Del Puente, now cast for Valentine. Campanini returned as a mellifluous Faust, and, in the rôle of Marguerite, appeared an American (Mrs. Hutchinson), who chose to sing under the pretty name of Alwina Valleria, a name indeed under which she acquired a fine popularity in this country, as in London.   She did not make here an immediate success, however, the Herald, on October 23rd, declaring her voice good, rounded, and even, and her appearance "pleasing."   Though not a great artiste, she was likely to please.   Others in the cast of Faust were last-year acquaintances — Mme. Lablache as Siebel and Mlle. Robiati as Martha.   At least Campanini, Galassi and Del Puente were in the company.

The third night of the season (October 24th) provided Rigoletto, with Mlle. Adini as Gilda, Mme. Lablache as Maddalena, Mlle. Robiati as Giovanna, Galassi as Rigoletto, Aramburo as Il Duca, David as Sparafucile, Monti as Monterone, &c.   And now the Herald (October 25th) openly expresses disapproval: "Mme. Ambre and Signor Runcio failed to carry 'Traviata' to a success on Monday.   Mlle. Valleria was a fair success in 'Faust,' but M. David, whom Mr. Mapleson had spoken of most highly, went down in a most melancholy failure as Mephistopheles. . . . Signor Aramburo was a partial success last evening, but Mlle. Adini was the most lamentable failure of the week by long odds . . . it is a wonder that the season is not doomed. . . . Valleria was really good and Aramburo acceptable, but if Mr. Mapleson supposed that New Yorkers were going to pay Nilsson prices to hear Ambre or Adini and be satisfied, the supposition was, to say the least, uncomplimentary either to his judgment or to the public's taste."   La Traviata was repeated at the matinée on the 25th, Campanini singing Alfredo.

This was a bad week for the redoubtable Mapleson; but experience had taught him to win losing battles.   He brought out Carmen, on October 27th — a daring thing to do, without Minnie Hauk.   In the title-rôle now appeared Selina Dolaro, whom, before the next season closed, we found disporting at Haverly's in a burlesque Carmen, which might be regarded as an offshoot of this October 27th.   Selina Dolaro will figure in many capacities before she leaves our history. Fortunately with her, at her début, were Campanini, Del Puente, Rinaldini (Il Dancairo), Grazzi, Bignardi, Alwina Valleria (a charming Michaela), Robiati and Lablache. This good cast, with Dolaro (not Hauk) reminds one of the attempt of Abbey and Grau with the same opera in 1894, when to atone for the absence of Emma Calvé, they put in Jean and Edouard de Reszke and Mme. Melba to support — whom? Zélie de Lussan! Both attempts met just about the success they deserved. Linda di Chamounix, on October 29th, brought into the fold Annie Louise Cary, very, very welcome as Pierotto, with Valleria as a satisfactory, if not brilliant Linda, Campanini, Galassi (a great Antonio), David (as Il Prefetto), and Tebaldo (Il Marchese). This was almost the first success of the season. On October 31st, Lucia enlisted Valleria, Aramburo and Galassi, and Carmen filled the matinée bill, on November 1st. Mme. Ambre was either ill or disappointed, and was not appearing.

Faust, repeated on the 3rd, had a delightful cast, with Campanini, Del Puente (again Mephisto), Galassi, Valleria, Lablache (as Martha) and Cary. Linda came once again on the 5th, and Il Trovatore, on the 7th, could hardly surpass performances of a great past, with (announced) Aramburo, Del Puente, Cary, and Adini; and, even so, Miss Cary was ill, and Mme. Lablache sang Azucena, Galassi (this of course was not so calamitous) replacing Del Puente as Di Luna. Faust was repeated at the matinée on the 8th, and on the 9th the Herald declared that Valleria "has become a popular favorite." Rather pleasing must have been Marta, on November 10th, with Valleria, Cary, Campanini and Behrens (a new basso, destined to a fair degree of public approval). Rigoletto, on the 12th, once more presented Aramburo, Galassi and Adini, Behrens now being the Sparafucile and Miss Cary the Maddalena. The Elks had a benefit matinée, on November 13th, at which appeared J. K. Emmet, in the second act of Fritz; the Tourists; Marie Bonfanti; Vernona Jarbeau and the Standard company, in Trial by Jury; Salsbury's Troubadours, in The Brook; Jennie Morgan, George Thatcher (in The Wrong House), the Herbert Brothers, Delehanty and Hengler, E. C. Dunbar, George R. Edeson, George Wilson, &c. Adini, Lablache, Behrens and Runcio sang.

The biggest production of Mapleson's season was an elaborate revival of Aïda, first heard on November 14th, with Emilie Ambre, Annie Louise Cary, Campanini, Galassi, Behrens and Monti. Mapleson provided new scenes, costumes and properties, and, for that time, the spectacle was gorgeous. Campanini and Miss Cary were magnificent as Radames and Amneris, parts they had created for New York in 1874. Mme. Ambre was a handsome, if not a great Aïda. The opera had several repetitions during the season. Il Trovatore was tame fare for the matinée on the 15th. And now Mapleson flowered in Sunday concerts; on November 16th, he gave the Stabat Mater, with Valleria, Cary, Campanini, Galassi and Behrens, a miscella-

MARIE MARIMON
(1879–1880)

ANNA DE BELOCCA
AS CARMEN

ALWINA VALLERIA
IN FAUST

ANNIE LOUISE CARY
IN MARTHA

EMILIE AMBRE

Photograph of Miss Cary by H. Rocher; others by Mora

neous group of songs filling out the programme. The rest of the week was devoted to repetitions, Faust (on the 17th, without Miss Cary), Aïda (19th), Il Trovatore (21st), and Marta (matinée, 22nd). On Sunday, the 23rd, a second Stabat Mater employed the same singers, except that Anna Drasdil substituted for Miss Cary. Mme. Ambre also sang in the miscellaneous concert accompanying the Rossini masterpiece. Aïda reached a third hearing, on the 24th, and, on the 26th, Mme. Ambre tried, as Carmen, to atone for the absence of Minnie Hauk. The Herald found her performance "neither good nor bad"; and Runcio's Don José was haunted by the auditor's memory of Campanini's. Mapleson seems to have possessed the enviable ability to freeze from his payroll singers who failed to attract. The Herald of November 27th carries news of the sudden departure for Europe of Aramburo and his wife, Adini. He was angry because of unflattering reviews in the Herald; besides, he had a contract at La Scala, a breaking of which, on his part, would result in a lawsuit. He modestly set himself down as one of the six leading tenors in Europe.

Having thus rid the house of two undesirables, we may return to the routine of Marta (28th) and Linda (matinée, 29th), the latter with Valleria and Campanini not in good voice, after their performance in Marta, the night before, and with Galassi and Mme. Lablache in other rôles. The Stabat Mater, with the singers of the 16th, came again on the 30th, Mme. Ambre taking part in the miscellaneous programme. Faust (without Miss Cary) once more exerted its spell, on December 1st, though Runcio was not a satisfactory substitute for Campanini. Aïda had a special performance, on Tuesday, December 2nd; it was again heard at the matinée on the 6th.

And on the 3rd appeared Marie Marimon, a coloratura soprano, who, it was hoped, would take the place of the sadly missed Etelka Gerster. She emerged in Gerster's great rôle of Amina, with Campanini to assist, and, to read the Herald, next day, one might almost assume that Gerster herself was singing; *almost*, because the lady, though fluent and gifted, had a slight voice and marked mannerisms. Marimon unquestionably made a hit, the first night audience going wild with joy over her trills and roulades. Mignon, on the 5th, had Ambre in the title-rôle, Mme. Valleria as Filina, Miss Cary as Federico, Campanini as Guglielmo, Del Puente as Lotario, and Rinaldini as Laerte. Campanini, Mme. Ambre and many of the company appeared in the Sunday concert of December 7th. On the 8th, Dinorah was to have enlisted Marimon, Galassi, Runcio, Cary and Behrens, but Marimon was ill, and Rigoletto was substituted, with Ambre, Cary, Campanini, Galassi and Behrens. La Sonnambula, announced for the 10th, was withdrawn, through Marimon's illness; Linda took its place, with Valleria, also ill, agreeing to sing the score somewhat curtailed. Runcio substituted for Campanini, who also was ill. On Sunday, December 14th, we were to have Rossini's Messe Solennelle, with Valleria, Cary, Lablache, Campanini,

Galassi and Behrens; alas! Lablache substituted for Cary, Runcio for Campanini, and Galassi did not carry through all his share of the score. The performance, according to the Herald, was disappointing to the audience as it must have been mortifying to the manager.

Meantime, let us remember that at the Academy were held the performances of the Philharmonic Society. On December 11th occurred the annual benefit of the Roman Catholic Orphan Asylum, under the direction of L. J. Vincent. The afternoon bill, as set down in the Herald of the 7th, offered N. S. Wood, C. L. Farwell and others in part of Poor Jo; J. K. Emmet in the second act of Fritz in Ireland; Clara Morris, Louise Muldener, Fritz Williams and Gustavus Levick, in the third act of Miss Multon; Harrigan and Hart in The Mulligan Guards' Christmas; Tony Pastor's company; specialties from Enchantment; and the Strategists. In the evening, Did You Ever? presented W. B. Cahill, Thomas Chapman, Alice Hastings, Nellie Taylor and Helena Cahill (her first appearance on any stage); Edwin Booth followed in the fourth act of Richelieu; the fourth act of Camille enlisted Charles R. Thorne, Jr., Signora Majeroni, Mrs. E. J. Phillips, J. A. Kennedy, A. Jacques and Harry Hogan; George Clarke recited Shamus O'Brien; Jennie Yeamans and Bonnie Runnells gave Lena's Birthday; Gustavus Levick and Helen Ottolengui appeared in the balcony scene of Romeo and Juliet; and Maude Granger, Emily Rigl, Evans and Sullivan finished the performance in the second act of The Galley Slave. On December 16th, the Jewish Festival of Chanucka (*sic*) was celebrated at the Academy by the Young Men's Hebrew Association, with tableaux arranged by Carl Marwig. And, on December 18th, Magda Irschick and the Germania Theater company acted there, in Der Fechter von Ravenna. On December 25th, Patrick S. Gilmore produced, after much preliminary advertising, his national ode, Columbia, words and music by himself. Algernon S. Sullivan made an address, George Vandenhoff read the poem, and Miss Thursby was soloist for the ode. The orchestra of Mapleson's opera, and that of Koster and Bial's, along with Gilmore's Band, participated, and a mighty chorus sang out the pæan of national joy. Levy also blew manfully into his cornet. The audience of three thousand joined in the last stanza of Columbia — the prayer — and, says the Herald of the 26th, they "rolled out with magnificent effect the stirring strain."

Much illness beset the singers this year, and one dare not trust the advertisements of coming joys; all one could do (and I did it) was to read the criticisms of operas on the days following the performances, to see how many of the promised delights were fulfilled. La Sonnambula was repeated on December 15th, Dinorah given on December 17th, and, on the 19th, La Figlia del Reggimento, with Marimon (of course), Lablache, Runcio, Del Puente, Grazzi, Rinaldini and Tebaldi. Aïda again spectacularly filled a matinée, on the 20th. We observe that Mapleson had profited by Marimon's success, in presenting her on all three subscription nights of the week. The Sunday offering, on the 21st, brought the customary Stabat Mater, and a miscellaneous concert, with Emilie Ambre and Howard Reynolds (cornet — his "début in America"). La Sonnambula (December 22nd), Aïda (Tuesday, the 23rd), and La Figlia del Reggimento (24th) were familiar matter of the last week of Mapleson's season; on December 26th he staged the difficult Il Flauto Magico, with Runcio, Del Puente, Behrens, Monti, Rinaldini, Bignardi, and Mmes. Robiati, Altona, Schor, Martini, Cary (as one of the Damigelle), Isidora Martinez (Papagena), Valleria (Pamina) and Marimon (Astrafiammante). The autumn season ended with the matinée, on December 27th, Faust enlisting the usual cast.

With the departure of the singers, the Academy was given over to social festivities. On January 5th occurred there a "Grand Masquerade Ball," and, on the 12th, another, this last by the Cercle Musical de l'Orphéon Français. And on January 16th, a French masquerade ball, with "Carnival Inauguration." The Old Guard Reception fell on the 15th. January 19th celebrated the ball of the Cercle Français de l'Harmonie, the Herald headlines, next day, stressing "A Fast and Furious French Fandango," "Tremendous Throng," and "Wit, Women and Song at Five o'Clock in the Morning." January 20th witnessed the Martha Washington Reception of St. John's Guild, with Gilmore repeating his Columbia, and with historical tableaux (arranged by L. J. Vincent) picturing Benjamin Franklin at the Court of France. The Charity Ball was danced on January 29th; the French Cooks' Ball, on February 3rd; the German Liederkranz Masquerade Ball fell on February 5th, and the fourth annual Children's Carnival and Ball made bright the evening of February 9th. On February 26th, the Purim Association gave a fancy dress ball. Well, I can invite the reader to no more dances.

Rather must I summon him to the spring season of opera, beginning on March 1st, and ask him to accompany me four times weekly to the noble Academy, each time hurrying unconsciously to see what changes, if any, have taken place in the announced programme. The opening bills went through without accident — Lucia, with Campanini, Galassi, Behrens, Robiati and Marimon (first time here as the heroine); Linda (3rd); La Favorita (5th, with Campanini, Del Puente, Behrens and Miss Cary); and La Sonnambula (matinée, 6th) were the delights of Mapleson's first week. On the evening of March 4th, a benefit for the Irish Relief Fund brought in Booth, in the third act of Hamlet; Ole Bull, in a violin solo; Galassi, Miss Cary and Campanini in operatic airs; Booth (Iago), J. C. McCollom, &c. in the third act of Othello; Behrens, in songs, Campanini, Miss Cary, Galassi and Valleria in the quartette from Rigoletto, and Mme. Valleria in a rendering of Kathleen Mavourneen; and Booth and Marion Booth in Katharine and Petruchio (entire). The Ninth Regiment Band also appeared. Surely that was a noble bill, and greatly to the credit of all concerned, especially Booth.

The opera went by on unruffled wing. Aïda (March 8th), Il Flauto Magico (9th), Lucia (10th), La Figlia del Reggimento (12th), and Faust (with a packed house, matinée, 13th) — these were the familiar offerings of a happy week, unmarred by illness or casualty of any sort. Anna de Belocca joined on the 15th, singing Carmen, with Campanini, Del Puente and Valleria — a fine cast, if only Belocca had been Minnie Hauk. On the 16th, that voice from the past, Brignoli, sang Edgardo to the Lucia of Marimon and the Aston of Galassi. This assuredly was a bridging of the decades between the old Academy and the new. And no one could pretend that time had not taken something from Brignoli; but the mere thought of that tenor-idol of the past in the same company with Campanini, the idol of the present, warms the imagination. La Favorita, become a great favourite, returned on the 17th, and Faust on the 19th, with Carmen as matinée attraction, on the 20th. Il Trovatore, on the 22nd, brought back the Manrico of Brignoli (he had "created" the part for New York in 1855!); his associates now were Alwina Valleria, Anna de Belocca (substituting for Mme. Lablache), and Del Puente. La Forza del Destino had, on March 23rd, its first performance in New York, with Campanini (Don Alvaro), Galassi (Don Carlo), Del Puente (Fra Melitone), Behrens (Padre Guardiano), Monti (Il Marchese), Annie Louise Cary (Preziosilla), Mlle. Robiati (Curra), and Marie Louise Swift (Leonora). This last selection enfeebled the cast; Mrs. Swift was only a fair singer and a poor actress. Yet, as Mlle. Dotti, she became a fixture for years in Mapleson's company. Campanini and Galassi created the usual furore with the famous duet, Miss Cary was excellent in her rôle, and Del Puente contributed a fine character study as Fra Melitone. Dinorah danced once more with her own shadow on March 24th. On Good Friday, March 26th, Mapleson piously gave, instead of an opera, Stabat Mater, with the usual quintette, Valleria (her last appearance), Cary, Campanini, Galassi and Behrens, and a concert employing Belocca, Brignoli and Del Puente — a notable array of singers. Aïda lured for the matinée, on the 27th. La Forza del Destino (March 29th), La Favorita (30th), Marta (31st, with Brignoli, Behrens, Belocca and Marimon) — these were the offerings of some earnest evenings; yet, on April 1st, the Herald assures us that, in Marta, Brignoli and Belocca were not at all equal to Campanini and Miss Cary, in their rôles, "in vocal or dramatic ability." Marimon, however, "looked and acted charmingly," in the part heretofore sung by Valleria. The cast of Les Huguenots, on April 2nd, included Campanini, Del Puente (De Nevers), Galassi (St. Bris), Behrens, Marimon (Marguerite), Belocca (substituting for Miss Cary, so frequently "indisposed"), and Ambre (Valentine). For the matinée, on the 3rd of April, Mapleson suddenly found all his tenors ill; he luckily discovered Lazzarini in town and brought him in for Lucia, with Marimon and Galassi. Lazzarini sang again, on April 5th, as Elvino to the Amina of Marimon, and the Count of Del Puente (*vice* Behrens). Mapleson's benefit, on the 6th, promised three acts of Aïda, a bit of Carmen, the shadow song from Dinorah, and the last act of La Favorita. Readers of the Herald of the 7th and later will be amused at the account of the quarrel between the prima donnas, Marimon positively refusing to share the star dressing room with Ambre, even though a partition-screen was introduced; she left the theatre in temperamental fury, returning only after a threat sent to her hotel to break some of the terms of her contract. Well, this really was sad — two prima donnas out of amity! Campanini sang, though ill, in Aïda and La Favorita. Les Huguenots was again billed for April 7th. On the 9th, Le Postillon de Lonjumeau, for the benefit of the French Benevolent Society, enlisted Capoul, Duplan, Jouard, and Mme. Leroux-Bouvard; Paola Marié also gave the second act of Le Petit Duc. The afternoon of the 10th provided La Favorita, with Belocca (Miss Cary again ill). The evening of that day brought a Seventh Regiment Entertainment of "tragedy, farce and minstrelsy." They actually performed Othello, with Virginia Brooks as Desdemona, Cora Goodall as Emilia, John H. Bird (of the Veterans) as Othello, Henry S. Spelman as Iago, and with, in other rôles, W. J. Underwood, Jr., C. T. Beeckman, Spencer H. Green, Edward F. Dumas, Edward C. Ray, Jr., Steele, Flanagan, Valentine and Sherman. Soldiers brave enough to attempt that feat might be depended on to win a war!

Mapleson was so successful that he extended his season; Aïda once more pined and died, on April 12th, and Don Pasquale, on the 13th, gave opportunity for fun and melody to Marimon, Papini (as Don Pasquale), Del Puente (as Malatesta), and Lazzarini (as Ernesto). La Forza del Destino (April 14th), Faust (15th, with Lazzarini, Del Puente, Galassi, Cary, and Marimon — her first appearance here as Marguerite) carried us to Campanini's benefit, on the 16th, with Carmen (second act), La Favorita (third act), Il Trovatore (third act), and Lucia (second act). Les Huguenots ended the season, at the matinée on April 17th — assuredly an interesting year, prospering from a very bad beginning. According to Mapleson, Marimon received $500 for each performance. A Sunday concert (April 25th) was to enlist Joseffy, Ambre, Marie Louise Swift, Mme. Lablache, Mlle. Lablache (her first appearance in America), Brignoli, Behrens and Rialp (director); the Herald, next day, states that the illness of Mrs. Swift and Behrens caused non-fulfilment of the scheme. Ole Bull and Emma Thursby co-starred, on the 26th. On April 30th came a benefit (probably needed) for Max Strakosch, with Ole Bull, Campanini, Marie Litta, Charles Adams, Mme. Lablache, Tagliapietra, George Conly, L. G. Gottschalk, Catarina Marco, Frida de Gebele, Teresa Carreño, a chorus and an orchestra, directed by Max Maretzek and S. Behrens. The programme included the first act of Lohengrin, the third of Il Trovatore, and the second of William Tell.

And now, on May 3rd, Maurice Grau's triumphant French singers entered the sacred precincts of the Academy, in Mignon; on the 4th they gave Le Pré aux Clercs, on the 5th Giroflé-Girofla, on the 6th and at the matinée on the 7th, Le Postillon de Lonjumeau, on the 7th (evening) La Princesse de Trebizonde ("first time in seven years" and for the benefit of Paola Marié), and on the 8th this same revived opera. After the lapse of a week, the company returned on May 17th, for a "farewell" visit; it is terribly hard to say good-bye when dollars are pouring in. On the 17th and 18th we were offered La Vie Parisienne; on the 19th, La Fille de Mme. Angot. For the benefit, on the 20th, of Fritz Hirschy, the assistant treasurer, a double bill offered Pomme d'Api (by Offenbach) and Les Chevaliers du Pince-Nez, the latter with Angèle as Fauvette and Mezières as Chabannais. On the 21st and 22nd, La Camargo was given, and, on the 24th, for the benefit of Mezières and Duplan, Les Cloches de Corneville. At Capoul's benefit, on the 25th, we heard Le Pré aux Clercs (first act), Le Postillon de Lonjumeau (second act), and Mignon (second and third acts). If the world was too much with us, in 1879–80, so, I feel, was opéra-bouffe, even of the excellent quality offered by Paola Marié, Angèle, Capoul and their comic confrères. To remind the reader of those colleagues, let me give the cast of the oft-deferred La Camargo of Lecocq:

La Camargo	Mlle. Paola Marié	Pontcale	M. Mezières
Juana	Mlle. Angèle	Saturnin	M. Juteau
Colombe	Mlle. Gregoire	Le Philosophe	M. Duplan
Ecureuil	Mlle. Raphael	Fournevis	M. Poyard
Mandrin	M. Jouard	Peruchot	M. Vilano

This ends 1879–80 at the Academy — on the whole, an interesting season.

THEATRE COMIQUE, 1879–1880

Harrigan and Hart may be said to have come into their own; the Mulligan Guards series was making them. Their popular theatre, the Comique, re-opened on August 11, 1879, with "Volume the Third" of the Mulligan progression — The Mulligan Guards' Chowder. Many favourites were greeted in the first cast of the season:

Dan Mulligan	Edward Harrigan	Mr. Hershaw	John Shay
Tommy Mulligan } Mrs. Welcome Allup }	Tony Hart	Mr. Hog-Eye	William West
		James Jarme	James Fox
Captain Simpson Primrose	John Wild	Danny Daly	J. McCullough
Rev. Palestine Puter	William Gray	Cordelia Mulligan	Mrs. Annie Yeamans
Young Dublin	John Queen	Bridget Lochmuller	Annie Mack
Gustavus Lochmuller	H. A. Fisher	Katy Mulligan	Jennie Yeamans
Walsingham McSweeny	M. Bradley	Mrs. Gilmartin	Mary Bird
Snuff McIntosh	Edward Burt		

In this diversion, the Skidmore Guards, that unconquerable negro band, were represented by John Wild, John Shay, Michael Foley, Charles Schaeffer (*sic*), Edward Goss, James Fox, William West, James Tierney, Timothy Cronin, Joseph Buckley, John Mealey, Thomas Ray, Eugene Rourke and James Fitzsimmons.

We need worry no more for Harrigan and Hart; they were pursuing the pleasant paths of prosperity. On September 1st, I find Mary Bird down as Katy Mulligan (Jennie Yeamans had played the part), with Annie Howard in Miss Bird's former rôle. In addition to the very edible Chowder, John Wild, in The In-Toe-Natural Walking Match, in October, satirised the current craze for those crazy feats of "pedestrianism," then devastating ill-nourished minds; the fourth week of the Harrigan skit began on October 20th. November 5th celebrated the hundredth serving of the Chowder; no "olio" had been advertised. The last night of the Chowder came on November 15th, and, on the 17th, Harrigan had ready the Fourth Volume of his famous series — The Mulligan Guards' Christmas, of course a revision of an earlier working of the same theme. In this volume, Planxty McFudd (Welsh Edwards) comes from Ireland, to visit his sister, Mrs. Lochmuller, and, on the way, marries Dan Mulligan's sister, Diana, at Albany. In the new piece Harrigan as Dan and Hart as Mrs. Welcome Allup had familiar rôles, as did John Wild as Captain Simpson Primrose, Billy Gray as Rev. Palestine Puter, Harry Fisher and Annie Mack as Gustavus and Bridget Lochmuller, Michael Bradley as Walsingham McSweeny, and Annie Yeamans as Cordelia Mulligan. Newer characterisations were offered by Welsh Edwards as Planxty, Edward Burt as Macaulay Jangles, the crazy man who misquotes, Billy West as Orlando Tucker, Charles Scheffer (or Schaeffer) as the Reverend Ferguson Clinton, John Mealey as Paddy Campbell, Master Husel (or Heusel) as Gustavus Lochmuller, Jr., Marie Gorenflo as Diana McFudd, Mary Bird as Rosy McFudd, and Julia Deen as Ellen McFudd. Braham's songs in the Christmas were The Skids are on Review, The Sweet Kentucky Rose (sung by Tony Hart), The Pitcher of Beer (sung by Harrigan), The Mulligan Braves, and Tu-ri-ad-i-lum, or Santa Claus Has Come (sung by Harrigan). In an "olio," on November 17th, appeared Jennie Morgan, Goss and Fox, and Edwin Barry. The reader will be interested to learn that all this fun cost but 35 cents in the dress circle, 15 cents in the gallery, 50 cents in the parquet, and 75 cents for an orchestra chair. Boxes were held at $4 and $6. Perhaps real fun is never expensive.

The Mulligan Guards' Christmas, with its bustle, its songs, and its popular contests between Germans and Irish, with the negroes standing by, ran easily up to and including February 14th — a wonderful holiday gift for all concerned. The Fifth Volume of the Mulligan Guards Series — The Mulligan Guards' Surprise — came forth on February 16th, with Harrigan still as Dan and Hart as Rebecca (now *sic*) Allup, Wild, Gray, Welsh

[99]

Edwards, Harry Fisher, Bradley, Annie Mack, Mrs. Yeamans, and May (*sic*) Gorenflo in the characters they had sustained in Volume IV. Edward Burt was now Roger Dunleavy, John Queen was both Dick Dublin and Mrs. Dublin, Edward Goss was Dr. Algernon Winterbottom, William West Ichabod Carper, Miss Mordaunt Rosy McFudd, Emily Yeamans Ellen McFudd, and Mary Bird Jenny. Braham's songs for this "Volume" were Linger Not, Darling, I'll Wear the Trousers, Oh! Hark, Baby, Hark, Dat Citron Wedding Cake, Never Take the Horseshoe from the Door, and Whist! the Bogie Man. This piece deals with the moving of the Mulligans uptown, and employs material used much more skilfully in Harrigan's later play, Cordelia's Aspirations.

The Surprise was a surprise, perhaps, in more than title; it ran cheerily to the end of the season, on May 15th. The hundredth performance fell on May 12th, when every lady attending received a satin programme. How one cherished such satin programmes given of old on special occasions! And how eagerly collectors buy them today!

Tony Pastor's, 1879–1880

At Tony Pastor's, during the week of September 1, 1879, were present the London Burlesque Company, with S. J. T. Pinafore, in which delectability Adelaide Campbell was Sir Joseph Cypher and Christine Percy Ralph. No impersonators of mere females were advertised in that rosebud garden of burlesque; Buttercup, however, was localised as Aunty Tammany, with a burlesque song. Marie Lentz's Minstrels were here during the week of September 15th.

Thereafter Pastor's remained closed to the public until the expansive Tony himself returned, on October 27th, with an array including Niles and Evans, Fred Bryant and Billy Hoey (Music in a Pawnshop), Georgie Kaine, Kelly and Ryan, Reynolds and Cogill, Flora and Jennie Weston, Sheehan and Jones, John Morris, the French Twin Sisters (Minnie and Lena), Frank Girard, Jennie Satterlee, Bonnie Runnells and Harry Budworth. That group makes us feel almost as much "at home" as was Tony himself. And, on November 3rd, in came Delehanty and Hengler, whom we are always pleased to greet, along with Harry and John Kernell, Fannie Beane and Charles Gilday, Kate Castleton and Kitty O'Neil, all equally welcome. Others were the Stuart (*sic*) Sisters (Mattie and Alice), Bothwick Reid ("wizard swordsman"), Bonnie Runnells (Dutch comedian), the French Sisters and Georgie Kaine ("prima donna").

I like the breeze that blew in, on November 10th, with Dashing Dunbar ("greatest of all England's comic singers"), and the Three Brazziers ("Les Trois Demons — only rivals of the great Majiltons"). In addition, Herrmann dispensed magic, and Flora and May Irwin added to the joys. A "new team," Paul Allen and Bob Slavin, gave (or were) The Dizzy Coons from Tobacco-land, and Tony sang The Turkish Reveille, as he continued to do for weeks.   Burt Clark and Charles Edwards appeared in Invited to the Sängerfest, and the Irwin Sisters, Tommy and Annie Dayton, Jennie Satterlee, Manchester and Jennings and Harry Budworth rounded out a full evening that, in the reading, seems promising.   Do we imagine that Harrigan and Hart could remain single in the field?   Perish the thought!   On November 17th, Pastor staged the well-known Murphy's Wedding, and The Parade of the Rafferty Blues, with songs by John and George Murphy, and with the variety teams, Murphy and Shannon and Murphy and Mack, at the helm.   The cast included John Murphy as Thomas Ryan, George Murphy as Peter Baum, Phil Mack as Mrs. Margaret Ryan, George Shannon as Seltzer Meyers, Otto Burbank as McKeon Setter, Jennie Satterlee as Katie Ryan, and Frank Girard as Mr. Murphy.   In the olio, Tony still sang The Turkish Reveille, Herr and Frl. Ordey appeared as equilibrists, and other entertainers were the "great" Dunbar, Flora Moore, Haley and West, Don Ferreyra, Manchester and Jennings, Bryant and Saville, Maggie Foster and Raymond and Murphy.   Murphy's Wedding Day (sic) lasted into the week of November 24th, and then also Maggie and Jennie Benson gave Money Matters.   One observes "Variety" merging into drama, to disappear almost, in later years, until it revived as "Vaudeville."   In the bill of November 24th were also John W. Ransome (or Ransone) and Emma True, "Professor" Sawyer and his Copophonium, Crumley and De Forrest, Belle Clifton, Sheehan and Jones, and Tony Pastor, with The Turkish Reveille.

The American Four (Pettingill, Allen, Dailey and Hoey), Niles and Evans, the Freeman Sisters, Harris and Wood, and Johnny Allen made bright (presumably) the week of December 1st–6th, along with a dash of J. K. Emmet's specialties in the accompanying farce of Schneider, or, the House on the Rhine, with John Allen as Schneider, Otto Burbank as Dick Fairchild, Frank Girard as Robert Thornton, William Campbell as Tom Cranshaw, John Burke as Brattles, Lizzie Freeman as Lowesa Schneider, and Jennie Satterlee as Mary Cranshaw.   Mlle. Cerito danced on December 8th, and other specialists for the week were Flora Moore, Mlle. Tournour (sic), Frank Jones and Alice Montague, Harry Bryant, Merritt Brothers ("elegant balladists"), Wilkinson Brothers (Irish), Charlie and Lewis (sic) Dockstader, and Niles and Evans.   Tony spread a rich table.   Perhaps there was excitement at Pastor's, during the week of December 15th, when Tom Sayers, "son of the late champion of England," appeared.   In addition, the Baldwin Brothers and Mlle. Lottie executed pyramids, posturing, and somersaults, and the Wilkinson Brothers gave From the Lakes of Killarney and Boys from Mullingar.   The playlet was Servants' Holiday (descended remotely, I suppose, from High Life below Stairs), with Sam and Carrie Swain.   Jennie Engel, the Parker Sisters, John and Lea Peasley (in Mollie's

[101]

Victory), and Charles Gardner, Jr. were added attractions of a bill which also included N. G. Pinafore, or, the Men who Bounced the Sailors. Gentlemen, in your ears: I have had enough, for the present, of Pinafore, in any shape. Christmas week (December 22nd-27th) poured a cornucopia of gifts in the Royal Marionettes (in Humpty Dumpty's Christmas), the Lawrence Sisters (trapeze) Tom Sayers, Bryant and Hoey, the Werners (Maud Stanley and Edward), Minnie and Lena French, the Irwin Sisters, &c. Mrs. Driscoll's Party, on December 29th, enlisted John Sheehan and Bobby Jones. William Hoey, Fred Bryant, Louise Montague, Georgie Kaine, Bob Slavin and Sawyer's Copophone Glasses helped to dispel December gloom.

Mrs. Driscoll's Party continued through the week of January 5th, when new to the olio were the St. Felix Sisters (Henriette, Clementine, Leonora and Charlotte), in Sweethearts. Others in the bill were the Rankins, Mlle. Barretta (in songs and dances), Harry Woodson ("great old man negro"), Bonnie Runnells, John Till's Marionettes, and the pantomime, Little Red Riding Hood. John Hart's Specialty Company were visitors, during the week of January 12th-17th, with Malony's Visit to New York; Harris and Carroll also gave School vs. Mischief. Kate Castleton, William Carroll (banjo), "Dutch" Dick Gorman, Jacques Kruger, Elise Kruger (dancer), Jennie Christie, Edith Crolius, and Fred Carroll kept alive the fun and frolic.

And now, on January 19th, came what I have been praying for — a hit that, by continued run, could save my pen from these long lists of weekly changes in personnel. The Emigrant Train, or, Go West! was obviously founded on the style of Fun on the Bristol and other such bits of jolly frivolity. It was said to have been written by William Carleton, author of Fritz in Ireland, and in it appeared Sheehan and Jones as the Irish Emigrants, Mulraney and Bridget; Lena (or Lina) Tettenborn (fresh from Aberle's) as the Dutch emigrant; Bonnie Runnells as Hans Munchausen and the Dutch Conductor; Billy Courtright as the Tramp; the Sparks Brothers as the Italian Emigrants; Mose W. Fiske as the Policeman; Nellie Hadfield as the Italian violin girl; and Perry and Hughes and Curdy and Magrew ("the four Eccentrics") representing the Negro Exodus. One sees that in one emigrant train were herded all sorts of dialect comedians that might be expected to appear in any "Variety" bill; and here they were gathered in a kind of dramatic thing suggestive, perhaps, of Harrigan and Hart, the Tourists, and other popular groups. And Pastor's offering succeeded; it ran for weeks, frequently under the single title of Go West! Nevertheless, my pen must record the olio on February 2nd — Harry Bennett (Irish comedian), Lina Tettenborn, Sheehan and Jones, Harry Woodson, Flora Moore, the Three Rankins, Bonnie Runnells, Idaletta and Wallace ("eating, sleeping, drinking, sewing, reading, writing, under water"), Merritt Brothers, Nellie Hadfield (violin solos) &c. The Sullivan Street

Brigade doubtless had an eye to the Mulligan Guards.   But Go West! was the word of the evening.   The irresistibly funny Billy Sweatnam was featured on February 9th, as were Hallen and Hart, Fannie Beane and Charles Gilday, and the Milton Jaspers ("acrobatic astonishments").   The Dutch Students, burlesque of the Spanish Students, then popular at Booth's, entered Pastor's, on February 16th; Go West! remained, and the Merritt Brothers sang the song written for the New York Herald, then trying to raise funds for relief ships to starving Ireland — the song, Hush, My Darlings, Do not Weep, a song supposed to express the lament of the Irish mother.   A matinée for the starving Irish brought to Pastor's, on the afternoon of the 18th, Emma Howe, the San Francisco Minstrels, Jennie Hughes, and members of the week's regular performers.

The big Four (Pettingill, Gale, Dailey and Hoey), Harry and John Kernell, Lena (*sic*) Tettenborn, W. Henry Rice (female impersonator), Bonnie Runnells, Minnie Lee, Nellie Hadfield, the French Twins, the Merritt Brothers, Bob Slavin, and Tony Pastor appeared in the week of March 1st, along with a skit called, at first, The Jays from Woonsocket, and afterward The Jays of Weehawken, a name with connotations still rich, fifty years later.   This was set down as the last week of The Emigrant Palace Car. On March 8th, Pastor re-worked the formula of Go West! into The Steerage, or, Fun on the Briny Deep, with Harry Kernell as Patsy O'Dowd, and the Poet, and the cockney, Theodoric Sapps; with Bonnie Runnells as Herman Himmelspink, Lina Tettenborn as Wilhelmina Himmelspink, and with Bob Slavin, John Kernell, Frank Girard, William and George Merritt and Jennie Satterlee standing by.   This lasted through the week of March 15th, set down, by the way, as the last week of Billy Sweatnam; John, Mike and Steve Crimmins, Sam Holdsworth ("primo tenor" and "lightning change") and Mollie Wilson were in the bulging olio.   And now, reader, here is more worry for us — a revival, on March 22nd, of Canal Boat Pinafore, with Lina (*sic*) Tettenborn as Josephine, William Cronin (of Scanlon and Cronin) as Buttercup, Georgie Parker as Hebe, George Merritt as Ralph, Bonnie Runnells as Dick Deadeye, Frank Campbell as the Dutch Admiral, &c.   The Big Four, McIntyre and Heath ("first time in New York, and positively the greatest negro performers in the world"), Mlle. Barretta, and Laura Russell (cornet) were part of the lure.   For March 29th, Pastor poured out a cornucopia of "Variety" — Harry and John Kernell, the Four St. Felix Sisters, Fannie Beane and Charles Gilday, Flora Moore, in Camp Meeting Songs, Charles Diamond (harpist, vocalist and dancer), Bonnie Runnells, Lina Tettenborn and Tony, himself.   And Go West on the Emigrant Train was once more the cry.

Another of those things, on the now popular pattern, was The Tramps, played on April 12th, with Dan Kelly as the Worn Down Tramp, Dan Collyer as a negro tramp, &c.   The Dockstaders, Beula Merton ("lady cornetist"), Kitty O'Neil, Harry Bennett and the American Four also participated in the evening's festivities. The burlesque of April 19th (rather late, it would seem) was Penn's Aunts among the Pirates; Tony Pastor had departed for a tour of anxiously expectant centres, and it was the Rentz-Santley troupe that staged this burlesque of the Gilbert and Sullivan operetta, and that kept it going for two weeks. On May 3rd began Fanny Herring, Barlow Brothers' Novelty Company, Julia Sheldon, the Fieldings, &c.

Hyde and Behman's Company came to Pastor's, presenting, on May 10th, Billy Barry (in Muldoon's Picnic), Hugh Fay, Charles T. Ellis, Niles and Evans, Clara Moore, Kitty O'Neil, Sheehan and Jones, Jennie Satterlee, Frank Wills, William T. Dwyer and Lou C. Lingard — largely a Pastor array; this good entertainment lasted for two weeks. On May 20th, a benefit was arranged for the widow and mother of W. H. Delehanty, of Delehanty and Hengler. That death saddens me. On May 26th, was to occur a testimonial to Blanche Selwyn, who, for reason I cannot specify, always bores me. It must be her photograph. A burlesque, Mrs. Joshua Whitcomb, figured in the bills of late May and early June; the Parisian Folly Troupe was responsible. On June 14th, Constantine's Dramatic Pantomime Novelty Company gave The Dumb Man of Manchester. Mlle. Saroni's Burlesque Troupe added, on June 21st, to what seems to me the pitifulness of this "off" season at Pastor's.

ABERLE'S NEW THEATRE, 1879–1880

Aberle, whose Tivoli, in Eighth Street, we might heretofore have attended, provided himself, in 1879–80, with a new house and, to some extent, a new policy. Between Broadway and Fourth Avenue, on Eighth Street, stood St. Anne's Roman Catholic Church, which had once been largely attended, but whose congregation had drifted to other parts of the city. In April, 1879, Aberle bought the property, remodelled it, and turned it into a variety theatre. These facts I learn from Allston Brown.

This new establishment opened on September 8, 1879, blandly advertising itself as "the most Commodious and Beautiful Variety Theatre in the City," and with a list of entertainers including Lulu Delmay and H. R. Archer, Cool Burgess, Maggie Weston, the Grinnells (Hattie and Bennie), Bonnie Runnells, the Ross Sisters (Emma and Ida), Professor William Pillaire ("will catch a ball fired from a cannon"), Mlle. Georgia, Larry Tooley, Paul Allen, Fanny Sandford (sic), Andy Leavitt, Jr., the Gschwanders Tyrolean Troupe, Sadie Meehan and Frank Nelson — certainly a generous provision. Levantine and Earle, Lizzie Daly (Lancashire clog) and Fred Lloyd were additions for the week of September 15th, as was the dramatic offering A Florida Belle, or, the Secret Marriage (with

[104]

Frank Nelson, George W. Johnson, Paul Allen and Sadie Meehan).   Charles Gardner, Ruttini (French illusionist), Webster Brothers (Ned and James, in The Strike on the Pittsburgh Road), Viro Farrand, Kitty Sheppard (sic), Milo Millard, Jennie Mitchell (soubrette), Maggie Weston, Andy Leavitt, Jr., Bonnie Runnells, Fanny Sanford (sic), Paul Allen and Frank H. Nelson constituted the array of friends old or new on September 22nd.   The concluding play was Home Again, or, Sunlight and Shadow.   Let us hope no shadow kept the sun from the venture.

The house now began to end its evening of "Variety" with a dramatic offering.   Sid C. France served this laudable purpose, on September 29th, in his familiar Marked for Life; he remained two weeks, in one or both of which the olio presented John Pierce, Bonnie Runnells, Harry F. Seymour, A. Leavitt, Jr. and Kitty Sheppard (in Servants by Legacy), Fanny Sanford, Andy Collum, Whitfield and Harry Lavarnie (in The Yankee Duelist), Geyer and Mackie, Whitfield (character impersonator and mimic), Allie Drayton, and Avery and La Rue (horizontal bars).   The bills for October 13th–18th opened with No Pay No Cure (John Pierce, Runnells, Leavitt, Lavarnie and Aline Gray), and followed with Croly McCarthy (Irish character songs), Barlow Brothers (James and William, in their burlesque fight), Dan Nash ("first appearance in America" — character sketches), and concluded with C. T. Nichols's drama, The Shadow Detective, the cast including Nichols in three parts, Harry F. Seymour as Jem Sharkey, the convict, Charles L. Farwell as Bill Rattle, a London bruiser, John Pierce as Johnny Hardfist, and Maggie Weston as Maggie Jordan.   Newcomers for the week of October 20th–25th were Belle Fairmont (serio-comic), and the Courtland Sisters (Helen and Carrie).   The play of the week was Keen Eye, the Ranger, which made us look out, with Harry Morland as Keen Eye, Ida Quigley as Prairie Flower, Farwell as Persimmon Bill, Dan Nash as Terry O'Farrell, and with, in other rôles, Leavitt, Johnson, Maggie Weston, Kitty Sheppard, and Aline Gray — to mention only the leaders.   The olio of October 27th–November 1st provided Tom Harper (one legged dancer), "Professor" M. O'Reardon (tumbleronicon), Andy Leavitt, Jr., Jessie Merton, Ella Mayo, Sullivan and Harrington, Levanion and Watson, and Harry F. Seymour; the dramatic offering was E. W. Marston, in Solon Shingle. I am amused, on November 3rd–8th, by William Conrad and his "College of Canine Graduates"; less so by Archie White and Ella Esmond, and Charles and Annie Whiting.   For plays, we had Charles L. Farwell as Job Armroyd, in Lost in London, supported by Seymour as Gilbert Featherstone, E. W. Marston as Benjamin Bunker, Maggie Weston as Nellie Armroyd, and Lizzie Gale as Tillie Dragglethorpe; also, Sarah's Young Man (with Marston and Johnson).   Of course there were Sunday concerts.   Jules Friquet, Carrie Boshell, Frank A. Gibbons ("king of the air"), and the play of Roving Jack, or, Saved from the Wreck, were prominent in the bills for

[105]

November 10th–15th. In Roving Jack, J. Z. Little, as star, had the support of Harry Elliston, Seymour and the regular company of olio actors. During the week of November 17th–22nd, Little appeared in Old Sleuth, the Detective; Leavitt and James Mulligan acted in Hard Cheek, and the "olio" gave turns by Kitty Sheppard, Alfred Liston, Lena Aberle ("first appearance in eight months") and William H. Delehanty, who, because of the illness of his partner, Hengler, was compelled to act alone. As we know, Delehanty died during this season. The programme for November 24th–29th began with The Mistaken Fathers, or, a Bull in a China Shop (acted by Marston, Leavitt, Johnson, Seymour, Maggie Weston and Kitty Sheppard, apparently the regularly established dramatic corps of the house); in the olio were Levanion ad Watson, Josephine Walby (skipping-rope dance), Maggie Weston (male impersonator), Renrut and Mme. d'Omer (he in the "William Tell act," she as a boxer), and Lena Aberle; and the closing spectacle was The French Spy (with no less a star than Marie Zoe, the Cuban Sylph of the '60s). The feature of December 1st–6th was N. S. Wood, in Nan, the Newsboy, that real character of the times who, according to the programme note, "had saved over 20 from drowning, and is now protégé of Captain Paul Boynton and Captain of the Volunteer Life Saving Force." As this brave hero, Wood had the support of Kitty Sheppard, Isabella Wilson, May Preston, Maggie Weston, Farwell, Johnson, Seymour and John Hogan. In the olio were Alice Daily, Foster and Hughes and Fred Levantine.

Wood, during the week of December 8th–13th, reverted to The Boy Detective, in which he assumed, according to the protean tendency of that period, eight characters; in the olio were Marie Désirée, John Hogan, Stella Newton, Alice Daily, Murray, Runnells and Aymar ("kings of the Carpet"), Mons. Bushnell (aerial juggler, and trainer of pigeons), Professor Fox (imitations of birds), &c. At the concert, on December 14th, "Professor" Wieffenbach played solos on sixteen drums, and any one who could do that almost deserved the title of "Professor." C. Eschert also performed on the xylophone. During the week, Lena (or Lina) Tettenborn appeared (in English) in Tina, the Milk Vendor, supported by M. W. Fiske, Mrs. Brennan and the usual acting force of the house; the olio featured the Brennans and Laible, De Witt Cooke ("king of clubs") and John Morris ("mystic change artist"). On the 17th, Aberle celebrated the hundredth night of his new theatre. For the Christmas week of December 22nd–27th Miss Tettenborn continued in Tina, and Sid C. France also played three rôles in Dead to the World, assisted by Seymour, Marston, Farwell, John C. Walsh, Johnson, William Beekman, Kitty Sheppard and Maggie Weston. Devlin and Tracy came into the olio. The week of December 29th–January 3rd presented Marston and Seymour (in The Artful Dodger), Billy Buckley, Master Rice, and ended with The Poor of New York (adapted "from Les

Pauvres de Paris, by J. Sterling Coyne, under the name of Fraud and Its Victims"). The cast:

Tom Trumper	W. J. Fleming	Joe	James Mulligan
Warrington	J. C. Walsh	Bob	Billy Buckley
Captain Seaborne	G. W. Johnson	Isabelle	Dollie Thornton
Morton	W. Beekman	Mrs. Seaborne	Mrs. W. G. Jones
Mark Valmore	C. L. Farwell	Marian	Lena Aberle
Alfred Seaborne	H. F. Seymour	Mrs. Pennypot	May Montalo
Mr. Pennypot	E. W. Marston		

This, it will be observed, was not the Boucicault version of Les Pauvres de Paris, then played so constantly by Frank Mayo, under the title of The Streets of New York. The piece remained at Aberle's for two weeks, though Mayo, alleging that he was sole owner of the play, tried, according to the Herald of January 11th, to enjoin Fleming.

Ireland as It Is, on January 12th, presented C. L. Farwell as Dan O' Carolan, supported by Mike Gallagher (as Ragged Pat), Marston (as Slang), Mrs. Jones, Maggie Weston and Ione Lang; in the olio were Delehanty and Hengler, Ione Lang, Julius Turnour (equilibrist), the Hogan Brothers (Harry and Gus) and May Diamond. The bill began with Did You Ever Send Your Wife to Brooklyn? N. S. Wood returned, on January 19th, in both Poor Jo and The Boy Detective; Rose Hall, May Diamond, Devlin and Tracy and Butler and Leslie did "turns" between those two Wood offerings. The bills for January 26th–31st presented The Convict's Fate (with Farwell, Marston, Mrs. Jones, Maggie Weston, &c.) and an olio richly caparisoned with Maud Sheppard, Devlin and Tracy, Virginia Stickney, Wingfield and Gregory, Delehanty and Hengler (in Blackberries in the South), Gibson and Binney, and ended with Bounce, acted by Delehanty and Hengler, Wingfield and Gregory, Gibson and Binney, Maggie Weston, Maud Sheppard, Virginia Stickney, Marston, Johnson and Mulligan — an imposing group. For the week of February 2nd–7th, Marston and Mrs. Jones revived Toodles for a generation that knew not Burton and Mrs. Hughes; Andy Leavitt, Jr., John B. Wills and May Adams, Ada Forrest and Jules Friquet did their "turns," and the serious business began with Neck and Neck, of course with E. T. Stetson, assisted by the regular Aberle force, Mrs. Jones playing Peg, the old witch, and Lena Aberle returning as Carrie Freeland.

The Black and Tan Picnic (with Delehanty as Priscilla Murphi and Hengler as Sunrise Henderson) merrily began the fun for February 9th–14th, which carried on with Cooper and Edwards, Lillian Forrest ("queen of serio-comics"), Foster and Hughes, Ada Forrest, P. C. Foy (Emblems of Ireland), Pell and Lewis, and finished all with His Last Crime, or, Vell, Vot of It? (with Farwell, Marston, Mrs. Jones and others). Did You Ever Send Your Wife to Brooklyn? started the questionings of February 16th–21st; Geyer and Mackie, Mons. Jules (character baritone), James T. Powers (of

[107]

Kearney and Powers, in "delectable song and dance"), Ada Fields (song bird), Barney and Ada McCreedie, and a three-act play, A Voice from the Streets (with O. B. Collins, as star, and with Mrs. Jones, Farwell, Marston, Ada Forrest, Maggie Weston, &c.) ran the gamut of emotional or cachinnatory joys for the rest of the evening. Thompson Brothers (Al and Charles), Lucy Adams and Guy Linton, Delehanty and Hengler, and Hernandez Foster, in his very usual Jack Harkaway, made up the sum of joy for the week of February 23rd–28th. Delehanty and Hengler ("positively their last week") and dear Mrs. Jones opened the budget of mirth for March 1st–6th, in Fun in the Kitchen; Charley McCarthy (the California character comedian, in Grogan's Chinese Laundry), Mlle. Georgia ("holding a cannon of 350 pounds in her teeth"), and George France, in A Block Game (with Ethel Earle, and the dogs, Bruno and Don Cæsar) ended it as beseemed the occasion. The Sunday concerts, recently, had featured Mons. Jules and Mme. Lodi; on Sunday, the 7th, appeared Cool Burgess, "Ella" Courtland and Winifred North. During the week of March 8th–13th, Julian Kent acted in Wild Bill, King of the Border Men, with G. W. Johnson as Old Sloat, Ella Mayo as Emma Reynolds, Mrs. Jones as Mrs. Reynolds, Maggie Weston as Betty, Farwell as Captain Huntley, &c. The new Aberle's was, in a way, dividing honours with the Windsor Theatre, as purveyor of true Bowery thrills. In the course of Kent's play occurred a bowie knife fight between Kent and Farwell, and a wrestling match with the bear, Julia; also a "sublime, realistic representation of Indian Warfare." What more could Shirtsleeves have demanded in the old Bowery now Teutonised into the Thalia Theater? The bill this week began with James T. Powers as Patrick Moriarty, in A Slippery Day.

Fayette Welch, Frank West, Mlle. A. Tissot and her living automatons, May Diamond and Jackits-Chy's Japanese Troupe were preliminaries (March 15th–20th) to the stirring drama of Prairie Flower, or, the Deed of a Dark Night, with Rose Goodall, the star of eve, as Vivia, Farwell as Robert Castlemaine, J. Walsh as Mandrake, Beekman as Oswald Brooke, Mrs. Jones as Meg, the Wildcat, and Maggie Weston as Kitty. The week of March 22nd–27th brought back or brought in James T. Powers, Ella Mayo, Dick Sands, the Crimmins Brothers, Charles Morosco, and the Four Italians (Fayette Welch, Crimmins Brothers and James T. Powers). George France was star in Wide Awake, supported by Sands, Ella Mayo and the established regulars of the house. Many of the artists recently listed in our chronicle remained for March 29th–April 3rd; the play of the evening was Daniel Boone, with Joseph P. Winter in the title rôle, W. Jackson as Squire Boone, Farwell as Simon Gerty, Marston as Dr. Busey, James T. Powers as Blackfish, King of the Shawnees (a characterisation the very thought of which with the irresistible Powers makes me laugh), Mrs. Jones as Rebecca Bryan and Bessie Boone, &c. Dave Foster and Artie Hughes, Kitty Stevens (in

McINTYRE AND HEATH   LINA TETTENBORN   THE WHITINGS

CHARLES DOCKSTADER   LENA ABERLE   LEW DOCKSTADER

BENNIE GRINNELL   HATTIE GRINNELL   ALICE DAILY

melodies), Mark Murphy ("Irish"), Nellie Byron, Mlle. Lottie and the Baldwin Brothers, with E. T. Stetson in Neck and Neck, made up the total joys of April 5th–10th; on the 8th, Lena Aberle had a benefit. The "great favourite," James T. Powers, returned for April 12th–17th, and other newcomers were Mackin and Bryant (the "Hibernian Twins"). Charles Foster had featured place in the bills, in Saved at Seven, playing the Major, with G. W. Johnson as Mr. Elwood, Farwell as William Elwood, Marston as Pete Perkins and Powers as Mike Mulligan — these two returned convicts — W. Jackson as Fred Verney (fortune's football), Mrs. Jones as Florence, a waif, called the Wildcat, Nellie Byron as Meg (keeper of a den), Maggie Weston as Lady Abigail (the Major's wife), and Nellie Hague as Emily Wilton (the heiress) — all of which sounds to me like serious business for an April evening. The week beginning on April 19th returned to us Fayette Welch (in High Jack, the Heeler) and staged General Grant's Trip around the World — then a burning topic — with Charles L. Banks as Geranium Gluebox, and with Johnson, J. H. Connor, Frank Lodge, Mrs. Jones and Maggie Weston as leaders in an enormous cast. There was nothing else in the bill. The next week retained the Grant performance (the Staats-Zeitung advertises for it a cost of $10,000), and opened the evening with Fayette Welch, in Scenes at Simpson's. And thus April went out easily for my weary pen.

The week of May 3rd presented "Variety" in persons of Ned Ryan, J. Clooney and James T. Powers (he as Policeman 3414) in Fits, Mollie De Mar, Lucy Adams and Guy Linton (in April Showers), the Callan Brothers (John and James), Bernard McCreedie, and Kearney and Powers (in Transmagnificandubandanciality, or, Anything You Play You Get). Following these delectable "turns" came that relic of an earlier day, Nick of the Woods, with Dollie Bidwell as Telie Doe, James T. Powers (I laugh as I write) as Big Tom Bruce, with Farwell as the Jibbenainosay, &c. The concert on May 9th favoured us with the the American Troubadours, and, on the 10th, Nick of the Woods yielded the stage to further Western thrills — E. T. Goodrich and his horse, Ginger Blue, in Grizzly Adams, Lena Aberle playing Lady Amaranth. It ended the bills for two weeks, during one or both of which the "olio" treated us to A Big Mistake (with Frank White and Agnes St. Clair), to Kitty Sheppard, the Crimmins Brothers, Lucy Adams and Guy Linton, Andy Collum, the Sparks Brothers, John Hogan, Murphy and Shannon (in Amalgamation), Ada Forrest, Frank and Lillian White, Keating and Sands, and Sam Roberts (motto singer). This brings us reverently to Sunday evening, May 23rd, when H. Cooke and Selome Crawford, ever on the move, gave their popular exposition of Spiritualism, "without the aid of Spirits." The only novelty of importance in the olio for May 24th–29th was Lizzie Mowbray ("Champion Lady Pedestal Club Swinger" — her first appearance). The finishing stroke of drama was supplied by E. T. Goodrich, in Just His Luck, or, the Winning Hand. And May slipped easily into June (May 31st–June 5th) with How I Used Casey (Saunders, Fash and Emma Devoy), Harry Cereni, Nellie Hague, Down on the Tom-Big-Bay (with Saunders and Fash), the Devoy Sisters (Emma and Josie, jig and Irish reel), and, for concluding drama, George B. Radcliffe in Life for Life, or, a Brother's Oath (with a support including William M. Paul, Farwell, Cereni, Charles Banks, Saunders, Fash and Pearl Seymour). Devoy, Devoe, De Voy — which spelling, dear reader?

Plays seem to be the most interesting items in the June bills: Rightmire and Lena Aberle, in The Two Wanderers (June 7th–12th); Hernandez Foster, in Jack Harkaway Afloat and Ashore (14th–19th); N. S. Wood, in The Boy Detective (21st–26th); and G. C. Charles and Kate Moffett (sic), in The Skeleton Hand (June 28th–July 3rd). The popular Zanfrettas filled for that month the highest points in the olio — Alexander, especially, on stilts or on the tight-rope. The pantomimic specialties for which they were responsible included The Arrival of a French Traveller, The French Dancing Master, The Arrival of Offenbach and The Village Torment. Arrivals, each for at least a week, in the olio included the Crimmins Brothers, Nellie Byron, Ed Sheehan and Ed Lynch (in The McShanes), Etta Morris, Charley Shay (juggler and necromancer), Bobby Newcomb and John Pendy. Aberle's now advertised itself as the "only open air theatre in the city" — a cooling thought in a hot summer, such as 1880 proved to be. The Zanfrettas, the Devoys, Saunders and Fash, and other favourites lingered in the bills. Harry Constantine and Charley Wright began, on July 5th, in The Stage-Struck Domestics, and a unique cast (for July 5th–10th) of Uncle Tom's Cabin gave us Bobby Newcomb as Topsy, Farwell as Uncle Tom, Pendy as George Harris, John Walsh as Phineas Fletcher, Pearl Seymour as Eliza and Cassy, Josie Devoy as Eva, and Flora Zanfretta as Miss Ophelia. The play for July 12th–17th was Nenemoosha, or, the Sweetheart, a production that fails to catch my imagination, though doubtless the cast did its best — H. W. Ellis, C. T. James, Mark Murphy, Charles Saunders, Flora Zanfretta, Farwell, Larry Smith, Charles Fash, and Andy Hughes, some of them mighty big chiefs in the Indian story. For a few weeks the theatre had brought in but few new performers; the week of July 19th–24th, though it retained the Zanfrettas, the Devoys, the Crimminses and Sam Roberts, added novelty with Ben Gilfoil, Carrie Lavarnie, Lizzie Derious, and Novissimo and Felicita Pasta (these two in a ballet, The Devil's Auction). The play was Chris, with Jule Keen, Lizzie Derious, &c.

Erba Robeson and Watson and Levanion entered the olio for July 26th–31st, and W. J. Fleming revealed The Six Degrees of Crime, aided and abetted by a support including J. and S. Crimmins, Levanion, Farwell, Sam Roberts, Alexander and Flora Zanfretta, Erba Robeson and the Devoys — names I gladly cite to show how easily the olio transformed itself into a

body of actors.   Rightmire, on August 2nd, began a week in his own play,
The Boss, or, Living for Vengeance.   For the week of August 9th–14th, five
Zanfrettas tried to revive the glory of Nicodemus, so long a treat of the
Ravels; Della Turner, Parker and his dogs entered the olio; and Ireland's
Struggle for Liberty was exemplified by Millie Sackett as Bridget, Maurice
Pike as Denis O'Leary, and by members of the olio in support.   C. L. Far-
well's benefit occurred on the 14th.   During the week of August 16th–21st,
Aberle's Mammoth Minstrels sat before us, in persons of Billy Bryant, J. M.
Norcross, Johnny Allen, Sam Roberts, Dave Reed, Bobby Newcomb, Ben
Gilfoil, George Levanion, W. D. Corrister, John, Stephen and Michael
Crimmins, &c.   George W. Woods and the Grimes Brothers also appeared
in the show.   Next week (August 23rd–28th), the Zanfrettas returned, as
did the Ripleys, Lucy Adams and Guy Linton, and Goodrich and Lena
Aberle and Ginger Blue, in Grizzly Adams.   The last gasp of summer
(August 30th–Sept. 4th) breathed on the heated air the efforts of the Zan-
frettas, May Vincent (serio-comic), John Hogan and Lizzie Mowbray (in
Mixed), Harry Mills ("Dutch"), Sam Roberts, Minnie Farrell, and Ed
Cleary (as the Old Apple Woman), the programme ending with E. T.
Goodrich and Dollie Thornton, in Just His Luck.

VOLKSGARTEN, 1879–1880

I begin the history of the Volksgarten for 1879–80 with a bill at Harvard
for September 16th (Tuesday), which promised Larry Tooley, Sam Norman
and Hannah Birch, in On the Beach, and provided thereafter "turns" by
Katie Ziegrist (songs), Williams and Sully, Susie Byron, George Carey,
Paul Hamlin and Ada Newcomb (clog-dancing); also Minnie Oscar Gray,
with W. T. Stephens, Norman, Tooley, Billy Williams, Hannah Birch and
Minnie Clyde, in Saved from the Storm, that rescue so popular in theatres
of this rank.   During the following week, beginning with September 22nd,
Miss Gray and Stephens appeared in Jack Sheppard and His Dogs, the
preceding items in the bill including W. C. Cameron (in The Crushed
Comedian), John F. Byrnes ("grotesque acrobatic," in Nonsense), Harry
Lloyd, Burton and Smith (in Going to the Picnic), Carrie Boshell, Frank
Carr and Lulu Wentworth (in The Happy Pair), and Edwin Smith (high
pedestal clog).   The week of September 29th–October 4th gave us, in addition to some I have just listed, Joe Johnson, H. J. Campbell, Jessie Forrester,
Kennedy and Magee, Moore and Lessenger, the farce of Bibbs and Bibbs
(with Norman), and Mlle. Lucille (in The Little Dutch S.).

A modification of the Lady Minstrel act appeared in the announcement
for October 6th–11th of a Part I cumbrously named Le Moult's Hear Me
Shout Pinafore Lady Minstrels, with "Captain" Bob Crumley as bones,
John De Forrest as Deadeye, H. J. Campbell as the Admiral, with W. C.

Cameron (Buttertub) as "Tambo," and with Jessie Forrester and Mlle. Lucille among the minstrels. The olio included Emma and John Whitney (in Rehearsal in the Parlour), the Sparks Brothers (in Callahan's Academy of Fun), Miss Lou Edwards, Crumley and De Forrest (high kickers, in The Coloured Jubilee), and Mlle. Lucille (in Fascination). New, in the week of October 13th–18th, were Harry Constantine, Hattie Richmond, Maude Leigh, Johnny Mackin, Rosie Lonsdale (songs), Mabel Florence, Nellie Hadfield (violin), and B. C. Taylor (in Hans's Adventures in America). The next week (October 20th–25th) introduced Winfield and George Shedman, Dick Edwards and Bill Gaylor, Jen Powers and Georgie Macy (these two in Susie's Serenade) and ended the programme with some sort of Uncle Tom's Cabin (with George Middleton as Legree and George Harris, Rosie Palmer as Topsy, Little Frederica as Eva, Isabella Wilson as Miss Ophelia, and Jen Powers as Uncle Tom). This version of the old classic ran through the week of October 27th–November 1st, newcomers in the olio of that semaine including Harry and Gus Hogan (in Nigs on the Mozambique), Annie and Joe Burgess (in Trouble in the Kitchen), and Frank Jones and Alice Montague (in Musical Mixtures).

Bills at the Volksgarten, as in many of the "Variety" houses, were now showing a lack of faith in the chief ingredient of the programme. More and more character sketches and farces were driving to the rearward the simpler songs and dances and acrobatic feats of the earlier years; and now long plays were demanded as concluding features of a lengthy bill. The Volksgarten, in 1879–80, advertised in the Staats-Zeitung usually only those closing dramas; but thanks to the file of bills at Harvard I can gratify the reader's desire to know what happened in the weekly olio. The drama for November 3rd–8th was The Ticket of Leave Man (with George Middleton, W. C. Cameron, C. Taylor, Josie Rathbone (sic — as May), Jessie Forrester (as Emily St. Evremond) and Rosie Palmer (as Sam.) Other features of the bill were the opening farce, The Civil Rights Bill (with Cameron, Gus Hogan, Taylor, Norman, Harry Lloyd and Jessie Forrester), Harry P. Welston (California vocalist), George H. and Nettie Wood (in the Anglo-German burletta, German Innocence), Fanny V. Reynolds, Mlle. Georgia ("the woman with the iron jaw"), "Professor" William Pillaire (who caught — and I know many professors who cannot do it — who caught a ball fired from a cannon loaded with powder, in presence — the ambiguity is in the printed programme — of the audience). During the week of November 17th–22nd, Billy Williams and W. J. Sully, Nellie Hague, Moore and Lessenger (the Eccentric Shoemakers) and Minnie Rainforth and Ned Campbell (in Kitty and Tim) appeared in the olio, and the concluding drama of Foiled had in its cast W. H. Langdon, P. M. Allison, Cameron, Norman, Campbell, Lloyd, Minnie Rainforth and Nellie Germon.

The bills for November 24th–29th began with Is a Clerk Responsible?

acted by Norman, John J. Lessenger, Cameron and J. S. Moore, and entered on engagements with Nellie Thorne, Frank Geyer and James Mackie, Wingfield (*sic*) and Gregory (horizontal bars), Fred Hallen and Enid Hart — a popular team (in Pinafore in Fifteen Minutes), Charles Gregory (on the dancing barrel), Professor Lorento (illusionist and mimic, with his Punch and Judy) and closed with Norman and others from the olio, in The Convict's Vengeance.   On December 1st, Tom and Henrietta Murray began a week, in Love and Liquor, and other features included J. F. Sherry, Tom Hedges (piccolo), Butler and Leslie (acrobatic songs and dances), Carrie Lewis, Harry Martin (in The Dancing Grenadiers), Winetta Craven and Tom Hedges (in Parlour Pictures, in course of which she was to make nine changes of costume), Emma Brennan, the sketch Geese! Geese! *vs.* Goose! Goose! (with Martin, Sam Butler and Rob Leslie), and the concluding thriller, The Black Hand, or, The Lost Will (with Frank Jones in five parts, assisted by Alice Montague).   An exciting railroad scene was part of the machinery involved in the play.   Many of the players just named figured in the bills of earlier December, with additional strength in John J. Carroll, Nellie Byron, the Woods (in The Rent Day), Fred Sharpley (late of Sharpley Brothers), H. Harman ("strength of arm and jaw"), Professor White and his dogs, Harry and Minnie Wood, and H. M. S. Pinafore (December 8th–12th), with Tom Murray as Sir Joseph Ale, Harry Wood as Corcoran, Hedges as Ralph, Norman as Dick Deadbeat, Carrie Lewis as Josephine, Henrietta Murray as Buttertub, and Winetta Craven as Hebe.   The week of December 15th–20th gave Jessie Merton (serio-comic), Brevarde and Sawtelle (in Peaches and Honey), Mabel Florence, Tom Harper, Frank George ("original Irish sayings," etc.), Master George Ellsworth (performances with musket and bayonet), and the play, The Pirate and the Faithful Ape (with Frank Donaldson and Frank Livingston).   The pantomime of The Red Knight, or, the Magic Trumpet, began the festivals for Christmas week (December 22nd–27th), with Charles Mauritius, Mons. Leopold, Larry Smith, Nellie Thorne and Kate Richards.   Minnie Oscar Gray and W. T. Stephens returned, in Saved from the Storm; and the olio embraced Ada Lanier, Smith and Butler ("two of the youngest song and dance artists in the world"), Leopold and Mauritius, Watson and Levanion (aerial evolutions, gymnastics, etc.), W. C. Cameron, Favor and Shields and B. C. Taylor. New Year gifts (December 29th–January 3rd) included Sol and Julia Aiken, Clooney and Ryan, Law and Excitement (with Ned Ryan, Ed Shields, Sol Aiken, Norman and Ned Favor), and Jack Sheppard and His Dogs (with Minnie Oscar Gray and Stephens).

January 5th–10th assembled Sam Weston and Ben W. P. Brown, Charles Foley ("Irish"), Frank and Fannie Davis (in Fogarty's Night On), Arthur Johnson ("eccentric acting and funny sayings"), Edwards and Gaylor (The Darkies' Jubilee), the Aikens, Bothwick Reid (ancient and modern feats of

[113]

claymore and Scottish exercise), Guy Linton and Lucy Adams (in Second Sight at a Discount), Mlle. Lottie (*sic*) Belmont (trapeze), and the concluding play, Irish Landlords, with Mike Gallagher (usually now so spelled), Aiken, Johnson, Foley, Mary Barker, and Julia Aiken. Harvard bills failing, I turn to the Staats-Zeitung, where I find, for January 12th–17th, merely the play, The Bowery Boys, or, Life in New York; from the same source, I learn that, during January 19th–24th, Vic and Harry Leonzo and their dogs appeared in Rupert's Dog, or, the Mexican Bandit. A Harvard bill shows the same Leonzos and their dogs concluding the performances for January 26th–31st, with The Dog Spy, features in the olio including Charles Peltier (in Cotton Belles), Nellie Hague, Ella Edna (a sweetly pretty name, in serio-comic songs), J. Tissot and a troupe of living automatons, and Harry Lloyd. February 2nd–7th provided The Scranton Bush Rangers (with S. S. Pettit and J. W. White), Harry Constantine, Billy and Nellie Hasson (in Just from Arkansaw), Jeffreys Warner, Sellou and Byrnes (in The College Students), and William H. Rightmire's play, Poison and Knife, or, the Boss (with Rightmire and Maude Osmond). Further delights of February included L. E. and Mary Barker (in The Yankee Duelist), Archie and Den Delmanning, Achille Phillion (magical séance), J. B. Wills and May Adams (in Larks), Minnie Clyde, Emma Phillion ("aerial suspension"), and the concluding drama, The Boy Avenger (with Maude Osmond in six parts, with Rightmire as Sam, Mary Barker as Beatrice, and with members from the olio in remaining rôles) — all these delicacies for the week of February 9th–14th; Crooked Whiskey (with Cameron, Barker and Harry Lloyd), the Arnold Brothers, Miss Ceni Havre (singer), Paddy Hughes, Lillie Ross and Carrie Edwards, Bobby Daily, Irene Kerns, Charles Morgan and Harry Mullen, with Minnie Clyde (in Christmas Eve), Slattery's Boarding House (with Morgan and Mullen) — precious items for February 16th–21st; John D. Griffin (in Irish Justice), Mabel Florence, the Hogans, the Olympia Quartette ("first appearance in New York"), Ned and Maud Stanley Werner, Ada Forrest, Frank Bolton and Ada Bradford (in The Enchanted Statue), and A Devil of a Scrape (with L. E. Barker, W. C. Cameron, Hugh Mack, W. M. Keough, M. J. Sullivan, Mary Barker, Ada Forrest, Ada Bradford, and Minnie Clyde) — these constituting the *summum bonum* for February 23rd–28th.

The veteran minstrel, Sam S. Sanford, began the week of March 1st–6th in the old minstrel farce, Oh, Hush! Barney and Anna McCreedie, the Werners, Ida Showers ("aerial artist"), Gibson and Binney, Rel Mueab, and Andrew J. Showers (with performing dogs and monkeys) led up to the familiar closing play — The Hidden Hand (with Mary Barker as Capitola and Dick, the Newsboy). Newer faces for March 8th–13th were Kennedy and Magee, Minnie Loder ("queen of song"), Howard and Sanford ("German comiques"), Cooper and Edwards; and the glad excitement closed with A

Tale of a Tar (with L. E. Barker and Frank Livingston in leading rôles). Idaletta, the water queen, and Wallace, the man fish, pleased, during the week of March 15th–20th, all beholders who liked to see that kind of queen and that sort of fish; dryer members of the olio were Alice Morosco (songs), Clark and Watson, Henrico (Indian clubs), Mark Murphy and Foster and Hughes, McAvoy and Emma Rogers (in Jealousy), Renrut and Mme. d'Omer (swordsmanship, and he shooting an apple from her devoted head), Charles H. Duncan (comic vocalist), &c. The Devil of a Scrape was once more concluding drama. The following week (March 22nd–27th) introduced or haply re-introduced Sam S. Sanford (now director of amusements, in A Ghost in Spite of Himself), the Dutch Mendels (Harry and Leonie), Winetta Craven and Tom Hedges (in Parlour Pictures), Tom and Henrietta Murray (in Brogue and Blarney), Charles Foley, The Mischievous Monkey (with Charles O'Brien as the weary traveller, and Tom O'Brien as the monkey), Lottie (sic) Belmont, and ended with the play, Holiday Picnic (cast with Tom Murray, Tom Hedges, Lou Barker, Winetta Craven, Henrietta Murray, Mary Barker, Cameron, Minnie Clyde, S. S. Sanford, &c.). March 29th–April 3rd gave us the American Triplets (Harry and Blanche Morton and Eddie Brennan), Weston and Woods, Carrie Boshell, Morgan and Mullen (the Irish Holiday), and the ever-during Rip Van Winkle (with Joseph Keane and Lizzie Gale, supported by a cast picked from the olio).

And April showers of blessings, sometimes, I fear, very much in disguise? Well, what thinks the reader of a procession, in single file or perhaps in "teams," consisting of Ada Lanier, Hines and Blossom (song and dance), Mme. Anderson (pedestrienne, in costume changes), Morgan and Mullen (in The Mighty Dollar), Minnie Clyde, Gus H. Saville (formerly of Bryant and Saville) now "teaming" with John H. Byrne (late of Shirley and Byrne), Minnie Oscar Gray and W. T. Stephens (for a third visit, April 5th–10th, in Saved from the Storm), of Nora Campbell (serio-comic), Jimmy Emerson ("Irish"), Kate Montrose and John McVeigh (in Spirits Frumenti), of Campbell and Burke, of the Emersons (James and Dolly), Fred Roberts, M. F. Tierney (contortionist), of W. C. Cameron (on April 12th–17th, in Rightmire's play, Our American Boys), of the Mackie Brothers (James and Billy), Ada Sanborn, Joseph A. Kelly (in Levy in a Fix, with imitations of Jules Levy), of J. W. McAndrews (the Watermelon Man), Joe and Annie Burgess (in Trials of a Dancing Master), Satsuma (Japanese feats of strength, skill and muscle), Minnie Lawton, and of the concluding drama (week of April 19th–24th) Ranger (by A. Z. Chipman, with J. W. McAndrews as Major Smutt, one of the Cullud Troops, and with Cameron and Barker in other parts? Whatever he thinks of it all, the reader has now arrived at the week of April 26th–May 1st, when William H. Rightmire acted in his own drama of The Beggar's Daughter, supported by Mary Barker, Lew (or Lou) E. Barker, Clarence Boyd, W. C. Cameron, Edith Crolius, Claudia Ripley and others. A Kiss in the Dark began the bills (with the Barkers, Cameron and Edith Crolius), and between the two dramatic pieces an olio exploited Miss Reno Stedman (singer), Boyd and Sarsfield, Paddy and Ella Murphy, Edith Crolius ("beautiful home ballads"), Brevarde and Sawtelle, Ceni Havre, and William and Claudia Ripley (carpet athletes and acrobats).

A New Way to Pay Old Debts began the festivities of May 3rd–8th (the cast including Mike Gallagher, Lew and Mary Barker and Cameron); thereafter Miss Lou Arnott sang, and we enjoyed, in succession, Foster and Hughes, Florence Sherwood (petite song and dance), J. H. Graham (motto singer, "with the most rapid changes of character costumes ever accomplished"), Mike Gallagher (in "his great Presidential Recitation"), Dave Foster, Artie Hughes, Cameron, Barker and Lou Arnott (all in The Baby Elephant), Jennie Ward (with "seven distinct changes of dress before the audience"), John M. Turner (banjo). The bill concluded with a return engagement of Leonzo and the dog, Tiger, in Rupert's Dog. Visitors later in May were Della Turner, Jen and Georgie Powers (in Susie's Serenade), Frank Melrose (one-legged gymnast), Harry La Rose (Indian club act), the Four Emeralds (Gibbons, Russell, Kennedy and Magee), the Aikens, Charles Constantine (as Strop, in Two Tramps), Virginia Stickney, T. F. Grant (one-legged specialist, another victim, presumably, of the Civil War), the Olympia Quartette, Alice Daily, with Harry Fielding and Maggie Walker (in Back to Erin), &c. The week of May 10th–15th ended the bills with Vic Leonzo's play, Rescued by a Dog, or, Found at Last, the cast including Leonzo, Tiger, Cameron, Lew E. Barker, Jen Powers and Mary Barker. To this day (1939) cinema-lovers attest the spell of dog drama. The return of Charles Constantine (May 17th–22nd) permitted of the production of The Dumb Man, or, the Felon's Heir (with Constantine, Barker, Hugh Mack, Harry Fielding, W. C. Cameron, Keough and Randalls, Julia Aiken, Maggie Walker and Mary Barker.

Female Minstrels were actively flirting at that time with "Variety," which, in turn, regarded them with auspicious eye. On May 24th–29th the Volksgarten succumbed and brought in (or possibly organised) the International Mastodon Minstrels, with, as participants, Tillie Lewis, Virginia Stickney, Jennie Fairbanks, L. E. and Mary Barker, May Clark, Nellie Hasson, J. D. Roome, Cameron, Ned Ryan, Hugh Mack, and the Olympia Quartette. Others in the bill were Nellie Germon, Roach and Fash (Ethiopians), the Hassons, Elmer E. Grandin (baritone), Clooney and Ryan, and Diff Diff in a Well (with J. D. Roome). And, thanks to that bill, I can inform the eager reader that the Olympia Quartette consisted of Hugh Mack, William Keough, M. J. Sullivan and P. Randalls. Newcomers of the week of May 31st–June 5th were Ed Lynch and Max Arnold (in A Slippery Day), Ward and Wells ("fine Irish gents"), Dan Leavitt (motto), the Jolly Three (Frank E. McNish — certainly very "jolly," when I saw him in later years

[116]

— and Rose and Jennie Leland, in Stolen Fun), Joseph Kelly (cabinet of musical instruments), and the play, That Boy of Dan's (with Addie Rogers, William C. Cameron, Lew Barker and Nellie Germon).

Blithely we pick June roses in the Volksgarten — blithely, perhaps, because the season nears an end. The week of June 7th–12th gives us Boyhood Days (with Billy Williams and Billy Sully), Kitty Gardner, Charles Allen and Joe Hart, Fanny V. Reynolds, the Jeromes, Alf Barker (in Flewy Flewy), and the concluding drama of Simon Kenton, or, the Spirit of the Kenawha (with Charles Thornton, and written for him by F. D. Skiff). Blue Glass (on June 14th–19th) enlisted Ned Thatcher and Dick Hume, William Hasson and George Bing, the olio skimming along gaily with the Hassons, the Jeromes, the Prescott Sisters (Lizzie and Carrie, in a very protean piece, The Mystery), John Pendy, &c. The concluding thriller was a military drama, Tried for Treason (with Charles Thornton, Pendy, Lew E. Barker, Charles Jerome, W. C. Cameron, Mary Barker, Ella Jerome, Lizzie Prescott, &c.). Other June accessions were numerous and good — J. J. Lessenger and J. C. Moore, Nellie Hague, the Russell Brothers, William T. Dwyer (motto vocalist), the Hayles (Billy and Lou, "the greatest clog dancers in the world"), Clara Cushman, Clams (with James T. Powers as Demosthenes Higgins, an actor of no talent, but great nerve, and with the Barkers and Cameron in other rôles). James T. Powers ("late of Kearney and Powers") also gave a single "turn," and was set down in the programme as "the versatile comedian, vocalist, dancer and mimic," in a "delectable song and dance. For neatness, style, and execution, he stands without a rival." Even thus early in his career was the excellence of this incomparable comic genius recognised. The play of that week (June 21st–26th) was Backwoods Heroes (with Dick Gorman). For June 28th–July 3rd, the newer arrivals were Minnie Emery (serio-comic), Landis and Steele (acrobatic song and dance skaters), Ada Sanborn, Maggie Nichols (wire-walker), Charles Banks, the Four Diamonds (Clark, Watson, Brevarde and Sawtelle), Little Todd ("the greatest one-hand balancer in the world"), Frank M. Wills, &c.

The Staats-Zeitung supplies no information for July, and the Harvard Theatre Collection lacks bills for that heated month. Four bills for August are stored in the latter institution — for the 2nd, 9th, 16th and 25th, covering practically all of the activities for the dog days involved. William C. Cameron's Combination was there on the 2nd, and in it were Cameron, the Barkers, Larry Tooley, Hattie Richmond, Hogan Brothers, Fanny V. Reynolds, the Four Emeralds, the Grinnells, Hannah Birch, Della Turner, Ned Barry, and Charley McCarthy. Monday, August 9th, yielded Jessie Forrester, Jen and Georgie Powers, Minnie Farrell, and The Rehearsal, or, John Russell's Old Man (with Frank Gibbons, John J. Magee, John Russell, Lew E. Barker, Mary Barker, and Jessie Forrester). Since the bill for August

[117]

16th (Saturday) specifically proclaims that date as the re-opening of the fall and winter season of 1880–81, I will leave it and subsequent bills till I pick up the flying leaves for that interesting year.

BOWERY GARTEN, 1879–1880

The week of September 1st–6th provided, at the Bowery Garten, the Deveres (in That Rascal Thomas) Albertine Wolgrath (German vocalist), Kelly and Weston, Frank Melville (female impersonator), Archie White and Ella Esmond, Lucy Adams and Guy Linton (in Dibdin's Jealousy), King Sarbro, Don Ferreyra (the man flute, making sound with his naked hands), and the concluding burlesque, Pinafore. The week of the 15th–20th added Susie Ulm (Tyrolean warbler), Lester Howard and Lizzie Hunter (in Fritz's Return), Julius Turnour (gymnastic clown, his "first appearance in this country"), Thompson (late of Howard and Thompson) and Waldron (in Hebrew specialties), Emma Brennan, Viro Farrand ("first appearance on the Bowery"), Roselle ("the wonder soprano, in female impersonations"), the Martelle Brothers (Harry and Willie, in a parlour entertainment), Houssaboura (*sic*) Sam (the "Japanese wonder," in balancing and juggling), and Love in a Tub (with Turnour, Ed Mills, Clara Cushman, &c.). Finally, so far as Harvard bills inform us, the week of September 22nd–27th brought to us Foster and Hughes (song and dance), George S. Garland and Cherry Chapman (German comedy team), Thompson and Waldron, Ada Lanier, John H. Carle (banjo), Senator Frank Bell, John M. Turner (challenge banjoist), George Garland (Our German Cousin), and Tommy Devere (in A Slippery Day).

The Staats-Zeitung carries almost no advertising, in that season, for the Bowery Garten; indeed I see no reason why a German newspaper should notice a place become linguistically so Anglicised in its offerings. Harvard has for October only two bills — one for the 8th and one for the 23rd. The first promises performances by Billy and Tommy Devere and Charles F. Seabert (in Actor *vs.* Singer), by Nellie Nelson ("serio-comic effusions"), the Russell Brothers, the Shedman Brothers (Winfield and George, acrobats), the Grinnells, the Rays (Billy and Maggie, plantation artists, in Home Again), Larry Tooley (in The Dutchman's Ghost), Master J. Roberts, the Martell (or Martelle) Brothers, and the concluding Our Old Cabin Home (with the Rays, Seabert, Ed Mills, the Russells and Tooley). Newer, on the 23rd, were Irene Kerns (song and dance), Minnie Rainforth and Ned Campbell (in The Moral Husband, or, I've Only Been Down to the Club), John Goodman (bone player), Ed Howard and Mike Coyne (in Family Affairs), Ward and Wells ("Irish"), Fred Sharpley and John Carroll (in Musical Contrabands), Mlle. Josephine ("female Sampson" ever so spelled for "Variety"), A. W. Sawyer, and the concluding New York Upside Down.

[118]

The week of November 3rd–8th presented The Scarecrow (with Harvey Collins, T. Devere, Seabert, Ed Mills and Jennie Leland), followed with "turns" by Smith and Waddie ("musical specialists"), the Leland Sisters (Rose and Jennie, in songs, dances, recitations), Everett and Daly (acrobatic song and dance), Marie Désirée, the three Milo Brothers (horizontal bar), Ione Lang (songs), the three Zanfrettas (Alexander, Flora and Leopold, in A Good Night's Rest), Nellie Nelson, Dick Sands, King Sarbro, Harvey Collins (as Daniel Bandmann in The Modern School of Acting), and ended with Zanfretta (in The Skeleton Witness).   John Schroder was now proprietor of the Garden, and, for the week of November 24th–29th, provided the Deveres and others in A Slippery Day, Rose Lonsdale (seriocomic), the Budworths (Harry and Emma), Bob Lindley ("first appearance in New York in sixteen years" — a banjoist and comedian), Mackin and Bryant (Irish song and dance), Lucy Adams and Guy Linton, Gonzales ("California sensational gymnast"), George Reynolds and C. W. Cogill (in April Fool's Day), Zanfretta (in The Mischievous Monkey), Kelly and Weston (in Less Talk and More Music), and Zanfretta in The Brigands. The spirit of the Ravels still walked abroad.

Billy and Tommy Devere opened the bills of December 8th–13th, in The Statue, followed in the olio by Joseph Stritter (German female impersonator), Brevarde and Sawtelle ("magnets of song and dance"), Nellie Thorne, Larry Tooley (in One Night in a Bar-room), the Grinnells, the Martells (sic), Clara Cushman, J. W. McAndrews, Lee Brothers ("Irish"), and a perversion (I suppose) of Pinafore (with Joe Burgess, the Deveres, Bennie (sic) Grinnell (Ralph), and Clara Cushman (Josephine).   Most of the performers just mentioned figured during the week of December 15th–20th, as did Bobby Williams (with Billy Devere, in The Huckleberry Party), Josephine Howland (ballads), and Harry Sheldon, with Pinafore still sailing in the rear of the evening's delights.   Christmas week (December 22nd–27th) opened the programmes with The Devil of a Scrape (the cast including Harvey Collins, T. Devere, Ed Mills, Joe and Annie Burgess, Alice Montague, Stella Newton and Bobby Williams), and ended with Johnny Allen as Jake Schneider, in Schneider, or, Dot House on der Rhine, with about the same persons in support.   In the olio between the two plays were George La Rosa (equilibrist), Joseph Stritter, Thompson and Waldron (in The Troubles of the Levi Brothers), Mons. Bushnell ("the world's champion aerial juggler"), Stella Newton, and Frank Jones and Alice Montague (in Mixtures), the Excelsior Three (in dances), the La Rosa Brothers, and King Sarbro.   And thus I pass into the New Year (1880) at the Bowery Garden (or Garten).

And I do it by means of A Good Square Shave, which began the bills for January 5th–10th, with Billy Devere, Edward K. Mills and Bobby Williams; the olio rewards were Fanny Sanford (sic), Love in the Country (with

[119]

Harry Slate), P. C. Foy (Irish vocalist), Tom Harper (the one-legged skater and acrobatic spade dancer — "his first appearance in America in three years"), Jessie Merton (vocalist), A. Zanfretta (in The Mischievous Monkey), the Cahill Brothers, "Professor" Pilliard (*sic* — the "modern Hercules") and Mlle. Georgia ("lady gymnast"), Satsuma, Harry and Pete Slate (in 1776, or, the Old Veteran's Birthday) and the Zanfretta spectacle, The Magic Book. The next week (January 12th–17th) proffered the Deveres (in The Siamese Twins), Allen and Hart (in Ethiopian duos), Alice Audley (jig), Jen and Georgie Powers (in Susie's Serenade), Dick Sands, Mackin and Bryant, Fayette Welch, the Zanfrettas (Alexander, Frank and Flora, in Smith and Brown, and also in the concluding The Skeleton Witness), Sharpley and Carroll, &c. Welch and Devere's Minstrels began the bills for January 26th–31st, in persons of Sherman Steele, Archie Hughes (bones), Allen (interlocutor), Fayette Welch (tambourine), E. W. Nichols, Frank St. Clair, &c. The olio gave us Watson and Haley, Paddy Hughes ("after two years absence in England, Ireland and Scotland"), the Four Italians (Welch, Hughes, Allen and Welston), Joe Redmond and Ada Clifton, the three Zanfrettas (in The French Dancing Master and in the concluding Nicodemus), Somerville and Cohen, &c.

February 2nd–7th had Sawdust Bill (with Frank Livingstone, Brevarde and Sawtelle), Little Daisy (songs), Lulu Wentworth (banjo), Billy Devere and Bobby Williams (in The Cottage Serenade), Maude Florette (song and dance), Harry Clark (*sic*), Frank Livingstone (equilibrism and head-balancing), King Sarbro, Annie Hindle ("King of Fashion, the Apollo Belvidere of the American Stage, in swell songs"), and the three Zanfrettas (in The Magician, as well as in the concluding Four Lovers). The next week (February 9th–14th) retaining Brevarde and Sawtelle, Bobby Williams, Billy Devere, Annie Hindle and others, added Mlle. Désirée, Harry La Rose (club act, juggling), Hughey Haggerty, Frank Bolton and Ada Bradford (in The Enchanted Statue), the French Clodoche Quadrille (with Alexander, George and Frank Zanfretta and Burt Allen), Frank Melrose (one-legged gymnast), John Williams and Willis Pickert (clog dancers) and ended the bill with Zanfretta's arrangement of Vol-au-Vent. It certainly is interesting to notice the survival of the old Ravel specialties in these different Bowery "Gardens." Specialists for February 16th–21st were Tommy Cooper and Harry Edwards ("vocal and terpsichorean feats" — a more grandiloquent way of saying "song and dance"), Nellie Hasson (in Way up Yonder), Sam S. Sanford (in an act of Uncle Tom's Cabin — as Uncle Tom), the Hassons (in Just from Arkansaw), Old Josh Carter (with S. S. Sanford), Mme. Anderson ("champion lady pedestrian of the world"), Eurardo and Zanfretta, to end the bill, in Jocko. The week of March 1st–6th re-introduced J. W. McAndrews (in The Watermelon Man and in Gus, the Slasher), Sharpley and West (Mirth and Music), Minnie Gough (her last appearances in America), and the concluding Zanfretta adaptation, The Coopers. March 8th–13th began the performances with Zanfretta's The Brigands, and, after an olio including Kate Montrose, McAndrews (in The Dutch Pedler), Nellie Parker, W. Allen, Add Weaver, Frank Montrose, and a few others, ended with something like a real play, at least in the old Bowery sense — Hernandez Foster, in Jack Harkaway Afloat and Ashore.

The Harvard collection (almost my sole source of information for details of these Bowery shows) supplied nothing further for March.   For April 5th–10th the bills promised Etta Morris (serio-comic), Joe and Annie Burgess (in Family Quarrels), Matt Gallagher and Billy Mack (in The Johnson Coterie), Charley Shay (as an Oriental necromancer, and also in an act with his dogs), Fields and Leslie (the Two Irish Gents), Leslie and Avalo (on the horizontal bar), Fayette Welch, Zanfretta (in The French Dancing Master), Ajax (contortionist), and the Zanfretta show, The Village Torment.   The entertainments for April 12th–17th ring pleasingly to the fancy — Harry Sheldon (necromancy), the Milo Brothers (James and John) and Joe Marcella ("in their Roman Brother acts, somersaults on shoulders, backward and forward in every conceivable manner"), Nellie Germon (motto vocalist), Fayette Welch (in High-Jack, the Heeler), Williams and Sully ("Ethiopians"), Fields and Leslie, the Four Italians, and Zanfretta (in Humpty Dumpty).   The remaining fortnight of April hurried across our fevered vision Alice Morosco (motto), La Rosa Brothers, Thompson and Mack (Hebrew team), Libby Ross and Carrie Edwards ("female athletes"), Fred Roberts, Conroy and Daly (in The Irishman's Home), The Enchanted Statue (with Frank Bolton, Alexander Zanfretta, and — in four parts — Ada Bradford), John Williams and Willis Pickert, a second week of Humpty Dumpty, How I Used Casey (with Tom and Flora Zanfretta and Charles Saunders), Maude Florette, Kain and Thompson ("Dutch" and Hebrew team), Ben Gilfoil, the Russell Brothers, Alfred Liston, Fred Roberts, the farce, The Arrival of Minnie Hauk, and the Zanfretta concluding act, The Magic Trumpet.

Harvard is rich in May blooms from the Bowery Garden (*sic*).   Among earlier aspirants for popular favour were Kitty Stevens (serio-comic), Elmer E. Grandin (songs), Max Arnold ("Dutch" Senator), Charles Morgan, Harry Mullen and Kittie Stevens (these three, in Christmas Eve), Campbell and Burke (in Clippings, and also in Dutchie in a Fix), Nellie Collins, the Four Planets (McDermott, Sheehan, Kennedy and Haley), the Weston Brothers (Sam and Morris), Alexander and Leo Zanfretta (in The Mischievous Monkey), Nellie Collins, the Zanfretta arrangement of The Coopers, Fooling The Old Man (May 10th–15th, with Ben Brown, Flora Zanfretta, Ed Mills and Billy Hasson), Nellie Hasson, O'Neil and Conroy, the Morello Brothers (acrobats), Little Daisy, Sharpley and West, The Brigands (with Zanfretta), &c.   Later May put up other candidates — Mas-

[121]

ter Alexander Green (character changes), Williams and Watson, the Hayles (Billy and Lou, "the greatest clog dancers in the world"), Jimmy Ross and his "Canine Wonders," and (May 17th–22nd) Among the Mormons, by George B. Densmore, "author of Colonel Sellers," and with a cast including John Sutherland, Andrew Jacques, W. Hasson, Ben Brown, Billy Devere, Edith Crolius, Mary Collins and many others. The week of May 24th–29th brought back Miss Ceni Havre, Thatcher and Hume, and James T. Powers, in capital letters, if you please, on the bills, and set down as "the great versatile comedian, in Irish songs and dances and sayings." Ormiston Dixon (an "English star ventriloquist") also was here, and Ben Brown and Edith Crolius acted Barking up the Wrong Tree. Charles Foster ended the programmes with Saved at Seven, acting the Major, a manufacturer of pills, and supported by Dick Hume, W. T. Dulaney, Ed Carpenter, James T. Powers (as Mike Mulligan, a returned convict), Edith Crolius, Ben Brown, Lizzie Gale and Ceni Havre. Our patience, I hope, will last till June roses revive our drooping spirits.

The next fortnight (May 31st–June 12th) gave variety (in both senses) with Minnie Chapin (serio-comic), A Live Subject (acted by Dan Kelly, Dan Collyer, Ben Brown, and Edith Crolius), Little Diamond (song and dance), John Carroll ("musical genius"), Mealey and Mackey (character artists), Dan Collyer (as Cæsar, in The Fright), the play of On the Trail, or, the Demon of the Border (acted May 31st–June 5th, with George A. Hill as Ralph Thornpath and the Trailing Serpent), Billy Devere and Ben Brown ("The Twin Brothers"), Kitty McDermott, the De Alve Sisters (vocalists and banjo players), the Four Planets, Ben Brown (in A Trip to Paris), and The Italian Padrone (with D. A. Kelly, Dan Collyer and others from the olio). The week of June 21st–26th brought back Bobby and Alice Daily, John Pendy, the Four Diamonds, and the Bowery's own Fanny Herring, who, for the first three nights, acted The Tigress of the West, and, on the 24th, mounted the high heroics of Jack Sheppard. On June 28th she began what the bills described as the second week of The Tigress of the West, the preceding olio supplying Haley and Boyd (song and dance), the Moore Sisters (Eunice and Laura), "Professor" Austin and his trained dogs (all these trainers of dogs are set down as "professors," and possibly justly, if one takes a broad view of education), and Mike Drew (with Lillian Doane, in Irish songs and dances). July 5th–10th was the last week of the season, and provided, as novelties, Dave Oaks (or Oakes) and George Reynolds (in The Militia Boys' Parade), William Cronin and J. P. Sullivan (in Life in a Tenement House), and—to crown all—Fanny Herring in The Dumb Boy of Manchester. The reader may be surprised to learn that any Bowery hall of "Variety" could close for even a brief spell; he may be interested to know that, when the place re-opened, in early August, it had been re-christened in English the Novelty Theatre.

NATIONAL THEATRE, BOWERY, 1879–1880

Though one of these "Variety" houses seems distressingly like another (and certainly the bills were all constructed on a similar model) performers, on closer inspection, are seen to have been very different from house to house. Having just listed the entertainers at the Volksgarten and the Bowery Garden (*sic*), I am impressed by the novel names, in September, 1879, at the National. For the valued information involved I am, I need hardly say, indebted to bills at Harvard. In familiar farces or in the olio that those initial and concluding farces enclosed in the bills I will merely cite the list — the host — of persons that flitted in succession before the dazzled audiences. A. Denier, Charles West, Den De Courcey, Jessie Forrester, Neumann and Anna Roland (in Lucca and Wachtel), Otto Bellman, Das Mädchen vom Dorf, Soldatenliebe, Robert Story and Den De Courcy (in Sixty-four Years Old Today and in Oysters), Mons. Ventini and Bessie Randolph, Denier and West (in The Four O'Clock Train), Mons. Legab (trapeze), Ventini's arrangement of The Grand Duchess (with Bessie Randolph), J. H. Graham, Jennie Ward (with seven changes of dress), Nettie Carlyn, the Leland Sisters, Thomas Ryan, Gibbons and Russell (the Irish Twins), Eurardo, Chinese Musical Divertissements (with Denier, West and J. H. Graham), John Russell (Celtic songs and dances), The First Rehearsal, or, John Russell's Old Man (this, on September 16th, with Frank Gibbons, Tommy Ryan, John Russell, Denier, Graham, the Lelands, Charles West, now stage-manager, Jennie Ward, Nettie Carlyn and Agnes Evans), Carrie Banker, Blackford and Bye, Mike Drew, The Ambitious Actor (with J. O. Hall, Denier and Grimaldi Zeltner), Goodbye, Sunny Home (with Nagle and Wright), Robert Macaire (with Zeltner and Hall), &c. The reader must pardon my hurrying him so rapidly through the feast of the harvest month of September. Newcomers on October 1st were Allie Alden, Blanche Descond (operatic), Ruttini (French illusionist), &c.

A bill at Harvard for October 8th gives us tantalising glimpses of many of those just cited, as well as of Nellie Byron, Frank Melville (female impersonator, whom we must not confuse with the one-legged Frank Melrose), William Edwards and George Brazzier (Irish songs and dances), Hattie Wilson (songs), Billy Wells and Grace Sylvano (in Uncle Jasper's Birthday), Young America, Harry C. Holmes (Teutonic imitations), Carrie Lewis, and The Brigands, with Grimaldi Zeltner and Charles Chrisdie). The National now stooped to the lure of Female Minstrels, so popular in cheaper resorts. A bill at Harvard for October 15th is my first intimation of the change; it gives a first part of the programme under caption of Wit, Music and Song, with A. Denier and James Kennedy as bones, Charles West as interlocutor, and Billy Wells and John Magee as "tambos," aided by the orchestra of Philip Loerch (*sic*), and the specialties of Annie Howard,

Nellie Byron, Grace Sylvano and Carrie Lewis. Many of these minstrels were, of course, recruited from the olio, and, in it, also appeared John and Jennie Goodroy ("Irish"), the Howard Sisters (Annie and Mary) and all ended with the continuing Brigands.

The specialty of Wit, Music and Song carried on through all the weeks, except one, till March 1st, and, in the course of that time, shifting aggregations gave us, as bones, George W. Woods, A. Denier, Harry Bruno, Lawrence Allen, and Larry Tooley; as interlocutors, Charles West, William Marsh, James Emmerson (sic), George Goodman, Charles F. Seibert (or Seabert), George W. Woods and George Kurtz; and as "tambos" Billy West, John Magee, John Blackford, W. Dashington, Charles Wells, Billy Kay and A. Denier (who could serve anywhere in the row of minstrels). Associated with these heroes, as the weeks went by, were fair minstrels in persons of Rose Lonsdale, Lottie Blanchard, Clara Stuart, Addie Madden, Frank Melville (female impersonator, whose "fairness" we must take for granted), Dolly Emmerson (sic), Nellie Amon, Nettie Woods (or Wood), Nellie Vincent, Minnie Kaye, Tillie Bianca, Nellie Brooks, and others too numerous and too insignificant to notice. Having thus dismissed this (to me, at least) not very pleasing phase of the subject, I may state that the olio of remaining October and of early November gave us Rose Lonsdale (in the songs, Awfully Awful, Soft Sweet Waltz, etc.), William Marsh (top songs), John Gade ("musical, legitimate instruments" and the xylophone), George W. Woods, Lottie Blanchard (songs), Mlle. Mahretta (popular pictures and lightning changes), Frank Melrose (one-legged gymnast), Mat Livingston (clown and gymnast), Denier (in The Ghost in a Pawnshop), Wardell ("fire demon"), the pantomime, Nicky Nuvel (October 20th–25th), with Zeltner, Chrisdie, Denier and Mlle. Mahretta, Andrew Watrigant (sic), Jake Kemerson and Billy Kehoe (in The Reginskies' Troubles), Blackford and Bye, The Comanches (this for the fortnight of October 27th–November 8th, with Zeltner, Chrisdie and Denier), Harry Bruno ("original and laughable songs"), the Shedmans, the Halls (James and Ocie, "terpsichorean songs," and in The Mischievous Monkey), Julius Hanson (in Punch and Judy), Charles West (airs on wood and straw instruments), Maud Hamilton, Young America, Johnny Mackin (clog), and (as per bill of November 16th) B. C. Taylor and the olio personnel, in Murder at the Old Toll Gate. A bill at Harvard for Sunday, November 23rd, presents, among other features of the olio, May Arnott, George Goodman ("sensational and motto songs"), Lottie Grant, Frank Bush, and The Charmed Cross (with Frank Wardell, Signor Diablo, May Arnott, Young America, Denier, Jerry Dashington and Lottie Grant.

For lack of evidence, I am forced to pick up the thread with a Harvard bill for December 15th and 16th, with promises of Julius Turnour (in "a comical chair act"), Tom English (as the coloured musician, with banjo,

FRANK McNISH
ND THE LELAND SISTERS

WILLIS PICKERT

EMMA ROGERS AND
HARRY McAVOY

ALICE MONTAGUE

RUSSELL BROTHERS

LITTLE TODD

FAYETTE WELCH

FOSTELLE

PADDY MURPHY

Several of these Pictures from the Harvard Theatre Collection

bones, cornet, violin and "tambo"), Miss Lou Arnott, Wells and Sylvano, and Rupert's Dog (with Vic and Harry Leonzo).   This last named exciting specialty remained for a second week (December 22nd–27th) and may have been the only Christmas joy of some poor, gallery boys — if boys were admitted to those heights of Olympus.   With the dog drama of that festal week we were treated also to Irene Kerns, Carl Neumann and Marie Vestvali (in Lucca and Wachtel and in Kurmärker und Picarde), Billy and Minnie Kaye ("Ethiopians") and some of the steady occupants of that Bowery stage.   During the week of December 29th–January 3rd, Tillie Bianca sang Our Hallway Door and How Ashamed I Was, Hugh Nixon and Lawrence Allen "teamed" in song and dance, Neumann and Vestvali gave 1,500 Dollars and Rothschild aus Frankfurt, and the Leonzos and their dog, Tiger, thrilled with their other special excitement, The Dog Spy.   The week of January 12th–17th saw the return of Ventini and Bessie Randolph, in The Grand Duchess, and the engagement of Williams and Morton, Landis and Steele, Emma and Louis Alfredo and Frank Bush, most of whom continued into another week (19th–24th).   According to the Staats-Zeitung, the week of January 26th–31st gave a play in three acts, entitled Fritz, and an olio weighty with Frank Bush, the Grinnells, W. and Claudia Ripley, Laura Russell, Jimmy and Dolly Emmerson, and Bryant and Belmont.

The week of February 2nd–7th alone in that series of winter nights neglected to provide the opening attraction of Wit, Music and Song; instead, the bills began with Family Jars (Charles F. Seabert, Etta Morris and A. Denier) and continued with Ada Raymond, Ed C. Smith (late Smith and Byrne, on various instruments), Frank Melville (in his sneezing song, etc.), Mackin and Bryant, Mlle. Lottie and the Baldwin Brothers (the "wonders of the acrobatic universe"), May Vernon (songs), the Grinnells, Mons. Henrico (equipoise, and juggling with balls, knives, cannon-balls, eggs, paper, plates, bells and burning torches), Etta Morris ("refined motto songs"), and the play of The German and the Waif (with B. C. Taylor, Seabert, Hattie and Bennie Grinnell, &c).   Subsequent February evenings (beginning early and ending at late hours) brought (in addition to the restored Wit, Music and Song), George Kurtz and Nellie Brooks (in Karl and Gretchen), Rose Lonsdale (in the songs, Dancing round with Charlie and The Skidmore Fancy Ball), the Morello Brothers, the farce of Oh! Boys (with Kurtz, Denier and Lawrence Allen), and a return visit of the Dog Spy (February 9th–14th); the three O'Brien Brothers (tumbling and somersaults), Billy and Minnie Kaye (in Cincinnati Hams), Harry Bruno (Rapid Transit Vocalist), Frederick Guy (English prestidigitateur), the Grinnells, Dooley and Tenbrook (the "Black Ambassadors"), Larry Tooley, and The Hidden Hand (February 16th–21st, with Nellie Brooks as Capitola and George Kurtz as Wool, and with other parts in the hands of the olio); Callahan and Collins (Irish clog-dancers in Just from Omaha), Kurtz and Nellie Brooks (in The

[125]

Orphan Chile), Christie and Williams (the "original Shamrocks" and also in blackface), the Grinnells (in The Apple Girl and Paper Boy of New York), and Arthur Sprague and George Douglass, with members from the olio, during the week of February 23rd–28th, in Hawkeye, the Scout.

This last-named delectability warmed the hearts of auditors for a second week (March 1st–6th), during which glad time Billy Mendel (Teutonic songs), Charles E. Johnson ("the world's greatest juggler"), Kurtz and Nellie Brooks (in The Emigrant's Lament), Morton and Miles ("the Irish Boys from Kerry"), Burt Queen (vocal ventriloquist, and his figures, Tom and Joe), Dick Sands (clog, and imitation of a railroad train), Kitty Stevens and the Grinnells did their best to sustain the olio. Later in March we had the Nelsons (George and Marie), the Thompson Brothers (Irish songs), the Grinnells as Bessie and Willie (in The Two Orphans), Alessandro (who performed with 160 and 200 pound dumb-bells as easily as I perform with this, my trusty pen), the play of The Old Cabin Home (March 8th–13th, with Seabert, Billy Kaye, Nelson, &c.), Blue Glass (March 15th–20th, with Seabert, now stage-manager for the whirling hosts), Marie Désirée, Joseph A. Kelly (in Levy in a Fix), the Burnell Brothers (Sam and Billy, in My Carolina Home), the Grinnells (in Jack's Farewell to Polly), Frank Bush, and Life for Life (15th–20th, by and with W. H. Rightmire, supported by Seabert, Nelson, the Grinnells and the Kayes), &c. Here Harvard bills again fail us, but the Staats-Zeitung advertised Norah Creina for March 29th–April 3rd. That week, judging from a bill at Harvard for April 4th (Sunday) gave us Dick Berthelon (banjo and comedian), Herr and Frau La Roche (in Dienstboten-Wirthschaft and in Was sich liebt das neckt sich), Florence May (in song and recitation), Howard and Sanford, J. H. Graham, Laura Russell, D. B. Emery, Julius Hanson (prestidigitateur, and also with his Punch and Judy), A. Denier, Billy Blair (as the aged negro), and the farce, Come Down, We'll Make It Pleasant for You. These attractions I assume to have blessed the week just mentioned, because the bill at Harvard for April 5th starts the week of April 5th–10th with a return to the opening specialty of Wit, Music and Song, with Tom Murray and Tom Hedges, S. S. Pettit, Nellie Vincent, Henrietta Murray, and provides later for specialties by these and by Tillie Bianca, the Murrays (in Brogue and Blarney), Pettit and White (African eccentrics), Laura Russell, Emery and Winetta Craven and ends the festive proceedings with Rupert's Dog barking up the tree of melodrama — of course with the Leonzos and Tiger. Wit, Music and Song began all bills in April, newcomers in that National feature or in the olio including Tillie Bianca, Julius Turnour, Andy McKee (eccentric dancing), Louis Alfredo and Turnour (as a team), the National Four (McKee, Denier, Pettit and White), Nellie Vincent, Susie Byron, the Crimmins Brothers (John, Steve and Mike, in songs and dances), Room 36 (McKee's extravaganza), Annie Hindle ("le roi de la mode" — fancy!),

[126]

Hedges and Winetta Craven (in Domestic Difficulties) and, for two weeks (April 12th–24th) our old familiar thriller, The Dog Spy. For April 26th–May 1st, our nerves were attuned to the antics of Wit, Music and Mirth, A. Denier as bones, Murray and Hedges as interlocutors, and Archie White as "tambo," leading the rosebud garden of Susie Byron, Nellie Vincent, Henrietta Murray and Winifred North (operatic vocalist), all of whom, male and female, figured, later, in the olio; Archie White and Ella Esmond gave Always on the Move; Annie Hindle showed male styles; Hotel Runners enlisted Arthur Sprague, Denier and McKee; and H(edges), M(urray), S(chooner), Pinafore, not quite as intended by Gilbert and Sullivan, had Thomas Murray as Sir Joseph Ale, Thomas Hedges as Ralph, Sprague as Dick Deadbeat, Susie Byron as Josephine, Henrietta Murray as Buttertub, and Winetta Craven as Hebe.

If, cries my distracted reader, if only two weeks in these "variety" houses could remain identical in offering! But no! the kaleidoscope must change into ever shifting patterns and we must weary our nerves with constant attempt at unity of design. Pinafore lasted through the week of May 3rd–8th, and the week of the 10th–15th give us A Life's Revenge, deeply, darkly serious, no doubt, with the author, William H. Brent, in the cast. All a Mistake, or, the Arrival of Gilbert, closed the show during the next week (May 17th–22nd) with Larry Tooley, Arthur Sprague, Dan Nash, Denier, Nellie Vincent, Kate Cooper and May Arnott in the cast.' Low Flats began on May 24th, and After Dark (in one act) performed the closing function during the week of May 31st–June 5th. Harvard has two bills for the month — May 12th and 20th — and these show Bud Granger, Arthur Sprague and Dan Nash (in Les Misérables), Désirée, Ward and Wells, Carrie Lewis, Dan Nash, Landis and Steel (or Steele), John Williams (late of Williams and Pickert — "champion clog-dancer of England and America"), Dan Nash and Kate Cooper (in The Rose of Killarney), A Life's Revenge, J. H. Graham, May Arnott, Larry Tooley, Gus Saville (late of Bryant and Saville) and Byrne (late of Smith and Byrne) in The College of Music, &c.

In June and July, Wit, Music and Song resumed the position at the head of the bills, and led programmes that, in successive weeks, gave us for longer or shorter stays the "art" of Harry and Emma Budworth, the Howard Sisters, Howard and Sanford (German song and dance), the Nelsons (George and Marie — "Ethiopians"), Elmer E. Grandin and Josephine Shanley (in Won at Last), Winifred North, Neil Conway (Irish Union bagpiper), John Egan, Pomp, or, a Nigger in Ireland (with Harry and Emma Budworth, Sprague, the Nelsons, &c.), Irene Kerns, Hawley and Manning, Mlle. Désirée (evidently desired of many halls), Julius Hanson (sic), Joe and Annie Burgess, Hattie Grinnell, Harry Mullen, Little Daisy (songs), Master Lew (banjo), Saunders and Fash, Georgie Lingard, Alice Evans (ballads), Bessie Randolph and Ventini (June 14th–19th, in Life in Turkey).

[127]

From two July bills at Harvard — 12th–18th and 19th–24th — I attempt to "eternise" the names of Denier, Sprague, Tom Cooper and Jessie Forrester, Hattie Grinnell, Annie and Joe Burgess, Marie Désirée, Wendell, Punch and Bessie Walton (who sang Come where My Love Lies Dreaming and What are the Wild Waves Saying?), La Statue Blanche (with Denier and Mlle. Mahretta), A Night of Terror (with Larry Tooley), George W. Callahan (ventriloquist), the Ringlers (Add and Minnie, in The Happy Irish Pair), the Cooper Brothers (Tommy and Will, in Just from Arkansaw), Moore and Lessenger (The Eccentric Shoemakers), The New Delivery (with Jessie Forrester, Denier and Sprague), and A German's Troubles (with Tooley, Hattie Grinnell, Sprague, Ringler and Tommy Cooper). Neither Harvard nor the Staats-Zeitung helps me further. And now, having determinedly done my duty by the persistent reader, I leave the National for 1879–80.

London Theatre, Bowery, 1879–1880

The London, without a summer's intermission, continued, during the week beginning on September 1, 1879, the engagements of the popular Delehanty and Hengler, and of the Murphy and Mack-Murphy and Shannon quartette, in Murphy's Wedding. The quartette of Emerson and Clark and the Daly Brothers, Georgie Melnotte, the Peasleys (John and Lea) and Minnie Lee were also in the generous bill of fare. Murphy's Wedding lasted for five weeks, ending its run on September 27th. Murphy and Mack, during the week of September 8th–13th, appeared also in the sketch, The Resurrectionist, and, during the week of the 15th–20th, in I Have Business with You; in the first of those two weeks Murphy and Shannon gave He Would Be an Actor, and, in the second, Just from Germany. Others, in addition to those just mentioned, were Kennedy and Clark, Tillie Antonio, Kelly and Weston, Ned Wambold, Frank Traynor and Otto Burbank (these in the farce of Cremation), the O'Briens (Charles and Dan, contortion act), Miss Lou Sanford, and the Brennans (in Trifles). Newcomers, during the week of September 22nd–27th, were Viola Clifton, Fayette Welch (impersonations of the Southern darkey), Mlle. de Granville ("the woman with the iron jaws"), Geyer and Mackie (in Down where the Cotton Grows), Mlle. Barretta, Weston, the Walkist (played by Murphy and Shannon), and the concluding piece, Base Ball, Our National Game (with Dick Parker, Murphy and Shannon, Murphy and Mack, Fayette Welch, Viola Clifton, Georgie Melnotte, &c.). The bills for September 29th–October 4th opened with The Man from Bay Ridge (Murphy and Mack, and Mlle. Barretta), and proceeded through an olio enlisting George W. Woods ("late of Moore and Burgess's Minstrels, St. James Hall, London, in imitation of drum corps," &c.), John Pendy and Miss Jeffreys Warner (in Here and There), Miss Reno Stedman (vocalist), Fayette Welch, the Barlow Brothers (James and

William), Fields and Hanson (in Music Conquered), O'Reardon, &c., till they arrived at a new Murphy playet — Murphy's Divorce, of course with the Murphys, Mack and Shannon, and with Burbank, Pendy, Woods and others.

Murphy's Divorce lasted till October 18th, some of its associates in earlier October being Murphy and Shannon (in and as Dick Turpin and Tom King), Harry McAvoy and Emma Rogers (in Jealousy, or, Two Can Play at that Game), Jennie Southern, Kitty Whitland (song and dance), the Suydams (Frank and Eugene, double bar), the Halls (James and Ocie), Ed Sylvester and William Everett, Our Boarding School (with Fayette Welch, Dick Parker, Burbank and George W. Woods), Which is Which? (with Murphy and Mack), the Le Clair Sisters, Raymond and Murphy ("chaste and unique portrayals of the refined Irish gentlemen"), Maud Morrissey (songs of the day, including Harrigan's Mountain Dew and W. J. Scanlon's (of Scanlon and Cronin) McDonald's Ould Tin Roof), Flora Moore ("queen of mimic vocalists"), and Carlos Dashway and Frank Monroe ("greatest gymnasts of the age").   The two weeks of October 20th–November 1st supplied newcomers in Burt (*sic*) Allen and Joe Hart (in The Rival Lovers), Dan McCarthy, Troubles in America (with Murphy and Mack), Alice Hale ("vocal gems"), Raymond and Murphy (in Casey's Old Fiddle), Fayette Welch (in A Ghost in a Pawnshop), Foster and Hughes (grotesque songs and dances), Africa *vs.* Ireland (with Dick Parker, Murphy and Mack, and Burbank), Tom Maclean ("London's mimic"), Kerrigan and McCarthy ("from Longford, Ireland"), Yank Adams ("royal emperor of the ivories — champion billiardist of the world"), Out All Night (with Murphy and Mack), Ella and Paddy Murphy (in Irish Felicity), Minnie Lee, the Original Irish Four (Williams, Edwards, Miles and Daly), George Murphy and Burbank (in He Would Be an Actor), John and James Russell, Emily Sylvester, the Four Diamonds (Thomas, Watson, Callan and Haley), and (week of October 27th–November 1st) Murphy's Campaign (with John and George Murphy, Phil Mack, Fayette Welch, Burbank, Ella Murphy, &c.).

Murphy's Campaign lasted for three weeks, ending on November 15th. Its associates, during one or both of its last two weeks, were Viro Farrand, The McMullen Family (with Murphy and Mack), Diplomacy (with Paddy and Ella Murphy — plenty of Murphys in the London!), Andy Collum, Charles A. Gardner ("Dutch"), the French Troupe Davene, Fayette Welch, Flora Moore, Murphy and Shannon (in Our Happy German Home), Mlle. Magerald (songs in French, German and English), The Two Dromios (with Murphy and Shannon and Phil Mack), Paddy Hughes (change artist), A. C. Moreland and John Foster (in The Modern School of Acting), Williams and Sully, Charles A. Foster, Ella Mayo, Clara Moore, the Brennans, The Dutch Indian (with Gardner, Moreland and Mack), Dr. Colton in Trouble (with Moreland, Murphy and Mack and Murphy and Shannon) and Fred F.

[129]

Levantine (equilibrist). Kitty Robinson, Tom English ("greatest musical artist living" — banjo, cornet, tambourine, bone solo), the Russell Brothers, Watson and Ellis (in Dutch Deception), Clara Moore, Dodging the Gang (with Gardner, Ella Mayo, Dick Parker and Moreland), Campbell and Burke (in Clippings), Klein's Visit to New York (with Gardner, Moreland, Tom English, John and James Russell, and Ella Mayo) — lo! the lure for November 17th–22nd. Harvard supplied no bill for the week of November 24th–29th.

Familiar to followers of "Variety" were the entertainers for December 1st–6th — Susie Byron, Parker, Moreland, Tommy and Maud Morrissey, Quilter and Goldrich, the French Twin Sisters (Minnie and Lena), **Maggie Foster** (motto songs), the K. H. K's (Emerson, Clark, and the Daly Brothers, in The Four Fascinating Coons), Yank Adams, and the returned Murphy's Dream. Later in December one might have greeted Charles White (as Cupid, in The Fellow that Looks like Me), Mary Rice ("vocal gems"), the three Milo Brothers (muscular feats on the horizontal bars), Manchester and Manning ("black Apollos of song and dance, acrobatic feats," etc., in The Two Eccentrics), Irving Jackits-Chy's Male and Female Japanese Troupe, That's My Trick (with Bobby Manchester, John J. Jennings and George Shannon), the Dalys (Bobby and Danny), Raymond and Murphy, Greenbriar's Troubles (with John Hart, Moreland and Ella Mayo), Professor A. W. Sawyer, Delehanty and Hengler (these two in capitals, large and looming, to denote the stars they were), and Murphy's Christmas (another of that unending string of Murphy episodes) which began a four-weeks run on December 15th. Bobby Newcomb, ever welcome, entered on an engagement on the 22nd, as did the Peasleys (in Jerry's Fortune), Mlle. Baretta (*sic*), and Harry Bennett; Delehanty and Hengler continued, and John Hart gave The Last of the Utes. The Morello Brothers (Max and Will, "premier gymnasts of the world"), Minnie Leigh (or Lee), Lillie Ellis, Pettit and White, Hart, the Pedestrian (with John Hart) — these were specialties of December 29th–January 3rd.

Am-u-let (with John Hart, Moreland and J. O. Hall) began the bills for January 5th–10th, other features being Emma Bretto, the Parker Sisters (Georgie and Lizzie, in song and dance), Charles and Ella Jerome, the Irish Agitator (with Murphy and Mack), Murphy and Shannon, &c. Thereafter January thawed lovers of "Variety" with appearances of Howard and Coyne (in Family Troubles), J. E. Green (veteran minstrel), Wingfield (*sic*) and Gregory (double horizontal bars), Ida Morris, Reynolds and Cogill, John B. Wills and May Adams (in Larks), Louise Stetson (skipping-rope dances), The Invaded Studio (with John Hart, George Reynolds and Moreland), John Morris ("mystic change artist"), Bobby Newcomb, the French Twins, William Courtright (in Flewy! Flewy!), Harry Bryant (ventriloquist and mimic), Harry and John Kernell, Dick Hume, the Suydam Brothers, Ella

Mayo, R. G. Allen (banjo), Alice Bateman (dancer), Allie Drayton, Gus Hill (feats of strength), Thatcher and Hume (in Just from Arkansaw), &c. The last week of January (26th–31st) gave us, in addition to many just cited, Morgan, Mullen and Lizzie Conway (in Christmas Eve), Minnie Chapin (character songs), Dolph Levino (tumbler-harmonicon and xylophone), Al W. Filson (comic vocalist), Charles and Carrie Moore (skaters), Edward McAvoy (equilibrist), Mme. Anderson (now in character songs), Paddy and Ella Murphy, "Professor" Charles Moore's school of educated dogs, the Bent Brothers (cornetists), and The Black Statue (with John Hart, Bobby Newcomb, Moreland, Cogill, Lizzie Conway, and George Reynolds).

Pell-mell I hurl at the reader the blessings of February — Alice Daily, the Arnold Brothers, J. O. Ward (baritone), Devlin and Tracy ("refined Irish comedy"), Clara Moore, A Quiet Evening (with Louise Montague and Bobby Newcomb), the Sparks Brothers (John and Joe), Baretta (sic), Paddy and Ella Murphy, Charles Frey and Florence Marshall (in Chips), Kerrigan and McCarthy, Minnie Lee, Bryant and Hoey, Captain George Laible, The Masquerade Ball (February 9th–14th, with Hart, Bobby Newcomb, Frey, Moreland, Charles and "Lewis" Dockstader, Fred and Lon Leslie, Louise Montague, Florence Marshall and Minnie Lee), the Dutch Mendels (Harry and Leonie), Daisy Remington, Hines and Blossom (Ethiopian song and dance), Louise Montague ("the Venus Aphrodite of the stage"), Fred Hallen and Enid Hart (in Pinafore in Fifteen Minutes), Viola Clifton, Kelly and Ryan ("the bards of Tara"), and Cremated by Wholesale (week of February 16th–21st, with Hart, Moreland, Lizzie Conway, Lew Dockstader, Fred Hallen and Harry Mendel). New or returned, during the week of February 23rd–28th, were Mlle. Eugenia (song and dance), T. F. Grant (one-legged song and dance), Pauline Batchelor, Manchester and Jennings, Jackits-Chy's Japanese, Charles Diamond (Milanese minstrel), Bryant and Saville ("mammoth cabinet of musical instruments"), &c.

March began with a gale of newer faces — Professor Logrenia (magic), Williams and Morton (Irish songs and dances), Fernando Fleury (lightning change artist), the Brennans (with Captain Laible), Mary Rice, the Sparks Brothers, the Ripleys (William and Claudia, acrobats), Charles Diamond, Joe and Annie Burgess, Harry Bennett, Bryant and Hoey, and Pompey's Patients (with John Hart). The week of March 8th–13th presented Jennie Ward ("with seven changes of dress in presence of the audience"), Ben Gilfoil, W. O'Dale Stevens (slack rope), McIntyre and Heath (in Skedaddle — possibly our first meeting with these later stars of musical comedy), J. H. Graham (topical motto and change artist), Murphy and Shannon, Linda Jeal ("Globe Roulantist and Aerial Slack Wire Artist"), Murphy and Mack, and For Better or Worse (with Hart, Lizzie Conway, Georgie Melnotte, and Moreland). The week of March 15th–20th presented Jim Crow Alive (with John Hart and John E. Murphy), Charles Redmond and Georgie Blake ("the genteel Irish couple"—lightning changes, songs, etc.). Carrie Davenport (light and heavy Indian clubs), Murphy and Shannon (in Preparation), Sellou and Byrnes (songs and double clog), Alice Daily, Hallen and Hart, the African dwarf, Tommy, Sheehan and Jones (in An Everyday Occurrence), the Rankins, and another Murphy sketch — Murphy's Uncle (with both Murphys, Mack, Shannon, Fred Hallen and others). Certainly the Murphys were serving the Murphys as devotedly as the Mulligans served Harrigan and Hart; but Murphy's Uncle remained only a week in the bills. The fortnight from March 22nd to April 3rd brought Geyer and Mackie (in The Centennial Traveller), Andy Collum, the Brazziers (William, George and Rufus, "grotesque elastic dancers"), the French Twin Sisters, Sheehan and Jones (in The Stage-Struck Daughter), Mollie Wilson, the three Leotards (athletes), Sam Holdsworth (in "a beautiful lyric act"), the Dockstaders, the three Rankins, Jim McIntyre and Tom Heath, Gibson and Binney, Dick Rowe, Murphy and Mack (in Troubles in America), Campbell and Burke, Cardella (*sic*) and Victorelli (gymnasts), Ira A. Paine, and The Rivals (with both Murphys and their respective partners, Mack and Shannon).

The April bills added to the procession of "Variety" figures and features Helen Courtland, the Reynolds Brothers (George and Steve, in Darkies on the Levee), The Mulberry Street Flats (with Murphy and Mack), Bingham (young ventriloquist), the Four Star Grotesques (Seamon, Somers and the Girard Brothers), Fun at Coney Island (with Murphy and Mack, Murphy and Shannon, Moreland, Hart, Misses Helen Courtland and Conway, and Daisy Remington), Guy Linton and Lucy Adams, the Peasleys, Charles T. Ellis (late of Watson and Ellis) and Clara Moore (in Eureka), Niles and Evans (in Reportorial Repartee), the Hassons (in Home Again), Minnie Lee, Charles Harris and Billy Wood (California "Dutch" team), Kelly and Ryan, and the Four Planets (McDermott, Sheehan, Kennedy and Haley). Harvard, my sole source of information for the London Theatre, has but two bills for May. On the 10th (and, presumably through the week of the 10th–15th) Mississippi Jim (with Bobby Manchester, Jennings and Moreland), Young Hercules, Healey and Conway (acrobatic song and dance men, in Disunited), Ella Mayo, the "great" Fostelle, Gus Hill (club-swinger and juggler), Mollie Wilson, Master Barney, the trio of Healey, Conway and Ella Saunders, the "K. H. K's" (Emerson, Clark and the Daly Brothers) led the way to the concluding Hassenbad, or, the Pretty Prince (with Lillie Hall as Hassenbad, and Fostelle as Jazabel). A bill for May 18th shows The Good Servant (with Frank Bell, Moreland and Lizzie Conway), the Russell Brothers, Lillie Howard (serio-comic), the Peasleys, Harry C. Lansing (male burlesque prima donna), Favor and Shields, Dave Oakes (in Tony, the Tailor), Yank Adams, &c. To conclude the festivities, members of the company (i.e., the olio) acted Trouble in French Flats (this was the

season of French Flats, at the Union Square Theatre).   On May 21st, Yank
Adams "contested" with Randolph Heiser.   The bill for June 2nd may also
cover the week of May 31st–June5th; in any case, it promises Alice Bateman,
Paddy and Ella Murphy, Fred Roberts ("author, composer and musician"),
Sheehan and Jones, J. Brevarde and C. Sawtelle (in The Baby Elephant),
Baretta (*sic*), the Four Diamonds (Clark and Watson, Brevarde and Saw-
telle), and Mrs. Driscoll's Party (with Sheehan and Jones).

For June 7th–12th, we were treated to "turns" by Frank and Clara Mara,
Lillie Howard, Everett and Daly, Fred Roberts, Jacques Kruger (as the
Great Uncrushed, in The Arrival of Gilbert, with Joe Sparks as Pinafore
Gilbert), the Hayles (the Arkansaw Travellers), Louise Montague, The
Stage-Struck Daughter (with Sheehan and Jones).   Novel faces or features
for June 14th–19th were George Carey, Paul Hamlin and Ada Newcomb,
William H. Chace and Charles H. Yale (in Merry Moments and in Wine
and Bivalves), Kitty McDermott, the sketch, Gilsey (with Seamon, Somers
and Girard Brothers), Minnie Lee, and Sallie Mason and Robert V. Ferguson (in Masquerading).   The next week (June 21st–26th) presented Sallie
Mason and Ferguson (in Love's Decision), Belle Cushing (songs), Maggie
Nichols ("queen of the aerial wire"), Mayo and Talbert (novelty team),
the three Lorellas, Seamon, Somers and the Girards, and McGilligan's Luck
(with Kruger, Chace and others). The bills for July 5th–10th began with The
College of Music, presided over by Gus Saville (late of Bryant and Saville)
and John H. Byrne (late of Smith and Byrne).   Newcomers in that week were
Nellie Parker, Elise Kruger, the American Four (Pettingill, Gale, Dailey and
Hoey), Max Arnold, Pat Rooney, Add Weaver and Ada Forrest.   The only
other bill for 1879–80 that I discovered at Harvard bears the date of August
27th, and lists as performers John Robinson, Sheehan and Jones, Lillie
Howard, the Four Grotesques (Seamon, Somers and the Girard Brothers),
Sanford and Wilson, Mollie Wilson, Ada Forrest, John Hart (in Where Is
He? and also in Buffalo Bill Outdone) and Pat Rooney — one of the most
popular "kings" or "emperors" or "dukes" of "Variety."   The reader will
pardon my use of the extravagant language of that special field of amusement.

Miner's Theatre, Bowery, 1879–1880

The first two weeks of September, at the new Miner's, rushed before our
critical eyes the Courtland Sisters, Curry and Hall, Maud and Tommy
Morrissey, the Parker Sisters (Georgie and Lizzie), Press Eldridge, Mullen
and Magee, O'Reardon, Scanlan (or Scanlon) and Cronin (in O'Donovan's
Victory), the Brothers Valjean (jugglers and balancers), A Slippery Day,
Press Eldridge as Napoleon (in Hemmed In), Nellie Germon, the Le Clair
Sisters ("dazzling stars of refined song and dance"), William T. Dwyer
("the ne plus ultra of motto, comic and character vocalists"), Albert Duncan

(ventriloquist), the St. Felix Sisters, Fields and Leslie, Mlle. Cerito (panto-mime and dance), and The Wrecker's Oath (with A. H. Sheldon).

Several of these, I need hardly say, carried into later September, but the cooling nights then brought to us in addition Charles Redmond and Georgie Blake, Whitfield (dialect comedian), the Jeromes, Kerrigan and McCarty (*sic*), the three Milos, Webster Brothers (Ned and James), Cellini's Novelty Troupe of Ten, Robert Brower and Tillie Malvern, The Rogue, the Ring and the Rope, Kitty Allyne (actress and vocalist), the Martell Brothers (Harry and Willie), Jessie Merton, Favor and Shields (in The Lackawanna Spooners), Tom Harper, Sawyer's Black Diamond Quartette (in hymns, refrains and camp meeting shouts), Fred J. Huber ("the oyster can moke") and Kitty Allyne (in Something), Sheldon (in The Scarecrow), the Daytons (Tommy and Annie), and Texas Jack (September 22nd–27th, in The Black Hills). The transition week (September 29th-October 4th) gave novelty with Maggie Foster ("California's serio-comic"), Dan Mason ("Dutch"), Goldie and Steele ("breakneck originalities"), Dan Sully ("Celtic mon-arch"), the La Rosa Brothers (Frank and George) Fred Roberts, Sallie St. Clair, Charles Morgan and Harry Mullen (in Christmas Eve), and Dan Mason and Dan Sully (in The Crowded Hotel).

Since the Harvard Theatre Collection contains a complete file of bills for Miner's, in the year now under examination, the harried reader knows that I will spare him but few details. I will, however, try to pass as rapidly as possible through the maze. If only October will let me name the enter-tainers, without too much need for describing casts of plays! The earlier weeks of that pleasing month brought Charles and Ella Jerome (in A Dilemma), Lester Howard and Lizzie Hunter (in Fritz's Return), Bobby Newcomb, Levantine and Earle, Goldie and Steele, Gussie Leach, Alice Bateman ("best lady clog dancer in the world"), Topack and Moore, and their "fiery untamed steed, Spot," Sallie St. Clair, Young Hercules, Dwyer and Sweeny, Sheldon (as Strop, in The Escaped Jail Birds), Howard and Saville (in The Somnambulist), Nellie St. John, Lizzie Mulvey and Barney Fagan (in American Lads), Ada Lanier, Jennie Hughes (her "first appear-ance on the East Side"), the Carrolls (R. M., E. H. and Master Richard, in The McFaddens), Bryant and Saville, and Lost at Long Branch (with Sheldon and Tillie Malvern). The later nights of October (October 20th–November 1st) saw the return of Fannie Beane and Charles Gilday (in When the Cat's Away), the Dockstaders, McVickers and Saunders, The Mas-querade and Peel Yourself (those two specialties of the Carrolls), the ar-rival of Dilks and Wade ("Ethiopians"), and a production of The French Spy (with Jennie Hughes) which lasted through the two weeks involved. Belle Fostelle, Morton and Miles ("Celtic"), the Clipper Quartette (Robert McIntyre, F. T. Ward, G. F. Campbell and Charles Heywood, in original songs and camp meeting hymns), Thatcher and Hume (in Just from Arkansas — *sic*), the Four Planets (Kennedy and Clark, McDermott and Sheehan) — these were the latest scintillants of the month.

The Dutchman's Ghost (with Larry Tooley, Robie, Hughes, Charles Diehl and Tillie Malvern) ushered in the week of November 3rd–8th, with newcomers immediately following, in persons of Nellie Parker, John and Amy Tudor, Add Weaver, Sam Lang and Dollie Sharpe (in German Love), Linda Jeal, Master J. Roberts (imitator of Pat Rooney), W. O'Dale Stevens (equilibrist), Alfred Liston, and The Scamps of New York (with Sheldon). The week of November 10th–15th had Professor John Till's Royal Marionettes (in Beauty and the Beast), Kitty Allyne, Bobby Newcomb, Harry C. Stanley (Hebrew delineations), Hines and Blossom ("Coloured Ambassadors"), Kitty O'Neil ("champion jig and clog dancer of the world"), Daisy Remington ("petite blonde vocalist"), Huber and Allyne, Harry and John Kernell ("originators of the North of Ireland style of entertainment"), the Four Eccentrics (Perry, Magrew, Curdy and Hughes), and Harry Miner's Pinafore, with Louise Montague as Josephine, Sheldon as Sir Joseph Buckbier, Bobby Newcomb as Ralph, Myron Calice as Captain Corcoran, Louis Robie as Deadeye, Daisy Remington as Buttercup, and Tillie Malvern as Hebe. This parody of Gilbert and Sullivan lasted for six weeks, passing out of the bills on December 20th. In the olio during those weeks appeared at one time or another Dave Reed, Bonnie Runnells, Erba Robeson, Pell and Lewis, Clark and Edwards, Fred J. Huber (in The Other Fellow or in The Senator from Louisiana), John B. Wills and May Adams, Bobby Newcomb, George Kurtz, as Erin, and Nellie Brooks (*sic*) as Columbia (in The Dawn of Liberty), Bingham (ventriloquist), Joe and Annie Burgess, Linda Jeal, Kelly and Ryan, Bryant and Hoey, Sallie St. Clair, O'Dale Stevens, Bob Milligan and Ada Adair (in Just Over), Goldie and Steele, Fred Huber and Kitty Allyne (in Stricken), Jean Benosser (French wrestler and athlete, and his performing and wrestling Swiss bears), Harry Constantine, Belle Clifton, Edward Banker and Florence Wells (in an operatic sketch), Dolph Levino, and the K. H. K's (Emerson, Clark, and the Daly Brothers). December went out with the mirth occasioned (22nd–January 3rd) by the De Alve Sisters (Lillie and Gussie, medley and banjo artists), Ida Morris ("the Golden State's most popular serio-comic queen"), Guy Linton and Lucy Adams (in Second Sight at a Discount), Kerrigan and McCarty (*sic*), the Richmond Sisters (Josie and Lulu), the Daytons (Tommy and Annie), the Carrolls (in Niches from Nature), Awata Katsnoshin, Edward and Maud Werner, Laura Russell and D. B. Emery ("late of Spaulding's Bell Ringers"). On December 22nd was staged a revival of The Naiad Queen, which, until January 24th (a period of five weeks) closed all the bills at Miner's, its cast at first including Nellie Brooks (*sic*), Sheldon, Lucy Adams, Myron Calice, Tillie Malvern, Louis Robie, Belle Clifton, Kurtz and many others. There was a great deal of scenery.

[135]

Acquisitions from January 5th to the 17th included the Leland Sisters (Rose and Jennie, in songs, dances and recitations), the Mortons (Harry K. and Blanche M., in a German comedy sketch, Old Mr. Knuckle and Wife), Viola Clifton, Joe Redmond and Ada Clifton, the three Brazziers ("first appearance in New York since their return from Cuba"), Harry Osborne and Fanny Wentworth, John F. Sheridan and Alicia Jourdan (in A Moonlight Flirtation), Clooney and Ryan (in I Tink Yah Ve Should Smile), Ada Lynwood, Lillie Western ("lady musician"), Turner, Welch and Harris, and Bryant and Hoey.   From January 19th to the 31st we might have seen or heard (at least for one week) Mackin and Bryant (in Ireland's Farewell), Kate·Montrose, the Boisset Family and Oscar Avalo, the St. Felix Sisters, Alf Barker (in Flewy Flewy), Sheridan and Alicia Jourdan (in Heindrick and Lena), Charles Redmond and Georgie Blake, Edith Lyle, Minnie Gough, Charles Glidden ("coloured senator"), Kennedy and Magee, F. F. Thomas and Ed Neary (assisted to the height of his ability by the dwarf, Captain Erb, in O'Donohue's Arrival), Mlle. Etta ("serpentine wonder"), and Knights of the Jimmy (with Sheldon and the regular company).

The bills for February 2nd–7th began with Sheldon in Snozzle! Bozzle! Wozzle! and continued blithely with "turns" by Eloise Allen (vocalist), Lester and Williams ("Mimetics and Saltatorial Artists"), Nellie Nelson (vocalist), "Professor" John Pidgeon's "great original" Punch and Judy, Men of Nerve (with Mullen and Magee), Charles Redmond and Georgie Blake, A High Time in Dixie (with Morris and Green), Minnie Gough, the Three Nondescripts (Cerini, Leslie and Byrnes), "Professor" Rhinehart and his six dogs, and A Slippery Day (with Mullen and Magee).   More newcomers graced the bills for February 9th–14th — Gorman and Gallagher, Mollie Wilson, the Daytons, Billy Lester ("originator of all the Big Fours"), Jennie Hughes, Shirley and Byrne, Maud Stanley Werner and Edward Werner, John H. Murray's Pony Circus, the Richmond Sisters, and Tony Farrell. McVickers (sic) and Saunders returned on February 16th, and in came for that week (16th–21st) a host including George Beane, Jr., Matt Gallagher, the Milton Jaspers (Newton, Thomas and Clinton), the Seamons (Charles O. and Gertie), Fred J. Huber and Kitty Allyne (in One Night's Rest), Katsnoshin, Marie Jasper (in five characters, in Anxious to Please), Young Hercules, and Jennie Hughes once more in The French Spy.   New for the last week (23rd–28th) of February were Dave Reed, Fannie Beane and Charles Gilday, Fanny Davenport, Goldie and Steele, Dilks and Wade, the Leslie Brothers (Louis and Fred, equilibrists and antipodeans), Ida Morris, and the Only Little Four (McCue, Finnick and the Carroll Brothers); Jennie Hughes for a second week ended the show with The French Spy.

March in the course of its first two weeks gave us Lillie Western, Dave Reed, Virginia Stickney, Nellie Parker, the St. Felix Sisters, Add Weaver, the Boissets, Nellie Parker, Fanny Davenport, Murray's Pony Circus, Oliver

Twist (March 1st, with Sheldon as the Artful Dodger, Little Dorritt as Oliver, W. H. Danvers as Fagin, Robie as Bill, and Tillie Malvern as Nancy), Alice Gleason, Clark and Edwards, Mons. Henrico ("Indian club exercises, juggling three clubs at a time"), Georgie Lingard ("most popular of lyrical celebrities"), Jennie Reese (operatic songs), Beane and Gilday (in Our Picnic), William Henry Rice ("first appearance on the East Side"), Flora Moore, Ten American Students, the American Four (Pettingill, Gale, Dailey and Hoey) and New York in Slices (by and with Sheldon). The week of March 15th–20th gave The Lion and the Lamb (with Sheldon), clog and jig dancing by George Carey, Paul Hamlin and Ada Newcomb, gymnastics by the Milton Jaspers, and specialties by Jennie Reese, W. H. Rice, Marie Jasper (in Anxious to Marry), Nellie St. John, the American Four (in Our Boys), Kerrigan and McCarthy, and the Ten American Students.

Josh Hart's Matchless Novelty Combination, from the Howard Athenæum, with William Harris as manager, took the stage at Miner's for the week of March 22nd–27th, its personnel including Sheldon (in Stuffin vs. Montague), Nellie St. John, Levantine and Earle, Dan Collyer, Dan Kelly and Jacques Kruger (these three in Fits), Dick Gorman, George Carey, Paul Hamlin and Ada Newcomb, Kate Castleton, William Harris and William Carroll (in School vs. Mischief), Master Barney, ending with Malony's Visit (cast including W. F. Carroll, Master Barney, Dan Collyer, Jacques' Kruger, Harris, Gorman, Billy and Fred Carroll, and Jennie Christie). The next week (March 29th–April 3rd) let March go out on the fun of Weston, the Walker (with Ned Ryan, James Clooney and Tillie Malvern), followed in olio procession by Carrie Howard, Sergeant George W. Labbree (bugle calls in the barrel of a gun), Belle Clifton, the three Rinaldos (George, William and Harry, in acrobatic dances), George Kurtz and Nellie Brooks (sic), the "great" St. (?) Leon ("whose style, wardrobe and general make-up surpass many of our elegant, aristocratic ladies"), Young Hercules, Cronin (late of Scanlon and Cronin) and J. P. Sullivan (in McCormick, the Copper), Sergeant W. H. L. Hamilton (lightning Zouave drill), Katsnoshin, the Four Diamonds (Clark, Watson, Brevarde and Sawtelle) and The Mystery of the Devil's Swamp (with the ever-present Sheldon).

The week of April 5th–10th brought in the important Bob Slavin ("formerly of Pastor's"), as well as the Olympia Quartette (negro hymns and jubilees), the Peasleys (in Mollie's Victory), the Carrolls (in Carroll's Masquerade and Peel Yourself), Frankie Johnson (serio-comic), Frank West (banjo), Nellie Germon, Sheldon (in his own A Nightmare, introducing Young Hercules, Williams and Sully, Georgie Lingard, Awata Katsnoshin, and Clark, Watson, Brevarde and Sawtelle — all in the fourth scene of the play). The next week (12th–17th) began its nightly offerings with Bob Slavin and Max Arnold (in The Rival Conductors), introducing in the olio

[137]

White and Ella Esmond (in Always on the Move), Walter Mack ("mystic change artist"), Max Arnold ("Dutch" song and dance), Bernard McCreedie (in Transmagnificandubandanciality), the Fieldings (John and Maggie), Slavin, the Ronaldos (*sic*), Delehanty and Hengler, Georgie Lingard, Neil Smith and his dogs, Young Hercules (the "serpentine wonder"), the Four Diamonds, and ending the bill with Sheldon in Landsharks and Sea Gulls. The eternal mystery lies in how the management, at the low prices of admission, could afford, even with all the "refreshments" sold during the show, to provide so vast a concourse of "Variety" notables. The latter half of April gave us Bob Slavin, Mealey and Mackey ("change from neat to rough"), the "Great" O'Brieno ("man serpent"), Ella Mayo, the McKain Sisters (Gussie and Emma), Kurtz and Nellie Brooks (in Domestic Felicity), Cool Burgess, Max Arnold, the Great Novelty Four (Emma and John F. Whitney, Lizzie Hunter and Lester Howard, in Rehearsal in the Parlour), Dick Sands, Boyd and Sarsfield, T. M. Hengler (poor Delehanty was passing from the earthly scene), Nellie Germon, the Four Emeralds (the "ne plus ultra of Irish Comedians," Gibbons, Russell, Kennedy and Magee), J. D. Roome, Morgan and Mullen, the Olympia Quartette, the Megatherian Eight (Gibbs, Kelly, O'Brien, Lyons, Magrath, Parks, Leary and Sherman — American clog dancers), Emma Bretto, Keating and Sands, Georgie Parker, James Carling, Bob Slavin, Seamon and Somers and the Girard Brothers, the Ten American Students, and Slattery's Boarding House (with Charles Morgan and Harry Mullen). Again I am overwhelmed by the quantity and quality of the entertainment offered for so trifling an entrance fee.

Most of these performers remained into at least a part of May, newcomers in that month including Charles and Gertie Seaman (or Seamon), Nellie Nelson, the Jeromes, Saville and Byrne, the American Four, Miss Lou Sanford, Ida Morris, Tillie Antonio ("dashing comique"), Johnny Carroll, Mattie Vickers and Charles S. Rogers (both — in the week of May 10th–15th — in protean rôles in The Players), Sallie St. Clair, Ella Mayo, Dan Mason, the Richmond Sisters (Josie and Lulu), Dan Sully, the Delmannings (Archie and Den, minstrel team), Press Eldridge, Goldie, Steele and Sallie St. Clair (as a trio), &c. May 17th–22nd showed Bob Slavin (in Blue Glass), Mattie Vickers and Rogers (in The Débutante), and Mason and Sully (in The Crowded Hotel).

Bob Slavin remained into June, arrivals for May 31st–June 5th including the Weston Brothers (Sam and Morris, "the refined and most perfect musical team in the profession"), the Merritt Brothers, the Werners (Edward and Maud), the Crimmins Brothers (clog, jig, reels), the De Alve Sisters, William Henry Rice, Cronin and Sullivan (in Life in a Tenement House), &c. That week also exhibited Mattie Vickers and Rogers in The Attic Thespians, Bob Slavin and Tillie Malvern in Tricks, and Sheldon in Dodging for a Wife. Vic Reynolds and the Fieldings were featured for June 7th–12th, and the bills ended with W. J. Thompson, in the "hit of the age," For a Life, or, the Orphan's Trust, Thompson playing Leopold to the Lawyer Graves of Sam Norman (new at Miner's); others in the cast were Harry B. Bell, W. T. Johnson, Dick Gorman, Tillie Malvern, Louis Robie, George Beane, Jr., &c. June 14th–19th featured Lucy Adams and Guy Linton, the two Haleys (their second week), Press Eldridge, the Original Big Four (Smith, Allen, Morton and Martin), the three Brazziers, A Big Mistake (with Bob Slavin), and Humpty's Frolics (with George Richards). A new force occupied the stage for June 21st–26th — George and Lizzie Derious, Lou Sanford, "Jim" O'Neil and Jack Conroy (in Mixtures), Quilter and Goldrich, the "original" Four Emeralds (Gibbons, Russell, Kennedy and Magee), Vic Reynolds, Press Eldridge, the Original Big Four, and Sheldon (in The Wrecker's Oath).

A. H. Sheldon and T. W. Moore's Monster Variety Combination possessed during the week of July 5th–10th, the ingredients consisting of John McVeigh and Kate Montrose, Johnny Carroll, Jeppe and Fannie Delano, Carrie Boshell, Murphy and Shannon, the Four Emeralds, Billy Carter, Murphy and Mack (in Our Irish Flats), Fanny Davenport, the Four Star Grotesques (Seamon, Somers and the Girard Brothers), and the concluding play, Behind the Footlights (with Gibbons, Magee, John Russell, &c.). The Harvard Theatre Collection ceases at this point, and I assume that Miner's closed about at that time for the season. It re-opened in August.

American Theatre (Third Avenue), 1879–1880

Thomas Canary became proprietor of this place (a storm-vext Bermoothes, if ever theatre-land knew one), and his bill, on September 1st, included Ben Brown, Kate Montrose, Bryant and Saville, Harry Mullen and C. Morgan (in Christmas Eve), Campbell and Burke, Allie Drayton, the American Four (Pettingill, Gale, Dailey and Hoey, in Boyhood Days), Annie and Joe Burgess, &c. The Herald, for September 8th-13th, announced the "Second Week of First Class Variety," featuring Jennie Hughes, the Hennessey Brothers and Lizzie Daly. In later September the bills at Harvard show a taking procession including Minnie Lawton, Frank and Fannie Davis, Kate Montrose, John McVeigh, Sol and Julia Aiken, the Four Planets (McDermott, Sheehan, Kennedy and Clark), Fannie Beane and Charles Gilday (in When the Cat's Away, the Mice Will Play), John and James Russell, Maggie Pearl, Kerrigan and McCarthy, McVickers (sic) and Saunders, John Pendy and Jeffreys Warner, Larry Tooley, the Clipper Quartette (McIntyre, Campbell, Heywood and Ward), John Reilly, John M. Turner (banjo), the American Four, Frank George and Tillie Antonio.

October 6th ushered in a reconstructed Uncle Tom's Cabin, with Abbie Hampie (sic in the Herald) as the only "coloured" Topsy (late of Jarrett

[139]

and Palmer's Company), Little Eva French (once in A Celebrated Case, at the Union Square), the Jolly Four, and with fifty men, women and children, in the plantation scene. There are no more bills at Harvard till December 1st. The first three weeks of that wintry month proffered Billy and Maggie Ray, Harry K. and Blanche Morton, Paul Allen, Nellie Nelson, Belle Clifton, Mike Drew, Dan Nash, Neil Smith, Ella and Charles Jerome, Grace Garland, Quilter and Goldrich, Campbell and Burke, Bobby Newcomb, Kerrigan and McCarthy, the Aikens, Fanny Sandford, the Morrisseys, May Diamond, Ward and Lynch, and Harry McAvoy and Emma Rogers.

From December 22nd (according to the Herald) the house was under management of Dick Parker and thenceforth was known as Dick Parker's American Theatre. He began with a fine array, including Delehanty and Hengler, the Irwin Sisters ("without any exaggeration, the finest in their line in the world"), Otto Burbank, the Brennans (with Captain Laible), Nully Pieris, John Morris, Manchester and Jennings, Sallie St. Clair, Goldie and Steele, Levantine and Earle, Mike Gallagher, Emma Granger and Dick Parker.

In January rapid changes brought in Bessie Bell (in "A Vocabulary of Serio-Comic Melodies"), Moore and Lessenger (in Ulrich's Troubles), Belle Celeste and Frank Monroe (trapeze), the Kayes (Billy and Minnie, in Cincinnati Hams), Charles A. Gardner, Manchester and Jennings, Dick Sands, Karoli and Augusta Ordey, Mullen and Magee, along with Dashway and Moore, the Murrays (Tom and Henrietta, in Love and Liquor), Tom Hedges (piccolo), Frank Girard, Bob Slavin, Jennie Satterlee, Devlin and Tracy, the burlesque No Pinafore (January 14th), George F. Slosson, Paddy and Ella Murphy, De Witt Cooke (juggler), Favor and Shields, the Brennans and Laible, Viola Clifton, Harry Bryant, Kelly and Ryan, Yank Adams, Otto Burbank, T. F. Kerrigan and Dan McCarthy, Harry Mack, John and Joe Sparks, Lucy Adams and Guy Linton, Ella Mayo, Retlaw and Alton, Nully Pieris, and the concluding Third Avenue after Dark. Manchester and Jennings remained for several weeks. For the first half of February, Harvard bills promise, in addition to some of those just cited, Tom English, Lenton Brothers (tumbling), Foster and Hughes, Andy Collum, the Three Boisset Brothers, Frank Bush, Joe and Annie Burgess (Trials of a Dancing Master), Quilter and Goldrich, Ella Mayo (very popular, one sees), Gibson and Binney (high pedestal clog), Manchester and Jennings (still functioning), Charles Redmond and Georgia Blake, Morgan and Mullen (in Christmas Eve, and in The Third Avenue Boarding House), "Professor" Rhinehart's dog circus, and Crossley and Elder.

The Herald advertises but little for this house, and now the bills at Harvard are scattering. On March 1st, were promised Ben Gilfoil (in farce), Healey and Conway, Dan Regan, James S. and Katie Edwards, Fayette Welch, Paddy and Ella Murphy, the Barlow Brothers (in a bur-

[140]

BILLY BIRCH   DAVE WAMBOLD   CHARLES BACKUS

THE SAN FRANCISCO MINSTRELS, CORNER OF TWENTY-NINTH STREET AND BROADWAY.

AN IDEA OF THE SAN FRANCISCO MINSTRELS
From a Print in the Harvard Theatre Collection

lesque prize fight); and, on March 8th, we were to have Mike Gallagher, the Hassons, Mollie Wilson, Manchester and Jennings, John Sheehan and Robert Jones (in An Every-day Occurrence), Emerson, Clark and the Daly Brothers (in the Fairest of the Fair), Conway and Eagan and Sheehan and Jones's play, Mike Riley, the Wrestler. Skipping, for lack of matter, to April 21st, I find Parker's American providing Lea and John Peasley, Georgie Melnotte, Manchester and Jennings, Murphy and Shannon and Murphy and Mack — the last four in the olio and in Murphy's Dream. The same lively four began the bill of May 6th with Dr. Colton's Laughing Gas, and ended it with Murphy's Dream; the olio was rich with John McVeigh and Kate Montrose, R. E. Wilson (baritone), the K. H. K's (Emerson, Clark and the Daly Brothers), Boyle and Malone, Georgie Melnotte and Master Prime. Later May brought (13th) The Rivals (with Murphy and Shannon and Murphy and Mack), and a concluding farce, Blue Glass (with Slavin and Burbank); Ada Forrest and Kelly and Ryan were in the olio. On May 18th we had Alexander and Flora Zanfretta, with George Kane (in The French Dancing Master and The Mischievous Clown), the Novelty Four (John and Emma Whitney, Lizzie Hunter, Lester Howard), and Harry and Emma Budworth. On the 24th, Mackin and Burns (Hebrew), the Zanfrettas, Mollie Wilson, Ned West, Harry and Minnie Wood (in Barney's Return) and Bobby Newcomb spread joy (I hope) to a weary world. Harvard provides but three more bills for 1879–80. On July 1st, Kate Montrose's benefit was enriched with the art of John Pendy, Paddy Nugent, Sheehan and Jones, and Jim McIntyre and Thomas Heath (in The Arrival of Gilbert). On August 18th, we were invited to the feast provided by the Four Emeralds (Gibbons, Russell, Kennedy and Magee), Mollie Wilson, Wood and Beasley, the Four Diamonds (Clark, Watson, Brevarde and Sawtelle), Parker and his dogs, and Pat Rooney — an excellent array, not to say brilliant, with those Emeralds and Diamonds. And August 30th topped our joys with the De Voy Sisters, Frank Jones (banjo), "Jim" O'Neil and Jack Conroy (in City Life), the Electric Three (Callan, Haley and Callan), Gus Hill, Kitty Gardner, and Alice Bateman and Willis Pickert (in a combat clog). Certainly Dick Parker's was advancing toward the higher altitudes of "Variety."

MINOR RESORTS, 1879–1880

The Folly Theatre, that old establishment at Greenwich and Eighth Streets, re-opened on September 8, 1879, under "new management." A Children's Pinafore, with "Variety," constituted the lure of September 29th–October 4th.

The barest mention must suffice for resorts long familiar to our annals and too familiar, some of them, to a certain kind of visitor. Shall I begin with the Clarendon Society Hops, Clarendon Hall, 114 East 13th Street, advertised in the Herald as opening on September 6, 1879? And let us not overlook the American Mabille, 59 Bleecker Street, near Broadway, which, in later September (22nd), gave a testimonial concert and "élite social" to John A. Runnett and Frank Fagan, all with "a host of musical talent." So late as April 4th, it was boasting that it was "the most popular and social resort of Beauty and Fashion in the City." And, on May 25th, Sause's closing *soirée* brought in the highly respectable cornets of the Bents. The Tivoli Winter Garden, once the Tivoli Theatre, held forth, from time to time, in Herald and Staats-Zeitung advertisements; on September 1st, it boasted of a new Berlin Lady Orchestra. Mme. Anderson, "champion lady pedestrienne of the world," was hoofing it there, from October 4th, trying to do 4,236¼ miles in 4,236¼ consecutive quarter hours. I suppose this entitled her to a niche in the hall of fame.

Buckingham Palace, on September 1st, was still boasting that it was the American Mabille, with Élite Sociables, nightly, and with an Electro-Magnetic Elevated Railroad, "one of the greatest novelties ever exhibited." Here on November 27th (Thanksgiving Night) was held a "Grand Parisian Costume and Prize Ball." On May 4th, 6th and 8th, the place advertised in the Herald "Le Premiers Nights de la Vie Parisienne (I am not responsible for their French) and Costume à la Turque" — the reigning sensation at the London Alhambra. A "grand summer garden" was part of the glory in July, 1880. And the Cremorne Gardens, 104-108 West 32nd Street, lured throughout the season, with the same old cries. "Fifty beautiful lady cashiers" were advertised on Thanksgiving Day (November 27th). The Atlantic Garden, Bowery, had Sunday concerts in February, with a band of Spanish Students — of course not the band, then so popular, at Booth's. On March 17th, it fell in line with a benefit for the Herald Irish Relief Fund. The Lexington Avenue Gardens, between 32nd and 33rd Streets, promised, in the Herald of October 5th, a popular concert every evening. The Sultan Divan advertised frequently in the Herald, boasting, for instance, on December 8th, of fifty "beautiful Lady Cashiers in attendance." Like in spirit was Gunther's Pavilion, 283 Bowery, with "Lady Cashiers," according to the Herald of January 5th. I do not see why one should become excited over lady cashiers. Spanish Students were here in March. And, of course, the Haymarket fittingly ends our paragraph, with its usual lure for flaming youth; or would end it, if I were not under necessity of calling attention to the Windsor Gardens, 120 West 14th Street, with, on April 19th and later, "Grand Concerts" every evening. But, after all, I will end with the Haymarket's self-description, a "Bijou of Terpsichore," launched in the Herald of July 12th.

At Theiss's concerts, 14th Street, near Sixth Avenue, one could have heard, in early May, the cornet of Fred W. Bent; and at other times, just music unspecified for drinkers of the entertainment bought and paid for. Here, on August 4th was held the "first Grand Anniversary Concert."

Harry Hill's, so coy in non-advertising, may be "smoked" by a bill at Harvard, for January 1, 1880, when as Harry Hill's Variety Theatre it was offering Minnie Harrison (operatic songs and ballads), Fattie Rush ("age 16, weight 217," and therefore in one sense at least "the greatest comic singer of the age"), Jennie Jerome and Clara Maxwell, a female boxing match (by Nettie Burt and Miss "Gertie" — Fattie Rush), Lu Arnold (songs and dances), Mary Howard (songs), M. F. Tierney (contortionist), a Sparring Match (Billy Fields of New York *vs.* Pete McCoy of New Jersey), Murphy, Kline and McNiece, &c. If my reader insists, tourist-wise, on a visit to this sporting palace, he might do so on April 17th (afternoon), when Edward Bibby, of Lancashire, England, and Albert Ellis, late of London, but now of New York, were to engage in a manly bout for a prize; at the end, Ellis defaulted, and the money was given to Bibby. Something educational may have been intended on Sunday, May 16th, when "Professor" De Soto's "magnificent" Sun Pictures or Transformation Scenes gave visions of "beautiful" statuary and "views from all parts of the world." And, on Sunday, the 23rd of May, Sawyer's Bell Ringers edified the gentry. A confusing place, this!

The American Dime Museum, 298 Bowery, boasted in late October that it had five large stories of curiosities. Tom Thumb and his wife, with their troupe, spent several weeks here from January 19th. The Horrible Chelsea Guillotine, "just received from Boston," was advertised on May 3rd, along with "two Immense Living Wild Gorillas" — much more impressive from their awesome initial capitals.

SAN FRANCISCO MINSTRELS, 1879–1880

The only resident band of negro minstrels, in a city once overrun with black-face art, began, on September 1st, the season of 1879–80, with Birch, Wambold and Backus still in control, and with a company including Add Ryman, Edwin French, Ricardo, Johnson, Powers, J. G. Russell, H. W. Frillman, W. Raymond, Charles Stevens, and Mullaly's orchestra — this last composed of W. S. Mullaly, J. Morelli, R. Ward, J. H. Ross, I. G. Withers, F. Myring, W. Schwab and Charles Gibbons. So welcome home, my merry men all!

No Pinafore began a run on September 29th, and, on October 27th, George Thatcher made his first appearance for the season. Before me lies a programme for November 4th, advertising the place as "The Family Resort! The Greatest Show on Earth!" Part I, the traditional black face row of minstrels, began with an overture, arranged by Mullaly, followed by the bass solo, Rocked in the Cradle of the Deep (sung by Frillman), and

[143]

the ballad, Till the Clouds Go By (sung by W. Raymond). Then Backus rendered the comic ballad, My Baby, and T. B. Dixon (a tenor, taking the place of Wambold, ill and ordered South) sang Sally in Our Alley. Billy Birch carried on with Dem Golden Slippers, and J. G. Russell gave When the Moon with Glory Brightens. The finale, Reine Indigo, introduced a xylophone solo, Whoa Emma, They All Do It, Nightingale Polka, Wine, Wife and Song, and Walking for Dat Cake. This finale, arranged by Mullaly, called into play the entire minstrel band, vocal and instrumental. As I write the names of those songs, my youth comes back to me, and I can hear, in fancy, every one of them as we used to sing or whistle them in the innocent parlours of long ago — girls and boys together. The second part of the bill for November 4th began with Edwin French, the famous banjo player, and proceeded to Governor Ryman, in Labour *vs.* Capital, and thereafter introduced Johnson and Powers in Uncle Abe and Sister Ruth. Then came the Great Ricardo (famous female impersonator) in Flirting in the Twilight, with George Thatcher ending the olio in his Carpet Bag of Fun. The evening concluded with No Pinafore (last week of it), with Add Ryman, as Max Grau, a manager in trouble, Billy Birch as Jim, a servant, Backus as Little Buttertub, à la margarine, Charles Gibbons as Richard Badeye, Esq., James Johnson as Captain Co-co-co-s'an, and Edwin French as Ralph. This introduced the Enchanted Ballet from Niblo's, with Ricardo as Cassati, Powers as Cornalba, Raymond as Zattis, Stevens as Cappelani, Frillman as Carnio and Russell as Orlosi, the whole including a "Grand Tableau, showing the penalty of any one heard singing Pinafore." The bill warns: "Trouble begins at 8. Street Cars may be ordered at 10. Police Regulations — Carriages taking up Parties must form at the Battery, facing Broadway and 29th Street." O spirit of Mitchell's Olympic, thou walkest still!

No Pinafore was succeeded, on November 10th, by a revival of His Mud Scow, Pinafore, and that, in turn, on the 17th, by Mother-in-Law-Phobia. French Flats, at the Union Square Theatre, drew from the lively San Franciscans, Thompson Street Flats, in Two Stories, on the Level. This first faced the lamps, on November 24th, along with The Turkish Patrol (sung also by Tony Pastor at his own theatre), and The Skids are Out Today (sung by permission of Harrigan and Hart). This lucky bill lasted a long while. With the three choice bits just cited were given, during the week of December 15th, The Hardback Family, The Villain Still Pursued Her, etc. With this combination we slipped joyously into January, 1880. On February 2nd came a new skit, Blue Fishing, or, the Pirates of Sandy Hook, certainly nearer home than The Pirates of Penzance, then operating at the Fifth Avenue Theatre; The Hardback Family and The Skids are Out Today were still in the bill — a bill which lasted for three weeks.

A programme for February 27th gives, among other things in Part I,

EMMA LAKE

EDWARD P. WESTON

ELISE DOCKRILL

CHARLES ROWELL

A. P. BURBANK

SIDNEY WOOLLETT

BELLE COLE

HENRIETTA MARKSTEIN

ANNA GRANGER DOW

Frillman's bass song, The Exile; Raymond in the ballad, When Jamie Comes Over the Sea; Backus's rendering of the comic The Galley Slave; T. B. Dixon's singing of Mullaly's song, Erin's Prayer (more Irish relief!); Birch in another comic song, The Widow Dunn; and a finale embracing The Turkish Patrol and The Skids are Out Today.   In Part II, Ricardo sang Come to Me, Darling; Add Ryman spoke On Fish; Sea Foam, or a High Old Time in a Bake Shop, enlisted Johnson, Powers, Gibbons and French; George Thatcher sang Grandpapa's Pants; and Edwin French played the banjo. Ryman's new piece, Blue Fishing, ended all, with Backus as Benjamin Thomas Winslow Smith, Ryman as Major Warefield Bluster, Birch as Dinkey, the yacht steward, George Thatcher as Port-hole Johnnie, Powers as Mr. Lighthead, Ricardo as Miss Jennie, James Johnson as Miss Fannie, and with Gibbons, Frillman, T. B. Dixon, Stevens, Raymond and Russell in other rôles.   On March 1st, Love's Endurance, Sea Foam and Grandpapa's Pants were specially stressed in Herald advertisement.

I fancy that Blue Fishing had failed as a burlesque of The Pirates of Penzance.   Far more amusing, in title at least, was Beadle's Pirates for Ten Cents, "with a realistic boat scene, and the arrival of the pirates"; this was in the bill on March 22nd and beyond.   Birch was Captain of Police, Thatcher General Stanley, Ricardo Mabel, and big, comic Backus was Fairy, an ethereal beauty.   A benefit to the veteran Dave Reed occurred here on the afternoon of April 15th, at which he appeared for the first (?) time in several years.   During the last week but one of the season (April 12th–17th) appeared Arthur Cook, tenor.

Minnie Palmer entered the hall of the San Francisco Minstrels almost as soon as they departed.   She brought out (May 3rd) Minnie Palmer's Boarding School, with William J. Scanlon (formerly of Scanlon — or Scanlan — and Cronin, and for some years thereafter a very popular star in Irish plays), John E. Ince, Emma Jones, Mrs. W. S. Harkins, and George C. Davenport.   Miss Palmer's beauty and her lively personality brought success, and she remained for a fair run, closing, on May 31st, with a benefit, at which she appeared in The Boarding School and The Little Treasure.

Koster and Bial's; Aquarium, 1879–1880

The variety of Koster and Bial's consisted largely in its shifting groups of visitors — perhaps the fore-runners of present-day (1939) visitors to night clubs.   Jules Levy played here for a long time, during the winter, and was, as always, a choice attraction.   A benefit to Levy, on January 15th, brought volunteers in Jacob Graff and Gilmore, "who will conduct his National Anthem"; in other words, Koster and Bial's hailed Columbia.   The first anniversary of the hall, under the Koster-Bial régime, was celebrated on May 5th, with a monster concert.   In later June, Wilhelmj played here on several evenings, beginning on the 22nd.   S. Liebling, pianist, appeared frequently in July and August.

The Aquarium was more odd than many a fish exhibited in its tanks; one never knew just what to expect there outside of the aquarial display. We left Pinafore, on August 31st, safely harboured in its hall; Marie Harvey was Josephine in later September.   Pinafore, in the week of September 29th–October 4th, had post of honour every evening and Wednesday and Saturday afternoons; on other afternoons one heard The Merry Tuners, by E. H. Harvey.   Rose Manning was, on the 29th, a new Josephine, in Pinafore, though Marie Harvey almost immediately returned.   The cast otherwise was good, including Haydon Tilla, Myron Calice, George Gaston, Charlotte Hutchings and Maude Branscombe.   On October 29th, the popular Gilbert and Sullivan opera gave place to The Bohemian Girl, who might dream that she dwelt among the fishes.   The cast included Marie Harvey, Mrs. Gonzales, Charlotte Hutchings (Gipsy Queen), S. P. Strini (Arnheim), Tilla (Thaddeus), W. P. Bown (Devilshoof), George Gaston (Florestan), &c.

Fanny Herring, long past her Bowery glory, came into the Aquarium, on November 10th, with a pantomime show, every afternoon and evening; in addition, Marie Harvey and Haydon Tilla gave operatic selections, and Maude Branscombe re-appeared, in exactly what capacity the Herald advertisements fail to specify.   The reader who has seen the countless photographs in countless poses of the cherubic Miss Branscombe now perceives that she really did have a stage career of a sort; hitherto, like me, he might have thought that her sole profession in life consisted in being photographed. But I re-assert that I once saw her, in Newburgh, New York, with Robert McWade, in his version of Rip Van Winkle.   Till's Royal Marionette Troupe came, in November 17th, for afternoon and evening showings daily. W. C. Coup's Broncho Horses were the proud offering of the week beginning on November 24th.   The Snow Brothers exhibited on December 8th.

Uncle Tom's Cabin — I cannot understand the confounding vogue of this thing, unless it is, as I suspect, a really dramatic show — entered the Aquarium, of all places in the world, on December 15th, and remained until January 10th.   In January 4th, the Herald lists Jennie Yeamans as Topsy and Little Amy Slavin as Eva.   On the 12th, the Aquarium took another astonishing plunge — this time into the Imperial Parisian Circus, whose personnel strongly suggests the group recently departed from 728-30 Broadway. At any rate, Robert Stickney, Frank Melville and John W. Hamilton were managers of the force at the Aquarium, and the performers included William Gorman (hurdle riding), Lenton Brothers ("Sports of the Carpet"), Robert Stickney (equestrian), William Burke (clown), Lottie Moranda (trapeze and ascension act), Pauline Lee (juggling equestrian), Charles McCarty (clown), Viola Rivers (equestrienne), James Cooke (clown), Frank Melville (bareback), "Professor" Showers and his performing dogs, Sam Stickney (clown), Annie Carroll (equestrienne), and Fred Aymar ("the riding Cynocephalus"). Of course there were leaping and tumbling acts by the company. This seems a good aggregation for the home of solemn-eyed fish. On January 19th, The Brigand was "laughable afterpiece." On the 26th, Avery and Forepaugh (triple-bar performers), M. Ajax, Mlle. Belmont, Satsuma, "Professor" White's performing dogs, and the equestrian afterpiece, Jack, the Giant Killer, were novel to the beholders. The Circus remained here for several weeks, even till March blew gusty in the streets. On March 29th, the Aquarium was advertising a "full-grown ant bear, the only one ever brought alive to this city."

On April 19th and later, Tom Thumb and his wife, Major Newell, a Water Queen and Punch and Judy divided attention with the imprisoned fish. Tom Thumb remained until May 15th, always a welcome curiosity, though no longer the smallest.

A dramatic company presented here, on May 17th, Our Bijah, or, a Double Life; on the 21st, Ten Nights in a Bar-room was substituted. And, ye gods! on May 31st, back came Pinafore, with the Burnand-Sullivan Cox and Box; the Norcross Fifth Avenue Opera Company was the exploiting agent. That company and Elma Delaro sang here (June 21st–26th) in Giroflé-Girofla, and, beginning on June 30th, Germania, a spectacular tragedy, was going forward. July 12th featured Logrenia's trained birds, cats and white mice, as well as "Professor" Parker and his seven "canine wonders," good hot-weather entertainment. Beginning on August 2nd, the Norcross English Opera Company for two weeks gave The Chimes of Normandy, Lisetta Ellani, Haydon Tilla and Belle Girard bearing chief rôles. Pinafore again sailed in, on August 16th, ballasted by the art of Tilla, Ethel Lynton, Frank Parmental and Sydney Smith. This lets us out of the Aquarium for 1879–1880.

LENT'S NEW YORK CIRCUS, 1879

L. B. Lent, on October 13th, housed his Circus in that home of many names and many sorrows — 728-730 Broadway. Among the earliest specialists were Harry Lambkin (exercises on a barrel), Lizzie Marcellus (equestrienne), Emma Lake, Pauline Lee (juggling on horseback), Levantine and Earle, Millie Tournour (aerial act), Robert Stickney, and Sebastian (rider). On November 17th first appeared Frank Ashton and Charles Geyer ("lofty leapers"), and educated dogs and "charming" ponies. It was also the first week of Fred Levantine, and his "enchanted Barrel, Table and Chair," of the three Mette Brothers (acrobats) and of William Du Crow ("high-leaping hurdle rider"). Robert and Emma Stickney, Jennie and Charles Ewer, and the Japanese King Sarbro, in his Slide for Life, were features of November 24th.

[147]

A holiday season was inaugurated on December 22nd, with Robert Stick-ney as manager, and John H. Murray as director. Robert Butler's panto-mime, Humpty Dumpty, figured in the bill, and circus folk were Robert Stickney, Frank Melville, Emma Lake, Mlle. Lottie, Jennie Tournour, Lenton Brothers, Murray and Runnells, Geyer and Ashton, and Butler and Cary. On Saturday afternoon and evening, January 3rd, Stickney and Melville had a joint testimonial. And this ended the Circus at 728-730 Broadway; it transferred to the Aquarium.

BARNUM'S 1879–1880

On April 8th, Barnum's Greatest Show on Earth, after a grand street parade on the afternoon of the 6th, opened at the American Institute Build-ing. The great star act — how well I remember it! — was Zazel, in her aerial dive, or "eagle swoop." There was also a group of native Zulus, awesome to behold. Mme. Dockrill ("bareback on four or six horses"), Emma Lake, M. Dockrill, with twenty imported royal stallions, Mme. Nel-son ("la Charmeuse des Colombes," with her flock of trained doves), the fire-horse Salamander, "surrounded by a blaze of fireworks," Mme. Martha and Herr Neygaard (in "a charming double four-horse Acte de Menage"), Signor Sebastian ("sensational bare-back act"), Signora Marcellus, Mlle. Leone, the Nelson Family (five in number), the Leotards, the Carroll Brothers, two performing oxen, a huge Hippopotamus, and Queen Mab, a tiny dwarf — such an array should have left the small boy breathless. Some of these performers, we note, had been earlier at 728 Broadway or the Aquarium. The fiery steed, Salamander, early in the visit, was appar-ently burned by bad management of the scene; Henry Bergh, of the Society for the Prevention of Cruelty to Animals interfered, and Salamander for a time left the bill — but only for a time. He was again advertised for the last week (April 19th–24th).

MADISON SQUARE GARDEN, 1879–1880

Suppose we begin our jaunts to the big Madison Square Garden on Sun-day evening, September 7, 1879, then and there to hear a concert by Marie Aimée, Mlle. (*sic*) Gregoire, Juteau, Jouard, Henrietta Markstein and others. On the 14th, Aimée, Mlles. Raphael and Gregoire, and Haydon Tilla joined Dodworth's Band. The Madison Square was becoming more and more athletic in its offerings, and we are not surprised, therefore, to find there, on September 13th, a "Grand Gymnastic Exhibition" by the New York Turn Berzirk, along with a "Grand Musical," by a male choir of two hundred and fifty from the Arion Society, the Sängerrunde, the Schillerbund, the Eichen-kranz and the Turner Liedertafel. A six-days walking match, "go as you

[148]

please," started here on September 22nd, for the Astley Belt. Some of the contestants were Edward Payson Weston, of New York City, "champion of the world, and holder of the belt," Charles Rowell, of Chesterton, Cambridge, England, "ex-champion and challenger," George Hazael, of London, "champion runner of England," John Ennis and George Guyon, of Chicago, Peter J. Panchot, "mail carrier of Buffalo," Samuel Merritt, of Bridgeport, Connecticut, Norman Taylor, of Vermont, Hiram Jackson, of New Bedford, Massachusetts, Frederick Krohne, of Hoboken, New Jersey, and William Dutcher, of Pelham, New York. Doubtless these names were heroic to the side-lines. Rowell won, with 530 miles, Merritt, following with 515, Hazael with 500, Hart with 482, Guyon with 470, Weston (completely broken down) with 455, Ennis and Krohne with 450 each, and Taylor with 250, the others all discreetly withdrawing before the contest closed. Doubtless many thousands grieved that the belt went back to England.

Another such contest — this time for the O'Leary Belt — ran its course from October 6th to October 11th, the belt "representing the Long Distance Championship of America." Blower Brown, "champion of England," Peter Crossland, "three-day champion of the world," James McLeavy, "champion runner of Scotland," P. Fitzgerald (alias Johnny Wild), "champion runner of America," C. Walker, "champion runner of Canada," J. J. Dickinson, "champion of Pennsylvania," F. L. Edwards, "champion of California," H. Behrman, "champion of Germany," E. Davis, "champion of Ireland," A. Pierce, "negro champion," J. Allen, "champion of Massachusetts," S. P. Russell, "champion of Illinois," and C. Faber, "champion of New Jersey," were among the numerous heroes willing to sacrifice themselves for — what grand end? This contest was won by Murphy, of Haverstraw, who, on his return to his home town, was greeted by a civic demonstration that rang all the way down the river to the excited columns of the New York Herald. He became Haverstraw's "idol" because he walked 503 1/3 miles in less than six days — a feat possible not even to Plato (I believe) or Emerson or even Adelina Patti. On October 20th and 21st, an O'Leary Tournament (which began the week of October 20th–25th) included a twenty-mile run, and a "grand wrestling match" between Edwin Bibby, "champion of England," and André Christol, "champion of the Pyrenees." I am proud to introduce the reader to all these glorious "champions." And to a billiard contest, at the Garden, now scene of many contests, between Jacob Schaefer, "champion of the world," and George F. Slosson, for a prize of $4,000 for 3000 points — 1000 points to the evening! This great event was carried out on October 23rd, 24th and 25th; Schaefer won. A Græco-Roman Wrestling Match, on the evening of December 4th, again involved Edwin Bibby and André Christol. On December 9th, one passed to another kind of contest and another "championship," when American-bred Durham cattle and American-bred sheep were exhibited for a stay of a few days.

[149]

Alas! another "Six-day Go as You Please" began on December 22nd, with Nick Murphy, of Haverstraw, S. Merritt, the Panchot Brothers, and other heroes. Charles Stewart Parnell, on Sunday, January 4th, addressed a mass meeting, on The Case of Ireland Stated; and another Irishman, Gilmore, played his own Columbia. A big night for the Irish! On January 19th, Muldoon and Bauer wrestled for the championship of the world. February 7th found here the First Annual Winter Meeting of the Manhattan Athletic Club. The Elks had a reception here on February 9th, and the Dress Parade of the Ninth Regiment was colourful and stirring on February 23rd. The ball of the Arion Society fell on February 19th. On the 26th of February was celebrated the Bal Masqué de l'Opéra and a Carnival. And a "Grand Athletic Benefit" for the Irish fund came, on March 4th, at this Garden. But much more "grand" were the three "Grand Concerts" on March 17th, at 11, 3 and 8 o'clock, for the Irish Relief Fund, concerts involving Levy, Arbuckle and Reynolds in a cornet trio, Belle Cole, Isabel Stone, Emily Spader, Henrietta Markstein, Mme. Chatterton-Bohrer, George S. Weeks, Harry Allen, a band of one hundred, a choir of six hundred, a performing of Columbia, the Anvil Chorus (with a chime of bells, etc.). Miller and Muldoon were the heroes of a Græco-Roman wrestling match on March 23rd. But, on Sunday, March 28th, a huge concert promised Joseffy, Anna Ackerman-Jaworska, a choir of males, and an orchestra of sixty, led by Carlberg. G. W. Colby was director, and R. Langenbach conducted the chorus. And another six-days pedestrian contest for the O'Leary belt, waged in early April (5th–10th). In this, Hart won, with 565 1/10 miles, followed by Pegram, 543½ miles, Dobler (530), Howard (534), Allen (525), Krohne (516), Williams (509), Hansaker and Jaybee — this record of Hart beating the record. And the Hahnemann Hospital Fair, in later April, opening on the 12th, enjoyed the co-operation of Downing's Ninth Regiment Band. A dog show of the Westminster Kennel Club filled the dates of April 27th, 28th and 29th.

HARLEM MUSIC HALL, 1879–1880

Let me call attention to a performance here, on October 22nd, of Max Maretzek's opera, Sleepy Hollow, given for the benefit of the Y. M. H. A. November 13th brought Billy Burt's Amateur Minstrels — "No Vulgarity."

From a playbill at Harvard I discover that, on November 26, 1879, the Mirth Makers appeared in Mischief, chief entertainers including Bertha and Ida Foy, Annie Wood, Alonzo Schwartz, W. Paul Brown and James H. Alliger. That same bill bristles with notes of pleasures past and pleasures pending. Marian Mordaunt had played here, on November 24th, in Our Girls, and, on Thanksgiving, the 27th, instead of a Fatinitza, originally scheduled, W. H. Higgins appeared in Tramps. November 29th brought the Metropolitan Blind Troupe of sightless vocal and instrumental musicians. I do not recognise the Units Comedy Company which, on December 1st, began a week in the Harlem hall, in My Awful Child. Less notable players from Augustin Daly's new company had Christmas day (afternoon and evening) in his well-liked Divorce, Helen Blythe playing Fanny, Mabel Jordan Lu, Zelma Valdimer Mrs. Ten Eyck, Estelle Clayton Grace, Isabelle Evesson Kitty Crosby, Regina Dace Flora Penfield, Charles Fisher Burritt, and, in other rôles, G. Morton, Hart Conway, W. Edmunds and E. P. Wilks. I deem this worthy of a trip to Harlem by the new Elevated Railway.

The playbill at Harvard promises for New Year's Day, 1880, a "probable" visit of the Georgia Minstrels. On January 13th, I learn from the New York Herald, the Warren Comedy Company, including Mrs. E. L. Davenport and Nina Varian, were to enter the Music Hall, Third Avenue and 130th Street, with Sacrifice and The Widow's Victim; Mrs. Davenport also read. And Uncle Tom's Cabin was scheduled for Washington's Birthday. On March 29th the Shakespeare Dramatic Society of New York invaded the hall, with a charity performance of a play, and with singing by Annie E. Beeré, Mina Geary and the Madrigal Boys.

Miscellaneous Entertainments, 1879–1880

The reader has met what I should call "entertainments" in various forms and in various places — particularly in "Variety" houses — during the discussion of activities in 1879–1880 at separate theatres; it remains, however, to group scattered incidents. I am almost reluctant to include here the Moody and Sankey meetings, in September and October, at Cooper Union; but they were really a large part of the excitement then prevalent in all directions in our city life. On September 23rd, at Chickering Hall, Laura D. Fair lectured on Chips from California. I trust that the reader will not grieve at my refusal to accompany him, on the afternoon of September 27th, to the amateur athletic games held on the New York Athletic Grounds, 150th Street and Mott Avenue, Mott Haven. There were 220 entries from Montreal, Toronto, San Francisco, Boston, etc. At Cooper Union on October 2nd, occurred a Literary and Musical Recital, by Mme. Ivan C. Michels (or Michaels), Frederick Mollenhauer, Leone Frost (soprano), Henry Hall (cornet), Master Willie Mollenhauer (soprano), and Clara E. Colby (accompanist). Perhaps I should include in this section the Walking Matches which I have regretfully treated elsewhere. And I will mention the show at Fleetwood Park, on October 10th, in which Colonel Thomas Butler gave an exhibition of hounds pursuing a running negro, as in the ante-war days. I do not know what purpose all this fleetness of foot was supposed to serve.

On October 16th, at Cooper Institute, Mme. Michels presented the Sherlocke Family of English Troubadours, an item that perhaps should be listed in the division of concerts, as possibly should be Max Maretzek's Sleepy Hollow, on October 22nd, at the Harlem Music Hall, for the Y. M. H. A. But in this present section at least belong A. J. Requier's lecture, on October 16th, at Chickering Hall, on The House that Jack Built, and readings by Settie Blume; also James E. Murdoch read, on October 24th, at Association Hall. And here assuredly must be enshrined the record of six successive Saturday mornings with Dickens, beginning on November 8th, and carried through by George Vandenhoff, almost the last of "the giant race before the flood" of the Civil War. On November 10th, 13th, 17th and 20th (evenings), Professor Richard A. Proctor lectured, with pictures, in the same hall on Astronomy. And in latest October and early November, a New York Miniature Opera Company gave on certain afternoons, at Chickering Hall, an idea of what children could do to and for Pinafore, the long-suffering and long-enduring; the last of these performances fell on November 4th. At the Lexington Avenue Opera House were to appear, on November 6th, 7th and 8th, the St. Cloud English Opera Company in Pinafore, with Heloise Giraldeau as Josephine. Beginning on November 7th, we had four Friday evenings at Chickering Hall devoted to the Romance of English History, with Reverend J. C. Eccleston descanting. And another billiard tournament waged between November 11th and 25th at Tammany Hall, the contestants being Garnier *vs.* Daly, and Schaefer *vs.* Carter.

On November 11th, Mirza Schaffy, at Steinway Hall, described in German his political development; on the 15th (matinée) he gave a lecture (his third) "in English"; why, and on what, the Herald advertisement failed to state.

But all know Wendell Phillips, who earnestly lectured at Steinway Hall (December 4th) on The Press: Its Power for Good and for Evil, the very thought of which draws me back from yearnings for the frivolous and the gay. And here, on the 5th, at Association Hall, is Tod Ford's lecture, Go West, Young Man; on the 12th, C. T. Winchester discoursed there on London a Hundred Years Ago. The Elks, on December 7th, offered at Chickering Hall a Dramatic and Musical Entertainment. George Augustus Sala, distinguished Briton, lectured, on December 20th, at Chickering Hall, on Shows I Have Seen. Vale, at that time a busy *entrepreneur*, advertised an interesting "Chickering Hall Series," in which were to participate R. J. De Cordova (January 12th), George Vandenhoff (19th), Charles Roberts, Jr. (January 30th and February 9th), and A. P. Burbank (February 2nd) — good, wholesome entertainment, as I know, and perhaps more professional than the Oratorical Contest, on January 9th, at Chickering Hall, under auspices of the Intercollegiate Association. Sexton and Schaefer again competed, on the 10th, at Tammany Hall. But heels and toes, if not heads! The New York Skating Rink, Madison Avenue and 58th Street, opened

CARLOTTA PATTI
AND DE MUNCK

HATTIE LOUISE SIMMS

AMY SHERWIN

FRANZ RUMMEL

RAFAEL JOSEFFY

MAX PINNER

ANNIE E. BEERÉ

ADOLPHE FISCHER

MARIE LOUISE SWIFT

on January 12th, with "artificial ice." We must go, by all means! A public meeting, held on January 16th, demanded protection of the law for the American Indians; Chickering Hall housed the demonstration. The Rev. R. S. Storrs presided, and, among the speakers, were Joseph Cook, of Boston, Seth Low, the Rev. Arthur Brooks, T. H. Tibbles, Standing Bear and Bright Eyes; interesting, I think. An evening of English glees brightened January 15th at Chickering Hall. On January 17th, a Bicycle Tournament dashed into the American Institute Building, and, on the 20th, a magical séance, for charity, introduced at Chickering Hall Edgar S. Allien and E. J. Dale, but failed to keep them prominently before the public eye. Henry Ward Beecher, on the 17th, lectured before a crowd, in Cooper Institute, on Amusements. On the 26th, Mrs. Maria Isabelle Hammond, of Baltimore, read in the New York Hotel parlours. John Fiske, on January 21st, 24th, 28th and 31st, lectured at Chickering Hall, on America's Place in History — decidedly worth hearing. J. S. Burdett and the Young Apollo Club of New York came, on the 29th, to Association Hall. Mrs. Jarley's Waxworks entered Steinway Hall, on February 3rd. The Doctor of Alcantara was a pleasing opera, in 1880, and therefore it was sung, for the benefit of St. John's Guild, on February 7th, at the Union League Theatre; Fred Harvey, J. G. Pierson and Julia Greer had leading parts. On the 9th, in the same theatre occurred an amateur performance for charity. On the 7th, at Chickering Hall, Dr. S. M. Landis would expound The Fallacies of Spiritualism.

And here is Vale with a series of Lenten Matinées, at Chickering Hall. The Reverend Newland Maynard was to lecture (with stereopticon views) on the Cathedrals of Europe, his dates being February 14th, 21st and 28th, and March 6th and 13th; George Vandenhoff's readings from Dickens and Shakespeare were to come on February 12th, 19th and 26th, and March 4th, 11th and 18th; on February 26th he was ill, and A. P. Burbank took his place. And Sidney Woollett would recite from memory (that newer form of the art elocutionary) The Merchant of Venice, Henry V, Macbeth, King John, Much Ado about Nothing and Hamlet, his dates being March 1st, 8th, 15th, 22nd and 29th, and April 5th. After this anticipated delight, I fear the entertainment, in Chickering Hall, on February 20th, for the relief of Ireland, might seem a bit flat, though Mrs. Rice Knox, Marie Conron, S. B. Mills and others were listed to appear; and certainly Ireland should have been grateful to New York theatres and players in that season of its distress. A ball for the Coloured Edmonians was featly danced through, on February 27th, at Tammany Hall. On March 8th, at Caledonia Hall, Scotsmen could have heard a lecture and concert, by Alexander Robertson (in Highland costume), on Bonnie Prince Charlie, the programme including old Jacobite songs, rendered by Jeanie Thorburn, J. R. McDonald and B. Drysdale. On the 9th, at Chickering Hall, Charles Roberts, Jr., recited,

[153]

and a chorus of one hundred and fifty — the choir of the American Temperance Union — sang. One sees my perplexity; should such entertainments be listed as miscellany or concerts? And what of Clara M. Spence (elocutionist) and W. R. Johnson (organist) at Chickering Hall, on the 20th? Well, I let the prevailing note or import of the offering decide the issue. And there can be no doubt of good George Vandenhoff, scheduled for March 20th, 24th and 27th, at Lyric Hall. I believe it would hardly pay us to travel, on March 20th, to the Union League Club Theatre, to see Etta Farrar in East Lynne. On April 1st (afternoon), at Chickering Hall, Professor Nathan Sheppard lectured on Dickens's Great Characters; on the 8th, on Thackeray's Social Satire; and, on the 15th, on Why Did She Marry Him? or, the Matrimony of the Novels and of Life. Walter R. Johnson played the organ, prior to the talks.

Vale's New Series (Chickering Hall) promised Charles Roberts and the Philadelphia Club (April 1st); George Vandenhoff (April 2nd); Sidney Woollett, with organ (April 7th); the Young Apollo Club, A. J. Knight and Florence Auld (April 10th); a trio of humourists (A. P. Burbank, W. S. Andrews and Josh Billings, April 19th); Mme. Chatterton-Bohrer, Anna Granger Dow, Antonia Henne, Ch. Fritsch, Gaston Blay (*sic*), W. R. Johnston and Jessie Couthoui (April 22nd), and the New York Miniature Opera Company in Pinafore (April 26th). Meantime, on April 5th, John L. Stoddard began at the same busy hall his series of lectures on foreign scenes; for years he was an institution of learning for the untravelled. Russia, Spain and the Orient were, this year, his themes. For several weeks Tom Thumb and his wife had been exhibiting at the American Museum, Bowery — a great drop from Barnum's of old; their last week began on March 15th. On March 20th, Dr. Baralt lectured and recited at Steck Hall. A billiard tournament for the Herald Irish Relief Fund carried on all the week of March 22nd–27th at O'Connor's Hall, East Fourteenth Street, the participants being Schaefer, Sexton, Daly, Carter, Rudolphe and Heiser — men of note in that day. And George Vandenhoff was at Lyric Hall, on the 27th. I recall to the reader's attention the "spiritual" evenings of Professor Cooke, Selome Crawford and (sometimes) May Leyton held in March at the Grand Opera House, the Standard Theatre, and elsewhere. Entertainment at any price and in any guise! Even Married Life, by amateurs, on April 3rd, at the Union League Theatre! or Humorous and Dramatic Recitals by H. G. Chapman, on April 12th (afternoon), at the same hall! Verily, the season is wearing thin. But Kate Field brought hope to Chickering Hall on April 9th, 14th (afternoon), 16th and 24th, with her musical monologue, Eyes and Ears in London. Henry Ward Beecher also exalted the tone, on April 15th, in his lecture, at Steinway Hall, on The New Profession; on the 21st, in the same room, Mrs. J. H. Hackett lectured on What is Cruelty? On the 22nd (afternoon) Chickering Hall, seldom idle, housed Mr. and Miss Adelaide Sydney's Drawing Room Entertainment, including a comedietta from the French, A Soup Tureen, without a Cover; also recitations by the Sydneys. They gave a second recital on the 29th. On the 22nd, also, Tammany Hall burgeoned in a Schaefer-Sexton billiard match. April 23rd brought to Chickering Hall a Columbia College Entertainment — Idala, on the plan of Pinafore, with words by a graduate, and music by R. H. Warren; in the show were W. H. Taylor, H. G. Paine, F. F. Flagg, W. Waller, G. H. Taylor, J. A. Oudin, and W. Seaman, Jr. Professional help came from Eugene Oudin and G. W. Warren (organist). On the 29th, the students of the polyglot St. Louis College presented plays in four languages — Una dé Tantas (by Don Manuel Breton de los Herberos), acted by Paul J. Rifflard, Antonio Montaloo and Leon Delmonico; Auf Tod und Leben, with R. C. Nichols, Charles Knoedler, Thomas J. Jarvis, Paul Rifflard and Edmond Knoedler; Les Deux Sourds, played by E. La Montagne, Jr., Charles Knoedler, Rifflard (a very linguistic youth), George A. Plumb, Albert La Montagne and Leon Delmonico; and One Too Many for Him, with Nichols, E. and A. La Montagne, Vinton Murphy and Garner West.

Burbank's Polytechnic was at Chickering Hall on May 3rd, 4th, 5th, 7th and 8th; on the 10th, in the same hall appeared Florence Rice Knox, A. King and Homer Bartlett, in a Literary and Dramatic Entertainment. About this same time (May 6th), at Standard Hall, Broadway, two doors above 42nd Street, Dr. F. L. Ritter lectured on Chamber Music, illustrated by the Standard Hall Quartet. And H. Cooke was, on May 2nd, at Harry Miner's Theatre, in the Bowery — still exposing Spiritualism. And let us recall Robert G. Ingersoll's lectures, on May 16th and 23rd, at Booth's. On May 21st, the busily operative J. S. Vale presented, at Chickering Hall, the Columbia College Opera Company in Pinafore; Mrs. Scott-Siddons preceded with an hour's reading. Under his management, afternoon and evening, on the 22nd, Mrs. Scott-Siddons read, in conjunction with the Swedish Ladies' Quartet. Society Sociables, inaugurated at the American Institute Rink, on May 30th, should allow me to close this section on a high plane. But, alas! Tammany Hall, in early June, ticks away with an astronomical clock, which I must ask the reader to hear explained, once in every hour. And, on May 30th, the New York Athletic Club celebrated Decoration Day, in far-off Mott Haven.

After this I dismiss the impatient to concerts at Manhattan Beach, or at the West Brighton Beach Hotel, or at the Metropolitan Concert Hall, or at Elm Park or Lion Park or heaven knows where; perhaps to Orrin Brothers' Circus at Brighton Beach, opening there on July 3rd. At Coney Island, in early August, at the new Iron Pier, Idaletta and Wallace were walking the ceiling, head downward, like a fly. Steamers to Coney Island or Rockaway Beach plied regularly, and the steamer, Plymouth Rock, took one seaward every day. Let me introduce the Spanish Society, La Nacional, with its picnic, on June 26th, in Jones Wood. Why visit theatres and entertainments indoors? Or shall we look in, on July 29th, at the Bal Champêtre of the Club Français de l'Harmonie, held at the American Institute Rink? Or, in the same rink, on August 9th, shall we attend the Summer Night's Festival and Games of the Manhattan Elevated Railway Athletic Club? Perhaps it would be wiser to await the twenty-fourth Annual Games of the Caledonian Club, on September 2nd, at Jones Wood.

CONCERTS, 1879–1880

The division of Concerts becomes more and more complicated, as more and more theatres opened for music, on Sunday nights, necessitating our placing their musical offerings in the chronicle of their seasonal activities. And, of course, the reader does not wish me to repeat here all that information, especially as he has had a surfeit of it in the account of the offerings of each theatre. All I can do, in this case, is to remind that reader, from time to time, of joys he has already indulged in, especially at the Madison Square Garden in early September, 1879.

CARLOTTA PATTI; RAFAEL JOSEFFY

I will start the season of music, then, with Carlotta Patti, who returned, on September 25th, after a long absence abroad, an absence so lengthy that it had, I fear, brushed some of the bloom from her lovely voice. At her first concert, at Chickering Hall, she rendered Eckert's Swiss Song (Jenny Lind's great glory), the Bolero from Verdi's Vespri Siciliani, and with Ciampi-Cellaj (baritone) a duet from Don Pasquale. In her company were Henry Ketten (pianist), de Munck (her husband, a 'cello player), and L. A. Phelps (tenor). The Herald declares (September 26th) that de Munck was the best 'cellist yet heard in America. Mme. Patti appeared again at Chickering Hall on the 26th and the 29th and on October 1st, 3rd and 4th (matinée). The "last" night was the 9th, and the "last" matinée the 11th. And, naturally, Mme. Patti and her company went right over to Booth's Theatre, on the 12th, for the concert I have elsewhere recorded. On October 6th, Theodore Thomas, fresh from a year in Cincinnati, gave an orchestral concert at Steinway Hall, Franz Rummel assisting; he gave another on the 9th, with Abbie Carrington as soloist.

And, on October 13th, first appeared a pianist — the excellent Rafael Joseffy — who became, for several seasons thereafter, a prominent figure in the musical life of New York. He gave Bach's Chromatische Fantasie and Fugue, a Boccherini Menuet (transcribed by Joseffy), an Étude on Chopin's Waltz in D-flat (also by Joseffy); and (with orchestra, led by Damrosch)

[156]

he played Chopin's Concerto in E minor and Liszt's Concerto in E-flat. The Herald of October 14th highly praises him: "His touch is almost perfect, being brilliant, clear and crisp, and he appears to almost equal advantage in forte or piano passages; . . . his technique was brilliant," and "the evidence of soul and thought" apparent.   His playing of Beethoven's concerto in E-flat, on the 15th, was that of "one great master interpreting another"; it was "his crowning glory."   Later in the evening he "played Bach's fugue in A minor incomparably."

The new artist appeared again on the 17th and 18th (matinée), on the 21st, 24th and 25th (matinée).   The Herald soon began to complain of a monotony in his programmes — he gave the same compositions very frequently.   For variety, we might have gone to Mina Geary's concert, on October 23rd, at Steinway Hall, when Harrison Millard, W. F. Mills, W. J. Hill and Mira Lucas (contralto) also participated; and Carlotta Patti and her company, with Gilmore's Band, had another "last" night at Booth's, on Sunday, October 26th.   On that same 26th, Paola Marié and Grau's artists gave, as we remember, a "first and only" concert, at the Fifth Avenue Theatre; and at Lion Brewery Park, on the same Sunday, occurred Eben's first Sunday concert.   On October 30th, A. Kessels (pianist), performed at Chickering Hall, with Cordelia Heraty (contralto) and Mrs. Grahn (soprano).   And we must remember those concerts, every Sunday night at the Grand Opera House (q.v.).   The Philharmonic Concerts, under the *baton* of Theodore Thomas, I have treated separately; likewise those of the Symphony and Oratorio Societies.

At Chickering Hall, on the 5th, the New York Philharmonic Club (Richard Arnold, Emil Gramm, Julius Gantzberg, Eugene Wiener, Charles Werner and Emanuel Manoli) had their first concert, assisted by Antonia Henne and Florence Copleston.   On November 14th, at Chickering Hall, Mme. Chatterton-Bohrer (harpist) was down for a concert (her début here), with Emily Winant and Agramonte; on the 16th, Gilmore's Band and several soloists made Sunday sacred at the Grand Opera House. November 21st was to bring to Chickering Hall Miss B. Reidy, Canadian soprano, along with Bignardi, Emil Senger, F. and H. Carri, G. W. Morgan, and Martinus Van Gelder (accompanist).   I am unmoved by this intelligence, as by the further news that, on November 25th, 28th and 29th, W. H. Sherwood, Boston pianist, would give at Steinway Hall, afternoon recitals.   I am mildly interested in the concert of the Misses Conron, on November 22nd, at Steck Hall, with Franz Remmertz, Jacob Graff and Constance Howard assisting.   The afternoon of that day promised, at Steinway Hall, Miss Henne, C. Fritsch, C. Richter, &c.   The New York Vocal Union Concert fell on November 25th; John White's organ recital at Chickering Hall, on the 26th.   After Carlotta Patti and Joseffy all these later announcements seem thin.   On November 25th, however, at

[157]

Steinway Hall, appeared, for the benefit of the English Church of St. James, Alwina Valleria, Mme. Ambre, Runcio, Del Puente, Behrens, Franz Rummel and Martinus Van Gelder, and, on December 1st, Maurice Strakosch presented at Steinway Hall Emma Thursby, returning from foreign triumphs; assisting in that glad festival were Emily Winant, Rummel, G. W. Colby, and an orchestra under G. Carlberg. Perhaps the Herald summed up adequately in stating that Miss Thursby "charms but does not thrill." For the relief of sufferers by the floods in Spain, the Spanish Choral Society appeared, on November 29th, along with Estelle Buzzetti, Gaston Blay (violinist), Villanova, Rosalba Beecher, Annie E. Beeré, Salcedo, and the French choral society, L'Espérance. America was called on, frequently, even then, to help Europe — famished Ireland, especially. Levy was now playing nightly at Koster and Bial's. Let us not forget the Sunday concerts at the Academy, by Mapleson's singers. On December 2nd occurred at Chickering Hall the second concert of the New York Philharmonic Club, with Franz Rummel and Franz Remmertz (again in good form) assisting. And the Reverend Dr. W. D. Godman's (what a name for a preacher!) University Singers of New Orleans were at the Presbyterian Church, West 35th Street, on December 4th.

The Church of the Disciples, Madison Avenue and 45th Street, welcomed, on December 6th, Rafael Joseffy and Anna Drasdil — a combination of unusual excellence for such a function. If advertisements were fulfilled, Chickering Hall devoted itself, on December 11th, to a concert of English glees, by the New York Glee Club, Miss Beebe and Anna Bulkley Hills, and, on the 12th, at Chickering Hall appeared Kate Vashti Hill (pianist, daughter of W. J. Hill), Henrietta Beebe, W. J. Hill, W. H. Beckett, &c. On the 11th, also, the Hutchinson Family brought the Granite State to the 24th Street M. E. Church; on the 13th, Steinway Hall housed the powerful voices of the Arion Society, in a concert conducted by Leopold Damrosch, with Anna Bock (pianist), Jacob Graff, and Remmertz. At about this same time, at Parepa Hall, one might easily have attended a performance of the cantata, Esther, rendered by members of the St. James Methodist Episcopal Church, of Harlem. The suburbs are crowding into our history.

And music crowds our pages uncomfortably. Mme. Chatterton-Bohrer (harpist) advertised for December 13th, at Chickering Hall, a concert, in company with Mme. Lablache, Runcio and Del Puente; on the 16th, at a concert for the Seventh Regiment New Armoury Fund, she again appeared, this time at Steinway Hall, along with Emilie Ambre, Campanini, Runcio, and Behrens. And here is Joseffy again, with promised recitals, at Chickering Hall, on the evenings of December 15th and 19th, and the afternoons of the 17th and 20th (the last date with Letitia Fritsch). On the 15th, Gertrude Franklin was to have appeared with him, but he was too ill to play.

[158]

He came forward, on the 17th.   On the 16th, the excellent Mendelssohn Glee Club began, at Chickering Hall, its fourteenth season, with the aid of Mary (*sic*) Louise Swift, Giuseppe Del Puente and Franz Rummel.   The soloists on February 17th were Annie Mac Collum (contralto) and Adolphe Fischer ('cello).   The ladies in that garden of men, on April 20th, were Henrietta Maurer and Isabella Palmer Fassett — a diminished glory, one suspects.   At Association Hall, on the the 16th of December, we heard the University Glee Singers from New Orleans, and, on December 22nd, at Chickering Hall, Joseffy and Letitia Fritsch.   On the 20th, at Steinway Hall, the Teachers' Association met, with Florence Copleston, Antonia Henne, Remmertz, Levy and George Vandenhoff in a rich programme.   Joseffy was back again on the 26th, and on the afternoons of the 24th and 27th.   Meantime, on December 23rd, the Harvard Glee Club was at Chickering Hall, and, in the smaller auditorium at Steinway Hall, Wilhelm Müller and associates gave a concert of chamber music.   Let us recall that other Christmas joy, December 25th, at the Academy — Patrick S. Gilmore's glory — Columbia.   And Levy every night at Koster and Bial's!   What a town, this of ours — amusing, yet so serious withal!

The Sunday concerts at the Grand Opera House went steadily on, as did Joseffy, whose "last" evening at Chickering Hall fell on December 29th, with a "last" matinée on January 3rd.   The third "soirée" of the New York Philharmonic Club came on January 6th, at Chickering Hall, Anna Bock assisting; on the 7th, the Yale College Glee Club had and possibly gave a good time at the same place.   On the 10th, at Steinway Hall, appeared Franz Remmertz, T. B. Buxton, Emma Dearborn, Ludwig Dingeldey, Ida Kleber, and Mme. Cappiani.   On January 11th, at St. Stephen's Church, one might have heard Annie J. Borie, Romeyn, Eugene Oudin, Elizabeth Sloman (harp), E. R. Mollenhauer and Agatha Munier.   And on the same evening Franz Kaltenborn led the Young Philharmonic Orchestra, at the Thalia Theater.   Anna Bock had her concert, at Steinway Hall, on the 13th, assisted by Arnold, Müller, Gramm and Dulcken; every minor musician must have his or her concert annually, and Miss Bock begins the weary progress for 1879–80.   And there were going on, since January 7th, organ recitals at the Five Points House of Industry, to show off a new organ, $2,800 in value, "given by a gentleman to Calvary Chapel, attached to that place."   Sometime soon we should attend, especially as the organists are from leading churches of New York and Brooklyn, and therefore good.

January 27th was musically busy.   The New York Quintet Club gave at Steinway Small Hall its third chamber music "soirée," with Wilhelm Müller ('cello), and Max Pinner; at Chickering Hall appeared the New York Vocal Union.   On January 29th, the Young Apollo Club and J. S. Burdett functioned at Association Hall, and, on the 31st, at Steck Hall, J. N. Pattison was master of a concert including Marie Harvey, Henry (tenor), Madeline

Jerolamon (contralto), Mrs. J. W. Harbeson (pupil of Pattison), J. C. Taylor (tenor) and S. P. Strini (baritone). These were but minnows compared with Belle Cole (replacing the ill Miss Beebe), Emily Winant, and William Courtney, who appeared on the same evening at the Saalfield-Sullivan concert (Steinway Hall), along with Mrs. J. Remington Fairland and Mortimer Weed in a programme of works by the composer of H. M. S. Pinafore. On February 2nd, at the same Hall, under auspices of St. Andrew's Society, could have been heard a programme of Scotch music, with Gilmore's Band and William Cleland, piper; singers included Miss Beebe, Miss Henne and W. H. Beckett. On the 3rd, the New York Philharmonic Club was again at Chickering Hall. February 4th ushered into Masonic Temple the Drummond Family and the Swiss Staff Bellringers.

For the stricken Silesians, on February 8th, appeared at Tammany Hall Johanna Meta (prima donna), and Timothée Adamowski, Polish violinist, afterward beloved of Bostonians resident in the Back Bay districts. Verily, in music, as in the drama, the stars of the '80s appear in this last season of the '70s! On February 9th, at St. Francis Xavier's Church, came a first performance of Tamaro's Grand Mass, dedicated to Cardinal McCloskey, who was present; and I must again remind of the Booth's Theatre concert, on February 15th, with Christian Fritsch, C. E. Pratt, the Spanish Students, Teresa Carreño, Levy, Amy Sherwin and H. Wannemacher — a host indeed! On the 18th, G. W. Morgan and his daughter, Maud, held at Chickering Hall the first of five organ and harp recitals. Harrison Millard had his concert on February 18th, at Chickering Hall, with Mme. Bouvier, Annie Beeré, Marie Millard (soprano), Homer Bartlett, &c. And the Fisk University Jubilee Singers were in the same auditorium, on the 21st. These last had been, on the 17th, at the Harlem Congregational Church, 125th Street and Second Avenue. Another Saalfield-Sullivan Concert, on the 21st, at Steinway Hall, was rich in the singing of the English Glee Club, Henrietta Beebe, Julie de Ruyther (or Ryther), Belle Cole, the Misses Conron, Aiken, W. C. Baird, Haydon Tilla, M. M. Weed and others — truly a notable array of fine talent. On the 22nd, at St. Stephen's Church, appeared Hattie Louise Simms, H. R. Romeyn, Eugene Oudin, Agatha Munier, and Edward R. Mollenhauer, in Rossini's Stabat Mater. February 28th brought into Chickering Hall Carlberg, directing all of Meyerbeer's music for Struensee; Genevieve Stebbins, Ch. Fritsch and Mme. Chatterton-Bohrer assisted. On the same evening, in Steinway Hall, a concert for the Silesian sufferers enlisted Amy Sherwin, Anna Drasdil, Anna Bock, F. Steins, Edward Mollenhauer and Wilhelm Müller. Joseffy, on March 1st, gave a Chopin recital at Chickering Hall; he appeared again, on the 3rd, in compositions by Schubert, Reinecke, Bach, and Beethoven — the Kreutzer Sonata, with H. Brandt (violin) and W. Müller ('cello). On the 2nd came the fifth "soirée" of the New York Philharmonic Club, and, on the 4th, we had a testimonial to

Carl Alves, Steinway Hall opening expectantly for the eagerly desired throngs. Joseffy was again at Chickering Hall on the evening of March 6th, for a Chopin recital; on the 7th, Marzo's Messe Solennelle was sung at St. Agnes' Church, East 42nd Street. On the 8th, Joseffy gave at Chickering Hall a Liszt night, and another — his "last" was to come on the 15th, but his illness forced postponement. On the 13th, at the Union League Theatre, Marie Benchley, Jacob Graff and K. Alfonso gave scenes from operas. And will the reader look back to the three concerts at Madison Square Garden, for Irish relief? The Yale Glee Club came, on March 18th, to Steinway Hall; and the third Saalfield concert brought to the same hall, on March 20th, Belle Cole, Emma Watson Doty, Haydon Tilla, Lencioni and M. M. Weed. Joseffy had been announced for further concerts, but illness prevented his appearing, even on March 19th. In later March, pray remember the concerts by Paola Marié and her colleagues, at the Fifth Avenue Theatre; and let us hear Joseffy, on the 31st, at Chickering Hall.

On March 29th, Charles Roberts, Jr., and the New York Philharmonic Club were at Chickering Hall. On the 30th, at Steinway Hall, were gathered Max Pinner, Amy Sherwin, Adolphe Fischer, Richard Arnold, and, presumably, an audience. The Church Choir Quartet (Fanny Pollak, Jennie Dickerson, Henry Brandeis and Adolph Sohst) held the same hall, on the 31st.   That ever-ready hall, on April 1st, hospitably took to its bosom Ida W. Hubbell, Mrs. Emma Henry, Mrs. Barron Anderson, S. B. Mills, G. W. Morgan and Liberati. On the 30th of March, also, at Chickering Hall, the Vocal Union appeared, with Emily Winant and J. N. Pattison. I have already spoken of the fine concerts, on April 1st and 8th, at the Madison Square Theatre. On April 2nd came Joseffy's Liszt night at Chickering Hall. And what of the Stock Exchange Glee Club, on the 3rd, at Chickering Hall, especially since Antonia Henne and Adolphe Fischer assisted? Chickering Hall, on the 6th, heard the last concert for the season of the New York Philharmonic Club, and Steinway Hall opened, on the 8th, for a testimonial to Franz Rummel (with Mrs. Swift, Miss Henne, Del Puente, Fritsch, A. Fischer, &c.). At the testimonial to Evelina Hartz (Steck Hall, April 7th) appeared Mme. Lablache and S. G. Young. On the 10th, Richard Arnold's concert, at Chickering Hall, employed Letitia Fritsch, Mrs. Richard Arnold (pianist) and the New York Philharmonic Club (to which we said good-bye only on the 6th); on the 10th, also, at Steinway Hall, Emma Thursby, Belle Cole, Pease, and H. L. Farmer appeared, in the last Saalfield concert. The 12th assembled in the same hall, for John Lavine's concert, Thomas and his orchestra, Miss Thursby, Max Pinner, and Adolphe Fischer (replacing the ill S. B. Mills). And what a drop to Annie J. Borie's concert, on the 15th, at Masonic Temple, with Sarah Barron Anderson (contralto), Fred Jamieson (tenor), Adolph Sohst (baritone), and Oscar M. Newell (pianist). Of such as these was our musical fabric composed — not of your Joseffys, Pattis and other visiting and money-exhausting stars. The musical chain is as strong as its weakest links.

On April 19th, Campanini arranged a charity concert, at which were to appear, in Steinway Hall, himself, Miss Cary, Mme. Ambre, Belocca, Marie Louise Swift, Miss Sheppard, Florence Copleston, Tagliapietra, Oudin, Behrens and Brignoli. And they all actually appeared! The Sunday concerts still dragged on at the Grand Opera House, and the opera singers had done their best, on Sundays during their spring visit, to fill the Academy with song and audiences. On the 13th, the Atalanta Boat Club felt that it, too, must have a concert, and gave, it, at Chickering Hall, with C. Fritsch, Eugenie C. Hummel (soprano), Anna B. P. Hall (soprano), Lena Little (contralto), and others; on the same evening, at Steinway Hall, the Bank Clerks' Musical Association held forth with A. Sohst, W. F. Mills, Ada Elkins and Annette Windt (sopranos), Bertha Frank (contralto), C. H. Thompson (tenor), and G. U. Hopkins (buffo). A "testimonial" to Carrie Moses, on the 14th, at Steinway Hall, enlisted Mme. Maretzek (harp), Christian Fritsch, Richard Arnold, Jennie Bach (soprano), and H. Buongiorno (baritone). The Fisk Jubilee Singers came to Steinway Hall on the 16th, and, on the 17th, a testimonial to Lillie A. Barry (not only everybody must have a concert, but anybody, apparently, could and did) enrolled, at Chickering Hall, the New York Philharmonic Club, Jennie Dickerson, Christian Fritsch, W. C. Baird, Emil Senger, and William R. Case (pianist). On April 20th, Adolphe Fischer, Ida Kleber, Teresa Carreño and Werner were at Steinway Hall; on the 22nd and 27th (afternoons) Mme. Chatterton-Bohrer was at Chickering Hall, with Anna Granger Dow, Antonia Henne, Gaston Blay, Charles Werner, and G. W. Colby. On the evening of the 22nd, F. V. Marckwald, Arbuckle, Belle Cole, and others held a concert, in Steinway Hall, of Irish and Scottish music.

Will they never stop? On April 23rd, Maurice Strakosch presented at Steinway Hall a glittering host — Emma Thursby, Ole Bull (how seldom the old gentleman now appears!), Emily Winant, Mme. Chatterton-Bohrer, Anna Bock, Brignoli, Ferranti, Adolphe Fischer, and Maurice Strakosch (conductor). Emma Thursby and Ole Bull were at the Academy on the 26th. On the 26th, at Standard Hall, were Bergner, whose concert it was, W. C. Baird, Brandt, Matzka, &c., and, on the same date, Jerome Hopkins's Springtide Lecture Concert engaged the aid of Emil Mollenhauer. On the 27th, a "testimonial" to Professor Simon of Fordham College brought into requisition at Chickering Hall a lesser array in Henriette Corradi, Émile Guyon, Octavie Gomien, James Pech (organist), A. Rivarde, and a full orchestra conducted by Felix Simon. Better were it to wait for Franz Rummel's recitals, at Steinway Hall, on the afternoons of April 27th and 29th, and May 1st, 4th and 6th; or Caryl Florio's concert, on April 29th, at Chickering Hall, when appeared from the past Maria Brainerd, with Henrietta Beebe, Mme. Lasar-Studwell, Baird, Aiken, Mrs. Barron-Anderson, &c.   I rather like (though my pen is utterly exhausted with recording these concerts) — I rather like the promise of Annie Beeré's concert, on April 27th, at Steinway Hall, when Emma Watson Doty, Florence Rice Knox, Ch. Fritsch, W. F. Mills, J. Caulfield (organist), Charles E. Pratt, Charles Werner, and S. G. Young (baritone) helped with whatever talent each possessed.   About this time came (May 6th) to Chickering Hall the Mendelssohn Club of Philadelphia, W. W. Gilchrist, conductor; on that 6th, Franz Rummel gave his last matinée at Steinway Hall.   On May 1st, Steinway Hall heard Schubert's The Maid of the Mill, with Franz Remmertz and Franz Merry.

On May 6th, Jerome Hopkins, who had been there on April 26th, gave us his second and last organ recital at Chickering Hall; I rejoice that it is finished.   Joseffy's last appearances began on May 12th, when, at Chickering Hall, he played a huge programme of pieces by Bach, Beethoven, Scarlatti-Tausig, Kirnberger, Schumann, Mozart, Henselt, Joseffy (four), and Liszt (five); on the 14th, he rendered compositions of Schumann, Mendelssohn, Chopin (three preludes, an impromptu, a mazurka, a waltz and four études), Rubinstein and Liszt.   On May 12th, the New York Stock Exchange Glee Club came to Chickering Hall, with Miss Beebe, George E. Aiken (their leader), Teresa Carreño, and Caryl Florio.   On the 18th, Belle Cole, Mrs. Rice Knox, Anna Granger Dow, Miss Beebe, Remmertz, Arbuckle and Miss Winant were listed at Chickering Hall, for the benefit of the Manhattan Hospital.   Lencioni, Brignoli and others were at Steck Hall on May 22nd.   A benefit to Brignoli, on May 24th, brought to Chickering Hall a performance of Don Pasquale, with Brignoli, Papini, Tagliapietra and Mrs. G. Robertson (unfamed); between the acts appeared in concert Teresa Carreño, Mme. Chatterton-Bohrer and Nina Marcy.   On the 26th, Joseffy had a farewell benefit; just why he felt entitled to a benefit, I cannot conjecture.

Surely they will begin to have mercy on us!   Here, at least, are hints. The Metropolitan Concert Hall, on May 27th, began its summer concerts, under Rudolph Aronson.   That new hall, at Broadway, Seventh Avenue and 41st Street was going all summer, with just the kind of nightly concerts suitable to the heat and the tired business world, with a fine orchestra (under Rudolph Aronson), popular music, café and restaurant.   And the West Brighton Beach Hotel gave the first of L. Conterno's concerts, on May 23rd, from two to seven o'clock.   Music and dashing waves! who would prefer to sit in stuffy Steinway or Chickering Hall?   Yet Mr. Parson Price had a concert at the latter hall, on May 28th.   And an Olde Folkes Concert, on the 25th, at the Church, 47th Street and Madison Avenue, was to offer, in addition, Maria Brainerd, Dr. and Mrs. A. B. Hills and Jennie Strong.   And Wilhelmj, idol of last year, gave several concerts, beginning

June 22nd, at Koster and Bial's! This seems too extreme a drop in artistic importance. Karl Jöhmus (harpist from Prague) appeared on June 1st at Steinway Hall; on the 3rd, at Chickering Hall, Henry Yzquierdo played the flute, and Mme. Carreño the piano. But the "great outdoors" called mightily. At Wendel's Elm Park, Ninth Avenue and 92nd Street, Sunday concerts (and drinks) attracted; on June 6th, one heard there Louise Linden (saxophone), Fred W. Bent, and Justus W. Koch (pianist). And, of course, Gilmore's Band, with Levy, was at Manhattan Beach every afternoon and evening during those hot summer hours in July and August. The dear old days, gone forevermore! And we could sail, if we pleased, to the Bal Champêtre and Festival of the Arion Society, held at West Brighton Beach, Coney Island, on July 22nd. Thus, with the Metropolitan Concert Hall playing Strauss, Schubert, Schumann, Lecocq, Ambroise Thomas, Gounod, Suppé and Genée at 41st Street, and Gilmore's Band at Manhattan Beach, not to mention concerts at Fort Lee, across the river, we were led into the open, quite unconsciously weaned from concerts in accustomed winter halls. Brignoli, on August 12th, sang at the Oriental Hotel, Manhattan Beach. So good-bye, concert season of 1879–80!

Philharmonic Society, 1879–1880

The season of this institutional body began on November 20th and 21st, with the expected public rehearsal and concert, Theodore Thomas conducting. The opening programme proffered Berlioz's overture, King Lear; Franz Rummel in Tschaikowsky's piano concerto, op. 23; The Ride of the Valkyries and Siegfried's Death; and Beethoven's Fifth Symphony. December 19th–20th brought Beethoven's Consecration of the House; Valleria and Galassi in a duet from Le Nozze di Figaro; Reinhold's new suite for string orchestra; Valleria, in Ocean, Thou Mighty Monster; Schumann's Symphony No. 1, in B-flat; Galassi in The Evening Star, from Tannhäuser; and the Vorspiel to Die Meistersinger. The offering for January 23rd and 24th comprised Cherubini's Anacreon overture; Prelude, Adagio, Gavotte and Rondo, by Bach, adapted for string orchestra by S. Bachrich; Joseffy's playing of Beethoven's piano concerto, No. 5, E-flat, op. 73; and Rubinstein's Ocean Symphony. On February 20th and 21st, we heard compositions by Mozart (Adagio and fugue), Beethoven (Fourth Symphony), Wagner (Introduction and Finale, Tristan und Isolde) and Chopin (Concerto in F minor, played by Joseffy). The March gift (19th and 20th) bore promise of spring; it began with Haydn's Symphony in B-flat, No. 8; proceeded with Mendelssohn's Midsummer-Night's Dream music, entrusting the songs to Jennie Dickerson and Fanny Pollak; and ended with Schubert's Ninth Symphony, in C major. The season closed, on April 23rd and 24th, with a programme composed of a chromatic fantasia and fugue of Bach, arranged

[164]

by G. F. Bristow; Act III of Die Götterdämmerung, with a heterogeneous group of soloists in Amy Sherwin, Mrs. T. Buxton, Antonia Henne, Campanini, Remmertz and C. Steinbuch; and Beethoven's Seventh Symphony. I must admit my surprise to find the luscious tenor of Campanini so often ringing out in the heroic measures of Wagner.

Symphony and Oratorio Societies, 1879-1880

The first public rehearsal and concert of Dr. Damrosch's Symphony Society, on November 6th and 8th, had as chief features Beethoven's Seventh Symphony and Liszt's Festival Sounds (first time); Anna Drasdil was soloist, and, as usual, Steinway Hall housed the harmonies. On December 4th and 6th, mainsprings of delight were the Jupiter Symphony, and Goldmark's overture, Penthesilea (new); Miss Thursby was to sing in the concert. On January 15th and 17th, the society played Beethoven's Pastoral Symphony; a Saint-Saens concerto for violoncello (with Adolphe Fischer, from Paris — his début); the prelude and finale to Tristan und Isolde; and Fischer in solos — a nocturne by Chopin and a Tarantella by Fischer. The reader perceives that the first performances here of Wagner's later operas, did not, thanks to Thomas and Damrosch, fall upon ears wholly unacquainted with their harmonies.

The fourth delight (February 12th and 14th) was Berlioz's La Damnation de Faust, with Amy Sherwin, Julius Jordan, Remmertz, and F. G. Bourne; this was an outstanding event of the year. Of course the Oratorio Society participated. On March 11th and 13th the programme included Beethoven's "Heroic" Symphony, Goldmark's Penthesilea overture, Dvorak's new Slavonic Rhapsodie, No. 2, and Liszt's Tasso. On April 1st (afternoon) and 3rd, the Symphony Society repeated La Damnation de Faust, Sohst replacing Remmertz (ill) and the Arion and Oratorio Societies participating. The rehearsal and concert of April 15th and 17th gave the third act of Siegfried and the Ninth Symphony of Beethoven. And who, think you, sang in Siegfried? Campanini, no less, with Mrs. Swift, Mrs. H. Norman, and Remmertz, the ever-useful.

The offering of the Oratorio Society, on November 28th (rehearsal) and 29th, was the Elijah, with Marie Louise Swift, Amy Sherwin, Anna Drasdil, C. Fritsch and F. Remmertz. Remmertz, suffering at the matinée from a severe cold, was superseded in the evening performance by the admirable Myron W. Whitney. On December 26th and 27th came the expected Christmastide performances of The Messiah, Miss Thursby, Miss Drasdil, George Simpson and Remmertz forming, one would suppose, an admirable quartette; the Herald, however, in its review of the rehearsal, found fault with Miss Thursby and Remmertz. The Creation lured, on February 6th and 7th, with Letitia Fritsch, Jacob Graff and Whitney. For reasons difficult to understand, unless religion were at the base of the scheme, Damrosch went, on March 17th and 18th, to St. George's Church, Stuyvesant Square, for his rendering of Bach's Passion Music, with the Oratorio Society, Anna Granger Dow, Mathilde Phillipps, W. J. Winch (tenor), John F. Winch (bass) and G. E. Aiken (baritone).

CHAPTER III

BROOKLYN, WILLIAMSBURGH, QUEENSBOROUGH, STATEN ISLAND, 1879-1880

AT the Park Theatre, Colonel Sinn began again, on September 1, 1879, with The Banker's Daughter, acted by a company seen at various houses in New York, in the next season, with Louis James as John Strebelow, Marie Wainwright as Lillian, Mr. and Mrs. Charles Walcot as Phipps and Florence St. Vincent Brown, Mrs. Farren as Mrs. Holcomb, Harold Forsberg as Babbage, Gustavus Levick as Harold Routledge, E. L. Tilton as Lawrence Westbrook, G. W. Farren as Dr. Watson, and J. W. Collier as Carojac — seemingly as good a cast as one could desire. Next week they gave The Danicheffs, at the Novelty Theatre. Two graduates from Vaudeville (Harry Richmond and Acland von Boyle) followed (week of September 8th–13th) as, respectively, Hon. Josephus Grimwig and Shang-Hi, the Chinaman, in Levin C. Tees's play, Our Candidates; with them were Alfred McDowell, Sam Norman, Florence Stover and Mrs. S. K. Chester. This production will not live long in our annals. Emerson's Megatherian Minstrels (September 15th–20th), under management of R. M. Hooley, featured Schoolcraft and Coes, Arthur Cook, Thomas and William Daly, W. and E. Girard, and C. Seamon.

Emma Abbott had the week of September 22nd–27th, her excellent company including Pauline Maurel, Walter Temple, Marie Stone, Ellis Ryse, Tom Karl, A. E. Stoddard, Zelda Seguin, William Castle, W. H. Macdonald and Edward Seguin. On the 22nd and 27th, Miss Abbott sang Virginia, in Victor Massé's Paul and Virginia; on the 23rd, and at the matinée on the 24th, Marie Stone relieved her, in the rôle. The cast also included Mrs. Seguin, Ryse and Tom Karl. On the evening of the 24th, Miss Abbott, Tom Karl and Mrs. Seguin gave The Bohemian Girl; on the 25th, Mignon presented Miss Abbott, Miss Stone and Mrs. Seguin in the three female rôles (if one may so designate Federico). Miss Abbott sang in Faust, on the 26th, and Marie Stone and Pauline Maurel, in The Bohemian Girl, on the afternoon of the 27th.

The "fall and winter season" opened, on September 29th, with Lester Wallack, in A Scrap of Paper, his support being partly from his own theatre, but mostly from the former company at the Park; it included Rosa Rand, Stella Boniface, Nellie Mortimer, Kate Bartlett, Gertie Johnson, Mrs. J. B. Sutton, Ed Lamb, James Dunn, N. S. Wood, John Z. Little, Con T. Murphy and Joseph T. Leonard. For the second half of his week (October 2nd,

[167]

3rd, 4th), Wallack played My Awful Dad. The next star, Joseph Jefferson, brought, for Rip Van Winkle (October 6th–11th), his own support, including Charles Waverly, James Galloway, William Burton, Henrietta Vaders and Little Maggie Gonzales. Fred Marsden's play, The Kerry Gow, was Joseph Murphy's medium for the week of October 13th–18th, with, for support, Luke Martin, Belle Dickson, Charline Weidman, &c.

Adelaide Neilson; Maggie Mitchell; Fanny Davenport

And here comes the most exquisite actress then known to America, to begin what was alas! to be her last American tour. Just why Adelaide Neilson waited till the next spring (1880) to make her re-appearance in New York, I cannot say; at any rate she began her tour with a week in Brooklyn, supported by "Max Strakosch's Metropolitan Company of Shakespearean Actors." She opened (October 20th, 22nd), as was to be expected, in the rôle that she had made peculiarly her own — Juliet, supported by a pleasing new English actor, Edward Compton, as Romeo, and with H. A. Weaver, Nellie Morant and J. H. Miller in her company. On the 21st and 25th, she played her exquisite Viola, with Nellie Morant as Olivia, Compton as Malvolio, F. W. Sanger as the Duke, and Reynier as Sebastian; the evening of the 23rd provided As You Like It, and, for her benefit, on the 24th, Miss Neilson appeared as Julia, in The Hunchback. There was no Wednesday matinée, and by request she gave Twelfth Night, at the matinée on the 25th. The Eagle critic was ecstatic in admiration of the lovely actress; from a charming letter Miss Neilson wrote to Colonel Sinn, on concluding her engagement, I learn that many auditors came from New York to enjoy the rare privilege of seeing her in her famous rôles. She had not been in this neighbourhood since the close of her engagement at Daly's Fifth Avenue Theatre, in the spring of 1877.

Maggie Mitchell was next in line, playing Lorle, on October 27th, 28th, 29th and 30th, and Fanchon, on the 31st, and on November 1st; with her were William Harris, R. F. McClannin, Julian Mitchell (her son), Rufus Scott, Lettie Allen, Marion P. Clifton and Annie Mortimer. Max Maretzek's English Opera Company entered for a week, giving Sleepy Hollow (November 3rd and 5th and matinée, 8th), Pinafore (matinée and evening of the 4th, Election Day), Il Trovatore (6th), and The Bohemian Girl (7th and 8th). The curiously assorted company, in that oddly chosen list included Florence Rice Knox (who should not have left the concert field), Minnie Palmer, Lillie West, Rachel Samuels, Ada Whitman, Charles H. Turner, Alonzo Hatch, James Peakes, L. Fink, &c. This business duly dispatched, Fanny Davenport, whose beauty still caused her photographs to sell largely, appeared, on November 10th and 12th, in Pique, with Edwin Price as Captain Standish, Emma Maddern as Raitch, E. K. Collier as

Matthew Standish and Harry Hawk as Sammy Dymple; on the 11th, and at the matinée, on the 15th, Miss Davenport played Fanny Ten Eyck, in Divorce. As You Like It (in which, of course, she challenged comparison with Miss Neilson) had, on the 13th, in support of her Rosalind, Price as Orlando, Emma Pierce as Celia, Harry Hawk as Touchstone, and Collier as Jaques. The School for Scandal (14th) and a double bill of London Assurance and Oliver Twist (a favourite bill with Miss Davenport) ended (15th) the busy week of the popular star.

Robson and Crane; Goodwin-Weathersby; Sothern; Kate Claxton

The rapid progression of the best stars dazzles our imagination; what must it have done to living, playgoing Brooklyn? On November 17th, 18th, and 19th, Robson and Crane presented Our Bachelors:

Bachelor Bangle	Stuart Robson	Bachelor Snug	William Morris
Bachelor Jowler	W. H. Crane	Spinster Blythe	Alicia Robson
Bachelor Waring	Frazer Coulter	Widow Clinton	Agnes Proctor
Bachelor Bruce	A. S. Lipman	Widow Mouser	Mary Myers
Bachelor Muldoon	John Marble	Spinster Courtney	Nellie Boyd

For the remainder of the week (November 20th, 21st and 22nd), the stars revived The Comedy of Errors, in which, of course, some show of verisimilitude consisted in having Crane imitate the piping squeak of Robson's voice. This attraction made room for the Weathersby-Goodwin Froliques, in Hobbies (November 24th-29th) with Eliza Weathersby as Minnie Clover, Nat C. Goodwin as Professor Pygmalion Whiffles, Venie Clancy as Miss Constance, Jennie Weathersby as Miss Euphemia Bang, Charles Bowser as Major Garroway Bang, and Raymond Holmes as Arthur Doveleigh. A burlesque, acted by these characters, was incorporated, as in the Salsbury Troubadours offering of The Brook; and Goodwin gave his now familiar imitations of Booth, Barrett, Fechter, Jefferson, Raymond, Robson and Mayo. The next week brought E. A. Sothern, in Lord Dundreary (December 1st, 2nd, 3rd, and matinée, 6th), The Crushed Tragedian (4th and 6th, evenings), and David Garrick (5th). The star's company appeared without him, for the Wednesday matinée (3rd), in Everybody's Friend. For December 8th, 9th and 10th, Kate Claxton gave The Double Marriage; The Two Orphans (11th, 12th, 13th) presented Miss Claxton as Louise, Josie Batchelder as Henriette, Margaret Cone as Marianne, Fyffe as Jacques, Stevenson as Pierre and the Chevalier, and H. B. Phillips as the Count.

Bandmann; McCullough; Emmet; Gus Williams; Frank Mayo; Rankins

A quintette of male stars, one after the other, flitted across our vision. Daniel E. Bandmann, no raging lion of popularity, gave, for the week of

December 15th-20th, his well-known Narcisse, with Amelia Herbert as the Pompadour, and Miss Bennison (*sic*) as Doris Quinault; Raising the Wind also was in the bill. A week followed of John McCullough in familiar repertoire — Virginius (22nd), Othello (23rd), Damon and Pythias (matinée, 24th), Richard III (evening, 24th), The Gladiator (Christmas, afternoon and evening), Payne's Brutus (26th), The Honeymoon and A Conjugal Lesson (congruously joined, in regard to titles, matinée, 27th), and Jack Cade (evening, 27th). With McCullough were F. B. Warde and Kate Forsyth (*sic*). J. K. Emmet came for New Year's (December 29th–January 3rd), and, since he did not play at the Wednesday matinée (December 31st), Wallack's company travelled from New York to present Old Heads and Young Hearts, with John Gilbert, Harry Beckett, Gerald Eyre, Maurice Barrymore, Harry Edwards, Charles Rockwell, Ada Dyas, Mme. Ponisi and Rose Wood — an extraordinary treat for Brooklyn. During the week of January 5th–10th, Gus Williams, out of "Variety" into Drama, presented Our German Senator, himself playing J. Adolph Dinkel, with C. Collins as Colonel Bruce, H. Liston as Judge Jere Spruce, Archie Boyd as Captain Dionysius Puff, Maggie Arlington as Louise Granville, Duchess of Katcherkerchow-Kistan, Jennie Harold as Flora Bruce, Katie Blancke as Fanny and Dora Stuart as Mrs. Dinkel. On January 12th, Our Girls, not very successful at Wallack's, began a week at the Park, with Edeson as Potter, J. A. Kennedy as Judson, W. H. Collings as Clench, H. S. Duffield as Aspland, Rosa Rand as Mabel, Annie Edmondson as Clara, Virginia Buchanan as Mrs. Clench, and Gertie Johnson as Jane. Mr. and Mrs. McKee Rankin then entered the Park (January 19th–24th), of course in The Danites; with them were W. E. Sheridan (as the Parson), Cora Tanner, Emma Marble, Ben Maginley, Lin Harris, Frank Budworth, Alexander Fitzgerald, George B. Waldron and Isabel Waldron.

ADA CAVENDISH

What a delightful season! The New York Criterion Comedy Company now gave us a week (January 26th–31st) without a star but with an excellent ensemble, in the comedy, Freaks; the cast included F. F. Mackay, De Wolf Hopper, A. H. Canby, T. F. Egbert, W. A. Whitecar, Louise Sylvester, Mattie Earle, Mary Davenport and Helen Gardner. On February 1st (Sunday) a concert for Beth Israel Congregation brought to the Park stage Jules Levy, Charles Werner, Minnie Cummings (elocutionist), Henrietta Markstein, Evelina Hartz (soprano), Lena Luckstone (contralto), Christian Fritsch, F. Remmertz and Caryl Florio. The dignified, artistic, but not quite great Ada Cavendish next presented an interesing repertoire: Much Ado about Nothing (February 2nd and matinée, 4th); Lady Clancarty (4th, 5th, 6th, and afternoon of the 7th); The New Magdalen (evenings of the 3rd and 7th). With her were Samuel Piercy, Eberle, Hagan, Adelaide Cherie, and Miss Matthews. On the 9th began a week of The Strategists, with Clinton Hall, T. J. Hind, Sol Smith, F. S. Meredith, Thomas Chapman, Sam E. Ryan, Alice Brooks, Mrs. Sol Smith and Lizzie Newell. Wives, seen during the autumn, at Daly's new theatre, came to the Park (February 16th–21st), with a cast including George R. Edeson, W. H. Collings, John Z. Little, Otis A. Skinner (as Horace de Chateauroux), O. H. Barr, W. Davidge, Jr., J. A. Kennedy, Joseph T. Leonard, Adelaide Detchon, Pearl Eytinge, Effie Vaughan, Annie Edmondson, and Mrs. J. P. Sutton. With that production, Sinn for a time abandoned the star system, in what looks like an effort to re-establish a stock company. Next week (February 23rd–28th) he brought out a new play by Leonard Grover (author of Our Boarding House). This novelty, My Son-in-Law, or, a Day at Brighton, was thus cast:

Sarah Trueheart	Henrietta Vaders	Daisy Uppers	Gertie Johnson
Mrs. Uppers	Mrs. E. L. Davenport	DeWitt C. Uppers	G. R. Edeson
Joaquina Bisbon	Meroe Charles	Cholmeley Stuart	Otis A. Skinner
Florence	Pearl Eytinge	Jean Bisbon	Leonard Grover
Ann Maria	Annie Edmondson	Blifilk	Walter Bronson
Biddie Nanine	Effie Vaughan	Mike	T. F. Brennan

For the week of March 1st–6th, we had Kiralfy Brothers' spectacular The Black Crook, the ballet presenting Mlles. de Rosa and Zallio, with Arnold Kiralfy, and the specialists including the three Rinaldo Brothers ("the modern Majiltons"), the three Herbert Brothers, and Master Carling (boy caricaturist). The mere actors included J. F. Peters, Willis H. Page, C. G. Craig, George R. Edeson, Sadie Bigelow (Amina), Mrs. Brutone and Nellie Larkelle (Stalacta).

BOUCICAULT; MARY ANDERSON; FATINITZA; EMMET;
JOHN T. RAYMOND; BARRETT

Two stars of magnitude made bright the March stage. Boucicault (March 8th–13th) appeared in The Shaughraun, with O. H. Barr as Molineux, J. A. Kennedy as Robert, George R. Edeson as Harvey Duff, Edward O'Brien as Corry Kinchela, George F. De Vere as Father Dolan, Pearl Eytinge as Claire, Annie Edmondson as Arte O'Neale, Mrs. E. L. Davenport as Mrs. O'Kelly, and Alice Hastings as Moya. And then the beautiful Mary Anderson for the first time played at the Park, presenting a repertoire that Ellen Tree or Fanny Kemble might, with one exception, have offered forty years earlier — Evadne (March 15th), Ingomar (16th, and at a matinée benefit, 17th, for the Herald Irish Relief Fund), The Hunchback (17th), Romeo and Juliet (18th), Meg Merrilies (19th), The Lady of Lyons (matinée, 20th), and Love (evening, 20th). With Miss

[171]

Anderson were Milnes Levick and Atkins Lawrence. She was succeeded (March 22nd–27th) by the Mahn Comic Opera Company, from the Fifth Avenue Theatre, in the new raging hit, Fatinitza, with Jeannie Winston (whose rise to stellar rank had been phenomenally rapid), with Alice Hosmer, Hattie Richardson, Vincent Hogan, W. A. Morgan, Adolph Franosch, A. H. Bell and Fred Dixon. After a week of that melodious work, Wives returned (March 29th–April 3rd), the company showing changes in a personnel now including George Edeson, J. Southerland, J. Z. Little, J. Leslie Gossin, George Gaston (replacing Otis Skinner), W. Davidge, Jr., George Jordan, Joseph T. Leonard, and Misses Eytinge, Edmondson, and Adelaide Detchon. Emmet (April 5th–10th) again gave Fritz in Ireland, and, for the Wednesday matinée, (7th), the great Wallack company repeated Old Heads and Young Hearts. The next week fell to John T. Raymond, in Wolfert's Roost, with Affie Weaver as Katrina, and George Holland as Baltus (April 12th, 13th, and 14th), and in Colonel Sellers (15th, 16th, 17th). Solon Shingle, Lord Dundreary, Rip Van Winkle, Bardwell Slote, Colonel Sellers, Davy Crockett — how big a part they play in American theatrical annals of the years we are now traversing!

Lawrence Barrett began the last lap of the season in his usual repertoire, with one important addition — Yorick's Love — which formed the bill on April 19th, 20th, 21st and 22nd, and for the matinée, on the 24th; his David Garrick filled the matinée bill, on the 21st; on the 23rd, he gave Richelieu, and, on the evening of the 24th, Shylock and David Garrick. With him were Ellen Cummens (sic), F. C. Mosley, Fred Bock, J. R. Grismer and Gustavus Levick. The Colville Opera Burlesque Company held the next week, with The Magic Slipper (April 26th and 27th, and afternoon of the 28th); Ill-Treated Il Trovatore (28th and 29th); Oxygen, and Ill-Treated Il Trovatore (Act I) for the benefit of Eme Roseau on the 30th, and for evening performance on May 1st. For the afternoon of the 1st we were moved by all of Ill-Treated Il Trovatore, and only that. The company included Eme Roseau, Kate Everleigh, Roland Reed, Ella Chapman, R. E. Graham, A. W. Maflin, Carrie McHenry, Ed Chapman, Rose Leighton, William Forrester, Annie Deacon, H. Amberg, J. W. Rosenquest, and Emma Carson, nearly every one of whom has now (1939) a small niche in the hall of fame. Sinn, perhaps wisely, let his season die in mirth. Tony Pastor's travelling company came in for the week of May 3rd–8th, with Tony himself, the Kernells, Bryant and Hoey, the Four Eccentrics, the St. Felix Sisters, Lina Tettenborn, Fannie Beane and Charles Gilday, the French Twins, the three Rankins, Charles Diamond, Bonnie Runnells, and Frank Girard — excel it who could! I wonder if we shall ever revive such care-free shows.

We are used to the idea of Brooklyn as a trying-out place for new plays, and are therefore not surprised to find (May 10th–15th) J. W. Shannon, "late of Wallack's," testing at the Park a play by himself and George R. Edeson, and exploiting the title of A Golden Game:

Max Strauss	J. W. Shannon	Chevalier Carnioli	Walter Kelly
Bob Sampson	G. R. Edeson	Baron Mobetski	Otis A. Skinner
John Larkspur	G. F. De Vere	Adelaide	Annie Boudinot
Oliver Thorndyke	G. C. Jordan	Mrs. Strauss	Mrs. Fred Williams
Old Peck	Walter Bronson	Clara Strauss	Estelle Mortimer
Cyril Brinkworth	Archie Cowper	Suzanne	Wilda Forrest

This the advertisement declared to be "the most complete cast the work has yet received," but it did not carry A Golden Game to longevity in the theatre. Augustin Daly contributed, for the week of May 17th–22nd, a success of his recent New York season — An Arabian Night — with Maggie Harrold as the circus girl, originally played by Catherine Lewis, and with, in other parts, Ada Rehan, John Drew, Harry Lacy, George Parkes, William Davidge, Jr. (sic), Georgine Flagg, Mrs. Charles Poole and Blanche Weaver. Another contingent of the Daly force, headed by Catherine Lewis, was, during that same week, playing The Royal Middy, at Haverly's new Brooklyn Theatre. Harrigan and Hart were at the Park, during the week of May 24th–29th, in The Mulligan Guards' Surprise, bringing with them John Wild, Billy Grey, Goss and Fox, Annie and Emily Yeamans, and Jennie Morgan. The next week (May 31st–June 5th) presented Milton Nobles for three days in The Phœnix, with E. L. Mortimer, M. B. Curtis (as Moses Solomons), Fannie Lewis Burt, Josie Langley, &c. On the 3rd, 4th and 5th of June, the offering was A Man of the People. This brought to a close what for the greater part of its course had been a very brilliant season at the Park.

HAVERLY'S BROOKLYN THEATRE, 1879–1880

During this season Colonel Sinn had encountered serious opposition. J. H. Haverly, who, as we know, was attempting to establish a chain of theatres in our neighbourhood, built a new house on the site of the calamitously destroyed Brooklyn Theatre — I must say this seems a bit gruesome — and opened it, after delays usual in such cases, on October 6, 1879. He tried to make of this a festal occasion, and expended all his resources to accomplish that end. Clara Morris, who had not acted in Brooklyn for over a year, was the first star, and, to add importance to the opening, she was to appear in a new play. Miss Morris, furthermore, was to deliver a dedicatory address by George Jessup; but, after the orchestra had played Bach's Inaugural Overture, and a male quartette had sung The Star-Spangled Banner, not Miss Morris, but Charles Wheatleigh read the Jessup lines. Audiences were always indulgent toward the ill, nervous Miss Morris, and patiently waited for her advent in the new play of the evening. This was another version of the Jane Shore story, entitled The Royal Favourite, with

[173]

Don Piatt as author; and it was most elaborately mounted (costumes and scenery) with this cast:

Gloster	Samuel Piercy	Sir Mortimer de Greville	B. T. Ringgold
John Shore	Charles Wheatleigh	Witthold	Charles McManus
Edward IV	George Metkiff	Queen Elizabeth	Lillian Cleves Clark
Cardinal St. John	Edwin Varrey	Lady Alice	Little Miss Croly
Lord de Greville	George Jordan	Jane Shore	Clara Morris

As we know, Genevieve Ward and Ada Cavendish had both acted recently in W. G. Wills's version of Jane Shore, but in good sooth Nicholas Rowe's famous old play on the subject of the errant Shore has never been surpassed. In 1875, we remember, Clara Morris herself at Booth's Theatre had essayed the Rowe tragedy. The Don Piatt version was a failure, Miss Morris acting draggingly with occasional flashes of her accustomed fire. It ran at Haverly's for a week, and was not again exhibited in New York or Brooklyn. Miss Morris being unable or unwilling to play twice in one day, her company, on Saturday evening, October 11th, gave Craiga Dhoul, with Piercy as Gerald, McManus as Dennis, and Lillian Cleves Clark as Rose. This was repeated on Monday, the 13th, and, on October 14th, 15th and 16th, Clara Morris again appeared as Constance, in Conscience, with Piercy as Eustace Lawton, Varrey as Dr. Mordaunt, Ringgold as the lover and victim, Wheatleigh as Judge Van Cort, Miss Lamierre as Tabitha, and McManus as the Irish servant. Camille, on the 17th, and on the afternoon of the 18th, allowed Miss Morris to appear in one of her strongest rôles, with Joseph Wheelock (specially engaged) as Armand.

It was a clever stroke to engage for the opening so great a Brooklyn favourite as Miss Morris, but somehow I receive the impression that matters were not running smoothly, not settling down comfortably for auditors. The second attraction of the new house (October 20th–25th) was The Mighty Dollar, with Mr. and Mrs. Florence in their famous rôles, assisted by the cast seen on September 29th, at the Grand Opera House, New York. Next in order (October 27th–November 1st) came O'Gorman's Church Choir Company (James H. Meade, manager), which had been at the Broadway Theatre, New York; it, of course, gave Pinafore:

Sir Joseph Porter	Louis de Lange	Josephine	Emma Henry
Captain Corcoran	A. N. Palmer	Buttercup	Miss A. V. Rutherford
Ralph	M. F. Donovan	Hebe	Miss E. Cameron
Dick Deadeye	G. T. R. Knorr	First Aunt	Mrs. S. Beatty
Bill Bobstay	J. J. Knox		

I know the reader will wish to store the cabinet of memory with every cast of this classic work. Personally, I find more interest in Engaged, presented during the week of November 3rd–8th, by James Lewis, J. E. Whiting, W. F. Owen, William Cullington, T. G. Riggs, Agnes Booth, Rachel Sanger, Sydney Cowell, Mrs. G. H. Gilbert and Marie Chester—the original New York distribution intact, except for the substitution of Rachel Sanger for Minnie Palmer. Salsbury's Troubadours made fun (November 10th–15th) in The Brook; during the week of November 17th–22nd, The Galley Slave (seen the week previously at the Novelty Theatre) had a strong cast, including Maude Granger, Emily Rigl, Helen Vincent, Frank Evans, J. J. Sullivan, and C. A. McManus. On November 24th, The Tourists in a Pullman Palace Car began a week of fun, with W. A. Mestayer, W. H. Bray, Ethel Lynton, Rosa Cooke, &c. The week of December 1st–6th brought J. N. Gotthold's company in The Octoroon, with the cast seen in late November at Haverly's Fourteenth Street Theatre. In fact the transition of attractions between Haverly's two theatres is marked.

It is apparent that Haverly was offering no such array of stars as those now making brilliant the stage of Sinn's theatre. But of great interest was the offering for the week of December 8th–13th, no less a thing than the first production in our vicinity of Steele MacKaye's play, An Iron Will, the earlier version of his Hazel Kirke, which, in January, 1880, was to establish a record for runs at the new Madison Square Theatre, New York. The cast in Brooklyn was almost identical (except for Ringgold) with that later seen in New York:

Dunstan Kirke	C. W. Couldock	Hazel Kirke	Effie Ellsler
Aaron Rodney	Frank Weston	Mercy Kirke	Blanche Galton
Arthur Carringford	B. T. Ringgold	Marie Marteau	Gabrielle du Sauld
Pittacus Green	Thomas Whiffen	Lady Travers	Cecile Rush
Barney O'Flynn	Edward Coleman	Clara	Annie Ellsler

The reader notes the absence in the *dramatis personæ* of Met Miggins, a character which Percy MacKaye says his father wrote in for Joseph Frankau; and Dolly Dutton, afterward so delightfully played by Sydney Cowell, is here a French niece of the miller, named Marie Marteau, doubtless to fit the foreign accent of Gabrielle du Sauld. Despite that accent, the character, when the Madison Square Theatre opened in January, had been transmuted into the English lassie, Dolly Dutton. And I, for one, am charmed to make the acquaintance of Effie Ellsler, talented daughter of John A. Ellsler, an actress whose lovely voice and sweet face lent distinction to several "talking" pictures in the early '30s of this century!

The Eagle of December 9th dwells on the lack of originality in the strong scenes of the play, especially the resemblance of the passage between Lady Carringford and Hazel to that between Duval, *père*, and Camille. And the "difficulty of sustaining interest in a drama increases with every borrowed factor." But the dialogue is "uniformly good"; "the scenes are telling and above all the characters are mainly well conceived and outlined." Of course Dunstan Kirke suggests Tennyson's Farmer Allen, and Squire Rodney has a touch of Ham Peggotty. The big scene at the end of Act III, with the

[175]

now blind miller unable to save the daughter he had driven from his home, gave Couldock a great opportunity. "Miss Ellsler . . . is a charming little actress. Bright, *petite*, full of animation, with a most sympathetic face, large bright eyes and a soft, silvery voice. . . . That she possesses dramatic ability and intuition she showed in her love scenes . . . in the silent scene at the window and the unspoken eloquence of her acting in the presence of the blind old miller."

This assuredly is engrossing; and to think that Brooklyn saw Hazel Kirke before we across the river knew of its existence! The next week (December 15th–20th) brought the Grau French opera troupe (Paola Marié, Angèle, Capoul, Leroux-Bouvard, Juteau, Jouard, Duplan and Vilano) in an expected repertoire — La Fille de Mme. Angot (15th, and matinée, 20th), La Périchole (16th with Mlle. Gregoire substituting for Paola Marié, very hoarse), Les Cloches de Corneville (matinée, 17th), Mignon (evening, 17th, with Paola Marié, Leroux-Bouvard, Angèle, Capoul), Giroflé-Girofla (18th), La Camargo (19th), and La Grande Duchesse (evening, 20th). Oh, those blessed, un-Europeanised '70s, thus vicariously sipping the cup of Parisian gaieties! The Parisian group gave way (December 22nd–27th) to something supposedly Wild-Western — Aldrich and Parsloe, in My Partner, with Henry Crisp as Ned Singleton, Frank Mordaunt as Major Henry Clay Britt, A. D. Billings as Matthew Brandon, J. W. Hague as Josiah Scraggs, Walter Lennox, Jr. as Sam Bowler, May Ulmer as Mary, Laura Thorpe (at last grown up) as Grace, and Josephine Laurens as Posie Pentland. Neil Burgess also was very native, during the week of December 29th–January 3rd, in Widow Bedott, assisted by George and Annie Stoddart (his relatives-in-law), Harry Rich, Effie St. John, and Charles S. Dickson — this last-named a favourite light comedian of the '80s. Haverly's Mastodon Minstrels filled the week of January 5th–10th; Frank Mayo and Laura Don began, on the 12th, a week of Davy Crockett.

Rice's Evangeline (January 19th–24th) now presented Verona Jarbeau in the title-rôle, Louise Searle as Gabriel, Fortescue as Catherine, Dora Wiley as Hans Wagner, Rose Dana as Eulalie, Edwin S. Tarr as Basil, Richard Golden as Le Blanc, Harry Hunter as the Lone Fisherman, Charles Rosine as Captain Dietrich, and George Cohen (*sic*) and F. Turner as the Deserters. All the Rage (by William D. Eaton), "Chicago's great success," and seen the week before at the Novelty Theatre, came to Haverly's (January 26th–31st):

Dr. Goodwin	F. Hardenberg	Star 547	C. Moriarty
DeWitt C. Briggs	W. Davidge	Sophronia	Meta Bartlett
Horatio Braney	J. C. Padgett	Julia Briggs	Lizzie Kelsey
Charley Granger	Charles Harkinson	Cleopatra	Julia Coventry
Will Goodwin	Harry Taylor	Mrs. Goodwin	Mrs. Owen Marlowe
O. D. Clinton Briggs	Charles Dade	Annie Goodwin	Clara Hyatt

This play had a pleasing run, during the spring of 1881 at Daly's Theatre, New York. And, if Haverly's could not compete with the Park Theatre in stars, it was now providing interesting productions and amusing comedies. During the week of February 2nd–7th, the autumn success of the Union Square Theatre, French Flats, exhibited at Haverly's, with a company composed in considerable part of members of the home force not employed in the current attraction — The False Friend — in 14th Street:

M. Blondeau	W. J. LeMoyne	Anna Blondeau	Maud Harrison
M. Bonay	C. Wheatleigh	Baroness	Helen Tracy
Rifflardini	E. M. Holland	Mme. Bonay	Nellie Mortimer
De Barameda	M. V. Lingham	Bianca	Emma Grattan
Billardo	Edwin Morris	Manette	Roberta Norwood
Tancredi	W. H. Wilder	Mme. Blondeau	Lizzie McMahon
Old Martin	J. H. Burnett	Frozine	Courtney Barnes
Ernest Vallay	Walter Lennox		

Le Moyne, it is seen, was now assuming the rôle done at the Union Square by John Parselle, but Brooklyn's own Maud Harrison was still Anna Blondeau. What a charming actress she was!

Again Haverly's received a prize exhibited the week before at the Novelty, in Williamsburgh. Bartley Campbell's play of Fairfax had (February 9th–14th) nearly its original New York cast:

Fairfax	J. E. Whiting	Willie Wagstaff	F. E. Bond
Guy Gaylord	Frederic Robinson	Mrs. Marigold	Agnes Booth
James Marigold	L. F. Barrett	Diana	Sydney Cowell
Webster Wynne	James Peakes	Mrs. Dorsie	Mrs. G. H. Gilbert
Uncle Ben	Eugene Eberle		

Nellie Whiting and Little Effie Barrett were also in the cast. An Arabian Night, from Daly's Theatre, employed (February 16th–21st) John Drew, Harry Lacy (they were not needed in The Royal Middy, then so successful at Daly's), J. F. Brien, George Parkes, Ed Wilks, Annie Wakeman (as Mrs. Louise Sprinkle), Margaret Lanner (as Kate Sprinkle), Mrs. Poole, Mabel Jordan (as Rosa Maybloom), Mrs. Blythe (as Mrs. Portley) and Miss Georgine (Flagg?) as Susan. For the Mayor's Committee on Relief in Ireland, the Philadelphia Chestnut Street actors were to come on to act The Wife, with J. M. Hardie, Harry Lee, George Hoey, and Katherine Rogers. I found no record of their having done so.

This interesting series of weeks garnered into the past, February ended (23rd–28th) with Tony Denier's Humpty Dumpty, presenting George H. Adams (Grimaldi). Herrmann, Mlle. Addie, and "those elfin sprites," the Lorellas, started March on its way (week of 1st–6th). Then, on the 8th, that Collier Combination which, in September, began the season at the Park Theatre, came to Haverly's in the same play, The Banker's Daughter, still featuring Louis James, Marie Wainwright and Mr. and Mrs. Charles Walcot. Lizzie Hudson, whom I saw later as Lillian, played the maid,

[177]

Lizette; as Lizzie Hudson Collier she won a good place in our later annals. J. W. Collier, having met with an accident, resigned his part (Carojac) to George Farren. The Tourists in a Pullman Palace Car returned for the week of March 15th–20th. And a similar bit of frivolity succeeded (March 22nd–27th) — J. J. McNally and Dexter Smith's Company, in Revels, employing a big, merry band, including Alice Atherton, Lena (*sic*) Merville, Henry E. Dixey (at last free from the legs of the heifer, in Evangeline), Florence Baker, Marion Elmore, Dora Wiley, George W. Howard, Willie Edouin, Louis Harrison, Donald Harold, David P. Steele, Carrie Perkins, Marion Singer, Emma Burgess, Jennie and Jessie Calef, Pauline Hall, &c. That aggregation, at 1930 salaries, would be prohibitive for any manager; nearly every person in the list made a place for himself or herself in comic opera or extravaganza. On the evening of the 26th, and the afternoon of the 27th, the company shifted to Babes in the Wood and Robinson Crusoe; on the evening of the 27th, they gave Prince Achmet. On March 29th, John A. Stevens began a week, in Unknown, assisted by W. H. Bailey, W. H. Southard, Ralph Delmore, George R. Sprague, George F. Ketchum, Lottie Church, and Angie Griffiths. Decidedly Sinn had won the battle of the stars.

Salsbury's Troubadours again brought The Brook, for the week of April 5th–10th; and now came a star of renown in Fanny Davenport, seen earlier in the season at the Park. Her repertoire included Leah (April 12th, 13th, and matinée, 17th), Divorce (matinée, 14th), Cymbeline (14th, evening, and 15th), As You Like It (16th), and the double bill of London Assurance and Oliver Twist (evening, 17th); in her support were Price, Emma Pierce and George F. De Vere. Denman Thompson followed (April 19th–24th) in his unvarying Joshua Whitcomb. Lotta appeared, on April 26th, for a week of The Little Detective, her company still including P. Augustus Anderson, Clement Bainbridge, Ed Marble, Mrs. G. C. Boniface, Julia Hanchett and Lulu Jordan; for the Wednesday matinée (28th), this company, without the star, gave Checkmate, and Father and Son, or, Naval Engagements. For her second week Lotta revived her old favourites — Zip (May 3rd, 4th, 5th, and matinée, 8th), and Musette (6th, 7th, and evening, 8th). The company on the afternoon of the 5th acted Toddlekins and Aurora Floyd. I wonder how many attended such matinées, when the visiting star did not appear? Annie Pixley, an actress of Lotta's class, followed (week of May 10th–15th) in her inevitable M'liss, J. E. McDonough still playing Yuba Bill. It is interesting to note that as Sinn's stars became less scintillant (no pun intended!), Haverly's advanced in brilliancy. On May 17th, however, stars were omitted, and Augustin Daly's company gave The Royal Middy, with Catherine Lewis, May Fielding, Alonzo Hatch, John E. Brand, John Hart, Charles Fisher, Sara Lascelles, Georgine Flagg, Emma Hinckley, Sallie Williams, Isabelle Evesson, &c. It will be remembered that, in this same week, another Daly company, with John Drew and

[178]

Ada Rehan, was giving An Arabian Night, at Sinn's Park Theatre. The San Francisco Minstrels came, for the week of May 24th–29th, to Haverly's, with a force including Birch, Wambold, Backus, Edwin French, Add Ryman, Johnson, Powers, Gibbons, and George Thatcher (with the song Grandpapa's Pants); Beadle's Pirates for Ten Cents was in the show.

J. B. Polk brought (May 31st–June 5th) A Gentleman from Nevada, "written especially for him," by George H. Jessup, but not successful in Brooklyn or in New York; in it, Polk played Christopher Columbus Gall (a name possibly suggested by George Washington Phipps, Polk's hit, in The Banker's Daughter), W. F. Edwards was Alfred, Fourth Earl of Egerton, Frank Losee was John Castle, and L. A. Eastman Captain Vereker. Others were Frank Willard as Ah Tye (one must have a Chinese in plays of that time), Emma Pierce (who flitted from star to star) as Lady Alice Lester, Minnie Monk as Countess of Egerton, and Carrie Vinton as Lady Edith Lester. W. C. Mitchell's Pleasure Party, during the week of June 7th–12th, presented their unexpected success, Our Goblins, with Augustus J. Bruno, Amy Gordon, Francis Wilson (his first appearance in a play in our neighbourhood), Elinor Deering, William Gill, and Clark Sidman (musical director). This sort of entertainment, as we know, was a passion of play-goers at that time — a novelty that drove the "legitimate" farther and farther afield. Next week (June 14th–19th) Our Goblins showed at Haverly's New York. Another of the new breed followed (June 14th–19th) at the Brooklyn Haverly's, with Angie Schott (late "Variety" star), in Trifles, her support including Jessie Greville, Sydney Smith, Andrew Waldron, Charles Wilson, and Master A. Janes, who played the Monkey.

I have no doubt the reader wishes that Haverly's would close for the season. Well, the end is near. Annie Ward Tiffany, during the week of June 21st–26th, gave The Child Stealer, her associates including Amy Lee and William Leake; in the course of the action appeared Charles S. Rogers and Mattie Vickers, with other specialists. A new play by Frederick Percy, glorying in the title of Carrick a Rede (Irish, I suspect) filled the week of June 28th–July 3rd, with George C. Davenport, Sam Ryan, A. H. Hastings, David M. Murray, Sol Smith, Harry Sinclair, Sedley Brown, Effie Johns, Mrs. Sol Smith, Miss Newcomb, Laura Phillips, and Annie Deland. Haverly's Minstrels, on point of sailing for Europe, appeared at the new theatre of their manager on Monday and Tuesday, July 5th and 6th, with a matinée on the 5th. And that parting was the last thing at Haverly's till the season of 1880–81 edged its way into the chronicle.

ACADEMY OF MUSIC, BROOKLYN, 1879–1880

It is rather strange to find Brooklyn's once so sacred temple of music opening profanely, so to speak, on Monday, September 22nd, for a week's visit of Rice's Surprise Party, in Horrors, the jolly entertainers including Alice Atherton, Marion Singer, Lina (*sic*) Merville, Marion Elmore, Florence Baker, Pauline Hall, Nellie Beaumont, Emma Burgess, Jennie and Jessie Calef, Rose Wilson, Carrie Perkins, Willie Edouin, Louis Harrison, Henry E. Dixey and George W. Howard, most of whom we saw later in the season at Haverly's Theatre. More in line with the traditions of the house was the appearance, on October 2nd, of Carlotta Patti and her company, including Henry Ketten (pianist), Ernst De Munck ("the king solo violoncellist"), L. A. Phelps (tenor), Ciampi-Cellaj (baritone), and Marzo (accompanist); the famous soprano sang Eckert's Echo Song and an aria from The Sicilian Vespers, as well as in a duet (with Ciampi-Cellaj) from Don Pasquale. Redpath's Elysian Nights (James Redpath, manager) began, on October 6th, a series of Monday showings. The Strakosch Italian Opera Company came for three performances: on October 10th it gave Faust, with Mlle. La Blanche (Blanche Davenport), Miss Lancaster, Lazzarini (Faust), Gottschalk (Valentine), and Castelmary (new, as Mephisto). I learn from the Eagle, next day, that Miss Davenport was ill, and unable to do herself justice, and that Castelmary's Mephisto was "the best ever heard in this country, except Faure's." On the afternoon of the 11th, Lucia enlisted Marie Litta, Baldanza and Gottschalk; in the evening of the same day Teresina Singer was Aïda, with Anna de Belocca as Amneris, Petrovich as Radames, Storti as Amonasro, Castelmary as Ramfis, and Lafontaine as the King. According to the Eagle, the houses were very small. On October 16th, the Royal Arcanum concert presented Henrietta Beebe, Louise Finch, the English Glee Club (Ellard, Baird, G. E. Aiken), H. E. H. Benedict, Alessandro Liberati, G. W. Morgan, W. M. Jelliffe, John Oakey, and Conterno — certainly generous measure.

A concert complimentary to David Taylor gave us, on October 22nd, Annie Louise Cary ("the nation's favorite"), Gertrude Franklin (first appearance in Brooklyn), Diaz Albertini (Cuban violinist), S. B. Mills, and the Temple Quartette of Boston. Six hundred "ladies and gentlemen" took part in the tableaux appertaining to The Great Republic, all on the evenings of October 23rd, 24th, and 25th. Joseffy and Giuditta Galassi were here on the 28th. Mapleson announced for October 30th the appearance of Emilie Ambre in La Traviata, but, by practice not unusual with him, especially in Brooklyn, substituted Il Trovatore, with Mlle. Adini, Annie Louise Cary, Campanini and Galassi. On November 6th, Rigoletto had a cast including Adini, Mme. Lablache (Miss Cary did not sing), Aramburo and Galassi — certainly a feeble array, except for Galassi of the ringing baritone. What was called The Frog Opera introduced, on November 7th and 8th, W. S. Daboll, Mrs. J. K. Draper, Mrs. Cortada, Isabel Rockwell, and Messrs. Elliott, Ellard, C. H. Parsons, John G. Hill, Belcher, Duncan, Laurie and Hoffman. At Haverly's Theatre, this year, we met Francis Wilson, later

[180]

to be the incomparable Cadeaux, in Erminie; here, now, is his fellow in that famous pair of rogues, Ravennes — no less a person than W. S. Daboll. Lucia di Lammermoor, on November 11th, had an interesting heroine in Alwina Valleria and a poor hero in Aramburo. On the 19th, the Amaranths gave Love's Sacrifice, with John H. Bird and Ada Elmer as the sad Elmores, Sophie Osburn as Herminie, C. S. Withington as Paul, W. E. Wilson as Eugene, E. J. Wilkins as Morluc and Charles Bamburgh as St. Lo.

On November 20th, Campanini, Alwina Valleria, Behrens and Miss Cary appeared in Martha; Mrs. Howard, on the 22nd, gave two performances of Uncle Tom's Cabin, and Denman Thompson filled the entire week of November 24th–29th, with, I need hardly say, Joshua Whitcomb. I am attracted by the concert, on December 2nd, with Emma Thursby, Emily Winant, Florence Copleston (pianist), Maud Morgan and G. W. Colby. Miss Thursby sang the polacca from Mignon, and the finale of L'Étoile du Nord, and in a duet with Miss Winant from Mefistofele, all, I am sure, in impeccable style. December 9th found the Brooklyn Apollo Club (Dudley Buck conducting) in a concert including Buck's Saga of King Olaf, with, as soloists, Alwina Valleria, and Fred Harvey, tenor, of Holy Trinity Church. On the 10th, Magda Irschick and the Germania Theater actors from New York performed, for the German Ladies' Association, The Narratives of the Queen of Navarre. On the 11th, Campanini, Galassi, Behrens, Monti, Miss Cary and Emilie Ambre sang Aïda, the hit of the opera season in New York. Of course the reader will look elsewhere for my account of the Philharmonic Concerts of 1879–80. But he will be pleased to attend with me, on December 18th, a performance of Linda di Chamounix, with Valleria, Miss Cary, Campanini and Galassi. He might also be interested in the concerts of the English Glee Club, advertised for December 22nd, January 26th and February 23rd, at which the club (A. D. Woodruff, George Ellard, W. C. Baird and G. E. Aiken) would have the assistance of Henrietta Beebe, Anna Bulkley Hills and Caryl Florio. These functions occurred in the Academy Assembly Rooms. The fine Boston Ideal Opera Company were at the Academy for the week of December 22nd–27th, in the everlasting Pinafore, the list of brilliant singers including Adelaide Phillipps, Mary Beebe, Adelaide Detchon, M. W. Whitney, H. C. Barnabee, W. H. Fessenden, George Frothingham, and Gus Kammerlee, with Napier Lothian, of the Boston Theatre, directing. Joseffy, Letitia Fritsch and G. W. Colby were here on the 30th. On January 10, 1880, P. S. Gilmore's anthem, Columbia, which he took very seriously, brought together a chorus of several hundred, a band, and an orchestra. Abbie Carrington was soloist, and Mrs. J. H. Hackett recited the anthem, which Miss Carrington sang.

On January 14th, the D'Oyly Carte company, from the Fifth Avenue Theatre, came to the Academy, with The Pirates of Penzance; when they gave a second matinée, on the 22nd, Rosina Brandram substituted, as Ruth, for Alice Barnett, ill. We know that Miss Brandram, a few years later, created Katisha and other great contralto rôles of Gilbert and Sullivan, at their London Savoy Theatre. In New York she was merely one of the daughters in The Pirates. On January 21st came the forty-second annual ball of the Emerald Association. The Strakosch Italian Opera Company gave Mignon, on January 24th, with Mlle. La Blanche, Marie Litta, Berta Ricci (afterward a singer in comic opera), Lazzarini, L. G. Gottschalk, Lafontaine, and Ferrario, S. Behrens conducting. On the 31st, the Strakosch forces sang Carmen, with Anna de Belocca (soon to join Mapleson), Miss Lancaster, Ida Valerga (also later with Mapleson), Mlle Arcone, Baldanza, Storti, Papini, Barberis, Lafontaine. The masquerade ball of the Brooklyn Sängerbund possessed the Academy on February 2nd; on the 5th, the Charity Ball. On the 6th, Gatling Battery N had a review, drill and reception. And, in late January (28th), the Amaranth Society acted The Ladies' Battle, with J. H. Bird, A. de Cordova, Mrs. Grace Clark and Virginia Brooks. Henry Ward Beecher lectured, on February 12th, on Amusements, the Amaranth Society, on the 18th, trying to illustrate that theme with a performance of The Hunchback, in which William Luske appeared as Master Walter, Charles Bamburgh as Clifford, E. J. Wilkins as Tinsel, W. W. Lambert as Wilford, Lillian McDonald as Julia, and Virginia Brooks as Helen. The Athenian (or Athenean) Society followed, the next night, with Led Astray, acted by H. M. Ferris (Rudolphe), Deane W. Pratt (Hector), R. C. Hilliard (de Lesparre), Alice Chapin as Armande, Ida Waller as Mathilde, &c. For the widow and children of William Baldwin of the Brooklyn Fire Department, Frank Mayo and Laura Don, on the 20th, acted Camille. On the 21st, the Strakosch singers hopefully gave William Tell, with Marie Litta, Miss Lancaster, Mlle. Ricci, Petrovich, Storti and Castelmary, and, on the 23rd, the Boston Ideals began another week of Pinafore.

E. C. Phelps's "historic" symphony, The Emancipation, was given, on March 2nd, in conjunction with Mendelssohn's Athalie, the participants being Henrietta Beebe, Miss S. L. Tooker, Emma Wilkinson, James L. Farley, a chorus of 150, and E. C. Phelps and E. J. Fitzhugh (conductors). Much preliminary puffing had inflated the Emancipation prospect. When the Mapleson company re-appeared, it was under the management of J. H. Haverly, a rather intriguing contract. On March 4th, La Sonnambula introduced Marie Marimon, with Brignoli, Del Puente, and Mme. Lablache. The Fifth Avenue company filled the week of March 8th–13th, in The Pirates of Penzance, except on the evening of the 11th, when the Mapleson artists again gave Aïda with the cast seen earlier in the season. The critic of the Eagle is invariably iconoclastic. On March 9th, he says that, in the Pirates, Pfau succeeds Talbot as Frederic; he speaks and acts better than Talbot, "but his appearance is unromantic and his singing is bad."

"Miss Roosevelt also remains as *Mabel,* much to the surprise of everybody, since, while she is extremely pretty and graceful, her articulation is so bad that her words are inaudible, her voice is weak and piping, and she sings usually out of tune. Miss Jessie Bond, who plays the part of *Kate,* is far better fitted to be the *prima* of the company than the present charming incumbent."

March 18th brought a performance of Dinorah, with Galassi, Runcio, Behrens, Miss Cary, Mlle. Robiati, and Marie Marimon, and, on the 25th, Carmen had a cast including Belocca, recruited from the Strakosch forces, Alwina Valleria, Runcio (substituting for Campanini, originally promised) and Del Puente. The week of March 29th–April 3rd transported from Booth's Theatre the Abbey-Hickey Dumpty Dumpty, with Mlle. Barretta, Levantine, Valjean (juggler), Bonfanti and Menzelli (*sic*), along with the much-vaunted Spanish Students. On April 5th, Ole Bull, Anna Granger Dow, Marguerite Selvi (alto), Teresa Carreño, Agramonte, and the Temple Quartette of Boston, united in musical profusion; on the 6th, came Joseffy, with an orchestra conducted by C. Carlberg, giving a Chopin-Liszt programme. The reviewer in the Eagle says that he first heard Ole Bull in London forty-four years before; no one else has his control over the feelings of an audience. Paola Marié came back, on April 8th, as La Belle Hélène, with Mlle. Angèle as Orestes; at a matinée, on the 10th, these two, with Capoul and Mlle. Leroux-Bouvard, repeated Mignon, and, on the evening of the 10th, Paola Marié appeared as Le Petit Duc. On the intervening 9th, the Mapleson company gave an extra, a "gala" performance of Les Huguenots, with Campanini, Del Puente, Galassi, Monti, Behrens, Mlle. Marimon, Miss Cary, and Emilie Ambre. Strange to say, especially strange for Brooklyn, the performance went through, with all those stars, exactly as announced; perhaps Haverly had been a corrective influence on the temperamental singers. Amaranth and other amateurs, on the afternoon of April 17th, gave Pygmalion and Galatea (with William Luske and Mattie Balch in the title-rôles) and in the evening The School for Scandal (with Luske as Sir Oliver, J. H. Bird as Sir Peter, and Miss Osborne as Lady Teazle); this display was a testimonial to Bamburgh, high in amateurdom. On the 20th, back came Ole Bull, this time with Miss Thursby, Miss Winant, Brignoli, Ferranti, Mme. Chatterton-Bohrer, Anna Bock, Fischer (cello), and Maurice Strakosch (conductor). Then Henry E. Abbey announced ten performances of Edwin Booth, with Mrs. D. P. Bowers and McCollom in casts that allowed them to appear. These three began (April 30th) in Macbeth; on May 1st (matinée), Booth was Iago, Mrs. Bowers Emilia and McCollom Othello. In the evening of that day, Booth was Richard III, Mrs. Bowers Queen Margaret, and McCollom Richmond. In Hamlet, on May 3rd, Ellen Cummens (*sic*) was Ophelia, McCollom the Ghost, and C. G. Craig the King. The week went by with

Richelieu (4th), The Fool's Revenge (5th), Macbeth (6th), Othello (7th, with Booth as Othello), Hamlet (matinée, 8th), and (evening of the 8th), The Merchant of Venice and The Taming of the Shrew.

I go back to May 4th, when, in the Assembly Rooms of the Academy, Miss Tooker, Agnes Lasar, and Messrs. Dennison, Bray, Cameron and Yates gave the first act of Martha, and Emma Wilkinson, Mrs. E. Sproul (pianist) and E. J. Fitzhugh (conductor) appeared in concert. The entire week of May 10th–15 saw the Academy once more housing the Fifth Avenue Company, in The Pirates of Penzance, with Alfred Cellier directing a cast including Brocolini, Ryley, F. Clifton, Jessie Bond, Rosina Brandram and Alice Barnett in their original rôles. Sallie Reber was now the Mabel, and Wallace Macreery the Frederic, with J. E. Nash as Samuel, and Miss Barlow as Isabel. Anthony Reiff conducted. Mrs. Scott-Siddons and the Swedish Ladies Quartette co-operated on the 20th. In the Academy Assembly Rooms, on the same date, appeared Burbank, Mme. Lasar-Studwell, Ellard, Baird and John H. Brewer in a "Complimentary" to Agnes Lasar. On May 29th occurred the farewell matinée of Joseffy, and our farewell to the Academy, for 1879–80.

Court Square Theatre, 1879–1880

The Court Square (once Hooley's) re-opened, on August 4th, with "Mlle. Marie D'Est's Famous Burlesque Combination. Twenty-five beautiful and gifted lady artists. Youth, beauty, talent. An entertainment containing wit, merriment and elegance"; also a game of base ball "in which two nines of young ladies appear in uniform, presenting a pretty spectacular effect." If that would not draw the impressionable, what would? During the next week (August 11th–16th), "Variety" contributed Lou Sanford, Lizzie Parker, Captain Ebb ("the smallest negro comedian on the stage"), Annie Wood (serio-comic), Thomas and Watson, Lillie Lehmann, and Press Eldridge. I leave the reader to judge for himself of this feature of the bill — the original burlesque, The Nine Beauties, "in which will appear Mlle. Circe's Sylphs and Sirens." August 18th brought The Grand Dutch S., James Roome, Gussie Leach, &c. S. Robertson was set down as manager, on August 25th, when Ella Mayo and Kennedy and Clark were in the olio, and the drama, Justice for a Day, was featured. During the next week appeared Ione Lang, Cahill and Regan ("musical mokes, performers on nineteen different instruments"), Ella Mayo, Florence May (songs, jigs and reels), Geyer and Mackie (grotesque acrobatic comedians).

Failure pursued this once popular house. It closed for a time, to re-open on September 29th, under "entire new management," with Viola Clifton's Female Minstrels, and Henry J. Byron's extravaganza, The Female Forty Thieves. Adelina Gasparini appeared, during the week of October

6th–11th, in Hearts and Dollars, "a domestic drama."   Mlle. Lou Delmar's Parisian Follies and Megatherian Minstrels, with "fifty beautiful ladies, living art pictures, and Love in Turkey" let us, I believe, by sheer announcement, into the secret of their appeal; they were here during the week of October 13th–18th.   The next week (20th–25th) brought Mlle. Henri's Congress of Beauties and Tito Cellini's Great Ballet.   The week of November 3rd–8th reverted to "Variety," with Zuila and Loyal, Cool Burgess, Freeman Sisters, the Courtland Sisters, the Hennessey Brothers, Bernard McCreddie (*sic* — musical magician), Nat Livingston (clown), Frank Melrose (one-legged gymnast) and Young Barbadoes.   Sharpley and Clarke's Mississippi Serenaders filled the week of November 24th–29th, with the alluring slogan, "The Home of Minstrelsy Revived!"   But, alas! revived not for long.   On December 8th, Blanche Corelli's Superb Burlesque Company and Viola Clifton's New Mastodon Combination and Arnold Brothers' Troupe and a Female Pinafore made, so to speak, a doubtful "foursome." Viola Clifton played Ralph, and Blanche Corelli was Josephine, as she had been in reputable Broadway performances.

The week of December 15th–20th proffered Gypsy, or, Wolves and Waifs, with Woodruff's Sensational Dramatic Combination; next week (December 22nd–27th) appeared Tom Harper (one-legged dancer), Jessie Merton, May Arnott, Frank Livingston, Edward Banker, and the Woods.   Harry Wood's Variety and Comedy Company (December 29th–January 3rd) gave us Bothwick Reid (Scottish swordsman), Fayette Welch, Mabel Florence, Arthur Johnson, and the concluding A Trip to the Moon.   I found no more matter for this unhappy place till February 9th–14th, when Slavin's Original Uncle Tom's Cabin was there, with the Georgia Cabin Singers; and after that, nothing except for a benefit, on May 15th, to Dave Oakes, till June 17th, when the Eagle bears message that the place is open every night and Wednesday and Saturday afternoons.   Poor Hooley's!

OLYMPIC, BROOKLYN, 1879–1880

So early as July 14th, the Olympic re-opened for a summer season, under management of W. B. Freligh, late of the Bowery Theatre, and with N. S. Wood, in The Boy Detective.   The week of July 28th–August 2nd brought Sid C. France, of course in Marked for Life.   Prices ranged from 15 cents to 50 cents.   Fanny Herring appeared during the week of August 4th–9th. The fifth week of the summer season (August 11th–16th) gave a great Bowery combination — N. S. Wood, in Nan, The Newsboy, and Fanny Herring, in The French Spy.   Wood, for his benefit, on the 15th, presented Nan and The Boy Detective.   John McMahon and James Owens, "champion wrestlers of America," were here (September 1st–6th), in Lost in London.   A benefit for Gus Hill was scheduled for the 5th, and, on the

6th, the bill included Lost in London, and La Tour de Nesle, a pretty exciting Saturday night. During the week of September 29th–October 4th, was played the "sensational" drama, Love and Labour, "founded on the railroad strike in Pittsburg," and calling for four hundred supernumeraries. The Eagle resurrects the place (for me, at least), on December 29th, with Señor Renrut and Mme. d'Omer (in feats of swordsmanship), Ward and Lynch, Artie Ardell, J. D. Roome, Archie Hughes, Matt Morgan's Historical Pictures, Frankie Lameraux, Lou Delmar, and the burlesque, Si Salem. For January 5th–10th, the list included Grimaldi Morris and Frankie Georgeson, Belle Winters, Harry Jacobs, Kittie Foster, and Lou Delmar. The Quaker City Serenaders, and a farce, Rapid Transit vs. Slow Coaches, emerged during the week of February 2nd–7th. On February 23rd, N. S. Wood began, in The Boy Detective, Mrs. W. G. Jones and Aberle's New York Combination also appearing, and the bill ending, for Brooklyn delight, with Did You ever Send Your Wife to New York? Advertisements for the Olympic are, in the Eagle, very scattering; on March 22nd–27th, however, the paper bore note of the Victoria Loftus Troupe of British Blondes, of the Richmond Sisters, Ida Morris, Dashway and Aubrey, Kate Montrose and John McVeigh. The next week (March 29th–April 3rd) proffered Fayette Welch's Minstrel Troupe, Zanfretta's Pantomime Company, and Andy Collum's Variety Troupe (the last with Ben Gilfoil, Alice Gleason, Harry Mack, George Kane, the Olympia Quartette, &c.). For April 5th–10th we had promise of Lillie Hall, Leonora Bradley, Vic Reynolds, John D. Germon, and the Novelty Four, with the extravaganza, Ixion. I "can no more" for the Olympic for 1879–80.

Hyde and Behman's, Brooklyn, 1879–1880

The Brooklyn Volks-Theatre, Hyde and Behman, managers and proprietors, re-opened on August 25, 1879, "rebuilt, refurnished and decorated in a superb manner," and advertising itself as a "Ladies' Theatre and Family Resort." It became the leading "Variety" theatre in Brooklyn, and tried to maintain a standard of respectability. The entertainers for the first week were Watson and Ellis, "Governor" Add Ryman, Billy Barry, Jennie Hughes, Little Mac, Delmay and Archer, the McDermott Sisters, Mullen and Magee, Jennie Satterlee, Fostelle, Curry and Hall, Ward and Wells, and A. C. Moreland, stage-manager — an unexceptionable list. Matinées fell every Tuesday and Thursday, and prices ranged from 15 cents to 50 cents.

The next few weeks presented an interesting procession of performers: Alice Bateman and Billy Noonan, Fred Huber and Kitty Allyne, Sparks Brothers, Watson and Ellis, Clara Moore, the Peasleys, Billy Barry, Mlle. Lea, Favor and Shields, Merritt Brothers, the American Four (Pettingill, Gale, Dailey and Daly), Jennie Morgan, the Milos, Tillie Antonio, Little

[186]

Mac, the Jeromes, Fields and Leslie, Jennie Satterlee (who remained for a long while), Moreland, Minnie Lee (serio-comic), McVickers (*sic*) and Saunders ("Irish"), Don Ferreyra (the man flute), Pettit and White ("Ethiopians"), Suydam Brothers, Wood and West, De Witt Cooke, Netta Keller, &c. Many of these remained but a week; others were temporary "fixtures."

The week of October 6th–11th put on, with their permission, Harrigan and Hart's new sketch, The In-Toe-Natural Walking Match; other features of the bill were provided by Mlle. Baretta (*sic*), Dashway and Monroe, the Daytons, Williams and Pickert, Le Clair Sisters, Frank Bell, Mullen and Morgan, W. T. Dwyer, and the abiding four — Little Mac, Moreland, Jennie Satterlee, and Billy Barry. On October 13th Hugh Fay returned, and Flat Boat Pinafore drifted into the bill. For the next fortnight the Eagle specifies no performers. On November 3rd–8th, however, we find the names of E. D. Gooding, Kelly and Ryan, May and Flora Irwin, Goldie and Steele and Sallie St. Clair, James Messenger, Hugh Fay, A. C. Moreland (his last week), Minnie Lee, Billy Barry, and Williams and Pickert. The group for November 17th–22nd included several notables — Bobby Newcomb, Sheridan and Alicia Jourdan, Hendricks and Lena, the Clipper Quartette, the Peasleys, Favor and Shields, Josephine Shanley, Wingfield (*sic*) and Gregory, Cooney and Ryan, Hugh Fay, Billy Barry, Dave Oaks (*sic*) and Gooding — in fact notables all. The afterpiece was Muldoon's Trip to Coney Island, featuring Hugh Fay. Next week (November 24th–29th) came Kitty O'Neil, the Kernells, Ella Mayo, Clara Moore, Add Weaver and Nellie Parker, certainly the cream of vaudeville. The Mulligan Guards *vs.* the Skidmores was a feature of December 1st–6th, as was Jennie Morgan. Emmerson, Clark and the Daly Brothers ("the four high-kickers"), George Reynolds and C. W. Cogill, John F. Sheridan and Alicia Jourdan, Minnie Lee, Levantine and Earle, Della Morgan, Hugh Fay and Billy Barry (these for December 8th–13th); Muldoon's Trip to Boston by Boat, with Hugh Fay as Muldoon, and Billy Barry as Bob Short (week of December 15th–20th); the second week of this skit, with an "olio" including Louise Montague, the Leotards, Turner and Collins, Florence Newman, Fanny Herring, Hugh Fay, Billy Barry (December 22nd–27th); and John F. Poole's new piece, Seeing the Sights, with Barry and Fay (December 29th–January 3rd) — lo! how easily December slips into icy January!

Muldoon's Picnic (with Barry and Fay), Delehanty and Hengler, Kelly and Ryan, the Richmond Sisters, the Peasleys, Ida Morris and the Union Quartette were the big features for January 5th–10th, Muldoon's Picnic continuing into the next week, and, indeed, starting Barry and Fay on a starring career in minor theatres. Muldoon's Picnic went to Boston for the week of January 19th–24th, and, in return, Boston sent to Hyde and Behman's its cherished company from its own Athenæum. Next week (Jan-

[187]

uary 26th–31st), Brooklyn welcomed back its own regulars, including Barry, Fay, Fanny Herring, Dave Oakes, Goldie, Steele and Sallie St. Clair, Minnie Lee, Sam Norman, and many others.   Another of the Muldoon series — The Chain Gang at Sheepshead Bay — was very local, during the week of February 2nd–7th; on the 16th came Charles Gilday and Fannie Beane, the Barlow Brothers, Clara Moore, Belle Clifton, Dave Reed, Thomas and Neary, and Muldoon's Flats (of course with Barry and Fay).   Evidently Muldoon was becoming as much of a creation as was Mulligan at Harrigan and Hart's.   For the week of February 23rd–28th, we had Seamon, Somers, and the Girard Brothers, constituting a quartette of "grotesque comiques," Clark and Edwards, Mlle. Baretta (sic), Kearney and Powers (the famous James T. Powers of the '80s), Barry, Fay, and Minnie Lee.

March 8th brought in Murray's Lilliputian Circus, Lucy Adams and Guy Linton, Charles Diamond, Kitty McDermott, Pell and Lewis, T. F. Grant (one-legged clog-dancer), the Martell Brothers, and, of course, re-tained Barry, Fay, and Minnie Lee; also we were treated to The Pirates of Sandy Hook.   Pat Rooney and Company (under direction of Harry Miner) held the week of March 15th–20th, with Jeppe and Fannie Delano, Georgie Kaine, Reynolds and Walling, Wood and Beasley, Lamont and Ducrow, Morris and Fields, Josie Granger and Billy Carter; for the 22nd–27th, March favoured us with John Hart, A. C. Moreland, Harry and John Kernell, the four St. Felix Sisters, the Fieldings (John and Maggie), Daisy Remington, Donaldson and McAdow, and the four Milton Jaspers — another interest-ing aggregation.   The next week (March 29th–April 3rd) proffered the American Students, Cool Burgess, Helen Courtland, the Leotards (acrobats), the Wilkinson Brothers (in an Irish sketch), Fred Hallen and Enid Hart (in Pinafore in Fifteen Minutes), Harry Bennett, Williams and Pickert, Add Weaver and Nellie Parker, Minnie Farrell, the Haleys, John Hart and A. C. Moreland.   Muldoon's Christening (April 5th–10th) restored to us Barry and Fay; in the "olio" were Kelly and Ryan, Jennie Satterlee, Dave Oakes, Lucy Adams and Guy Linton, and Minnie Lee.   New, during the week of April 12th–17th, were the African Students, the Philharmonic Quar-tette, Allie Drayton, the Murphys (Paddy and Ella) and the La Rosa Brothers; The In-Toe-Natural Walking Match was revived.

The Old Toll House began the bills for April 19th–24th, and the olio presented Seamon, Somers and the Girard Brothers, Charles T. Ellis and Clara Moore, Billy Barry, Lou Sanford, Press Eldridge, William T. Dwyer, Ella Chace, Fields and Leslie, Young Hercules, Jennie Satterlee, Cool White, Frank M. Wills, and Dave Oakes, and concluded with Bibbs vs. Bibbs. April 26th–May 1st had The Maloney Family in A Wagner Palace Sleep-ing Car (one sees the origin of that piece), the four Carrolls, Little Rosebud, the American Four, Mollie Williams, Billy Barry in the burlesque, The Queen and Her Babe, Jennie Christie, Cool White and Dave Oakes.   The

Eagle of May 7th announced that, on May 10th, Hyde and Behman's company would begin a fortnight's engagement at Tony Pastor's Theatre, with Muldoon's Picnic, Niles and Evans, Kitty O'Neil, Charles T. Ellis and Clara Moore, &c.   Meantime, May 10th–15th brought to the Volks Theatre J. Z. Little, in a play by the ever-ready J. J. McCloskey, entitled Nuggets, or, Lost and Won.   "Variety" returned in force, on May 24th, with Sam Devere, Kelly and Conlon, Charles Banks, George Reynolds (the "Zulu Chief"), Wood and West, Cool White, Kitty McDermott, Clara Fostelle, Hogan Brothers, the Werners, Friel and Rogers, Billy Carter, and A Night at Coney Island.   The regular company had gone a-touring.   For the week of May 31st–June 5th, Maude Forrester and her horse, Lightning, with O. B. Collins and an "Amazonian march of 40 beautiful ladies," gave Brooklyn a taste of Mazeppa.   On that fiery promise (and its fulfillment) the season of 1879–80 seems to have closed.

Mozart Garden (Brooklyn Opera House), 1879–1880

The Mozart Garden, on the old basis, was doomed.   For September 29, 1879, it offered a sparring match and an athletic exhibition tendered to Mike Donovan.   And that was the last I heard of it till, on November 10th, it opened as the Brooklyn Opera House (George F. McDonald, manager). Sheehan and Jones, Jennie and Maggie Benson, Bryant and Hoey, Crumley and De Forrest, Kate Castleton, Paddy and Ella Murphy, George F. McDonald and Hannah Birch were in the bill.   Next week (November 17th–22nd) came Georgie Kaine, Harry McAvoy and Emma Rogers, Emily Sylvester, Fayette Welch, &c.   For the week following (November 24th–29th) appeared the Brennans, Alfred Liston, Professor William Pillare (sic) and Mlle. Georgia (in a cannon act), the Dockstaders, Hannah Birch, Harry Clark (sic) and the sketch, Kitty and Her Baby.

I found no more for this enterprise till March 1st, when, as the Brooklyn Opera House, the place re-opened, with William C. Budlong as manager. He offered the French Family Davene, the grotesque Brazziers, also the Ladies of Mystery (the Prescott Sisters), Ella Mayo, Lester and Williams (eccentrics), Dilks and Wade ("musical coons"), Geyer and Mackie ("Sable Grimaldis"), the "refined" May Marshall, Minnie Chapin ("the Irish girl"), Addie Farwell, Frank Marson, Jennie Gary and J. F. Crossen.   Thereafter, for visits of greater or less duration, came Barney McNulty, the French Twins, Miss Joyce Martelle, Mlle. de Granville, Sharpley and West, the Boisset Family, the three Brazziers, Ella Mayo, the "Powers," George Richards, Shirley and Byrne, the Thompson Brothers, Dan Nash and Kate McCarthy, Murphy and Mack, Murphy and Shannon, the "Wonderful Nondescripts," Ada Stanwood, Sellou and Byrnes, Clark and Edwards, Georgie Lingard, J. F. Crossen, Maggie Burshall, Sylvester and Lester, the

[189]

American Four (Pettingill, Gale, Dailey and Hoey), Nellie St. John, the Jeromes, the Moore Sisters, Ward and Lynch, Master Roberts, Frank Marion, William Rouse and Fanny Denham — all these mind you, in March! The closing night of the season (April 12th) — the season must have failed — was devoted to a benefit for Harrison, Bell and Nolan. But E. D. Gooding advertised a benefit for April 17th.

GERMAN ACTIVITIES IN BROOKLYN, 1879–1880

The Germans advertised but little in the Staats-Zeitung in the season of 1879–80 for our sister city across the bay. The Brooklyn Sängerbund, on September 4th, had an Italian night, at the Club House, 198-200 Court Street, and, on November 11th, gave a concert and a ball and the operette, Hans Dampf. The Brooklyn Schützen Corps disported, on September 25th, at the West Brighton Beach Hotel. The Brooklyn Club-Haus (*sic*), on December 4th, advertised Mamsell Rosa, Die Kunst geliebt zu werden, and our old friend, Frau Schreiner-Kronfeld. At the Academy of Music, on December 10th, for the benefit of the Frauen-Verein, Magda Irschick, as we saw, acted Die Erzählungen der Königin von Navarra. The Abend-Unterhaltung of the Brooklyn Männerchor rang through Association Hall, 221-223 Washington Street, on the evening of December 14th; they gave H. Kipper's opera, Fidelia. Gothic Hall, on March 28th, opened for the ball and Stiftungsfest of the Independent Schützen-Compagnie. At 198-200 Court Street, on June 15th, the Brooklyn Sängerbund held its first Sommernachtsfest and concert; at the same place, on June 21st was the Sommernachtsfest of the Frauen-Verein. And the Sängerbund advertised its "first" again for the 22nd. July 26th, 27th, and 28th took the German Volksfest-Verein to the West Brighton Beach Hotel, for concerts by Conterno's Band, fireworks by Hatfield, &c.

BUNNELL'S DIME MUSEUM; AMERICAN DIME MUSEUM, 1879–1880

In spite of warnings of departure and incorporation in a Bowery museum, Bunnell's Dime Museum was again operative (now in Washington Street, opposite the Post Office) on November 17, 1879, when it advertised in the Eagle P. T. Barnum's Tattooed Man, a giantess, a bearded girl, a talking bird, a white Moor, Everett (prestidigitateur) and Whiston (humourist) — quite the list expected for that sort of place. Here, during the week of December 15th–20th was on view Miss Ethel Guy's Second Vision, set down as a "Weird Wonder." At the New Year, in addition to giants and midgets, Bunnell's advertised Fred Guy, magician, and a Man Fish and a Water Queen.

A rival institution, the American Dime Museum, at 424 Fulton Street, a branch of the American Dime Museum, 298 Bowery, was advertising, during the week of January 19th–24th, in the Eagle; there were gathered Hannah Battersby, "largest Woman in the World," Wild Men of Borneo, the Fan Child, &c.   Frederick and Ethel Guy were then at Bunnell's, in tricks of second sight.   During the week of February 23rd–28th, Bunnell's exhibited Commodore Nutt (his "first appearance in Brooklyn") and the Indiana Midget.   March 1st bears tidings, glad to many, that Bunnell's *only* Museum, 325 Washington Street, was exhibiting the Texas Giant Boy, Commodore Foote and Comical Brown.   Beginning on March 22nd, Tom Thumb and his company were at "Uffner's" Museum — the American Museum, in other words; also there were other abnormal specimens — Colonel Goshon, and Isaac W. Sprague, the living skeleton.   The "last two weeks" of Bunnell's Museum began on March 22nd; "positively" the "last week" was that of April 12th–17th.   And that was the last week, also, of Tom Thumb and his troupe at the rival museum.

Miscellany and Music, Brooklyn, 1879–1880

And what of miscellaneous entertainments, musical or otherwise, aside from Academy attractions?   During the week of September 8th–13th, the Young Apollo Club was again doing Pinafore, with Julia Thompson Corden — a name hauntingly like the Juliette Corden of the '80s — as Josephine. The week of September 15th–20th presented the Norcross Fifth Avenue Opera Company "on board a full rigged ship deck," in the same devastating opera, their scene of operations being the Brooklyn Rink.   On September 22nd began at the Athenæum (or Atheneum) J. C. Padgett, Belle Norton, Cora E. Daniels, Jedediah Bassett, with Frederick Intropodi (musical director), in Bric-a-Brac, and Love and Rain; Oscar M. Newell also played the piano.   September 25th showed the season getting under way: A. P. Burbank, on that evening, was at the Strong Place Baptist Church; J. Jay Villers talked, at the Washington Street M. E. Church, on Funny People We Meet, on that evening and on October 2nd.   And the Young Apollo Troupe returned (September 29th–October 4th) to the Athenæum for another week of Pinafore.   They remained for at least two months.   The New Orleans University Singers, on October 1st and 2nd, at the Johnson Street M. E. Church, gave a programme of Old Plantation Songs.   And on October 7th Burbank at the Tabernacle recited, from memory, Rip Van Winkle, more of a feat, methinks, than a blessing; he was at the Greene Avenue Presbyterian Church, on October 2nd, and at the Washington Avenue Baptist Church, on October 15th.   On the 16th, Avon C. Burnham was scheduled to read at the Simpson M. E. Church.

Forepaugh's Circus pitched tents, for the week of October 6th–11th, at the corner of Atlantic and Carlton Avenues, promising six acres of pavilions

[191]

and "three times the largest show in the world," with nine elephants at one time in the ring, with Robert Stickney and twenty male riders, twelve equestriennes "inspired" by Miss A. Carroll, and one hundred "peerless arenic stars." Lest we might suspect these boasts, the Eagle advertisements mentioned no other names of performers. On October 7th, at the Sands Street M. E. Church (how many Methodist churches were there in Brooklyn? one vainly asks), Allan Latham offered an evening of elocution, music and the stereopticon; on the 7th, also, Ashton's exhibition of wax figures (some automatic) opened at 325 Washington Street. On the 9th Villers was again at the Washington Street M. E. Church, this time talking on All for Fun. The Hanson Place Baptist Church, on the 13th, presented the Reverend J. A. Spurgeon — brother of the famous Spurgeon — in My Brother and His Work. Geraldine, "written by Ringgold McCay," gasped and nearly died, on October 16th, at Bedford Hall, under the auspices of the Everett Literary Association. And Ashton's Wax Works were exhibiting at 325 Washington Street. Meantime, the Young Apollo Club persisted at the Athenæum. For the week of October 20th–25th, they joined Pinafore with The Rose of Auvergne. Miss Corden and Bessie Louise King were alternating as Josephine, Macy was Deadeye, Drew Sir Joseph, Robitsek the Captain, Master Black Ralph, and Master Hanau the Boatswain. For October 27th–November 1st, they gave evening performances of The Bohemian Girl and Poor Pillicoddy (the latter with J. W. Macy), and confined their exertions in Pinafore merely to the matinées, on Wednesday and Saturday. Verily, in America, Pinafore was a gold mine to every one concerned, except — I blush for shame as I write — Gilbert and Sullivan. The fifteenth week of the Young Apollo Club exertions fell on November 17th–22nd. During the week of November 24th–29th, they combined The Bohemian Girl and Offenbach's Breaking the Spell, for evening delight, and repeated Pinafore at the matinées on the 27th (Thanksgiving) and 29th. This was, for the present, the last I heard of them. But what a success! and at the expense of the author and the composer!

I go back to November 10th, for a performance at the Athenæum of Sweethearts and Aunt Charlotte's Maid, carried through by the Gilbert Dramatic Association, with casts including Maud Evans, Adele Oakley, Delapierre, Harry Bishop, Julia Mines, Edith Knowles, T. C. Hammill and John W. Noble. A concert scheduled for the 16th at St. Stephen's Church, with Isidora Martinez, G. W. Morgan and E. A. Lefebre, was postponed, on account of the death of the sexton, to the 23rd; on the 19th, Henry Eyre Browne, organist of Plymouth Church, offered at that liberal institution a concert involving Werrenrath, Clara Stutsman, Annie Lockwood, Alberto Laurence, George Edelheim, Wilhelm Müller and G. W. Morgan. An Old Folks Concert, on the 18th, invaded the Simpson M. E. Church. At the Washington Avenue Baptist Church, on the 19th, were harmoniously assembled Mme. Lasar, Agnes Lasar, F. A. Guild, L. B. Dean (organist), Carl Richter (violinist) and Harvey C. Camp (conductor). The Auld Sisters graciously presented themselves on the 20th in the same sacred edifice. November 25th discovered Carrie Cristadoro, Mrs. S. Christianson (*sic*), Miss J. T. Losee (organist), F. Backus (tenor), R. Bragee (bass), Professor J. P. Silvernail (elocutionist) and H. E. H. Benedict joined in a concert to Fannie L. Jarvis, held at the Warren Street M. E. Church. During this same week the McEvoys were at Music Hall, for the benefit of St. Augustine's Church. And Mme. Anderson, "champion lady pedestrian of the world," was walking at Central Pedestrian Hall, doubtless to the applause of the idle. In the De Kalb Avenue Church on November 27th, the choir of three quartettes gave a glee and ballad concert; on that same evening (Thanksgiving), my reader may be retrospectively grateful for a reading by Charles Roberts, Jr., in the Fleet Street M. E. Church, and for the Lambert Family and Edith Watrous, in the First Baptist Church, Pierrepont Street. At this season Henry Ward Beecher was lecturing in Association Hall and elsewhere, Dr. Hebbard was doing the same thing at the Brooklyn Institute, and in the Art Association Rooms one might have heard those then acclaimed authorities, Richard A. Proctor and John Fiske.

On December 1st, the Scandinavian Singing Society of fifty male voices showed its skill, at Music Hall, with assistance from Minnie Spieker (soprano), Werrenrath (a Dane, as we know), C. Lanzer (violinist) and Albert Rudvall (pianist). On the same evening, an amateur Il Trovatore (the very worst kind of Trovatore, *me judice*) introduced at Bedford Hall E. C. M. Cronan, Henry Brandeis and Susie Tooker, whose very names seem to wilt before the ordeal. Nettie Taylor, elocutionist, on the 4th, was at Greene Avenue M. E. Church. Plymouth Church, on the afternoon of December 6th, proffered a programme including Clara Morris (who was to read), Isabel Stone (soprano), Nella F. Brown (dramatic reader), Alfred Cellier (at the organ), F. C. Harriot (humorous reader, and husband of Clara Morris), Del Puente, George W. Colby and A. H. Pease. The Eagle did not inform me as to whether all these celebrities appeared. On the same afternoon, at Music Hall, Bertrand Clover gave a piano recital. On December 8th and 9th, the University Singers of New Orleans, with their Plantation Songs, were at Plymouth Church. John B. Gough lectured, on the 9th, in the Lafayette Avenue Presbyterian Church. On the 10th, the Gilbert Dramatic Association acted, at the Atheneum, Palgrave Simpson's Time and the Hour; on the 11th, at Music Hall, H. S. Renton lectured on Thirty Minutes in a Volcano, Kilauea, Sandwich Islands, and H. W. Foote gave Thirty Minutes with American Humourists.

We may now become military, and attend, on December 11th, a "Grand Bouffe Militaire," held by the 13th Regiment at its Armoury, Flatbush Avenue and Hanson Place (music by Dodworth's Band); on the 13th, we might hear the band concert of the 23rd Regiment, at its Armoury, Clermont Avenue; and, thus attuned, we might, at the Athenæum, on the 18th, attend the entertainment of Company D, 23rd Regiment, providing Harry L. Sands (amateur prestidigitateur), with E. J. Dale (assistant), and also providing Rafael Navarro, J. L. Farley and the Eclectic Glee Club in its bill. A. P. Burbank, nearly ubiquitous in those days, held forth, on December 15th, at the Sands Street M. E. Church, with Henry H. Nast at the organ; on the 17th, he was at the South Congregational Church, Court and President Streets. And here, on the 16th, at Music Hall, was an attempt made to resuscitate Ringgold McCay's drama, Geraldine. Del Puente was announced to sing at morning mass and at vespers, on the 21st, in St. Peter's Church, Hicks and Warren Streets. On the 17th, a testimonial to Ernest Felix Potter supplied numbers by Carrie Cristadoro, Fred Steins and Liberati; on the 22nd, at the First Presbyterian Church, Henry Street, Henry Galt read from Dickens, and, on the same evening the Young Apollo Club returned, giving this time Pinafore and Breaking the Spell every evening and Thursday (Christmas) and Saturday matinées, in the larger spaces of the Music Hall; for their second week (December 29th–January 3rd), their bill comprised The Two Buzzards, Poor Pillicoddy, and Breaking the Spell. The New Orleans Jubilee Singers held sway, on the 24th, in Association Hall.

The Brooklyn Caledonian Club, on Christmas eve, gave a concert and hop, in their hall, 200 Clinton Street; on Christmas night, at the Tabernacle, Mapleson offered the Stabat Mater and a miscellaneous concert, with Mmes. Valleria, Cary and Ambre, and with Campanini, Galassi, Behrens and G. W. Morgan, at the organ. On Sunday, the 28th, at St. Stephen's Church, Mlle. Martinez, Mrs. Christianson (sic) and the choir carried through a special musical programme. Quite different in tone was the elocution of Mattie Balch, on the 30th, at the De Kalb Avenue Church, or W. Howard Doane's Christmas cantata, Santa Claus, by the Bedford Reformed Sabbath School, on the 30th, in the Bedford Avenue Church, or the Stag Athletic Racket, on New Year's Eve, of the 23rd Regiment; "no ladies admitted," and "the Gates Ajar at 7.30."

Thus we erase 1879 from the calendar, and with hope approach the new year. On January 5th, Lotti, "formerly of the German Opera Company," gave his "grand annual concert," at Music Hall, assisted by Louisa Marley and Sophia Maurer (his pupils), Fred Steins, Charles Schweneke and S. B. Mills. On the 8th, the Hutchinson Family, Alice L., Carrie W., O. D. (baritone) and Mrs. O. D. Hutchinson (accompanist), with T. S. Guise (bass), were at the De Kalb Avenue M. E. Church; and to show you that Hutchinsons cannot change their type of programme, from generation to generation, I will say that they sang The Voice of Spring, The Hunter's Song, The Fisherman's Wife, Nearer, My God, to Thee, Barbara Frietchie, Robin

Redbreast, Be Thou with Me, Nobody Knew de Trouble, Mrs. Lofty and I, Johnny, Don't Tickle the Baby, The Old Oaken Bucket, When 'tis Moonlight and The Old Granite State.   Some amateurs — the Athenean Society — on the 8th, played Alone, at Bedford Hall, Tompkins Avenue, promising Henry Dunbar for the 21st.   And at the Athenæum, every evening of the week of January 5th–10th, one might have seen experiments in Mesmerism by Professor Carpenter, who remained, except for January 13th, 14th and 30th, to the end of the month.   On the 16th, at Unity Chapel, Classon Avenue, De Cordova discoursed on The Pipley Family in Europe.   Simple talks for simple listeners!   At the Athenæum, on January 14th, Mary W. Barrows (pianist) and George Ellard appeared; in the evening of the 21st, Ida K. Hinds read at Music Hall, assisted by the English Glee Club (Ellard, Baird, &c.).   Better still was the benefit of Company G, 13th Regiment, on the 14th, at Plymouth Church, with Remenyi, Emma C. Thursby, Edith Abell, Isabella Palmer Fassett (contralto), Edmund de Celle (tenor), and Julian Heinze (pianist and conductor).   On January 15th, Laura D. Fair lectured, at Music Hall, on Chips from California; Burbank was funny at the De Kalb Avenue M. E. Church (he seemed to favour Methodist churches, or they him, or both); and, at the York Street M. E. Church, James L. Farley, Josephine T. Losee (piano) and A. D. Fohs (cornet) abstracted whatever joy they could from appearing before such as chose to hear them (I cannot state this more cautiously).   The James H. Perry Post, No. 89, G. A. R., came to Bedford Hall, on January 17th, presenting Little Florence Auld and Caste, with William H. Friday as Eccles, George E. Hogg as Sam, Andrew Chamberlain as D'Alroy, Kate Earle as Polly, and Mrs. Reynolds as Esther.   The 18th (Sunday evening) provided at St. Stephen's Church a sacred programme of music, with Isidora Martinez, Mrs. Christianson, C. G. Lockwood, and J. M. Loretz, Jr.   On January 20th, scholars of the Academy attached to St. Peter's Roman Catholic Church gave Pinafore, in St. Peter's Hall; on the 23rd, the fourteenth annual ball of the Caledonian Club made festive the City Assembly Rooms; and, on the 24th, the Twenty-third Regiment gave a "grand" promenade concert.   Of course skating prevailed at Capitoline Lake.   In late January McNevin's Panorama, introducing Dan Nash and Kate Cooper, was at the Wigwam, Classon and Putnam Avenues, and Dr. Hebbard, at Music Hall, was lecturing on problems of health, a kind of amusement for hypochondriacs.

Thus in various ways Brooklyn resisted the stinging blasts of winter. On January 27th, a concert to Emma Wilkinson, at the Lafayette Avenue Presbyterian Church, enlisted Charles Belfort (violin), Ch. Fritsch, Mary Louise Swift, and W. F. Mills.   And Burbank was funny, on the 31st, at Duryea Chapel, Clermont Avenue.   A private concert (if I may be pardoned the intrusion) offered at the Tompkins Avenue Church (February 2nd) the Bedford Vocal Society, W. A. M. Diller, Emma Howe, Emma Wilkinson and F. Steeb. On February 5th, Henry Ward Beecher lectured in the Brooklyn Rink, on The Reign of the Common People; on the same evening, the Clermont Vocal Society, which had given one concert to R. S. True, gave another, assembling for the purpose, in St. Matthew's English German Lutheran Church, True, J. P. Silvernail, Thomasine Dennithorne (a pleasing name), Mrs. Lillie Crane Nickolds, Nellie Nash, A. G. Nickolds, and Alice Waltz. The Eagle for February 2nd states that "Miss Edith Kingdon, of Downing Street, a dramatic pupil of Professor Philip Lawrence, will take the part of Grace Harkaway in 'London Assurance,' at the Atheneum, Thursday evening, February 5. It is said that Miss Kingdon gives promise of brilliant dramatic talent. The play will be produced by members of the Garrick and the Social Literary Society, under the auspices of Company C, Twenty-fourth Regiment." So this introduces to us the beautiful Edith Kingdon, later of Daly's Theatre. On the busy evening of February 5th, the Sunday School Room of the Church of the Messiah housed, in concert, Mme. Niemann-Dorini, Pasquale Dorini, Liberati and Master Mollenhauer ('cello). Il Jacobi, an opera by John M. Loretz, Jr., had trial at the Athenæum, on February 9th and 10th; on the 11th, at the Marcy Avenue Baptist Church, one might have found out what a Japanese Kettledrum should be. At the Athenæum, on the 13th, the Gilbert Dramatic Association played Black Sheep, founded on Edmund Yates's novel of the same name. The University Singers of New Orleans were, on February 11th, at the Franklin Avenue Presbyterian Church, and, on the 17th, at the Reformed Presbyterian Church, Duffield Street. University Jubilee Singers were at Plymouth Church, on the 16th; on the 18th, Mrs. E. J. Grant and Mrs. J. K. Draper appeared at the Strong Place Church. On Tuesday, February 17th, another Pinafore began in the Athenæum, this time by the Excelsior Miniature Opera Company, composed of "the best materials of Haverly's, the New York Juvenile Pinafore Companies, and the Young Apollo Club"; Emmett Drew as Aunt Penelope was "the only adult in the cast." They were here also on the 23rd and 24th. George Vandenhoff, sole survivor of the "palmy" days, read at the Washington Avenue Baptist Church (February 18th), with J. M. Loretz, Jr., assisting at the organ. And Burbank was at the First Baptist Church, Pierrepont Street, on the 19th, an evening which also heard, at the Rink, the Clermont Vocal Society, Levy, Alice Waltz, and Mattie Balch. On the 23rd the De Kalb Avenue M. E. Church gave a Bird Concert with Belle and Nettie Cooke, Thomasine Dennithorne, W. A. M. Diller and others, representing odd birds of musical note.

The Tabernacle was to open, on the 23rd, for a testimonial to Professor P. Ali (cornet) and Professor A. J. Powell (organist); Gertrude Franklin, Florence Rice Knox, F. Remmertz, Henry Eyre Browne (organist of Plymouth Church) and George W. Morgan (organist of the Tabernacle) were promised as participants. For the benefit of Post Rankin, G. A. R., were listed (February 25th) at the North Reformed Church, Clermont Avenue, Mrs. S. B. Tuthill, Mr. and Mrs. Furey, John Evans and Dr. Tuthill.   February 26th overflowed in blessings: the Fisk University Jubilee Singers were at the Hanson Place Baptist Church; Bedford Hall housed a charity performance of the operetta, Laïla; the Purim ball danced at the City Assembly Rooms; the Scandinavian Singing Society once more held forth, at Music Hall, with, as assistants, Geraldine Nelson (soprano), August A. Wolff (violin), and Albert Rudvall (piano); and a concert to Mrs. C. R. Williams, at the South Congregational Church assembled Clementine Lasar, George Ellard and ₃E. W. Bray (basso).   On the 27th, at the Athenæum, Henry Mollenhauer's pupils tendered him a testimonial.   At the Music Hall, on the 28th, a concert for the relief of the Irish famine enlisted Levy, Mills, Vitale, Coletti, Lotti, and Henry Mollenhauer.   On the same evening in the Art Rooms, Montague Street, Kortheuer began a series of four piano recitals, one a month; Henrietta Markstein, in Association Hall, was to give three recitals on the piano, on February 27th and 28th, and March 1st.   Verily a crowded February!   March 2nd was vocal in three places, and in different ways: the Fisk University Jubilee Singers gave their "last" performance at Plymouth Church; at the Tabernacle J. Harry Shannon, the "Wonderful Ten Year Old Orator—the Marvel of the Nineteenth Century" had an "Introductory and Complimentary Levee," all for an admission of 25 cents; and an "Elocutionary and Musical Entertainment," at the Chapel, Monroe Street, near Classon Avenue, consisted of Allan Latham's Illuminated Recitals, along with Emma Henry (soprano), Mme. A. C. Tomaselli (pianist), L. P. Atkinson (French horn virtuoso), and Frank Chichester (flautist). On the 3rd, at the Herkimer Street Baptist Church, James L. Farley read, and Professor Miller performed on his baby guitar; on the same evening, at the Bethel of Plymouth Church, Hicks Street near Fulton, were to appear Clementine Lasar Studwell, Agnes Lasar, Mrs. O. N. Payne, Mr. and Mrs. J. C. Bostelmann, Henry Eyre Browne and John Morgan.   And, still, on the 3rd, Mrs. E. J. Grant and others rehearsed, at the Athenæum, L'Elisir d' Amore.   Finally, that crowded evening provided, at the East Congregational Church, Tompkins Avenue, a Japanese Kettledrum and concert.   On the 4th, the 14th Regiment had, at its new Armoury, North Portland Avenue, a reception, rifle match and review; and Stewart L. Woodford gave at Adelphi Academy, My Impressions of the South.   On the 9th, the Caledonian Club held a concert and hop, at their hall, 200 Clinton Street.

J. Henry Shannon, that "wonderful" boy orator, went to the Rink, on March 10th, in hope of filling it with eloquence and an audience; perhaps he did so.   He was at the Middle Reformed Church, Harrison Street, near Court, on the 17th, and at the Reformed Church, Duffield Street, on March 18th.   To me a boy orator is unspeakable.   On the 12th, the Church, corner of State and Hoyt Streets, proffered a Japanese Kettledrum, Belle Melville (elocutionist), Kate K. Fowler (soprano), Lottie E. Kempton (alto), Henry Gorham (basso), and Frank W. Meachem (accompanist). At a matinée, March 13th, and on following evenings, Rossini's opera, Cinderella, was given at Music Hall, by Heloise Giraldeau, Marie Gurney, Alice Hutchings, &c. And, on Sunday, the 14th, that other work of Rossini's, Stabat Mater, was again heard at St. Stephen's Church, Summit and Hicks Streets, with Amy Sherwin, Fanny Pollak, Mrs. Christianson, Lockwood, a male chorus of sixteen, a full chorus of thirty-six, the Eclectic Glee Club, and with Albert S. Caswell, organist and musical director. It was repeated on the 21st. On March 16th, Frank Beard gave his Chalk Talk at the Y. M. C. A. Hall; on the 17th, McEvoy's Hibernicon returned to the Athenæum. The second Kortheuer piano recital came on March 19th, at the Art Rooms; the New York Philharmonic Club assisted him. And the boy orator (wonderful! marvellous! miraculous!) was, on the afternoon of the 20th, at the Rink, and, on the 23rd, at the Middle Reformed Church, Harrison Street, near Court. That 23rd found Mrs. O. N. Payne reading at Y. M. C. A. Hall. March 24th divided allegiance between a Japanese Kettledrum at the First Baptist Church, Pierrepont Street, and an Old Folkes Concert at Dr. Cuyler's Church, Lafayette Place and Oxford Street. And March 29th also gave choice between Henry Ward Beecher's lecture on The Reign of the Common People, at the Park Avenue P. M. Church, and a concert at the Middle Reformed Church, Harrison Street and Tompkins Place, at which appeared Belle Cole, Lizzie Bouvier (soprano), Mr. and Mrs. F. V. Marckwald, Le Grand White (cornet and xylophone), W. M. Weed (bass), and W. B. Tremaine (organist). The 29th also staged Alberto Laurence's concert at the Simpson M. E. Church. I found no exact date for a concert at about this time at the Music Hall, with Clementine and Agnes Lasar, Mattie Balch, A. P. Burbank and John H. Brewer; but March 30th was set for a concert, at the Tabernacle, to Florence Rice Knox, at which with her were to appear Imogene Brown, Brignoli, Galassi, C. Fritsch, Remmertz, Levy, Florence Copleston, C. E. Pratt, Agramonte, &c. The six vocalists rendered the sextette from Lucia di Lammermoor, and Mrs. Brown and Mrs. Rice Knox sang, as a duet, The Mocking Bird. That evening found also Mrs. A. B. White, with a fairy operetta, at Bedford Hall. With a battalion drill and dress parade (April 3rd) of the 23rd Regiment, I close this surcharged paragraph. The entire week of April 5th–10th (Thursday excepted) found at the Athenæum Aunt Polly Bassett's Singin' Skewl and Jedediah Bassett's Bric-a-Brac.

At Bedford Church, on April 7th, Anna Morgan read and Lucy Pratt played the piano, both, no doubt, in search of the elusive bird, Fame; on that evening appeared at the Baptist Church, Pierrepont Street, Mattie Balch, Anna Phelps, Lillian Blauvelt (violin), Charles Roberts, Jr., Irene Backus (elocutionist) and Miriam Blauvelt (pianist). On the 8th, W. W.

Davies gave a dramatic reading at Adelphi Academy, and Bert Meafoy, at the Athenæum, appeared in dramatic, poetic and humorous readings, with Mme. Lasar, Navarro, Caswell and the Eclectic Glee Club to render assistance in music.   On that same 8th, the Brooklyn Athletic Club and the 13th Regiment played a burlesque polo game at the Armoury of the regiment.   And, that busy date also brought to the Hanson Place Baptist Church the "original" Fisk University Jubilee Singers; on the 13th, they were at the Lafayette Avenue Presbyterian Church.   On April 11th, St. Stephen's Church performed Gounod's St. Cecilia Mass, with Rudolf Himmer, Amy Sherwin (she had not been able to sing at the Easter services), and the Eclectic Glee Club.   At the Pilgrim Chapel, Henry and De Graw Streets, Sidney Woollett, on April 13th, recited from Longfellow and Shakespeare, with music of the zither, xylophone, piano, soprano and contralto.   On the 15th, the Hutchinson Family sang farewell at the Washington Avenue Baptist Church, and, on the 17th, the 23rd Regiment had a battalion drill and dress parade of the left wing.   At the Music Hall, on the 15th, 16th and 17th, Mr. and Mrs. G. C. Howard appeared in Uncle Tom's Cabin, with Laura Linden as Eliza, George Maddox as George Harris, George McDonald as Uncle Tom, and Lydia Corduan as Eva.   On the 15th, Jeanie Thorburn, Thomasine Dennithorne, James L. Farley, Frank Gilder and others were scheduled to appear at Uris' Dancing Academy, 611 Fulton Street.

At Plymouth Church, on April 21st, the choir appeared in "ye songs and costumes of a hundred years ago."   Squire Camp would "sound ye pitch at 8 by ye Towne Clocke," and among the celebrants were Miss Simms, Miss Dennithorne, Miss Stutsman, Werrenrath, Broderick and Arbuckle. At the Music Hall, on the same night, Professor H. Cooke was exposing Spiritualism.   On the 22nd, Dr. James L. Farley, at the Athenæum, recited from Hamlet, all to honour Shakespeare's birthday eve; on that date, also, at the Church of the Messiah sang in The Creation Maggie Mitchell, George Simpson and W. C. Baird, with Mrs. L. G. Nickolds.   The last concert at St. Stephen's Church fell on the afternoon of April 25th, with a fine group, including Amy Sherwin (soprano of the church choir), Fanny Pollak, Mrs. Christianson (ever *sic*), Miss A. M. Judge, Lockwood, E. S. Grant, the Eclectic Glee Club and Juan Salcedo.   For the benefit of the Church of the Incarnation, April 27th brought to the Music Hall Arbuckle and a group of church choristers.   And from this it is a great leap in mood to Barnum's Greatest Show on Earth, exhibiting for the week of April 26th–May 1st, with Zazel, Mme. Dockrill, Emma Lake and Signor Sebastian as chief performers.   With the Gilbert Association's performance of Caste (Emma Toedteberg as Esther, W. B. Vernon as D'Alroy, George W. Cogan as Hawtree, J. J. Darling as Eccles, N. Campbell as Sam, Bella Murray as the Marquise, and Minnie Hall as Polly), at the Athenæum on April 29th, and with

Professor H. Cooke's exposé of spiritualism, in the same auditorium, on April 30th and May 1st, I pass as easily as possible into the month of flowers.

A concert to Anna P. Sanger came on May 3rd at the Clinton Avenue Congregational Church (I suppose that Brooklyn churches were not built solely for concert-givers), with W. Dennison (tenor), W. C. Baird, C. B. Hawley (bass), Wilhelm Müller ('cello) and John H. Brewer. And, during the week of May 3rd–8th, the Miniature Opera Company presented at the Athenæum no less an antique than Uncle Tom's Cabin. On May 6th, members of the Amaranth Society, with other amateurs, were at Bedford Hall, with Our Boys. And Kortheuer's fourth piano recital occurred, on May 8th, in Art Hall. The London Circus and Sanger's Menagerie tented, May 4th–8th, on the Capitoline Grounds. May 10th brought to the Hanson Place M. E. Church the lingering New Orleans University Singers; on the 11th and 13th, at St. Peter's Academy, one might have heard Loretz's comic opera, Il Jacobi, interpreted by Maggie Mitchell (soprano), Mrs. Corinne Moore, James A. Furey, R. A. Breesee and a chorus. Burbank's Polytechnic and Gallery of Illustration began, on the 10th, a fortnight's visit to the Music Hall, Nellie Fargis (pianist) and Florentine (vocalist) assisting. On the 12th, a concert to Ada H. Fuller (who was she?) at the Middle Reformed Church enlisted Mrs. A. Mixsell, Mrs. C. F. Furey (alto), Mrs. L. Payne (elocutionist), J. Fletcher (tenor), J. A. Furey (baritone), Charles Osborne (bass), Belfort (violin), Loretz (piano) and Rafael Navarro (conductor). I can only suggest, once more, that musicians made a precarious livelihood by giving one another concerts. On the 12th, the non-commissioned staff of the 23rd Regiment staged a minstrel show at the ever-welcoming Athenæum. Of higher quality, however, was the testimonial to G. W. Morgan, on May 15th, at the Tabernacle, with Teresa Carreño, Emily Winant and Tagliapietra. The Tennessee Jubilee Singers were to "repeat," on May 18th, their concert at the Rink. St. Stephen's Church changed its mind, and gave another concert, on Sunday afternoon, May 30th, with Fanny Pollak, Mrs. Christianson, Henry Brandeis, Grant, Cartwright, and A. S. Caswell. I close the season with three events of minor importance: a performance of the juvenile cantata, Flora's Festival, under direction of E. C. Phelps, on June 1st, at the Music Hall, with Florence Auld, elocutionist, assisting; a ".complimentary" to J. M. Loretz, Jr., on June 3rd, at the Athenæum; and a "testimonial" to J. W. Macy, of the Young Apollo, on June 12th, also in the Athenæum. Then ho! for picnics, strawberry festivals, garden parties, church entertainments, school "commencements" and splashing in neighbouring surfs. The ninth season of concerts in Prospect Park also invited on Saturday afternoons from 3.45 to 5.45, Conterno's Band still officiating. And the United Caledonian Athletes were, on August 6th, at Brighton Beach Race Course.

Brooklyn Philharmonic, 1879–1880

The Philharmonic increased, that season, the number of its concerts and decreased the number of public rehearsals preliminary to each concert, contenting itself with an afternoon rehearsal, with soloists, on the day preceding the concert. It also changed the evenings of the concerts to Tuesdays. On Monday, November 17th, it held the public rehearsal, and, on the 18th, it offered the first concert for 1879–80, with the Overture to King Lear (Berlioz); Tschaikowsky's piano Concerto in B minor, played by Franz Rummel; Siegmund's Love Song (with Campanini, in that day before the German opera movement here); the Ride of the Valkyries and Siegfried's Death; and Beethoven's Fifth Symphony. The Eagle almost screamed its enthusiasm over Campanini's singing. The second concert (December 16th) provided Beethoven's overture, Consecration of the House; an air (sung by Galassi) from Spohr's Faust; a Prelude, Minuet and Fugue (new), op. 10, for string orchestra, by Hugo Reinhold; aria, Infelice (Mendelssohn), sung by Alwina Valleria; Symphony No. 1, op. 38 (Schumann); a duo from The Flying Dutchman (Valleria and Galassi); and the Vorspiel to Die Meistersinger.

The concert on January 20th had for attractions Cherubini's overture, Anacreon; a Prelude, Adagio, Gavotte and Rondo, by Bach; Beethoven's *Ah! perfido*, sung by Amy Sherwin; a concerto for 'cello, by Saint-Saëns, played by Adolphe Fischer; and Rubinstein's Symphonie Dramatique. That programme might be given a half-century later by our best orchestras. The fourth concert (February 17th) provided Mozart's Adagio and Fugue, in C minor, for string orchestra; Beethoven's Fourth Symphony; Goldmark's overture, Penthesilea; and the Introduction and Finale to Tristan und Isolde. Anna de Belocca sang an aria from Handel's Ezio, and Baldanza the immortal *Il mio tesoro*, from Don Giovanni. The fifth concert (March 16th) proffered Schubert's Symphony in C; Bruel's piano Concerto, in F major, played by Richard Hoffman; the Midsummer Night's Dream music of Mendelssohn, with vocal parts entrusted to Fanny Pollak, Jennie Dickerson (contralto), and a chorus of twenty women; and Dvorak's Slavonic Rhapsody, No. 3. The sixth and last concert (April 20th), had a programme including Bach's Chromatic Fantasia and Fugue; the third act of Die Götterdämmerung, with Amy Sherwin, Mrs. Buxton, Antonia Henne, Campanini, Remmertz and Steinbuch (Campanini singing in Italian, the others in German); and Beethoven's Seventh Symphony. As I read these programmes (almost identical, as to orchestral numbers, with the offerings of the New York Philharmonic), I cannot find it in my heart, O ye young! to pity and despise concert-goers of 1879–80.

NOVELTY THEATRE, WILLIAMSBURGH, 1879–1880

Theall's Novelty Theatre began its second season on September 1, 1879, with a week's engagement of Haverly's Genuine Coloured Minstrels. For the week of September 8th–13th, Collier's Union Square Theatre Company, seen the week before at the Park, in The Banker's Daughter, came to the Novelty, in The Danicheffs, with Louis James as Osip, A. P. Haughton as Vladimir, Charles Walcot as Roger de Taldé, Harold Forsberg as Prince Walanoff, E. L. Tilton as Father André, Mrs. Farren as the unyielding Countess, Mrs. Walcot as Princess Lydia, Sadie Bigelow as Baroness Dozene, and Marie Wainwright as the gentle, afflicted Anna. Lizzie Eaton (sic) Hudson was Nathalie. September 15th–20th brought John P. Smith's Tourists in a Pullman Palace Car; and September 22nd–27th proffered the Frayne and Tiffany Combination, in Si Slocum, Annie Ward Tiffany playing Ruth. Agnes Herndon, "the distinguished Southern actress," appeared, during the week of September 29th–October 4th, in Bartley Campbell's "sensational society drama," Fate.

None of this (except The Danicheffs) sounds attractive; but one gladly greets (October 6th–11th) Kate Claxton and Josie Batchelder, in The Two Orphans, and, if one cared for "Variety," Tony Pastor's Travelling Troupe, in the week of October 13th–18th. Salsbury's Troubadours brought their ever-running Brook (October 20th–25th), as precursor of Rice's Surprise Party, a band of similar purpose and accomplishment, in Horrors (October 27th, 28th, 29th), and Revels (October 30th, 31st, and matinée, November 1st); on the evening of the 1st, the company, headed, as we know, by Willie Edouin and Alice Atherton, arranged a special programme. Later in the season, this group was at Haverly's Brooklyn Theatre, as before that it had opened the doors of the Academy for 1879–80. The New York Church Choir Company "of nearly fifty performers" gave us a week (November 3rd–8th) of Pinafore, with Louise Leighton as Josephine, and T. Wilmot Eckert as Ralph. The Galley Slave, seen during the next week at Haverly's, was at the Novelty (November 10th–15th), with Maude Granger, Emily Rigl, Frank Evans, J. J. Sullivan and C. A. McManus. Charles R. Thorne, Jr., not acting in French Flats, at the Union Square Theatre, came to the Novelty, in The Marble Heart (November 17th, 18th, and 19th) and Camille (20th, 21st and 22nd), supported by Laura Don, O. H. Barr, Charles Rockwell, George S. Robinson, H. W. Montgomery, Nina Varian, Marie Wilkins, Carlotta Evelyn, Nannie Egberts (sic) and Lillie Thorndyke. In Our Boarding House (November 24th–29th) appeared Rosa Rand and W. H. Lytell; and, on December 1st, the ever-desired Denman Thompson began a week, in Joshua Whitcomb. Robson and Crane followed (December 8th–13th) in The Comedy of Errors, giving way, for the New York Criterion Company, which presented (December 15th, 16th and 17th) Freaks, and

[202]

(18th, 19th and 20th) Our Daughters.   The reader remembers that this company included F. F. Mackay, De Wolf Hopper, T. F. Egbert, Louise Sylvester, Mary Davenport and Mattie Earle.   Fun for Christmas week arrived (December 22nd–27th) with Neil Burgess as Widow Bedott and George W. Stoddart as Elder Sniffles; Aldrich and Parsloe, in My Partner, filled the week of December 29th–January 3rd, and Frank Mayo and Laura Don that of January 5th–10th, in Davy Crockett.   One observes that Williamsburgh had, at the Novelty, most of the stars and combinations seen to the westward, in Brooklyn, or, indeed, in Manhattan.

Haverly's Mastodon Minstrels (January 12th–17th), All The Rage (January 19th–24th, as enjoyed next week at Haverly's), Robert McWade in Rip Van Winkle (26th–31st), Fairfax (February 2nd–7th, with the cast which I have transcribed for the following week at Haverly's), French Flats (February 9th–14th, with the distribution the reader may find for the preceding week at Haverly's) — these things allow us to travel easily to February 16th, when began two weeks of silence in papers to which I have access.

Perforce I transfer the reader to the New York Herald, which obligingly continues the story.   On March 1st–6th, we had Humpty Dumpty, with George H. Adams (Grimaldi), and, on March 8th, we began a week of The Tourists, in A Pullman Palace Car.   The Banker's Daughter (March 15th–20th) brought that now familiar cast, headed by Louis James and the Walcots.   The bill for March 22nd–27th was filled by Pat Rooney's New York Star Combination, and that for March 29th–April 3rd by Joseph Murphy, in The Kerry Gow.   Stars that glittered for a week only to make room for others differing in glory were Fanny Davenport, in Pique (April 5th–10th, the week before her visit to Haverly's); Lawrence Barrett, opening in Hamlet, April 12th, and appearing next week at Sinn's Park); Gus Williams, in Our German Senator (April 19th–24th), and Annie Pixley, in M'liss (April 26th–May 1st); John T. Raymond, in Colonel Sellers (May 3rd–8th), and Tony Pastor's Specialty Troupe (May 10th–15th).   The San Francisco Minstrels filled the week of May 17th–22nd, and Milton Nobles, in The Phœnix, that of May 24th–29th.   The season ended with a week (May 31st–June 5th) of Harrigan and Hart.   Practically all of these attractions were seen during those later months at either the Park Theatre or Haverly's; to my account of those two houses I refer the reader curious as to details of the productions.

Berry's Theatre, Williamsburgh, 1879–1880

Berry's Theatre, Broadway and Fourth Street, E. D., was offering, on October 9th, 10th and 11th, an "entire change of bill," including The Ambassador's Lady, Ten Nights in a Bar-room, and The Mysterious Ghosts.

On October 13th, the Brooklyn Times advertisement asserted that the house was "crowded nightly with ladies and gentlemen." The Howard Variety Combination were there and Mr. and Mrs. Selden Irwin, in Uncle Tom's Cabin. This attraction lasted till October 17th, when J. P. Winter and Mr. and Mrs. Irwin gave Lost in London, and J. S. Berry and Belle Berie (*sic*) acted The Young Widow. This seems to me a cheap thing, and I am not surprised to learn that when, on October 20th, J. S. Berry's "original" drama, Leona, or, Trapped at Last, came forth, it did so at an admission of 10, 15 and 25 cents. All the week of October 27th–November 1st, the Brennan Combination appeared, with Mr. and Mrs. Brennan, Captain George Laible, the Morrisseys, May Arnott, Frank Melrose, King Sarbro, John Reilly, Bessie Bell, and a full band of Female Minstrels. The Brennans and Laible and the Female Minstrels were featured for November 3rd–8th, along with Dooley and Tenbrook, Ward and Lynch, Clooney and Ryan, Bertha Eschert, Nellie Hadfield (*sic*), Nita Gerald, Ada Lanier, and Sadie Connolly. Mlle. Delmar's Original Folly Burlesque Company was here for November 10th–15th, and a Japanese Troupe for the following week. Belle Berie now takes the centre of the stage. The Thanksgiving bill (November 24th–29th) included Belle Berie's Jolly Duchess, Archie Hughes and the Female Minstrels.

Belle Berie's Burlesque Opera Company, in The Brigand Daughter, Cooper Brothers and Frank and Fannie Davis began December (1st–6th); for December 8th–13th came The Happy Man and His Monkey, Nellie Vincent ("Erin's Nightingale"), George Harris (negro comedian), Annie Griffin (comic vocalist) and the abiding Female Minstrels. The bill for December 15th–20th included the Novelty Four, Ada Castleton, Georgie Bell, Gilbert Long, and the "sensational" drama, Betrayed. December 22nd–27th proffered Steel Arm, the Avenger, The Charmed Cross and Laughing Gas, and an olio with Cooper and Golden, J. A. Kelly, James Mott, Harry Mack, Nellie Steele, Eva Dobson, Nellie Amon, Signor Diablo, and the Female Minstrels. January entered (December 29th–January 3rd) with The Black Crook, Roman Statues, Nellie Amon, Sadie Dunbar, Dick Turner and J. S. Berry. Advertised for January 5th were the Leonzo Brothers, in Rupert's Dog.

WILLIAMSBURGH MISCELLANY, 1879–1880

It is pleasing to enter September, 1879, with the Suabian Volksfest, on the 7th, 8th, 9th and 10th, at Ridgewood Park. Thence we pass to Burbank's recital from memory of Rip Van Winkle, on September 27th, at Old Bushwick's New Sunday School; why any one should recite this piece, in the heyday of Joseph Jefferson, I cannot see, or, indeed, why any one should wish to hear it done! At Turnhalle, on the 28th, occurred a performance by the Brooklyn Arbeiter Bühne.   And that, eager reader, is all I can supply for September.   Cool October is richer in autumn fruitage.   The Times of October 6th says that O'Leary was walking at Browne's, Fourth and South Fourth Streets; on the 6th, also, the Times apprises of a concert at the First Baptist Church, Fifth and South Fifth Streets, with Belle M. Rankine, Miss Hazlett, William Featherstone and W. Nash (tenors), Fannie and Frank Leonori, the Euterpean Glee Club, and E. H. Ducharme, W. Shute and J. Delong (basses).   A concert of the 9th, at the Second Street M. E. Church brought in Belle Rankine, Ella Fox (pianist), Frank Mulligan (organist), Zilpah Hazlett, Jennie Figgis and the Lyceum Glee Club — a double quartet.   Baptist or Methodist — Belle Rankine would recite for either.

An Old Folks Concert (not yet may we escape from this craze) came to pass, on October 13th, at the Cedar Street M. E. Church, near Bushwick Avenue, Professor J. H. Hall and Company organising the platitude; and, on the 15th, came Little Pinky to Masonic Temple, with Ada Drummond, Johnny A. Silva and Gracie Clifford, Sammy Roberts (two years old, with Bertie Phillips), Misses Wheeler and Whittingham and Messrs. McMunn and Upham — almost a round dozen of talented nonentities.   But let us hasten to Lee Avenue and Lynch Street (on October 13th and 14th) to enjoy the Forepaugh Show, deploying twenty male riders "headed" by Robert Stickney and twelve equestriennes "inspired" by Miss A. Carroll; also there were one hundred "peerless arenic acts!"   Laura Wheeler, elocutionist (I hate this word), was at the Grand Street M. P. Church, on a busy October 23rd that gave us also to enjoy, at the South Third Street M. E. Church, both Burbank and J. A. Van Kuren (organist); or the singing of the Coloured Jubilee Singers at Old Bushwick's New Sunday School (I see possibilities for topic songs in this address).   On the 22nd, at Christ Church Chapel, J. Jay Villers had once more described Funny People We Meet. Truly exciting must have been (if carried out) the spectacle on October 25th and 27th, at Euler's Broadway Park, Brooklyn, of the Fire King, William Sparker (certainly an appropriate name), appearing "in a house-high burning pyre, soaked with petroleum," and staying there "till the fire extinguishes."   October 27th brought choice between the performance of Box and Cox, played at the Lyceum by the Mite Society of All Souls' Church, and a "humorous and instructive magic lantern exhibition" by J. M. Craig, at the North Fifth Street M. E. Church.   North or south these numbered streets bore testimony to the strength of Methodism.   I pass to an orchestral concert directed by Professor Ortloff, at the Central M. E. Church, and end October findings with a concert at the Cedar Street Church, at a date I cannot exactly supply, with Kittie and Jennie Johnson, Lena C. Foster and the Chickering Harmonics.

We advance rapidly.   A "complimentary" to Jennie Figgis made cheery, on November 18th, the Church of Christian Endeavour, with the aid of Maggie Stewart, Florence Boyle, Annette (once Nettie) L. Read, A. F. Bowers and P. J. Smith — a collection of no epochal impressiveness. On the 24th, the Hutchinson Family, "Tribe of Asa," were at the North Fifth Street M. E. Church. Father Blake's Original (of course!) Old Folks were announced for the 26th and 27th, at the Leonard Street M. E. Church; and, on the 27th, Samuel W. Murphy, elocutionist, held forth at the Second M. E. Church, Grand and Ewen Streets. The Zöllner Männerchor, on the 23rd, invaded Turn-Halle, Meserole Street. The everlasting Hutchinsons must be our first winter bouquet, on December 3rd, at the First Presbyterian Church, South Fourth and Sixth Streets, but George McMunn follows on their heels, on the 4th, acting The Spectre Bridegroom, at 146 South Fourth Street. On the 7th, the Odd Fellows Männerchor concert and ball made Sunday sacred at Germania Hall, and the Wilhelm Tell Männerchor operated at Baumgartner's Military Hall. The 8th was bright with De Cordova's The Pipley Family in Europe, illustrated humorously at the New England Church; on the same date, at the Lyceum, the Young Apollo Opera Troupe were down for The Bohemian Girl and Poor Pillicoddy, performers including Bessie Louise King, Masters John Hanau, John W. Black, Joseph Craig and J. B. Budworth, and Messrs. J. W. Macy, J. Drew, T. B. Cooper, W. Robitsek and C. Mackenzie — a group that has sent no name down to posterity. The 9th again exploited the ever-welcome Burbank, at Christ Church Chapel. Roller skating was the brisk device daily at Lefferts Park. James S. Burdett, on December 17th, was main feature of a concert at the Grace Congregational Church, Lewis Avenue and Monroe Street; on the same date appeared at the Lyceum Priscilla Whittingham, the Lambert Children, Charles Ames (cornet), Maggie Drummond, and actors in The Spectre Bridegroom; and also, on that 17th, Dr. W. P. Godman's University Singers of New Orleans lifted up their voices in the Leonard Street M. E. Church (a rapidly advancing amusement hall, if I may speak without irreverence). Perhaps churches should be centres — on week days — of jollity; I am not trying to decide this interesting question.

The Coloured University Singers of New Orleans were, on December 22nd, at St. John's M. E. Church, competing with a superb concert on the same evening at the Bedford Avenue Reformed Church, with (promised, at least, by Maurice Strakosch) Emma Thursby, Emily Winant, Anna Bock, Adamowsky (Polish violinist and later loved in the Boston Symphony orchestra) and Blumenberg ('cello). The Ross Street Presbyterian Church housed, on the 27th, a lecture by Richard A. Proctor, on Other Worlds and Other Suns. And the 30th proffered pleasing fare provided, at St. John's M. E. Church, by Settie Blume, Imogene Brown (a good soprano, popular in the '80s), Emma Wilkinson (who must have been good) and Salcedo (cornet). This closes my December inducements. The pupils of Mrs.

[206]

Louisa Taylor's Dancing Academy were, on January 26th, to offer some form of Cinderella; and then for six months (January–June) I found no Brooklyn Times in the several libraries and even in the warehouse that guards the treasured news of 1880. I pass perforce to July, merely to find excursions, athletic meets, beach fun, and bicycle races. On August 18th, Euler's Broadway Park contained the mirth of the Williamsburgh Arion. The Canstatter Volksfest was held, on August 22nd, 23rd, 24th and 25th, at Myrtle Avenue Park. And that is all!

GREENPOINT, 1879–1880

The record for the season under review will be another mosaic put in such pattern as I may evolve from items in the Brooklyn Times, the Greenpoint Globe and the Long Island Star (both daily and weekly issues).   On September 13, 1879, the Greenpoint Athletic Club carried through their second annual games at their grounds, Van Cott Avenue, between Eckford and Oakland Streets. On Sunday evening (the 14th) the Germania and Social Quartette Clubs joined forces in a "dramatic concert" and ball at Passe's Germania Hall. On October 15th we revelled in the Forepaugh Show, Circus, etc. And October 17th brought to the Primitive Methodist Church the anomaly of a Grand Olde Folkes Concert by "ye little olde folkes" of the congregation. At Eckford Hall, on October 22nd, the Amphion Choral Society wiped out that freak with performances of Dearer than Life and A Quiet Family; or, if they could not accomplish that sweet purpose, Burbank, on November 1st, at the Noble Street Presbyterian Church, might be depended on to do so.

November 12th brought to Whitestone blessing of a concert by Mrs. Alonzo Foster, Annie Mooney (soprano) and Rachel Mooney (pianist). Harry T. Bryant (humourist) came forth, on November 18th, at the Presbyterian Church; on the 20th, at Eckford Hall, a musical and dramatic entertainment exploited F. W. Zeiner and his classes, in Mrs. Willis's Will, The Duchess of Mansfield and Grass Widows — an enjoyable show, doubtless, to friends and relatives of the pupils. On November 25th, the Amphion Choral Society gratified with performances, at Smithsonian Hall, of music and Ici on Parle Français. On the grounds of the Greenpoint Athletic Club, on the 27th, occurred an amateur twenty-mile walk. The everlasting Hutchinsons, hewn out of the granite of their native hills, were at Association Hall, on December 1st, and the Chickering Harmonics, on the 2nd, at the Christian Church of the Evangel, Leonard Street, near Meserole Avenue. J. Jay Villers followed in the wake, on December 3rd, at the First Baptist Church. December certainly was lively in Greenpoint. On the 6th, Company I, 47th Regiment, indulged in a "soirée," and the 9th carried to Smithsonian Hall the Brooklyn Operatic Club (C. Mortimer Wiske directing) in

[207]

Pinafore. A concert, on December 11th, to G. W. Foster, chorister of the church, brought co-operation, at the Noble Street Baptist Church, from Nellie Blauvelt, E. J. Mayers and the Chickering Harmonics. The Tabernacle, on the 12th, heard (according to the Star) the University Singers of New Orleans; and the same paper brings to the same hall, on the 18th, the Jubilee Singers of Louisiana. December also gave an evening of music as a testimonial to F. A. Bower, with Marie Boyce, Jennie Figgis, Kathrene Cavannah and Linden L. Parr participating, at the Noble Street Baptist Church. On the 29th, at Smithsonian Hall, the busy Amphion Choral Society acted The Belle of the Kitchen. Much of the social life of Greenpoint centred in churches — festivals, fairs, choir concerts, etc.

I enter January through the gateway of the 16th, when J. M. Craig's Magic Lantern revealed, at Smithsonian Hall, Gabriel Grub, or, the Man Stolen by the Goblins in the Graveyard on Christmas Eve (seventeen views), and Annie and Willie's Prayer (nine views); also Bible scenes and miscellaneous. The Social Quartette Club was at Eckford Hall on the 18th. On the 19th, Father Blake's Old Folks restored us to the then usual fare, at Association Hall. The Continental Glee Club of Greenpoint functioned, on January 22nd, at Eckford Hall; and the Chickering Harmonics entertained, on the 27th, at the Christian Church of the Evangel. January abounded in church and club entertainments, but with very little of importance for us. The Reverend William H. Boole (husband of Mrs. Ella Boole, worker for fifty years in the cause of prohibition) lectured once on temperance and once on Men and Things. Passing into bleak February, I find a concert on the 2nd, at the Tabernacle, with Mrs. Alonzo Foster, Marie Boyce, Annie Mooney, Lillie Distler (contralto) and S. F. Richardson (bass). Fortified by this, I venture, on the 5th, into Eckford Hall, for a musical and dramatic entertainment of the Amphion Choral Society; if I had been a German of Greenpoint I might have waited till the 9th, for the masquerade, at Passe's Hall, of the Germania Singing Society. On the 10th (postponed from January 29th), Murphy and Welch's Mastodon Minstrels appeared at Eckford Hall; the same evening promised for Smithsonian Hall a musical and athletic entertainment by the Greenpoint Athletic Club.

I begin the March flurry with Variety and Music at Temperance Hall, provided by I know not what band of Rip Van Winkles, roused from slumber, all on the evening of the 8th. On the 15th, a testimonial to Ida Percy enriched the night with a visit by Father Blake's Old Folks. In my haste to reach this Ides of March I overlooked a sweetly pretty thing on the 11th, at the Christian Church of the Evangel — Grandpa's Birthday, no less, performed by children and adults. Chaplain McCabe also had an evening in March at the First M. E. Church, showing The Bright Side of Life in Libby Prison. And let us not forget the merry masked balls, in February and March, of the German societies. On March 17th, the Amphion Choral Society, ever busy, ever breaking into these Annals, gave at Smithsonian Hall an entertainment including His Last Legs and The Plague of My Life. On March 24th an Old Folks Concert could have been a novelty to none at the Church at Leonard and Conselyea Streets. The Germania Singing Society again busied itself, on March 28th (Easter Sunday), at Germania Hall, as did the Greenpoint Social Quartette Club at Eckford Hall.

After a drowsy winter, Greenpoint awoke in April. On the first three evenings of that month, we find, at Smithsonian Hall, Miss Kingsland ("the only lady magician"), Henry Hatton ("preternaturalist"), and J. S. Allerton ("prestidigitateur premier"). If their stage magic was as marvellous as their magic of language, they must indeed have reduced their audiences to a state of wonder and amaze. On April 7th, at the Church of the Ascension, the Ariel Vocalists and Entertainment Combination of John G. Pierson and Tom Ellison were listed for performance; and Eckford Hall, on the 12th, gave us local entertainers in the Walters and Morgan Combination. One could hardly believe that this village life was just across the river from New York of the '8os. At Eckford Hall, on the 7th, the Black Prince Association of the Knights of Pythias gave, appropriately to its title, tableaux of Damon and Pythias. Aunt Polly Bassett's Singin' Skewl held sessions, on April 15th and 16th, at Smithsonian Hall; the same hall, on the 21st and 22nd, exhibited McNevin's Panorama of Ireland, with Dan Mack and Kate Cooper. A small house for this show, on the 21st, led the Star on the following day to exclaim, "The indifference of the residents of Greenpoint to all entertainments outside of the churches is indeed remarkable . . . nothing but a circus or a free show will draw a crowd." My suspicion as to this state of affairs I have gently insinuated in the narrative preceding. Nevertheless, "Professor" Henry T. Bryant (ventriloquist and humourist) tried his luck, on the 29th, at the Presbyterian Church. On the 28th, the Noble Street Presbyterian Church presented Greenpoint's favourites, Mrs. Alonzo Foster and Marie Boyce.

Without the slightest pang of regret I leave April for flowery May, finding, on the 10th, the Amphion Choral Society acting, at Eckford Hall, Anything for a Change and That Rascal Pat. On the 13th, the "Original" Jubilee Singers of New Orleans were at the Presbyterian Sunday School, and, on the 16th, the Germania Singing Society celebrated Pfingst-Sonntag at Passe's Hall. The cantata of Red Riding Hood's Return and singing by the Continental Quartette accomplished results, on May 19th, in the Reformed Church Chapel, Java Street; on the 27th, the Ariel Vocalists, J. G. Pierson and Tom Ellison were at the Ascension Chapel; on May 30th, the Greenpoint Musikverein's last concert made Sunday sacred at Passe's Hall. May died, on the 30th, in the throes of the second annual spring games of the Greenpoint Athletic Club. Thenceforward strawberry festivals, excursions, harvest home festivals, regattas and other joys of a community

[209]

untortured by complexes filled the summer of 1880 — a summer of course ruffled by a presidential campaign as between Garfield and Hancock.

FLATBUSH AND ITS NEIGHBOURS, 1879–1880

Oddly enough, amusement items for the vicinity indicated by my caption diminished yearly in the local Gazette. The towns reached out toward Brooklyn, which in turn stretched out to them thrice-welcoming arms; and traffic conditions rendered it easier to visit real plays and concerts in Manhattan and Brooklyn. But "crazes" of given years excited smaller communities; for instance, the Gazette of November 1, 1879, is epic with walking matches in New Utrecht, Bay Ridge and other seats of highest respectability. Gladly the Hutchinson Family restored the older order, on December 8th, in Flatbush Town Hall. May Melville, elocutionist, was, on January 8, 1880, at the M. E. Church, Flatbush, and, on February 14th, the Flatbush Choral Society functioned in the Chapel of the Reformed Church in that quiet town.

And now let Bay Ridge of 1939 look back with pride to February 10, 1880, when a pretty pre-valentine came to the Athenæum, a hall so often sedately closed. On the date in question, the Literary Union acted there Our Boys, with no less a celebrity of years immediately following than Edith Kingdon, as Mary Melrose; others in the cast were John Billings and Mrs. W. S. Howson. St. Patrick's Day appropriately gave for sufferers in Ireland a "grand" ball at Town Hall, Gravesend. And Town Hall, Flatbush, set up, on April 19th and 20th, McNevin's Panorama of Ireland, with Dan Nash and Kate Cooper to assist. Surely the Gazette failed to report some amusements of 1879–80 in "rural" Brooklyn; or possibly my eye failed to detach such items from a closely printed context in that veracious chronicle of former times.

LONG ISLAND CITY, 1879–1880

I begin on September 11th, with John Denier openly walking the tight-rope in this city across the river. On the afternoon of September 28th, the New York Männerchor appeared at Mrs. Albert's Hall, Astoria, and, in the evening of that day, the Ueberall Society gave there a dramatic performance. Cousin Jonathan's Old Folks, on October 17th, gratified those who liked that sort of thing, in the Astoria Presbyterian Church. In German farces, on November 23rd, appeared, at the Astoria Assembly Rooms, the Apollo Dramatic Association and the Ueberall. The Astoria Liederkranz, on November 25th, indulged, at the Astoria Assembly Rooms, in its third anniversary ball and musical entertainment. On December 11th, the young ladies of the R. C. Church of Astoria, were at the Astoria Assembly

Rooms, in farces and other entertainments. I found thereafter for December only Christmas festivals in churches. On December 30th and 31st, at the Hunter's Point M. E. Church, the cantata of The Four Seasons presented Miss Graham as Spring, Miss Grimes as Summer, Miss Edith Woodruff as Autumn (she sang The Last Rose of Summer; as, indeed, why not?), Miss Nellie Whitman as Winter, G. Miner as Father Time, and Mr. Turner as the Old Year. On December 29th, in the school room of the Church of the Redeemer, Astoria, Professor Hawkins exhibited Dissolving Views of the Holy Land. In the hall at Woodside, the Women's Association of St. Paul's Church, of that community, presented in this season of the year, an entertainment with singing by Misses Hollingsworth and Morris and a scene from Lytton's Money.

On January 12th the Seneca Dramatic Association gave a "Grand" Entertainment and Hop at Albert's Astoria Assembly Rooms. A benefit performance, on January 27th, at those Rooms, had the assistance of Murphy and Welch, of the minstrel troupe. A. P. Burbank, on February 7th, came to Washington Hall, Astoria; on the 9th, the young men of St. Patrick's Church, Dutch Kills, sponsored a "Grand Variety Entertainment" in Schehr's Assembly Rooms; and, on February 10th, a double delight divided the mind as between Hart's Variety Troupe at Wagner's Assembly Rooms, Laurel Hill, and the University Singers of New Orleans, at the M. E. Church, Astoria. On February 15th, the Ueberall Dramatic Society of Astoria gave, at the Astoria Assembly Rooms, the ever-popular Der verwunschene Prinz. February 21st also distracted with a double duty, bringing choice between the ball, at the Astoria Assembly Rooms, of the Long Island Sängerrunde and a performance of farces (Sally McNally and Joe vs. John, or, the Long Island Returning Board — this latter a satire on the mayor, the aldermen and the supervisors) holding forth at Koch's Broadway Hall, Astoria. Possibly the duty was a triple one, since, on the 21st, "Professor" Wendel displayed his magic for the benefit of the German School, at the school house, Middle Village.

My sole offering for March is the masquerade at the Astoria Assembly Rooms, of the Astoria Männerchor, a lighter matter of the 6th. The young men of the St. Vincent de Paul Society of St. Mary's Church were at Schehr's Hall, on April 5th and 6th. On April 7th, the Astoria Liederkranz resumed their weekly sessions at Rassiga's Hall; the Astoria Athletic Club gave, on April 12th, at Washington Hall, a dramatic and musical entertainment. On the 14th, in the same hall, came a Kindersymphonie, along with Professor Heerwagen, Frank E. Blackwell, Mme. Rebecchini and Ferdinand Dulcken. The Continental Quartette appeared at a fire-laddies' entertainment, on April 19th, at Woodside, Addie Hollingsworth of Astoria also pleasing Woodside on that allotted evening. Hattie Cole's début occurred, on the 20th, at Washington Hall, with Kitty Coates and Otto Heerwagen to support

[211]

her in the ordeal. At the Reformed Church, Dutch Kills, on the 22nd, Misses Cole, Coates and Hollingsworth, Heerwagen, Mrs. L. Steward and E. B. Sperry must have seemed to that little community a veritable starry host. The Ueberall Dramatic Society did its best, on May 9th, at the Astoria Assembly Rooms, with Der Goldbauer; on the 16th, at Koch's Assembly Rooms, the Frohsinn of Long Island City acted 1733 Thaler und 22½ silber Groschen. And "Professor" Seppel Gschwandner's Tyroleans, in native costume, gave, on the 16th, at the Astoria Assembly Rooms, a "sacred concert." The Annex Association concert, on May 19th, presented at Smithsonian Hall, Hunter's Point, Oscar M. Newell (pianist) and Edith Woodruff.

I leave Long Island City with just a few summer items conscientiously recorded. The Junior Friendship Coterie attended the opening Summer-Night's Festival, on May 3rd, at Schwalenberg's Jackson Avenue Park; Henry Galt visited Astoria, on May 24th; on the 30th, Scharnowitzky's Park gave a Sunday afternoon concert to a sparse congregation. On that same 30th, Caulfield of New York appeared in an organ recital at the Church of the Redeemer, Astoria. On June 5th, the Astoria Männerchor celebrated, at Albert's Assembly Rooms, their seventeenth anniversary, presenting Der Nachtwächter; for the benefit of C. Jaeger, a destitute invalid, they gave a ball and concert, on June 26th. Then strawberry festivals in June, and excursions in July and August, sang of a small community life. Yank Adams, finger billiardist, was, on July 2nd, at Schwalenberg's Billiard Parlours, and, on July 25th (Sunday) the Revel Variety Troupe appeared at Rassiga's Bowery Bay Garden and Pavilion, singing before a good attendance in English and German. Well, Long Island for the Germans! some natives may have thought. The Ninth Annual Harvest Home at Miller's Hotel, Little Bayside, was postponed, because of a severe storm, from July 20th to August 17th.

FLUSHING AND ITS NEIGHBOURS, 1879–1880

The Flushing Journal, on August 16th, bears note of the opening, on the 26th, of the "pleasant little theatre" at Fort Willets, for the fall and winter season. Assisting the officers, in Byron's comedy, Weak Women, were Emma Rich, Marie Gorenflo and Isabella Preston. The offerings of the post on October 21st were to be To Oblige Benson and The Irish Tutor. Meantime, on September 5th, amateurs acted Our Boys, at the College Point Institute. Those who cared might have heard Mary F. Eastman lecture in Town Hall, on September 26th or October 3rd (the Journal, as so often, leaving me dubious in dating), on The Relation of Women to Business — a theme certainly pertinent in the half century that has since supervened. Clark's Fifth Avenue Uncle Tom's Cabin (with Little Dot as Topsy and

Charles Mestayer, the "original" Uncle Tom) came to Town Hall, on September 29th; on the same date, the University Singers (coloured) sang at the Methodist Church. The Bayside Quartette Club concert occurred on October 11th, the farce, Don't Lend Your Umbrella, closing the programme. For the benefit of St. Paul's Church, a concert at Poppenhusen Institute, College Point, gave patrons the Harmonie and the Krakehlia Männerchor. And, on the 11th, Our Boys, at the Opera House, Flushing, presented the actors seen on September 5th at College Point. Long Island was very neighbourly, when it came to matters of amusement. A series of concerts and hops began, on November 15th, at Freygang's Hall, College Point, with "Professor" Fink, of New York, as master of ceremonies. There, on January 16th, appeared those beautiful voices, Henrietta Beebe and Emily Winant. And plays were given, on December 4th and 22nd, by the military gentlemen at Willet's Point. On December 4th, likewise, the Bayside Quartette Club gave a second concert and entertainment at Literary Hall; and at this time, at the Flushing Opera House, Harry L. Sands presented his Rêverie du Diable. On either December 18th or 25th (the same vagueness of dating in the Journal leaves me uncertain of the exact evening) Aberle's Troupe, from Aberle's Theatre, New York, came to the Flushing Opera House, Fanny Davenport, the deep-voiced contralto, being in the olio. On the 13th, says the Times of December 18th, Rip Van Winkle was played at the Flushing Opera House before a mere fifty auditors.

Those two native flowers, Nonie L. Wright and Mamie Lowerre, combined their charms, on January 16th, at the Poppenhusen Institute, and another play by Breath — Cast Away, or, the Island of Pearls — figured, on January 27th, at the Flushing Opera House.

February yielded only three meagre items: the Flushing Musical League's Minstrel Show, on the 9th, at the Flushing Bank Building; Byron's comedy of Wrinkles, with Betsey Baker, on the 10th, at Willet's Point; and "Professor" Nichols's Glass Blowing Exhibition, on the afternoon of the 28th, at the Opera House. For March only two offerings detain us: a concert, on the 16th, at the Congregational Church, with Guild, F. Ingraham, Mrs. Pelton, Miss Walker and Miss Leggett; and the fourth concert of the Bayside Quartette Club, on the 24th, at Literary Hall. April 1st brought a concert, at the Flushing Opera House, to Albert Steinfeld, organist of St. Paul's Chapel, College Point, and, on the 6th, the Willet's Point performance of Old Soldiers and Bamboozling, with Sara Courtney and Emily Lewis (their first appearance) aiding the officers. Amateur theatricals illumined the Opera House, on April 19th, and on the 24th, "a celebrated New York prestidigitator" was advertised to hold that harassed stage. Clinton Burling's entertainment of music and recitations fell due in Town Hall on April 27th, with A. L. King to assist. Nellie Balmor, advertised, did not arrive, saith the Times. For May 10th and 11th were promised The Two

Orphans and Uncle Tom's Cabin — those deathless images of fear and pity turned melodramatic; on May 27th, the Opera House opened for an entertainment (theatrical) in aid of the Flushing Library. During the week of May 30th–June 4th a concert at the Congregational Church promised Fred Guild, Fred Ingraham, Miss Jennings, Mrs. Kenman and Miss Rockwell, whoever they may have been in art. On June 10th, the Flushing Amateur Dramatic Club gave Buckstone's old play, Leap Year; on July 1st, at the Post Theatre, Willet's Point, one might have seen Who Killed Cock Robin? A Happy Pair and His Last Legs.

At Harry Hill's Pavilion, Monday, July 5th, was celebrated gaily with boxing, wrestling, walking and running matches, with yacht races arranged by the redoubtable Harry, proud owner of the yacht, Avalon (pretty name). Miller's Harvest Home Festival, July 20th and 21st, at Little Bayside, was spoiled, as we know, by bad weather; he tried again on August 17th. A stage ran, in that summer, every Sunday, from Flushing to Harry Hill's Pavilion. On August 15th, the Arion Society of New York, 800 strong, invaded and possessed Columbia Grove, Cold Spring Harbour. I end with Led Astray, performed on August 18th, at the Willet's Point Theatre, by a company of New York actors, for the benefit (why?) of the Willet's Point Dramatic Club.

JAMAICA, 1879–1880

We begin the Jamaica season with Clark's Fifth Avenue Uncle Tom's Cabin, given at Town Hall, on September 20th, with Little Dot, Little Lulu, and Charles Mestayer. At the Uptown Hotel, Jamaica, appeared, on October 4th, the "Coloured Troupe" of John Farmer, then showing for the second time; the same hotel housed, on October 11th, Joseph Nichols's Minstrel Troupe, "late of The Fayette Welch Pavilion, Rockaway Beach." The aging Bernard Covert, with H. M. Rogers (singer) came to East Jamaica, on October 23rd, and arrived at the Jamaica Town Hall on the 27th. On either November 10th or 17th, the Town Hall again welcomed Bernard Covert, then with the Tremaine Brothers and H. M. Rogers. Clark's Fifth Avenue Company returned, on November 26th, presenting Mary Brimer, in East Lynne — of course at the Opera House; on the next evening, in the same hall, came a "Variety" troupe, including John B. Wills and May Adams, Edwards and Gaylor ("Coloured Ambassadors"), Annie Hart, Lillie Howard (songs) and Mark E. Ryder (comedian). The Uptown Hotel was offering regular Saturday evening entertainments through November and December. Largely of local talent was the concert for Richard H. Bagott (director of music at the Reformed Church, Jamaica) proffered on December 17th, at the Town Hall, with Misses Jennie and Nellie Spader, Helene Taylor, J. G. Pierson (of Tremaine Brothers), Thomas Short, and Bagott himself (tenor). For the 20th (afternoon and evening) the Young Apollo Club of New York gave Pinafore and Poor Pillicoddy.

Well, that sends 1879 off the calendar. On January 23, 1880, the Jamaica Opera House sheltered the New York Operetta and Cox and Box Company, in the opera, Felina, by Charles Barnard and H. N. Sawyer, and a reconstruction of Box and Cox under title of The Jolly Bachelors. Jamaica was then in throes of ten lectures, chiefly by reverend speakers, presented at the Methodist Church. The University Singers of New Orleans, "now making a second tour of Long Island," were "expected" on February 4th, at Jamaica Town Hall. The Jamaica Town Hall, on February 10th, had a concert for the Irish sufferers, and February 16th found the Sängerbund masquerade at John Distler's Hotel. The Democrat of March 2nd speaks of a recent lecture by Dr. Talmage for the Irish sufferers. It netted $120. The Opera House, on April 20th, thrilled to "Professor" H. Cooke ("monarch supreme of spirit mysteries") and Selome Crawford ("modern mediums eclipsed"). On May 30th, Fritz in Ireland engaged an ambitious band of amateurs. Atlantic Garden, corner of Fulton Street and Van Wyck Avenue, Jamaica, advertised for the afternoon and evening of May 31st a "grand opening." With this I leave the rather uninteresting season of 1879–80 at Jamaica; I know the reader would not care to attend the strawberry festivals in June, or patronise the excursions and picnics of July and August.

STATEN ISLAND, 1879–1880

Twice in September, 1879, the Staten Island Sentinel summons us to Temperance Lyceum, New Brighton; on the 6th to hear the Father Mathew Dramatic Club in Kathleen Mavourneen, and, on the 17th, to enjoy the Humorous Sketches provided by Miss Nellie Casely (sic) and "eminent" assisting "artists." Conflicting reports in the Sentinel leave me in doubt as to whether it was on September 24th or the 27th that the German Club Erheiterung had at the German Club Rooms a concert and ball, for the former of which it promised the co-operation of Emily Winant and Martinus Van Gelder (violin). Moore's choir (in costume) repeated Pinafore, on October 1st, at the Temperance Lyceum; on October 4th, the Union Square Combination (M. J. Vinton, manager) gave no greater novelties than Uncle Tom's Cabin (afternoon) and The Octoroon (evening) with actors no more distinguished than Bella Martin ("the only colored Topsy in the world"), J. V. Melton, James F. Peters, A. W. Levison, Tom Owens, Marie Davidson, Mrs. M. A. Beuil (sic) and Little Ada. I could not believe that Staten Island, so near New York, could be so provincial. On October 27th, Josh Billings was scheduled for a lecture in Odd Fellows Hall.

On November 20th, at the German Club Rooms, Uncle Tom's Cabin

[215]

presented Mrs. G. C. Howard — "her first appearance in Stapleton, notwith-standing unscrupulous persons had tried hitherto to deceive." In the same rooms, on the 24th, the burlesque Fidelia proffered H. Methfessel as Fidelia and E. Lieck as Florian. On the 27th at the Temperance Lyceum appeared Mr. and Mrs. Harry Osborn, in The Ticket of Leave Man and The Colleen Bawn. Reader, I know as well as ever thou canst, that these things were not worth the inconvenience of a journey to the island — unless one were bent on the study of social conditions. Certainly, unless one were of nearer Brooklyn, and devoted, like so many good Brooklynese to the amateur cult, it would hardly re-pay one to go over on the cold evening of December 29th to see the Father Mathew Dramatic Club of New Brighton in Above the Clouds and a shadow pantomime. Later in the season this society threat-ened to revive The Golden Farmer, and fulfilled its promise on January 24th.

I go back to the Richmond County Gazette, which, on November 26th, announced the dates of the forthcoming concerts of the Philharmonic Society, the Sextette to be as last year, and including Richard Arnold, Charles Werner, and Eugene Wiener. At the first concert (on December 19th) were to appear Antonia Henne and Richard Hoffman. The Union Square Combination returned to the Temperance Lyceum, on January 10, 1880, with The Two Orphans, Marion Booth (her, at least, we have heard of) as Louise, and Marie Davidson as Henriette, with other rôles entrusted to J. V. Melton, Fred Kent, J. S. Rooney, Lew Baker, W. C. Donaldson, George E. Fenno, J. F. Fay, H. J. Levison, &c. This seems to have been given again on the 17th. On the 13th of January something more local was the concert of the Staten Island Vocal Society, at the German Club Rooms, the assisting artists being George E. Aiken, Fannie Kellogg (of Boston), George Ellard and Carl Feininger (violin). The nobly-striving Philharmonic con-cert of January 23rd presented as soloists Letitia Fritsch and Morgan (pianist). The Union Square Combination, on January 31st, gave Caste. And, on February 9th, at the German Club Rooms, society revelled in the big charity ball — function of functions. I take the reader to Edgewater Sunday School, on February 19th, not for the concert at which appeared Belle Cooke (coloratura soprano), Nettie Cooke (contralto), Doubleday (tenor) and Leach (baritone), but merely for the pleasant duty fulfilled of taking him to Edgewater. On February 21st, the Union Square Combina-tion — something of a fixture, apparently, at the Temperance Lyceum — gave Box and Cox and The Factory Girl, J. F. Crossen, F. C. Wells, Mrs. Wells and Alice Landon being newer names in the force. The Black Sheep by Palgrave Simpson was announced as "in rehearsal." The third Phil-harmonic concert (February 27th) presented Richard Arnold, Emily Wi-nant, Charles Werner, Julius Gantzberg and Emil Gramm. The fourth con-cert fell on April 2nd (according to the Gazette), with, as soloists, Evelina Hartz, Theodore Toedt, Wiener and Hagedorn, and with the Staten Island

Philharmonic Sextette establishing the basic and tonic pitch of the proceedings. On April 6th, at the German Club Rooms, the Staten Island Vocal Society did its best to justify its existence, with the willing help of George E. Aiken, A. D. Woodruff (tenor), Caryl Florio, William Müller ('cello), and Hermann Rietzel (pianist). And I gladly mention the Richmond County Dramatic Association, which gave in March (the Sentinel review gives not the exact date), at Oddfellows' Hall, West Brighton, Box and Cox and Handy Andy, and, on April 23rd, at Griffith's Hall, Port Richmond, appeared in further dramatic and musical performances. On the 29th of April, the fearsomely named Chippewa Council, O. U. A. M., had an amateur minstrel show. At the York Avenue Temperance Lyceum, on April 21st, the Father Mathew Dramatic Association presented The Irish Emigrant, The Coal Heavers, and A Night in a Medical College.

After all, Staten Island was then the pretty island across the bay, with a fine winter colony, and many pleasant summer homes. For theatrical and musical entertainments, the inhabitants could ferry to Brooklyn or New York. Therefore, we find but little further, germane to our subject, in 1879–80. On May 20th, at Calvary Presbyterian Church, a concert enlisted Nova (violin), and Miss Figgis (soprano from Brooklyn). On May 25th, the last concert of the Staten Island Vocal Society had the assistance of Henrietta Beebe, W. C. Baird, Charles Belfort (violin) and Caryl Florio. June on the island supplies me with nothing entertaining but roses and strawberries, and I leap, therefore, into the burning zone of July. July 5th celebrated the athletic games of the West Brighton Athletic Club. For the 7th and 8th of that torrid month, the German Club Rooms advertised a *return* (I found no trace of the initial visit) of the Norcross Fifth Avenue Opera Company in Trial by Jury and the all-conquering Pinafore. On the 10th of July, the South Beach Pavilion (open since June 2nd) indulged in fireworks and a "hop." And, on the 19th, the Staten Island Quartette Club held its Summer Night's Festival at "Supervisor" Bechtel's Park; beer, one observes, had got into politics. With a "musical soirée," on August 10th, at the Pavilion, New Brighton, I leave the island for 1879–80; the function was for the benefit of Niethamer, pianist of the pleasant resort, and to his assistance flocked several nonentities including Mrs. Clark, Bourne, Hilliard (if Harry or Robert Hilliard, not a nonentity), and the McNamee Brothers. Belfort, the violinist, was a better known contributor to the delights of the occasion.

[217]

CHAPTER IV

WALLACK'S, UNION SQUARE, DALY'S, MADISON SQUARE, BOOTH'S, FIFTH AVENUE, HAVERLY'S (LYCEUM), PARK, STANDARD, BIJOU OPERA HOUSE, NIBLO'S 1880-1881

A PRELIMINARY season at Wallack's began on August 5, 1880, with the very last kind of offering one would have expected in that historic house — unless one remembered summer incursions of Lydia Thompson and other purveyors of fun and frivolity. The new production was a "Grand Pantomimic Burlesque Extravaganza" — Grim Goblin — by George Conquest and H. Spry, "introducing many of Mr. George Conquest's most famous original creations." Conquest, "from the Alhambra Theatre, Crystal Palace, Gaiety Theatre, Alexandra Palace, and Grecian Theatre, London," had come to us to stage the piece, and he put it on with a large cast, himself appearing as Hic-Hac-Hoc, the Grim Goblin, as Prince Pigmy, the Dwarf, as Nix, the Demon Head, as Rokoko, the Rock Fiend, and as the Vampire Bat; M. W. Fiske was Boohbeigh, the 1,000,000th King of Noodledum, Harry Allen was the Widow Grizzlegrief, and Maude Stafford, A. W. Maflin and Ed Chapman the Widow's sons, Hopeful, Gobble and Guzzle, respectively. George Conquest, Jr., was cast for Tallbones, a gentleman of high standing, and Lillian Lancaster essayed Waspino, a swell demon. Mlle. Etheria, "the flying fairy," was the Fairy Honeydew, Queen of all the Bees, and Laura Conquest Princess Melodia. R. M. Nichols was Shekeigh Shank, Lord Chamberlain. In the vast army of pages, lords and ladies and body guards, all named in the bill, I have room to mention only H. and G. Ricketts, W. Elliott, Elsie Deane, Bessie Temple, Alice Wright, Louise Loring, Susie Parker and Sophie Hummel. How many of them can the diligent student identify?

The great scene of the show was the Cobweb Cave of the Grim Goblin, with sight of the Vampire Bat and the Rock Fiend, and with "the Great European sensation of The Flying Fairy and the Wonderful Phantom Flight, introducing those marvellous flights from stage to roof, for which the Conquests (father and son) stand unrivalled." According to later playbills, the feat "consists of the performer flying from floor to ceiling, where he grasped a swinging trapeze, to which a rope was thrown, and by which he descended to the stage as quickly as possible." On the first night, a rope broke, and the elder Conquest fell from the flies to the stage, breaking his left leg in

[218]

two places. He could not appear again during the engagement, but the run of the show, temporarily suspended, resumed on August 9th, with the younger Conquest in his father's parts, and with W. H. Manley replacing the son. Even then, according to the Herald of the 10th, young Conquest was caught in the flies, and Manley fell fifteen or twenty feet to the floor. The Herald wonders if the game, with the entailed nervousness of the audience, was worth while; Conquest and Manley reassured the audience, on the 9th, by taking curtain calls at the end of the show. The piece ran, without further serious trouble, up to and including September 11th. Yet, on September 8th, Mlle. Etheria was slightly injured in a fall before the end of the performance. George Conquest, Jr., in the Herald of the 9th, says this was the fourth accident since the engagement began, and he would gladly hail the end of the visit at Wallack's. The financial results had not been good; solace from the box-office had not mitigated the pain of the calamities on the stage.

Last Season of Wallack at the Second Wallack's, 1880–1881

The final appearances of the Wallack company in the Thirteenth Street house, a house mellowed in memory by their many matchless performances, began on September 30, 1880, with a careful revival of As You Like It, a play last seen there, with Ada Cavendish, in the spring of 1879. Perhaps that earlier performance suggested this of 1880. The reader notes that As You Like It was only the second Shakespearian play ever revived by Lester Wallack in the theatre he was now deserting for a new Wallack's at Broadway and Thirtieth Street; not since Much Ado about Nothing, in February, 1869, had his regular company, of and by itself, produced any Shakespearian comedy — a fact very surprising, when one comes to think of it. Perhaps, after all, perfection in the acting of Sheridan does not necessarily entail perfection in rendering the romantic charm of Shakespeare.

As You Like It introduced to our public three new actors of importance, though no one of them succeeded in the pastoral comedy. Osmond Tearle, the Jaques, was fourth in a line of handsome, talented leading men who latterly had decked Wallack's stage, his three predecessors, of course, having been H. J. Montague, Charles Coghlan and Maurice Barrymore; in addition, Harry M. Pitt, himself almost a leading man, came forth as Orlando. Both these actors became greatly admired by our playgoers; William Elton (Touchstone) had many successes in modern farce or comedy before he retired to his native England. Of course all three of the new actors were English; no one expected Lester Wallack to engage or to train American players. Note the difference from Augustin Daly, to whose teaching the American theatre owes many of its most highly esteemed performers. But to the cast of As You Like It:

[219]

Jaques	Osmond Tearle	Jaques du Bois	W. H. Pope
Adam	John Gilbert	William	C. E. Edwin
Orlando	Harry M. Pitt	Charles	J. M. Laflin
Touchstone	William Elton	Dennis	H. Pearson, Jr.
Banished Duke	Harry Edwards	Eustace	G. C. Sherman
Oliver	Gerald Eyre	Louis	T. Morgan
Le Beau	J. H. Gilmour	Rosalind	Rose Coghlan
Duke Frederick	James Harrison	Celia	Stella Boniface
Amiens	James G. Peakes	Audrey	Effie Germon
Corin	W. J. Leonard	Phebe	Marion Booth
Sylvius	Albert Roberts		

It will be seen that Rose Coghlan, after her unsatisfactory journeys, in 1879–80, to Booth's and the Madison Square Theatres, was back in the fold of America's most famous theatre; her return was very welcome. We observe, also, that Wallack had engaged a real singer (Peakes) for the songs, and a real wrestler (Laflin) for Charles. Furthermore, the names of the un-Shakespearian characters, Louis and Eustace, would indicate that Wallack had used an old stage version, rather than Shakespeare's undiluted text. The "new and beautiful scenic illustrations of forest glade and sylvan dell" were by J. Clare and J. Mazzanovich; Thomas Baker arranged the music.

William Winter (Shakespeare on the Stage, Second Series) states that the production "was tasteful and pleasing. An effect of morning twilight, broadening into dawn and then the light of day . . . was, at that period, novel, and it was beautiful." The Jaques of Tearle "impressed by correct, even exquisitely smooth elocution," but it was "merely a specimen of respectable acting." Pitt, as Orlando, "pleased by intrinsic manliness, earnest feeling, and a specially clear and effective delivery," while Elton's Touchstone "evinced neither the quaintness, sapience, satiric drollery, kindly feeling, nor quizzical manner" of the jester. And Miss Coghlan's Rosalind was "agreeably piquant, but neither poetical in spirit, nor flexible in style. . . . Her voice, which she knew how to use, was strong and melodious," and in her boy's "garb of slate-colored cloth and leather, with a red cap, she was a bewitching figure." J. Ranken Towse (Sixty Years of the Theater) also felt that this Rosalind "had brilliancy and charm . . . but was deficient in poetic imagination and tenderness of feminine spirit." And this leads me to inquire what the "poetic" quality of Rosalind may be, since critics almost invariably accused actresses of being lacking therein. Perhaps Modjeska came nearest to it, of all the Rosalinds of the last fifty years; but her foreign accent! Towse felt, also, of Tearle's Jaques that it was "Victorian, demonstrative and shallow." Finally, Elton, a "graduate" from burlesque, "interpreted Touchstone after the burlesque method." So much for Wallack's new actors (in Shakespeare) and for Wallack's carefully staged As You Like It.

Wallack kept the comedy going through Monday, October 18th. On

[220]

Tuesday, he brought out a great minor success of his management, E. C. Lankester's comedy, The Guv'nor, presenting in it some new actors and some older favourites in their season's first bow:

Mr. Butterscotch	John Gilbert	Mr. Vellum	W. H. Pope
Freddy	Osmond Tearle	Ullage	George Conway
Theodore Macclesfield	William Elton	Gunnel	H. Pearson, Jr.
Theodore	Harry M. Pitt	Aurelia	Effie Germon
The MacToddy	Gerald Eyre	Kate	Stella Boniface
Jellicoe	W. J. Leonard	Mrs. Macclesfield	Mme. Ponisi
Gregory	W. L. Gleason	Carrie	Adelaide Detchon
Cab Driver 3407	C. E. Edwin	Barbara	Emma Loraine
Cantle	Albert Roberts		

John Gilbert made a great hit as Butterscotch, the retired confectioner, as did Tearle as his son, "of the Iex Rowing Club." Photographs of Gerald Eyre as the MacToddy and of Mme. Ponisi as Mrs. Macclesfield, the boat-builder's wife, show how funny they were, and how remarkable their "make-ups"; Sarony's photographs of Stella Boniface as Kate Butterscotch revive for us her girlish charm. Alas! the good old days, the rare old actors!

The last consecutive performance, for the present, of The Guv'nor came at the matinée, on Saturday, December 18th. In the evening of that day, Wallack staged the London success of Herman Merivale and F. C. Grove — Forget Me Not — in which Genevieve Ward had greatly succeeded at the London Lyceum. Miss Coghlan, at Wallack's, was also very successful in the character of Stéphanie, Marquise de Mohrivart, one of those adventuresses attempting to work her way upward, in society, by means of a hold on another's past, but defeated, in the end, by her own past, typified, in this case, by a Corsican vendetta, and what the playbills shiveringly described as "the Face in the Garden." The cast at Wallack's included, besides Miss Coghlan as the witty, resourceful, but finally fear-stricken Stéphanie, Osmond Tearle (whose great versatility was beginning to show itself) as Sir Horace Welby, Harry Edwards as Prince Maleotti, who really defeats Stéphanie, Gerald Eyre as Barrato, the vengeful Corsican, Harry J. Holliday as Roberts, H. Pearson, Jr., as Luigi, Mme. Ponisi as Mrs. Foley, Stella Boniface as Alice Verney, and Agnes Elliott as the Vicomtesse de Brissac.

Forget Me Not was a great success, and might have continued for a very long run had not Genevieve Ward, claiming sole right to the play, instituted legal proceedings, which resulted unfavourably for Wallack. On January 13th, his bills carried announcement that "in obedience to an order of the Superior Court," he was "compelled to announce the discontinuance for the present," of the play. The Guv'nor, which had been given at Wednesday matinées, on December 22nd and 29th, January 5th and 12th, was restored to the evening bills, on January 14th, and continued through the matinée of January 22nd. On the evening of the 22nd, Wallack fell back on the great pillar of the house — The School for Scandal — one of the glories, as he presented it, of our stage. Osmond Tearle, as his photographs in this part show, was one of the handsomest and best-dressed representatives of the part of Charles ever seen in New York; his acting lacked the elegance of Coghlan's, but it had charm and ease of its own. I remember him well in the auction scene, especially. Gerald Eyre was the Joseph (and a good one), Adelaide Detchon Maria, Elton Moses, Dan Leeson Crabtree, Albert Roberts Sir Benjamin, and Wilmot Eyre Careless. H. R. Humphries (the singer) was engaged for the songs of Sir Harry Bumper. And, of course, Gilbert, Harry Edwards (best, I believe, of all Sir Olivers of a half-century), Rose Coghlan and Mme. Ponisi constituted the quartette of supreme excellence in their rôles. This delightful revival ended with the performance on Saturday afternoon, February 5th.

On the evening of the 5th, Wallack's met failure with Where's the Cat? James Albery's adaptation of a Schönthan comedy, produced with a cast including Horatio Saker (new here) and Rose Wood (her first appearance this season):

Sir Garroway Fawn	Osmond Tearle	Second Guide	H. Pearson, Jr.
George Smith	William Elton	Stella	Rose Wood
Percival Gay	H. M. Pitt	Mrs. Smith	Effie Germon
Scott Ramsay	Horatio Saker	Dagmar	Adelaide Detchon
Fritz	C. E. Edwin	Madge	Stella Boniface
First Guide	H. J. Holliday	Nan	Emma Loraine

Two weeks sufficed for this piece, and proved that the Cat was at least not in the box-office. On February 21st, The School for Scandal once more chattered its witty way, and, on the 22nd, The Guv'nor had another showing. On the 23rd, a second failure perplexed an anxious management — H. J. Byron's comedy of The Upper Crust, with Harry Edwards as Lord Hesketh, Osmond Tearle as Sir Robert Boobleton, Elton as Barnaby Double-chick (proprietor of Doublechick's Diaphanous Soap), H. M. Pitt as Walter Wrentmore, C. E. Edwin as Tibthorpe, Miss Detchon as Norah Double-chick, Miss Boniface as Kate Vennimore, and Mme. Ponisi as Lady Boobleton. With the matinée on Saturday, March 5th, The Upper Crust ceased to be — at Wallack's.

The School for Scandal again held its session on the evenings of the 5th, 8th, and 10th, The Guv'nor replacing it on the 7th and 9th. Another long-cherished tradition of Wallack's stage was revived on March 11th, when The Rivals, with Gilbert, Mme. Ponisi, Miss Coghlan and Miss Boniface in their accustomed rôles, had specially interesting new features in the Captain Absolute of Osmond Tearle, the Acres of Elton, the Faulkland of H. M. Pitt, the Sir Lucius of Gerald Eyre, the David of Dan Leeson, the Fag of C. E. Edwin and the Lucy of Emma Loraine. During the next few evenings it divided with The School for Scandal the honour of holding Wallack loyalists, one or the other of the Sheridan classics being in the bill until

March 24th, when Old Heads and Young Hearts enlisted Gilbert, Tearle (Littleton Coke), Harry Edwards, Elton (Bob), Gerald Eyre (Tom Coke), Wilmot Eyre (Lord Charles Roebuck), Dan Leeson (Earl of Pompion), Rose Coghlan, Mme. Ponisi and Stella Boniface — still a glorious Wallack array, though many of the members were new here, in their rôles. Doubtless talk between acts at this theatre ever harked back to Broome Street and the '60s at Thirteenth Street.

On March 29th, Wallack, who had, as we shall see, played several weeks at various threatres in New York and Brooklyn (he was then an energetic travelling star) came back home in A Scrap of Paper, with John Gilbert, Rose Coghlan, Miss Germon, Miss Boniface, Kate Bartlett and Miss Blaisdell in the parts created by them in 1879. Harry Edwards was now Baron de la Glacière, Tom Jefferson Anatole, C. E. Edwin Baptiste, H. J. Holliday François, and Emma Loraine Pauline. This play, achieving its usual success, ended its run on April 11th, when Lester Wallack made his farewell appearance on the stage he had so long managed and so frequently adorned. It was an epochal night and merited celebration in an ode; but, like most events of this sort in the theatre, it passed quietly into history.

Wallack's at Thirteenth Street went out in melodrama of the kind then popular at the London Adelphi or Drury Lane. The World, one of the most worthless of the school, but full of stage tricks and marvellous scenic thrills, was put together by Paul Merritt, Henry Pettitt and Augustus Harris, every one of whom knew every device of melodramatic invention. Wallack's staged it, on April 12th, with wonderful scenery by J. Clare and J. Mazzanovich, and with machinery beyond anything yet seen here. The bill acknowledged in this latter respect, "the valuable assistance" of Charles Harris, of Covent Garden, a brother of Augustus Harris, of the tripartite authorship. The cast:

Sir Clement Huntingford	Osmond Tearle	Locksley	Harry Gwynette
Harry Huntingford	H. M. Pitt	Rushton	John Irwin
Mo Jewell	William Elton	Lawrence	Albert Roberts
Martin Bashford	Gerald Eyre	Captain Pearson	W. H. Pope
Blackstone	Wilmot Eyre	Marshall	F. Alberts
Lumley	D. Leeson	Joe	H. Holliday
Owen	W. J. Leonard	Commissioner	H. Pearson, Jr.
Ned	Emma Loraine	Detective	Robert Warren
Dr. Wyndham	C. E. Edwin	Mabel Huntingford	Stella Boniface
Dr. Hawkins	G. W. Conway	Mary Blythe	Adelaide Detchon

The Herald, next day, ventures the suggestion that the three authors may have partaken too freely of Welsh rarebits, gone home, and dreamed, each, one of the impossible scenes of the play. But "the harbor at the Cape with its shipping; the explosion of the dynamite machine on the ship at sea, followed by the bursting of flame through numerous traps in the stage, which is realistically set as the saloon deck of a steamer; the raft,

[223]

with its living and dead cargo, floating on the 'boundless sea,' which is the most perfect scenic illusion of its kind ever seen within a theatre — the private Insane Asylum and the River Thames, with its panoramic effects; the Great Hotel, with its realistic passenger elevator and many other details, are all such masterpieces of the stage carpenter's and scene painter's art that whenever they claim the attention of the audience they do so thoroughly and completely. The play itself, as a literary effort, is dramatic rot." The Herald might also have credited, as one of the reasons for success, the mightily persecuted hero, the machinations of villains, and the final triumph of the good. But this was Wallack's, and the very last offering of Wallack's company on a stage supposed to be the upholder of the finest traditions of Sheridan, Robertson and their worthy successors (though few). But, of course, even Wallack's, had, in previous years, gloried in the success of Rosedale and The Shaughraun, a success the harvest of which it was now reaping in the way of The World. The new thriller ran till July 2nd, when Wallack's actors left forever the theatre which for exactly twenty seasons (1861–62 to 1880–81) they or their predecessors had made, I believe, the most elegant to that time in the history of the New York stage. A matinée benefit, on May 18th, presented the matchless Old Heads and Young Hearts, of Wallack's. On June 1st, Rose Coghlan took her first benefit, and appeared as Camille, with Osmond Tearle as Armand, Harry Edwards as Duval, William Elton as Gaston, Gerald Eyre as de Varville, Wilmot Eyre as Gustave, Effie Germon as Olympe, Louisa Eldridge as Prudence, and Stella Boniface as Nichette. Surely another odd thing for the passing of the second Wallack's!

In recording this passing, I cannot refrain from recalling the names of the glorious leaders for twenty years in the famous house — W. R. Blake, William Reynolds, Lester Wallack, W. R. Floyd, John Sefton, John Brougham, Mark Smith, Charles Fisher, John Gilbert, Owen Marlowe, E. L. Davenport and J. W. Wallack, Mrs. Hoey, Mrs. Vernon, Mary Gannon, Fanny Morant, Miss Henriques, Rose Eytinge, Harry Beckett, Harry Montague, Charles Coghlan, Ada Dyas, Mme. Ponisi, Mrs. John Sefton, Jeffreys Lewis, Rose Coghlan, Stella Boniface, Effie Germon; when or whence comes there such another list? When Wallack's Theatre at Thirteenth Street reopened, in September, 1881, it was a German house, directed by Adolph Neuendorff; when Wallack's company returned next season, it was to open the new Wallack's, at Broadway and Thirtieth Street.

UNION SQUARE THEATRE, 1880–1881

And the glorious reign of A. M. Palmer, at the Union Square, was drawing to a close, though the end was not quite yet. During this very season, the Herald had notice, now and then, of Palmer's intention to move up-

AGNES ELLIOTT

MARION BOOTH

ADELAIDE DETCHON

OSMOND TEARLE
AS CHARLES SURFACE

ROSE COGHLAN
AS ROSALIND

STELLA BONIFACE
IN THE GUV'NOR

GERALD EYRE
IN THE GUV'NOR

WILLIAM ELTON

H. M. PITT
(OF WALLACK'S)

town.   The beginning of the new season, however, found him still comfortably ensconced in the familiar quarters in Fourteenth Street.

We begin our annals for this term, on August 16th, when Two Nights in Rome, a crude but powerful drama by A. C. Gunter, introduced Maude Granger as a star on the stage that had witnessed her début in 1873.   Two Nights in Rome dealt with the machinations of a heartless Corsican adventuress, who almost ruins the life of her English-speaking husband and the "nice" girl whom he should have met before the Corsican crossed his path, the whole ending very much as Forget Me Not ends, with the defeat of the adventuress and a return for the others to final-curtain happiness. The play succeeded, with this cast:

Gerald Massey	Joseph Wheelock	Waters	M. B. Curtis
Abija Peabody	Frank Mordaunt	Beppo	John Morgan
Herr Franz	Harry Edwards	Antonia	Maude Granger
Captain Warmstres	J. R. Grismer	Evelyn Aubrey	Julia Stewart
Louis Benedetti	J. B. Studley	Lilly Davenant	Katie Gilbert
General Aubrey	G. F. De Vere	Mme. de Montalvan	Adelaide Thornton
George Seeley	J. W. Thorpe	Tema	Genevieve Mills
Ferdie Fortescue	Harry B. Bell		

This cast is striking as to actors, weak as to the women in support of the star. Miss Granger made a hit as the wicked Corsican, frightened by a Corsican vendetta (as Stéphanie de Mohrivart had been) into ultimate decency, but evidently she did not like to fit her beauty and talents into the despicable character; on September 7th, she resigned the part to Laura Don, and took up the gentler virtues of Evelyn Aubrey; W. J. Leonard replaced J. W. Thorpe.   The engagement closed on September 11th.

On Tuesday, September 14th, Blanche Roosevelt, a wandering fire since she used to sing, in The Pirates of Penzance, "Poor Wandering One," introduced to a public none too eager for it Alfred Cellier's operetta, The Sultan of Mocha, which the composer himself directed, and which had a cast including William Hamilton as the Sultan, Fred Dixon as "Admiral" Sneak, Harry Allen as Captain Flint, Eugene Clarke as Peter, Mills Hall as the Lord Chamberlain, G. W. Reynolds as the Chief Scribe, G. B. Synder as the Grand Vizier, Leonora Braham as Dolly, Carrie Reynolds as Isidora, Miss L. Feltner as Eureka, Emma Guthrie as Jenny, and Pearl Everleigh as Moggy.   It hardly survived its birth pangs, and passed peaceably, on September 25th, through the portals of oblivion.   Blanche Roosevelt, this year, tried much, and accomplished little; she did not, herself, appear in this opera.

The preliminary skirmishes at the Union Square, except for Two Nights in Rome, are hardly worth recording.   John Habberton's play, Deacon Crankett, came in, on September 27th, with Benjamin Maginley as the Deacon, "a jolly old fellow, who understands a good many things besides religion," and with Joseph Wheelock as Joe Thatcher, "a thorough man." Other parts were played by George Wilson as Tom Curtis, a Maine logger,

[225]

by Harry Eytinge as Heatherton, a New York capitalist, Frank Roberts as Egbert Gray, a young banker, W. Henderson as Weazel, a village ne'er do well, by Helen Sedgwick as the heiress, Eleanor Heatherton, Annie Ware as Mrs. Crankett and Stella Chapman as Polly Peekin, "help" to Mrs. Crankett. Well, this was rural drama to the life (of the stage). Three weeks sufficed for it; but the play did not expire when it left the Union Square after the matinée performance on October 16th.

DANIEL ROCHAT; THE BANKER'S DAUGHTER; CLARA MORRIS MATINÉES, 1880–1881

Palmer's regular season began on the evening of October 16th, with a production of Sardou's fine drama, Daniel Rochat, a play dealing with the eternal conflict between two diametrically opposed natures — a free thinker and a deeply religious woman. Yet these two loved, at the time of their marriage; but love could not prevail over differing views, and the play ends with a separation of two broken hearts. The man, the free-thinker, offered to sacrifice his principles, but the woman, realising the motive, refused a compromise repugnant to her beliefs. There was some fear that, in 1880, so frank a discussion would offend patrons of the theatre, but the magnificent acting of Palmer's company, and the beautiful presentation of the play won over any possible opposition. Sara Jewett was sweet as the loving girl, and the inflexible wife, and Charles Thorne, in a rôle very much finer in grain than those usually assigned to him, achieved a great success, even if the most delicate phases of the character escaped him. Perhaps Daniel Rochat was the most artistic offering of Palmer's management of the Union Square:

Daniel Rochat	C. R. Thorne, Jr.	Kelly	Mr. Ayling
Guillaume Fargis	John Parselle	Julien	William Moss
Dr. Bidache	J. H. Stoddart	Verley	James W. Thorpe
Casimir Fargis	Walden Ramsay	Antoine	W. S. Quigley
Charles Henderson	Joseph Whiting	Robert	S. Du Bois
Laurent	T. E. Morris	Lea Henderson	Sara Jewett
Rev. Septimus Clarke	Charles Collins	Esther Henderson	Maud Harrison
M. Turler	Owen Fawcett	Mrs. Powers	Mrs. E. J. Phillips
M. Clavaron	H. F. Daly	Arabella Bloomfield	Florence White
Andram	Alfred Becks	Ellen Bloomfield	Netta Guion
Pierson	Andrew Jacques		

As I read the advertisements in the Herald, I had an impression that Palmer was proud of this performance and was rather coaxing his public not to be hard on the religious, or, rather, what they might esteem the anti-religious aspects of the play. He managed to keep it going till December 15th, when he revived the safe and sane theatricalities of The Banker's Daughter, that huge success of 1878–79. In this, of course, Thorne and Miss Jewett (she had had a benefit, on December 7th, in Daniel Rochat) were once more John Strebelow and Lillian, also an ill-assorted married pair, finally united for a final curtain; doubtless many preferred that more conventional ending. Stoddart, Parselle, Walden Ramsey, LeMoyne, Sarah Cowell and Maud Harrison resumed their original rôles; but now Frederic de Belleville (first appearance here) was de Carojac, Owen Fawcett was George Washington Phipps (not nearly so good as Polk had been), and Little Eva French played Nathalie in one phase of her childish career. The revival lasted only for a month.

Palmer, with a keen eye to Clara Morris's recent success at the Park Theatre in a series of special matinées, engaged her for a similar experiment at her old home in the Union Square. On January 4th and 6th he revived, at matinées, his former triumph, Miss Multon, with Miss Morris, John Parselle, J. H. Stoddart and Marie Wilkins in their great original rôles. Sara Jewett was at first announced for her former character of Mathilde de la Tour, but Eleanor Carey (her first appearance with a company she long thereafter adorned) assumed the part, and played it forcefully, if without the elegance that was inherent in all of Miss Jewett's work. Frederic de Belleville, also long connected with this theatre, was Maurice de la Tour, Roberta Norwood was Kitty, Netta Guion Louise, Charles Collins Gravesend, W. Morse Wopping, Leila Granger Jane and Eva French Paul.

We always relish comment on Clara Morris; therefore without apology I quote from the Herald of the 5th. The actress has great "power," but "her acting lacks the subtle refinements, the delicate grace, the exquisite detail of method, which go to make up the accomplished, finished artiste. It is not that something of these last named qualities is not now and then apparent in her impersonations, but that they are so often lacking — their presence is so infrequent and fitful — that she cannot be said to be ever really and fully possessed of them; in consequence, her acting, through her gestures, her posing, her intonation, even in her very pronunciation of the English language, is often extremely crude; but when called upon to give expression to deep human emotion she does so with a wonderful realism, not by any carefully worked out artistic method, but by an instinctive latent dramatic power, of which she seems hardly conscious, which she uses crudely, but with grand results." With all her "want of dramatic refinement," she can give to her parts "a truthfulness to nature, a depth of feeling, a mighty passion, that . . . sweeps aside and defies just criticism of the actress, and leaves us in tearful wonderment."

I wonder if the recent visit of Sarah Bernhardt, with its revelation of the finest technical perfection, influenced judgment in regard to Miss Morris, whom it was now popular to compare with the great French actress? The juxtaposition of these two noted emotional players, if fortuitous, was at least very advantageous for students of the stage. The Clara Morris matinées on Tuesdays and Thursdays became a great feature of the season, and Palmer was fortunate to have adopted the scheme. On January 17th,

Palmer produced A. R. Cazauran's adaptation of a play by D'Ennery, which he called The Creole, and in it appeared Eleanor Carey as another of those adventuresses bound to ruin the lives of gentlemen with a past. In this case, young Maillepré is her victim, unless his father will do as she demands. "Those papers" finally confute her, and, utterly foiled, she departs. Miss Carey was good in her part, and Charles Thorne as the harassed father, who thinks he kills her in his sleep, was excellent in his; but the play was impossible and not even the following excellent cast could save it:

Count de Maillepré	C. R. Thorne, Jr.	Lorain	Owen Fawcett
Count de Malesherbes	John Parselle	President	T. E. Morris
Count de Lavarde	F. de Belleville	Denis	Charles Collins
Armand	Walden Ramsay	Diana	Eleanor Carey
Chevalier de la Tourette	J. H. Stoddart	Henriette	Maud Harrison
Baron d'Armagny	H. F. Daly	Countess de Maillepré	Mrs. E. J. Phillips

This was the worst failure for several years in the regular seasons of the Union Square; but Palmer could felicitate himself on the Tuesday and Thursday matinées of Clara Morris. Miss Multon ran its course, and, on February 1st, Camille succeeded it, with Miss Morris as an American heroine, to be contrasted with the Polish Camille of Modjeska, the French of Sarah Bernhardt and (soon) the German of Marie Geistinger. Charles Thorne was once more the Armand, with Parselle as the elder Duval, de Belleville as de Varville, Owen Fawcett as Gaston, Walden Ramsay as Gustave, Eleanor Carey as Olympe, Maud Harrison as Nichette, Louisa Eldridge as Mme. Prudence (a part she had made entirely her own), and Netta Guion as Nanine. This excellent cast (superb, in the powerful impersonations by Thorne and Miss Morris) kept Camille on the stage for Tuesday and Thursday afternoons, and the evening of February 5th, the last performance falling on March 10th.

Meantime, on February 8th, The Danicheffs, prominent in the season of 1876–77, came back, with Charles Thorne still in his touching characterisation of the noble, self-sacrificing serf, Osip, with Parselle and Stoddart in their former parts of Prince Walanoff and Sakaroff, and with H. F. Daly still as Father André. In all other important respects the cast was new, Sara Jewett even resigning the pretty part of Anna to Maud Harrison, who played it very pleasingly; in fact Miss Harrison was charming in the expression of gentle pathos as in light, bright comedy. She was an exquisite actress. Frederic de Belleville succeeded James O'Neill as Vladimir Danicheff and Eleanor Carey was now the Princess Lydia Walanoff (vice Katherine Rogers and Linda Dietz, who had played it, successively, in 1877); perhaps both of the new interpreters were better than those of the original cast. But no one could expect Mrs. Phillips, good routinière, to replace the magnificent Fanny Morant as the Countess Danicheff, a part in which Miss Morant had been superb in the expression of haughty pride and iron insist-

[228]

ence on her feudal rights of domination in the lives of her son and her dependents; nor is it likely that Walden Ramsay could equal W. R. Floyd as Roger de Taldé.   Others of the 1881 cast were Nellie Morant as Baroness Dozene, Mrs. F. A. Tannehill as Anfissa, Louisa Eldridge as Marinna, Netta Guion as Nathalie, M. Howard as Paul Danicheff, T. E. Morris as Ivan, Charles Collins as Nikifor, and G. Glover as Herr Linder.

It would seem that the failure of The Creole found Palmer unprepared. The Danicheffs endured only to February 26th.   On Monday, the 28th, Rose Eytinge returned, after an absence of five years from this company, for a special engagement in Cazauran's adaptation of Adolphe Belot's drama, Le Fils de Coralie, here called Felicia, or, Woman's Love, and brought out with a compact cast of great strength and attractiveness:

Captain John	C. R. Thorne, Jr.	Mme. Dumont	Rose Eytinge
M. Mornay	John Parselle	Dolores Mornay	Sara Jewett
M. Ferri	J. H. Stoddart	Eleanor Mornay	Mrs. E. J. Phillips
Claude Clavarel	Owen Fawcett	Mme. Doricourt	Estelle Clayton
Cassagnac	F. de Belleville		

Any one who knows the fame of the actors in that group realises the excellence of the cast, individually and collectively.   In spite of the superb assignment, the play itself was not over-successful, though it kept the stage through the matinée performance on April 23rd.   Miss Eytinge made the last hit of her career (*Eheu fugaces!*) as Mme. Dumont, the farmer woman, forced by fate to reveal her shady past, in order that her illegitimate son (the fine Captain John) might marry the girl of his choice (Dolores). Nothing could have been sweeter than Sara Jewett's performance of Dolores, or more youthfully pleasing than Thorne's Captain John (he did not look a day over twenty).   Of course, whatever Stoddart and Parselle played, their audiences regarded their work as perfect, and indeed it usually was.

We must not forget the popular Clara Morris matinées.   On March 17th she appeared for the first time in Manhattan as Constance Harewood, in Conscience, a part which illness had prevented her playing at the Union Square in the spring of 1876, but which she had since played in Brooklyn and elsewhere.   In power she quite surpassed Kate Claxton, who was Constance on this stage in 1876, but she could not equal her in sweetness, in beauty and in an innate refinement of manner.   Thorne, Parselle and Stoddart resumed their original rôles, and Mrs. Phillips replaced Marie Wilkins, now under contract with the Madison Square Theatre.   Mark Pendleton was Cyril Harewood, and Owen Fawcett the lawyer.   Illness prevented Miss Morris's appearance on March 24th; and the series of special matinées came to an end on March 31st.   An alarming incident in the run of Felicia occurred on the evening of April 2nd, when a defective flue in the Morton House, which was built round the theatre, filled with smoke the auditorium

[229]

of the Union Square, and sent the panicky audience into the night spaces of the square outside. Holders of coupons for this evening were allowed to replace them for later performances of the play.

Felicia, passing at the matinée on April 23rd, left the stage on the evening of that day for a single rendering of Camille, with Miss Morris and Thorne and the winter cast; both performances were crowded, as they might well have been, considering the splendid casts. Bernhardt had played Camille, that afternoon, at Booth's. Verily a juxtaposition! The last week of the regular season (April 25th–30th) was devoted to Raymonde, a revised version of Dumas's play, Monsieur Alphonse, which we remember at Daly's Fifth Avenue Theatre in 1874, with Ada Dyas, Fanny Davenport, Charles Fisher, George Clarke, Frank Hardenberg, and, above all, that marvellous child, Bijou Heron. At the Union Square Clara Morris was the distressed heroine, another lady with a past and an illegitimate child; Effie Germon (loaned by Lester Wallack) was the vulgar but kindly Mme. Guichard, Eva French was the child, James O'Neill (courtesy of Henry E. Abbey) was de Montaiglin (so nobly played at Daly's by Charles Fisher), de Belleville was Octave, W. J. LeMoyne Rémy, the comic sailor, and T. E. Morris Dieudonné. Except for Miss Morris, I doubt if the cast was as good as that at Daly's; in any case the six evenings announced (there was no matinée) sufficed for the public demand. The regular season closed on the 30th of April, a term, except for Daniel Rochat and the Morris matinées, not among the most glorious in the history of the Union Square.

A supplementary season, starting on May 2nd, re-introduced the Vokes Family, returning after an absence so long as to be felt, and alas! without their most popular member, the delightful Rosina. To fill her place they brought Bessie Sansone, who simply could not qualify in that hazardous undertaking; who in the world could be expected to fill the void created by the departure of Rosina Vokes? And especially as the company began in The Belles of the Kitchen and Cousin Joe (the Rough Diamond), in the first of which Rosina had been so irresistibly comic! The cast of the latter piece included Fred Vokes as Cousin Joe, Victoria Vokes as Margery, J. H. Howland and Jessie Vokes as Lord and Lady Plato, Archie Cowper as Sir William, E. H. Warren Wright as Captain Blenheim. This cast I copied from the Herald review of May 3rd. Even without Rosina, the famous family kept that bill afloat until their last week (May 23rd–28th) when with Cousin Joe they presented The Wrong Man in the Right Place. And then the curtain fell at the Union Square, for 1880–81.

DALY'S THEATRE, 1880–1881

If Wallack's and the Union Square companies were entering on their final days of acclaim, Augustin Daly, with a fresh outlook and an overpowering ambition, was training young actors to take up the burden and to surpass in brilliancy, if not in finish, the work of the declining elements. Daly's Theatre was forging ahead, and, within a year or two, was to be the acknowledged first theatre of America. His first year (1879–80) had been one of trial and experiment, but better times were ahead, with the growing reputation of his theatre and his actors.

He began the season of 1880–81, on August 18th, with what might have been expected to be a great success — a "picturesque" drama adapted by himself from Fred. Williams's translation of a French play, — La P'tiote of Maurice Drach — the New York version glorying in the mystifying and unpronounceable name of Tiote. For the title-rôle, Gwendolen or "Tiote," Daly engaged Emily Rigl, whom he had trained at the old Fifth Avenue, and Fanny Morant, noble actress, rejoined his forces for the part of Lady Normant, a much maligned but finally vindicated lady. Both were warmly welcomed back into the fold, though Miss Rigl's stay was unfortunately brief. Ada Rehan made a hit as the gipsy queen, and John Drew was delightful as Sidney Ferrers, "a biblio — sometimes known as Jack Ferrers, an itinerant philosopher, and sometimes as the Gul Eray, a gipsy fine gentleman." Charles Leclercq gave a remarkable melodramatic study of a halfmad sexton. The scenes of gipsy life were counted on to attract, and the story of Gwendolen, Lady Normant's daughter, who, on hearing the false tale of her mother's sins, jumps from the castle window, only to be rescued by gipsies, and restored at last to her ancestral home, certainly was of a romantic charm exactly suited, one might suppose, to the simpler dramatic tastes of 1880. But, alas! the play, as Judge Daly says (Life of Augustin Daly), "succumbed to hot weather and that undefinable something that will so often baffle theatrical hopes." Yet how well I remember the scene of Emily Rigl's hiding behind the curtains of the bed, to surprise her mother, and overhearing to her horror the story of her mother's alleged crimes; and the entrance of the stately Fanny Morant, just after her daughter's reckless attempt at suicide! It was all acting of the fine, finished quality one would expect from those two actresses. I preserve the cast:

Sidney Ferrers	John Drew		Crook-Fin	E. P. Wilks
Darrel Crofton	Harry Lacy		Gwendolen	Emily Rigl
Cecil Asper	George S. Robinson		Lady Normant	Fanny Morant
Sir William Howden	J. H. Swinburne		Dame Crofton	Mrs. Charles Poole
Sir Hugh Morgan	W. H. Bokee		Nancy	Blanche Vaughan
Daddy Cadvan	Charles Leclercq		Gwillian	Sallie Williams
Jenkson	W. H. Beekman		Rosy	Isabelle Evesson
Owen	E. Sterling		Issopel	Ada Rehan
Sanpriel	John E. Brand		Ursula	May Sylvie
Synfye	Mr. Macdonough			

I also reproduce the names of the "girls of the village" and of the gipsies and farmers involved in the action — Emma Hinckley, Ellie Vinton, Nellie Howard, Kitty Maxwell, Fanny McNeil, Ada Featherstone, Misses Ham-

[231]

ilton, Donaldson, Porter, Brooks, Barton, Kirwin and Kirkland, Messrs. Roberts, Lawrence, Burnham, Milton, Murphy, Stultz and Palmer.

Tiote, then, failed to meet expectations, and Daly, with his usual promptitude to detect defeat, withdrew it after the performance of September 11th. On September 21st he began his second regular season in the new theatre, with a comedy by Edgar Fawcett, entitled Our First Families. Prior to the play, Fanny Morant delivered a graceful prologue dedicating that stage hereafter only to comedy, to the utter banishment of tragedy and more serious plays, and threatening (humorously) with instant dismissal any member of the company who in the remotest degree suggested in action the tricks of the tragic or the melodramatic player. After this the play proceeded, with five sterling members of Daly's old Fifth Avenue company (Fisher, James Lewis, Drew, Mrs. G. H. Gilbert and Fanny Morant), and with Ada Rehan in the van of the newer recruits. The return of Mrs. Gilbert and James Lewis brought unmitigated joy, but most of the players in the cast could now be greeted as old or newer friends:

Leonardo Tompkyns	James Lewis	Mrs. Pomeroy Stanhope	Fanny Morant
Geoffrey Knickerbocker	John Drew	Mrs. Van Rensellaer Manhattan	Mrs. Gilbert
Van Horn Knickerbocker	Charles Fisher	Eva Manhattan	Ada Rehan
Rafael Angelo Ludovici	Charles Leclercq	Celestine Ludovici	Maggie Harrold
Grigg	Hart Conway	Amelia	Blanche Weaver
Van Cortlandt	F. V. Bennett	Sophie	May Sylvie
Ten Eyck	E. Sterling	Kitty Keteltas	Nellie Howard
Rutgers	Mr. Macdonough	Lu Pleasanton	Ellie Vinton
Timothy	W. H. Beekman	Ellie Van Dam	Emma Hinckley
William	E. P. Wilks	Sue Murray	Virginia Brooks
Hebe Joscelyn	Laura Joyce	Grace Joscelyn	Georgine Flagg

It will be seen at a glance that, interesting as the company, by fine additions, had become, it had suffered a serious loss in the departure of the sprightly Catherine Lewis; Laura Joyce could not take her place in the line of sprightliness. And Davidge, so long of Daly's force, had now left it. But Ada Rehan forged ahead. Miss Joyce's scene, in the play, pretending to be deaf and dumb was an exhilarating bit of comedy full of promise for her future on Daly's stage. Our First Families served merely to start the season; it was not really a success. But Daly's next production was a delight — another of those lively comedies from the German (this one from J. Rosen's play of Starke Mittel), which was brought out, on November 9th, under the title of Needles and Pins:

Nicholas Geagle	James Lewis	Box	Mr. Lawrence
Christopher Vandusen	Charles Fisher	Mrs. Vandusen	Fanny Morant
Kit Vandusen	John Brand	Dosie Heffron	Mrs. G. H. Gilbert
Tom Versus	John Drew	Silena Vandusen	Ada Rehan
Sergeant Macdonald	Mr. Roberts	Mary Forrest	May Fielding
Jonah	E. P. Wilks	Caroline	Maggie Harrold
Blot	W. H. Beekman	Hannah	Miss Levere

JAMES LEWIS
(CINDERELLA AT SCHOOL)

MRS. G. H. GILBERT
(CINDERELLA AT SCHOOL)

ADA REHAN
(CINDERELLA AT SCHOOL)

MAY FIELDING
(CINDERELLA AT SCHOOL)

ROSE EYTINGE
IN FELICIA

F. DE BELLEVILLE
(UNION SQUARE THEATRE)

BESSIE SANSONE

JOHN E. BRAND

LAURA JOYCE

In the Masque and Nursery Cotillion, incidental to the play, appeared a host of pleasing young members of the corps — Misses Evessen, Vinton, Maxwell, Kirkland, Williams, Vaughan, Howard, Featherstone, Weaver, McNeil, Donaldson, Trevelyan, Hinckley, Flagg, Levere and Brooks, and Messrs. Wilks, Sterling, Macdonough, Lawrence, Bennett, Hewitt, and Mlle. Malvina (who directed the dance).   In this comedy, as Judge Daly points out, James Lewis, John Drew, Mrs. Gilbert and Ada Rehan were "first recognized as the famous quartet which for so many seasons endeared Daly's Theatre to the public."   Mrs. Gilbert played a ridiculous spinster, "got up" in girlish guise, and regarding her niece (Ada Rehan) as a thorn in the flesh.   Miss Rehan was simply delightful as what the Restoration playwrights regarded as the "fausse ingénue" or something approximating thereto; and James Lewis, of course, was finally "caught" by the designing Dosie (Mrs. Gilbert).   It was all very good fun, and it spun merrily down the road of success till January 15th, when, by previous contracts for other shows, Daly was forced to withdraw it.

The theatre was closed on Monday, January 17th, for rehearsal of Zanina, or, the Rover of Cambaye, an operetta adapted from Genée, in the hope, doubtless, that it would duplicate the success of the same composer's The Royal Middy, which Catherine Lewis had made so merry in the preceding season.   Laura Joyce was now called on to show what she could do in the difficult task of replacing Miss Lewis, and Digby Bell (afterward Miss Joyce's husband) was called in to add comedy and vocal accomplishment to the score.   Thus cast, Zanina opened on the 18th:

Monteil	John Brand	Delamanna Moro Khan	J. Macdonough
Booma Poota	Digby Bell	Allabad	W. Paul Bown
Strakoschino Mapello	James Lewis	Zanina	Laura Joyce
Simmondson Rinaldo	Charles Leclercq	Muttra	Ada Rehan
Rinaldini	E. P. Wilks	Nuna	May Fielding
Captain Trafalgar	Harry Lacy	Maeda	May Sylvie
Africanus	T. Hengler	Nauchida	Maggie Harrold

Through the efforts of Harry W. French (author of Art and Artists) Daly engaged a force of performers from India — Nautch dancing girls, magicians and snake-charmers (these last-named with cobras and a policeman mongoose).   The scenery was fine, and a success might have been anticipated. As a matter of fact, Zanina was an acute failure, and it breathed its last on February 12th.   The Indian contingent returned to their native shores, with the loss of one dancer, a girl of fourteen or fifteen, who died in New York prior to the opening of Zanina.   Judge Daly gives an interesting account of these exotic performers, their demand for heated living apartments, "the shuffle, shuffle, shuffle, of the bare feet of the dancers," etc.   And what thinks the reader of the presence in the cast of T. M. Hengler, of the team Delehanty and Hengler, a team now dissevered by the death of Delehanty?

[233]

Needles and Pins came back on February 14th and reached its hundredth performance on March 2nd; its last playing was at the matinée on March 5th. On the evening of the 5th Daly put on a musical farce, founded on Robertson's popular comedy of School, with music by Woolson Morse, orchestrated by Edward Mollenhauer, conductor of the Daly orchestra. Though much of the dainty charm of the Robertson play evaporated in this new version, enough broad humour took its place to make a great popular success. James Lewis as Syntax, with a marvellous academic make-up, and Mrs. Gilbert as Zenobia Tropics, head-mistress of the Papyrus Seminary, made stunning hits, and, as Judge Daly says, Mrs. Gilbert "marshalled her fun-loving scholars not only with Amazonian firmness, but with a terpsichorean grace which had no equal. As for Lewis, he was a figure that might have stepped out of Rolandson's eccentric drawings." But we must write down the leaders of the cast, if only for the sake of the bright array of school girls:

Arthur Bicycle	Harry Lacy	Niobe Marsh	May Fielding
Jack Polo	John Brand	Merope Mallow	Laura Joyce
Lord Lawntennys	C. Leclercq	Psyche Persimmons	Ada Rehan
Professor Kindergarten	Paul Bown	Zenobia Tropics	Mrs. G. H. Gilbert
Syntax	James Lewis	Miss Globes	Agnes Perring
Dr. Porous	H. Roberts	Circe Slatepencil	Georgine Flagg
Jenkinson	E. P. Wilks	Lotis Slatepencil	Sallie Williams

A great array of young men and women served as chorus to the merriment. This gay trifle ended Daly's productions for 1880–81; he carried it till April 30th, when his season closed with a mixed bill including acts from the three best things of the year — Our First Families (which had been played fifty-six times), Needles and Pins (one hundred and three times), and Cinderella at School (sixty-five). No one could place this season at the head of Daly's achievements; but it had helped to establish his company in the high tide of popular favour. After the departure of his actors, a combination under management of J. M. Hill brought in a farce that had had a year's success in various cities, including Brooklyn; this was W. D. Eaton's All the Rage, and on May 2nd, at Daly's, it enlisted a cast of actors two of whom, at least, had won much of their New York reputation in Daly's Fifth Avenue Theatre:

Dr. William Goodwin	F. Hardenberg	Sophronia Briggs	Meta Bartlett
DeWitt C. Briggs	W. Davidge	Julie Gale	Lisetta Ellani
Horatio Braney	J. C. Padgett	Cleopatra	Blanche Moulton
Charlie Granger	W. Richardson	Mrs. Goodwin	Mrs. G. C. Germon
Will Goodwin	A. Z. Chipman	Annie Goodwin	Clara Hyatt
D. Clinton Briggs	Edward Milliken		

This summer trifle was rather liked, and continued for four weeks at Daly's; on May 30th, it moved to Niblo's Garden for one week more (and only one) of sweet metropolitan ministration. Daly's remained dark till August 9th, when Cinderella at School again enlivened the heated city.

[234]

Madison Square Theatre, 1880–1881

We left Hazel Kirke in possession of the stage (or, to be exact, the double stage) of Steele MacKaye's drawing-room theatre, the beautiful Madison Square. Even before September 1st, changes, as we saw, had come into the cast, Georgia Cayvan having replaced Gabrielle du Sauld as Dolly Dutton. On August 21st, the Herald states that Daniel Frohman, business manager of the Madison Square, had left to assume a simliar position at Haverly's Fifth Avenue Theatre; the Madison Square Company had presented him with a handsome gold watch and chain by way of fond farewell. The 250th performance of Hazel Kirke fell on October 8th. On October 11th, Steele MacKaye assumed, for a time, the rôle of Dunstan Kirke; I fancy that he was less adapted to it than had been the accomplished C. W. Couldock. A ripple on the surface and possibly the surfeit of success came on October 13th, when a musical matinée brought to the little theatre Constantine Sternberg, a Russian pianist recently arrived, Anna Drasdil, the ever-reliable, Poznanski, Theodore J. Toedt and G. W. Colby. All things came to us then, as now, and, on the 20th (matinée), Sternberg tried again, with the assistance of Mlle. de Montello (soprano), Jeanne Chastel (mezzo-soprano), Roberto Stantini (tenor — first appearance in America), Giorgio Castelli (basso — début here), Hermann Brandt (violinist), Grecco (or Greco, accompanist) and G. W. Colby (director). The reader may judge the merits of the concert by the subsequent oblivion into which the performers were immersed. But we have all heard of the London writer, Joseph Hatton, who, on October 21st, read a dramatic version of his novel, The Queen of Bohemia. For the musical matinée of the 27th, Sternberg's associates were Henrietta Beebe, Toedt, Brandt and Colby. That ended music as a sole provision at the Madison Square, and Hazel Kirke was left in sole possession — almost.

"Almost," because, on October 28th, Nelson Waldron, machinist and worker of many of the mechanical wonders of the new theatre, had a benefit (why?), when, to my surprise, I find that William H. Gillette gave an act of his play, The Professor, one day to succeed Hazel Kirke on this stage. C. W. Couldock recited The Vagabonds, and Osmond Tearle did the same thing for Grace Darling. The Wallack company gave an act of As You Like It, the Madison Square actors played the second act of Hazel Kirke, and Kate Claxton appeared in the last act of The Two Orphans. An exhibition of the working of the double stage concluded the show. The Madison Square advertised but sparsely in the newspapers, and its pretty, souvenir programmes bore no dates; it is therefore somewhat difficult to follow accurately its frequent changes of cast; the Brooklyn Eagle of November 7th states that Jeffreys Lewis, Sydney Cowell, George Clarke and Steele MacKaye were in it. At a benefit for the Elks, held at the Academy of

[235]

Music, on December 2nd, one act of Hazel Kirke was promised with the actors presumably then carrying on at the Madison Square; Steele MacKaye was Dunstan, Dominick Murray was Aaron Rodney, George Clarke Lord Travers, Whiffen Pittacus Green, Joseph Frankau Met, Louis F. Massen Joe, Harry Hogan Dan, Jeffreys Lewis Hazel, Sydney Cowell Dolly Dutton, Flora Livingston Lady Travers, and Mrs. Whiffen Mercy Kirke. Shortly after, Jeffreys Lewis fell ill, and Jean Burnside came out of the past to play Hazel for a few nights. The reader may wish to know that some of the original cast of the play (Couldock, Miss Ellsler, Cecile Rush, Annie Ellsler) were now carrying to outlying districts the glad message of Hazel Kirke; on February 7th they began a week at the Park Theatre, Brooklyn; another company, headed by Lillian Spencer and Charles Wheatleigh (as Dunstan) was, according to the Herald of March 13th, touring our Eastern cities. By this time, Georgia Cayvan was acting Hazel (she had begun to do so in January), in the home theatre, with Dominick Murray (the original Aaron Rodney here) as Dunstan, George Clarke as Lord Travers, Mr. and Mrs. Whiffen as Pittacus and Mercy, Sydney Cowell as Dolly, Flora Livingston as Lady Travers, Maude (or Maud) Stuart (a pretty girl later admired as the blind girl, in Young Mrs. Winthrop) as Clara, William F. Clifton as Aaron Rodney, Frankau as Met, W. B. Cahill as Barney O'Flynn, Louis F. Massen as Joe, &c. On April 17th, the cast in Herald advertisements gave Eben Plympton as Lord Travers and George Clarke as Aaron Rodney. A list of all the performers who ever played in Hazel Kirke would be a museum-piece fit to be placed side by side with a similar list for Uncle Tom's Cabin or The Two Orphans. On February 4th, the Madison Square celebrated the anniversary of the production, with flowers and with bronze plaques to lady visitors; on April 25th the four hundred and fiftieth performance of its grandly successful play. On the next afternoon (April 26th), an amateur performance of Old Love Letters and A Wonderful Woman attracts us, because in the latter appeared that beautiful society woman, Mrs. James Brown Potter, destined within a few years to win much notoriety on the stage. Other performers were Miss D. E. Ingersoll, Dr. Curtis, and Major Bedlow, of Newport.

Hazel Kirke finally ran its allotted course, and finished on May 31st, the occasion of its four hundred and eighty-sixth performance — the longest run up to that time achieved in an American theatre. Before the end of the run, the author of the play and the designer of the lovely little theatre had, as might have been expected, differed hopelessly with the cleric, Dr. Mallory, and Mr. Marshall Mallory; he withdrew from the theatre, and the brothers removed his name from the bills, first as manager, and then as author of Hazel Kirke. MacKaye, like most dreamers, an unpractical business man, had signed a contract with the managers, to give his services as author, actor and manager for $5,000 a year; when, therefore, he left the

SYDNEY COWELL
AS DOLLY DUTTON

W. H. GILLETTE

W. B. CAHILL
AS BARNEY O'FLYNN

HAZEL KIRKE (ACT II) IN THE MADISON SQUARE THEATRE
From a Print in the Harvard Theatre Collection

establishment, the courts decided that he gave up his rights in Hazel Kirke, which he had supplied as part of his services for that yearly stipend. Though for many years thereafter the play coined money for the Mallorys, they never, according to Percy MacKaye (Epoch) paid his father a penny in royalties. It seems incredible; whatever the legal aspect of the matter, there was the human, Christian side to be considered.

The successor to Hazel Kirke was William H. Gillette's comedy, The Professor, thus produced on June 1st:

Daisy Brown	Georgia Cayvan	Professor Hopkins	W. H. Gillette
Mrs. Elliott	Mrs. Nellie Taylor	Mr. Thomkins	Leslie Allen
Estelle	Nellie Morant	Gustavus	C. W. Butler
Grace Gay	Marie Chester	Moses Brown	E. L. Tilton
Susy Sundown	Belle Melville	Henry Marston	Harry Lacy
Annie Timms	Josephine Bailey	Fred Bangs	D. H. Chase
Dotty Pinney	Belle Jackson	Jack Topley	A. Waldron
Minnie Moss	Maud Stuart	Sheriff	C. Eldridge
Molly Merry	Helen Ottolengui	Thomas	Harry Hogan

The Professor, with its troupe of pretty students, carried on the custom established by Cinderella at School; and oddly enough, in it Harry Lacy, as one of three Yale students roaming the pretty romantic glades of The Professor's scenic investiture, was engaged in much the same kind of work he carried on in the earlier piece at Daly's. To Daly's he never returned, alas! One notes the progress of the talented Georgia Cayvan; in fact, from Dolly Dutton to the May Blossom of 1884, Miss Cayvan was one of the outstanding figures in Madison Square plays. And, of course, in The Professor, we are delighted to greet William Gillette, as author and actor; in both capacities he is one of the best-loved, the most acclaimed persons in the last half-century of the American theatre. Like Daly's, the Madison Square brought prominently forward and developed many of the best players of their time. That can be said for the Mallorys, even after MacKaye retired. Let us, however, remember that in their force was the young David Belasco. On August 15th, the Herald informs me, Helen Ottolengui replaced Marie Chester, ill. The Professor had one hundred and fifty-one performances, and was therefore a minor success, compared with Hazel Kirke and Esmeralda, the latter of which followed it on this stage, in October, 1881.

BOOTH'S THEATRE, 1880–1881

Does the reader remember the excitement in 1880 about Dr. Tanner's attempt to fast for forty days? Well, on September 9th, after the ordeal, he was down for a lecture at Booth's, on What I Know about Fasting. With this preliminary, I begin. Except for the visits of two of the most famous

[237]

European players, the season of 1880–81 at Booth's, under Henry E. Abbey's management, was not particularly important. Yet a bit of interest attaches to the first engagement of the autumn, that of the Boston Ideal Opera Company, which opened on September 13th, in The Pirates of Penzance, with several singers of high repute on the concert stage in leading rôles:

Richard	Myron W. Whitney	Mabel	Mary Beebe
Samuel	W. H. Macdonald	Edith	Clara Merivale
Frederic	Tom Karl	Kate	Lizzie Burton
Major-General Stanley	H. C. Barnabee	Isabel	Miss Mitchell
Sergeant of Police	George Frothingham	Ruth	Adelaide Phillipps

On the 15th, Marie Stone appeared as Mabel, and, on the 16th, W. H. Fessenden as Frederic, and thereafter divided the responsibility of those rôles with Miss Beebe and Tom Karl. Beloved names are in that aggregation — Whitney, Barnabee, Macdonald, Frothingham, Adelaide Phillips (or, as recently printed, Phillipps) stand high in our musical annals. On September 14th, the Herald declares: "Certainly some of the parts were better sung than they were by the English company, although the acting suffered somewhat by comparison. Voices like those of Messrs. Whitney and Barnabee are seldom heard on any stage, except in grand opera, and they are rare even there. . . . Miss Phillips has not the voice of Miss Barnett, but she excels that lady in the dramatic work of her part." Miss Beebe created "a grand furor by her work in the duet that comes early in the second act." This all sounds attractive.

The Pirates carried through September 25th, and, on the 27th, Fatinitza presented Miss Phillips (or Phillipps), graduate of grand opera, in the title-rôle, Marie Stone as Lydia, Whitney as Count Timofey, Barnabee as Izzet Pacha, Tom Karl as Julian Hardy, Gus Kammerlee as Osip, W. W. Tuttle as Captain Vasil, George Frothingham as Sergeant Stepan, Lizzie Burton as Dimitri, and H. F. Dixey as Mustapha — assuredly the best interpreters by far the opera had yet had in New York. On October 7th, the everlasting, ever-sailing Pinafore had a delightful singing cast in Barnabee as Sir Joseph Porter, Marie Stone as Josephine, George Frothingham as Dick Deadeye, Mary Calef as Hebe, Adelaide Phillipps (sic) as Buttercup, W. H. Fessenden as Ralph, and M. W. Whitney as Captain Corcoran. On the 8th, Tom Karl was Ralph. In these performances Adelaide Phillipps appeared for the last times in New York. The accomplished Bostonians departed on the 9th. They were succeeded, on October 12th, by H. C. Jarrett's aggregation, in Cinderella, or, the Little Glass Slipper, the cast including Catherine Lewis (now a star, since her great success last season at Daly's), Elma Delaro, Jennie Hughes, Annie Shaffer, Katie Seymour, Mark Smith (son of the great Mark Smith of the '6os at Wallack's), W. H. Seymour, James Vincent, Edward Connell, and Arthur Germon, and with Anthony Reiff as conductor (the music was partly from Rossini). In the specialty acts figured Lizzie Simms, dancer from the London Alhambra. Lilliputian ponies and a "fairy" palace were part of the spectacle. Thanks to Miss Lewis and the scenic effects, this production lasted through November 6th, four weeks in all.

SARAH BERNHARDT; TOMMASO SALVINI

And now, on November 8th, came the great event for which the press agents had awakened thrills and longings of expectation. For months, prior to her appearance here, the name of Sarah Bernhardt had been bandied back and forth in speculative discourse, her eccentricities (sleeping in a coffin, for instance), her "scandalous" conduct, her "break" with the Comédie Française, her extraordinary slimness and height (in an age before girls worked for slim figures) — all these things were current in talk, and helped wonderfully to arouse curiosity. Of course, Mlle. Bernhardt was hailed as the greatest of actresses since Rachel, and, in America, there was a desire to compare her emotional powers with those of Clara Morris. Excitement ran high, and a great mob besieged the box-office, buying in short time, on the opening day of the sale, ten thousand dollars' worth of tickets, at prices for that day very exalted. On the opening night single seats sold for $3 in the orchestra, orchestra circle and balcony; for $2.50 in the dress circle; and for $2 in the family circle. For other perfomances $2 would admit to the dress circle, and $1 to the family circle. Season tickets (twenty-four performances) brought sixty dollars.

And the great night arrived. The famous actress appeared, on November 8th, in Adrienne Lecouvreur, that part written for Rachel, and beautifully played here, more recently, by Ristori, Marie Seebach and Helena Modjeska. Bernhardt's company was but passable, but it was naturally assumed that all interest would centre in the star:

Adrienne Lecouvreur..Mlle. Sarah Bernhardt		Princesse de Bouillon.......Mlle. Colombier	
Maurice de Saxe.................M. Angelo		Duchesse d'Aumont............Mlle. Sidney	
Prince de Bouillon.............M. Bouilloud		La Marquise................Mlle. Carpentier	
Michonnet.................M. Chamounin		La Baronne...................Mlle. Martel	
Abbé de Chazeuil.................M. Théfer		Mlle. Jouvenot.................Mlle. Pacra	
Quinault.....................M. Deletraz		Mlle. Dangeville................Mlle. Jane	
Poisson.........................M. Piron			

Of course critical knives were sharpened, and the reviewers vied with each other in analysis, dissection, and juggling of terms. The Herald, on the 9th, states that Mlle. Bernhardt has "a musical voice, an expressive face, a command of appropriate gesture, a wonderful facility in expressing the tenderest womanly emotions or representing with startling reality the most agonizing physical suffering," but "she is lacking in that power, which, com-

[239]

bining dramatic and physical force, enables an actress to rise to the demands of the grandest climax and produce the profoundest effects by the impetuous outburst of uncontrolled human passions in a moment of intense emotion. In the expression of all the tenderest, most fascinating charms by which a loving woman can woo or win affection — in the music of her voice, the touch of her caress, the fond, loving and earnest look from her eyes, the sweetness of her smile" she "is an absolute mistress of her art." "In depicting human suffering she seems to absolutely control every organ of her body — her cheek blanches, tears come at her bidding, and in the famous death scene there is a ghastly resemblance to the real in the feigned dissolution . . . but where her lines call for the grand and imposing effects of concentrated passion, such as the scene between the Princess and the actress in the third act . . . Mlle. Bernhardt lacked breadth, force and passion."

William Winter, of the Tribune, never granted the highest qualities to Bernhardt; to him, also, she failed in grandeur, but he felt (The Wallet of Time, Volume One) that Adrienne was "one of the most agreeable and admirable of her many performances." Adrienne was repeated on the 9th, and at the matinée, on the 13th. On the evenings of the 10th, 11th and 12th, Mlle. Bernhardt appeared as Gilberte, in Frou-Frou, that hectic tale by Meilhac and Halévy, of the light-minded wife who learns too late. In this she had the support of Angelo as Sartorys, of Gally as de Valréas, Deletraz as Baron de Cambri, Chamounin as Brigard, Théfer as Pitou, Mlle. Colombier as Baronne de Cambri, Mlle. Sidney as Louise, Mlle. Jane as Zanette, and Mlle. Martel as the Gouvernante. The Herald, of the 11th, notes the excellence of the star's acting, her presenting the heroine as less frivolous and childish in the early scenes, etc. William Winter (The Wallet of Time) regards her Gilberte as "one of the most expert, sparkling, and effective achievements of 'natural' acting ever shown on our stage . . . a perfect image of winning prettiness, unconscious coquetry, and exquisite, if irrational, sensibility, a passionate woman and . . . a fascinating child." Her fiery, jealous rage, when at last "she seemed to lose all control of herself and liberated the storm of passion which thrilled her slender, delicate, fragile person was as splendid . . . as any professional exploit of hers in the whole range of her long career."

La Dame aux Camélias was inevitable and came duly on November 15th, 16th and 17th, the Marguerite of the star being associated, of course, with the Armand of Angelo. The public could now compare the French Camille with the American Camille of Clara Morris and the Polish Camille of Modjeska. Needless to say, it was more like Modjeska's than Miss Morris's, in delicacy of finish, in beautiful detail, in pathos; as William Winter said, there was in it "no reek of the medical dispensary or of the brothel." Sarah Bernhardt's performance of this not wholly pleasing rôle is, of course, a

TOM KARL
AS RALPH RACKSTRAW

GEORGE FROTHINGHAM
AS DICK DEADEYE

H. C. BARNABEE
AS SIR JOSEPH PORTER

MATHILDE PHILLIPPS
(OF THE BOSTON IDEALS)

MARIE STONE
IN FRA DIAVOLO

ADELAIDE PHILLIPPS
IN FATINITZA

MYRON W. WHITNEY

W. H. MACDONALD

MARY BEEBE

classic of stage history. The evenings of the 18th and 19th allowed the new luminary to shine as Doña Sol, with Angelo as Hernani and Gangloff as Don Carlos. Frou-Frou was matinée lure, on the 20th. The star did not play on Saturday evenings.

On Monday, November 22nd, Mlle. Bernhardt repeated Frou-Frou (evidently a favourite with her), and on the 23rd gave that test of the French tragic actress, Phèdre, in which it must be confessed, she fell below the grandeur of the lamented Rachel. Her Phèdre, according to William Winter, was lacking "in majesty and tenderness"; she applied to the character "the passion of *Camille*, with the method of *Adrienne* — the 'natural' style to a subject entirely unnatural." She "revealed the ravaged condition of Phèdre's mind at the outset, and thus at once excited pity. But she never attained to majesty; she but dimly gave the idea of an impelling, inexorable fate; and there was more of self than of anybody else in her attempted portraiture of the operation of love. The most startling moment . . . was that in which *Phèdre's* frenzy precipitates the disclosure of her fatal secret to *Hippolyte*. The alternations of self-pitying lamentation with explosive protest were made with intense power." Yet the portrayal failed in majesty and tenderness, and "in spiritual remorse." One can believe this; grandeur comes only from grandeur of soul. On the next evening, Bernhardt returned to Camille, and on the 25th and 26th of November, again gave opportunity of comparison with Clara Morris (who, by the way, had been appearing at the Park Theatre) in the hateful part of Blanche de Chelles, in The Sphinx. The matinée, on the 27th, reverted to La Dame aux Camélias. On November 29th, the celebrated actress repeated Doña Sol, Frou-Frou on the 30th, Camille on December 1st, Phèdre on the 2nd, The Sphinx on the 3rd, and Hernani at the matinée on the 4th. On the evening of the 4th, appearing, for the first time here twice on one day, she took a prosperous farewell in the second and third acts of Frou-Frou, in Le Passant, and in the fourth and fifth acts of Camille. Thus ended the four-weeks excitement; many doubtless believed they had now seen the greatest of all actresses. And, whatever one may think of the tragic powers of Sarah Bernhardt as compared with her sensational and emotional utterance, one realises that for theatrical expertness, for infinitude of detail, for finish of style, she has probably never been surpassed. She was not Mrs. Siddons or Rachel or Charlotte Cushman; but she showed that, if she lacked the heartbreak of Clara Morris, she also lacked the crudity of that popular representative of physical and mental suffering. The kind of drama in which each excelled is today (1939) out of vogue.

The next great figure on the stage of Booth's was Tommaso Salvini, but in the week (December 6th–11th) that intervened between Barnhardt's departure and his arrival, A Celebrated Case was tried, with James O'Neill (as Jean Renaud), Rose Wood, Lewis Morrison, Gabrielle du Sauld, Harry

[241]

Edwards, W. Scallan and the everlasting Little Eva French. There had been promised for that week a much-advertised Passion Play, arranged by Salmi Morse, with James O'Neill as Christ. Public clamour prevented its production. Salvini, after an absence of several years, re-appeared on December 13th, in his great rôle of Othello, supported by an English-speaking company, including L. R. Shewell as Iago, Henry Crisp as Cassio, W. F. Owen as Roderigo, A. D. Billings as Brabantio, T. M. Hunter as the Duke, J. H. Ring as Gratiano, Ellie Wilton as Desdemona, and Marie Prescott as Emilia. John Stetson was manager for the Italian actor; hence the large proportion of Boston actors in the cast. Othello was repeated on the 15th; Hamlet came on the 17th, and on the 18th, La Morte Civile, Giacometti's pathetic play, with Ellie Wilton as Rosalie. Salvini appeared but four times a week, and on the other evenings the house remained dark. For his second and last week, the tragedian repeated Othello, on Decembr 20th and 25th (evening), gave Sullivan (known to us as David Garrick) on the 22nd, and The Gladiator (Saumet's tragedy, not Bird's) on the 23rd. In later plays his support had included also H. A. Weaver, Mrs. E. L. Davenport and Athena. And that was all New York, growing faster toward its doom of frivolity, could stand of the greatest tragic actor of his time; his audiences had not been large or enthusiastic.

I advise the reader to turn to J. Ranken Towse (Sixty Years of the Theater) for a superb analysis of all these performances. Dramatic critics reared on the English ideal of Othello and conceiving of him, despite his complexion, as a gentlemanly European, considered Salvini's Moor brutal, barbarous and un-Shakespearian. Mr. Towse, ignoring such cavilling, says that there was "no limit" to the range of the Italian's "emotional expression. He exhibited the power of an Edwin Forrest in combination with the delicacy and subtlety of a Duse. He could overwhelm with a thunderous outburst — free from all suspicion of rant — or electrify with the mute manifestation of suppressed passion."

The portrayal of Conrad, in La Morte Civile, was unalloyed pathos, as distinct as possible from Othello; the death scene, with the pitching forward, head-foremost from his chair, was one of Salvini's most stirring effects. Towse thinks Salvini's Sullivan more perfect in all its aspects, collectively, than the David Garrick of Lawrence Barrett or E. A. Sothern; whereas his Niger, in The Gladiator, was "tremendous" at first, and later even greater when, in the arena, he recognises in the girl who was to be left to the lions the daughter for whom he was seeking. "He seemed," says Towse, "the center of a veritable hurricane, a whirlwind of emotions." "There was no rant, no aimless, hysterical contortion or shrieking. The actor was always master of himself and of his art. As I survey the theatrical firmament as I have known it," says Towse, "Salvini shines among the constellations *velut inter ignes luna minores.*"

[242]

After eight performances, then, Salvini left Booth's Theatre to — Uncle Tom's Cabin! This was revived by H. C. Jarrett and H. J. Palmer's company, and ran from December 27th to January 29th, in a house that had not always been crowded for a beggarly eight performances by Salvini. Those were the "palmy" days, or at least their degenerate offspring. The cast of Uncle Tom's Cabin was somewhat better than that of many recent revivals:

Simon Legree	Lewis Morrison	Topsy	Marie Bates
Uncle Tom	A. H. Hastings	Eva	Zoe Tuttle
Fletcher	Charles Wheatleigh	Miss Ophelia	Mrs. W. A. Rouse
Marks	Harry Courtaine	Cassie	Jennie Carroll
George Harris	Ogden Stevens	Eliza	Blanche De Bar
St. Clair	Nelson Decker	Emeline	Josie Wilmere
George Shelby	L. F. Barrett	Mrs. St. Clair	Mabel Lozier
Haley	George Mordaunt		

One notes with interest the name of Blanche De Bar; one remembers, also, that Uncle Tom's Cabin was current, in part of this Booth's run, at the Academy of Music. It is simply inexplicable, until one recalls the exciting melodramatic character of many of the incidents in the play.

On January 28th (not December 28th, as Allston Brown has it), came a benefit for M. V. Lingham, at which were to appear Herrmann; Willie Edouin and company in an act of Dreams; Charles R. Thorne, Jr., in a recitation of Sheridan's Ride; the Union Square company, in an act of French Flats; Goss and Fox in a sketch; the Rankins, in the fourth act of The Danites; Catherine Lewis and John Howson, in selections from Olivette; John Gilbert and Rose Coghlan, in the quarrel scene from The School for Scandal; the Wallack Company, in the third act of The Guv'nor; Charles Drew and Amy Gordon; C. B. Bishop, in the third act of Widow Bedott; Harry Edwards, in a recitation; and the trial scene of Bardell vs. Pickwick, with G. F. Rowe as Buzfuz and H. M. Pitt as Sergeant Snubbins, and a jury composed of Charles Gayler, Steele MacKaye, Osmond Tearle, William Elton, George Clarke, Harry Edwards, Joaquin Miller and others.

Salvini returned, on January 31st, in The Gladiator, which he repeated on February 2nd, 3rd, and at a matinée on the 5th of February; his associates were W. H. (Harry) Crisp as Flavian, H. A. Weaver as Origen, A. D. Billings as the High Priest of Juno, F. Kilday as Octavius, W. Warren as Lucius, T. M. Hunter as Albino, Marie Prescott as Faustina, and Julia Stewart as Neodamia. On February 1st, 2nd (matinée), 4th and 5th, Enoch Arden tried to fill Salvini's "off" nights, with James O'Neill as Enoch, Agnes Booth as Annie Leigh, Mrs. E. L. Davenport as Miriam Lane, Harry Crisp as Philip Ray, A. D. Billings as Reuben, and W. F. Owen as Peter Lane. According to the Herald of February 2nd, the audience was so small on the preceding evening that Mrs. Booth and her colleagues were chilled into an

[243]

almost fatal lack of ability to carry out their rôles. Yet how much the reader and I might have enjoyed such a cast in that once popular play! On February 7th, Salvini was again Othello; on the 9th, Ingomar; on the 10th and 12th, Macbeth (for the first time in America, and with Marie Prescott as Lady Macbeth). At other performances of the week, Enoch Arden struggled on against an undesired return to the stage on which Edwin Adams had once been so admired in the title-rôle. On February 14th, Salvini offered a professional matinée of Othello.

Seventeen performances, then, were all that Salvini gave that season in Manhattan; it seems incredible. On February 11th, a great benefit matinée was carried through for the presentation to the Metropolitan Museum of a life-size alto-relievo, in bronze, of Edgar Allan Poe; A. M. Palmer was director, and Leon Vincent stage manager. H. J. Widmer began with an orchestral performance, followed by Gilmore's Band, with the redoubtable Gilmore. Charles Roberts, Jr. recited The Bells, and the farce of Betsey Baker presented John T. Raymond as Mouser, Cecil Yorke as Mrs. Mouser, Lewis Baker as Crummy, and Louise Sylvester (replacing Mrs. McKee Rankin, originally announced) as Betsey. Locke Richardson next recited the Wooing Scene, from Henry V, Signor Tagliapietra sang, and Clara Morris, Louisa Eldridge and Thomas Chapman gave the sleep-walking scene from Macbeth. A violin solo by Carlos Hasselbrinck led to the screen scene from The School for Scandal, by John Gilbert, Osmond Tearle, Gerald Eyre, Rose Coghlan and Harry J. Holliday; this, in turn was succeeded by Kate Field, in selections from Eyes and Ears in London. Next came a scene from Sullivan, with Salvini, H. A. Weaver, Owen, T. M. Hunter, Ellie Wilton, Mrs. T. E. Morris and Mrs. E. L. Davenport. Nellie Holbrook read Poe's Annabel Lee and his Dream within a Dream, the Hatton Quartet following with a singing of Caryl Florio's setting of the second of those poems. The first and second acts of The Colleen Bawn enlisted Agnes Robertson and Charles Wheatleigh in their original rôles of Eily O'Connor and Danny Mann, with William Elton as Myles, Nelson Decker as Hardress, T. E. Morris as Father Tom, and Louisa Eldridge as Shelah. The trial scene from Colonel Sellers, with a jury of celebrities, was to have ended this rare and lengthy afternoon, but instead we were treated to the second act of Our Boarding House, in which appeared J. B. Polk, Leonard Grover, Georgie Dickson (Mrs. J. H. Rowe), Josie Batchelder, &c. Catherine Lewis and John Howson were to have appeared in a scene from Olivette, but, though they were present, failed to do so; something about the situation of the orchestra under the stage, I learned from the next day's Herald. Mr. and Mrs. Rankin, originally announced, did not participate. This assuredly was a generous and a pleasing bill.

The week of February 14th–19th lapsed from Salvini to DeWolf Hopper and the Gosche-Hopper Company, in One Hundred Wives:

[244]

Confucius McGinley........De Wolf Hopper	Hutchings...................Frank J. Rolfe
Edward Bradford.............Frank Weston	Jack Sykes...............George R. Sprague
Elder Bezum..........Alexander Fitzgerald	Sophronia McGinley...........Ada Gilman
Hung Li.....................John E. Ince	Elsie Bradford.....Georgie Drew Barrymore
Spriggins.....................John Ogden	Bessie...................Little Vivia Ogden
Dickson....................Charles Rolfe	Mrs. Andrews.............Mrs. J. Wheeler
Nick Culver............Lawrence Eddinger	Mrs. Broody, No. 1............Adele Wright
Broody..........................J. Perry	Mrs. Broody, No. 2.........Mary Richards

This trifling device lasted for three weeks.

JANAUSCHEK; SARAH BERNHARDT

On March 7th, Fanny Janauschek, a grand relic still striving to maintain a former leading position, entered in her great rôle of Brunhild:

Brunhild..................... Janauschek	Volker.......................J. L. Carhart
Siegfried..................Harry Meredith	Chriemhilde................Florence Noble
Gunther.................George W. Wessells	Sigrun.................Mrs. J. L. Carhart
Giselher..................Charles Herman	Gerda.......................Miss Fletcher
Hagen.....................James Taylor	Maiden.......................Miss Gordon

Brunhild was repeated on the 9th; on the 8th, 10th and 12th (matinée) Janauschek gave her superb performance of the Countess of Mansfeldt, in Mother and Son, an emotional play founded by Janet Tuckey, of London, on Frederika Bremer's novel of The Neighbours. In this Janauschek's rôle was that of an iron-willed mother who casts out her beloved son, whom she believes guilty of theft. She was very powerful, as I remember, in the scenes of reviling of this supposedly criminal son (in reality he was assuming the guilt of another) and she was simply magnificent in the scenes of gradual dissolution and death. By this time, so long after her début in America, audiences needed to be reminded that Janauschek was really one of the great actresses. The cast included Charles D. Herman as Bruno and Harry Meredith as Stephen, sons of the Countess, George W. Wessells as Andrew, Shirley Smith as Parson Newman, J. L. Carhart as Palmer, James Taylor as Stromer, Miss Jewell as the Baroness Wenderfels, Mrs. Carhart as Margaret, and Florence Noble as Franziska. On March 11th, Janauschek gave her great performance of Medea, and, on the evening of the 12th, Lady Macbeth, with Harry Meredith as Macbeth, Herman as Malcolm, and Wessells as Macduff. For her second and last week, Janauschek acted Mary Stuart on the 14th and 18th; Bleak House (as Lady Dedlock and Hortense) on the 15th and 17th, with a matinée on the 19th; Medea on the 16th; and Deborah, as a farewell, on Saturday evening, March 19th. I hazard the guess that business was not large.

Voyagers in Southern Seas, or, the Children of Captain Grant, came to Booth's on March 21st, all the way from Boston and with the company from the Boston Theatre; it was a concoction of Jules Verne and D'Ennery, and its production necessitated the engagement of Marie Bonfanti, Ernestine Bossi, and "the flying wonder," Ariel. Here is the cast:

[245]

Captain Grant	Frank Weston	Dick	A. E. Chase
Paganol	Leslie Allen	Forster	E. Y. Backus
Bob	D. J. Maguinnis	Guide	R. D. Moss
Ayrton	Mark M. Price	Hotel Keeper	Arthur Moulton
Lord Glenarvon	Otis Skinner	Lady Arabella	Mrs. M. A. Pennoyer
Thalcave	George R. Parks	James Grant	Rachel Noah
Burck	M. J. Jordan	Robert Grant	Master Harry Woodruff
Mulray	John T. Craven	Mary Grant	Mary Tucker
Captain Wilson	H. A. Cripps	Elmina	Charline Weidman

If New York may have said that this did not seem a glittering array of actors, Boston could proudly have answered that Boston liked them very well indeed; and that would have meant more than appears on the surface. The piece was no great contribution to our joys, but it kept afloat until April 16th, which, after all, made a pleasant trip for those Boston Voyagers in Southern Seas.   A benefit was advertised for the Provident Dispensary for Working Women and Girls.   Listed for the afternoon of March 31st, it promised John T. Raymond, in an act of Fresh, the American; a musical programme by certain of Mapleson's artists, by Florence Rice Knox, Liberati and A. H. Pease; and the screen scene from The School for Scandal with Sara Jewett, Osmond Tearle and Welsh Edwards (Sir Peter).   Another benefit, on the afternoon of April 7th, was for the ever-benefiting Charles White, at which were scheduled J. K. Emmet, James O'Neill (in two recitations), A. C. Moreland, the Russian Athletes, Mlle. Ariel, Anna Theresa Berger ("the invincible cornetist"), Ella Wesner, Annie Rennie, Bernard Sloman, John and Maggie Fielding, Gus Phillips, Stirk's Bicycle Riders, Parker and his dogs, Ferguson and Mack, the quintet from the San Francisco Minstrels, and poor old White, himself; others scheduled may not have appeared, if the Herald review, on the 8th, lists all participants.

And, on April 18th, Abbey began his last two weeks as manager of Booth's, with a return of Sarah Bernhardt.   She appeared in La Princesse Georges, a newer play by Dumas; her rôle was that of Séverine, Princesse de Birac, and associated in the cast were Angelo as Prince de Birac, Bouilloud as Galanson, Deletraz as Comte de Terremonde, Gally as le Baron, d'Orsay as de Foudette, Théfer as Cervières, Joliet as Victor, Jeanne Bernhardt as Comtesse de Terremonde, Mlle. Mea as Mme. de Périgny, Mlle. Sidney as la Baronne, Mlle. Carpentier as Berthe, and Mlle. Jane Mea as Rosalie.   Bernhardt's two weeks were varied in offering; on the 19th, La Dame aux Camélias (repeated at the matinée on the 23rd), Hernani (on the 20th), Frou-Frou (on the 21st), and Adrienne (on the 22nd), might have appealed, singly or collectively, to almost any taste.   In addition, the famous actress gave, on April 21st, a professional matinée of La Princesse Georges, attended, according to the Herald of April 22nd, by Clara Morris, Sara Jewett, Ada Rehan, Jeffreys Lewis, Agnes Robertson, De Wolf Hopper and a host of rare notables.   From this Gallic emotionalism, one could pass, on Sunday, the 24th, to a lecture by Robert G. Ingersoll, on The Reasons

Why. Bernhardt's last week provided mostly repetitions — La Princesse Georges (April 25th), Camille (26th), L'Etrangère (her first time here as Mrs. Clarkson, 27th), Frou-Frou (28th), La Dame aux Camélias (29th), and Frou-Frou (farewell matinée, on the 30th). In the evening of April 30th, the star shone in the Brooklyn Academy, as Frou-Frou. And that was the last of the Gallic star here until 1886; and, as I have said, it ended Abbey's tenancy of Booth's. It also closed the season of 1880–81 at this house, a season distinguished only by the visits of Bernhardt, Salvini, and possibly Janauschek and the Boston Ideal Opera Company.

FIFTH AVENUE THEATRE, 1880–1881

The Fifth Avenue Theatre re-opened, on August 23, 1880, under the management of J. H. Haverly, who was already in control of the Fourteenth Street Theatre (late Lyceum) and of Niblo's Garden, as well as of Haverly's Brooklyn Theatre. This kind of wholesale management had been exemplified in 1873 by Augustin Daly, but Haverly ramified beyond the ambition of any previous operator here. His opening attraction for his most recently-acquired house was that newer style of company and play — The Tourists, in A Pullman Palace Car, an amusing trifle already familiar:

Miss Baby	Carrie Swain	James Winkerton	T. W. Eckert
Isabella	Louise Paullin	Sir Henry Cashmore	J. N. Long
Pamela	Jeannette Reiffarth	Rich	Samuel Swain
Marie	Alice Hutchings	George Flamer	Will H. Bray
T. Henry Slum	W. A. Mestayer	Hans	Harry Watson

FANNY DAVENPORT; JOHN McCULLOUGH; MARY ANDERSON

I always think and speak and write, with great pleasure, of Fanny Davenport; perhaps my boyhood memories of her prevail over my more mature judgment of her work. And some of Sarony's photographs of her, in the '70s, were so pretty! She entered her old home, the Fifth Avenue Theatre, with a clever play (clever in dialogue, at least) by the irrepressible Anna Dickinson; under the rather colourless title of An American Girl, this novelty was seen on September 20th:

Kate Vivian	Fanny Davenport	Dr. Camp	F. Chippendale
Mrs. Cranford	Mrs. G. F. DeVere	Allyn Cromarty	Henry Lee
Stella Camp	Dean McConnell	Julian Reirdon	M. V. Lingham
Lucy	Vera Vere	Fred Gower	Felix Morris
Lawrence Vivian	R. G. Wilson		

The play was by no means so attractive as had been several of Miss Davenport's successes on the same stage when Augustin Daly controlled it; and certainly her present company could not compare with Daly's fondly-remembered aggregation. Yet An American Girl had a fairly good run, not clos-

[247]

ing until October 30th. Miss Davenport, who had always been noted for sumptuous and fashionable dressing in her characters, quite eclipsed her former record in that regard; her costumes were veritable sensations and were alleged to have been concocted by Worth. They were so numerous as almost to confuse the audience, and some were perhaps too rich for certain scenes in which they came trailing clouds of silken glory. So much for Anna Dickinson and Fanny Davenport, noted women of that day.

On November 1st came an actress, striving for fame, and failing of the goal. This was Lillian Spencer, who offered herself in a play called Norah's Vow, her associates including Gabrielle du Sauld, Helen Just, Little Eva French, Hamilton Harris, E. A. McDowell, B. W. Turner, J. Winston Murray and James R. Keene. If the "combination" system did nothing else, it brought into New York and other large cities players who could never have hoped in the "stock" days to enter the envied portals of leading theatres. Of course, also, it litters our pages and our indexes with names of innumerable nonentities.

And now began a few weeks of the "legitimate," doubtless inspiring to older persons, who could not see that the "legitimate" was dying. John McCullough entered the Fifth Avenue, on November 15th, in one of his finest characterisations — Virginius, a rôle the costume and carriage of which exactly suited his handsome face and splendid figure, while the heroics of the verse and the scenes allowed him to show how absolutely he was of the school of Edwin Forrest. He had an excellent support, including Frederick B. Warde, E. K. Collier, Harry A. Langdon, John A. Lane, W. C. Barton, Kate Forsyth, Mrs. Augusta Foster, and Mittens Willett. Salvini honoured the performance by attending on Saturday evening, November 20th; and the public, seemingly, honoured it by keeping it on the stage for two solid weeks, or through the evening of November 27th. For his third week, McCullough turned to Shakespeare, enacting Othello (one of his best rôles), on November 29th, 30th, December 1st and 4th (matinée), King Lear, on December 2nd, and Richard III, on the 3rd and 4th (evening). His last week gave us (December 6th, 7th and 11th) The Gladiator (not the tragedy in which Salvini was to appear on the 23rd, at Booth's, but a Forrestian survival fitting indeed for McCullough); Othello (8th) and Virginius (9th), with Brutus and Katharine and Petruchio (10th), and The Lady of Lyons (at the Saturday matinée, December 11th). I can imagine John McCullough, certainly in physique the noblest Roman of them all, in almost any of the characters he portrayed during these interesting four weeks; in some no living actor could have surpassed him. But as Claude Melnotte! His company included Edward Dee (young E. H. Sothern), who was down for Lucius (in Virginius), Roderigo (in Othello), King of France (in King Lear), Prince of Wales (Richard III), Gellius (in The Gladiator), and Gaspar (Lady of Lyons)—a fine training in versatility. In Brutus, then a rarity

[248]

SARAH BERNHARDT
AS PHÈDRE
(Photograph by
Sarony)

SARAH BERNHARDT
AS CAMILLE
(Photograph by
Sarony)

EMMA ABBOTT IN FAUST
From a Photograph by Anderson

GENEVIEVE WARD (FORGET ME NOT)
From a Photograph by Mora

TOMMASO SALVINI
From a Photograph by T. H. Burnham

on our stage, McCullough was assisted by F. B. Warde as Titus, Collier as Tarquin, Langdon as Valerius, Lane as Collatinus, Kate Forsyth as Tarquinia, Mrs. Foster as Tullia, and Mittens Willett as Lucretia. Warde had played Iago, Edgar, Petruchio and Richmond.

This interesting engagement was followed by a term of Mary Anderson, who had not been on the stage in Manhattan for two years — why, I cannot imagine, unless, as I suspect, Tourists and Troubadours and Surprise Parties, with their trifling wares, and comic opera generally were killing the taste for serious plays. Old-fashioned, even for 1880, may have seemed her first-week offerings — Evadne, on December 13th, 14th and 15th, and Ingomar, on the 16th, 17th and 18th. In the former of these Milnes Levick assisted as Colonna, Robert L. Downing as Ludovico, T. L. Coleman as King of Naples, Atkins Lawrence as Vicentio, Joseph Anderson as Spalatro, F. J. Currier as the Page, and Laura Clancy (a graduate of Rice extravaganza) as Olivia. Another relic of the past, Love, was Miss Anderson's play on December 20th, 21st and 22nd; in this her haughty Countess loved the seeming serf, Huon, of Atkins Lawrence; John McDonald was Sir Rupert, Downing Ulric, T. L. Coleman Prince Frederick, Joseph Anderson Sir Otto, Mrs. M. L. Berrell the kind Empress, and Laura Clancy Christina. The Hunchback was the bill for December 23rd, 24th and 25th (matinée and evening). Miss Anderson returned to us after three years of hard work since her début here, in the same theatre, in 1877. Critics now judged her with more discriminating and judicial eye, and found her still lacking in ease and power of dramatic insight; lacks that usually denote the amateur or one who comes late to the stage. She was beautiful, her voice was rich and melodious, albeit still prone to sudden changes of register and of power, she still dressed unbecomingly, and — she still had much to learn. She was, perhaps, just beginning to learn the last needful things when she suddenly left the stage in 1889. Artistically, Miss Anderson never quite filled the place left vacant by Adelaide Neilson; perhaps no one did, from that day to this, nearly sixty years later.

Nevertheless, this season of hers was interesting. Her third week brought Fazio (December 27th and 28th), Evadne (29th), The Hunchback (30th), Love (31st and January 1st), and The Lady of Lyons (matinée, January 1st). These parts were all associated with the fame of Ellen Tree, Julia Dean and their successors. But the rôle with which, possibly, the lovely Ellen Tree of the '30s was most identified was Ion, in Talfourd's play of that name, and this part Miss Anderson added to her list, on Monday, January 3rd; in the cast were Milnes Levick as Adrastus, H. B. Norman as Medon, John McDonald as Agenor, T. F. Brennan as Timocles, F. J. Currier as Cleon, Atkins Lawrence as Phocion, R. L. Downing as Ctesiphon, T. L. Coleman as Crythes, Joseph Anderson (the star's not very talented brother) as Cassander, Emma Maddern as Clemanthe, Mrs. Berrell as Abra, and

[249]

Laura Clancy as Irus. This piece was repeated on the 4th and 5th (it was said not to have been played previously in New York for thirty years). The Herald of January 4th is not keenly excited by the star's portrayal of the leading rôle:

> Miss Anderson's Ion is a pretty, charming, delightful dramatic portrait to look upon, but when critically considered it lacks perfect symmetry and at times vigor of touch in many of its outlines and details. In all branches of art youth and inexperience are ever present drawbacks, no matter how great are natural talents . . . and as Miss Anderson possesses a generous share of both youth and inexperience, it cannot be expected that she shall in the spring of her artistic life exhibit the ripe dramatic ·results that only time can bring. . . . In the first interview with the King Miss Anderson was very good and delivered her lines with feeling; in the scene where . . . Ion draws the lot . . . to kill the King she was less effective. In her parting, prior to her own death, with Clemanthe, whom she loves [one would gather from this critic that Ion was a woman], she again gave to the lines much sweetness and gentleness of utterance; but in the last act, while she led up well to the final climax, she rather failed to sustain the power to the close, allowing the curtain to fall on a comparatively weak finale.

For the balance of that week, Miss Anderson repeated The Hunchback (January 6th), The Lady of Lyons (7th), and Ingomar (8th, matinée). By particular request, for her farewell, on the evening of the 8th, she revived Meg Merrilies, a part in which some found her always quite inferior to Charlotte Cushman. All things considered, this engagement of Miss Anderson is very interesting, especially in light of history, more than a half-century later. She was followed, on January 10th, at the Fifth Avenue, by another ambitious person — Frederick Paulding, who came out in a poor piece, Salviati, or, the Silent Man, adapted from the French by William Seymour. In this it was his duty to portray Raphael Salviati and Lazarus, and with him were Hamilton Harris as Julian Salviati, Milton Rainford as Cosmo di Medici, L. M. McCormack as Judial di Medici, Frank Norcross as Matheo, M. Leffingwell as Battista, Miss M. Loduski Young as Nativa, Emma Lathrop as Sylvia, and Nettie Myers as Meta. Collectively, these actors were no more striking than their play, and after a week they departed in peace (I hope).

EMMA ABBOTT; CATHERINE LEWIS; MARIE RÔZE; GENEVIEVE WARD

With Mary Anderson departed, I feel, much of the glory of the Fifth Avenue season. I cannot become greatly interested in Emma Abbott, who, on January 17th, began a season of opera in English; though she doubtless was a fair singer, and though some of her company were good, her advent

[250]

usually leaves one cold. Perhaps it was a matter of personality. At any rate, the Herald, during this engagement, takes to task those who maintain that one should admire Miss Abbott because she was American; as if, says the Herald, art was a matter of nationality. On January 17th and 22nd, The Bohemian Girl presented Miss Abbott, Pauline Maurel, A. E. Stoddard, Henry Peakes, and (if you can possibly believe it) Brignoli, of the once silvery voice and still an agreeable singer. On the 18th and 20th, and at the matinée on the 22nd, Paul and Virginia was announced, with Misses Abbott and Maurel, Stoddard, Lithgow James and William Castle; in Fra Diavolo, at the Wednesday matinée, January 19th, Julie Rosewald, Maurel, Stoddard, Tams and Castle united in the score. The evening of the 19th promised Martha, with Miss Abbott, Clara Bonheur, Tams, Frank Augustine and Brignoli; Gounod's Romeo and Juliet was originally announced for the 21st, but Lucia di Lammermoor, with Miss Abbott, was substituted. The second and last week began with Rosewald in The Chimes of Normandy (24th), repeated The Bohemian Girl (on the 25th), Martha (matinée, 26th, with Rosewald, and evening of the 29th, with Abbott), and Lucia (with Brignoli and Abbott, 28th). Faust, on the 26th, presented Miss Abbott, Miss Maurel, Castle, Stoddard and Peakes; Mignon, on the 27th, had Miss Abbott, in the title-rôle, Julie Rosewald as Filina, Miss Maurel as Frederic, with Castle, Stoddard and Peakes as male support. The Chimes of Normandy rang out for the matinée on the 29th.

After this fortnight of native exotics, so to speak, patrons of the Fifth Avenue were regaled, on January 31st, with the lively Olivette, Audran's operetta, transferred from its earlier triumph at the Bijou Opera House, and with Catherine Lewis, John Howson and the merry band associated with it at the other theatre. It remained for four weeks at the Fifth Avenue, yielding the stage, on February 26th, for grander flights in music. On February 28th came the Max Strakosch-C. D. Hess English Opera Company, headed by the beautiful Marie Rôze, in an English version of Boito's opera, Mefistofele, which had been a feature of Mapleson's recent season at the Academy of Music. Mme. Rôze doubled the parts of Margherita and Helen (as Valleria had done at the Academy and as Christine Nilsson had done in London). Others in the cast were Lizzie Annandale as Marta and Pantalis, Giovanni Perugini (born Chatterton) as Faust, George Conly as Mefistofele, and Tilla as Wagner. On March 1st, William Tell enlisted Abbie Carrington, Laura Schirmer (later to be an international figure, though not in art), Arthur Byron, Carleton, Conly and Gustavus Hall; the Herald, on the 2nd, intimates that the performance was not superlative. Carmen was the offering of March 2nd and 5th (matinée) with Marie Rôze, Laura Schirmer, Perugini (overweighted), and Carleton. And a surprise of March 3rd reintroduced (in Il Trovatore) Ostava Torriani, for the first time in several years, and still possessing much of the fine voice and the fine art of yore.

[251]

Mignon, on the 4th, had, of course, Marie Rôze as the heroine, and, in other rôles, Miss Carrington, Miss Annandale, Perugini, Conly, Hall and Tilla. On the evening of the 5th, with Torriani, Annandale, Perugini, Carleton (Valentine) and Conly, Faust was sung. S. Behrens and Signor Novellis were conductors of the force, and regular theatre prices prevailed. Since Mapleson was again operating at the Academy, this Rôze season would seem to be somewhat supererogatory. Nevertheless, a second week (March 7th) began with Carmen, and changed, on the 8th to Fra Diavolo, with Miss Schirmer, Miss Annandale, Perugini, Peakes, Conly and Hall. Aïda was performed, on the 9th, for the first time here in English, with Marie Rôze, Miss Annandale, Byron, Conly and Carleton; it was to be given again on Saturday afternoon, March 12th, but Marie Rôze was ill and unable to sing. March 10th and 12th (evening) gave us the saccharine delectabilities of The Bohemian Girl, with Misses Carrington and Annandale, Perugini and Conly. And so this operatic host went its way. These offerings were not all as originally advertised.

On March 14th New York had what it loves — something sensational, something new to discuss. We remember that Wallack had produced, in December, 1880, Palgrave Simpson's really brilliant Forget Me Not, and that, after a too brief success with it, he was compelled by law to withdraw the comedy from his stage. Genevieve Ward was sustained by the courts in her claim to sole rights in the play, and now, on the 14th, she brought it out at the Fifth Avenue Theatre, enacting Stéphanie de Mohrivart, in which she had so richly succeeded in London. The cast included, besides, Frank Clements (who had been here in 1878–79, with Modjeska) as Sir Horace Welby, Cora S. Tanner (later a star of some note) as Alice Verney, Laura Le Claire as Mrs. Foley, Charles Dade as Barrato, Horace Lewis as Prince Malleotti, Percy Campbell as the Servant, and Walter Morgan as the Porter — a distribution quite inferior (except for Miss Ward) to that at Wallack's. The Herald of March 15th expresses something of that sort:

> The lady was welcomed most heartily by a very good audience, which she speedily impressed with a sense of great power and consummate art. Comparing the performance ... with that which another company has so recently given ... it must be said that the general effect was not as satisfactory, although the title *rôle* was rendered with greater power.... Miss Ward's conception of the part of Stéphanie does not materially differ from Miss Coghlan's.... For clearness of conception, consistency in presentation, artistic finish and a never wavering impression of tremendous earnestness ... Miss Ward's rendering of the part demands the highest praise.

In fact Miss Ward made this part entirely her own, so far as America was concerned. Who can forget her icy sarcasm, in the earlier scenes, her magnificent style, and the cry of fear as she recognised the enemy face, seen

[252]

SELINA DOLARO

OSTAVA TORRIANI

KATE FORSYTH

LILLIAN SPENCER

CATHERINE LEWIS
AS OLIVETTE

TOPSY VENN

ENNIE WEATHERSBY

M. B. CURTIS
AS SAM'L OF POSEN

ROBERT DOWNING

in the garden, by moonlight?   I can still see her clutching the curtains that shut her in from that mortal terror.   Of the old school, we might say, sixty years later; but I know of no one today who could produce so tremendous an effect.   I remember Rose Coghlan, also, in that last great scene, but not in so graphic, so piercing a way.   Yet Miss Ward remained now but two weeks at the Fifth Avenue; perhaps previous engagements prevented a longer visit.

She was succeeded (on March 28th) by the excellent John E. Owens in as poor a play — a "rural" drama — as he had had for many years.   This was That Man from Cattaraugus, the usual type of rural honesty, eccentric but helpful; Piercy Wilson adapted it from the German:

Allan Trueman	John E. Owens	Sweatham	Oliver Wren
Adolphus Trueman	F. S. Hartshorn	Professor Müller	J. H. Brown
Edgar Livingston	George Parkes	Mrs. Adolphus Trueman	Virginia Buchanan
Solomon Stockman	Joseph Arthur	Rose Trueman	Frankie McClellan
Hon. Edward Grayson	Edward Powell	Ellen Trueman	Georgie Knowlton
Henry Grayson	W. S. Harkins	Jerusha Trueman	Marie Bates
John Felton	Russell Bassett		

That all was not prosperous with this production, I learn from the Herald of April 12th, which states that, on the 11th, two actors walked on in Act I for the part of Solomon Stockman; the original actor declined to be superseded by a more recent recruit.   A "row" in the lobby alarmed visitors to the theatre, but, in later scenes, only the new actor appeared.   Owens finished his engagement on April 16th, and back to the fold came, on the 18th, Catherine Lewis, John Howson and their colleagues, in the exceedingly popular Olivette; Marie Jansen, I learn from the Herald, was prevented by illness from acting, until April 23rd.   On the afternoon of May 3rd, Catherine Lewis took a benefit (my pen is a-weary of these long benefit bills), with a fairly attractive bill.   Harry Edwards recited A Showman's Story; Carrie Burton, Vernona Jarbeau, Rose Chappelle, J. H. Ryley and W. Hamilton rendered scenes from Billee Taylor, that great success of the Standard Theatre; Cyril Searle recited; John Howson gave a character song, and J. H. Ryley did the patter song from The Pirates of Penzance.   Miss Lewis and her sister, Jeffreys Lewis, were down for a scene from The Hunchback.   The last two acts of Olivette completed the programme; in Act II, Miss Lewis sang the drinking song, from Giroflé-Girofla, and, in Act III, A. W. F. McCollin sang the very popular All on Account of Eliza (from Billee Taylor).   I am quoting from the Herald advertisement of May 3rd; I found no review.   Olivette finally bowed herself out on May 14th, after a long, if somewhat interrupted season in New York.

The last production of 1880–81, at the Fifth Avenue, was H. B. Mahn's presentation, beginning on May 16th, of von Suppé's operetta, Donna Juanita:

[253]

René Dufaure	Jeannie Winston	Picador	Arthur Van Houten
Petrita	Janet Edmondson	Dolores	May Booth
Gaston Dufaure	Wallace Macreery	Aguador	Joseph Hans
Donna Olympia	Rose Leighton	Tepa	Clara Douglas
Don Pomponio	Ellis Ryse	Fitzroy	Harry Dale
Colonel Douglas	Arthur H. Bell	Duplan	S. Battle
Don Riego	W. A. Morgan	Marco	Marie Somerville
Gil Polo	Vincent Hogan		

This failed to reap the success of Fatinitza or Boccaccio, though it ran until the end of the season at the Fifth Avenue, on June 4th. The performers would have been surprised to learn that Donna Juanita would be given fifty years later (1931) by "grand" opera singers at the Metropolitan Opera House, a shrine for which plans were then (1881) taking shape in the minds of its original projectors.

HAVERLY'S FOURTEENTH STREET THEATRE, 1880–1881

Another venture of Haverly's, the Fourteenth Street Theatre, once the Théâtre Français and later the Lyceum, will now demand attention. It had fallen by 1880 far below the hopes of its first owners, and not soon again would it house such geniuses as Ristori, Fechter, Adelaide Neilson and Edwin Booth, to mention only a few of those who once graced its stage. Rather did Haverly attract by light, ephemeral entertainment, and it would seem that in the season now under review he may have reaped something of a harvest.

He started on August 9, 1880, with the former favourite, Fun on the Bristol, or, a Night on the Sound, with John F. Sheridan still as Mrs. O'Brien, with Kate Castleton as Dora, Agnes Hallock as Norah, Marion Fiske as Bella, Henry Saville as Captain Cranberry, Frank Tannehill, Jr. as Tom Cranberry, Mark Smith as Count Menaggio, George Topack as Pinkerton Hawkshaw, William Courtright as Jerry Thompson, and Master Linden as Jerry Thompson, Jr. This was just another of those things — a combination of variety, singing and dancing, with a weakly strung plot — that had made, of recent months, so devastating an inroad on the more stately drama. From them, of course, came such entertainers as N. C. Goodwin, Henry E. Dixey, Willie Edouin, George S. Knight, and heaven knows how many more of the leading fun-makers of the '80s; but those years produced no successors to Edwin Booth or Lawrence Barrett. Fun on the Bristol ran through August 28th, and was followed, on the 30th, by another and similar plant of American growth — E. E. Rice's never-dying Evangeline, revised by J. J. McNally, and with at least a fairly new cast, including Vernona Jarbeau in the title-rôle, Louise Searle as Gabriel, Rose Dana as Eulalie, George K. Fortescue as Catherine, Jennie Calef as Felicien, Ed. Chapman as Le Blanc, Charles Groves (his first — but not his last — appearance in

[254]

America) as Peter Papyrus (a new character, in which Groves made a hit), J. W. Ransone as Captain Dietrich, Max Figman as Basil, Harry Hunter as the Lone Fisherman, and the sumptuous Pauline Hall as Hans Wagner; in smaller rôles figured Mattie and Ella Winner, Jessie Calef, Jessie Johnson and H. M. Morse.

After two weeks Evangeline gave way, on September 13th, to M. B. Leavitt's Grand English Operatic Burlesque Company, in Carmen, or, Soldiers and Seville-ians, "written for this company by Frank W. Breen, author of the Christmas Pantomimes at Covent Garden," and produced with scenery by Voegtlin, music by Frank Musgrave, and a "Grand Transformation" by Professor Hughes, of London. All was under the direction of James A. Meade; and this was the cast:

Carmen	Selina Dolaro	Escamillo	James A. Meade
Don Jose	Marie Williams	Pasquillo	Alma Stanley
Zuniga	Fanny Wentworth	Gomez	Lizzie Mulholland
Morales	Daisy Ramsden	Dancairo	J. W. Bradbury
Michaela	Mat Robson	Remendado	Frank Hind
Juanita	Adelaide Praeger	Concho	C. H. Spiller

We remember that, in the season of 1879–80, Mme. Dolaro sang Bizet's Carmen, at the Academy of Music. Minor helpers in the burlesque were Minnie Marshall, Camille d'Elmar, Lena French, Clara Maybel, Grace Leaver and Marie Clifton. The show ran for three weeks, closing on October 2nd. On the 4th came an English version of La Fille du Tambour Major, heard in French only two weeks earlier at the Standard Theatre. At the Fourteenth Street Theatre, Selina Dolaro was Stella, Marie Williams Griolet, the drummer boy, Fanny Wentworth Claudine, Alma Stanley, the statuesque beauty, was Duchesse della Volta, James A. Meade the Drum Major, Mat Robson the Duke, Lewis Finke Captain .Robert, Louise Leighton Raoul, Laurie Trevor Gabriel, Camille d'Elmar Henri, Adelaide Praeger the Abbess, &c. After a week of this the company betook itself elsewhere.

October 11th raised the standard, but possibly reduced the attendance. Dudley Buck brought in his opera, Deseret, conducted by himself, and cast it with Julia Polk as Rosamond, Belle Cole (a pleasing singer) as Arabella, Kate French as Sally, Charles F. Lang as Major Clemm, W. J. Cogswell as Joseph Jessup, J. Evarde as Elder Scram, W. D. Marks as Lieutenant Montgomery, Eugene Eberle as Setting Hen, and H. A. Stuart as Corporal Riley. W. A. Croffut wrote the libretto (if any one cares to know). Two weeks were all of Deseret in Fourteenth Street. On October 25th, Rice's Surprise Party entered Haverly's theatre with a bit of fun entitled Revels, or, Bon Ton George, Jr., in which appeared Topsy Venn, a popular English actress, Marion Elmore, Lena Merville, Vic Reynolds, Emma Burgess, Carrie Perkins, May Livingston, Henry E. Dixey, John Gourlay, John A. Mackay, George W. Howard and other funny or shapely purveyors of the spirit of

[255]

burlesque and exquisite nonsense. Most of these performers were known in the '80s, and photographs of the ladies adorned the studies of college boys of the time. Revels provided five jolly weeks at the Fourteenth Street Theatre, and gave way, on November 29th, to Prince Achmet, with Topsy Venn, Marion Singer, Venie Bennett, Ada Lee, and most of the popular performers just listed for Revels. Hiawatha came in due course, on December 13th, with Topsy Venn in the title-rôle, John A. Mackay as William Penn Brown, Henry E. Dixey as Romulus Smith, John Gourlay as Remus Brown, George W. Howard as Mr. Lo, Lena Merville as Yenadizzi, Rose Wilson as the District Telegraph Boy, Carrie Perkins as Honeydew, Lavinia Bennett as Hazel Dell, Marion Singer as Minnehaha, Marion Elmore as Mrs. Lo, and Victoria Reynolds as Sally Bohee. One of the surprises of Rice's Surprise Party was the length of its present stay, but its last week began, finally, on December 27th, with a revival of its long-popular Babes in the Wood, Topsy Venn appearing as the Bad Man, and Henry E. Dixey as Takeit Sneak.

The Fourteenth Street Theatre was obviously committed, at least for the present, to the lightest kind of entertainment. On January 3, 1881, Salsbury's Troubadours returned in their favourite success — The Brook, which ran on till January 15th, with Nate Salsbury, John Webster, C. A. Stedman, Nellie McHenry and Ray Samuels; it yielded the stage to Widow Bedott, played on January 17th, with C. B. Bishop, an excellent comedian, in the title-rôle, with J. O. Barrows as Elder Sniffles, C. S. Dickson as Fred, Helen Vincent as Melissa, &c. This also had two weeks. And now, on January 31st, the theatre reverted to its former success in serious drama, The Galley Slave, which remained for three weeks, with a cast including Gussie De Forrest, Signora Majeroni, Frank Evans, Junius Brutus Booth, Thomas H. Burns, Edwin F. Knowles, Nellie Barbour, Mrs. Clara Stoneall, &c. Another favourite returned on February 21st, when N. C. Goodwin (temporarily without Eliza Weathersby) presented Hobbies, in which he gave imitations of Henry Irving (new), Jefferson, John McCullough (new), Sothern (new), Stuart Robson, Lawrence Barrett, J. T. Raymond, Frank Mayo, and a London comic singer in the latest English sensation song. Goodwin was very clever, but in due time he became a fine actor in comedy. With him now were Daisy Ramsden, Jennie Weathersby, Elma Delaro, Charles Bowser and Frank Lamb. On March 9th, Goodwin tried a new piece — The Marionettes:

Bob Crump	N. C. Goodwin	Georgina	Effie Vaughan
Wilfred Blount	W. S. Harkins	Angelina	Jennie Weathersby
Mr. Babbage	C. W. Bowser	Constantine	Belle Jackson
Sardanapalus	Frank E. Lamb	Evelina	Carrie Milton
Burke	De Los King	Arabella Minks	Daisy Ramsden
Seraphina Sphinks	Mme. Ivan Michels		

CHARLES PLUNKETT
IN YORICK'S LOVE

F. C. MOSLEY
IN YORICK'S LOVE

BEN G. ROGERS
IN YORICK'S LOVE

AYMOND—MISS CREESE
(FRESH, THE AMERICAN)

LAWRENCE BARRETT
IN YORICK'S LOVE

LAURA DON
(FRESH, THE AMERICAN)

SOL SMITH RUSSELL

SAMUEL W. PIERCY

JAMES T. POWERS

The bill began with Goodwin in the popular farce, To Oblige Benson. This closed on March 12th, and, on the 14th, back from their European tour came Haverly's Mastodon Minstrels, one of their specialties being Ill-True-Bad-Doer, with Billy Emerson as Man-Wreak-Oh, E. M. Rayne as Count Di-loony, Paul Vernon as Lean-O'er-Her, Billy Rice as Captain of the Guard; others in the vast company were Sam Devere, J. W. McAndrews, Barry Maxwell, James Adams, George H. Harvey and W. T. Raymond. Billy Rice and Sam Devere figured in a black ballet. Doubtless everybody before and behind the curtain was happy at this glad home-coming; yet the mighty host remained but two weeks. Haverly then went back (March 28th) to the kind of thing he had most persistently purveyed in this season; he called in W. C. Mitchell's Pleasure Party in their excruciatingly funny Our Goblins. The cast now included William Gill, J. M. Norcross, Francis Wilson, William Forrester, Elinor Deering, Emma Carson and Mira V. Barrie. With Francis Wilson and Emma Carson we realise that the hosts of comic opera are gathering for the decade of the '80s. Our Goblins dispersed merriment till April 9th.

On the 11th, Fun on the Bristol carried on the same mood, with, of course, John F. Sheridan and about the same fun-makers who started the season at this theatre in August. They remained until April 30th. On May 2nd, Mr. and Mrs. George S. Knight began a two-weeks engagement in Otto, a German. And that might be said to be the last of a season that had flourished on frivolity and, except at rare occasions, banished serious drama from its purlieus. Then, on May 16th, what I venture to call a summer season began with M. B. Curtis, launched into stellardom, in a piece that lasted him for years — Sam'l of Posen:

Samuel Plastrick	M. B. Curtis	Uncle Goldstein	R. O. Charles
Mr. Winslow	Welsh Edwards	Folliot Footlight	Walter Eytinge
Frank Kilday	Frank Losee	Celeste	Albina De Mer
Jack Cheviot	Nelson Decker	Rebecca Dreyfus	Gertie Granville
West Point	Ed Marble	Ellen	Carrie Wyatt
Con Quinn	Charles Rosene	Mrs. Mulcahy	**Mrs. Fanny Rouse**
Fitzurse	Gerald Elmar		

According to Allston Brown, Albina De Mer was Mrs. Curtis; Gertie Granville became Mrs. Tony Hart. Allston Brown also assigns both Con Quinn and Uncle Goldstein to Charles Rosene; perhaps R. O. Charles is a sort of metathesis of his letters. Sam'l of Posen was a Jewish commercial traveller, with most of the brass required by his profession, and the play involving his activities went into the group of pieces that had carried to fortune such performers as W. J. Florence, John T. Raymond, Lotta and others — pieces that had but little merit as drama, but a happy knack of hitting off national traits in their leading characters. Curtis was able to keep his lucky hit at the Fourteenth Street Theatre until August 6th, when the theatre closed for a very few nights preparatory to the operations of 1881–82.

[257]

ABBEY'S PARK THEATRE, 1880–1881

The quaintly amusing Sol Smith Russell began the season, on August 23, 1880, at the Park Theatre. Known originally as a platform entertainer, somewhat in the style of Dr. Valentine, he had, we remember, served in modest rôles in the company of Augustin Daly for a season in the mid-Seventies. A more engaging personality seldom meets one in the theatre. I can still see his lean, angular figure, his sharp-featured face, his slow, sunny smile, his large, expressive eyes, all so effective in the types of gentle, diffident country lads he affected. He became, especially in smaller towns, one of the best-liked and most prosperous of stars. But now, in 1880, he was at the beginning of that career, when he brought out at the Park J. E. Brown's comedy of Edgewood Folks:

Tom Dilloway............Sol Smith Russell	Wilson........................Z. Williamson
Rev. Arthur Melville......Charles Rockwell	Faith Hardewick...........Carrie McHenry
Ferguson....................J. W. Lanergan	Phoebe......................Mrs. Sol Smith
Fitz-Altamont..............B. T. Ringgold	Annie Dilloway................Mattie Earle
Deacon Hardewick................Sol Smith	Hulda Hardewick.............Nellie Taylor
Fosdick Skinner........Walter Lennox, Sr.	Matilda Bates...............Jennie Wharton
J. Adolphus Gilson..........W. Warmington	Little Sylvia................Belle Wharton
Mr. Springer..................Harry Davis	

Perhaps to make the transition from platform to stage less abrupt, Mr. Russell introduced into his acting of Tom Dilloway "several of his famous songs and characters." He remained for four weeks, I hope with appreciable profit.

On September 20th, the Comley-Barton Company introduced us to Lawn Tennis, a concoction of B. Woolf, author of The Mighty Dollar. In this John Howson appeared as Cornwallis Algernon Prout, Digby V. Bell (later in the season at Daly's) as Alfred Puddifoot, James Barton as Captain Dowton, J. C. Armand as George Farleigh, F. W. Lennox as Datchett, Hettie Tracy as Mrs. Prout, Lillian Brooks Bell as Bella Stanley, Marie Jansen (slowly working toward her popularity in the late '80s) as Cicely Fay, Adelaide Carleton as Laura Doll, and Mrs. J. H. Rowe (Georgie Dickson) as Mrs. Doll. In the second act of Lawn Tennis, Woolf introduced an "operettina," Djack and Djill. I fear the production was not a success; it disappeared on October 2nd, a short period for any game of Lawn Tennis on the stage of that day. And the next production failed to set the surrounding rivers afire. This was A Baffled Beauty, founded by Townsend Percy on Frank Lee Benedict's novel, Her Friend Laurence. The theatre was closed on October 4th and 5th, and presented the new play on the 6th. In the very interesting cast Rose Eytinge made her first appearance in New York in two years, as Giulia, Duchesse da Rimini; Ellie Wilton, a very clever actress, was Violet Cameron, an American heiress; Gabrielle du Sauld was Marchesa Magnoletti, Josephine Baker Mary Danvers, and Louisa

Eldridge Eliza Bronson — a remarkable group of actresses. Among the men were Mark Pendleton as Laurence Aylmer, Barton Hill (his "first appearance in this city in eight years") as Sabakine, a Russian prince, Harry Courtaine as Diogenes Schmidt, M.D., Joseph R. Grismer as Ion Dimitri, a Greek adventurer, J. G. Saville as Marchese Magnoletti, Edwin Cleary as Captain Gherardi, Richard Brennand (*sic*) as Harry Stanhope, L. A. Eastman as Gilbert Warner, D. Robertson as Antonio, &c. This cast, I repeat, is excellent in good names, but it could not carry the play to success. On October 18th, Emily Rigl succeeded Rose Eytinge in the leading rôle. The last night of the play was scheduled for October 25th.

CLARA MORRIS; THE LEGION OF HONOUR

On Tuesday, October 26th, Clara Morris, after a considerable absence, returned to New York as Alixe, in a new adaptation of The Countess de Somerive, assisted by Mark Pendleton as Henri, A. D. Billings as the Marquis de Césaranne, J. G. Saville as Duc de Mirandola, J. W. Bankson as Joseph, Edwin Varrey as Count de Somerive, Emily Jordan Chamberlain (sister of C. R. Thorne, Jr., and once the wife of George Jordan, of Burton's and Laura Keene's) as Marquise de Césaranne, Mrs. J. J. Prior as Mme. Valory, Josephine Baker as Lucienne, and Eva Garrick as Claudine. It was a considerable time since Miss Morris had acted Alixe in New York, and the critics were again impressed by her impersonation of the hapless child for whom there was no place in the accepted scheme of things. Yet the Herald, on October 27th, animadverts on Miss Morris's provincial speech, "exceedingly disagreeable to refined ears" — as indeed it was — but admits without reservation the strong appeal of her emotional acting. She was still in poor health, and able to play but sparingly, forgoing Saturday matinées. On November 1st she revived that other great Daly success, Article 47, newly adapted and omitting the court-room scene; in this she was assisted by Mrs. Prior, Eva Garrick, Josephine Baker, Rose Parker, Mark Pendleton, George Parkes, J. G. Saville, A. D. Billings, Russell Bassett, Edwin Varrey and Mason Mitchell. This she played for six evenings, omitting the Saturday matinée, and closed on November 6th, having no doubt made a renewed sensation by her tremendous impersonation of the vengeful Cora, in Article 47. The scene in which this unhappy woman gradually goes mad, until, a raving maniac, she falls exhausted to the floor, will ever remain in my mind as one of the most extraordinary exhibitions of dramatic power it has been my privilege to witness. I saw it during this autumn at the Park, and I still see Miss Morris in that sweeping red dress, clutching at the veil that conceals her disfigured face, until, pulling it away, she fell a-heap with that shriek of maniacal laughter. It was terrible. And all this was, fortuitously, on view a fortnight or more before Sarah Bern-

[259]

hardt came out at Booth's. I wonder how Bernhardt would have acted Cora. It is interesting to find in that period, in New York, four of the best graduates of the school of Augustin Daly's Fifth Avenue Theatre — Miss Morris, Fanny Davenport, Kate Claxton and Sara Jewett; and a new group, including Ada Rehan, in the making, at Daly's new theatre.

A new play called The Legion of Honour was revealed on November 9th, at the Park:

Raoul de Lignières	S. W. Piercy	M. Pinkie	G. W. Barbour
Gaston de Lignières	Mark Pendleton	François	J. Elliott
Count de Maubraye	Lewis Morrison	Elise	Agnes Booth
Viscount Distrait	Harry Courtaine	Baroness	Emily Jordan Chamberlain
Edmond de Rochfort	J. G. Saville	Mathilde	Louise Dillon
Picard	Charles Mason	Maid	Rose Parker
M. Laroche	Mason Mitchell		

It will be seen that the Park had, in its recent offerings, been maintaining something like a stock company, and a very good company it was in the present play. The Legion of Honour dealt with the distress of a husband who learns that his reputed son is really not his, with resultant agony and melodrama, the wife and mother meantime standing by in anguish beyond relief. But all finally ends happily. Piercy retained the play in his repertoire until his early death in 1882; Agnes Booth (appearing by courtesy of Steele MacKaye) was excellent, as always in such rôles, as the frightened, sorrowful mother. Meantime, on November 11th, Clara Morris began a series of Tuesday and Thursday matinées, in Article 47, an idea suggested by her delicate health and her inability to act regularly throughout the week. These she continued until Thursday, December 2nd, her last two afternoons being devoted to Alixe. Lewis Morrison and Mark Pendleton were now in the cast of Article 47. As we know, the famous actress returned on January 4th, to the Union Square Theatre, for matinées of Miss Multon, Camille and Conscience. New York almost rediscovered Clara Morris in those interesting days. And The Legion of Honour continued at the Park, finally departing on December 18th, after a reasonably successful run.

Lawrence Barrett; John T. Raymond; Lotta

Lawrence Barrett had not graced the stage in Manhattan since the season of 1876–77, at Booth's; am I right in assuming that New York had become a bad centre for the "legitimate"? Certainly recent events pointed to that conclusion. And when Barrett emerged at the Park, on December 20th, he appeared in something newer, if not quite new to the town — W. D. Howells's adaptation of a play by Tamayo y Baus, which he called Yorick's Love, and another version of which Daly had produced in 1874, with Louis James, Charles Fisher and Sara Jewett in the leading rôles. Curiously enough, Louis James was in Barrett's company, though he now acted Master Edmund, no longer, of course, Yorick:

Master Yorick	Lawrence Barrett	Thomas	Charles Hawthorne
Master Edmund	Louis James	Philip	R. C. Hudson
Master Walton	F. C. Mosley	Tobias	P. Hacquett
Master Woodford	Charles Plunkett	Mistress Alice	Marie Wainwright
Gregory	B. G. Rogers	Mistress Dorothy	Addie Plunkett

Barrett always, in those years, had a good company. Louis James had proved his worth with Daly. Marie Wainwright, though she was not a favourite of mine, was a dependable actress, F. C. Mosley was a personable leading man, and Ben. G. Rogers was almost in the class of John Gilbert and Charles Fisher as the "old man" of classic drama. Barrett as Yorick, the elderly husband, maddened by jealousy as he sees his young wife's affections turning to the inevitable young and handsome lover, played with a pathos, a gentle wistfulness that endeared him to his audiences whenever he chose to enact the part. The plot of the play is, in essentials, not unlike that of Pagliacci, long so popular in our opera houses; but, of course, the characters are of higher moral tone, and sympathy goes out to all three angles of the triangle. I am surprised to find that Yorick's Love endured for four weeks in this engagement of Barrett's at the Park; could it be that it was profitable, especially in the Christmas depression usual at all theatres?

Yorick's Love departed on January 15th, and, on the 17th, J. C. Duff staged a seemingly unnecessary production of Audran's new operetta — Olivette; unnecessary because for several weeks Catherine Lewis had been winning the town in this very piece at the Bijou Opera House. Nevertheless, two Olivettes are not so extraordinary as were five or six Pinafores in 1879. The cast of Olivette at the Park included Marie Conron in the title-rôle, Julia Polk as Bathilde, Sara Lascelles as Veloutine, Ed Marble as Captain de Merrimac, Charles Lang as Valentin, Edward Connell as Marvejol, Harry Courtaine as Duc des Ifs, Henry Dixon as Postiche, W. Davidge, Jr., as Coquelicot, and various nonentities (from the view of posterity) in minor rôles. It could not stand the rivalry with the all-conquering Olivette of Miss Lewis and the Comley-Barton force at the Bijou, and withdrew from the Park, on February 5th, after a stay of only three weeks. In its later evenings, Hart Conway joined the cast.

The theatre had a big hit in its next production, A. C. Gunter's play of Fresh, the American, dealing with the adventures of a resourceful American in the Orient, his marriage to a lady of the harem, and their escape from pursuing vengeance, all treated in the manner of farce. John T. Raymond met in this bit of nonsense his greatest success, perhaps, since Colonel Sellers, and, with the following cast he kept the play on the stage of the Park until April 9th:

[261]

Ferdinand Nervy Fresh......J. T. Raymond		Water Lily.................Charles Parham	
Baron Boskovitch..............E. J. Buckley		Erema Almi.....................Laura Don	
Mahomet Ali..................Walter Kelly		Flora.........................Lizzie Creese	
Achmet Pacha.................G. F. DeVere		Helene.....................Laura Bascomb	
Mathias Manassah...........W. Cullington		Zenora.....................May Gallagher	
Zazarack......................C. W. Butler		Lalla..........................Julia Everts	
Adolph.......................Lewis Baker		Miriam........................Lillie Yale	
Doria.......................J. W. Archer		Sadia.......................Miss Andrews	

Possibly Laura Don reached in this play her highest pitch of popularity in a stage career unfortunately short.

The irrepressible Lotta entered the Park, on April 11th, in her always popular Little Nell and the Marchioness, in which her Nell was, of course, far from Dickens, and her Marchioness a mad scramble of exaggerated burlesque. She was assisted by W. H. Wallis as Grandfather Trent, C. H. Bradshaw as Dick Swiveller, P. Aug. Anderson as Quilp, H. B. Bradley as Sampson Brass, Fred Percy as Ned Trent, Julia Hanchett as Sally Brass, Lulu Jordan as Mrs. Quilp, and Mrs. G. C. Boniface as Mrs. Jarley — all of which sounds attractive. This play was enjoyed for two weeks (Lotta still had her inalienable admirers, and many of them), and gave way, on April 25th, to Musette, with C. H. Bradshaw as a fat Billy Bokus. The Herald review (April 26th) asserts that Lotta's character had "no more to do with unfolding the story than it has with solving a problem in Euclid." But it displayed her roguish face and her feet. La Cigale constituted the delight of the little star's last week, ending on May 7th. On the afternoon of May 5th, James H. Palzer, treasurer, and Maze Edwards had a joint benefit, at which appeared Lotta, John T. Raymond, John Howson and Catherine Lewis, in acts, respectively, of Musette, Fresh, and Olivette. Louise Linden also assisted, and Mr. and Mrs. Knight were down for an act of Otto. I quote from Herald advertisements; I cannot guarantee that all appeared.

The last attraction of the season came in, on May 9th, the Grayson-Norcross Opera Company, in The Mascot, that other opera of Audran's, already familiar here. At the Park, Helen E. H. Carter was Bettina, Seth M. Crane Pippo, Sydney Smith Lorenzo XVII (sic), Lizzie Harold Fiametta, Helen Grayson Frederic (Act I), and W. Haydon Tilla (Frederic, in later scenes), William Allen Rocco, Charles J. Ross Parafanti, and James E. Miller Matteo. The Park had not been particularly fortunate this year in its Audran productions; after three weeks of The Mascot, the theatre closed on May 28th, for the season of 1880–81. All in all, the term had been interesting, if not overwhelmingly important.

STANDARD THEATRE, 1880–1881

One did not expect, in the Standard Theatre, to thread the dizzying mazes of intellectual drama; especially since the great success of Pinafore, the house had lured more and more with musical shows.   It began the offerings of 1880–81 with Our Gentlemen Friends, presented on August 14th, with George and Joseph Holland, sons of the famous George Holland, so long popular on our stage:

Joseph Moorhouse	George Holland	Helen Gillespie	Agnes Proctor
Walter Morton	Harry Rainforth	Mrs. McPepper	Mrs. Farren
Augustus Doolittle	J. J. Holland	Belinda	Ida B. Conway
Frank Gillespie	H. S. Duffield	Mrs. Moorhouse	Mrs. J. J. Prior
George Jones	E. D. Tannehill	Rose	Nellie Boyd
Dr. Chapman	Charles Waverly	Caroline	Dean McConnell
Mike Hooligan	J. Lant	Minnie	Nanita Lewis
Lizzie	Jennie Boyd		

This effort carried through but two weeks, and, on August 30th, A Golden Game, or, Spider and Fly, took its place, with J. W. Shannon, George R. Edeson, Samuel K. Chester, Lawrence Eddinger, John W. Bankson, George Parkes, H. S. Duffield, Charles Dade, B. Wharton, Annie Boudinot, Cora Tanner and Laura Le Claire in rôles which it seems, in view of the short life of the play, unnecessary to force into this already overcrowded narrative. A Golden Game took a leaden retreat, on September 11th.

Maurice Grau's French Opera Company, headed by the very popular Paola Marié, presented on September 13th, for the first time in New York, Lecocq's La Fille du Tambour-Major:

Stella	Mlle. Paola Marié	Duc della Volta	M. Mezières
Claudine	Mlle. Mary Albert	Griolet	M. Tauffenberger
Duchesse	Mlle. Delorme	Marquis Bambini	M. Poyard
Prioress	Mlle. Choquet	Clampas	M. Vilano
Monthabor	M. Duplan	Sergeant Morin	M. Vinchon
Robert	M. Nigri	Gregorio	M. Illiet

This was the first appearance of Mary Albert, Nigri and Tauffenberger, and all were good, especially the last-named.   Charles Almeras directed the music, including a grand military band on the stage.   Oddly enough, considering the usual frequent changes of bill, recently, with these French organisations, La Fille du Tambour-Major ran uninterruptedly for three weeks.   On October 4th, 6th and 8th, with matinée on the 9th, however, Paola Marié reverted to Serpolette, in Les Cloches de Corneville, others being Mlle. Merle as Germaine, Nigri as the Marquis, Tauffenberger as Grenicheux, Duplan as the Bailiff, and Mezières as Gaspard, the miser. Le Petit Duc, with Paola Marié in the title-rôle and Mlle. Merle as the Duchesse, filled the evenings of October 5th, 7th and 9th.   On October 11th, 12th, 15th and 16th (matinée), Paola Marié sang and acted Mignon, with Mlle. Josephine Schaeffer (début) as Philine, Mlle. Merle as Frédéric, Mauras (first appearance) as Wilhelm Meister, and Bernard (also new) as Lothario; on the 13th, 14th and 16th (evening) the inevitable and desired Giroflé-Girofla exercised the charming talents of Paola Marié.   Mlle. Albert

[263]

re-appeared, on October 18th and 19th, in La Fille du Tambour-Major;
Paola Marié being in Brooklyn, on the 20th, Mlles. Albert and Gregoire
gave, at the Standard, Les Cloches de Corneville.

Another novelty bloomed on October 21st, 22nd and 23rd — de Rille's
pastoral opera, Babiole, "written for Paola Marié and Mary Albert, and
presented by them for one hundred consecutive nights at the Théâtre des
Bouffes Parisiens." In this Paola Marié assumed her original rôle of
Babiole, and Mlle. Albert her original rôle of Madeleine; others in the cast
were Mlle. Merle as Arabelle, Mlle. Vallot as Georgette, Mezières as Mira-
belle, Duplan as the Bailiff, Nigri as Carcassol, and Tauffenberger as Alain,
with Mlles. Estradère, Armand and Malvina and M. Vilano in smaller parts.
On October 25th and 26th, Paola Marié sang La Périchole, with Nigri as
Piquillo. An Offenbach Memorial characterised (October 27th) the fiftieth
and last performance here of this French aggregation; the bill included the
first act of La Belle Hélène, the second of La Grande Duchesse, the second
of La Périchole, and the third of La Fille du Tambour-Major, assuredly a
generous provision; and, in addition, Mary Albert sang an air from another
Offenbach opera — Maître Petronitta.

Another wholly unnecessary play came forth on Thursday, October 28th
— The Upper Crust (not Byron's comedy of the same name acted later in
the season at Wallack's, but something from the French of Heron and Belot):

Marie Hagar	Annie Graham	Paul Lamb	Raymond Holmes
Count de Rives	Lewis Morrison	Lillian	Pearl Eytinge
Count Legave	J. R. Grismer	Gertrude	Amy Northcott
Germain	W. A. Lavelle	Cornelia Walpole	Maude Mowbray
Baron Lasman	W. Scallan	Mme. de Rives	Mrs. Charles Poole
Duc de Noise	Charles Loveday		

This was another quickly vanishing thing, the third in the Standard history
for the early weeks of 1880–81. And I am not sure that the next comedy
production was much more successful — Sharps and Flats, presented on
November 8th by Robson and Crane, and attributed to Clay M. Greene and
Slason Thompson as authors:

Cutler Sharp	Stuart Robson	Marion Pemberton	Agnes Proctor
Dullstone Flat	W. H. Crane.	Lydia Lowndes	Alicia Robson
Captain Everton	A. S. Lipman	Mrs. Flat	Mrs. Mary Myers
John Pemberton	R. J. Dillon	Nellie Flat	May Gallagher
Rattle	John Marble	Mrs. Edwards	Miss M. Skippington
Reverend Percy Gosling	F. M. Burbeck	Mrs. Decker	Miss A. Townley
Harvey Singe	F. E. Ambrose	Miss Guppy	Mrs. Harriet Digges
Richard Blaze	Seldon Mitchell	Miss Prim	Miss A. Bart
Reuben Craze	Mr. Fessenden		

Sharps and Flats lasted through December 4th, four weeks in all. It was
followed, on December 6th, by another short-lived play, seen only the week
before at Haverly's Theatre, Brooklyn. This, one of Bartley Campbell's

TAUFFENBERGER
(FILLE DU TAMBOUR-
MAJOR)

DUPLAN
(FILLE DU TAMBOUR-
MAJOR)

MAURAS
AS DON JOSÉ IN CARMEN
(1881-1882)

MLLE. PAOLA MARIÉ
AS CARMEN

CÉCILE GRÉGOIRE

KATE CLAXTON
IN THE SNOW FLOWER

ALFRED CELLIER

JACQUES KRUGER
IN DREAMS

FANNY WENTWORTH

failures, was called Matrimony, and introduced Edwin F. Thorne as Dick Seabright, J. Newton Gotthold as Ralph Vannotte, Edwin F. Knowles as M. de la Tour, William Maurice as Littleton Dyke, Charles A. McManus as Colonel Playford, Clarence Gibson as St. John, Louise Muldener as Laura Vannotte, Emily Baker as Madeline, Mrs. Edwin F. Thorne as Alice Playford, Emma Skerrett as Dorcas Doran, Charlotte Neville as Sophia, Sarah Goodrich as Nora, and Lillian B. Conway as Maude. This important theme of Matrimony lasted only two weeks, and passed on the 18th. The house remained closed on the 20th, and, on Tuesday, the 21st of December, a company including many of those lately participating in Matrimony were seen in another new play by the prolific Bartley Campbell. This piece, called My Geraldine, had been the victim of much preliminary puffing, and it failed with this seemingly good cast:

Maurice Arden	E. F. Thorne	Terence	C. A. McManus
Squire Arden	John Jack	Geraldine	Louise Muldener
Larry Loane	W. M. Maurice	Mary Carroll	Emily Baker
Phil Carroll	J. N. Gotthold	Nora Brophy	Mrs. E. F. Thorne
Teddy Cregan	W. Scallan	Little Geraldine	Little Elko
Mike McShane	Frank Lawlor	Mrs. Bebee	Emma Skerrett

It is sad to chronicle so many ephemeral things, most of them utter failures. On January 17th came another, one of the poorest of all — a play by Ettie Henderson and Fannie Aymer Matthews, entitled Bigamy. Perhaps if Matrimony had failed, Bigamy might succeed? Well, Manager Henderson engaged a fine cast for his wife's play, and launched it with hope:

Miriam Strafford	Ada Dyas	Judge Ashton	J. W. Shannon
Adele Delville	Louise Sylvester	Henri de Valence	Nelson Decker
Mrs. Adams	Mrs. M. A. Farren	Abraham	Henry Chanfrau
Lulu	Ernestine Floyd	Alfred Thornton	W. Fitzgerald
Annie	May Maurice	Edward Flynn	Charles W. Day
Ada	Lillian Westbrook	Lawrence Girard	A. Tavernier
Marie	Charlotte Adams	Dr. Paine	J. J. Spies
Philip Dacron	Eben Plympton		

Alas! two weeks sufficed also for Bigamy, and, on January 31st, the distracted management took to Drink, evidently quite oblivious of the failure of Augustin Daly's venture, in the spring of 1879, with his version of L'Assommoir. The present adaptation was Charles Reade's, nicely refined and expurgated for English taste, and with Rose Eytinge as Gervaise and Cyril Searle as Coupeau. It was played nightly for two weeks, except at the Saturday matinées on February 5th and 12th, when East Lynne (with Rose Eytinge) was tried, and repeated on the evenings of February 14th, 15th and 16th. And that ended the long period of doubt and perplexity and ill-directed effort. The theatre was closed for rehearsals on February 17th and 18th, and on Saturday evening, February 19th, burst into extreme popular favour with Billee Taylor (book by H. P. Stephens, music by Edward

Solomon), which had been seen in earlier weeks of the season in London, and was now presented by D'Oyly Carte and E. E. Rice, with this cast:

Captain Felix Flapper	J. H. Ryley	Arabella Lane	Alice Burville
Sir Mincing Lane	W. H. Seymour	Phœbe Farleigh	Carrie Burton
Ben Barnacle	A. W. F. McCollin	Susan	Miss R. Chappelle
Christopher Crab	William Hamilton	Eliza Dabsey	Nellie Mortimer
Billee Taylor	Arnold Breedon		

Alfred Cellier was musical director, and Ernest Neyer conductor, with Charles Harris (from Covent Garden, a brother of Augustus Harris, and also part director, later, of The World, at Wallack's) as stage-manager. There was a hornpipe by the French Twin Sisters. T. M. Hengler (of Dele-hanty and Hengler) and Major Burke also gave specialties. Billee Taylor was a great success, and soon everybody was whistling or singing its music, especially the killing song, All on Account of Eliza, which probably divided the honours in popular suffrage, with Olivette's In the North Sea Lived a Whale (The Torpedo and the Whale). The dear old times! On May 19th, the D'Oyly Carte and E. E. Rice Companies arranged a benefit matinée for Helen Lenoir, at which were given Act I from The Pirates of Penzance, the second act of Pinafore and the first of Billee Taylor, sung chiefly by the artists then engaged at the Standard.

An entirely new cast appeared on May 23rd, in Billee Taylor, including Brocolini, Eugene Clarke, Standish, Wilkinson, Miss F. Guthrie, Vernona Jarbeau (she had succeeded Alice Burville, on April 25th), Miss E. Guthrie, and Miss Hughes; they were labelled as the Standard Opera Company. The run of the operetta (more than a hundred performances) terminated on May 31st. On May 30th, W. F. Morse had a benefit, A. P. Burbank adding to Billee Taylor. Less successful was Elfins and Mermaids, staged on Satur-day, June 4th, with Haydon Tilla as the Admiral, J. Beaumont as the Earl of Tudor, Belle Cole as the Viscountess, and with L. M. Florin, J. Furey, H. H. Howard, J. Phillips, H. R. Humphries, Bella Floyd and Lottie Ince in other rôles. This lasted so short a time that I almost blush to record its ephemerality. Well, except for Billee Taylor, the Standard, in 1880–81, had had an uphill journey.

BIJOU OPERA HOUSE, 1880–1881

The Bijou Opera House had at last nosed its way among the leading pro-ducing theatres of New York, and in this new capacity deserves a place among the foremost centres of amusement at that time in our city. It re-opened on August 30, 1880, with Willie Edouin's Sparks, in Dreams, or, Fun in a Photograph Gallery. This, of course, was another aggregation similar in make-up and intent to Salsbury's Troubadours, Rice's Surprise Party, etc., and its offering differed in no way from that of its rivals, except per-haps in results achieved in fun and foolery. Edouin and Nat Childs were authors of the piece.   Edouin was an extremely comic actor, and in Dreams he appeared as John Antonio Binks, Ralph Haberson, a villain, and Foo Shung.   Frank W. Sanger was Otis Verydizzy and Jack Shivermytimbers, and Jacques Kruger extracted fun from the part of Pickleback Grabiball, the photographer.   James T. Powers, one of the most naturally funny comedians I ever saw, was Chip Cheeky and Policeman 128; George Le Claire completed the male contingent as Harold.   Alice Atherton (Mrs. Edouin) was very protean as Ruby Chillington, Mary, the Child of Misfortune, a City Swell, and a Flower Girl; Lotta Belton was Violet Parachute and an opera tenor; Ida Shapleigh gloried in the part of Lillie Succotash, a name that delights me; Julia Edouin was Mrs. Chillington and Annetta du Mare was Hortense.   Reader, if thou smilest not at the mere reading of the names of the *dramatis personæ* of that merry trifle, I condemn thee to attendance at melodramas or thesis-plays for the rest of thy life.

Dreams had a pretty run of six weeks, closing on October 9th.   The theatre remained dark for a few nights, and re-opened on October 13th with Kate Claxton in a revival of Dion Boucicault's old play, Pauvrette, now renamed The Snow Flower, and set with fine scenery and particular attention to the avalanche, for which, indeed, the Bijou stage was a trifle too small.   The avalanche scene was designed and executed by Nelse Waldron, of the Madison Square Theatre.   Miss Claxton, who was rather charming in the rôle of Pauvrette (created in 1859 by Agnes Robertson), seemed doomed to wander about in stage snow-storms, but this one did not last for many weeks.   The public was unwilling to accept Kate Claxton in any play but The Two Orphans.   Her support in The Snow Flower included Dollie Pike as the Duchess de Beaulieu, Margaret Cone (Miss Claxton's sister) as Louise, Alice Mansfield as Marie, Gertie Johnson as Thérèse, Charles A. Stevenson as Maurice de Granval, Edward Arnott as Bernard, W. F. Owen as Michel, R. J. Dustan as Martin and J. T. Burke as the Intendant.   I regret to say that The Snow Flower drooped and died out of the bills, on November 18th; it has left to us Mora's pretty photographs of Miss Claxton in act of climbing the mountain-side, in a snow-storm, photographs sometimes mistakenly ascribed to the actress's rôle in The Two Orphans — merely because snow figured in both plays.   For the last three performances of her engagement, November 19th and matinée and evening of the 20th, Miss Claxton reverted to The Two Orphans, with Marie Wilkins (by permission of Steele MacKaye) in her famous impersonation of La Frochard, with Ida Vernon in her original rôle of the Nun, with Dollie Pike as the Countess, Margaret Cone as Henriette, Stevenson as both the Chevalier and Pierre, Arnott as Jacques, and H. B. Phillips as Count de Linières — a good cast.

On November 22nd, the Comley-Barton Company brought in their specialty, Lawn Tennis, with D'jack and D'jill, seen a few weeks earlier at the

[267]

Park, and with the same players, except that H. W. Montgomery was now in the list. Perhaps this piece was better than its short run at the Park would lead us to believe; at any rate, it continued at the Bijou, now, for over four weeks, finally ceasing on December 22nd. The company, with the important addition of Catherine Lewis, was announced to appear on December 24th in what proved to be a raging success — Olivette, an operetta by Audran, then first to be staged here, by arrangement with R. D'Oyly Carte (whose visit to New York, with Gilbert and Sullivan, in 1879–80, had indeed resulted in his placing several important irons in the fire). Olivette was not heard until the matinée on the 25th, and then it settled into one of the great successes of the season:

Captain de Merrimac	John Howson	Postiche	F. W. Lennox
Coquelicot	Digby Bell	Olivette	Catherine Lewis
Duc des Ifs	James Barton	Bathilde	Hetty Tracy
Valentine	J. C. Armand	Veloutine	Marie Jansen
Marvejol	W. J. Cogswell	Moustique	Helen Stuart

This merry thing filled out five weeks at the Bijou, and, as we know, was transferred, on January 31st, to the Fifth Avenue Theatre, there to continue its round of pleasing delight. Catherine Lewis made in this opera the most notable success of her career; it is cause for wonderment that she did not maintain the vogue she established by her Olivette. In reality, she had but a brief period of stellar glory.

On January 31st, Our Boarding House opened for two weeks at the Bijou, with J. B. Polk and Leonard Grover (author of the play) in the rôles created by Robson and Crane, respectively; with Herbert R. Archer (whom many of later years remember as playing the villain in E. H. Sothern's earlier pieces) as the villainous Fioretti, Lillian Cleves Clark as Beatrice (created by Maud Harrison), Sidney Drew (Mrs. John Drew's younger son) as Clarence, Virginia Buchanan as Margaret (her original rôle), and Little Eva French, who seemed in danger of never being allowed to grow up, as the child of Beatrice. Belle Mackenzie, Georgie Dickson, Josie Batchelder, W. J. Percival and Arthur Collins were also in the cast. Another favourite, tried and true, succeeded, on February 14th — Neil Burgess, in Widow Bedott, assisted by his parents-in-law, Mr. and Mrs. George Stoddart, by Harry Rich, Walter Fessler and May Taylor. This also ran its appointed fortnight, and, on March the 1st, Edgar Fawcett, author of the fairly successful plays, A False Friend and Our First Families, met with a decided reverse of fortune in his new play, Sixes and Sevens:

Isabel Suydam	Jeffreys Lewis	Julian Suydam	Herbert Archer
Mrs. Vandervoort	Henrietta Irving	Lemuel Oilington	Henry Linden
Angelica	Belle Mackenzie	Walsingham Spinner	A. H. Canby
Tapioca Tomlinson	Mrs. Georgie Rowe	Smilie Mild	Sidney Drew
Mrs. Ezekiel Spanker	Lizzie Hight	Watkins	George Parker
Susan	Nellie Dickson	Dr. Delehanty	J. B. Polk

Some of the critics were very severe on the piece, but it held the boards for nearly two weeks, closing on March 12th.

Perhaps because of this demise of high hope, the Bijou remained dark until the evening of March 19th, when the Acme Opera Company tried its fortunes with another production of the recently successful Olivette. Now Selina Dolaro was Olivette, W. T. Carleton was Valentine, Henry Peakes Captain de Merrimac, J. H. Jarvis Duc des Ifs, James Peakes Coquelicot, George Olmi Marvejol, Fanny Wentworth Bathilde, Belle Girard Veloutine, Nellie Clifton Moustique, and Henrietta Irving Jayouf. Vocally the male aggregation probably surpassed that of the Comley-Barton group; and Olivette was so popular that the Acme troupe kept it going at the Bijou — despite the rivalry of Catherine Lewis and her colleagues at the Fifth Avenue — for four weeks.

Steele MacKaye, frozen out of the Madison Square Theatre, brought to the Bijou, on April 18th, his never very successful Won at Last. He enacted John Fleming, with F. F. Mackay as Professor Tracy, Mark Pendleton as Will Tracy, Harry Courtaine as Major Bunker, Clinton Hall as Baron von Spiegel, Herbert Archer as Dr. Sterling, Belle Archer (wife of the last-named, and a very pretty girl) as Grace Fleming, Louise Sylvester as Mrs. Bunker, Mrs. H. Courtaine (Emma Grattan) as Mrs. Tracy, and Helen Ottolengui as Flora Fitzgiggle. This excellent cast kept the play afloat for two weeks, with what financial profit I know not. On the first night, the sympathetic audience called MacKaye before the curtain; he spoke, almost breaking down with emotion, of the great desire and aspiration with which he had begun the work of the Madison Square Theatre, and expressing the hope that he would, before very long, have a new and even finer theatre ready to be dedicated to the art of the stage. That hope was realised in the beautiful Lyceum Theatre, at Fourth Avenue and 24th Street.

The last venture of the Bijou Opera House for 1880–81 was hugely successful — a companion piece to Olivette, and by the same composer. The triumph of Olivette led to a contest for priority of production of Audran's newest operetta, La Mascotte; in this effort the Bijou won by four nights, and produced the piece on May 5th, with Harry Brown as Lorenzo XIV (*sic*), C. H. Thompson as Prince of Pisa, John Brand (late of Daly's) as Pippo, W. Paul Bown as Rocco, G. M. Palmer as Parafanti, J. T. Craven as Matteo, Emma Howson (announced as the original London Josephine in Pinafore, and known in New York in the '70s) as Bettina, and Lillie West as Fiametta. Thompson, the tenor of Dr. Cuyler's Church, in Brooklyn, sang his part, at the last moment, reading and singing it from the libretto and the score; the tenor, J. E. Conly, originally announced for the rôle was enjoined from appearing. La Mascotte (the management kept the French form of the title) reached its hundredth performance on August 5th, and closed on August 13th. By that time, or before, the Gobble duet had taken its place with All on Account of Eliza and The Torpedo and the Whale as among the great song hits of the year.

NIBLO'S GARDEN, 1880–1881

Niblo's had not yet ceased making original productions, such as they were, and I therefore still include it in the chapter of front-line theatres. It very much favoured the style of entertainment it had inaugurated, in 1866, with The Black Crook, and we shall not be surprised to find the season of 1880–81, beginning on August 30th, with the Kiralfy Brothers' revived Around the World in Eighty Days, alleged to be put on at the cost of fifty thousand dollars, and with Helen Tracy as Aouda, Harry Meredith as Fogg, E. J. Buckley (a good actor) as Myles O'Pake, and E. A. Locke ("Yankee" Locke) as Passepartout. In the cast also were Carlotta Evelyn, E. S. Tarr, L. F. Rand, Alice Sherwood and Russell Bassett. The ballet, so important for such journeys into spectacle, was led by Mlles. de Rosa and Cornalba, and Arnold Kiralfy. The scenery, of which much was made, included a Palace of the Porcelains, with a ballet of Bric-à-Brac. My unwearied pen rests delightedly during the five-weeks run of this voyage spectacular and thrilling.

The attraction for the evenings of the week of October 4th–9th was Adele Belgarde as Hamlet (if any one could be attracted by a female Hamlet). Her support included W. H. Bokee and Mrs. E. M. Post as the King and the Queen, Harry Meredith as the Ghost, J. P. Sutton as Polonius, George C. Jordan as Laertes, G. R. Boaler as Horatio, Genevieve Stebbins as Ophelia, John Daily and Charles Summers as the Actors, and James Cooper and J. M. Humphreys as the Gravediggers — a cast that may possibly have been better than it sounds. For the Wednesday and Saturday matinées, Miss Belgarde played Parthenia, to the Ingomar of Meredith. And worse remained behind, when, on October 11th, The Duke's Motto came in, with, to be sure, that excellent actor, W. E. Sheridan, as Lagardère, but with W. H. Lytell as Carrickfergus, George F. De Vere as Gonsagues, W. L. Gleason as the Regent, John F. Herne and Mrs. J. J. Prior as the Duke and Duchess of Nevers, Harry Colton as Æsop, Alice G. Sherwood as Blanche, and Blanche Mortimer as Zillah. This is not, perhaps, so weak a cast, but the world must have become tired of the Duke and his motto and his heroics. A play fresher, but still growing familiar, came in, on the 18th — My Partner, a visitor to several theatres during this season. Aldrich and Parsloe, of course, headed the cast, which included also Oliver H. Barr (as Ned Singleton), Frank Mordaunt, J. F. Dean, J. W. Hague, Dora Goldthwaite, Lizzie Goode and Mrs. Louisa Morse. It remained for four weeks, celebrating, on November 5th, its hundredth performance in New York, and its three hundred and thirty-third anywhere. After all, this was only

[270]

the second season of the popular drama.   It left Niblo's on November 13th.

Then, on November 15th, the house could revert to a revival of Enchantment, which enjoyed the services, in its cast, of Blanche Corelli, Adelaide Cherie, Jennie Yeamans, Miss Reynolds, Goodwin, Hoyte, Henri Laurent, Felix Morris, W. Davidge, Jr., Turner and Hoyt, and in its ballet such celebrities as Adele Cornalba, Eugenie Cappalini, Mlle. Carnis, &c.   Among the specialists now necessary for such shows were the Herbert Brothers, the Comic Staircase Band, the Russian Athletes, and the Japanese prince, Awata Katsnoshin.   On December 4th, Enchantment dimmed its glories, and, on the 6th, Haverly's Genuine Coloured Minstrels, "one hundred in number," began once more to arrest the attention of the crowd; two weeks were, apparently, enough of these, and, on December 20th, Abbey's Humpty Dumpty extravaganza came in, piloted by Maffit, Fraser, Albert Valjean, Belle Gabrielle, the Martinetti Family, the Davenes, the Rajade Troupe, the Tyrolean Warblers, and, above all, Zazel, who was shot from a cannon and literally grasped the air in her daring flight.   She was a great sensation for years, in one company or circus, or another.   Humpty Dumpty amazed until January 8th.

On the 12th, Black Venus, founded on a piece by Adolphe Belot had this cast:

Baroness de Guéran	Gabrielle du Sauld	Mr. Lex	E. S. Tarr
Beatrix	Miss F. Simmons	Rodar	C. J. Toole
Branda	Belle Melville	Black Venus	Emmie Wilmot
M. de Moran	Harry Dalton	King Monza	R. M. Henry
Dr. Delange	J. H. Howland	Nazzar	Harry Meredith
Perriers	Alfred Horton	Ali Bembe	A. H. Denham
Baron de Guéran	D. R. Young	Mazourka	S. M. Burton
Joseph	W. H. Lytell	Ameri	Emily Reed

This cast makes me wonder if I am justified in providing space for it in an overcrowded volume.   And often does the doubt beset me, as antiquarian zeal hurries me on.   Important for the management was the fact that Black Venus exerted its attraction through the hardest of the winter months; on February 7th, the Herald advertised as part of the show a caravan of wild animals, some Bengal tigers, and three grand ballets.   What did mere actors count in such company?   The satisfactory run terminated on February 19th.

I am delighted to welcome, on February 21st, The Tourists in a Pullman Palace Car.   The cast was about the same as that which opened its season at Haverly's Fourteenth Street Theatre, except that Theresa Vaughn, one of the sweetest of ballad singers and "Dutch" character actresses, was added to the list, which now included W. A. Mestayer, J. N. Long, John Gilbert, Will H. Bray, T. Wilmot Eckert, Samuel Swain, Carrie Swain, Jeannette Reiffarth, Louise Leighton, and, as musical director, Fred A. Müller.   Two weeks were granted to the Tourists, and, on March 7th, Niblo's brought back once more

[271]

its love of loves, its heart of hearts, its glory beyond compare — The Black Crook. Pauline Markham returned to the part of Stalacta, and the ballet displayed the art and the nimbleness of Mlles. de Rosa and Cappalini and Arnold Kiralfy, as well as the mystifying exploits of Prince Awata Katsno-shin. One could count on audiences for that spectacle, and it ran for five weeks — up to and including April 9th. On the 11th, back came My Partner, with the leaders of the earlier visit, and again squeezed a week from the public purse. Dion Boucicault followed, on the 18th, with The Shaughraun, with Charles Stanley as Molineux, J. W. Shannon as Father Dolan, W. H. Fitzgerald as Robert, W. H. Lytell as Harvey Duff, J. J. Sullivan as Corry Kinchela, Mrs. Charles Poole as Mrs. O'Kelly, Mrs. H. J. Sargent as Claire Ffolliott, Emily Oldfield as Arte, and Lizzie McCall as Moya. This ever-delightful play remained for two weeks.

On May 2nd moved in a real sensation — "the original company" in Hazel Kirke, that most talked-of play, still running at the Madison Square Theatre. Couldock, Cecile Rush and Effie Ellsler did indeed remain in their original rôles, and Annie Ellsler, the original Clara, was now Dolly Dutton; but the others, except Edward Coleman (Barney), were not "original," though they were acclimated in their parts — Gustavus Levick (Lord Travers), W. J. Ferguson (Pittacus Green), Henry Aveling (Aaron Rodney), Edward H. See (Met), Carrie Jamieson (Mercy Kirke), and Maude Osborne (Clara). After a week of this popular offering, Castles in Spain, by Arturo Cuyas, presented (May 9th) Pauline Markham as Mother Gafas, Amy Lee as Clara, Louise Paullin (keep your eye on her) as Lucinda, Mrs. Owen Marlowe (one of the daughters of the late John Nickinson) as Monica, Hart Conway (last season at Daly's) as Henrique, W. H. Fitzgerald as Lorenzo, James C. Dunn as Granada, Harry H. Pratt as Don Candido, E. M. Porter (according to the Herald review) as Sinecuro, Eugene Eberle as Counsellor Verba, and Robert Brower as Dr. Plasta and Grifo. In the ballet were Signor Giovanni Lepri, Mlle. Aurelia Lepri (good names for ballet in Castles in the Air) and Mlle. Leonilda Ortori. This show crumpled in a few nights, leaving Niblo's as a deserted castle of indolence.

On May 30th, All the Rage was transferred from Daly's to Niblo's, where it lasted for a week; Billee Taylor, by the "original Standard company" came in, on June 6th, and managed to live out a not unusual fortnight, with J. H. Ryley, H. A. Cripps, McCollin, Hamilton, Eugene Clarke, Rachel Sanger, Rose Chappelle, Nellie Mortimer and Carrie Burton. On June 20th, Niblo's opened its hospitable stage to Jay Rial's Uncle Tom's Cabin company, with Arthur W. Gregory as Tom, H. S. Duffield as George Harris, L. R. Stockwell as Marks, Sid Hicks as Phineas Fletcher and Legree, Blanche Newcomb as Eva, Sallie Partington as Topsy, and Mrs. Jay Rial as Eliza; a "comical star donkey, Jerry," was part of the show, which closed the season at Niblo's on July 4th.

[272]

CHAPTER V

GRAND OPERA HOUSE, WINDSOR THEATRE, GERMAN THEATRES, ACADEMY OF MUSIC (NEW YORK), THEATRE COMIQUE, VARIETY THEATRES, MINSTRELSY, CIRCUS, MISCELLANY, CONCERTS, 1880–1881

NEW YORK and outlying districts were developing a circuit of theatres in which travelling stars and combinations could spend several weeks, with the metropolis as a homing centre; very much indeed like what the "profession," a half-century later, denominated the "subway circuit." The Grand Opera House and the Windsor Theatre in Manhattan, the Park and Haverly's in Brooklyn, the Novelty in Williamsburgh, not to mention houses in Jersey City and Newark, could keep actors circling from week to week with possibility of sleeping every night, if desired, in what was then New York City. Thus these various theatres frequently housed in successive weeks the same attractions, thereby, on the whole, greatly simplifying our narrative.

The Grand Opera House, like the Windsor Theatre in the Bowery, had by 1880 become merely a "stand" for stars or combinations; it almost never made an original production — in fact, it was ever ready to receive second showings of plays previously successful on Broadway. Historically, therefore, it sinks to second place in our narrative, and consequently I relegate it to the second chapter of the yearly doings in the New York theatre. It had, however, an enormous clientèle and gave admirable returns for the reasonable prices of admission to its roomy and comfortable auditorium.

The season of 1880–81 began on August 23rd, with the ever attractive J. K. Emmet in Fritz in Ireland; he was to remain for three weeks. Since Emmet did not appear at the Wednesday matinées, his company acted Our Mother-in-Law. According to the Herald of September 4th, Fritz ceased ahead of its appointed date, because of Emmet's lapses; he had gone on a protracted drinking spree and was unable to act. An application for his arrest as an habitual drunkard brought him to the Tombs, with $1,393 pinned in a waistcoat pocket, but with his watch gone. At Counsellor Hummel's request, he was committed for examination and turned over to Warden Finn, who was to watch him until he was restored to normal condition; Our Mother-in-law finished the week, and, on September 6th, John T. Raymond entered as a stop-gap, to keep the theatre open for the third of the

[273]

weeks for which Emmet had been originally engaged. Raymond gave Colonel Sellers, his company including Harry Lee (soon to be seen with Fanny Davenport, in An American Girl), Davenport Bebus, Frank Wise, George C. Boniface, Jr., William Cullington, R. T. Runyon, Frankie McClellan, Courtney Barnes (Mrs. Raymond), Mrs. Baker and Mrs. Duffield. The (to me) very interesting Ada Cavendish, who seldom appeared in Broadway, but frequently at the Grand Opera House, was the star on September 13th, as Mercy Merrick (the rôle by which, probably, she is best remembered in America), in The New Magdalen; George C. Boniface was not the most youthful Julian Grey conceivable. J. H. Miller was Horace Holmcroft, Mr. and Mrs. Eugene A. Eberle were Ignatius Wetzel and Lady Janet Ray, and Sara Stevens, the charming Mary Meredith of Our American Cousin at Laura Keene's, in 1858–59, and still in 1880 rather youthful in appearance, was Grace Roseberry. For her second week, beginning on September 20th, Miss Cavendish essayed A. C. Gunter's The Soul of an Actress, a piece presented by Clara Morris in the West — at least so says the Herald of the 21st. As a novelty in New York, its cast clamours for inclusion in the chronicle:

Josephine Clairon............Ada Cavendish		Henri de Soubise.................J. H. Miller
Chevalier de Crevecœur......G. C. Boniface		Domestic......................Mr. Dickens
Charles de Moncrief............J. F. Hagan		Mimi.........................Sara Stevens
Gaston Lenoir.................Hugh Fuller		Countess de Crevecœur.........Mrs. Eberle
Prince de Rohan..............E. A. Eberle		Julie.......................Laura Bascomb
Gerald Fitzgerald..........Harry Harwood		Madelon....................Mrs. Harwood

Miss Cavendish certainly had a superior support, in those days of poor companies for "stars"; it is a pleasure to greet Harry Harwood in those, his apprentice days.

Tony Pastor, who travelled in lengthy seasons from his own theatre, had a week, beginning on September 27th, at the Grand Opera House; with him were the clever male impersonator, Ella Wesner (her first appearance after five years in Europe), Harry and John Kernell, Bonnie Runnells, Charles Diamond, Fred Bryant and William Hoey, Charles Gilday and Fannie Beane, Flora Moore, Lina Tettenborn, the St. Felix Sisters, the French Twin Sisters (Minnie and Lena, with Eva) and the three Rankins (William, Richard and Carl). On October 4th, Mr. and Mrs. George S. Knight (Sophie Worrell) returned "from their European triumphs," in their very familiar Otto, a German, and perhaps had a New York "triumph" of two weeks. The Mahn Opera Company presented, on October 18th, the much desired Boccaccio, with Jeannie Winston (almost identified with the leading rôle), Charles Starelle, Francesca Guthrie, Ellis Ryse, W. Morgan, A. H. Bell, Vincent Hogan, Sidney Barnes, Sophie Hummel, Miss M. Summerville (sic), Rose Leighton, and very many minor prophets of joy. This feast of fun and melody had the (by that time) unusual run of three weeks, except that, for her benefit, on November 5th, Miss Winston reverted to Fatinitza, which she repeated for both performances on Saturday, the 6th. Sallie Reber again played Lydia. Herrmann, beginning on November 8th, gave a week of magic, supported for "Variety's" sake by Val Vose and the Lorellas, these last-named in High Life in Impland. On November 15th, Joseph Jefferson brought the greater magic of his perfect art in Rip Van Winkle, and carried through for what was still the almost customary two weeks of visits to this popular theatre; with him were Adine Stephens as Meenie, and Rosa Rand as Gretchen. He had just revived The Rivals, at Mrs. John Drew's Arch Street Theatre, Philadelphia.

Maggie Mitchell, by that time almost as much of an American institution as Jefferson, followed, on November 29th, in Fanchon (of course), with R. Fulton Russell as Landry, Julian Mitchell (her son) as Didier, R. F. Mc-Clannin (much esteemed in Boston) as Father Barbeaud, Annie Mortimer as Old Fadet, Marion P. Clifton (whom we shall grow to admire) as Mother Barbeaud, and Lettie Allen as Madelon. For the Wednesday matinée and on the evening of December 4th, Miss Mitchell gave Little Barefoot. Her second week presented Jane Eyre, except for the Wednesday matinée, which again proffered the somewhat easier Little Barefoot. I need hardly apprise the reader of the interesting fact that Maggie Mitchell was not, in 1880, quite so youthful as when, in 1862, she first fascinated the town in Fanchon; yet time dealt very lightly with this charming little sprite. She was succeeded at the Grand Opera House, on December 13th, by another actress of presumably the same school, but assuredly of less charm (though she had many admirers) — Annie Pixley, in her greatest success, M'liss; this attraction also lasted for a fortnight, with a supporting cast including J. E. McDonough, Lin Harris, M. C. Daly, Florence Robinson, Lillian Reeder, William Johnson, and G. S. Robinson — certainly not an array famous, individually, to the last syllable of recorded time. I simply cannot place Miss Pixley in the class where Maggie Mitchell still remains, a captivating spirit of eternal youth and charm. That abiding gift of the Rankins — The Danites — came in for two weeks of holiday trade, on December 27th, with a cast greatly reduced in importance from that which offered it at the Broadway Theatre (now Daly's) in 1877; the reader is to be congratulated (or pitied?) if he can thrill at the names of J. E. Nugent, Charles Chappelle, Harry Hawk, G. J. Henderson, Eva Randolph and May Nugent. But the company also included E. M. Holland, one of our best comedians of later years, and Emma Marble, daughter of the once famous Dan Marble. Their parts were William Wise and Henrietta Dickson. And this carries to January 8th, and the beginnings of 1881.

Our German Senator, "in three acts and a telephone," made a star of Gus Williams for two weeks, beginning on January 10th; this was advertised as the "début of the telephone on the stage." What would dramatists do without it in the 1930s? The cast of Our German Senator included Wil-

[275]

liams as J. Adolph Dinkel, J. F. Stevens as Colonel Bruce, Hudson Liston as Judge Jere Spruce, Archie Boyd as Captain Dionysius Puff, Albert Murdock as Bertie Benson, Maggie Arlington as Louise Granville, Emily Bigelow as Flora Bruce, Julia De Young as Fannie, and Dora Stuart as Mrs. Dinkel. We rose, on January 24th, to the high comedy of Ours, enacted by Lester Wallack, J. W. Shannon, H. M. Pitt (as Angus), Julian Magnus (as Perovsky), Russell Bassett, Kate Bartlett (as Mary Netley), Marion Booth and Mrs. Fred Williams. And, on the afternoon of the 27th, we might have attended a benefit for Frank Whittaker, "the disabled showman," who had met with "a terrible accident"; in the bill were Tony Pastor, Lillian Russell, the St. Felix Sisters, Flora Moore, the Herbert Brothers, and contingents from Harrigan and Hart's and from the San Francisco Minstrels. Ours continued for three gala weeks. On February 14th, Wallack began a week of Rosedale, assisted by Mark Pendleton as Matthew Leigh, Russell Bassett as Bunberry Kobb, Shannon as Myles McKenna, Lillie Eldridge as Lady Florence May, Kate Bartlett as Rosa, Mrs. Fred Williams as Sarah Sykes, and Mrs. W. A. Rouse as Tabitha Stork. A benefit, on the afternoon of February 17th, was for the mother of Ella Mayo (recently deceased); Tony Pastor, Pat Rooney, Sam Devere, Ferguson and Mack, Kelly and Ryan, John Hart, Ella Wesner, Harry Kennedy, A. C. Moreland, Jennie Yeamans, the St. Felix Sisters, Jennie Morgan, Fred Levantine and Harrigan and Hart contributed their services.

The Banker's Daughter, so recently seen in revival at the Union Square Theatre, now filled a week (February 21st–26th) at the Grand Opera House, with Sara Jewett (she was not acting in The Danicheffs, at the home theatre), Louise Sylvester, Estelle Clayton, Eva French, Kate Denin, J. B. Polk (again in his original rôle), M. J. Pendleton (as Harold Routledge), J. E. Whiting (as John Strebelow), Herbert Archer, W. J. LeMoyne, Julian Magnus, Alfred Becks, F. F. Mackay (as Babbage), H. F. Daly (as Lawrence Westbrook), and W. S. Quigley — a very interesting group. One is amazed to see how many irons Shook and Palmer now had in the fire. On February 28th, Denman Thompson began a fortnight, in Joshua Whitcomb.

Lawrence Barrett, who returned to us earlier in the season, at the Park Theatre, came, on March 14th, to the Grand Opera House, with a company including Louis James, Marie Wainwright, and the same aggregation that had supported him at the Park. He began with Richelieu (March 14th, 15th and matinée, 16th), and during a busy week played Yorick's Love (evenings, 16th and 17th); Julius Cæsar (evenings of the 18th and 19th, with himself as Cassius, Louis James as Brutus, and Frederick Bock as Antony); and eased the burden of heavy leads by acting, for the Saturday matinée, The Marble Heart. For his second week, the earnest actor played Hamlet (March 21st and 22nd), The Merchant of Venice and David Garrick (23rd and 24th), Yorick's Love (matinée, 23rd), Richard III (evenings of the

[276]

25th and 26th), and The Lady of Lyons (matinée, 26th). At least, Marie Wainwright's Pauline may have been interesting, whatever one might think of Barrett's Claude. J. K. Emmet came back, on March 28th, in Fritz in Ireland; this time, tendency to drink kept in check, he remained for three weeks, surely one of the most popular of stars. His smile and his singing enraptured his audiences. A remarkably pleasing personality! Joseph Murphy, also popular and pleasing, but in Irish vein, succeeded Emmet, on April 18th, in The Kerry Gow. A re-arranged Shaun Rhue, by Fred Marsden, filled the week of April 25th–30th:

Larry Donovan	Joseph Murphy	Summerville	John Murphy
Gerald Kavanagh	Nelson Decker	Lawyer Waddy	Murry Woods
Brian Calligan	Hugh Fuller	Tim	Belle Dickson
Morris Donovan	Welsh Edwards	Kate Donovan	Genevieve Rogers
Patrick Kavanagh	Harry Harwood	Dora Kavanagh	Libbie Noxon
Peter Calligan	J. F. Hagan		

Fanny Davenport came in, on May 2nd, in her compelling rôle of the haughty Mabel Renfrew, in Pique, J. B. Studley playing Matthew Standish; on the afternoon of the 7th, Miss Davenport appeared, for one only performance, as, I fear, a too-too solid Camille, but pretty withal, Joseph Wheelock assisting as Armand. She was succeeded, on May 9th, by the funny Louis Harrison, with his sister, Alice Harrison, in Photos, another of those specialty pieces then so popular; Carrie Daniels assisted. On May 16th, Tony Pastor, footloose again from his own theatre, began a week at the Grand Opera House, with a company including Ella Wesner, Lillie Western, the French Sisters, the Irwin Sisters, William Lester and Paul Allen, Harry MacAvoy and Emma Rogers, Bernard Ferguson and Richard Mack, Frank Girard, Dan Collyer, Frank E. McNish, and Rose and Jennie Leland. The "New" Evangeline brought joy on May 23rd, with Rose Dana as Evangeline (she had been Eulalie at the Fourteenth Street Theatre, in September, 1880), Louise Searle as Gabriel, Jessie Calef as Eulalie, Jennie Calef as Felicien, Pauline Hall as Hans Wagner, George K. Fortescue still as Catherine, George A. Schiller (new) as the Lone Fisherman, Max Figman as Captain Dietrich, Ed Chapman as Le Blanc, Horace Frail as Basil, &c. The last week of the season (May 30th–June 4th) brought The Child of the State, George Hoey's adaptation from D'Ennery, with James M. Hardie, Hoey, Will H. Sands, H. Rees Davis, M. B. Snyder, Frank Willard, Ellen Cummens (sic), Minnie Monk, Eva Glen Barker and Katie Baker as a not very promising cast, especially for those who remembered Emily Rigl and the Wallack distribution in the spring preceding. Of course the treasurer, William McCoy, must have his benefit. On the afternoon of May 30th, he offered acts (I quote from the advertisement in the Herald) from The Child of the State, La Tour de Nesle (the last-named with J. B. Studley and Kate Meek), The Rough Diamond (with Ben Maginley and Mrs. Fred Williams), A Pleasant Neighbour (with J. H. Ryan and Mrs. E. L. — sic — Barker),

[277]

Mr. and Mrs. George S. Knight, Herrmann, Frank Boudinot and Frank Mockabee (Asleep at the Switch). The season of 1880–81 closed here on June 4th.

WINDSOR THEATRE, 1880–1881

The Windsor Theatre, formerly the Stadt-Theater, and now a very respectable "combination" house, offered its patrons an English *menu* very superior to any met with, for several seasons preceding, in the Bowery. It re-opened, on August 16th, with A Celebrated Case, still exciting, with E. K. Collier as Jean Renaud, Anna Boyle as Madeleine and the adult Adrienne, Emily Baker as Valentine, and W. Scallan as O'Rourke. Buffalo Bill shot true Bowery, on the 23rd, in The Prairie Waif, in which a band of Cheyenne Indian chiefs added verisimilitude in scalp and war dances, doubtless horrific indeed; Harry Clifton and George T. James assisted as Danites, Jule Keen was Hans, and other actors included R. C. White, C. Wilson Charles, Ralph Delmore (whose cast of feature doomed him to villains always), Robert Neil, E. Booth, Lizzie Fletcher and Connie Thompson. The Herald, on the 24th, tells us gravely that "their parts were simple, and they sustained them well." Much more sophisticated, in the eyes of 1880, was East Lynne, on August 30th, with Ada Gray, then the best-liked representative of Lady Isabel and her ruined shadow, Mme. Vine; on September 2nd, A Friend Indeed was presented, with Miss Gray as Milly, and Isidore Davidson as the cripple. "One merit," says the Herald, unkindly, "the piece . . . possesses in a high degree — everybody in it is doing something all the time; they never stand still and begin to talk." Annie Ward Tiffany introduced herself, on the 6th, as Nemo, the actress, in a play by Elliott Dawn, entitled Prejudice; J. Leslie Gossin was Elliott Dare and Jennie Yeamans was Rose. For the second half of her week, beginning on September 9th, Miss Tiffany gave Lucille Western's old play, The Child Stealer. Thus far, the Windsor season — in spite of what I said a minute ago — seems flat to our more fastidious taste.

Oliver Doud Byron, on September 13th, again tried Across the Continent, which had for so many seasons satisfied his not too exacting audiences; for the latter half of his week (16th–18th) he went even farther, in 10,000 Miles Away. And a novelty of an un-Bowery character came in, on the 20th, with Mrs. F. S. (Henrietta) Chanfrau and Harry Courtaine. This was Christie Johnstone, adapted from Charles Reade's novel, and thus cast:

Christie	Mrs. Chanfrau	Charles Gatty	H. D. Gale
Lord Ipsden	Harry Courtaine	Saunders	George Woodward
Lady Barbara	Ethel Greybrooke	Sandy Liston	W. N. Griffith
Jean Ramsay	Ada Hamilton	Flucker Johnstone	R. L. Tayleure
Widow Rutherford	Mrs. Kate L. Littel	Robert Carnie	A. V. Ranous
Beenie Carnie	Rose Keene	Mr. Oldfield	J. H. Alliger
Mrs. Gatty	Victoria Cameron		

I warn all and sundry that the "combination" system will fill our pages and (alas!) our indexes with many such forgotten worthies. Frank I. Frayne was the star of the week beginning September 27th, in his well-known Si Slocum, his featured support including Master Freddie, Little Clara, and "the wonderful trained dog," Jack. John A. Stevens and Lottie Church, on October 4th, gave us Unknown, certainly known to my reader, however unknown the supporting actors — William H. Bailey, Angie Griffiths, George F. Ketchum, Mamie Wilson, Charles Abbott and Spencer Pritchard. Have I rated the Windsor too highly? All my mind is clouded with a doubt, as I write the attraction for October 11th — Anthony and Ellis's Famous Ideal Company, in Uncle Tom's Cabin, with Kate Partington as Topsy, and with "one hundred on the stage," including, of course, jubilee singers.

Then, on October 18th, came a surprise to the Windsor and to me — Ada Cavendish and George C. Boniface, in The New Magdalen, seen only a few weeks earlier at the Grand Opera House; The Four Seasons, with C. L. Graves's Combination, did what it could, during the week of October 25th, to fill the roomy spaces of the Windsor. The show boasted of a carnival skating scene and a rehearsal in a barn. J. B. Studley, on November 1st, began a week in Monte Cristo, and began, also, an upward grade in the quality of the offerings. Charlotte Thompson, then slipping quietly out of our ken, appeared at the Windsor, on November 8th, in The Planter's Wife, a play by James M. Tillotson, in which she acted Edith, with Rose Keene as Angie, and Walter L. Dennis as Arthur Blake. Later we shall see elsewhere Emily Rigl in this rather hectic play. F. S. Chanfrau filled the following week (October 15th–20th) with his everlasting Kit, supported by Griffith as Suggs, and Woodward as Squiggs, those amusing rogues. A "sacred" concert, on the 21st, provided the Apollo Club, the Bent Brothers and others. Miss Markstein was announced "without authority," as she states in the Herald of the 22nd. And, on November 22nd, entered Kate Claxton and Charles A. Stevenson in their recent *quasi*-success from the Bijou — The Snow Flower; this they gave for the first three days of their visit, and for the last three inevitably reverted to The Two Orphans. Was not the Windsor at last attaining to something like the glory of the Grand Opera House? Let us hope the audiences responded cheerfully to the rising temperature (artistically). But we drop, possibly, on November 29th, when Marie Wellesley, Marie Bates and W. E. Sterling presented Old Cross, with a large cast including Russell Bassett, Edgar L. Davenport, W. Singleton, Louise Loring, J. H. Rowe and J. B. Howard, along with the dogs, Sultan and Cæsar, useful in a play dealing, as did Old Cross, with the Hospice St. Bernard. The aggregation of actors seems somewhat above the average "combination." The old Bowery flame of delight, Jack Sheppard, presented, on December 6th, the youthful star, N. S. Wood, with the old

Bowery favourite Mrs. W. G. Jones, in support, and also Maggie Weston and Joseph P. Winter. A special feature was "the old London stage, drawn by four splendid horses." For his benefit, on the 10th, young Mr. Wood (the original Anatole in A Scrap of Paper, at Wallack's) gave The Boy Scout of the Sierras and Dora, the Detective; I hope that enough of the old Bowery spirit remained to pack the galleries with whistling, stamping boys. This same Boy Scout started on the 9th and departed on the 11th. I am amused at the idea of Nellie Holbrook's Hamlet, on December 13th and 14th, and the quick change of the star to East Lynne, on the remaining nights of her week; she was supported by no less a person than D. W. Waller, once of the palmy days at Booth's, who played the Ghost. Lewis Baker was Laertes, Julian Magnus Horatio, and Nellie Boyd Ophelia. On Saturday evening, December 18th, Miss Holbrook was to play both Hamlet and East Lynne. Nick Roberts's Humpty Dumpty (with three clowns) made merry during the week of December 20th–25th, and Led Astray (with Katherine Rogers as star) made sad the New Year, during the week of December 27th–January 1st). With Miss Rogers were Harry Meredith, J. W. Summers (as Hector Placide), Albert Tavernier (as Mount-Gosline), Lottie Church (as Mathilde), Angie Griffiths (as Suzanne O'Hara), Florence Vincent (as the Countess), Mrs. Le Brun (as the Baroness), and Charles Abbott (as de Lesparre). J. B. Studley returned on January 3rd, as Mathias, in The Bells, with W. H. Bailey as Walter, J. L. Ashton as Dr. Franz, J. W. Summers as Heinrich, J. V. Melton as Christian, A. Tavernier as the Mesmerist, T. Blake as the Judge, Alice Chandos as Annette, Mrs. W. G. Jones as Catherine, and Miss Jackson as Lois. A farce, He Must Be Married, eked out the bill. And actually, straight from their two weeks at the Grand Opera House, the Rankins shifted south-southeast, to the Windsor, on the 10th, for a week of The Danites. One observes that supporting actors in the offerings cited above passed from star to star, with a haunting suggestion that they may have been regularly connected with the house.

Perhaps for fear of too much refinement, the management brought back, on January 17th, Buffalo Bill, in The Prairie Waif. Gus Phillips (Oofty Gooft) held the week of the 24th, in Under the Gaslight, rewritten in part for him by Augustin Daly; Snorky now became a German veteran. Others in the cast were G. W. Farren as Ray Trafford, J. Winston Murray as Byke, Frank McGraw as Justice Bowling, Frank Budworth as Bermudas, Lillian M. Joyce as Laura, Edith Florence as Pearl, Louise Fox as Peach Blossom, and Mrs. Gus Phillips as Old Judas and Mrs. Van Dam. This is certainly one of the least notable aggregations my conscientious pen has ever transcribed. Perhaps it is well that we cannot always unearth supporting casts of those years. Salsbury's Troubadours, on January 31st, brought in their ever-flowing Brook. And, on February 7th, the company recently seen at Booth's transferred to the Windsor their Uncle Tom's Cabin.

The Rentz-Santley Novelty Company could not be certified to raise the artistic standard, when, on February 14th, they came into the Windsor, with Lisa Weber, Mabel Santley, Rosa Lee, James Vincent, Lew Benedict, Quilter and Goldrich, J. E. Henshaw, Harry Woodson, Mark Heintz, and the Española Ballet, in Skiptomania. Yet many of these were notable in "Variety." A farce, Don Juan, Jr., or, Leporello, the Naughty Fellow, may have pleased the kind of persons who, fifty years later, like "sophisticated" comedies. Gus Williams, on the 21st, introduced his recent offering, Our German Senator, from the Grand Opera House. And, on the 28th, that fine success from the Park Theatre, The Legion of Honour, brought to the Windsor S. W. Piercy, Annie Graham and Lewis Morrison. Certainly the quality of the offerings was again showing an upward tendency. The Mahn Company, with Jeannie Winston, appeared, on March 7th, in Boccaccio, and the elegant Lester Wallack came to the Windsor, on the 14th, in Rosedale, possibly remembering those far-off nights, about thirty years before, when he had appeared at the Bowery Theatre, as the youthful heroes of romance. After this fine flight, the Windsor settled back, on March 21st, on Frank I. Frayne's new play, Mardo, the Hunter, in which appeared a lion, Chio, the dog, Jack, and the horse, Rocket. James O'Neill and Lillian Glover were here, on March 28th, to begin a Bulwer-Lytton week, in which they tried Richelieu and The Lady of Lyons; their support(?) included George Gordon, Charles Pfyffe, Louis Haywood, Hart Conway, De Los King, Welsh Edwards, S. Du Bois, Fred Lotto, and Cassie Troy. How many of these can my reader identify?

Tony Denier's Humpty Dumpty, in the week of April 4th–9th, advertised George H. Adams as "the greatest of living clowns," believe it who listed; the company also included J. O. Hall as Pantaloon, W. Eunice as Harlequin, Miss V. North as Columbine, and Rosina Cooke as the Fairy Queen. Herrmann, Mlle. Addie, the three Lorellas and Val Vose constituted the lure for the week of April 11th–16th. On the 18th, the Gosche-Hopper company presented One Hundred Wives, a recent production at Booth's; the cast included De Wolf Hopper, Ada Gilman, Margaret Cone, William H. Harris, Alexander Fitzgerald and Lawrence Eddinger. Annie Pixley, in M'liss, was here on the 25th. Joseph Murphy, having completed two weeks at the Grand Opera House, came to the Windsor, for the week of May 2nd–7th, in The Kerry Gow. Neil Burgess followed, on May 9th, in his very funny Widow Bedott; and Mr. and Mrs. George S. Knight brought Otto to the Bowery establishment in the week of May 16th–21st. For the closing week of the season (May 23rd–28th), Baker and Farron, that team in comedy not so very refined, appeared in The Emigrants, seen shortly before in Brooklyn.

A supplementary season began on May 30th, with B. H. Butler as manager, and with William Stafford and Anna Boyle as stars. On the 30th and 31st, and on June 1st, with matinées on June 1st and 4th, they gave The

[281]

Lady of Lyons to a public not over-eager to accept; on the evenings of June 2nd, 3rd and 4th, their medium of self-exploitation was The Merchant of Venice, with John T. Malone as Bassanio. On June 6th they essayed Fanchon, without permanent injury to the fame of Maggie Mitchell. With their Othello and Desdemona, on June 13th, they joined the acceptable Iago of Fred B. Warde, with John Malone as Cassio, J. F. Hagan as the Duke, F. Chippendale as Brabantio, and Mrs. W. G. Jones as Emilia, a very respectable Bowery cast for early summer. The stars went out in a kind of glory, presenting Romeo and Juliet at matinées on June 18th and 22nd, and on the evenings of June 23rd and 24th, and Hamlet on the three preceding evenings of their last week, June 20th, 21st and 22nd, with Frank Roberts as the Ghost, Chippendale as Polonius, Mrs. Jones as the Queen and Malone as Laertes. They departed on the 25th, with repetitions of The Merchant of Venice, afternoon and evening. A pretty ambition gratified, at what cost I know not! With this burst of Shakespearian representations, the Windsor lapsed to the management of William Freligh, long manager of the old Bowery, who, on June 27th, brought out Charles Foster as Dick Phillimore, in "his great California success," Tripped and Trapped, with J. H. Rowe as Dr. Walter King, Randolph Murray as Fred Randall, Josephine Crocker as Kitty Wilton, Lillian Westbrook as Minnie Adams, and Mrs. W. G. Jones as Mrs. Adams. What a treat it would have been to talk with Mrs. Jones of her life in the theatre! The last week of the season began on July 4th; on the afternoon of that day we had The Sea of Ice and The Buccaneer of the Gulf, with Abe, the Pioneer, in the evening.

THALIA THEATER, 1880–1881

The Thalia had, unquestionably, the more interesting season of the rival German houses; austere chroniclers, believing, apparently, that a German season should consist only of Schiller and the classics might impugn my judgment. But the reader will, of course, decide for himself. The term began with performances on September 16th, 17th and 18th, of Wilhelm Tell, with Joseph L'Hamé, stage-manager of the house, making his first appearance here as an actor, in the title-rôle; his associates were Schönfeld as Arnold, Wohlmuth (first appearance in America) as Werner, Hauser as Gessler, Varena as Ulrich, and, in other characters, Schnelle, Adolfi, Meyer, Frl. Holzapfel, Frl. Heller, Frl. Beeskow, and Julie Heller. On the 20th, for the début of Marie König (who did not make a hit), came Genée and Zell's opera, Die Porträtdame, with music by Max Wolff. In this, Lube and Adolfi, in comic rôles, were declared by the Herald to be very funny, but, though Frl. König, as Charlotte, was starred, the honours, according to the same paper, fell to Frl. Holzapfel, in Amalie, a minor part! Frl. Kuster was the young Friedrich August.

[282]

Die Porträtdame was heard again on the 20th, 21st and 22nd, with recurrence, on the 23rd and 24th to Wilhelm Tell; on the evening of the 25th, Die Hexe, a tragedy by Arthur Fitzger (a name declared by the Herald to conceal the identity of the author, an essayist and government official), presented Frl. Reinhold as the free-thinking persecuted Thalea, Frl. Beeskow as Almuth, her sister, L'Hamé as Edgard von Wiarda, Bojock as Lubbo, Schönfeld as Xavier, the Jesuit, and Hauser as the Pastor. Others were Wohlmuth, Meyer, Schmitz, Lehmann, Frl. Heller, &c. It was repeated on Monday, the 27th.

On the 28th, the exuberant Mathilde Cottrelly inaugurated a season of light entertainment and opera, with Jacobsohn's and Lehnhardt's Der jüngste Lieutenant (*sic*):

Von Alden	Herr Bojock	Eva	Frl. Beeskow
Majorin von Alden	Frl. Hartmann	Bernhard	Frl. Cottrelly
Hedwig	Frl. Kelly	Traugott Michael	Herr Adolfi
Mitscherlich	Herr Schnelle	Bertha	Frl. Holzapfel
Demmler	Herr Puls	Strunk	Herr Schmitz
Bumke	Herr Lube	Ursula	Frau Lube
Schönland	Herr Varena		

This had a few repetitions, as did Giroflé-Girofla (first heard on October 4th) and Ein Russischer Beamter and Die Zillerthaler (brought out on the 7th). Boccaccio enlivened the evening of the 9th, and several succeeding nights. On the 16th came the spectacular trifle named 500,000 Teufel, which brought, on the 17th, from the Herald reviewer a severe rebuke. The piece abounded in "broad jokes," and "outrageous puns," and flaunted a "luridly painted hell, with fine limbed female denizens in attractive tights." "Tuneless comic songs by voiceless comedians and soubrettes," and "that general farcical hullabaloo in which German audiences seem to delight," obviously annoyed the reviewer. Lube was "very funny," but "Cottrelly seems to be becoming as much stouter in physique as she is becoming thinner in voice." With all these drawbacks, "the snap and merriment of the farce appeared to carry the audience with it."

The Thalia was now committed to the course of operetta which it pursued for the rest of the season, especially after the advent, in January, of the delightful Marie Geistinger. 500,000 Teufel made merry several ensuing evenings, though its course was interrupted on the 23rd by Boccaccio (matinée) and Bajazzo und seine Familie (evening). On the 26th, Franziska Raberg made her first appearance as Fiametta, in Boccaccio. The evening of October 29th brought the première here of Johann Strauss's delightful opera, Prince Methusalem, with Frl. König in the title-rôle, Adolfi as the Duke of Trocadero, Frl. Kuster as Pulcinella, Bojock as Marquis Carbonazzi, Puls as Count Vulcano, Lube as Duke of Rikarak, Frau Lube as Sophistika, his wife, and Schnelle as Trombonius, the composer. Needless to say, this was a great success; Frl. Raberg entered the cast, on November 8th, in the title-rôle. Meantime, since, after all, the Thalia was a repertoire theatre, 500,000 Teufel came back for the matinée on the 6th, and, on the evening of the 4th, Hedwig Hesse and Edouard Härting entered as stars, in Faust. On the 10th, these stars gave Maria Stuart, and, on the 13th, Das Glas Wasser. Der Seecadet (*sic*), that huge success of the preceding winter, was revived on the 15th and 16th. The Thalia was now giving Sunday concerts, its attractions in that field, on the 14th, including Arbuckle's Band, Henrietta Markstein, A. Wohlmuth, Lube, Hedwig Hesse, Emma Kuster, Adolfi, &c. Prince Methusalem still had certain performances, and, on the 18th, Frl. Hesse and Härting revived Feenhände. Die Fledermaus fluttered in, on the 20th, after a matinée, on that day, of Das Glas Wasser.

Does not the reader, if he can detach himself from the usual academic demand for nothing but the classics, find these promises interesting? On November 23rd, Frl. Hesse and Härting said farewell, in Der Kaufmann von Venedig. The undying Lumpaci Vagabundus made holiday on November 24th and matinée, 25th (Thanksgiving); also on the evening of the 27th. Die Fledermaus and Prince Methusalem still edged their way into certain evenings. Der Sonnenwendhof came on the 29th and 30th, to be followed, on December 1st, 2nd and 3rd, by Fatinitza, with Franziska Raberg as Vladimir, Emma Kuster as Lydia, Edouard Schmitz as Kanschukoff, Max Schnelle as von Golz, Gustav Adolfi as Izzet Pacha, &c. Der Seecadet, on the 4th, rounded out a week of fun, if not of the highest musical delight.

On Tuesday, December 7th, R. Genée's opera, Nisida, was introduced with Mathilde Cottrelly as the much-travelling heroine, with Adolfi as the Corregidor of Havana, Frau Lube as his sister, Miguela, Marie König as Donna Mercedes, Schnelle as Don Montiel, her brother, F. Lenoir as Don Rodrigo Sandoval, O. Meyer as Don Grajiano, Lube as Barnacle, Frl. Raberg as Carmen, F. Varena as Spartaco and Puls as Luna — these last two characters being members of a negro minstrel troupe. The place was Havana, and the time the present. This had a long run, interrupted by an occasional Prince Methusalem or Seecadet. A concert, on Sunday, December 19th, exploited the Swedish Ladies' Quartet and members of the regular stock company of the house. One might be surprised to find Die beiden Waisen produced (December 20th and a few nights subsequently) by arrangement with Shook and Palmer, and with this cast in leading characters:

Graf von Linières	Herr Bojock	Henriette	Frl. Beeskow
Gräfin Diana	Frl. Reinhold	Louise	Frl. Bernard
Chevalier	Herr Schönfeld	La Frochard	Frl. Heller
Picard	Herr Schmitz	Jacques	Herr L'Hamé
Marquis de Presles	Herr Meyer	Pierre	Herr Wohlmuth
Lafleur	Herr Steppes	Marianne	Frau Lube
Doctor	Herr Wagner	Schwester Genoveva	Frl. Kelly

[284]

Nisida was soon back in the bills. The benefit of Carl Schönfeld, on December 30th, gave us Around the World in Eighty Days. Children, beginning on the 27th, gave matinées of Bibi, oder der Gänzekönig. At the New Year's matinée, Nisida was again the attraction, but, in the evening of that holiday, Robert and Bertram had a performance. At the Sunday concert, January 2nd, appeared Nahan Franko, with Rachel and Jeanne of the same family. Prince Methusalem re-emerged on the 3rd, and, on the 4th, the theatre was closed, in preparation for the great event of the year.

Marie Geistinger

On the 5th, appeared one of the most attractive German artists seen up to that time in New York — Marie Geistinger, from Vienna, a woman of sparkling charm, whose versatility allowed her to range from Boccaccio to Camille. Perhaps such variety of talent was unparalleled in modern times. She came out, on the 5th, as the Grand Duchess of Gerolstein, assisted by Frl. Kuster as Wanda, Schnelle as Fritz, Lube as Prinz Paul, Adolfi as General Boum, and Bojock as Baron Puck. The Herald, on the 6th, says that those who had seen Schneider, Tostée, Irma, Aimée and Paola Marié as the Duchess were surprised at Geistinger's performance. "She does not give to it the *abandon*, the *verve*, the spirit of rollicking fun of the bouffe stage, but plays it, rather, in a tone of high comedy. Hers is a duchess who is full of animal spirits, no doubt, but is still a Duchess, and retains always something of the dignity of the position. There is humour in the part, but she never indulges in any of the coarseness of the bouffe stage."

After four nights of triumphant success as the Duchess, Geistinger, on Monday, the 10th of January, came forth as Mme. Favart, with Frl. Raberg as Suzanne, Lube as de Pontsable, Adolfi as Favart, Bojock as Cotignac, and Schnelle as Boisrepreau. The Herald of the 11th confirms our suspicion that the company did not sing well, if it could really be said to sing at all. Mme. Geistinger, in the title-rôle, was "quieter" than Aimée, and the *doubles entendres* were touched on so delicately that "they lost their coarseness, without being robbed of anything of their questionable brilliancy" — surely something of a feat of suggestiveness. Mme. Favart ruled the evenings of January 11th, 12th and 14th, and, on the 13th and 15th, Mme. Geistinger won a great success as Boccaccio, a performance which was directed by Rudolf Bial, who then first conducted for the triumphant new star. The cast of Boccaccio included, in addition to Mme. Geistinger, Schnelle as Pietro, Schmitz as Scalza, Frl. Kuster as Beatrice, Lube as Lotteringhi, Mathilde Cottrelly as Isabella, Frau Lube as Peronella, Adolfi as Lambertucci, and Frau Raberg as Fiametta, with, of course, a large array of minor players in minor rôles. By this time the Herald had discovered that the guest-star sank her personality in every character she essayed; in fact, that Mme.

Geistinger was a great artist. She was acclaimed by the German press, until the German critics awoke to the fact that her success in operetta forced Schiller into the background; then the German critics became sad indeed. Alas! operetta in all countries was giving the classics what is known as a close run for life.

The third week of the new star repeated Boccaccio on the 17th and 21st of January, and the Grand Duchess on the 20th; on the 18th, 19th and 22nd, Die Fledermaus winged its way into the bills. The reader will not desire the dates of all repetitions of these favourite operettas; suffice it to say that such repetitions were numerous. On January 27th, 28th and 29th, came Drei Paar Schuhe, an amusing piece, in which the star played the part of Leni, a shoemaker's wife, who, by carrying shoes to three discontented or careless women, managed to get them into worse difficulties than they had previously feared. Her support included Schnelle as Lorenz, Bojock as Stangelmeier, Lube as Julius, Meyer as Wappenknopf, Cottrelly as Irma, Frl. Kelly as Clara, and Frau Raberg as Laura. For her first matinée, on the 29th, Mme. Geistinger offered Am Clavier and Versprechen hinter'm Heerd; between these trifles, Cottrelly acted Madame Flott, in a farce of that name. The only novelty of the fourth week was Barbe Bleue, or since it was sung in German, I suppose we must say Blaubart; this was offered on February 3rd and 4th. Already, one sees, Mme. Geistinger had translated into German several successes of the French *opéra-bouffe* almost too familiar to our stage. For her second matinée, on February 5th, the brilliant actress repeated Drei Paar Schuhe, and for her third, on February 12th, Boccaccio. On the 14th, 15th, 18th and 19th, she first slipped the bonds of operetta, and came out, with perfect success, as Therese Krones (a piece of course with music), filling the interstices of a busy week with Boccaccio (16th), Drei Paar Schuhe (17th) and Die Fledermaus (matinée, 19th). Therese Krones was repeated on the 21st and 24th, with a matinée, on the 26th; on the evening of the 23rd (for the benefit of Herr Schönfeld) and again on the 26th, Mme. Geistinger appeared as Anna, in Der Pfarrer von Kirchfeld. For those desiring, I can now supply part of the cast of Die Fledermaus, of those days; Schnelle was Gabriel, Geistinger Rosalinde, Mathilde Cottrelly (lately much eclipsed) Adèle, Frl. Kelly Ida, Lube was Frank, the prison warden, Lube Prince Orlowsky, Lenoir Alfred, Adolfi Frosch, Varena Dr. Blind, Meyer Dr. Falk, and Schmitz Iwan.

On March 1st, the new artist displayed her remarkable range by enacting Camille (Die Cameliendame). Next day the Herald was enthusiastic, asserting that this performance would be remembered when most of her other parts were forgotten; the actress was very, very versatile. New York, in that season, one remembers, could compare this German lady of the camelias with the French one of Sarah Bernhardt and the American version of Clara Morris; and, only a season earlier Modjeska had played the part here.

[286]

Camille suffered and died, also, on March 4th and 5th. On March 7th and 9th, Graf Essex filled the bill, with Geistinger magnificent in the robes of Queen Elizabeth; Camille again wept on the 10th, and Therese Krones came back on the 11th; Boccaccio and Drei Paar Schuhe relieved the tension of the week.

On Sunday, March 13th, appeared at the Thalia in concert, Mme. Geistinger, Dengremont, A. H. Pease, Ch. Fritsch, Max Treumann (baritone), Emma Kuster, and Hubert de Blanc. On March 14th, 16th and 17th, with the matinée on the 19th, Mme. Geistinger acted in Der Verschwender, Maurice Dengremont playing a violin solo in the second act; Camille was repeated on the 15th and 19th. On the 18th, Mme. Geistinger enacted Donna Diana, with Hauser as Don Diego, Schönfeld as Don Cäsar, Meyer as Don Luis, Puls as Don Gaston, L'Hamé as Perin, Mathilde Cottrelly as Florette, Frl. Kelly as Donna Laura, Frl. Beeskow as Donna Luisa, &c. Between the acts, Dengremont played. One might well have asked, in amazement, where were the operettas of yester-eve? or was this a German Modjeska? The favourite Max Schnelle suddenly died, and for the benefit of his family, on Sunday, March 20th, a concert introduced the hard-working Geistinger, Leopold Lichtenberg (violinist), Fanny Albert (pianist), Liberati, Max Lube, C. Schönfeld, and Emma Kuster.

The week following exemplified the versatile talent of the all-conquering Geistinger, with Camille (March 21st, 24th and 26th); Drei Paar Schuhe (22nd); Donna Diana (23rd); Versprechen hinter'm Heerd, Ich Speise bei meiner Mutter and Die Schöne Galathée (for her seventieth appearance, on the 25th); and Donna Diana again, at the matinée on the 26th. On the 28th, she repeated the triple bill of the 25th, and, on the 29th, gave her last rendition of Therese Krones. Camille suffered and died on the 30th, followed, on the 31st by Drei Paar Schuhe (last time), and on April 1st by Strauss's Der Carneval in Rom. The cast included Geistinger, Fritsch, Adolfi, Lube, Frl. Kuster, &c. The bill for the matinée on the 2nd was Der Pfarrer von Kirchfeld. The week beginning on April 4th was also interesting, including as it did Der Carneval in Rom, on April 4th and 6th and Boccaccio on the 7th, the popular triple bill on the 5th and at the matinée on the 9th, and a novelty on the 8th and 9th (evening). This latter was Ludwig Held and Edouard L. Jacobsohn's Die Näherin (The Seamstress), "written expressly for Mme. Geistinger," who, of course, played the part of Lottie Griesmeyer. Her associates were Urban as Leopold Hoch, Herr and Frau Lube as Schombar and Ilka Schombar, Meyer and Frl. Ahl (from San Francisco) as the young Schombar "paar," Frl. Heller as Frau Weber, &c. This also was successful, and was repeated every evening "till further notice," except on April 15th, when The Grand Duchess once more sprang to life in the bills. This last-named specialty came again, on the 18th, for the benefit of Emma Kuster; on the 20th, Max Lube, for his benefit, revived

[287]

La Belle Hélène, acting Menelaus, with Mme. Geistinger in the title-rôle, and with F. Urban as Paris — a delight repeated on the 21st, 22nd and 23rd. The undying Camille once more coughed and passed out, at the matinée on the 23rd. For her last week, the reigning favourite offered constant changes of bill. On the 25th, she acted Therese Krones, for the benefit of the German Hospital; Die Näherin sewed and chattered on the 26th; La Belle Hélène was offered on the afternoon of the 27th, and Camille in the evening; Boccaccio on the 28th, led to Mme. Favart, on the 29th, for Adolfi's benefit; La Grande Duchesse was the matinée fare on the 30th, and, on the evening of that day, Geistinger said farewell, in La Belle Hélène. It was her hundredth performance in New York. What a woman and what a season! The German stage in New York had known nothing like it. The complaint of certain austere critics, then and since, that Geistinger's success in less worthy things helped to kill the taste for Schiller and other classic playwrights may be set down as a German variant of the familiar cry in America about musical shows and Shakespeare.

GERMANIA THEATER, 1880–1881

The older establishment, the Germania Theater, began its season on September 16, 1880 — an evening which brought the re-opening of the rival Thalia. Neuendorff started his campaign with Hugo Bürger's play, Auf der Brautfahrt:

Frau Delmont	Frl. Setti	Sophie	Frl. Bensberg
Robert	Herr Lichtenthal	Hildegard	Frl. Wagner
Marie	Frl. Necker	Miss Cragg	Frl. Schmitz
Paul Gersdorff	Herr Sauer	Franz Hollmann	Herr Meery
Von St. Foye	Herr Raberg	Benedict	Herr Fortner
Heinrich Potter	Herr Kierschner	Eine Wirthin	Frl. Umlauf

This was the first appearance for several years of Kierschner.

After three performances, the play just cited gave way (September 20th) to L'Arronge's comedy, Hasemann's Töchter, in which Claudius Merten, who had been absent for three years, returned to a gratified public, in the character of Hasemann. "A more enthusiastic audience," says the next day's Herald, "never gathered in a New York theatre." Ehrliche Arbeit, on the 21st, provided the début of Georgine von Januschowsky, a pleasing person, afterward known to frequenters of our English-speaking stage. Interestingly enough, the music of this piece was by our recently well-known leader, Rudolf Bial. Kalte Seelen, by G. von Moser, had, on the 22nd, what was set down as "its first performance in America." The cast included Kierschner as Consul Wendt, Meery as Georg, Raberg as Professor Reinau, Frl. Necker as Johanna, "dessen Tochter," Frl. Bensberg as Wittwe von Western, Sauer as Max Kleeberg, Lichtenthal as Herr von Zieburg, Frl. Umlauf as Ludmilla, Kummer as Holm, Rank as Paul, Frl. Schmitz as Frau

[288]

Herzlich, and Heinemann as Wilhelm.   The theatre was closed, on the 23rd, because of a mass-meeting in Tammany Hall, adjoining; but, on the 24th and 25th, Kalte Seelen once more gladdened the auditors.

The rivalry between the theatres grew tense.   On the 27th of September, the Germania brought out Der jünge Lieutenant (sic) by Mannstädt and Görtz, with music by Hübner-Trams, and, the very next night the Thalia retorted with Jacobsohn's vaudeville, Der jüngste Lieutenant (sic).   Neither piece had a protracted run, and, on October 4th, and for several succeeding nights, the Germania staged Gute Zeugnisse, by Mallachow and Elsner, as well as Hanni weint, Hansi lacht.   After repetitions of both Ehrliche Arbeit (8th and 9th) and Kalte Seelen (11th and 12th), Der Zugvogel, by Moser and Schönthan, on October 13th, inaugurated a brief run, terminating on the 18th, when Berg and Jacobsohn's Das Mädel ohne Geld replaced it in the bills for eight successive performances:

Baron von Sontheim	Herr Kierschner	Frau Kiebitz	Frl. Schmitz
Eduard	Herr Meery	Franz	Frl. Wagner
Marie	Frl. von Januschowsky	Teltow	Herr Rank
Moritz	Herr Lichtenthal	Pschiworsky	Herr Merten
Merkl	Herr Raberg	Betty	Frl. Umlauf

Der G'wissenswurm, Anzengruber's comedy, was the next production (October 29th), and met with success (I surmise), since it continued till November 9th and 10th, when Das Mädel ohne Geld had further showings, Merten, Raberg, Kierschner, Frl. von Januschowsky and Frl. Schmitz heading the cast.   Julius Rosen's comedy, Sauere Trauben, began on November 11th, running sweetly, with Merten, Frl. Bensberg, Raberg, Frl. Necker, Frl. Schmitz, and Frl. von Januschowsky, until Der Diplomat der alten Schule drove it (November 17th) from the programme.   Von Moser's Der Elephant came in, on the 20th, Der G'wissenswurm, on the 24th; on the 25th, Hans Lonei, by L'Arronge, began an apparently prosperous career, the cast including Frl. Setti, Sauer, Raberg, Frl. Schmitz, Frl. Necker, Lichtenthal, Merten and Kierschner.   On December 3rd, Hugo Müller's comedy, Heydemann und Sohn, with music by Rudolf Bial, had its first performance, with Raberg, Meery, Frl. Necker, Frl. Bensberg, Lichtenthal, Sauer, Rank, Merten and Frl. von Januschowsky.   For the benefit of Eugenie Schmitz, on the 8th, Der Meineidbauer was performed.   This clever actress then celebrated the twenty-fifth anniversary of her first appearance in New York, and, according to the Herald, she received, at this benefit, an ovation of heartfelt proportions, not to speak of masses of flowers heaped on the stage.   Kalte Seelen was revived on December 13th, and, on the 14th, Neuendorff brought out an operetta, Der Rattenfänger von Hameln, with music by himself and with words by Herr H. Italiener, also resident here.   This ran, or possibly was forced to run continuously to January 3rd, a heartwarming experience in cold winter evenings.   In the cast were Stein-

[289]

buch, Frl. Janson, Frl. Schmitz, Kummer, Frl. von Januschowsky, Pönitz, Hahn, Janitzky, Munnecke, Rank and Merten (he in the title-rôle).

CARL SONTAG

On January 4th, Carl Sontag, said by the Herald, next day, to be a younger brother of the great Henrietta Sontag, appeared at the Germania, as Robert, in Die Memoiren des Teufel's, his support including Kierschner, Raberg, Reinau, Frl. Bensberg, Frl. Setti, Frl. Necker, Rank and Merten, and Frl. Schmitz. Sontag also, on the same evening, gave Ein Knopf (A Button), by Rosen. The Herald, on the 5th, speaks of his great versatility. In the first piece, he portrayed a shrewd, polished young assistant to an attorney; in the second, he was an absent-minded college professor who could not remember even where the buttons were on his clothing. "An actor," sums up the Herald, "of rare finish and spirit, with a voice so musical as to render even the 'achs' pleasing to foreign ears."

Sontag's long term at the Germania ran synchronously with the remarkably successful engagement of Marie Geistinger at the Thalia; both seem to have been very profitable. His opening bill was repeated on the 5th, and another double bill, on the 6th, including Dir wie mir and Dr. Wespe. In the latter piece, Sontag had the name-part, with Frl. Bensberg as Elisabeth, Frl. Necker as Thekla, Frl. Schmitz as Theudelinde, Reinau as Ludwig, Lichtenthal as Welstein, Wachsner as Schreiner, Rank as Adam, and Kierschner as Christoph. In this piece, according to the Herald, of the 7th, Sontag "as the brazen, pretentious, 'cheeky' journalist, who thrusts himself ahead of everybody until the aged and angular poetess who makes love to him appears on the scene, the actor was simply inimitable. The characterization was marked by a sprightliness, an ease of carriage, and a reckless, irresponsible dash that won the audience." In Dir wie mir, "his manner" was "at times suggestive of Lester Wallack." This double bill came again on the 7th, and, on the 8th and 10th Sontag played Bolingbroke, in Das Glas Wasser, in association with Frl. Bensberg as Queen Anne, Frl. Setti as Duchess of Marlborough, Frl. Necker as Abigail, Meery as Mascham, Kierschner as Marquis de Torcy, Kummer as Thompson, Lichtenthal as the Member of Parliament, and Frl. Umlauf as Lady Albemarle. The Herald, on the 9th, asserts that Haase and Sontag were almost identical in conception of the character of Bolingbroke, "but in the execution there is a marked difference. Mr. Haase was perhaps the most finished and the most artistic in his studious attention to detail, but there is a spontaneity, a naturalness and an unstudied bonhommie in the personation of Mr. Sontag that carried the audience by sympathy."

Die Journalisten, on January 11th and 12th, had a cast including Kierschner as Berg, Frl. Setti as Adelheid, Frl. Necker as Ida, Reinau as Oldendorf,

Sontag (of course) as Conrad Bolz, Rank as Bellmaus, and Frl. Schmitz as Lotte. Gutzkow's Der Königslieutenant filled the evenings of the 13th, 14th and 15th:

Graf Thorane	Herr Sontag	Seekatz	Herr Rank
Althof	Herr Meery	Frau Seekatz	Frl. Schmitz
Rath Göthe	Herr Kierschner	Belinde	Frl. Wagner
Frau Rath Göthe	Frl. Setti	Mack	Herr Merten
Wolfgang	Frl. Bensberg	Gretel	Frl. Necker
Miller	Herr Raberg	Alcidor	Herr Lichtenthal

Dir wie mir and Dr. Wespe returned on the 17th. On Tuesday, the 18th, and for the remaining evenings of the week, the star was brilliant as Fabricius, in Wilbrandt's Die Tochter des Herrn Fabricius, assisted by Kierschner as Eulenstein, Reinau as Rolf, Frl. Setti as Ida Reinhold, Frl. Bensberg as Agathe Stern, Julie Heller as Hugo, Frl. Schmitz as Frau Wohlmuth, and Rank as Demmler. Repetitions of plays already listed carry us to February 1st, when came Moser and Schönthan's comedy, Krieg im Frieden, a merry thing on which, next season, Augustin Daly based his great success, The Passing Regiment. It was also a fine success, running consecutively through the 16th, with Sontag, Raberg, Frl. Setti, Frl. Necker, Frl. Bensberg, Merten, Frl. Schmitz, Kierschner, Sauer, Lichtenthal and Meery in leading rôles. Dir wie mir and Dr. Wespe came back on February 17th. On February 18th, the lucky star played Orgon, in Tartuffe, with Raberg as Tartuffe, Kierschner as Cléante, Sauer as Valère, Meery as Damis, Merten as Loyal, Frl. Schmitz as Mme. Pernelle, Frl. Bensberg as Elmire, Frl. Wagner as Marianne, and Frl. Necker as Dorine. With this was given Schneider's one-act Die Unglücklichen — a double bill several times repeated. Pechschulze came on the 21st, for the benefit of Rank, and without Sontag and, on the 28th (with several repetitions on days immediately following) Sontag gave a double bill, including von Moser's one-act Ein moderner Barbar (with Sontag as Constantin von Horst, assisted by Frl. Bensberg, Meery, Frl. Janson and Kessler) and the three-act Die Frau im Hause, with Kessler and Frl. Schmitz as Counsellor Sanders and wife, Sontag and Meery as Friedrich and Roderich, their sons, Frl. Bensberg as Margarethe, and Frl. Necker as Alma Rosen. Pechschulze was repeated on March 7th and 10th, and, on the 8th, 9th, 11th and 12th, another double bill united Frauen-Emancipation (by Sontag himself), and Kotzebue's Die Beiden Klingsberg. Certainly, if long runs were changing the policy of Wallack's and others of our American stock theatres, the German actors suffered no surcease of change of bill. Richard's Wanderleben, on the 14th, presented Sontag as Richard and Frl. Bensberg as Sophie.

Lockere Zeisige was the offering on March 18th, 19th, 21st; it was played by the company alone, Sontag flitting, on the 21st, to the Brooklyn Athenæum in Die Memoiren des Teufels and Ein Knopf; on the 22nd and 23rd he renewed earlier triumphs in Dir wie mir and Dr. Wespe (22nd) Der

Königslieutenant (23rd). Ein glückliche Familienvater was promised for the 24th, alas! without the star. A novelty (for Sontag's engagement), on March 25th and 26th, was Dr. Klaus, on which, we remember, was founded Dr. Clyde, seen at the Fifth Avenue Theatre in 1878–79. At the Germania, Sontag was Dr. Klaus, with Rank as Leopold Griefinger, Frl. Bensberg as Julie, Sauer as Max von Boden, Frl. Necker as Emma, Frl. Setti as Frau Klaus, Frl. Schmitz as Marianne, Merten as Lubowski, and Frl. Stöbner as Auguste. On the 30th, Ein Lustspiel allowed Sontag to appear as Bergheim, assisted by Frl. Bensberg as Franziska, Frl. Necker as Ernestine, Kierschner as Brömser, Meery as Karl Fichtenau, Lichtenthal as Dr. West, Frl. Schmitz as Frau Waltrop, Frau Kierschner as Agnes, and Rank as the valet, Tümpel. Sontag also played Moritz, in Glückliche Flitterwochen (by Georg Horn). On April 2nd (set down as the first time), a triple bill gave Frauen-Emancipation, with Sontag as Anton Walter; Ein Knopf, with Sontag as Dr. Rudolf Bergen; and Der Topfgucker, with Sontag as Spurlein. The popular star's last week brought Krieg im Frieden (April 4th), Das Glas Wasser (6th), Die Journalisten (7th), Dir wie mir and Dr. Wespe (8th), and Der Königslieutenant — the benefit and farewell and seventy-seventh performance of Sontag. For the 5th, Sontag was advertised to give Die widerspenstige Frau at the Academy of Music. It will be seen that Sontag's term was somewhat shorter than that of Marie Geistinger, the rival star at the Thalia; nevertheless, it was an extraordinary duration at that time for a stellar visit.

On April 11th, 12th, 14th and 15th, Neuendorff repeated his own opera, Der Rattenfänger von Hameln; on the 13th, came the ever-popular Ultimo (The Big Bonanza), and, on the 16th, Dorf und Stadt. Der Rattenfänger filled the week of April 18th–23rd, and slipped into the evening of April 25th. On the 26th, we had, surprisingly, a return to the classics, with Minna von Barnhelm; and, for Reinau's benefit, on the 27th, Egmont, with Reinau and Frl. Bensberg. Die Verlobung bei der Laterne and Ein glücklicher Familienvater (28th), Lockere Zeisige (29th), and Hasemann's Töchter (30th) finished an interesting week, without stars. Dorf und Stadt (May 2nd), Hans Lonei (3rd), Das Mädel ohne Geld (4th), Der Veilchenfresser (5th and 6th), and Das Stiftungsfest (7th) provided another. And that ended it; the Germania had carried on a week longer than its rival theatre — perhaps a matter of satisfied pride to certain breasts.

OTHER GERMAN PLAYS, 1880–1881

The Concordia Halle, 20-30 Avenue A, was, in early October, 1880, announcing two sacred concerts, on Sundays. The Eröffnungs-Ball, for the season, occurred there on October 6th. On October 13th and 14th, the Staats-Zeitung advertises for the place a new programme, involving twelve performers, and, to close the show, the Posse, 1733 Th, 12½ Slbgr. On the 16th, the bill comprised Lumpaci Vagabundus and Versprechen hinterm Herd. Thence followed, in autumn nights, Kurmärker und Picarde, Aus Liebe zur Kunst, Ein Frühstückstündchen, Die Räuber, Wer ist mit? Im Vorzimmer seiner Excellenz, Pechschulze, Schneider Fips, Die falsche Sarah Bernhardt (Sarah having but recently appeared at Booth's Theatre for that memorable first engagement), and a Kindervorstellung, on December 25th, of Schneewittchen und die sieben Zwerge. Performers announced in early November were Frl. Albertine Wollgrath, Frl. Hermanus, and Herren Neumann, Hermanus, Paul Gern, and Hugo Kladivko, manager. Variety mingled in at least some of these bills, and performances seem to have occurred only on Saturdays and Mondays. Don Ferreyra, man-flute, astonished in certain bills.

The Concordia specified but little in advertisements and I could find no bills of its plays; therefore my record is scant. January and February moved on their appointed course with Der Sohn auf Reisen, Stille Liebe mit Hindernissen, Studentenstreiche, Lehmann's Jugendliebe, Der Goldonkel, Theodor Wachtel und Pauline Lucca, Schulzen's Heimkehr aus Paris, Der Kesselflicker, Dr. Eisenbart, Einer muss heirathen, Lady Beefsteak — old farces long known to my reader. In the olio of March 5th and 7th were Minnie St. Clair, Clara Leonhard, Albertine Wollgrath, Joseph Stritter, Carl Neumann, and Herr and Frau La Roche; the concluding farce was In Friedenszeiten. Later weeks gave Saturday and Monday performances of Studentenstreiche, Eine komische Geschichte, Die Heimkehr, Man soll den Teufel nicht an die Wand malen, Ein Mädchen vom Ballet, Er ist Baron, Seine Dritte, Der Goldonkel, Eine gefährliche Liebe, Der Kesselflicker, Selbstmord aus Liebe, Stille Liebe mit Hindernissen, Schulzen's Heimkehr aus Paris, Lehmann's Jugendliebe, Die Eifersüchtigen, Folgen einer Zeitungs-Annonce, etc. The theatre closed in later summer, to re-open on September 3, 1881.

But other minor theatres opposed the Concordia. The New York Turn-Halle, 66-68 East Fourth Street, opened with a ball, on October 14, 1880. October 17th displayed Das Porträt der Geliebten. And the German Veterans were here on the 31st. On November 25th (Thanksgiving Day) a Kinder-Theater proffered Rochus Pumpernickel; in the evening came Namenlos and Frish, gesund und meschugge. In early December we celebrated Das Stiftungsfest. On January 16th, Dr. Klaus restored our spirits, and, on January 30th, Des König's Befehl. Richard's Wanderleben and Hasemann's Töchter were staged in May. But, on February 9th, the children of Frau Lang's school acted Preciosa.

I have recorded elsewhere certain proceedings at Terrace Garten, and will here merely record performances that seem of special significance. The Germania Quartett Club, on November 13th, gave there a concert and a comic "operette," Die Barden (by Julius Freudenthal). In the concert ap-

[293]

peared Emma Juch, Frl. Beaupain, &c. On November 28th, the first Abend-unterhaltung of Harmonia promised Mathilde Cottrelly, Franziska Raberg, Emma Kuster, Gustav Adolfi, Carl Lanzer (violin), S. Liebling (piano), Wohlmuth and Carl Schlesinger — surely a dignified array. As stated elsewhere, the New York Männerchor concert fell here on December 25th; and the Harmonia proffered a second Abendunterhaltung, on December 19th, with Cottrelly, Marie König, Josefine Lube, and Herren Lube, Schnelle, Schönfeld and Liberati. For charity, Neuendorff's actors appeared on December 16th in Ein grosser Redner. The Yorkville Männerchor operated vocally on February 27th. Let us not forget the testimonial to Professor Fanciulli, tendered on April 29th. The Dramatic Verein, Wir, gave us, on May 14th, Ehrliche Arbeit.

OTHER GERMAN ACTIVITIES, 1880–1881

The more I try to crowd together the far-flung line of German operations in those New York years, the more details escape into ever-widening battalions; I am almost in despair, and I scramble together the heterogeneous elements into a disorganised array of facts. In earliest October, Gunther's Pavilion, 283 Bowery, boasted of Sunday concerts in its Spiegelhalle; on the 2nd, to close its season, Turtle Bay Park, First Avenue and Forty-third Street, gave a belated Sommernachtsfest — let us hope not frost-bitten. Frl. Marie Roller throughout the season of 1880–81 was directing, at Atlantic Garten, an "Elite Kapelle" of fifteen "Damen."

And now let us sing! The Mainzer Carneval-Verein opened its season, on October 3rd, at Beethoven Männerchor Halle; the opening ball in that room occurred on the 4th. The Sängerrunde, on the 3rd, were at the Germania Assembly Rooms, and the Schleswig-Holsteinischer Verein at Turn-Halle. On Sunday, the 10th, the Beethoven Männerchor celebrated its "erste Abend-Unterhaltung"; the New York Männerchor, on the same sacred evening held, at the Teutonia Assembly Rooms, a concert and Stiftungsfest, and the Marschner Männerchor was in Beethoven Halle, 431 East Sixth Street. Wendel's Elm Park was vocal and instrumental, on those Sundays, with "sacred" concerts; and Wendel's Assembly Rooms (334-344 West Forty-fourth Street) were frequently busy with concert and dance of happy Germans. Prospect Garden, 106-108 East 14th Street, was now featuring Don Ferreyra; and Jacob Schloeder's Weinhandlung, 166 First Avenue, had Sunday zither-concerts to make musical the imbibing of drinks, Carl Zima being chief executant on that instrument apparently beloved of our Teutonic citizens.

The Turtle Bay Assembly Rooms, 45th Street, between First and Second Avenues, and also the Harmony Rooms, Essex Street, gave, on October 7th, an "Eröffnungs-Ball," as did Walhalla, 48-52 Orchard Street, on the 14th.

[294]

On the 10th, the Gesangverein Oestreich held in the Germania Assembly Rooms a fifth Stiftungsfest, concert and ball; the same evening listed an Unterhaltung of the Bloomingdale Turn-Verein at 341 West 47th Street. The M. G. V. Eichenkranz, on the 17th, edified its friends with a concert, held at the Teutonia Assembly Rooms, the Arminia opened its season "im Vereinslokal," West 4th Street, and on the same Sunday evening the Arion Quartett Club gave its ninth Stiftungsfest, concert and ball. The Mainzer Carneval-Verein, on the 17th, carried out a benefit for Julius Bledong, blind and lame. I simply must omit the balls, shooting-matches and other social activities of the various clubs of brewers, butchers, bakers, piano-makers and other purveyors of the necessities of life; seldom, if ever, musical, they hardly enter my scheme. But we might drop in at the Eröffnungs-Ball, on October 14th, at the New York Turn-Halle, 66-68 East Fourth Street, or at the Grosse Eröffnung of L. Schuler's "elegant" Winter Palmgarten, on October 16th, at 132-144 East 14th Street. I merely attempt to give an idea of German amusements in those far-off years. For that laudable purpose, I must recall to memory the sacred concerts, with Eben's orchestra, held on Sundays, at Löwen-Park, at 109th Street, between Eighth and Ninth Avenues, and invite, on October 24th, to the opening Musikalische Abendunterhaltung (*sic*) of the Gesangverein Schillerbund. The opening ball at Empire Hall, 613-615 Third Avenue, fell on October 25th.

I return to music, heavenly maid. The Allemania Männerchor was at the Germania Assembly Rooms, on October 24th, and the concert of the New York Zither-Verein, in the Teutonia Assembly Rooms, on the 31st, enlisted Frau Bertha Bremer, Frl. J. Laubenheimer, and the same devoted Schillerbund; the Verein Cordialia, on that same exit night of October, held its eleventh Stiftungsfest, concert and ball, in the hall of the Beethoven Männerchor, and the Badischer Männerchor was at the Germania Rooms. But the great feature of dying October was the benefit, at the Teutonia Assembly Rooms, for blind Adolf Schmidt, the announced participants including Emma Juch, Carl Steinbuch and Arbuckle.

So much for October, blithely scurrying to its doom. November showed the Germans in full pursuit. One could dine any night at Goebel's Restaurant in his Central Park Brewery and hurry thence to endless amusement. The highly respected Liederkranz, on November 6th, held its first Geselliger Abend in its quarters, East Fourth Street, and, on the 7th, one was distracted by sheer *richesse* of offering — the twenty-sixth annual Stiftungsfest, concert and ball of the Mozart Männerchor, held at the Germania Assembly Rooms; the tenth Stiftungsfest und Ball des Orden Germania, at Beethoven Männerchor Halle; the Erste Abendunterhaltung (now so printed) of the Heinebund, at Wendel's Assembly Rooms; the meeting of the Gesangverein Euphonia; that of the Schillerbund; that of the Verein Bruder Zirkel, at Teutonia Assembly Rooms; that of the Kreutzer Quartett Club, at Turn-

[295]

Halle; and that of the Liedertafel Social Reformer, at Geib's Walhalla, Orchard Street — not to mention the continuing Damen Elite Kapelle of Marie Roller, at Atlantic Garden. At Prospect Garden, East 14th Street, Lena and Charles Lovenberg, violin and xylophone, were listed in Staats-Zeitung advertisements. Between November 7th and 30th, inclusive, nineteen balls were scheduled for nimble Germans, at Wendel's Assembly Rooms. Let us end the paragraph with the opening ball (November 10th) at the Teutonia Assembly Rooms (152-160 Third Avenue).

At their hall, 19-21 St. Mark's Place, the Arion Society, on November 14th, gave a concert under direction of Dr. Damrosch, with the assistance of Katie Nuffer (contralto), Marie Geist ('cello), Jacob Graff, S. B. Mills, and Franz Remmertz; on the same evening, the New Yorker Sängerrunde proffered a concert and ball, at the Germania Assembly Rooms. Most interesting, perhaps, for that same crowded evening, was the concert at Männerchor Halle of the Mainzer Carneval-Verein, with Emma Juch, O. Schmittbauer (violin), G. Faust (piano), &c., in compositions by Auber, Lortzing, Bizet, Haydn, Mattei, Verdi and others. Other November activities of German societies will be found under caption of Concordia or Terrace Garten. I close November with a scurry of delights: the Stiftungs-fest of the Rheinischer Sängerbund (on the 21st) at the Concordia; the Invitation Concert and Ball of the Bismarck Quartett Club, on the 22nd, at the Germania Assembly Rooms; the first Stiftungsfest of the Schalloden-bacher Männerchor, on the 23rd, at Concordia Halle; the concert of the Deutscher Männerchor, on the 24th, at Karl's Germania Hall, 46 Avenue A; the Abendunterhaltung (sic) und Tanz-Kränzchen (sic) of the Sänger-lust, on the 25th, at Beethoven Halle, and other activities of that same evening — with concert and ball of the Schwäbischer Sängerbund, at Beethoven Hall (with, to assist, the Schwäbischer Sängerbund of Williamsburgh), and the twenty-fifth Stiftungsfest of the New York Sing-Akademie (with Mary Hindle, soprano, Jacob Jung, tenor, and George Weiss, baritone) at Metropolitan Assembly Rooms, 64 East Fourth Street. On the afternoon of the 25th, a children's performance occurred at Turnhalle — a function elsewhere listed. On the 26th, at Turnhalle, Max Mansfeld read from Fritz Reuter's works, and, at Teutonia Assembly Rooms, the Aschenbrödel-Verein did what it was expected to do. A concert of the Liederkranz (November 28th) decidedly raised the tone of our recent history with assistance of Emma Juch, Graff, S. B. Mills, and an orchestra directed by A. Paur. On the 28th, Professor Schenkewitz gave, in Gothic Hall, a plattdeutsche Vorlesung. I end the paragraph with an appeal to the reader to remember the nightly ministrations at Atlantic Garden of Marie Roller's lady orchestra, the concerts at Prospect Garden by the Spanish Students, and Theiss's Concerts every night in his well-known resort in 14th Street.

This brings on snowy winter. Wendel's Assembly Rooms were devoted nearly every evening in December to gladsome balls.   On December 4th, the Teutonia Assembly Rooms housed a concert by the Helvetia Männerchor. Sunday, December 5th, hurries us hither and yon to varied enterprises: the concert and ball of the Haydn Amateur Musical Society, at Wendel's Assembly Rooms; the concert of the Beethoven Quartett at Beethoven Männerchor-Halle; a zither concert at Schloeder's Weinhandlung, 166 First Avenue, and another at Simon von Brunn's Weinhandlung, in the basement at 6 Rivington Street, near the Bowery, and still another at Künstler-Halle, 167 Chrystie Street; a concert and ball of the Franz Abt Schüler, at the Germania Assembly Rooms.   On the 6th, Max Mansfeld lectured, at Steinway Hall, on Judenhetze in Deutschland; on the 10th, in the same hall, the Arion Society concert called in the aid of Lillian Bailey, Max Pinner, Jacob Graff and Remmertz, with Dr. Damrosch to conduct.   The Liederkranz held, on December 18th, its first Abendunterhaltung (*sic*), following the second Abendunterhaltung (*sic*), on the 12th, of the New Yorker Sängerrunde.   The New York Männerchor and Harmonia went, as we saw, to Terrace Garten, for rather elaborate celebrations.   Meantime, every evening brought to Prospect Garden an orchestral concert, with Achille Laguardie (cornet) and Leo (tumbleronicon and xylophone).

And in January came multiplication of the Carneval-Sitzung; that of the Verein Frohsinn, in Terrace Garten, on the 9th, with its erste grosse Narresitzung; that of the Arion Society, on the 8th, at its own hall; that of M. G. V. Eichenkranz, on the 15th, at Terrace Garten, with another there on the 29th; that of the Beethoven Männerchor on the 16th, and another on February 6th; a second of the Arion Society, on the 22nd, with a third on February 5th.   But concerts edged into the vacant spaces.   On January 9th, the first Stiftungsfest of the New York Zither Verein came to pass at the Teutonia Music Hall; on the same evening the Mainzer Carneval Verein held Beethoven Männerchor Hall.   January 16th (Sunday) allowed the Sängerrunde and the Liederkranz to hold forth in social wise.   The Jubiläum for its twenty-fifth anniversary excited the Sing-Academie, on the 22nd, in the Teutonia Rooms.   And then the season of masked balls, so dear to German hearts: that of the Schillerbund (on January 24th) at the Germania Assembly Rooms; that of the Gesangverein Fidelia, the same date, at Geib's Walhalla, and that of the Heinebund, on February 2nd, at Wendel's Assembly Rooms; that of the Harlem Turn-Verein, in February (date uncertain) in Sulzer's Harlem River Park; that of the Schleswig-Holsteinischer Verein on the 7th, at Geib's Walhalla, and that of the Haydn Amateur Musical Society, on the same date, at Wendel's Assembly Rooms; also, on the 7th, Euphonia at Turn-Halle; that of the Allemania Männerchor, on the 12th, at the Germania Assembly Rooms; that of the Frauen-Verein Fortuna, at Harmony Hall, on the 14th, and that of the Liedertafel Social Reformer, also on the 14th, at Geib's Walhalla; that of the Schwäbischer Sängerbund, on

[297]

the 14th, in Beethoven Männerchor-Halle; and still on the 14th, that of the Sängerrunde, at the Germania Rooms, and that of the Concordia, in the Teutonia Rooms; that of the Mozart Männerchor, on the 15th, at the Germania Assembly Rooms; that of the Liederkranz, on the 17th, at the Academy of Music; that of the Gesangverein Arminia, on that same 17th, at Beethoven Männerchor Hall; that of the Beethoven Männerchor, on the 21st, in its own hall; and that of the Arion Society, on the 21st, at Madison Square Garden; that of the Bloomingdale Turn-Verein, on the 22nd, at Wendel's; that of the M. G. V. Eichenkranz, on February 28th, at Terrace Garten, and that of the New York Turn-Verein, on that date, in its own hall. But let us not forget the concerts and balls. On January 23rd, the Social Männerchor went to Terrace Garten to sing and dance, assisted in the former function by Anna Hill (soprano), H. Bersin (tenor), Schwicardi (bass) and Leiboldt's orchestra; for the same date, at Turn-Halle, Heinrich Maret arranged a concert and ball, enlisting Mathilde Cottrelly, Elise Unger, Gretchen Herz, Isabella Maret, Tilly Unger, Alfred Kierschner, F. Hildebrand and P. Steppes. January 27th found the concert of the Frauen-Verein at Steinway Hall, with assistance from Anna Drasdil, F. Steins, Henschel, Adolphe Fischer, Dengremont and the Liederkranz — assuredly a fine array. A few nights later (January 30th), the Liederkranz entertained, with A. Fischer, Marie Schelle (contralto), Franz Rummel and the Philharmonic Club. And also, at that time, J. L. Krische's Spätze-Häuschen, 299 Bowery, delighted its patrons with zither-concerts. February 6th brought to Künstler-Halle, 167 Chrystie Street, a "Grosses Zither-Guitarren und Vocal Concert," with Professor Hinco (zither), Charles Krumm (guitar), Mme. Majerino (soprano), and Professor La Roche (piano), Eintritt (if not beer) frei. The Bloomingdale Turn Verein, on the 9th, heard Dr. Limpert's lecture on Die Judenhetze im 19 Jahrhundert. On the 10th, one might have attended, at Steinway Hall, a benefit for the Swiss Hulfs-Gesellschaft, at which appeared Mme. Rossie (soprano), J. Graff, Remmertz, Bersin, and A. Sohst — talent somewhat above that often heard to the eastward in Kleindeutschland. The Melodia Männerchor held its third annual concert and ball, on February 26th, at Pythagoras Hall, 134-136 Canal Street, assisted by the Chor Lætitia, the Bismarck Quartett and the Hudson Männerchor. On the 27th, the Yorkville Männerchor was at Terrace Garten, and, on March 1st, the Marschner Männerchor held a masked ball at the Germania Assembly Rooms. On February 28th, the South Brooklyn Turn-Verein came to Turn-Halle. Meantime the Damen Elite Kapelle still charmed at Atlantic Garden, Günther's Pavilion kept going, and Theiss's concerts held those who liked them in 14th Street.

In early March, one might have heard at Künstler Halle, Chrystie Street, a zither, guitar and vocal concert, featuring Mme. Majerino; at Parepa Hall (corner of 86th Street and Third Avenue), a concert one evening pre-

[298]

sented the Chor der Immanuele-Gemeinde. Later, the popular Joseph Kaiserino was at Künstler Hall, and the Purim Masked Ball was carried through at Irving Hall. Almost all the societies listed thus far in 1880–81 functioned bravely till Pfingst-Montag, when, I need hardly say, they went to neighbouring parks and groves for a thoroughly good time in the true German manner. Newcomers into our story were the West Side Liedertafel, with a ball on March 21st, at Lyric Hall, Sixth Avenue, below 42nd Street; the Jahres-Fest der Deutschen Patrioten von 1848–49 was at Wendel's Elm Park in late May (24th). Elm Park, by the way, began its Sunday concerts early in April. A concert and ball of the New York Männerchor enlisted, on April 17th, at Terrace Garten, Caroline Schulte (soprano), Wilhelm Schwicardi, Herman Bersin, George Prehn (bass), and F. Bergner ('cello). The Hudson Männerchor functioned, on the same date, at Dramatic Hall, East Houston Street, as did the Bloomingdale Turn-Verein at Wendel's. And the Beethoven Männerchor concert invited with S. B. Mills, Lotte Simpson, &c. The Mozart Musical Union, on April 29th, tendered to Professor Fanciulli, at Lexington Avenue Opera House a testimonial concert and reception. In April, at Atlantic Garten, Liberati was added to the existing attraction of the.Damen-Kapelle. On April 17th, the Liederkranz gave a Kinderfest, and the Arion Society worked up a Kinder-Maskenball, with tableaux and a Festzug. The same 17th found the Gesangverein Germania functioning. On the 19th, the twenty-sixth Stiftungsfest of the mixed choir Lætitia enjoyed the assistance of the Bismarck Quartett Club, the Hudson Männerchor and the Melodia Männerchor; the Teutonia Assembly Rooms housed this concentrated joy. In Wendel's Assembly Rooms, on April 24th, the Haydn Amateur Musical Society held forth in concert, assisted by Clara Boucsin (soprano) and Lorenz See (tenor), with an orchestra of twenty-five. On that evening the Sängerrunde had, in the Germania Rooms, a Schlusskränzchen and a big zither concert of the Zither-Verein called to the Teutonia Rooms. And Katy Schalm appeared in concert, on April 25th, at the Germania Assembly Rooms (small hall), with a Tanzkränzchen to follow. A lecture, by Friedrich Schünemann-Pott "über die Entscheidung des Kultur-Kampfes" may, on April 26th, have filled Arion Hall with enthusiasm and other returns. At any rate, Lula Kissel (pianist) and Charles Eschert (xylophone) were at that time featured in Theiss concerts.

On May 1st, the Liederkranz performed Das Lied von der Glocke, with, as soloists, Emma Juch, Miss Henne, J. Graff and Sohst. On that same Sunday, Ferdinand Goebel's Sommergarten opened at the foot of East 57th Street, Leopold Fünkenstein directing the orchestra. About that time were in operation Held's Hamilton Park; Turtle Bay Park; Karl's Park (147th Street and Third Avenue); Jones Wood Colosseum; Löwen Park (107th Street and 8th Avenue); Sulzer's Harlem River Park (125th Street and

Second Avenue — this last the scene of many German picnics and summer-night outings); Wilhelm Schwab's Harlem River Bridge Garden (2387 Third Avenue, between 129th and 130th Streets); Funk-Georgi's Union Park, Morrisania (formerly Hartung's Park); Wendel's Elm Park; Löwen Park Belvedere; Fritz Kiar's Grove Hill Park (Hüpfel's Brauerei, 161st Street and Third Avenue, Morrisania); Pavilion Pier, No. 1, North River; Washington Schützen Park (69th Street and East River); Morrisania Schützen-Park (170th Street and Boston Avenue); Euler's Broadway Park, Long Island; Henri Zeltner's Park and Brauerei (170th Street and Third Avenue); the Germania Garten (291-293 Bowery, "verbunden mit Germania Assembly Rooms"); Fritz Jagau's Halle und Sommer Garten (130 Third Avenue); Schuler's Palm Garten (with Bertha Ravené and Haydon Tilla singing); and Conrad Stein's Sommer-Garten (57th Street, near Tenth Avenue).   To these friendly shades went eager Germans to quench their thirst for beer and music, and to view in some cases a little stage entertainment.   At Goebel's Sommergarten, for instance, in late July and early August, appeared Alfred Liston; Bertha Ravené continued at Schuler's Palm Garten, Liberati and the Damen Elite Kapelle at Atlantic Garten, and Don Ferreyra at Goebel's, at which last named place appeared in August Emma, Lula and H. Kissel.   But some preferred the neighbouring beaches and sought refreshment of wave and wind at Coney Island, or Manhattan, or Long Beach or Far Rockaway; perhaps eyed rather favourably the Wasserfahrten of the various German societies to Staten Island, College Point or other adjacent retreats.

Something rather fine came to Washington Schützen Park, Jones Wood. There, on June 12th, 13th and 14th, amid flowers and illuminations, appeared Dr. Leopold Damrosch, "hero of the late Music Festival," with a group of German musical societies, the Schillerbund, the Allemania, the Sängerrunde, the Rheinischer Sängerbund, the Uhlandbund, the Liedertafel, and the Yorkville male chorus.   Grandly, I suppose, rolled through the bosky shades the lusty voices of those earnest Teutonic hosts.   And Damrosch was again director, when, on August 18th, the Arion Society held a concert and Summernight's Festival at Washington Park and Jones Wood Colosseum; fire-works and tableaux beautified the scene.   And let us not forget that, every evening of summer one could hear a "grand concert" at the Atalanta House, 155th Street and Eighth Avenue.

FRENCH MISCELLANY, 1880–1881

I begin, as often I must, with Paul Juignet, whose concert, on November 7, 1880, Tammany Hall, was to enlist Hélène Leroux, Zélie de Lussan, Blanche de Lussan (contralto), Brigiotti, A. F. Périn (baritone), Nahan Franko (violin), Désiré (*chanteur comique*) and the inevitable Max Schwab.

FRANCO NOVARA
IN FAUST
(Photograph by
Mora)

RAVELLI IN
LUCIA
(Photograph by
Mora)

ALWINA VALLERIA AS AÏDA
(From a Photograph by Scholl)

MARIE GEISTINGER
(From a Photograph by Mora)

CARL SONTAG

On November 14th, the eighth anniversary of l'Espérance brought to Irving Hall a concert and ball. Thenceforth we danced. On December 18th, at Irving Hall, the Huron and Idaho Tribe, 35 and 36, held a *bal d'invitation, paré et masqué;* on the 19th our allegiance was divided between a concert at the Church of St. Vincent de Paul, and a concert and ball of the Cercle Musical et Philanthropique de l'Orphéon Français, directed at Irving Hall, by F. Groux.

January 8th starts us on the new year, at Irving Hall, with a *bal d'invitation paré et masqué* of the Union Fraternelle Française; on the 11th, at the Metropolitan Concert Hall, came the ball of the Société Française L'Amitié. January 22nd found at the Ferrero Assembly Rooms Gaieté Française (réunion de famille); and on the 24th, the Cercle Français de l'Harmonie utilised for its grand masquerade and costume ball not only the Academy of Music but Irving and Nilsson Halls as well. And Max Schwab directed the music. And the Société Culinaire also needed, for its ball, on February 1st, both the Academy and Irving Hall. La Concorde more modestly betook itself, on February 11th, to Tammany Hall. I could not discover, from the Messager, where the Société Helvetienne, *avec le concours du choeur mixte,* La Cécilienne, carried through, on February 26th, its concert and ball; but L. Conterno directed the orchestra. At the Metropolitan Concert Hall, on March 1st, the *bal masqué de Carnaval du Mardi Gras* was advertised as the last masked ball of the season. On March 9th, however, the Société Israelite Française possessed Irving Hall with a *bal d'invitation paré et travesti;* on the 24th, l'Association Culinaire Cosmopolite gave in the same place a *mi-carême* ball; and on *Lundi de Pâques* we passed merrily out of Lent (April 18th) with a ball, review, parade and *présentation des drapeaux* arranged at the Metropolitan Concert Hall by the Bataillon des Gardes Lafayette.

On May 10th a benefit for the defunct French opera company fruitlessly exploited at the Academy of Music promised at the Metropolitan Concert Hall the co-operation of Campanini, Mmes. Lablache and del Prato, Jourdan, Otto, Garnier and the orchestra of the stranded troupe. At French Lyric Hall, 21 South Fifth Avenue, a benefit for M. and Mme. Etienne Levy, of the French company, was to enjoy the assistance of Beauplan and many amateurs and professionals. July 14th aroused the patriotic enthusiasm of all Franco-New York. Certain *sociétés* held Lion Park, with *jeux divers, danses, musiques, chants patriotiques, discours,* and a *fête de nuit, feu d'artifice, bal* and *tombola;* another group, in Jones Wood Colosseum and Washington Park, celebrated with similar festivities, including a *représentation théâtrale.* I end with September 6th, and the annual fête of the Bataillon des Gardes Lafayette, held at Lion Park, with the band of the battalion, directed by Max Schwab, and with *tir à la cible, tombola* and varied sports. Of course, we must not forget the engagements in New York theatres of Sarah Bernhardt and Paola Marié.

ITALIAN PLAYS, 1880–1881

We have hitherto enjoyed the acting of Italy's greatest stars, Ristori and Salvini; now comes into our ken a group of native players presenting in far-off halls what may have been performances of an amateur basis. The Eco d'Italia informs us that, on September 26, 1880, the Società Filodrammatica Italiana of New York was to meet in the Sala dei Signori L. Jorio e G. Gazzoli, 69 South Washington Square. And lo! on October 17th this prettily named organisation presented, in Dramatic Hall, Maria Giovanna. On Sunday, December 12th, it played Bruno il Filatore and the farce La Contessa è di Russare; also Lopez gave *diversi giuochi di prestigio,* and the orchestra was to be composed "di buoni professori." This performance and those that follow were staged in Dramatic Hall. On December 19th, another group, the Società Filodrammatica Tommaso Salvini, under the direction of the *artista-comico,* Venturoli, produced I Postiglioni del Villagio d'Albi and the farce, Un Numero Fatale; in the first of these we were assured that the rôle of Mme. Leblanc *è stata affidata alla Signora Argia Catarsi* — a statement perhaps more modest than re-assuring. Christmas night brought the gift of the "brillante commedia," Il Segretario del Segretario d' un Segretario — a performance set down as the company's sixth "recità"; this was the offering of the Società Filodrammatica di New York. The Salvini group, on January 8th, made *"un secondo esperimento con la brillante commedia,"* Un Gerente Responabile, adding thereto *"lo scherzo comico,"* Lucrezia Borgia.

Thereafter the Eco d'Italia admits us only to performances by the Società Filodrammatica di New York. With the reader's permission I will catalogue their winter offerings. January 9th brought Dopo la Tempesta la Calma and Pulcinella geloso della Moglie; on the 16th we had our old friend transmuted into Una Camera affittata à Due, along with Pulcinella Prestidigitore e l'Alloggio Militare ossia la Cena Infernale. January 30th brought La Battaglia di Tolosa, ovvero la Colpa del Cuore; on February 6th, we had I due Sordi, Pulcinella Prestidigitore, Charles Diamond, from Tony Pastor's, and La Tazza di Tè, matter familiar from French and English theatres; on the 13th, for the benefit of the Italian School of Vineland, came a repetition of La Battaglia di Tolosa, along with Il Flauto Magico con Pulcinella. The play of February 27th was Roma e Tolosa (*"brillante dramma"*); March 13th repeated Il Segretario del Segretario d'un Segretario, along with L'Alloggio Militare. I scent collapse of the scheme. For March 20th the advertisement is very vague, without specification of plays; on the 27th, however, we were promised I due Ladri and Il Flauto Magico con Pulcinella Servo Fedele, as well as selected music by L. Conterno. On April 2nd, the society invited to a ball, but nevertheless advertised In Manica di Camicia and

Lucrezia Borgia. The last I found for the enterprise was the double bill of April 10th — La Macchia di Sangue and L'Alloggio Militare.

ITALIAN MISCELLANY, 1880–1881

The docket thus cleared of plays, I may go back to October 12, 1880, for the annual celebration of the discovery of America, carried out, this year, in Bender's Schützen Park by the Guardia Colombo. The Firenze ball came, on January 15th, at Tammany Hall, and, in the same rooms, on January 28th, that of the Società di Unione e Fratellanza Italiana. The Teutonia Assembly Rooms opened, on February 5th, for the eleventh annual ball of the Società Ticinese, and the Ferrero Assembly Rooms, on February 12th, for the fifteenth of the Associazione del Tiro al Bersaglio Guardia Colombo — also, on March 19th, for the seventh of the Società Legione G. Garibaldi.

June carries us to the open spaces. At Sulzer's Harlem River Park, 126th Street and 2nd Avenue, on June 12th and 13th, came the fifteenth annual celebration by the Associazione del Tiro (Guardia Colombo) of the Festa Nazionale dello Statuto. June 28th was gay, at Elm Park, with the first *festa compestre* of the Società Italiana Mazzini di Mutuo Soccorso. And, in June, Lazzari's Cottage, at Williamsbridge, kept calling us to its alluring promise of "Conforto, Ristori e Passatempo." The Società di San Antonio di Padova went as usual, on July 4th, to Dittmar's Bellevue Park, West Hoboken, there to celebrate American independence. The Società Firenze, on July 17th, sailed up the Hudson to Iona Island (and, I suppose, back therefrom). On August 6th, the Società Operaia Italiana journeyed no farther afield that Elm Park, 92nd Street, for its *festa campestre estiva, diurna e notturna*.

The Società Filodrammatica Salvini re-emerged, on July 26th, in the Teatro Vercelli, 152-154 East 42nd Street, playing Leopold Marengo's drama, Giorgio Gandi, with Edoardo Majeroni in the title-rôle, Giovanni Venturoli as Papa Stefano, L. L. Ventura as Michelino, M. Maurie as Conte di Prado, Angiolo Villa as Petronino, Santina Pernigotti as Sandrina, and Signora Giulia Majeroni as Margherita. This is an unexpected re-introduction into our story of Signora Majeroni. On August 1st, the Teatro Vercelli was advertising Pinafore (with Marie Gurney) and the farce, Gennarine. I close the Italian account with the celebration, on September 7th, at Jones Wood, of the entrance of Garibaldi into Naples, this pious festival being staged, of course, by the Società Legione Giuseppe Garibaldi.

ACADEMY OF MUSIC (NEW YORK), 1880–1881

The temple of music and of social display began the season of 1880–81 with a concert, on October 7th, to introduce Constantine Sternberg, "the

[303]

great Russian pianist," assisted by an orchestra of seventy, directed by Gotthold Carlberg. The débutant played Scharwenka's Concerto in B-flat minor, Grieg's Aus dem Norwegischen Volksleben, and a Rhapsodie Espagnole, by Liszt. The orchestra performed Meyerbeer's overture, Struensee, and the Procession of the Gods, from Das Rheingold. I must again call attention to the great amount of Der Ring des Nibelungen our public had heard before the operas were staged at the Metropolitan Opera House. Sternberg repeated his opening programme at an Academy matinée, on the 9th. Thereafter, as we know, he gave some matinées at the Madison Square Theatre. He may have been "a great Russian pianist," but he was not a great American success. He had digital expertness and other valuable assets, but he was not a mature student.

Mapleson began his third autumn season of opera here on October 18th, with a return of the beloved Etelka Gerster (sadly missed during 1879–80) as Lucia, assisted by the excellent Antonio Galassi as Ashton, and with a delightful new tenor, Ravelli, as Edgardo; the minor rôles fell to Monti, Rinaldini, Grazzi and Mlle. Valerga, all trustworthy artists in minor parts. The Herald of the 19th asserts that Gerster's voice was even more mellow in the middle and lower upper register, though the power was small. Ravelli, as so often happens, was not highly praised, at first, but he grew in popularity, and was the only tenor Mapleson ever introduced who could stand comparison with the idolised Campanini. The second night of the new season inaugurated a period of bad luck. Miss Cary and Campanini were to re-appear in their favourite of the preceding season, La Favorita; the lady was ill, and Mlle. Belocca substituted as Leonora, and Campanini, though he sang, was in so wretched a condition, vocally, that but little enjoyment was derived from his efforts. Under these circumstances, chief honours fell to the dependable Del Puente. Monti and Isidora Martinez sang the other rôles. More disappointment came on October 22nd, when the wholly unsatisfactory Lazzarini sang Faust, instead of Campanini, too ill to appear, and when Bertha Ricci, an inexperienced girl, was hurried into the rôle of Siebel, to take the place of Miss Cary, still indisposed. The audience had expected much, and in these dampening disappointments, it hardly enjoyed even the Margherita of Alwina Valleria, returning to a public that had acclaimed her last year. A new basso, Franco Novara, came forth as Mephistopheles, and established himself as a royal favourite for several years ensuing. Del Puente was Valentino, and Mlle. Valerga Marta. Lucia was repeated at the matinée on October 23rd.

Mapleson's wretched luck followed him into Monday of his second week, and then stopped. Linda di Chamounix was announced for Monday, October 25th, with Campanini, Galassi, Monti, Baldassare Corsini (an excellent new buffo), Belocca and Gerster; Campanini was still unable to sing, and Ravelli took his place. The announced Carmen of the 27th was sung with its promised quartette — Campanini (in poor condition), Del Puente, Valleria and Belocca. Gerster, on the 29th, made her first appearance here as Gilda, in Rigoletto, others in the cast being Ravelli, Galassi and Belocca. At the Saturday matinée, October 30th, Miss Cary struggled bravely through the music of La Favorita (the Herald states that her admirers could hardly recognise her voice or style), Campanini again assuming the rôle of Fernando. The artists who had thus far appeared in the season were the most beloved, the most popular Mapleson ever brought to this country; one still loves to think of them and of the charming surroundings, the delightful audiences associated with their performances here. Gerster, Campanini, Cary, Del Puente, Galassi, Valleria—it is a joy even to write their names. On November 1st, Gerster reverted to the rôle in which she is best remembered — Amina, in La Sonnambula — her associates being Campanini, Del Puente, Isidora Martinez (Lisa), and Ida Valerga (Teresa); both these latter young women were New Yorkers. In Un Ballo in Maschera, on November 3rd, were listed a new soprano, Bianca Montesini (owner of a tremolo), as Amelia, Miss Cary (in better voice) as Ulrica, Marie Louise Swift as Oscar, the page (and, according to the critics, a poor page, ever, in Mapleson history), with Ravelli, Galassi and Novara in chief male rôles. On the 5th, Aïda grouped the valued services of Campanini, Galassi, Novara, Monti, Cary and Valleria (the last-named not good, according to the Herald). The company was then singing once a week (Thursdays) in Brooklyn. Linda was repeated at the matinée on the 6th, Campanini now assuming the rôle of Carlo. On Sunday, the 7th, a concert introduced Campanini, Valleria, Cary, Swift, Ravelli, Galassi, Belocca and Novara.

The fourth week began on Monday, November 8th, with La Traviata (Gerster, Martinez, Valerga, Ravelli, Galassi, Monti), and brought repetitions of La Sonnambula (10th), Faust (12th, with Campanini, Novara, Del Puente, Cary and Valleria), and Rigoletto, cast as before (matinée, on the 13th). On Sunday, the 14th, Mapleson gave Stabat Mater (with Valleria, Cary, Campanini, Novara and Galassi), and a miscellaneous concert, with Mrs. Swift (almost the only unsatisfactory singer in his company), Belocca and others in solos. The popularity of Gerster is shown by the fact that she sang on every subscription evening of the fifth week — as Lucia, on the 15th; as Elvira, in I Puritani, on the 17th, with Campanini, Galassi and Novara; and in La Traviata, on the 19th. Carmen, with the cast of the earlier season, and with Campanini in good voice, filled the matinée bill on Saturday, the 20th; the performance was honoured by the presence of Salvini.

On the afternoon and evening of November 16th came the annual benefit of the Roman Catholic Orphan Asylum. The afternoon bill included acts by Rice's Surprise Party, in Revels; by Harrigan and Hart's company, in The Mulligan Guard Picnic; from As You Like It, by the Wallack Company; and W. F. Owen and W. Davidge, Jr., in Two Gentlemen in a Fix.

Gilmore's Band, Harry Kennedy, the French Twin Sisters, and the Bent Brothers also appeared. In the evening, Annie Ward Tiffany gave the fourth act of East Lynne; Cool as a Cucumber followed; a scene from The Marble Heart led to the sleep-walking scene from Macbeth, with Julia Evarts; Geraldine Morgan, a twelve-year-old violinist, Harry Edwards, S. A. L. Bently (in songs), and W. J. Scanlan furnished specialties. I have seldom recorded a less interesting entertainment for the particular charity involved.

On November 22nd, Campanini, again ill, could not sing, and Lazzarini took his place in La Sonnambula — a very poor substitute, enough to take the life out of Gerster's Amina. On the 24th and 26th were promised performances of Boito's much-discussed opera, Mefistofele, a recent success in Mapleson's London season, with Christine Nilsson, Mme. Trebelli, Campanini and Novara. Here, Campanini and Novara were again to sing Faust and Mefistofele, and Alwina Valleria was to double the rôles of Margherita and Helen, with Miss Cary as Marta and Pantalis. Of course the music was listened to with reverence, but it cannot be said that the new work swept our public off its critical feet. Nevertheless, we were glad to hear Mefistofele, the much discussed. La Traviata (Ravelli, Galassi and Gerster) filled the afternoon of the 27th. A Sunday concert, on the 28th, repeated Stabat Mater, and presented Mrs. Swift, Ravelli and Belocca in a miscellaneous concert. The seventh week brought only repetitions, with casts already cited — Linda (November 29th), Mefistofele (December 1st), Aïda (December 3rd), and La Sonnambula (4th). The actors from the Germania Theater played (for charity) on November 30th, Heydemann und Sohn. A benefit for the Elks, on the afternoon of December 2nd, promised singing by Ravelli, Swift, Corsini, Belocca and Del Puente; the quarrel scene from Julius Cæsar, by John McCullough and John A. Lane; the third act of Hazel Kirke, with Steele MacKaye, Jeffreys Lewis, Sydney Cowell, &c.; Rice's Surprise Party, in Prince Achmet; Agnes Booth in an act of The Legion of Honour; Anna Teresa Berger; a bit from Enchantment; the Davene Troupe, Stirk's Bicycle Riders, the Skidmore Guards, Sheridan and Mack, and other "variety" performers in their special "turns." Osmond Tearle and Harriet Webb recited, and Welsh Edwards, by permission of Steele MacKaye, was stage-manager.

Etelka Gerster, on December 6th, made her first appearance here as Marta, with Miss Cary, Campanini and Del Puente; Mefistofele was down for a special performance, on the 7th; I Puritani fell on the 8th, Rigoletto on the 10th, and Faust, at the matinée on the 11th. The week of the 13th promised repetitions of Marta (with Ravelli), Mefistofele (15th), Lucia (17th, with Ravelli) and Aïda (matinée (18th). On the 18th, however, Valleria was ill, and Campanini and Miss Cary gave, instead of Aïda, La Favorita. At the Sunday concert, on the 19th, besides the usual Stabat

Mater, without its fine quartette, since Mrs. Swift took the part of the indisposed Valleria, we had Gerster, in the variations on The Carnival of Venice and in the polka cantabile of Arditi, Fior di Margherita. On December 20th, the last week of the opera began with La Sonnambula; on the 22nd, Il Trovatore was announced, with Valleria, Cary, Campanini and Galassi, but La Favorita was substituted to the distress of the audience. Marta had a special performance, on Thursday, the 23rd. Don Giovanni, advertised for the 24th, with Ravelli, Del Puente, Swift (Donna Anna), Valleria (Elvira) and Gerster (Zerlina) was withdrawn because of Valleria's illness, and Lucia took its place, with the great trio of Campanini, Galassi and Gerster. Perhaps Gerster's overwhelming popularity, and her taking Linda and Marta from Valleria's last year's repertoire was a determining factor in Valleria's state of health — mental, at least. I go back to the evening of December 14th, when Dr. Damrosch revived La Damnation de Faust, with Valleria, Fred Harvey, Remmertz, Bourne, the Oratorio and Arion Societies, and the Symphony Orchestra. Of course, the Philharmonic concerts were held, as usual, at the Academy.

Beginning on Christmas afternoon and evening (Saturday), the Academy dropped from those days and nights of the dear old operas to Jay Rial's Uncle Tom's Cabin, which was staged for a run. And the same piece was put on, at the same time, at Booth's. I leave the reader to work off his own astonishment at this coming of the old play, blood-hounds, plantation songs and sports, and all, into an auditorium recently filled with the fine flower of New York society and with the voices of some of the finest singers of their generation. The cast of Uncle Tom's Cabin included Arthur Gregory as Uncle Tom, L. R. Stockwell as Marks, Harry Duffield as George Harris, Sidney Hicks as Legree and Phineas Fletcher, J. N. Drew as St. Clair, Sallie Partington as Topsy, Baby Blanche as Eva, Hattie Lewis as Aunt Ophelia, Mrs. Jay Rial as Eliza, and Florence Elmore as Cassy. The visit of these not brilliant interpreters of the moral earnestness of Mrs. Stowe was brief.

Midwinter, as usual, filled the Academy with fleetness of the dance. The Cercle Français de l'Harmonie held there, on January 24th, its annual ball, and utilised, in addition, Irving Hall, across Irving Place, as well as Nilsson Hall nearer the Academy. On the 26th, the Academy housed the Old Guard reception and ball, always a social function of importance. The Société Culinaire Française, for February 1st, possessed both the Academy and Irving Hall. The charity ball, acme of delight to many, came on February 3rd. On the 7th, we had the fifth annual Children's Carnival and Ball, with Aronson's orchestra. And the Martha Washington Reception and Ball came on the 9th, the Elks' ball, New York Lodge No. One, holding the Academy and Nilsson Hall on the 14th. The Palestine Commandery danced on the 15th. The Liederkranz ball, with tickets at $10 for a gentleman and a lady, functioned German-wise on the 17th. The French responded, on February 28th, when the Cercle de l'Orphéon Français entered the Academy and Nilsson Hall.

RETURN OF THE OPERA, 1881

Mapleson's delightful singers returned on March 7th, for the spring season, usual throughout his régime. And I am sorry to say that some of them appeared to be in very bad vocal condition. Campanini, for instance, announced for the opening night, was forced by illness to yield his place, in Marta, to the useful and now popular Ravelli; otherwise the cast, as before, included Gerster, Cary, Del Puente and the excellent new buffo, Corsini. Don Giovanni, which Valleria's illness had stopped in the autumn season, now emerged, on the 9th, with Ravelli, Del Puente, Corsini (Leporello), Marie Louise Swift (absurdly overweighted as Donna Anna), Valleria, and Miss Cary (certainly a weighty Zerlina, vocally and physically; both of Zerlina's lovely airs were transposed to the contralto range). Mefistofele, announced for the 11th, could not, because of Campanini's continued illness, be sung, and Faust was substituted, with Lazzarini, Novara, Del Puente, Cary and Valleria — Faust without Faust, indeed. Rigoletto, with Ravelli, Galassi, Monti, Belocca and Gerster finished the uncertain week, at the Saturday matinée, March 12th.

Better luck attended the second week. La Sonnambula, on the 14th, presented Ravelli, Del Puente and Gerster; on the 16th, Gerster for the first time here sang Rosina, in Il Barbiere di Siviglia, introducing in the lesson scene the famous coloratura Carnaval de Venise and Arditi's Fior di Margherita; Ravelli, Del Puente (a delightful Figaro), Monti (Basilio) and Corsini (Dr. Bartolo) completed the cast of principals. Linda, on the 18th, had Ravelli, Galassi, Cary and Gerster as chief executants, and finally, at the matinée on the 19th, Campanini could return to his devoted public in Carmen, Del Puente, Valleria and Belocca again appearing in their well-known characters. On the 15th, I pause to say, occurred at the Academy the Purim Ball. And warningly to the ears of Mapleson and directors and stockholders of the Academy came a notice in the Herald of that date to the effect that the site at Broadway, Thirty-ninth and Fortieth Streets, had been selected for the new Metropolitan Opera House. With the building of that temple of song, the doom of the Academy was sealed as a home of opera. An elegy might be written on all the things that passed out of New York with the going of that old order and the beginning of the new.

Marie Rôze, having finished her season with Max Strakosch's Opera Company, joined her father-in-law at the Academy, and was announced, on March 21st, for Pamina, in Il Flauto Magico; illness prevented her appearance, and I Puritani was substituted, with Gerster, Campanini, Galassi and

Monti.   The amusing thing is (see the Herald of the 20th) that both Rôze and Valleria were at the Academy for the rehearsal of this opera, both in friendly mood, and confused by directions from Mapleson.   Mme. Rôze was able to essay Mignon, on the 23rd, in association with Valleria (her last appearance), Novara (substituted for Del Puente), and Campanini.   The Herald of March 24th states that a perfect ovation followed Valleria's singing of the polacca, and that "a magnificent jewel case on a beautifully worked velvet cushion" was presented her as a farewell tribute.   She quite took the honours from Marie Rôze.   I can remember her Filina during the first season of the Metropolitan Opera House (1883–84), and I can assert that it was one of the most beautiful bits of singing that I ever heard, and lives in my ear, though some of Christine Nilsson's Mignon, on the same occasion, has left my storehouse of memory.   Valleria was a delightful artist.   Repetitions of La Favorita (25th) and Lucia (matinée, 26th) presented familiar casts, Ravelli singing Edgardo.   Il Barbiere di Siviglia, on the 28th, endured the substitution of Bellati for Del Puente, and, on the 30th, Lohengrin enlisted Campanini (in bad voice, but always the artist), Galassi, Novara, Monti, Gerster and Belocca.   Il Flauto Magico finally came, on April 1st, with Lazzarini, Del Puente, Novara (Sarastro), Monti (Il Sacerdote), with Belocca, Valerga and Ricci (Tre Geni), Swift, Cary and Martini (Tre Damigelle), Marie Rôze (Pamina), Mlle. Dotti (really the uninteresting Marie L. Swift, as Papagena), and Etelka Gerster (Astrafiammante).   Except for the tenor and Mrs. Swift (or Mlle. Dotti), that is a very fine collection of singers.   Marta delighted at the matinée on April 2nd.   On April 3rd (Sunday), Stabat Mater had Rôze, Cary, Campanini, Galassi and Monti, and Gerster in a miscellaneous concert rendered the Shadow Song, from Dinorah, and the Polka Cantabile, Fior di Margherita.   Ravelli, Galassi and Mme. Sacconi, the gifted harpist of the opera orchestra, also appeared. The last week of the opera began on April 4th, with La Forza del Destino, sung by Campanini, Galassi, Del Puente (Fra Meletone), Novara (Padre Guardiano), Monti (Marchese), Cary and Swift.   The Herald, next day, states that Campanini was hoarse, that Miss Cary sang badly and was too "kittenish," and that Galassi carried off the honours; but why, O why, asks the anguished critic, why Marie Louise Swift?   Lohengrin (April 6th), Il Trovatore (April 8th, with Marie Rôze, Miss Cary, Campanini and Galassi), and La Sonnambula (matinée 9th, with Gerster, Ravelli and Del Puente, all in poor voice, says the Herald, on the 10th) ended what, in spite of too frequent illness of artists, I am almost inclined to believe Mapleson's most attractive opera season at the historic Academy; certainly it was the season of Gerster's greatest glory in our town.   When next she appeared in opera ·at the Academy (1883–84) she was pitted against the incomparable Adelina Patti in the same line of parts.   To vie with Patti, one must be a second Patti.   Meantime, on April 5th, Carl Sontag, Frl. Bensberg and the Germania Theater company acted, in German, Die widerspenstige (*sic*) Frau and Die Unglücklichen.

On April 17th, Mapleson's artists again sang Stabat Mater, with Gerster, Ravelli, Rôze, Belocca, Del Puente and Mme. Sacconi following in miscellaneous numbers. April 18th brought a benefit for the patient Mapleson, with Campanini, Novara, Galassi, Cary and Swift, in the third act of Aïda; Cary and Gerster in the second act of Dinorah, terminating with the shadow song; Campanini, Del Puente, Belocca and Valerga (replacing Marie Rôze) in the third act of Il Trovatore; Gerster, Ravelli and Galassi, in the third act of Lucia; and Marie Rôze, Campanini, Del Puente and Galassi in the fourth act of The Huguenots. Naturally, the house was densely packed with admirers of the singers appearing. On the 19th, Henry W. Pope, for reasons hard to fathom, acted Dr. Pangloss. April 20th promised Joseffy, Theodore Thomas, and an orchestra of one hundred from the Philharmonic.

A benefit for the Poe fund, on April 23rd, promised Charles Roberts, Jr., in a reading of Byron's The Corsair; Rafael Joseffy; Locke Richardson in a recital of Longfellow's King Robert of Sicily; Blanche Roosevelt singing The Nightingale's Trill; Sara S. Rice, of Baltimore, in a reading of William Winter's At Poe's Grave; Pelayo, read by Roberts, accompanying a tableau; Lester Wallack, Rose Coghlan and Harry Edwards in a scene from The Wonder; an address by Algernon S. Sullivan; a reading of The Raven, by William Fearing Gill; Maud Morgan in a harp solo; and scenes from A Midsummer Night's Dream, "by young ladies and gentlemen and children." *Tableaux vivants* figured frequently in the programme. Florence Rice Knox and Adelaide Phillipps, originally announced, did not appear.

De Beauplan's Grand French Opera Company from New Orleans began an unnecessary season at the Academy, on April 25th. The opening performance, for the benefit of the French Benevolent Society, presented Les Huguenots, with Tournie as Raoul, Utto as Nevers, Feitlinger as St. Bris, Jourdan as Marcel, Mlle. Lagye as Marguerite, Mlle. Pilliard as Urbain, and Emilie Ambre (of all people in the world) as Valentine. The ballet, incidental to the opera, introduced Mlles. Hennecart, La Bella, and Gossi. In La Juive, on the 26th, were to appear Tournie as Eleazar, Jourdan as the Cardinal, Pellini as Leopold, Mlle. del Prato as Rachel, and Mlle. Villeray as Eudoxie. Faust, on the 27th, with Pellini, Feitlinger (Mephisto), Mange, Mlle. Pilliard, Mme. Courtade and Emilie Ambre was set down by the Herald, next day, as a complete failure; the performance included the Walpurgis ballet. And that about ended the fiasco; Ambre and Tournie, I learn from the Herald of a few days later, disappeared from the situation, and the unfortunate singers were stranded here. Why they thought, after the fifteen weeks of Mapleson's opera, the town needed them, one cannot even conjecture. It may be they were on their way home and were not averse to the idea of collecting more American dollars to ease the pain of parting.   From this heroic fiasco, we move on to Jerome Hopkins's Springtide for the Orpheon Fund, at which (April 28th), he offered Blanche Roosevelt, Lencioni, S. B. Mills, Nahan Franko, and the "first Pianists' Tournament of America."   May 1st found Robert G. Ingersoll lecturing on The Great Infidels.

On May 9th, the great Salvini, for whose mighty art no theatre seemed too large, came to the Academy for a farewell engagement.   On the 9th, and at the matinée on the 14th, he gave Othello; Macbeth was the offering on the 11th, and The Gladiator, on the 13th.   Ellie Wilton, Marie Prescott, Henry Crisp and H. A. Weaver still supported him, speaking English in answer to his sonorous Italian.   And, on May 10th, another foreign tongue rang through the auditorium, when, for the benefit of Adolph Neuendorff, Was Ihr Wollt had Reinau as Orsino, Frl. von Januschowsky as Sebastian, Kierschner as Antonio, Rank as Junker Tobias von Rulp, Meery as Junker Andreas von Bleichenwang, Raberg as Malvolio, Sauer as Fabio, Merten as Narr, Frl. Setti as Olivia, Frl. Bensberg as Viola, and Frl. Necker as Maria. Well, Shakespeare has suffered many changes since first he wrote Twelfth Night.   A farewell benefit to Campanini, on May 16th, presented Il Trovatore, with the beneficiary, Orlandini, Broderick, Mme. Lablache (absent all season, though promised with the recently stranded French company) and Ostava Torriani, the original Aïda here, in 1873–74.   Time, the mystery, baffles one in imagining these re-appearances of so long ago.

Theatre Comique, 1880–1881

Harrigan and Hart, if we may judge by the lengthy runs of their plays, enjoyed about the most prosperous season known in New York in 1880–81. The Mulligan Guards marched from success to success.   The first offering in the series was (August 9th) The Mulligan Guard Picnic, set down as "Volume I, reconstructed":

Dan Mulligan............Edward Harrigan		Mrs. Dublin..................John Queen
Rebecca Allup...................Tony Hart		Judge Cohog...................Robert Hall
Lemons..........................John Wild		Gipsy Jack.......................M. Foley
Tommy Fagin...............William Gray		Farmer Armyworm.............J. Buckley
Gustavus Lochmuller..........Harry Fisher		Hezekiah Swift..............James Tierney
Roderick O'Dwyer................Ed Burt		Gussy Lochmuller...............Emil Husel
August Bimble..............Harry Sinclair		Bridget Lochmuller............Annie Mack
Walsingham McSweeny..........M. Bradley		Cordelia Mulligan......Mrs. Annie Yeamans
Captain Primrose................James Fox		Jennie Lantry...................Mary Bird
Rev. Ferguson Clinton.............Ed Goss		Delia Darcy................Belle Mordaunt
Theophilus Grasp............William West		Phœbe Casey..............Emily Yeamans

Since the songs of Dave Braham were so important a feature of these productions (of course Harrigan's words to the "lyrics" also counted heavily), I may state that these extra inducements in The Mulligan Guard Picnic included The Second Degree Full Moon Union, All Aboard for the M. G. P.,

[311]

Mary Kelly's Beau, Locked Out after Nine, and Sandy-Haired Mary in Our Area. It is interesting to observe Harrigan thus enlarging and improving the slighter Picnic of 1878. With the new version now, John Wild and Billy Gray added a slight sketch, Dr. Tanner Outdone. Of course that fasting gentleman of the late summer could not expect to escape the satire of the comedians. What fun William Mitchell would have had with him at the Olympic of the '40s! A farce preceding the successful Picnic, in the week of October 4th, was My Wife and My Mother-in-law, with Wild and Jennie Morgan. During the week of October 11th, Wild appeared in The Happy Family, and Jennie Morgan, "the American linnet," sang new ballads. All happy at the Comique! On November 3rd, occurred the hundredth performance of The Mulligan Guard Picnic; previous to the performance, as usual of late, Wild gave a farce and Jennie Morgan still sang ballads.

The Mulligan Guard Picnic closed on November 20th, and, on the 22nd, Harrigan had ready another "Volume" of the famous series — The Mulligan Guards' Nominee:

Dan Mulligan	Edward Harrigan	Tip Molony	Eugene Rourke
Rebecca Allup	Tony Hart	Carl Robecker	Robert Hall
Captain Primrose	John Wild	Cromwell	John Mealey
Rev. Palestine Puter	William Gray	Pedro	James Fitzsimmons
Gustavus Lochmuller	Harry Fisher	Officer Sudden	J. McCullough
Snuff McIntosh / Humphrey Down	Ed Burt	Officer Soon	Joseph Buckley
		Officer Stop	John Coffee
Caroline Melrose	James Tierney	Gus Lochmuller, Jr.	Master E. Husel
Wentmore Cinders	William West	Bridget Lochmuller	Annie Mack
Oliver Bullwinkle	Edwin Barry	Cordelia Mulligan	Annie Yeamans
August Bimble	Harry Sinclair	Diana McFudd	Emily Yeamans
Walsingham McSweeny	M. Bradley	Lucretia Crowley	Mary Bird
Mrs. Honora Dublin	John Queen	Henrietta Dempsey	Belle Mordaunt
Dandeline Douglas	M. Foley	Annetta McSorley	Susie Byron
Dick Dublin	Fred Queen		

These lengthy casts at the Comique drain even the most willing pen. According to A. H. Quinn (A History of the American Drama) this new piece was "an amusing satire on politics, on women's organizations, and on the British fear of American interposition in Irish affairs. When the play opens, they are at the Cunard docks, waiting for Bridget Lochmuller to come home. Oliver Bullwinkle, an English spy, comes on the same ship. He is trying to obtain evidence of Irish conspiracies here and in Sligo. There is a delightful meeting of the Nightingales, 'a society of Irish ladies who are working for Irish freedom.' Bridget Lochmuller has brought back a cipher letter and Bullwinkle is very anxious to get it. There is a contest on for Alderman-at-large, and Dan Mulligan and Lochmuller are rival candidates. Mulligan's crowd meet in Lyric Hall; there is a speech and a fight with the Lochmuller contingent, till the police come, and Rebecca tells them loftily, 'I'm a member ob de Baptist church — don't push me!'" Mr. Quinn quotes with gusto a bit of dialogue in which Dan secures the release of his follower, McSweeny, just arrested for a fight in a barber shop.   "Raylease him," says Dan.   "I'm 200 votes ahead of Lochmuller, and I'll say no more."   To which the police officer replies, "Anything, Mr. Mulligan, to oblige *you*."   The songs were Down in Gossip Row, Hang the Mulligan Banner Up, Mulligan's Promises, The Skidmore Masquerade, The Skids are Out Tonight and A Nightcap. Harrigan and Braham forever!

The scenery for the new piece was by "our artist," Charles W. Witham. The play ran uninterruptedly till February 21st, when the third and last production of Harrigan and Hart's season brought The Mulligans' Silver Wedding:

Alderman Mulligan........Edward Harrigan	Luminary Soot.................John Oberist
Dennis Mulligan.................Tony Hart	Shepherd of the Fold.............James Fox
Captain Primrose................John Wild	Gussy Lochmuller...............Emil Husel
Rev. Palestine Puter..........William Gray	Brien McQuirk...............J. Fitzsimmons
Lochmuller.....................Harry Fisher	Dr. McGinn....................Robert Hall
Edgar de Angelles.............Edward Burt	Officer Late.................James O'Rourke
Washington Irving Crumbs........M. Drew	Honora Dublin..................John Queen
Caroline Melrose............James Tierney	Clorinda Perkins...............Annie Mack
Walsingham McSweeny..........M. Bradley	Cordelia Mulligan...........Annie Yeamans
Timothy Heaves..............Edward Goss	Winsome Winnie...........Emily Yeamans
Mr. Hog Eye.................William West	Celia Quigley....................Mary Bird
Jolly Johnson...............Edward Barry	Edith McGarrigan..........Belle Mordaunt
Crabbs.....................George Merritt	Camille O'Hara................Susie Byron
Satellite Fresco..............Michael Foley	

The songs (music, of course, by Braham) were The Castaways, Don't You Miss the Train, Boys, The Mirrors the Cause of It All, John Reilly's Always Dry, South Fifth Avenue, The Third Degree Full Moon Union, and Wheel the Baby Out.   In one of the later scenes of the play, Mrs. Yeamans, as Cordelia, in a fit of jealousy of Dan, drinks, as she supposes, a poison from a bottle which Dan had filled with whiskey, and then, to keep it from Rebecca Allup, had labelled "Rat Poison."   Mrs. Yeamans made an even greater hit with this scene, when Harrigan reworked it (1883) into perhaps the greatest of his Mulligan plays — Cordelia's Aspirations.   The Mulligans' Silver Wedding lasted until the end of the season on April 30th; with it the Theatre Comique, at 514 Broadway, passed out of existence, a large store being soon after built on the site.   When Harrigan and Hart returned to New York for 1881–82, they were established in the hitherto variously-named 728 Broadway, which they refurbished and remodeled, and renamed the Theatre Comique.

Tony Pastor's, 1880–81

Tony Pastor's comes again into the record, on August 23, 1880, with a "variety" troupe including Alf Lawton (negro comedian), Campbell and Burke, Hannah Birch, and Nellie Richards.   The favourite skit, Murphy's Dream, cast John and George Murphy, Phil Mack and George Shannon in familiar rôles. This last-named quartette remained a second week, the three Gorman Brothers, Florence May and Bernard McCreedie being also stressed in Herald advertisements. The skit was now The Rivals. I found no more for Pastor's until September 24th, when a Græco-Roman match, for $2,000, was arranged between Edward Bibby, "champion of England," and Thiebaud Bauer, "champion of France."

The theatre re-opened for the regular season, on October 18th, Tony Pastor returning after his autumn tour, with an array including Ella Wesner, the St. Felix Sisters, the three Rankins, the French Twin Sisters and Eva French, Bryant and Hoey, the Kernells, Flora Moore, Bonnie Runnells, Lina Tettenborn and Frank Girard — also the Four Eccentrics, Perry, Hughes, Curdy and Magrew. Doubtless all were rapturously acclaimed by their loyal public. The farce, beginning on October 25th, was Fun on the Stage, or, a Manager's Trials, written years ago for Pastor's use by John F. Poole. Parker's Dog Circus made itself heard and seen. The company for November 1st–6th was almost completely changed — Lester and Allen, Minnie Farrell ("lightning change"), the American Four, Charles Fostelle, the Olympia Quartette (Keough, Sullivan, Andrews and Mack), Ada Forrest, Dan Collyer (Ethiopian), Frank Girard, the Three Crawfords (acrobatic grotesque dancers), Jennie Miaco, Allie Smith, Jennie Christie, and Edith Crolius; of course Tony was always present, with his crush hat and his pseudo-elegant air. Fun on the Stage still prevailed in the bills for November 8th–13th, and then Add Ryman, Harry and Emma Budworth, George and Marie Nelson (in jubilee songs, these two), Reynolds and Walling, Andy and Annie Hughes, Alice Bateman, Willis Pickert, the Burtons, John Lottie, Donnelly and Drew, Edwin French, Lizzie Derious, Lester and Allen, and Edward Mealey formed a veritable host of entertainers. Herald Personals was a feature of the week beginning on November 15th; and then Pastor brought out, for the first time, Our Second Families, of course a burlesque of Our First Families, at Daly's. In the olio appeared the Irwin Sisters, Leonard and Jones (Irish comedians), Lester and Allen, Ferguson and Mack, Add Ryman, The Four Daisies, William Henry Rice, the Lawrence Sisters, the "Dutch" Mendels, &c. Going to Germany was another skit. November 22nd presented an immense bill, in which shone resplendent for us, in light of her later fame, the name of Lillian Russell, "prima donna contralto in superb vocal efforts." This is the first time I have found any record of that famous woman. Others in the "olio" were the Stirk Bicycle Riders, Ella Wesner, Henry Whalen (baritone), Harry McAvoy and Emma Rogers and Paddy and Ella Murphy. A timely skit was The Arrival of Sallie Burn-Hard; and Table d'Hote, or, Fun at Dinner, a sketch by Add Ryman, presented the author as Abner Mapes, Dan Collyer as Digwaleper Dumps, Frank Girard as George Porgie, William Lester as Brass, Paul Allen as Buster, Harry McAvoy as A. Dollar

Note, Paddy Murphy as Jerry Gindipper, Emma Rogers as O'Dear, Lillian Russell as Rachel Reacht, "our first to the table boarder," Ella Murphy as Sallie Slaughter, Jennie Christie as Mrs. Splutter, and Edith Crolius as Mrs. Dumps. I wonder if Lillian Russell had at that time the remotest idea of her future fame? The most famous beauty of her day in a "Variety" hall! November 29th brought in William Carroll (banjoist), the Nondescripts (Cereni and Leslie) and Minnie Lee, and retained the Stirk Bicycle Riders, Lillian Russell ("the elegant balladist") and Fun in a Hotel (*sic*). Needles and Hairpins, on December 6th, pointed directly to Daly's great success, Needles and Pins; in it were Ryman, F. Girard, Collyer, Jennie Christie, Lucy Adams and Edith Crolius. The Peasleys, the Four Shamrocks and Guy Linton brightened the olio.

The features of the bill, on December 13th, were Krausmayer's Rival (with Henry Watson and Alice Hutchinson), the Irwin Sisters, Kelly and Ryan (Bards of Tara), Florence Merton ("the most elegant balladist in America"), the La Verde Sisters (Belle and Lillie), the Daly Brothers (Bobby and Dan), Charles and Annie Whiting (in The Music Teacher), and, above all, for us of later years, the "return of the favourite ballad vocalist," Lillian Russell. The promises for December 20th embraced Sheehan and Jones, Sheridan and Mack, Harry Watson, the Kernells, the French Twin Sisters, Lillian Russell, Joyce Martelle, Reynolds and Walling, Niles and Evans, Kitty O'Neil, Florence Merton, Frank Girard and Dan Collyer. On December 27th, a new piece by James A. Barnes — Pastor's Evening Party — introduced John Sheehan, Johnny Jones, Ferguson, Dick and J. W. Mack, Billy Hoey, Collyer, Girard, Ada Boshell (wife of J. W. Mack), Georgie Blake, Lena French and Jennie Christie. Lillian Russell was featured in the olio — *the* feature of it for us. The Evening Party continued to January 15th, and in the week of January 3rd–8th, Lillian Russell, Florence Merton, Till's Royal Marionettes, Ella Wesner, Andy and Annie Hughes, Harry Woodson, Mr. and Mrs. R. A. Brennan, Sheehan and Jones and Captain Laible appeared in a very strong olio. Beginning on January 10th, Lillie Western did what few of my readers could do — she played on forty different instruments. Beside that marvellous feat, what could hope to avail the Jolly Three (Frank McNish and the Leland Sisters), the Virginia Trio (Turner, Welch and Harris), Frank Bennett and Lida Gardner (in Capers), the ever-lasting French Twin Sisters, or Harry McEvoy (*sic*) and Emma Rogers (in Caught at Last)? What even Lillian Russell and Florence Merton, or Morgan and Mullen (in The Irish Holiday)? Lester and Williams, Major Burke, "the wonder musketeer," Dan Collyer and Frank Girard completed an extraordinary array for that week.

Pastor was apparently striving to get away from the older type of bill; I have no doubt the success of Harrigan and Hart piqued and baffled him.

[315]

At any rate, on January 17th, he brought out a burlesque on Robertson's School, which he called Our School Girls:

Amos Sourspring	John Morris	Nettie Dash	Lida Gardner
Charley Whiting	Charles Edwards	Tilly Orville	May Irwin
Harry Lawrence	Frank Girard	Emma Ray	Flora Irwin
Fred Pyne	Paddy Murphy	Lou Allyne	Ella Murphy
Henry H. Hopkins	Dan Collyer	Grace Hall	Kitty McDermott
Barney	Mr. Fields	Dolly Pitt	Florence Merton
Sally Smithers	Fannie Beane	Lottie Babbett	Lillian Russell
Jennie Roberts	Jennie Christie	Fannie Jones	Edith Crolius

I wonder if any spectator, on that night, casually reading those names, picked out May Irwin and Lillian Russell as likely to be two of the best-known and most prosperous stars of our stage in years not far in the future? Above all, did any one realise that oblivion would engulf practically all the other members of that cast? What a thing is life with all its chances! With Our School Girls, during the week of January 24th, the olio included Parker and his dogs, Flora Moore, May Arnott, the Daly Brothers, the St. Felix Sisters, and Harry Woodson. Fun in the Police Court, the Big Four (Smith, Waldron, Martin and Cronin), Lester and Allen, Ella Wesner were here on the 31st.

The Pirates of Penn-Yan, on February 7th, had Flora Irwin as Little Freddy, W. D. Marks as Peter, King of the Prowlers, Samuel Holdsworth as Richard, his viceroy, John Morris as Brigadier Stanislaus, Lillian Russell (rapidly forging ahead) as Maria, May Irwin as Ruthy, Florence Merton as Katie, &c. On the 14th, with this burlesque, Sara, "the great dancer of the Soldene Troupe," figured in the olio. In addition to the successful burlesque, the bill for the week beginning on February 21st featured Frank McNish and the Leland Sisters (in Stolen Fun), the "elegant prima donna," Lillian Russell, Louis and Emma Alfredo ("wonder acrobats"), the Irwin Sisters, Huber and Allyne, and Bernard Sloman ("ventriloquial wonder," in imitations of birds and animals). Since Harrigan and Hart had branched out into lengthy plays, Pastor's was about the only "legitimate" theatre of "Variety" in the city — uptown, that is. The week of February 28th–March 5th ended the depredations of The Pirates of Penn-Yan, and also introduced Lizzie Simms, "the great dancer from England." Another burlesque was ready on March 7th, Olivette, with Flora Irwin as Valentine, Signor Olmi as Duke of Ifs and Buts, John Morris as Merrymac, George W. Palmer as Marvejol, Dan Collyer as Ko-Ko, Frank Girard as Matelot, Lillian Russell (now a reigning favourite) as Olivette, May Irwin as the Countess, and Bessie Gray as Velveteen. In the olio were Lizzie Simms, Eugene (the former "prima donna" of the minstrel halls), Louise and Florence Murio (vocalists), Victoria ("the flying woman of the skies"), and Lester and Williams. With Olivette, on March 14th, appeared Kitty O'Neil, Clooney and Ryan ("Dutch") and the Kernells; its surrounding celebrities,

DAN COLLYER

WILLIAM HENRY RICE

BARNEY McNULTY

LILLIAN RUSSELL

MAY TEN BROECK

DOLLIE THORNTON

J. E. HENSHAW

FLORA AND MAY IRWIN

F. F. LEVANTINE

on the 21st, were Pastor, Lizzie Simms, the St. Felix Sisters and the Big Four (Smith, Waldron, Martin and Cronin).   Olivette still ran during the week of March 28th–April 2nd; in addition, Tony Pastor's The Slave's Dream, or, Plantation Life before the War, featured a jubilee chorus of forty.   The Big Four, Lillian Russell, the Irwin Sisters, Harry Woodson and Lizzie Daly, "elegant dancer," added to the joys of the olio.

A change of plan gave, on April 4th, the French Twin Sisters, the Irwin Sisters, Barney Ferguson and Dick Mack, Lester and Allen, Lester and Williams, Ella Wesner, Lillie Western, Frank McNish and the Leland Sisters, McAvoy and Rogers, and Dan Collyer, all from the very heart of "Variety."   And then Tony and his satellites retired to the Grand Opera House, surrendering the theatre to the Rentz-Santley company, who, on April 11th, presented a burlesque, Billy Taylor, or, the Lass Who Stuck to the Sailor.   In the company were Frank Bennett and Lida Gardner (in Capers), John Henshaw and May Ten Broeck (in comedy sketches), Keating and Sands (musical team), the Whitings, Quilter and Goldrich, and Rosa Lee, Mabel Santley, Fanny Florence, Lulu Mortimore (sic), Helen Courtland and Louise de Luisi.   During their second week (April 18th–23rd) they gave their own burlesque of The Pirates of Penzance, with May Ten Broeck as Richard, Rosa Lee as Frederick, Capitola Forrest as Sammy, Laura Bennett as Whippersnapper, Peter Goldrich as Arthur Pinafore Sullivan, Lew Benedict as the Major-General, D. Quilter as Captain of Police, Mabel Santley as Ruth, Lulu Mortimer (sic) as Mabel, &c.   After all, these are "headliners" of "Variety"; perhaps I have underrated Mmes. Rentz and Santley.   Mabel Ledgerwood's Novelty Queens brought lower the dignity of Pastor's, presenting on April 25th, along with their own attraction, Sanford and Wilson, Master Barney and Barney McNulty, Nellie Richards, Allie Drayton, and Howard Dorr and Son.   These also frequently appeared on the best "Variety" stages; possibly the feminine gender, so to speak, of the titles of the aggregations misled one.

On May 2nd, Pastor's was announced as "the Only Vaudeville Theatre open on Broadway."   The company then included Maggie Weston, as Bedelia Maloney, in Dan Maloney's Raffle, introducing the "Grand Parade of the South Fifth Avenue Rangers" and some "Great Stilt Wonders."   This sounds like an attempt to bore into the popularity of Harrigan and Hart.   Thatcher and Ryman's Minstrels were here on May 9th, offering the skit, Sara Heart-Burn.   The theatre now opened, apparently, to any one who would hire.   "Professor" H. M. Parker's Combination of forty performers had the week of May 16th, and Victoria Loftus' Troupe of British Blondes began a four-weeks tenancy on Mary 23rd; on June 6th, they stressed the St. Felix Sisters and four Nautch dancers.   The Nautch dancers, the Kernells and the Garnellas were starred on June 13th; with them, on the 27th, were featured the Dockstaders, the British Blondes, Charles Reed, Harry

[317]

Clarke (*sic*) and Wood and Beasley. One glances askance at Pastor's during the absence of Tony, himself. The week of July 4th–9th was the last of the Bouquet of Beauty — Victoria Loftus's British Blondes, and fifth week of the "Charming Houris" — the Nautch Dancers. The Kernells kept us to the level of the ground. On July 11th returned Mabel Ledgerwood's Novelty Queens, to match with the Naughty Nautch Girls; Lulu Delmay and Georgie Lingard were in the olio, on July 18th, as was Joseph Massey, "champion light-weight wrestler of the world." The Novelty Queens and the Nautch Dancers were still here (August 8th–13th), when they were alleged to be a "decidedly voluptuous and bewitching sensation." Chalet, Bob Slavin and George H. Wood were, in that last week, extra attractions. Add Weaver, Nellie Parker, Chalet ("the world's wonder"), Kitty Wells and Wood were here, on August 15th, the Nautch Dancers and the Novelty Queens remaining. The last week of the Novelty Queens began on August 22nd, when Irene Worrell, Charles Reed, Florence French, Chalet and the Nautch Dancers shared with them the doubtful glories of the bill.

The Rentz-Stantley Novelty Company, likely to show up in any "off" season at Pastor's, came in, on August 29th, with a burlesque Haze L. Kirke, which ran a second week, with Rosa Lee as Haze L. Kirke, the Mascot, Robert Manchester as Dolly Dutton, Lizzie Payne as Lord Travees, disguised as a gentleman, Fannie Florence as Oh, Mercy Kirke, Harry Wood as Dunstan Kirke, called Iron Will for short, William Buckley as Airy Rodney, the great American sacrifice, William H. Chace as Pettigang Green, and Pat Murphy as Barney. This sounds funny. On September 12th, the Hopkins-Morrow "Grand" Combination brought in Ben Gilfoil, the Daytons, Miss Lou Sanford, Dan Mason, John D. Griffin, Crosby and Martin, J. H. Surridge, Lulu Newton, and the burlesque, All I've Ate. With the entrance, on the 19th, of M. B. Leavitt's "Great" Specialty Company, I close Pastor's for 1880–81. And I look back in doubt at the seemingly questionable offerings of the summer.

728 BROADWAY, 1880–1881

That unhappy site, 728 Broadway, again piped up, on September 6th, as the "Broadway Theatre, late Globe," the managers being Fleming and O'Brien. Its offering was The Hand of Providence, with a cast including C. G. Craig, J. F. Peters, T. F. Egbert, W. L. Gleason, D. W. Van Deren, Bertha Welby (a rather interesting, if not thrilling addition to our caravan), Ada Trimble, and W. J. Fleming, that ever-recurring obligation of our theatre. The prices of admission were 50 cents, 35 cents, 25 cents and 15 cents, with "no extras for reserved seats." Even so, The Hand of Providence grasped no success; during its second week it was made more enticing by a second title — The Mysterious Murder, or, the Hand of Providence, a name

[318]

worthy of the cinema a half-century later. I doubt if that second week carried through to a concluding Saturday.

I once more pick up the place as the Broadway Novelty Theatre, when, on December 20th, J. Z. Little appeared there in Nuggets. Allston Brown seems to place this not very impressive, and very brief engagement in the December of 1879; I have followed advertisements in the Herald. On Sunday, the 26th, that journal advertises the second week of Nuggets; Mme. Nelson and her doves were showing, as well as Professor Nelson and his sons.

The Manhattan Opera House, 305 and 307 West 54th Street, and 915-919 Eighth Avenue, advertised in the Herald, during the week of July 11th–16th, 1881. J. L. Molloy, Jr., was listed as proprietor, and May Roberts's Combination was in its third week, H. J. Byron's play of Blow for Blow serving as lure for an easy-going public. On July 18th, Annie Ward Tiffany and Minnie Doyle were featured in Led Astray.

ABERLE's NEW THEATRE, 1880–1881

Thanks once more to bills in the Harvard Theatre Collection, I can invite the reader to a full season's repast, at Aberle's Eighth Street house, of combined melodrama and "Variety." The offering for the week of September 6th–11th (1880) began with Poverty vs. Riches (acted by Harry Clifford, George A. Bailey, Sam Roberts, Dollie Thornton and Flora Zanfretta); thereafter the intervening olio gave us William Wells and Grace Sylvano (in Uncle Jasper's Birthday), Ada Forrest, Charles Allen and Joe Hart (banjo, etc.), Polly Daly, and F. F. Levantine; the concluding feature was Marie Zoe, in The French Spy. Who ever dreamed that the Cuban Sylph could last so many years? She remained through the following week (September 13th–18th), in Eline, the Girl Detective, supported by C. L. Farwell, Bailey, Clifford, Harry Constantine, Flora Zanfretta and Dollie Thornton; in the olio for that week were Sanders and Dean, Nellie Hague, Minnie Farrell, Harry Constantine (female impersonator), &c. Most of the entertainers just listed remained for the week beginning on September 20th; but, Marie Zoe departing, Charles Foster awakened surmise in a play called The Old Straw Man of New York. Newcomers for "Variety" were Sarah (or Sara) Beryl (character change), Kemerson and Kehoe (a "Hebrew" team), Maude Sheppard, Rose and Harry Franklin (in Fighting for a Wife), and Carroll and Walters. The week of September 27th–October 2nd provided bountiful fare in Howard and Sanford (sangs, dance, and witty sayings), Arnold Brothers (Amos and Frank), Georgie Lingard, Fayette Welch (in The Hominy Man), and the concluding play, The Young Avenger, or, Thrown upon the World, with the protean William H. Rightmire as Harry Thornton, a cripple, Dick Ruby, a bootblack, Augustus De Rose, a Broadway swell, Bob Warren, a jolly tar, Jacob Schmidt, a German emigrant, and

[319]

Moses Solomon, a Jew peddler; Fayette Welch essayed the faithful negro, Sam.

The plays for October 4th–9th were The Coopers (with Fayette Welch) and The Prairie Flower (with Rose Goodall, Farwell, Bailey, &c.); October 11th began a week of No Pinafore (with the Arnolds, Bailey, G. W. Clifford, &c.) and Across the Atlantic (with John W. Ransone in five characters). "Variety" for that fortnight enlisted the Crimmins Brothers, Elmer E. Grandin and Josephine Shanley (in Won at Last), Lizzie Derious, George Derious (who stood, head downward, for eight minutes), Murphy and McAloon (songs and dances), the La Verdes, the Arnolds, O'Neil and Conroy, and Watson and Levanion — several of them for one week only. Later October brought in Lulu Arnott (vocal), Morton and Miles (Irish comedians), Charles and Annie Whiting, Etta Morris, Alice Bateman and Willis Pickert (clog dancers), and Marie Sherman. The concluding drama for October 18th–23rd was Yacup, or, the Peddler's Story, with George W. Thompson; for October 25th–30th, we had The Lily of Poverty Flat, in which Lena Aberle made her first appearance of the season, assisted by Farwell, the Arnolds, Dollie Thornton, M. Friquet, and the regular olio-dramatic corps.

One sees that for the melodramas Aberle maintained a stock company. The week of November 1st–6th gave us Farwell and Dollie Thornton, in Black-Eyed Susan, an olio comprising Mons. Bushnell (aerial juggler and equilibrist), Andy Collum and Annie Florence, John Burke and Larry Smith, Stella Newton, and Andy and Annie Hughes, and Farwell and the stock actors in Lost in London. George W. Woods was here on November 8th, as were the not very exciting balladist, Emmeline Cole ("her first appearance in America"), Emma Bretto, Parker and his dogs, and the old favourite, The New York Fireman (with Lena Aberle, Farwell, G. W. Johnson and Dollie Thornton). A funny thing, by intention at least, was The Arrival of Bernhardt, which began the bills for November 15th–20th, with Clifford as Henry E. Abbey, Farwell as Jac Aberle's Manager, Bailey as Harry Jarrett, J. Morton as Ed Gilmore, Sailor West as Harry Sergeant, and Dollie Thornton as Bernhardt; other features for that week were Harry Lamonto and Archie Baldwin (The Zulu Twins), Lena Rosa (the fire queen), Morton and Miles, Marie Sherman, Maude Sheppard, Watson and Levanion, Charles Diamond, and the "thrilling" play, Wild Bill, with Julian Kent, of course, as star. J. J. McCloskey's play, Pomp, or, Way Down South, presented, on November 22nd, Harry Clifford as the faithful Pomp; in the olio, for that week, were the Hull Twin Sisters (Effie and Emma), Harry Horton (male soprano), James Hearne (sic — "the spirit of Irish comedy"), Bernard McCreedie, Tom Sayers, and George Parker. John Allen, Lottie Winnett ("queen of Terpsichore"), Nellie Hague, Nellie Edwards (serio-comic and motto), the Winnetts (in Love in Broken German) and The Two Wanderers (with Rightmire and Lena Aberle) allowed November to die gracefully (week of November 29th–December 4th) in the lap of winter.

Many of the celebrities of Aberle's autumn shows grouped in an attractive olio for the week of December 6th–11th, but most febrilely were stressed in the advertisements Harry Cerini and George Leslie, "electric, elastic, agile, india-rubber, serpentine grotesques," who were to "turn somersaults over chairs and tables, fire guns while turning in the air," and indulge in "grotesque dancing, high-kicking," etc. After all that excitement Marie Zoe, returning in The French Spy, may have seemed a lame and impotent conclusion to the evening's delights. Newer features of the olio were Nellie Hague, Martha and Max Miller (in Going to the Picnic), Little Venus, and Fred Carroll (banjo). On December 13th, James Messenger began a week in his act of cannon ball and club juggling, and, doubtless very welcome, the amusing Carrolls (R. M., E. H. and Master Richard) appeared in Nonentities and also in The Italian Padrone. During the week of December 20th–25th, the Carrolls reverted to their popular The McFaddens. Others in that Christmas bill were Charles A. Loder, Lucy Adams, May Antonio (slack wire), J. M. Johnson (in his stump speech, Our Country), Awata Katsnoshin, and Rose Lisle (once, if briefly, at Wallack's) in The Circus Rider, supported by Farwell, Bailey, Richard Carroll, E. F. Sylvester, T. V. Watson, Dollie Thornton and Lucy Adams, the olio, as usual, coming bravely to the assistance of drama. The last week of the year (December 27th–January 1st) brought to our notice W. S. Higgins, in the drama, The Tramps. A feature of the bill was a bout between John McMahon ("champion of the world") and William Kennedy ("champion of Connecticut"), who strove to rate his native state above the habitable globe.

In January Aberle turned even more definitely toward dramatic ingredients. The week beginning on the 3rd offered an opening farce, The Nervous Clerk (with J. M. Johnson, Woods and Bailey), provided "turns" by the Millers and Fannie Bernard, and staged Mazeppa, with Maude Forrester and Harry F. Seymour (Abder Khan). Mamie Ogden (song and dance), Johnson, Fannie Bernard, Charles Diamond, and the Four Shamrocks (Dave Conroy, Matt Daly and the Webster Brothers) were but preliminary, in the week of January 10th–15th, to Ten Nights in a Bar-room (Seymour, Bailey, George W. Johnson, J. M. Johnson, Sylvester, Miss Bernard, Alice Carroll, and Mme. Odeon). On January 17th, Billy Bryant, Georgie Lingard and Sailor West subserved the interests of "Variety," and W. J. Thompson (with the dogs, Hero and Hector) ended the programme excitingly in For a Life, or, the Orphan's Trust. The week of January 24th–31st began with The Serpent's Sting, or 'Twixt Angel and Devil, provocative indeed, with George A. Hill as star; in the olio were Rita Keller (melodies), Andy and Annie Hughes (in Irish Servants), Arada Brothers ("direct from South America," in juggling, equilibrism, etc.), and Frank and Lillian White (in A Big Mis-

[321]

take). On January 31st, Rightmire once more returned in The Boss, or, Living for Vengeance, supported by most of the "Variety" performers recently mentioned. In the same bill Frank and Lillian White gave That Rascal Tom and Andy and Annie Hughes presented Norah's Birthday. Features for February 7th–12th were J. M. Johnson ("late of Johnson and Bruno"), Charles Redmond and Georgie Blake, Billy Devere and Bob Williams (in The Drum Major), and J. J. McCloskey's concluding play, High, Low, Jack and the Game, featuring J. Winston Murray. I do not know how the house dared so flagrantly to suggest Boucicault, in the offering of February 14th–19th — The Shaughaun, with John T. Hinds as Con Mc-Carthy and James O'Connell, the piper, and with Miss Ivian Lawrence as Mrs. McCarthy (Con's wife) and Marie Lismore; members of Aberle's force assisting were Seymour as Redmond O'Hara, of the Queen's Own; Mike Gallagher as Felix O'Flanagan, a broth of a boy, with songs; Ella Murphy as Nellie O'Toole; Sylvester as Lord Lismore; Bailey as Roger de Lacy, &c. Maude Forrester returned for the week of February 21st–26th, in Mazeppa; on the 24th, however, Lena Aberle took a benefit, enacting Camille (fourth act), with Winston Murray as Armand, and Seymour as de Varville.

Then the house went back to "Variety." Hasaboura (sic) Sam, Fields and Leslie, Nellie Parker, Wood and Beasley, Morris and Fields, Add Weaver, the Novelty Four (the Whitneys, Lizzie Hunter and Lester Howard), The Coloured Conductors (with Frank White and J. M. Johnson), Lottie Winnett, Lillian White, &c. were some of the entertainers in latest February or earlier March. The Staff of Diamonds ended the bills for February 28th–March 5th; the concluding melodrama for March 7th–12th was The Vision of Death, or, the Soldier's Dogs, acted by W. J. Thompson (with the dogs, Hero and Hector), J. Winston Murray, Ed H. Lay, Sylvester, Dollie Thornton and Frank and Lillian White. No "Variety" interfered with the unmitigated joys of March 14th–19th, when sole and singular in the field Around the World in Eighty Days presented George Metkiff as Phileas Fogg and Lena Aberle as Aouda. And the offering of March 21st–26th also was merely one play — the old One o'Clock, or, the Knight and the Wood Demon, the cast including Bailey, John C. Walsh, Neil Grey, A. Dumond, Marie Grandin, May Darling, Ada Forrester, Dollie Davenport, E. F. Sylvester, &c. Novissimo and Florence Barrett danced a ballet, Slave and Wood-Nymphs, and another ballet, likewise incidental to the piece, was entitled North American Indians. Beginning on March 28th, we had a week of The Three Guardsmen, starring W. J. Fleming. Is not this easy for my pen, devoted reader? For April 4th–9th, Larry Smith, John Burke, Jennie Engel, Dollie Davenport and George W. Callahan (ventriloquist) contributed to the olio, and Fanny Herring (alas! for her former glory) ended the bills with Little Buckshot, or, Brought to Light. W. J. Fleming was star of the following week, with Custer (April 11th, 12th and 13th), and The

[322]

Ticket of Leave Man (14th, 15th and 16th).   In the latter play, his Bob had the support of Lillian Drew as Sam, Ada Forrester as May, and Seymour as Hawkshaw.   On Saturday evening (the 16th), Fleming added to The Ticket of Leave Man a performance of Black-Eyed Susan (with himself and Ada Forrester).   Maggie Weston, fresh from "Variety," enacted, during the week of April 18th–23rd the eight characters of a protean part in D.D., or, Dora, the Detective.   Earlier in the evenings of that week "Prof." Chris Schiebel and Isabella Ward extracted operatic selections from thirty-seven pieces of wood — a feat suggestive of certain singers in opera; on April 25th, Fleming, Lena Aberle, May Seaton, Dollie Davenport, Grandin, &c. gave The White Crook — and never a suggestion of "Variety" in the bill.   To this paly Crook, during the next week (May 2nd–7th) Fleming joined The Lost Ship.   I also feel like a lost ship, seeking a path of fact as between the Ada Forrester of this paragraph and the Ada Forrest ante.

"Vaudeville," as later ages term it, had gone, temporarily, by the board. The Sea of Ice, under title of The Wild Flower of Mexico, or, a Thirst for Gold, filled the bills of May 9th–14th, with Fleming as Carlos, A. S. Caspar as Raoul, Miss Aberle as Louise and Ogarita, May Setoun (sic) as Diane, &c. Life in New York (really Falconer's version of Les Pauvres de Paris) had, on May 16th, Fleming as Tom Trumper.   Alice Adams, on the 23rd, began a week of Mazeppa; on the 25th, Jacob Aberle gave to himself a benefit. For the week of May 30th–June 4th, Mr. and Mrs. Harry Seymour appeared as, respectively, Quasimodo and Esmeralda, in Quasimodo, or, the Dancing Girl of Paris, with Caspar as Frollo and Allen Dumond as Phoebus.   Beginning on June 6th, we had a week of Joe Buckley, in The Crushed Tragedian, and E. T. Goodrich and Lena Aberle, in Grizzly Adams.

"Variety" seeped back into the bills for June 13th–18th, with Joe Buckley, Allen Dumond and May Seaton (in Don Pedro), Mons. Bushnell, Fannie Bernard, Morton and Bryant, Stella Newton, and Frank Bush (Hebrew act); C. L. Farwell ended the offering in Cartouche, or, the Highwayman of Paris. Levanion and McCormick joined the olio for June 20th–25th, and Kate D. Pell emerged in The Child Stealer.   Lily, or, California in '49, presented Lena Aberle as Gracie, the Lily of Poverty Flat, Farwell as Poor Joe Mercer and Harry Clifford as Tom Flynn, as concluding feature (June 27th–July 2nd) of a bill embracing, in olio, Joe Buckley, C. Burt Clark (of Clark and Edwards), Miss Jeffreys Warner, Ronaldo and Baldwin, and Georgie Lingard.

Billee the Tailor of course burlesqued the recent operetta success, Billee Taylor; it began the bills for July 4th–9th, which ended with W. S. Higgins in five characters, in Out of the Fire, with, in support, Farwell, G. W. and J. M. Johnson, Burt Clark, S. Swain (late of Sam and Carrie Swain), Larry Smith, Fannie Bernard and Lulu Delmay, most of whom had participated in a returning olio.   Newcomers in later July were John Pendy and Jeffreys

[323]

Warner (in Here and There), Frank M. Wills and Charles H. Sheffer (in Troublesome Sheriffs), the Devoy Sisters (Emma and Josie), Murphy and Miles (The Gentlemen from Kerry), Harry Irving, Minnie Farrell, the Four Luminaries (the Devoys, Larry Smith and John Burke), and the Four Shamrocks (Dave Conroy, Matt Daly, Mike Thompson and Joe Brock). Concluding plays were Just in Time (with W. J. Russell, Harry Le Clair and Lena Aberle, July 11th–16th), Out of the Dark (with E. T. Goodrich and Miss Aberle, July 18th–23rd), and Jack Harkaway (with Hernandez Foster, 25th–30th). The big feature of August 1st–6th was Long Branch, or, Five Millions of Money (with selections from La Mascotte, Billee Taylor, Olivette and Patience), acted by M. W. Fiske, G. W. Johnson, Ellsworth(?) Grandin, Farwell, Larry Smith, H. L. Bascombe, Rosa Lee, Kate Peabody and Mamie Wallace. For two weeks (August 8th–20th), Sights in New York City enlisted most of these actors, and a number of "Variety" persons in a minstrel scene; the "lightweights," Jerry Murphy and Jimmy Kelly, also gave a "grand assault at arms." The week of August 22nd–27th exhibited Joe Buckley (in The Coming Man), William and Claudia Ripley, William Johnson and Steve O'Sullivan (in wrestling), and W. J. Thompson and Lottie Forrest, and the dogs, Hero and Hector, in For a Life. So much for Aberle's New Theatre in its second season (1880–81). Despite my weary distaste for the epidemic "Variety," this season rather interests me.

VOLKSGARTEN, 1880–1881

According to a date written in on a playbill at Harvard, the Volksgarten began its fall and winter season on August 16th, 1880. Entertainers were William C. Cameron, Georgie Lingard, the three Milo Brothers, Howard and Sanford (a German team), Fanny V. Reynolds, Magee (late of Mullen and Magee) and Dan Tracy (late of Devlin and Tracy) in Men of Nerve, Add Weaver and Nellie Parker (in The Policeman's Troubles with a Bootblack), the three Lorellas, Wood and Beasley, &c. The farces were The Coming Man, and a concluding Come Down and We'll Make It Pleasant for You (this last with Larry Howard, Frank Sanford, and Lew E. and Mary Barker).

The floods of "Variety" inundated this Garden. Week by week the bills changed almost entirely, and I have space merely for the vast influx of latest August, of September and October; in order of appearance during the weeks involved, the hosts included William Devere, Al W. Decker, Lottie Grant, M. F. Drew (as Bob, the Bootblack, with negro songs, Dutch recitations, Irish song and dance, etc.), Frank E. McNish, accompanied by the Leland Sisters (in Stolen Fun), Paddy and Ella Murphy, Weston and Hanson, George Reynolds (formerly of Reynolds Brothers), Clooney and Ryan, Ed H. Banker, Florence Wells, Frank and Fannie (now sic) Davis (in The

[324]

Veteran), the Ripleys (William and Claudia), Saville and Byrne, the Maxwells (in Poverty *vs*. Wealth), William T. Dwyer (motto songs), Emma Rice, Jim O'Neil and Jack Conroy (in City Life), Fields and Leslie, Fannie Bernard, Frank Campbell and C. Burke (in Clippings), Alice Daily, the Grinnells (in Jack's Farewell to Polly), Ripley and Reed (a musical team), Fenton and Frain (English and Irish songsters), Daisy Norwood, Minnie Lawton, Sailor West, the Four Comets (Hawley, Manning and Cooper Brothers), May Arnott (in The Sculptor's Studio, or, Mephistopheles' Cabinet), the Gregory Brothers, Frank George (Irish comedian), the La Rues (John and Willie), Mullen and Cline (Muscle *vs*. Science), Bernard McCreedie, Charles Morgan and Harry Mullen (in The Irish Holiday), Lawrence Allen (songs and funny sayings), Ned Barry (motto), Georgie Lingard, the Hassons, Young Athol (boneless marvel — "first appearance in this city"), Favor and Shields, Larry Tooley, Mlle. Georgia ("woman with the iron jaw"), Minnie Clyde, Professor William Pillare (— *sic*, "real" cannon act), Fayette Welch (the "Hominy Man"), Frank Hennessey and Sallie Mason, Carrie Brower, Hennessey Brothers (song and dance), the three Mette Brothers, and Joe Norton.   If the reader's head is dizzy, so must have been that of the weekly visitor trying to catalogue the pleasures of the two early autumn months.   Few of these performers remained for more than a week; and, of course, there was practically a new concluding play for every week, in which visiting stars and members of the olio participated, along with a seemingly permanent stock company.   The week of August 23rd–28th presented George C. Charles and Kate Moffett, in Irish Assurance; on August 30th, Jerry Cohan came forth in The Molly Maguires, with Lottie Grant (not Mrs. Cohan) in chief support.   The week of September 6th–11th gave us Charles Thornton, in Simon Kenton, or, the Spirit of the Kanawha, Thornton beginning, on the 13th, a week of Tried for Treason, with Ben W. Brown, M. F. Drew, Charles Burke, Tom Maxwell, Sallie Mason, Emma Rice and Clara Maxwell in leading rôles.   Swift and Sure for two weeks (September 20th–October 2nd) ended the bills, with Minnie Oscar Gray as Ragged Nell of the Mines, W. T. Stephens as Percy Todd, and William H. Langdon as Walter Downing, gambler; prominent in the cast of leading characters were the dogs, Romeo, Zip and Hero.   The play for October 4th–9th was Wrestling Joe, or, Life in the Mines, with W. H. Langdon (in four parts), E. S. Goodwin and Sallie Mason; October 11th–16th spread shivers with The Skeleton Hand, acted by George C. Charles and the leaders of the olio.   The Black Hand, or, the Lost Will, gave us (October 18th–23rd) Frank Jones and Alice Montague.   Jones and Miss Montague, during the week of October 25th–30th, brought out a piece called The Creole Slave, very like The Octoroon, with themselves as Jonathan Cartwright, the Yankee overseer, and Eph, he, and as Creole Lulu, she; others were W. C. Cameron as Tecumseh, M. F. Drew as Richard Darke, and Hattie Richmond as Saul.

[325]

If the olio changed its personnel from week to week, the Volksgarten retained the stock actors who helped the stars of melodrama.

The olio for November and December presented in rapid procession Harry Fielding and Maggie Walker (in Mike's Fortune), Harry La Rose (clown gymnast), Ada Burnett, Gibson and Binney (double pedestal clog), John M. Turner ("classical solos on the banjo"), Frank Melrose (the one-legged gymnast), Jennie Southern, Lucy Adams and Guy Linton (in April Showers), J. L. Manning, Clooney and Ryan, Sharpley and West (in Music and Mirth), Jerry Kennedy and Ed Heeney (in O'Donoghue's Arrival), Emma Rice, Donnelly and Drew, Charles Allen and Joe Hart, Frank and Fannie Davis (in Fogarty's Night Out, or, in Love in Ireland), Minnie Lee, Paddy Murphy, Morton and Miles, Frank Lewis, Thompson (late of Howard and Thompson) and Brock (late of Webster Brothers), John H. Byrne and Major Burke, Charles and Annie Whiting (in The Music Teacher), Orndorff and McDonald, Harris and Wood (in Katie Grousemier — sic), Belle and Lillie La Verde, Sheldon and Barry (in Connolly's Troubles), Mackin and Bryant ("the Hibernian Twins"), Sage Richardson and Charles W. Young (in Fat and Thin), Charles H. Hoey (swinging and juggling), Paddy and Ella Murphy, Professor Lorento (The Devil's Doctor and Satan's Physician), Charles A. Pettit and James W. White (in Splinters), Campbell and Burke, John W. Gibbons (motto and comic songs), Clara Cushman, Watson and Levanion, Nellie Hague, the three Mette Brothers, Mlle. Carrie Voos, Howard and Coyne, Ward and Lynch, John F. Fenton, Charles Diamond, &c. And the concluding "thrillers"? Let us list them in order: Jerry and Helen F. Cohan (parents of George M. Cohan) in The Molly Maguires (week of November 1st–6th); Minnie Oscar Gray and W. T. Stephens, in Jack Sheppard and His Dogs (November 8th–13th); A Devil of a Scrape, or, Who Paid for the Supper? with Frank Lewis, Lucy Adams, and W. C. Cameron (November 15th–20th); Rose Lisle in Naomi, or, the Moonshiner's Daughter, with E. S. Goodwin, Irene Kerns, and Sallie Mason (November 22nd–27th); The '49ers, or, the Pioneer's Daughter, with T. W. Hanshew and Jennie McClellan (November 29th–December 4th); Hanshew and Norbert Malger, in Tiger Hunter, or, Back from Death, a romance of the Mexican War (December 6th–11th); Faith, or, a Daughter's Wrongs, with Mabel Florence, Ward L. Horton and Harry Lloyd (13th–18th); Lillian Drew, E. S. Goodwin, &c. in Caught at Last (20th–25th); and Through by Daylight (by J. J. McCloskey), with Russell Bassett as George Glenroy, assisted by Goodwin, M. F. Drew, Thomas H. Ward, W. C. Cameron, Sallie Mason, Lillian Drew, Ella Murphy, Carrie Lewis, Joseph Pell, and James Lewis — names that I cite merely to convince the reader that the "stock" remained firm, though the olio shifted almost from week to week. Trying to bring order out of the chaos of names exhausts me.

January began (3rd–8th) with George Kurtz and Nellie Brooks (in

Booked), Sam Martin ("performing more with one leg than other artists do with two"), J. W. Mack (formerly of Sheridan and Mack) and Ada Boshell (Mrs. Mack) in character changes, Dick Gorman, three St. Felix Sisters, Andrew Gaffney (performer with cannon balls), and Joseph H. Keane in Rip Van Winkle.   In later January we had Donnelly and Drew, Minnie Farrell, the popular Fred Hallen and Enid Hart (in The Pirates of Pinafore), the Lamartine Brothers, W. J. Fleming (ending the bills of January 10th–15th, with his gory play, Custer, the interesting cast of which included Drew, W. C. Cameron, Hallen, Dick Gorman, F. J. Post, Ada Boshell, Enid Hart, Joe Donnelly, Goodwin (as Sitting Bull) and J. W. Mack); Charles A. Loder, Guy Linton, Sam Holdsworth, the Hull Twin Sisters (Emma and Effie — sketch artists), Tom and Maud Morrissey, May Antonio ("queen of the aerial slack wire"), Julian Kent, in Wild Bill, King of the Border Men — all these for the 17th–22nd; the Dutch Mendels (Harry and Leonie, in Going to Germany), Carrie Boshell, Charles Redmond and Georgie Blake, the Morello Brothers (Max and Will), the Lorellas (William, John and Thomas — legerdemain, grotesque dancers, "the only successors of the Majiltons"), and Charles Thornton (January 24th–29th), ending the bills shiveringly with The Headless Horseman, or, the Trail of the Lasso, "a Mystery of the Texas Plains," in which the olio bravely shared to the top of its dramatic ability.   The week of January 31st–February 5th gave A Connubial Dilemma (by the regular stock actors), Fannie (sic) V. Reynolds, Sailor West, the Brennans and Captain Laible (in Double Tonguing), and Charles Thornton in F. D. Skiff's play, Simon Kenton, seen this year also at Aberle's.

February ran with bright array of talent: the Brennans, with Captain Laible (in Trifles, or, Fun in the Parlour), Harry Lloyd ("young motto and topical vocalist"), George Derious (balancer — "stands eight minutes with his head downwards"), Fannie (sic) Reynolds, the La Rues (John and Willie), the Jeromes (Charles and Ella), the acrobatic Ripleys (William and Claudia), Lizzie Derious (operatic songs), the play of Conrad, or, the Hand of a Friend (week of February 7th–12th, with Dick Gorman, Drew, &c.), Frank Budworth (in A Visit South), James Gilson and James Welch (breakneck specialties), Lucy Adams, Leonard and Jones (clog and reels), Lillie and Belle La Verde, Murray, Snow and Runnells ("Kings of the Carpet"), Frank Jones and Alice Montague, in On the Brink, or, the Creole Slave (returning February 14th–19th), Harris and Wood (California team), Mealey and Mackey (Irish), Fanny Davenport (baritone-contralto), Charles Diamond, T. W. Hanshew in The '49ers (February 21st–26th), Levi's Arrival (with Micky Thompson, E. S. Goodwin, Ned Howard, Sallie Mason, Cora Everett), Minnie Clyde, the Ross Sisters (Emma and Ida), the Mette Brothers, Williams and Sully (in Our Wedding Day), Howard and Thompson ("Celtic Kings"), Gus Hill and Hanshew, with Helen Adell, W. D.

[327]

Chalpin, Post, Sallie Mason, &c. in Lucretia Borgia — this poisonous thriller to end the bills of February 28th–March 5th.

Features of later March olio were George Kurtz and Nellie Brooks (in The Soldier's Orphan Child, and, later, in Booked), Maude Leigh, the St. Felix Sisters (in A Rehearsal in the Woods), Lucy Adams, Harry Woodson (The Happy Southern Negro), the two Wesleys, Minnie Clyde, Harry Lloyd, Charles Saville and Ben Bennett (in Our Southern Home), W. C. Cameron (in Bibbs and Bibbs), Housabura (sic) Sam, the Garnellas, Charles McCarthy and George W. Monroe (in Grogan's Chinese Laundry), J. D. Roome, Howard and Sanford, Miss Earle Remington, William E. Hines and Nat Blossom (in T.T.T.), Sailor West and Gus Hill. Concluding plays were Rip Van Winkle, with Joseph H. Keane (March 14th–19th); Solon Shingle, also with Keane (21st–26th); and The Two Wanderers (March 28th–April 2nd), with W. H. Rightmire, Cameron, Minnie Clyde, Chalfin, E. S. Goodwin, Sallie Mason, Earle Remington, &c.

April blessings were plentiful, with George W. Woods, John H. Mack (banjo), the Hayles (William and Lou), William Gaylord (equilibrist), Harry Lloyd, Sheehan and Coyne (in An Everyday Occurrence), Hanshew and Jennie McClellan (in Lucretia Borgia, April 4th–9th); Kitty and the Baby (with Fayette Welch, Goodwin, Harry Lloyd and Minnie Clyde), Nellie Germon (in New Year's Day), Zegrino and Moulton (gymnasts), Charles L. Banks ("will make a few unnecessary remarks"), Williams and Sully, Lizzie Mulvey and Barney Fagan, and W. H. Langdon, in Foiled (11th–16th); Harry and Minnie Wood (in Going to the Picnic), Ned West (black face), Allie Drayton, the Martell (sic) Brothers, Lou Vavasour, the Leonzo Brothers, and the dogs, Tiger and Lion, in Avenged, or, the Dogs of the Sierras (18th–23rd), Sage Richardson (in The Clockmaker's Hat), Ada Forrest, Joe Redmond and Ada Clifton (parlour sketches), the Four Planets (McDermott, Sheehan, Kennedy and Clark — in Danger Alley Ball), Gus H. Saville and John H. Byrne (in The College of Music), Sage Richardson and Charles W. Young (in Fat and Thin), and the Leonzo Brothers and their canine cast and others in The Dog Spy (April 25th–30th). And May also bloomed luxuriantly in the parterres, with a succession of entertainers including the Hogan Brothers (Harry and Gus, in Happy Boys from Borneo), Dollie Davenport, Coleman and McCarthy, Kitty Sheppard, Cogill Brothers (Charles W. and Harry P., in Chit Chat), Fanny (sic) V. Reynolds, Matt Green and Dick Rowe ("crême de la crême of all contortionists"), George C. Charles and Katie Moffett, in the four-act thriller, The Skeleton Witness (May 2nd–7th), James Brevarde, Charles Sawtelle and W. S. Gilmore (in Animal Education), Harry Mullen and Minnie Chapin (in Love in Irish), Lucy Adams, the Four Diamonds (G. W. Watson, W. S. Gilmore, Brevarde and Sawtelle), Yank Adams ("greatest of all living billiardists"), Adelina and Ida Gasparini, in the concluding drama, Meg

(May 9th–14th), the Great Thorn (prestidigitateur), Carrie Boshell (song and dance), Campbell and Burke (lightning changes), Harry Lloyd, John Pendy and Jeffreys Warner (in The Wrong Man in the Right Place), Clooney and Ryan, Fanny Herring in Jack Sheppard (May 23rd–28th) and in Little Buckshot (May 30th–June 4th), Harry Mullen, Matt McCormick, the Russell Brothers, Campbell and Burke, Minnie Chapin, Levanion and Matt McCormick, &c. Roses of June included Magee ("late of the Four Emeralds") and Taylor ("late of Taylor and Powers," in Contrasts), Carrie Davenport ("champion club swinger of the world"), Dick Gorman, Lucy Adams, Martell Brothers (acrobats), Nellie St. John, the Two Wesleys, Fred Roberts, W. C. Cameron (as Toodles) — these for the 6th–11th; Dan Tracy and Will Goldsmith (Irish song and dance), Fred Hallen and Enid Hart (in Billy, the Taylor), T. W. Hanshew and Jennie McClellan (in Lucretia Borgia or in The '49ers — week of June 13th–18th), The Illicit Distillery (with Goodwin and Harry Lloyd), Fanny Davenport ("the peerless descriptive and bravoura singer"), Lizzie Daly (clog, jig, reel), the Olympia Quartette (Mack, Sullivan, Keough and Randalls, in Gip Liza), Williams and Sully, Rightmire, in The Boss (June 20th–25th); the Johnsons (Virgie and Arthur, in All-of-It), Charles Glidden (banjo), the Four Emeralds (Gibbons, Russell, Conway and Kennedy), and Black-Eyed Susan (Chalfin and Cameron), &c. — these in the week of June 27th–July 2nd.

The week of July 4th–11th gave us The Wrong Man (with Thomas H. Ward, Con Lynch and Goodwin), Lucy Adams, the Jeromes (Charles and Ella), Carroll and Walters (in In and Out), Gus Hill, John H. Fenton ("champion dancer of the World"), the Martells (bicycle performers and acrobats), and the farce of Turn Him Out. On Monday, July 11th, W. C. Cameron took a benefit. Later July performers were Lizzie Conway, Max and Martha Miller, the Carrolls (in The McFaddens and in The Italian Padrone), Pollie Dale, Magee and Taylor, and Kate Montrose. Harvard has but one bill for August; under date of the 23rd it lists Frank and Fannie Davis (in The Veteran), the Winnetts (Thomas and Lottie, in Found at Last), Kitty Sheppard, Delvan and Tracy ("the Irish Lords"), Billy and Nola Forrest (acrobatic clog), the La Porte Sisters, and T. W. Hanshew, in The Marble Heart. From the Staats-Zeitung of mid-August I learn that the house, refurbished to the tune of $5,000, re-opened at that time with Alice France Adams and her horse, Sensation, in Mazeppa. In the olio were the Maxwells, Daisy Norwood, Mullen and Miles, the De Bar Brothers, Lucy Adams, &c. Perhaps I might include here the bill for Thursday, September 1st — Dick Morosco and Kitty Gardner, Fanny Sandford, J. J. Mullen and Kitty Mills ("Irish"), Daisy Norwood, Clara and Thomas Maxwell (in The Jolly Old Couple), Joseph H. Brindis ("Cuban violin virtuoso, the second Ole Bull"), and Hanshew, in The '49ers. Thus we leave the Volksgarten for 1880–81.

[329]

NATIONAL THEATRE, 1880–1881

In October, 1880, were appearing at one time or another at the National Theatre, Bowery, Carrie Brower (serio-comic), De Witt Cooke (juggling three clubs at the same time), Tom and Clara Maxwell (in Poverty *vs.* Wealth), the Martells ("parlour gymnasts"), the Moore Sisters (Laura and Eunice), Ned Barry ("greatest of all motto vocalists"), Campbell and Burke, Kitty O'Neil, Emerson, Clark and the Daly Brothers, and, in farces, Ben Brown, Bobby Johnson, and W. T. Dulaney; also, Minnie Chapin (Irish ballads), Harry Fielding and Maggie Walker (in Back to Erin), William and Lou Hayle (clog), Billy Devere and Bobby Williams, Scott Hanley (wire-walker on stilts sixteen inches high), Tom Sayers (only son of the famous fighter), Barney Ferguson and Dick Mack, Larry Howard and Frank Sanford (*sic*), the Zanfrettas (Alexander, Tom, Leo and Flora, with George Kane, in The Skeleton Witness, Vol-au-Vent, etc.), Gibson and Binney, Everett and Daly (in Mixtures), the Hassons, William Bryant and Lizzie Richmond (in Opera Buffers), the Peasleys (in Mollie's Victory), C. J. Gregory (dancing barrel, cross and electric tables), Belle La Verde and Fannie Bernard.

Newcomers in November were Fayette Welch, Jennie Southern, Watson and Levanion, Ed Banker, J. L. Manning (in Silly Bill and Old Aunt Sally), James O'Neil and John Conroy (the Jolly Irish Sports, in City Life), Florence Wells (society sketches), Ten American Students, Fanny Herring (in Daring Dick, the King of Highwaymen — November 8th–13th), Katie Foley's Birthday Party (with Ed Howard, M. T. Coyne, Dave Posner, Virgie Johnson), Ned Barry, Eugene Blitz, the Hull Twin Sisters, The White Statue (with Billy Devere, Ben Brown, W. T. Dulaney, &c.), Going to the Races (with James Tighe, Minnie Clyde and Devere), the Rice Brothers (as Roman Gladiators), Parker's Dog Circus, the French Twin Sisters, the Four Italians (Fayette Welch, George Meagill, Brown, &c.), Kelly and Ryan, Fanny Herring in The French Spy (for two weeks — November 15th–27th), Bob and Alice Daily, Niles and Evans, C. E. Johnson, School (with Fayette Welch, E. W. Marston, &c.). In December Georgie Lingard joined, as did Lucy Adams and Guy Linton (in April Showers, or, Katy Did), Master Charles Lovenberg, John T. Kelly, Thomas J. Ryan and James Tighe (in Senator McFee), Julian Kent (in Wild Bill, week of November 29th–December 4th), Don Ferreyra, Andy and Annie Hughes, Eurardo, Charles E. Emmett (*sic* — with Alice Placide, in Dashing Charlie — week of December 6th–11th), George Kurtz, Kitty Sharpe, Nellie Brooks, the three Gorman Brothers, Bernard McCreedie (in Transmagnificandubandanciality — *sic*), Fritz and Robinson (gymnasts), Ajax, Johnny Allen, Burt Queen and Kitty McDermott, the Jaspers (Thomas and Clinton), Ada Forrest, Harry Lamonto and Archie Baldwin (in The Happy Hottentots), &c. Plays of later December were Moll Pitcher, or, the Fortune Teller of Lynn (December 13th–18th), with Alice Placide, C. E. Emmett (*sic*), E. W. Marston, and members of the olio; and Cigarette, the Little Leopard of France (December 20th–25th), with Amy Stone in three characters.

January gave us two weeks (3rd–15th) of the German Charles Konollman in farces, along with Nellie Hague, Charles and Annie Whiting (in The Music Teacher), Kelly and Ryan ("the Bards of Tara," in Senator McFee), Houssabura (*sic*) Sam, Campbell and Burke, Minnie Clyde, E. W. Marston as Solon Shingle, Nellie Brooks, Annie Hindle, Hearts of Steel (January 10th–15th, with W. T. Dulaney, E. W. Marston, Tighe, Minnie Clyde, Nellie Brooks, Sadie Dulaney, and Nellie Hague), Lew Barker, Ada Lanier, Ernest (or Earnest) and Healey (vocalists and banjoists), Morello Brothers, Frank Jones and Alice Montague (in The Black Hand, 17th–22nd, and also in On the Brink, or, the Creole Slave, 24th–29th), Max and Martha Miller, Foster and Hughes, the three Vidocqs (John, William and Jacques), Dick Sands, Bernard Sloman, the O'Brien Brothers, Daisy Remington, Hines and Blossom, Red de Jalma (fire king), E. W. Marston (in The Jolly Cobbler), and the Leonzo Brothers, in Avenged, or, Dogs of the Sierras (January 31st–February 5th). The next week (February 7th–12th) carried on the Leonzo thrills in The Dog Spy, and began the evening's diversion with Did You Ever Send Your Wife to Brooklyn? The Hull Twins, the Four Planets (McDermott, Sheehan, Kennedy and Clark), Ajax, Bobby and Alice Daily (in May and December) and Tom Sayers were also in the interesting programme. Other February specialties included He Would Be a Doctor (with J. M. Johnson, Ben Brown and L. E. Barker), Charles Redmond and Georgie Blake, "Professor" Phillion (illusionist), Carroll and Walters, the Leotards, the play of The Workingman's Strike (with a telegraph scene, and acted, February 14th–19th, by Marston, Dulaney, Tighe, L. E. Barker, Maggie Ferris and Emma Phillion), Cupid's Frolics (with Ben Brown, Redmond and Georgie Blake), the La Rues, Sailor West, Nettie Carlyn, Emma Phillion ("aerial"), and Julian Kent (in Wild Bill — February 21st–26th). Zoe Gayton appeared (with her horse, Fearless), on March 7th–12th, as Mazeppa; in the olio were Ben Brown, Emma Hoffman, Al and Charles Thompson, the Megatherian Four (Kelly, Gibbs, Lyons and Leary), the Ripleys, Landis and Steele, and Fred Roberts. Miss Gayton's Mazeppa endured a second week (March 14th–19th), with Tobin and Reed, Louis and Emma Alfredo, Dick Sands, Emma Hoffman, J. H. Graham, the Virginia Trio (Turner, Welch and Harris), and Jennie Ward attending to the duties of the olio. The last days of March provided Donnelly and Drew, Tommy Harpin, Hallen and Hart (always welcome), Gus Hart, the Virginia Trio, Pauline Batchellor, Sailor West, the Carroll Brothers (as the Merry Clowns), Ford and Knowles, Laura Russell and D. B. Emery, Lizzie Derious, Lucy Adams, Dan Tracy and Will Goldsmith ("late Devlin and Tracy"), and

[331]

Frank Bush. The week of March 21st–26th ended its bills with Uncle Tom's Cabin (Little Gertie as Eva, Dot Aborn as Topsy, W. T. Dulaney as Uncle Tom, and Marston as Phineas Fletcher); the concluding play for March 28th–April 2nd was the deceiving The Shaughaun, acted by John T. Hinds and Miss Ivian Lawrence — an offering not unknown to our pen. It is to be hoped the reader will distinguish it from The Shaughraun of Boucicault.

The Harvard files provide full measure for showery April. The week of the 4th–9th is interesting for the appearance of J. J. Wallace as Bob Gilstone and Frisco Bob, in Wallace's own "typical American drama," Destroying Angels; his support included Dulaney as Tom Blanchard, outlaw of the Sierras, Marston as Sut Fungus, Harry Cogill as Red Dick, Laura Russell as Betty Suret, and Maggie Ferris as Rose Harland. The olio for that week presented Pendy and Jeffreys Warner, Morton and Miles, the Cogill Brothers (C. W. and H. P.), D. B. Emery and Laura Russell, and Ada Forrest. Newcomers, later in the month, were John B. Wills and May Adams, Coleman and McCarthy, Minnie Farrell, Edwards and Gaylor, the Monumental Quartette (Hammond, Earle, Hawley and West), Eurardo, John T. Hinds (as Rip Van Winkle — April 11th–16th), Charles A. Saville and Ben Bennett, with James Tighe (The Three Hunters), the Hayles (in Fun on the Farm), the Winnetts (George and Lottie, in Love in Broken German), the Four-in-Hand (Mayo, Talbert, Sullivan and Smith), the Two Barneys (Barney McNulty and Master Barney), Joseph P. Winter (in Dan'l Boone, April 18th–23rd), Emma Hoffman, Minnie Lee, the Novelty Four (John and Emma Whitney and Charles and Ella Jerome, in Rehearsal in the Parlour), and Julian Kent, in Wild Bill, King of the Border Men (week of April 25th–30th).

The bills for May 2nd–7th began with Lolly Pop, the Brave (Ben Brown, W. Brazzier, C. Talbert and Martha Miller), proceeded to an olio including the Six American Students, in reels and jigs, Emma Hoffman, the Original Little Four (Talbert, Owens and the Carroll Brothers, in The Coloured Party and The Burlesque Circus), Max and Martha Miller, the Two Brazziers, the Martell Brothers (Harry and William), Campbell and Burke, and Minnie Lee, and closed with The Ticket of Leave Man (Joseph P. Winter as Bob, Mlle. Sylvia as May, Tighe as Hawkshaw and Dulany as Dalton). In later May, we endured the treat of the Great Thorn ("royal illusionist"), Great Nonpareil Coloured Troubadours (Mme. J. M. Zara, W. A. Fernandez, Miss C. C. Thomas) and Frank Jones and Alice Montague (in The Black Hand, or, the Lost Will — May 9th–14th, and in On the Brink, May 16th–21st), the De Bar Brothers, May Arnott, Saville and Byrne (sic), Fernando Fleury, Tom Sayers, Mad Life (with Mons. Ventini, Bessie Randolph, Ben Brown and Maggie Ferris — May 23rd–28th), Nellie Amon ("operatic gems"), Fred Sharpley and Charles West (in Smiles), Ventini and Bessie Randolph ("champion hat spinners"), Alice Bateman and Willis

[332]

Pickert, the Garretta Troupe, the Leonzos and Tiger (in Avenged, May 23rd–28th, and in The Dog Spy, May 30th–June 4th), Old Mother Fussy (May 30th–June 4th, with John Denier as Africanus, the Ape), Polly Dale (songs), the Two Wesleys, the Hermans (La Rose and Charles), Nellie Amon, and the Big Four (W. H. Smith, Dan Waldron, Tim Cronin and Master Martin). This quartette gave, for the week of June 6th–11th, Justice pro Tem; others in the bill were Ada Lanier, Punch Walton, John McVeigh and Kate Montrose (Spirits Frumenti), Parker and his dogs, Gallagher and Mack, and Frank Doud (in Buffalo Bill, the Monarch of the Plains, with Marston as Snake-Root Sam). Verily attendants at these Bowery houses masticated life in the raw.

N. S. Wood was here for two weeks, ending the bills for the week of June 20th–25th with The Boy Detective, and those of June 27th–July 2nd with The Boy Scout of the Saharas (Sierras?); in the latter piece he employed the steeds, Hassan and Abdallah. Other features of that fortnight were Grimaldi Zeltner and Charles Chrisdie as Jacques Strop and Robert Macaire (first week) and in The Brigand's Doom (for the second); also the Grinnells, the Hogan Brothers, Frank M. Wills and Charles H. Sheffer (in That Troublesome Sheriff), the Four Emeralds (Gibbons, Russell, Conway and Kennedy), Grace Burton, John F. Fenton, Sheehan and Coyne (in An Everyday Occurrence), Luigi dell'Oro, the Four Planets, and the Great Nonpareil Coloured Troubadours. The holiday week of July 4th–9th presented The Stratagem (with Larry Tooley, Ben Brown and Carrie Brower), Varney and De Bar (acrobats), Minnie Hall (songs), Barney Reynolds (of Reynolds and Walling) and Jennie Miaco (in The Old Arm Chair), the Four Diamonds (Watson, Gilmore, Brevarde and Sawtelle), and Leonzo in his popular play, Avenged. Next week (July 11th–16th) Bud and Annie Granger, Alfred Liston, Frank Campbell (late of Campbell and Burke), the Four Comets, Dan Williams and Joe Morton, the Martell Brothers, and the Leonzos in The Dog Spy made a pretty feast for perspiring customers. July 18th began a week of Hob-be-de-Hoy (with Zeltner, Chrisdie and Annie Howard) and, in the olio, Edna Markley, the Big Four (Billy Smith, Dan Waldron, Saville and Bryant), Morton and Bryant, Alma Curry ("aerial"), and N. S. Wood, with J. P. Winter and Kate Estelle, in Life and Adventures of Jack Sheppard. At the beginning of August (1st–6th), Ada Forrest, D. B. Emery and Laura Russell, Herr Otto von Brandesky (vocal and terpsichorean), Gus Hill ("the greatest club swinger and juggler"), and N. S. Wood (in The Boy Detective) appealed to tastes not too delicately refined. The Harvard file misses two mid-weeks in August, and lets us out of the National in the week of August 29th–September 3rd, with an olio comprising Kate Montrose and John McVeigh (in Spirits Frumenti), Fannie (sic) V. Reynolds, Harry Leslie, the Weaver Brothers, the Grinnells, Master Roberts, the Four Diamonds (Watson, Gilmore, Sawtelle and Brevarde), Isabel

[333]

Ward, and Joseph H. Keane and Kate Estelle (in Rip Van Winkle). The National seems to me to lack a kind of distinction in "Variety."

NOVELTY THEATRE (BOWERY GARDEN), 1880–1881

The Bowery Garden (113 and 113½ Bowery) had several names in the season we are now reviewing. As the Novelty Theatre it presented in earliest August the farce, Uproar in the Family (with T. F. Thomas, Heeney, Maggie Walker, and Ed Mills), Little Todd (set down as "making" his first appearance in this country, in his act, The Pillar of Gold), Sallie Mason and Rob V. Ferguson (in Masquerading), Harry Fielding and Maggie Walker (in Back to Erin), the Original Four Diamonds (Clark, Watson, Brevarde and Sawtelle), Thomas and Heeney (in Modern Actors), the three Brazziers (William, George and Rufus — "dancing, apparition-like dervishes — mystic and eccentric gyrations — they seem like animated shadows"), Keating and Sands (in The Tenants), Cronin and Sullivan (in Life in a Tenement House) and a final Humpty's Frolics (with the Brazziers, Brevarde, Charley Sawtelle, &c.). Later in August we might have revelled in the antics or the comic ebullience of Everett and Daly (contortion and acrobatic song and dance — The Happy Hottentots), Charles Redmond and Georgie Blake (Irish songs and dances), Billy Devere, Campbell and Burke, the Big Four (Smith, Waldron, Cronin and Martin), Sallie Mason and R. V. Ferguson (in Man and Wife), Ollie Audley ("champion jig dancer"), John B. Wills and May Adams (in Larks), Thompson and Waldron, Hawley and Manning, the Carrolls (in The Masquerade and Peel Yourself), Dick Rowe, Frank Bennett and Lydia Gardiner (in Kitchen Domestics), and various sketches by the performers I have cited. John Schroder was proprietor of the resort, and Billy Devere business manager. Perhaps Lydia Gardiner was Lida Gardner.

September — a crowded month — brought in its golden course a huge array of players and farces: Fanny Sandford, the La Rues, Levanion and La Rosa (ring performers), Gibson and West (acrobatic song and dance — "first appearance in New York"), Harry Mills ("Teutonic celebrity"), Landis and Steele ("the two icicles"), the Olympia Quartette (Hugh Mack, M. J. Sullivan, William Keough, and Peter Randalls), Matt Green, Frank Bush, A Slippery Day, Harry Franklin (as Cupid, in The Fellow that Looks like Me), Sara Beryl (London change artist), Charles and Annie Whiting (in The Music Teacher), the Four Star Grotesques (Seamon, Somers, and the Girard Brothers), Laura Russell and D. B. Emery (duets on silver bells and cornets), the Franklins (Rose and Harry, in Fighting for a Wife), the American Four (Pettingill, Gale, Dailey and Hoey — a big attraction, in Our Boys, etc.), Sim Dipsey (with Charles Seamon), Larry Howard and Frank Sanford (German team), Kate Montrose, Ada Lanier (serio-comic),

[334]

Lottie and George Winnett (in Love in Broken German), the Sheehan Brothers (Dan and John, in The Longshoremen), the Three Grotesques (Seaman, Somers and Eddie Girard, Ethiopian song and dance), Billy Lester and Paul Allen (in Nonsense), the American Four (Joe Pettingill, Pete Gale, James Hoey and Pete Dailey — in Blue Glass), John McVeigh, George Campbell, Joe Hart, Charles Allen (these four in Too Many Visitors), William and Claudia Ripley ("carpet athletes and acrobats"), Mary Rice (serio-comic), Lucy Adams and Guy Linton, Frank Jones and Alice Montague (in Music and Notions, they using various instruments), J. H. Graham (electric transformation vocalist), Charles Allen and Joe Hart (banjo, etc.), Frank George (Irish), the American Four (in Looking for Dates), Reynolds and Walling, Mlle. Georgia ("the woman with the iron jaw"), and "Professor" William Pillare (*sic*).

The talented and popular American Four remained (October 4th–9th) in School, other entertainers of that week including Kitty Gardner, Mary Antonio (hoop bell dance), Saville and Byrne (in College of Music), John M. Turner (banjo), Dick Gorman, the Carrolls (in The McFaddens), Joseph Donnelly and James Drew (in John and Ellen Magee), Ernest Haven ("from the Conquest Troupe, late at Wallack's"), Frank Lewis ("first appearance in this city for three years"), &c. Later in the month came, progressively, Nellie Hague ("the only lady baritone on the American stage"), the Hogan Brothers (in The Hottentots), Murphy and Shannon (in Bound for Germany), Andy Butler (Hebrew impersonator), Murphy and Mack (in Our Irish Flats), Bernard McCreedie ("primogenial Musical Phenomenon and Symphonium Wonder"), the Carrolls (in The Masquerade and Peel Yourself), Murphy's Dream (with the very popular Murphy and Mack and Murphy and Shannon — this for October 11th–16th), William E. Hines and Nat Blossom (in Manœuvring), Dan Nash (in The Irish Schoolmaster), John Carroll ("musical wonder"), May and Charles Diamond, Fields and Leslie (Irish character changes), Murphy and Mack (in The McMullen Family), Murphy and Shannon (in Just from Germany), and these four — Murphy and Mack and Murphy and Shannon in The Rivals (October 18th–23rd). The same inimitable four gave us next week (October 25th–30th) The Christening; Murphy and Shannon also presented Turning the Tables, and Murphy and Mack appeared in O'Shaughnessy Guards. Others in that last week of October were Weston (late of Weston and Woods) and Hanson (in So You Say), Pat Doody ("youthful prodigy"), John Walsh ("greatest living patriotic singer"), the Four Grotesques (Seamon, Somers and the Girard Brothers), John Hogan and Lizzie Mowbray (in Mixed), the Thompson Brothers (Irish song and dance), and John McVeigh and Kate Montrose. If the reader thinks "Variety" very monotonous, I agree with him. The Bowery Garden (or Novelty) was charging, at this time, 15 cents admission, 20 cents for balcony chairs, 25 cents for orchestra chairs, $3 for lower boxes, and $2 for upper boxes; seats in the upper boxes were held at 50 cents, and 10 cents admitted to the boys' gallery. One could not expect much, at that rate.

The week of November 1st–6th began with the Arrival of Nielson (Nilsson? or Neilson? played by James Dalton, McVeigh, Ed Mills and Kate Montrose) and followed with Boyd and Sarsfield, Clara Wagner (Clockworking jig), Mickey Thompson (Hebrew), James Dalton (as the aged darkey, in Funny Old Man Essence), Charley Shay ("juggler, sorcerer, necromancer and equilibrist"), the Four Shamrocks (Dave Conroy, Matt Daly and the Webster Brothers), the three Vidocqs ("contortionists from the Folies Bergère"), and ended with Who's the Candidate? played by the Shamrocks. November went on and out with a procession composed of the above, Ripley and Reed (musical team), Fenton and Fraine (— sic, "first appearance in New York" — English and Irish songsters), Apple and Willis (Hebrew specialties), Dan and Gussie Hart (in Uncle Pete's Return, she changing in ten seconds from white face to black), the popular American Four (returning, on November 8th, in Blue Glass), McVeigh and Kate Montrose (in Spirits Frumenti), Minnie Farrell, Young Ajax ("gymnastic wonder of the world"), Emma Rice ("petite stature, beautiful face and style — queen of serio-comics"), Ella Loyal ("walking in mid air on an ordinary piano string, and a great dive for life from the dome of the theatre to a net below"), Martha and Max Miller (in their German sketch, Going to the Picnic), the Weston Brothers (Sam and Morris, in Going to Join the Minstrels), Master Clifton (Irish specialty), George Vance (motto singer), Clooney and Ryan (German team), the Loyals (Ella, Victoria and George, on the trapeze), The Surprise Party (with Jerry Kennedy, Ed Heeney and Emma Rice) — all this to November 27th. The week of November 29th–December 4th began its bills poetically, with Verona Carroll ("bird of beauty, in her wonderful double voice, baritone and soprano"); other newcomers were the Lamartine Brothers ("Classical Parlour Entertainments of grace, strength and muscular developments"), Sage Richardson and Charles W. Young (Fat and Thin), Paracletes (with McVeigh and Kate Montrose), Alice Bateman and Willis Pickert, Frank Lewis (returning) and The Enamelled Face (with Sage Richardson, Young, &c.).

And December, with its wintry blasts? The week of December 6th–11th presented Billy Devere and Bobby Williams (in Family Troubles), Saville and Bennett (in Our Southern Home), the Loyals, Kerrigan and McCarthy ("the Boys from Longford, Ireland"), and W. J. Lawrence (in Life in New York — from Les Pauvres de Paris, with himself as Tom Trumper). Harvard has but one other December bill — that for December 20th–25th, the Christmas joys including Etta Morris, King Sarbro, Saville and Bennett, the Big Four (Smith, Dan Waldron, Tim Cronin and Master Martin, in The Freshman Class), and Joseph P. Winter (in Daniel Boone, assisted by

[336]

Charles Saville, Harry Lavernia, Fred Arlington, W. Donaldson, Ed Mills, Bobby Williams, May Preston, and Hannah Birch).   The Novelty was now, like other "Variety Halls," ending its programmes with a melodrama, or a drama of some sort and length.   The play of that function, for January 10th–15th, was The Chain of Guilt, or, a Life's Revenge, with Charles E. Emmett (*sic* — Dashing Charlie), as Ralph Raynor and Long Jim.   For January 17th–22nd, however, H. J. Campbell appeared as General Boum in some kind of version of The Little Dutchess (from Offenbach), Mlle. Lucille enacting the title-rôle, with C. Saville as Baron Puck, Ben Bennett as Fritz, and Hannah Birch as Wanda.   January 24th began a week of The New York Newsboy (with Lucille Campbell and Harry J. Campbell).   And the week of January 31st–February 5th ended the evening's delights with The Princess Tott (Lucille Campbell and Harry J. Campbell in the lead). I hope the reader finds this interesting.

Meantime I go back for the olio of those bright weeks: James O'Neil and John Conroy, Nettie Carlyn ("queen of song"), Andrew Gaffney ("finest cannon ball performer in America"), George Ellsworth (performance with musket and bayonet), Red de Jalma ("King of all Fire Kings and Human Salamander"), Professor L. Quadinfield (in parlour rifle shooting, assisted by Carrie Stuvers), Humpty Dumpty (with John and Connie Denier — January 17th–22nd), Mickey Thompson and Joe Brock (dialect artists), C. Saville (motto songs), John Denier (stilt act), Joe Redmond and Ada Clifton (in Parlour Sketches), Fayette Welch's Male and Female Minstrels (January 24th–29th, with Welch, H. J. Campbell, J. D. Roome, Maggie Murray, Maud Webber, &c.), the Monumental Quartette (Hammond, Earle, Hawley and West), Millie Malburg and Rosa Blair (duets), Ada Boshell and J. W. Mack (Irish and German Lovers), J. W. Boyle (song and dance), Clooney and Ryan, Harry W. Lederer ("the world's greatest rifle shot")— surely a list to excite orchestra sitters (at 25 cents a night) and boys' gallery (at 10 cents a treat).

Harvard owns for February only the bill for the week of the 14th–19th; it begins with Ventini and Bessie Randolph (in Bobby Bowlegs), provides an olio with Houssabura Sam ("the glory of Japan"), Alfred Liston, T. J. Warren and Elfie de Rock (in Dot Old School House), and Sanders and Dean (in the plantation sketch, Jubilee Day), and ends all with Joseph H. Keane in Rip Van Winkle.   The bill for March 7th–12th opens blithely with The Farmer's Frolic (George L. Gregory, Frank Cransel, Elfie De Rock, George Derious and Charles Worley), passing thence to "turns" by Lottie Grant, the Martell Brothers, Lizzie Derious, Ed Howard and M. Coyne (in Kitty Foley's Birthday), George Derious, John Rice (clog and jig), Mamie Ogden (song and dance), T. J. Warren and Elfie De Rock (The Servants' Holiday), United States Mail (with Worley and Lucille Campbell), Uniac and Walker (song and dance), and ends with Our Hash House (with several

[337]

of these olio performers, Billy Bryant, J. Mackin, &c.). As March thawed into April, successive weeks gave us, in addition to certain of the performers just listed, such favourites as Nellie Amon, Lottie Grant, Annie Worley, Robert Butler (clown), in The Three Dwarfs (with John Foster as Pantaloon, Young Ajax as Harlequin and Lucille Campbell as Columbine — this to end the bills of March 14th–19th). Those bills began with Robinson Crusoe ("as presented by Lydia Thompson's Troupe," and with Elfie De Rock, T. J. Warren and H. J. Campbell in the lead). Butler remained for The Magic Cabinet (ending the bills for March 21st–26th; others in the bills were Jerry Kennedy and Henry G. Clark (contortion negro singers, in Happy Nigger Pete), McGill and Ryland (Irish songs), the Three Russian athletes (Fredericks, Gloss and Lavin), Isabella Ward ("gifted musical artist"), C. Ryland, Worley, Campbell, &c. The week of March 28th–April 2nd presented Rooney and Thompson (Irish), Nellie Amon (still a feature), Charles Saville and Ben Bennett (in Our Southern Home), James O'Neil, Charles and Carrie Moore, and a revival of The Little Dutchess (still with the Campbells). It is fortunate that this O'Neil is distinguishable by a single final *l* from James O'Neill, the "legitimate" actor.

The week of April 4th–9th bristled with novelties: H. W. Eagan, Saville, Campbell, May Clark (in A Night of Terror), the Two (*sic*) Brazziers, Jessie Warner ("queen of clubs, in a complete change of the finest wardrobe of any female on the American stage"), Harry Cereni and Ada Page (in the burlesque German sketch, Snaps), Lord and Von Leer (in We Are so Glad), Nora Campbell (serio-comic), Herr D. M. Zalto (wire-walker), Ricketts Brothers (Harry and Georgie, "late of the Conquest Company, at Wallack's" — dancers, skaters, etc.), Andy Amann (Teutonic and American delineator) and the play of Seth Grit (with Eagan, Amann, Saville and Lucille and Nora Campbell). Later incitements in April were Jim Rooney, Pete Thompson, Lillie Morton, Nellie Webber, Lew and Lena Cole, Signor Demonio, Harry Constantine (female impersonator), the Shamrock Four (Dave Conroy, Matt and John Daly and Mickey Thompson), "Professor" Alexander Davis, the burlesque Pocahontas (with Harry Constantine, Lucille Campbell, Lena Cole, and an enormous cast — April 18th–23rd), Howard and Sanford ("German eccentrics"), the Enterprise Four (A. Baldwin, J. K. Foster, H. S. Wayne and A. Cumings, in The Rival Lovers), J. Sanderson (motto songs), the Shamrock Four, and the old favourite, The Forty Thieves (with Viola Clifton and Lucille Campbell — April 25th–30th). Harvard possessing but one bill for May (that for the week of the 23rd–28th), I can gratify the reader merely with the fare for the feast-nights of that week. George J. Kraus was now set down as manager, and Harry F. Seymour as director of amusements. The opening farce, Matrimonial Quarrels, enlisted Charles Worley, and H. J. and Lucille Campbell; in the olio were Ada Clifton, Harry Lamonto and Archie Baldwin (these two in

[338]

The Zulu Twins), Lucille Campbell (songs), T. J. Warren and Elfie De Rock (in The Servants' Holiday), Minnie Lawton (song and dance), Worley and Campbell (in Shakespeare Rehashed), Joe Redmond and Ada Clifton (song and dance), Fanny (*sic*) Bernard (serio-comic); and all ended with the play of Uncle Alick Slocum, acted by performers from the olio. For May 30th, the Staats-Zeitung lists Alice Adams and her horse, Napoleon, in Mazeppa.

In late May the place resumed its old name of the Bowery Garden; by June 25th it was Aberle's Bowery Garden.   Here, in that delightfully balmy month appeared the Four Ethiopians (Arnold, Harvey, Fletcher and Allen), Ned West (Ethiopian), Lucille Campbell, Billy Bryant ("old man specialties"), the Ricketts Brothers (Harry and George — pantomimists), Alice Adams and Ed H. Lay (in Mazeppa — May 30th–June 4th), John Pendy and Jeffreys Warner, Mullen, Murphy and Kitty Mills, May Vincent (serio-comic), Melville and Bunnell (Melody in a Music Shop), J. J. Mullen (late of Mullen and Magee) and Tony Murphy (late of Raymond and Murphy), Frank Bush, Henry R. Scott and H. F. Seymour (in Hezekiah Perkins, or, True to Life — played in the week of June 6th–11th), Fanny Sanford (*sic*), Ernest Haven ("late of the Conquest Company" — in Irish songs), Carrie Davenport (club exercises), Fanny Herring (in Little Buckshot, for the week of June 13th–18th, and in The Tigress of the West, for the following week), Archie Hughes, William Ronaldo (*sic*) and Archie Baldwin (in The Zulu Twins), John Hogan and Lizzie Mowbray, Morton and Bryant, John B. Wills and May Adams (in The German Mashers), John Burke (clog), and E. T. Goodrich (in his never-dying Grizzly Adams — week of June 22nd–27th).

The reader will be shocked and bitterly disappointed to learn that I could unearth for him no bills for July, and, for August, only those for the last two weeks — August 22nd–September 3rd.   Among the last roses of the summer as shown by those August offerings were Carroll and Walters ("musical geniuses and comedians"), Foster and Hughes (in The Two Aldermen), the La Rosa Brothers (Frank and George, gymnasts), Howard and Sanford, Bud and Annie Granger (in Mixtures, with change from white to black face), Young Hercules, Ada Farnham (songs), Delvan (Devlin?) and Tracy, the Spanish Students, Red de Jalma (fire king), "Professor" Gorman ("king of ventriloquists"), Nelson Curry (gymnast), &c.   The concluding play for August 22nd–27th was The Hunter's Dogs, with Vic and Harry Leonzo, Tiger and Lion, and players from the olio; for August 29th–September 3rd, we were regaled with Golden Guilt, played by G. A. Henderson (as star), Neil Grey, L. Robie, Joe Hurley, John Carroll, Maggie Ferris, &c.   The place was now called the Bowery Theatre.   Like the reader, I fear that "Variety" will sink our delicate craft — at least cause it to drift, in utter weariness.

[339]

London Theatre, 1880–1881

For some reason difficult to explain, the London Theatre and Miner's seem to me the most interesting of the Bowery homes of "Variety"; difficult to explain, because, after all, the same performers flitted from house to house, so that one could imagine their being but rarely called on to leave New York. The London, in 1880–81, retained its best performers for considerably more than the week usually allotted individuals or "teams" in the run of such theatres, and to that extent chronicling the story of its offerings in that season becomes rather easy.

In September, 1880, appeared there John Hart in farces, Bibbs and Bibbs, A Kiss in the Dark, A Nocturnal Wedding, etc. Schoolcraft and Coes had the week of September 6th–11th, in Music vs. Elocution, and that of the 13th–18th in their famous Mrs. Didemus' Party; in addition, George H. Coes appeared singly in Irish and Scotch ballads, with banjo accompaniment. Other entertainers of the month were Campbell and Burke, the Gregory Brothers (Charles and George, on double horizontal bars), Ada Forrest, Lillie Howard, Kerrigan (Irish piper) and McCarthy (jigs, reels, etc.), Sheehan and Jones (in An Everyday Occurrence), Mollie Wilson, the Big Four (Smith, Waldron, Cronin and Martin), Fred and Lillian Chamberlain (in The O'Donovans' Rehearsal), Lizzie Derious (song and dance), George Derious (with his head downward for eight minutes, whatever good that did to him or to anybody), the Peasleys, Kitty O'Neil, Harry Parker and his dogs, Fred Sharpley and West (late of Bryant and West, with all kinds of musical instruments), Campbell and Burke, William Griffin, Theodore F. Dausche (piccolo solo), Kelly and Ryan (in The Hod Carriers, etc.), Lucy Adams and Guy Linton (in I've Only Been Down to the Wigwam, or in Dibdin's Jealousy), John and Willie La Rue, the Megatherian Eight (Kelly, Manning, O'Brien, Lyons, Parks, Magrath, Leary and Arnold — American clog dancers), Niles and Evans, Minnie Lee, &c.

Alexander Zanfretta, in the week of September 27th–October 2nd, appeared in The French Dancing Master and also walked the "high rope"; John Hart, John Robinson and Lizzie Conway acted in Box and Cox; Maloney's Visit to New York enlisted Barney McNulty, Master Barney, Hart, &c., and olio "turns" introduced May Antonio ("vocal electric change act"), Charles A. Loder (German comique), May Barretta (songs and dances), Ferguson and Mack, the Two Barneys (in Troubles of a Ballet Girl), &c. October wore on with contributions from Reynolds and Walling (in Dot Turnpike Gate), Sanford and Wilson (in Nick Nax), the Barneys (in Swearing Off), Fred Hallen and Enid Hart (in Penzance Pirates in a Nutshell), Ferguson and Mack, the farce of Maloney's Supper (October 4th–9th, with the Barneys, and Sanford and Wilson), Dan McCarthy (in a North of Ireland specialty), John Hart, in The Three Graces, Hemmed In,

[340]

Helen's Babies, etc., a return of Schoolcraft and Coes (in Our Alabama Home, in the week of the 11th–16th, and in Oh, Well, It's no Use, for the next week, 18th–23rd), Ella Mayo, Jennie Miaco (skipping rope act), Sheehan and Jones, the farce of Jim Crow Alive (October 18th–23rd, with Hart, Robinson, J. H. Surridge and Lizzie Conway), The Hester Street Serenaders (during that same week, with Schoolcraft and Coes, Wilson and Sanford), Nellie Richards ("queen of all serio-comics"), Frank B. Carr (motto vocalist), Tom Granger, the Love Sisters (Ella and Kitty), and the farce of The Mounted Police (with Sheehan and Jones).

Many of these favourite artists recurred in November; newer faces were those of H. P. Cogill (motto songs), May Irwin (her first appearance here), The Cogills (C. W. and H. P., in Chit Chat), Cardello and Victorelli, the French Troupe Davene (this for three weeks), Charles T. Ellis and Clara Moore (in Swiss Courtship), the French Twin Sisters, Harry and John Kernell, Etta May, Harry Bryant (ventriloquist), Yank Adams, Tom Sayers, Kitty McDermott, Major Burk (sic — "military sensation"), Reynolds and Walling (in The Old Arm Chair), Master James Callan ("the little Pat Rooney"), Barney Reynolds (motto songs), Ira A. Paine, the Electric Three (Callan, Haley and Callan, "Ethiopians"), Ferguson and Mack, &c. Among the skits or pantomimes of the month were The O'Gradys at Rehearsal (with Sheehan and Jones), Greenbriar's Troubles (with John Hart), Robert Macaire and The Brigands (with Alexander Zanfretta), a burlesque Daniel Rochat (with Hart, Surridge and Robinson), and also a burlesque The World (with the same performers). John Hart appeared, during the week of November 29th–December 3rd, in both Money and Court of Appeals. In that week the Irwin Sisters made their "first appearance on the East Side," and Dan and Gussie Hart rendered Uncle Peter's Return (in "Variety" sketches, somebody was always "returning," to the tune of either tears or hilarity). Helene Smith, The Coming Man (with Hart), Reynolds and Walling and Ferguson and Mack in the same week helped November to pass peacefully into December. Thereafter, in December, came Charles and Thomas O'Brien (in The Mischievous Monkey), Jennie Engel, J. W. Mack (late of Sheridan and Mack) and Ada Boshell (Mrs. Mack), James O'Neil and John H. Conroy, Clark and Edwards (Swiss delineators), the delightful Irwin Sisters (May and Flora), Sam Holdsworth (in The Pirate's Dream), the American Four (Pettingill, Gale, Dailey and Hoey), Gallagher and Mack, Kitty O'Neil, Lester and Allen, Charles T. Ellis and Clara Moore (in Swiss Courtship), the French Twins, Harry and John Kernell (in Krousemeyer's Visit to New York, December 13th–18th), George and Lizzie Derious, Jessie Boyd ("queen of song"), Sage Richardson and Charles W. Young (a "black" specialty), the Peasleys (in Mollie's Victory), Andy Collum, the Grinnells, John Hart (in Ham-u-let), Walter Phœnix (in song and dance), the Brothers Arada ("Egyptian wonders"), the Four Emeralds

[341]

(Gibbons, Russell, Kennedy and Magee), &c. The bills for the week of December 27th–January 1st, ended, appropriately, with New Year's Calls (Hart, Surridge, Robinson, Lizzie Conway, and Lizzie Derious). One sees that, for its farces, the London, like some other "Variety" houses, maintained a permanent stock company.

These same stock players, with a new Mamie Conway, began the bills for January 3rd–8th, in The Jealous Wife, and ended with Monkey Jack, or, Pirates of San Domingo, with Master Martin as the Monkey; the olio, in that week, boasted of Maud Morrissey, the Brothers Arada (Albert and Max, necromancers), the French Twins (in The Living Photographs, songs, dances, reels, jigs), Wood and Beasley (cornet soloists), the Lamartine Brothers, the Big Four, the Morrisseys, Sailor West, the Abyssinian Dwarf (Tommy), the Irwin Sisters, and Harry Watson ("Dutch") and Alice Hastings. Later in January we enjoyed the Collins Brothers (Lew and Frank, in song and dance), Andy and Annie Hughes (in Irish Servants), Mlle. Baretta (sic —"Empress of Song and Dance"), Tom Sayers, Sheehan and Jones (The Ash Box Inspector), the Nondescripts (Harry Cereni and George Leslie), Dick Gorman ("Dutch"), J. D. Roome, Kerrigan and McCarthy, Harry McAvoy and Emma Rogers (in Caught at Last or in Jealousy), Carrie Boshell ("This lady's elegance and style are most recherche"), the Nelsons (including Mme. Nelson's flock of trained doves), Ferguson and Mack, the Big Four, Mr. and Mrs. Augustus J. Bruno (in The Voyagers, or, Fun on the White Star Steamer, Celtic — obviously "Variety's" response to the challenge of Fun on the Bristol and others of its kind), the Herbert Brothers (stilt act), Clark and Edwards, Campbell and Burke, &c. The Brunos remained a second week (January 31st–February 5th) in Voyagers, and in the bills were also Ira A. Paine, the London's Troupe of Gymnasts (in The Staircase Band), McAvoy and Rogers (in Matrimonial Difficulties), Clark and Edwards (The Merry Swiss Couple), the French Twins, Billy Buckley (in Ginger Snaps), Dick Gorman, Trudell and Rowan ("bone duett statue clog"), and Murray, Snow and Robinson (acrobats and tumblers).

February kept up the bright procession with Carrie Lavarnie ("this lady's style and appearance is most recherche"), Parker and his dogs, Donnelly and Drew, Fred Roberts, Carl Hertz ("California necromancer"), Sid C. France (in Dead to the World, February 7th–12th), Andy Amann ("musical son of Momus"), the Three St. Felix Sisters (Clementina, Henrietta and Charlotte), Hart and Robinson (in Booth vs. Jefferson), the Leslie Brothers (Louis and Fred, equilibrists), Dick Gorman, the Four Shamrocks (Dave Conroy, Matt Daly, and the Webster Brothers), the Female Forty Thieves (February 14th–19th, with Viola Clifton, the regular actors, and, for one scene, the Jackits-Chy's Company). In later February appeared Harry Woodson, Elise Kruger, the Four Shamrocks (in A Strike on the

[342]

Narrow Gauge Road), Lillie Howard, Lester and Allen, Dick Gorman, the Three Leotards, &c. For the week of February 28th–March 5th, Hart, Robinson, Lillie Howard and Lizzie Conway began the proceedings with The Henpecked Husband, and John T. Kelly and Thomas J. Ryan ended them with Senator McFee. Fred Hallen and Enid Hart returned (in I'm an Actor), and McCarthy and Monroe gave Grogan's Chinese Laundry. The Four Planets (McDermott, Sheehan, Kennedy and Clark), the Davenport Brothers (athletes), Harry Bryant, Kelly and Ryan ("Bards of Tara"), and Lester and Allen fed a fat olio. John B. Donniker, "recovered from the effects of a severe accident," resumed, in late January, his work with the orchestra; he had been absent for two months.

In March we could greet, progressively, Murray and Murphy, Billy Devere and Bobby Williams (in The Drum Major), Hallen and Hart (in Things that Are Seen Every Day), the Monumental Quartette (Hammond, Earle, Hawley and West), Bryant and Hoey (in a "new nautical spasm," All-of It and Billy the Tailor), McGill and Ryland (in The Gas House Micks), the Ricketts Brothers ("late of the Conquest Troupe at Wallack's," in Pantomimical Absurdities), Mollie Wilson, Sailor West, Varney and De Bar (acrobatic gyrations), Sam Holdsworth ("great English tenor"), the old minstrel, Dave Reed, Mlle. Victoria (trapeze), the Daly Brothers (Irish songs, dances, jigs, reels), the Kernells, Charles T. Ellis and Clara Moore (in Love's Labour), Lester and Williams, William Gaylord (acrobatic equilibrist), Barney Ferguson and Dick Mack, and the stock actors and members from the olio in skits and farces. The week of March 28th–April 2nd brought in Robert Nickle, Schoolcraft and Coes (Mrs. Didemus' Party, etc.), and the concluding farce, The Arion Ball (with John Hart and others).

Lapses in the Harvard files carry me to the week of April 11th–16th, when Hart, Surridge and Lizzie Conway began the fun with 3 A.M., and Dan Sully, Lew Cole, Robinson and others concluded the bills with Unneighbourly Neighbours; between these provocatives to mirth, the olio congregated Howard Dorr and Son (somersaults, gymnastic doings, etc.), the Miramichi Family (Mlles. Geraldine and Lavinie, and Louis and Edouard, in The Clodoche Quadrille of the Four Hunchbacks), Nellie Richards, Add Weaver, Nellie Parker, Mattie Vickers and Charles S. Rogers (in Antony and Cleopatra), Pat Reilly, Four Onofri Brothers, and James Sanford and Charles Wilson — a brave array. Ma, Look at Him opened the proceedings for April 18th–23rd, with Dick Gorman, Lizzie Conway, Surridge and Robinson; Nellie St. John, Richardson and Young, Mattie Vickers and Rogers (in The Débutante), Minnie Chapin, Fayette Welch (in School), Donnelly and Drew were other ingredients of the olio. April went out (25th–30th) with Melville and Bunell (instrumental comedy sketch), Frank and Fanny Davis (in Fogarty's Night On), Al Emerson and Ruby Brooks (bone and banjo), the Four-in-Hand (Mayo, Talbert, Sullivan and Smith),

[343]

Goss and Fox (black face), Parker and his dogs, Vickers and Rogers (in Protégé de Français), Gorman, Nellie St. John, Maggie Weston (in Dan Maloney's Raffle for an Eight Day Horse), &c.— again a dazzling host for lovers of the "halls."

May blooms came thick and fast as one could desire: Charles T. Ellis and Clara Moore, William Gaylord, the Four Eccentrics (O'Brien, Magrew, Curdy and Hughes), Dick Gorman, John Hart (as Cupid, in The Fellow that Looks Like Me), Tom Sayers, Mills and Warren (in Schneider, how You Vas?), the Carrolls (Richard M., Edwin H. and Master Richard, in Nonentities), Lillie Wood, Avery and La Rue (parlour acrobats), Alfred Liston (xylophone and many other musical instruments), A. J. Talbot (a discourse on topics of the day), Fannie Lucille, T. M. Hengler, the Carrolls (in The Italian Padrone), D. B. Emery and Laura Russell (medleys on the silver bells and cornets), Gus Hill (club swinger and juggler), the Two Wesleys ("the Long and the Short of It"), Mollie Wilson, the Suydams (acrobats), the Johnsons (Arthur and Virgie, in a German sketch), Hart, Robinson, Lizzie Conway and others (in farces, Booth vs. Jefferson, The Double-Bedded Room, The Rivals, The Dead Alive, etc.), the Grinnells, Frank M. Wills and Charles H. Sheffer (in The Troublesome Sheriff), Hallen and Enid Hart (in Billy, the Tailor), the Martell Brothers, and Hassenbad, or, the Pretty Prince (May 23rd–28th), with Lillie Hall, the "Great" Fostelle, John Hart, Ada May, Lizzie Daly, and many more. A benefit to James Donaldson, Jr. and Edwin A. Bull, treasurers, signalised May 26th. The regular season ended in the week of May 30th–June 4th, special features including Dick Gorman, Hart (in The Coming Man), Hallen and Hart, Hines and Blossom, Mollie Wilson, Jennie Miaco, Bryant and Hoey, and Cam-o-Mile, or, the Big Bokay, with Lillie Hall, Charles Fostelle, &c.

A special season of two weeks began on June 6th, with Maggie Weston's Dan Maloney's Raffle Combination, component elements of which included Frank and Fanny Davis, the La Porte (sic) Sisters, Tony Watson, the Four-in-Hand (Will H. Mayo, Harry C. Talbert, Joe Sullivan and Billy Smith), Lou Sanford and "Governor" Add Ryman. During the week of June 13th–18th were featured Press Eldridge, Ellis and Clara Moore, the Four Grotesques (C. V. Seamon, E. M. and W. H. Girard and T. E. Somers, in The Flat Boat Ball), Pat Rooney, and (still) Dan Maloney's Raffle (with, of course, Maggie Weston as Bedelia). What was set down as the third and last week of the special season (June 20th–25th) gave us Sim Dipsey's Visit to New York (with Seamon, Somers and Add Ryman), Maggie Weston (in male impersonations), the Four-in-Hand, the Grotesque Four (in Children from the South), Hughey Dougherty, and a third week of Dan Maloney's Raffle. For June 23rd, John B. Donniker announced his benefit. An interesting season, this, at the London.

[344]

Harry Miner's Theatre, Bowery 1880–1881

The new season at Miner's began on August 23, 1880, with a glittering array — Frank Jones and Alice Montague (in Music and Notions), William West, Lizzie Derious, Paddy and Ella Murphy (in Irish Felicity), Ella Mayo, Harry Bloodgood ("minstrel star and unapproachable king of sable low comedy," in Uncle Rufe's Home), Add Ryman, Charles and Ella Jerome, the Olympia Quartette (Hugh Mack, William Keough, M. J. Sullivan, and P. Randalls), Morris and Fields, McIntyre and Heath (in Skedaddle), Cronin and Sullivan (in O'Hare's Ambition), the Shamrock Four (Conroy, Daly and the Webster Brothers), the Ten American Students, and A. H. Sheldon (in his own play, Red Star, assisted by Tillie Malvern, William Lansing, J. R. Lewis, Charles Diehl, Charles Jerome, G. Low, George Beane, Jr., and Kate Dennison); so large an aggregation at so small an entrance fee! But, of course, beer and drinks and refreshments swelled the house-receipts.

Newcomers, in the week of August 30th–September 4th, were Billy Carter, Pat Reilly, Jeppe Delano, Louis and Emma Alfredo, E. C. Dunbar ("Milanese Minstrel"), Lamont and Ducrow, the Novelty Four (the Whitneys, Lizzie Hunter and Lester Howard, in Rehearsal in the Parlour) and the Daytons; the concluding play was The Miser of the Five Points (with Sheldon and the regular actors). I scurry through September, merely listing Jessie Forrester, the Seamans, Alice Bateman and Willis Pickert ("American and Lancashire dancing"), Morris and Fields (in The Clockmaker's Hat), Sheldon (in Vice and Poverty), the New York Vocal Quartette (Amberg, Welling, Dalton and Pelham), Lillie Western, Wills and May Adams, Tommy Granger, Nellie St. John, Murphy and Mack (in Our Irish Flats), the Delmannings, Georgie Kaine, the Three Nondescripts (Cerini, Leslie and Kennedy), the Four Comets (Hawley, Manning and the Cooper Brothers), the popular combination of Murphy and Mack and Murphy and Shannon (in Murphy's Dream, played for the week of September 13th–18th, to be followed by a week of Murphy's Wedding, and that, in turn, by a week of Murphy's Christmas, the engagement ending — October 4th–9th — with a week of The Christening), Charles Redmond and Georgie Blake, Helene Smith, Ned Barry (motto and character singer), the three Milo Brothers, Charles T. Ellis and Clara Moore (in Swiss Courtship), the Electric Three (Callan, Haley and Callan), Billy Hayden (English trick clown), Valjean (juggler), Master James Callan (in When Hancock Rules the State), Kitty Gardner, Gibson and Binney (pedestal clog dancers), Carrie Howard, John Hogan and Lizzie Mowbray (in Mixed), Murphy and Mack (in The Mullen Family, or in The O'Shaughnessy Guards), Bernard McCreedie, Murphy and Shannon (in The Two Pompeys) and the Hogan Brothers (Harry and Gus). Ye gallery gods — even ye boys' gallery — what a list!

[345]

Sheldon, Tillie Malvern, Lansing and the other members of the dramatic corps were relegated, during the incumbency of the Murphy-Mack-Shannon quartette, to opening farces — A Jolly Cork's Pleasure Trip (September 27th–October 2nd), or The Dissecting Table (October 4th–9th). Miner's retained olio favourites for more than the formerly customary week's engagement; with this warning I mention only newcomers to the October ranks — Favor and Shields, Polly Daly, Fred F. Levantine, W. H. Rice, the Comedy Quartette (Harry and Emma Budworth, George and Marie Nelson), Landis and Steele (skating champions), Lucy Adams and Guy Linton, Clooney and Ryan ("Teutonic"), Everett and Daly (the Happy Hottentots, acrobats and contortionists), Sid C. France (October 11th–16th, in Marked for Life, assisted by Sheldon, Lansing, Guy Linton, Hugh Mack, Tillie Malvern and Miss Sackett), Alexander Davis (ventriloquist), Professor Abt's Grecian Mystery and Dissolving Statues (October 18th–23rd), Mabel De Verne ("England's double-voiced vocalist"), Needham and Kelly ("rough and tumble Irish"), Andy Collum, the Russell Brothers (welcome! thrice welcome to me), Ella Mayo, Seamon, Somers and the Girard Brothers, Sheldon's play, Scarlet Dick, or, the King of the Road (with Tillie Malvern as Dick — October 18th–23rd), Louise Murio, Donnelly and Drew (in John and Ellen Magee), Alice Gleason, Minnie Lee, Gussie Webster (change specialty), the Crimmins Brothers (John, Stephen and Michael), Bernard Sloman (imitations of birds), the Lamartine Brothers (gymnasts and acrobats), Al Emerson ("the greatest living bone-player"), Harry Cereni and George Leslie (now set down as the *Two* Nondescripts), and A. H. Sheldon (in his own play, Knights of the Jimmy).

The fluttering, scurrying leaves of November fell thick and fast on Miner's populous stage — Dr. Knox and his Putnam County performing pigs, the Alba Sisters, Wills and May Adams, Fanny Davenport, James Goodwin ("Dutch"), the Brennans and George Laible (in Double Tonguing, etc.), T. M. Hengler, Minnie Lee, the Fieldings, the St. Felix Sisters, Pat Reilly, the Mette Brothers, Fannie Beane and Gilday, Awata Katsnoshin, Kitty Sharpe, Neil Smith and his dogs, the Boisset Brothers (Fred, Hugo, Frank and Willis), Ella Wesner, the Gorman Brothers (James, George and John, in The Old Kentucky Home), the Kine Brothers (James and Barney, bone, banjo, etc.), the Megatherian Four (Kelly, Gibbs, Lyons and Leary, in The Coloured Fancy Ball), Sheldon (in Glimpses of City Life — November 8th–13th), Alice Bateman and Willis Pickert, Charles and Annie Whiting, Fannie Beane and Charles Gilday (in Rural Felicity), the Rankins (William, Carl, and Richard, in The Amateur Rehearsal), Ada Forrest, Dave Reed, the Novelty Four, Sheldon (with Little Marion Russell, Tillie Malvern, &c., in Oliver Twist, week of November 15th–20th), Mackin and Bryant, Nellie Parker, the Four Comets, Wally Raymond and John Leslie (vocal duets), Luigi dell' Oro ("the most miraculous musical genius on the face of the earth"— under management for one year to Miner), the Albion Brothers (William, Frank and Charles, acrobats), the Four Eccentrics (O'Brien, Magrew, Curdy and Hughes), the Monumental Quartette, Sheldon (in The Adventures of a Rogue, November 22nd–27th), the Dutch Mendels (Harry and Leonie, in Going to Germany), Little Venus, the Chappelle Sisters (clog dance), Kurtz and Nellie Brooks, Harry McAvoy and Emma Rogers (in Jealousy, or, Two Can Play at that Game), Redmond and Georgie Blake, "Governor" Add Ryman, Mealey and Mackey, William Henry Rice, Foreign Cousins (with William Hayle, Will H. Mayo, Lou Hayle and Harry Talbert), Bryant and Hoey, &c.

Dell'Oro, a man of wonder, carried into bleak December, and to warm chilly applausive hands in the theatre came a progression of newcomers in Frank Ashton, Frankie Johnson, Georgie Parker, Dick Gorman, Burt Queen (ventriloquist), Jennie Morgan, Redmond and Georgie Blake, Bryant and Hoey, Mlle. Morlacchi (of all people in the world, for a week — December 6th–11th — of The French Spy), J. W. Mack and Ada Boshell (Irish and German sketches), Edith Sinclair and Ed F. Barnes (in Faint Heart never Won Fair Lady — not, of course, the famous old play of that name), Murphy and Mack (in Our Irish Flats), Murphy and Shannon (in Just from Germany), Crossley and Elder (Caledonian Sports), Jackits-Chy's Male and Female Japanese Troupe, Charles Foster (December 13th–18th, in his own play, Bertha, the Sewing Machine Girl, with Tillie Malvern, Sheldon and Lansing), Fred Hallen and Enid Hart (in The Pirates of Pinafore, very protean for both performers), Lizzie Mulvey and Barney Fagan, the Olympia Quartette, the Four Boissets, Maude Leigh ("a lady possessing a faultless voice, superb form, and gifted by nature with remarkable musical ability"), the Fieldings, the Wesleys (John and Louis, eccentric song and dance), Lottie Elliott (skipping rope dancer), Andy Collum, the American Four (Pettingill, Gale, Dailey and Hoey), The Demon of Gold (December 20th–25th, by and with Sheldon), the Catletts (Lew and Lulu, clogs), Fannie Beane and Gilday (in Spices), and Awata Katsnoshin (returned). The Demon of Gold lasted for three weeks, and many of the performers listed above settled on Miner's hospitable stage for visits of greater or less protraction.

The new year lavished, of course, copious blessings — Leonard and Jones (Irish change act), the abiding dell'Oro, Hettinger and Nibbe (German Emigrants), the Monumental Quartette (Hammond, Earle, Hawley and West), the Murrays (Tom and Henrietta), Beane and Gilday, Minnie Lee, Redmond and Blake, Williams and Morton, the Comedy Quartette, the Cogill Brothers (in Chit-Chat), Bertha Rowe, the Brennans and Laible, Mlle. Magerald Davene ("songs in German, English and French"), Alice Bateman and Willis Pickert, Gallagher and West, Bryant and Hoey, Bernard Sloman, the French Troupe Davene, Harry Budworth, the Carroll

[347]

Brothers, Pat Reilly, Reynolds and Walling, the Jeromes, the Three Rankins, the Virginia Trio (Turner, Welch and Harris), the Three Vidocqs, Valjean, the play of Scamps of New York (by and with Sheldon, January 17th–22nd), Fields and Leslie, Frank B. Carr and the Love Sisters (in Budding Talent), Lucy Adams, Ella Wesner, Ada Forrest, Manchester and Jennings ("Black Apollos of song and dance, grotesque acrobatic feats"), Frank E. McNish and the Leland Sisters ("The jolly Three"), the Three Gorman Brothers, and Sheldon, in his own play of Forgery. The week of January 31st–February 5th yielded N. B. Shimer and Flora Bingham (musical and change act), Fred J. Huber and Kitty Allyne, Annie Boyd (serio-comic), Reynolds and Walling (in Sweet Home of Flowers), Frank Bennett and Lida Gardner (in Capers), Flora Moore, the Four Comets, and Sheldon (in Lost at Long Branch). Of course favourites remained from the previous week.

Newcomers or returned treats in February were Fanny Davenport, George Kurtz and Nellie Brooks (in The Soldier's Orphan), Helene Smith, Neil Smith's dogs, Frank M. Wills and Charles H. Sheffer (in That Troublesome Sheriff), Lester and Williams (in The Actors), John C. Hughes ("champion 6 day walker"—for one night only, February 9th), the Ten American Students, Sheldon and Tillie Malvern (in Dick Turpin), Goldsmith and Tracy (Celtic songs and dances), F. F. Levantine, Maude Leigh, Polly Daly (*sic*), Bonnie Runnells, the Four Boissets, Minnie Lee, Morris and Fields, the Two Wesleys, Flora Moore, the Original Little Four (Talbert, Owens and the Carroll Brothers), Sheldon and Tillie Malvern (in his play —The Red Scar—February 14th–19th), Millie Dean (lyric), the Barlow Brothers (song and dance), Belle Fairmont (serio-comic), T. M. Hengler, Cogill (or Coghill) Brothers, the Three Vidocqs, The Robbers of Genoa (adapted by Sheldon—February 21st–26th), Burt Queen, Crandall and Eastwood (a California team), Belle Clifton, the Peasleys, Jennie Morgan, Emma and Louis Alfredo, Della Turner (serio-comic), McAvoy and Rogers, the Troupe Davene, Ella Wesner, the Four Eccentrics, and the play of Scarlet Dick. Thus we have skidded, with no glance right or left, to the evening of Saturday, March 5th, 1881; the rapid going leaves us dizzy, blindly clutching at names and the tags appropriate to them, all and sundry.

Earlier March moved on, with Sheldon (in Sarah's Young Man), Joe Redmond and Ada Clifton, the Peasleys, Burt Queen, Fannie Beane and Charles Gilday (in When the Cat's Away, or in Spices), Crandall and Eastmond, Della Turner, the Brennans and Laible, the Comedy Quartette (the Budworths and the Nelsons), Ella Wesner, Lottie Elliott, the Four Eccentrics, The Arrival of Bernhardt (March 14th–19th, with Joe Pettingill, Pete Gale and Carrie Howard), the Parker Sisters, the Fieldings, Murphy and Mack (in Our Irish Flats), Murphy and Shannon (in Amalgamation), also these two famous teams united (March 14th–19th, in Murphy's Dream,

[348]

and, 21st–26th, in The Christening), the Weston Brothers, Cardello and Victorelli, Frank Lewis, Ajax, the Burtons (Johnnie and Lottie), Annie Boyd, Hawkins and Kelly ("dialect emperors, banjo, and all sorts of musical instruments"), the Olympia Quartette, Edith Sinclair and Ed F. Barnes, Carrie Lavarnie, John and James Russell (in both black and white face), Minnie Lee, McNish and the Leland Sisters (in Stolen Fun), and Sid C. France (in Marked for Life).

The reader perceives that I am trusting for his satisfaction merely to a catalogue of rapidly shifting groups. The April delights included Thorn and Darwin (illusionists and prestidigitateurs), Lizzie Derious (so long that season at the London), Lottie and George F. Winnett (in Love in Broken German), Annie Boyd, the Hogan Brothers (in Happy Boys from Borneo), the Seamans, Fred Carroll (banjo), Morris and Fields, the Russells, the Stirk Family (bicyclists), the Virginia Trio, Sheldon (in Adventures of a Rogue), Georgie Kaine, Tommy and Annie Dayton, E. C. Dunbar, Billy Carter, Jeppe Delano, Pat Rooney, Lamont and Ducrow, Larry Tooley, the Little Four, Sheldon (in his own play — April 11th — Slave Life in Brazil, or, April 18th–23rd, in his own The Irish Outlaw of '98), Mealey and Mackey (sic), Harris and Wood, Dan Tracy and Will Goldsmith, Belle Clifton, the Three Razillias (William, George and Edward, "Leg-Mania Artists"), Lucy Adams, Beane and Gilday (in Rural Felicity), John F. Fenton ("English swell song and dance"), Jessie Boyd (songs), Wood and Beasley, Flora Moore, the Four Diamonds, and The Naiad Queen (with Sheldon, Tillie Malvern, Eva Byron, Annie Boyd, Lucy Adams, Lansing, Belle Clifton, J. R. Lewis, and many others). This carries April to its very last evening.

Newcomers in May were Charles Frey and Florence Marshall (in Chips — parodies, medleys, duos, etc.), Connors and McBride ("the true Irish gentlemen"), Harry Watson and Alice Hutchings (in Dutch Deception), Kelly and Ryan, Fred Sharpley and Charles West (in their musical sketch, Smiles), the Four Diamonds, Dave Reed, Clark and Edwards, the Cogill Brothers (in Points), the Onofri Brothers (Achille, Charles, Forteen and Oreste, in Offenbach's Quadrille), Fred J. Huber and Kitty Allyne (in Dreams, or, in The Banker's Daughter), William H. Rice, Alice Bateman and Willis Pickert, Sheldon (in A Female Blubeard), Crandall and East-wood (in Echoes from Germany), Maggie Bursel (skipping-rope songs and dances, and hoop clog), the Brennans and Laible (in The Coopers), Galla-gher and Mack (in Music), Leonard and Jones (The Telegraph Lads, clog and reel), John J. Sellou and John J. Byrnes (in The College Students, or in Our Style is Irish), the Four-in-Hand (Mayo, Talbert, Sullivan and Smith), Punch Walton, the Stirk Family, Sheldon (in The Innocent Vic-tim), Beane and Gilday, Billy Carter, the Electric Three (Callan, Haley and Callan), William Cronin and J. P. Sullivan (in Life in a Tenement

[349]

House), Bessie Bell, the Moores (Charles and Carrie, on roller skates), the Ryans (Perry and Lulu, in Strolling in the Woodland), Cronin and Sullivan (in McCormick, the Copper), the Dehas Sisters (Emily and Clara), Max and Martha Miller, Fred Roberts ("splendid wardrobe, rich baritone voice, original songs"), the Great Nonpareil Coloured Troubadours, Charles Moore's School of Educated Dogs, and Larry Tooley (in On the Beach). This transports me thankfully through the week of May 30th–June 4th.

The Comedy Four and the American Four Consolidated Shows united in splendour (weeks of June 6th–18th) such stunning celebrities as Pettingill, Gale, "Pete" Dailey, Parker Sisters, Andy Collum, Murphy and Mack, Murphy and Shannon, the Weston Brothers, Frank Lewis, and Cardello and Victorelli. Murphy's Dream ended the bills for the first week, and Murphy's Wedding those for the second. Entirely new talent emerged in the later weeks of June — the Delmannings, Alfred Klein (motto songs), Mills and Warren (in Schneider How You Vas?), Ada Forrest, Carroll and Walters, Minnie Hall, the Carrolls (R. M., E. H., and Master Richard, in Nonentities), Cora Cardigan ("greatest flute, piccolo and violin soloist among her sex in the world"), Irene Santella (skipping rope), the De Bar Brothers (Charles and William, in "serpentine manipulations"), the Four Comets (Frank Hawley, Walter Manning, Bobby Williams and Charles Hague, in Fragments), Sheldon (week of June 20th–25th, in A Tailor's Luck, No. 10,001), Sailor West ("vocalist, dancer and pantomimist, as danced by him in England, Austria, New Zealand, China, Japan, East and West Indies, and the United States"— a roaming sailor indeed), J. M. Johnson and S. C. Swain (in The Jealous Darkies), the California Quartette (T. B. Dixon, H. C. Wyatt, Harry W. Roe and H. W. Frillman), the Bohee Brothers (James and George), D. B. Emery and Laura Russell (medleys and duos), George W. Woods ("duke of the bones") and John H. Mack ("king of the banjo"), Grimaldi Gregory (in Flick and Flock)— all to the glory of June and its roses.

In July we might have enjoyed progressively the turns of Sheldon (in A Trip to Coney Island), Minnie Lavenia (vocalist and actress), the Hermans (Charles and La Rose, in The Fireman's Spree, "introducing five styles of dancing"), Morton (late of Morton and Miles) and Bryant (late of Mackin and Bryant), James Hoey, Bryant and Saville, Cronin and Sullivan, John Walsh, the Three Ronaldos (sic), Murphy and Shannon (in The Two Pompeys), the Little Four, "Professor" H. Monroe and his troupe of cats, Daisy Norwood ("queen of the footlights"), Bud and Annie Granger (in Mixtures), Minnie Farrell, Thomas and Clara Maxwell (in The Jolly Old Couple), Pat Rooney, Fannie Beane and Gilday, Charles McCarthy and George W. Monroe (in Grogan's Chinese Laundry), Ramirez's Spanish Troubadours ("first appearance in New York"), the Two Wesleys, "Professor" Anella (aviary of performing birds), Polly Dale, Charles Gilday and

Charles Turner (in The Thespian Pedestrians), Carrie Swain (acrobatic song and dance), Irene Santella, Delvan and Tracy, the De Bar Brothers, and Sheldon in various farces.

And now August will round out for us the distracting year at Miner's. In that heated month we basked in the fun of Charles Weston and Charles Hanson, Eddie Vernon (young female impersonator), John E. Sanders and Charles H. Dean (in Jubilee Day, a sketch of Southern life), Jeppe and Fannie Delano (in Strolling by the Old Mill Stream), Murphy and Shannon, Beane and Gilday, Fred Roberts, the Johnsons (Virgie and Arthur, in All-of-It), the Forrests (Billy and Nola), the Electric Three, and Sheldon (in The Happy Neighbours)—all of this vast and excellent array for the week of August 1st–6th. Newcomers of later weeks were "Professor" M. J. Gorman (ventriloquist), Fanny Davenport, Ward and Lynch (Irish comiques), the Werners (Ed and Maud Stanley), the Delanos, Sailor West, the Benner Brothers (Ernest, William and Jacob), the California Quartette, Parker and his dogs, James Huey, the Four Comets, Murphy and Shannon (in Turning the Tables), Frank Woodson, Mollie Wilson, the Ramirez Troupe, Pat Rooney, Daisy Ramsden, Little Katie Rooney, Murphy and Mack, Carrie Swain, Minnie Lee, Wood, Beasley and the Weston Brothers, Keegan and Wilson (grotesque song and dance, and boneless wonders), Carrie Howard, Huber and Kitty Allyne (in Stricken), Clark and Edwards (The Merry Swiss Couple), Murphy and Miles, the Cooper Brothers, Sheldon (August 15th–20th, in The Actor's Boarding House, and, in the following week, Buffalo Bill's Last Shot), Billy Carter, the Brennans and Laible, Boyd and Sarsfield, the Jeromes, the Little Four, and Murphy's Dream (August 22nd–27th, with John E. Murphy as Grady Murphy and Mrs. Crowley, with Phil Mack as Mrs. Gradus Murphy, Grady Murphy, Jr. and Literary John, George Murphy as Jake Krouse, landlord, George Shannon as Captain of Gendarmes and Hobby Horse Jo, and, in other rôles, Ella and Charles Jerome, Captain George Laible, Frank Lewis, Allie Hall, and Mrs. A. Cummings). The week of August 29th–September 3rd presented Sheldon (in Minnie Ha Ha), Flora King (English vocalist), Crandall and Eastwood (in Echoes from Germany), the Cogill Brothers, Sharpley and West, Pat Rooney, John and James Russell (in The Friendly Neighbours, Burlesque Ballet, etc.), Fred Hallen and Enid Hart (in Billy, the Tailor, in 15 Minutes), Flora Moore, Lamont and Ducrow, the Stirk Family, the Megatherian Four (now composed of Kelly, Sherman, Lyons and O'Brien), Cronin and Sullivan (in Life in a Tenement House), &c. The question again gaspingly arises as to how so much could be offered for so slight an admission fee; surely much beer and liquid refreshment must be sold to make up the expenditure! Well, here we are at the end of Miner's long, long season, and we may leave perplexing questions and pass to other abodes. If I ever learn to spell, infallibly, the names of these "Variety" experts, I shall be happy.

[351]

Dick Parker's American Theatre, 1880–1881

Harvard is richly supplied with bills for 1880–81 of the Cinderella theatre in Third Avenue. Under the management of Dick Parker, it was presenting in September, of course in progression, and not all together, Jennie Leland, Laura Russell and D. B. Emery (silver bells and cornet), Ella Mayo, the Chappelle Sisters (Grace and Jeanne), Larry Tooley (in The Dutchman's Ghost), the Three Gorman Brothers, Frank Jones and Alice Montague, McNish and the Leland Sisters (he also in his inimitable Silence and Fun), Frank and Fannie (*sic*) Davis, John Hogan and Lizzie Mowbray, May Irwin, William J. Gibbons (motto), John and Lea Peasley, the Maxwells (Tom and Clara), the Carrolls (in The McFaddens), Schoolcraft and Coes, Emerson, Clark and the Daly Brothers, and Lizzie Derious. In October came another interesting procession of favourites, Sharpley and West (one formerly of Sharpley Brothers, the other formerly of Bryant and West), Tommy Granger, Charles Redmond and Georgie Blake, the Russell Brothers, Charles T. Ellis and Clara Moore, the Peasleys, the Four Comets (Hawley, Manning and the Cooper Brothers), Ada Burnett, Gibson and Binney, the Comedy Four (Harry and Emma Budworth, George and Marie Nelson), Johnny Allen (in The New York Hackman), Paddy Nugent, Lulu Wentworth, the American Four (Pettingill, Gale, Dailey and Hoey), Helene Smith, and for the week of October 26th, Minnie Oscar Gray and W. T. Stephens (in Dogs of the Storm).

This is good matter, and, in fact, superior to the talent of November, which wore to its close with visits from Bob Harrison, Frank Traynor and Ella Mayo (these in Going to the Races), the Hennessey Brothers, Lucy Adams, Favor and Shields, "Hen" Graham (in Solomon Levy), W. H. Rightmire (on November 6th, in The Boss), Rose Goodall (in The Prairie Flower), Genie Webster (Irish character change), Trudell and Rowan (bone duet, statue clog, juggling, etc.), Miss Dell Trudell ("accomplished double-voiced singer"), the Novelty Four (Emma and John F. Whitney, Lizzie Hunter and Lester Howard — in Rehearsal in the Parlour), Larry Tooley, the Four Shamrocks (Dave Conroy, Matt Daly and Webster Brothers), the Four Diamonds (Watson, Gilmore, Brevarde and Sawtelle), the Hull Twin Sisters, Ella Wesner, George Derious ("stands eight minutes with head downward"), Gregory Brothers (Charles and George — horizontal bar and dancing barrel), and W. J. Fleming (in Life in New York, or, Tom Trumper — this on November 20th), Dan and Gussie Hart (in Uncle Peter's Return), "Hen" Graham ("Dutch" and Hebrew), the Grotesque Four (Seamon, Somers and the Girard Brothers), Alice Bateman and Willis Pickert, Clark and Edwards (in The Merry Swiss Couple), Jennie Engel and (November 27th) W. J. Fleming in Six Degrees of Crime. The bills, one sees, were now closing with melodrama.

[352]

From December 11th to 25th the Harvard files show appearances of Bernard McCreedie, Levantine, Earle and Wilton (acrobats), Frank and Fannie (*sic*) Davis (Love in Ireland), Ella Mayo, the Chappelle Sisters (clog dancers), Cogill Brothers (C. W. and H. P., in Chit Chat), the very popular Kitty O'Neil, Charles Diamond (Milanese Minstrel), Harry and John Kernell (A Sidewalk Convention — *sic*), Rightmire (11th) in Thrown upon the World, Bob Harrison (in The Coming Man, The Live Nigger, etc.), Foster and Hughes, Minnie Lee, Ferguson and Mack, Julian Kent and the bear, Julia (in Wild Bill), Belle LaVerde, Cahill and Martin, and N. S. Wood (in The Boy Scout of the Sierras). On Christmas afternoon every child present received a gift.

January, 1881, brought to our attention Tobin and Reed (song and dance), Georgie Lingard, Reynolds and Walling (in Con a Moore), the Carrolls (in Nonentities and also in The Italian Padrone), Harry Woodson ("the master negro comedian of America"), Lucy Adams, the Four Shamrocks, Neil Smith and his dogs, Millie Sackett and Maurice Pike (in Ireland's Land League), Charles White (in funny negro characters), Georgie Melnotte, George W. Woods and John H. Mack (bones and banjo), Gertie Webster, Manchester and Jennings (in Just Dropped In, and The O'Malleys), Minnie Lee, John and Maggie Fielding, Jackits-Chy's Male and Female Japanese Troupe, Ella Wesner, and Lost in London (with Charles L. Farwell as Job Armroyd, and Addie Farwell as Tilly Dragglethorpe — this for the week ending January 22nd). But two February bills survive at Harvard — that for the week ending on the 12th, with Frank and Fannie (*sic*) Davis, Billy Robinson (laughable pathetic ballads), Retlaw and Allen, Nellie Hague, the Comedy Quartette (Harry and Emma Budworth and George and Marie Nelson), Mackin and Bryant (Hibernian Twins), and The '49ers, with T. W. Hanshew and C. L. Farwell); and the bill of February 21st–26th, with John Pendy and Jeffreys Warner (in Here and There), Harry Mills and Tom Warren (in Schneider, How You Vas?), Williams and Sully (in Our Wedding Day), Emma Hoffman, the Russell Brothers, and The Two Wanderers (with Rightmire and Farwell).

And only three bills for March! The week ending March 5th presented Harry and Minnie Wood (in Barney's Return), Emma Hoffman, Ned West's negro sketch, Clams, Lucy Adams, the Brennans and Laible, Marie Gurney, and The Boy Detective (with N. S. Wood, Farwell, &c.); the next week brought in Billy Robinson (in The Darkies' Stratagem), Amy Nelson, Clark and Edwards, Manchester and Jennings, Donnelly and Drew, and the Leonzo Brothers (in their famous Avenged, or, the Dogs of the Sierras); and the week of March 21st–26th proffered the Novelty Four (the Whitneys, Lizzie Hunter and Lester Howard), Dan Sully, Nellie Parker, the Barlow Brothers, Charles and Ella Jerome, Morris and Fields, Ella Wesner, Wood and Beasley and Neighbourly Neighbours (with Dan Sully and Harry

[353]

Morris). In April, Harvard bills allow us imaginatively to observe from time to time the turns of Minnie Chapin (serio-comic), Ned West, Carroll and Walters (in The Serenaders), Harry Mullen and Minnie Chapin (in Irish Love), Daisy Kernell, and the concluding Roving Jack, or, Saved from the Wreck (with J. Z. Little, Scott Davis and Farwell — this for the week ending on the 9th); the Hennessey Brothers, the Cogill Brothers, T. J. Warren and Effie (or Elfie) De Rock (in The Servants' Holiday), and Fanny Herring and Farwell, in the week of April 11th–16th, in The Tigress of the West); Charles Austin and his dogs, the Great Thorn (illusionist), W. J. Scott (banjo), the Vampiers (Jean, Ella and Julian, in Elastication, "leg gyrating folly"), Hawkins and Kelly, and (for April 18th–23rd) The French Spy (with Fanny Herring, A. Glassford, Florence Bell, Farwell, and Charles Seabert); finally, from April 25th–30th, N. S. Wood (in The Boy Detective) began a bill which included William Davis (one-legged acrobat), the Virginia Trio (Turner, Welch and Harris), The Jealous Husband (with John Hart, Lizzie Conway and Florence Bell), Williams and Sully (Ethiopians), Ned West (Jockey clog), Pat Reilly (cartoon artist), Yank Adams ("billiardist"), Edna Markley and Alfred Davis (ventriloquist). At this time Parker exercised the manager's privilege of taking a benefit.

I hurry through May, merely noting by the weekly route Harry and Minnie Wood, Harry Mullen and Minnie Chapin, N. S. Wood (in Life and Adventures of Jack Sheppard, with Maurice Pike as Blueskin, W. L. Gleason as Jonathan Wild, and with, in other parts, May Nugent, Andrew Glassford and J. V. Arlington), The Boy Detective (with N. S. Wood), Miss Earle Remington (in songs of the day), the Laporte Sisters, the Hogan Brothers (in Happy Boys from Borneo), Morton and Mack (High Kicking), Frank and Fannie (*sic*) Davis (in Four o'Clock in the Morning), Ada Forrest, Sanders and Dean (in Jubilee Day), Ward and Lynch, and John T. Hinds (in his deceptively named The Shaughaun). Thanks to a full file at Harvard I need spare the reader no details of June, with its shifting of talent from week to week: Charley Worley (in The Skeleton Witness), Kane and Graham ("Dutch" and Hebrew), Gallagher and Mack (Southern Chimes), Harry Wood, George W. Woods (or Wood) and John H. Mack (bones and banjo), Rightmire (week ending on the 4th, in The Boss); the John Hart Combination (June 6th–11th), bringing fresh talent in John Hart, Lizzie Conway, Fred Hallen and Enid Hart (in Billy, the Tailor), Pat Reilly, Wood and Mack, &c. And for the week of June 13th–18th came, with no olio whatever, The Two Orphans:

Jacques......................J. P. Winter	Picard.....................George T. James
Pierre.........................Maurice Pike	Louise......................Maggie Morgan
Chevalier...................George Maddox	Henriette....................Ray Alexander
Count de Linières.............T. J. Quinn	Countess....................Jessie Morgan
Marquis de Presles...........Horace Cone	La Frochard..... ....Marie Vernon
Doctor........................H. Warner	Marianne.....................Sadie Jones

Reader, by all that's merciful, compare that cast with the three glorious distributions of years gone by at the Union Square!

The Harry and John Kernell Combination filled the week of June 20th–25th, presenting, besides the proprietors, Larry Tooley, Hannah Birch, Rose and Lillie La Porte, Virgie and Arthur Johnson (in All of It), Dave Reed, Hines and Blossom (in The Political Coons), Sailor West, Minnie Farrell, &c.   For the week ending on July 2nd Uncle Tom's Cabin had Joseph P. Winter as George, Adele Saunders as Topsy, Ray Alexander as Eliza, Marie Vernon as Ophelia, Maddox as Legree, and Ward Swift as Uncle Tom.   In July the Four Comets (Bobby Williams, Walter Manning, Frank Hawley and Charles Hague), Andy Collum, Polly Dale (vocalist), Dan McCarthy and Kitty Coleman, and Ten Nights in a Bar-room (with George A. Bailey as Joe Morgan) began a procession that passed through ensuing weeks with N. S. Wood (in The Boy Scout of the Sierras), the Original Four Shamrocks (Dave Mealen, Tommy Mackin and the Webster Brothers, in The Hod-Carriers' Strike), Blanche Webster, Kennedy and Clark, and The Creole Slave, or, the Staff of Diamonds (with, for the week ending July 23rd, Maurice Pike as Tom Trunnion and May Estelle as Nahmettah).   Only three bills for August survive at Harvard; the week of August 15th–20th presented Delvan (*sic*) and Tracy, Mollie Wilson, Lottie Elliott, and J. P. Winter in the play Abe, the Pioneer, or, the Mad Hunter of Arizona — written by Maggie Weston.   For the week ending August 27th, Harry Le Clair and W. J. Russell appeared in Just in Time.   And August 29th–September 3rd gave us a week of Harry Clifford and May Estelle (in A Pleasant Neighbour), Myles Morris, Harris and Wood, Florence French, the Wesley Brothers (The Long and Short of It) and Hernandez Foster (in Jack Harkaway).

METROPOLITAN CONCERT HALL, 1880–1881

The hundredth concert in this new hall occurred on September 21, 1880; throughout the winter it remained a place of popular resort.   In September Rudolf Aronson was conducting, nightly, concerts of lighter classics or selections from operettas and current successes.   On Sunday evening, September 19th, artists from Maurice Grau's French Opera Company, then appearing at the Standard Theatre, came to the Metropolitan for a concert; participants were Paola Marié, Mary Albert, Vilano, and A. Bernard (his first appearance in this city).   On the 26th, appeared, in addition to Paola Marié and Mlle. Albert, such attractive newcomers as Nigri, Tauffenberger and Bernard; of course, Aronson's orchestra was a powerful support.   During the week of October 4th–9th, Levy played his famed cornet.   Sunday, October 10th, again gave Paola Marié, Mlle. Albert, and Tauffenberger in an evening of Gallic airs and graces.   A flower and fruit show was sweet on September 22nd, 23rd and 24th.

[355]

A winter season was inaugurated, on October 13th, by no less a person than Theodore Thomas; on Sunday, the 17th, the French contingent included Paola Marié, Mlle. Schaeffer (the new soprano), Mauras (who was too hoarse to sing) and H. Brandt, with Levy's cornet to fill the intervals with golden brass, so to speak. On the 24th, Paola Marié, Mary Albert, Bernard and Mauras appeared. We see now why the French singers did not give Sunday concerts at the Standard Theatre, during their long engagement there. As a matter of fact, the Metropolitan and Koster and Bial's, with Mapleson's Sunday nights at the Academy, seem to have put a stop, definitely, to Sunday concerts in our theatres. Observe the record at the Grand Opera House and at Booth's, both former purveyors of "sacred" concerts on Sundays. On Sunday, the 31st, soloists at the Metropolitan were to be Hélène Leroux, Jeanne Chastel, Georges Castelli and Stantini; on Sunday, the 7th, appeared Hermine Lorenz, Armandi Villa (tenor), and Orlandini. November 14th presented, with Thomas's orchestra, Florence Davidson D'Arona (contralto from the Italian opera houses), Charles Belfort (violin), and Armandi Villa.

On November 16th, Carl Feininger (violinist) appeared, and, on the 21st, the "original" Spanish Students, Emma Howe, and the Weber Male Quartette. And actually Rafael Joseffy, the best pianist we then knew, was at the Metropolitan, with Thomas and his orchestra, on Sunday, December 5th, perhaps to offset a remarkable trio on the same night at Koster and Bial's — Wilhelmj, Letitia Fritsch and Constantine Sternberg. A Hebrew Fair occupied the Metropolitan in mid-December; they had a concert on the 19th, with Antonia Henne, Miss F. Hirsch, Christian Fritsch, Remmertz and Miss Feist, along with Thomas's orchestra. The Von der Alm Tyroler Quintet were here, on January 2nd; it was then announced that Aronson's orchestra would play several of Jullien's celebrated compositions. And then fell the blow: this building, once dedicated to music, was secured for roller skating — patinage, "the highest form of skating." This was a recent craze in our city of rapidly shifting crazes.

If, however, patinage prevailed during the week, Sunday concerts could still be arranged; on January 16th, therefore, Teresa Carreño, Tagliapietra (her husband), and the Swedish Ladies' Quartet (Ingeborg Lofgren, Inga Eckstrom, Anna Cedergren, and Emma Larson) raised the standard of music. As a matter of fact, Carreño and Tagliapietra were there also on the 9th. On the 23rd, the soloists, with Aronson's orchestra, were Amy Sherwin, Carlos Hasselbrinck, and Henriette Maurer, pianist. And Catherine Lewis, star of Olivette, was advertised for January 30th; on February 6th, Aronson left, Dengremont was the star, and Rudolf Bial's orchestra began a series of Sunday concerts. The annual ball of the New York Commandery, No. 55, K. T. occurred in earliest February (the 3rd, in fact), with Arbuckle's Ninth Regiment Band, and, on February 9th came a reception of the Lincoln Union, Ninth Ward; but skating ruled the general run of evenings at the Metropolitan.   Dengremont and Hubert de Blanc (pianist) assisted at Rudolf Bial's concerts here, on February 13th, 20th and 27th.   On March 1st came a masquerade and mardi-gras festival.   Anything for variety!

On April 3rd and 10th, Joseffy appeared, Bial's orchestra continuing as centre of gravity.   On Easter Monday, April 18th, the Bataillon des Gardes Lafayette held here a review, parade and ball.   Campanini, for May 10th, arranged a concert in aid of the unfortunate singers from New Orleans, some of whom sang, as did Mme. Lablache and her daughter, Louise.   Bial's orchestra continued for Sundays, far into the summer.   On Sunday, July 3rd, we might have heard compositions by Johann Strauss, von Weber, Wagner (Bridal March from Lohengrin), Gounod, and Bial himself.

Koster and Bial's, 1880–1881

This popular hall was still offering, in September, 1880, concerts by an excellent orchestra, assisted by S. Liebling, pianist.   The five-hundredth performance, on September 15th, was turned into a benefit for Rudolf Bial, and on that occasion we were brightened by "the first night of electric illumination."   Lest the reader imagine that Koster and Bial's was entirely frivolous, I should like to quote the musical programme for September 30th, with a first part devoted to Beethoven, in which Hamm played the violin Romance in F major, Florence Copleston the piano concerto in C minor and the orchestra of fifty, conducted by Bial, gave the Consecration of the House and the Pastoral Symphony.   The second part was lighter, with selections from Auber, Johann Strauss, R. Bial, Gounod, &c.   Or consider the list for October 1st, including as it did, Mendelssohn's Overture to Ruy Blas; the Prize Song from Die Meistersinger; a valse by Saint-Saëns; Finale, Act I, of Verdi's Macbeth; the Carnaval Romain of Berlioz; a scherzo by Goldmark; Meditation, by Gounod; a "Grand Ensemble" from Rossini's William Tell; the Overture to Auber's Fra Diavolo, etc.   I do not believe a similar establishment today would offer anything better, or, indeed, as good.   A Wagner night was Rudolf Bial's contribution, on October 12th, to the rising tide of Wagnerism in our city.   Bial's fifth Wagner concert occurred there on November 9th.

Koster and Bial's did astonishing things; certainly their offering for Sunday, December 5th, seems phenomenal — Wilhelmj, Constantine Sternberg and Letitia Fritsch; on the same evening, Joseffy was advertised for the Metropolitan; the great trio were again at Koster and Bial's on December 12th, 14th, 15th, 16th and 17th.   The six hundredth concert fell on December 21st.   The last weeks of Bial's leading the orchestra were soon announced; on January 9th, P. S. Gilmore's famous band began a season of considerable

[357]

duration. Just before that date, on January 5th and 6th, to wit, the recently imported sensation, the boy violinist, the Brazilian Maurice Dengremont, was to have displayed his art for the delectation of frequenters of the house; illness prevented his appearance until January 11th. Rudolf Bial had gone to the Thalia Theater, to lead the operettas given there by Marie Geistinger, though he gave, as we saw, Sunday concerts at Metropolitan Hall. At Dengremont's second concert (January 13th) at Koster and Bial's, Signora Trafford Sabbatini (soprano) and Sabbatini (tenor) appeared, as did also Hubert de Blanc (pianist). Dengremont (or d'Engremont) continued, along with Gilmore's Band; his last appearance was listed for January 30th. On that night, also, Walter Emerson played on the cornet. On February 20th, S. Liebling, the pianist, re-appeared. On Sunday, February 27th, we were promised Jullien's Exhibition Quadrille, a quartette for saxophones, and S. Liebling. And Walter Emerson, "the young American cornetist," began on February 6th, a long and triumphant engagement, suitable, as to his medium, for solo work with Gilmore's Band, still the mainstay of the establishment.

March 20th was labelled Koster and Bial's America to the Front. Dudley Buck's overture on The Star-Spangled Banner, and G. F. Bristow's The Great Republic, along with Gilmore's Band, were depended on to awaken patriotic fervour, if not artistic delight. The seven-hundredth concert at this popular resort, on March 31st, was devoted to a benefit for Gilmore. On April 3rd and 10th, Gilmore and Walter Emerson were twin-stars of the brassy instruments tuned to golden harmonies. On the 17th, Gilmore gave his Columbia, and, on the 24th, for the first time, his Trip to Manhattan Beach. The hundredth performance here of Gilmore's Band (May 1st) presented A Tour of the Nations. E. A. Lefebre, "the first to introduce the saxophone to Europe," was here, on June 5th, to swell the resonance of Gilmore's concert. Neuendorff, having finished his season of German plays, was leading the orchestra at Koster and Bial's, from June 11th. Open-air concerts were arranged there for the summer, and, on June 20th, Henrietta Markstein was soloist.

I believe the reader might have enjoyed the concert on Sunday evening, July 3rd, the programme embracing the March from Tannhäuser; the overture to Maritana (by Wallace); a cornet solo by Robert Ward; Strauss's waltz, Fusionem; air composed for the violin, in 1660, by Alessandro Stradella, and played by Wilhelm Müller; a saxophone solo by Bertha Linden ("the charming lady saxophonist") of variations (by herself) on The Carnival of Venice; Tausig's Invitation to the Dance, played by Henrietta Markstein; and a concluding "Selection" from La Mascotte. On July 17th, Edouard Remenyi began an engagement that carried him through several nights (not consecutive) of summer; for his benefit, on August 30th, he appeared as soloist, composer and conductor.

[358]

MADISON SQUARE GARDEN, 1880–1881

The garden just off of Madison Square became, in 1880–81, a mere home for big shows, athletic and otherwise; gone, at least for the present, was its former musical glory.   The week of February 28th–March 5th indulged in a walk for the O'Leary belt.   On March 7th, a six-days walking match began, the exciting causes including Dan O'Leary against Henry Vaughn of England ("heel and toe") and Charles Rowell, "champion of the world," against James Albert, "the unknown," in a "go as you please."   The 9th Regiment Dress Parade celebrated Washington's Birthday, with Arbuckle and music to set the march; on the 24th of February came a "Bal Paré et Travesti de l'Opéra."   And the New York Athletic Club was here, on March 14th and 15th, with promise of Rowell, "champion of the world."

And Barnum's Greatest Show on Earth housed itself here, on March 28th, with a truly royal host of entertainers — Tom Thumb and his wife, Chang, the Chinese giant, a Baby Elephant, twenty "grand" elephants, twenty Ute Indians, a Giant Black Rhinoceros, a Giant Black Ostrich, Giant Black Camels, Giant Giraffes broken to harness, Racing Dromedaries, hundreds of Monkeys, a Juvenile Fife and Drum Corps, Georgia Jubilee Shouters, Highland Bagpipers, all in generous profusion.   In the rings were Barnum's performers (first ring), the Great London Circus (second ring) and the International Circus (third ring), and among the stars were Elise Dockrill, Mme. Adelaide Cordona, Emma Lake, Louise Boshell, the Claire Sisters, Frank Melville, Awata Katsnoshin, W. H. Bachellor, Frank Gardiner, the Troupe Davene, the Boissets, 20 educated stallions, William Guyer, Edwin Bibby and Charles Hoefler (these two in Græco-Roman wrestling), &c.   Surely this great show would have satisfied old and young, surfeited many.   The glittering array passed from our ken on the sad, sad evening of April 16th.

On May 9th, at the American Institute, nine pedestrians were to start a Go-as-you-please, in the Ennis Tournament.   John Hughes, George Hazael, Daniel Burns, John Sullivan, Edward Geldert, Ephraim Clow, Phil Mignault, George Barbour, and Henry Weekman were those great heroes of old. Another Contest for the O'Leary belt began at 12.05 A.M. on Monday, May 23rd, under management of Daniel O'Leary.   The names of contestants (to me unknown) may be found in the Herald of May 22nd.   Among the features was a ten-mile "go-as-you-please," on the 26th, for police, letter carriers and firemen, useful public servants whom I am sorry to find in such undignified proceedings.

AQUARIUM; HARRY HILL'S, 1880–1881

On September 6, 1880, the Aquarium was still advertising Pinafore and Trial by Jury, two hardy plants of recent years.   On the 13th, however, it

[359]

gloried in Giroflé-Girofla, with a cast including Haydon Tilla, Belle Girard, C. A. Gilbert, Helena Taylor and E. Neville; the popular French piece flourished nightly, with matinées Wednesday and Saturday. The Chimes of Normandy rang out during the week of the 20th–25th. On October 4th, the Aquarium proudly advertised "a New Stage, a New Proscenium, and New Private Boxes." H. Wayne Ellis was manager, and Sydney Smith stage-manager. The opening attraction had the not too pleasing title of The Frolicsome Oysters (in a stew)—the Adventures of the Whipple Family on Board the Susan Jane. Entertainers in this concoction included Sydney Smith and J. H. Burnett (comedians), Marie Gurney (soprano), Theresa Newcomb (contralto), Lillie De Grey (soubrette), W. B. Newborough (tenor), and Luigi Lencioni (buffo-baritone, whom we have met in concert halls). During the week of October 11th–16th, we had, in addition to this unnatural phenomenon of The Frolicsome Oysters, "two wonderful baby elephants, covered with hair four inches long, purchased for $20,000"; they were, in height, but twenty-eight and thirty-four inches, respectively. The ant bears were also still on exhibition, as well as a chimpanzee. One could learn at the Aquarium; but I do not know to what practical use one could put an education in ant bears and woolly elephants.

I suppose it had to come—Uncle Tom's Cabin among the fishes; on October 18th, the Aquarium bowed to the inevitable, and produced the neoclassic, with J. H. Burnett as Marks, Lillie De Grey as Topsy, Traynor as Gumption Cute, Sidney (or Sydney) Smith as Uncle Tom, Charles Kidder as St. Clair, and Amy Slavin as Eva. But the stay was brief; the Aquarium, on November 8th, presented Baron Seeman (prestidigitateur), and Mlle. Seeman. The baron remained for several weeks, to the complete effacement of drama. On December 20th, John H. Murray's New and Best Show invaded this retreat of bashful fish; in the company, I learn in the Herald, a week later, were Katie Stokes, William Hayden ("King of clowns") and Frank Melville. "Professor" Knox and a pair of educated pigeons, "the lovely and intrepid Katie Stokes," Johnny Patterson (Irish clown), and Herr Naaygard (sic) and Mlle. Martha, "from Rentz's Circus, Germany," figured in the bills of January 3rd–8th. Charles W. Fish entered the ring on January 17th, other performers being about as before. Mlle. Victoria, equestrienne, was new on February 21st, and Philo Nathans, "only four-horse rider," thrilled along the course. Katie Stokes, Fish, Neygard (sic) and Martha, in their "double act de menage" were still chief wonders of the ring. This circus remained throughout March; newcomers in the week of February 28th–March 5th were the Leotard Brothers.

Harry Hill's place still advertised its wares for Sundays in the New York Herald; on September 26, 1880, appeared the "Great English Trio, in their elegant entertainment"; on December 5th, it offered the "Original Coloured Georgia Jubilee Singers," and also in early January. The Harvard Theatre Collection has four bills for this season: that for the week ending February 26th provided Ricardo and Ramon (Spanish athletes, on the horizontal bar), Julia Bennett, Maggie Nichols ("aerial queen"), Kitty Smith, Lillie Boyer, Blanche Morton, Fattie Rush, Female Jig Dancers, and Johnny Keegan and Billy Wilson (grotesque, acrobatic songs and dances); for the week ending March 12th, we might have enjoyed Frank Livingstone (balancing), Billy and Mary Milton ("jig of defiance"— they challenge the world), a comic Chinese ballet, Maude Barnes, and several of those listed for February 26th; for the week ending July 2nd appeared Alice Martyne (ballads and operatic), Paul Hamlin and Ada Newcomb (lightning change), Annie Devere, John Welch (Walsh-"Irish"), a "Great Dance of All Nations," Frank Livingstone, James O'Neil and John Conroy, Bertha Waring, Fatty (now *sic*) Rush, May Smith (serio-comic), and The Salvation Army (acted by four or five comedians).   James L. Ford (Forty-Odd Years of the Literary Shop) asserts that the first meeting in America of the Salvation Army occurred at Harry Hill's (with his consent) and that the rounders present, convinced of the sincerity of the evangelists, "passed the hat"— and gave them the financial encouragement accruing therefrom.   And the week ending July 30, 1881, presented Sophie Thorne (songs and jigs), Keegan and Wilson, Amy Nelson, John Walsh, Kitty and May Smith, and others, and a sparring match between Jimmy Kelly and Jerry Murphy.   I go back to April 3rd, for a lecture by Mary Fisk, on Beecher's and Talmage's Private Hell, as Given to Her Personally; on May 1st, her intriguing theme was Friends that Are Enemies, and Enemies that Are Friends.   June 19th brought a concert by "the beautiful lady vocalists," "the great male quintet," and a "supurb (*sic*) orchestra."   On Sunday, July 31st, and subsequently, were to appear the "Original" Spanish Students.   There were doubtless far worse places than Harry Hill's.

MINOR RESORTS, 1880–1881

The reader will desire but scant information concerning the places of questionable entertainment in the bypaths of the city; hardly more than the mere statement that they persisted.   On Sunday evenings, the Atlantic Garden (not questionable) advertised, in September and October, 1880, the Ladies' Elite Orchestra.   The Sultan Divan operated throughout the season, in ways already known to the reader.   Buckingham Palace was still blatant in advertising of its dance propensities, and of its being the only American Mabille, and the Cremorne opened its doors to the easily entertained.   All these places helped to build up the taste that now (1939) revels in the wares and the shows of night clubs.   Sause's Soirées fell every Tuesday, at Clarendon Hall.   And let us not forget the Haymarket, not quite a lily bed of pure enjoyment.

[361]

The Cremorne, in the Herald of December 5th, dazzled its admirers by advertising itself as the "Palace of Mirrors — Most Magnificent Concert Garden in the World — 75 Pretty Barmaids." And the St. Lawrence Music Hall, 35th Street, west of Broadway, was in the running, during the week of December 13th–18th, with its "Second Fancy Dress Ball," and with the Kiralfy Lady Dancers. I suppose, even today (1939) some persons might prefer this sort of thing to a perfect performance of Hamlet. Buckingham Palace, on January 13th, lured with a Fancy Dress and Costume Ball.

The St. Lawrence Music Hall, on January 16th, advertised new management, with Eugene M. Phillips leading the orchestra. Furthermore, in spite of "fabulous reports" about closing the place, it was still open, for "Fun, Folly, Fashion and Beauty." New York was still New York. The reader may be amused by the grandiloquence of the Haymarket, which set itself down, on January 17th, as a "Bijou of Terpsichore," a tag which may have made more feat the dancing of the *habitués*. And now Huber's Prospect Garden, 106 and 108 East 14th Street, cries its wares — a free concert every evening, with the "original Spanish Students." Perhaps here I should include mention of Theiss's concerts, going all the year, in 14th Street. Does the reader wonder that my pen almost wearies in the search?

A "Grand Fancy Dress and Carnival Ball" distinguished St. Patrick's Day at the St. Lawrence; on April 21st, Buckingham Palace indulged itself and its patrons with a "Grand Costume Bal de l'Opéra Comique." The Buckingham loved its highfalutin; and on the floodtide of its rhetoric I withdraw, for 1880–81, from the night life of the less staid Manhattan.

SAN FRANCISCO MINSTRELS, 1880–1881

Birch and Backus (alas! Wambold was gone from the San Francisco host) opened their new season on August 30, 1880, with Mullaly and an enlarged orchestra, with the Madrigal Singers and Boy Choristers (who appeared throughout the greater part of the season), with Stanley Grey, an English alto balladist (his first appearance in America), with A. C. Moreland (interlocutor), Harry Kennedy, W. F. Bishop (baritone), Frank Dumont (author and tenor), Joseph White (musical artist), George Thatcher (a host in himself), James Johnson, George Powers, T. B. Dixon, Edwin French, H. W. Frillman, Ricardo, and, of course, with Birch and Backus themselves, as storm-centres of fun. Frank Dumont's "absurdity," Pleasant Companions, was a feature of the bills in the week beginning on September 13th. The first week of Our Torchlight Parade (it was the year of the Garfield-Hancock presidential campaign) began on October 4th; the skit continued for several hilarious weeks, the moral being that you could always have a big political parade, if you could find enough small boys to march in it. Pleasant Companions was also a hit.

[362]

Dumont's new musical burlesque, The Cannibals of Barren Island, figured on October 18th, along with Our Torchlight Parade. I fear the new piece was not successful; on October 25th, the advertisements again stressed Our Torchlight Parade and Pleasant Companions. William H. Hamilton, baritone, also, on the 25th, made his début in this house, as did Bryant and Hoey, on November 1st. The establishment, one perceives, had grown far away from the earliest trend of negro minstrelsy; it seems in many ways, especially after the first part of the evening's entertainment — the minstrel row, with its songs and its wit — to have become merely "Variety" in black face. Of course the minstrels must salute Sarah Bernhardt; on November 15th, Sarah Heart-Burn began to rage in heart-breaking or at least side-splitting comicality. Our Torchlight Procession still marched to applause and laughter. The last week of Bryant and Hoey began on November 22nd; they were succeeded, on the 29th, by Lester and Allen. On the 29th, also, came a successful skit, Rogers Peet and Company's Clothing Emporium. About this time, The Railroad Car Conductor's Parade broke into the bills. William Carroll and Richard Gorman were fresh entertainers, beginning on December 13th.

Sarah Bernhardt having bowed to the minstrel yoke, Salvini took his punishment, beginning on December 20th, when Signor Charles Salvini Backus appeared as Othello, supported by Signor A. C. Vermicelli Moreland as Iago, Signor Billy Maccaroni Birch as Desdemona, Signor Frank Garibaldi Dumont as Cassio, and Signor F. M. Spermaceti Ricardo as Emilia. I fear we must admit that this sounds funny; and audiences for weeks thereafter revelled in the burlesque. Wood and Beasley came in, on the 20th, and Scenes at Rogers Peet and Company's Emporium still delighted the customers. How nearly minstrelsy had encamped in the field of "Variety" may be learned from an engagement, of December 27th, with "Professor" Parker and his dogs; Wood and Beasley remained, and Signor Salvini Backus still thrilled in Othello, with "English and Italian Hashed." Frank Dumont's skit, A Hot Night in the City, made one forget the chill outside, on January 3rd; during its second week, Harry G. Richmond and Parker and his "wonderful mastodon dog circus" were part of what I venture to call the olio. Harry Kennedy, the well-known ventriloquist, seems a little out of the minstrel line, beginning on January 24th. Bryant and Hoey were here from the 31st. Salvini Backus's Othello, A Hot Night in the City, Bryant and Hoey, Harry Kennedy and Harry Woodson (his first appearance) in The Old Negro, constituted chief lure during the week of February 7th. On the 14th came a new burlesque, Olivette Condensed, along with first appearances of Harry W. Roe and Billy Buckley; Othello and A Hot Night persisted, as did the Boy Choristers, very popular this year. This constant change of entertainers, this constant dependence on novelty, most of it out of the proper minstrel field, leaves me apprehensive of what actually happened a few years later — the utter collapse of minstrelsy, and the passing of the San Francisco Minstrels.

Daly's success, Needles and Pins, had a belated compliment, on February 21st, with Needles and Clothes Pins (*sic*), by Frank Dumont; Othello, Olivette Condensed, Harry Kennedy, Bryant and Hoey, Johnson and Powers, were among the featured attractions. Bernard Sloman, the "bird man," joined the array on February 28th, and Fred Roberts (motto and topical vocalist) on March 7th. Harry Woodson, Parker and his dogs, Bernard Sloman, and Harry Kennedy, all on a gay 7th, made the San Francisco Minstrels more than ever like, say, Tony Pastor's. And look at the list for March 14th — Roberts, Leonard and Jones (clog dancers), Bernard Sloman, Parker, Ricardo, and Johnson and Powers. Needles and Clothespins still reminded of Daly's.

Thompson Street Flats came back on March 21st, along with the remaining specialists just cited, and Olivette Condensed. New offerings of April 4th were Billy, the Tailor, and Frank Moran; All I've Eat reminded of Olivette. The last week of the season (April 18th–23rd) had Frank Moran, Harry Kennedy, Johnson and Powers, and Billy, the Tailor. On the 25th, Herrmann entered for a month of magic, accompanied by Mlle. Addie, Val Vose, Louise Linden, and the Garetta Family. This group departed on May 21st, and the house remained dark until September, 1881.

Bunnell's New Museum; Middleton's, 1880–1881

Some citizens and more strangers in New York may have gladly attended the opening of Bunnell's New Museum, at Broadway and Ninth Street; as many as four giants were exhibiting there during the week of December 20th–25th. By January 10th, Bunnell's had attracted from Middleton's Museum, the mighty Chinese giant, Chang; Neil Smith's Dog Circus, and a whole Congress of Curiosities also piqued the imagination of such customers as had imagination. A group of "genuine" Chinese musicians joined Chang, on January 17th; on the 31st, Bunnell's branched out, offering Alf Burnett, Helen Nash, funny farces, Chang and Goschen, the largest men in the world, and Dot and Atom, the smallest. Miss M. Kingsland, "empress of magic," Burnett and Helen Nash were here in the week of February 21st–26th. On March 7th began a cat show, or, as it magnificently called itself, a Cat Congress; it lasted for two weeks. Arnazulu, daughter of Cetawayo, showed us, beginning on March 21st, how different some parts of the globe were from Broadway. This Zulu princess was still exhibiting on March 28th, along with a Zulu baby (just to show that Zulus sometimes were just babies), a pair of midgets, and "a World of wonders." Che-Mah, a Chinese dwarf, set down as "a pig-tailed pigmy pet," was here from May 23rd, proving that Chinese may be small as well as gigantesque. And a

[364]

LIZZIE MULVEY AND
BARNEY FAGAN

AMY STONE

JAMES FOX — ED GOSS
(GOSS AND FOX)

TOM SAYERS

ST. FELIX SISTERS

GEORGE W. MONROE

GEORGE SHANNON
MURPHY AND SHANNON)

CHARLES T. ELLIS

JOHN MURPHY
(OF MURPHY AND MACK)

From Photographs in the Harvard Theatre Collection

Monkey Circus, beginning on June 13th, taught us to see oursel's as ithers see us.   A Bird Show and a band of Gipsies attracted on June 27th; Bunnell's, in its way, was educational.   Fortune-telling Gipsies amazed the credulous, during the week of July 11th–16th, and a "snake enchantress" excited us for some time after the 18th.   A girl with two heads, four arms and one body awakened uncomfortable sensations, beginning on August 1st.

During December, 1880, Chang, the Chinese giant, was exciting surprise at Middleton's Museum, 298 Bowery; alas, for Middleton! the oriental wonder passed anon to Bunnell's Museum, newly housed at Broadway and Ninth Street.   A Giant Zulu Chief was flaunted in the face of merely normal visitors, beginning on January 31st.   In March he gave way to Princess Nenemoosha and her troupe of war chiefs and papooses; but he was back again in mid-April.   And the first week of May brought "the Wonderful Child"—the "last extraordinary engagement for the season."   But the Spanish Students were here in May.

Miscellaneous Entertainments, 1880–1881

Suppose we start our season of miscellany with a week (beginning on September 6, 1880), at Masonic Temple, of Primier's "beautiful illusion," Cremation, given with Frank Beard's Chalk Talk, the Lambert Children, and Professor Lambert's organ concert.   From this it seems a long jump in time and in content to a lecture by Alexander Robertson, Scotch "geologian," on Ingersoll Confuted by Geology; Republican Hall, 33rd Street and Broadway, housed this portentous manifesto.   On October 13th, Archibald Forbes, the famous English war correspondent, lectured at Chickering Hall, on a subject dear to American hearts—Royal People I Have Met.   And, as we know, on October 31st, another distinguished English journalist, Joseph Hatton, read at the Madison Square Theatre, from his novel, The Queen of Bohemia.   The audience for this last treat was, the Herald informs me, rather small.

On October 25th, J. S. Vale began a series of thirty popular entertainments at Masonic Temple, at which were to appear Helen Potter (she remained, with her Pleiades, for a few nights), Abbie Sage Richardson, Robert Collyer, George Vandenhoff, Frank Beard, B. F. Taylor, De Cordova, Nathan Sheppard, Vale's Lyceum Comedy Company, Rev. J. H. Carroll, A. P. Burbank, Minerva Guernsey, Jay Villers, Olive Logan, Eli Perkins, and Charles Roberts, Jr.   One attending the series would have heard some of the best platform entertainers of that time.   Throughout the autumn weeks, that wonder of the past season, the American National Astronomical Clock, kept working and amazing, at 733 Broadway.   For one week only, Vale's Lyceum Comedy Company began, on November 8th, at Masonic Temple, performances of those aging pieces, The Serious Family and The

[365]

Day after the Wedding. Dr. James L. Farley recited from Hamlet, on November 17th, at Chickering Hall; why, in an age that could still see good stage performances of the play, it is difficult to understand. On the 19th, one might have attended a Græco-Roman wrestling match, staged at Lyric Hall, between Edward Bibby ("champion of England"), and Clarence Whistler ("better known as Peter Snyder") for a purse of $500. At Masonic Hall, on November 15th, Campbell's Comic Coterie began a week, with matinées on Tuesday, Thursday and Saturday, in Tit for Tat, or, a Lover's Frolic; this was part of that gigantic series of J. S. Vale. And, during that same week, Sarah Bernhardt's Art Exhibition was shown daily, from ten to five o'clock, at the Union League Theatre; the self-exploiting actress, then at Booth's, would fain reveal to New Yorkers the treasures of her sculpture and other forms of art. Sarah really was a wonder. With that thought, I pass, on the 22nd, to John Denier's Humpty Dumpty, at the Harlem Music Hall.

Charles F. Underhill, on November 29th, read at Memorial Hall; on the same date, George Rooke, Jack Stewart, Bibby, Bauer, Gus Hill and other heroes appeared for the benefit of Rooke. On the 11th of December, John L. Stoddard, at Chickering Hall, described the Passion Play, with illustrations from Oberammergau, continuing for a time and profiting, doubtless, by the ban on the piece at Booth's Theatre. In November and December, at Chickering Hall, Reverend Dr. Maynard delivered a series of twelve illustrated lectures on foreign lands. I hardly know whether or not to include in the record a complimentary entertainment for Professor and Mrs. Frobisher, arranged for December 7th, at their College of Oratory, or Edgar S. Allien's magic, on the 5th, at Chickering Hall, for the New York Athletic Club. At Temple Hall, Masonic Temple, during the week of December 6th–11th, appeared Bassett's Bric-à-Brac. And, on December 15th, occurred the Inauguration Ball, at the new Seventh Regiment Armoury.

Locke Richardson, in a series of afternoon recitals (not readings), at the Union League Theatre, gave us renderings of Shakespeare's text — Julius Cæsar (December 13th), The Merry Wives of Windsor (20th), King Lear (27th), Romeo and Juliet (January 3rd), Othello (10th), and The Merchant of Venice (17th). And, on December 22nd, R. D'Oyly Carte presented, at Chickering Hall, Archibald Forbes in a lecture on The Inner Life of a War Correspondent. That week found Professor Carpenter, mesmerist, at Masonic Temple. During the week of December 27th–January 1st, we were told that there was Good Skating at the domain of the Manhattan Polo Association, 110th Street to 112th, between Fifth and Sixth Avenues. On January 6th, one might forego this tingling rapture for the doubtful pleasure of listening to Edwin Lawrence, "elocutionist," at Chickering Hall. At the Lexington Avenue Opera House, on December 28th, Henry Ward Beecher lectured on The Reign of the Common People.

[366]

On January 7th and 8th, amateurs acted, at the Union League Theatre, The Heir of Greylock; my best wishes go with those who attended.   Memories of their youth will recur to many as they read of Dr. John Lord's series of twenty-five lectures, beginning on January 17th and continuing on succeeding Fridays and Mondays until the educational scheme had worked itself to a conclusion.   Charlemagne, the subject of the first lecture, started the progression of great figures with dignity and force.   Carpenter's Mesmerism, in January, attracted to Masonic Temple.   A curious and unaccustomed "Variety" group were assembled at a benefit in Chickering Hall, on January 13th — Julia Polk, Tony Pastor, Ella Wesner, the Irwin Sisters, the French Twin Sisters, Lillian Russell, Lillie Western, Harry McEvoy (*sic*) and Emma Rogers, and L. J. Vincent (stage-manager)— all for the benefit of New York Lodge No. 330, F. and A. M.   On the 14th, in the same hall, Adela Rankin read and recited, and Lillie A. Barry, A. D. Hubbard and Müller supplied some music.   On the same day, at Association Hall, Locke Richardson recited bits of The Rivals.   I fear I cannot invite the reader to the entertainment of the Maimonides, on January 19th, at Steinway Hall, with Felix Adler lecturing in English, nor may I ask him to the Bachelor Club Ball, on January 24th, at the Metropolitan Hall, or the Invitation Ball of the Albion Society on January 25th, the latter being held at Tammany Hall; but I may lead him to Mrs. George Vandenhoff's literary and dramatic entertainment, given with the aid of her pupils, on January 20th, at Chickering Hall.   They acted A Pretty Piece of Business, and Mr. and Mrs. Carl Feininger gave music.   And I must really urge him to attend at least some of the new recitals of Locke Richardson at the Union League Theatre — The Rivals (January 24th), Macbeth (31st), Enoch Arden, Locksley Hall, and The Charge of the Light Brigade (February 7th), As You Like It (14th), and a miscellaneous list from Scripture, Scott and Dickens (21st).   The reader must follow his own inclination as to the Græco-Roman wrestling match, on January 26th (Terrace Garden) between William Muldoon and Clarence Whistler.   For myself, I shall go, instead, to Daly's or Wallack's.   But I mean to attend De Cordova's evening, at this time, in Grace Hall (opposite the Academy of Music, in 14th Street); his topic was Our New Clergyman.   My more frisky readers could have gone in later January to Madison Avenue and 58th Street, for roller skating, an exciting evening's diversion.

At the Harlem Music Hall, 130th Street and Third Avenue, afternoon and evening, February 3rd, appeared, in aid of the Library of the Young Men's Hebrew Association of Harlem, a fine array, including the Madison Square Theatre company, Katherine Rogers, Nard Almayne, Catherine Lewis, Lillian Cleves Clark, Florence Rice Knox, Mrs. James H. Hackett, Charles Roberts, Jr., J. S. Burdett and Nelson Decker.   On February 14th, at Chickering Hall, Miss Hunt gave a recital of Juliet, with Lavinia Dempsey as Romeo; Miss Hunt's pupils also appeared. On February 9th, at the Metropolitan Concert Hall, the Lincoln Union, Ninth Ward, held a reception, and, as we know, in January and February, many balls, some of them grand and stately, others not so stately, occupied the Academy of Music. In later February (24th), J. E. Frobisher and amateurs, including Nestor Lennon (afterward a pleasing, minor professional) and Sara Goldberg, acted, at the Union League Theatre, Henry Bergh's play, Love's Alternative. For several weeks previously, Professor Carpenter had been exhibiting feats of mesmerism, at Masonic Temple; into Chickering Hall, on February 28th, March 2nd, and 5th, and subsequently, came Hartz, the magician, "recovered from his four-years unparalleled sickness," and exhibited his magic, "with no machinery and no assistant." Shortly afterward he began a long tenancy of Masonic Hall. March 9th found George Martinez, with Mrs. Jarley's Waxworks, at Caledonian Hall, Horatio Street, near Eighth Avenue. A mixture of music and magic brought to Steck Hall, on March 17th, Professor John Goldberg, magician, Sara Goldberg, dramatic reader, J. N. Pattison and Isabella Stone. And, on the 17th, Riverston's "Colossal Exhibition of the Moon" began at Steinway Hall. At Chickering Hall, John L. Stoddard lectured, with illustrations, on the evenings of March 21st, 24th, 28th and 31st, and April 4th, and on the afternoons of March 22nd, 25th, and 30th, and April 5th and 8th, his subjects being The Country of the Moors, Saunterings through Spain, La Belle France, Between Two Seas, or, Travels in Northern Italy, Gems of German Travel, and The Sultan's Paradise, or, Life along the Bosphorus. I am especially interested in a Chinese Festival, held on March 21st, in the school-room under the Spring Street Presbyterian Church, and rather wild, according to the Herald of the 22nd. I blush to include a wrestling match between Bibby and Muldoon, held on the afternoon of March 2nd, in the old Post Office Building, Nassau and Liberty Streets. On March 24th, Mrs. Jessie S. Yenni gave an afternoon of vocal and literary entertainment which I have listed among the Concerts. Hartz's Illusions still mystified at Masonic Temple, but Riverston's Moon went out on March 28th. Our next item is not unrelated — Professor Richard A. Proctor's three lectures on Astronomy, beginning at Chickering Hall, on April 1st. The apparently very popular Locke Richardson continued at the Union League Theatre; I find him reading The Merchant of Venice, on March 21st, and Othello on the afternoon of April 4th. And, beginning on April 6th, Professor E. B. Jennings presented, every evening, at Masonic Hall, The Marvels and Fun of Mesmerism. The "last grand ball of the season" — so advertised — was that of the Bataillon des Gardes Lafayette, on April 18th, at the Metropolitan Concert Hall. At Association Hall, on the 22nd, Sidney Woollett recited Enoch Arden, and, according to the Brooklyn Eagle, Bjornstjerne Björnson was to speak, in Norwegian, on the 20th, at Teutonia Hall, 16th Street and Third Avenue, on The Foundation and the Causes of the Moral Development of the Human Race — certainly a problem big enough for any hour's talk.   On the 26th, Professor Robert Houston, of Belfast, recited at Association Hall, and, on the 28th, Nellie Kline presented herself, Mrs. Rice Knox, W. R. Case, MacGrane Coxe and others, at Steck Hall, for a literary and musical entertainment; I feel that I am beating out, very, very thin, the golden plates of spring amusement.   A dog show barked its way into the consciousness, on April 26th to 29th, at the American Institute Building.   On April 26th, also, began to exhibit at Republican Hall, John Banvard's original panorama of the Mississippi. Where did amusement-seekers in New York find all the money they poured out for the balm of self-forgetfulness?   Keeley Motor Views, full-size, "wonderful machinery, strongest in the world," were exhibited and explained, on May 18th and 20th, at Chickering Hall; O. M. Babcock, of Philadelphia, was the lecturer.   About this time, at 109 West 34th Street, Dr. S. M. Landis did Hamlet, assisted by the Landis Dramatic Club.   Under the caption of Concerts, the reader will find account of Hurle Barvardoe, "the only colored, talented and cultivated Shakespearian," who appeared, on May 31st, at Chickering Hall, along with musical celebrities(?) from Baltimore.   On June 27th, the May Roberts Combination entered the Manhattan Opera House, in The Two Orphans.   Thereafter, excursions to beaches and groves supplied most of the miscellaneous entertainment demanded by a voracious public; some of these, since music held sway, I have treated in the next section.   Here, however, I record for August 23rd the excursion, by Steamer Long Branch and convoying barges, of the Young Men's Hebrew Association of Harlem, to Pleasant Grove, on the Hudson, and "no malt or spirituous liquor sold on board."   With the twenty-fifth annual games of the New York Caledonian Club, held on September 1, 1882, at Jones Wood, I featly pass to other themes.

AMATEURS AT LEXINGTON AVENUE OPERA HOUSE

Craving indulgence, I will here, as tag to miscellany, note the activities of the Amateur League, which began its third season, in the autumn of 1880, with Our Boys, the cast including J. Anderson, W. E. Wilson, Deane W. Pratt, I. J. Wilkins, Jessie Randall, Mrs. W. H. Seaich, Mrs. Jennie and Annie Hyde.   In Fred Marsden's play of Clouds appeared J. W. Scott, A. R. Whytal, R. C. Nichols, G. W. Suydam, A. Beaumont, Helen Russell, Mabel Rossmore, Mrs. Seaich, Jessie Villiers and Evelyn Forster.   Doubtless they had fun, back there in 1881; I wonder how many of them are alive today (1939)?   On March 29th, the League gave Maud's Peril, and, on April 20th, Lend Me Five Shillings, this last with both Whytal and Helen Russell in the cast.   A few years later, Miss Russell was acting at Wallack's, and Russ Whytal has only recently (1939) passed from the scene after a

[369]

long and honourable stage career. The Mimosa Society acted here, on January 28th.

CONCERTS, 1880–1881

The reader has attended with me, or will attend, concerts by the Philharmonic, Symphony and Oratorio Societies, or by the orchestras in the Metropolitan Concert Hall or at Koster and Bial's. The Academy of Music, the Thalia Theater and the Madison Square Theatre proffered their quotas of concerts of varying degrees of merit. Even Sunday concerts in minor theatres have been noted. All these activities I will ask those who may be interested to carry with them as I traverse the field of musical events furnished by vocalists and instrumentalists in Steinway Hall, in Chickering Hall and in many more humble quarters. Before we are summoned to a public performance, I introduce the Harlem Mendelssohn Union, Leopold Damrosch, conductor, which began its tenth season on September 27th with a rehearsal, in the Mount Morris Baptist Church (126th Street and Fifth Avenue), of Handel's Acis and Galatea.

I will invite to the "first grand concert of the season," given on October 5th, at the Church of the Disciples; in it were exploited Henry Galt, Florence Rice Knox, Kate Percy Douglas, Fred Harvey, S. B. and W. F. Mills, and F. G. Bourne (basso)—an impressive aggregation. Marie Pauline Ninninger next summons us, on October 14th, to Chickering Hall, for a concert at which her assistants were Knudson Nilsson (tenor), Adolf Unger (flute), Carlos E. Hasselbrinck (violinist — his first appearance), and Carlberg, with his orchestra. We remember Sternberg's matinées, at the Madison Square, on October 13th and 20th, following his début at the Academy, on October 7th. October 21st brought to Steinway Hall Marie Schelle, the possessor, according to next day's Herald, of "a rich mezzo-soprano"; Franz Rummel and Adolphe Fischer, with an orchestra conducted by William G. Dietrich, supported her in the ordeal. She and her assistants appeared again on the 23rd. In the same auditorium, on the 28th (matinée), H. R. Humphries (tenor) held forth, with the capable assistance of Henrietta Beebe, Antonia Henne, Jacob Graff, S. G. Young, Richard Arnold and W. F. Mills. Standard Hall, on October 23rd, introduced Hermine Loretz, soprano, with, as associates, Constantine Sternberg, Remmertz and C. Fritsch. The Dobson Brothers twanged their banjos before a small audience, on October 25th, at Chickering Hall.

Saalfield, on November 8th, started a series of twelve ballad concerts, at Steinway Hall, with a remarkable array of artists — Campanini, Belocca, Florence Copleston (who replaced Joseffy), Marie Geist, Jeanne Franko, and the Philadelphia Quartet Club. On the 9th, at Chickering Hall, the New York Philharmonic Club gave its first concert of the season, S. B. Mills assisting. On that same evening, Gilmore conducted a "grand military concert," at the Seventh Regiment Armoury, with the New York Choral Union abetting him in a performance of his Columbia, a composition of which he seemed proud. Emily Spader, Fritsch, Constantine Sternberg, De Carlo (piccolo) and Raffayolo (euphonium) also appeared. And let me remind the reader of the seasons of the Philharmonic, the Symphony Society, and the Oratorio Society, beginning in this same windy November.

Florence Copleston, that season a pianist in demand, gave, at Steinway Hall, three matinées, on November 9th, 16th and 23rd; at the first, she had the promised assistance of Florence Rice Knox and F. Rummel; at the second, of Richard Arnold; and at the third, of Joseffy (one of the most uncertain artists ever known to our town; but he actually appeared on this occasion). On November 13th, another pianist, Anna Bock, appeared at Steinway Hall, with H. Brandt and W. Müller; she promised to come forth again, on the 18th and 20th. Still another pianist, Albert D. Hubbard, played at a matinée in Chickering, with Miss M. Louise Segur, vocalist, to vary the bill. Steinway Hall opened hospitably, on November 19th, for a concert provided jointly by Mme. Donaldi (soprano) and the well-liked Rummel. Levy assisted, as did Marie Schelle, Bellari (tenor), Giorgio Castelli (basso), Filoteo Greco (accompanist), and an orchestra conducted by Dietrich. On the 19th, at Chickering Hall, Mlle. Rionda (soprano) came forth, with Tracie Wadsworth (contralto), Adele Barker (pianist of twelve years), Leon Hayman (violinist), and Alfred d'Hubert ('cellist). She was to appear again on the 24th. As I write these names, I cry in despair, "Where, oh! where, are now (1939) those snows of 1880?" On the 20th, the leader was to give a second promenade concert at the Seventh Regiment Armoury, but his illness caused postponement to the 27th. On the 27th also, Gilmore and his band played at the 22nd Regiment Armoury. Sunday, the 21st, brought to St. Teresa's Roman Catholic Church, Rutgers and Henry Streets, a truly splendid array from the opera — Campanini, Valleria, Cary, Ravelli, and Gerster were all scheduled to appear, but the Herald review, next day, omits reference to most of these, mentioning only Belocca, Ravelli, Galassi and Mrs. Swift. On the next evening (22nd), Saalfield's second concert promised, at Steinway Hall, Ravelli, Galassi, Belocca and Marie L. Swift; Mrs. Swift was ill, I fancy to the regret of but few, and Mme. Sacconi, the brilliant harpist of the Mapleson orchestra, took her place. Saalfield's next concert, on December 11th, lured with the beloved names of Annie Louise Cary, Galassi and Arditi, along with Lazzarini and Lucia Violante (pianist).

I go back to December 2nd, for the second concert (Chickering Hall) of the New York Philharmonic Club, with Richard Hoffman and Minna Jonas (soprano) as co-operating soloists. George Henschel, on the 7th, gave at Steinway Hall the first of four vocal recitals, Lillian Bailey (Mrs. Henschel, then or later) assisting. On the 8th, at Steinway Hall, appeared the Franko Family — Sam and Nahan (violinists, and both extremely well known, later), Jeanne (pianist), and Rachel (soprano). On that same date, at Steinway Hall, in the afternoon, Mme. Constance Howard offered a piano recital, in conjunction with S. B. Mills, H. Brandt, Mrs. T. B. Buxton and Caryl Florio. On the 8th (evening), a concert for the Union Boat Club promised Anna Granger Dow, Mrs. Rice Knox, Teresa Carreño, J. Graff, F. Remmertz, Liberati, W. E. Mulligan (organ) and C. Florio. The Mendelssohn Glee Club began its season on the 14th, at Chickering Hall, assisted by Lillian Bailey and Camilla Urso. February 15th found the club presenting W. W. Gilchrist's Ode to the Sun, awarded the first of three prizes offered by the club for a work for male voices; George Henschel and William G. Morgan (pianist) were in the programme. George Henschel's The King and the Poet, written especially for the club, was sung on April 19th; also W. W. Gilchrist's In Autumn, awarded the second of the club prizes. Adolphe Fischer and Antonia Henne were the dignified soloists of the occasion.

On December, 14th (evening) 16th and 18th (afternoons) and 21st (evening), Joseffy and Thomas's orchestra were to appear at Steinway Hall — and did! W. C. Tower sang at the first and Brandt played on the 16th. A very interesting experiment was that of December 20th, at Chickering Hall, a performance of Handel's Acis and Galatea ("for the first time in New York") by the Harlem Mendelssohn Union, Leopold Damrosch conducting, and with George Henschel (as Polypheme), Maggie Mitchell (soprano), A. D. Woodruff and Albert King (tenors), Emil Schenck ('cellist), and Charles R. Rutenber (accompanist). On the 19th, at the Church of St. Vincent de Paul, we had the Stabat Mater and a group including H. Brandeis, H. Prehn, Gaston Blay, Maggie Mitchell, Octavie Gomien, and the choir from St. Stephen's Church, Brooklyn. Albert Rosse gave a "third" concert, on the 21st, at Chickering Hall. At the Saalfield concert, Steinway Hall, on December 27th, appeared Amy Sherwin, Miss Winant, Ferranti, Alexander Lambert, and F. de Leauhodu, zither (début in America) and the New York Philharmonic Club. And the dependable Herald, of January 2nd, informs us that last week (December 27th–January 1st) Sophia Priestley, pianist, drew a large audience to Chickering Hall, her abettors being Emily Spader, Belle Cole, Henry Brandeis and Summers; the 28th was the allotted evening. Carl Feininger's first chamber music concert occurred, in the same week, at Steinway Hall; his string quartette consisted of Feininger, Roebbelin, Risch and W. Müller. His next concert fell on January 12th, in the same auditorium, with Joseffy and Miss Winant to assist. George Henschel, more and more appreciated as a great lieder-singer, gave a second vocal recital, on January 4th, at Steinway Hall. On the 6th, at Edwin Lawrence's elocution showing at Chickering Hall, appeared Belle Cole, F. T. Liliendahl (organ), and W. Y. Vandewater (baritone). January 7th brought to Steinway Hall a Saalfield concert involving Remenyi, Emily Spader, Alexander Lambert,

[372]

Signor La Villa and the New York Philharmonic Quartet Club.   On the 11th, at Steck Hall, the Standard Quartet played, with Harry Lauterbach at the piano.   On the 14th, the Misses Thomas gave an entertainment of music and poetry, luring to Chickering Hall on that afternoon, not only by their own art, but by that of Florence Rice Knox, Albert L. King (tenor), Carlos E. Hasselbrinck (violin) and C. E. Pratt.   These Thomas ladies (Julia and Annie) were teachers of elocution.   On the same evening at Steinway Hall, under auspices of the Coloured Citizens' Association, occurred a concert by St. Philip's Protestant Episcopal Church.   The Mozart Musical Union, on January 19th, held, at the Lexington Avenue Opera House, the second rehearsal of its tenth season, Miss Geist ('cello), Mrs. Jucht (*sic* — soprano), and Nahan Franko assisting.   On the 20th, at Steinway Hall, Eugenie Simonson gave a piano recital, aided by the violin playing of Richard Arnold.   January 24th brought another Saalfield Concert, with Brignoli, Emma Watson Doty and Emma De Land, in selections from Sullivan's ballads.   On the 21st, Julia and Annie Thomas, now setting themselves down as teachers of elocution, offered at Chickering Hall, a notable array including Henrietta Beebe, Florence Rice Knox, Florence Copleston, Franz Remmertz and C. E. Pratt.   A terrible storm kept Miss Beebe and Remmertz away, and Julia Thomas, Mrs. Rice Knox and Miss Copleston carried on without them.   At Chickering Hall, on the 22nd (afternoon), Frederic Archer, organist and music director at the Alexandra Palace, London, and music examiner of the University of Glasgow, appeared in concert with Emma Howe.   J. N. Pattison's concert, on the 25th, provided the helping art of Isabel Stone, Zélie de Lussan, Arbuckle, Alberto Laurence, Harry Stanfield (tenor), and Mrs. J. W. Harbeson (pupil of Pattison).   George Henschel's third recital (Steinway Hall, January 27th) enlisted Lillian Bailey (soprano).   And let us turn back to the concert of the Frauen-Verein (elsewhere treated) on the evening of that day.   The soloists at a third and last entertainment of Julia and Annie Thomas (Chickering Hall, January 28th) included Miss Beebe, Mrs. Rice Knox, King and Pratt.   On the same evening, Miss Spader sang and Miss Markstein played to the convicts on Blackwell's Island.   January 30th offered, at Steinway Hall, Angela Munier (contralto), with Emma J. Lathrop (soprano), E. R. Mollenhauer, Christian Fritsch, and F. Remmertz; the same 30th heard the second concert of the Liederkranz, assisted by Marie Schelle, Rummel and the New York Philharmonic Club.   On February 1st, the New York Vocal Union was at Chickering Hall, with Miss Hubbell and C. H. Thompson (tenor).   Ferdinand Hiller's cantata, Lurline, was part of the lure.

A very old friend came to Chickering Hall, on February 4th — Stephen Massett ("Jeems Pipes of Pipesville"), long absent from our story.   The seventh Saalfield concert, on February 7th, brought to Steinway Hall another from the long-ago, Mme. Anna Bishop ("who has been persuaded to appear"), with Remmertz, Signor Godoy, Mrs. Delano (contralto) and Mme. Pupin (pianist). The New York Philharmonic Club was at Chickering Hall, on the 8th. On the 9th, 16th and 23rd of February the nervous, uncertain Joseffy was scheduled for piano recitals at Steinway Hall, in aid of charity. The third seems really to have fallen on the afternoon of the 19th. And Franz Rummel, also an admirable pianist, gave recitals at Steinway Hall, on the afternoons of February 17th and 24th, and March 10th and 24th. At Carl Feininger's third concert of chamber music, on February 16th, at Steinway Hall, appeared Florence Copleston and George Henschel; Saalfield's concert, on the 19th, re-introduced Marie Litta, whose absence, if truth must out, had not been tearfully regretted. Jerome Hopkins, whom we cannot lose, promised for February 19th, at the German Masonic Temple, Stuyvesant Square, a second piano recital; he followed with another on the 26th. St. Stephen's Church offered, for the benefit of African Missions at Dahomey, a concert, on February 20th, with Emma Lathrop, C. Fritsch, E. J. Savage (tenor) and Prehn, as a group of slight carrying power for so far-flung an assistance. On the same 20th Manhattan Hall, 54th Street and Eighth Avenue, gave a "grand" concert, with Zélie de Lussan, Miss Markstein, Bignardi, Lencioni and Tamburello (director); on the 27th, the Manhattan summoned again, with Miss de Lussan, Miss Markstein, Lencioni, Liberati and Father Ryan, the latter using America, as usual, for propagandising, with his lecture on Ireland and the Land Question. February 25th brought a "grand inauguration concert" of the Republican Central Club of New York, with, as contributors to the musical scheme, Lizzie B. Ross (soprano), Mrs. G. W. Delano (contralto), C. Fritsch, Charles Belfort (violin), Liberati and the Central Campaign Club Chorus.

On the 24th, at Steinway Hall, came a concert of George Mangold, with the Arion Society of Newark, and the Schillerbund and the Heinebund of New York, and with, as soloists, Graff and Althaus (tenors), Steinbuch and Fuchs (bassi), Katie Nuffer (contralto), and Fanny Pollak (soprano). John Lavine's sixth annual concert (February 28th, Steinway Hall) gave us Emily Winant, Louise D. Reynolds (soprano), C. Fritsch, Rummel and the New York Philharmonic Club. On March 3rd, Ella Hayes held at Clarendon Hall, 13th Street, "a Grand Concert and Reception." The fifth "soirée" of the New York Philharmonic Club, on the 8th, at Chickering Hall, had the aid of Marie Schelle and S. B. Mills, with one or two others of little note. And, on the 6th, Manhattan Concert Hall, at Eighth Avenue and 54th Street, and rather far uptown, opened with a concert at which appeared Zélie de Lussan, Liberati, Mrs. McIlvaine, Lencioni, and Morosini, pianist. On the 8th, a benefit for the paralysed dancer, Mlle. Venturoli, enjoyed, at Steinway Hall, the services of Liberati, Orlandini and Minnie Hands (pianist).

Carl Feininger's fourth and last fell on March 9th; March 10th restored once more Anna Bishop (still a fine artist) at Steinway Hall, with Florence Rice Knox, Christine Rossée (soprano), Florence Copleston, Julia Thomas, A. L. King, Ferranti, C. Roberts, Jr., W. H. Dayas (organist) and Caryl Florio. The proceeds were to benefit the New York Medical College. Mme. Bishop appeared on the afternoon of the 10th, at the organ and harp recital of G. W. and Maud Morgan, at Chickering Hall. Blanche Roosevelt, an interesting woman, who seemed not quite to find her place, had a concert on March 11th, at Chickering Hall, along with C. Fritsch, G. Papini (basso), Carlos Hasselbrinck (violinist), E. Wiener (flutist), and W. R. Case (pianist), with the usual C. E. Pratt to accompany. Saalfield's ninth concert, on the 12th, gave us Emma Dearborn and Mlle. Rubini. On the 13th, as we remember, appeared at the Thalia Theater, Marie Geistinger, Dengremont, Fritsch and others; but Thalia concerts will be found in the discussion, elsewhere, of the year's doings at that house. On March 19th, at Chickering Hall, appeared the Princeton College Glee Club, doubtless to the delight of musical young ladies. The Cooper Union Free Entertainments for Self-Supporting Women were, this year, at times, of unusual promise; on March 14th, for instance, appeared there Eugenie Simonson, Arbuckle, Geraldine Morgan (violinist), Clara Stutsman (contralto), and Mrs. Yenni and Miss Swayze (elocutionists). Mina Geary's annual concert fell on the 15th, at Steinway Hall, Liberati, W. F. Mills and Tom Bullock assisting. On the 15th, also, at Steck Hall, Herman Brandt, Max Schwartz, G. Matzka and F. Bergner gave a chamber-music concert, with Herman Rietzel at the paino. On March 17th, at four o'clock, in Chickering Hall, G. W. Morgan and his daughter, Maud, offered an organ and harp recital, the second of several this spring; Emily Winant sang. On the evening of the 17th, at Chickering Hall, came forth the Philadelphia Glee Club, with Dora Henson (soprano), Mrs. A. H. Darling (contralto), &c. On the 18th, at Chickering Hall, another evening of English glees presented Henrietta Beebe, Mrs. Louise Finch Hardenbergh, Minnie Thurston, T. J. Toedt, George E. Aiken, Walter R. Johnson and Caryl Florio. Another entertainment for Self-Supporting Women brought to Cooper Union, on March 21st, Mme. Gage-Courtney, Belle Cole, Miss Markstein, the Frobishers, and Mrs. Yenni. On the 28th appeared there Ella Plummer (soprano), Misses Bacon and Hill, Godoy, Lanzer and Villa.

Carrie Moses hired Steinway Hall, on March 22nd, for a concert. On the afternoon of March 23rd, William R. Case (pianist) and M. Louise Segur had a joint concert at Chickering Hall, and in the evening of that day David Small gave, in the same auditorium, a literary and musical entertainment based on the works of Burns and Scott; Florence Rice Knox and Florence Tyler assisted him. According to the Herald of the 24th, Small sang six songs "extremely bad." On the afternoon of March 24th, Mrs.

[375]

Jessie Yenni promulgated, at 3 East 14th Street, the third of her musical recitals, congregating therefor Belle Cole, the Misses Conron, Julia Thomas (elocutionist), H. R. Humphries and George Kyle. The reader sees the perplexing combinations, recently, of music and declamation; under which heading should they be listed? Our task is not simple. At Chickering Hall, also on the 24th, George W. Morgan, Maud Morgan and Mrs. Helen Norman gave another concert, at four o'clock; at Steinway Hall, on that afternoon, occurred Franz Rummel's farewell recital. And, on March 26th, at Chickering Hall, Henrietta Beebe, admirable artist, had a farewell concert, prior to her departure for Europe. Local talent turned out in force, and one heard, on this notable occasion, besides Miss Beebe, the very popular Emily Winant (whose rich contralto some still living remember with delight), Mrs. Finch Hardenbergh, Mrs. Sarah B. Anderson, Mme. Chatterton Bohrer, Theodore J. Toedt, George Ellard, W. C. Baird, W. H. Beckett, G. E. Aiken, and Frederic Archer (London organist). My heart warms as I write those names.

The tenth Saalfield concert, on March 28th, gave us a local list in Belle Cole, Lizzie Bacon, Carl Lanzer, Weed, and Signor Godoy. March went out (none too soon for my weary pen) on the 31st, with Jessie Yenni's last recital, which assembled at Steck Hall, 11 East 14th Street, Mme. Gage-Courtney, Miss Simms, Florence Rice Knox, William Courtney, S. B. Mills, and, for "elocution," Mrs. Yenni, Mrs. Van Horn, and "Sam" Ellison. In the afternoon of that day, at Chickering Hall, the organ and harp recital of the Morgans had the additional attraction of the singing of that charming soprano, Hattie Louise Simms.

Blanche Roosevelt again forges to the front. On April 4th, she was at the fourth entertainment, at Cooper Union, for Self-Supporting Women, along with Russell Case (pianist) and Anna Randall Diehl and Harriet Webb (elocutionists); on the 9th, she appeared at the eleventh Saalfield concert at Steinway Hall, her associates then being Emily Spader, William Courtney, Romeyn, Lencioni, Liberati, Carlos Hasselbrink (sic), and Mme. Delviniotti (pianist). Meantime, on April 5th, the persistent New York Philharmonic Club was at Chickering Hall, with Mrs. Leslie Lowerre (contralto), Richard Hoffman, Henry Kayser (clarinet), Carl Pieper (horn), Adolph Sohst (bassoon — sic), and Max Liebling (accompanist). And, on the 7th, a "Gala and Testimonial" to Sophia J. Neuberger does not seem very "gala," with only the Arion Society, W. F. Mills, Herman Breitschuk (harpist) and Jacob Graff to assist in the festivities. On the 11th, Arbuckle's Ninth Regiment Band played at Steinway Hall, assisted by Lizzie E. Arbuckle ("her first appearance in New York"). On the same evening, the fifth Free Concert at Cooper Union presented Hattie Louise Simms, Charles Werner ('cellist), H. R. Humphries, and Jessie Yenni.

The raging concert epidemic began to thin its fires. On April 18th, Amy

Sherwin's farewell, at Steinway Hall, had the artistic co-operation of Emily Winant, Constance Howard, Christian Fritsch, Oscar Steins, Pietro Ferranti and Constantin Weikert.   Richard Arnold, on that night, had a concert at Chickering Hall, with Miss Henne, A. Fischer and Rietzel.   At W. R. Case's concert (Chickering Hall, 19th), Blanche Roosevelt sang the great air from Hamlet and The Nightingale's Trill.   On the 20th the Bank Clerks' Musical Association come to the same hall, along with Mrs. James Bogle, Mary Wernecke, Florence Copleston, Carl Bergstein and A. F. Ottmann — surely not a glittering host.   At Chickering Hall, on the 20th, the Yale Glee Club sang, and, at Steck Hall, Lencioni, Zélie de Lussan, Florence d'Arona, Brignoli, Godoy, La Villa and Mme. Delviniotti joined in musical accord.   On the 21st, at Chickering Hall, sang the New York Vocal Union, Miss Simms and Emma Wilkinson.   I blush to offer the reader the annual concert of Mr. Parson Price, on April 22nd, at Chickering Hall, even though his pupils and a male quartet assisted.   Far more attractive was the concert, at this time (April 2nd), of Mme. Murio-Celli's pupils, because Emma Juch, one of the pupils who appeared, became almost a famous singer, in years about to be.   On April 23rd, Toulmin (harpist) arranged a concert for Chickering Hall, with Miss Winant, Maud Morgan, Mary Wernecke, Toedt, Feininger, and G. W. Morgan.

If the reader is rather weary of Saalfield, so am I; yet his artists, on April 25th, are interesting — Marie Rôze, Amy Sherwin, Constance Howard, Sybella McIlwaine, La Villa, Zippora Monteith, and William Courtney; more interesting, indeed (to me, at least), than Emily R. Spader, whom Saalfield presented, on April 29th, at Steinway Hall, or, indeed, Agramonte's concert, on the 25th, at Chickering Hall; Annie Beeré's concert, in this hall, promised Fritsch, W. F. Mills, Arbuckle and Lizzie Arbuckle.   On the 26th, at Steinway Hall, Emma Juch had a concert, with Mme. Vanoni, Miss A. Stoffregen, Miss Copleston, H. Brandeis and Oscar Steins, with Justin Juch as accompanist.   The Carri Brothers said farewell, on the 28th, at Steinway Hall, with the Misses Conron, F. Remmertz, H. Mollenhauer, &c.   On the same evening Emily Spader had a concert.   And a complimentary benefit to Theodore Thomas, on the evening of April 30th, in Steinway Hall, presented Joseffy and Annie Louise Cary (the latter in scenes from Orfeo).   On the 29th, at the Lexington Avenue Opera House, the Mozart Musical Union did what it could; perhaps we, indefatigable though we be in concertgoing, may be pardoned for missing this one.   The operatic concert of John Lavine, at Steinway Hall, on the afternoon of April 30th, offered an astonishing array — Etelka Gerster, Blanche Roosevelt, Florence Rice Knox, Florence Copleston, Campanini, Courtney, George H. Broderick (basso), Eugene Weiner (or Wiener, flute) and Adolphe Fischer.   How could he afford it?

An astounding return was staged on April 29th, at Chickering Hall.

[377]

We marvelled, during 1880–81, at the re-emergence of Anna Bishop, first heard in New York in 1847; and now, on April 29th, came "after her extended residence in Europe," Cora de Wilhorst, the young operatic star of 1857. She came forward, with the aid of Lena Little, Maud Morgan, Mary Wernecke, Signor A. Torriani (flute), Orlandini, Montegriffo, McGrone (*sic*) Coxe and William Berge (organist). Next day the Herald stated that "though her voice is somewhat worn, she possesses some excellent high notes, which more than once came out with fine effect. Her execution was marvellously brilliant, the most difficult passages being given with a clearness and finish that is only found in first rate artists. Her trills were especially well executed." She sang Air de Rossignol, by Massé, Waiting, by Millard (as an encore), an air from I Puritani, and, with Orlandini, a duet from L'Elisir d'Amore.

I sadly drop to a "soirée" of zither playing, offered at Steck Hall, on May 8th, by F. de Leauhodu; on the same night Settie Blume made what was advertised as her "début" in New York, assisted by the New York Philharmonic Club, and, at Steinway Hall, W. E. Mulligan offered Fred Harvey, Miss Munier, Remmertz, &c. At this time the "wonderful man flute" appeared afternoons and evenings at Burlington Music Hall, 600 Sixth Avenue. On the 9th, Rosa Silverstädter, Emma Juch and others were at Steinway Hall. At the Union League Theatre, on a rather busy 11th, the Euterpe Club presented itself in association with the Mozart Musical Union; and Charles Roberts, Jr. read at the Spaight Street Baptist Church, corner of Varick. At Steck Hall, on the 12th, Dr. L. Baralt took it upon himself to lecture on True Art, and added a concert at which appeared Hasselbrinck and that beautiful-voiced singer, Ella Earle. On the 12th, at Chickering Hall, Francis Korbay had the concert absolutely inescapable for every singer, and, on the 14th, Mlle. Delviniotti (Greek pianist) came forth at the same place, along with Constantine Sternberg and Frederic Archer. May 17th continued the progression of concerts, with Florence Rice Knox, Fred W. Jameson, Magrane (*sic*) Coxe (baritone), A. P. Burbank, A. H. Pease, William Withers (violinist), James S. Burdett and a male quartet, all at Chickering Hall. Kate Percy Douglas, Lina Luckstone, and others, were, on May 22nd, at the Lexington Avenue Opera House. The Crescent Lodge, at Chickering Hall, celebrated their anniversary (June 8th), with Belle Cole, Miss Henne, Montegriffo, Hasselbrinck and W. R. Johnson (organist). At the Y. M. C. A. Association Hall, on June 9th, Ernest Eberhard, director of the Grand Conservatory of Music, had his bout with public support, in a testimonial concert tendered by his friends and pupils.

Now, surely, it was time to dismiss us to the open spaces. Union Park, 133rd Street and Southern Boulevard, opened its season, on May 29th, with a "Grand Concert" by Wannemacher and an orchestra. But, on the

31st, curiosity doubtless led one again indoors, to hear, at Chickering Hall, Mr. Hurle Barvardoe's "Grand Recital and Operatic Concert." He set himself down as "the only colored, talented and cultivated Shakespearian in America," and to his assistance gathered a group of superlatives, including Mme. Mahoney, "Baltimore's Black Swan," J. T. Meredith, "Baltimore's favorite tenor," and Professor J. H. B. Dungee, "Baltimore's grand pianist." And, on June 6th, at Chickering Hall, occurred Miss Hunt's Society Matinée of Costume Recitals and Songs. And now we really may go outdoors for our music. I have elsewhere listed the German picnics and excursions. Gilmore and his popular band began their concerts, on Saturday afternoon and evening, June 11th, at Manhattan Beach; Walter Emerson was solo-cornetist. Stodder's Orchestra made music, at this time, at Fort Lee Park, and, at Rockaway Beach, one could hear the playing of Deverell's 47th Regiment Band. Why, then, enter stuffy concert halls? And, beginning on June 15th, afternoon and evening, Cappa's Military Band and Liberati could be heard every afternoon and evening, on the pier of the Iron Steamboat Company—Pier No. 1, North River. Verily, it was music, music everywhere.

PHILHARMONIC SOCIETY, 1880–1881

Thomas began the season of our venerable orchestra on November 12th and 13th, with performances of the Eroica of Beethoven, Joseffy's playing of Henselt's Concerto, op. 16, the introduction to Act III of Die Meistersinger, and Berlioz's Harold in Italy (violin obbligato by Max Schwartz). The second programme of the series gave us (December 10th and 11th) Beethoven's Coriolanus overture, Schubert's Unfinished Symphony, W. C. Tower's singing of the Welding of the Sword, from Siegfried (Max Treumann was Mime), and Liszt's Faust Symphony. On January 14th and 15th the orchestra played Mozart's G minor Symphony; George Henschel sang a recitative and air from Handel's Siroe, and later one from Euryanthe; the orchestra also contributed the introduction to the third act of Cherubini's Medea, and Schumann's Symphony No. 2, C major, op. 61. Thomas was a remarkable programme-maker, as, later, was Walter Damrosch.

Most interesting was the offering of February 11th and 12th—Bach's A Stronghold Sure and Beethoven's Ninth Symphony, assistants including Ida Hubbell, Emily Winant, Christian Fritsch, Franz Remmertz, the New York Chorus and the Brooklyn Philharmonic Chorus. This sounds tempting, but the Herald thought Miss Hubbell and Fritsch not quite up to the music; how many have been? On March 11th and 12th, we returned to the instrumental, with Rheinberger's Overture to Schiller's Demetrius; Bach's Concerto No. 3, in G major, for string orchestra; Joseffy, in Schumann's Concerto, in A minor, op. 54; Svendsen's Fantasia, Romeo and Juliet; and Beethoven's Pastoral Symphony. The sixth and last programme

(April 8th and 9th) provided Brahms's Symphony in D major, Wagner's Faust Overture, and three "scenes" from Berlioz's Romeo and Juliet; Miss Winant sang Rubinstein's Hecuba and Beethoven's *In questa tomba* — beautifully, I wager.

SYMPHONY SOCIETY, ORATORIO SOCIETY, 1880–1881

The first rehearsal (November 4th) and the first concert (November 6th) of Dr. Leopold Damrosch's Symphony Society introduced, at Steinway Hall, George Henschel, the very accomplished baritone, who was among the first to prove to New York that musical taste and exquisite art are almost more important for a singer of songs than is a great voice. This was Henschel's début in New York, and he sang an air from Handel's Alexander's Feast, and an air from Euryanthe. The orchestra played Beethoven's Egmont overture, Brahms's Symphony in C, Liszt's Mazeppa, etc. Henschel, in time, became something of a fashion among musical experts. On December 2nd and 4th, the society repeated La Damnation de Faust, with Alwina Valleria (*vice* Amy Sherwin of last year's performance), Harvey and George Henschel (Mephistopheles). Mme. Valleria thus sang in 1880–81, Marguerite in the operas of Gounod, Boito and Saint-Saëns, a feat accomplished years later at the Metropolitan Opera House by Geraldine Farrar.

On January 6th and 8th, the Symphony Society played Beethoven's Fourth Symphony, Bronsart's Spring Fantasy, and the Overture to Tannhäuser; Wilhelmj gave a Max Bruch concerto and a Chaconne by Bach, with the Meistersinger Preislied as an encore. The fourth rehearsal and concert came on February 3rd and 5th, Maurice Dengremont serving as soloist, and playing a concerto by Mendelssohn and a nocturne of Chopin, arranged for the violin by Sarasate. The orchestra rendered Schumann's Symphony in D minor, Beethoven's Leonore No. 3, and Liszt's March of the Three Kings. On March 3rd and 5th, Franz Rummel played Saint-Saëns Concerto in G minor, Emily Winant sang, and the orchestra gave Schubert's Symphony in C. Antonio Galassi and a male chorus appeared at the concert on April 2nd, in bits from The Flying Dutchman. Berlioz's Carnaval Romain and Cinq Mai (first time) and Beethoven's Seventh Symphony were in the programme.

The Oratorio Society began its season on November 25th (rehearsal) and 27th (concert), singing the Elijah, assisted by Anna Drasdil, Marie Louise Swift, George Simpson and George Henschel. Dr. Damrosch assuredly was a busy man and a valuable factor in our musical life. Of course the second rehearsal and concert (December 28th and 29th) were devoted to the expected Christmas-tide Messiah; Lillian Bailey, Anna Drasdil, Simpson and Henschel helped to spread its message of joy. On

ISIDORA MARTINEZ

MR. AND MRS. HENSCHEL

EMMA HOWE

IMOGENE BROWN

MME. CHATTERTON-BOHRER

ELLA EARLE

MAX HEINRICH

ISABEL STONE

THEODORE THOMAS

February 25th and 26th, the Society rendered Handel's L'Allegro, Il Penseroso ed Il Moderato, with Julie Rosewald, Abbie Whinnery (soprano), Emily Winant, Theodore Toedt, George Henschel, and Walter Damrosch (organist — his first appearance in our story).

During the winter Dr. Damrosch had been busily arranging a grand music festival to be held at the new Seventh Regiment Armoury, which was transformed into a gigantic and somewhat poorly provided music hall.   The best available soloists appeared, and a great main chorus of 1200, a young ladies' chorus of 1300, a boys' choir of 250, and an orchestra of 250 showed how big a thing a musical festival could be.   The first concert, on the evening of May 3rd, presented Handel's Dettingen Te Deum, with Miss Cary, Campanini and Myron W. Whitney as soloists, and Rubinstein's sacred opera, The Tower of Babel, with Campanini, Whitney and Franz Remmertz, Walter Damrosch, a handsome, talented youth, assisting as organist.   New York was excited about this festival, and the surrounding towns and villages poured in visitors for the afternoon concerts.

On the afternoon of May 4th, the programme began with Spontini's Overture, Olympia; followed with Etelka Gerster and Annie Louise Cary in a duet from Handel's Giulio Cesare; gave Beethoven's Fifth Symphony and Wagner's Ride of the Valkyries; presented Campanini in Siegmund's Love Song, and Miss Cary in La Captive (by Revere); advanced with Gerster, in the great aria from L'Étoile du Nord, and concluded with Liszt's second Hungarian Rhapsody.   On the evening of the 4th, Damrosch played his own Festival Overture, presented Berlioz's Requiem, and ended with Wagner's Kaisermarsch.   The assisting sextet included such excellent singers as Imogene Brown, Antonia Henne, Campanini, Theodore J. Toedt, A. E. Stoddard and Max Heinrich.   Beginning at two o'clock, on May 5th, G. W. Warren gave an organ solo, Damrosch conducted the overture to Euryanthe, and Campanini sang the romance from that opera.   Hamerik, an American composer, was represented by a folksong from his Norwegian Suite; Gerster sang Sweet Bird that Shun'st the Noise of Folly, and, as an encore, *Ah, non credea;* Mendelssohn's overture to A Midsummer Night's Dream led to the quintette from Tannhäuser, with Campanini, King, Toedt, Remmertz, Stoddard, Heinrich and Sohst.   Two Hungarian Dances, by Brahms, Gerster's singing of the *Casta Diva,* and the playing of the Rakoczy March (from La Damnation de Faust) ended the generous programme.

The evening of May 6th was devoted to The Messiah, with Mme. Gerster, Miss Cary, King, and Whitney.   According to the Herald of the 7th, Miss Cary was inferior to the accustomed Anna Drasdil, King's voice was entirely lost in the vast auditorium, and Whitney made a good, but not a great impression.   It is surprising that Damrosch should have chosen so familiar a work for his vaunted festival; but The Messiah with nearly three thousand performers might appeal, and actually brought the largest audience thus

[381]

far, of the series. On Saturday afternoon, May 7th, Imogene Brown sang Ocean, Thou Mighty Monster; Miss Cary gave Divinités du Styx; F. Bergner, the 'cellist, played Boise's Ballroom Scene from Romeo and Juliet; Gerster, Cary, Campanini and Stoddard rendered selections from the Manzoni Requiem; Gerster and Campanini sang a duo from Rienzi; the orchestra played Damrosch's orchestral arrangement of Schubert's Marche Militaire; Etelka Gerster gave (as I, who heard it, know) a perfectly scintillant performance of *Gli angui d'Inferno*, from Il Flauto Magico; and Liszt's Les Préludes closed the concert. The great festival ended on the evening of the 7th, with selections from Die Meistersinger, in which appeared Gerster, Cary, Campanini, Toedt and Stoddard, and with Beethoven's Ninth Symphony, Gerster, Cary, Campanini and Stoddard constituting, as a whole, as famous a quartette as ever in this city appeared in that difficult music. And that ended a breath-taking five days of music on a gigantic scale.

CHAPTER VI

BROOKLYN, WILLIAMSBURGH, GREENPOINT, QUEENS COUNTY, STATEN ISLAND, 1880–1881

ON August 30th, the Brooklyn Park Theatre presented Leavitt's Vaudeville and Specialty Company, including Nellie Larkelle, S. Holdsworth, the American Four (Pettingill, Gale, Dailey, and Hoey), Nimmie Kent, the Jeromes, Wood and Beasley, Lizzie Daly, Moore and Lessenger, Louise Linden, the Morello Brothers, the Garnellas, and something called The Mighty Dollar — surely not an impressive beginning for a first-class theatre in staid Brooklyn. Minnie Palmer's Boarding School Combination was the feature of the week of September 6th–11th, the vivacious little star being supported by W. J. Scanlan, G. C. Davenport, Sadie Bigelow, Ella Hatton, Lillian Vane, J. E. Nagle, Jr., and Matthew Holmes. Agnes Leonard (for a short time, next season, at Daly's), in Woman's Faith, or, Oregon Life in '55, seems to me to have provided, on the 13th, questionable fare for Brooklyn, city of culture and of churches. But the season still was young, and her support not bad, including, as it did, Frank Weston, Edwin Varrey, C. T. Nichols, Oliver Wren, Ralph Delmore, C. J. Fyffe, Lizzie May Ulmer, and Mrs. Brutone.

And the week of September 20th brought our reward for waiting. The beautiful Mary Anderson began on that date as Juliet, and filled a rich week with The Lady of Lyons (21st), Evadne (22nd), Ingomar (23rd), Love (24th), The Hunchback (matinée, 25th) and Fazio (evening, 25th). Milnes Levick was her leading man, and Hamilton Griffin, her stepfather, astutely managed the organisation. Miss Anderson not acting at the Wednesday matinée, her company rendered Still Waters Run Deep. Since the star had not appeared in New York during 1879–80, and since she was not to act there till December of this year, perhaps some New Yorkers ferried to Brooklyn on the still balmy evenings of later September, to appraise her advance in art, especially when she essayed for the first time in this neighbourhood Sheridan Knowles's comedy of Love. The supporting casts were about identical with those seen a few weeks later at the Fifth Avenue Theatre.

On the 27th, Cinderella, with some at least of Rossini's music, and with Annie Shaffer in the title-rôle, began a week's engagement, prior to appearing at Booth's, on October 11th; in the company were Marie Bates, Elma Delaro, Lizzie Simms and Mark Smith. October 4th brought to the Park Lester Wallack, in Ours; his support included Kate Bartlett, Adelaide

[383]

Detchon, Mme. Ponisi, Harry Lacy, G. F. DeVere, &c. On the 11th, Ada Cavendish and G. C. Boniface presented The Soul of an Actress, seen on September 20th at the Grand Opera House. Sol Smith Russell, fresh from the New York Park, gave Brooklyn, on the 18th, his funny Edgewood Folks.

Maude Granger, on October 25th, began a week of her recent Union Square success, Two Nights in Rome; Henry Crisp, Katie Gilbert, Charles Stanley and George D. Chaplin assisted. On November 1st, we might have seen James A. Herne's Hearts of Oak. On November 8th, the Emily Soldene Opera Company, which did not venture into Manhattan, offered Chilperic and Trial by Jury; on the 9th, and at the matinée on the 13th, Genevieve de Brabant revived memories of an earlier Soldene; on the 10th and 13th (evening) Naval Cadets (by R. Genée) held the stage; on the 11th, La Fille de Mme. Angot, and, on the 12th, a repetition of "Monday's great success." The week of the 15th gave N. C. Goodwin's amusing Hobbies; November 22nd–27th brought dear little Maggie Mitchell, in Fanchon, her support including, as at the Grand Opera House, in the following week, R. Fulton Russell, Julian Mitchell, Marion P. Clifton, Annie Mortimer and R. F. McClannin. Her busy week involved The Pearl of Savoy (23rd and 25th); Fanchon (matinée, 24th); Lorle (evening, 24th); Little Barefoot (Thanksgiving afternoon, 25th, and evening, 27th); Jane Eyre (26th); and Lorle (matinée, 27th). Lawrence Barrett, just prior to his re-emergence on December 20th, at the New York Park Theatre, came to the Brooklyn house of the same name, for a week of the "legitimate." He began, on November 29th, as Richelieu, with Louis James as de Mauprat, and with Marie Wainwright, Anna Warren Story, Archie Cowper, Frederick Bock and Ben G. Rogers in other rôles. Richelieu was repeated on December 3rd and 4th (matinée). Hamlet came on November 30th; The Marble Heart at the matinée on December 1st, and Othello (Barrett as Iago), on the evening of that day. Julius Cæsar (2nd) and the double bill of The Merchant of Venice and David Garrick (4th) also graced the bills.

For the week of December 6th–11th, Robson and Crane played Sharps and Flats, immediately after their four-weeks engagement in the same play at the Standard Theatre. And Kate Claxton, not long after its production at the Bijou Opera House, brought to the Park, on December 13th, 14th, and 15th, The Snow Flower; of course, for the remaining three days of the week, Brooklyn received what it probably expected, The Two Orphans, a play which, with Miss Claxton as Louise, must have awakened many memories of the holocaust of December 5, 1876. A Child of the State, seen in the spring preceding at Wallack's, was the attraction of December 20th–25th, at the Park; Ellen Cummens, Katie Baker, Eva Glen Barker, Carl Ahrendt, Minnie Monk, J. M. Hardie and George Hoey (as Gros-René) were in the cast. Willie Edouin's Sparks, in Dreams, made lively the mid-holiday season of December 27th–January 1st. And Denman Thompson, during

KATIE BAKER

KATIE GILBERT

LILLIE GLOVER

CARRIE WYATT

EDWIN F. THORNE

MRS. E. F. THORNE

LAWRENCE BARRETT
AS HAMLET

DORA WILEY

MINNIE MONK
AS MRS. CANDOUR

the week of January 3rd–8th, continued the happy, holiday mood, with Joshua Whitcomb, Julia Wilson still playing Dot, the crossing-sweeper, and other excellent assistants including Ignacio Martinetti, Eugene Jepson, George Beane, Isabelle Coe, Walter Gale, Mrs. D. Nourse and Alice S. Logan.

The attraction for the next week consisted of the Emma Abbott Opera Company, just prior to their fortnight, previously chronicled, at the Fifth Avenue Theatre.   At the Park they promised The Bohemian Girl (January 10th), Paul and Virginia (11th), Maritana (matinée, 12th), Lucia (evening, 12th), Il Trovatore (13th), Romeo and Juliet (14th), The Chimes of Normandy (matinée, 15th), and Martha (evening, 15th).   The company, of course, was that heard, so soon thereafter, at the Fifth Avenue.   Herrmann followed for the week of January 17th, assisted as usual by Mlle. Addie, the Lorellas, Val Vose and the Onofris.   And, on January 24th, Joseph Jefferson, known then to younger playgoers merely by his performance of Rip Van Winkle, presented for the first time in our vicinity his subsequently popular and violently debated rendition of Bob Acres, in a much curtailed version of The Rivals.   This he had produced in Philadelphia, with the great Mrs. John Drew, whose career we have followed since 1828, as an incomparable Mrs. Malaprop, and he presented the play, now, in Brooklyn, with her invaluable assistance in that character.   The cast, otherwise, was excellent, with Frederic Robinson as Sir Anthony, Maurice Barrymore (Mrs. Drew's son-in-law) as Jack, Charles Waverly as Sir Lucius, H. F. Taylor as Faulkland, Thomas Jefferson (son of the star) as Fag, J. Galloway as David, Rosa Rand as Lydia, and Adine Stephens as Lucy.   Jefferson had, to the horror of men like John Gilbert and William Warren, entirely deleted the part of the sentimental and, it must be confessed, tiring Julia.   "Sheridan twenty miles away," was Warren's comment on his cousin Jefferson's version of the classic; Gilbert called the work sacrilegious, and hoped Sheridan's ghost would haunt the desecrator.   But the public liked Jefferson's Bob (which purists declared not in the least like a British squire) and flocked for years to his performance, especially when the grandly unctuous Mrs. Malaprop of Mrs. Drew — possibly the greatest Mrs. Malaprop of all time — was associated with it.   Now, in this Brooklyn visit, Jefferson gave his version of The Rivals only for three days; for the final three days of his week (beginning on the 27th) he restored Rip Van Winkle to his public. All the Rage, that success of the following spring at Daly's, came to the Park on January 31st with Frank Hardenberg, William Davidge, J. C. Padgett, A. Z. Chipman, Mrs. Owen Marlowe, Clara Hyatt, W. Richardson, Susie Winner and Meta Bartlett.   More interesting was Hazel Kirke, still running at the Madison Square, and now played (February 7th–12th) at the Park by C. W. Couldock, Effie Ellsler, Cecile Rush and Annie Ellsler, in their original rôles, and with Gustavus Levick as Lord Travers, W. J. Ferguson as Pittacus Green, Henry Aveling as Aaron Rodney, Edward Coleman as

[385]

Barney O'Flynn, E. H. See as Met, Dora Leigh as Dolly, and Mrs. Carrie Jamieson as Mercy Kirke. Gus Williams followed, on the 14th, in Our German Senator.

On February 21st, Augustin Daly's company appeared in Needles and Pins, with Harry Lacy as Tom Versus, Henry Rainsforth as Geagle, and May Sylvie as Miss Dosie, certainly a cast of diminished splendour, though Charles Fisher, Mrs. Charles Poole (whom I am surprised to find still with Daly) and Laura Joyce participated. On the 28th, came The Banker's Daughter with a new and interesting distribution, including F. C. Bangs (not recently in our eye) as John Strebelow, Mr. and Mrs. Charles Walcot as Phipps and Florence, Anna Boyle as Lillian, Signor Majeroni as Carojac, E. L. Tilton as Mr. Westbrook, Harold Forsberg as Babbage, Alexander H. Stuart as Harold Routledge, and Lizzie Hudson as Lisette. The attraction for the week of March 7th–12th was Chanfrau as Kit.

The Mahn Comic Opera Company, with Jeannie Winston, treated us, on March 14th, 15th and 16th, to Boccaccio, and, on the 17th, 18th and 19th, to Fatinitza; verily the deluge of comic opera is upon us! But comedy, though not of the highest, was restored, on March 21st, 22nd, and 23rd, with Robson and Crane, in Our Bachelors; The Comedy of Errors was their offering for the 24th, 25th and 26th. On the 28th, Lawrence Barrett returned, in one of his very best parts — Harebell, the Man o'Airlie, a masterpiece of pathetic acting; this he repeated at the matinée, on the 30th. On the 29th and 31st, and at the matinée, on April 2nd, he gave Yorick's Love. Julius Cæsar was the offering on the evening of the 30th, Richelieu on April 1st, and The Merchant of Venice and David Garrick, as a farewell, on the evening of April 2nd. Barrett was not a great, compelling tragedian, but his ideals were high, and his influence prevailingly good. It is of fine augury to see him returning into a theatre-world of frivolity and purposeless cachinnation. And, as I have said, it is always a pleasure to welcome Fanny Davenport, who came in, on April 4th, as Camille (repeated on the 8th and at the matinée on the 9th), with Henry Lee as Armand, with her brother, E. L. Davenport, as Gustave, and with, in other rôles, George Morton, R. G. Wilson, David H. Chase, Leonore Harkins, Jessie Lee Randolph, Mrs. L. F. Barker and Ada Wernell — how different from her former associates at Daly's Fifth Avenue! She essayed Leah, on the 5th, Pique for two performances on the 6th (her brother playing Thorsby Gyll), The Lady of Lyons on the 7th, and London Assurance and Oliver Twist for a farewell on the 9th. Miss Davenport's best work, at that time, was done in comedy, or in parts of pathetic appeal; she was less successful in the emotional utterance of Camille, or the fiery invective of Leah. But her Nancy Sykes was, externally at least, an effective performance. From her exciting week, it was possibly a relief to some to turn to the hearty humour of Neil Burgess, who, on April 11th, disported as the sententious Widow Bedott. The week of April 18th–23rd brought the Acme Olivette Company, including William Carleton, Henry and James Peakes, Selina Dolaro, and Fanny Wentworth, a good list.

Baker and Farron, "the original Chris and Lena," presented, on April 25th, a piece called The Emigrants, with P. F. Baker as Ludwig Vinkelstein-hausenblauser and Aunt Jemima, T. J. Farron as Dennis McGraw and Christina Waldhauser, Ralph Delmore as Arthur Sidney, James Dunn as Abel Hogg, T. J. Martin as Bill Holland, Walter Adrian as Philip Worth, Harry Hotto as D'Arcy Brown, H. C. Beryl as Waldhauser, W. Barrett as Heinrich, Ettie Baker as Agnes Sydney, Georgie Dickson as Mrs. D'Arcy Brown, and Sadie O'Brien as Little Katie. We must keep our eye on Baker and Farron, soon to be registered among the minor luminaries. On May 2nd, John T. Raymond brought from the Park Theatre, New York, his recent success, Fresh, the American. The advent, on the 9th, of Tony Pastor and his company, along with his burlesque, Our School Girls, showed the closing of the season to be near. Harrigan and Hart followed, on May 16th, in The Mulligan Guards' Nominee; they remained a second week, presenting The Mulligans' Silver Wedding. On May 30th, Cinderella at School had most of Daly's original cast, in Harry McDonough, James Lewis, Digby Bell, Charles Leclercq, H. Roberts, May Fielding, Laura Joyce, Ada Rehan, Mrs. Gilbert and Nellie Howard. That ended what I think we must regard as the finest single season in Brooklyn for 1880–81. A testimonial to A. R. Samuels, on June 11th, assembled "Professor" Goldberg, Brocolini, Rogers and Mattie Vickers, John Wills and May Adams, Oofty Gooft, Jennie Satterlee, Bonnie Runnells, Charles Reed, Arthur Cook and Fanny V. Reynolds — quite the headliners of "Variety."

HAVERLY'S THEATRE, BROOKLYN, 1880–1881

Except for the greater excitement of journeying to New York, or for the desire to see a new play during its Broadway run, it was hardly necessary in the '80s for Brooklynites to ferry to New York for stage entertainment. Haverly's Theatre and the Park provided, from week to week, much stimulating theatrical attraction. Haverly's, on August 23rd, began the season of 1880–81 with Haverly's Genuine Coloured Minstrels, whose recent season at Niblo's Garden will be fresh in our minds. On the 30th, The Galley Slave, a success of 1879–80, and still potent everywhere, entered Haverly's for a week, with Gussie De Forrest, Signora Majeroni, Nellie Barbour, Mrs. Clara Stoneall, Eda Clayton, Frank Evans, J. J. Sullivan, Thomas H. Burns, Charles A. MacManus and Charles B. Waite, some of them of the original New York cast. Across the Continent served Oliver Doud Byron, during the week of September 6th. The new Evangeline, on the 13th, began a week of fooling, with Vernona Jarbeau, Louise Searle, Rose

[387]

Dana, the Calefs, Pauline Hall, Charles Groves, J. W. Ransone, Max Figman, Harry Hunter and George K. Fortescue.

On September 20th, the Meade and Maginley Combination appeared in John Habberton's play, Deacon Crankett, anticipating by only a week its introduction at the Union Square Theatre, and with the same cast, except that Helen Sedgwick at the Union Square supplanted Marion D'Arcy as Eleanor, and the Union Square bill prints Stella Chapman for the Brooklyn Stella Congdon. Fun on the Bristol, after fun, in August, at Haverly's Fourteenth Street Theatre, came to Haverly's in Brooklyn, for the week of September 27th–October 2nd. The Union Square company, in Led Astray, with C. R. Thorne, Jr., Owen Fawcett (as Hector), Walden Ramsay (Mount Gosline), J. E. Whiting (de Lesparre), W. J. LeMoyne (O'Hara), Lillian Glover (Armande), Sarah Cowell (Suzanne), Mrs. E. J. Phillips (Baroness), was the attraction on October 4th; according to the Eagle review, on the 5th, Maud Harrison, ill, could not play, and Kate Claxton obligingly re-assumed her original rôle of Mathilde — a gracious act of courtesy to her former managers, highly appreciated by the audience. Later in the week, Margaret Cone was to attempt the part. Grau's French Opera Company (a second combination, not the group at this very time playing at the Standard Theatre, or perhaps an offshoot from it) gave, during the week of October 11th–16th, a list including La Fille du Tambour Major (11th, 12th, 13th and 16th), Les Cloches de Corneville (14th, and matinée, 16th), and Giroflé-Girofla (15th). In the casts were Mary Albert, Mlle. Gregoire, Duplan, Mezières and Tauffenberger. Rice's Surprise Party, in Revels, fresh from Haverly's Fourteenth Street Theatre, was lively, on the 18th, 19th, 20th and 21st, with Topsy Venn, Lena Merville, and the others from New York; on the 22nd and 23rd, they gave Prince Achmet. Deseret was the attraction during the week of October 25th, with Julia Polk, Belle Cole, C. F. Lang and W. J. Cogswell. And Rice's Bijou Opera Company came in, on November 1st, with a reminder of their success, last spring, in the same bits — The Spectre Knight, and Charity Begins at Home. On the 8th, appeared A. M. Palmer's The False Friend combination, seen the week before at the Novelty Theatre, Williamsburgh; in the cast were Frederic de Belleville (in Thorne's former rôle of Lucien Gleyre), G. F. De Vere (in Harry Courtaine's part of Cuthbert Fielding), W. J. Le Moyne, John Wilson, Hart Conway, E. L. Davenport, Eleanor Carey (in Sara Jewett's rôle of Edith), Sara Lascelles, Kate Denin, Alice Brooks, Nellie Mortimer and Nellie Morant, a goodly offshoot from the parent tree in Union Square, then performing Daniel Rochat. Miss Carey and De Belleville had not yet appeared in the home theatre, though they were, as we remember, soon to do so. A Celebrated Case, another former glory of the Union Square, followed, on November 15th, with Harry Lacy (just from Daly's), Lillie Glover and the cast seen the week before in Williamsburgh. On the 22nd, The Tourists in a

[388]

Pullman Palace Car, presented a lively party in Carrie Swain, Louise Paullin, Jeanette Reifferth (*sic*), W. A. Mestayer, J. N. Long, T. Wilmot Eckert, &c.

The week of November 29th–December 4th gave us Matrimony, just a week before it failed at the Standard Theatre, and with about the same cast, including E. F. Thorne, J. Newton Gotthold, E. F. Knowles, W. Maurice, C. A. McManus, Clarence Gibson, Louise Muldener, Emily Baker, Charlotte Neville, Mrs. Thorne, Emma Skerrett and Madge Butler. Annie Pixley, on December 6th, brought in M'liss, with John McDonough figuring as Juba Bill. On the 13th, Mr. and Mrs. George S. Knight revived the fun of Otto. And, on December 20th, John McCullough, having finished his engagement at the Fifth Avenue, brought to Brooklyn a week's heavy repertoire, comprising Virginius, Othello, The Lady of Lyons, King Lear, The Gladiator and Richard III; F. B. Warde, Kate Forsyth and Edward Dee in support. But the patrons of Haverly's relaxed, during the week of December 27th, under the songs and the smile of J. K. Emmet, in Fritz in Ireland. Kiralfy's Around the World in Eighty Days filled the week of January 3rd, and, on the 10th, came Lester Wallack, still debonair, though aging, in Rosedale, with a company including George F. De Vere, H. M. Pitt (he was announced, though I do not find his name in the playbill), J. W. Shannon, Lillian Cleves Clark, Kate Bartlett, Mrs. Charles Poole, and Isabella Thornton. Salsbury's Troubadours, in The Brook, gaily floated in, for the week of January 17th. And, on the 24th, the ubiquitous Mr. and Mrs. McKee Rankin returned with the ever-during The Danites. Buffalo Bill, who had passed the week before at the Novelty Theatre, Williamsburgh, now treated Haverly's adherents to the dramatic values of The Prairie Waif; let us hope they enjoyed it!

The Union Square Company began, on February 7th, a week of Daniel Rochat, that recent centre of animated discussion; in the cast were J. E. Whiting, Le Moyne, F. F. Mackay (as William Fargis), Owen Fawcett, Nelson Decker, Sara Jewett, Louise Sylvester (as Mrs. Powers), Estelle Clayton (as Arabella), and Florence White. On the 14th, Haverly's Mastodon Minstrels, returned from Europe, reached Brooklyn in their travels; and, on the 21st, Charles B. Bishop appeared as Widow Bedott, supported by J. O. Barrows, John Sutherland, Charles S. Dickson, Helen Vincent, Nellie Peck and others. The Meade and Maginley Combination, for the week of February 28th–March 5th, favoured Haverly's with a second visit of Deacon Crankett. On March 7th, the Gosche-Hopper Company, with De Wolf Hopper and Georgie Drew Barrymore, began a week, in One Hundred Wives, recently at Booth's; on the 14th, the Smith and Mestayer Combination gave a novelty, Pour Prendre Congé, or, Seeing Switzerland, with William and Thomas Daly, Morton Emmerson, Willis Clark, Richard Golden, W. H. Bartholomew, Charles Rosene, William Sturges, J. V. Melton, Dora Wiley, Vinie Daly, Josephine Potter, Ida Whiting, May Raymon and

[389]

Marie Zoel, no glittering host; the piece was a failure, so far as getting to Broadway was concerned. Furthermore, the production was enjoined. On the 21st, Our Goblins, that merry joke, gave us still the fine aggregation of William Gill, J. M. Norcross, Francis Wilson (whom my pen wishes to get into something new), William Forrester, Elinor Deering, Emma Carson and Miss V. Barrie. On the 23rd, afternoon and evening, Charles L. Andrews, acting manager, had a benefit. And here, on March 28th, comes Emily Rigl, whom I love to greet, in Only a Farmer's Daughter, seen earlier in the season at the Novelty. Now I can supply the cast at Haverly's: Miss Rigl as Mme. Laurent, and the Adventuress (the kind of thing this actress did so well); Carrie Wyatt as Justine, the farmer's daughter; Mme. Ivan C. Michels as Mother Stark, the terror of Poverty Hollow; Lydia Yeamans as Nance, the black beggar; Nellie Jones as Mollie, Little Mamie Gilroy as Nelly, mamma's treasure; W. F. Burroughs as Harold Lennox, the famous author; Delancey Barclay as Farmer Marion; Elliott Barnes (author of the play) as Philip Bertram, "a handsome face, but a wicked heart"; Charles Stanley as Sammy Green, "whose heart was broke"; Harry Pratt as Higgins, the butler; and Frank Wise as Joe Bates. We remember the brief life of this play, in 1878–79, at 728 Broadway. I give the character-tags with edification; I feel that I am in the rich domain of melodrama undefiled.

I am surprised to find the once highly rated Mrs. Scott-Siddons acting at Haverly's, during the week of April 4th–9th; I had thought the platform had won her entirely from the stage. She began, on the 4th, as Rosalind, with Luigi Lablache as Orlando, George D. Chaplin as Jaques, James Cooper as Touchstone, Leo Cooper as Oliver, L. F. Rand as the Banished Duke, Charles C. Jordan as Frederick, Harry Pearson (once so popular) as Adam, Virginia Bray as Phebe, Isabel Morris as Celia, Lily Stone as Audrey, Harry Haven as Le Beau, F. O. Savage as Corin, Edwin Cleary as Sylvius, George Gray as William, and R. L. Lott as Charles, the wrestler. For the balance of her week, the star appeared in Blind Iolanthe and The Honeymoon (April 5th, and matinée, on the 9th), As You Like It (matinée, on the 6th), The School for Scandal (evening of the 6th), Twelfth Night (7th), Romeo and Juliet (8th) and Macbeth (evening, 9th). I wonder how many found the earlier beauty of the famous lady impaired by time and, if the truth must out, by neglect of the public. During her engagement at Haverly's that other beauty, Fanny Davenport, was at the Park. Olivette, by the Comley-Barton Company, filled the week beginning on April 11th, and Tony Denier's Humpty Dumpty that beginning on the 18th. The Vokes Family were here from April 25th to April 30th, just the week before they opened at the Union Square Theatre.

On May 2nd, Boucicault began a week in The Shaughraun, and, on May 9th, and 10th, Lotta acted Little Nell and the Marchioness; on the 11th and 12th, she frisked in La Cigale; and, on the 13th and 14th, she disported, to delight of her audiences, as Musette. Well, Brooklyn thought there was only one Lotta. The Legion of Honour, progressing through regions contiguous to Broadway, reached Haverly's, Brooklyn, on May 16th, with Piercy, Lewis Morrison and Annie Graham, supported by Forrest Robinson (a personable young man), Herbert Ayling, G. C. Davenport, Sarah (*sic*) Bigelow, Louise Dillon, and Marion Lawrence. The last week of the season (May 23rd–28th) brought Aldrich and Parsloe, in My Partner. The reader observes that one play — My Partner, The Danites, etc. — would last a star or stars for several seasons in those far-off travelling days of our theatre. Haverly's, one also observes, had entertained Brooklyn decidedly well, during 1880–81.

ACADEMY OF MUSIC (BROOKLYN), 1880–1881

A week of the Musical Phalanx, managed by Palmer (formerly of Jarrett and Palmer) began on September 13th, with Christine Dossert, Janet Edmondson, Charles Bovey, Helen Dudley Campbell and J. Williams Macy. It died, on the second night, of utter inanition. For the week beginning September 30, 1880, Inez de Leon advertised performances of Norma, Il Trovatore and Lucrezia Borgia, her assistants comprising Anna de Berlan, Annetta Venturi, Giuseppina Logani, Ida Benedetti, Signori G. Coda and N. Galloni (tenors), Orlandini, and others unknown to a luckless posterity. Whether or not this plan got itself writ into Academy annals, I cannot say. More like the offerings of Manhattan was Constantine Sternberg's concert, on October 7th, with Gotthold Carlberg as chief aid, a joy fulfilment of which I could not verify in the Eagle; and I mention a presentation of colours (October 9th — postponed from September 29th) to the Young Men's Hancock and English Glee Club — how many remember that Hancock was then running for president? — merely because assistants included Allan Latham, Isidora Martinez and Marguerite Selvi. Hager's allegory, The Great Republic, exhibited at the Academy on October 14th, 15th and 16th.

Surely this is a feeble start for the Brooklyn temple of music; but good Colonel Mapleson rescued us from the doldrums, on October 28th, with Linda di Chamounix, sung by Campanini, Galassi, Monti, Corsini, Etelka Gerster and Anna de Belocca (the last-named substituting for Annie Louise Cary, originally announced). The reader will be amused to learn that for seven nights of opera by this fine galaxy and others subscribers could secure a parquet seat for $17.50. On November 4th, Ravelli, Del Puente and Gerster appeared in Lucia di Lammermoor — a delightful trio, still fondly remembered. The activities of the Philharmonic Society, beginning on November 4th, will be treated separately. November 18th gave to the Academy a performance of Carmen, with Campanini, Del Puente, Alwina Valleria (a charming Micaela) and Anna de Belocca (never accepted here

[391]

as equivalent to Minnie Hauk in the title-rôle). On November 23rd, La Sonnambula brought back the delightful Gerster, with Del Puente and Lazzarini (he replacing Ravelli, ill).

A lighter note prevailed on November 25th, 26th and 27th, when The Pirates of Penzance enlisted Sallie Reber, Maude Branscombe (whom I always think of as merely a photograph or, to be exact, as hundreds of photographs by Mora or Sarony), Helen Stuart, Miss Bearman, George Brown, J. Donovan, E. Gillow, George Reynolds, and others of even less note. Meantime, I had learned from the Eagle of September 9th, that the Amaranth Society of good amateurs was to give six performances at the Academy, one a month, beginning on November 17th. Duly on that date, The Rivals enlisted Luske as Sir Anthony, Mrs. St. George as Mrs. Malaprop, Miss Longstreet as Lydia, Bamburgh as Jack and Wilson as Bob. The Amaranths were but a shrunken host; G. de Cordova and his sympathisers had erupted in wrath over an election of officers that suited not their pride, and lo! they established a new Kemble Society, which soon made the parent stem look to its prestige in Brooklyn affections. On November 19th, then, the Kembles began their first campaign with Fred Marsden's play of Clouds, preceded by an opening address delivered by R. J. de Cordova and two members of the society. The cast of the play included William Penny, W. B. Vernam, James Cloherty, Charles S. Withington, G. H. Beuermann, Will H. Butler, Julia W. Reid, Emma Gilbert, Annie L. Hyde, C. C. Ayres, and Edith G. Knowles. The irate G. de Cordova (irate, that is, as to the Amaranthine group) directed the performance. At David Taylor's concert (he was manager of the Academy) appeared a fine group — Campanini, Del Puente, Belocca, Fanny (*sic*) Kellogg (of Boston), the "celebrated" Temple Choir of the same charming city, Mme. Chatterton-Bohrer, Teresa Carreño, Marie Geist ('cello), and Agramonte; this a rich treat of November 29th. Mapleson presented, on November 30th, I Puritani, with the indispensable Gerster, Ravelli and Galassi, and, on December 9th, the interesting Mefistofele, with its excellent New York cast — Valleria, Cary, Campanini and Novara. And, on December 11th, a concert of the Grenadier Band of the 23rd Regiment summoned to its assistance those good singers, Henrietta Beebe, Louise Finch, Aiken and Woodruff, of the English Glee Club. And, on the 16th, the tuneful Marta brought to the welcoming hearts of Brooklyn Etelka Gerster, Miss Cary, Del Puente, Corsini and Ravelli (replacing the announced Campanini). The frequent indisposition of Campanini and Miss Cary caused foreboding in 1880–81; their operatic careers were finishing, had one but known it.

A Peasants' Festival in aid of the Sheltering Arms Nursery brought (December 13th) to the Academy Gilmore's Band; on the 14th it availed itself of the assistance of the United States Marine Band, and, on the 15th, of the Grenadier Band. The Amaranth flowered, on December 21st, in

META BARTLETT

TONY DENIER

SARA LASCELLES

MARION P. CLIFTON

GERALDINE ULMAR

MRS. CHARLES WALCOT

WILLIAM GILL

OWEN FAWCETT

J. E. WHITING

Pygmalion and Galatea, and the offshoot from that society — the Kembles, to wit — followed, on the 21st, with Love's Sacrifice, casting Mrs. Imogene Brown and John H. Bird as the unhappy Elmores, Sophie Osburn (*sic*) as Herminie, Withington as Paul Lafont, Will Butler as St. Lo, Robert C. Hilliard, later an esteemed professional, as Eugene, and Annie Hyde as Manou. On the 25th, Mrs. D. P. Bowers twice acted East Lynne, with McCollom, Lewis Baker and his daughter, Josephine. On December 27th, Salvini gave his superb performance in La Morte Civile, substituted by request for the previously announced Sullivan; on the 28th, he thrilled and stormed as Othello. January 11th allowed us to dance off this tragedy at the Charity Ball, and, on the 15th (afternoon and evening), Hager's Great Republic invited us for the benefit of the building fund of St. John's Hospital. Major-General Judson Kilpatrick lectured, on January 17th, on The Irish Soldier in the War of the Rebellion. According to a file of playbills now before me, the Boston Ideal Opera Company filled a week here with Fatinitza (January 24th and 25th, and matinée on the 29th, with Adelaide Phillips (*sic*) as Vladimir, Marie Stone or Geraldine Ulmar, in alternation, as Lydia, M. W. Whitney as Count Kantchukoff, H. C. Barnabee as Izzet Pasha, Gus Kammerlee as Osip, Lizzie Burton as Dmitri, and George Frothingham as Stepan); The Chimes of Normandy (26th, 27th and 29th, with Marie Stone, Miss Phillipps, May Calef, Fessenden, Whitney, Barnabee and Frothingham; and The Bohemian Girl (28th, with Miss Ulmar). Let me complete this paragraph of miscellany with record of the forty-third annual ball (February 1st) of the Emerald Association, and with grudging account of C. H. Rivers's exhibition of his pupils in fancy dances (February 2nd). But I must not forget the masquerade ball of the Sängerbund, held on February 7th.

That huddling of unexciting events allows me to recur to January 19th, when the Amaranth Society presented The Serious Family, with P. H. Bowne as Sleek, A. S. Wightman as Charles, W. E. Wilson as Captain Maguire, W. H. Greenland as Frank, Edith Kingdon as Mrs. Charles Torrens, Mrs. G. H. Parkhurst as Lady Sowerby Creamly, and Mrs. E. F. Beecher as Mrs. Delmaine. Since this is the début-year in our story of the beautiful Edith Kingdon, I give the reader the verdict of the Brooklyn Eagle of January 21st: "The grace and beauty of Miss Kingdon and Mrs. Beecher were specially noteworthy, and their performance of the characters was quite a revelation in contrast to what is often seen at the hands of lady amateurs." Shortly after, as the world knows, Miss Kingdon joined the company of the Boston Theatre, and, in 1884–85, appeared at Daly's Theatre for two years of success prior to her marriage to George J. Gould. The Amateur Opera Society of Brooklyn, on February 3rd, honoured their conductor, Frank A. Howson, with a performance of Fra Diavolo, Mrs. James Bogle, Mrs. E. J. Grant, James T. Walker, Charles H. Parsons, Henry Gor-

[393]

ham and John G. Hill contributing their art to that end. On February 8th, appeared the Apollo Club and Lizzie B. Ross; on the 10th, Henry Ward Beecher lectured before the Young Men's Central Republican Club of King's County. Amateurs, again, were responsible, on February 17th, for an Academy performance of The Colleen Bawn. And, from February 21st to the 26th, Jay Rial's Uncle Tom's Cabin set up for a week of bloodhounds, jubilee singers and actors. The week of February 28th–March 5th gave us the Comley-Barton performance of Olivette, with Catherine Lewis and John Howson. And back again, on March 10th, came the glorious exemplar of *bel canto*, Etelka Gerster, with Ravelli and Galassi, in La Traviata, to be followed, on the 17th, with Il Trovatore (Campanini, Galassi, Cary and Valleria), and, on the 24th, by Il Barbiere di Siviglia (Gerster, Ravelli, Bellatti — Del Puente not appearing, though announced — Corsini and Monti). Brooklyn was subjected to much disappointment always, in Mapleson days, by failure of advertised artists to live up to Mapleson promises; I wonder, sometimes, that the public bought seats in advance. Probably, so long as Gerster sang, all was forgiven. Let me end March opera, on the 31st, with Campanini, Galassi, Monti, and Miss Cary, in La Favorita. Thus I can recur to the Stoddard lectures (Paris, La Belle France, Northern Italy, Germany, and the Sultan's Paradise), on, respectively, March 23rd, 30th, April 5th, 8th and 11th; also to Ingersoll's lecture on Liberty (March 29th). On April 1st, and for two performances on the 2nd, the J. C. Duff Company presented Olivette, with Julia Polk, Marie Conron, Sara Lascelles, Ed Marble, Charley Lang, Hart Conway, Edward Connell and W. Davidge, Jr.— a good cast; but in truth, Olivette without Catherine Lewis was something like Carmen without Minnie Hauk. On April 4th, I jump to a lecture by John B. Gough, on Platform and Personal Experiences.

On April 7th, Mapleson promised Il Flauto Magico with the big New York cast — Lazzarini, Del Puente, Novara, Monti, Valerga, Ricci, Belocca (these three as the Geni), Marie Swift, Martini and Cary (as the Damigelle), Marie Rôze, Dotti (Papagena) and the divine Gerster (as Queen of the Night), and, for a great wonder, in Brooklyn, it carried through as advertised. Mr. and Mrs. George Henschel (Lillian Bailey) were here on the afternoon of the 8th. Somewhat in harmony with the magic of Mozart, Professor Richard A. Proctor lectured, on April 12th, on The Birth and Death of the Worlds. Arbuckle's Ninth Regiment Band and Lizzie E. Arbuckle filled a niche of their own, on April 16th. That company from New Orleans, which failed so signally in New York, tried a week in kind Brooklyn, opening, on April 18th, with Les Huguenots (Tournie, Jourdan, Utto, Mlle. Lagye, Mlle. Pilliard and Emilie Ambre, she last year almost a failure with Mapleson). Subsequently, these ambitious singers tried La Juive (19th), L'Africaine (20th), and Guillaume Tell (21st) — surely Paris opera in little. Singers not already cited were Garnier (tenor), Mlle. del Prato (dramatic soprano), Mme. Lablache (our old Mapleson friend), and Mlle. de Villeray (as Eudoxie, in La Juive). Everything pales before a real star, and I admire as I record the concert (April 25th) of Etelka Gerster, assisted by Emily Winant, S. Liebling, Pietro Ferranti and the New York Philharmonic Club. This was the year of Gerster's glory, in Brooklyn as in New York. And, what a drop, my masters, to the Floral Matinée (April 30th) of C. H. Rivers' masters and misses, and to the performance of Maritana (May 2nd), by the recently established Brooklyn Amateur Opera Association, with Emma Henry as scintillant star of eve. But, on April 30th, the overpowering Sarah Bernhardt had made her "last appearance" in America, as Gilberte, in Frou-Frou, and said good-bye again, on May 3rd, in Camille. Perhaps tears flowed, also, on the evening of May 6th, when a testimonial to Luciano Conterno enlisted the sympathetic co-operation of Levy, Ferranti and members of the Kemble and Amaranth societies. A complimentary concert (May 7th) to Dudley Buck assembled the Apollo Club of Brooklyn, Joseffy, Henry S. Brown and Antonia Henne.

And now, spring being fully in the blood, the grandmotherly Academy had her fling. The Boston Ideal Opera Company, as we met it that season, in Manhattan, gave us a week of good comic opera, with Fatinitza (May 9th and 13th), Olivette (10th, 11th, 12th), and Pinafore (afternoon and evening, May 14th). In D'Oyly Carte's cast for Billee Taylor (May 16th–21st) appeared Brocolini as Christopher Crab, Charles Groves (whom I am surprised to meet here) as Sir Mincing Lane, W. O. Wilkinson as Ben Barnacle, Eugene Clarke as Billee, George Thorne (can this possibly be the Ko-Ko of 1885–86?) as Felix Flapper, Rachel Sanger as Arabella Lane, Emma Guthrie as Susan, Jennie Hughes as Eliza, and Francesca Guthrie as Phœbe — certainly a most interesting cast, especially if Charles Groves was the Charles Groves of Wallack's, in 1886–88, and if George Thorne was the great D'Oyly Carte Ko-Ko of 1885–86 and later.

On May 23rd a benefit for Detective Charles Chambers brought in a "society drama," Time and the Hour, with T. W. Hanshew, W. D. Chalfin, Frank Dunbar, A. Glassford, G. J. Maddox, Laura Linden, and Julia Sheldon, with specialties by Liberati and Annie Wakeman; Perfection ended the bill. Possibly the motive was more praiseworthy than the offering.

On the 24th (afternoon) came The Mascot, from the Bijou Opera House, repeated cheerfully on June 2nd. The evening of the 24th arranged a benefit for the family of W. A. M. Diller, deceased. Miss Simms, Miss Wilkinson, Ellard, Bray, the Brooklyn Vocal Society and the New York Philharmonic Club were promised. May 26th brought Emily Spader, Liberati and Charles Roberts, Jr., in a free entertainment for working women. So far as I know, this closed the Academy for 1880–81, a season that had given good opera and some other interesting features.

[395]

HYDE AND BEHMAN'S, 1880–1881

The Volks Theatre, during the week of August 30th–September 4th, presented Our Country Boarders. On September 6th–11th, the house was renamed after its proprietors, Hyde and Behman, and thereafter took its position as the leading "Variety" hall in Brooklyn; for that week of its rechristening, it promised a new farce, The Table's Spread, and gave specialties by Add Ryman, Murphy and Shannon, Kitty McDermott, Frank Lewis, Fields and Leslie and Billy Barry and Hugh Fay — these last two the bright stars of the establishment, where they continued to scintillate for weeks thereafter, in Our Aldermen (September 13th–18th), Primary Election (September 20th–25th), Muldoon's Trip to Boston (September 27th–October 9th), Solon Shingle (October 11th–16th), Muldoon's Wedding (18th–23rd) and Muldoon's Trip to the West (25th–30th). During those happy months of early autumn, the olio presented, progressively, Bowery favourites like Valjean (Egyptian juggler), Louise Sherwood, the Milo Brothers, John Till, Mlle. Baretta (sic), Mollie Wilson, John and Lea Peasley, Parker's undying dogs, Bruno, Schoolcraft and Coes, Redmond and Miss Blake, Little Rosebud, Suydam Brothers, the La Rues, Ned Barry, the Chappelle Sisters, Ella Mayo, La Rosa and Levanion, Goldie and Steele, Harry Bryant, Laura Le Claire, Sheehan and Jones, Reynolds and Walling, Niles and Evans, Pell and Lewis, Georgie Kaine, Charles Diamond, and the delightful May Irwin.

Muldoon's Trip to the West lasted two weeks, and yielded the stage thereafter to other Barry-Fay delights — Servants, The Arrival of Sarah Bernhardt, Our City Politics, etc. "Turns" significant to patrons were provided by Larry Tooley, Burbank, the Rankins, Louis Morton, the Harts, the Love Sisters, Jennie Satterlee, Jennie Morgan, the Irwin Sisters, the French Davene Family, Seamon, Somers and the Girard Brothers, the Comedy Quartette (the Budworths and the Nelsons), the Olympia Quartet (Riley, Barry and the Murphys), Clooney and Ryan, Mamie Riggs and Lew Spencer — a procession that brings us, shivering with joy, to December 4th. But that first month of winter warmed our hearts with the bright presences of Niles and Evans, Sheehan and Jones (in The Ashbox Inspector), Lottie Elliott, the French Twin Sisters, Barnes and Mack (Japanese necromancers), Dave Reed, McAvoy and Rogers, Otto Burbank, Jennie Satterlee, Jennie Howard, Barry and Fay (ever this popular pair), the farce of Our Ball (December 13th), Luigi dell'Oro, the four Boisset Brothers, Parker Sisters, Mollie Wilson, the Peasleys, the Lynn Sisters, Little Rosebud, Weston and Hanson, Harry G. Richmond, C. T. Ellis and Clara Moore, Murray, Snow and Runnells, Elise Kruger, Fannie Beane and Charles Gilday, Louise Murio, and, for the week of December 27th–January 1st, the Nick Roberts Humpty Dumpty Company.

Barry and Fay now went a-starring, and Hyde and Behman, to atone, gathered (January 3rd–8th), a mighty host, including Harry G. Richmond (in Dime Heroes, or, Pirates of the Far West, which suggests "debunking" of the ballyhoo of the 1930s), Ferguson and Mack, Charles Diamond, Manchester and Jennings, the La Rues, Hayden (English trick clown), and Charles A. Loder.   On January 17th, "Variety" yielded the stage to Maude Forrester and Mazeppa.   Thereafter that bleak month gave tribute of Charles Sheffer, the Four Planets, Mealey and Mackey, Wood and Beasley, Little All Right, Frank Wills, Clooney and Ryan, Tom Sayers, Annie Hindle, the Jackits-Chy's Japs, &c.   For the week of January 31st–February 5th, Barry and Fay returned in Muldoon's Picnic, along with Harry and John Kernell, C. T. Ellis and Clara Moore, Kitty O'Neil, Mollie Wilson, Little Rosebud, Al W. Filson, Jennie Satterlee, Otto Burbank, and Niles and Evans — as good a group as one could desire either in the Bowery or in lower Broadway.   On February 7th, the theatre put on a juvenile Pinafore and Trial by Jury, which failed so badly as to be withdrawn after one performance.   But a good olio included Alice Bateman, the French Twin Sisters, the Boissets, Fannie Beane, &c.   Snelbaker's Majestic Combination, during the week of February 14th–19th, presented Maggie Cline, Little All Right (in a slide for life), Press Eldridge, Lou Sanford, Magee and Allen, the "beautiful" Hindoos, the Clipper Quartette, the Nautch Girls, the Till Marionettes, &c.   The week of February 28th–March 5th was rich in promise of "turns" by Ferguson and Mack, Luigi dell'Oro, three St. Felix Sisters, Dave Oaks, Manchester and Jennings, Young Ajax, Lizzie Derious and Lottie Elliott.   The house gave itself for the week of March 7th–12th to the dubious ministrations of the Rentz-Santley Novelty and Burlesque Combination, which by many years antedated "Flo" Ziegfeld with promise of a "stage crowded with lovely women."

Back to "Variety" blustered remaining March with Morris and Fields, Wood and Beasley, Add Weaver and Nellie Parker, Pat Reilly, the Novelty Four (John F. and Emma Whitney, Lizzie Hunter and Lester Howard, in Rehearsals in the Parlour), Reynolds and Walling, Barlow Brothers, Fields and Leslie, Charles and Ella Jerome, and Dan Sully (in Unneighbourly Neighbours), Kelly and Ryan (in the comedy, Senator McFee), Ten American Students, the Four Eccentrics (O'Brien, Curdy, Magrew and Hughes), Jennie Morgan, Gilday and Fannie Beane, Parker's dogs, Lucy Adams, the Martell Brothers, Bonnie Runnells, Helen Adell, &c.   The company from the London Theatre, New York, occupied the week of April 4th–9th, with the imposing array of John Hart, the Kernells, the Big Four (Smith, Waldron, Cronin and Martin), W. T. Bryant and Lizzie Richmond, C. T. Ellis and Clara Moore, Howard Dorr and Son, T. M. Hengler, Mollie Wilson, Lottie Elliott, John Robinson, Lizzie Conway, and John Hart's farce, The Henpecked Husband.   For the week of April 11th–16th we revelled in Maze Martini's ballet show, 80 Days around the World, "with a carload of scenery." The two biggest "Fours" in "Variety"— the Comedy and the American — united to make eight for the week of April 18th–23rd; Pettingill, Gale, Dailey and Hoey, with Murphy and Mack and Murphy and Shannon constituted an octette sufficient to sink Brooklyn into the harbour of delight; also in the bills were the Weston Brothers, the Parker Sisters, Cardello and Victorelli, Frank Lewis and Andy Collum. All this seems too much for so moderate an admission fee.

And the show for April 25th–30th also boasted of celebrities in the "great" Thorn, Cronin and Sullivan, Beane and Gilday, Morris and Fields, E. C. Dunbar, Billy Carter, Reynolds and Walling, Lamont and Ducrow, and the concluding Life in a Tenement House. For May 2nd–7th George Thatcher and Add Ryman's Minstrels presented, not only the proprietors, but Seamon and Somers and the Girard Brothers, Beane and Gilday (oddly placed in a minstrel troupe), the Olympia Quartette, Charley Rice, Arthur Cook, Charles Heywood, and William Henry Rice (early and accomplished female impersonator). And the beloved Barry and Fay brought back, May 9th–14th, the ever-during Muldoon's Picnic, in a bill providing Charles Rogers and Mattie Vickers, Minnie Lee, Harry Watson and Alice Hutchings, Bryant and Hoey, Niles and Evans, the Peasleys, Jennie Satterlee, Nimmie Kent, Little Rosebud, and Muldoon and Mulcahey. Certainly Hyde and Behman were kind and generous purveyors. They gave us, for May 16th–21st, Pat Rooney's company, including, besides Pat and his daughter, Katie, the Barrettas (revolving globes and trained doves), the three Russian athletes, and Alice Bateman and Willis Pickert. And Muldoon in Russia carried Barry and Fay afar, in the week of May 23rd–28th, outstanding figures of the week also including the Stirk Family of bicyclists, Rogers and Mattie Vickers, Nimmie Kent, the Peasleys, Bryant and Hoey, Jennie Satterlee and Otto Burbank. On the shrill high C of that week's achievement, I end the tune of 1880–81 at Hyde and Behman's now thoroughly established theatre.

COURT SQUARE (WAVERLEY) THEATRE, 1880–1881

The Court Square Theatre, once a home of innocent merriment yclept Hooley's, re-opened on Monday, August 23, 1880, with a "Grand Pyramid Female Minstrel Scene," suggestive, in title at least, of Ziegfeld's Follies of the great years to come. "Variety" unspecified in the Eagle eked out the bill. That is all I found till a clarion call summoned us to a newer opening, on October 25th, the house "greatly altered and improved," and renamed the Waverley Theatre, under guidance of Luske and Bamburgh, amateur actors, lessees and managers. The company from the Thalia Theater, New York, gave Boccaccio, on November 13th. A. P. Burbank, popular humourist, was here on November 15th, and, for the evening of the 20th, the Thalia actors in Feenhände. For the week of November 22nd–27th, somebody presented Pinafore. The company, from the choirs of the city, included J. G. Hill as the Captain, George S. Weeks as Sir Joseph, George L. Ellard as Ralph, Edwin W. Bray as Deadeye, H. S. Brown as the Boatswain, Ida S. Cortada as Josephine, Isabel Rockwell as Hebe, and Emma Wilkinson as Buttercup, with Rafael Navarro as director. Most of these singers were well known on the concert stages of Brooklyn; they remained a second week at the Waverley.

The Brooklyn Vocal Society promised three concerts — on December 15th, February 23rd and April 27th; for the first of these, at the Waverley, Gade's Cantata, The Crusaders, enjoyed the aid of Emma Wilkinson, T. J. Toedt, F. Remmertz, and Robert Thallon (accompanist). On December 18th, "the greatest living prestidigitateur," Baron Seeman, with Mlle. Seeman, gave the first of several exhibitions that carried him, with intermissions, to January 8th. One such intermission occurred on December 24th, when the Thalia company again came from New York. Teresa Esmonde advertised a reading for January 25th, David Small assisting in baritone songs. The Rivals, on January 17th, enlisted William Luske as Sir Anthony and Charles Bamburgh as Jack Absolute; so one sees that the managers of the house were those two well-known amateurs. The Rivals was given under the auspices of the Heights Amateur Association. On January 26th, the Gilbert Association brought out London Assurance, with John W. Noble as Sir Harcourt, Melville Ross as Charles, John Billings as Dazzle, C. H. Macklin as Max, James Jordan Darling as Mark Meddle, William S. Howson as Dolly, Maggie Hall as Lady Gay, Edith Kingdon, who only the week before had appeared with the Amaranths, as Grace, and Mrs. John W. Noble as Pert. And interest in Miss Kingdon induces me to quote from the Eagle of the 28th: "The feature of the performance was the success of the ladies who were assigned the parts of Lady Gay and Grace Harkaway." Let us pass, on February 7th, to the New York Miniature Opera Company, which then began a fortnight in The Pirates of Penzance. And, on February 21st, Gustav Schütz's German opera, Prince Eugene, had Carl Prox to lead to whatever success accrued. Thence we hurry to March 8th, for the New Orleans University Jubilee Singers. On March 10th, afternoon and evening, a benefit to Levi J. North, of long ago, brought the mercy of amateurs (Luske, Oakey, Southard, Violet Montague, &c.) in Pygmalion and Galatea and Awata Katsnoshin in magic of the east. Callender's Minstrels raised the average for two weeks, beginning on March 28th. A minstrel show of the Columbian Glee Club, on April 18th, ended with The Enchanted Cask, a bit of nonsense "translated at great expense from the inscriptions on the Obelisk," by Allan Forman. Goldberg, in magic, made April 26th significant. And about this time (April 20th) William Luske, manager, took a benefit with (I suppose) an amateur School. With a testimonial to Miss Anna Wilson tendered, on June 9th, by the Lincoln Dramatic Club, I close

[399]

the Waverley for 1880–81; the testimonial brought the priceless novelty of East Lynne — and by amateurs.

OLYMPIC THEATRE, BROOKLYN, 1880–1881

This house advertised but sparingly in the Eagle. The week beginning November 22nd presented Maggie Weston and Joseph P. Winter in D. D., or Dora, the Detective, which we have met in Boweryland of "Variety." May Fisk's British Blondes filled the cup of joy from December 27th to January 1st. John T. Hinds, in The Shaughraun (*sic*, in Eagle advertisements), figured during the week of January 31st–February 5th. I wonder if this was the Boucicault play, or Hinds's own Shaughaun?

William B. Freligh, once of the Bowery Theatre, opened the Olympic, on Saturday, June 11th, for a summer season of plays. Charles Foster, in Saved at Seven, and also in Ups and Downs, began the festivities, and, during the week of June 13th–18th, Leonzo Brothers presented their everlasting Avenged — at least were advertised so to do.

BROOKLYN NEW MUSEUM, 1880–1881

The issue of the Brooklyn Eagle for October 5, 1880, promises the opening, on the 11th, of the New Museum, 424-426 Fulton Street. There, during the week of October 11th–16th, appeared Tom Thumb and his wife, Major Newell, and an illusion, The Grim Goblins. The Lilliputian Opera Company was attraction for the last days of October, with, as features, Admiral Dot, Major Atom, Amy Reed and Sadie Belton. Grim Goblins continued, but the stars of the midgets were the Texas twins, of a combined weight of thirty-five ounces; they carried the weighty names of General Hancock and General Garfield. These twins brought wonder and amaze into the week of November 1st–6th. Little Jim, the Collier's Son, was here in early December, with "five beautiful tableaux." The New Museum, during the week of December 6th–11th, veered to a faculty of big men, presenting Colonel Orr, the Ohio giant, along with "Professor" Velos and his trained monkeys, "Professor" Goodson (in magic), Eva Celeste (Albino), and "Professor" Rodgers and his Punch and Judy. In later December, we were treated to The Spectre of the Forest, and Fun in a Hotel — surely a wide range of dramatic possibilities.

A cat show was here in later March, exhibiting among others, the cats owned by Edward Rhinehardt, the Silver Lake Murderer, certified to by the Sheriff of Richmond County and his deputy. "Poor Katie and Snookson will miss me tonight," were alleged, in the Eagle advertisement, to have been

Rhinehardt's last words. There was also a cat that hatched chickens. From April 11th, we could view Princess Nenemoosha and her Indian Chiefs and Warriors; Langlois, the Lorenberg Family and other curiosities also gladdened April. A poultry show began on April 25th, accompanied by the Lorenberg Family of Spanish Students.

Allen's Mechanical Dime Museum was another temptation for the coins of the unwary. Thither, in the week of October 25th–30th, we wended our way, to see Automatic Wonders, the Crystal Stage — surely a novelty — and suffered while Lottie, the infant elocutionist, did what an infant elocutionist may. The resort was at 325 Washington Street, and had recently come to town from Rockaway Beach. In latest December we saw Harry Sheldon (juggler), Wright (ventriloquist and escomateur), the Royal Marionettes, and Edwards (change artist). The Museums were passing from "freaks" to "Variety," or, perhaps I should say, joining them. An Iowa giantess (450 pounds, with a luxuriant beard), a tattooed man, and Sheldon's Royal Marionettes enlivened early January. On January 13th came Whitfield ("the man of many faces"), La Petite Millie, and the Royal Marionettes.

George B. Bunnell took over this place on January 24th, the long hair of the Sutherland Sisters being part of the show; and he was offering there, during the week of February 14th–19th, the diversities of Admiral Dot, Major Atom and the mighty giant, Chang. On March 2nd, Nellie Keeler, midget, was strongly contrasted with the enormous Chinese. Neil Smith's dog circus performed during the week of March 7th–12th, and Giovanni's performing canaries and musical glasses during that of the 14th–19th. A Zulu giant and twin midgets made men wise during the week of March 28th–April 2nd, and the weeks of April 11th–23rd gave us a baby show, with eighty prizes and a grand prize for the finest pair of twins. Later came a coloured baby show. Apparently Bunnell was out of the concern. But he was back again on July 18th, when Bunnell's Broadway Museum opened at 325 Washington Street, with Che Mah, a Chinese dwarf, "the smallest and homeliest man in the world," who was to sing a Chinese love song; with Zulus in "startling savage scenes"; and stage entertainments by "popular and pleasing artists." Furthermore, there were "mechanical cooling appliances," and "Pure Fun" and "Pure Amusement" were to prevail. This advertisement lasted in the Eagle for about two weeks, then ceased to be. But on August 1st Hungarian gipsies, "queer people who foretell the future," were in Bunnell's Annex Museum, at the Washington Street address. Later in August, Major Tot ("the smallest man in the world") and the Zulus gave what measure of joy they could. Frank Bush, Jewish comedian, also dispensed pleasure to those he pleased. In late August we were treated to the Zulu chief and "his pretty bride," an idea new and strange to me, in relation to Zulus.

[401]

German Plays in Brooklyn, 1880–1881

The Germania Theater company acted this season, as before, at the Brooklyn Athenæum. Das Mädel ohne Geld was there on Tuesday evening, October 26th. The Thalia Theater actors were at this period performing occasionally at the Newark Academy of Music; of course those activities are beyond the sphere of my obligations. They set up rivalry, however, to the Germania players in Brooklyn in "Waverley's neues Opernhaus," Court and Remsen Streets, where, on November 13th, they produced the lively Boccaccio. On February 21st, Carl Sontag and the Germania players gave Das Glas Wasser; they had appeared, on the 13th, at the Hoboken Deutscher Club, in Der G'wissenwurm, of course without Sontag.

The first performance of G. Schmidt's Prinz Eugen was advertised in mid-February (21st) at the Waverley Theatre; Carl Prox conducted. And in Dir wie mir and Dr. Wespe, the Athenæum, on March 7th, presented Sontag and the Germania company; on the 10th, Sontag and the company performed at the Newark Academy of Music. On March 21st, at the Brooklyn Athenæum, Sontag enacted Robert, in Die Memoiren des Teufels, and Dr. Bingen, in Ein Knopf; on the 28th, he was Friedrich, in Die Frau im Hause, and Moritz, in Glückliche Flitterwochen.

Other German Activities in Brooklyn, 1880–1881

We may begin the foreign season on October 11, 1880, with the Concert and Kränzchen of the Brooklyn Männerchor, at its new hall, 406-410 Fulton Street; thence the transition will be easy to the opening of the season of the Brooklyn Sängerbund, on October 25th, at the much-used Club House, 198-200 Court Street; on November 14th, the Männerchor carried a Musikalisch-dramatische Abend. And, on November 25th, we might go, if invited, to 187-189 Adams Street (Gothic Hall) for some kind of festivity carried through by the Amt Stolzenauer Verein. The second Abendunterhaltung of the season for the Brooklyn Sängerbund had brightened the evening of the 22nd of November. Obviously the Germans were singing their way through a wide radius.

Other feats were displayed on November 28th, at Gothic Hall, when Professor Schenkewitz read from the works of Fritz Reuter; another Reuter reading or lecture occurred in the same hall, on December 5th, and, on December 15th, the Club House advertised a Platt-deutsche Vorlesung aus Fritz Reuter's Werken — Schenkewitz again being ministering agent therefor. On January 17th, the Brooklyn Sängerbund enjoyed its masked ball at the accustomed Court Street Club House, and a regular Abendunterhaltung and concert, in the same hall, on April 26th. Brooklyn assuredly was becoming partly Teutonised; and the Sängerbund blithely hired the

Academy of Music for a masked ball on February 7th, with tickets held at three dollars, with an extra charge of a dollar for an extra lady. The Männerchor again offered, on February 28th, a play and a Kränzchen. The South Brooklyn Turnverein and the Gesangverein Thalia, S.B., united in a Schauturnen, on August 11th, at Ocean Pavilion, Coney Island. And that reminds us that the beaches are calling and that we must end the Teutonic strain for 1880–81. If we go to the Stuttgart Hotel, Rockaway Beach, we may have the ineffable pleasure of listening to Don Ferreyra, the man-flute — hardly worth the cost and trouble of a journey thither!

BROOKLYN MISCELLANY, 1880–1881

It remains to collect scattered amusements of the Brooklyn season now under review. George de Gross, a coloured tragedian, appeared on September 20, 1880, at the Athenæum, as Macbeth and the Chevalier de St. George; his support also was "coloured," including Miss Savelle, "the only living coloured Jenny Lind." At Music Hall, Professor A. E. Carpenter began, on October 4th, an engagement of several weeks in mesmeric mystification. In contrast, open as day, at the Hanson Street Church, on the 12th, was Acland von Boyle, on The Use and Abuse of Humour, or, indeed, the reading of A. P. Burbank, on the 14th, at the Fleet Street M. E. Church. At the Athenæum, Elmendorf's company of actors assuredly proffered the familiar in Uncle Tom's Cabin (November 5th and 6th, and repeated "by request" for the week of the 8th), with Julia Sheldon as Topsy. On November 11th, George Werrenrath was down, at Plymouth Church, for a recital of folk-songs. And now I list, to be free of them, the course of entertainments at St. Ann's Hall, Clinton and Livingston Streets, including (November 16th) Henry Ward Beecher's lecture on The Reign of the Common People, with a cornet solo by Harvey Major; Frank Beard's Chalk Talk (November 23rd); brightened, possibly, by a duet of Nettie and Lottie Smith; Sidney Woollett's readings (December 14th), with two violin solos by W. M. Pope; a concert (January 11th); a lecture by E. P. Ackerman (January 25th), on Mrs. Fitz Samuel's Cosmopolitan Club; and D. G. Eaton's lecture on Astronomy (February 8th), made palatable by Annie Thornton's piano solo. So much for the Heights in its more serious moods. On November 16th, Burbank read or recited at the Duryea Chapel.

The opening of a new organ at the Church of St. Charles Borromeo, Sidney Place, provided, on November 10th, singing by Imogene Brown, Anna Buckley Hills, Christian Fritsch, H. Bersin, Buongiorno (baritone), and Bergstein; selections from Rossini's Stabat Mater added to the solemnity of the occasion. St. Augustine's Literary Society staged at the Athenæum Caught by the Cuff and something grandly entitled The Freedom of the Press. Kindred in religiosity was the panorama of Our Saviour's Life, exhibited, on November 25th, at the Athenæum. That same 25th was excessively busy: the Æolian Dramatic Association acted at the Lyceum; at Plymouth Church, Robert R. Raymond read, and Nettie and Lottie Smith sang; Charles F. Underhill read at the De Kalb Avenue M. E. Church; and the University Singers of New Orleans held sway at the Simpson M. E. Church. We must remember that the 25th was Thanksgiving, and be appropriately grateful for these accumulated blessings. At the Hanson Place Baptist Church, Olive Logan, on December 9th, lectured on The American Abroad, with, as musical coadjutors, Arbuckle, E. L. Merriam and J. M. Loretz. The 29th opened Music Hall for Adelaide Bangs (reciter), Mrs. Wiswell, and F. F. Powers. The Young Men's Hebrew Union, on the 30th, presented, at Music Hall, To Oblige Benson and The Hunchback; players included Jacob Brenner, Henry and Jenny Manne, Simon Metzger, Dora Seckle, Josephine Koch, Josie Leopold, William V. Hirsch, B. B. Indig, Myron J. Furst and Oscar J. Harris. On the same date appeared at the Y. M. C. A. Rooms the Misses Nettie Cooke and Helen Griffing and T. Y. Pemberton — small beer, indeed. On the 30th, also, as if they could not let November die in peace, Laura C. Holloway lectured, at the Temple Lecture Room (formerly the Rink), on the much-debated Charlotte Brontë. December 1st allowed Company H, 23rd Regiment, to present at Music Hall a programme including Harry L. Sands (prestidigitateur) and Eliza Wilson (soprano).

The cantata of The Haymakers, at Bedford Hall, on December 2nd, 7th and 9th, enlisted Maggie Mitchell (soprano), Mrs. Lillian G. Nickolds (contralto), Rudolf Himmer (tenor), and Charles H. Oliver (baritone). On December 8th, Plymouth Church opened for an exhibition (the second in Brooklyn) of O. W. Pond's company of native Palestine Arabs; and, on December 9th, the Warren Street M. E. Church promised Charles Roberts, Jr., and several vocal lights since extinguished by conquering time. A goodly evening must have been that of December 13th, at Plymouth Church, with A. P. Burbank, Mrs. Cortada, Agnes Lasar, George L. Ellard and Edwin W. Bray; pleasing also the reading of Sidney Woollett, on the 14th, in the St. Ann's Course, previously cited. On December 21st, at the Temple (formerly the Rink) an evening of music gave us Alice Waltz (soprano), Mrs. Nickolds, and J. P. Davis. And the Willoughby Avenue Baptist Church housed, on December 16th, the eloquence of the elocutionary Henry Galt. A. P. Burbank, on the 17th, showed his Polytechnic at the Summerfield Chapel. On December 19th, the Church of St. Vincent de Paul offered the Stabat Mater, with Maggie Mitchell and Albert Caswell (organist). Almost equally impressive was Henry Ward Beecher, on the 22nd, at the Tompkins Avenue Congregational Church, with his favourite lecture on The Reign of the Common People. On December 25th, the Fleet Street M. E. Church promised Agnes Lasar, Alice Waltz, &c. And appropriate to the

[404]

season was Cinderella, with Charles E. Perrine's Juvenile Company, visible twice daily at the Athenæum, from December 25th to January 8th, with several players from Haverly's Juvenile Pinafore Company, Lisle Leigh, later an actress of some note, figuring in the proceedings. And Beecher's Church, ever alert to keep its congregation in the sacred temple, presented, on December 28th, a Christmas Cantata, with Hattie Louise Simms, George Edelheim, Georgie Nelson, Martha Solomon, Belle Nash, Amy Buck and a large army of juveniles. And General (ex-President) Grant was announced to review, on January 12th, the 13th Regiment. Interesting should have been John Fiske's lectures in the new lecture room of the Long Island Historical Society, on The Historical Development of American Political Ideals: The Town Meeting (January 3rd); The Federal Union (10th); and Destiny of the English Race (10th).

On January 11th and 12th, the Swedish Ladies' Quartet were at Music Hall, and, on the 13th (postponed from the 12th), Frederic Archer, of the Alexandra Palace, London, played the organ in Plymouth Church, with Emma S. Howe singing. The Brooklyn Quintet Club had its first chamber music concert, on January 14th, at the rooms of the Brooklyn Conservatory of Music, Clinton Street. And, on January 11th, at the Tompkins Avenue Congregational Church, appeared the Bedford Vocal Society, with Henrietta Beebe and Emma Wilkinson, two trustworthy daughters of song. David Small, baritone and reader, was moved to offer, on January 13th, A Night with Robert Burns, at which he was assisted by Eliza Wilson (soprano), and Robert Thallon (accompanist); that venture safely past, he appeared, on the 20th, in A Night with Sir Walter Scott, Eliza Wilson and George Werrenrath aiding. The Second Presbyterian Church, Clinton Street, housed both entertainments; Brooklyn was on Sundays and weekdays indeed a city of churches. On January 16th, St. Stephen's Church (corner of Summit and Hicks Street), provided a solemn vespers and a repetition of its Christmas music, with Fanny Pollak, Mrs. A. Christianson, Henry Brandeis (tenor), R. Cartwright (bass), a chorus, and Albert S. Caswell (organist). Of different appeal were the tableaux and art studies, on January 25th and 26th, arranged for church charity, at the Athenæum, by G. B. Bartlett, of Boston; and decidedly different that of R. J. De Cordova's evening (January 28th), at Unity Church, Classon Avenue, where he entertained with Miss Jones' Wedding — No Cards. Adelphi Academy Lectures were now going, with Chauncey M. Depew, James L. Farley, Irene Backus, and others less germane to our theme; and the first promenade concert of the 23rd Regiment was duly soul-stirring, on January 29th. On February 1st, the Clifton Society acted, at Everett Hall, The Spectre Bridegroom; on April 26th, they enlisted, at Rivers' Academy, for Naval Engagements.

Thus I pass into February with its varied pleasures. At Plymouth Church, on the 2nd, the Classon Avenue Presbyterian Church gave to Jose-

[405]

phine T. Losee, organist, a testimonial, in which were advertised to figure Joseffy, George W. Morgan, and the New York English Glee Club (Henrietta Beebe, Louise Finch Hardenbergh, W. H. Beckett, G. L. Ellard, A. D. Woodruff, George E. Aiken — names I have grown almost to love). On the 3rd, at All Saints' P. E. Church, were to appear Ida Requa, Nettie Cooke, James L. Farley, E. W. (*sic*) Bray, C. H. Requa, and others even less notable. The second concert of the Brooklyn Quintet Club occurred on the 2nd, with aid from A. Schotte (pianist), Mrs. Chadwick and Marie Geist; the third of these affairs fell on February 23rd. On the 8th of February, at Music Hall, Kate E. Moon staged Love's Strength, R. J. Chappelle later impersonating The Tramps of the Present Day, and Miss Moon and J. F. Crossen closing the festivities with Twenty Minutes under an Umbrella. James L. Farley emerged with humorous and dialect readings, on February 10th, at the Greene Avenue Presbyterian Church, and, on the 15th, at St. Matthew's Church, Throop Avenue, near De Kalb; in the latter, Francis F. Powers sustained him musically, as did Harvey Major's cornet. The 23rd Regiment operated socially, on the 12th. On February 14th, at the Brooklyn Art Association Rooms, Marie Benchley's musicale presented Emily Spader, Carlos Hasselbrinck, H. E. H. Benedict, &c. George Werrenrath's three song recitals were scheduled for February 17th and 24th and March 3rd, at the Long Island Historical Hall, Robert Thallon and S. Liebling assisting. The Sands Street M. E. Church, on the 17th, promised Helen Dudley Campbell, and the New York Quartet (George White, David Drewry, I. N. Soper and Burr Edwards, vocalists all); and on the same evening, at Bedford Hall, the Bulwer Club tried to act New Men and Old Acres. The Washington Avenue Baptist Church, on the 21st, presented J. M. Loretz, Jr., Adela Rankin, Clementine Lasar Studwell and Emma Wilkinson — very good Brooklyn, musically. And February 22nd allowed the Music Hall to offer a minstrel and variety show of the Æolian Dramatic Association, and opened the Classon Avenue Presbyterian Church for a Columbian Festival, with, as celebrants, Paul Primier (prestidigitateur), Josephine Losee, Miss Iveagh Maginnis (pianist), G. Vitale (violin), and F. Eben (flute); to the Warren Street M. E. Church it brought a Japanese Kettledrum; and at a Hanson Place Church the entertainers were Evelyn Hegeman (soprano), Carl Feininger (violin), Richard S. True (baritone), A. D. Fohs (cornet), and Florence Copleston. On the 23rd, Dr. John Lord's farewell course of lectures began at the Long Island Historical Hall, with Charlemagne as the inspiring theme. Carrie E. Mason was to profit by a testimonial, on the 24th, at the Strong Place Baptist Church, and the Bric-a-Brac Club appeared in Bedford Hall in The Land of Nod and A Pretty Piece of Business. And here, on March 3rd, at the Hanson Place Baptist Church, sang the delightful Hattie Louise Simms, with the saxophone quartett from Gilmore's Band (a treat not so delightful to me).

On the 1st, the New Orleans Jubilee Singers were at St. Matthew's German Lutheran Church, Amity and Clinton Streets.

Thomas Kinsella, on the 7th, lectured at the New Temperance Hall, Kent Avenue, on Irish Wit and Humour; on the 8th, T. De Witt Talmage talked at his Tabernacle; on the 16th and 17th, Moore's Calcichromopticon, polysyllabic and puzzling, appeared at St. Peter's Hall, with pictures of Ireland and Irish melodies. On March 22nd, Allan Latham's Illuminated Recitals and Tableaux may have attracted to St. Matthew's English Lutheran Church persons interested in such an offering; others may have attended the fourth concert of the Brooklyn Quintet Club. On the 21st, the second concert of the Southern Jubilee Singers led willing slaves to the Willoughby Avenue M. E. Church. And the 23rd Regiment gave its fifth concert, on March 26th. March 28th proffered at the First Baptist Church, Clinton and Pierrepont Streets, a concert of the Philharmonic Chorus, with Joseffy, and with Theodore Thomas directing. Far different was the Old Folks Concert, on March 30th, at the Union Congregational Church, State Street, near Hoyt, with Mrs. Christianson, Mr. and Mrs. R. A. Breesee, and Nellie Hall ("the original Yankee girl of Bosting Town"). I am about weary of Old Folks concerts, and pass with anticipations of pleasure to a concert, on April 1st, of Blanche Roosevelt, Florence Rice Knox, Montegriffo and Hasselbrinck, held at the Historical Society Rooms. St. Stephen's Church, on the 3rd, offered the Stabat Mater, with Maggie Mitchell, Mrs. Christianson and Fritsch. A concert on April 4th, for the De Kalb Avenue M. E. Church brought in Marshall P. Wilder, R. S. True, Nellie Decevee, and several inconspicuous artists. On the 7th, some Jubilee Singers were at St. Matthew's English Lutheran Church, Clinton and Amity Streets; and, for the week of April 11th–16th, Ribiston's (*sic*) Colossal Moon shone at the Athenæum.

This brings me to April 18th and the Hanson Place M. E. Church, then and there to hear Loretz, Mrs. Rice Knox, Settie Blume and Signor Bellari. On the 19th, one might have enjoyed Frank Beard's Chalk Talk, at the Christian Endeavour Church, or, at Music Hall, the bell-ringing of the Drummond Family, with their precious Baby Pinky; and, on the 20th, at the Athenæum, have judged the début of Susie L. Tooker, whose kind assistants included Ida and Henry Mollenhauer, Mrs. K. H. Cavannah and the Harmonic Club. The 20th also brought to Music Hall a "complimentary" to Annie Whipp (soprano) and Tillie Crane (contralto). On the 21st, at the First Baptist Church, Clinton and Pierrepont Streets, one enjoyed the art of Clementine and Agnes Lasar, Toedt, F. F. Powers and the Dudley Buck Quartet. These stately or pious duties performed, one might have gone to the patient Athenæum, on April 23rd, for Mrs. J. W. Peters's performances by children, or have heard, on the 25th, the concert of the Harmonic Society, at Music Hall, or have attended, on the same 25th, at

[407]

Plymouth Church, the "complimentary" to Clara E. Stutsman, with her talented coadjutors, Hattie Louise Simms, George Werrenrath, Leopold Lichtenberg (violin), Mme. Chatterton-Bohrer, and Henry Eyre Browne — Brooklyn's very best. That crowded 25th also gave us May Wallace's benefit, at the Athenæum, with proud amateurs in Our Boys. Again, on the 27th, at Plymouth Church, Miss Simms appeared in E. J. Fitzhugh's concert, other participants including Miss Winant, W. Dennison, George Ellard, Bray, G. W. Morgan, the Brooklyn Vocal Society and the Vocal Society of Plainfield. The 27th found also the Flatbush Choral Society operating in the Chapel of the Reformed Church, with assistance from W. S. Leggat, F. L. Dallon, Mollie Martense (elocutionist) and F. Kipp. On the 28th our allegiance wavered as between a concert at Pilgrim Chapel of the Amherst College Quartet (with A. P. Burbank) and one of the Rutgers College Glee Club at Music Hall.

This is for me sufficient music. I turn to James L. Farley's dialect and humorous readings held, on April 26th, at the Sands Street M. E. Church; or to Wilbur F. Rushmore's readings and recitations, on the 28th, at the Greene Avenue M. E. Church. On May 3rd, Eli Perkins, at St. Matthew's English Lutheran Church, expounded The Perkins Family — Philosophy and Fun. And a week of Barnum's and the London Circus, beginning on May 9th, at the Capitoline Grounds! But I must go back for more music and more seriousness, and with May flowers calling abroad! On May 1st, James Redpath, at the Athenæum, lectured for the benefit of the Nun of Kenmare, on the subject of The Irish Land War and Boycotting. At the Hanson Place Baptist Church, on May 3rd, a complimentary concert to Giuseppe Vitale gave us Hubert de Blanc (piano), the Dudley Buck Male Quartet, Clementine Lasar Studwell, Emma Wilkinson, F. V. Marckwald (tenor), and W. B. Firman (baritone) — just as Brooklyn as Brooklyn could be. Also, Nettie Taylor and C. F. Underhill read. Henry Mollenhauer's pupils functioned, on the 4th, in the Athenæum. On the 6th, the 13th Regiment Band played, with Liberati, at its Armoury; at the same season (May 5th) Laura C. Holloway lectured at 398 Fulton Street, on Ladies of the White House, then, at least, a sweetly pretty subject. On May 10th at Music Hall were to appear Jeanie Thorburn, the Jarley Uniques, &c. On the 11th, Henry George, at the Long Island Historical Rooms, spoke on The Next Great Struggle; and, on the 16th, at Plymouth Church, a "complimentary" to Albert S. Caswell congregated the talents of Maggie Mitchell, Herman Bersin, Mrs. Julia F. Draper, George Prehn, the overworked Dudley Buck Quartet Club, George W. Morgan, Rafael Navarro and Henry Mollenhauer — again good Brooklyn. Nella F. Brown, the famed Boston elocutionist, emerged on the 18th, in the rooms of the Historical Society, Florence Rice Knox and A. H. Pease assisting. On the 19th, the second concert of the second season of the Mozart Vocal Society

[408]

brought to the Baptist Church, Fourth Avenue and Fifteenth Street, Green-wood, Hattie Louise Simms, Nettie Cooke, George Werrenrath, and Henry Eyre Browne.   And, on June 7th, a benefit to Gabriel Harrison assembled in the Athenæum Misses Tooker and Meafoy (sopranos), Mr. Meafoy, Mrs. Cutter, &c.   That ended it.   The beaches and the great outdoors called us. In June, Conterno held forth at Brighton Beach, with Levy; on July 1st was to occur (weather permitting) the first fireworks display.   The Scandi-navian Singing Society of Brooklyn went, on July 7th, to Feltman's Ocean Pavilion, Coney Island, there to sing with the Norwegian Singing Society of New York, the Swedish Singing Society of New York, Hans Lechner's Tyroler Quintet from Switzerland, and Charles Metzger's orchestra.   Also for games!   Evidently in New York everyone sang except Americans.

Now beaches and excursions held the advertising columns of the Eagle, except for such diversions as the International Concert Company, holding forth, on July 13th and 16th, at the Club House, 198-202 Court Street.   At Paul Bauer's West Brighton Hotel, on August 6th, appeared the Opleska Agiosco (translate who can!), or, a Trip around the World by Moonlight, which, it was alleged, had been at the Crystal Palace, London, and at the Paris Opera House.   In August (weather permitting), fireworks at Brighton Beach represented the Horseshoe Falls, Niagara; it was to be shown for the ninth time, on August 26th.   The tenth and last concert in Prospect Park fell on the 27th, Eben directing.   And, on Sunday, August 28th, on the Observatory Plaza, Brighton Beach, Arbuckle's Ninth Regiment Band was to render (entire) Rossini's Stabat Mater.   The last fireworks display at Manhattan Beach, postponed from September 10th to 13th (weather per-mitting) was to employ a "grand set piece," by Pain, of London, represent-ing Westminster Abbey, the Houses of Parliament, and Big Ben, with 2,500 large coloured rockets.   At Brighton Beach, on September 24th, in memory of the late President Garfield, Conterno's Band and Levy were to render The Dead March from Saul, Selections from Rossini's Stabat Mater, Men-delssohn's O Rest in the Lord (played by Levy), the overture to Donizetti's The Martyrs, the Inflammatus (with Levy), and the Hallelujah Chorus.

Brooklyn Philharmonic, 1880–1881

The Philharmonic, this season, attempted the scheme of presenting at least one preliminary public rehearsal before the regular rehearsal and concert; at these earlier concerts, merely the orchestral numbers of the concert-bill were proffered, without the appearance of soloists engaged for the perfected scheme — though extra soloists were occasionally utilised.   For instance, on November 5th, the orchestral rehearsal gave us Beethoven's Eighth Symphony, the Siegfried Idyll and Berlioz's Harold in Italy.   These were repeated at the full rehearsal and concert (November 19th and 20th), with Joseffy playing a piano concerto by Henselt, and Miss Cary singing *Divinités du Styx*, from Gluck's Alceste. A lovely bill!

With the permission of my indulgent reader, I will carry on the narrative with mention only of the full regular rehearsals and concerts, proffering, on that understanding, the bill for December 17th and 18th which promised Handel's Ode on St. Cecilia's Day, Schumann's Fourth Symphony, the Welding of the Sword (from Siegfried), Liszt's symphonic poem, Orpheus, and Beethoven's Ruins of Athens, with chorus, etc. Concerned in the proceedings were Henrietta Beebe, W. C. Tower (tenor), Max Treumann (baritone), and a chorus that Theodore Thomas, perhaps with an eye to Damrosch's Oratorio Society across the river, had been assiduously training in Brooklyn. For the initial orchestral rehearsal (January 7th) of the third concert, Joseffy was engaged by special request, to repeat the Henselt concerto, and the orchestra performed Mozart's Symphony in G minor, Wagner's Faust overture, a Septet from Beethoven, the ball scene from Berlioz's Romeo and Juliet. At the rehearsal and concert (January 21st and 22nd), George Henschel sang The Two Grenadiers and an air from Euryanthe. The preliminary rehearsal on February 4th presented Mauricio Dengremont with Mendelssohn's violin concerto, opus 64, and allowed the orchestra to render the first three movements of Beethoven's Ninth Symphony, the Waldweben from Siegfried, and Spohr's Consecration of Sounds. The reader knows that at the rehearsal and concert of February 18th and 19th, the Beethoven Symphony would be given entire; soloists were Ida Hubbell, the rapidly and deservedly advancing Emily Winant, Christian Fritsch and Franz Remmertz, along with a choir of 300. Bach's cantata, A Stronghold Sure, also figured.

The rehearsal and concert of March 18th and 19th gave us Haydn's Symphony in B-flat, No. 8 (Breitkopf and Härtel), Joseffy in Schumann's concerto, Schubert's Unfinished Symphony, Joseffy in the fantasia on The Ruins of Athens (Beethoven-Liszt) and bits from La Damnation de Faust. The last offerings of the season (April 22nd–23rd) included Beethoven's Pastoral Symphony and scenes from Gluck's Orpheus, the latter with Amy Sherwin, George Werrenrath, Miss A. Sessions, N. Callan, Jr., Fred Steins, and Annie Louise Cary, the last of whom must have been simply unrivalled in America in the exquisite music of the title-rôle. Thomas's chorus assisted.

NOVELTY THEATRE, WILLIAMSBURGH, 1880–1881

The Novelty, a theatre which interests me, re-opened on August 30, 1880, "remodelled and redecorated, with a new drop curtain, a new exit and iron stairs from the gallery." Barlow, Wilson, Primrose and West's Minstrels supplied light summer entertainment. For September 6th–13th, Frank I. Frayne, Little Clara Frayne, the dog Jack, and Morris and Gray's

Specialty Company appeared in Si Slocum. The first real drama for epicures came with the week of September 13th–18th, when Maude Granger entered as Evelyn, in Two Nights in Rome, resigning her original rôle of the hateful Antonia to Laura Don. In the supporting cast were Katie Gilbert, Adelaide Thornton, Genevieve Mills, Joseph Wheelock (replacing Harry Crisp, ill, originally announced for Gerald Massey), George Chaplin (as Herr Franz), Charles Stanley (as Abija Peabody), George S. Robinson (as Captain Warmstree), M. J. Jordan (as Benedetti), Harry B. Bull, George De Vere, J. W. Thorpe and M. B. Curtis (the last-named to become a star of the '80s). Reserved orchestra seats at the Novelty cost but 75 cents.

The Novelty then entered on a reign of familiar things: Anthony and Ellis's Uncle Tom's Cabin, with Kate Partington as Topsy (September 20th–25th); Kate Claxton in The Two Orphans (September 27th–October 2nd); Jarrett and Rice's Fun on the Bristol (October 4th–9th); Corinne and her Merry Makers (Lelia Farrell, "Dannie" Daly, Bobbie Daly, Bessie Louise King, &c.) in The Magic Slipper (11th–16th); N. C. Goodwin's Froliques, in Hobbies, with Goodwin, Charles Bowser, Jennie Weathersby, Alice Burville, Jean Delmar and Harry Vaughn (18th–23rd); and Miss Multon (25th–30th), with Katharine (*sic*) Rogers in the title-rôle, Leslie Gossin as Maurice de la Tour, Gabrielle du Sauld as Mathilde, George F. De Vere and Mrs. I. Michaels (*sic*) as the Osbornes, Hattie Thorpe as Kitty and E. H. Stephens as M. Belin — certainly a good utility cast. Another Union Square attraction, The False Friend, must have been acceptable (November 1st–6th) with the cast seen next week at the Brooklyn Haverly's. Again I say one finds most interesting history in these Brooklyn visits; here, for instance, is Eleanor Carey playing for A. M. Palmer several weeks before her début as a regular member of the Union Square forces at the home theatre. And I am pleased to find those former mainstays of the Daly Fifth Avenue company, Mr. and Mrs. De Vere (Nellie Mortimer) enrolled under the Palmer banner.

With James A. Herne, in Hearts of Oak, appeared (November 8th–13th), Frank E. Aiken, Harry Mainhall, W. H. Crompton and Genevieve Reynolds, all of whom I am pleased to find placed for the season. Aldrich and Parsloe followed (15th–20th), of course in My Partner; and another Union Square success — A Celebrated Case — filled the week of the 22nd–27th, with Harry Lacy as Jean Renaud, Lillie Glover as Madeleine and Adrienne, Mrs. J. J. Prior as the Chanoinesse, Eva French, the inevitable, as the child Adrienne, Etelka Wardell as Valentine, J. Winston Murray as the bad Count de Mornay, Frank Little as Raoul and John T. Hinds as O'Rourke. Certainly a bond of interest must have stretched across the East River from Brooklyn to the Union Square Theatre. For November 29th–December 4th, however, we changed to The Tourists in a Pullman Palace Car, with

W. A. Mestayer, Carrie Swain and Louise Paullin.   A play by William Seymour, entitled Long Branch, enlisted for December 6th–11th Catherine
Lewis, who was not at present living up to her Daly successes of 1879–80, as
well as Susie Parker, Moses Fiske, Murry Woods and Charles Lang.   Only
a Farmer's Daughter was announced for December 13th–18th, with Emily
Rigl, Constance Hamblin, Lillie Eldridge, Mrs. Ivan C. Michaels, Blanche
Mortimer, Lydia Yeamans, George C. Jordan, E. Murray Day, Ed Marble
and G. J. Henderson; Miss Rigl was ill and Constance Hamblin replaced her
as Mme. Laurent, with promise of Miss Rigl's re-appearance on the 15th, a
promise whose fulfilment I cannot vouch for.   J. B. Studley and Ida Vernon,
in Monte Cristo, were scheduled for December 20th–25th, and Annie Pixley's
M'liss for the 27th–January 1st.   The Legion of Honour, with Piercy and
Constance Hamblin, filled the week of January 3rd–8th.

And Willie Edouin, seen during the preceding week at the Park Theatre,
Brooklyn, carried his Dreams, on January 10th, to the Novelty; A Child
of the State held the week of January 17th, of course with the Hardie-Hoey
company seen earlier at the Brooklyn Park.   Buffalo Bill and The Prairie
Waif doubtless pleased some tastes, during the week of January 24th–29th.
The Harrisons (Louis and Alice, a funny pair) were here, on January 31st,
in B. E. Woolf's trifling piece, Photos — a piece which served them for a
few merry seasons.   On February 7th, Frank Mayo tried, unsuccessfully,
it would seem, a new play by Bartley Campbell, entitled Van, the Virginian; the reader may never hear of it again.   Samuel Reed and Affie
Weaver were in the cast.   On the 14th, Mayo reverted to that sure-fire hit,
Davy Crockett.   The Galley Slave, with Gussie De Forrest, Signora
Majeroni, Frank Evans and E. F. Knowles, entered the Novelty, on February 21st, yielding the stage, on the 28th, to F. S. Chanfrau, in his seemingly immortal Kit.   Another long-lived entertainment, Joseph Murphy
(with Genevieve Stebbins) in The Kerry Gow, was the feature of March
7th–12th; somewhat more novel, though not exactly new, was the offering
of the 14th — the Gosche-Hopper Combination (with De Wolf Hopper), in
One Hundred Wives.   On March 21st came A. M. Palmer's Union Square
Company (Whiting, Le Moyne, Cyril Searle, Ramsay, Nelson Decker, Miss
Carey, Maud Harrison, Virginia Buchanan), in Daniel Rochat, intellectual
matter that may have stimulated some minds in Williamsburgh.   If so, they
could sink back, during the week of March 28–April 2nd, into the fun and
frivolity of J. H. Haverly's Mastodon Minstrels, which my pen would not
have wept to find remaining even longer amid their European "triumphs."

I am pleased to greet a return of Hazel Kirke, this time (April 4th–9th)
with an entirely new cast, including Charles Wheatleigh, Alfred S. Phillips,
W. H. Gillette (the famous Sherlock Holmes of the future, then playing
Pittacus Green), John Wilson, E. L. Walton, Albert Tavernier, Lillian
Spencer, Genevieve Mills, Kate Denin, Mrs. Sara A. Baker, and **Josie Wil-**

mere. We shall meet many casts of this play, before we finish. Tony Denier's Humpty Dumpty, on the 11th, wiped away the tears that Hazel Kirke's woes had set running from sympathetic eyes. On the 18th, Neil Burgess began a week of Widow Bedott.

Fanny Davenport, who had been skirting the centre of things, as represented by Broadway, reached the Novelty, on April 25th, for a week of Pique, still her best asset; J. B. Studley was the iron Matthew Standish. H. B. Mahn's Company sang the merry tunes of Boccaccio, beginning on May 2nd; the cast included Jeannie Winston, Janet Edmondson, Marie Somerville (*sic*), Maud Allison, Rose Leighton, W. A. Morgan, Vincent Hogan and Ellis Ryse. May 9th brought kindred matter, with the New York Comedy Company, in Billee Taylor. Harry Miner's Grand Novelty Constellation, booked for the week of May 16th–21st, leaves me with the feeling that the winter glories have passed; but Daly's company (May 23rd) in Needles and Pins, pricks my drooping courage, to go once more to see James Lewis, Leclercq, Digby Bell (as Kit), John Drew, Ada Rehan, Mrs. Gilbert, Laura Joyce and Mrs. C. W. Poole (trying to replace the gifted Fanny Morant). The last week of the season (May 30th–June 4th) at the Novelty provided the rich celebration of The Mulligans' Silver Wedding, with Harrigan and Hart, who for two weeks before, had been at the Park, Brooklyn, with successively, The Mulligan Guards' Nominee and The Silver Wedding. Altogether, the Novelty had provided good entertainment for Williamsburgh, thereby reducing the necessity for ferrying to New York for an evening's enjoyment, or even taking a street car to Brooklyn in the west. We see that Brooklyn sent to the Novelty much of the attraction of that season at the Park or at Haverly's; and sometimes the Novelty sent the attraction to Brooklyn.

BERRY'S BROADWAY THEATRE, WILLIAMSBURGH, 1880–1881

Berry's Broadway Theatre, then so called, re-opened on September 11, 1880, with Andy Morris, Tom Granger, Ida Maussey and Sadie Gomersal conspicuously listed; on Saturday, the 18th, the Electric Three and the Four Comets were numerically strong. I found no more in the Brooklyn Times till November 8th, when "a grand opening for the season" brought Jerry Cohan and Miss Nellie F. Cohan (Mrs. Helen Cohan, of course) in their exciting The Molly Maguires; Belle Berry (*sic*) headed a group of minor celebrities in the olio. On Saturday, November 20th, the Times advertises for every evening and Tuesday and Saturday matinées, Muldoon's Picnic, with performers including Ned Barry, Ione Lang, Harry Mack, Grace Arnold, F. A. McClane and George Shepherd (*sic*). This must have been the last of a week's engagement; on Monday, November 22nd, Addie Ryan was to play That Boy of Dan's. November 29th–December 4th gave us

[413]

Larry Tooley, in Night Scenes in New York, and Belle Berri (*sic*) in A Human Fiend, or, the Ways of the World; Mamie and Billy Williams, Fostelle and Forrest, Ione Lang, Grace Arnold, F. A. McClane and J. W. Macready made up an olio. Bell Berri next (December 6th–11th) essayed Mazeppa, George Harris, in the same bill, giving Alexander Mayblossom's Visit to New York; others in the bill were Will C. Matthews, Lottie Grant and Nellie Harris. For December 13th–18th, W. H. Rightmire was engaged in The Boss, and other attractions were Bobby and Alice Daily, Arthur Sprague ("young American tragedian"), Ira Paine (the "champion marksman of the world") and F. A. McClane; the next week (December 20th–25th) scheduled Charles Thornton in Simon Kenton, the Parker Sisters, Nellie Collins, Edwards and Gaylor, and McClane's negro act, Broadway Milliners. I cannot recommend Berry's to a fastidious lover of "Variety." The bill for December 27th–January 1st bore promise of Tommy Granger (in Zipp and My Wife), Monroe and King, Hart and Collins, The Ambassador Lady (with Belle Berrie, now so spelled) and McClane in The Black Statue. Poor Rose Lisle, "late of Wallack's Theatre," but at present sunk, sunk from that proud position, was to appear in The Moonshiner's Wife.

The week of January 24th–29th also tried to impress with the dignity of its stars. Laura Phillips ("late of the Boston Museum") and Rose Lisle ("late of Wallack's") appeared in an Irish play, Sleive na Garry; and the olio certainly was improved, with Georgie Melnotte, the Garnella Brothers, Frank King, Monroe and Sheparde (*sic* — German team) and McClane's farce, Cummings, or, the Other Fellow. Frank Jones and Alice Montague (in The Black Hand), Alice Daily, the "wonderful" Phillions, the merry Swiss Warblers, and McClane's "funniest" negro act (Hackman 47) tested the range of adjectives for the week of January 31st–February 5th. Denier's Humpty Dumpty was welcomed for February 7th–12th, along with Minetta and Kincade (the "modern Samsons"), Howard and Coyne ("Celtic eccentrics"), Sullivan and Smith (song and dance), Amy Hoey (serio-comic), Connie Hanlon ("song and dance lady") and F. A. McClane, in The Crushed Tragedian. No, I really cannot recommend Berry's. Nor am I impressed with the offerings for February 14th–19th; the Leonzo Brothers and their dogs (in Avenged), Idaletta and Wallace ("man and woman fish"), Maggie Nichols (aerial queen, for another of the four elements), E. C. Edwards ("electric change") and F. A. McClane's farce, The District Telegraph, acted by "our great stock company." The Leonzos remained a second week (21st–26th), in Rupert's Dog, and the olio gave O'Brien Brothers (gymnasts), Max and Martha Miller, Didway Brothers ("eccentric instrumentalists") and The Mischievous Monkey. Only my zeal as an historian keeps me going to Berry's. There, for February 28th–March 5th, W. S. Higgins, and the child actress, Lulu, ap-

[414]

peared in Tramps; the Four-in-Hand (Sullivan, Smith, Mayo and Talbert), James A. Kennedy, Nellie Amon and F. A. McClane (in The Dog Next Door) did what they could for the olio.   March 1st brought a benefit for "struggling Ireland."   Rightmire returned (March 7th–12th) in Thrown upon the World, and the olio improved, with James O'Neil, Dick Sands, the Four-in-Hand, Nellie Amon, Belle Berrie and McClane.   N. S. Wood (in The Boy Detective, supported by J. P. Winter), H. A. Wallington and "his talking figures," and Addie (*sic*) Farnham (change artist) were chief lure of March 14–19th; the drama of Retribution, or, a Life for a Life, proclaimed its stern message (March 21st–26th) in connection with an olio comprising Sheldon and Barry (Irish sketch artists), Grace Arnold, Davis Brothers (lofty tumbling), Andy Bryant, and Frank McClane (in Room 44).   And here for March 28th–April 2nd is our old friend, Fanny Herring, in Little Buckshot, other entertainers being Charles Siebert (*sic*) and A. S. Caspar ("the talented actors"), Lena Cole (vocalist), P. C. Melrose (balancing trapeze), Monroe and King (acrobatic song and dance) and McClane (in A Taxpayer's Vicissitudes, certainly an intriguing title to our day in 1939). Berry's seems to be taking on a tang or a flavour of something more palatable.   For April 4th–9th it offered Adelina Gasparini, in Meg, supported by the child actress, Ada (*sic*); McClane's farce, The Wrong One; and an olio with La Rosa Brothers, Cooper Brothers, and George S. Garland and Cherry Chapman.   Johnny Allen, in "his great drama," Schneider, was exploited for April 11th–16th, the olio including Lester Brothers (trapeze), Griffin and Marks (song and dance), and Georgie Melnotte.   Belle Berrie's benefit, on the 12th, promised N. S. Wood, in the first act of The Boy Detective, and a huge olio.

   G. C. Charles reached out (April 18th–23rd) with The Skeleton Hand, but did not grasp much of an olio, with Jennie Ward and J. H. Graham (sketch artists), P. C. Melrose (contortionist) and Minnie Bryant (serio-comic).   Sam Ryan came next (25th–30th) in Faithful and True, in association with an olio offering Martha and Max Miller (ladies now first, one sees), Carroll and Walters, and the Four Kings (Conklin, Lee, Sullivan and Quick).   Frank Jones and Alice Montague (again in The Black Hand), "Professor" Phillion (French illusionist) and Emma Phillion (aerial suspension), Vampier and Vidocq (grotesque dancers), and Sophie Thorne (May 2nd–7th); Leonzo Brothers and dogs (in The Dog Spy), John B. Wills and May Adams, the Four-in-Hand (Mayo, Talbert, Sullivan and Smith), during the week of May 9th–14th; George C. Charles and Kate Moffett (in The Poor of Ireland), Lottie Grant, Joe Norton, Griffin and Mack and McClane (16th–21st); N. S. Wood and J. P. Winter (in The Boy Detective), Wheeler and Colbert, Lottie Grant, Byron and Coffee, Ned Rodgers (23rd–28th); A. A. Wallace (in The Hangman of Paris), Archie Hughes, Tommy Granger, Annie Cummings, Gus H. Saville, and John H.

[415]

Byrne (May 30th–June 4th); there, in staccato outline is the history of the last nights of Berry's for 1880–81. I apologise to the reader for dwelling on the unimportant details of the offering.

WILLIAMSBURGH MISCELLANY, 1880–1881

The weary reader and I must start on a long trail through the Williamsburgh Miscellany of 1880–81. Beginning on August 22nd, 23rd, 24th and 25th, with the Canstatter (*sic*) Volksfest in Myrtle Avenue Park, we pass to the exhibition of the Williamsburgh Athletic Club (Saturday, August 28th), at their new grounds on Wythe Avenue; thence, on the same night, to the fifteenth anniversary of the Brooklyn Arion, at Euler's Broadway Park; on September 5th, to a charity concert and summer-night festival, at Myrtle Avenue Park, provided by the Williamsburgh Turnverein, the German Liederkranz, the Williamsburgh Sängerbund, the Haydn Männerchor, the Arion, the Schwäbischer Sängerbund and the Brooklyn Musical Union — a function worth attending, if only for the purpose of estimating the German vote in the Eastern District; thence to the Schwaben Volksfest, on September 12th, 13th and 14th, carried out at Ridgewood Park by the Schwäbischer Sängerbund; and, finally, to get out of this open-air activity and my very long sentence, announce the opening of the Williamsburgh Bicycle Track, on September 11th. On the 28th, 29th and 30th, the New York Standard Combination in Aurora Floyd was scheduled for the Lyceum Theatre, South Eighth and Fourth Streets; midway of that engagement the Old Bushwick Church lighted up (September 29th) for a visit of the ubiquitous A. P. Burbank, a popular figure in Williamsburgh.

Either entertainment was scarce in Williamsburgh, during that autumn of a presidential election (poor Garfield!) or my eye or the Brooklyn Times failed in the crisis. Andrew Halliday's drama, Daddy Gray, came to the Lyceum, on October 13th, and Blind Tom was, on the 18th, at Dr. Porter's church. On the 21st, a literary and musical testimonial to Wilbur F. Rushmore promised, in the lecture room of Calvary Church, D. B. Thompson (flute), Priscilla Whittingham (elocutionist, as she almost must be with that name), Florence N. Lethbridge (pianist), the Lyceum Glee Club and Sarah Spender (singer). The fall meeting of the Williamsburgh Athletic Club opened their grounds, on the 23rd. Doubly blest was October 28th, with Charles Roberts, Jr., at the Central Baptist Church, and the concert, at the Lyceum, of the Euterpean Club of Williamsburgh, assisted by George Law, George McMunn (reciter), and E. H. and Ada Ducharme. Post-election November likewise yields but meagre harvest — as a ribald wit might say, very small pumpkins. On the 9th, at the Clinton Lyceum, 118 Myrtle Avenue, E.D., Clinton Lodge No. 97 played The Drunkard's Warning and Browne the Martyr, educational, I suspect, rather than exhilarating.

A testimonial to Robert A. Johnson, librarian of the Brooklyn E. D. library was to bring to Dr. Porter's church, on November 10th, Nella F. Brown, Florence Rice Knox and the tenor King.   The Drummond Family of Bell Ringers played, on the 17th, at the Lyceum, and, on the 23rd, at the First Presbyterian Church, South Fourth and Sixth Streets, the dramatic Rev. T. DeWitt Talmage held forth on Big Blunders.   At Dr. Porter's Bedford Avenue Church, on the 25th, Settie Blume was chief attraction and was pitted, on the same date, against Betty Terwilliger and Her Troublesome Tramps, settling for the nonce in the lecture room of Calvary Church.   The same busy 25th found at the Kent Street Dutch Church, E.D., Henry Galt, Florence Rice Knox, F. G. Bourne, W. F. Mills and Miss L. Florence. On December 2nd, 7th and 9th, The Haymakers, at Bedford Hall, enlisted Maggie Mitchell (soprano), Lillian G. Nickolds (contralto), Rudolf Himmer (tenor) and Charles H. Oliver (bass).   At Grace P. E. Church, on December 21st, a large group included Katherine (*sic*) Cavannah, Priscilla Whittingham, George Law, the Lyceum Glee Club, George McMunn, Samuel Murphy, Minnie Watson and Jennie Cabble.   Charles Beam, on the 28th, gave a concert at the Lyceum, and the 29th found the Lee Avenue Baptist Sabbath School promising Charles Roberts, Jr. and Christmas trees and Santa Claus and all things appropriate for Christmas in a "Sabbath" School.   On the 29th, also, and apparently on the 30th, the Drummond Family operated at the Leonard Street M.E. Church; Dr. Porter's church, on the 30th, displayed fifty stereopticon views of Venice, the Bride of the Sea, all to illustrate Rev. Newland Maynard's lecture on that fascinating theme. And, on an evening in early January (the 8th), at the Ross Street Church, we were invited to buy tickets for a concert by Florence Rice Knox, Florence Copleston, Franz Remmertz, Henry Galt, and William Edward Mulligan (organist).   On January 27th, at Dr. Porter's Church, the Amphion Musical Society started its public career, with, as soloists, Hattie Louise Simms, T. J. Toedt and Florence Copleston.

On January 28th, the Souvenir acted, at Turn Hall, Time Tries All, with Robert Seligman, Joseph Rosenblatt, R. M. Masur, H. and J. M. Benjamin, B. Rosenbaum, Tillie Wolff and Mrs. C. Kodieson.   Is this our first Hebrew play?   Beginning on January 31st, Abbie Sage Richardson was to deliver a course of lectures on English literature, at the Woman's Club, 80 Willoughby Street.   February by excess of entertainment atoned for a meagre autumn.   On the 2nd, The Land of Nod, at All Souls Church, had scenery, costumes, and music.   February 9th was distractingly busy: Kate Hill's concert, at Dr. Porter's Church, promised Emma Wilkinson, Fred Steins, Grace Wade and August Victor Denham; at the Lyceum appeared Priscilla Whittingham, Mrs. M. A. Davis, Wilbur F. Rushmore, the Euterpean Glee Club, the Meigs Sisters (a delightful quartet) and Ortloff's orchestra of nineteen performers; the Brooklyn Liedertafel, the Euterpe, the

[417]

Wilhelm Tell Männerchor, and the Choir of St. Matthew's Lutheran Church co-operated at Germania Hall; Mrs. Delia Stewart Parnell, mother of the Agitator, asked, at the hall of the Spread the Light Club, 365 Fulton Street, Shall Women Engage in the Land Movement? And February 10th had a bursting cornucopia: Lillian Latham delivered a musical and literary entertainment at Latham's Hall, Ninth Street between Hope and Ainslie; the ball of the Bowronville Plattdeutsche Club was danced at Jansen's Germania Hall. And about this time, in Lyceum Hall, Dr. and Mrs. Uriah Clark attempted to expose spiritualism, challenging any medium on earth to do anything that could not be duplicated or explained as fraud or psychological phenomena, "without the agency of any kind of spirits, good or bad."

I pass to the mask ball of the Zoellner Männerchor, danced, on February 14th; to the calico ball of the Williamsburgh Benevolent Society, on the 21st; and to the Arion Masquerade, on the 25th — all celebrated in Turnhalle, Meserole Street. On February 14th, the Amphion Musical Society gave a concert in their rooms; and the Young Men's Hebrew Union gave, at the Athenæum, their fourth play and reception. Y. M. C. A. concerts at the Lyceum employed (on the 14th and 15th) Florence Auld, William Nash and Mary Keech. Let us proceed to Dr. Porter's church, on February 22nd, to hear Settie Blume, Maud Morgan and A. Miller, journeying, thence, on the 24th, to a concert, in Library Hall, of the Euterpean Glee Club. Williamsburgh during this period was very busy with church concerts, lectures, sociables and all harmless diversions that take one from home; also with balls, as I have shown above. Hughes and Allen's Minstrels were, on February 23rd, at Turn Hall Theatre; on the 24th, the "Wallack" acted Love, at Association Hall. The Drummond Family and Gracie F. Wade ("favorite" elocutionist) were at the Lyceum, on February 23rd. But I must insert here some performances at Turn-Halle, Meserole Street, by the actors from the Thalia Theater, New York, all given as Sunday "sacred" concerts: Einer von unsere Leut' (February 20th); and Boccaccio (March 6th).

February was for me a hard, terrifying month; so much so that I lack energy to drag myself, on March 1st, to the masquerade of the Williamsburgh Turnverein, in their Meserole Street abode, or to that of the Arndt Männerchor, on the same night, at Wardell's Sängerhalle, 89 Grand Street; it might refresh my mind to watch the sparring, wrestling and fencing at the "stag" party, on the 4th, at the Lyceum, by the Williamsburgh Athletic Club. On the 7th, Thomas Kinsella lectured, at Temperance Hall, Kent Avenue, on Irish Wit and Humour; Herbert S. Renton, President of the Hawthorne Literary Association, talked, on the same date, in the Faith Mission Chapel, on A Day and Night in a Volcano. For March 8th we had, at Sänger Hall, the celebration of the fifteenth anniversary of the Cecilia Singing Society of Grand Street; on the 8th, also, the Chickering

Harmonics were at the North Fifth Street M.E. Church.   Turnhalle gave itself, on the 9th, to an athletic entertainment and ball of "Professor" Herman Hattenhorst, at which were to appear "Professor" McClellan and Mike Donovan in, I suspect, something to do with physical prowess.   On the 10th, Locke Richardson, at All Souls Church, was to read bits of The Merry Wives of Windsor, strange matter for a sacred edifice.   On the 12th, Philip Phillips and his son gave an evening of song at the Church of Christian Endeavour; on the 14th, the Schwäbischer Sängerbund danced the merry hours away in masquerade.   Henry Firth Wood (elocutionist) and Lydia Jefferies were, on March 24th, at the Second Reformed Presbyterian Church, North Street, near South Second.   I wonder if they had a paying audience, or expected one. That question applies, also, on the 24th, to W. F. Rushmore and Ada Gleason, at the New England Church.   The Thalia actors from New York completed their engagement, on March 27th, at Turnhalle, with H. Greiner and Miss Kuster, in Prince Methusalem.   On the same evening, at the Lyceum, a "complimentary" was tendered to Lena Bungert.   The 30th brought the humour of Burbank to the Tabernacle M.E. Church and a Zoellner Männerchor show at Sänger Hall; on the 31st, at South Bushwick Reformed Church, the first of a series of musical and literary entertainments enlisted the choir of the church, Alice K. Decevee (contralto) and Settie Blume.

It is going to be difficult to thread the mazes of April Miscellany, but with the kind indulgence of my reader I shall hope to win through.   The third concert of the Loreley Zither Club, at Jansen's Germania Hall may draw whoever listeth, on April 3rd; I prefer the annual concert of the Williamsburgh Arion, held on the same evening at Turnhalle.   On April 4th, 5th and 6th, "Professor" M. J. Voxie, of England, "King of All Spiritual Mediums and Exposer of the Most Startling Phenomena of This Age," lured to the Lyceum.   Another wonder, Chang, the Chinese Giant, began, on the 6th, a visit of a few days at Masonic Temple.   Also, at this time (April 9th and 11th), Reverend Charles P. McCarthy was to exhibit at Library Hall, South Eighth and Fourth Streets (next to the Lyceum), his "marvels of mesmerism, as given at Exeter Hall, London."   April 7th, 8th and 9th, and again the 14th and 15th allowed "Professor" Thomas Mitchell to exploit at the Lyceum his Mental Dynamics. Locke Richardson, on the 10th, possessed All Souls Church, South Ninth Street.   Carried to April 13th, I report a performance, at the Lyceum, of Among the Breakers, given by the Nelson Association, under the auspices of All Souls' Young People's Association.   On the 19th, Frank Beard gave his Chalk Talk at the Church of Christian Endeavour.   I offer a bouquet of beauties for April 21st: Burbank, at the South Bushwick Reformed Church; the Amphion Choral Society, at Dr. Porter's church; at the Lyceum, Forster Backus (tenor), Mrs. M. A. Davis (soprano), Priscilla Whittingham, the Lyceum Glee Club, J. Nova

[419]

(violin) and Belle M. Rankine; and, at the Christian Endeavour, General Kilpatrick's lecture on Sherman's March to the Sea. At the Lyceum, on the 26th, we had the Drummond Family and Baby Pinkey (*sic*). The 27th brought to the Lyceum promise of Lena Bungert (her benefit), with Rose and Annie Bungert (pianists), Mrs. A. K. Decevee, George D. Bungert (bass) and James L. Farley (reader). The St. Aloysius Dramatic Society had an evening, at this time, presenting in German both Panto and Mino and Mr. Faustgerecht.

After all, we have arrived safely into the haven of May. The "Bulwer" closed its season, on the 5th, with Meg's Diversion and Who Killed Cock Robin? On the 6th, friends of Jacob Nova tendered him a reception and testimonial at Turnhalle; on the 10th, a testimonial to C. Mortimer Wiske promised the Amphion Musical Society, the charming Hattie Louise Simms and Carlos Hasselbrinck. Father Obadiah's Young Old Folks may have amused, on the 11th, at the Leonard Street Church. The Young Men's Hebrew Union acted, on May 15th, at Turn Hall, Our Boys, as it had previously done at the Brooklyn Athenæum. On the 16th, Carter's Novelty Concert Company gave a dime concert at the Lyceum, with Ada Gleason and Lizzie Anderson, and, on the 17th, Frank Beard's Chalk Talk made its mark at Association Hall, and Robert Duncan Elder read at Calvary Church. Double entertainment for the 18th brought James L. Farley to the New England Church, and the Zöllner Männerchor to Masonic Temple. On the 29th, at Turnhalle, the Thalia actors from New York acted Hasemann's Töchter. And thus May flowers turned to June roses and picnics and strawberry festivals. On June 1st, the Avonian Association went to the Lyceum with W. S. Gilbert's Sweethearts and F. W. Morton's A Husband to Order; on the 4th, the Williamsburgh Athletic Club held their games at their grounds, Penn Street and Wythe Avenue. Then came the call of Brighton and Manhattan Beaches and other neighbouring retreats. On June 16th, 17th and 18th, with a matinée on the 18th, Mr. and Mrs. Jerry Cohan and Frank A. McClane were at Turnhalle, in The Molly Maguires, preceded by an olio including Andy Leavitt, Jr., the Delmannings and Maude Leigh.

A progression in June carried us from the acting at the Lyceum, on the 21st, of The Rising Man and Domestic Difficulties, given by the Parnell Dramatic Association, to the Drummond Family, on the 23rd, at the Second R. P. Church; on the 27th, to St. John's M. E. Church, with a concert by Emily Winant, Eugene Wiener (flute), Charles Werner ('cello), Henry Eyre Browne (organ) and the Dudley Buck Quartet Club; and, finally, to the Fourth Street M. P. Church, on the 30th, where were to appear the Euterpean Glee Club, Priscilla Whittingham, and De Nori (violin).

This was not indeed a sequence to be proud of. In early July, Nicholas Hasenzahl's Orchestrion Hall, 34 Grand Street, was advertising Fred Roberts, Lottie Blanchard and Josie Howland; in mid-August Polly Dale,

Thomas Maxwell (motto) and Robert McIntyre ("invincible tenor").   July 4th brought to the Bedford Avenue Church Reformed (Dr. Porter's) the Amphion Society's morning celebration, with James Tanner, orator, and Wiske supplying the music; the same holiday witnessed, at Broadway Park, the fifteenth annual gathering of the Brooklyn Caledonians, and, at the club grounds, Wythe Avenue, the third annual summer meeting of the Williamsburgh Athletic Club.   The busy Zoellner Männerchor assembled, on August 17th, at Myrtle Park for that function so dear to Germans — a Sommernachtsfest.   With Hasenzahl's offering of August 27th, I close the season; his features were John Whitney, Emma Johnson, Clara Donaldson and George Jackson (also set down as an "invincible" tenor).

GREENPOINT, 1880–1881

As usual, I make up my record for the "Point" from journals cited for the chronicle of the former years.   The popular Tennessee Jubilee Singers start us on the gladsome foray, on September 8th, at the First Presbyterian Church; on October 5th, at Association Hall, Ed P. Ackerman must have tried to be like De Cordova in a humorous lecture, Mrs. Fitz-Samuel's Cosmopolitan Club.   October 27th promised an entertainment at the Tabernacle, with Annie Mooney and Mary E. Cherry (elocutionist), and, on the 28th, the Apollo Union of Greenpoint gave its first entertainment of the season at Eckford Hall.   Murray's Circus was at Greenpoint, on October 28th; I find it at Hunter's Point on October 7th.   At Passe's Germania Hall, on November 14th, the Germania Singing Society celebrated its thirteenth anniversary.   The Lambert children, John Lane (elocution and xylophone) and Professor Roberts were in Greenpoint on November 22nd.   Thanksgiving evening (November 25th) found Florence Rice Knox, Henry Galt (elocutionist) and W. F. Mills at the Kent Street Reformed Church, with opposing attraction at the Tabernacle Sunday School of an Old Folks Concert by young people.   The Amphion Choral Union of Greenpoint went, on November 22nd, to the Williamsburgh Lyceum.

At Eckford Hall, on December 2nd, the young people of the Noble Street Baptist Church gave a repetition of Mother Goose and Her Goslings; in that Noble Street holy fane, on December 9th appeared Florence Rice Knox (a hearty contralto), Nettie Taylor (elocutionist), Albert King (tenor) and Carl Walter (pianist).   The Continental Quartette Concert Combination did as it did (I am ignorant of details) on December 13th, at Smithsonian Hall; in Eckford Hall, on December 22nd, one might have attended a Variety and Athletic Entertainment, unless one preferred, on that evening to go to the Kent Street Baptist Church for Mrs. Jarley's Waxworks.   Christmas evening found the Social Quartette Club celebrating at Eckford Hall, and the Arion group joyfully doing the same thing at

[421]

Kineste's Arion Hall. The Tabernacle yawned wide its welcoming doors, on December 29th, for another Old Folks Concert; on the same evening the Apollo Union, at Eckford Hall, staged A Kiss in the Dark and Caught by the Cuff. I end December, on the 30th, with J. W. Jarboe's concert at the Presbyterian Church. In general the chronicle has been of small beer indeed.

Persons who cared to do so could have ventured, on January 12th, into the Noble Street Presbyterian Church, there to judge Mrs. Alonzo Foster and her pupils; some may have preferred to cross the river to attend a performance at Wallack's Theatre or Daly's. The Greenpoint Musikverein concert and "hop" came duly, on January 23rd, at Germania Hall. The Universalist Church, on January 31st, piped up with T. Mason Tier's concert, supported by such glittering celebrities as Mrs. Ella Tier Baker, Mort M. Weed, and the Rossini Quartette of New York. February 1st promised for Eckford Hall the annual entertainment of the Social Quartette Club; on February 9th, Company I, 47th Regiment, filled its armoury in Calyer Street with the combined talents of Mrs. Alonzo Foster, Alexander Elder, Kathrene Cavannah, George W. Foster, and the Chickering Harmonics. I am, the reader perceives, omitting church lectures, concerts, fairs and entertainments of purely local interest; I feel foolish in repeating, on February 10th, Mother Goose and Her Goslings, in the Presbyterian Sunday School. It would be cruel to suggest that the audience contained many Mothers Geese of the community thoroughly enjoying the heaven-sent talent of their goslings. Mrs. Martha Marshall, on February 23rd and 24th, brought forth, at the Sunday School of the Kent Street Reformed Church, her brand of entertainment by children. I recur to February 17th, when, at Smithsonian Hall, the Shakespearian Association of Greenpoint provided an evening of music and scenes from the plays of the great one from whom they took their name; the same evening allowed the Apollo Union to act, in Eckford Hall, Betsey Baker and My Turn Next. The Amphion Choral Association functioned, on the 24th, at Eckford Hall. It is difficult to take these proceedings with becoming seriousness, or the battalions of church entertainments marching bravely through the snows and icy winds of winter. Masquerades of German societies flourished mightily in February and March.

March advertised most sparingly in the Star and the Globe; all I found was an evening of readings and music, at the Union Avenue Baptist Church, carried through by Mrs. Braman, "Professor" Allmuth, and the Misses Adelia and Emma Bigelow — names that to me mean absolutely nothing. But April showers were richer in promise. Company I, 47th Regiment, provided at its armoury, on April 7th, A. P. Burbank, Lena Bungert, and Ida Percy; on the 14th entertainers under the same auspices were Burbank, Miss Bungert, and Mrs. Mattie Balch (reader). Andrew McLean's lecture on Robert Burns (April 20th, at the Presbyterian Church was rendered more palatable by the singing of Jeanie Thorburn and (I hope) of David B. Drysdale. On the 21st, the Amphion Society, at Eckford Hall, acted To Oblige Benson and Barney, the Baron; in the same hall, on the 27th, the "Bulwer" closed its season. The Apollo Musical Union was at Eckford Hall on April 28th and May 18th, and Burbank was humorous, on April 29th, at the Tabernacle. At the First Baptist Church, Noble Street, beginning on May 7th, one was treated to several afternoons — one weekly — of a Stereopticon Exhibition, Punch and Judy and music; the evenings of May 17th and 24th digested the same varied feast. On May 9th an entertainment of the Sagoyewatha Tribe occupied Eckford Hall; on the 10th, at the Union Avenue Baptist Church, a notable concert introduced Anna Bishop, Florence Rice Knox, Fannie J. Lovering of Boston (who made a great hit), C. E. Pratt and (at the organ) A. E. Gosling and Edward Jardine. Frank Beard's Chalk Talk was the attraction, on May 17th, at Association Hall; Gracie Haskell (child soprano) filled the evening of the 24th at the First Baptist Church. On Decoration Day, the Barbara Frietchie Post, No. 11, held forth at the Tabernacle. Graham J. Henderson hired Smithsonian Hall, for a performance, on June 23rd, of Our Boys and His Highness the Duke; the audience was so small (less than $7 having been taken) that money was refunded and no performance given. Greenpoint preferred its fun and its entertainments in churches. Strawberry festivals, excursions, baseball games and water sports carried from early June to late September. But the Star of August 27th imparts the news that the Continental Glee Club (Jones, Dunphy, Dunham and Alvord) was rehearsing weekly.

Flatbush and Its Neighbours, 1880–1881

The record for Flatbush and its environs is very, very thin, hardly repaying research in the Kings County Rural and Brighton Gazette. Christmas and holiday "exhibitions" in churches exhausted in January, 1881, the vocabulary of praise. A New England Supper in the Town Hall, Flatbush, made Washington's Birthday digestible for pious pilgrims. Acland von Boyle, in the hall of the Y. M. C. A. of New Utrecht welcomed spring (I cannot supply the exact date) with an exposition of The Use and Abuse of Humour, set down as the fourth lecture in the Young Men's course. And, on March 16th, in residential, charming Bay Ridge, an Entertainment Literary and Musical entered the portals of the M. E. Church; "if stormy, the next fair evening" was the rural note of the advertisement. A Bay Ridge item in the Gazette of April 30th assures us that the German given last week by the officers at Fort Hamilton was a "decided success" — surely a cheering message to us of 1939. More startling is the news from Canarsie in that same issue of the 30th, to the effect that "John Denier startled our

[423]

citizens by a rare tight-rope performance this week." Happy citizens, say I!

The Flatlands Neck Vocal Society entered the Chapel, on June 2nd, for a concert of I know not what musical importance (though I can guess); and, on June 14th, the Midwood Dramatic Society, at Town Hall, was to act, under direction of Mr. and Mrs. Harley Merry. So successful were these brave spirits that they repeated their performance on October 14th, their quarry then including Merry's play of The Argonauts of '49 and the familiar The Rough Diamond.

LONG ISLAND CITY, 1881–1882

Hart and Collins's Variety Combination was listed for September 27th, at Wagner's Laurel Hill Assembly Rooms. October 7th brought to Hunter's Point two performances by John H. Murray's New Show, embracing Ellen Cooke (bareback equestrienne), W. H. Morgan (hurdle rider), Mlle. Annie (hurdle), Mlle. Miaco (trapeze), Alta Hallet (flying rings), Levantine and Earle (acrobats and barrel acts), "Professor" John White's dogs, Delevanti Brothers (acrobats and leapers), Dan O'Brien (champion tumbler and athlete), R. O. Libby (gymnast), Grimaldi Miaco (clown), Aubrey and Dashway (bar gymnasts), six clowns, Lilliputian "equines," &c. At ten o'clock Miss Hallet was to make an ascent "from the ground to the centre pole," and, at one, Aubrey was to perform his feat of "aeronautic oscillation." "Variety" and the circus loved their polysyllables.

On November 10th, Addie Hollingsworth and Miss Hiller (reciter) appeared at St. John's Church, Hunter's Point. The New Orleans University Singers collected toll from an audience, on November 24th, at the Hunter's Point M. E. Church, and from another, on the 29th, at Washington Hall, Astoria. The School House, Woodside, was scene of an entertainment, on December 1st, given to Addie Hollingsworth, soprano of the Church of the Redeemer, Astoria, with Raggett (singer) and E. A. Cadwell (in black face, as Professor Snow, just from Carolina). January 4th was, I opine, merry and bright at St. George's P. E. Church, Astoria, under the ministration of A. P. Burbank. On the 8th, Rassiga's Franklin House, Hunter's Point, opened with the artistic co-operation of Frohsinn. January 28th staged a benefit, at Albert's Assembly Rooms, Astoria, at which one heard Hattie Cole, Mamie Andrews (reciter), Nellie M. Stearns (piano), Josephine Nelson (singer), Orlando (sic) Heerwagen (violin) and Mrs. L. Stewart (banjo). The days are of a far distant past when young ladies would announce themselves publicly as "Mamie."

With that sad thought I pass into February, recording for the 5th the appearance of B. Frank Leo, "America's Young Elocutionist," in his "popular acts, songs and character sketches." Since this was a "grand free entertainment" at the Astoria Assembly Rooms, with tickets procurable "at any of the drug stores," I can but wonder at the cause.   Further February events were the exercises, on the 8th, at the New Chapel of the First Reformed Church, Astoria, of Mortimer ("prestadigitist," humourist and magician); Mrs. Jarley's Waxworks, St. John's Church, Hunter's Point, on the 9th and 10th; an evening (that of the 14th) at the Reformed Church Sunday School, Astoria, with the ever-welcome De Cordova, telling us of Miss Jones's Wedding, Cards or No Cards; the cantata, Little Red Riding Hood, directed by Mrs. Marshall (16th and 17th) at the East Avenue Baptist Church, Hunter's Point; the University Singers of New Orleans, on the 22nd, at the Methodist Church, Hunter's Point; and Mrs. Jarley's Waxworks, on the 24th, at Albert's Assembly Rooms, Astoria.   Most germane to our subject, however, were the performances at Scharnowitzky's National Variety Hall (late Singleton's Hall), Vernon Avenue, between Third and Fourth Streets. Leo was there, on February 21st.   During the week of February 28th–March 5th, we were invited to enjoy the work of Minnie Lawton ("song and dance lady"), Grace Arnold (serio-comic), James O'Neil, Sanders and Ward ("Dutch"), Frank Melville (female impersonator), and Charles Konollman (comique and also stage manager).   The evenings of Saturday and Monday (March 12th and 14th) were to be made bright with Sanders and Ward, Cora Campbell (melodies), Lew Barton (comedian), the Sanders Brothers (statue clog), Melville, Frank Budworth and Anna Montague (ballads). After this I found no more of the ambitious National.

Henry T. Bryant, ventriloquist, was to be, on February 23rd and March 7th, at the Reformed Church School Room, Astoria.   Washington Hall, Astoria, set March in motion, on the evening of the 1st, with a concert involving James Caulfield (organist), W. F. Mills, the Misses De Lussan, Fred A. Guild, John B. Montell, Addie Hollingsworth, and Master Willie Caulfield.   The masked ball of the Frohsinn Singing Society danced away the late hours of March 12th, at Koch's Broadway Hall, Astoria; at the Methodist Church, Hunter's Point, on the 15th, Alfred E. Pearsall tried his luck in humorous and dramatic readings.   On March 30th, in the Chapel of the Reformed Church, Astoria, the concert of the Idlewild Quartette promised to avail itself of the assistance of Kitty Coates (soprano) and Miss A. H. Lancashire (elocutionist, a pupil of Roberts).   Except for the May Festival (May 22nd) of the Germania Singing Society, at Schwalenberg's Jackson Avenue Park, my attentive eye caught no amusements in columns of the trusty local papers for April, May or June.   Of course excursions abounded in summer heat, and the Long Island Daily Star bears warning of a circus at Astoria, on July 20th.   And that is all — positively.

FLUSHING AND ITS NEIGHBOURS, 1880–1881

Clarke's (sic) persistent Fifth Avenue Company came back to Flushing, on September 18, 1880, with Little Dot as Topsy, in Uncle Tom's Cabin.

[425]

For Irving's Novelty Troupe, on November 27th, the Opera House held, according to the Journal, an audience of about one hundred. On November 30th, the New Orleans University Singers were at Union Church, Great Neck. The College Point Alpenroeschli Club, on December 28th, invited to a concert and dance at Freygang's Pavilion. And before Cornucopia Lodge, F. and A. M., Judge Edward H. Frame, beginning on January 17th, delivered (with stereopticon) a series of lectures on foreign architectural wonders. This Judge Frame was apparently a versatile genius; he painted the scenery for a romantic drama, For Honour's Sake, written by the intriguingly named James Breath, Jr., "an author," according to the Journal, "of considerable local repute," and presented, on February 10th, at the Opera House, by the Sythia Dramatic Troupe of Flushing. This emanation of Breath was a story of the Civil War, still an engrossing topic to those who had participated in it.

If my reader is surprised at the paucity of entertainment for this year in Flushing, I might assuage his curiosity by quoting from the Journal of February 5th: "Imported amusements are at a discount. Local talent holds the boards, and their entertainments are all good and liberally supported." Besides, we must remember that these snug havens of Long Island were near New York and Brooklyn, and at the inconvenience of short railway and ferry trips one could reach a real theatre in either of those more favoured cities. On March 4th, however, the Young Apollo Club, "formerly of Gilmore's Garden," gave, at the Flushing Opera House, The Pirates of Penzance; on the 7th, Fred A. Guild and Fred Ingraham sang in that house, and Eglee mystified with magic. On March 16th (postponed from the 10th) an amateur minstrel show delighted those who cared for it. Meantime, on March 8th, Judge Frame gave his lecture on Poems in Stone, at the Willet's Point Theatre, repeating it, on April 21st, at Newtown Association Hall. He gave a talk on Rome, at Roslyn, on May 9th. The Dudley Buck Quartet was in Flushing, on April 5th; on April 18th, amateurs played, at the Opera House, David Garrick, etc. On April 25th, the pupils of the Flushing Institute acted Kit, the Arkansas Traveller, and, according to the Journal, a son of the original Kit (Chanfrau) and a son of Maggie Mitchell appeared in the cast. On the 29th of April, the Opera House again suffered Sythia's Revenge. For June 1st one might choose a concert of the United Church Choirs, at the Congregational Church, with a chorus of seventy-five, J. B. Grant, Miss M. E. Jennings (soprano), Mrs. A. B. Kennan, F. A. Guild and George (sic) Ingraham (bass). For June 10th and 11th, at the Opera House, Hager's allegorical play and tableaux, The Great Republic, enlisted many pupils from the Flushing schools. Then came the Harvest Homes — on July 28th, at the Crocheron Bayside House, and, on August 3rd, at Miller's Hotel, Little Bayside. On August 29th, Harry Hill's Regatta enlivened Flushing Bay, and, on the 30th, the McEvoys were at the Opera House, Flushing. And where, recently, has been the circus of yesteryear?

JAMAICA, 1880–1881

The Long Island Democrat, that serviceable little weekly of the village of Jamaica, informs us that the attendance at the "concert" in "our Opera House," on September 14th, was "very large, and the receipts exceeded any show ever given in the above Hall." The attraction was that glittering novelty, Uncle Tom's Cabin, as given by Clarke's Fifth Avenue Company of New York. A genuine concert followed, on September 21st, when a portion of the Long Beach orchestra, residents of Jamaica, played in Town Hall, La Guardina, the cornet player, being declared by the Democrat of the 26th, to be "worth the price of admission, as he is fully up to either Levy or Arbuckle." The orchestra promised another concert for October 4th. For charity, the Hon. John Kelly, of New York, lectured (October 14th), in Town Hall, on The Sisters of Charity, Their Works and Their Labours. And, in the afternoon of October 16th, the Opera House was cheery with H. M. S. Pinafore, performed by the New York Miniature Pinafore Opera Company, "from the New York Sunday School Chorus, the Madrigal Club and the Young Apollo Club."

Memories of those joys of the autumn of the year of the presidential election must suffice us till November 23rd, when Clarke's Fifth Avenue Company assailed our purses, this time with The Two Orphans, "creditably performed," says the Democrat of the 30th; but the attendance at the Opera House was small. Carlos A. Butler, "formerly of this village," proposed, in early winter, to exhibit for Sunday Schools of Jamaica, The Tabernacle of Israel, or the House of God in the Wilderness — the large room in Town Hall holding the treasure. Twenty cents would admit an adult, and ten cents a child. With a fair by the ladies of St. Monica's Church, in Christmas week, and with lack of details about Christmas festivities in churches and skating and sleighing in the icy air outside, I erase 1880 from the budget of entertainments in Jamaica. The annual lectures of the town's M. E. Church began on January 20th; the Reverend D. A. Goodsell was to open the series with Leisure and Laziness — an intriguing title; this talk was apparently postponed to February 10th; but reverend gentlemen carried on the progression, doubtless to the satisfaction of all concerned.

Thenceforth readers of the Democrat could find advertisements in the paper of Haverly's Fifth Avenue Theatre, in New York, and of the new Madison Square Theatre, and think how nice it would be to travel to the big city and see those attractions — possibly even do so. Aside from that barmecide feast, I found nothing germane to our subject till February 21st and 22nd, when the ladies of the Jamaica Reformed Church carried through, at Town Hall, a "Festival and Bazar," to the immense profit of $260. How

[427]

well I remember such functions in that unbelievable period of social security! An amateur entertainment, on February 25th, brought to Town Hall, young men from Flushing, assisted by Wilbur F. Rushmore, of Hempstead, and the Misses Lottie Clary (reader) and Mary Semar (singer) — both of Jamaica. The proceeds were for St. Monica's School of Jamaica. The Democrat of March 1st assures us that the affair was a great success, clearing over $300 above expenses. Fancy! Cheered by this news, we could wend our way through the cold and ice of February 28th, to the Sängerbund masquerade, in Distler's Hotel. Or we might wait till March 5th, when the Young Apollo Club was scheduled for a performance, at the Opera House, of The Pirates of Penzance; possibly even, till March 16th, when Mrs. Dewey, a teacher of music in the village, was to give a concert at "her residence, over the Atlantic and Pacific Tea Store, in Fulton Street, Jamaica." This primitive, happy life seems unbelievable in 1939.

I have not a single item for April; but May blooms are richly plentiful — Jamaica had thawed out of its iron wintry bands. On May 5th, Charlotte Barrett, "supported by Frank L. Yerance's Dramatic Company," gave, in the Opera House, a play with the designedly misleading title of A Banker's Daughter, or, Aurora Floyd's Secret. About two hundred villagers attended, and I quote from the Democrat of May 10th this singularly contorted sentence: "The piece gave general satisfaction and it indeed the best played piece ever yet was in Jamaica." Passing by a strawberry festival, on May 26th, in Town Hall, we may attend with edification a "grand" musical and variety performance vouchsafed to our rural consciousness by the Æolian Dramatic Association of Brooklyn, on May 30th, in the Opera House. And, at Town Hall, we might have celebrated the death of May, on the 31st, with Albert Ellery Berg's humorous lecture, We Americans.

After two postponements, James H. Alliger, "formerly of this village" and recently with Mr. and Mrs. Chanfrau, presented, at the Opera House, Caste, himself playing Hawtree, and offering a support worthy of minor New York theatres in Amy Lee as Polly, Regina Dace as Esther, W. H. Lee as D'Alroy, Arthur Moulton as Sam, and Horning as Eccles. I am surprised to find these people in a small village. The Æolian Association reappeared, on June 22nd, acting, I know not by whose permission, Fritz in Ireland. The Elks Minstrel Troupe occupied, on June 29th, the ever-ready Opera House. Bushnell's Show and Minstrel Combination, in Jamaica under canvas for two performances, on July 18th, was declared by the Democrat to be the first circus in the village for eight years; is it so long since I have recorded for the good little town a treat of such dimensions?

Picnics and excursions call in summer from the columns of the Democrat. That paper, on August 2nd acclaims the recent Harvest Home at Crocheron's Bayside House, "a great success"; and the twelfth Annual Queens County Harvest Home Festival and Midsummer Jubilee was scheduled for August

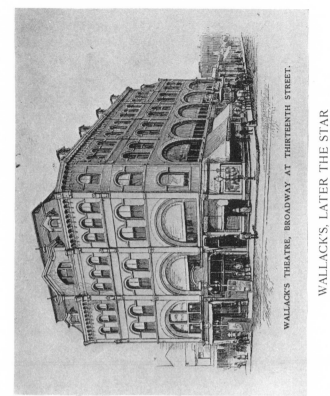

WALLACK'S THEATRE, BROADWAY AT THIRTEENTH STREET.

WALLACK'S, LATER THE STAR

OPENING PERFORMANCE (SCHOOL FOR SCANDAL)
WALLACK'S NEW THEATRE (1882)

3rd, at Miller's Hotel, Little Bayside.   Having been truly rural at these bayside retreats, we might go to the Opera House, on August 16th, for a concert by the Coloured Tennessee Cabin Jubilee Singers, or to Town Hall, on Sunday, August 28th, for a lecture, a revival and a séance on Spiritualism, with five efficient mediums to convey the message to our listening ears.

STATEN ISLAND, 1880–1881

I feel reasonably certain that none of my non-Teutonic readers would have ferried to Gebhardt's Park, Clifton, for the outing of the Staten Island Schützen corps, beginning on September 9, 1880; possibly not even for a concert, on the 18th, at the Pavilion, New Brighton.   J. C. Eccleston's series of illustrated travel lectures might possibly attract us for four successive Monday evenings, beginning on October 4th, at the Christ Church Sunday School.   And, on October 15th, Mrs. G. C. Howard, at the Temperance Lyceum, played her undying Topsy.   The concert of the Æolian Glee Club of Brooklyn was listed for October 20th at Grace M. E. Church, Port Richmond, with J. G. Kellinger, Signor Nova (violin) and W. T. Randall (conductor).   And, on November 4th, 5th and 6th, Professor J. M. Hager's allegory and tableaux, The Great Republic, was due at the Temperance Lyceum; bad weather forced postponement to November 12th and 13th, when, I hope, 150 young ladies and gentlemen were found to be worth waiting for.   The Staten Island Vocal Society, at its concert (December 7th) at the German Club Rooms, availed itself of the services of Ella C. Lewis (soprano), Mrs. S. B. Anderson (contralto) and Caryl Florio; this was the first concert of its second season.   At Tompkinsville, on December 21st, Dr. Eccleston lectured before the Young Men's Republican Club, on The Tower of London.   December 29th (postponement from the 22nd) brought to Temperance Hall Thespian Ambition, a comedy by S. R. Gildersleeve, of New Brighton.   It was repeated, according to the Gazette, on January 5th. I pass by the Y. M. C. A. course of lectures and entertainments beginning on January 25th with a concert by the North Shore Glee Club, and arrive, with interest, at a performance, on February 12th, at the Music Hall, New Brighton, involving George Holland and "a strictly first-class company," in Our Boys.   On February 17th, the Father Mathew Dramatic Club gave at the German Club Rooms Gildersleeve's Thespian Ambition, along with The Coal Heaver's Revenge.   And, on the 21st, at the same rooms, came to pass the Charity Ball.

I agree with my severe reader in thinking these events hardly worth chronicling.   What then shall I say of the fourteenth annual masquerade ball of the Staten Island Quartette Club, held on March 7th at the German Club House? or what of the North Shore Glee Club Concert, on April 7th, at Association Hall, West Brighton?   What indeed of the Amateur The-

[429]

atricals, on April 21st, at New Brighton Library Hall, with the Staten Island
Vocal Society assisting? What, finally, of the entertainment of Tompkins
Lodge, No. 471, F. and A. M., at Tynan's Hall, Stapleton, proffering on April
22nd Miss Cooke, the Orphean Glee Club of New York, and the readers,
Dr. Farley and Miss Bangs? All this is not only something too little
but also something entirely too much. In despair I omit several concerts by purely local talent. According to the Staats-Zeitung something
much better came on April 25th, when Carl Sontag played at the German
Club House both Dir wie mir and Die Frau im Hause. And, on May 10th,
the Staten Island Vocal Society gave, in the same rooms, a concert with
soloists so good as Mme. Carreño and Theodore J. Toedt. By this time the
island was bristling with concerts in churches, of which I note only that of
June 7th in the chapel of Calvary Presbyterian Church, in which figured
Jennie Figgis, Nova, and the Æolian Glee Club.

And the Princeton Glee Club, with Maud Morgan, came, on June 23rd, to
the Pavilion Hotel, New Brighton; there, also, on the 28th, Mrs. "Professor"
R. Ogden Doremus arranged a concert involving Maud Morgan, Louis
Schreiber, and the comedy A Happy Pair (with Mrs. Charles A. Doremus
and T. H. Brosman, of New York). The Pavilion Hotel was lively. On
July 7th it offered readings by George S. Hilliard, "of New York"; and, on
the 23rd, advertised a concert by Saalfield's "Grand Opera Company," including Brignoli, Carreño, Ferranti, Emily Spader and Sara Barton, a group
certainly worth the admission fee of one dollar. On August 6th, the same
Hilliard read at Peteler's South Beach Hotel; and at Bechtel's Park, on the
8th, one might have attended a concert and summer-night festival. I close
on August 24th with the second visit ("by request"), of the Hyers Sisters
Combination — "the only coloured comic opera company in the world."
Constituent elements, at the Pavilion Hotel, were Madah A. Hyers (soprano), Louise Hyers ("bewitching contralto"), Charles Bentley (tenor),
Fred Lyons ("comic banjoist"), and W. W. Keenan (pianist).

CHAPTER VII

WALLACK'S NEW THEATRE, THE UNION SQUARE, DALY'S,
MADISON SQUARE, BOOTH'S, FIFTH AVENUE, HAVERLY'S
FOURTEENTH STREET THEATRE, PARK, STANDARD,
BIJOU OPERA HOUSE, NIBLO'S, 1881–1882

WALLACK, we remember, joined the northerly procession, and arranged to leave his famous theatre (only twenty years old) at Broadway and Thirteenth Street. He built, on the northeast corner of Broadway and 30th Street (diametrically across from Daly's Theatre) a handsome playhouse, at a cost, says Allston Brown, of $247,-782.47; it had a frontage, on Broadway, of 105 feet, and extended along 30th Street for 122 feet. The front of the building, of not unpleasing design, was never completed beyond the second story. Tragic irony lurks in the terms of the land-lease, which had twenty-one years to run, with privilege of two renewals, each for twenty-one years. And, in 1887, Wallack retired, and his company, so far as he was concerned, went out of existence! Thus stage-history changes its scene from act to act.

But this is anticipating. There was no thought of failure on the night of the opening of the new house — January 4, 1882 — an opening much delayed by difficulties in completing the theatre. On that precious evening, the audience, still Wallackian in character, entered a handsome lobby, passed into a spacious crimson-furnished, luxurious promenade, and thence into an auditorium rich in red and gold decoration, not unlike the cozy, homelike interior of the house at Thirteenth Street. But somehow the auditorium of this last Wallack's was never quite homelike in effect on its patrons; one felt more remote from the stage and the actors. It was just the little more, or the little less that made all the difference. And, of course, times and taste were changing, and Wallack was growing old and less capable of coping with the difficult demands of playgoers. Wallack's was almost moribund when it moved, and, for its few remaining years, it might, possibly, better have remained at the old, well-known, well-loved site.

But, as I have implied, no one thought of this, on the opening night. Excitement reigned, the house was declared beautiful, and the favourites of the company were greeted with fond acclaim (they had been forced to travel during the weeks of uncertainty before the new home was ready). Best of all, Wallack began with that high specialty of his actors — The School for Scandal:

[431]

Sir Peter Teazle	John Gilbert	Rowley	H. Gwynette
Sir Oliver Surface	Harry Edwards	Trip	C. E. Edwin
Charles Surface	Osmond Tearle	Sir Toby	F. G. Kerr
Joseph Surface	Gerald Eyre	Lady Sneerwell's Servant	H. Pearson
Crabtree	Dan Leeson	Joseph's Servant	H. Holliday
Sir Benjamin	E. V. Sinclair	Lady Teazle	Rose Coghlan
Moses	William Elton	Mrs. Candour	Mme. Ponisi
Careless	Wilmot Eyre	Lady Sneerwell	Agnes Elliott
Sir Harry Bumper	J. C. Taylor	Maria	Stella Boniface
Snake	W. H. Pope		

I doubt if a better Sir Peter or a better Sir Oliver ever walked the stage than the two seen on that occasion at Wallack's; Tearle, Eyre, Miss Coghlan and Mme. Ponisi also were admirable in their parts. But I greatly doubt the excellence of the other actors compared with their predecessors in the same rôles at the earlier Wallack's. We note the name of F. G. Kerr, later well known here and in his native England as Frederick Kerr; his son, Geoffrey Kerr, graced the scene in 1937. A new act drop by Philip Goatcher shut out the players from act to act; after Act III Wallack addressed the audience, touchingly referring to his father, who had made a speech on the opening of the Thirteenth Street house. After Wallack's address, the audience called for John Gilbert, an honour richly merited; greatly moved, he acknowledged the call and delivered a few heartfelt words. According to Allston Brown, Lawrence Bardon, who had taken the tickets at both the earlier Wallack theatres, exercised the same function at the new house.

The School for Scandal was but a preliminary flourish — a gesture of notable promise. It ran till January 21st, when came to our stage the first play of Arthur Wing Pinero seen in New York — The Money Spinner, a recent success at the St. James's Theatre, London, with John Hare and Mr. and Mrs. Kendal. The cast at Wallack's included Osmond Tearle as Lord Kengussie, William Elton as Baron Croodle, gentleman crook and keeper of a gambling house, Gerald Eyre as Boycott, Harry Edwards as Jules Faubert, E. V. Sinclair as Mockett, W. H. Pope as Sobofski, S. Du Bois as the Porter, Rose Coghlan and Stella Boniface as Millicent and Dorinda, daughters of Croodle, Hattie Elliott as Mme. Montlouis, and the faithful Miss E. Blaisdell as Margot. Miss Coghlan's rôle called for much intensity of feeling; married to a weakling, whose financial dealings may lead to ruin, Millicent conceives the idea of using some of the underhand tricks of gaming learned in her father's establishment to raise money for the aid of that husband. She is caught at cheating in a game with her former lover, Lord Kengussie, and confesses all; of course he magnanimously aids her. According to the Herald of the 22nd, "The London success of 'The Money Spinner' was due to the tenderness and sweetness with which Mrs. Kendall [sic] invested Milly's character and the touching pathos with which she pleaded with Lord Kengussie for forgiveness. . . . Miss Coghlan was unequal to the task, for bright and charming as she is in crisp and sparkling comedy,

[432]

| WILMOT EYRE | OSMOND TEARLE | GERALD EYRE |

| OSMOND TEARLE | ALMA STUART STANLEY | HARRY EDWARDS |

| C. E. EDWIN | JOHN GILBERT | WILLIAM ELTON |

SARONY'S PHOTOGRAPHS FROM YOUTH (AT WALLACK'S)

she understands little of true pathos and consequently the pith and substance of the character were wanting."

Nearly ten years later, Mrs. Kendal was to be seen here in this rôle, one in which she made a great impression. Meantime, The Money Spinner held the stage of the new Wallack's for about a month. One remembers, with regret, that at this time, Wallack was acting at the Park Theatre, in The Colonel; it seems strange to find him away from the new house. The great success of the home season came on February 20th, when, encouraged by the acclaim last year of The World, Wallack put on another melodrama, one by Paul Merritt and Augustus Harris, with the attractive title of Youth:

Rev. Mr. Darlington	John Gilbert	Fowler	H. Holliday
Frank Darlington	Osmond Tearle	Waiter	H. Pearson, Jr.
Major Reckley	Gerald Eyre	Eve Malvoisie	Rose Coghlan
Colonel Dalton	Harry Edwards	Mrs. Darlington	Mme. Ponisi
Hon. Arthur Lavender	Wilmot Eyre	Mrs. Walsingham	Fanny Addison
Captain Loverton	C. E. Edwin	Alice Wenlock	Stella Boniface
Willie Spratly	Alma Stuart Stanley	Kitty Athol	Minnie Vining
Larry O'Phesey	William Elton	Amy Athol	Cecilia Edgarton
Detective	F. G. Kerr	Bessie	Emma Loraine
Tom Gardham	E. V. Sinclair	Mrs. Grummage	Miss E. Blaisdell

Of course, much of the appeal of these London melodramas lay in the scenery and the spectacle. Young Frank Darlington greatly offends his parents by marrying Eve Malvoisie; the father casts him off; Eve is a bad lot and by the aid and for the aid of her lover, Reckley, has poor Frank accused of forgery, and thus "breaks" him in his regiment. He enlists as a private, goes to the Sudan (always pursued by the terrible Reckley and officers of the law), achieves unheard of triumphs of bravery in face of awful odds, is decorated, forgiven, cleared of imputation of crime and also of Eve, who, if you can believe it, had a husband when she married Frank. Thus, Frank can at last wed the refined Alice. The scene of the sailing of the troops and the battle scenes surpassed anything of the kind yet placed on our stage. The spectacle was managed, as had been The World, by Charles Harris, brother of the resourceful Augustus. I am sorry to see Wallack's company in such business, but what would you? Sheridan and Shakespeare were waning lights, and up flared Paul Merritt and Augustus Harris in a blaze of melodramatic glory. The atrabiliar Herald declares, on February 21st, that "any gentleman with a bad digestion could conceive an equally entangled and unpleasant" story, "in an after dinner nap," but it admits that the scenery and groupings were wonderful, and the company fine. According to Allston Brown, Youth ran seventy-seven nights to receipts of $73,000, a big sum for 1882, if not for 1939. A matinée on April 3rd was for the benefit of the Actor's Fund, for which, on that day, practically every theatre in New York gave a performance.

The fourth and last production for this season at Wallack's came on

[433]

May 8th, David Belasco's drama, La Belle Russe, with Osmond Tearle as Captain Dudley Brand, Gerald Eyre as Sir Philip Calthorpe, John Gilbert as Monroe Quilton, C. E. Edwin as Roberts, Harry Holliday as Burton, Rose Coghlan as Geraldine, Mme. Ponisi as Lady Elizabeth Calthorpe, Mabel Stephenson (but recently a child reader) as Little Beatrice, and Cecilia Edgarton as Agnes. The play, melodramatic and improbable, nevertheless strong and brisk in action, ran until the end of the season on June 28th. It bore unmistakable resemblance to both Forget Me Not (as had Two Nights in Rome) and to The New Magdalen, especially in the leading character of Beatrice Glandore, a decoy for a gambling house, where she is known as *la belle Russe*. Former mistress of Captain Dudley Brand, she pretends to be her twin sister, Geraldine, wife of Sir Philip Calthorpe, she thinking both that sister and Sir Philip dead. Thus, like Mercy Merrick, she finds herself installed in a home of wealth and luxury, only to be confronted by her former lover, Brand, who routs her by showing her the figure of her sister — the real Geraldine — coming into view. The wicked woman, having been Mercy Merrick, now becomes Stéphanie de Mohrivart, and, finally leaves the stage to virtue and domestic bliss. According to the Herald, Tearle and Miss Coghlan practically re-enacted the best scenes of Forget Me Not, in all respects, except verbally, as they had given them previously at the late Wallack's at Thirteenth Street. Osmond Tearle played Brand in San Francisco and recommended the piece to Wallack. Jeffreys Lewis, who had created the false Geraldine in San Francisco, was most anxious to perform the part here; of course Miss Coghlan's right to the rôle was paramount. In his Life of David Belasco, William Winter states that Belasco and Thomas Maguire, of the Baldwin Theatre, San Francisco, had come to New York to place La Belle Russe, with Belasco determined to have it played at Wallack's, Maguire anxious to sell it to John Stetson. Finally, Maguire withdrew his support, leaving Belasco stranded. Belasco ultimately sold the play to Maguire's nephew, Frank L. Goodwin, for fifteen hundred dollars, a return ticket to San Francisco, and one hundred dollars more for expenses. The play was announced at Wallack's "by arrangement with Mr. F. L. Goodwin, the production of a new and powerful drama by David Belasco, Esq." "Fifty times the amount of money Belasco received for 'La Belle Russe' would have been," says Winter, "more like a fair payment for it than the sum he actually received." One may compare Belasco's experience with that of Steele MacKaye in connection with Hazel Kirke. I go back to state that, on the afternoon of May 11th, Oscar Wilde, our sensational winter's guest, lectured on Art Decoration. He was not setting the Hudson afire.

This is the history of the first season of the new Wallack's — interesting but not inspiring. Yet it is something to meet Belasco and Pinero. It must have been a profitable season, especially with Youth and La Belle Russe, and, to run six months with only four plays was something of a feat.

A company of juveniles acted Patience here, in August, but I will leave the discussion of that precocious beatitude until I reach the season of 1882–83.

Union Square Theatre, 1881–1882

Wallack, then, moved uptown, and Palmer, so long his neighbour round the corner, in Union Square, was in a season or two to do likewise. 1881–1882, however, found him still installed in the Union Square Theatre, as both proprietor and manager. That pretty, popular house had a long preliminary season of varied attractions. One is a bit dubious about the opening play (August 8, 1881), "the Five Act Emotional Domestic Drama, by George F. McDonald," entitled Coney Island, or, Little Ethel's Prayer, the subtitle of which is the last thing the reader would ever associate with the *locale* of the main title. But the scenery carries us from an Illinois homestead to Coney Island and thence to a garret in a New York tenement house. In the last act we have a view of City Hall and Printing House Square in a melodramatic snow storm and we end in a barn and stable above Harlem. The student of ways theatric perceives, therefore, that Little Ethel might have prayed in any one of a number of widely separated places. And the cast was rather promising for a warm August evening:

John Oakburn	Cyril Searle	Primrose Green	James H. Cummings
Henry Oakburn	Edwin Varrey	Larry	J. J. Sullivan
Richard Weyland	T. J. Martin	Fluke Morris	Charles Sturges
Dr. Wilbur	F. Chippendale	Adele Oakburn	Laura Wallace
Jasper Blunt	W. W. Allen	Arabella Wilkins	Mrs. W. A. Rouse
Hans von Blumenschmidt	E. A. Locke	Hetty Johnson	Marion Fiske
James McCormick	H. H. Pratt	Little Ethel	Fanchon Thompson
Budd	G. F. McDonald		

James W. Collier was responsible for the production of this novelty, which dealt with the old theme, so popular in recent London melodramas, of the son, misunderstood, falsely accused and cast adrift to encounter all kinds of hardship and danger before finally restored to parental favour. In this case his mother follows him out into the pitiless stage storm of thunder, lightning and sheeted rain. The charming Meigs Sisters sang in the Coney Island scene. We may laugh at the thing, but it held the boards at the still fashionable Union Square Theatre for three weeks, with what profit I know not.

Joseph Jefferson; Genevieve Ward; Mme. Janauschek

The house remained closed for a week, re-opening on September 12th, with Joseph Jefferson as Bob Acres, in The Rivals, then new to modern New York, though he had played it, during the last season, in Philadelphia and in Brooklyn. It would seem that he approached this addition to his narrow

[435]

repertoire tentatively and cautiously, as if he anticipated the criticism so often applied, that his Acres was wholly American and as little as possible like the Squire of Sheridan's imagining. Now Jefferson arranged for but two weeks of his revival, and he brought it out with the invaluable aid of Mrs. John Drew, a simply incomparable Malaprop, better possibly than the performances of the same part by either Mrs. Wheatley or Mrs. Vernon, both of which she must have studied. She now came forward to be acclaimed for one of the finest comedy portrayals ever seen on any stage. The elegance, the finish of her art remain as precious heritages in memory and in stage history. Compared with these two great leaders the rest of the cast was inferior; it was below that so often seen at Wallack's. Nevertheless, it was adequate, with Rose Wood as a pleasing and handsome Lydia, Mark Pendleton as Jack, Charles Waverly as Sir Lucius, Frederic Robinson as a rather heavy Sir Anthony, H. F. Taylor as what was left of Faulkland, with Julia ruthlessly cut from the *dramatis personæ*, with James T. Galloway as David, Thomas Jefferson as Fag, and Eugenia Paul as Lucy. Of course the battle waged anew in regard to Jefferson's cuts, but little doubt remains that he speeded up the action in a way that greatly facilitated delight and success. Julia is, if truth must be told, something of a bore, but the complete deletion of the part shocked and dazed old Wallackians.

    J. Ranken Towse, brought up on the English tradition of the character asserts (Sixty Years of the Theater) that Jefferson "never really played Acres at all. He did not in the least resemble the unsophisticated British country squire, vainly aping fashionable manners. . . . He was delectable, infinitely amusing, utterly unreal — Joseph Jefferson in delicious masquerade." And, really, William Winter (The Jeffersons) says the same thing, though his intent was, as always, to laud Jefferson to the height of praise: "Jefferson has considered that a country squire need not . . . reek of the ale-house and the stables; that his head is completely turned by contact with town fashions," etc. . . . "The interior spirit of Jefferson's impersonation, then, is humanity and sweet good nature; and the traits that he has especially emphasized are ludicrous vanity and comic trepidation." One would like to hear Burton or Harry Beckett on this analysis of the part.

    After two weeks of Rip Van Winkle (so to speak) as Bob Acres, Genevieve Ward, admirable actress, came (September 27th) to the Union Square, in her great success, Forget Me Not, her support being far from brilliant, with Frank Clements as Sir Horace Welby, Agnes Barnett as Alice Verney, George W. Wessells as Barrato, Bella Cuthbert as Mrs. Foley, William Farren, Jr., as Prince Maleotti, and Percy Campbell as the Servant. The theatre, like most theatres in New York, was closed on September 26th, the day of Garfield's obsequies at Cleveland. A matinée was given on October 5th for the benefit of sufferers by the Michigan fire. Miss Ward's impressive engagement ended on October 22nd.

    [436]

On the 24th, Mme. Janauschek, still a great actress, entered the Union Square in her dual rôle of Lady Dedlock and Hortense, in Bleak House; with her were James H. Taylor as Sir Leicester Dedlock, R. F. McClannin (that favourite of Boston) as Tulkinghorn, George B. Waldron as Bucket, Harry Rainforth as William Guppy, W. D. Chalfin as Rouncewell, Florence Barrett as Jo (a part played a few weeks previously at the Fourteenth Street Theatre by Jennie Lee), Anna Warren Story as Esther, and Henrietta Irving as Mrs. Rouncewell. For her second week (October 31st–November 5th) Mme. Janauschek, then the best tragic actress in America, presented herself as Maria Stuart, Schiller's play now called Mary Queen of Scots.

For her final week, beginning on November 7th, the actress brought out The Doctor of Lima, a "sensational play" by Salmi Morse, in which she appeared as the "Subject," restored to reason by James Austin, the Doctor of Lima (Alexander H. Stuart), whom she marries only to find her bad former husband (James H. Taylor) returning to make trouble. Of course some god from the machine brings a suitable solution to the difficulty. Others concerned were R. F. McClannin as the British Consul at Lima, Harry Rainforth as Sir George Tilton, a titled tourist, George B. Waldron as Jones, a merchant, W. D. Chalfin as Prescott, a lawyer, Isabel Waldron as Donna Inez, Henrietta Irving as Rosa, the housekeeper, and Little Dora Connor and Master Arthur Gay as Dr. Austin's children. Since the play lasted for but a week, I apologise for burdening the reader's memory with the cast.

REGULAR SEASON, 1881–1882

So much for the preliminaries. The season of the venerated stock company began late, on November 14th, with a revival of Sardou's fine play, Daniel Rochat, Charles R. Thorne, Jr., and Sara Jewett resuming the characters in which, last season, they had been so successful; others of the original cast appearing in their former rôles were Stoddart, Parselle, Walden Ramsay, Owen Fawcett, Quigley, Maud Harrison, Mrs. Phillips and Netta Guion. Frederic de Belleville succeeded Joseph E. Whiting as Charles Henderson, and other changes or re-adjustments now offered H. W. Montgomery (*vice* T. E. Morris) as Laurent, Julian Magnus (*vice* Charles Collins) as the Reverend Septimus Clarke, J. W. Thorpe as Clavaron, Lysander Thompson as Andram, S. Du Bois as Pierson, William Morse as Julien, Alfred Becks (who last year was Andram) as Verley, Estelle Clayton as Arabella, and Nellie Wetherill as Louise. I cannot afford to overlook even the most insignificant members of this important company; and how the older members of lesser rôles disappear and return — Montgomery, Thompson, T. E. Morris, H. F. Daly, &c.! But Marie Wilkins had at last left forever the comfortable nest which so long had cherished her art. On one

[437]

evening, Eleanor Carey played Lea, in place of Sara Jewett, temporarily out of the cast.

After two weeks of this provocative play, Palmer, on November 28th, staged for six performances Camille, "with the great cast of last season," including Clara Morris, Maud Harrison, Eleanor Carey, Netta Guion, Mrs. Phillips, Thorne, Parselle, De Belleville, Fawcett and Walden Ramsay. There was no matinée on Saturday, December 3rd, Clara Morris being unable to play twice in one day. And then the Union Square followed the Wallack example of The World and put on (December 5th), G. R. Sims's "powerful melodrama," The Lights o' London, designed and pieced together according to the prevailing formula for Adelphi or Princess Theatre thrillers. The falsely accused hero, the villainous cousin, the obdurate father, the long suffering wife, the comic relief, the elaborate scenery, the frequent change of scenes, virtue triumphant and villainy foiled — all these ingredients were mixed in The Lights o' London, as in The World or as in Youth, shortly to follow, as we saw at the New Wallack's. This crude thing was perhaps no less melodramatic than had been some of its French predecessors on the same stage, but it lacked the neat construction and the real emotional value of The Two Orphans or A Celebrated Case. I give the cast entire:

Harold Armytage	C. R. Thorne, Jr.	Mr. Miles	John Swinburne
Mr. Armytage	A. D. Billings	Policeman	Lysander Thompson
Clifford Armytage	F. De Belleville	Irish Policeman	H. W. Montgomery
Marks	T. E. Morris	Boxer	E. Elberts
Seth Preene	J. H. Stoddart	Tim	Little Eva French
Joseph Jarvis	John Parselle	Bill	F. W. Gretton
Shakespeare	Maud Harrison	Superintendent	Julian Magnus
Jim	W. Morse	Porter	W. S. Quigley
Skiffington	J. W. Thorpe	Bess Marks	Sara Jewett
Detective Cutts	G. S. Robinson	Hetty Preene	Eleanor Carey
Detective Watts	J. P. Winter	Mrs. Jarvis	Mrs. E. J. Phillips
Philosopher Jack	Owen Fawcett	Janet	Eloise Willis
Percy De Vere	Walden Ramsay	Annie	Netta Guion
Jo	Andrew Jacques	Sal	Nellie Wetherill
Mr. Bancroft	John Matthews		

This cast is long enough for the most greedy pen. The many scenes were by the capable Marston, and H. Tissington, as usual, directed the music.

The Lights o' London was a great success, and in it Thorne and Sara Jewett appeared for the last times together on this stage; Thorne left the company at the end of the season, and died a few months later. Stoddart made a hit of an accustomed kind as Seth Preene, the conscienceless wretch whose heart was softened when the man he was pursuing (Thorne) rescued him from the watery grave into which he had been cast by the polished villain (De Belleville). Parselle, in the Dickens-like character of Jarvis, "of Jarvis' Temple of the Legitimate" was also excellent, as was Maud Harrison in the boy-part of Shakespeare Jarvis, son of the aforesaid. Some must have missed Marie Wilkins as Mrs. Jarvis, a part she should have played admirably, whereas the competent, conscientious Mrs. Phillips lacked something of the required touches of broad comedy.   Eleanor Carey was very successful as the garish Hetty Preene, cause of much of the melodrama.

A benefit for the Poe Memorial Fund brought to this theatre, on the afternoon of December 8th, a remarkable array of talent.   Charles Roberts, Jr., recited The Bells, and Anna T. Berger did that unfeminine thing — she played on the cornet.   The Bijou Opera Company (with Selina Dolaro and Lillian Russell) gave an act of The Snake Charmer; Mr. and Mrs. W. J. Florence were advertised for an act of their new play, Professor Opstein, with a support including Annie Ellsler, Ada Tavernier, Frank Lamb, Lindsey Harris and others (I am not sure that this was given, since the Herald review states that Florence recited I Was with Grant); Agnes Ethel (of all people in the world), Eleanor Carey, George Clarke, Owen Fawcett, C. A. Stevenson, T. E. Morris, Louisa Eldridge and Mary Drake were down for an act of Frou-Frou; McCullough, Shewell, George Griffith and Kate Forsyth gave the wooing scene from Richard III; and Joseph Jefferson, H. F. Taylor, J. T. Galloway, Thomas Jefferson, Ida Vernon, and Lillian Lee appeared in Lend Me Five Shillings.

CLARA MORRIS; THE NEW MAGDALEN; ARTICLE 47

With the triumph of The Lights o' London, the nightly fare and that for the Saturday matinées was now set for practically the rest of the season. In view of the success of her last-season matinées, Palmer re-engaged Clara Morris for a similar series in 1882.   He first produced (January 5th) that great feature of the repertoire of Ada Cavendish, The New Magdalen, of course with Miss Morris as Mercy Merrick, the cast otherwise including Eleanor Carey (proving herself a most useful actress) as Grace Roseberry, Virginia Buchanan as Lady Janet Ray, James O'Neill (returned to the fold) as Julian, Walden Ramsay as Horace Holmcroft, Owen Fawcett as Surgeon Surville, John Parselle as Surgeon Wetzel, H. W. Montgomery (how sunk from his position in the early '70's!) as James, Lysander Thompson as the Special Officer, Julian Magnus as Captain Arnault, Robert Warren as the German Orderly, W. Morse as the French Sentinel, and the ever-serving W. S. Quigley as Max.   On the 6th the Herald states that the acting of all was "so thoroughly excellent as to call for the highest praise."   Miss Morris was "a less polished but far more natural and effective Mercy than Miss Cavendish"; in fact, J. Ranken Towse (Sixty Years of the Theater) declares that Miss Morris simply eclipsed the English actress.   The New Magdalen was played on Tuesday and Thursday afternoons until February 16th. According to the Herald of January 13th, Oscar Wilde, then our latest sensation, attended The New Magdalen, on the 12th, and declared (though the Herald thought this might be "æsthetic taffy") that "Miss Morris is the

[439]

greatest actress I ever saw, if it be fair to form an opinion of her from her rendition of this one rôle. . . . We have no such powerfully intense actress in England. She is a great artist, in my sense of the word, because all she does, all she says, in the manner of the doing and of the saying constantly evokes the imagination to supplement it. That is what I mean by art. She would be a wonderful success in London. . . . She is a veritable genius. We have no one like her."

There was no matinée on February 21st, the stage being required for rehearsal of Article 47, brought out, on the 23rd, in a slightly altered version, and with this excellent cast:

Georges Duhamel	Alexander Salvini	Hotel Porter	Robert Warren
Mazilier	Walden Ramsay	Cora's Servant	H. W. Montgomery
Dr. Coombes	Welsh Edwards	Dr. Coombes' Attendant	W. S. Quigley
De Breve	John Parselle	Mme. Gerard	Virginia Buchanan
Potain	Owen Fawcett	Marcelle	Eleanor Carey
De Lille	G. S. Robinson	Louise	Mollie Revel
Lauristot	Julian Magnus	Miss Dowson	Miss McKee
Hotel Clerk	W. Morse	Countess	Miss Abbott
Paul	Clinton Stuart	Cora	Clara Morris

This was the first appearance on our stage of Alexander Salvini, son of the great Tommaso Salvini; he won a fine position before his early death a few years later. Miss Morris had her accustomed success as the vengeful, finally insane Cora, and needed no further change of bill before the extra matinée season closed on March 30th.

Meantime, The Lights o' London had brightened the box office. The hundredth performance of the work (no literary masterpiece) occurred on March 20th, and its flame flickered out on April 15th — after one of the longest runs recently achieved by this home of successes. On April 3rd came the matinée, usual at all theatres on that afternoon, for the benefit of the Actors' Fund. The last production of the regular season arrived on April 17th, with A. R. Cazauran's adaptation of Hardy's novel, Far from the Madding Crowd. Under the same title, it employed this cast:

Bathsheba	Clara Morris	Farmer Boldwood	H. A. Weaver
Fanny Robbin	Netta Guion	Joseph Poorgrass	John Ince
Liddy Smallbury	Mollie Revel	Henery Fray	Julian Magnus
Mary Ann	Mrs. J. Wilder	William Smallbury	F. Lotto
Temperance	Mrs. Hattie Thorpe	Cain	Alfred Becks
Soberness	Mrs. H. A. Weaver	Andrew Candle	W. H. Eiling
Mrs. Tall	Miss Cameron	Laban Tall	Charles Wilson
Sergeant Troy	F. de Belleville	Matthew Moone	J. J. Secor
Gabriel Oak	Charles Vandenhoff	Jacob Smallbury	C. Heritage

This was not one of Cazauran's successes, nor, indeed, one of Clara Morris's; the delicate humour of Hardy evaporated among the minor actors employed for the wise rustics of the story, and Miss Morris seems not to have dis-

MRS. JOHN DREW
AS MRS. MALAPROP

JOSEPH JEFFERSON
AS BOB ACRES

THOMAS JEFFERSON
AS FAG

EUGENIA PAUL

JOSEPH JEFFERSON
AS BOB ACRES

EUGENIE LEGRAND

MAUD HARRISON
(THE LIGHTS O' LONDON)

SARA JEWETT

ELEANOR CAREY
(THE LIGHTS O' LONDON)

covered the essential charm of Bathsheba, as Ada Rehan discovered that of Kate Verity, in Pinero's play on practically the same theme — The Squire — produced at Daly's on October 10, 1882. And how fine was Mrs. Kendal as Kate Verity, both in the original London cast, and a few years later in America! Far from the Madding Crowd endured but for two weeks at the Union Square, and then disappeared forever.

On April 28th occurred at this theatre a benefit to Genevieve Ward, tendered by the Mayor and Judges of the city, in celebration of her six hundredth performance in Forget Me Not; this sounds pretty formidable, but ardour cools on learning that John H. Bird and other "distinguished" amateurs took part in the cast.

The glory (if any) departed for 1881–82. A supplementary season began on May 1st, with the first appearance in New York (though she had essayed the "provinces") of Eugénie Legrand, who came forward in a piece by George Darrell, entitled Solange. In this Miss Legrand appeared first as Elinor, and later in the action as Mme. Solange, "the reigning favourite"; George Darrell, the author, was Walter Vaughan, a ruined gamester, and subsequently Gerald Vaughan, an American gentleman. Others in the cast were B. T. Ringgold as Dr. Falkner, H. A. Weaver as Beal Brock, a disgraced divine, H. W. Montgomery as Fitz MacQuarrie, John Matthews as Wash Wimple, a coloured servant, Mary Maddern as Dr. Dorothea Dibbs, and Netta Guion as Maud Marryatt. The play was a dreadful failure; the Herald of May 2nd, referring to Darrell's acting in it, says that his appearance "gave the spectators a view of the person who had the assurance to inflict this fearfully and wonderfully constructed play upon an unoffending actress and a too patient public.... The play proved to be irretrievably, irredeemably bad."

We are not surprised, then, to learn that one poor week sufficed for Solange. On May 8th, Miss Legrand changed to the long-suffering Camille, supported by Lewis Morrison as Armand and the inevitable Louisa Eldridge as Mme. Prudence, other parts falling to Ringgold, Montgomery, Weaver, Herbert Ayling, Miss Guion and Eliza Long, an array very inferior to that which appeared here in this drama, in November, with Clara Morris. Nevertheless, Camille now died as per schedule for two weeks, and gave way, on May 23rd, to The Lady of Lyons, with Miss Legrand, of course, as Pauline. The allotted four weeks of the engagement closed on May 27th; the new star had at least had an opportunity to shine. Allston Brown says that Miss Legrand in 1884 married Kyrle Bellew, though "they never lived together, the wife going her way and Mr. Bellew his, immediately after the marriage." She obtained a divorce in 1888.

Another dead failure, and the last of the year, was Frederic (*sic*) Bock's "Magnificent Illustration" of the "American Pictorial Melodrama," The Living Age, brought out on May 30th:

[441]

Jules Labourdonais..........Lewis Morrison	Marie Durant.................Ellie Wilton
Arthur Mackenzie............B. T. Ringgold	Little Moses..............Charline Weidman
Charles Durant....................D. Leeson	A Couple...........Mr. and Mrs. Donnelly
Jacob Baumgartner............W. M. Fiske	Mat...........................John Irwin
Timothy O'Donnell......H. W. Montgomery	Nick....................Thomas Brannick
Ikey Swain....................John E. Ince	Pete.........................A. Deerfoot
Adam Peterson...............Frederic Bock	Hotel Porter.................Mr. Anderson
Cora.....................Ellen Cummens	Hotel Waiter...............Mr. Broughton

Bock, we shall find, was this season a member of Lawrence Barrett's company. In his play the scenes carried us from the French Market in New Orleans to the Great Snow-ball Chamber of the Mammoth Cave, Kentucky, to the Horseshoe Bend on the Pennsylvania Railroad, with the Great Locomotive, 317, to an Opium Den in New York, and finally to a Library on Brooklyn Heights, with a View of New York, by moonlight — a long journey, and naught profiting. Even the stage moonlight, usually your great solvent of dramatic difficulties, failed to keep The Living Age alive. It died quietly on June 10th, bringing peace to the Union Square until, in August, The Black Flag was run up to herald the beginning of a new season. The term just closed had been notable for the appearance of Genevieve Ward, Jefferson, Janauschek and Clara Morris (her last appearances here, by the way, with the still splendid stock company); but the productions with that company must have set older patrons fondly ruminating on the former glories of Led Astray, The Two Orphans, A Celebrated Case, The Banker's Daughter, etc. And Charles R. Thorne, Jr. was never again to act on the stage he had so long adorned!

DALY'S THEATRE, 1881–1882

One sometimes wonders how Augustin Daly managed to weather the storms of his earlier seasons at his new theatre. So many failures, really, he had, despite the seeming prosperity of protracted runs; but 1881–82, after a bad start, would seem to have brought him some success. He began on August 9th, with a revival of his last spring hit, Cinderella at School, the cast, but little changed, including Laura Joyce, Ada Rehan, May Fielding, Agnes Perring (replacing Mrs. Gilbert, ill), Digby Bell (*vice* John Brand), H. Macdonough (in Harry Lacy's former rôle), Charles Leclercq, and, of course, James Lewis. It was proudly announced that the schoolgirls would wear new Kate Greenaway costumes — then greatly in vogue.

Cinderella made sport until September 7th, when Daly met with a severe reverse in the failure of Quits, or, a Game of Tit for Tat, "by the authors of Needles and Pins, Lemons, etc." The cast included James Lewis as Buttles, John Drew as Bob Cayses, Digby Bell as Clive Quincy, W. J. LeMoyne (new here and replacing Charles Fisher, now supporting Fanny Davenport) as Horatio Hickory, E. P. Wilks (a quaint, funny little actor) as Tops,

Harry Macdonough as O'Mooney, W. H. Beekman (a standby in minor rôles) as Dixie, Laura Joyce (not her first appearance at Daly's, as Judge Daly states) as Gabrielle Prince, Ada Rehan as Thisbe Mestic, Mrs. Gilbert (fortunately able to reappear) as Mrs. Mariah Mestic, Helen Tracy (her first bow with this company) as Mrs. Amelia Hickory, Emily Denin (also new here) as Lizzie, Lillie Vinton as Sarah, Miss K. Denin as Susan, and Miss Hapgood as Sally. Fanny Morant had gone to the Boston Museum, and Charles Fisher was a strong pillar in Fanny Davenport's touring company. Daly kept this failure afloat for four weeks. On September 20th, the day of President Garfield's death, he closed the theatre, but his house was one of the very few open on the 26th, the day of the final funeral service in Cleveland.

At the matinée on Wednesday, September 28th, Daly introduced a new actress, Agnes Leonard, in Raven's Daughter, adapted by Fred Williams from the German of Wilbrandt, and acted by Miss Leonard, H. M. Pitt (the débutant of last year at Wallack's), John Drew, Charles Leclercq, George Vandenhoff, Jr., J. W. Nowlan, Agnes Perring, May Sylvie, Georgine Flagg, Isabelle Evesson and Blanche Weaver. This was repeated on October 5th. Meantime, Quits was shelved with the performance on October 3rd, and, on the 5th, Daly met another heartbreaking failure with Edgar Fawcett's comedy, Americans Abroad, produced with one of those enormous casts then not unusual at his theatre:

Silas K. Wilks	James Lewis	Mrs. Livermore	Laura Joyce
Charles Wilks	John Drew	Pauline de Beausejour	Ada Rehan
Archie Vanvelsor	H. M. Pitt	Lucy Wilks	May Fielding
Hughie McLaughlin	Digby Bell	Maria	Marie Williams
Marquis de Bric-à-Brac	W. J. LeMoyne	Mrs. Silas Wilks	Mrs. G. H. Gilbert
Vicomte de la Rivière	Charles Leclercq	Bobby Wilks	Nellie Howard
Count de Beausejour	G. Vandenhoff, Jr.	Countess Molikoff	Blanche Weaver
Aristide	E. P. Wilks	Miss Jones	Georgine Flagg
J. Jenkyns Smythe	H. Macdonough	La Fiordilisa	Lillie Vinton
W. Wilkyns Smythe	E. Sterling	Violet	Isabelle Evesson
John	H. Roberts	Marquise	Helen Bancroft
Zachary Slye	W. H. Beekman		

Emily Denin, Virginia Brooks, Miss A. Hapgood, Miss M. Parkhurst, and Sally Williams added youthful charm to the huge cast. We note the names of George Vandenhoff, Jr., and Marie Williams, the latter well-known to us as a sprightly interpreter of extravaganza and musical burlesque; Daly, as we know, was always looking for fresh talent, and took it where he found it.

He must have been bitterly disappointed at the failure of Fawcett's comedy, but, being Daly, he kept dauntlessly on his way. On Saturday evening, October 22nd, he staged, with rich settings and costumes, a version of Dumas's play, The Youth of Louis XIV, which he called Royal Youth, and thus cast:

[443]

Louis XIV......................John Drew	Count Daugeau..............W. J. LeMoyne
Mazarin....................Charles Leclercq	Charles II.....................Emily Denin
Duc d'Anjou................Virginia Brooks	Marie de Mancini...........Ada Rehan
Comte de Guiche.........G. Vandenhoff, Jr.	Anne of Austria..........Mrs. G. H. Gilbert
Bouchavannes.................George Parkes	Princess Henrietta.............May Fielding
Captain Guitant...............H. Roberts	Mlle. de la Motte...........Helen Bancroft
Paquelin.......................E. P. Wilks	Mlle. Charlotte..............Isabelle Evesson
Molière........................Digby Bell	Georgette.....................Laura Joyce

This is certainly an interesting cast, among other reasons, because of the appearance of the later famed Helen Bancroft, the newest recruit in Daly's famous rosebud garden of girls. Royal Youth was perhaps the greatest of three successive failures, and there was nothing to do but send its archæological splendours to the storehouse. On October 26th, at a matinée for the benefit of the Michigan sufferers, Daly had staged Frou-Frou, with Agnes Leonard in the title-rôle, Ada Rehan as Louise, Mrs. Gilbert as the Baroness, Marie Williams as Pauline, H. M. Pitt as Sartorys, James Lewis as the Baron, George Parkes as Valréas, Le Moyne as Brigard, &c. He now put it, on the 29th, into the regular bill, and ran it till November 3rd, when once more he gave Cinderella at School, repeated up to and including November 9th.

All this was discouraging, but, on November 10th, the eager manager at last met success, perhaps the greatest, thus far, of his new theatre. On that date, he brought out The Passing Regiment, adapted from von Moser and von Schönthan's comedy, Krieg im Frieden, already known in New York to frequenters of plays in German. "The incident of a regiment billeted upon a rural town, was," says Judge Daly, "neatly transferred to America." And Drew and Miss Rehan made delightful successes as Adjutant Paul Dexter and the Russian girl, Telka Essipoff:

Linthicum Winthrop........W. J. LeMoyne	Telka Essipoff....................Ada Rehan
Hofmeister, Jr..................James Lewis	Mrs. Winthrop..........Mrs. G. H. Gilbert
Peregrine Bunker..........Charles Leclercq	Milly Merritt..................May Fielding
Colonel Van Kleek...........George Parkes	Linda......................Marie Williams
Adjutant Dexter.................John Drew	Mrs. Bunker....................May Sylvie
Lieutenant Suydam..............H. M. Pitt	Sophie........................Emily Denin
Surgeon Van Tassel..............Digby Bell	Mary Anne...............Blanche Weaver
Solomon......................E. P. Wilks	

Unfortunately, Allston Brown gives for·this important production not the actual first cast, as above, but the cast of a travelling company sent out later by Daly to carry the glad message to outlying communities.

Daly, I am pleased to state, was now launched on a successful course. The Passing Regiment was billeted on his stage until February 6th, reaching the ever-desired goal of a hundredth performance on February 3rd. I rejoice with Daly and his busy cohorts. And, on February 6th, the theatre had another success in the last sort of play one would have expected to find in this house, devoted, one remembers, in the prologue so nobly delivered by Fanny Morant, at the opening of the season of 1880–81, to comedy, and

JAMES LEWIS—MRS. GILBERT HELEN BANCROFT ADA REHAN—JOHN DREW
(THE PASSING REGIMENT) (THE PASSING REGIMENT)

BIJOU HERON HENRY MILLER AGNES LEONARD

CHARLE LECLERCQ MAY SYLVIE WILLIAM GILBERT

comedy only. The surprising novelty, on the 6th, was Daly's adaptation of Sardou's Odette, and in it Ada Rehan was cast for the tearful, tragic heroine, a part wholly unlike anything she had hitherto attempted on this stage. Again an immense cast participated:

Count Clermont-Latour	H. M. Pitt	Jacques	J. Hamilton
General Clermont-Latour	W. J. LeMoyne	Narcisse	C. Jackson
Philippe La Hoche	John Drew	Laurent	Mr. Saleon
Bechamel	James Lewis	Odette	Ada Rehan
Duke de Meryan	Henry Miller	Berangère	Hélène Stoepel
Vicomte de Frontenac	George Parkes	Juliette	May Fielding
Anatole Morizot	Charles Leclercq	Baroness	Mrs. G. H. Gilbert
Dr. Oliva	John Moore	Mme. Morizot	Nellie Howard
Eustache	W. H. Beekman	Princess de Gorta	Emma Hinckley
Ignacio Esteban	E. Sterling	Miss Sarah	Agnes Perring
Sir Henry Pecock	H. Roberts	Olga	Isabelle Evesson
Chevalier Carvani	W. Bedell	Jeannette	Emily Denin
Infant Berangère	Little Angelica	Mlle. Bertin	Lillie Vinton

Odette had features expected in French drama of that time — the suspected wife, driven from home and child; her sinking to the position of *appanage* of a gambling resort; her refusal, years later, to gratify the demands of the husband in certain matters that will permit the marriage of their daughter, unless she be permitted to see the girl; her tearful interview with the daughter, who takes her for a friend of her mother, a mother long believed by the daughter to be dead; and her final self-sacrificing departure from the scene, not to drown herself, as in Sardou's original, but to enter a convent, as in Daly's version. One sees how far this is from Ada Rehan's usual line of hoydenish maidens. I suppose the Herald could not have been far out, on the 7th, in its summing up of the situation: "It was suggested ... that there was a likelihood of Miss Rehan's filling the place occupied long since by Miss Ethel and Miss Morris in Mr. Daly's company. There was no real evidence of this, last evening, although Miss Rehan showed much cleverness in being able to make anything at all of a part decidedly out of her best line of characters, and at times was really excellent. Her pathos was not artificial, but it was frequently girlish and shallow; it was not the awful anguish and terrible misery of a woman in such a position as Odette's. She struggled bravely against terrible odds, and showed an earnest intention that deserved more substantial rewards. She played the part with refinement of art, and nice finish in almost all directions, but she lacked the womanly depth of feeling and passion that the part demanded. She was not a failure at any time, but she simply continued on a moderate plane of merit where she might have touched sublime heights. Miss Heron gave a delightful interpretation of ... Berangère." The Tribune, however, asserts that "in the stormy interview of Odette with her hostile husband in the gaming house Miss Ada Rehan put forth unexpected powers with surprising effect, and embodied with overwhelming force the ideal of a desperate woman

[445]

hunted down and turning at bay"; whereas the Evening Post thinks that, "in the final scene between mother and daughter, Miss Rehan gave forth a suggestion of tearless grief which was genuinely pathetic."

In the character of the daughter, Hélène Stoepel (daughter of Matilda Heron) returned to the Daly management, under which, several years before, she had been so very successful as the child, Bijou Heron; it is interesting to note also in the cast the name of Henry Miller (his first appearance in New York). Shortly after this occasion, the two young people married, and Mrs. Miller left the stage. Of course Henry Miller is an outstanding figure in our theatrical history. Pitt falling ill, during the run of Odette, Miller succeeded him for a time as the wronged husband, and, says Judge Daly, "acquitted himself with dignity and discretion." Odette attained seventy-seven performances, passing from the scene on April 12th; on the 3rd of April, it was given at the matinée for the benefit of the Actors' Fund.

Daly's last production for 1881–82 was a light musical piece by Caedes, adapted by Fred Williams and Robert Stoepel, and called Girouette, or, the Weathercock. The leading members of the company had gone on tour, and the cast of the new attraction (April 13th) included William Gilbert (new at Daly's and thenceforth for several seasons a prominent comedian there) as Baron Papin de Birmenstorff, sometimes known as the Weathercock; E. P. Wilks as Captain Colardo; Signor Montegriffo as the true Eustache; Harry Macdonough as the false Eustache; May Fielding as Princess Frédérique; Francesca Guthrie (also new at Daly's) as Suzanne; Marie Williams as Pelagie the Proud; Agnes Perring as Lieutenant Bragonette, and Isabelle Evesson (who was not advancing fast, after three years at Daly's) as Corporal Lucette. This made light, pleasing entertainment for early spring, and lasted until the season closed on May 20th; Girouette had revolved in all weathers for forty-four times.

It has been interesting to watch Daly's determined energetic struggles during these early years of his since so celebrated theatre; The Passing Regiment and Odette are the only noteworthy gleanings for 1881–82, and even they were nothing to boast of in a season that throughout the city was far from stimulating to the historical imagination.

Madison Square Theatre, 1881–1882

We left the beautiful little Madison Square Theatre, in September, 1881, repeating its summer success, The Professor, with which, both as author and as actor, William H. Gillette first came prominently into notice. This attraction reached, on September 8th, its hundredth performance, and passed from the home theatre with the matinée on October 29th. Georgia Cayvan had latterly been out of the cast.

On the evening of October 29th came another sweet, harmless play, of the theatric-religious cast affected by the Mallorys; a play indeed that might be said to be the only rival Hazel Kirke had in the history of the Mallory régime at the home theatre and throughout the country, whither travelling companies were to make it familiar to all and sundry. The piece in question was Esmeralda, built up by the popular novelist, Frances Hodgson Burnett, from one of her stories, and fashioned into a drama by her and William H. Gillette. In the title-rôle came forth a very young girl, Annie Russell, who had appeared earlier in the city in a juvenile Pinafore company, and who now began a career that for a quarter of a century was to rank her among the foremost American actresses, both in popularity and in art. All who saw Miss Russell know how sweet she was either in comedy or in pathetic plays, and will recall gratefully her charm, her grace, her exquisite voice, her genuine dramatic power. I have seen few actresses more appealing than Annie Russell, and the Mallory management deserves great credit for bringing her forward. She made a big hit as the little Southern girl, whose family was suddenly enriched, by the discovery, as was supposed, of oil on the farm, and who was carried by an ambitious mother to Paris, there to forget her honest Dave Hardy, and marry an unworthy scion of the nobility. Leslie Allen, in the original cast, played poor, doddering Elbert Rogers, father of Esmeralda, utterly confused by Paris, and longing for the dear old home in the South; Kate Denin Wilson was the hard, ambitious mother. Another family group, this time in Paris, and devoted to art study, consisted of E. A. McDowell as Jack Desmond, and the brilliant Agnes Booth and the winsome May Gallagher (their first appearances at the Madison Square) as his sisters, Nora and Kate. Thomas Whiffen, a landmark in that earlier Madison Square record, was Estabrook, whose business it was to help get the family of Rogers to America and to have several delightful comedy scenes with Mrs. Booth. Lesser parts fell to Davenport Bebus as Marquis de Montessin, Edwin Knowles as George Drew, the oil prospector, and Clara Hyatt as Sophie. And, of course, honest Dave Hardy must be played very well; the part was entrusted to the vigorous Eben Plympton. The reader may wish to know that, after all, the enriching oil was really on Dave's place, and that Lydia Ann Rogers was forced to swallow her pride, give up her graceless marquis as a possible son-in-law, and let the curtain fall on a happy Dave and Esmeralda. Certainly this was sweet, and our innocent Americans of the '80s loved it.

Esmeralda ran throughout the winter, spring, summer and early autumn of 1882. The reader sees, thus, how easy is this section of our chronicle, for him and for me. The hundredth performance was celebrated on February 3rd, the same night as the hundredth of The Passing Regiment at Daly's. The original cast continued until February 27th, when John E. Owens, the famous Solon Shingle and Caleb Plummer of former seasons, first assumed the congenial rôle of Elbert Rogers; Mrs. Whiffen then replaced Kate Denin

[447]

Wilson as Lydia Ann. A break in the sameness of the record occurred on the afternoon of March 2nd; George Riddle, who had recently, at Booth's, acted (in the original Greek) Œdipus Tyrannus, came to the Mallory house in a series of recitations and readings, including a selection from the Sophoclean tragedy. Esmeralda pursued its serene road of success; the hundred and fiftieth performance fell on March 24th. The afternoon of April 3rd brought at this theatre, as elsewhere, a performance for the Actors' Fund. On the 13th (afternoon) came to the Madison Square the Hasty Pudding Club of Harvard, with a performance of Dido and Æneas, "by Owen Wister, of Harvard." Well, if Fanny Kemble's grandson might not write a play, who might? And is it not pleasing to encounter thus, for the first time, the later so celebrated author of The Virginian?

During the week of April 17th–22nd, on a given evening or so, Eben Plympton was ill, and Harry Lee, at short notice, played Dave Hardy. Plympton soon returned, and the cast, with Owens and Mrs. Whiffen, continued, so far as I can learn, unchanged till May 12th, when the two hundreth performance brought souvenirs and felicitations. The 250th rendering of the pretty, innocuous play fell on July 1st. The cast, as printed in the Herald advertisement for July 3rd, now showed Owens, E. A. McDowell, Davenport Bebus, Mrs. Whiffen and Annie Russell in familiar rôles, but with Edward J. Buckley (a manly actor) as Dave Hardy, Harry Lacy in Whiffen's character of Estabrook, Fanny Reeves replacing Agnes Booth as Nora Desmond, and Louise Dillon as Kate. On July 4th, however, Leslie Allen resumed his original rôle of Elbert Rogers, with Mrs. Allen as Lydia Ann, and with Viola Allen, their daughter (her first appearance on any stage) as Esmeralda. Of course Viola Allen, like Annie Russell, became, in later years, a notable star; like Miss Russell, also, she was a sweet Esmeralda. For several weeks, now, the cast of the Burnett-Gillette play included, besides the Allens, Buckley, Lacy, Bebus, McDowell, Fanny Reeves and Miss Dillon (an excellent *ingénue*). Annie Russell, however, returned on July 31st, and John E. Owens on August 7th. These permutations and combinations of the Mallory régime require wary treading. The cast printed in the Herald for August 21st included Owens, Buckley, Lacy, Horning (as Jack Desmond), Louis F. Massen (as George Drew), Bebus, Fanny Reeves, Mrs. Whiffen, Annie Russell and Louise Dillon. Here I leave the famous little theatre for 1881–82, warmed by memories of both of its plays for that season.

BOOTH'S THEATRE, 1881–1882

If the season of 1881–82 was not brilliant in the four "stock" theatres just discussed, it was also disappointing to a great degree in the "combination" houses now to be considered, especially as three or four comic operas

LESLIE ALLEN AND
ANNIE RUSSELL

EBEN PLYMPTON

THOMAS WHIFFEN AND
AGNES BOOTH

MAY GALLAGHER

AGNES BOOTH

KATE DENIN WILSON

JOHN E. OWENS

DAVENPORT BEBUS

E. A. McDOWELL

ANDERSON'S PHOTOGRAPHS FROM ESMERALDA

were repeated and shifted from one theatre to another in utterly damnable iteration. I am not sure that, except for a few outstanding attractions, the dramatic history of 1881–82 is not as little interesting as any we have studied for some years preceding.

Booth's, under management of John Stetson, began the new term on August 31st (the opening having been postponed from the 29th) with an elaborate spectacular production of the Jules Verne-Adolphe d'Ennery melodrama, Michael Strogoff — a piece much advertised, and presented, in some form, in rival showings, at the same time in the Academy of Music and Aberle's Tivoli, in Eighth Street. The cast at Booth's:

Michael Strogoff	F. C. Bangs	Passport Agent	Charles Torrence
Ivan Ogareff	J. N. Gotthold	Telegraph Clerk	T. F. Atkins
Governor of Moscow	A. D. Billings	Tartar Chief	Z. Tailraf
General Kiezoff	John Swinburne	High Priest	W. H. Pope
Richard Hunt	Isidore Davidson	Grand Duke	Frank Beresford
John Philpot	Felix Morris	Wassil	John T. Burke
Emir of Bokhara	George Robinson	Fugitive	Thomas Barton
Chief of Police	Delancey Barclay	Marfa Strogoff	Eliza Bates
Innkeeper	George Rowson	Sangarre	Florence Robinson
Aide-de-Camp	Walter Eytinge	Nadia	Rachel Sanger
General Verouzoff	John Bright		

Michael Strogoff was, I fear, a failure. The Herald, on September 1st, informs us that "it failed to make the success that had been prophesied for it in America." The stage management was bad, bombs and guns did not explode on time, a carriage broke in two, the horses walking off with just the tongue, etc. On September 5th, W. J. Ferguson replaced Isidore Davidson as Richard Hunt, the American reporter, and doubtless brought out far more of the comic element in the part; Felix Morris as the British correspondent had been one of the successes of the piece — a piece, however, that depended for its appeal on the flight of Michael Strogoff, the Imperial messenger, through all kinds of danger by fire and flood, including a harrowing scene of his blinding by red-hot irons. Booth's, like most theatres in the city, closed on September 20th and 26th, the dates, respectively, of the death and of the funeral of President Garfield. And Michael Strogoff, the much lauded and much desired, passed out of Booth's on October 1st.

EDWIN BOOTH; ROSSI; MLLE. RHEA

Edwin Booth came back, on October 3rd, to the theatre he had with such hope inaugurated. He began as Richelieu (a part played on the same evening by Lawrence Barrett, at the Fifth Avenue Theatre), and repeated it on October 4th and 8th; on the 5th and 6th, he essayed Macbeth; on the 7th, he was Othello; and, at the matinée on the 8th, Iago. In his company were Bella Pateman (returned after several seasons to the scene of her

[449]

former activity), Samuel Piercy, Cyril Searle, D. C. Anderson, Robert Pateman, F. C. Huebner, Will A. Whitecar, L. F. Barrett, Edwin Cleary, Mason Mitchell, W. Chisnell, Frank Lander (later a pleasing leading juvenile), Henry Bristol, W. Carpenter, Mrs. Charles Calvert (the distinguished Rumour in Henry V, with Rignold), Miss A. Calvert, Louisa Eldridge, and Eva Garrick — on the whole a better aggregation than Booth had recently employed. Booth had been in London during the preceding season, a fact that may account for the English players now supporting him. Henry E. Abbey was manager of the Booth season.

One knows what to expect of these later engagements of our famous tragedian; what one never received or expected was novelty. On October 10th, 11th and 15th, we suffered with Bertuccio, in The Fool's Revenge; on the 12th, 13th and 15th (matinée) we enjoyed Booth's golden Hamlet. The Herald found this performance perfect in every detail, but without a spark of inward fire. Booth played Iago, on the 14th. On the afternoon of the 14th, also, he appeared for the benefit of the sufferers from the Michigan fires, acting Iago, to the Othello of Lawrence Barrett, the Cassio of Louis James, the Emilia of Bella Pateman, and the Desdemona of Marie Wainwright — a cast of enduring distinction. The third week of Booth's visit gave us King Lear (October 17th and 18th), Katharine and Petruchio and The Merchant of Venice (19th), Richard III (20th, 21st and 22nd), and Richelieu (matinée, 22nd); the fourth and final week repeated matter already seen and enjoyed — Hamlet (October 24th, and matinée, 29th), Richelieu (25th and 28th), The Merchant of Venice and Katharine and Petruchio, 26th and 29th, and Richard III, 27th. Thus departed our leading actor, leaving us with memories refreshed by his great art, and with renewed pleasure at again meeting Bella Pateman and Mrs. Calvert. This last-named lady had played Emilia, Goneril, Queen Margaret, &c.

After this month of the English "legitimate," we turned to the Italian muse, and became acquainted with Ernesto Rossi, one of Italy's most distinguished actors. He had the temerity to present himself, on October 31st, in Othello, possibly the best-known impersonation of his great compatriot, Salvini. Like Salvini, during the season of 1880–81, Rossi was supported by an English-speaking company, including Milnes Levick as Iago, Leslie Gossin (Cassio), H. A. Weaver (Brabantio), Charles Kent (Duke), E. A. Eberle (Roderigo), J. H. Ring (Gratiano), H. A. Weaver, Jr. (Montano), Louise Muldener (Desdemona), and Constance Hamblin (Emilia). Rossi had made his American début, on October 3rd, in Boston, playing King Lear. He made his way slowly in New York. Says the Herald of November 1st:

> Signor Rossi is a little over fifty years of age, though upon the stage he looks at least a dozen years younger. He is tall, of commanding figure, and possessed of an intellectually handsome countenance. He is

graceful but not forcibly eloquent in his gestures and carries himself when in repose with ease and dignity.   His voice is not entirely satisfactory, his articulation not being distinct, and though his Italian is pure and refined, his intonation is not always well chosen.   Nor is his voice as round and full, as sweet or musical as is Salvini's. . . . It is impossible to look upon his Othello and dissociate it . . . from Salvini's. . . . It was impossible to listen to Signor Rossi last evening and fail to recognize the great talents of the man and the frequent bursts of genius which illumined the picture. . . . But it was not in all directions . . . evenly sustained. . . .

In the earlier scenes . . . it lacked the finish, the dignity, the imposing power with which Salvini invested the Moor, and there was a restlessness, an uneasiness of movement, almost a flippancy . . . that is foreign to all accepted views of the character.   His was a laughing, buoyant, good-natured, almost happy-go-lucky soldier of fortune . . . and his meeting with Brabantio's friends, his address to the Senate and his meeting with Desdemona were disposed of in an off hand, almost thoughtless manner that offended English views. . . . In the scenes with Iago and Desdemona later, when his jealousy is roused, he vastly improved, and at times rose to positive grandeur, the finale of the third and fourth acts resulting in enthusiastic triple calls before the house. . . . The final chamber scene was well begun, but the good results first promised were not fulfilled owing to a false judgment, which, in its desire to produce absolute realism, allowed Signor Rossi to enact Desdemona's murder in full view of the audience, in an almost brutish fashion, by strangling her with his hands after twisting her long hair about her neck, as he shook her violently and then dragged her about the bed and finally tossed her down upon the pillows.   The scene was simply revolting . . . and murmurs of dissatisfaction were audible in the house.

The new star gleamed as Othello again on November 2nd and at the matinée on the 5th; on November 1st and 4th he acted Romeo, and, on the 3rd essayed Hamlet.   A little over fifty years of age, he could not have been a captivating Romeo; but, from what I remember of Louise Muldener, a few years later, I hardly see how her Juliet could have inspired even the most ardent youth.   Rossi's second and last week repeated Hamlet (November 7th and 10th, and matinée on the 12th), Othello (on the 8th), and Romeo and Juliet on the 9th; the only new offering was King Lear (on the 11th).   Since he would not, usually, perform twice in one day, the two Saturday evenings of his term (November 5th and 12th) were devoted to a concert by Camilla Urso (not recently heard in New York) and the Carreño-Donaldi Company — rare musical treats, I opine.   Rossi's engagement was not a huge financial success, apparently, but artistically it scored well; critical opinion seemed to be that he progressed steadily in stature from part to part, and that it would have been wise for him to open in Lear, rather than in Othello.

William Winter, whose analyses of Shakespearean performances must ever awaken respect and admiration, did not like Rossi's Othello or his Hamlet, on the score that they were wholly Italian in conception, with very little of the spiritual quality inherent in Shakespeare's heroes. "His Othello," writes Winter (Shakespeare on the Stage, First Series), "was a common man, at first intoxicated by sensual passion and afterward infuriated by demoniac jealousy." But "that *Othello* is a poetic creation, a consummate type of nobility and magnanimity," with its idolising love of Desdemona, was "not comprehended by Rossi," any more than by Salvini, and his performance was, therefore "radically wrong and supremely repulsive." The tragedian's Hamlet was "heavy and muscular...massive and portly.... There was not the slightest indication of the essential spirit of *Hamlet* in any part of his performance, except in the delivery of the soliloquy on suicide." The reader is referred to Winter's illuminating account of the novel details of Rossi's interpretation, and to his summing up that the actor "applied what is called 'realism' to poetry; and realism, applied to 'Hamlet,' is desecration."

After this serious business, we may lightly turn to thoughts of Patience. The Gilbert and Sullivan satirical operetta was a raging epidemic in the season of 1881–82, only a trifle less devastating to other theatrical ventures than had been Pinafore in 1879. And Oscar Wilde, against whose "æsthetic" cult the satire had been directed, was in New York to accentuate the killing nature of the attack. Things were too "utterly utter" to escape the notice of the most unobservant. Well, the reader of this veracious chronicle must expect to find Patience at almost any theatre during the season now under review. It was played first, on September 22, 1881, at the Standard Theatre, but thenceforth, for months, it sprang up unexpectedly in many a fallow field. And here, following Booth and Rossi, we welcome it to the roomy stage of Booth's, where, on November 14th, Edward E. Rice's Comic Opera Company presented it with A. W. F. McCollin as Bunthorne, Eugene Clarke as Grosvenor, Gustavus Hall as Colonel Calverly, George A. Schiller as Major Murgatroyd, Henri Laurent as Lieutenant the Duke of Dunstable, Thomas Sage as the Solicitor, Vernona Jarbeau as Lady Angela, Irene Perry as Lady Saphir, Fannie Hall as Lady Ella, Rosa Cooke as Lady Jane, and Rose Temple as Patience. This was not the best cast, by far, that Patience enjoyed that season in New York, but with New Yorkers it was anything so long as it was Patience. The company remained at Booth's for two weeks, and, on November 26th, departed for other stages.

It was succeeded by Mlle. Rhea, a handsome, ambitious actress, who never quite fixed herself in our affections, though on the "road" she attained a certain vogue. She had appeared, on November 14th, at the Park Theatre, Brooklyn. At Booth's she came out (November 28th) as Adrienne Lecouvreur, repeating the part on the 29th and 30th, and at the matinée on

December 3rd; on December 1st, 2nd and 3rd (evening) she gave the expected, the inevitable Camille. In her company were J. Newton Gotthold, J. L. Carhart, J. H. Howell, Edwin Varrey, W. F. Clifton, Isabel Morris, Mrs. J. W. Brutone, Grace Hall, Josie Robinson, and Lillie Moses — certainly not, as a whole, a glittering array. The poor lady had but a week of it, and litigation pursued her, for one reason or another, into the outer spaces of the road. Nevertheless, Mlle. Rhea persisted; we shall meet her again. But not often!

MR. AND MRS. FLORENCE; VOKES FAMILY; KATE CLAXTON

On December 5th, the admired Florences ("first appearance since their return from Europe") began two weeks of The Mighty Dollar, yielding the stage, on December 19th, to the Vokes Family, in their favourite Belles of the Kitchen and Cousin Joe. The Vokes Family, but, alas! without the merry, irresistible Rosina, and with Bessie Sansone doing her best (a fairly good best) to replace the absent, regretted star of the family.

It would seem that Booth's had entered on a long term of short exploitation of stars. The Vokes Family having served their week, Kate Claxton, of whom one always thinks with affection, entered, also for one week (December 26th–31st), in her never-flagging vehicle, The Two Orphans. She made a special effort to present the familiar play in worthy style, and engaged James O'Neill, Marie Wilkins, Ida Vernon and T. E. Morris for parts they had so often acted with her at the Union Square Theatre; Edwin F. Thorne appeared as the Chevalier de Vaudrey, so frequently portrayed by his famous brother, C. R. Thorne, Jr., and the handsome C. A. Stevenson shifted from Pierre and the Chevalier, both of which he usually played, to the villainous Jacques. Others in the cast were Henrietta Vaders as Henriette, Florence Robinson as the Countess, H. B. Phillips as the Count, R. J. Dustan as Picard, Walter Eytinge as the Marquis de Presles, and Josie Batchelder as Marianne, altogether an interesting distribution.

MARY ANDERSON; ETELKA GERSTER; DION BOUCICAULT

And now followed a month of the beautiful Mary Anderson in a severely "legitimate" repertoire. She began, on January 2nd, as Juliet, with William Harris as Romeo, J. B. Studley as Mercutio, Robert L. Downing as the Friar, J. G. McDonald as Tybalt, T. L. Coleman as Paris, Joseph Anderson (her young brother) as Benvolio, H. B. Norman as Capulet, F. Currier as Peter and the Apothecary (a not unusual "doubling"), Grace Logan as Balthasar, Mrs. M. A. Pennoyer as the Nurse, &c. This favourite play was acted on the 2nd, 3rd, 4th, 5th and 6th. At the matinée on the 7th, Miss Anderson for the first time in New York acted Galatea, in W. S. Gilbert's

[453]

satirical Pygmalion and Galatea; in the evening she was Julia, in The Hunchback.

If there was ever a more beautiful vision than Mary Anderson as the statue in Pygmalion and Galatea, or in the classic draperies of the statue come to life, my eyes have not been blessed with it. I speak now of that glorious picture, not as presented in 1881–1882, but as seen in 1885, after the actress's return from London, where the great Academicians had vied with one another in designing costumes and draperies adapted to her classic beauty. How wonderful, then, her Galatea! Her support in the Booth's season now reviewing consisted of William Harris as the sculptor, Robert Downing as Leucippe, H. B. Norman as Chrysos, Coleman as Mimos, F. Currier as Agesimos, Alice Brooks as Cynisca, Mrs. Pennoyer as Daphne, and Grace Logan as Myrine.

The Herald had cooled from its earliest eulogy of the actress, and on January 8th, spoke but with a tempered joy of her Galatea, which, "while marred here and there by the blemishes noticeable in all that Miss Anderson does," had "decided merits." "These merits were chiefly in her posing, which was artistic and effective; her gestures, which were usually well chosen and gracefully accomplished, and a pleasing and winning sweetness and a seemingly unconscious archness. The blemishes were caused by a faulty and stilty (sic) enunciation of certain lines . . . to which she tried to give a highly dramatic and almost tragic earnestness, at once robbing the character of its greatest beauty. . . . Her appearance . . . was strikingly handsome, and she managed her draperies with great and apparently unstudied skill."

The first five evenings of her second week (January 9th–13th), Miss Anderson devoted to The Hunchback, in which, as Julia, she was assisted by Studley as Master Walter, Harris as Clifford, McDonald as Modus, and Alice Brookes as Helen. At the matinée, on the 14th, she repeated Galatea, and, on the evening of that day she played The Daughter of Roland, from the French of Count Henri de Bournier:

Berthe	Mary Anderson	Richard	Joseph Anderson
Gerald	William Harris	Hardre	Oliver Doud
Charlemagne	T. L. Coleman	Hugo	T. Melbourne
Ragenhardt	R. L. Downing	Geoffrey	F. Currier
Neathold	W. Lavelle	Count Amaury	J. B. Studley
Duke de Nayme	J. G. McDonald	Theobald	Grace Logan
Radbert	H. B. Norman		

This play served Miss Anderson well, and it figured frequently in her repertoire for a season or two. She made a personal success in the character of the proud Berthe, yielding at last, in love, to the slayer of her kinsmen. She repeated it, now, on January 16th and 17th, revived Love, on the 18th, 19th and 20th, and, on the 21st, reverted to Galatea, for the matinée, and

Juliet, for the evening performance.   One likes to think of the earnest, ambitious young woman steadily forging ahead to her ultimate renown.   Her last week shows the growing popularity of her Galatea, with performances on January 23rd, 24th, 25th and 26th; it was given, also, for Miss Anderson's benefit, on Friday, the 27th, when to it was added the third act of The Daughter of Roland.   The last day of the engagement (January 28th) gave us The Lady of Lyons, in the afternoon, and Ingomar, in the evening. This was one of the few inspiring engagements of the season.

On January 30th, Booth's Theatre opened to an unusual experiment, a performance of Œdipus Tyrannus, in which George Riddle, who had directed and acted in the play at Harvard, in the original Greek, now performed the leading character in the same language, in association with a cast of English-speaking players.   If Salvini and Rossi could do a similar thing in Italian, why might one not do it in Greek?   Well, Riddle tried it for a week, with a stage set according to archaeological dictates, with appropriate Greek costumes, and with a cast including the youthful, talented Georgia Cayvan as Jocasta (surely a strange choice), Lewis Morrison as Creon, J. F. Hagan as Teiresias and the Messenger from Corinth, J. J. Hayes as Priest, P. C. Hagar as the Messenger from the Palace, and Preston Wilcox as Coryphæus.   G. Lyon, of Harvard, served as stage-manager, G. W. Chadwick as musical director (with music by Professor Paine), and Frank Millet as designer of costumes, after Harvard models.   The play was produced under the management of E. H. Ober, of Boston, and Daniel Frohman.   It was certainly a dignified experiment, but I greatly doubt its financial success.   It brought George Riddle into prominence.

And after that intensely serious week, came in, on February 6th, another Boston offering — performance of operetta by the delightful Boston Ideal Opera Company.   They opened on the 6th, in Fatinitza, with Mathilde Phillips (or Phillipps) as Vladimir, Marie Stone as Lydia, Lizzie Burton as Dimitri, May Calef as Ivan, Tom Karl as Julian, W. H. Macdonald as Izzet Pacha, Myron W. Whitney as Count Timofey, and George Frothingham as Sergeant Stepan.   In The Chimes of Normandy, on the 7th, Miss Stone was Serpolette, Geraldine Ulmar (whom we shall love, in 1885, as Yum Yum, in The Mikado) was Germaine, Zephie Dinsmore Gertrude, May Calef Jeanne, Lizzie Burton Manette, Marie Coleman Suzanne, Tom Karl Henri, W. H. Fessenden Jean Grenicheux, Myron W. Whitney (a magnificent basso) Gaspard, Macdonald the Bailli, and Frothingham the Notary — perhaps the best singing cast the opera ever had in New York.

The offering for the 8th was Czar and Carpenter, alleged to be for the first time here in English; on the 9th, The Mascot (heard that winter in many New York theatres) presented Miss Ulmar as Bettina, Miss Burton as Fiametta, the richly humorous H. C. Barnabee as Lorenzo XVII, Fessenden as the Prince, and Frothingham as Rocco.   The Pirates of Penzance

[455]

delighted on the 10th, and, for the matinée, on the 11th, Olivette, another epidemic of the winter, presented Miss Stone in the title-rôle, with Miss Ulmar as the Countess, Macdonald as De Merrimac, Karl as Valentine, and Barnabee as the Duc des Ifs, all combining for "one of the very best performances," declares the Herald of the 12th, "that we have seen in this city." Pinafore, on the evening of the 11th, closed the busy first week of these brilliant visitors. For their second and last week they repeated some of the rich fare of their first: Fatinitza (February 13th and 18th), The Pirates of Penzance (14th), Olivette (16th), The Mascot (17th), and Pinafore (matinée, 18th). They attempted a flight slightly higher, musically, on the 15th, with The Bohemian Girl.

These performances, attuned to music's lighter moods, prepared the way for the more serious musical feast that began on February 20th with Max Strakosch's Grand Italian Opera Company. Strakosch had tempted from Mapleson's forces the brilliant and beloved Etelka Gerster, who since autumn had been travelling throughout the country and was now presented, on the 20th, in Lucia di Lammermoor, assisted by artists far less acceptable than those who had formerly appeared with her at the Academy of Music. At about this same time the peerless Adelina Patti was singing in opera, wretchedly supported, at the Germania Theater (late Wallack's). One can only reflect sadly on the idea of how perfect Mapleson's company at the Academy would have been, if these two great sopranos had been enrolled under his banner. Three Italian companies at about the same time in New York would seem to be just a little too much. It is interesting to note that the Edgardo of Mme. Gerster's opening night was Francesco Giannini, reminding us of Dusolina Giannini, of a half-century later. He had a light, pleasing tenor voice, and was respected, if not acclaimed in his initial performances here. Others in the cast of Lucia were Massimo Ciapini as Aston, G. F. Hall as Raimondo, Bardini as Arturo, and the faithful S. Behrens as conductor.

On February 21st, Maria Leslino sang Aïda, with Maria Prasini as Amneris, Giannini as Radames, Ciapini as Amonasro, Mancini as Ramfis, and Maina as Il Re. La Sonnambula, on the 22nd, enlisted Gerster, Miss Lancaster (as Lisa), Miss Arcone (as Teresa), Lazzarini, Mancini and Maina. Il Flauto Magico was advertised for the 23rd, but Rigoletto was substituted, with Gerster, Lazzarini, and Ciapini. Un Ballo in Maschera, on the 24th, was weakly cast, with Leslino, Prasini, Miss Lancaster, Giannini, Ciapini, G. F. Hall, Maina, Tagliapietra and Bardini. Gerster appeared at the matinée (February 25th) in Il Barbiere di Siviglia, and Faust ended a busy week, on the evening of the 25th, with Leslino, Van Arnheim (as Siebel), Hall (Valentino), Mancini (Mephisto) and Giannini (Faust). A concert on Sunday evening, February 26th, enlisted Carolina Zeiss, a good contralto recently imported, Abbie Carrington, Katharine Van Arn-

RHEA AS ADRIENNE
LECOUVREUR

HENRI LAURENT
AS RALPH RACKSTRAW

EUGENE CLARKE
AS GROSVENOR

ROBERT PATEMAN

ROSSI AS HAMLET

BELLA PATEMAN

GEORGE RIDDLE
AS ŒDIPUS

MARY ANDERSON
AS GALATEA

GEORGIA CAYVAN
AS JOCASTA

heim, Lazzarini, L. G. Gottschalk, Perugini, &c. According to Herald reports the house, on Gerster nights, was crowded.

The beloved Gerster had returned in exceptionally fine voice, with her exquisite art unimpaired; perhaps the rivalry with Adelina Patti, whose brief opera season began on February 27th, put Mme. Gerster on her mettle. She drew fine houses, lavish with their applause. The second and last week of the season began on February 27th, with Ambroise Thomas's seldom-heard Hamlet, in which Mme. Gerster for the first time here sang the difficult rôle of Ophelia; Lazzarini was Laertes, Ciapini Hamlet, Mancini the King, G. F. Hall the Ghost, Bardini Horatio, Maina Marcellus, Della Vedova Polonius, and Maria Prasini the Queen. It needs no ghost come from the grave to tell us that this was a very undistinguished cast. Of course Gerster sang the mad scene very brilliantly. Il Trovatore, on the 28th, assembled Leslino, Carolina Zeiss (a satisfactory Azucena), Giannini and George Sweet. On March 1st, La Traviata had Gerster, Giannini and Ciapini as chief interpreters. Only three nights earlier (February 27th) Patti had sung Violetta at the Germania Theater, and had been declared by the Herald, next day, to be "incomparable in her exquisite vocalization." "Her glorious voice came forth with marvellous beauty." And what of Gerster, in the same part? The Herald, on March 2nd, says she "gave her music in exceptionally fine style and was several times enthusiastically recalled." She acted "with good taste and much feeling." One now could compare the two Violettas, not, one conjectures from the Herald accounts, to the advantage of Gerster. The reader may be interested to find from the Herald that Giannini "just missed making a great success of Alfredo; several times he rose to absolute excellence, but did not manage to sustain the good standard he aimed at and often reached." Admirers of Dusolina Giannini will observe a note similar to mature consideration of her art. One reflects sadly on the great artist a more patient study might have made of the latter.

Gerster, on March 2nd, repeated Il Barbiere di Siviglia, sung on the same night at the Germania by Patti; Ernani, on the 3rd, fared as it might, with Abbie Carrington, Giannini, Sweet and Mancini. Gerster sang farewell as Amina before a crowded matinée audience, on the 4th, and on the evening of that day, instead of Aïda announced, Giannini's illness forced a substitution of Il Trovatore; even so, Ciapini grew hoarse in Act I, and G. F. Hall needs must replace him in later acts as Conte di Luna. This season interests one, but chiefly because of Etelka Gerster, who, it will be observed, performed the unusual feat of singing four times a week, and — let me repeat — before crowded houses.

Booth's, on March 6th, returned to drama. Dion Boucicault, a somewhat waning attraction, presented then his new play, Suil-a-Mor, or, Life in Galway, really a revision of Daddy O'Dowd, seen at Booth's on March 17, 1873:

[457]

The O'Dowd..............Dion Boucicault		Mat..........................W. F. Falls
Bertie Talboys..................Henry Lee		Sligo Dan....................G. D. Mackey
Mike O'Dowd................Ogden Stevens		Morrisey................Henry A. Clarke
Colonel Muldoon................T. W. Ford		Lady Rose Lawless............Helen Tracy
Lord Ossidew..............T. J. Galloway		Mrs. O'Dowd..............Lizzie Anderson
Lord Borromore............P. W. Coolidge		Kitty........................Pearl Eytinge
Ramsey Leake..............E. M. Holland		Molly......................Hattie Treville
Chalker........................Sol Smith		Mrs. Foster................Minnie Upham
Wilcox........................J. H. Ring		Maud..........................Miss Volair
Mr. Daly..................Robert Archer		Sheelah................Henrietta Wallace
Barney....................J. J. Williams		

One feels rather sad in comparing this cast, largely of nonentities, with the aggregations that appeared with Boucicault, in the '50s and '60s, at Wallack's, Laura Keene's and the Winter Garden, and, in the '70s, at Wallack's. Boucicault's Daddy O'Dowd was one of his finest characterisations, and acted for two weeks, ending on March 18th.

The season at this house was frittering away in scattered engagements. On March 20th, in came the Boston Comic Opera Company (a rival to the Boston Ideal Opera Company, seen a few weeks previously at Booth's). Many of the singers of this present organisation had, indeed, played Patience at the same house, on November 14th. They began again with The Pirates of Penzance, on March 20th, 21st, 23rd and 24th (this was then current at the Bijou); at Booth's Gertrude Franklin appeared as Mabel, Rosa Cooke as Ruth, Rose Dana as Kate, Fannie Hall as Edith, Mollie Fuller as Isabel, Brocolini in his original rôle of Richard, J. E. Nash as Samuel (also his well-known character), Henri Laurent as Frederic, William Hamilton as the Policeman, and A. W. F. McCollin as the Major General. On the 22nd they gave Patience, and, for the matinée and evening of the 25th, Pinafore. For their second week, Billee Taylor, every evening and Saturday matinée, enlisted Brocolini, Laurent, Hamilton, McCollin, T. M. Hengler, James A. Gilbert, Hattie Moore, Vernona Jarbeau, Fannie Hall and Rosa Cooke. Thus ended a fortnight of the Boston Comic Opera Company.

Mr. and Mrs. Florence filled the week of April 3rd–8th with their old success, The Ticket of Leave Man, Lin Harris, A. Tavernier, Maurice Pike, Frank Lamb, Annie Ellsler (as Sam), Ethel Greybrooke (as May), and Miss L. Novello (as Mrs. Willoughby) supporting as best they might. On April 3rd, for the Actors' Fund matinée, the stars gave The Mighty Dollar. Bronson Howard's comic piece, Green Room Fun, brought in, on April 10th, Salsbury's Troubadours, with John Webster as Captain Opdyke, U. S. A., John Gourlay as Reverend Ernest Duckworth, Nate Salsbury as Booth McC. Forrest, Nellie McHenry as Kittie Plumpet, and Ray Samuels (Mrs. Nate Salsbury) as the young widow, Mrs. Camilla Westlake. The gist of the piece consisted in the rehearsal by these characters of an amateur show — always a funny theme. The piece had been seen previously in Brooklyn. Brooklyn had recently launched several cargoes of hopes, not all fulfilled.

EDWIN BOOTH

And now dramatic consistency once more gave us solid footing. Booth returned, on April 17th, for a two-weeks engagement, prior to his departure for Europe. Of course he gave nothing new, and since his company was somewhat near that which supported him here in November, I will content myself with stating that he drew his loyal public on April 17th, at the matinée on the 22nd, and on the evening of the 26th, in Richelieu; on the 18th, he acted Othello, and, on the 19th, Macbeth. The Fool's Revenge filled the evenings of the 20th, the 22nd and the 28th; on the 21st, Booth gave his incomparable Iago. Hamlet, without which any Booth season would be inconceivable, brooded on the evenings of April 24th and 27th, and at the matinée on the 29th; King Lear stormed and suffered on the 25th, and Richard III ended the engagement the evening of the 29th. The cast of Hamlet included F. C. Huebner as the Ghost, Barton Hill as the King, D. C. Anderson as Polonius, Robert and Bella Pateman as the Grave-digger and Ophelia, and Mrs. Charles Calvert as the Queen. With but few exceptions, this is a chilling group.

The theatre remained dark for a week, but, on May 8th, Rice's Surprise Party relighted it with the fun of Daly's recent hit, Cinderella at School, with Henry E. Dixey as Dr. Syntax and George K. Fortescue as Zenobia Tropics, the parts so comically filled at Daly's by James Lewis and Mrs. Gilbert. Others in the cast at Booth's were Rose Temple, Nellie J. Prescott, Irene Perry, Jennie Calef, Flora Pike, Eugene Clarke, George A. Schiller, W. H. West, Donald Campbell, Edwin Aiken, &c. On Saturday, May 20th, Dixey's benefit offered the second act of Patience, with Dixey as Bunthorne and Fortescue (doubtless funny, if not Gilbertian) as Lady Jane, and Rice's Surprise Party's burlesque of La Mascotte. With that, the season of 1881–82 came to an end at Booth's. With the engagements of Booth, the Florences, Rossi, Etelka Gerster, Mary Anderson, Boucicault, and the Boston Ideal Opera Company, one must pay to it something like a tribute of respect; but there had been intervals that made one look back, regretfully, to the palmy days of this theatre, built with such hope, and now nearing its doom. A year hence, Booth's Theatre would pass out of existence.

FIFTH AVENUE THEATRE, 1881–1882

And that other theatre founded in hope — the defeated hope of Augustin Daly — pursued a scattering course in 1881–82. The Fifth Avenue, still under the management of J. H. Haverly, re-opened, on August 22nd, with a play by George Fawcett Rowe, entitled Smiff (surely a name to repel customers):

[459]

Philander Smiff	G. F. Rowe	John Genessee	G. C. Davenport
Albert Smiff	James Cooper	Jason Pegrim	Murry Woods
Thaddeus Smiff	J. E. Nagle, Jr.	Miss Cadwallader	Mary Stuart
Daphne Smiff	Louise Balfe	Pipes	Harry Reeves
Laurelia Smiff	Alma Stuart Stanley	Parsons	A. Henderson
Mimosa Smiff	Kate Gurney	Alonzo Brown	Charles S. Dickson

Allston Brown states that on this occasion Louise Balfe and Kate Gurney made their American début; I am interested in the re-appearance of the old favourite of the Bowery, George C. Davenport, and in the name of young Nagle, evidently the son of that other Bowery hero, J. E. Nagle. Charles S. Dickson acted with acclaim during Daniel Frohman's Lyceum season of 1887–88. Smiff had but two weeks at the Fifth Avenue, closing on September 3rd. On the 5th, the Wilbur Opera Company appeared in La Mascotte, a work that might emerge, during that season, in any theatre in New York, except the four homes of stock companies discussed at the beginning of this chapter. How New Yorkers endured the constant repetition of this opera and of Olivette, I cannot even conjecture. In the Fifth Avenue version now in debate, Louise Searle was Bettina, Lillie West Fiametta, Harry Brown Lorenzo XIV (sic), W. Bishop Pippo, J. E. Conly Frederick, and Ed Chapman Rocco. Two weeks ended the run here, but at the Bijou The Mascot went merrily on.

CATHERINE LEWIS; LAWRENCE BARRETT; ROBSON AND CRANE

Catherine Lewis had only a short period of stellar acclaim; her success in The Royal Middy was followed by greater triumphs as Olivette, and that really was the extent of her glory. But a candle sputters, often, before its light is extinguished, and now, on September 19th, Miss Lewis and the Comley-Barton Opera Company entered the Fifth Avenue Theatre in an English version of Mme. Favart. Other notabilities appeared in the opera, as the cast shows:

Mme. Favart	Catherine Lewis	Pierre	Jennie Boyd
Favart	Frederick Leslie	Nicholas	Alice Cooper
Marquis de Pontsable	John Howson	Sans-Souci	Maud Beaumont
Major Cotignac	William Hamilton	Joli-Coeur	Eme Lascelles
Hector	J. C. Armand	Fracasse	Minnie Le Rue
Biscotin	Richard Golden	Vespre	Lulu Carter
Suzanne	Marie Jansen		

John Howson, Richard Golden and Marie Jansen loom rather high in our theatre annals of the '80s, and Frederick Leslie, a very funny comedian, who here made his début in New York, was later a tower of strength in the musical shows of the Londan Gaiety Theatre. By popular suffrage, he took stellar honours from the famous Nelly Farren, when the London Gaiety Company came to America in 1888. One sees, then, that the cast of Mme. Favart was interesting, if not, from French standards, wholly good. The Herald, for instance, thought Catherine Lewis, as Mme. Favart, unsatisfactory vocally and from the point of view of understanding of the character. Nevertheless, the opera continued (closing, of course, on September 26th) until October 1st.

Lawrence Barrett, sincere and ambitious, if not always magnetic, had now begun to return to New York, with constantly increasing store of novel plays. Unlike Edwin Booth, whose repertoire was becoming more and more crystallised, Barrett, perhaps feeling his limitations as a tragic actor in the great Shakespearian rôles, put on the stage during the next few years several newer poetic and high-intentioned dramas for which the public should have been, and I believe was, profoundly grateful. And he generally brought with him a good company, well trained and directed under his personal supervision. His present engagement, however, was confined almost entirely to "legitimate" plays, and, beginning on October 3rd, he gave a week of Richelieu, on the opening night encountering the rivalry of Booth in the same character at Booth's Theatre. Barrett had the support of Louis James as de Mauprat, Frederick Bock as de Baradas, F. C. Mosley as Louis XIII, Ben G. Rogers (a very fine actor) as Father Joseph, Charles Plunkett as de Beringhen, Otis Skinner as François, Nestor Lennon as Second Secretary, Addie Plunkett as the Page, Marie Wainwright as Julie, and Clara Flagg or Miss Maddern (Herald advertising and review are in conflict here), as Marion de Lorme. How delightful the memories awakened by the names of Louis James, Rogers, Skinner, and even of Nestor Lennon and F. C. Mosley (the last two of promise never quite fulfilled)! Barrett's Richelieu was esteemed by discriminating critics.

For his second and last week, the star gave Hamlet (October 10th and 11th), Yorick's Love (12th, and matinée on the 15th), The Merchant of Venice and David Garrick as a double bill, on the 13th, and Cassius, in Julius Cæsar, with sonorous Louis James as Brutus, Bock as Antony and Kate Meek as Portia, on the 14th and 15th. Barrett will always be cited as the perfect Cassius. He left the Fifth Avenue, now, on October 15th, but he was to return for a most interesting engagement later in the season. Robson and Crane succeeded him, on October 17th, in Joseph Bradford's amusing comedy, Our Bachelors. In this they continued for two weeks, and, on October 31st, revived Twelfth Night, under the valued direction of Charles Webb, one of the famous Webb Brothers, who, as we have seen, had acted The Comedy of Errors in London, in 1863, at the time of the three hundredth anniversary of Shakespeare's birth. One would know what to expect of the Sir Andrew Aguecheek of Robson, with that actor's squeaky voice and his decided mannerisms; likewise what to look for in the Sir Toby of Crane, whose blunt direct manner and hearty personality were capable of few overtones in characterisation. Nevertheless, superficially, the stars

[461]

must have been amusing in this pair of Shakespearian comics. The play had been cut and re-arranged in order to make Sir Andrew and Sir Toby more prominent than they had been, say, when Ellen Tree or Adelaide Neilson played Viola; but the cast seems so uninteresting that one is inclined to think that the less one saw or heard of some of them the better:

Orsino	A. S. Lipman	Sir Andrew Aguecheek	Stuart Robson
Sebastian	Grace Thorne	Sir Toby Belch	W. H. Crane
Fool	John Marble	Viola	Alicia Robson
Antonio	Charles Webb	Olivia	Adele Waters
Curio	F. E. Ambrose	Maria	Lizzie Goode

In spite of Webb's direction, and of elaborate scenery and costumes, one week sufficed for the revival; after all, without a lovely Viola, what is Twelfth Night? On November 7th, Robson and Crane reverted to Sharps and Flats, and closed their engagement on the 12th.

John McCullough; Fanny Davenport

After all, towering figures marked the season we are chronicling; it may be that excess of comic opera everywhere dulled our perception of the occasional fine things in the more serious drama. Lawrence Barrett and Edwin Booth had upheld the standard, in October, and now, on November 14th, John McCullough entered the Fifth Avenue for six weeks of very ambitious productions. He had what Lawrence Barrett lacked — a winning, handsome, magnetic personality, and his magnificent physique and wonderful voice, as has so often been said, allowed him to carry on the Forrest plays and the Forrest tradition. He began, on November 14th, in a typically Forrest character — Virginius, and, I fancy, was the finest Roman, in appearance, of all the great actors who ever attempted the part. One need only look at his photographs as Virginius, to be convinced of this. Like Barrett, he brought with him a good supporting company, including Edmund Collier as Appius, H. C. Barton as Caius Claudius, John A. Lane (a fine classic actor) as Icilius, J. H. Shewell as Numitorius, H. A. Langdon as Dentatus, H. T. Chanfrau as Marcus, Frank Lane as Lucius, Kate Forsyth (a handsome, accomplished actress) as Virginia, Mrs. Augusta Foster as Servia, and Mittens Willett (whose first name I marvel at) as the Slave. This sturdy play held the stage for two weeks, except for the matinées, on the 24th (Thanksgiving) and 26th, when McCullough eased the burden by changing to Ingomar, of course with Miss Forsyth as Parthenia.

For his third week, McCullough varied the bill, from King Lear, on November 28th and 30th, and December 2nd, to Richard III, on November 29th, December 1st and 3rd; Ingomar was again the matinée offering on the 3rd. He was wholly in the Forrest vein, during the week of December 5th–10th, with The Gladiator; and, like Forrest at times, he ill-advisedly essayed Claude Melnotte — this as lighter matinée fare, on the 10th. I cannot imagine Macready or Forrest or Edwin Booth or McCullough in this sentimental rôle. On December 12th, McCullough brought out The Bondman, a new version, by Lewis Wingfield, of Conrad's old play, Jack Cade. This was one result, and not the most fortunate, of McCullough's recent engagement in London. He made a careful production of The Bondman, with this cast:

Jack Cade	John McCullough	Egbert	H. S. Harris
Kenneth	Edmund Collier	Bishop	J. H. Shewell
Earl of Suffolk	Frank Lane	Oswald	Frank Little
Henry de la Poole	John A. Lane	Mildred	Kate Forsyth
Basil Cade	H. A. Langdon	Gwyllin	Mrs. Augusta Foster
Owen	William Bower		

C. H. Kidder, also, appeared as the Captain of the Sussex Rebels, H. T. Chanfrau as the Captain of the Essex Rebels, and George Griffith as an Officer of the King's Guard. The new version of the Cade legend was regarded as far less satisfactory than the old, and, on the 17th, McCullough again enacted the Conrad Jack Cade, for a single performance. For his last week he played Lucius Junius Brutus (December 19th and 20th); Othello (he was, says William Winter, the best Othello of his time) on the 21st; The Gladiator, on the 22nd; Virginius (I always think of McCullough in a Roman toga), for his benefit, on the 23rd; Iago, at the matinée, on the 24th; and Virginius again, as a farewell character, on the evening of that same day. This certainly was one of the most dignified engagements of that season in the New York theatres.

Fanny Davenport, somewhat older than in her youthful heyday of beauty in this very theatre, and perhaps not vastly advanced in art, came to the Fifth Avenue, on December 26th, as a somewhat buxom quite moral and elaborately dressed Camille, supported by May Davenport (her pretty, talented sister), Mrs. Charles Fisher, Mary Shaw, Minnie Monk, George Clarke, Charles Fisher, W. F. Edwards, Harry Hawk and Lewis Baker, a good array for a travelling troupe. This bill lasted till Saturday, December 31st, when Miss Davenport acted Lady Gay Spanker and Nancy Sykes (in the evening of that day and on January 2nd). On January 3rd and 4th, the star reverted to Rosalind, a part she always, apparently, longed to play to the satisfaction of critical taste — an ambition never quite fulfilled. Her support included George Clarke as Orlando, Edmund Tearle (brother of the leading man at Wallack's) as Jaques, Fisher as Adam, Harry Pearson as the Banished Duke, W. J. Hurley as Frederick, Lewis Baker as Le Beau, Harry Hawk as Touchstone, May Davenport as Celia, Mary Shaw (years later famed as Mrs. Alving, in Ghosts) as Audrey, and Mrs. Charles Fisher as Phebe. This reads like a good cast, but the Herald, on the 4th, declares that Clarke was "peculiarly ill suited" to Orlando, and Edmund

[463]

Tearle as Jaques "abominably oratorical." Fisher's Adam, however, was "capital," and May Davenport's Celia "graceful and sympathetic." Fanny Davenport's costumes were "triumphs of the dressmaker's art, and they were not less admired than her acting."

On the 5th, Miss Davenport again essayed Leah, and, on the 6th, for her benefit, she brought out a new play by Dumas — The Princess of Bagdad — which she renamed Lionette, and in which she played the name-part, with George Clarke as Victor de Beriac, Charles Rockwell as Nourvady, Charles Fisher as Godler, Lewis Baker as de Treville, W. F. Edwards as Richard, W. J. Hurley as Commissary of Police, and Little Lydia Corduan as Raoul. The play was not a success, though it was repeated twice on Saturday, January 7th.

CATHERINE LEWIS; LAWRENCE BARRETT; ANNA DICKINSON

The Comley-Barton Opera Company came back, on January 9th, in (ye gods!) Olivette, with Catherine Lewis and John Howson in their accustomed rôles, and with Fred Leslie as the Duc des Ifs, F. H. Frear as Coqueliquot, Armand as Valentine, and the vivacious Marie Jansen as the Countess. Alfred Cellier was director of the music. According to the Herald review, Marie Jansen as the Countess was not so good as she had been in the part of Veloutine; she sang out of tune, still an offensive fault in 1882, whatever it may be fifty years later. Olivette ran for two weeks, giving place, on the 23rd, to Mme. Favart, cast about as in September. This also endured for a fortnight in that season of craving for operetta. I recur to the afternoon of January 13th, when a benefit bill presented the Standard Theatre Company in an act of Patience, and the Park Theatre Company in an act of Mother-in-law. George Edgar gave an act of Othello, supported by Joseph Wheelock as Iago, Maud Harrison as Desdemona and Ada Neilson as Emilia, and Maude Granger offered an act of Camille, with Henry Lee and Charles Rockwell. The Tourists also promised a scene of their farce. W. T. Carleton and Fred Leslie sang songs. All this was at least promised.

A novelty came on February 6th — Manola, from Lecocq's Le Jour et la Nuit; it was "presented on a scale of great magnificence, at an outlay of over $20,000," and with Catherine Lewis as Manola, John Howson as Prince Calabazas, Fred Leslie as Don Brasiero, Marie Jansen as Beatrice, C. J. Campbell as Miguel, F. H. Frear as Pablo, Rose Chappelle as Sanchita, Emma (sic) Lascelles as Tessa and G. Paxton as Christoval. It was produced under the direction of James Barton, and lasted only one week, though, on the 13th, it opened at Haverly's Brooklyn Theatre.

Lawrence Barrett began, on February 13th, a highly important engagement, his opening play being Pendragon, or, the Knights of the Round

Table, fashioned by William Young from the inexhaustible legends of King Arthur and his court:

King Arthur	Lawrence Barrett	Gaheris	F. P. Barton
Sir Launcelot	Louis James	Edyrn	Charles Hawthorne
Sir Modred	Frederick Bock	Sir Agravaine	A. T. Riddle
Sir Pelleas	Otis Skinner	Sir Lionel	L. Brown
Dagonet	B. G. Rogers	Sir Tor	J. Garrison
Sir Lucan	J. W. Thompson	Guinever	Marie Wainwright
Sir Bedevere	F. C. Mosley	Vivien	Kate Meek
Sir Gawain	Charles Rolfe	Cicely	Addie Plunkett
Lamiel	D. Garrison	Abbess	Clara Flagg
Colgrevaunce	G. Davidson		

This ambitious effort remained on the boards for two weeks, or more, without, I fear, greatly enriching any one concerned. The last performance fell on February 28th; Yorick's Love filled four evenings, March 1st–4th, with a matinée on the last-named day. For his last week Barrett went back to the tried and true: Richelieu (March 6th), Julius Cæsar (7th), Harebell, the Man o' Airlie (one of his greatest assumptions, 8th and 9th), The Merchant of Venice and David Garrick (10th), The Marble Heart (matinée, 11th), and Richard III (evening, 11th). Lawrence Barrett was fast becoming a dominating figure on our stage.

The Comley-Barton company filled another week (one sees how popular they were), with Manola (March 13th and 14th), Olivette (15th, 16th, 17th, and both performances on the 18th). Then the determined Anna Dickinson, bent on becoming an actress, began an engagement, on March 20th as Hamlet, with a support of unknown players, including Charles Overton (whom we shall hear of, later) as the Ghost, L. F. Rand as the King, Bennett Matlock as Laertes, Percy Hunting as Horatio, H. N. Wilson as Polonius and First Gravedigger, Lillie Joyce as Ophelia, and Carrie Jamieson as the Queen. I defy the reader to recall, offhand, a less distinguished cast for Hamlet in any reputable theatre. Miss Dickinson still played the hero, says the Herald of the 21st, in purple, "under the idea, evidently, that when he refers to his 'inky' cloak, purple was then, as now, a fashionable article of stationery. . . . She still shows an utter lack of talent for the dramatic stage." A Crown of Thorns, announced for the 27th, was postponed to the 29th. The engagement closed on April 1st, a rather significant date, if one cared to make jokes at Anna Dickinson's expense.

On Monday, April 3rd, James O'Neill, so frequently in those years a stopgap of a week's duration, began a fortnight's stay as Jean Renaud, in A Celebrated Case, with Maude Granger as Valentine, Carrie Turner (soon to be a recognised leading lady) as Adrienne, William Scallan as O'Rourke, Lewis Morrison as the villainous Lazare, J. H. Fitzpatrick and Florence Robinson as Count d'Aubeterre and the Countess, Mrs. Farren as the Chanoinesse, and Forrest Robinson as Raoul — seemingly a very good cast.

[465]

This attraction gave way, on April 17th, to Hazel Kirke, its fifteen-hundredth performance, with Effie Ellsler, Sydney Cowell (how long these two had played Hazel and Dolly), Mrs. Sol Smith, Kate Denin Wilson, Perle Dudley, C. W. Couldock, Henry Lee, Frank Weston, Charles Bowser, W. B. Cahill, Edward Milliken and Frank Colfax.

Maurice Grau's ever-recurring French Opera Company returned on April 24th, in the inescapable La Mascotte; the cast included Paola Marié, Mlle. Grégoire, Nigri (Pippo), Mezières (Laurent XVII), Tauffenberger (Fritellini), and Duplan (Rocco). Les Mousquetaires au Couvent entered on the 25th; on the 26th, Mignon enlisted Paola Marié in the title-rôle, Mlle. Dalmont (new) as Philine, Mlle. Vallot as Frédéric, Mauras as Wilhelm Meister, Mauge as Lothario, Poyard as Laerte, Mussy as Jarno, and Millet as Aloyisius. On the 27th, Les Dragons de Villars gave us Mme. Privat as Rose Friquet, Mlle. C. Grégoire as Georgette, Mauras as Sylvain, Mauge as Bellamy, and Duplan as Thibaut. The rest of the week was devoted to La Fille du Tambour Major (28th), La Mascotte (matinée, 29th), and Si j'étais Roi (evening of the 29th) — the last-named with Mmes. Privat and Grégoire, and MM. Mauras, Mauge, Dangon, Tauffenberger and Poyard.

Lecocq's Le Jour et la Nuit, on May 1st, 3rd and 6th (matinée), had a cast including Paola Marié as Manola, Mlle. Grégoire as Beatrix, Mezières as the Prince, Duplan as Don Brasiero, and Nigri as Miguel. On May 2nd, Carmen ("in its original form") presented Paola Marié (sister of Galli-Marié, who created the rôle in Paris) as the gypsy, Mme. Dalmont as Micaela, Mlle. Grégoire as Frasquita, Mlle. Vallot as Mercedes, Mauras Don Jose, Mauge as Escamillo, Nigri as Zuniga, and Poyard as El Dancairo — a very different thing, I fancy, from the Carmen seen at the Academy of Music, with Minnie Hauk, Campanini and Del Puente, but a vivaciously French Carmen withal. On May 4th and 6th, Mauras and Mme. Dalmont sang Paul et Virginie; Les Noces d'Olivette, on the 5th, enlisted Paola Marié, Mlle. Grégoire, Tauffenberger (Valentin), Mezières (Duc d'Ifs), Nigri (Merrimac) and Poyard (Marvejol). It is interesting to find these actors dropping (on May 8th) the music of their accustomed choice, and playing straight comedy in Sardou's delightful Divorçons, in which Alice Dunning Lingard had been scoring at the Park Theatre. At the Fifth Avenue, Paola Marié was the flighty Cyprienne, Mezières the wise des Prunelles, Nigri Clavignac, Tauffenberger Adhemar, and Poyard Joseph. "By request," Carmen again lured, on the 9th; La Périchole came on the 10th, and actually, on the 11th, La Favorite, the last-named employing (not very successfully) Mmes. Privat and Grégoire, and MM. Mauras, Mauge, Dangon and Poyard. Just such variety of comedy, operetta and "grand" opera the famous New Orleans artists used to provide, in the long ago, during their summer visits to the old Park Theatre. La Fille de Mme. Angot, on the 12th, brought Grau's singers back to their normal field.

Carmen and Divorçons were the afternoon and evening bill, respectively, on May 13th.   This closed the French season, except for a concert on Sunday, the 14th. After much anxious cogitation, I have restored to Mlle. Grégoire the accent on the first vowel of her name — an accent of which playbills and newsprints of the time deprived her.

The season of the Fifth Avenue was waning.   A Checkered Life, by A. Z. Chipman, met failure, on May 15th:

Ernest Lenwood	A. Z. Chipman	Puffie	S. P. Norman
David Lenwood	W. J. LeMoyne	Harold	W. R. Falls
Thomas Warrington	Frank Roberts	Dora Lenwood	Kate Mayhew
Switzilbocher	Frank M. Wills	Kittie Lee	Lisetta Ellani
Henry Fenton	S. P. Norman	Emily Lenwood	Lizzie Anderson
Tommy Gray	John E. Nash	Florence	Julia Stewart
Leonard Dawson	C. A. McManus	Angie Dawson	Etelka Wardell
Samuel Skidder	Arthur Moulton		

The Herald of May 16th complains that the play "gave no sign of knowledge by its author of the primary rules of dramatic art. . . . It was clumsy, tiresome and windy."   One week ended the run.   On June 10th, Ada Gray began, in a new version of East Lynne (her great specialty), her associates including Mrs. S. A. Baker, Carrie Vinton, Mrs. S. B. Duffield, Fannie McNeil, Lindsay Harris, W. F. Edwards, S. C. Dubois, Little Tommy Russell (young brother of Annie Russell, the winning Esmeralda), and others even less known.   And, if the reader can believe it, she kept the thing going until July 1st!   I don't see how it was done.

On June 29th, came a benefit to Gerald Eyre, who was leaving Wallack's. Herrmann was advertised to appear, as were Osmond Tearle and Rose Coghlan (in A Happy Pair).   Gerald Eyre played as Grosvenor, in the second act of Patience, with Lillian Russell, Augusta Roche and Ed Temple; and Selina Dolaro, Harry St. Maur and others gave The First Night.   The season at the Fifth Avenue, except for the engagements of John McCullough and Lawrence Barrett, was not very interesting or important; too much comic opera of a monotonous sameness sagged it down.

Haverly's Fourteenth Street Theatre, 1881–1882

The former Lyceum Theatre in Fourteenth Street began its new season on August 15, 1881, with Sayre's play of The Strategists, "in four acts and a thousand laughs," the company, under management of Haverly, carrying the piece to success:

Jack Ruttledge	J. B. Polk	Terence O'Flam	Sam E. Ryan
Arthur Ruttledge	F. E. Aiken	Sergeant Gumbleton	L. F. Howard
Major Abijah Howard	Harry Linden	Nellie Howard	Katie Gilbert
Rev. John Mildman	A. H. Canby	Mrs. Major Howard	Marie Bates
Capsicano Peppers	Harry Bell	Araminta	Lizzie Hight

[467]

The Strategists was another of those nondescript things put together merely for entertainment — of close kinship to Dreams, Fun on the Bristol, etc., though more solid in plot, more like a play. It succeeded in its purpose; though it remained now but two weeks at the Fourteenth Street Theatre, it returned there for a fortnight in October, and exhibited elsewhere in our neighbourhood in months to come.

On August 29th, Jennie Lee, once popular here in burlesque, made her *rentrée* in J. P. Burnett's adaptation from Bleak House, entitled Jo. In the character of the persecuted boy, Miss Lee had made a great success in England, and indeed had played it previously in New York. Her present cast was as follows:

Jo	Jennie Lee	Mr. Bucket	J. P. Burnett
Sir Leicester Dedlock	J. L. Carhart	Lady Dedlock	Constance Murielle
Tulkinghorn	J. A. Howell	Esther	Ethel Grey
Snagsby	E. L. Walton	Mrs. Rouncewell	Ada Wright
Chadband	Thomas E. Jackson	Jenny	Edna Vernon
Guppy	F. M. Kendrick	Rosa	Josie Langley
Coroner	J. E. Dodson	Guster	Miss C. Lewis
Beadle	Thomas F. McCabe	Mrs. Snagsby	Mrs. E. M. Post
Mercury	J. Edwards	Hortense	Isabel Morris

We note the name of J. E. Dodson, later a most successful comedian here in the company of Mr. and Mrs. Kendal and of the Empire Theatre. The reader remembers that, shortly after this production of Jo, Mme. Janauschek played Lady Dedlock and Hortense, at the Union Square Theatre. Miss Lee remained at the Fourteenth Street house only two weeks, and yielded its stage, on September 12th, to Oliver Doud Byron in his everlasting Across the Continent, assisted by J. P. Johnson as the merchant price, Harry Hudson as the villainous Adderly, and Kate Byron as the broken-hearted wife of the drama.

On September 19th, Mr. and Mrs. McKee Rankin, making a brave effort to escape from the shackles of The Danites, brought out, "for the first time in America," W. G. Wills's new version of Black-Eyed Susan, under the title of William and Susan, in which Mr. and Mrs. Kendal had recently had success in London. The New York cast:

William Bowling	McKee Rankin	Robert	Luke Martin
Captain Crosstree	J. H. Barnes	Master at Arms	W. B. Murray
The Admiral	J. J. Holland	Old Man	Tom Leigh
Lieutenant Pierce	William Lee	Susan	Mrs. McKee Rankin
Slater	Archie Boyd	Polly	Lizzie May Ulmer
White	George Ulmer	Dame Green	Mrs. F. A. Tannehill
Truck	Cyril Searle	Little Bill	Lulu Teson

It is interesting to find here the name of J. H. Barnes, handsome Romeo, in 1874, to Adelaide Neilson's Juliet (in this very same theatre, by the way); and in the Rankin company also Joseph J. Holland, youngest son of the late George Holland, so long of Wallack's, is beginning to attract our attention.

[468]

William and Susan carried on for nearly two weeks, except on the evenings of September 20th and 26th, when the theatre closed out of respect to the memory of President Garfield.

On Saturday evening, October 1st, the Rankins produced '49, a play the authorship of which was made more or less of a mystery, speculation ascribing it all the way from Rankin himself to Joaquin Miller. It was another Western piece, and in it Rankin appeared as "'49," a relic of bygone days, wrecked by the villainous taking off of his wife and child, back in 1857; now, in the play, in the year 1871, he is a pitiful, broken creature. Mrs. Rankin was "Carrots," a "red-haired waif but a true woman," bless her, and, of course, the lost child of the preliminary tableau. Well, supporting the stars were J. H. Barnes as Arthur Dennison ("of St. Louis"), J. J. Sullivan as Tom Bradshaw, Ed Lamb as Solomon Kane ("a General by courtesy, but dry as a powder horn, and a total wreck"), George Ulmer as Colonel James ("a lawyer who never makes a mistake"), Luke Martin as Anthony Cousins (his clerk), Archibald Boyd, as the old negro, Ned, W. Lee as Bedrock, J. J. Holland as Colonel Broadstreet, of the Vigilantes, Lizzie May Ulmer as Belle ("a lady she is"), Miss Wallace Brittain as Mississippi, and Emma Marble (daughter of Dan Marble) as Mrs. Dennison (Arthur's mother). Though '49 had never the great success of The Danites, it nevertheless served the Rankins for a few years. It remained now at the Fourteenth Street Theatre until it was superseded, on October 17th, by a second visit for two weeks of The Strategists. This trifle gave way, on October 31st, to Haverly's Mastodon Minstrels, they, in turn, yielding the stage, on November 7th, to Deacon Crankett, with Benjamin Maginley still in the title-rôle, James O'Neill as Joe Thatcher, E. J. Buckley as Egbert Grey, Harry Eytinge as Heatherton, T. F. Brennan as Werzel, Miss M. Loduski Young as Elinor Heatherton, Annie Ware as Mrs. Crankett, and Blanche Vaughan as Polly Peekin. I am rather surprised to find this revival persisting for three weeks.

A week (November 28th–December 3rd) of John F. Sheridan as the Widow O'Brien in Fun on the Bristol, led to a three-weeks engagement, beginning on December 5th, of J. K. Emmet ("the world's favorite"), in Fritz in Ireland, that source of abiding joy to countless thousands here and throughout the country. The piece was advertised as "entirely rewritten by W. Carleton, Esq.," and its cast included Emmet as Fritz Shultz, De Los King as Lawyer Priggins, W. Standish as Baron Hertford, H. C. Albaugh as Hercules O'Dowd, W. Christie Miller as Lord Seaton, W. J. Donnelly as Charles Seaton, J. H. Ryan as Thomas Goldfinger, W. J. Donnelly as Patrick Blackeye, an Irish negro, Little Annie Smith as Master Herbert and Lena Shultz, Miss Vandenhoff as Lady Amelia, Kate Blancke as Louise Hertford, Jennie Harold as Mme. Shultz and Pollie Poland as Judy Callahan. During the play Emmet introduced songs written by himself — The Bells are

[469]

Ringing, The Swell, The Cuckoo Song, The Shamrock, Wilheidrick Strauss, The Brother's Lullaby, and I Know What Love Is. Of course Emmet's songs swept the country to the heart of its remotest farms. He was a great personality. Allston Brown states that these three weeks at the Fourteenth Street Theatre brought to the box-office "a trifle over $30,000 . . . undoubtedly . . . the largest amount of money ever played to by any dramatic star in the same length of time at the prices prevailing."

F. S. Chanfrau began on Monday, December 26th, with a Christmas matinée, and continued for two weeks, his vehicle being the undying Kit. How the actors of that time could continue, year after year, in the same play, is one of the mysteries; even we, who lived through the period, cannot account for the annual visits for so many seasons, of Rip Van Winkle, Fanchon, The Two Orphans, The Danites, The Mighty Dollar, Colonel Sellers, Fritz, and Kit, with many more. Of course, playgoers became attached to these offerings and attended repeatedly, as one does today with favourite operas. In Chanfrau's company were O. H. Barr as Manuel Bond, S. H. Verney as Wash Stubbs, Harry Barfoot as Major Squiggs, F. M. Wills as Judge Suggs, Regina Dace as Alice, Ernestine Floyd as Mrs. Stubbs, Victoria Cameron as Mrs. Temple, &c. At the matinées, December 28th and 31st, and January 4th and 7th, Mrs. Henrietta Chanfrau, the great favourite of the '60's, appeared in a new East Lynne by Clifton W. Tayleure. On January 9th, The Tourists in a Pullman Palace Car began a fortnight's stay, introducing into the show music from Olivette, Patience, Billee Taylor and The Musketeers. The next fortnight (January 23rd–February 4th) brought once more into view All the Rage, Frank Hardenberg, William Davidge and Meta Bartlett retaining their former rôles, along with J. C. Padgett, George N. Dalton, A. Z. Chipman, S. P. Norman, Lisetta Ellani, Blanche Moulton, Annie Douglas and Helena Coe. This comedy lasted surprisingly.

It would be a starved theatre that could not, in that season, provide Patience. Haverly's Opera Company gave the all-pervasive satire on February 6th, with Emma Howson, again brought forward from the '70s, as Patience, Gertrude Orme as Lady Jane, Louise Manfred as Lady Angela, Pauline Hall as a statuesque Lady Saphir, W. H. Seymour as Bunthorne, C. M. Pike as Grosvenor, Lithgow James as Colonel Calverly, Alonzo Hatch as the Duke of Dunstable, Richard Golden as Murgatroyd, &c. I know the reader cherishes these many casts of Patience. The Gilbert and Sullivan delight ran through February 15th; on the 16th, 17th and 18th, The Mascot, of which my reader may be weary, employed Emma Howson as Bettina, Alonzo Hatch as Frederic, J. W. Norcross, Jr. as Lorenzo, Richard Golden as Rocco, and Pauline Hall (at last advancing) as Fiametta. On February 20th, M. B. Curtis began a four-weeks engagement in his last-season great success, Sam'l of Posen. On March 13th, he gave a matinée for the Actors'

Fund. I next chronicle a fortnight of Haverly's Mastodon Minstrels, beginning on March 20th; negro minstrelsy increased greatly in size as it decreased in public demand for its dying formula. In Haverly's huge company were Lew Dockstader, E. N. Hall (banjo), Leon (imitation of operatic artists), Harry Robinson (burlesque trapeze acts), Billy Rice, &c. Among the sketches were Thompson Street Æsthetes, and Patience Wilde; in the latter Leon was Miss P. Wilde, "who takes the sunflower," and Billy Rice was Milady Jane. I dare say this was funny, in its dusky way, in that year of Patience and Oscar Wilde.

THE WHITE SLAVE; OLD SHIPMATES; ONE OF THE FINEST

The house now escaped from the very usual into a period of novelty. Bartley Campbell presented, on April 3rd, a stirring melodrama, very reminiscent of Boucicault's The Octoroon; he called it The White Slave, and, really, the poor persecuted girl proved to be white; but before that welcome *éclaircissement* she had gone through dreadful tortures, including the perils of an exploding river steamer (a great stage trick). The cast was good:

Lisa	Georgia Cayvan	P. H. Stieb	M. C. Daly
Daphne	Emmie Wilmot	Clem	Charles Webster
Nance	Etelka Wardell	Jack Hazelton	F. De Vernon
Mrs. Lee	Mrs. G. C. Germon	Bancroft	D. E. Ralton
Letty Lee	Frances Kemble	Captain Stryker	T. E. Bowen
Martha	Marie Bates	Natchez Jim	Scott Davis
Clay Britton	Gustavus Levick	Jamison	W. H. Smith
William Lacy	Frank Roberts	Count Strain	Jay Hunt
Judge Hardin	Welsh Edwards	Little Jim	Master La Forrest
Job	W. J. Scanlan		

The play had vital interest despite its antiquated theme, and lasted during this, its first New York engagement, for five weeks. One sees that Georgia Cayvan, since leaving the Madison Square casts, had reaped a reward in many parts, none, I fear, of lasting value. The next offering at the Fourteenth Street Theatre was (May 8th), the Madison Square specialty, The Professor, with William Gillette, Nellie Taylor (as Mrs. Elliot), Belle Jackson (as Daisy), Nellie Morant (as Estelle), Blanche Weaver (as Minnie), Helen Ottolengui (as Molly), Harry Allen, Charles W. Butler, C. W. Stokes, Ramsay Morris, &c. This attraction had the almost customary two weeks.

The next novelty came on May 22nd, Robert Griffin Morris's comedy drama, Old Shipmates. In this Frank Mordaunt was Captain Marline Weathergage, "of the whaling Ship, Aurora Borealis, loving, generous, a man afloat, but an infant ashore," and Georgia Cayvan, printed on the bill in the large type that marks a star, was Harriet Lane, "Captain Ned's niece and ward, gentle, self-denying, passionately fond of sailors because her father had been one of them." Miss Cayvan, a rapidly rising actress, appeared "by permission of the Madison Square Theatre." Others in the new play were J. F. Hagan as Captain Ned Witham, an old shipmate of Captain Lane, and "a daring, unscrupulous old rascal"; Charles B. Waite as Dan Denny, Weathergage's staunch friend; G. J. Henderson as Counsellor Witham; E. C. Coyle as One-Armed Johnny; Addie Eaton as Mrs. Cherry Jones; Mrs. J. H. Rowe as Abigail Coffin, "the Commodore"; and Louise Dillon as the pert housemaid, Jenny Hunter. Joseph M. Buell, Tom Atkinson and Frank Gilsey filled minor rôles. Old Shipmates lasted up to and including June 17th.

On June 19th, Gus Williams, a graduate from vaudeville, opened for a long run in a new comedy, One of the Finest:

John Mishler	Gus Williams	Superintendent	Harry Linden
Hugh Hickman	J. N. Gotthold	Quincy Veal	Louis Howard
James Eastman	Nelson Decker	Dick	Master Renner
Officer Burns	Albert Hall	Officer Elterich	L. O. Rand
Ruth Hickman	Isabel Waldron	Officer Muldoon	T. H. Smythe
Mrs. Mishler	Dora Stuart	Katie Mishler	Rachel Booth
Edgar Weeks	E. S. Tarr	Jennie Eastman	May Bardell
Mart Devine	William Gilbert	Miss Livingston	Jennie Harold
Robert Weeks	Frank Rose	Miss Van Buren	Kate Durand
Fred Eastman	Sidney Drew		

Gus Williams made a hit as Mishler, the policeman, "one of the finest"; and his company included interesting personalities in Newton Gotthold, Nelson Decker, William Gilbert, Sidney Drew and Rachel Booth (the present Mrs. James T. Powers). One of the Finest ran until August 5th, when the curtain rang down for 1881–82, a season not rich, at this house, in striking plays or players.

ABBEY'S PARK THEATRE, 1881–1882

The Park Theatre, like Booth's, was very near the end of its life; after the present season (1881–82) and a few weeks in the autumn of 1882, it ceased to be. But no one could have foreseen this when, on September 12, 1881, it re-opened with a really novel show, the Hanlons (or the Hanlon-Lees, as they were announced) in a Parisian "absurdity," entitled Le Voyage en Suisse, adapted for our market by Henry Pettitt, the English playwright.

The six Hanlon Brothers were here, at Niblo's Garden, in 1860, with Cook's Circus, and made a great sensation with their daring acrobatic feats. A good account of the exploits of the family will be found in Allston Brown's History of the New York Stage (Volume III, pages 204 ff). The show, Le Voyage en Suisse, was, of course, spectacular, and employed astounding athletic feats by the Hanlons (only five were now here); altogether it suggested the Ravel pantomimes of years gone by. Rough and tumble skirmishes, exploding engines and wrecked hotel furnished the brothers with

[472]

opportunities for falls, tumbling, somersaults, leaps, etc. The cast printed on the playbill for the 12th (it is on my desk as I write) was as follows:

Captain Maguire	T. H. Glenney	Peter Porter	J. Berri
Frank Maguire	Nelson Decker	Tipp	R. Jones
Dwindledown	W. S. Penley	Juliette	Miss A. Randolph
John	William Hanlon-Lees	Marie	Daisy England
Bob	Frederick Hanlon-Lees	Euphrasia	Miss E. Kean
Ned	Edward Hanlon-Lees	Anastasia	Miss Gonzales
Harry	George Hanlon-Lees	Ambrosina	Lillian Taylor
Jack	Alfred Hanlon-Lees	Alice	Miss Merritt
D'Escargot	Francis G. Wyatt	Adelaide	Miss Barton
Crevasse	Percy Meynall		

In Act II, on the sleeping car, the Hanlon-Lees appeared, in addition to characters in the programme, as Car Attendants and Custom House Inspectors; in Act III, "At the Rigi-Kulm Hotel," George, Edward and Alfred Hanlon assumed various disguises, and Wyatt that of a Gendarme. According to Allston Brown, H. Reeves Smith (in later years one of our best actors) came here to play the part of Frank Maguire, but "at rehearsals he was found to be incompetent, and his return to his native land quickly followed. Nelson Decker was engaged" and was the only American in the company, except the ballet. This is interesting, but the name of H. Reeves Smith is opposite the part of Frank, on October 1st. One is tremendously impressed by finding in the bill the name of T. H. Glenney, the original Shaun the Post, here, in Arrah-na-Pogue; and lo! to our great surprise, here also is the name of W. S. Penley, the original of Charley's Aunt in England, a part that he played for many years. Until I saw the cast of Le Voyage en Suisse, I did not know that he had ever graced our stage. After a few weeks, Emily Kean replaced Miss Randolph as Juliette, and Daisy England took up the rôle of Euphrasia.

Abbey now had on his hands a success of magnitude, which carried through smoothly till November 26th, and then transferred to two other houses in succession. It was succeeded on November 28th by Maurice Grau's French Opera Company, which began in Mme. Favart, with Paola Marié in the title-rôle, with Nigri as Favart, Mezières (the ever-dependable) as Pontsable, Tauffenberger as Hector, Poyard as Cotignac, Mussy as Biscotin, Mlle. Grégoire as Suzanne, Mlle. Vallot as Jolicœur, Malvina as Sans Quartier, &c. On the 29th and December 3rd, Si j'étais Roi enlisted Mlle. Leroux, and Mauras, with the début of MM. Mauge and Dangon and Mlle. Lentz. The inescapable La Mascotte, on the 30th, and at the matinée on the 3rd, presented the vivacious Bettina of Paola Marié, that same attractive singer on December 2nd essaying Simone in Les Mousquetaires au Couvent, with Mlle. Lentz as Marie, Mlle. Delorme as the Mother Superior, Nigri as Brissac, Tauffenberger as Gontran, Duplan as Bridaine, &c. La Fille de Mme. Angot, on the 1st, was matter more familiar, and gave us Paola Marié

[473]

as Clairette, Mlle. Leroux as Mlle. Lange, Mlle. Delorme as Amaranthe, Mezières as Larivandière, Mauras as Ange Pitou, Poyard as Pomponnet, and Duplan as Louchard.

Three nights more ended the visit of these French artists; was New York tiring of opéra-bouffe, in the light of Gilbert and Sullivan and Audran in English? On December 5th, Les Cloches de Corneville rang merrily with Paola Marié as Serpolette, Mlle. Lentz as Germaine, Mezières as Gaspard, Nigri as Grenicheux, Dangon as the Marquis, and Duplan as the Bailiff. Les Noces d'Olivette (with Paola Marié) on the 6th, and La Fille du Tambour-Major, on the 7th, carried the French contingent to other stages. We remember they came back later in the season to the Fifth Avenue. I end the paragraph with a charity matinée (December 8th), with acts of Patience, by the Standard Theatre Company, and of The Snake Charmer, by the Bijou company; Anna T. Berger, Fanny Addison, W. T. Carleton, Jacques Kruger, Pastor's company, and the San Francisco Minstrels also were promised. And Bessie Byrne was to render Leah's curse.

On December 8th (evening) came a farce, Mother-in-Law, by George R. Sims, "of England," which had a respectable run:

Talfourd Twigg	W. J. Ferguson	Mrs. McTurtle	Nellie Mortimer
John Pownceby	John Dillon	Topsy Grey	Laura Don
Major McTurtle	E. M. Holland	Rosa Matilda	Marie Chester
Percy D'Almaine	Henry Lee	Mrs. Pownceby	Mrs. G. C. Germon
J. Jarraway	Felix Morris	Susan	Jean Delmar
Jorrocks	J. T. Burke		

This strikes me as an admirable, compact cast. The bill for December 31st puts down E. A. Locke ("Yankee" Locke) as Dr. Jarraway. A good deal of forcing and funny advertising carried Mother-in-Law to and through January 14th. Oddly enough, Lester Wallack, whose own new theatre had just opened on the 4th, and who might have been expected to appear about this time on its stage, came out instead on January 16th, at the Park, in a new play by F. C. Burnand, editor of Punch, a play satirising the current "æsthetic" craze with a fair degree of success. This piece, The Colonel, presented Wallack as Colonel Woothweel W. Woodd, U. S. Cavalry, Eric Bayley as Richard Forrester, C. P. Flockton (an excellent new character actor, prominent thereafter) as Lambert Streyke, E. T. Webber as Basil Georgion, Lilford Arthur as Edward Langton, Ian Robertson (brother of Forbes Robertson) as Mullins, William Royston as Parkes, Leslie Edmonds as Romelli, Maria Davis as Lady Tompkins, Mindha Bayley as Olive, Theresa Waldron as Nellie, Rachel Sanger as Mrs. Blythe, and Helen Hewitt as Goodall. One thinks regretfully of the finer cast this play could have had at his own theatre, if Wallack had carried out an earlier intention (as I read in the Herald) of producing it there. Nevertheless, The Colonel ran until February 25th, and injected into current speech the catch expression, "Why cert'nly."

[474]

NAT C. GOODWIN; ALICE DUNNING LINGARD; MINNIE MADDERN

On February 27th, Mr. and Mrs. Nat C. Goodwin (Eliza Weathersby) appeared in another play by George R. Sims, entitled The Member for Slocum, in which Goodwin played Onesimus Epps, "the young and dashing member for Slocum," and Eliza Weathersby was Arathusa Smith, with J. G. Saville (a very good actor, at least in later years) as Bill Smith, a friend of Epps, and separated from Arathusa. Others were W. H. Herbert as Gunning, Emie Weathersby as Madelin, wife of Mr. Epps, Jennie Reiffarth as Mrs. Jeffs, Madelin's mother, Anna Brevoor as Fanny and Lillian De Garmo as Betsy — both maids in waiting. This had been seen previously in Brooklyn, and endured for two weeks at the Park, without, I honestly believe, hastening the vernal showers and flowers near Madison Square.

The beautiful Alice Dunning Lingard attempted, on Tuesday, March 14th, the character of the charming, light-headed Cyprienne, in Sardou's latest comedy success, Divorçons — a piece something like Dance's once very popular Dangerous Ground, with a wise, patient husband curing his wife's infatuation for a silly lover, by proposing divorce and arousing her jealousy by apparent preference for another woman. Many actresses were to play Cyprienne, before Divorçons left the stage. The cast at the Park included, besides Mrs. Lingard (who had tried Cyprienne in California), Nellie Mortimer as Mme. de Brionne, Clara Cole as Mme. de Valfontaine, Elizabeth Andrews as Mlle. de Lusignan, Eliza Long as Josephine, Frederic Robinson as M. des Prunelles, Charles B. Welles as Adhémar, W. T. Harris as Clavignac, Herbert Ayling as Bafourdin, Louis Barret as Commissioner of Police, Max Freeman (later noted in comic opera) as Joseph, and G. Montserrat as Bastien. Of course a benefit for the Actors' Fund occurred on the afternoon of April 3rd. On the evening of Saturday, April 22nd, Mrs. Lingard appeared in a play by A. C. Gunter, author of Two Nights in Rome; this piece, entitled After the Opera, was put down as a "midnight comedy," and enlisted Mrs. Lingard as Mrs. Alice Montague Marvin, "the most bashful widow in New York"; Louise Dillon as Maria Pierson, "the Connecticut floweret"; Elizabeth Andrews as Lavinia Backsetter, "devoted to religion and the keyhole"; Charles Walcot as Harvey Kelsey, director of the Consolidated Bank; Charles B. Welles as "Chawles" Livingston, an anglomaniac; E. M. Holland as Probity Pierson, professor of theology; J. O. Barrows as Jobson Johnson; J. G. Saville as Jack De Lacy, clerk in the Consolidated; H. Williams as Policeman 44, and George Castle as Hackman 95. The run ended on May 13th.

And here, on May 15th, is Minnie Maddern, a very young girl, whom we have not met since she was a small child, in the early '70s. She came out now as Chip, in a piece by Charles E. Callahan called Fogg's Ferry, which she carried on for two weeks, with Atkins Lawrence as Gerald White, C.

Russell Blake as Bruce Rawdon, William Cullington as William Still, William Herbert as Zebulon Fogg, R. C. Wilson as Judge Norwood, A. H. Hastings as Jim Bolter, Miss M. Loduski Young as Blanche Norwood, Mme. Ivan C. Michels (*sic*) as Samantha Fogg, and Alice Brooks as Martha Blodgett. The reader will be interested to know that Miss Maddern (the since famous Mrs. Fiske) pleased the critic of the Herald, who, on May 16th, declared she "made a decidedly pleasant impression . . . but the play was anything but a success. Miss Maddern is . . . apparently about twenty years of age. She is petite . . . has a bright and interesting face, decided dramatic talents and an abundance of animal spirits, which altogether make her an exceedingly vivacious little actress who cannot help being popular. All that she has to do is done with a merriment that is charming."

It is good to find Minnie Maddern thus early in her career starting on the road to success. She was followed at the Park Theatre, on May 29th, by another débutante, Julia A. Hunt, who failed, in a piece by Sydney Rosenfeld, entitled Florinel:

Florinel	Julia A. Hunt	Marquis de Runières	W. J. Hurley
Countess	Constance Hamblin	René	C. B. Welles
Duchess d'Arolles	Alice Grey	Jules Clarence	Edwin Hammond
Marcelle	Georgine Flagg	Abbé St. Maur	B. W. Turner
Normand	Adelaide Thornton	Bertrand	C. W. Butler
Madelaine	Mme. Ivan C. Michels	Doctor	Edward Powell
Claudine	Jennie Kennark	Servant	Charles Poore

A very few performances sufficed for a sated public and for the discouragement of Miss Hunt. The Park Theatre closed for the season, beginning again on September 2nd for the few weeks prior to its destruction by fire, on October 30th. I cannot say that the season just recorded strikes me as a gain for art.

STANDARD THEATRE, 1881–1882

The Standard Theatre during the season under review was, possibly, the most successful in the city; its history needs fewer words than that of any other except the new Theatre Comique. It re-opened on Saturday, August 20th, with Barney McAuley in his popular rural drama, A Messenger from Jarvis Section, in which his associates were Charles Mason, J. H. Stuart, Alexander Fisher, Sedley Brown, William Morris, Lizzie Evans, Mrs. Charles Peters, and Jessie Randolph — certainly an undistinguished group. McAulay's genuine performance of Uncle Dan'l kept the play at the Standard until September 17th.

On Thursday, September 22nd, the theatre entered on one of the great successes of its career. R. D'Oyly Carte's Company produced the latest Gilbert and Sullivan operetta, Patience, that undying satire on the æsthetic craze of its time, and still (1939) regarded as a perfect satire on affectation

THE HANLONS
(VOYAGE EN SUISSE)

CARRIE BURTON

MINNIE MADDERN
(FOGG'S FERRY)

DIGBY BELL
AS GROSVENOR

ADELAIDE RANDALL

J. H. RYLEY AS
BUNTHORNE

W. T. CARLETON
AS BUNTHORNE

HARRY HAWK

JAMES G. PEAKES
AS CAPTAIN CORCORAN

in general.   Patience was, is, and probably ever will be, a joy, musically, and in its witty dialogue and lyrics.   The first cast here of the exquisite delight does not especially impress one:

Colonel Calverly	W. T. Carleton	Lady Angela	Alice Burville
Major Murgatroyd	A. Wilkinson	Lady Saphir	Rose Chappelle
Duke of Dunstable	L. Cadwallader	Lady Ella	Jenny Stone
Solicitor	William White	Lady Jane	Augusta Roche
Bunthorne	J. H. Ryley	Patience	Carrie Burton
Grosvenor	James Barton		

Arthur Wilkinson, Cadwallader and the sonorous Augusta Roche were specially imported from the London Opera Comique.   The opera was produced under the direction of Charles Harris, and conducted by W. P. Halton and Ernest Neyer.   It had, according to Allston Brown, the greatest financial success the house ever knew, making about $100,000, as opposed to the $60,000 during the first run of Pinafore.

Patience ran uninterruptedly (except for the sad night of September 26th) until March 4th, and even after that, it was sung for three nights weekly until March 25th.   The Standard Patience was, despite efforts elsewhere with the opera, the oustanding performance of the classic for that season; but Lillian Russell later, especially at the Bijou, won great acclaim as the artless milkmaid.   The Herald, on November 14th, advertised a changed cast; Carleton was then down for Grosvenor and William Hamilton for the Colonel (Carleton's former rôle); Jeannette (?) Edmondson was Lady Angela, and Miss Stanley Lady Ella.   The hundredth performance of the all-conquering Patience occurred on December 29th; shortly after, the San Francisco Minstrels and Tony Pastor were very successfully burlesquing the opera.

All good things reach an end.   The Standard was under contract to produce Edward Solomon's opera, Claude Duval, and, after repeated delays, caused by the success of Patience, it staged the new work, on March 6th:

Claude Duval	W. T. Carleton	Blood Red Bill	J. H. Ryley
Charles Lorrimore	L. Cadwallader	Constance	Carrie Burton
Sir Whiffle Whaffle	A. Wilkinson	Rose	Marie Hunter
Martin McGruder	W. Hamilton	Betty	Jennie Hughes
Captain Harleigh	J. A. Furey	Dolly	Victoria Reynolds
Boscatt	F. Dixon		

Even so, as I have said, the new piece was sung only on Mondays, Tuesdays, and Wednesdays, with Wednesday matinée; for the remaining evenings of the week and Saturday afternoon, Patience blithely survived.   The last of Patience occurred on March 25th, Claude Duval thereafter forming the staple of entertainment for the entire week, and closing on April 29th.   A special Duval matinée fell on April 3rd, for the Actors' Fund.

And then what?   What, indeed, but the inescapable La Mascotte, presented on May 1st, by the C. D. Hess Acme Opera Company, with the mellow-voiced Adelaide Randall as Bettina, Henry Peakes as Lorenzo, Mark Smith (son of the popular Mark Smith of the '60s and early '70s) as Pippo, Alfred Wilkie as Frederic of Pisa, James Peakes as Rocco, Josie Renner as Francisca, Blanche Adorni as Paola, Kate Griffiths as Planquette, Kate Bauer as Audran, and Emma Elsner as Fiametta. On the 8th came a new work, The Widow, by Frank Nelson, with music by Calixa Levellée, the cast including Zelda Seguin Wallace, Adelaide Randall, Emma Elsner, Emma Pressey, Louise Searle, Alfred Wilkie, Mark Smith, James Peakes, H. F. Fairweather, Herbert Jones and William Castle, a fine aggregation. But the opera did not succeed, and, on the 12th, with a matinée on the 13th, we had again La Mascotte, with The Chimes of Normandy on the evening of the 13th, and for the week following. On May 22nd, Emma Elsner sang Olivette, and, on the 25th, H. M. S. Pinafore once more sailed the ocean blue on the stage of its first New York success; Mark Smith was Sir Joseph, Wilkie Ralph, James G. Peakes the Captain, H. C. Peakes Deadeye, Henri Leoni the Boatswain, Adelaide Randall Josephine, Emma Hagger Hebe, and Emma Elsner Buttercup. This revival lasted until June 1st, when The Chimes of Normandy rang out the season.

On June 5th, a summer term began with the rising Baker and Farron in a comicality entitled Max Müller:

Max and Emil Müller	P. F. Baker	O'Neil	Harry Rich
O'Connell	T. J. Farron	Keeper Hawes	Charles Wilson
Blackburn	Frank Losee	Keeper Jones	F. N. Lee
Luke Dowling	J. W. Summers	Rita Müller	Mrs. W. G. Jones
Sheriff	E. D. Tannehill	Little Mina	Elsie Loane
Dr. Renard	De Los King	Mina Müller	Victory Creese

Victory Creese later acquired some repute as Victory Bateman. Max Müller lasted two weeks, and, on June 19th, what came back but Patience, with Marie Hunter as the milkmaid, John Howson as Bunthorne, Gertrude Orme as Lady Jane, and Charles J. Campbell as Grosvenor? One week sufficed, and in the following week Howson joined a new array in the same opera, at the Bijou Opera House. We shall always gratefully remember the Standard Theatre, in 1881–82, for its protracted Patience.

BIJOU OPERA HOUSE, 1881–1882

The major part of 1881–82, at the Bijou, was devoted to performances of the then raging element of comic opera. Nevertheless, it began, on August 15th, with a farce (by Edward Holst and Herman Lee) entitled Rooms to Rent, with W. J. Ferguson as Henry Huccleman, author, penny-a-liner and general Bohemian; others in the cast were Edward Coleman as Colonel Bombast, W. L. Gleason as Sam Cutler, Edward Holst as Fred R. Dahl (ballet master), Clarence Gibson as Albert Raymond, Joseph Waters as John, W. Alfred as a Telegraph Boy, Genevieve Reynolds as Mlle. Ross-kella, Mina Crolius as Mrs. Cutter, and Fannie McNiel as Alice. The Herald, on the 16th, was mordantly sarcastic; "it is just such plays that make not alone 'rooms for rent' at the Bijou, but will make the entire house vacant, if the proceedings are persisted in." Yet by dint of feverish adver-tising, the thing kept on for a short time.

On September 5th, La Mascotte returned with, for the first time here, "the composer's original orchestration." The Audran Opera Company put it on, with Selina Dolaro as Bettina, Blanche Chapman as Fiametta, George W. Denham as Lorenzo, Alonzo Hatch as Frederic, Lithgow James as Pippo, Joseph Greensfelder as Rocco, Bessie Temple as Francesca, Emma Ducha-teau as Antonia, &c. Jessie Williams conducted, and A. J. De Fossez was manager. Again it ran, as if luck had no ending; and, we remember, it was revived, on the same evening, at the Fifth Avenue. The hundred and fiftieth performance of the opera in New York was advertised for September 14th, and the two hundredth (and last) on October 27th. The house was closed on the 28th, and presented, on the 29th, The Great Mogul, or, the Snake Charmer (a new work of Audran) with no less a celebrity (of the future) than Lillian Russell, last year merely a "freshman," so to speak, at Tony Pastor's:

Prince Mignapour	Selina Dolaro	D'Jemma	Lillian Russell
Nicobar	G. W. Denham	Bengaline	Blanche Chapman
Astrakan	J. W. Greensfelder	First Vender	Bessie Temple
Tao Tsin	F. W. Lennox	Second Vender	Emma Duchateau
Grand Brahma	Mr. Cardoza	Third Vender	Kate Livingston
Officer	C. Tucker	Ministers	W. P. Hampshire, J. C. Smith

The reader will be delighted to receive from the Herald of October 30th his first review of Lillian Russell: "Miss Russell, who graduated at Tony Pastor's, seemed afraid of her audience at the beginning, and promised little, singing faultily and acting ill at ease, but later in the evening she sang charmingly, and received much well-earned applause.... Miss Russell has a beautiful face, a rare figure and a delightful voice that has not been suffi-ciently trained. If this lady learns to bring her acting up to the level of her other accomplishments, she will be invaluable in comic opera." Excel-lent prophecy! She never became a good actress, but she was certainly "invaluable" in her chosen field. And her beauty is still (1939) a tradition of the American people. The Snake Charmer lasted through December 17th, Raymond Holmes ultimately cast as Nicobar; on Monday, the 19th, back came Olivette, with Selina Dolaro in the title-rôle, Lillian Russell as Bathilde, Emma Duchateau as Veloutine, Kate Livingston as Moustique, Raymond Holmes as Duc des Ifs, W. F. Hampshire as Valentine, Greens-felder as Merrimac, Fred W. Lennox as Coquelicot, and E. S. Grant as Marvejol. Jesse Williams, of course, still conducted. On December 29th,

[479]

Selina Dolaro took a benefit, with the second act of Olivette, the third of The Snake Charmer, and an original comedietta, The Reading of a Tragedy, in which Harry St. Maur made his first appearance in America. The company departed, on the 31st, after a performance of The Snake Charmer. On the afternoons of December 29th and 30th, and at 11 A.M., on the 31st, little Corinne (daughter of Jennie Kimball) made her appearance in The Magic Slipper, supported, for fun's sake, by big George K. Fortescue as one of the proud sisters, Susie Parker as the Prince, Lizzie Hunt as Dandini, Herbert Crosley as Thisbe, &c. Corinne for years was tenderly regarded by provincial audiences.

On January 2nd, John A. McCaull was advertised as proprietor and manager of the theatre, and the attraction was Haverly's The Strategists, with J. B. Polk and F. E. Aiken still in the leading rôles. Corinne and The Magic Slipper attracted on several afternoons and on Saturday morning. On January 9th (matinée) and subsequent afternoons, she tried Bettina, in The Mascot. On the 13th the infant wonder had a benefit, with acts of The Mascot, Olivette and The Magic Slipper; Lillian Russell also appeared. On January 16th, Willie Edouin's Sparks scintillated in the well-known Dreams; Willie Edouin, John A. Mackay, James T. Powers, Alice Atherton, Marion Elmore and Sylvia Gerrish, notable all in the later '80s, were among the funmakers. On January 30th (not 23rd, as in Allston Brown) a new opera by W. C. McCreery, L'Afrique, enlisted Fred W. Lennox as Captain Fitzhugh Montague-Jones, Philip Branson (first appearance in New York) as Lieutenant Geoffrey Plantagenet Hamilton De Bracy, Joseph S. Greensfelder (busy man!) as Sergeant Tops, Harry Standish as Mynheer Van Zwickenboot, E. S. Grant as Corporal Hops, Marie Glover (first appearance in New York) as Georgiana Montague-Jones, and Lizzie Keiler (also her début here) as Alice, her maid. The scene was on the border of the Transvaal, and much danger lurked in the bush. This was an amateurish affair, and the first failure, for some considerable time, at the Bijou; nevertheless, it struggled through three hard weeks.

On February 20th, the Emilie Melville Opera Company presented The Royal Middy, the company including Miss Melville (as Fanchette), Lilly (sic) Post (as Maria), Tom Casselli (as Don Januario), Fred Lennox (as Mungo), Charles Dungan (as Don Norberto), Wallace Macreery (as Don Lamberto), Elma Delaro (as Antonia), &c. On the 25th, Apajune, the Water Sprite, a feature that season on our German stage, employed the combined companies of Emilie Melville and the Bijou Opera House:

Natalitza	Emilie Melville	Yosa	J. S. Greensfelder
Princess Heloise	Elma Delaro	Alexandri	Charles W. Dungan
Ilinka	Lilly Post	Ivan	W. H. Stanley
Prince Prutchesko	William Gilbert	Jacob	Harry Standish
Marco	Tom Casselli	Milhailo	E. S. Grant
Captain Nitchano	Fred Lennox	Katinka	Miss T. Valerga

The piece did not achieve the expected success, and, on March 13th, the Pirates of Penzance was resuscitated, with Blanche Roosevelt in her original character of Mabel, with Joseph Greensfelder as the Pirate King, with Harry Standish as Samuel, Wallace Macreery as Frederic, William Gilbert as the Major General, Tom Casselli as the Sergeant of Police, Lilly Post as Edith, Tilly Valerga as Kate, Susie Winner as Isabel, and Augusta Roche as Ruth (her original character in London).   Miss Roosevelt, forced by previously arranged concert engagements, was out of the cast on March 20th, 21st and 22nd, her place being filled by Sallie Reber; she returned on the 23rd, and continued to the end of the run on April 1st.   On March 16th, Julie De Ruyther (*sic*) began as Ruth.

The next attraction was the master-magician, Herrmann, who entered, on April 3rd, with Mlle. Addie, Awata Katsnoshin, E. D. Davies ("Premier ventriloquist of the world"), and Howell and Darwin.   He was succeeded, on April 17th, by Louis and Alice Harrison, in Photos, a very amusing bit of nondescript fun, of the kind then so eagerly devoured; their assistants were Virginia Ross, Dickie Martinez, E. J. Connelly, W. C. Mandeville, Jerome Mills, E. D. Stone and Arthur Shewell.   After two weeks of this, we could return (May 1st) to the genial humour of Neil Burgess, in Widow Bedott, of course with George W. Stoddart as Elder Sniffles; one week (May 1st–6th) was all that was vouchsafed us of this native product.   Selina Dolaro began, on May 8th, a sort of "parlour entertainment," with two comedies, A Lesson in Love and The First Night, her supporting company including Harry St. Maur (who had played at the Bijou on December 31st), Clinton Stuart, E. M. Holland, Nellie Mortimer, Eva Barrington, Edward P. Temple, and Minnie Lee; this experiment lasted, with the same plays, for four weeks, closing on June 3rd.

On June 5th, hither came Patience, beloved of the muses, with Lillian Russell, who had recently appeared as the milkmaid in a very successful burlesque of the opera at Tony Pastor's, now cast for the character in the genuine work; with her were Edward P. Temple as Bunthorne, Harry St. Maur as Grosvenor, John E. Nash as the Colonel, Harry Pepper as the Duke, William Gillow as the Major, William Ridgeway as the Solicitor, Augusta Roche as Lady Jane, Marion Lambert as Lady Angela, Emily Lawrence as Lady Saphir, and Miss G. Bowler as Lady Ella, a cast chiefly distinguished by the presence in it of Miss Russell and Miss Roche.   On June 26th, an entirely new cast presented Lilly Post as Patience, Laura Joyce as Lady Jane, Emma Guthrie as Lady Angela, Victoria Reynolds as Lady Saphir, Susie Winner as Lady Ella, John Howson as Bunthorne, Digby Bell as Grosvenor, Charles Dungan as the Colonel, and Alonzo Hatch as the Duke, decidedly, except for Miss Russell and Miss Roche, a change for the better; and Laura Joyce and Lilly Post were doubtless good.   With this cast the opera ran through July 29th.

[481]

On July 31st, a revived Olivette brought back Selina Dolaro, with Lilly Post, Victoria Reynolds, Greensfelder, Charles Campbell, George Gaston and Fred H. Frear; after two weeks, it yielded the stage (August 14th) to The Snake Charmer, Selina Dolaro, Lilly Post (*vice* Lillian Russell), Emma Guthrie, Greensfelder, Gaston, and Frank Budworth filling the leading rôles. This also endured for a fortnight, giving us, on August 28th, another former delight in Billee Taylor, with Carrie Burton as Phœbe, Emie Weathersby as Arabella, Amy Harvey as Susan, Jennie Hughes as Eliza, Albert Henderson as Sir Mincing Lane, C. J. Campbell as Billee, Edward Chapman as Captain Flapper, Ed. Connelly as Crab, and A. D. Barker as Ben Barnacle. This lasted until Patience began another run on September 9th, with Lillian Russell and most of the performers who had appeared here from June 26th. The Bijou had weathered the heat of the entire summer with Patience, Olivette, Billee Taylor and Patience once more; I leave it, on September 9th, to begin at that date for the season of 1882–83. I hope the reader is not tiring of comic opera; if so, let him remember the passing of other popular crazes. It is easy to be Cassandra, in matters theatrical.

NIBLO'S GARDEN, 1881–1882

The famous old Niblo's Garden, still sturdy, if less aristocratic than in earlier days, re-opened on August 15, 1881, under management of John F. Poole and Edward G. Gilmore. The first attraction was My Geraldine, with the ever-interesting Emily Rigl, assisted by Emily Baker, Emma Skerrett, Susie Winner, Little Maude, Charles Webster, E. A. White, Theodore Balfour (from the London theatres), W. J. Scanlan, Frank G. Cotter, Charles A. McManus and S. C. Du Bois. It remained for three weeks. Next came the great success of the last season at Wallack's — The World; in this, on Sepetmber 5th, appeared Henry Crisp as Sir Clement Hungerford, George Morton as Harry Hungerford, Roland Reed (a funny man, later a star, and father of Florence Reed of the '30s) as Mo Jewell, M. J. Jordan as Martin Bashford, G. W. Conway as Blackstone, W. H. Collings as Lumley, W. J. Leonard (once of Wallack's) as Owen, Miss Tiny Hilleker as Ned, Helen Sedgwick as Mabel, and Alice Mansfield as Mary Blyth. This distribution, doubtless inferior to that at Wallack's (though we are always pleased to meet Harry Crisp) carried the very popular and exciting melodrama for four weeks, closing on October 1st.

On October 3rd, down from Booth's came that disappointed hope, Michael Strogoff, which had been expected to do so much, but which had apparently been buried under a mass of heavy scenery and unmanageable spectacle; the actors were as at the more fashionable house uptown. The play would seem to have won greater success, comparatively, at its new home; it ran there up to and including November 5th. During the last

week a benefit matinée was offered for the Michigan relief; the police department aided by selling tickets.

Niblo's, one sees, had fared well, needing only three plays for a period of
eleven weeks.   A change of *menu,* on November 7th, provided H. B. Mahn's
Comic Opera Company, in Donna Juanita, of course with Jeannie Winston
in the title-rôle.   During their second and last week, the singers gave, on
November 14th, 15th and 16th, Boccaccio; on the 17th, 18th and 19th, The
Mascot.   And, on November 21st, The World came back in triumph for
another four weeks.   Fortunate Niblo's!   It was succeeded, on December
19th, by the very great hit from the Park Theatre, but more recently at the
Casino — the Hanlon-Lees, in Le Voyage en Suisse.   And J. K. Emmet, one
of the very most popular entertainers of his day, who had recently closed a
remarkably prosperous three weeks at the Fourteenth Street Theatre, came
to Niblo's for one week, beginning on January 2nd; of course he gave Fritz
in Ireland.   The weeks of January 9th and 16th and 23rd offered Billy
Barry as Michael Mulcahy and Hugh Fay as Michael Muldoon in Mul-
doon's Picnic — "the authors and creators in their original characters."
With them were the Electric Three, The St. Felix Sisters, the Garnellas,
Fields and Hanson, &c.   Of course Harrigan and Hart and Salsbury's
Troubadours with various merry parties must expect to be imitated.   Even
Muldoon's Picnic was followed, next week at Pastor's, by Muldoon's Coterie.
Imitation may be not only the sincerest form of flattery, but good business
withal.   At any rate, three weeks accrued for Muldoon's Picnic.

A. M. Palmer was sending a rather strong company through neighbour-
ing districts in several of the past successes of the Union Square Theatre.
This aggregation entered Niblo's, on January 30th, with The Banker's
Daughter, the cast including James O'Neill, Maude Granger, Owen Fawcett,
Netta Guion, Walden Ramsay, Virginia Buchanan, M. W. Fiske and Little
Effie Barrett in rôles easily assigned by the reader.   On February 6th, The
Danicheffs enlisted O'Neill as Osip, Walden Ramsay as Vladimir (originally
played at the Union Square by O'Neill), Fiske, Charles Seymour, Fawcett,
Julian Magnus, Lysander Thompson, J. H. Fitzpatrick, Miss Granger, Ida
Vernon (as the Princess Lydia), Netta Guion, Virginia Buchanan, Mrs. Far-
ren (as the Countess), Hattie Thorpe, &c.   This, if not so fine as the orig-
inal cast at the Union Square, was nevertheless an excellent distribution.
A Celebrated Case began, on February 13th, for two weeks, O'Neill's Jean
Renaud being associated with the Lazare of Lewis Morrison, the Raoul of
Nelson Decker (his original rôle at the Union Square), the d'Aubeterre of
J. H. Fitzpatrick, the O'Rourke of M. W. Fiske, the Valentine of Miss
Granger, the Adrienne of Netta Guion, the Madeleine of Ida Vernon, the
Chanoinesse of Mrs. Farren, the Duchesse of Virginia Buchanan and the
child Adrienne of Effie Barrett — really a heart-warming cast, almost as
moving as the original in the home-theatre.   In fact the glory of the Union

[483]

Square seems almost at that time to have transferred itself to Niblo's while the mother theatre was partially eclipsed by The Lights o' London. I bore the reader by informing him that, on February 23rd, Frank de Vernon played Raoul. Of course this series of revivals would have seemed incomplete without The Two Orphans; that melodramatic classic duly came on February 27th:

Pierre	James O'Neill	Louise	Netta Guion
Jacques Frochard	Lewis Morrison	Countess	Virginia Buchanan
Count de Linières	J. H. Fitzpatrick	La Frochard	Mrs. Farren
Chevalier de Vaudrey	M. W. Leffingwell	Marianne	Etelka Wardell
Picard	Owen Fawcett	Sister Thérèse	Hattie Thorpe
Marquis de Presles	Julian Magnus	Julie	Estelle Clayton
Doctor	T. E. Morris	Sister Geneviève	Ida Vernon
Henriette	Maude Granger		

The reader observes that Ida Vernon and T. E. Morris played the rôles they had carried in all three runs of the play at the Union Square, and that Maude Granger, the Marianne of the greater part of the first run and James O'Neill, the Pierre of the second, were also of this interesting Niblo assignment. We note, as well, that Owen Fawcett, Walden Ramsay, Lysander Thompson, Julian Magnus and Netta Guion, originally cast for smaller parts in The Lights o' London, had been drafted for better work in these Niblo performances. The very pleasing reminder of Union Square hits ceased, in the week beginning on March 6th, when George Fawcett Rowe came in as Micawber, in Little Em'ly, some of his support consisting of Clinton Hall, Etelka Wardell, Netta Guion and Julian Magnus.

An entirely new force took possession on March 13th. Frank Mayo played Badger, in The Streets of New York, and with him were Mrs. E. L. Davenport as Mrs. Fairweather, and two of her children, May and Harry, respectively, as Lucy and Bob, the street urchin. Others in the cast of the popular play were Mary Young (Mrs. Puffy), Mattie Earle (Alida), Harold Forsberg (Gideon Bloodgood), T. M. Hunter (Captain Fairweather), C. Russell Blake (Mark), John T. Malone (Paul), Carl Ahrendt (Puffy), Edwin Frank (Dan), &c. M. B. Curtis, as Sam'l of Posen, filled the weeks of March 20th and 27th. And, on April 3rd, Niblo's, which seems to me to have had thus far a most interesting season, fell back on earlier loves in producing The Black Crook, with J. B. Roberts (ambitious tragedian of yore), D. H. Andrews, W. F. Wallis, George R. Edeson, Fanny Barry, Mrs. Berrell, and Nellie Larkelle in the "drama," and with specialties by the Martens (or Marten) Family (Styrienne, cat duet, etc.), and the Herbert Brothers, and with a ballet led by Mlles. de Rosa and Bazzano. As usual, this old piece was staged in spectacular splendour, but it lasted only two weeks.

Mr. and Mrs. McKee Rankin, who, as we remember, had tried two new plays, in the autumn, at the Fourteenth Street Theatre, nevertheless reverted to The Danites, on April 17th, at Niblo's. Allston Brown, unfortunately, seems to indicate an engagement at about this time at Niblo's, with John McCullough; an item has become misplaced, perhaps, in the printing of his book. At any rate, it was the Rankins who held the stage for the week of April 17th. On the 24th, the Madison Square actors presented Hazel Kirke, with the cast but recently seen at the Fifth Avenue; Allston Brown again errs in saying that the Kiralfys presented Excelsior on April 21st — he is a year ahead of the story. Well, we are all only too liable to error. May 1st brought the third visit to Niblo's of The World; Clinton Hall replaced Henry Crisp, now alas! dead. On the 8th, J. K. Emmet, after three weeks at the Grand Opera House, returned in Fritz in Ireland. John T. Raymond, on the 15th, began as Fresh, the American. With him were Charles Rockwell, G. F. De Vere, Harry Pierson, Sedley Brown, Agnes Proctor, Lizzie Creese, Katie Baker, and Mattie Ferguson. And, behold! on the 22nd, Uncle Tom's Cabin presented Frank Tannehill as Legree, Sam Lucas as Uncle Tom, and Nellie Scott, "the famous shouter and leader," in the plantation scenes. Daisy Markoe was Topsy No. 1. There were two Topsys, but only one Eva. This lasted for two weeks.

Frank I. Frayne, whom we associate only with one play — Si Slocum — brought out a semi-novelty (to us) on June 5th, a piece called Mardo, some of the excitements of which make one think of Michael Strogoff, excitements consisting of Nihilists, a Burning Bridge, Siberian Snow, a great Fire Scene, a Realistic Conflagration, etc. In his company were Annie von Behren, S. K. Chester, Lillian Vane, Harry Gwynette, Jessie Deagle, Annie Chester, Bessie Borry, George C. Wood, George A. Beane, Jr., H. M. Markham and Andy Mallon. The new drama at the end of two weeks gave way to Si Slocum, revived on June 19th. On June 26th, Lillian Russell and Augusta Roche, and others, who had been playing in Patience, at the Bijou Opera House, came to Niblo's, in the same opera, a new company, as we saw, continuing the run at the Bijou. Patience, on July 1st, closed what seems to me a rather interesting season at Niblo's.

CHAPTER VIII

GRAND OPERA HOUSE, WINDSOR THEATRE, GERMAN THEATRES, ACADEMY OF MUSIC (NEW YORK), THEATRE COMIQUE, VARIETY THEATRES, MINSTRELSY, CIRCUS, MISCELLANY, CONCERTS, 1881–1882

THE Grand Opera House, firmly fixed in the affections of the west side, threw open its doors on August 15, 1881, to a loving public that entered to hear once more (surely they must all have heard it before) the never-dying The Banker's Daughter, with a very interesting cast:

John Strebelow	J. E. Whiting	Harold Routledge	Archie Cowper
G. W. Phipps	Charles Walcot	Brown	J. H. Burnett
Count de Carojac	W. S. Daboll	Lillian	Adele Belgarde
Lawrence Westbrook	E. L. Tilton	Florence St. Vincent	Mrs. Walcot
Babbage	Joseph A. Wilkes	Mrs. Holcomb	Rose Graham

If one could not see the original players, this substitute group might well suffice; it certainly would have been interesting to observe Daboll, in later years the great Ravennes of Erminie, in the rôle of the wicked Count de Carojac. Two weeks of this favourite drama led to another Union Square success, My Partner, Louis Aldrich, of course, appearing (August 29th) as honest, manly Joe Saunders, and Parsloe as the "Chinaman," with Walter L. Dennis as the careless Ned, George D. Chaplin as Major Britt, J. F. Dean as Matthew Brandon, J. W. Hague as Josiah Scraggs, Dora Goldthwaite as Mary, Louise Fuller as Grace, and Josephine Laurens as Posie Pentland. This also fulfilled its allotted destiny of two weeks.

On September 12th, Mr. and Mrs. George S. Knight (Sophie Worrell), fresh from Europe, produced a play by Bronson Howard, entitled Baron Rudolph, a version of an earlier piece by Howard, Only a Tramp, copyrighted in 1877. Written for Mr. and Mrs. Florence, Baron Rudolph was never acted by them, and fell into the repertoire of the Knights, who, according to Arthur H. Quinn, would "seem" to have performed it at Hull, England, on August 1, 1881. And here, just a few weeks later, they gave it to New York:

Rudolph Wiegand	G. S. Knight	Owen	Albert Morrill
Whitworth Lawrence	W. J. Cogswell	John H. Thomas	T. J. Jackson
General Metcalfe	J. L. Ashton	Mrs. Dashwood	Mrs. G. S. Knight
Judge Merrybone	E. A. Locke	Rhoda	Charlotte Cobbe
Geoffrey Brown	W. H. Young	Ernestine	Josie Wilmere
Allen	A. Lindsay		

This story of a drinking, good-hearted ne'er-do-well, who is deserted by his wife, tramps about, becomes *deus ex machina* in his daughter's life, and finally inherits a German baronetcy, is certainly not one of Howard's best plays, but it lasted the Knights for a few seasons. They kept it, at that time, at the Grand Opera House for two weeks. It will be observed that the cast here set down, as copied from the Herald, differs entirely from that given by Allston Brown, who evidently has in mind some production (I know not where) by the Union Square Theatre travelling company.

Tony Pastor and his company filled the week beginning on Tuesday, September 27th (the house was closed on the 26th, in honour of the funeral, that day, of President Garfield). With Pastor were Ferguson and Mack, Lester and Allen, Frank E. McNish, the Leland Sisters, Lester and Williams, Dan Collyer, Harry McAvoy, Frank Girard, Lizzie Simms, Ella Wesner, Lillie Western, the French Sisters, and Emma Rogers. The attraction for two weeks, beginning on October 3rd was the Emma Abbott Opera Company. On the 3rd and 5th, we might have heard Fra Diavolo, with Miss Abbott, Miss Maurel, George Conly, Alonzo Stoddard, Tams and William Castle. On the 4th, Martha enlisted the same group, excepting Stoddard. A changed group, on the afternoon of the 5th and the evening of the 6th, presented Olivette; Julie Rosewald, Miss Maurel, Mlle. Zelna, A. E. Stoddard, Appleby and Castle were the leaders. The bill for the 7th enabled Miss Abbott to soar into the vocal feats and the mad scene of Lucia di Lammermoor, her assistants being Conly, Stoddard, Appleby and Fabrini. Maritana was matinée fare, on the 8th, and The Bohemian Girl, in the evening of that day, once more dreamed of marble halls; Miss Abbott sang in the first, and Miss Rosewald in the second. Olivette, of which the public could not tire, had on the 10th, 11th, and 12th, with a matinée on the 12th, a cast including Miss Abbott as the Countess (she did not sing at the matinée), Julie Rosewald as Olivette, George Olmi as Merrimac, Alonzo Stoddard as Duc des Ifs, A. W. Tams as Coquelicot, William Broderick as Marvejol, Annetta Zelna as Veloutine, and William Castle or Fabrini as Valentine — nearly a "grand" opera cast for an operetta, but, according to the Herald of the 11th, sadly lacking in comedians. Catherine Lewis and Howson were singing Olivette at the same time at the Metropolitan Casino. On the 13th, Paul and Virginia enlisted Miss Abbott, Miss Maurel, Marie Hindle, Annetta Zelna, George Olmi, Stoddard, George Weeks, Harry Harvey, Walter Temple and Castle. Miss Abbott's benefit, on the 14th, brought a gift no more fresh than The Bohemian Girl. The Saturday (15th) bills were (matinée) The Chimes of Normandy, with Miss Rosewald, and (evening) Faust, with Miss Abbott. We in New York hardly realised the popularity of Miss Abbott "on the road."

But there was no doubt, latterly, of the great vogue of John T. Raymond, who, on October 17th, began two weeks of Fresh, the American; and no

[487]

possible question of the personal appeal of Lotta, who once more, on October 31st, gave us the vivacious Musette, assisted, as usual, by P. Augustus Anderson, H. B. Bradley, C. H. Bradshaw, Clement Bainbridge, Mrs. G. C. Boniface, Florence Noble and Lulu Jordan. Louis and Alice Harrison, in Photos, held the week of November 7th–12th. On November 14th, Joseph Jefferson began two weeks in Rip Van Winkle, supported by Mark Pendleton, Charles Waverly, Rose Wood and Josephine Baker. Lester Wallack (his new theatre not yet ready) came in, on November 28th, in Rosedale, with J. F. Hagan, Walter Eytinge, W. H. Lytell, Milton Rainford, H. V. Donnelly (later a well-known comic actor), G. W. Herbert, Julia Hanchett, Kate Bartlett, Carrie Jamieson, Mrs. Fred Williams and Mrs. M. L. Berrell. This attraction also stayed two weeks. Rip Van Winkle and Rosedale — one could write an epic on those plays!

Herrmann and magic held sway during the week of December 12th, Mlle. Addie, the Lorellas, Howell and Darwin (illusionists) and Awata Katsnoshin participating. On the 19th, Annie Pixley began a two-weeks engagement in M'liss. The Danicheffs was here for the week of January 2nd–7th, with James O'Neill, Walden Ramsay (as Vladimir), Owen Fawcett (as Paul), H. F. Daly, Julian Magnus, Alfred Becks, Lysander Thompson, Somers (as Roger de Taldé), Maude Granger, Ida Vernon, Mrs. Farren, Ida Jeffreys (as Baroness Dozene), and Virginia Buchanan — much the same cast that acted the play, on February 6th, at Niblo's. Mr. and Mrs. McKee Rankin appeared, from January 9th to 21st, in '49, as recently tried at the Fourteenth Street Theatre. Certainly *habitués* of Niblo's, the Grand Opera House and the Windsor saw nearly everything, and, at cheaper prices, if they had the patience to wait awhile. A Child of the State, which lasted longer than I ever dreamed it could, had the week of January 23rd–28th, with J. M. Hardie, George Hoey (its author), H. Rees Davis, Mark M. Price, Signora Majeroni, Emma Pierce, Mrs. J. J. Prior, and Eva Barker.

And lo! here for the first time in New York at popular prices is the beautiful Mary Anderson, immediately after her month at Booth's Theatre. With J. B. Studley, William Harris, R. L. Downing, and the same support as at Booth's, she began, on January 30th and 31st, as Juliet, following on February 1st and 2nd, with Ingomar, and, on the 3rd and 4th, with Evadne; for the matinée, on the 4th, she presented her lovely Galatea. At the Wednesday matinée, at which she did not appear, J. B. Studley, sturdy actor of an older day, enacted Mathias, in The Bells. For her second week, Miss Anderson gave The Lady of Lyons (February 6th, and matinée, 11th), Evadne (7th), Galatea (8th), The Daughter of Roland (9th, 10th, 11th); and this week she acted Galatea at the matinée on Wednesday, the 8th. On the 13th, Denman Thompson, long absent, returned for two weeks of Joshua Whitcomb, his support still including Julia Wilson, Mrs. D. Nourse and Ignacio Martinetti, along with Isabelle Coe, Eugene O. Jepson,

[488]

Walter Gale and George Beane. How long they had played together! Somehow their long fellowship appeals to the imagination. Another perennial flower emerged on February 27th — Maggie Mitchell, who gave us, on the 27th and 28th, and, on March 1st, the expected Fanchon, reverting, on the 2nd, 3rd and 4th, to Jane Eyre. With her were L. R. Shewell (a favourite of Boston), R. Fulton Russell, James Taylor, Julian Mitchell (her son), W. H. Burton, Rufus Scott, Laura Le Claire, Carrie Wyatt and Mrs. D. B. Vanderen (*sic*). On March 6th, 7th and 8th (matinée) we might have laughed and wept with The Pearl of Savoy. On the evening of the 8th, Miss Mitchell brought out a new play, The Little Savage, and continued it till the close of her term, on March 11th. The World, that great success of Wallack's and Niblo's, came to the Grand Opera House, on March 13th (not 20th, as in Allston Brown), and left on April 1st; Henry Crisp, George Morton, Russell Bassett, W. J. Leonard, Amelia Watts and Hetty Tracy were in the cast.

Our Boarding House opened on April 3rd, with Virginia Buchanan as Mrs. Dalrymple, Leonard Grover as Fioretti, W. H. Lytell as Colonel Elevator, Leonard Grover, Jr. as Gillipod, J. C. Burrows as Walter Dalrymple, George W. Farren as Matthew Eligible, Mrs. Fred Williams as Maria Colville, Mattie Earle as Beatrice Manheim, Fanny Gonzales as Little Florence, &c. On the afternoon of the 3rd, for the benefit of the Actors' Fund, Clara Morris acted Article 47, assisted by the artists who had supported her at the Union Square. On April 10th, Joseph Murphy began a week of Kerry Gow, J. K. Emmet succeeding him, on the 17th, in Fritz in Ireland, which remained (its popularity could not wane) for three delightful weeks. From my early recollections of her, it is always a pleasure for me to record the name of Fanny Davenport. She entered the Grand Opera House, on May 8th and 9th, in The School for Scandal, assisted by Charles Fisher as Sir Peter, George Clarke as Charles, Frederick Paulding as Joseph, Edgar L. Davenport as Sir Benjamin, Harry Pearson as Sir Oliver, Harry Hawk as Crabtree, Minnie Monk as Candour, Mary Shaw as Lady Sneerwell, and Mrs. Charles Fisher as Maria. She acted Leah, on May 9th (afternoon) for the benefit of the Actors' Fund, repeating it on the 10th and 11th. Her usual double bill of London Assurance and Oliver Twist made versatile her benefit night, on the 12th; this she repeated on the evening of the 13th. Charles Fisher was Sir Harcourt and Fagin — surely a sweeping versatility. For the matinée, on the 13th, the star gave The Lady of Lyons. This week was advertised as the last of Miss Davenport prior to a European tour. She actually appeared in London, later, but without great success. Her beauty, one of her greatest stage assets, was no longer as fresh as in the early days of the Daly company at the Fifth Avenue Theatre.

Tony Pastor came in, on May 15th, with Lizzie Simms, Mattie Vickers, the Irwin Sisters, the French Twin Sisters, Elise and Jacques Kruger, William Carroll, Lester and Allen, Wood and Beasley, Sam and Morris Weston, Frank Girard, C. S. Rogers, and Donnelly and Drew — a notable array. The skit, Fun on the Stage, added to the fun in the audience. Willie Edouin, on the 22nd, brought in his never-lagging Dreams, and with it ended the season on May 31st. On May 30th, occurred a farewell benefit (matinée) for McCoy, treasurer of the house; volunteers included J. B. Studley, George Clarke, R. E. Graham, Marshall Wilder, Kate Meek, Sallie Williams, Louisa Eldridge, and Hattie Anderson. John F. Poole was retiring from the management (Henry E. Abbey succeeding in 1882–83) and hence the "farewell" note of the treasurer's bespeak.

WINDSOR THEATRE, 1881–1882

The Windsor Theatre assuredly brought to playgoers resident near the Bowery far higher entertainment than had been provided by the old Bowery Theatre in its later days. The season of 1881–82 began, on August 15th, with the popular The Galley Slave, acted by Maude Granger, Gussie De Forrest and Frank Evans, each of whom had long been identified with it. Evangeline, in the week of the 22nd, presented Nellie Larkelle as Gabriel, Hattie Richardson as Evangeline, Jennie Weathersby as Catherine, Masters Cohen and Turner as the Heifer, Cohen as Deadshake, Charles Burke as Leblanc, Joe Harris as the Lone Fisherman, and Harry Morton as Basil — certainly not the most arresting aggregation ever assigned to the burlesque.

The interesting P. F. Baker and T. J. Farron had the week of August 29th–September 3rd, in a piece written for them by R. G. Morris, and entitled Up Salt Creek. In this Baker appeared as Herman Krauss, a young German, with musical, emotional and political tendencies, and Farron as John Shay, an Irish lord, with strong diplomatic, saltatory and amorous inclinations. Of the supporting cast only two (Mrs. Jones and Ada Boshell) awaken chimes in my memory:

Herman Krauss	P. F. Baker	Bill Hunting	George Arthur
John Shay	T. J. Farron	Chris Olsen	G. D. Davies
Hon. P. A. Myers	R. C. Hudson	Nicolai	Richard Ames
Cannibal Jack	Alfred Beverly	Bridget Gonzaga	Ettie E. Henry
Jake Blum	W. H. Bryan	Eleanor Myers	Mrs. W. G. Jones
Harry Austin	Joseph Hewes	Ottilie Krauss	Ada Boshell
Lew Simmons	Frederick De Vere		

In this list of characters I seem to scent the morning air of Harrigan and Hart farces. James A. Herne's Hearts of Oak offered the lure for the week beginning on September 5th; his support included Harry Mainhall as Ruby Darrell, Sydney Smith as Owen Garroway, Katharine Corcoran (Mrs. Herne) as Crystal, Mollie Corcoran as Tawdry, and Henrietta Bert as Aunt Betsey. James M. Hardie and George Hoey, on September 12th, offered their familiar A Child of the State. The Legion of Honour, that Park Theatre success of 1880–81, came on September 19th, with a cast including

Samuel Piercy, Lewis Morrison, Annie Graham, Forrest Robinson, George C. Davenport, Sarah Bigelow and Louise Dillon.   Oliver Doud Byron gave us, on September 26th, Across the Continent, changing on the 29th to Ten Thousand Miles Away, which continued till his departure on October 1st. On October 3rd, George Clarke appeared in Connie Soogah, and, on the 10th, Around the World in Eighty Days boasted of a monster live elephant and of a ballet led by Mlles. de Rosa and Carnis.   The Knights, on October 17th, brought from the Grand Opera House their recent offering, Baron Rudolph; on the 24th, Aldrich and Parsloe did the usual thing with My Partner.   The Madison Square Theatre Company followed, on October 31st, for a week of Hazel Kirke, the cast including Effie Ellsler, Sydney Cowell, Mrs. Sol Smith, Flora Livingston, Mary Rivers, C. W. Couldock, Gustavus Levick, Frank Weston, Charles Bowser, E. H. See, W. B. Cahill, Frank Colfax and E. M. Roberts — and a very good cast it was.

De Wolf Hopper came to the Windsor, on November 7th, in his comedy, One Hundred Wives, his assistants being Alexander Fitzgerald, George R. Sprague, John Ogden, Lawrence Eddinger, Frank Budworth, Joseph Herman, Helen Gardner, Lillie Eldridge, Mrs. J. Wheeler, and Little Vivia Ogden.   Barney McAuley, in A Messenger from Jarvis Section, attracted (I hope) during the week of the 14th; on the 21st, Jeffreys Lewis began a week of Two Nights in Rome, as the malevolent Corsican — the part originated by Maude Granger.   The usual cast of Deacon Crankett (Maginley, Buckley, Hart Conway, M. Loduski Young) gave that play for the week of November 28th–December 3rd; on the 5th of December came Jay Rial's Uncle Tom's Cabin.   Smith and Mestayer's Tourists in a Pullman Palace Car brought fun for a week beginning on the 12th, and tragedy ruled the week of the 19th, when the still great Mme. Janauschek gave Mary Stuart (19th and 22nd), Deborah (20th and 23rd), Bleak House (21st), Macbeth (24th), with Mother and Son for the matinées on the 21st and 24th.   And John A. Stevens, manager of the theatre, gave himself a Christmas present of a week's engagement, beginning on December 26th; of course he offered Unknown.   Tony Denier's Humpty Dumpty provided holiday joy for the week of January 2nd–7th, with Miaco, the "greatest living clown," and with a gift of $500 worth of toys at the matinée on the 4th.

J. K. Emmet, peregrinating through city theatres, reached the Windsor for the week of January 9th, in his usual vehicle, Fritz in Ireland; Buffalo Bill had the following week (January 16th–21st) in The Prairie Waif (by John A. Stevens), and with genuine Pawnee Indians in the ensemble, Chief Bear and Spotted Horse being two of the braves.   And lovely Kate Claxton followed in the wake of these horrors, opening, on January 23rd, in The Two Orphans, with Charles A. Stevenson, Marie Wilkins, Edwin F. Thorne, and others less notable.   She had had some difficulty about appearing in Stevens's Boston theatre, and at the Windsor in New York, but here she was,

[491]

all differences apparently smoothed away. Joseph Murphy, in Kerry Gow, entered on January 30th, and, on February 6th, Sol Smith Russell, in Edgewood Folks. Mr. and Mrs. McKee Rankin gave us '49, for the week beginning on the 13th. The Banker's Daughter constituted the refined fare of February 20th, with that company which opened the Grand Opera House in September. But Florence White, according to Herald advertisements, had replaced Adele Belgarde in the title rôle; yet the Herald review, on the 21st, states that Miss Belgarde appeared. On February 27th, Milton Nobles gave The Phœnix; All the Rage (with Hardenberg and Davidge) succeeded him, on March 6th.

An original production in this house of "combinations" was that of March 13th, a comic opera, The Jolly Bachelors, with libretto by John A. Stevens, and music by Edward A. Darling; the cast included Jeannie Winston, Amy Gordon, Leonora Bradley, Carrie Williams, E. M. Howard, W. A. Morgan, A. H. Bell, J. C. Cline, J. F. Raymond, and Charles H. Kimball, surely a poor support for Miss Winston. On the 20th came matter more familiar, The Galley Slave, which, we remember, re-opened the house on August 15th; Emily Rigl resumed her original character of Francesca, and Gussie De Forrest, who had played the part in August, to Maude Granger's Cicely, now succeeded Miss Granger in that rôle. Others in the cast were Frank Evans, Gabrielle du Sauld, Thomas H. Burns, and Junius Brutus Booth, brother of Edwin Booth and husband of Agnes Booth, then in Esmeralda. Joshua Whitcomb, with Denman Thompson and the cast so long associated with him, carried rural life to the Bowery for the week of March 27th. M. B. Curtis (with Harry Eytinge and Josie Wilmere) brought Sam'l of Posen, on April 3rd, to be followed, on the 10th, by Maggie Mitchell for a week divided between Fanchon and The Pearl of Savoy. Nearly everything came to the Windsor (often by way of the Grand Opera House), unless it happened to be rather new.

Jarrett and Rice's Fun on the Bristol (of course with John F. Sheridan) was the source of innocent merriment for the week of April 17th, and, on the 24th, F. S. Chanfrau impersonated the undying Kit. Annie Pixley and M'liss charmed, doubtless, for the week of May 1st, and actually Lotta, usually rather aristocratic in choice of theatres, came to the Windsor on May 8th, in Musette, her company exactly as before. She, Miss Pixley and Miss Mitchell had all filled engagements, during 1881–82, at the Grand Opera House; as a matter of fact none of them had been on "Broadway." On May 15th, James O'Neill began a week, in A Celebrated Case; on the 22nd, William H. Gillette eased the tension by the lighter matter of The Professor. James O'Neill, on the 29th, gave us The Danicheffs and caused us to wonder when he was to arrive at his appointed goal of stardom.

On June 5th, Charles L. Davis presented a piece for some time thereafter popular in smaller communities — Alvin Joslin:

[492]

O. H. BARR

CORINNE

ELMA DELARO

AUGUSTA ROCHE
(PIRATES OF PENZANCE)

LILLIAN RUSSELL
AS PATIENCE

JOHN HOWSON
AS BUNTHORNE

BLANCHE CHAPMAN

JESSE WILLIAMS

ALONZO HATCH

Alvin Joslin	C. L. Davis	Julia Ford	Josie Loane
Edwin Milton	Will J. Sherry	Clorinda	Dollie Thornton
Jim Dean	John Burnett	Ella Milton	Fannie du Coron
Theophilus	Harry C. Stanley	Florence	Marie Elliott
Joe Baxter	Charles Willard	Mother Cronin	Mrs. C. Washburn
Judge Lawrence	L. W. Harper	Clara	Florence Charles
Bob Ford	William M. Dell		

I wonder, good reader, if you recall a single member of that cast, the star alone excepted? Where did this rush of new actors come from? Of course the breakup of the stock system and the increase of "combinations" partly caused the influx into communities that some of the players under the older system could never have hoped to reach. Alvin Joslin ran for two weeks; it was followed, on June 19, by The Maid of Arran, adapted by Louis F. Baum from William Black's once famous novel, A Princess of Thule. The cast included Baum, Agnes Hallock, Myron Leffingwell, C. W. Charles, John H. Nicholson, Katharine Gray and Jennie Seeley. A theatre, in 1881–82, without The Mascot would be reft indeed; waiting long, the Windsor offered it, on June 26th, with Fay Templeton (Bettina), George Olmi, Ed Morris, W. M. Fuller, Pauline Hall (Fiametta), Harry Molten, Charles Sturges and William McPherson. The last week of the season (July 3rd–8th) gave us N. S. Wood, in The Boy Scout of the Sierras, with Maurice Pike, Joseph P. Winter, Mrs. W. G. Jones, four imported stallions, fifty soldiers, Indians, and a full brass band. It will be seen that the Windsor, more or less aping Broadway all season long, finished with a grand reversion to Bowery standards of a decade or more preceding; and Mrs. W. G. Jones, an excellent actress in better plays, was there to remind us of her later exploits in the famous old Bowery Theatre.

THALIA THEATER, 1881–1882

That old Bowery Theatre, now the Thalia, would never again be what it once was in the days of the b'hoys. Respectable to a degree, it opened its doors, on September 14th, for another season of performances by German players. Amberg and Herrmann were managers. The opening attraction was Demetrius, by Schiller and Laube, and the reader will scan the cast for names of players, old favourites and new candidates:

Demetrius	Herr Schönfeld	Der Thürsteher	Herr Metsch
Erzbischof von Gnesen	Herr Otto Meyer	Boris Godunoff	Herr Kierschner
Erzbischof von Lemberg	Herr Schäfer	Arinia	Frl. Brandmann
Fürst von Sendomir	Herr Malz	Fürst Schnisby	Herr Karl Meyer
Castellan von Lublin	Herr Frank	Patriarch	Herr Gotthard
Fürst Sapieha	Herr Schimke-Herrmann	Marfa	Frau Bersing-Hauptmann
Marina	Frl. Kelly	Olga	Frau Lube
Krongrossmarshall	Herr Prätorius	Xenia	Frl. Stäbner
Odowalsky	Herr Bollmann	Helena	Frl. Schlag
Komla..	Herr Schultze	Ein Fischer	Herr Schüler

[493]

Here we find two newcomers of note in Herr Schimke-Herrmann and Frau Bersing-Hauptmann, with names almost heavy enough to sink the ship or ships that brought them to our shores; but they seem to have won their way, despite those rather unprepossessing tags. Kierschner, the favourite of Neuendorff's Germania Theater, was now enrolled in the rival camp. After this serious opening, the Thalia management gave evidence of its preference for lighter offerings, a lesson learned in previous years and quite in keeping with habitudes in theatres along Broadway; it brought out on September 15th and for several nights following Gypsfigur (The Plaster Cast), by Theodor Taube, and with, as leaders of the cast, Müller, Link, Lube, Bollman, Mühlbauer, Frl. Lindemann, Frl. Schätz and Frl. Jules — the last two new to our stage.

The Thalia arrived at the full expression of its preference on September 21st, when it introduced Jenny Stubel (new) as Haiderose (Serpolette) in Die Glocken von Corneville; her chief associates were Frl. Seebold as Germaine, Herr Walter as Marquis de Corneville, Klein as Grenicheux, Müller as Gaspard, and Link as der Amtmann. According to the Herald, next day, a large audience greeted the production, as opposed to a small gathering for Don Carlos, at the new Germania Theater. What would you? German writers on the New York German theatres are, as we know, particularly severe on managers for indulging public taste for operetta rather than Schiller; those writers seem to think that, if the managers had persisted in presenting Schiller, audiences would have ceased to care for Lecocq and Offenbach and von Suppé. They fail to specify the source of income possible under such austere methods for managers and actors. Of course I admire the classics, but I also like my Offenbach and my Gilbert and Sullivan. Frl. Stubel made a hit, repeating her entrance-offering for several hearings. The German theatres closed on September 26th, as one might expect from their loyal patrons; the Thalia and Germania closed also on the 20th.

On September 27th, the long-desired Marie Geistinger returned, in von Suppé's Donna Juanita, in which, as the hero-heroine, she had the assistance of Müller as Don Pomponio, Frl. Jules as Donna Olympia, Link as Sir Andrew Douglas, Witle-Wild as Gaston, Klein as Riego, Otto Meyer as Gil Polo, Frl. Seebold as Petrita, Frl. Schamidatus as Marco, &c. On the 28th, the Herald states that as Mme. Geistinger "made her entrée as the roguish young cadet," she "was greeted with a perfect furore of enthusiasm. The vast audience rose to their feet, handkerchiefs were waved in all directions, hundreds of ladies and gentlemen shouted themselves hoarse in their cheers of welcome." Again I ask — who could blame the managers, as between Geistinger and Schiller? At any rate, Donna Juanita ran nightly through October 4th, Die Glocken von Corneville (with Frl. Stubel) furnishing matinée fare on October 1st and 8th, and evening delight on the 5th and

7th, and Geistinger reviving Donna Juanita on the 6th, and her dashing Boccaccio on the 8th, 10th and 12th.   On October 11th and 13th, the versatile star, abandoning von Suppé, appeared as Adrienne Lecouvreur, and, on the 14th and 15th, went to the Brooklyn Academy, leaving the home stage to Mathilde Kühle, who enacted Lorle, in Dorf und Stadt.   The range of Marie Geistinger always awakens amazement and admiration.   The versatility was noticeable during the following week: Boccaccio (October 17th), Adrienne (18th and 21st), a triple bill (19th), comprising Die schöne Galathee, Das Versprechen hinter'm Heerd and Eine wohlkomme Frau (she did not appear in this last), and (20th and 22nd), Die Näherin.   Loyal followers of the actress must have been in ecstasies of enthusiasm.   The triple bill was repeated on Saturday afternoon, October 22nd.   A concert graced the evening of Sunday, October 23rd, with Sternberg, pianist, and Emma Fleury from St. Petersburg (her "first appearance in America").

On the 24th, Mme. Geistinger repeated Die Näherin, and on the 25th and 27th, added Arria and Messalina to her extensive and varied repertoire; Boccaccio (26th), Adrienne (matinée, 29th), and Camille (evening, 29th) were her other offerings of the week.   On the 28th, she was out of the bill, and Jenny Stubel appeared in Die Fledermaus.   Die Näherin (October 31st), Camille (November 1st), Boccaccio (2nd) led the way to Millöcker's operetta, Das verwunschene Schloss (The Haunted Castle), on November 3rd, 4th and 5th, with the triumphant Geistinger as Regerl; this she repeated on the 7th, 8th, 9th and 10th, reviving, on the 11th and 12th, her last year's success, Drei Paar Schuhe, and appearing once more, at the matinee on the 12th, in Donna Juanita.   There is something stimulating in the thought of this versatile, vivacious, highly talented actress.   Das verwunschene Schloss (five times), Mme. Favart (November 18th), and Drei Paar Schuhe (evening, 19th) made the offerings of the week of November 14th–19th.   This varied offering dazzles one.

The following week, Mme. Geistinger played in Philadelphia, and Schiller raised his head on the 21st, in the Thalia, with a performance of Maria Stuart, enlisting Frau Kühle in the title-rôle, with Frau Bersing-Hauptmann as Elisabeth, Schönfeld as Mortimer, Schultze as Burleigh, Schimke-Herrmann as Leicester, and Kierschner as Shrewsbury.   Ihr Korporal (by Costa, with music by Millöcker) held the stage on the 22nd and 23rd; on Thanksgiving day, 24th (afternoon), this novelty was appropriately fitted to the holiday, and, in the evening, Heinrich Conried made one of his rare appearances as Dr. Klaus.   Lindner's Die Bluthochzeit (St. Bartholomew's Night) presented, on November 25th, Frau Bersing-Hauptmann as Catherine de Medici, Conried as Charles IX, Schönfeld as Henry of Navarre, Lenoir as Anjou, Steiner as Alençon, Bollmann as Duc de Guise, Kierschner as the Cardinal, Schimke-Herrmann as Coligni, Schultze as Rioux, Karl Meyer as Potrot, Otto Meyer as the Magician, Frau Kühle as

Marguerite of Valois, Frl. Kelly as Marquise de Fontanges, &c. Of course, the singing actors had accompanied Geistinger to Philadelphia, and the more serious element in the company now had an opportunity. But what of the paying public?

On November 28th, the beloved star returned, giving, once each, Das verwunschene Schloss, Die Näherin, Boccaccio, La Belle Hélène (evening of the 30th), Therese Krones (for her benefit, on December 1st). With these performances Mme. Geistinger departed for a long tour which was to lead her in triumph from city to city, as far as remotest California. On December 2nd and 3rd, therefore, Jenny Stubel attempted to carry on the tradition of operetta established by Geistinger, and gave us the tuneful Die Fledermaus. And, on December 5th, the far-reaching octopus, La Mascotte (Der Glücksengel), clutched the Thalia, with Frl. Stubel as Bettina, Alexander Klein as Pippo, Franz Müller as Lorenzo XVII, Hermine Jules as Fiametta, Adolf Link as Fritellini, and Gustav Adolfi as Rocco. And having seized, the popular operetta could not relinquish its hold until December, on the 24th, was about ready to fade into the arms of the New Year. For December 19th was advertised a benefit for sufferers by the fire of the Ring Theater in Vienna. On the afternoon of December 17th (and for a few afternoons thereafter) Max und Moritz formed the bill — a Christmas gift for children, old and young; Das verwunschene Schloss (with Jenny Stubel as Regerl) decked the evenings of December 26th, 27th, and 29th, La Mascotte that of the 28th, and Einer von uns're Leut' ended December, on the 30th and 31st. Repetitions filled the first evenings of January, La Mascotte still emerging from time to time, until January 12th, when Conried gave his admired performance of Franz Moor, with Schimke-Herrmann as Karl, and Frau Kühle as Amalia.

On January 13th came the first production of Apajune, der Wassermann (music by Millöcker, to a libretto by F. Zell and R. Genée), and with Jenny Stubel as Natalitza, Link as Fürst Vladimir, Frl. Jules as Heloise, Frl. Hecht as Ilinka, Walter as Manolle, Klein as Marco, Adolfi as José, Frl. Camara as Katinka, and Kierschner as Alexandri. It succeeded, and the fortunate Thalia, even without Geistinger, needed no change of attraction for several nights; its run ceased on January 28th. On Sunday evening, January 22nd, Remenyi appeared in concert. The bill for January 30th gave Bayer's Der Chevalier von San Marco, with Müller as Van Bock, Frl. Jules as Ludmilla, Frl. Seebold as Isabella, Klein as Camillo, Frl. Stubel as Fanny, Adolfi as Zephyrin, Link as Wenzel, &c.

The Thalia had already offered successful new players. On February 2nd, it presented two more in Katharina (Käthi) Schratt and Herr Bassermann; furthermore, they made their début in an entirely fresh piece by Sardou, the lively Divorçons, here called Cyprienne. As Cyprienne and des Prunelles, they were associated with Bollmann as Adhemar, Kierschner as de Clavignac, Frau Kühle as Mme. de Brionne, Frl. Brandmann as Mme. de Valfontaine, Frl. Jules as Mlle. de Lusignan, and the comic Link as Joseph. On the 3rd, the Herald speaks delightedly of Frl. Schratt's "youth (she is but twenty-six), her beauty, her exquisite elegance of manner, and the polish of her art." Bassermann, as the new *jeune premier*, seemed "destined to fill the situation left vacant by the secession of Herr Schönfeld. He seems a thorough artist and is of a fine presence." Divorçons also ran well; given at the matinée on February 8th, it yielded the stage on the evening of that day to Frl. Seebold, in Fatinitza, but came back on the 9th, 10th and 11th, with Fatinitza for the matinée, on the last-named date. On the 13th, Frl. Schratt appeared as Hedwig, in Durch die Intendanz (by Henle); with her were Schimke-Herrmann as Baron von Kuhn, Frau Bersing-Hauptmann as his Baroness, Frl. Lindemann as Maria, Bollmann as Hans Waldau, Bassermann as Captain Baron von Göben, K. Meyer as von Leonroth, and Adolfi as Strohberger. For the matinée, on the afternoon of the 18th, Frl. Schratt repeated Divorçons, and, in the evening Jenny Stubel sang La Mascotte. Fanchon (Die Grille) enlisted Frl. Schratt on the 20th, 22nd, and at the matinée on the 25th; Divorçons (or Cyprienne) still held the way on the 21st, 23rd and 25th (evening). For "off" performances, La Mascotte (afternoon of the 22nd and evening of the 24th) allowed Jenny Stubel to shine in her chosen field. Meilhac and Halévy's Die kleine Mama, with Frl. Schratt as Brigitte, was offered on February 28th, March 1st, 2nd and 3rd; on the evening of the 4th, Kierschner's benefit restored Der Pfarrer von Kirchfeld, with Kierschner as Vetter, Katharina Schratt as Anna, Conried as Wurzelsepp, Schimke-Herrmann as Count Peter, Bassermann as Heil, and Frl. Jules as Brigitte. Repetitions of this (6th), Fanchon (7th), and Divorçons (8th) led to the 9th, 10th and 11th, and "the first performance anywhere" of S. E. Schevitsch's play, Tania, with Katharina Schratt in the title-rôle, Kierschner as Count Alexander Namiroff, Bollmann as Andre von Dolgorsky, Link as Schindroff, Bassermann as Gregor, Frau Bersing-Hauptmann as Maria Petrova, Karl Meyer as Vater Cyrill, Schimke-Hermann as Iwanuschka, Stubel as Matwejeff, and Frl. Jules as Mutter Thekla. On the 13th came Sie hat ihr Herz entdeckt, Frauenlist, and Ein ungeschlissener Diamant, with Käthi Schratt in all. She said goodbye, on the 14th, in Cyprienne, but had another farewell at the matinée on the 18th, in the triple bill formerly listed. She shines, in my imagination, "like a rich jewel in an Ethiop's ear."

Johann Strauss's delightful Der lustige Krieg (The Merry War) had its first New York performance on March 15th, with Mlle. Jules as Artemisia, Jenny Stubel as Violetta, Link as Sebastiani, Adolfi as Balthasar Groot, Mühlbauer as Carlo, Klein as Umberto Spinola, Kren as Durazzo, Frl. Seebold as Else, Karl Meyer as Van Scheelen, and Frl. Schamidatus as Theresa Balbi. At the matinée, on the 16th, Maria Stuart formed the bill;

Minna von Barnhelm performed similar service on the 22nd, and Uriel Acosta on the 25th — this last with Bassermann and Frl. Brandmann. The Merry War was waged successfully for several weeks, ceasing on April 19th. For the Actors' Fund matinée, on April 3rd, a triple bill combined Der Raubmörder, Umsonst and Salon Pitzelberger. Heinrich Conried again, on the 17th of April, enacted Dr. Klaus. Jenny Stubel sang farewell, on the 19th, in Der lustige Krieg.

And then, on the 20th, back from conquering the hearts of German-America came the triumphant Marie Geistinger for eleven farewell performances. On the 20th, 21st and 22nd, she gave Der Seecadet, with Das verwunschene Schloss for matinée delight, on the 22nd. Her last week was devoted to Boccaccio (April 24th), Drei Paar Schuhe (25th), Die Tochter der Hölle (26th), Die Näherin (27th), Die Fledermaus (28th), Der Seecadet (matinée 29th) and Damenkrieg and Die schöne Galathee (evening of the 29th). On Sunday, April 30th, Mme. Geistinger said farewell, in a concert for the benefit of Victor Helly, "cashier." With Boccaccio, on May 1st, for the benefit of the chorus, and with Marie Seebold (first time in the title-rôle) the interesting season ended. On May 2nd, a supplementary season started, with Herrmann, Mlle. Addie, E. D. Davies, Awata Katsnoshin, and the Stirk Family of Bicycle Riders. This season closed on May 13th, leaving my pen free for other exercises till 1882–83 rang up again at the German Thalia; except that I must record a benefit, on May 30th, for Signor Lotti, at which Der Freischütz enlisted Emma Juch, Cecilia Hecht, Christian Fritsch and J. Weinlich, with Max Maretzek directing. When did we last meet either Lotti or Weinlich? And Martha was sung on June 10th, with Miss Juch, Bertha Ricci, Carl Sternberg, Weinlich and Michael Loé — certainly not a startling array.

GERMANIA THEATER (LATE WALLACK'S), 1881–1882

Wallack having moved his company from the seat of its great fame, his deserted mansion passed, by arrangement with Wallack, under the control of Adolf Neuendorff, who transferred to this large house the activities he had formerly pursued at the little theatre in Fourteenth Street. Renaming the old Wallack's, he opened it, with high hope, on September 15, 1881, as the Germania Theater. It was a gala occasion. Neuendorff, greeted with acclaim, led the orchestra in Beethoven's Consecration of the House. Then followed a Festspiel, or Festival Prologue, by Wilhelm Müller, with music by Neuendorff, in which Frl. Bensberg appeared as Columbia, Frl. Berg as Germania, Frl. Etienne as das Drama, Frl. Necker as das Lustspiel, Frl. von Januschowsky as das Singspiel, Raberg as die deutsche Industrie, Meery as der Ackerbau, and Kessler as Rip van Winkle. The play of the evening was Der Compagnon (by L'Arronge), with one of those long casts so usual

[498]

in German drama; but a repetition of it will apprise the reader of the personnel of the company:

August Bosz	Herr Merten	Friedrich	Herr Rank
Mathilde	Frl. Berg	Tante Röper	Frl. Umlauf
Adele	Frl. Bensberg	Gleichenberg	Herr Wachsner
Oskar Schumann	Herr Meery	Semmelmann	Herr Kummer
Bernhard Bosz	Herr Raberg	Der Prediger	Herr Lieb
Fanny Bosz	Frl. Etienne	Sturm	Herr Stultz
Betty Bosz	Frl. Gross	Dr. Lind	Herr Langenbach
Cäcilie Bosz	Frl. Lieb	Frau Lind	Frl. Langner
Ferdinand Winkler	Herr Sauer	Böller	Herr Müller
Wittwe Lerch	Frl. Schmitz	Frau Böller	Frl. Renicke
Louise Lerch	Frl. Wagner	Ein Arbeiter	Herr Heinemann
Marie	Frl. von Januschowsky		

This play, with the festival prologue, was repeated on the 16th and 17th; on the afternoon of the 17th and on Monday, the 19th, the prevailing craze for operetta brought La Fille de Mme. Angot, with von Januschowsky as Clairette, Frl. Schrötter as Mlle. Lange, Weiss as Ange Pitou, and Rank as Pomponnet.   But, on the 21st (he closed the house on the 20th), Neuendorff atoned for adherents of the classics and only the classics by reviving Don Carlos, with Philipp as the hero, Fischer as Philipp II, Frl. Bensberg as Elisabeth, Frl. Berg as Herzogin von Olivarez, Frl. Liebich as Prinzessin Eboli, Merten as Alba, and with, as the Herald stated, next day, a small audience.   On the 22nd and on the afternoon of the 24th, Frl. Wienrich appeared as Frou-Frou, with Frl. Bensberg as Louise, Resemann as von Sartorys, Philipp as von Valreas, Frl. Liebich as Baronin von Cambri, and Raberg as Brigard.   Mamsell Angot disported on the evenings of the 23rd and 24th.   The Germania closed on Monday, the 26th, and, on the 27th, revived Der Schleichhändler, giving with it Hoffänger for two evenings. On the 30th, came Unsere Frauen, by von Moser and Schönthan, good for a few repetitions, with Raberg, Frl. Berg, Frl. Necker, Frl. Wagner, Sauer, Meery, Frl. Bensberg, Frl. Wienrich, Resemann, Philipp, Merten, Frl. Gross and Frl. Umlauf — evidently a rose-bud garden of girls, with few men admitted.   Lortzing's opera, Der Wildschütz, presented, on October 5th, Steinbach, Frl. Schmitz, Weiss, Frl. Schrötter, Frl. Lorenz, Max Schultz, Georgine von Januschowsky (as Gretchen) and Rank (as Pancratius).   This, also, was repeated, till, on the 11th, Unsere Frauen came back.   On October 12th was promised, "for the first time on any stage," Julius Rosen's comedy, Ein Ideal, with Raberg as Karl von Kurzweil, Frl. Schmitz as his wife, Frl. Wienrich as Edith, their daughter, Merten as Josef Kurzweil, Frl. Liebich as Selma, his wife, Frl. Wagner as Ada, their daughter, Philipp as Otto Lebner, Kummer as Prettenhofer, Jonas as der junge Herr Prettenhofer, Frl. Umlauf as Frau Prettenhofer, Sauer as Hermann Schelle, Wachsner as Kohlweishing, Rank as Jacob, and Frl. Gross as Anna.   And this, likewise, had a few repetitions.

[499]

FRIEDRICH HAASE

If the Thalia was enriched by the performances of Marie Geistinger, the new Germania had reason to hope for great success with its autumn engagement of Friedrich Haase, not seen here since 1869. He appeared, on October 17th and 18th, as Narciss; on the 19th and 20th, as Harleigh, in Sie ist wahnsinnig, and as Siegel, in Der Vetter; on the 21st and 22nd, as Count Thorane in Der Königslieutenant (then still so spelled, despite our more modern usage). In Sie ist wahnsinnig, Frl. Bensberg assisted as Anna, Frl. Necker as Fanny, Raberg as John Harris, Philipp as Sir Henry Maxwell, and Sauer as Wilkens. Since Haase did not appear twice in one day, the regular actors presented for the matinée, on the 22nd, a triple bill consisting of Fortunio's Lied, with Rank, Frl. von Januschowsky, Frl. Schrötter and Frl. Schmitz; Ein Toilettengeheimniss, with Sauer, Frl. Wienrich, Rank and Frl. Necker, and Bei Wasser und Brod, with Frl. von Januschowsky, Frl. Schmitz and Rank.

The Herald, having judiciously withheld final criticism of Haase, published, on October 24th, an excellent review, from which I abstract essentials:

> Herr Haase's titles to distinction are founded, not on the fact that he presents one or two characters with overwhelming power, as Salvini, for instance, does Othello or the Gladiator, but rather because his peculiar talents enable him to enact a large variety of characters in such a manner that they do not bear the remotest resemblance to one another. To shine conspicuously on the stage in Germany versatility is the first and all important essential.... Herr Haase ... acts with nearly equal success in farce, melodrama, comedy, and the tragic *rôles* of Goethe, Schiller and Shakespeare, though it is doubtful whether as an interpreter of the latter author he would favorably compare with the best English or American tragedians.
>
> Herr Haase occupies a position of great eminence upon the German stage. He ranks with such artists as Ernst Possart, of Berlin and Munich, an actor who excels as Richard III, as Manfred, as Narciss, and other *rôles;* Barnay, the Hungarian . . . and with Lewinsky, the eminent actor of the renowned Vienna Burgtheater . . . Sonnenthal, the first actor of this same theatre, is, however, greatly Haase's superior, because to the intellect, finish and charm, which are the strong points of Haase's acting, Sonnenthal adds besides an intensity and passion which Mr. Haase possesses only in a moderate degree. But if in Adolf Sonnenthal the German stage possesses a genius superior to Friedrich Haase, the latter's individuality is so strong, so interesting, free from eccentricity, his originality so pronounced and his talent so versatile that his position on the stage of Germany is, if not the most eminent, at least unique. His personality is very magnetic, and one adjective, somewhat untranslatable, is always applied to him by Germans—*liebenswuerdig*.... In his acting he strives to establish a connection or balance between realism and idealism. In

[500]

supplying those distinguishing traits by which different characters are instantly recognized, such as 'make up' of figure and countenance, peculiarities of voice and oddities of manner, his method is like life almost to the last degree.

. . . So much of imagination, however, is coupled with these realistic touches that, despite their strict adherence to nature, one receives the impression that there is a strong element of idealism in Haase's acting. Thus in 'Narziss' the neglect of his person, the hollow gayety of his voice, the assurance of his manner, the explosive outbursts of speech, were realistic and life-like. . . . But there was now and again noticeable a wistful look in the eye, a sudden abstraction and as sudden a restlessness of manner that was very pathetic, and told the whole history of Narziss. . . . In scenes of passion, however, Herr Haase seems to follow his training, which, as already stated, was conducted by Tieck . . . when vehemence and an exaggerated loudness of voice in passionate scenes took the place of real intensity and depth of emotion. In this respect Mr. Haase is rather of that old school of which Irschick, who acted at the Thalia lately, is an exaggerated specimen. . . . Mr. Haase is hampered in tragedy by certain physical conditions, such as lack of voice. . . . The fact is that Mr. Haase is by nature destined to achieve the greatest artistic results in comedy and perhaps also in certain melodrama. His grace, finish, rare intelligence, the wealth of original detail with which he lights up the characters, the distinction of his manner and his colloquial naturalness, all these make his Seigliere, his Rochferrier (in 'Eine Partie Picquet'), his Thorane (in 'Königslieutenant'), his Klingsberg *père* and other characters of rather a higher artistic value than his Shylock, his Richard III, and other tragic characters. . . . In exhibiting acuteness of intellect rather than tumultuous passion lies Herr Haase's power."

We are now launched on the stream of Haase's varied impersonations. His second week brought (October 24th, 25th, 26th) a triple bill consisting of Ein feiner Diplomat (by W. Mejo, after Scribe), Eine kleine Gefälligkeit and Eine Partie Picquet (by Bahn, from the French), in which he acted, respectively, Gavigny, Dr. Holm and Rochferrier; on the 27th, 28th and 29th, he gave Raupach's Die Royalisten, oder die Flucht des Karl Stuart II, in which he portrayed Cromwell, with Resemann as Karl II, Meery as Wilmot, Fischer and Frl. Berg as Lord and Lady Windham, &c. We perceive again his great versatility and, possibly, his talent for *genre* sketching. The matinée, on October 29th, allowed the company to triple Fortunio's Lied, Er ist nicht eifersüchtig, and Des Löwen Erwachen. Haase, for his third week, repeated Der Königslieutenant, on October 31st, and combined, on November 1st and 2nd, Man sucht einen Erzieher and Der verbrochene Krug, in which he played Marsan and Adam, respectively. On the 3rd, 4th and 5th, he lapsed into melodrama, enacting Jean, in Der Lumpensämmler von Paris. Somehow, one might have expected from the three opening weeks of a famous star productions of plays of higher value. Der Lumpensämmler von Paris filled the first three nights of the fourth week (November 7th, 8th, and 9th), and the triple bill just cited for the second week emerged again on the 10th, 11th and 12th, with the substitution of Man sucht einen Erzieher for Ein feiner Diplomat. A Sunday concert (on the 13th) presented the Carreño-Donaldi concert troupe. Haase's fifth week began on the 14th, with, for the benefit of the Frauen-Verein, a repetition of Sie ist wahnsinnig and Der Vetter, and, on the 15th, 16th and 17th, gave us Im Vorzimmer seiner Excellenz and Die beiden Klingsberg; the 18th and 19th provided Lorbeerbaum und Bettelstab. Im Vorzimmer seiner Excellenz and Die beiden Klingsberg was repeated on the 21st and 24th, and newer matter (for this engagement) was Der alter Magister and Nach Sonnenuntergang, on the 22nd and 23rd. For a Thanksgiving matinée, on the 24th, Haase participated in a bill including Eine kleine Gefälligkeit, Eine Partie Piquet and Des Löwen Erwachen. And, at last, on the 5th, for his benefit, he ventured on something of international import — Hamlet.

And the Herald of the 26th shows why he had limited himself to lesser flames. He had played as Hamlet, before "the most brilliant audience ever gathered at a German theatre in this city, and so numerous as to fairly crowd much of the aisle space. His Hamlet was essentially that of the German stage, and had much about it that is unacceptable to English traditions." He had not "the physical attributes" necessary for Hamlet, but "his reading gave evidence of a carefully thought out conception of the part, and he was at all times intellectually forcible. Accepting his German views of Hamlet, his performance was consistent and artistic." Frl. Wienrich "played Ophelia charmingly." On the 26th, the star went back to Lorbeerbaum und Bettelstab.

On November 28th, the company gave Krieg im Frieden, and, on the 29th, Haase repeated his impersonation of the poet, Heinrich, in Lorbeerbaum und Bettelstab. On November 30th, and December 1st, 2nd and 3rd, he enacted the sentimental Marquis, to the Margarethe of Frl. Wienrich, in Der Roman eines jungen Edelmannes. The last nights of the distinguished star began on December 6th, 7th and 8th, when he played the Marquis von Seiglière, in Das Fräulein von Sieglière; and, for his farewell appearances (December 9th and 10th) he put on Der Kaufmann von Venedig, in which, as Shylock, he had the support of Frl. Bensberg as Porzia, Frl. Necker as Nerissa, Kren as the Duke, Meery as Arragon, Merten as Morocco, Fischer as Antonio, Sauer as Gratiano, Resemann as Bassanio, Jonas as Lanzelot, Philipp as Lorenzo, and Max Schultz as Old Gobbo.

And that ended an engagement from which much had been expected, but which, from all accounts, resulted in financial loss that terribly hampered the success of Neuendorff's ambitious venture in his newer, larger, more expensive quarters. Mr. E. H. Zeydel (The German Theater in New York City) states that Haase's visit "was a distinct disappointment.... His ar-

[502]

rogance rendered him deaf to Neuendorff's good advice . . . and he insisted on presenting old plays that had lost their popular appeal many years ago." And he received forty per cent of the net profits during his stay.   Like many other disappointed foreigners, he wrote letters, after his return to Germany, in which he "attributed to American audiences an utter lack of artistic sense and of appreciation for true art."   Only "frivolous entertainment" could hope for success, and "the name of Marie Geistinger echoed thru the country in tones that silenced the roar of Niagara."

On December 12th a benefit for the German Rechtsschütz-Verein brought back Der Rattenfänger von Hameln; it had renewed life through the 19th, and yielded the stage on the 20th, to Wilkens's farce, Hopfenrath's Erben, which then began a run of six nights, followed, on the 27th and subsequently by a renewed Rattenfänger von Hameln.   In the new farce appeared Resemann, Frl. Schmitz, Frl. Wienrich, Weiss, Merten, Rank, and, of course, Georgine von Januschowsky, a bright favourite in the company.   A matinée benefit for sufferers from the burning of the Ringtheater, Vienna, promised, on December 21st, Minnie Hauk, John McCullough, and members of the German force.   January 2nd provided — possibly to fit Drei Paar Schuhe — Die Galoschen des Glück's (The Lucky Overshoes), by Jacobsen and Girndt), with Frl. Wienrich as the Genius of Fortune, Resemann as the Genius of Sorrow, Rank as Kullrich, Frl. Schmitz as Lotte, Frl. Wagner as Marie, Georgine von Januschowsky as Helene, Frl. Lieb as Fritz, Merten as Muggelberg, Hartzheim as Charles, Weiss as Francis, and Müller as Wilhelm.   On the 9th, Neuendorff presented an operetta by himself (with text by H. Italiener) — Don Quixote, with Merten in the title-rôle, Weiss as Alonzo, Frl. Schrötter as Diana, Frl. von Januschowsky (a charming person) as Pasquillo, Hertzheim as Guggillo, Rank (a funny comedian) as Sancho Panza, Frl. Schmitz (also excellent) as Rapsode, Kren as Rufo, Frl. Lorenz as Dulcinea, and Steinbuch as Gabrielo.   When it came to a question of operetta, I fear that the Thalia Theater bore the palm; nevertheless, Don Quixote had several repetitions.   On January 20th we attended Das Stiftungsfest, and on the 21st, Die Räuber had Kessler as Maximilian, Resemann as Karl, Raberg as Franz, and Frl. Wienrich as Amalia.

On the 23rd, Der Leibarzt (The Prince's Physician), by Leopold Günther, employed a large cast, including Herren Resemann, Fischer, Raberg, Sauer, Meery, Schultz, Wachsner and Jonas, with Frl. Liebich, Frl. Wagner, Frl. Bensberg, Frl. Berg, Frl. Etienne, Frl. Röper, and Frl. Gross.   On the afternoon of the 26th, a benefit for the Lady Elks presented Marie Hunter (balcony scene from Romeo and Juliet), Daisy Ramsden, Patti Rosa, Henrietta Markstein, Lester and Allen, Ella Wesner, the French Twin Sisters and Jacques Kruger.   Die Prinzessin von Bagdad (seen previously in English, at the Fifth Avenue, as Lionette, with Fanny Davenport) enlisted, on January 27th, at the Germania, Frl. Bensberg as Lionette, Philipp as Jean

[503]

de Hun, Meery as Nourady, Raberg as Godier, Sauer as Treverle, Fischer as Richard, and Kessler as the Commissioner.

February 2nd repeated Hopfenrath's Erben, and the 3rd and certain following evenings presented a new piece, Der Erbonkel (by G. Henle). The benefit of Georgine von Januschowsky revived, on February 8th, Lumpaci Vagabundus, repeated on the 9th; and matter equally antiquated adorned Albert Kessler's benefit, on the 10th, in Rosenmüller und Finke, given again on the 11th. The Germania was a fine, large theatre, but its offerings were frequently very thin. Benefits now called, in cheerless February; Bernhard Rank's, on the 13th, gave Des Lebens Mai and Die falsche Patti — a bill repeated on the 14th; on the 15th, Claudius Merten, for his benefit, offered Inspector Bräsig. In Des Lebens Mai, Merten appeared as Läderitz, Frl. von Januschowsky as Adele, Meery as Fritz, Frl. Berg as Lena, Frl. Schmitz as Mme. Duval, Wachsner as Nöhlig, &c. On the 18th, Helene Bensberg profited (I hope) with her benefit offering of Die Tochter des Herrn Fabricius.

Franziska Ellmenreich; Adelina Patti

The period since the departure of Haase had been meagre and lean. On February 20th, hope revived with the début of a talented actress, Franziska Ellmenreich, who came forward in Die Valentine, Freytag's "rather musty" play, as the Herald called it, next day. On February 22nd and 23rd, the new star was Jane Eyre, and, according to the Herald, the part was "never more adequately presented in New York." She played, on the 25th and 26th, Die widerspänstige Frau (or Die bezähmte Widerspänstige), with Fischer as Baptista, Frl. Necker as Bianca, Meery as Lucentio, Reinau as Petruchio, Lichtenthal as Hortenzio, Raberg as Tranio, Merten as Grumio, and Rank as Curtis — this last part often played in English by a woman.

And now, on February 27th, descended on the Germania a glory in person of Adelina Patti. The great singer in November had arrived in New York, after an absence of twenty years, and had almost failed under a wretched management of which I shall speak under the caption of concerts; the efficient Henry E. Abbey had saved the situation, and now, after a successful concert tour, presented the *diva* in a short series of operatic performances. The vocal artists who had appeared with her in concert almost wrecked the artistic values of the operas now presented; but the incomparable Patti carried everything before her. The tenor was Nicolini, who would have been her husband, if her husband, the Marquis de Caux, had permitted a divorce; whatever he may once have been, vocally, Nicolini in 1882 was a drag that only Patti's affection for him could have endured. The audiences here generally suffered when he sang. The famous soprano made her first appearance in many years in the city that first recognised her greatness as a *prima donna* in one of her most famous rôles, that of Violetta, in La Traviata, a part in which, all things considered, she was incomparable, and in which no one has ever effaced her, at least in magnificence of song.   Her support was wretched, including Nicolini, Mlle. Montegriffo, Mlle. Dingeon, Salvati (as Germont), Pinto and Barili, with d'Auria as conductor.

I shall quote, under division of Concerts, critical opinions of Patti's *rentrée* in concert in the preceding November.   The Herald, on the 28th, states that the audience at La Traviata was "nothing like so select as that at her first concert," but it was financially "solid."   It was a "mistake to display her brilliancy against such a fustian background" as that offered by her support; Nicolini frequently sang off the key, despite Patti's efforts to keep him in tune.   Though she had sung Violetta better at Covent Garden, "Mme. Patti even a little tired is beyond comparison with other singers, and when she rose to the exigencies of the supreme moments . . . her glorious voice came forth with marvellous beauty and effect and she was greeted with long and loud applause."   When freed from concerted numbers with her inadequate support, she "was, as she always is, incomparable in her exquisite vocalization."   To all this, I who heard Patti many times, wholeheartedly cry Amen!

On the 2nd of March, the glorious one gave another of her most famous rôles, one that she seemed born to play — Rosina, in Il Barbiere di Siviglia. On the 3rd, the Herald states that her acting "was as light, graceful and animated as the music which she sings, and so her impersonation was in faultless harmony, vocally and dramatically.   Her singing was almost beyond criticism.   Mme. Patti has not only a lovely voice and a perfect style, but she has a superlatively fine taste and an artistic sense which — last night at least — prevented her even attempting anything which she could not perform to perfection.   Moreover, Rossini's sparkling music is peculiarly well suited to her style, and she renders it with an ease, a grace and a brilliancy which are unequalled by any other singer now on the operatic stage."

The Times, which this season backed and filled in critical opinion of Patti's singing (it could not forgive her for asking a ten dollar admission fee at her opening concerts) admitted, on February 28th, the vocal beauty of the diva's Violetta: "A voice of perfect evenness, of marvellous brilliancy, power, and flexibility, and absolutely true as to intonation, an enunciation of extraordinary distinctness, and a mastery of the art of phrasing" distinguished the performance, but Mme. Patti "moved over the boards as beautiful, as graceful, and . . . as unimpressed and unimpressive as a statue. . . . All Violetta's numbers were rendered with unimpeachable correctness and taste; not one of them sank into the hearts of her listeners." The critic proceeds to show the changes that twenty years had brought in Patti's voice — a voice at first "simply matchless" in "evenness of tone-color, a richness of quality, and a flexibility the like of which no living singer could boast of"; but, in passing from the lighter rôles of her youth into the more dramatic rôles of Verdi her limitations became evident. On March 3rd, however, this reserved voice of the Times yielded to the spell of Patti's incomparable Rosina: "It was a remarkable triumph. . . . In her action Mme. Patti was exceedingly felicitous, her by-play being amusing and graceful, and she was in superb voice throughout the evening . . . she showed a wonderful command of her voice and an absolute mastery of the art of vocalization. Her 'Una voce' was a delight to every hearer, and in the singing lesson, where she interpolated the 'Shadow Song' . . . and 'Home, Sweet Home,' she was all that the most exacting musician could ask. The singing was as perfect as if it had been mathematically arranged, and at the same time was neither cold nor unimpassioned. In a word Mme. Patti achieved a triumph."

With the reader's permission, I will gather into a posy the account of this Patti season. On March 6th, she sang in Faust, and once more I call on the enthusiastic Herald:

> The short phrase with which she makes her first entrance . . . was sung with incomparable beauty of tone and charmingly phrased. The "King of Thule" was sung with a graceful spontaneity and ease that are but rarely heard, and in the jewel song she surpassed in brilliancy of vocalization all others who have ever sung the part. The love duets . . . were sung with more feeling than is Mme. Patti's wont to sing. Here the truly golden timbre of her voice was of irresistible effect. But after that, in the church scene, and during the death of Valentin, Mme. Patti's emotion (passion there was none) was sincere. In the last act the "Anges Radieux" was superbly sung, first in devout *sotto voce* tones and then with a tragic abandon that was thrillingly effective.

Of course Patti was chiefly renowned as a *coloratura* singer, and her Margherita, charming as it was (I speak from personal recollection) was not one of her great rôles; neither, I fancy, was Leonora, in Il Trovatore, which she sang on the 9th (I never heard her in this). Her support in Il Trovatore included Florence Rice Knox, Nicolini and Salvati; no wonder that the audience, according to the Herald, was "not enthusiastic." For her last appearances Patti gave two of her most notable assumptions — Lucia di Lammermoor (March 13th), and Violetta, in La Traviata (16th). In Lucia, we remember, she began her great operatic career, in the Academy of Music, on November 24, 1859. The memory of Patti in those two rôles, as I heard her in them a few years later, is one of the delights of my life. With a repetition of Lucia, on April 3rd, before a crowded, almost hysterical audience, she said good-bye. Next year, she sang at the Academy, with Mapleson's company. The admission for the short term at the Germania was $8 for the orchestra and first three rows of the balcony; $5 for the remaining rows of the balcony; $4 for the first three rows of the second balcony, and $3 for the remaining rows.   For the appearance on April 3rd, $6 was the highest rate.   The houses were usually full, though not always crowded.   But, so far as Patti was concerned, such flawless singing had not been heard in New York since she left us twenty years before — and not then, since her art in those two decades had developed and matured.

I go bak to Franziska Ellmenreich, who appeared on evenings in which Patti did not sing.   On February 28th and March 1st, the new star played Leopoldine, in Der beste Ton, and Clothilde, in Eine anonyme Correspondenz.   On March 3rd and 4th, Die Fremde (L'Etrangère) enlisted Meery as the Duc de Septmonts, Frl. Ellmenreich as Catharine, Fischer as Mauriceau, Frl. Wienrich as Noemi Clarkson, Merten as Professor Dr. Remonin, and Frl. Berg as Marquise de Rumières.   The star, on the 7th and 8th, enacted Helena, in Die Feenhände.   On the 10th and 11th, in Emilia Galotti, she doubled the rôles of Emilia and Countess Orsina, with Fischer as Odoardo, Frl. Berg as Claudia, Meery as Gonzaga, Raberg as Marmelli, Merten as Angelo, &c.   Die Fremde figured again on the 14th, Emilia Galotti on the 15th, and, on the 17th, Frl. Ellmenreich acted Walburga, in Die Geier-Wally, supported by Kummer, Merten, Sauer, Frl. Schmitz, Raberg, Meery, Fischer, Reinau, Wachsner, Frl. Wienrich, Rank, and Frl. Wagner in leading rôles.   This had some repetitions.   Inspector Bräsig again did duty on March 22nd, and, on the 27th, Odette, that recent quasi-success at Daly's, came to the Germania, with Frl. Ellmenreich in the title-rôle, Reinau as Count Clermont-Latour, Frl. Necker as Berangère, Kessler as General de Clermont-Latour, Sauer as Philippe de la Roche, Merten as Bechamel, Lichtenthal as Cardailhan, Frl. Bensberg as Juliette, Frl. Schmitz as Mme. Morizot, Meery as de Meryan, Frl. Wagner as Olga, and Frl. Berg as the Baroness Conaro-Doria; many others appeared in minor rôles.   The Herald, next day was enthusiastic about Frl. Ellmenreich, who "played with marvellous power and a thorough consistency. . . . The almost tigerish anger and wild despair of the woman when driven at bay . . . the scene in the gambling hell, when she paints the picture of her lost home and with a moan of agony . . . lays bare to Philip her unhappiness and life of agony was as pathetic and deeply touching as it well could be. . . . The occasion showed most fully how accomplished an actress this lady is."   On March 29th and 30th, she played Gretchen, to the Faust of Reinau, the Mephisto of Raberg, the Valentin of Meery, the Martha of Frl. Schmitz, the Wagner of Fischer, the Siebel of Merten, and the Spirit of Earth of Kessler.   The dramatic performances, under the stimulus of Frl. Ellmenreich's visit, were certainly increasing in interest.   On April 4th and 5th, she acted Adrienne Lecouvreur, and, on the 6th and 7th Käthchen von Heilbronn.   For the Actors' Fund matinée, on the 3rd, a triple bill allured. In Maria Stuart, on April 8th, Frl. Ellmenreich had, of course, the title-rôle,

[507]

with Reinau as Leicester, Frl. Berg as Elisabeth, Raberg as Burleigh and Meery as Mortimer. In Kneisel's Die Tochter der Hölle, on the 10th, Frl. Ellmenreich was Clara Wallfried, daughter of Belial. The benefit of the star, on the 14th, presented her in the third act of Die Widerspänstige Frau (Die bezähmte Widerspänstige), and three acts of Faust. Hermann Raberg's benefit on the 17th revived Das Mädel ohne Geld.

Back to an admiring public had come, on April 18th, Carl Sontag, as Richard Weiss, in Dir wie mir, and as Dr. Wespe, two favourites of his last year's repertoire; on the 19th, he was again Conrad Bolz, in Die Journalisten. On the 20th, 21st and 22nd, Hazel Kirke enlisted Frl. Berg as Lady Travers, Sauer as Carringford, Merten as Rodney, Hans Meery (who translated the play) as Isocrates Grün (poor Pittacus!), Sontag as Dunstan, Frl. Schmitz as Margaret (Mercy), Frl. Necker as Lilly Linden (Dolly Dutton), Rank as Barney, and Frl. Ellmenreich as Hazel. Sontag and Frl. Ellmenreich appeared together, on April 24th, as Donna Diana and Perin; on the 25th they were Shakespeare's Benedick and Beatrice in German. Bürgerlich und Romantisch was offered on the 26th, and, on the 27th, Maria und Magdalena, a comedy by Paul Lindau, with Frl. Ellmenreich as Maria, and Sontag as Professor Laurentius. Decidedly, the Germania was looking up. Emilia Galotti, on the 28th, must have gratified sticklers for the classics, with Frl. Ellmenreich again doubling the rôles of Emilia and Gräfin Orsina, and with Sontag as Marinelli. On the 29th, Der Königslieutenant allowed one to compare Sontag with the departed Haase; Frl. Ellmenreich was Goethe. The stars again did Hazel Kirke, on May 1st, for the benefit of Eugenie Schmitz. Sontag and Frl. Ellmenreich said farewell, on the 4th of May, in Das Glas Wasser. Bertha Necker's benefit, on the 5th, presented Bassermann as Freund Fritz. The last night of German plays fell on May 6th, with Mein Leopold (benefit of the ushers and door-keeper).

ENGLISH OPERA AT THE GERMANIA

Thus ended Neuendorff's first ambitious season in his large, new home; a season we now know, of perplexity and financial doubt. He rented his house, beginning on May 8th, to the J. W. Norcross Opera Company, which began with the simply inescapable The Mascot. Dora Wiley appeared as Bettina, Ella Caldwell as Frederic, Pauline Hall as Fiametta, Richard Golden as Rocco, W. T. Carleton as Pippo, and J. W. Norcross, Jr. as Lorenzo XVII, a decidedly interesting cast. Henry Molten had been expected to sing Frederic, but did not arrive in time to do so; by May 12th, the Herald stated that he was in the rôle. The Mascot ran to June 24th, when a triple cast appeared in it, including Dora Wiley, Fay Templeton, Louise Brosi. Pauline Hall, Alice Vane, Maggie Duggan, Annie Gunter, W. T. Carleton, Henry McCreery, Henry Molten, &c.

[508]

KÄTHI SCHRATT

F. HAASE AS HAMLET

FRANZISKA ELLMENREICH

MINNIE HAUK
IN L'AFRICAINE

EMMA JUCH IN
FAUST

ANTONIO GALASSI
IN L'AFRICAINE

MADAME GALASSI
AS AMNERIS

WILLIAM RIGNOLD

PAOLINA ROSSINI
AS AÏDA

On June 27th came the first version here in English of Strauss's The Merry War, the cast including W. T. Carleton, Dora Wiley, Belle Cole, Louise Paullin, Richard Golden, Gustav Adolfi (the comedian from the Thalia, who made a great hit), and a ballet led by Adele Cornalba. It enjoyed a very successful run, ending on July 22nd; I sincerely hope that profit accrued therefrom for the harassed Neuendorff. The Merry War was carried, on July 1st, to the Metropolitan Alcazar, for a continuance of the town's favours. In closing the Germania for 1881–82, we may be pardoned a feeling of anxiety for Neuendorff.

OTHER GERMAN PLAYS, 1881–1882

The Concordia shall begin the record in this division with Das Fest der Handwerker (September 3rd and 5th) and with a bill whose concluding feature (September 10, 1881) was Ein alter Fuchs in der Falle. On September 18th, the New York Turn-Verein presented Königin Margot; on October 9th this latter organisation gave Rosenmüller und Finke, along with a concert by Josephine Jansen, Bertha Robert, Michael Loé and Gustav Bremser. During the rest of the season, the Concordia usually specifies nothing, in its advertisements in the Staats-Zeitung, as to the farces included in its programmes. But the Turnhalle is more than usually detailed in promises. There, on November 17th, a benefit for the widow and children of Heinrich Unger assembled Josephine Jansen, Helene Weingarten, Frau Schreiner-Kronfeld, Max Lube, and Gustav Schultz, and presented Die Macht der Arbeit, with Clara Schmager, Gustav Kahn and Isabella Maret. The play at this busy house, on November 20th, was Er muss auf's Land; and thither, on November 26th, came the Dramatic Verein, Wir, in Zehn Mädchen und kein Mann, Einer muss heirathen and Der gerade Weg der beste — assuredly an amusing collocation of titles. The Turn-Verein itself played Der Bibliothekar, on January 15th; Hans Dampf, a Schwank by Aug. Schaeffer, essayed this stage on February 5th. On March 9th, the pupils of Frau Lang's school bravely encountered the difficulties of Der Freischütz. If only the Concordia had been as specific in announcing its every Theatervorstellung!

On April 2nd, Dorf und Stadt came to the stage at Turnhalle, and, on April 30th, Die Karlsschüler. A benefit arranged by Elise Unger and the company brought us, on May 21st, Hasemann's Töchter; on the 3rd of June, a benefit for N. Rosenbaum offered as lure Von Stufe zu Stufe. Obviously a Hebrew company was here in late summer. The Staats-Zeitung carries advertisement for August 12th of a Hebrew Opera and Dramatic Company under direction of the seventeen-year-old "comic," Leon Golubok, who was to play the eighty-year-old witch, in the opera, Die Hexe — a performance for the benefit of ten poor families of Russian immigrants. In September

[509]

this company inaugurated Hebrew drama at the Bowery Garten Theater. The Hebrew invasion of our theatre began, so far as I know, with these performances.

Terrace Garden (Lexington Avenue Opera House), 1881–1882

Terrace Garden (or the Lexington Avenue Opera House, as it was frequently called) offered important attractions in the season we are discussing. On September 17th, the Schillerbund held its Sommernachtsfest. Anna-Lise, followed by a ball, invited on October 17, 1881, for ever-crying charity. The opening ball of the season came, in due course, on the 27th; the 30th brought the New York Männerchor for a Stiftungsfest, concert and ball. The Mozart Musical Union met here, on November 29th, for a concert and subsequent ball. On the 15th, the Amateur League acted an original Old Soldiers. On February 20th, the M. G. V. Eichenkranz danced here its masked ball; on the following night the Männerchor followed in like festivity. April 9th found here a benefit for the French Children's Society, with Marie Vachot, Marie Vanoni, Juignet, Blanche Roosevelt, &c. The farewell of G. Adolfi presented, on May 5th, Die 73 Kreuzer des Herrn Stützelberger, with a cast including Adolfi, Lube, Frl. Lindemann, C. Maier (sic), O. Meyer, Prätorius and Frl. Umberti; a concert followed, and the bill ended with von Suppé's operetta, Flotte Bursche, sung by Mathilde Cottrelly, Frl. Meyer, Frl. Hecht, Lube, Frl. Schamidatus and Adolfi. English performances here will be found under the captions of Miscellaneous Entertainments and Musical Miscellany.

And now came a summer treat to the place in shape of Neuendorff's company from the Germania Theater (late Wallack's). On June 9th it began with von Moser's one-act Kaudel's Gardinenpredigten, and Papa hat's erlaubt (by L'Arronge, with music by Bial). Fifty cents admitted to the show, with an extra quarter for a reserved seat. Performances were listed for Mondays, Wednesdays and Fridays. On June 14th we had Romeo auf dem Bureau and Der Hahn im Dorfe. The third night (June 16th) was devoted to Die Dienstboten and Mamsell Uebermuth (by Bahn, with music by Michaelis). The theatre, we learned, was connected with the garden, wherein Leiboldt's military "Musikchor" performed. Succeeding evenings brought Hector and Eine verfolgte Unschuld (June 22nd), Durch and Aus Liebe zur Kunst (24th), Die eifersüchtigen and Bei Wasser und Brod (June 30th), Er soll dein Herr sein (by von Moser) and Im Wartesalon III Klasse (July 5th), Ein moderne Verhängniss and Hermann and Dorothee (July 7th). In the last-named double bill appeared Frl. Bensberg, Raberg, Merten, Frl. Schmitz, Frl. von Januschowsky, and others of the regular Germania force.

Following offerings were In Hemdsärmeln (by Günther) and Durch's Schlüsselloch (by Salingré) — these two on July 12th; Eigensinn and Holz und Blech (July 14th), Ehemann auf Probe and Der Zigeuner (July 19th), Eine kleine Erzählung ohne Namen (by C. A. Görner), and Wer ist mit (July 21st), Sperling und Sperber and Der Bombardier im Feuer (July 26th), Ein amerikanischer Duell (by von Moser) and Guten Morgen, Herr Fischer (July 28th), Tante Lotte (by J. Stinde) and Des Löwen Erwachen (August 4th), Eine Ohrfeige um jeden Preis and Offenbach's trifle, Dorothea (August 9th), Ein grosser Zwist um eine Kleinigheit (by Görner) and Dorothea (August 11th), Ein amerikanischer Duell and Des Löwen Erwachen (August 16th), Ein grosser Zwist um eine Kleinigheit and Genée's one-act Der Musikfeind (August 18th), Ein empfindlicher Mensch (by Grandjean) and Der Musikfeind (23rd), Die Feuerprobe (by Günther) and Jacobson's Faust und Gretchen (25th), Eine kleine Erzählung ohne Namen and Fritzchen und Lieschen (30th) and Das Schwert des Damokles and Im Weinberg des Herrn (by Conradi) to end the season on September 1st.   All this is interesting, especially as it shows the inexhaustible repertoire of actors who, during the preceding winter, had played in much more serious works.

I close Terrace Garden for 1881–82 with account of the concert on August 14th, of the Beethoven Männerchor, and of the "Fest" of the Schillerbund, on August 26th.

Other German Activities, 1881–1882

Perhaps we might allow the sacred concerts on Sunday, September 11, 1881, at William Schwab's Harlem Bridge Garden, 2387 Third Avenue, solemnly to usher in our discussion of the German miscellany for 1881–82. On that date, also, Elm Park welcomed the song of the Hudson Männerchor, the Melodia, the Bismarck and the Lætitia.   And now enters our story the Atalanta House, 155th Street and Eighth Avenue, with concerts every Sunday afternoon and all evenings of the happy weeks.   John Kress's Sommergarten, 55th Street, between Second and Third Avenues, must not escape us.

I ask the reader to imagine the customary activities for this year of the almost innumerable singing societies of the town — activities especially stressing the autumn Stiftungsfest, Christmas, the Carneval-Sitzung, the masked balls of mid-winter, the Easter joy, the Pfingst-Montag outings, the Sommernachtsfest in leafy grove, and the Wasserfahrt to neighbouring havens.   Engaging in some or all of these festal celebrations — celebrations so similar from year to year — were, in order of their appearance for 1881–82, in advertisements in the Staats-Zeitung, the Orden Söhne der Freiheit, the Gesangverein Oesterreich, the M. G. V. Eichenkranz, the Gesangverein Euphonia, the Veteran Gesangverein, the Allemania Männerchor, the Sing-Akademie, the New York Männerchor, the Mozart Männerchor, the Cordialia Verein, the Arion Society, the Haydn Amateur Musical Society, the Mainzer Carneval-Verein, the Mozart Musical Union, the Helvetia Männerchor, the New Yorker Sängerrunde, the Schillerbund, the

[511]

Schleswig-Holsteinischer Verein, the Bloomingdale Turnverein (not, of course, necessarily musical in purpose), the Concordia Männerchor, the Kölner Carnevals-Gesellschaft, the Beethoven Männerchor, the Gesangverein Germania, etc. The list is impressive, if for no other reason, as a social document. The halls in which the organisations met were Wendel's Assembly Rooms, the Teutonia or Germania Assembly Rooms, Geib's Walhalla, the Beethoven Männerchor Rooms, Harmony Hall, Essex Street, and Turn-Halle, Fourth Street. Of course the reader knows the names of parks and groves in which the summer night festivals winged the happy hours away.

Some of these functions were too imposing to be shuffled into a mere catalogue. For instance, the concert and ball of the Cordialia Verein, availing itself, in November, at Beethoven Männerchor Hall, of the assistance of Marie Salvotti, Frl. Wolf, Frl. Hirsch and J. Flidig; or the regular concerts of the Arion Society and the Liederkranz, in their own quarters. The first concert of the Liederkranz, on November 20th, gave Max Bruch's Das Lied von der Glocke, Emma Juch, Miss Henne, Graff and F. Steins figuring in the bill; and I call attention to the concert and ball of the Haydn Amateur Musical Society, at Wendel's, on November 27th, with Steinbuch and Ida Klein. The greater functions of the Arion and the Liederkranz I have treated under the caption of Concerts; they became too universal to be confined to Kleindeutschland.

The Atlantic Garten, firmly fixed at 50 Bowery, offered, in October, Lena Ravené, C. A. Lefebre, Conrady (tenor), and Marie Roller's Damen-Kapelle; Liberati joined in January. The attractions in early February were Elsa Alberti (opera singer), Ignatz Conrady, Liberati and Marie Roller. And very minor functions sometimes opened Parepa Hall. Here I mention the twenty-fifth jubilee of Carl Sahm, conductor of the Mozart-Verein, who, on April 2nd, at the Germania Assembly Rooms, rested on the assured aid of Carl Alves, John Bolze, the Arion Quartett, Carl Steinbuch (baritone), the Mozart-Verein, the Cordialia, Frl. Anna Benziger (soprano), the Yorkville Männerchor, the Rheinischer Sängerbund, the Theodor Körner Liedertafel, the Bloomingdale Eintracht and the Badischer Männerchor — certainly Kleindeutschland strongly in evidence! At the Sängerrunde concert, on April 23rd, in the Germania Assembly Rooms, appeared Agnes Florence, Emile Berghold, Steinbuch, Bolze, &c. Miss Florence also sang for the Schillerbund. Ida Klein and Sophie See had assisted, on the 16th, the Haydn Amateur Musical Society.

And now for an early opening of the summer gardens or a continuance of the winter resorts into spring and summer, all offering refreshment musical and liquid — Theiss's Concerts, Huber's Prospect Garten, Günther's Pavilion, Schüler's Palm Garten, etc. Ferd. Goebel's Sommergarten (57th Street and the East River) was presenting in latest May the Austrian National Sänger-Gesellschaft Steiermarck. Künstler-Halle, Chrystie Street, with June zithers,

Germania Garten (with Bertha Ravené, Herr Mostroff, and Leiboldt's "beliebte" Kapelle), Wendel's Elm Park (with every Sunday a concert in both the Park and the upper hall, supplied by a Wiener Damen Orchester and the Military Band of Louis See), the Atalanta Casino (155th Street and Eighth Avenue), what a variety, my Herren! On July 2nd, at Jones Wood Colosseum, the twenty-fifth jubilee of Joseph Weinlich enlisted Christian Fritsch, Max Treuman, Emma Juch and Bertha Ricci — the best group in this section of my story. The Bloomingdale Liederkranz, whose name I would fain eternise, had its picnic and Sommernachtsfest, on July 24th, at Wendel's Elm Park. And, in mid-August Don Ferreyra was man-flute again at Goebel's Sommergarten. The Plattdeutsches Volksfest made glad August 14th, 15th and 16th, at Sulzer's Harlem River Park (126th Street and Second Avenue), and the Little Paradise, H. Bernhardt's Sommergarten, at First Avenue, between 117th and 118th Streets, was blandly advertised as the "most pleasing and popular family establishment in Harlem" — as, for aught I know, it may have been. The Arion Society held its Sommernachtsfest and *bal champêtre* on September 2nd, at Washington Park, Jones Wood, stressing living pictures, fireworks and illuminations; and the Bayerisches Volksfest took three days, at Sulzer's Harlem River Park, to work off its excitement — August 21st, 22nd and 23rd. I end this phase of my story with a reference to Morrisania Schützen Park and Club House, at 170th Street and Boston Avenue. We are moving uptown!

FRENCH MISCELLANY; ITALIANS, 1881–1882

The autumn of 1881 comes to us with a dying fall, as of almost nothing accomplished by the French, except, of course, in Paola Marié's opéra-bouffe. On October 23rd, at Irving Hall, the Helvetian choral society gave a concert and ball, with the assistance of Mme. Vanoni, Max Treumann, Miss Montegriffo and Antonia Henne. L'Espérance, on November 6th, in the same hall, also functioned in a concert and ball, A. Dupin directing; and there was to be a *"surprise extraordinaire pour les dames."* Irving Hall housed also, on December 3rd, the ninth concert and ball of the Cercle Musical et Philanthropique de l'Orphéon Français, F. Groux serving as director. We may dance more frequently in the early nights of the new year; at the ball of the Union Fraternelle Française (Teutonia Assembly Rooms, January 15th); at that of the Cercle Français de l'Harmonie (Academy of Music, January 16th); at that of the Huron and Idaho Tribe, 35, 36 (Irving Hall, January 21st); at that of La Gaieté Française, with its concert, involving Mme. Vanoni, Montegriffo, G. Galloni, Lencioni and Liberati (January 29th, at Ferrero's Rooms); at that of L'Amitié (Academy of Music, January 30th); at that of the Société Suisse Générale (Teutonia Assembly Rooms, February 2nd); at that of the Société Culinaire Philanthropique (February 7th, Academy of Music); at that of La Concorde

(Tammany Hall, February 18th); finally (March 2nd) at that of the Société Israelite Française de Secours Mutuels (in Irving Hall).

Thenceforward the Messager invites to nothing till the festival, concert and ball given by the Société des Ex-Refugiés de la Commune et l'Internationale, for the benefit of the French *asile laïque*, on the anniversary of the Revolution of Paris, March 18, 1871; Mme. Vanoni assisted. La Sincérité, aided by L'Harmonie Espagnole, had a ball, on March 25th, in Irving Hall. Where had Sincérité been, since last we met it? A union of French societies gave, on April 9th, at Terrace Garden, a concert for the Children's Asylum, at which we were promised Marie Vachot, the Montegriffos, Lencioni, Marie Vanoni, Juignet and Blanche Roosevelt; April 15th proffered, at Irving Hall, the *bal d'invitation* of the Bataillon des Gardes Lafayette. And April went off the calendar (24th–29th, inclusive) with a bazaar, at Irving Hall for the Société Française de Bienfaisance. Paul Juignet's concert and *bal de printemps*, on May 21st, at Irving Hall, advertised assistance from Mlle. A. Bettini, Henrietta Markstein, Marie Vanoni, the Family Martens (with, "first time in ten years," the Cat Duet), L. Gottschalk, Juignet, Carrano (flute), Max Schwab and S. Guerra (leader of the orchestra). And, on Sunday, June 25th, La Concorde sailed up the Hudson.

La fête nationale du 14 Juillet, in Lion Park, enlisted the Société Française de Bienfaisance, the Bataillon des Gardes Lafayette, the Cercle Français de l'Harmonie, L'Amitié, La Sincérité, O. F., La Union Alsacienne, the Société Chorale L'Espérance, the Union Franco-Américaine, the Union de Hudson County, New Jersey, the Clémente Amitié Cosmopolite, the Athénée Français and the Société Patriotique Alsace-Lorraine — an imposing list that leaves one wondering as to what French societies could have been left for the celebration, on the same day, in Jones Wood Colosseum and Washington Park, of the same patriotic 14th. Leaving that perplexing question, we may try our luck, on August 9th, in Irving Hall, at a *tombola* for a Sèvres vase, given by the French government for the benefit of the *hospice* of the Société Française de Bienfaisance de New York. And I end on a Spanish strain, with the festival, picnic and concert of the Société de Bienfaisance Espagnole La Armonia (I am quoting from the Messager) held on August 22nd, at Washington Park. Participants with La Armonia were L'Espérance, L'Orphéon Français, L'Helvétienne, Mme. Vanoni and *artistes polyglottes.*

ITALIAN PLAYS, ETC., 1880–1882

I must carry the reader to the Teatro Vercelli, East 42nd Street, there to witness performances of Italian actors whom we met, the season before, in Dramatic Hall, West Houston Street. The company of Fannie Wallack was advertised, in September, at the Vercelli, in "commedia, canto e danza," and as a "splendido successo," to quote from the Eco d'Italia. On Sunday,

September 25th, however, la Società Filodrammatica Tommaso Salvini acted La Legge del Cuore and La Figlia del Domenica.   The other group, the Campagnia Filodrammatica Italiana, was at the Vercelli, on October 2nd, in La Macchia di Sangue, advertised again for October 9th.   Later in October, the Italians advertised merely sacred concerts *"col concorso di parecchi artisti italiani.*   Alf Burnett was then occupying the week-day evenings. A benefit to Fannie Wallack, on November 13th, enlisted many performers of slight importance; Sunday, November 20th, brought back the Unione Filodrammatica Italiana Tommaso Salvini; on the 27th they acted Fuoco al Convent, Dopo la Tempesta la Calma, and Pulcinella geloso della Moglie. After this, I found no more for Vercelli's; but the Eco d'Italia advertises the Hotel di Roma, 152-154 East 42nd Street (the address of the Vercelli), run by G. Vercelli, where, every evening would be *rappresentazioni comico-umoristiche,* at popular prices.   This lure continued into January, but by March the Hotel di Roma was advertising merely wine, beer, liquors and billiards.

I go back to December 3rd for the concert and ball of the Società di Canto Helvetienne, held at Irving Hall, and to January 14th, for the ball of Firenze, at Tammany Hall.   January 30th found the Società di Unione e Fratellanza dancing in the Teutonia Assembly Rooms; February 4th threw open Tammany Hall for the annual ball of the Associazione del Tiro al Bersaglio (Guardia Colombo); and February 11th brought the twelfth annual ball of the Ticinese.   L. Conterno provided the music, on March 19th, at Tammany Hall, for the eighth annual ball of the Società Legione Giuseppe Garibaldi.   Very little in our vein appears thereafter in the file of l'Eco d'Italia for 1882.   The usual festa nazionale Italiana dello Statuto occupied, on June 5th, at Sulzer's Harlem River Park, the busy Tiro al Bersaglio (Guardia Colombo); the Società Mazzini, on June 22nd, had a *festa campestre* and a *ballo serale,* in Elm Park.   And, in late June, Vercelli was advertising garden concerts, at 152-154 East 42nd Street.   Of course, Rossi's acting made proud our Italian population.

ACADEMY OF MUSIC, 1881–1882

The Academy, home of opera, re-opened on September 3, 1881, with the unaccustomed attraction of a play, or perhaps it would be better to say a spectacular melodrama.   This was Kiralfy Brothers' production of Michael Strogoff; a piece which had been heavily staged, in another version, on August 31st, at Booth's, and had been seen, in some guise, even before that at Aberle's Theatre in Eighth Street.   The cast of the adaptation at the Academy presented William Rignold, brother of the handsome George Rignold, whose Henry V had for so many nights in America set maiden hearts a-flutter.   The complete distribution follows:

[515]

Michael Strogoff	William Rignold	Dombrosky	A. H. Denham
Ivan Ogareff	Charles Chappelle	Muravieff	J. Cox
Czar	Harry Gwynette	Telegraph Operator	J. W. Bankson
Feofar	George Harmon	Vladimir	L. Steele
Grand Duke	F. Monroe	High Priest	D. H. Adams
Ezekiah Sharp	George R. Edeson	Nadia	Ellie Wilton
Harry Blunt	A. Thomas	Sangarre	Ada Neilson
Dr. Wassili Fedor	S. Morton	Marfa	Mrs. J. L. Carhart
General Kissoff	H. Montgomery		

William Rignold and Ada Neilson were new to America; but their stay here was brief. The Herald, on September 4th, states that "the piece moved along so slowly at times as to be intolerably tedious, but the dresses, the scenery and the ballets proving to be rich and beautiful, and there being few mishaps in the scenic department [there had been several at Booth's] the performance may be set down as a satisfactory success." Rignold was "only a tolerably good Strogoff, with the rough earnestness of the old school melodramatic heroes whom the gods worship, rather than the handsome, elegant hero whom it was hoped by the 'box circle' that he would prove to be."

MAPLESON'S OPERA COMPANY

I fear Michael Strogoff à la Kiralfy was a failure; there is no trace of it at the Academy after September 17th. The house returned to its accustomed field, on October 17th, when Mapleson began his usual ten-weeks autumn term with Lohengrin, sung by Campanini, Galassi, Novara, Monti, Minnie Hauk (her first appearance in three years) and a new contralto, Climene Kalas, who proved to be hardly tolerable. Gerster, Valleria and Miss Cary were not in the company, and were dreadfully missed, as nonentity after nonentity strove, in the next few weeks, to supply their places. If it had not been for Campanini, Galassi, Del Puente and Miss Hauk, I cannot see what Mapleson could have done. The Herald, on October 18th, asserted that Miss Hauk's voice had deteriorated and her method as well; she had lost something of power and excellence in the upper notes, and an occasional roughness was observed. This impression passed, as the soprano undertook parts more suited to her style; one knows she could not have been an ideal Elsa. Of course Arditi conducted this and every opera of the season.

Miss Hauk passed, on the 19th, to the more congenial Carmen, assisted by Runcio (a poor stubstitute for Campanini), by Del Puente and by Mlle. Dotti, the latter as Micaela, a part in which as in most she was wholly unsatisfactory. The opera for October 21st was Mignon, with Virginia Ferni (a rather successful débutante) in the title-rôle, Emma Juch as Filina, Mlle. Lelia Lauri (who proved to be Mrs. Lowerre, a local concert singer) as Federico, Campanini as Wilhelm Meister, and Del Puente as Lotario. The week ended with a Saturday afternoon Lohengrin.

[516]

Faust began the second week, on October 24th, with Campanini, Novara, Del Puente, Kalas and Virginia Ferni, a cast strong in men and weak in women.   Martha, on the 26th, brought back the mellow-voiced Ravelli, and promised the début of Mlle. Brambilla, in the title-rôle; the lady was ill, and Emma Juch sang Martha.   Others in the cast were Del Puente, Corsini and Lelia Lauri.   Mlle. Ferni was advertised, on the 28th, for Leonora, in La Favorita, with Ravelli, Galassi, Monti and Ida Valerga.   Carmen, with the cast of the week before, except that Campanini now sang Don José, graced the matinée on the 29th.   Mignon again pleased (I hope) on October 31st; as Manrico, in Il Trovatore, on November 2nd, came Prevost, a tenor who at first won applause that diminished at later performances; with him, on the 2nd, were Galassi, Kalas and Minnie Hauk.   Il Barbiere di Siviglia, on the 4th, brought another débutante, Marie Vachot, at first acclaimed and then, as faults began to appear, merely tolerated; others in Il Barbiere were Ravelli, Del Puente, Corsini; in the lesson scene Mlle. Vachot introduced the Shadow Song from Dinorah.   La Favorita, cast as before, was offered for the matinée on the 5th.   A more ill-balanced company, as between men and women, had seldom sung on the Academy stage; subscribers and *habitués* must have longed for the return of Gerster (then a wandering star), Valleria and Miss Cary.   And with Adelina Patti soon to be singing at Steinway Hall!

A curious thing happened at a repetition of Carmen, on November 7th; Corsini could not appear, and the part of Il Remendado was deleted from the score, the quintette of Act II being reduced to a quartette!   Kalas was the Mercedes, and Rinaldini was now set down for Il Dancairo.   Il Trovatore again thrilled (?) on the 9th, and Martha was sweetly melodious on the 11th — this last hastily substituted for Lucia, which Vachot's illness rendered impossible.   Mignon, on the 12th, ended the fourth week of the ever uncertain Mapleson repast.

Mlle. Vachot was able to appear on the 14th, once more as Rosina; and now the Herald found her uncertain in intonation and afflicted with a vibrato of noticeable size.   The Herald, on the 17th, is simply scorching in its animadversion on a Lohengrin of the evening before; it had been announced with the cast of the opening night, but Minnie Hauk's illness forced the substitution, as Elsa, of the objectionable Mlle. Dotti!   Lucia, re-announced for the 18th, was again abandoned, and Faust instead had its cast of a few weeks earlier; Il Trovatore sang and suffered at the matinée on the 19th. Mapleson's prime donne were certainly a liability, rather than an asset.

I pause to record a benefit matinée, November 17th, for the B. P. O. Elks, at which appeared the San Francisco Minstrels; Mlle. Dotti, Mlle. Lauri, Novara, Galassi and Prevost; the second act of Engaged, with Agnes Booth, May Gallagher, Annie Russell, Mrs. Whiffen, Clara Hyatt, Thomas Whiffen, Eben Plympton, Leslie Allen, W. J. Ferguson (with William Seymour as stage manager); Anna Teresa Berger; John McCullough, reciting The Little Hero; Kate Monroe and Helen Dingeon, in bits from Les Cloches de Corneville; Rudolf Bial's orchestra; Dora Wiley in ballads; Maginley, Buckley and Hart Conway, in the fourth act of Deacon Crankett; Harrigan and Hart's company, in Clara Jenkins' Tea; Harriet Webb's recital, How We Saved St. Michael's; Julie de Bertrand; Billy Barry and Hugh Fay, in scenes from Muldoon's Picnic; John F. Sheridan, in a bit of Fun on the Bristol; ventriloquism by E. D. Davies, and Tyrolean Warblers. A full afternoon, well worth the admission fee! The Herald review fails to mention the Sheridan number. On Thanksgiving, November 24th, Tony Pastor had here, afternoon and evening, a grand jubilee.

I return to the opera, on the 21st, for Lucia, at last given with Campanini, Galassi, Monti and Mlle. Vachot, only to learn, if the Herald's ear did not deceive it, that the mad heroine sang terribly sharp! On the 23rd, Ravelli, Galassi and Minnie Hauk gave La Traviata, and, on the 25th, Carmen employed the usual cast, Il Barbiere di Siviglia also having its accustomed singers at the matinée on the 26th. On Monday, November 28th, Prevost sang Arnoldo in Guglielmo Tell, assisted by Galassi (the ever fine) as Tell, Monti as Walter, Costa as Gessler, Runcio as Il Pescatore, Emma Juch as Jemmy, Mlle. Dotti as Matilda, and with a ballet led by Cavallazzi (sic), daughter-in-law of the redoubtable Mapleson. This pretentious revival was repeated on December 2nd, when Isidora Martinez sang Jemmy at very short notice.

Aïda, on November 30th, introduced a novelty — a really successful prima donna. This was Paolina Rossini, a safe, satisfactory performer; no genius, no vocal wonder, but a dependable person, withal. After the fiascos of the past weeks, she seemed very good to the attendants. On the same evening appeared a new contralto, Mlle. Cobianchi, not quite so satisfactory. Campanini, Galassi, Monti and Costa filled the male rôles. Carmen, ever desired, gratified the ladies at the matinée, on the 3rd. The eighth week offered repetitions of Lucia (December 5th), Aïda (7th), and Tell (matinée, 10th, again with Emma Juch). Mefistofele, on the 9th, gave a cast inferior to that of the preceding year: Campanini, Novara, Lauri and Ferni.

On the afternoon and evening of December 6th, the Roman Catholic Orphan Asylum had its annual benefit. In the afternoon appeared Harriet Webb, the Meigs Sisters, John McCullough in an act of Julius Cæsar, Anna T. Berger, J. K. Emmet in an act of Fritz in Ireland, Harry Kennedy, Dora Wiley (the new singer), Edwin French, Edward Connell and the Catholic Protectory Band. The evening services began with A Glance at Married Life (by A. H. Sheldon and company), and followed with the Four Eccentrics (Perry, Magrew, Curdy and Hughes), Del Puente, Corsini, Minnie Hauk (she took the place of the undependable Marie Vachot), Ravelli and

[518]

Anna T. Berger. Kate Claxton, Stevenson and Marie Wilkins gave the fourth act of The Two Orphans, and Marie Prescott and Frank Roche appeared in an act of Camille. Other volunteers included the French Twin Sisters, Dr. Lynn, and the American Four (Pettingill, Gale, Dailey and Hoey). I cannot vouch for the appearance of this Four or of the Twins. Better bills had graced the benefits of this institution.

Again I pick up the operatic strain. Minnie Hauk's two hundredth performance of Carmen was stressed on December 12th, and, on the 13th (an extra night), Mlle. Rossini sang Margherita, in Faust, a performance found to be not so good as her Aïda; Runcio was the poor Faust, enough to take the high notes of enthusiasm from any prima donna. In La Favorita, on the 14th, Campanini, always admired in the part, succeeded Ravelli as Fernando. Guglielmo Tell again shot an arrow, on December 16th, and on the 17th (matinée), Aïda employed the recent cast, except that Del Puente was Amonasro, vice the fiery Galassi. A Sunday concert (18th) offered Hauk, Juch, Lauri, Dotti and Ferni (except for the two first-named a disappointing list of ladies), with Ravelli, Del Puente, Galassi, Monti and the ever-welcome Campanini. The last week of the subscription began on December 19th, with Runcio(!) as Radames, in Aïda, Galassi again as Amonasro; Les Huguenots, on the 21st, employed the tired Campanini, with Galassi, Del Puente, Novara, Emma Juch, Lelia Lauri and Paolina Rossini. Minnie Hauk's Carmen was to have ended the night performances, on the 23rd, with a kind of glory; the prima donna was ill, and Martha was substituted, with Campanini, Emma Juch and the recently eclipsed Kalas. In Les Huguenots, for the last matinée, on the 24th, Ravelli sang Raoul, replacing Campanini, who, one feels, was losing some of his youthful freshness of voice and of physical vigour. This is apparent in reading the criticisms of that season's performances. On December 22nd, Mrs. James H. Hackett, nothing if not ambitious, advertised for the Academy her appearance as Lady Macbeth, with Barton Hill as Macbeth, E. F. Thorne as Macduff, George Holland as Duncan, George F. Browne as First Witch, A. H. Hastings as Banquo, &c.

Well, Mapleson departed, till March gales would once more rage round the Academy, in imminent peril of singers' throats. On Monday, December 26th, Tony Pastor celebrated Christmas bringing in his own suave personality, along with the Irwin Sisters, Ferguson and Mack, Harry Woodson, William Carroll, Parker's dogs, Lillie Western and Jacques Kruger; his new theatre (the late Germania) was now but a stone's throw from the august Academy. Thereafter, in absence of opera, the Academy entered on its winter course of receptions and balls, seemingly in 1882 more numerous than usual. These I need, of course, merely to catalogue: the masquerade ball of the Cercle Français de l'Harmonie, on January 16th; the Old Guard Ball, on the 19th; the Martha Washington Reception and Ball, on the 20th; the ball of the Société Française de l'Amitié, on the 30th, and the Charity Ball, on the 31st. The 22nd Regiment held at the Academy, on February 2nd, its great annual dance, the Liederkranz on the 9th its masked ball, and the Elks Association came in, on February 6th. The French Cooks' Ball (La Société Culinaire Philanthropique) was a merry feature of the 7th. We must not overlook the Children's Carnival and Ball, on February 13th. The drill and reception of the Palestine Commandery graced the 15th, and the Sparkling Coterie possessed the Academy and Nilsson Hall, on the 14th. The Purim Ball was listed for March 2nd. And we must not forget that in the Academy were carried through the august concerts of the Philharmonic Society.

Meantime, this kind of festivity yielded briefly in January to a few performances of tragedy, with Rossi as star. He began, on the 17th, as King Lear, supported by the same company of English-speaking actors who had appeared with him shortly before at Booth's; in fact, he himself spoke a few of his lines in English. On the 18th, 20th and 21st (matinée), he played Edmund Kean, in a play of that name, somewhat like Sullivan, which we know as David Garrick; some great English actor's name was necessary for the hero:

Kean	Ernesto Rossi	Peter Patt	T. F. Kelly
Prince of Wales	Leslie Gossin	Manager	W. V. Ranous
Count Koefeld	H. A. Weaver	Servant	S. Jackson
Lord Melville	H. A. Weaver, Jr.	Helen	Louise Muldener
Solomon	E. A. Eberle	Anna	Carrie Turner
Pistol	W. J. Shea	Amy	Constance Hamblin
Constable	Charles Kent	Gidsa	Mrs. H. A. Weaver

In this play Rossi made a hit; and, in view of her forthcoming success on our stage, I am pleased to find the Herald of the 19th saying that "a good word must be said of Miss Carrie Turner's Anna. It was an exceedingly simple and tasteful bit of acting and won for the lady many hearty commendations." Next season we shall find Miss Turner at the Madison Square Theatre, creating the title-rôle in Bronson Howard's fine play, Young Mrs. Winthrop.

On January 24th, Rossi gave a professional matinée of Kean; the Herald advertised this play for every evening and Saturday matinée of his second week, but the plan changed to King Lear on the 25th, Othello on the 26th, and Hamlet on the 27th. There was no performance on Saturday, the 28th. A lull followed, except for balls previously cited, until, on Washington's Birthday, Tony Pastor again appeared at the Academy, with Wood, Beasley and the Weston Brothers ("the best musical quartet on earth"), the Irwin Sisters, Jacques Kruger, William Carroll ("Prince Imperial of the Banjo"), Susie Russell (sister of the fair Lillian), Donnelly and Drew, Flora M. Pike, Joe Buckley, and the burlesque of Patience, recently so successful at his theatre.

Return of the Opera

Mapleson's singers came back from their tour, and opened, on March 6th, with Mignon, with Minnie Hauk, Juch, Del Puente and Campanini. The artists in Les Huguenots, on the 8th, were Ravelli, Galassi, Del Puente, Novara, Monti, Marie Vachot, Lelia Lauri and Paolina Rossini.   An Italian Fidelio, on the 10th, presented Ravelli, Galassi, Novara, Emma Juch and Mlle. Dorani (new) as Leonora.   Carmen, on the afternoon of the 11th, ended the first week, a week that had gone through without harrowing substitutions of any sort.   Lohengrin (March 13th), Faust (15th, with Ravelli and Rossini), Carmen (17th), and Les Huguenots (matinée, on the 18th, with Emma Juch again as Marguerite) — behold the joys of the second week, also sailing through exactly as announced.   Outside of the subscription was a benefit (March 14th) for the building fund of the New York Press Club; volunteers were Campanini, Galassi, Arbuckle, Louis Blumenberg (cello), Henrietta Markstein, Minnie Hauk, Emma Juch, Ravelli, E. D. Davies, and the Musical Four.   The third week of opera passed without mishap; seldom had Mapleson been so fortunate.   Ravelli, Del Puente, Kalas (sunk to the small part of la Contessa), Mlles. Lauri and Rossini gave Rigoletto, on March 20th.   A very elaborate, spectacular revival of L'Africaine, on the 22nd and 24th, enlisted Campanini (decidedly showing signs of fatigue), Galassi (always excellent in parts like Nelusko), Novara, Rinaldini, Monti, Costa, Mlle. Dotti (as Inez) and Minnie Hauk (as Selika), with Mme. Cavallazzi leading a showy ballet.   The Mimosa Society broke in, on the 23rd, with a performance of School, before two thousand. Tom Ellison, a very clever amateur, played Beau Farintosh.   Aïda, at the matinée on the 25th, had a cast embracing Ravelli, Galassi, Novara, Monti, Mme. Lablache (as Amneris), and Paolina Rossini.   Mapleson certainly had not replaced Miss Cary or even Anna de Belocca; Mme. Lablache was a real artist, but of course she was no longer young.   On Sunday, the 26th, the singers appeared in concert; Campanini and Miss Hauk were announced, but neither appeared.   L'Africaine again delighted on the 27th and 31st, Ravelli, on the latter date, succeeding Campanini as Vasco di Gama; on the other hand, Campanini, on the 29th, first appeared as Arnoldo, in Guglielmo Tell (Prevost having left the company); I fear I shall bore the reader by telling him that Carmen again tempted to the matinée on April 1st.   The last week of the subscription brought (April 3rd) Il Trovatore, with Ravelli, Del Puente, Monti, Mme. Lablache (noble in style, if not fresh in voice, as Azucena) and Mlle. Rossini; L'Africaine, by request, and again with Campanini (5th), and (on Thursday, the 6th, since the 7th was Good Friday), Ernani, with Ravelli, Del Puente, Novara, and Rossini.   Faust closed the season (matinée, 8th) with Campanini, Galassi, Novara, Mlle. Lauri, Mme. Lablache, and Minnie Hauk.

[521]

The five weeks had been successful — with few substitutions, and with a fine revival of L'Africaine. Mlle. Vachot had departed, rather annoyed with the management, and Prevost, of the autumn season, had not appeared; but Paolina Rossini had edged forward, and Mme. Lablache had, for old times' sake, been welcomed. In view of results for his regular subscription season, Mapleson announced a supplementary season, at reduced prices ($2 to 50 cents, with boxes at $8, $10 and $12). Les Huguenots (April 10th), L'Africaine (April 11th, with Campanini and Minnie Hauk, and April 13th, with Ravelli and Rossini), Ernani (12th), and L'Africaine again at the matinée on the 15th, with Campanini and Minnie Hauk — these offerings showed no diminution of excellence in the casts. On Sunday, the 16th, Robert G. Ingersoll lectured on Talmagian Theology, without reducing to silence, I need hardly say, the Reverend De Witt Talmage, of Brooklyn.

Lohengrin, on April 17th, gave us Campanini and Minnie Hauk, with Mme. Lablache as Ortrud; in the oft-repeated L'Africaine, on the 18th, Ravelli and Rossini again had the lead. And actually, on the 19th, Mapleson mounted Roberto il Diavolo, with Campanini, Rinaldini (Rambaldo), Novara (Bertramo), Costa (Alberti), Bieletto (un Araldo), Corsini, Bieletto and Monti as Cavalieri, Mme. Cavallazzi as Elene, Minnie Hauk as Alice, and Emma Juch as Isabella. On the 20th, Aïda, which could not be given, as announced, on the 13th, limped into the bills, fearfully hampered by the illness of Ravelli, who was replaced by the hopeless Runcio, and also hurt by the illness of Mme. Lablache, replaced by Mlle. Cobianchi. Under these depressing conditions, Galassi, Novara and Mlle. Rossini did the best they could to lighten the gloom of the audience. Ill luck now descended on Mapleson; Runcio even had to sing Don José (Campanini being ill), on April 21st; and Ida Valerga also being indisposed, Mme. Lablache, in Act II of Carmen sang, where possible, the notes and words of both Frasquita and Mercedes. In such misfortune, Minnie Hauk's farewell was certainly far from gay. We remember that, in one performance in the autumn, the part of Il Dancairo was deleted from the same act. The matinée gave us L'Africaine (April 22nd), Campanini and Rossini as a new combination. On the afternoon of the 23rd, Ingersoll again lectured on Talmagian Theology, and in the evening Rossini, Galassi, Lablache, Campanini, Juch, Del Puente, and Mme. Sacconi (harpist of the company) were listed for a concert.

The last week of Mapleson's opera began on April 24th, with a testimonial benefit for Campanini, who, alas! was not to be with the company in 1882–1883. It was known that Adelina Patti had been engaged at (it was alleged) the enormous salary of $4,400 a performance. In an interview in the Herald, Campanini stated that he was very tired, the season just ending having been particularly hard, and he would, next year, take a complete rest; besides, since Patti insisted on singing only with Nicolini, and since she would be the sensation of the opera, Campanini had no desire merely to sing on what would be considered "off" nights.   For his benefit he offered acts of La Favorita, Il Trovatore and Ruy Blas; in the first and last of these Mme. Galassi appeared and won, says the Herald of the 25th, a great success.   The announced bill for the 25th (Martha, and the incantation scene from Roberto il Diavolo) was forced, because of Ravelli's illness, to be abandoned; Rigoletto, with Runcio, Del Puente and Rossini was substituted.   The last night of L'Africaine (26th) employed Campanini, Galassi and Rossini, the last-named, the Herald cruelly remarked, making Selika "a kind of tragic Topsy."   Mapleson, on the 28th, considerately gave himself a benefit, the bill including the garden scene of Faust, with Campanini, Novara, Lauri, Lablache and Rossini; a ballet divertissement by Mme. Cavallazzi; the fourth act of Ruy Blas, with Campanini and Mme. Galassi; and scenes from Carmen (without Minnie Hauk) and L'Africaine.   This differs materially from the programme originally announced; but Mapleson ran true to form in late-hour changes.   The Saturday matinée, April 29th, brought in Etelka Gerster, who, we know, had been touring the country with Max Strakosch's opera troupe; and here she came back home for a final Lucia di Lammermoor, with Ravelli (replacing Campanini, ill) and Galassi. The house was packed with her shrieking admirers.   Thus the regular opera passed for 1881–82; but, on May 10th, a grand "farewell" offered us Il Trovatore, with Campanini, Galassi, Mme. Lablache, and Paolina Rossini. Mme. Chatterton-Bohrer harped, and Rasori conducted.   Campanini could not really go; he was prominent once more on May 29th, at a benefit to J. W. Morrissey, in a mixed bill including the play of The World, with J. W. Morrissey in the raft scene; Campanini in *Spirto gentil, Salve dimora,* and *La Donna e mobile;* the balcony scene from Romeo and Juliet (with Eben Plympton and Jeffreys Lewis); Minnie Palmer in songs from My Sweetheart, &c.

The great Wagnerian soprano, Amalia Friedrich-Materna, who had come to America for Theodore Thomas's festival concerts in early May, had, on June 9th, at the Academy, a farewell concert, in which she sang an air from Rienzi, a lied, Meine Boten (by Gerecke), and (with Candidus) the duet from Tannhäuser, a curious selection for the original Brünnhilde, at Baireuth. On the afternoon of the 10th, a benefit for the family of George Conly, the operatic basso, recently drowned in company with Hermann Rietzel, brought a notable gathering of volunteers.   Zelda Seguin, William Castle and W. T. Carleton gave the second act of Maritana; Emma Juch sang, and Jeffreys Lewis recited The Bridge of Sighs; L. G. Gottschalk rendered The Toreador Song; in the fourth act of Il Trovatore appeared Clara Louise Kellogg (after three-years' absence), Mme. Lablache, Brignoli, Tagliapietra and W. Seaman; Teresa Carreño played the Second Rhapsodie Hongroise; Lichtenberg gave a violin solo; Emma Abbott, with Ellis Ryse, sang the mad scene from

Lucia di Lammermoor; John T. Raymond and Laura Don acted A Conjugal Lesson; Mlle. Rossini sang, and Arbuckle played on the cornet; Rossini, Lablache, Christian Fritsch and Gottschalk rendered the quartette from Rigoletto; and the proceedings ended with the funeral march from Donizetti's Don Sebastian. A remarkable bill!

NEW THEATRE COMIQUE, 1881–1882

The harassed and mysteriously unlucky premises at 728-730 Broadway entered on a final and more fortunate phase of existence, when Harrigan and Hart moved from their old quarters at 514 Broadway, and began a new career of success in an entirely rebuilt and refurbished auditorium on the sad old site further uptown. It was a great year for moving; Neuendorff had transferred his company, as we saw, from Fourteenth Street to the old Wallack's at Broadway and Thirteenth Street, and, as we shall see anon, Tony Pastor migrated from 585 Broadway to the house, just vacated by Neuendorff. Old playgoers must have rubbed their eyes; the moving of Wallack's alone would have seemed cataclysmal.

Harrigan and Hart advertised their new abode as "a gem of mechanical art — Acoustic properties perfect — 17 exits — Architects, Kimball and Wisedell — Builder, George T. Dollinger — new stock of scenery by Charles W. Witham — Dave Braham, musical director." These startling facts gasped out in staccato, the managers staidly announced their first play, which inaugurated the house on August 29, 1881. Harrigan deserted his Mulligan characters, and presented his company — the same favourites — in entirely new rôles in a play called The Major, in which he acted Major Gilfeather, a man, according to A. H. Quinn, "who lives on his wits," possesses "an extensive vocabulary," and "emerges from situations by his cleverness in hoodwinking other people." How rapturously the loyal audience must have greeted the members of the company as they came on the new stage:

Major Gilfeather	Edward Harrigan	Mr. Sole	Fred Queen
Enry Iggins	Tony Hart	Mr. Welt	George Merritt
Phineas Bottlegreen	John Wild	Ephraim Shroud	William West
Caleb Jenkins	William Gray	Mr. Plaid	Robert Hall
Granville Bright	Edward Burt	Clara Jenkins	James Fox
Mr. Spotem	Harry Fisher	Aunty Green	John Oberist
Percival Popp	M. F. Drew	Burnside Ruffle	Emil Heusel
John Murphy	John Queen	Slip Runner	Morgan Benson
Phadrig Murphy	M. Bradley	Policemen	Rourke, McCullough
Mr. Dip	James Tierney	Arabella Pinch	Annie Mack
Mr. Grab	Edward Goss	Miranda Briggs	Annie Yeamans
Mr. Pry	Thomas Ray	Henrietta	Gertie Granville
Steward	M. Foley	Amelia Bright	Marie Gorenflo
Henry Huxley	W. Merritt	Bridget Murphy	Mary Bird

[524]

EDWARD HARRIGAN
AND TONY HART

ANNIE MACK
AND TONY HART

HARRIGAN—ANNIE YEAMANS

JOHN QUEEN—HARRY FISHER

JOHN WILD
MORA'S PHOTOGRAPHS OF SCENES FROM THE MAJOR

With all that enormous cast to pay, and with other expenses, Harrigan and Hart charged only one dollar for admission to orchestra and balcony, 50 cents to the dress circle, 25 cents to the family circle, and $8 and $6 for boxes.   The Major was a hit, and registered its hundredth performance on November 25th.   By that time, Dave Braham's songs were whistled everywhere — Major Gilfeather, Clara Jenkins' Tea, The Veteran Guards Cadets, etc.   The theatre was closed on September 20th and 26th.   The last performance of The Major fell on January 7th (it had had about one hundred and fifty), and, on the 9th, it was followed by an even more successful play, Squatter Sovereignty, dealing, as Professor Quinn states, with the conflict between the owners of the land in the city lying adjacent to the East River and the "squatters" who had dwelt thereon unmolested, until the land began to have value.   Since Harrigan was the author, the initiated reader will expect a large cast:

Felix M'Intyre	Edward Harrigan	Horatio M'Intyre	W. West
Widow Nolan	Tony Hart	Wellington M'Intyre	James Fox
Darius Dauber	John Wild	Fred Kline	James Tierney
Salem Sheerer	William Gray	Paddy Duffy	Eugene Rourke
Captain Kline	Harry Fisher	Bella Parker	Annie Mack
Charles Parker	Edward Burt	Josephine Jumble	Annie Yeamans
George Parker	M. F. Drew	Nellie Nolan	Gertie Granville
Terence M'Intyre	M. Bradley	Emily Parker	Marie Gorenflo
Denny M'Guire	John Queen	Kitty M'Guire	Mary Bird
Pedro Donetti	John Oberist	Katrina Schwartz	Susie Byron
Tommy Darcy	George Merritt	Louisa Kringle	Emily Yeamans
Jimmy Casey	Edward Goss	Lena Stucke	Lizzie Finn

This lucky piece ran to the end of the season, on June 3rd, attaining its hundredth performance on April 4th, and its hundred and fiftieth on May 17th.   The songs, especially Paddy Duffy's Cart, gave Braham a short period of immortality; they certainly were tuneful.   Others songs were The M'Intyres, Widow Nolan's Goat, and Miss Brady's Pianoforte.   The first season of the new Theatre Comique had needed but two plays — a remarkable record, second only to that of the Madison Square.

TONY PASTOR'S NEW THEATRE (1881–1882)

Tony Pastor, as just stated, joined the great moving impulse, and transferred his activities from 585 Broadway to the former Germania Theater, recently vacated by Adolf Neuendorff.   As usual, Pastor spent the early autumn weeks in a tour of the country (we saw him earlier at the Grand Opera House), and his new theatre indulged in a preliminary season, beginning on October 10, 1881, with Nick Roberts's Humpty Dumpty Company, specialties including the Clipper Quartette, the Onofri Brothers, and the Peerless Pantomime Three — Grimaldi, Dromio and Pedro.

And then, on October 24th, the suave Tony himself came into his own, supported by practically the same artists who had appeared with him, during the week of September 6th, at the Grand Opera House. Specially stressed, on October 31st, were Jacques Kruger (in Our Professor), "Governor" Add Ryman, "Florence" Merton Pike, May Irwin, Redmond and Blake, Lester and Allen, Lester and Williams, "Professor" Harry Parker's dogs, Dan Collyer, Frank Girard, and Jennie Christie; Pastor sang That Hebrew Maiden of Mine, and I'll Give you a Pointer on That. Some of these features remained, but new, on November 7th, were Mattie Vickers and Charles S. Rogers, in The Débutante, Flora Moore, Frank Bennett and Lida Gardner, John and Lea Peasley, &c. The McGilligans, or, Mixing Oil with Water, the sketch of the week, would seem to curtsy to the new Theatre Comique. On November 14th, I come upon the name of the magnetic Maggie Cline, who for years thereafter was one of the greatest stars of vaudeville; she sang now in Mary Ann Kehoe; Jacques Kruger (a fixture of the house) tried Charley Duno. Susie Russell (sister of Lillian), the Grotesque Four (Seamon, Somers and the Girard Brothers), William Carroll (banjoist and comedian), E. D. Davies ("the world's premier ventriloquist"), the Karl Brothers (acrobats), Ed Baldwin (gymnastic clown), Flora M. Pike (she became a feature of the house), Dan Collyer, and Lester and Allen were featured in the gigantic bill. Clark and Edwards (Tyrolean warblers), the Garnella Brothers (Robert and Little Dick), May Irwin, Mealey and Mackey ("the Irish gents"), the St. Felix Sisters (Henrietta, Clementine and Charlotte) and Fields and Hanson ("musical mokes") joined, on the 21st, with Kruger, Ryman, Miss Pike, Susie Russell and Jennie Christie. No one could deny that Pastor supplied, at moderate admission, much Variety, in both senses of the word. But Lillian Russell, the beautiful "find" of the preceding season, was not here; Broadway had taken her.

And, for a time, Pastor carried on in the same generous way; specialists for the week of December 5th–10th were Jacques Kruger (as the Pedagogue, in Our School Girls), Fannie Beane and Charles Gilday, Lester and Williams, Frank McNish and the Leland Sisters (in Servants' Frolics), Charles Heywood (in The Arrival of Patti), the Original Four Shamrocks (Dave Conroy, John and Matt Daly and Micky Thompson), May Arnott, Dan Collyer, May Irwin, Flora Pike and Jennie Christie. Evidently Pastor was reaching for a programme more unified in effect; on December 12th, he revived Go West on the Emigrant Train, with Kruger, Mattie Vickers, Charles S. Rogers, Harry McAvoy, Emma Rogers, Lizzie Simms, Susie Russell, Kelly and O'Brien, James W. Bingham (ventriloquist), Flora Pike, Charles Heywood, May Irwin, Dan Collyer, Jennie Christie and Frank Girard as passengers contributing to the hilarity. On the 19th he staged Charity Begins at Home, announced boldly as an "operetta"; Alfred Beven, Kruger, Bessie Gray and Helen Morrell were depended on to prove the adage. The Great American Four (Pettingill, Gale, Dailey and Hoey) and

[526]

Charles Diamond were in the bill, and, at this holiday season, Pastor gave dolls on Friday afternoons to all nice little girls in the audience. We remember his grand entry, on December 26th, into the stately Academy of Music.

The chief attraction, on January 2nd, was Fun on the Stage, unless the re-union of the Irwin Sisters seemed more important. In the olio were Lester and Allen, Wood, Beasley and the Weston Brothers, the French Twin Sisters, Susie Russell, Flora Pike, Dan Collyer, William Carroll, J. W. McAndrews, and the Grotesque Four (Seamon, Somers and the Girard Brothers — lest the reader forget). Barry and Fay had played at Niblo's in Muldoon's Picnic; on January 9th, Pastor put on Muldoon's Coterie, with William F. Carroll as Michael Muldoon, and Jacques Kruger as Fitzdarlington. Cora Cardigan, in the olio, played the flute, and the Whitings entered the programme. Muldoon's Coterie lasted a second week (January 16th–21st), and then a companion in the bill was The Frenchman's Protégée, with Mattie Vickers and Charles S. Rogers. Hallen and Hart, in Over the Stile, gave bits of Pinafore and Patience; Mlle. Catherine exhibited her performing birds; the Durell Twin Brothers offered their specialty and the remaining Grotesque Four continued to give theirs; J. H. and Ida Jeffrey we shall need to know better, to assign them to their proper place.

LILLIAN RUSSELL IN PATIENCE

And now Pastor found the unity he had sought. On January 23rd he produced a burlesque of the raging Gilbert and Sullivan operetta, which he called Patience, or, the Stage-Struck Maidens. Lillian Russell, fresh from successes at the Bijou, returned to the Pastor fold in the rôle of Patience, in which she made a great hit — so great that she was soon singing elsewhere the part in the operetta itself. Of course Pastor laid on heavily the satire of the current æsthetic vocabulary; hence Jacques Kruger was Bun-Thorne, "sweetly sweet, neatly neat, charmingly charming"; May Irwin (and I will wager she was very funny) was Lady Jane Jemima, "saucily saucy"; Flora M. Pike was Lady Angelina, "pertily pert"; Bessie Gray was Lady Ella, "elegantly elegant"; Alice Reeves Lady Saphir "languishingly languid"; Flora Irwin Grosvenor, "prettily pretty"; Frank Girard Colonel Calverly, "dashingly dashing"; Vincent Aubrin the Major, "martially martial"; James Bernard the Duke, "courtingly courtly"; and Dan Collyer the Solicitor, "pleadingly pleading." Susie Russell was among the maidens "strikingly struck," and there was a chorus of dragoons "lovingly lovesick." In addition, William Carroll, Fannie Beane, Charles Gilday, the Grotesque Four and Pastor swelled the olio. Patience, I am pleased to report, was a hit, and continued for weeks. With it, on January 30th, were featured Lizzie Simms and Lew Baker, a "negro" comedian. On February 13th entered the olio Fred Wilson ("famous statue and protean artist") along with Lizzie Simms ("the world's greatest transformation dancer"), the French Twin Sisters, the Irwin Sisters, Joe Buckley ("negro"), Georgie Blake and Charles Redmond. But Patience was the thing; soon Herald advertisements stress little besides. Lillian Russell might almost be called the talk of the town; photographs of her beauty were in demand. With Patience, on March 6th, a piece alleged to be by Denman Thompson was brought out, under the title of Castle Garden, presenting Pat Nelson as the Widdy Malone, May Irwin (bless her!) as Huldah Ann Hopkins, of Brattleboro, Vermont, Flora Irwin as Pat O'Brien, Jacques Kruger as Frank Mortelle, "too utterly too," Emil Ames as Uncle Billy Miller, Dan Collyer as Aunt Nance, Frank Girard as Dougherty, and Charles Atwood as Murphy.

Castle Garden yielded (Patience still holding out, in the bills) on March 13th, to Our Claude Duval, a burlesque, of course, of the recently produced Claude Duval. Jennie Christie appeared as Sallie Robbins, afterward Claude Duval; Flora Pike was Lizzie Leslie, afterward Jack Sheppard; Susie Russell was Louise Leslie, afterward Dick Turpin, Edna McDonald was Hattie Foster, a country maid, afterward Blueskin, Eva Barrington was Josie Farwell, afterward Tom King, Mary Wyman was Mary Proctor, afterward Sixteen-String Jack, and Ena Donnell was Minnie La Rue, afterward Daring Dick. It would seem that this might have been funny; but one week ended its career.

Patience at last gave way, on March 20th, to a burlesque Billee Taylor, with Lillian Russell as Phœbe, Kruger as Barnacle, F. Girard as Sir Wellington Lance, Flora Irwin as William, Aubrin as Chris Lobster, Jennie Christie as Eliza, and Bessie Gray as Bella; May Irwin also appeared in Fun at School, as Sallie Smithers, the stupid scholar. Of course Tony Pastor sang. A benefit, during the week of March 27th–April 1st, to Harry S. Sanderson, business manager and treasurer of Pastor's, promised Frl. von Januschowsky and Rank from the Germania, in Hanni weint, Hansi lacht, and bits by Gerald Eyre, John Wild, Billy Gray, Harry Fisher, Cappa's Seventh Regiment Band, the California Quartette, Ed French, A. C. Moreland, Lillian Russell, the Irwin Sisters and Mlle. Barretta (sic). Billee Taylor ran on till, on April 10th, The Mascot succeeded it, with Fanny Wentworth as Bettina; Lillian Russell, not without anguish, publicly expressed, by the management, had left the establishment for more aristocratic quarters in Broadway operetta. In The Mascot, at Pastor's, J. H. Rennie was Lorenzo, W. J. Stanton Rocco, and J. A. Montgomery Pippo; on the 24th, Henri Laurent assumed the last-named rôle. Olivette came in, on May 6th. Pastor's company had long since departed, and J. H. Rennie was now directing genuine operetta; his cast for Olivette included Henri Laurent, James Sturgis (Merrimac), Harry De Lorme (des Ifs), W. J. Stanton (Coquelicot), W. Gillow (Marvejol), Fanny Wentworth (Olivette), Marion Lambert

[528]

(Bathilde) and Maggie Duggan (Veloutine).   The real Patience (not Pastor's burlesque) employed, on May 22nd, Fanny Wentworth as Patience, Maggie Duggan as Lady Jane, May Hill as Lady Angela, J. H. Rennie as Bunthorne, Alma Stuart Stanley (!) as Grosvenor, Laurent as the Colonel, and Harry Pepper as the Duke.   Two weeks sufficed; rather, less, since The Mascot came back on June 2nd and 3rd.

Pastor's had generally remained open during the summer, and often to shows of doubtful propriety; on June 5th, his new house advertised a musical and political fairy extravaganza, entitled Venus; and a burlesque of Barnum's recent importation, Jumbo, a Trick Elephant.   Venus was merely Gilbert a Beckett's The Happy Land, burlesque of Gilbert's The Wicked World; in it appeared Alma Stanley and Fanny Wentworth.   During the last week of Venus (June 12th–17th) Pat Rooney and Joseph Arthur were specially engaged.   For the week beginning June 19th, Pastor's advertised Two Medallions.   I am not sorry to announce that this was the last production for 1881–82; for good measure, however, I give the cast — Amy Lee, Emma Clavelle, Sara Lascelles, Mary Stuart, Harry A. Smith, T. J. Hawkins, C. B. Hawkins, and John H. Burnett.

ABERLE'S NEW THEATRE, 1881–1882

I will begin the season at Aberle's, on August 29, 1881, when, according to bills at Harvard, Michael Strogoff, seen two nights later at Booth's, and a few nights after that at the Academy of Music, was first produced in New York:

Strogoff	C. L. Farwell	General Kissoff	E. Doran
Czar	George W. Johnson	Emir	Max Miller
Harry Blount	L. W. Barker	Wassili	M. McCormick
Josivet	H. L. Bascombe	Nadia	Mamie Wallace
Ivan	Alf A. Wallace	Marfa	Addie Farwell
Grand Duke	J. W. George	Sangarre	Martha Miller

The names of the *dramatis personæ* I carefully copied from the bill.   Previous to the melodrama, Barker, Lottie Simmons and others acted Another Half Dollar and Max and Martha Miller did a "turn."   Michael Strogoff ran a second week, beginning on September 5th; indeed Allston Brown starts the run on that date.   Delvan and Tracy and the Millers figured in the olio.   On September 12th, J. H. Ryan was starred, in Fitz, a True Irish Friend; "Variety" reared its hydra head in shape of "turns" by the Millers, Josephine Walby (jigs and reels), Jennie Lindsay and the Carey Brothers (George and John, Irish song and dance).   "Variety," however, at this theatre retired to rearward, as concluding dramas lengthened and became more important.   Through September and October appeared, in addition to those I have mentioned, "Senator" Frank Woodson, Frank and

[529]

Fannie (*sic*) Davis, Jessie Merton, the Lamartine Brothers, Lottie Winnett, the London Athletes (McDonald, Snow, Greystone and Whalen), Fannie Bernard, Foster and Hughes, Isabel Ward, John H. Byrne (in Waiting for John), Melville and Bunell (Melody in a Music Shop), Harry Leslie (tight-rope), Mike Gallagher and Edith Andow, and Griffin and Marks. But the reader will care more for the plays produced: Ouida, or, a Woman's Vengeance (September 19th, with Lena Aberle and the regular dramatic corps, as seen previously in Michael Strogoff); Rightmire as Harry Saunders, with four disguises, in his own play of The California Detective (September 26th–October 1st); G. W. Johnson, in his own play, Steps to Ruin (October 3rd–8th); Maude Forrester in Mazeppa (10th–15th); The Idiot of the Mountain (17th–22nd, with Farwell as Claude Marcel, Bascombe as Jacques Caussade, and Addie Edgecombe as Mme. de Flavigneul); J. T. Hinds and Ivian Lawrence, in Rory O'More (October 24th–29th).

The bills for this last week began with Ed F. Sylvester and Johnson, in Hatter and Printer (Box and Cox); for October 31st–November 5th, festivities opened with the same pair in Slasher and Crasher; proceeded to an olio involving the Three Rinaldos (*sic* — "grotesques and king high kickers"), Blanche Webster ("the emerald gem, in songs, dances, flashes of fun"), Paddy and Ella Murphy (in Just from Ireland); and ended with George W. Middleton, in The Pirates' Legacy, or, the Wrecker's Fate.

If only "Variety" would go! But I must record, for November, George La Rosa (equilibrist and slack wire), Maggie Willet (in Good for Nothing Nan), Barney Reynolds, Ned West (in farces), Thomas and Clara Maxwell (in Trifles), Will H. and James Vane, Daisy Norwood, Nestor and Venoa (gymnasts), the Four Shamrocks, Emma Hoffman, the American Four (Pettingill, Gale, Dailey and Hoey), Carroll and Walters (in In and Out), Joyce (Irish piper) and Murphy (dancer), the Ramirez Spanish Troubadours, and Sophie Thorne (Lancashire clog, etc.). Having thus conscientiously fulfilled my duty, I may turn back to the plays, reporting two weeks (November 7th–19th) for a return of Lena Aberle, in Ouida; a week (November 21st–26th) of William H. Brent, in The End of the World; and an equal period (November 28th–December 3rd) for The Stranglers of New York, with Rose Lisle and Valentine Love each in three parts, assisted by the regulars and pickings from the olio of the week — G. W. Johnson, Alf Wallace, Murphy, J. W. George, Sylvester, Mamie Wallace, Maggie Willet, Sophie Thorne and Annie Edwards. Prices at this time ranged from 25 cents admission to 35 cents and 50 cents in the orchestra and 75 cents in the upper boxes. 10 cents admitted to the gallery, and $4 or $5 would buy a box.

Well, here we are in chilly December, greeting Ada (*sic*) Farwell in five rôles in Advertising for a Wife, and ending the bill (December 5th–10th), with a return of Maude Forrester in Mazeppa, for the tournament scene of which we were promised the Ripleys and the Ramirez Troubadours; later in the month Frank Morosco (in farces), Fannie Bernard, Maggie Romelli, Miss Earle Remington (parodist), Frank Morosco (of the "great" Morosco Family, in a contortion act, "devoid of all unpleasantness"), Emma Hoffman, the Hermans (Charles and La Rosa), the La Rosa Brothers, and Quilter and Goldrich.   The play for December 12th–17th was The Pirates of the Savannah, or, the Tiger Hunter of the Prairie, with Maude Forrester as Fabrico, "the tiger slayer, who makes sure of his aim, a stanch and noble friend," Farwell as Nick Lively, G. W. Johnson as Sarroda, and H. F. Stone as Don Salvatori, a pirate chief.   I hope the reader revels, as I do, in the melodramatic possibilities of those rôles.   Under the Lights of London (the old play of Lost in London) presented (December 19th–24th) Farwell as Job Armroyd and Christine Percy as Nellie.   The title of the play was changed, doubtless in hope of picking up some of the crumbs from the Union Square Theatre, which had won great success, on December 5th, with The Lights o' London.   Not all pirates sail the ocean blue, as Gilbert and Sullivan could well attest.

For the holidays, December 26th–31st, John Denier gave Humpty Dumpty, assisted by Gilbert Hanlon, Harry Leslie, Addie Farwell, Connie H. Denier and Carrie Lewis; specialists introduced were Frank and Fannie (sic) Davis, Walton and Victor (song and dance), Frank Morosco, "Josie" Walby, John Denier (on stilts), and H. F. Stone (army and navy dance). The week of January 2nd–7th revived Robert Macaire (with Farwell and Sylvester) and proffered in the olio the Maxwells, the Murphys (Ella and Paddy), Daisy Norwood, W. T. Dwyer, Frank Morosco, and a ballet. January 9th introduced The White Crook (postponed from the 2nd), with Farwell as Rupert, Lena Aberle as the Naiad Queen, and in other parts, J. F. Edwards and Effie (sic) De Rock, who appeared also in the olio.   J. W. McAndrews and the Saddleman Dancers ("first time in America") also fed "Variety."   In the second week of The White Crook (January 16th–21st), Fannie Bernard succeeded Lena Aberle; in "Variety" for that week appeared Mons. Bushnell and Kitty Thomas, Edith Andow, and Fannie Bernard.   For January 23rd–28th, Avenged, or, the Dogs of the Sierras, brought in the Leonzo Brothers, with Tiger and Lion; new to the olio were Frank de Forrest and his military dog, Danger, Alexander and King, and the La Rosa Brothers (returned).   The week of January 30th–February 4th ended its bills with H. James Seymour and Mrs. Carrie M. Seymour, in Esmeralda; the olio included Sarah Bernard ("queen of song"), the Quaker City Quartette (Frank Budd, Will (?) Laird, Sam Davis and Hi Graham), the Moore Sisters (Eunice and Laura), and "Professor" Abt and the Grecian Mystery — the Dancing Skeleton.

Fayette Welch (in School), Blanche Webster, Griffin and Marks (song and dance), the Quaker City Quartette, the Four Shamrocks, and The Flying Dutchman (with Farwell and Lena Aberle) got us (February 6th–11th) well

[531]

on in our wintry path. Later in the month, we had Morton and Bryant, Clara Cushman, Vanolar ("champion equilibrist"), Kitty Gardner, Harper Brothers (one-legged song and dance), the ballet, La Tarantella (with Mlle. Pasta, Jennie Emmerson, Ada Moore, &c.), the Devere Brothers, and E. D. Davies. The four-act play, Eviction (February 13th–25th) featured two weeks of Charles Frew and Gus Reynolds. And Michael Strogoff began a renewed life of two weeks, on February 27th, with Farwell and Lena Aberle. For March 6th–11th, its fellow in the bills was The Dog Spy, with the Leonzo Brothers.

In March also we had (13th–18th) Louise Foster and A. S. Casper (in Asphyxia), Belle and Lillie La Verde, the well-known quartette of C. V. Seamon, T. E. Somers and E. and W. Girard, Lester and Allen ("the Expressionists"), Karoly and Augusta Ordey, and W. F. Carroll, in Muldoon's Excursion. The week of March 20th–25th brought Nick Roberts's Humpty Dumpty (with three clowns, Grimaldi, Dromio, and Pedro), and with Louise de Luisi, and as specialists, in Act II, the great Rajade Troupe, King and Hildebrand, Tillie Van Buren (xylophone), Annie Hindle, the Onofri Brothers, Florence French, and Parker's dogs. A "new departure" began on March 27th, in a "new local, topical comedy drama," Bachelor's Frolics, with Lena Aberle, Annie Hindle, Myles Morris, A. S. Casper (or Caspar), G. W. Johnson, Harry G. Linesley, Jac. Aberle, Jr., Agnes Milburn, &c., in songs and specialties. For April 3rd–8th, we were treated to The Two Tramps (C. Constantine and A. S. Casper), Frank and Fannie Davis (in A Quiet Rehearsal), Sanders and Dean (in Jubilee Day), and a concluding thriller, The Dumb Man, or, the Felon Heir (with Constantine, Casper, and the regular company). Newcomers for April 10th–15th were Collins and Mack (in The Emeralds' Ball), Jessie Smithers (English serio-comic — "first apearance in America"), Four Ramirez Spanish Troubadours, and Charles E. Emmett ("Dashing Charlie"), with Alice Placide, in Dashing Charlie, or, the Prairie Flower, in which Jessie Smithers acted Mag Magrath, "a gem from the Emerald Isle." On Sunday, April 16th, May Fisk ("authoress, actress and blonde heroine, and cousin of James Fisk") lectured on Fallen Women! A more complete change of policy filled the week of April 17th–22nd with what was called the Bijou Opera Company, in The Mascot, leading rôles falling to Marie Martelle, Eva Featherstone, Signor Ravello, George Graff, Alfred P. Beaver (who also was manager) and Harry G. Linesley. During the next week (April 24th–29th), Fannie Louise Buckingham reverted to the tried and true, as Mazeppa, with James Ward as Premislaus, H. F. Stone as the Castellan and Thamar, H. G. Linesley as Drolinsko, Mamie Wallace as Olinska, and Albert S. Casper (or Caspar) as Abder Khan.

I suspect that Aberle's was none too prosperous. For the week of May 1st–6th it admitted May Fisk's English Blondes, with a "swinging first part," directed by Billy Blair (bones), May Fisk (interlocutor), and Frank McClane (our old friend from the National Varieties, and skilled in such shows, as "tambo"). The bills ended with Blondes on a Lark. Among the fair ladies were Bertha Bates, Nellie Boisset, Jennie Sinclair, Ada Moore, Lizzie Gonzales and Zilla Loton, whom I really dislike to "eternise." Jessie Garrett's English Blondes succeeded (weeks of May 8th–20th) with Joe Buckley as bones, A. S. Caspar as interlocutor, and McClane as "tambo." Many of the same "swinging angels" remained, but somewhere in the bills, one week or the other, figured Arnold Kiralfy and Mlle. Pasta in dances, G. W. Johnson, Caspar and others (in farces), Mike Gallagher, Georgie Arnott and Joe Buckley (in The Lively Coon). "Our Swinging Angels" continued, with name changed to "Our Swinging English Blondes"; bones, "tambo" and interlocutor varied from week to week, but, at this place, from time to time in May and June might have been seen Grace McClane, Edith Andow, the Brennans and Laible (in The Jolly Coopers), Frank T. Morton, My Way (with McClane, Caspar, Grace McClane), Kiralfy and Pasta (in ballets), Lena Aberle (in The Sleeping Beauty, weeks of May 22nd–June 10th), Frank and Fannie (still so spelled) Davis, John Hogan and Lizzie Mowbray (in Flirtations), Señor Lerch (imitation of musical instruments, animals, etc.), the Ramirez Family (Joseffy, Guillamo and La Belle Marie), Max Rostock (German character comedian), Charles Constantine's Une Nuit de la Joie, Billy Bryant, Lillie Hall, Luigi dell' Oro, Grace McClane (double-voiced), Les Jolies Grisettes (with Mlle. Pasta), Kitty McDermott, the Boston Quartette (Richard Parker, Edward Trutt, J. H. U. Harris and H. C. Chivers), &c. On June 26th, the Swinging Angels gave way to The Sultan's Harem, as opening delectability; this yielded, in turn, on July 10th, to a first part named The Shepherd's Festival. And, lo! on July 24th came back Our Swinging Angels, which continued to enrapture small boys and others till August died out of the calendar.

Meantime, I hurry through the weeks. Lillie Hall, Lena Aberle, Larry Smith, McClane, and others, in Hassanbad, lasted from June 12th to June 24th, and resigned the stage to Ixion (June 26th–July 1st) with Lillie Hall in the title-rôle, and Lena Aberle as Jupiter. The never-dying Forty Thieves began, on July 3rd, a three-weeks occupation as concluding farce, Irene Worrell appearing as Ganem, Lillie Hall as Abdallah, and J. O. Hall as Ali Baba — the last-named succeeded before long by G. W. Johnson. In one capacity or another, during those heated evenings, appeared Nellie Arthur, Jennie Sinclair, Ed Howard and J. L. Barry (in Connolly's Troubles), Billy Bryant ("nephew of Dan Bryant"), Kitty McDermott, the Boston Quartette, Mlle. Pasta (in La Cecilienne), Tommy and William Cooper, Georgie Parker, Irene Worrell, Ada (?) Edgecombe (serio-comic), St. George Hussey, Ada Forrest, Bobby Newcomb (most welcome to me), Arthur Stiles and Smith (in song and dance), Mlle. Pasta (in La Maja de Seville or Le Diable à Quatre),

[533]

M. Foley, Irene Carleton, John Callan, Ada Hulmes, Lizzie Miller, &c. Concluding the bills for two weeks (July 24th–August 5th) we had Bobby Newcomb's arrangement, Babil and Bijou, with Irene Worrell and Irene Carleton in the title-rôles, with Sadie Meehan as Orson, George W. Johnson as Sir Rupert, John Callan as Hogseye, &c. Irene Worrell was serving also as interlocutor or otherwise in the act of Our Swinging Angels. Late July and August entire favoured the olio with Lizzie Miller, Alice Lerners, Bobby Newcomb, the Brennans and Laible, Charles Worley, Arthur Stiles, Victor Koop (Le Postillon de Longjumeau), Levanion and Lexington (Spanish rings), Pasta and a ballet of thirty (in The Gathering of the Clans), John Walsh, the Muldoon Quartette (Willis, Harris, Maxwell and Green), Pettingill, P. H. Gale, Dailey, James Hoey (the American Four), Ada Forrest, Fanny Western (some not bad), Grace Arnold (serio-comic), Billy Diamond, &c. The concluding entertainment for three weeks (August 7th–26th) was R. A. Brennan's burlesque Pinafore, with Captain George Laible as Mr. Joseph Weisbeer, Irene Worrell as Josephine, Brennan as Captain Cork-a-ran, Bobby Newcomb as Jack Rackstraw, and Mrs. Brennan as Buttercup. The closing week of August 28th–September 2nd ended its bills with Atalanta, or, the Female Athlete, with Lena Aberle (as the runner), Irene Worrell (as Hippomenes), H. F. Stone, Larry Smith, Georgie Parker, &c.

METROPOLITAN THEATRE (LATE TONY PASTOR'S), 1881–1882

Of course, if Pastor moved from 585 Broadway, others would be ready to enter the house. As Tony Pastor's (still so named), it had remained open during the summer of 1881, the Rentz-Santley Company presenting there in early September its burlesque Haze L. Kirke. On September 19th entered M. B. Leavitt's Great Specialty Company, including Sanford and Wilson, Andy and Annie Hughes, Rudolf Levico and Susie Dillon, the Four Diamonds, Nellie Richards, the Two Barneys (Barney McNulty and Master Barney, in Malony's Visit), Val Vose, Bonnie Runnells, and Andy Collum.

Then, on September 26th, the Metropolitan Theatre (late Tony Pastor's) flew open with a flourish, presenting the Yannanabachi Gasha Dancers ("a quartet of beauteous Japanese maidens"), Little All Right, Flora Moore, Hassaboura Sam, Larry Tooley, Erba Robeson, the Vivian Sisters, William Carroll, &c. Here, during the next few weeks appeared, though, of course, not all together, Fanny V. Reynolds, the Three Rankins, Mlle. Catherine, Lizzie Byron, the Three Sisters Vivian, Chalet, William F. Carroll, Larry Tooley, May Hamilton, Charles Gilday and George H. Wood (these for the week of October 3rd–8th); George Spence and Minnie Sartelle, Perry and Lulu Ryan, Add Weaver and Georgie Melnotte (week of October 10th–15th); Allie Drayton, Moore and Lessenger, the Japanese dancers (here since their début), and Scenes at the Grand Central, with Allie Drayton, W. F.

Carroll and Larry Tooley (all this for the week of October 17th–22nd); Katie Cooper, Mealey and Mackey, Marlow and Plunkett, Bowman and Radcliffe, W. F. Carroll and Master Eddie, George H. Wood, Larry Tooley, Allie Drayton, the Japanese dancers, and Scenes at the Grand Central (October 24th–29th).

Thus October lapsed insensibly into November. The week of October 31st–November 5th gave us John L. Sullivan, of Boston, now matched to fight Paddy Ryan for $5,000; he would appear all week with Billy Madden. And in the bill was a St. Petersburg Ballet, directed by Alexander Blandowski, and with Viro Farrand and Florence Barrett as *premières*. The Metropolitan was feeling its way, and, on November 6th, advertised itself as "the Home of Sensationalism," specifying only its St. Petersburg Ballet, and its Louis XVI Minuet. The sketch, on November 21st was Piper Heidsieck, or, Lights of Gotham; in the olio were the Two Haleys, the Ordeys, Fred Hallen and Enid Hart, Bessie Bell, Chalet, Harry and Minnie Wood, and Dan and Gussie Hart. Along with the St. Petersburg Ballet, the Louis XVI Minuet and Piper Heidsieck we find on November 28th, Mme. A. Rudolf, Pauline Batchellor (*sic*), Smith and Leopold, Bothwick Reid, Sallie Mason, Fannie Lucille, and the abiding Harry and Minnie Wood. Few of these people established abiding reputations; nor did many of the lights of the following week (December 5th–10th), Emerson and Clark, Fanny (*sic*) Lucille, Louise Vavasour, George B. Radcliffe, the Woods (ever here), Quilter and Goldrich, Donnelly and Drew, &c. The Arion Ball was skit of the bill, and a Havanese ballet was depended on for lightsome grace — twenty-one Cuban Sylphs, and a genuine Cuban orchestra helped to that end. The place now advertised as "the Home of Seductive Sensationalism." The Cubans remained for the week of December 12th, vying with the St. Petersburg dancers. The Grotesque Four, the Villons (John, William and Elise), Jimmy Gough, John and Lea Peasley, and A Puff of Smoke were included in the lure. A third week glorified the Havanese (December 19th–24th), along with the Barlow Brothers, the Horseshoe Four (Four was the mystic number everywhere in Vaudeville), Larry Tooley, Radcliffe, Irene Worrell, Manning and Drew and the everlasting Woods. The week beginning on December 26th gave a cornucopia of Christmas delights — Viro Farrand, Fanny (*sic*) Lucille, Viola Clifton, Frank Bush, Pat Reilly, Irene Watson, Durell Twin Brothers, Delvan and Tracy, Larry Tooley, Jimmy Gough, and the skit of The Fortuitous Forty. The St. Petersburg Ballet, in its specialty of the Louis XVI minuet, was, of course, the chief feature, in weeks preceding, and in the weeks to come; with it, on January 9th, were listed Viro Farrand, Fanny Lucille and twenty-five "lovely coryphées." The olio included Add Weaver and Nellie Parker, Magee and Allen, George H. Wood, Crossley and Elder, Sallie Mason, Harry and Minnie Wood, Larry Tooley, George B. Ratcliffe, Karoly and Augusta Ordey and Donnelly and Drew.

[535]

The show concluded with Gotham by Night. With the same St. Petersburg Ballet, on January 16th came Lizzie Derious and Allie Smith, Kerrigan and McCarthy, the "Four Fair Feminine Paroxyamalists," Weston and Hanson, the Four Shamrocks, Howard Dorr and Son, Frank and Lillian White. Shades and Shadow, or, a Night's Adventure, gathered the loose ends of joy into a sketch.

And now the Metropolitan, on January 23rd, let itself go along the primrose path, announcing (I am not responsible for its "French") Les Cocettes Fantastiques in Les Bizarre Masque, "the latest sensualistic, terpsichorean craze in charming Paris, the home of riotous festivity." If that would not attract a certain type of visitor, what would? The dubious delectability figured next week (January 30th–February 4th), along with the abiding St. Petersburg Ballet, J. W. McAndrews, the Clipper Quartette, Capitola Forrest and Laura Bennett, William Gaylord, George H. Wood, Lizzie Hunter, Tillie Graham, Harry and Minnie Wood, Sallie Mason and George B. Radcliffe. And there was a questionable show named Nana, or, the Blonde Venus, which had a protracted life at the Metropolitan; with Les Cocettes Fantastique (*sic*) and the St. Petersburg Ballet, it carried through the week of February 13th–18th, when the olio boasted of John and Lea Peasley, Frank Bush, and others so often mentioned in this chronicle. Fleeting Follies joined the crew, on February 27th, as did Intrigue, or, Robes de Rouge. Maggie Cline was here, beginning on March 13th, as well as La Aragonaza (Castilian dancers) and the St. Petersburg Ballet; George H. Wood's sketch, Fascination, or, the Princess and Soldier, also tried to please. The olio presented Lester and Williams, Howard Dorr and Son, May Richards, Lizzie Hunter, Ten Roman Students, and Harry and Minnie Wood.

I plough on, as in duty bound. A group of Nautch dancers, Charles White, Th. Clark, Levanion and McCormick stood by (March 27th–April 1st) as warmer days began. On the 3rd, came George H. Wood's burlesque, Golden Pippins. A testimonial to R. Fitzgerald, on the afternoon of April 7th, leaves me cold. I pass, because of sparse advertising, to April 24th, when the St. Petersburg Ballet had, as première, Mlle. Peponelli, "the greatest can-can dancer living." With that exhibition I leave the Metropolitan, because I found no further details of its offerings for the season under review.

METROPOLITAN CONCERT HALL, 1881–1882

We attended many concerts, during the summer season, at the Metropolitan Concert Hall, with Rudolf Bial's orchestra discoursing sweet music, not too heavy in intent; the last concert of this season fell on September 25th, and took the form of a benefit for Bial.

[536]

As the Metropolitan Casino, the place opened, on October 10th, under management of E. G. Gilmore, with no less an attraction than the Comley-Barton Company, in Olivette, Catherine Lewis and John Howson heading the list of artists.   And "Grand Sunday Concerts" began on the 16th, with Gilmore's Band, Henrietta Markstein, H. M. Stanley (tenor), B. C. Bent (cornetist), Emily Spader, Raffayolo (euphonium) and Signor de Carlo (piccolo); the second concert (October 23rd) gave us Rudolf Bial's orchestra (Henry J. Widmer directing), Laura Stelzner (singer) and Anna Teresa Berger (cornetist).   Olivette departed on October 29th, and, on the 31st, Les Cloches de Corneville employed Kate Monroe, Helen Dingeon, Pauline Hall, Charles Campbell, William H. Seymour, Richard Golden, Edward Connell, &c.   It is well the reader does not expect me to account for the inexplicable craze then raging for repetitions of Olivette, The Mascot, Patience, The Chimes of Normandy, in theatre after theatre.   For the Sunday concerts, now, the Casino drafted talent from the Mapleson opera; on November 6th were promised Mlle. Lauri, Emma Juch, Novara and Anna T. Berger, and, on the 13th, Prevost, Lauri and Mme. Sacconi (the fine harpist). The soloists on the 20th were Virginia Ferni, Mme. Sacconi, Runcio and Del Puente.   And Les Cloches de Corneville ran on (it must have been partly due to Kate Monroe) till November 26th; Sunday, the 27th, brought Ravelli, Corsini, Lauri, E. Wiener and E. Belz.

On the 28th, the Hanlon-Lees transferred here from the Park Theatre their highly diverting Voyage en Suisse, Corinne, the child wonder, being announced to appear every afternoon at two, beginning on the 29th, in The Magic Slipper.   There was difficulty with the law, over the youth of the childish actress.   From November 28th, the house was known merely as the Casino.   The Sunday concert, December 4th, provided Paola Marié, Julie Lentz, Mauras, Maugé, &c.   On the 11th came Emma Juch and Prevost.   Le Voyage en Suisse journeyed, on December 17th, to Niblo's, and J. H. Haverly's company, on the 19th, entered the Casino with Patience, the cast including Dora Wiley, Gertrude Orme, Pauline Hall, William Seymour, Alonzo Hatch and James Dalton.   The concert, on Sunday, December 18th, gave us Jenny Stubel, Emma Seebold, Alexander Klein and Karl Walther, from the Thalia; the 25th enlisted Ravelli, Marie Vachot, and Mlle. Kalas (replacing Lelia Lauri); January 1st brought Carolina Zeiss, Anna T. Berger, Montegriffo and the Rudolf Bial orchestra.   Patience departed on December 31st.

One sees that the Casino had become a real theatre.   Hague's British Operatic Minstrels began, on January 2nd, with fifty performers, including the two Wises in acrobatic dances, Billy Richards (stump orator) and Professor Wallace (imitator of birds and animals); there was also a comic act, The Major.   For the concert, on Sunday, the 8th, were advertised Carolina Zeiss, Miss Berger, Montegriffo, and, if the reader can credit it, Cora de

[537]

Wilhorst (in the shadow song from Dinorah)! Hague's Minstrels, on Sunday, the 15th, gave a ballad concert, the singers including C. Samuels, C. Young, G. Dodd, C. Rubens, Edgar Wilson, C. Garland, T. W. Walton, W. B. Stoddart, J. M. Wood, T. Currie, W. S. Waud, and J. O'Keefe. Faithful C. E. Pratt accompanied. The minstrel band remained until January 21st, and gave another ballad concert, by way of farewell, on the 22nd. According to Allston Brown, Henry E. Abbey and E. G. Gilmore retired from the management on January 29th. On April 17th, the Zanfretta Troupe were advertised in The Brigands; the place was then called the Metropolitan Alcazar.

A long darkness settled on the place until it re-opened on June 17th, still as the Metropolitan Alcazar, J. Fred Zimmermann, manager. Adelaide Randall (a charming singer), Fanny Wentworth, Rosa Cooke and Signor Montegriffo sang Plighted by Moonlight, a version of Offenbach's Un Mariage aux Lanternes; there was also a ballet, involving Mlle. Amalia Lepri and the Misses Rose. Signor de Novellis conducted, and Juignet was stage manager. On June 28th, Marie Vanoni appeared. The last night of Plighted by Moonlight and the Tarantella ballet came on July 3rd. On the 4th, The Doctor of Alcantara and Delibes's ballet of Sylvia made delightful entertainment; in the former appeared Misses Randall, Wentworth and Cooke, and Messrs. Montegriffo, Ellis Ryse, Vincent Hogan and Harry Allen. Mlle. Lepri appeared in the ballet, and Marie Vanoni still gave her "polyglot" specialties. The Hungarian Gipsy Band only was stressed in advertisements of July 10th, but the opera and the ballet remained till July 28th. The Merry War transferred here, on July 29th, from the Germania Theater, with Dora Wiley, Fanny Wentworth (replacing Louise Paullin), Molly Powers (replacing Pauline Hall), W. T. Carleton, Richard Golden and Adolfi. It ran till August 18th; on the 19th, in came the inevitable La Mascotte, with Adah Richmond, of all people in the world, as Bettina, Pauline Hall as Fiametta, J. W. Norcross as Lorenzo, S. P. Norman as Frederic, C. W. Dungan as Pippo, and W. H. Crompton as Rocco. The Snake Charmer emerged, on August 28th, with some of the artists seen two weeks before — Selina Dolaro, Lilly Post and Emma Guthrie. Olivette, beginning on September 4th, ended this term of management, with Selina Dolaro as Olivette, Lilly Post as the Countess, Miss Guthrie as Veloutine, Joseph Greensfelder as de Merrimac, George Gaston as des Ifs, Louis Pfau as Valentine and Harry Standish as Coquelicot; the last night of the present Olivette clanged on September 16th.

KOSTER AND BIAL'S, 1881–1882

The reader may this year note the change of Koster and Bial's into a musico-variety hall. We carried the establishment through the summer of

1881, with performances by Remenyi, and may begin, on September 4th, with the twenty-seventh appearance of that virtuoso; S. Liebling also had been recently at the popular resort.   Sunday, September 11th, marked the last appearance of Neuendorff's orchestra, and the last appearance but three of Remenyi.   On the 12th, Carl Hamm took up the duties of musical director.   On Sunday, September 25th, came the "first appearance in America" of the Ladies' Philharmony, with Julia de Bertrand, leader, and an orchestra of "lady pupils" from the Conservatories of Leipzig, Prague and Vienna, and the "first" in America of the Rainer Family of Tyrolean Warblers, "three ladies and five gentlemen."   These attractions remained for many weeks.   They were joined, on October 30th, by Juliette Laurence, "chanteuse internationale," who also filled a long engagement.   The week of December 26th–31st united with those long-staying visitors Louis Blumenberg, 'cellist.   The last week of all these autumn entertainers was announced to begin on January 9th; Juliette Laurence said farewell on Sunday, the 15th, when a special engagement began with the Roman Students.

Sunday, January 22nd, brought in the Stettin Humoristen Sextet, and marked the début in New York of Patti Rosa, for long thereafter a popular music hall singer.   The occasion was also notable in that it was the thousandth concert given in the hall; and, though the Rainers and Juliette Laurence had departed, Julia de Bertrand and her Ladies' Philharmony still appeared.   The entertainers, beginning on Sunday, February 5th, were Mlle. Imbre Marthe, "from the Paris Opéra Comique," Patti Rosa, Julia de Bertrand, the Ladies' Philharmony, the Stettin Sextet and William Woodhead; I trust the reader sees why I denominated the hall a home of musicovariety.   On February 12th, Marie Hasslacher (prima donna), and Rudolphe Frische (comic actor), joined Patti Rosa, Julia de Bertrand, and the Ladies' Philharmony.   Mlle. Marie König was here during the week of February 19th–25th and later; and May Livingston began on March 5th.   On Sunday, March 12th, appeared Adolphe William Kirchner, "concert master of the King of Hanover," in his Comic Eccentric Concert.   The full list, on March 19th, and later, comprised Marie König, May Livingston, Frische, Julia de Bertrand, the Ladies' Philharmony, and I. Shukowsky (a basso excellently named in a sort of humorous way); the last appearance of Marie König came on March 23rd, but the others just cited remained, Theodore Hoch, cornetist, blowing in with the very last March gales, on the 26th.

A new combination began on April 10th, with Fred Roberts ("the Lion Comic"), the Ladies' Philharmony, Adrienne Trevais (cantatrice), Mlle. Nandl Hofer (Tyrolese warbler), Hoch and Frische.   Fred Roberts, and Mlles. Trevais and Hofer left on the 22nd, but E. C. Dunbar, Milanese minstrel, joined on the 17th.   Charles Heywood, the "male soprano" and female impersonator, long absent from our chronicle, was at Koster and

[539]

Bial's, in the week of April 24th–29th. On May 7th, a season of summer concerts began, with Arbuckle's Band, Carl Kegel (clarinet), Arbuckle (cornet) and Harry I. G. Frank (euphonium). Stabat Mater was in the bill for Sunday, May 21st; on Sunday, June 11th, Arbuckle rendered selections from La Damnation de Faust, and Mendelssohn's Midsummer-Night's Dream music. His engagement closed on the 17th. June 18th introduced a Hungarian Gipsy Band; with it, in early July, appeared Henrietta Markstein and the Rainer Tyrolean Warblers. Fred W. Zaulig was here, as were the Three St. Felix Sisters in later July. The week of July 31st–August 5th restored Marie Vanoni and brought in Adelaide de Smidt, prima donna soprano; Zaulig and the Tyrolean National Singers were part of the joy. The twelve hundredth concert occurred on August 13th. Malvina Renner, late of the Ring Theater, Vienna, was here for the last evenings of August; and Marie Vanoni still held the stage. With this announcement I pass for 1881–82 from Koster and Bial's.

MADISON SQUARE GARDEN, 1881–1882

The big garden in Madison Square reopened on Tuesday, September 6th, with W. C. Coup's Hippodrome, Triple Circus, Monster Menagerie and Automatic Museum. It promised "ten monster exhibitions," and "Lu Lu, a human being hurled through the air from a huge iron catapult — a distance of over 100 feet." Katie and Emma Stokes were in the force, and a mammoth street parade, on the 5th, initiated wide-eyed boyhood into a wealth of promised glories. Three weeks were all that Coup won of metropolitan custom; he departed on September 24th.

Scarce advertising necessitates a leap to January 26th, when the Grand Opera Ball invited the curious and the frivolous. On February 15th came the Twelfth Regiment Reception and Drill, and, on the 21st, the Arion Society seriously tried to be gay with its annual Grand Masquerade Ball. But the Garden reverted to its normal stride on February 24th, when the Manhattan Athletic Club winter meeting had L. E. Myers competing against time, or on the 27th when Gilmore's Band by a sacred concert inaugurated a Grand Six-Day Go-as-You-Please, for many champions, including Charles Rowell, P. Fitzgerald, J. Sullivan, Robert Vint, G. D. Noremac, George Hazael, W. H. Scott, John Hughes and P. J. Panchot (these at least were advertised), for a sweepstakes of $9,000, and the champion's diamond whip — "the handsomest trophy ever contended for." Peter Duryea was manager of this great walking contest, Hamilton Busbey referee and stakeholder. If this had happened in the 1930s, the radio would simply have burst with delight. Well, Hazael was victor, with a record of 600 miles, Fitzgerald coming second with 577, and Noremac third with 555.

And lo! on March 13th came Barnum's Greatest Show on Earth and

[540]

KATE MONROE

SIGNOR DE NOVELLIS

MONTEGRIFFO

PAULINE HALL

RUDOLF BIAL

ANNIE T. BERGER

PATTI ROSA

MARIE KÖNIG

MARIE VANONI

London Circus. Lu Lu, flying through air, a band of Zulus, trained serpents, a four-legged girl, twenty racing camels, ten towering giraffes, twenty-two trained elephants, Brustad (Norway giant), Chemah (Chinese dwarf), Zazel shot from a cannon (how well I remember the thrill of that episode!), Major Atom and Wild Men of Borneo — these were some of the wonders of the master showman. On April 10th, Barnum was able to announce that Jumbo, hugest of elephants, was at last here, and on exhibition with the circus. Tom Thumb, Jenny Lind, Jumbo — are these Barnum's three most famous contributions to American wonder and amaze? Ye gods, the talk that Jumbo caused! I still hear it in a kind of postprandial delight, since really I did not revel in the feast itself. But Jumbo certainly was advertised until imagination clutched in vain at greater marvels.

Barnum filled a month. On May 8th, began a week of a delectable show — "artists sketching from life as in their studios." Far different was the delight of July 17th, when I learn from the Herald that John L. Sullivan was, if not outslugged, at least chagrined, in a glove fight by Joseph Collins (Tug Wilson), champion of England. Wilson was adjudged winner because Sullivan failed to knock him out.

Aquarium (Equine Paradox and Cosmopolitan Theatre), 1881–1882

The puzzled Aquarium, at Broadway and 35th Street, that could never seem quite to make up its mind as to what it was or what its purpose, became, on October 24, 1881, the Equine Paradox, and there F. M. Comstock began, on that date, to exhibit educated horses for all and sundry who liked educated horses; these trained specialists were curvetting and prancing so late as early February.

On April 24th the Cosmopolitan Theatre (late Aquarium) opened under the management of Thorpe and Company, with a variety list including Emerson and Clark, Ella Wesner, Frank Gibbons, Powers Brothers, Lillie Raymond, Hattie and Bennie Grinnell, Prince Awata Katsnoshin, Celene Vareis, Frank King, C. W. Ravel and Harry Bryant. The place struggled on, and was advertising, on May 8th, "variety and sports," and Adrien and Revillo (magicians).

Vercelli's: Grand Central Theatre, 1881–1882

On the highest peak of the Matterhorn, we think not of little hills; I wish, almost, that it were not necessary to bring into the narrative that did more stately domes decree the record of Vercelli's Theatre, 152 and 154 East 42nd Street, between Third Avenue and Lexington, which we met in 1880. On August 8th, this theatre opened, with the Marie Gurney Opera

[541]

Company in Pinafore, and the Martinetti dancers. August 29th brought Fanny (or Fannie) Wallack and the Wallack Tripologue Company, in The Irish Heiress, or, Perfection, and Torturing Tame Turtles. Only three performers participated — Miss Wallack, Watty Wallack, and J. A. Ryder. With the farces a musical *mélange* spread (I hope) a kind of pleasure. The Herald advertises the entertainment for at least two weeks. The house, renamed the Grand Central Theatre, again re-opened, on October 17th, for a season of vaudeville, under the management of Burnett and Wittaker. The attractions were Alf Burnett's Tea Party and Fanny Wallack's Tripologue Company. I learn from the Herald of November 7th that Our Club, at this theatre, met with "roars of laughter." Under another heading, I have discussed Italian plays at Vercelli's.

VOLKSGARTEN, 1881–1882

I feel like a general lining up the cohorts of "Variety." From house to house they flit, in kaleidoscopic shiftings, leaving one thankful that it is not necessary to trace their individual migrations week by week, through the intricacies of a given season; think of following each and every one of them in the various combinations from one theatre to another for fifty-two weeks of the year!

Shuddering at the very idea of that, I invite the eager reader on Monday, September 12, 1881, to the Volksgarten, there to enjoy the "turns" of the Grinnells, Harry La Rose (or La Rosa), J. H. Byrne, Lillie Wood (cantatrice), Press Eldridge, Boyd and Sarsfield, Melrose and La Rosa, and the appearance of W. H. Rightmire and Hattie Grinnell in the play of The Two Wanderers. Subsequently in balmy autumn nights one might have seen Tommy J. Harpin (in a one-legged song and dance act), Georgie Melnotte, Geyer and Mack, the La Rosa Brothers, Amy Nelson, the Three Ronaldos (*sic*), Adelina Gasparini and her little sister, Ida (in Meg), De Lacey and Parker, John L. Manning ("transmogrification trapeze star"), Jennie Southern, Ward and Lynch, the Cooper Brothers, Williams and Morton, &c. The concluding play for the week of October 3rd–8th was The Molly Maguires, or, the Black Diamond of Hazelton, with Jerry Cohan as Mark O'Dare, the Black Diamond Engineer, W. C. Cameron as Banty Bob, E. M. Favor as Bernard McTurk, J. R. Gildersleeve as Nathan Lyford, E. S. Goodwin as Marius Duychink, Helen Cohan as Diana Duychink, the flower of Duychink House, and Lucy Adams as Pauline. As to this serious matter, read the note on the house-bill of October 4th: "Never has a play been written with so many startling situations as presented in this drama. The Grand Conflagration Scene of the Coal Mine Breaker and the charge of the Pennsylvania Regiment on that memorable night of blood and carnage, are of the most thrilling character. The play abounds in sentiment, elevating in its nature, showing how political intrigue, wire pullers and capitalists, used the secret order of the Molly Maguires to carry out their wicked and tyranical [*sic*] designs." Now we see where George M. Cohan (son of Jerry and Helen) obtained his sense of theatrical values.

Let us hurry through October and November, noting, as our chariot rolls along, such familiar (or mayhap such unfamiliar) figures as Clooney and Ryan, Edith Andow, the Four Comets, Belle Fairmount (singer), Charles Gilday, Fanny V. Reynolds, George C. Charles and Katie Moffett (in The Skeleton Hand, or, the Lost Diamond, a Tale of St. Louis, thrilling for October 10th–15th), Fred J. Huber and Kitty Allyne (in Pleasant Dreams), Lucy Adams ("our own comic singer"), Leonard and Jones (the Telegraph Lads), Jeffreys Warner (burlesque actress), the Two Clarks (Hen and Major, the latter set down as "the smallest comedian in the world"), Master Roberts (Irish comedian), Charles L. Howard (as Aunt Keziah, in Mrs. Joshua Whitcomb, assisted — October 17th–22nd — by Hattie Morris, Master Lorin, Cameron, F. J. Post, Ed Favor, Huber, Kitty Allyne, Lucy Adams, &c.), Max and Martha Miller, Ada Burnett, Binney and Fraine ("greatest living English and Irish songsters, dancers, and electric change artists"), Dick Gorman, Magee and Taylor, Fanny Herring (October 24th–29th, in Little Buckshot), Melville and Bunell, Harry Lloyd, Tony Williams and Andy Shields (late of Favor and Shields), Clara Cushman, Orndorff and McDonald, Charles Diamond, Dan and Gussie Hart (in Uncle Pete's Return), Charles Redmond and Georgie Blake, Maude Leigh, John F. Fenton, Boyd and Sarsfield, Nelton (Egyptian boy juggler), the Burtons (John and Lottie, in The Good Old Home), the Three Aubreys (gymnasts), Fannie Bernard, Sailor West, Foster and Hughes, and Dan McCarthy. Finishing the programmes for October 31st–November 5th came Frank Jones and Alice Montague, in The Black Hand, or, the Lost Will, with "a human being suspended between life and death on a Huge Derrick." And a great railroad scene! These stars remained for the week of November 7th–12th, in On the Brink, or, the Creole Slave. E. T. Goodrich, in Grizzly Adams, had the week of November 21st–26th.

Stars of the sparkling heavens of December were Sanders and Dean (in Jubilee Day), Georgie Melnotte, Sam Martin (one-legged dancer), Frank George, the Vanes (Will and James, "from the St. James Music Hall, London"), Jessie Merton (lyric), W. J. Fleming, with his dogs, Hero and Hector (December 5th–10th, in For a Life, with new scenery by Sailor West, "our excellent scenic artist"), the La Porte Sisters (Rose and Lillie), Carroll and Walters (in In and Out), Ford and Knowles (in What's the News?), Walsh and Dempsey (Irish), Hettinger and Nibbe (songs and dances), Emma Hoffman, the play, Held at Bay (with Nellie Germon, W. C. Cameron, Harry Linson, Sailor West and Lucy Adams — week of December 12th–17th). Perforce, Harvard bills failing, I leap to the week of January

[543]

2nd–7th, with a starry host composed of Ward and Lynch, Belle La Verde, Williams and Sully, P. C. Foy (Irish tenor), Fayette Welch, Fanny V. Reynolds, W. H. Rightmire and his pony, Little Nell, in The Two Wanderers. The files at Harvard become defective. One more for January and three for February yield the names of Joe Redmond and Ada Clifton, Ned Goodwin and Thomas Watson (in Just from Amsterdam), Madge Aiston, Shed Le Clair, Herr Drayton (juggling cannon-balls weighing thirty, forty and sixty-four pounds each), Hanshew and Jennie McClellan (January 9th, in Lucretia Borgia), Charles Harris and Billy Wood (in Grousemier's Brewery), Isabel Ward, Morton and Bryant, Dell Trudell (double-voiced singer), Trudell and Rowan, Gus Hill, Dick Gorman (in Conrad), Flynn and Euson (Irish song and dance), Williams and Sully, Lucy Adams, Nellie Abbott, the Quaker City Quartette (Frank Budd, Sam Burnell, Will Laird and Hi Graham, in camp meeting songs, etc.), Frank Lavarnie and Jessie Leseur (in Road Agents), Hen and Billy Clark, Den and Ella Howe (in Flirtation), Harry Lloyd, the Four Emeralds (in Out for a Stroll), Carrie Lewis and Carl Hertz, and the play (February 27th–March 4th) of Time and the Hour, with Hanshew, Cameron, Lucy Adams and Jennie McClellan.

The week of March 6th–11th provided novelty in Frank Peasley and Tom Vennetta (in Sallie, Will You Marry?), Myles Morris ("the Irish gentleman," in Just from Canada), Cavana and Mack (in Shakespeare Outdone) Theresa Girard (ballads), Paddy and Ella Murphy, and Harry Amlar in Counterfeit, in which he played Peter G. Washington Green, a "cullud" boy, assisted by Harry Lloyd, Den Howe, Cameron, Jerry Cavana, Dick Mack (evidently of the team of Ferguson and Mack), Myles Morris, Peasley, Vennetta, Andy Lynch, Lucy Adams and Ella Murphy — a cast selected entirely from the ranks of the olio. Fayette Welch (in School), Nellie Germon, John Pendy and Jeffreys Warner (in Anything You Like), Donnelly and Drew (in The Irish Strangers), Fayette Welch and Harry Lloyd (in The Two Italians), the Four Comets, Charles Constantine (March 20th–25th, in The Dumb Man, or, the Felon Heir), Jessie Merton, Joe Palles and John Cusick ("The Sunbursts of Ireland"), Graham and Butler ("champion all around shots of the world"), and W. J. Thompson, Lotta (sic) Forrest, and the dogs, Hero and Hector, in For a Life (March 27th–April 1st) — behold the offerings for March, the blustery and unkind! April varied with shiftings, in order cited, of Applicants for a Position (with Frank George, Lucy Adams, Lloyd and Goodwin), Lillie Raymond (serio-comic), Andy Shields and James Richmond (Irish — "first appearance in this city"), Naoni ("artistic juggler"), Leonard and Jones, Frank Jones and Alice Montague (in The Black Hand, for the week of April 3rd–8th, and, for the following week, in On the Brink), Fannie (sic) Sanford (sic), Hettinger and Nibbe (German Emigrants), Harry Edwards and Lew Morton, Charles Turner (banjo), Joe and Annie Burgess (in The Little Widow),

George Stansil and Ed Ryan (in Who Won Her?), Tony Farrell and Ned Ryan (in Slattery's Boarding House), the Favor Brothers (in The Lackawanna Spooners); Charles Weston and Charles Hanson (in Rehearsal in the Parlour), Lucy Adams, and the excruciatingly funny Russell Brothers. For the week of April 17th–22nd, N. S. Wood (with Maurice Pike, Sallie Mason, Ed M. Favor and Jennie McClellan) closed the bills in The Boy Detective; for the week of April 24th–29th he gave The Life and Adventures of Jack Sheppard.

The special artists in May were Cavana and Mack (in Shakespeare Outdone), Annie Hart, Clem Magee and Bob Allen (in Men of Nerve), Carrie Lewis, the De Bar Brothers, Andy Collum, Murphy and Miles (The Gentlemen from Kerry), Emma Marden (songstress), Morris and Fields (in Rudolph and Ricka Klein), the Olympia Trio (Keough, Mack and Randalls — formerly of the Olympia Quartette), Lamont and Ducrow (The Happy Hottentots), Crosby and Martin, Isabel Ward, Billy Moore (song and dance), Fannie (sic) V. Reynolds, Lizzie Mulvey and Alice d'Estelle (songs, dances, clogs), James D. Roome, Andy and Annie Hughes (in Norah's Birthday), McVicker (sic) and Saunders (in The Modern School of Acting), Charles A. Burke (lightning change), Lillie Western, and Quilter and Goldrich (in Ordinary Conversation). Concluding plays were Rightmire's The California Detective (May 1st–6th) and his The Two Wanderers (8th–13th); in both he was assisted by his pony, Little Nell. For the week of May 15th–20th, Dick Gorman appeared, with Joseph V. Arlington and Isabella (sic) Ward, in Conrad; the week of the 22nd–27th, gave us Dick Gorman and May Estelle, in My Hebrew Friend. For May 29th–June 3rd Henry Belmer starred as Lester Roland and Old Crazy Joe, in his own melodrama, To the End of the World, the assisting cast including W. C. Cameron, Ed M. Favor, Harry Lloyd, Ned Lang, Joseph Hart, Lucy Adams (now merely in the "stock"), Mrs. Brennan and Ida Gasparini; the olio for that week provided Lang and Rosa, Willis Pickert, the Brennans and Laible (in The Coopers), Marlow and Hart, and Fields and Leslie. The June incitements included the Maxwells, Daisy Norwood, Williams and Sully, Farrell and Ryan (in a German act), Frank McNish and the Leland Sisters (Rose and Jennie), Henry Belmer and May Estelle (5th–10th, in A Double Life), Magee and Allen (in The Two Extremes, and in Men of Nerve), "Professor" Hoefler ("champion heavyweight club swinger"), Hen and Billy Clark (song and dance), Allie Drayton, W. C. Cameron (in The Henpecked Husband), the Staffords (Frank and Al), Press Eldridge, Hoefler and Hen Killmer (wrestling), Dan Sully (June 12th–17th, in Mulcahey's Racket), the Zanfrettas (Alexander, Emma and Leo, June 26th–July 1st, in The Brigands, with George Kane, Andy Link and Julius Meyer; also, in A Frenchman's Troubles), Joe and Annie Burgess (in The Little Widow, etc.), Gus Hill, Parker and his dogs, and Crumley and De Forrest.

[545]

For the week of July 3rd–8th, Mme. Ellwood's Lady Minstrels broke in; where, I wonder, did female minstrels hibernate, since in New York their coming almost always indicated the approach of summer? Now with them in the bills were associated Dick Gorman, Harry Lloyd and Billy Williams as, respectively, bones, "conversationalist" and "tambo," May Arnott, George Wells, Gus Hill, Charles Turner, the Muldoon Quartette (Lloyd, Wills, Maxwell and Green), and the Zanfrettas (Alexander, George, Leo and Emma, in The Fat Man's Wedding). Billy Williams was also allotted the questionable honour of being "the greatest living wench performer." Jessie Garretta's Mastodon Lady Minstrels followed (July 10th–15th), with Lulu Wentworth, Jessie Garretta and Jessie Forrester; in the bill also were Georgie Parker, Lulu Wentworth (banjo), Ada Hulmes ("beautiful wardrobe, elegant style, and modest demeanor"), The Sunflower and the Wasp, or, Prince Popett and the Sweet Ruby that Was Lost at Sea (with Jessie Garretta, Lloyd, Cameron, and several from the olio). At Aberle's, a few weeks earlier, Jessie Garretta had been merely Jessie Garrett; but pride will sometimes swell in the passing of a short time. The attractions for July 24th–29th were more appealing, in persons of John Hart and Dan Waldron (in The Gripsack), Annie Boyd, Ward and Lynch, Harry Watson and Alice Hutchings (in Dutchy in a Fix), John Hart and Dick Gorman (in The First of May), Luigi dell' Oro ("playing two instruments at the same time, representing a brass band in full"), St. George Hussey, and The Arrival of President Grant, or, Patience Abused (with Thomas H. Ward and Con T. Lynch).

August flowers in the Volksgarten were hardy annuals or perennials — Dick Gorman, Lizzie Davis (serio-comic), Frank Budworth, Farrell and Ryan, George France and his dogs, Don and Bruno (in The Block Game, July 31st–August 5th), The New Post Office (August 7th–12th, with Billy Williams, Dick Gorman, E. S. Goodwin, Harry Lloyd and Annie Howard), Sallie Mason (serio-comic), Foster and Hughes, William C. Cameron ("first time in two years in a single specialty"), Ethel Earle and George France (August 7th–12th, in Wide Awake), the Novelty Four (Emma Whitney, May Adams, J. F. Whitney and J. B. Wills, in Rehearsal in the Parlour), Jessie Forrester, Frank Bush, E. T. Goodrich and Edith Crolius (August 14th–19th, in Grizzly Adams, with the celebrated Indian horse, Ginger Blue), &c. For the week of August 21st–26th, the Out of the Dark Combination held the Volksgarten. In the olio were Harry Lloyd (motto), the Hogan Brothers (in Nigs from the Mozambique), Mai Raimon (serio-comic — "first appearance in this city"), and Professor Hoefler and Hen Killmer (wrestling). The concluding thriller was Out of the Dark, with E. T. Goodrich as William Osmond, a detective, Nellie Germon as Lillian, a child of the streets, Harry Lloyd as John Hardy, a retired millionaire, Joe Hurley as Colonel Roland Peyton, an adventurer, W. C. Cameron as Rock

Hill, a New York rounder, E. S. Goodwin as Pedro, an Italian "Diego," and Annie Howard as Mother Nolan. I could not refrain from giving that list of characters and "tags." I gratefully leave the Volksgarten for 1881–82, with record of the performers for August 28th–September 2nd: the Maxwells (in Strolling by the Seaside), Daisy Norwood, Harris and Wood (the California team), and the play Across the Seas (with Rightmire, Mamie Wallace, Cameron, Goodwin, Daisy Norwood, Sophie Grove, and Isabella Preston). I am certainly pleased to set out for pastures new.

BOWERY THEATRE (BOWERY GARDEN) 1881–1882

The old Bowery Garden, now called the Bowery Theatre, had, on September 26, 1881, an array of entertainers including Annie Worley, George Vance, Annie Howard, "Professor" H. Monroe and his educated cats; it was also giving in some wise The Two Orphans, with Maggie Ferris as Louise, May Estelle as Henriette, Annie Howard as Marianne and the Countess, Katie Estelle as La Frochard, Fanny Sandford as Sister Genevieve, J. P. Winter as the Chevalier, J. R. Lewis as La Fleur and Picard, J. Hurley as de Presles, Louis Robie as Pierre, Neil Grey as the Count and as Martin, and Charles Marley as Jacques. Those orphans certainly wandered far.

The bills at Harvard are scattering. One for October 17th gives us Daniel E. Ralton, and a big cast, in The Convict's Daughter, as well as the Leonzo Brothers, with Tiger and Lion, A. S. Casper, Neil Gray, Andy Bryant, &c., in The Dog Spy. Intermediate olio featured Mollie De Mar, Ed Lynch (North of Ireland songs) and Josie Howland (operatic melodies). The Old General's Birthday began the programme on November 7th, with Ada Clifton, Billy Devere, Joe Hurley, Joe Buckley and Lottie Blanchard; the olio were Tom Harper ("one-legged artist, author, comedian and vocalist"), Redmond and Ada Clifton, The Crushed Tragedian (with Buckley, Hurley, James Thompson and Annie Howard), Spencer and Murphy (in A Room to Rent), Herr Schlam, Jennie Ward ("seven distinct changes of dress, in presence of the audience"), Signor Etano and his tropical birds, and J. J. Jones ("champion rifle shot of the world"). The concluding play of The '49ers, or, The Pioneer's Daughter, employed J. E. Howe, Charles Gray and May Hamilton, &c. On November 29th came George Vance (motto), Stokes and Henshaw (Rapid Transit Peddlers), Billy Devere and Harry Thompson (in Two Majors), Emma Warren (ballads), Professor Hoefler (club-swinging), Andy Bryant ("Dutch" songs), Nora Campbell (serio-comic), George Devere and Matt McElroy (banjo and bone solos), Conway and Egan (Irish pipers and dancers), Signor Costello (fire-king), and A Slippery Day (with Billy Devere). I pass to a bill for December

5th, introducing the Mountjoy Female Serenaders, with George Devere as bones, Joe Hurley as interlocutor, and Matt McElroy as "tambo," and with Emma Warren, Carrie Lewis and Minnie Belmont. Others in the bill were Guy Linton, Moore and Daly (in Cranky Poets), Allie Olden (serio-comic), the Three Invincibles (Maguire, Flynn and Welch), Alexander Wilson (ventriloquist), and the concluding Lurline (with Dot Auburn, Lillie Raymond, Guy Linton, &c.). Somehow I am sorry to see that Guy Linton and Lucy Adams have separated artistically.

This unhappy house now became the Folly Theatre, with S. Levy as business manager. Harvard possesses a bill with the date January 30th, written in, and promising performances by Charles Nelson, May Clark, Waldron and Kaine (formerly Thompson and Waldron), Matt McCormick (New Zealand equilibrist), Gertie Holden (singer), Albert Denier (song and dance), Isabella Ward, Frank Peasley and Tom Vennetta ("late of Haverly's Minstrels"), Miles and Nelson, Levanion and McCormick, and Lizzie Lanning. For February 20th, a Harvard bill with printed date provides Dick Turner and Sadie Dunbar (in The Darky's Promise), Haussabura (sic) Sam, the Winstanley Brothers (novelty duo), Fanny Reynolds, A. H. and Nellie Le Clair (in Shakespeare in the Kitchen), Carrie Lewis, Add and Maggie Ringler (in Heinrich's Courtship), Lawrence and Baldwin (in Zulu Twins), and The Grand Dutchess (with Carrie Lewis, William Miles, Charles Nelson, Lillie Raymond, Dick Turner, &c.). Farces featured a bill at Harvard for March 6th (date written in), with, as actors, Frank Kent, W. Fields, Nellie Vincent, Ida Robinson, Irene Carleton, &c. In addition an olio gave us Frank Wallere (trapeze), Miles and Kent (song and dance), Theodore Loranzo (dancer), Nellie Vincent, and Maude Florette ("queen of song"). The bill for March 13th shows the place once more glorying in the name of the Bowery Garden Theatre, with farces enlisting McCormick and Levanion, Nellie Vincent, C. Morgan, Amy and Frank Kent, Irene Carleton, &c. Many of these performers figure in the bill for March 20th, Our Chateau Mabille starting a show which included also John and Kate McVeigh in a delicately named John's Drunk Again. I fancy the place was in parlous condition, financially. In latest March, admission was "free," though many of the above cited performers remained in farces and "turns."

In April we might have seen, at one time or another, Charles and Annie Worley, William Hart ("the neat Irish gentleman"), Gertie White ("dashing vocalist"), McCormick and Levanion (gymnasts), Mme. Lavely (feats of strength), the Four Sunflowers, Costello ("drinks burning fluids"), Willie Hart ("lively as an eel"), Lottie Waters (dancer), Sophie Johnson (serio-comic), Byron and Fash (acrobatic song and dance), Kitty Bell, Leon (prestidigitateur), Maude Florette, Miss Leon (songs), and the farces, A Picnic at Jones's Wood and Troubles of a Door-Tender at a Masquerade

[548]

Ball.   It will be seen that the entertainment was worth just about the price of admission — nothing.

The "Variety" halls had vied with each other in inventing names for the female minstrel scene with which, when hard up, they began their revelry.   One is intrigued by the first offering here, on May 1st — Mrs. Campbell's Sewing Circle, surely an attractive suggestion for those times that delighted in Old Folkes Concerts and other quaint devices.   Participants in the Bowery Garden bill of May 1st were Phebe Shaw, Billy Hart, John Burns, Maude Florette, Byron and Fash (Ethiopians), and Sophie Johnson.   The concluding farce was Two Gentlemen from Verona (with James Thompson and Billy Fields).   Later in that month of blooms we had A Moonlight Picnic at Cape May, J. H. Graham, Jennie Ward ("in seven distinct changes of dress"), Miss Worley, Johnny O'Connor, Flora Willis, The Black Statue, The Arrival of Jumbo, Levanion and McCormick, Nellie Vincent, Carrie Herbert (vocalist), Ned Wilson ("Dutch" songs), John Holcomb (song and dance), Kate Montrose, Jennie Turner (dancer), Ettie Steele (songs of the day), Harry Mack and Ed Wilson (in The Sneiders), Frank Forrest (female impersonator), Billy Fields (silver clog), and the farce, The Arrival of Salvini.   And now, in June, the first part of the show was entitled The Elevated Blondes — 25 Beauties in Mid-Air, as the bill for June 19th printed it.   The "blondes" were, apparently, but the females of the lists cited above; other performers, in rose-bearing June, were Pete Shaw (female impersonations), Phebe Delmay, Mack and Wilson (in The Levy Brothers), the play of The Dog of the Lonely Mountain (with Harry Mack), Nellie Vincent, Charles Satelle (Sawtelle?), Nellie Clifford, Billy Lane, &c.; farces or sketches in latest June were Pink Dominos, and One Dollar a Kiss.   The first part was now even more suggestively named — Scenes in the Khedive Harem, in Cairo, Egypt.   This inciting caption lasted till mid-July, a month that brought in Costello, the Barron Brothers (Billy and Tom, in songs), The Ghost in a Pawnshop, The Brass Monkey, The Rehearsal, Jones and Madigan, Mamie Lee, Lew Delmore and Fred Wilson (in The Birthday Surprise Party), Jones and Madigan (in The Galvanic Battery), May Johnson, Nellie Vincent and Nellie Clifford.   The latest July nights gave us J. Lord, Carrie Herbert, Minnie Belmont, Murder at the Old Toll House, Minnie Bryant and Harry Thompson (in Old Mr. Schneider, and in Life), Fred Wenzel ("Dutch songs"), Hughey and Jennie Barton, The Comanches, &c.

A Trip to Glen Cove, beginning the bill for August 7th, was home-like and local; in the programme, besides, were Ada Forrest, Bill Buffalo, or, Buckets of Blood (with Hugh Barton), O'Connor and Willis, Frank Forrest, Wenzel and Barton (in South Carolina), and the sketches of The Safe Robber, The Coming Man and The Village Barber.   The week of August 14th–19th proffered A Trip to Starin's Island, Ada Williams (Irish character

[549]

songs), Manning and Marlowe ("Irish"), Jennie Turner and Bill Buffalo. In the final nights of August, Our Swinging Beauties again began the bills, with four end men, the olio proffering Retardo and Shaw (female impersonators), Kitty Bell, O'Connor and Flora Willis, Under the Lamp-post, Ella Leon, Jennie Turner, Joe Byron and Billy Barron (in Darkey's Holiday), and Slattery's Boarding House. I have given to the reader all I could find of the offerings of this decidedly diminished resort; if the reader thinks the story not worth chronicling, I agree with him, except as regards necessity for historical fulness.

National Theatre, Bowery, 1881–1882

Let us begin the season of 1881–82 at the National with the week of September 5th–10th, when the proffered blessings included The Jealous Husband (Tom Maxwell, Edith Crolius, Ben Brown, Manning, and Tommy and Robert Williams), Daisy Norwood, the Grinnells, the Morello Brothers, the Four Comets (Frank Hawley, Walter Manning, Bobby and Thomas Williams), the Maxwells (in The Jolly Old Couple), Cora Cardigan, the Clarks (Edward and Alice — "just arrived from Europe, initial performance in America"), and John T. Hinds and Ivian Lawrence (in The Shaughaun, which certainly sounded too much like The Shaughraun to be a mere coincidence). The next week (12th–17th) provided Davy Posner (as The Mischievous Monkey), Florence French ("petite nightingale"), Orndorff and McDonald ("the California boys"), Phillips Brothers (John and Charles), Grace Sherwood, the Ramirez Troubadours, Nelton, the Morellos, and Edwin Blanchard ("his first appearance in America in ten years") as the Indian slave, in the play of Cato:

Cato	Edwin Blanchard	Old Melrose	Ben Brown
Mrs. Melrose	Kate Estelle	Ora	Edith Crolius
Philip Gastineau	W. T. Dulany	Henry Melrose	John Phillips
Peter Simple	E. W. Marston	Little Henry Melrose	Davy Posner

Subsequently, in September, we were treated to Charles Worley, Andy McKee and Miss Crolius (in Rat-i-fi-ca-tion), Grace Belmont, Little Eddie ("Mexican wonder, in pedestal polandric equilibrisms"), McKee and Byrnes in (A Nigger's Ups and Downs), Gus Hill, Georgie and Emma Kaine, Jeppe and Fannie Delano, Frank Jones and Alice Montague (in On the Brink, week of 19th–24th), Billy Diamond (in Under a Southern Sun), Jennie Southern, John L. Manning, the De Voy Sisters, the Lamartine Brothers, the Four Luminaries (the De Voy Sisters, Burke and Smith, in Frolics), T. M. Hengler (in The Merry Minstrel), and J. J. McCloskey's play of The Bowery Boys, with Frank Jones, Alice Montague, A. S. Casper, Dulany, Marston, Edith Crolius and others of the regular stock company maintained by the house. Dulaney has now become Dulany.

[550]

October gave, in its first fortnight, Billy Diamond (in The Belle of the Bowery), Walsh and Dempsey, Hengler, Logrenia, Harry Clark, the Four-in-Hand, Carrie Brower, Fanny Herring, the perennial (in Little Buckshot and in The Dumb Boy of Manchester), Walter Mack, the Sparks Brothers, the Peasleys (in Sparking in the Park), Moore and Lessenger, the three Rankins (in The Amateur Rehearsal), &c.   And October went out with a final fortnight involving in its course J. H. Graham, Eddie Laiscell (contortions and gyrations), Paul Dresser (in Mirthful Morsels, songs and parodies), Parker and his dogs, the Lanier Sisters (Theresa and Ada), the Barlow Brothers (in Merry Trifles), the Laiscell Family of acrobats (Charles, Eddie and Belle), P. C. Foy, Boyd and Sarsfield, the Ripleys, the La Porte Sisters (Rosie and Lillie), Emma Hoffman, and Emerson and Clark (in Some Other Evening).   N. S. Wood, Joseph P. Winter and Kate Estelle were featured in the closing dramas — The Boy Scout of the Sierras (17th–22nd) and Life and Adventures of Jack Sheppard (24th–29th).   The week of October 31st–November 5th featured McGlone and Lacy, Houssabura (sic) Sam, Frank Bennett and Lida Gardner (in Kitchen Domestics), Tom Sayers, Six American Students (all twanging the banjo), and Flora Moore.   The play of the night was no less a thing than Under the Gaslight, altered to suit Gus Phillips (Oofty Gooft) who played Snorky, with Mrs. Phillips as Old Judas and Mrs. Van Dam, Dulany as the Old Signal Man, Tighe as Ray Strafford, J. M. Forrest as Byke, Marston as Bermudas, Lulu Dulany as Peachblossom, Edith Crolius as Laura, and Lida Gardner as Pearl.

More and more the National depended on its concluding dramas, but in the olio for November it provided interesting features involving the Four Shamrocks (Dave Mealen, Tommy Mack and the Webster Brothers, in a burlesque wrestling match, the Hodcarrier's Strike, etc.), Tom Sayers, Kelly and Ryan ("Bards of Tara"), the Virginia Trio (Turner, Welch and Harris), Mollie Wilson, Harry Le Clair and W. J. Russell, with Kate Estelle and Lulu Dulany (in Just in Time), Frank McNish and the Leland Sisters (in Stolen Fun), Billy Moore (late of Topack and Moore), Williams and Sully (in The Moonlight Picnic), Charles Diamond, Welch and Dempsey, Lester and Williams and the Novelty Four (Emma and John F. Whitney, Lizzie Hunter and Lester Howard, in Rehearsal in a Parlour).   The play for the week of November 14th–19th was Oliver Twist, with Kate Estelle and Joseph P. Winter as Nancy and Bill, Charles Foster as Fagin, Lulu Dulany as Oliver, Tighe as Brownlow, Miss Crolius as Rose, and Marston as the Dodger; for the week of the 21st–26th N. S. Wood returned, in The Boy Detective.   The bill for November 28th–December 3rd presented Tommy J. Harpin (Irish reel), the Irish Comedy Four (Reilly, Collins, Earl and Smith, in The Men from Galway, or, Life in the Scranton Coal Yard), Foster and Hughes, Trudell and Rowan (bone duett statue clog),

Dell Trudell (serio-comic and motto), Emerson and Clark (in Some Other Evening) and John W. Ransone in a very protean part in Across the Atlantic, with members of the stock or the olio as ladies and gentlemen of aristocratic nomenclature, native and foreign. I suspect they wore their rue and their titles with a difference.

December provides me with but two bills at Harvard; that for the 9th promises Earle Remington (in parodies), Waldron and Kaine (Hebrew specialties), the Percy Sisters (Christine and Anna), Hines and Blossom, the Winstanley Brothers (Lancashire act), and—of all things in the world!—Joseph Proctor in Nick of the Woods, with Edith Crolius as Telie Doe. Featured on December 23rd were Charles Moore's School of Educated Dogs (seven in number), Levantine and Earle, T. M. Hengler, the Peasleys (in Mollie's Victory), the Four Musical Kings (Wood and Beasley and the Weston Brothers), Charles and Carrie Moore, and W. H. Rightmire and Katie Estelle (in The Two Wanderers). And Harvard has but one bill for January—that of the 3rd; the entertainment began with Humpty Dumpty in Every Clime (John Denier, Gilbert Hanlon, Connie H. Denier, J. Smith and Louise Crolius), passed through an olio with Andy Collum, the Four Shamrocks (Conroy, Daly, Thompson and Daly), Connie Denier, the Four-in-Hand, and John Denier (tight-rope), and ended with Harry Amlar as the "cullud" boy in Counterfeit, with Al Kiel as chief of the counterfeiters, Tighe as the detective, Edith and Louise Crolius as feminine interest, &c. Thereafter the Harvard files are more satisfactory, supplying record, in February, of "turns" by J. H. and Ida Jeffreys, the Durell Twin Brothers, Manning and Drew, the Clipper Quartette (Robert McIntyre, F. T. Ward, George F. Campbell and F. A. Howard), Carrie Lewis, the Parker dogs, Charles and Thomas O'Brien (in The Centennial Weary Traveller), Delvan and Tracy ("Irish"), Hines and Blossom, Earle Remington, Clever Carroll (prestidigitateur), Smith and Leopold (in The Perplexed Manager), the Allen Sisters (May and Lillie), the St. Elmos (Harry, George and Haney, acrobats), Cavana and Mack (in Shakespeare Outdone), The Specialty Trio (Jennie Reese, soprano, Irvin Bush, baritone, and Charles Reese, tenor), and Lester and Williams. During the week of February 6th–11th, the pulsing concluding drama was Nobody's Daughter, with Amy Stone in three characters and J. Winston Murray as Andrew Larkspur, W. R. Hamilton as Victor Carrington, Ed Lay as Black Milson, E. S. Goodwin as Sir Oswald Eversleigh, &c. During the week of February 13th–18th Fanny Herring and J. Winston Murray acted in The French Spy, and, for the 20th–25th, these same featured players gave The Girl Detective. Winter passed into spring (February 27th–March 4th) with Winston Murray, Marston, Goodwin and the Misses Crolius in Ivan, the Hammer, or, Trapping a Tartar; with an olio made up of the Two Clarks (Hen and Billy), Donnelly and Drew, Charles and Annie Whiting, the Four-in-Hand,

Tommy Watson, and "Professor" Abt, and ended the joy with Maggie Weston and J. J. Sullivan in Dan Maloney's Raffle.

If we attend the National regularly in March, we shall see and hear Andy Bryant ("Dutch songs, sayings and parodies"), Mabel Vaughan, J. W. McAndrews, Fred Roberts, Lester and Allen, St. George Hussey, Oofty Gooft (March 6th–11th, in Under the Gaslight, with J. Winston Murray as Byke), Tommy Granger, Tommy and Annie Dayton (in Our New Postman), the French Troupe Davene, Sailor West, the Sparks Brothers, the play of Just in Time (March 20th–25th, with Harry Le Clair, W. J. Russell and Winston Murray), Harris and Wood (in Grousemier's Brewery), Johnny Patterson (Irish Clown, late of the Great Australian Circus), Parker's dogs, Rice and Barton, Paddy and Ella Murphy, W. T. Bryant and Lizzie Richmond, and Minnie Oscar Gray and W. T. Stephens (March 27th–April 1st, in Swift and Sure). The brighter evenings of April hurried along with, in due course, appearances of the Marr Brothers (John and Billy), Ned Lang and Viola Rosa, Bryant and Saville (in the farce, P. G. Gilmore), the Four Shamrocks, Emerson and Clark, N. S. Wood (3rd–8th, in The Boy Scout of the Sierras), Sol and Julia Aiken, Charles Weston and Charles Hanson, Frank and Fannie Davis (in The Old Veteran), The Horseshoe Four (the Love Sisters, F. B. Carr and J. J. Quinlan, in The Actor's Family), Andy Collum, the Four-in-Hand (Joseph J. Sullivan, John J. Keegan, John J. Sheehan and Henry C. Talbert), J. W. Ransone, in Across the Atlantic (10th–15th), Lew Baker, the Davises (in Fogarty's Night On), the Ordeys, Arnold Kiralfy in dances, the California Quartette of the San Francisco Minstrels (W. T. Morant, Harry C. Wyatt, Harry W. Roe and W. S. Frohman), C. W. Barry (17th–22nd, in Escaped from Sing Sing, with, in support, Charles F. Seabert, Marston, Lew Baker, George W. Whitford, James Tighe, the Misses Crolius, Frank and Fannie Davis, and Dot Aborn), N. B. Shimer (*sic*) and Flora Bingham (in the musical sketch, New Ideas), Joe Mealey and Harry Mackey, the Barlow Brothers, Charles and Carrie Moore, Fred Hallen and Enid Hart (in Over the Stile), and Henry Belmer (24th–29th, in To the End of the World).

Shrinkage in Harvard files reduces me to two dates for May — the 18th and the 22nd; promises therein list Harris and Wood, Gus Hill, Harry and George Booker, Kelly and Ryan, John B. Wills and May Adams, the Monumental Quartette (Charles Earle and Vic Hawley, tenors, G. Hammond, baritone, Walter West, bass), the Peasleys (in Jerry's Fortune), Kelly and Ryan (in That Man from Galway), A Trip on the Steamboat (with Marston, Tighe, and Edith Crolius), John and Emma Whitney (in Rehearsal in the Parlour), Emerson and Clark, Ferguson and Mack, the Four Diamonds (G. W. Watson, W. S. Gilmore, J. G. Brevarde and Charles Sawtelle, in The Darkey's Wedding), the Stirk Family and D. M. Zalto, and George W. Thompson (22nd) in Yacup. Harvard becomes bountiful with roses of

[553]

June: the Four Shamrocks (Dave Conroy, John and Matt Daly and Micky Thompson, in The Workingmen's Strike), William and Leoline Ripley and Claudia (Ripley?) Leslie (in a parlour acrobatic sketch, Exercises), the Big Four (Smith, Waldron, Cronin and Martin), Harry J. Myers (June 5th–10th, in Bill, Our Coloured Friend, supported by Allen Dumond, J. J. Edwards, Marston, Matt and John Daly, Ben Grinnell, Edith and Louise Crolius, and Claudia and "Leonie" Ripley), J. D. Kelly ("classical and comical instrumental performances"), W. T. Bryant and Lizzie Richmond, Paddy and Ella Murphy (in The Finnegan Coterie), Joseph P. Winter (12th–17th, in Dan'l Boone, the Hero of Kentucky) Marston (in A Bull in a China Shop), the Sparks Brothers, Fred C. Bryant and Hoey, Frank Campbell, Miss St. George Hussey, Minnie Oscar Gray, W. T. Stephens and the dogs, Romeo, Zip and Hero (June 19th–24th, in Saved from the Storm), the Electric Three (Callan, Haley and Callan), Dixey and Leyton, Lang and Rosa, and Fanny Herring (June 26th–July 1st, in her popular Little Buckshot). One could pity Fanny Herring, once the pride of the Bowery.

Two bills at Harvard (for "the week ending July 15th," and July 31st–August 5th) give us, in rapid survey, The Frisky Cobbler (with Marston, J. J. Edwards, George Schaeffer (sic), Annie Howard and Edith Crolius), Joe Morton and R. G. Knowles (parodies, local songs and grotesque dancing), D. B. Emery and Laura Russell, the Tissots ("a troupe of living automatons"), the Four Diamonds, Hallen and Hart (in Over the "Style"), N. S. Wood (in Nan, the Newsboy), Foster and Hughes, Isabel Ward, Hartz ("illusions without any apparatus"), Ella Wesner, and The Hunter's Dogs (with the Leonzo Brothers, the dogs, Tiger and Lion, Winston Murray and the regular corps). Finally, the year rounding full circle with August, Harvard files, again complete, bring before us Fattie Stewart (in Faint Heart Can't Win), Mabel Vaughan, Joe and Annie Burgess (in The Little Widow), Max Arnold, Professor Alexander Davis (ventriloquist, in Pleasant Moments), the Novelty Four (now composed of Emma and J. F. Whitney, May Adams and J. B. Wills, in Rehearsal in the Parlour), Alf A. Wallace (in A Big Mistake), Maggie Ferris, Harry Edwards and Lew Morton, John H. Byrne (in Waiting for John, with solos on the flunette, xylophone, dulcimer, bells, etc.), Georgie Parker, the Four Shamrocks, Murphy and Shannon (in Sullivan vs. Willon, and Bound for Germany), the Christie Brothers (Will and Frank, "Irish"), Maggie Bursel, the Two Wesleys, Lester and Williams, the American Four (perhaps the best of the countless "Fours"), Cooper Brothers (black face), and Len Shillito (musical clown). The plays, in that heated last month of the busy season were Gifford's Luck, C. H. Hoyt's "beautiful companion piece to My Partner," presented (August 7th–12th), with Frank Wright and Mai Estelle; Oofty Gooft, in Under the Gaslight (14th–19th); Queen's Evidence (21st–26th), with J. H. Rowe as Gilbert Medland and Philip Stanfield, Alf Wallace as

[554]

Isaacs, Allen Dumond as Matthew Thornton, and Mai Estelle as Kate Medland; and (August 28th–September 2nd) Jim Bowie, or, the Massacre of the Alamo, by and with W. H. Langdon as Jim, Alf A. Wallace as Davy Crockett, and with, in other rôles, George Sheparde, Chris Sheparde, Frank Campbell, John and A. Cooper, George Sheffer (*sic*), Mai Estelle, Annie Howard, Maggie Ferris, and Bowie's acting dogs, Pat and Fritz. And so, a glad good-bye to the National, for 1881–82!

London Theatre, 1881–1882

Perforce (earlier Harvard bills failing me), I begin the London season, on October 7th, with The Lawyer's Clerk (acted by Joe Buckley, John Robinson, Ed Mills, Lizzie Conway and Mattie Boutwell), with an olio comprising Erba Robeson, Hallen and Enid Hart (in I'm an Actor), Jimmy Kelly and Jerry Murphy ("in full ring costume, in a manly assault at arms"), Crumley and De Forrest (breakneck song and dance), Tom Sayers, Parker and his dogs, Edward and Alice Clark ("another importation from England — Miss Alice Clark is the only Lady High Kicker in the World"), Harry Cereni (eccentric dancer), Emerson and Clark (in Some Other Evening), Nestor and Venoa ("grandest gymnastic achievement the world has ever seen"), and the concluding farce of Smoked Out (Buckley, Robinson, &c.). Thereafter, in October, we had Kelly and Ryan, the Olympia Quartette, Maude Leigh (serio-comic), Morris and Fields (burlesque Germans), the Four Eccentrics, Ella Bordeaux ("captivating songs and dances"), Bessie Bell, That Man from Galway (with John T. Kelly, Thomas J. Ryan, and Hugh Mack), the Grangers (Bud and Annie, in Mixtures), Amy Nelson ("petite and beautiful serio-comic"), Geyer and Mack, Harry Bryant, Knock Me Down (with John Hart and John Robinson), William Dwyer (motto), the Four Shamrocks, Charles Heywood (soprano), William and Charles Landis (re-united after three years, in song and dance, on roller-skates), Dyllyn (in Moore's melodies and Irish idioms), the farce Bernhardt and Rossi in Tragedy (with Heywood as Mme. Boutwell, afterwards Bernhardt, and John Hart as John Westervelt, afterwards Rossi — this for October 17th–22nd), Chalet (ventriloquist), the Vanes (Will and James, musical performances), Bessie Bell ("queen of opera bouffe"), John Hart (in The Jealous Wife and in The Watch Dog), Zitella (in songs), the Ramirez Spanish Troubadours, May Irwin ("the most refined Song and Dance lady on the Vaudeville Stage"), the Novelty Four (Emma and John Whitney, Lizzie Hunter and Lester Howard), the Champion Collar and Elbow Wrestlers (John McMahon, of Vermont, "champion of America," and William Kennedy, of Montreal, "champion of Canada") — these for October 24th–29th.

Harvard is rich in the falling leaves of November, and, from its files,

[555]

I gather mementoes, as the weeks passed by, of the Suydams, Delvan and Tracy, Andy Collum, the Sparks Brothers, the French Twin Sisters, Kelly and Ryan, Morris and Fields, Walsh and Dempsey, Mills and Warren (Tyrolean sketch), Bessie Bell, Mlle. Barretta (*sic*), Ferguson and Mack, the Daly Brothers (Bobby and Danny, Irish clog and reel), Alf S. Gibson and Lizzie Davis (in Actors in the Kitchen), the Four Shamrocks, Lester and Williams, the concluding farce, The Political Candidate (November 5th–12th, with Barney Ferguson as Michael Strogoff, Richard Mack as Charley Rich, and with Lester, Williams and Dan Daly in the cast), Gregory Brothers, Jessie Merton, Kerrigan and McCarthy, Harry Clarke (*sic*), the Peasleys (in Sparking in the Park), Professor A. W. Sawyer (xylophone), Moore and Lessenger, Cora Cardigan, Master Dunn, Kelly and O'Brien, May Irwin, Jimmy Kelly and Jerry Murphy, Lester and Williams (in Can You Skate?), Richard Mack (as Casey, the Piper), &c. On November 21st began a week of M. B. Leavitt's Great Specialty Company, including the Davene Family, Bonnie Runnells, the Four Diamonds (Watson, Gilmore, Brevarde and Sawtelle), Nellie Richards, Annie and Andy Hughes, Val Vose (ventriloquist), Sanford and Wilson, Dolph Levino and Susie Dillon (in Love *vs.* Music), Barney McNulty and Master Barney (as Mike and Bridget Maloney (*sic*), in Maloney's Visit). The week of November 28th–December 3rd closed autumn with Alice Hale (songs), Hettinger and Nibbe (Hebrew dialect), Carl Hertz, George H. Wood (in The Culchaw of Colour), Hallen and Enid Hart (in Over the Stile), the acrobatic Garnellas (Dick and Bob), Fields and Hanson, the French Twins, the American Four (Pettingill, Gale, Pete Dailey and James Hoey), Alice Daily, and the farce, Married in the Dark (with Gale, Dailey, and others). In December (according to two Harvard bills, sole and singular) we had Poison (with Fayette Welch, John Robinson, and Lizzie Conway), Ada Burnett, the O'Brien Brothers, George H. Wood, Hallen and Hart (in Billy, the Tailor, in Fifteen Minutes), Binney and Fraine (*sic* — Irish songsters), the American Four, William Lester and Paul Allen (in The Expressionists), Mollie Wilson, the farce of Clara Simpson's Tea Party, John F. Blint ("the only correct imitator of J. K. Emmet"), the De Bar Brothers, Parker and his dogs, E. C. Dunbar, Robert Gilfort (equipoise), Sam Rickey (in Bad Whiskey), Georgie Kaine (vocalist), the Gilfort Brothers (athletes, "possessing the strength of the mythological Hercules, with the figures of Apollo and the grace of Adonis" — certainly a choice combination, rare even a half century later).

Thus we bid good-bye to 1881, and bravely call on January, 1882, for a full supply of treasures in "Variety." The week of the 2nd–7th of that wintry month provided J. H. and Ida Jeffreys (in The Pyramid of Gold, she "passing her body through a fourteen-inch hoop, while standing on his shoulders"), Nellie Hague, Mlle. Baretta (or Barretta, in The Scholar's Return, Howard Dorr and Son, the Durell Twin Brothers (in acrobatic

[556]

EDDIE GIRARD   COOL BURGESS   WILLIAM GIRARD

TOM DALY   CHARLES McCARTHY   BILL DALY

BILLY WEST   PRESS ELDRIDGE   JOHN SPARKS

song and dance), Lester and Williams, Harry LeClair and W. J. Russell (in Prima Donna for a Night), Emerson and Clark, the Garettas (revolving globe and juggling), Maggie Cline, and Robinson, Willis Clark and Morton Emerson (in New Year's Calls).   Subsequently a richly-provided January poured from the cornucopia "turns" by Andy Collum ("leading banjo player of the present day"), Charles Redmond and Georgie Blake (in An Actor's Luck), Moore and Daly (late of Topack and Moore, in Absurdities), Nellie Germon, the Peasleys (in St. Patrick's Day), the American Four (in That's What I Thought), Maggie Cline, Ferguson and Mack, The Two Jack Sheppards, Paddy and Ella Murphy (in Just from Ireland), and Kelly and Murphy in an Assault at Arms — all this for the week of the 9th–14th; for the 16th–21st, we had Langdon and Allison's Swift and Sure Combination, with Moore and Lessenger (in The German Shoemakers), Tillie Antonio, Ripley and Reade ("greatest of all musical teams"), Charles Redmond and Georgie Blake (in Theatrical Tramps), the Bookers (Harry and George A., formerly Canfield and Booker, in Tompkins' Surprise Party), Isabel Ward ("playing the most difficult airs on the largest and smallest wooden instruments ever seen — also steel bells"), the Davenport Brothers, and Langdon and Allison's play, Swift and Sure, written for Minnie Oscar Gray and W. T. Stephens, who now used it as a vehicle for the display of their art. The week of January 23rd–28th defied winter with Lester and Allen (in The Coming Man), Edith Andow, Hallen and Hart (in Over the Stile), the Sparks Brothers, the Hogan Brothers (Kickapoo dancers), the Davenport Brothers, J. W. McAndrews, Bernard Sloman, and Mulcahy's Excursion to Coney Island (with the Sparks Brothers, Lester and Allen, and Lizzie Conway).   Finally winter advanced (January 30th–February 4th) with Kerrigan and McCarthy, Kitty Coleman, Fred Wilson (Irish, Chinese, "Dutch" and Negro specialties), the French Twin Sisters (dances, skipping rope, etc.), Hallen and Hart (The Pirates of Pinafore), Lillie Western, Quilter and Goldrich (in Ordinary Conversation), Miss St. George Hussey (male impersonator), Frank E. McNish and the Leland Sisters (in Stolen Fun), and the Sparks Brothers (in Muldoon on a Lark).

And February gave the Novelty Four (now composed of Emma and John Whitney, Georgie Kaine and Lester Howard), P. C. Foy (Irish tenor), Weston and Hanson, the French Twins, Robert Nickle, E. C. Dunbar, the Australian Four (Kennedy, Richardson, Caselli and Rench, in Clara Simpson's Tea), the Gilfort Brothers, Hallen and Hart (in I'm an Actor), The Tourists (with Robinson, Weston, Mills, Hanson and Lizzie Conway), the Le Petres (Paus and Lillie, in Disturbance), John Fenton (clog), George H. Wood, Crossley and Elder (Athletic Games of the Highlanders), Dan Williams and Joe (sic) Morton ("Irish"), Williams and Sully, Val Vose, Farini's Zulus (Princess Ama Zulu and Chief Newcomo), St. George Hussey, Mr. and Mrs. Joe Allen ("England's premier artists"), Alice Hale, Gregory

[557]

Brothers (double horizontal bar), Morello Brothers (William and Max, parlour acrobatics), Carrie Lavarnie, Nestor and Venoa, Jimmy Kelly and Jerry Murphy ("art of self-defence"), Billy Moore ("late Topack and Moore"), the Four Shamrocks (Dave Conroy, Matt and John Daly, and Micky Thompson, in The Workingman's Strike), &c. The week of February 27th–March 4th presented Smith and Leopold (in The Perplexed Manager), Miss Earle Remington ("the aesthetic maiden, in songs and parodies written by herself"), Kerrigan and McCarthy, Harry St. Clair and W. J. Russell (in The Stage-struck Chambermaid), Ella and Paddy Murphy (in Just Out), Charles and William Landis, Harry Woodson, Karoly and Augusta Ordey (Hungarian jugglers), Tom Peasley and Tony Vennetta, Frank H. and Lillian White (in On the Frontier) and Le Clair and Vennetta (in She's Boss).

March in its long, blustering course gave us in due order the Rentz-Santley Novelty and Burlesque Company (M. B. Leavitt, manager), here for the week of March 6th–11th, with Dolph Levino and Rosa Lee, Lizzie Paine, the Bartlett Sisters, Eloise Linden, Billy Buckley, Manchester and Jennings, the Etzeltine Sisters, Minnie Farrell, Lizzie Daly, Billy Chase, Mlle. Catherine and her trained doves and pigeons, Lottie Elliott, and the farce Haze-L-Kirke, or, the Mascot's Revenge, with Robert Manchester as Dunstan Kirke, called Iron-Will for short, Billy Buckley as Airy Rodney, the great American sacrificer, Lizzie Paine as Lord Traveller, disguised as a gentleman, W. H. Chase as Petts Gawk Green, Minnie Farrell as Barney, Nellie S. Bartlett as Met, Rosa Lee as Haze-L-Kirke, the Mascot, John Jennings as Dolly Dutton, and Fannie Florence as Oh! Mercy Kirke. I hope this was as good as it sounds. Later in March we had Cardello and La Rose (horizontal bar), Harry Bryant, Clark and Edwards, the De Bar Brothers ("serpentine manipulations"), the French Twins, Pat Reilly, Harry Blakely, the acrobatic Siegrists (Thomas, Louis and Harry), Mollie Wilson, T. M. Hengler, the farce of Dodging the Gang, Frank and Fannie (*sic*) Davis (in The Old Veteran), Mabel Vaughn (*sic*), Hines and Blossom, Elise Kruger, Andy McKee and Alf Barker (in Mixed), Hallen and Hart (in Over the Stile), Maggie Cline (in Mary Ann Kehoe Ha! Ha!), Wood, Beasley and the Weston Brothers (in Going to Join the Minstrels), The Vagrants (with John Robinson, William Hines, Ed Mills, Nat Blossom and Lizzie Conway), Alexander Zanfretta (March 27th–April 1st, in The Brigands, and on the tight-rope), the Barlow Brothers, the Sparks Brothers, Dutch Daly, Frank Bolton and Ada Bradford (in The Crystal Fountain), William Gaylord (contortionist), Hallen and Hart (in Musical Mixtures), E. C. Dunbar, and The Galway Lawyers (acted by Joe and John Sparks, Fred Hallen, Lizzie Conway and Nellie Hague).

Courage, reader! spring creeps on a-pace, and Harvard has but two bills for April — that for the 3rd–8th, and that for the 10th–15th; Dan Collyer (in A Live Subject, and also in a few brief remarks), John Sheehan and Mike Coyne (in An Everyday Occurrence), Kelly and Murphy, A. W. Sawyer (copophone), Annie Hart, Mlle. Baretta (*sic*) and Zanfretta, the Garnellas, Dunbar, Miss St. George Hussey, and Robert Macaire (with Alexander and Emma Zanfretta and George Kane) — behold the lure of the first of those weeks! with Dalton and Watts ("art of manly self-defence"), Minnie Weber (serio-comic), the Peasleys (Sparking in the Park), Dan Collyer (in Thompson's Ghost), Sheehan and Coyne (in The Family Next Door), the Clipper Quartette (Robert McIntyre, F. T. Ward, George F. Campbell, F. A. Howard), Lester and Williams and Pat Reilly — lo! the delights of the second. In May, the London piled Ossa on Pelion.   For the week of the 8th–13th, Leavitt's All Star Specialty Company proffered Jeppe and Fannie Delano, J. Selbini and Mlle. Lily (bicyclists), Nellie Richards, the Lamont Family of Male and Female Acrobats, including Master John Lamont, "champion somersault thrower of the world — makes 40 consecutive revolutions." Alas! "in consequence of the interference of the authorities only two of the family will appear."   But Flora Moore, Val Vose, Sanford and Wilson (in The Trials of a Nurse) and the Two Barneys (in Maloney's Picnic) were there to console.   Later in May the cohorts of "Variety" included the Ordeys, Ada Forrest, Mlle. Barretta (*sic*) and Zanfretta, Kelly and Murphy, George W. Rice and Charles Barton (Ethiopians), Mollie Wilson, Hallen and Hart (in Over the Stile and in I'm an Actor), Zanfretta (on the high rope), Maggie Cline, Frank H. and Lillian White (in On the Frontier), Miss St. George Hussey, Dan Collyer (in A Little Misunderstanding), Mabel Vaughn, Dutch Daly, the Sparks Brothers, Crandall and Eastwood (in Echoes from Germany), F. H. and Lillian White (in A Big Mistake), Minnie Oscar Gray and W. T. Stephens and their dogs (May 22nd–27th, in Saved from the Storm), Gus, the Slasher (with J. W. McAndrews), the Winnetts (Lottie and Thomas, in Love in Broken German), George H. Wood, the Ramirez Family (four in number), Dan Collyer (in Murder in the Old Toll House), McAndrews (as the plantation darkey, in The Watermelon Man), Moore and Lessenger, Harry F. Dixey and May Leyton (in Tantrums) and the Sparks Brothers (in The Galway Lawyers).   Thus have we come cleanly through to Saturday, June 3rd.

For June 12–17th, Halleck's Muldoon's Picnic Combination possessed the stage, with The Comanches (Robert Fraser, C. W. Ravel, J. and A. Dashington, Ed Lamont and John Foster), Alice Gleason, Dan Collyer and George Campbell (in A Pleasant Evening), the Dashington Brothers (Jerry, Walter and Albert, in a black-face act), the Three St. Felix Sisters, Fred Roberts, the Clipper Quartette and Muldoon's Picnic (acted by W. F. Carroll, Dan Collyer, Alice Gleason, W. and J. Dashington, and all three of the happy St. Felix maidens).   June 19th–24th brought a week of Nick Roberts's Carnival, enlisting the Great Grimaldi, Frank King, Bertha Faber, J. C.

Tiernan, Frank Hildebrand, Dollie Davenport, Kelly and Ryan, Parker and those undying dogs of his, the Olympia Quartette (Keough, Randalls, Sullivan and Mack), the Vivian Sisters (Emily, Weavy and Bella), E. D. Davies, Awata Katsnoshin, and the farce, Blunders, or, that Man from Galway (with John T. Kelly, T. J. Ryan, Hugh Mack, &c.). From June 26th to July 8th, I can inform my anxious reader that the London offered progressively W. T. Dwyer, Chalet, Lillian Ramsden ("the English Nightingale"), Allie Drayton, Fields and Hanson, Master Dunn, Wheatley and Traynor (the "original Dublin boys"), William Cronin and J. P. Sullivan and Emma Rogers (in Life in a Tenement House), Alf Lawton, Charles Roach, George H. Wood, Charles Lord, Nat Blossom, Sol and Julia Aiken, Ada Castleton, Dan Tracy and Billy McMann (Irish melodies), Carrie Brower, and Larry Tooley (he gave Haley's Trip to Coney Island). And, since Coney Island itself was calling at that time, the London Theatre prudently closed for 1881–82.

MINER'S THEATRE, BOWERY, 1881–1882

I begin with the week of September 5th–10th, which assembled on the stage of Miner's, in the Bowery, the divergent talents of Sellou and Byrnes (in College Students), Annie Boyd, Mills and Warren (in Schneider, How You Vas?), Maggie Bursel, Edith Sinclair and Ed F. Barnes (in Faint Heart never Won Fair Lady), Press Eldridge, Georgie and Emma Kaine, Frank and Fannie (*sic*) Davis (in The Veteran), the Cawthorn (*sic*) Brothers ("first appearance in America in five years"), Dyllyn ("the autocrat of Irish comedy"), the Carrolls (in The McFaddens), Lamartine Brothers ("acrobatic marvels"), and A. H. Sheldon (in Married in the Dark). Many of these remained for the following week, when newcomers were Minnie Lee, John B. Wills and May Adams, the Ryans (Perry and Lulu), Miss St. George Hussey ("first appearance in America"), Charles McCarthy and George Monroe, Bernard Sloman, and the Megatherian Four. The concluding play presented Sheldon, in The Rogue, the Ring and the Rope. In later September novel faces and features were Professor Logrenia (with his educated dogs and mice), Fanny Davenport, Williams and Sully (in The Moonlight Picnic), McGlone and Lacy ("Emperors of Celtic Comedy," in Scraps), the Carrolls (in The Masquerade, and Peel Yourself), the Daytons (Tom and Annie), the Hermans, the Russell Brothers, Huber and Kitty Allyne (in Dreams), the California Quartette, and Sid C. France (September 26th–October 1st), in Marked for Life, assisted by the Miner stock company, including Tillie Malvern, Sheldon, Lansing, J. R. Gildersleeve, J. R. Lewis, Nellie Sandford (*sic*) and many more.

Entertainers lingered at Miner's for several weeks; October carried several such assets from September, particularly Sheldon in farces. Newer

[560]

in the bills of the chillier month were Billy Moore ("Irish"), Leonard and Jones (clog, reel, etc.), Melville and Bunell (musical divertissement), J. Selbini and Mlle. Lily, Frank I. Frayne and Annie von Behren, in Si Slocum (October 3rd–8th), De Ome and Amann ("Dutch" sketch and musical artists), Helene Smith, Sellou and Byrnes (in Our Style is Irish), the Moores (Charles and Carrie), Ada Forrest, the Fieldings, Thatcher and Hume (in Just from Arkansaw), Mattie Vickers and Charles S. Rogers, the Fieldings, Fanny (sic) Bernard, the Three Ronaldos (sic), Flora Moore, Charles Foster (October 17th–22nd, in Bertha, the Sewing Machine Girl), Orndorff and McDonald (in Irish Market Women), Frank Livingstone ("gymnastic and athletic star, late of Astley's"), Kitty Sheppard, Harry Cereni (Slow but Sure, somersaults, firing a gun while in the air, etc.), Clem Magee and Bob Allen (in Men of Nerve), Charles A. Loder (German sketches), Everett and Daly (in The Disappointed Lovers), Georgie Melnotte, the Comedy Quartette (the Budworths and the Nelsons), the Four Emeralds (Gibson, Russell, Kennedy and Conway), the De Bar Brothers, May Antonio, and Sheldon in various concluding plays — The Idiot Witness, Slave Life in Brazil, and The Robbers of Genoa. For the week of October 31st–November 4th came Harry McAvoy and Emma Rogers (in Love in a Letter Bag), Lizzie Simms (in transformation dances — "twelve changes of character and custume"), John Sweeney and Cliff Ryland (in Micks-tures), Ella Wesner, &c. Let me repeat that Miner's entertainers remained, frequently for several weeks.

The week of November 7th–12th was rich with Fits (James Russell as Gus Fitzpatrick, and John Russell, much the funnier of the brothers, as Gus Fitzpoodle), Trudell and Rowan (in bone duet statue clog, trick bone duets, juggling and imitations), E. C. Dunbar, the Russells ("in black and white changes, introducing the Two Servant Girls, Dutch and negro character specialties, burlesque dancing, and Dandy Colored Swells"), Charles McCarthy and George Monroe (in The Chinese Barber), and Sheldon (in Tailor's Luck, No. 10,001). Ada Forrest, the Fieldings, the California Quartette and the Cawthornes (or Cawthorns) remained in fulness of joy. Later November up to December 3rd gave us Houssabura (sic) Sam, Joe and Annie Burgess, McGlone and Lacy (in Pull the String), Huber and Kitty Allyne (in The Banker's Daughter), Keegan and Wilson, Dunbar, John Williams and Willis Pickert (clogs, etc.), Mattie Vickers and Rogers (in Stage Struck), Naoni (Japanese juggling — "first appearance in three years"), the Nonpareil Coloured Troubadours, Fred J. Huber (in The Senator from Louisiana), Capitola Forrest and Laura Bennett (songs, dances, skipping rope, etc.), McVickers (sic) and Saunders, Al W. Filson and Miss Lee Errol (in Kinks), Minnie Lee, E. D. Davies ("premier ventriloquist of the world"), the Hogan Brothers, Frank and Fannie (sic) Davis (in The Old Veteran), Ford and Knowles (in What's the News?), the Grotesque Four (Seamon, Turner and the Girard Brothers), the Horseshoe Four (the

[561]

Love Sisters, Frank B. Carr and J. J. Quinlan, in The Actor's Family), and Sheldon (in A Battle for Life). New, as one month faded into the next (week of November 28th–December 3rd) were Lulu Wentworth (banjo), Clark and Edwards, the Karl Brothers (William and Charles) and Edwin Baldwin (in acrobatic feats), the Two Wesleys, Mlle. Zittella (*sic*), Charles Glidden ("songs and comicalities"), the Four Eccentrics, and Sheldon (in The Midnight Lovers). From week to week, progressively, came these December blossoms — Mason and Titus (Shadowgraphs), Fanny Knight ("American song bird"), Peasley and Vennetta, Ward and Lynch, De Ome and Amann, Magee and Allen, Maude Leigh, William Carroll ("prince of funny fellows"), Ella Wesner, the Four Boisset Brothers, Dick Turpin (with Tillie Malvern and Sheldon), the Sheehans (James and Lydia, in America, Ireland, Germany, introducing "songs and characteristics of those nations"), the Ordeys (Karoly and Augusta, balancers and jugglers), the Four-in-Hand (Joseph Sullivan, William J. Smith, John P. Sheehan and Harry C. Talbert), Fanny Davenport, the Villon Troupe (Mlle. Elise, Signor Mendoza, and W. Villon, in bicycle feats), Jacques Strop in France (with Sheldon), Nelton (in Sports of Ancient Egypt — Enchanted Serpent, Magic Pagoda, Beautiful Fountain, etc. — "juggles huge torches of blazing fire"), Cooper Brothers (Tommy and Willie), Joseph Palles (Pelles?) and John Cusick (in Casey's Raffle), the Albion Brothers (William, Frank, Frederick and John, in a classic and athletic divertissement), the Clarks (Hen and Billy — "the smallest comedian in the world"), the Four Emeralds, &c. And December went out (26th–31st) with Professor Abt (Grecian Mystery), the Carrs (Walter, Norman and Lewis — the "Musical Three"), the Three Eltons (Albert, Frank and Samuel, acrobats), Lizzie Simms, Add Weaver and Nellie Parker (in A Policeman's Troubles), Ralph Pringle ("pronounced English star comic vocalist"), Herr Drayton (Modern Hercules, juggling, feats of strength), and a spectacular closing show — Mystic Star (with Tillie Malvern, Nellie Sandford, Helene Smith, and many, many others).

A. H. Sheldon was director of amusements, and, for January, 1882, he provided in large groups, each for its own special week or more, favourite performers known throughout the realms of "Variety" — Naoni, Manning and Drew, John B. Wills and May Adams (in The Fisherman's Home), Joe Mealey and Harry Mackey, Fannie Beane and Gilday, Charles Wayne and Alf de Vaney, John M. Turner (banjo), the Harts (Dan and Gussie), the Carrolls (R. M., Edwin H. and Richard, in Nonentities), Miss St. George Hussey, Charles Seeley's Troupe of English Acrobats (in Fun on the Axminster), The Mystic Star (continuing for January 9th–14th, written and adapted by Sheldon, with Tillie Malvern as Hero Harold, the sea king, Nellie Sandford as Sylvia, Sheldon as Mustapha Harold, Helene Smith as Hilda, Sorceress of Norway, &c.), Joe and Annie Burgess (in The Little Widow), Perry and Lulu Ryan (in Strolling in the Woodland), Charles and

[562]

Annie Whiting, Morton and Bryant, Ritta Keller, John and Maggie Field-
ing (in The Garden Wall), the Vanes (Will and James, musical artists),
Harry Blakely (Ethiopian), Magee and Allen, Lizzie Simms, Russell Broth-
ers, Ella Wesner, the Cawthornes (in The Rival Tradesmen), Ford and
Knowles, Dell Trudell (motto), Capitola Forrest and Laura Bennett, Wesley
Brothers, the Four-in-Hand, Trudell and Rowan, the Nonpareil Coloured
Troubadours (Mme. J. M. Zara, W. A. Fernandez, and Miss C. Thomas),
Len Shillito ("musical marvel"), the Clipper Quartette (Robert McIntyre,
F. T. Ward, George F. Campbell, F. A. Howard), the Three Monarchs
(Maura, Leondo and Bell), Joseph A. Burgess (as Turrell Tuttle Grub, in
A Banker's Luck, "written by a Boston journalist," and produced, in the
week of January 23rd–28th, with Annie Burgess, the Russells, George Beane,
Jr., J. H. Hazelton, J. R. Lewis, and Tillie Malvern).   For January 30th–
February 4th, we had Mason and Titus (Shadowgraphs), Delvan and Tracy
(the Irish Lords), Al W. Filson and Miss Lee Errol (in Kinks), Jessie Warner, Fanny Knight, Bryant and Saville, Griffin and Marks, Della Turner,
the Specialty Trio (Jennie Reese, Irvin Bush and Charles Reese), Carl Hertz,
the Virginia Trio (Turner, Welch and Harris), the Horseshoe Four (the
Loves, Carr and Quinlan), the Villon Troupe, and Muldoon in New York
(with Sheldon).   I still fail to see how they could provide so much for the
tiny admission fee.

Processionally, through February, passed before the vision of patrons
Waldron and Kaine (Hebrew), William Clifford and Frank Skelly (Empire
breaknecks), Leonard and Jones, the Ringlers (Add and Maggie, in Two
Little Shamrocks), Minnie Lee, Cavana and Mack (in Shakespeare Outdone), the Specialty Trio, the Winstanley Brothers (Lancashire act), James
Marlow and Joe Hart (late Allen and Hart), Thomas Ward and Con R.
Lynch, the Four Eccentrics (Perry, Magrew, Curdy and Hughes), the Milo
Brothers (John, James, Francis, vaulters and tumblers), Herr Drayton (jug-
gling), Edward Mealey (duet on 2 B-flat cornets at the same time), and Shel-
don (as Strop, in Robert Macaire) — all this for the week of February 6th–
11th; Charles and Carrie Moore (in The Troubles of an Amateur Skater),
John McVickers (sic) and C. Saunders (in A Perplexing Predicament),
Gallagher and West (in Nonsense), the Marr Brothers (Billy and John, in
Nationalities), Harry McAvoy and Emma Rogers (in Love in a Horn),
Leonard and Flynn, the Three Powers (Jen, Georgia and Dan — the Crescent
City Trio), Ralph Pringle, Charles Moore's Educated Dogs, Sheldon (in
The Idiot Witness) — these the priceless pearls of February 13th–18th;
Joe and Annie Burgess (in My First Drunk), the Two Sissons (Oscar and
Josie), McAvoy and Rogers (in Jealousy), Ada Forrest, Mattie Vickers and
Rogers (in Stage Struck), Sid C. France (in Marked for Life) — all to
brighten the week of February 20th–25th; and Boyd and Sarsfield (in Blue
Glass), Capitola Forrest and Laura Bennett (in A Summer's Vacation), the

[563]

Mortimers (Fred and Ida), Fannie Beane and Charles Gilday (in Spices, and in The Frenchman's Protégée), the Daytons (Tommy and Annie), Cavana and Mack, the Nonpareil Coloured Troubadours, James Kelly and Tom O'Brien, the Cawthornes (in Off for Australia), Simon Blackchief (Indian contortionist and hoof performer), and the play of Life in Leadville (with Jerry Cavana, Dick Mack, W. T. Dulany, J. R. Lewis, Tillie Malvern and Nellie Sandford) — to carry winter richly into spring (week of February 27th–March 4th).

And March lavished inexhaustible treasures for those who liked them: the Harts (Dan and Gussie, in Uncle Pete's Return), Mealey and Mackey, Ford and Knowles, Maud Morrissey, the Four Boisset Brothers, Pauline Batchellor, Fannie Beane and Gilday (in The Picnic), Ward and Lynch, Tommy Morrissey (jig), Leonard and Jones, Neil Smith and his dogs, Ella Wesner, the Megatherian Four (Kelly, Lyons, De Vaney and O'Brien), Sheldon (in The Actor's Boarding House), the Alwards (Gus and Nellie, illusionists, mind-readers, ventriloquists), the Bookers (Harry and George, formerly Canfield and Booker), Young Ajax ("serpentine wonder"), Kitty Gardner, George Homer and Georgie Lingard (in Our Pleasure Party), Dollie Davenport, E. D. Davies, George Kane, Lillie Western, Dick Morosco, Williams and Pickert, Naoni, Ward and Lynch (in The Arrival of General Grant) — all these before the Ides of that fatal month. The last fortnight gave us Kitty Sheppard, Frank Livingstone, Gilson and Welsh (acrobats), William Dolan and Mike Lynch (song and dance), Carrie Howard (serio-comic), Mattie Vickers and C. S. Rogers (in The Débutante), Frank I. Frayne and Annie von Behren, with H. M. Markham, Grace Foster, Andy and Katie Mallon, the African lion, Emperor, and the performing bears, Bruno and Chio — animals safely caged, and "there is no danger" — in Si Slocum (week of March 20th–25th), Murphy and Miles (Irish), Mason and Lord (Ethiopians), Filson and Lee Errol, Harry Blakely, Fannie Beane and Charles Gilday (in When the Cat's Away, the Mice Will Play), the Burlesque Trio (Cereni, Peters and Ada Page), the Specialty Trio (the Reeses and I. Bush), the Four Aces (Sherman, Wayne, Tierney and Owens), Ralph Pringle, Leopold and Wentworth (gymnasts), the Four-in-Hand, the St. Elmos (Harry, George and Haney, acrobats), and The Centennial Weary Traveller (with Charles and Vic O'Brien and Tillie Malvern). I sit in amazement, and my pen plods in despair, in the unending catalogues of names these "Variety" houses entail upon us.

The week of April 3rd–8th brought in Harry Miner and Pat Rooney's New York Star Combination — Flora King (serio-comic), Harry Crandall and Charles Eastwood (in Echoes from Germany), the Cogill Brothers (Charles W. and Harry P., in Chit-Chat), Charles and Annie Whiting, Pat Rooney, Sharpley and West (musical team), Ada Forrest, Lamont and Ducrow (in The Happy Hottentots), Stirk's Troupe of Male and Female

Bicycle Equestrians, the Two Wesleys, and William Cronin and J. P. Sullivan (in Life in a Tenement House).   Later in April we had Ripley and Reede ("perform on every known instrument"), McVickers and Saunders, the Two Coopers, the Dashway Brothers (Carlos and Hugo, horizontal bars, double pirouettes, double somersaults, forward shoots, double giant swing), John G. Hodge ("California's Italian dialect performer"), Dick Hume and Jennie Lindsay, Hanley and Logan ("the slender six-foot nigs"), the Allen Sisters (May and Lillie), Marlow and Hart (in Nick-Nacks and in Inspiration), the Quaker City Quartette (Frank Budd, Sam Burnell, Will Laird, &c., in Uncle Jasper's Invitation), the Cawthornes (ever *sic*), Sheldon (in The Female Gambler, or, the Harvest of Sin), Frazier and Hallam (musical eccentrics), James C. Vincent (Irish song and dance), Ned Lang and Viola Rosa ("Dutch," in Curious), Dan Williams and Tommy Morton (Irish), Charles H. Sheffer and Harry Blakely (in Our Wedding Day), the Onofri Brothers (Achille, Fortune and Oreste), the Cogill Brothers (in Points), Tillie Van Buren (xylophone), Vane and Vane (Will and James, from the St. James Music Hall, London, pony banjo, etc.), Annie Boyd, Little Todd and Lew Snow (equilibrisms), Charles H. Hoey (of Nantick, Mass., single, double, triple and quadruple Indian clubs), the Four Aces, New Year's Calls, "Professor" James Ross and his dog circus, Richards Brothers (song and dance), Walton and Edwards (in The Deitcher Fancy Ball), Minnie Lee, Crosby and Martin (songs, etc.), George W. Rice and Charles Barton (in Æsthetic Originalities), the Electric Quartette (Campbell, Chalfont, Young and Harris), Charles Diamond, the Wesley Brothers, the Horseshoe Four, and A. H. Sheldon (24th–29th, in his own play, A Battle for Life).   The reader is wondering if he will ever escape from this particular hall of "Variety"; I myself am almost prostrate before the task.   We may thank the Harvard Theatre Collection for this richness of information.   *Timeo Danaos et dona ferentes!*

May and June piled high the delights of the palace of pleasure that was Miner's in the Bowery; I can afford space only for newcomers and novel features that I fear will serve to heap high the lumber in my reader's storehouse of memory.   Harry Miner's Comedy Four — our old friends Murphy and Shannon and Murphy and Mack — gave (May 1st–6th) Stuffin *vs.* Montague, and Murphy's Dream; others in the bill were Billy Carter, Carrie Swain ("late of The Tourists," in The Western Union Telegraph Boy), Ella and Charles Jerome (in Comedy), the Blaisdell Family (Lancashire bell ringers), assisted by John Murphy, Valjean, Bryant and Hoey, Frank Lewis, and the Little Four (Talbert, Mack and the Carroll Brothers).   Subsequent weeks brought "Professor" Pidgeon's Royal Punch and Judy, the Marr Brothers, Roger Dolan and Mike Lynch (in rough Irish songs and dances), Duncan (ventriloquist), Max Arnold (in The Dutchman from Kahoos), Beane and Gilday (in Rural Felicity), Murray and Magrath

[565]

("Irish"), John Henshaw and May Ten Broeck (in Deception), Jennie Morgan, Morosco and Kitty Gardner (in The Schlum Family), Fred Mathews ("England's greatest facial comique and grotesque dancer"), The Arrival of Gilbert and Departure of Sullivan (May 8th–13th, with Max Arnold as Gilbert "forced to father Pinafore," Dulany as Barry Sullivan, "who has had sad experiences of Pinafore," and Tillie Malvern as the "keeper of the Pinafore Hotel"), Charles de Bixamos (feats of strength), Edward Werner and Maud Stanley (in My New Servant), Bryant and Saville (in P. S. Gilmore), Beane and Gilday (in Spices), Burt Queen (ventriloquist), Dick Hume and Jennie Lindsay (in Clipper Ads), Clem C. Magee and Bob Allen (in The Man of Nerve), Parker Twin Brothers (song and dance), Charles McCarthy and George Monroe (in Grogan's Chinese Laundry), the Allen Sisters, the Electric Three (Callan, Haley and Callan), Ten American Students (banjo), Sheldon (in Fun at a Picnic), John E. Sanders (or Saunders) and Charles H. Dean (in Jubilee Day), Joe and Annie Burgess (in The Little Widow), Belle Clifton and Louisa de Luisi ("rifle song and dances, changing to skipping rope dance, both ladies dancing in one rope, changing costumes, including tights, shoes, etc."), Wills and May Adams (in The Fisherman's Home), Werner and Maud Stanley (in After the Opera), Pat Rooney, Murphy and Shannon (in Mixtures), Murphy and Mack (in The Arrival of Mulcahey), Joe Burgess (in Oscar Wilder), Revillo (magic), James C. Vincent ("the neat Irish lad"), the Onofris, Max and Martha Miller, Tillie Van Buren, Orm Dixon (ventriloquist), the Price Brothers (Harry and Theo, in Two Boys from Old Virginia), Kitty McDermott, Harry Watson and Alice Hutchings (in Dutch Deception), Charles Turner, and A. H. Sheldon (in Lodgers! Inventors! Dodgers!).

Thus we have arrived breathless, dizzy, through Saturday, June 3rd, and plunge headlong into the seas of later June, with Dollie Davenport, J. F. Sherry (song and dance, clog and reel), Jeppe and Fannie Delano, the Electric Three, Ross and his dog circus, Murphy and Shannon (in Turning the Tables), Bryant and Hoey, Charles H. Hoey (of Nantick), the re-united Comedy Four (Murphy and Shannon, Murphy and Mack, in Murphy's Christening), Henshaw and Ten Broeck, Emery and Russell, Frank Livingstone, the Cooper Brothers, Sheldon in The Midnight Lovers, The Shoemaker's Ghost, and other farces, Annie Boyd, the Skatorial Three (W. H. Landis and Powers Brothers), Dan Williams and Thomas Morton (in The Dandy Jockeys), the Barron Brothers ("Crème de la crème" of Ethiopian Comedy, in Commotion), the Martell Brothers (acrobats), Charles and Ella Jerome, Flora Moore, Charles Diamond, Ella Wesner, Our German Cousin (June 19th–24th, with Max Arnold, J. R. Lewis, Dulany and Tillie Malvern), J. M. Johnson and S. C. Swain (in Leisure on the Levee), Ward and Lynch, William Walton's Whimsicality Company (June 26th–July 1st, in The Cow with the Crooked Horns, Walton as the cow), Lizzie Derious,

[566]

the American Four (in That's What I Thought), Twenty Minutes in Fishkill (July 3rd–8th, with Sheldon and the regular company), the Armstrong Sisters (Sidney and Ollie), Pat Rooney, the Four Aces (E. H. Talbert, late of the Little Four, Wayne, Tierney and Owens), John W. Gibbons (vocal) and Murphy's Dream again.

Harvard inexorably piles up its inexhaustible supply of bills for these minor theatres, and I blindly pace the sands of the salty sea of facts involved, bringing back to my reader flotsam and jetsam as follows, for July and August: "Professor" James H. Burton and his dogs, Ned Lang and Viola Rosa, Austin and Dale (zither, mandolin, chime bells), Foster and Hughes, Frank and Fannie (now the habitual spelling) Davis, Ripley, Leslie and Ripley, the Four-in-Hand (George Gilson, J. E. Welsh, T. F. Tobin, William F. Smith), Paul Hamlin and Ada Newcomb (rapid changes), Mabel Vaughn (*sic*), Carroll and Walters, Capitola Forrest, Wills and May Adams (in Larks), Pauline Batchellor, Leslie and Gentry (grotesques), Fred Roberts, Dan Lacy and Mike Lynch, Dutch Daly, the Four Shamrocks (Conroy, John and Matt Daly and Micky Thompson), Who Broke the Clock? (with J. R. Taylor), Sheldon (in Getting Rid of a Cousin), Ada Forrest, J. F. Hoey, Edwards and Morton, the Brennans and Laible (in The Coopers), Fattie Stewart (in Tricks), the Clarks (Hen and Billy), Maggie Cline (in Mary Ann Kehoe), Murphy and Miles (the Gentlemen from Kerry), the Four Comets (Frank Hawley, Bobby and Tommy Williams and Walter Manning, in Fragments), the Skatorial Three (now O. B. Steele and the Powers Brothers), Bessie Ventini, Lord and Lovely (Ethiopian grotesques), Annie Hart, Bree and Kirwin (in Musical Absurdities), Billy Diamond (the Black Diamond of the West), McAvoy and Rogers (in Jealousy), James T. Kelly, William Cronin and J. P. Sullivan (in The O'Gradys), George W. Kenway, the Four Aces, Christie Brothers (Frank and Will), the Onofris, Maude Leigh, Flora Moore, the Ten American Students, Oliver Twist (with Tillie Malvern as Nancy), Clem Magee and Bob Allen (in Ma, Look at Him, and in Bradley's Luck), Marie Whittingham, the Quaker City Quartette, Dan McCarthy and Kitty Coleman (Celtic act), the Burlesque Three (Cereni, Peters and Ada Page), the Four Comets, Parker Twin Brothers, the Four Diamonds (G. W. Watson, W. S. Gilmore, J. G. Brevarde and Charles Sawtelle), "Professor" Anella and performing birds, James Sweeney and Eddie Kearney, the Twilight Four (Hines, Hodges, Moore and Martin), Billy Moore and John Marr, Four-of-a-Kind (George Gilson, J. E. Welsh, T. F. Tobin, William F. Smith), the Four Emeralds (Russell, Magee, Kennedy and Conway), the Little Four (Watson, Mack, and the Carroll Brothers), A. H. Sheldon's farce, Rush-in Baths *vs.* .Supreme Court, "Professor" J. H. Burton and his dogs, Sullivan and Harrington (Ethiopians), Murphy and Mack (in The Two Nurses and in The Arrival of Mulcahey), the Monumental Quartette (Charles Earle, Vic Hawley, George Hammond

[567]

and Walter West) — lo! exhausted, we arrive at September 2nd, and, gasping for air, rush out of Miner's in the Bowery, for 1881–1882.

MINER'S EIGHTH AVENUE THEATRE, 1881–1882

And here is another Miner's. The ambitious manager shot an arrow into the air and built at 312-314 Eighth Avenue, above Twenty-sixth Street, another hall of "Variety," with himself and Thomas Canary as proprietors, Louis Robie as director of amusements, John Nickinson as treasurer, H. Higgins as leader of the orchestra, James Macklin as master machinist and William Schaeffer as scenic artist. The place was declared to have twenty exits and to have cost $80,000.

The opening bill (November 21st–26th) was of Miner's usual giant proportions: Perry and Lulu Ryan, the Daytons (Tom and Annie), McGlone and Lacy, Jeppe and Fannie Delano, Magee and Allen, Fannie Beane and Charles Gilday (in Spices and in Stage-Struck), Lillian Ramsden (opéra-bouffe), Miss Lavenia, McAvoy and Emma Rogers (in Courting in a Horn), Maggie Cline (in Mary Ann Kehoe, Ha, Ha), John Williams and Willis Pickert, the Two Wesleys, the California Quartette, and the Carrolls (R. M., E. H., and Richard F., in The Italian Padrone, assisted by olio performers including Harry McAvoy, Fred J. Huber, Clem Magee, Pat McGlone, Dan Lacy, Kitty Allyne, Fannie Delano, Annie Dayton, Eva Byron, and Miss Lavenia). Thus was the new venture launched. The week of November 28th–December 3rd brought in a host of other favourites tried and true — Judge Duffy's Substitute (with Dan Lacy, McGlone, Eva Byron, &c.), Al W. Filson and Miss Lee Errol (*sic* — in Kinks), Naoni, Fred Wilson (character portraits), the Peasleys (in Mollie's Victory), the Russell Brothers, Herr Drayton, Mlle. Elise, Griffin and Marks, E. D. Davies, and New York in 1881 (with Huber, Kitty Allyne, the Russells, &c.).

December rushed into the arms of January with a dazzling procession of Sellou and Byrnes (in College Students), Fanny Davenport, Fred Huber and Kitty Allyne (in Stricken and in The Banker's Daughter), Leonard and Jones (The Telegraph Lads), the Four Emeralds, Maggie Bursel, Mills and Warren ("German"), Jeppe and Fannie Delano, the Peasleys, the Ordeys, Lillie Wood ("who will afford the devotees of song a pretty face, rich voice, and handsome form, with the necessary adjuncts of tasteful dressing"), the Four Eccentrics, Bernard Sloman (the bird man), Joseph A. Burgess and Fred J. Huber (in A Banker's Luck), Mason and Titus (Shadowgraphs), Fanny Knight, Joe and Annie Burgess (in The Little Widow), C. and Thomas O'Brien (in The Centennial Weary Traveller), the Nonpareil Coloured Troubadours, Boyd and Sarsfield, Beane and Gilday (in When the Cat's Away), Dick Baker (motto and comic), Mr. and Mrs. Joe Allen (in The Terpsichorean Mania), The Senator from Louisiana (December 12th–

[568]

17th, with Huber, Robie, Kitty Allyne, &c.), Orndorff and McDonald, Helene Smith, Beane and Gilday (in Rural Felicity), Mealey and Mackey, Capitola Forrest and Laura Bennett, Delvan and Tracy, Cora Cardigan, John W. Ransone, and the stock actors (December 19th–24th, in Across the Atlantic), Effie (or Elfie) De Rock (ballads), McVickers (*sic*) and Saunders ("Irish"), Lizzie Mulvey and Alice d'Estelle (songs and dances), Charles A. Loder, Mattie Vickers and C. S. Rogers (in The Débutante), The Three Royal Russian Athletes, Minnie Lee, May Antonio, and Robert Fraser (in Cluck-a-luck). Most of these shining ones appeared during the season at Miner's Bowery; what could be more reasonable?

And so January breaks open a new calendar (week of 2nd–7th), with newcomers in persons of Professor Abt, Lizzie Derious, Allie Smith, Peasley and Vennetta, Ralph Pringle, Lizzie Simms, and thence advances toward February with the Daytons (in Our New Postman), the Lamartine Brothers, J. W. Kelly (extempore vocalist), E. D. Davies, Weston and Hanson, Mlle. Zittella (*sic*), Dutch Daly, Mason and Lord ("nonsense makers"), William Carroll, the Comical Cawthornes, Harry McAvoy (in his own play, The Metropolis After Dark, January 9th–14th), La Selle, the Water-Queen, Dell Trudell, Wills and May Adams, Leonard and Flynn, Elise Kruger, William Carroll, F. J. Huber and Louis Robie (in The Modern School of Acting), Trudell and Rowan, De Ome and Amann, the French Twin Sisters, Miss St. George Hussey, the Nonpareil Coloured Troubadours, the Four Emeralds, the Whitings, the Vanes, Carl Hertz (young California necromancer), Morton and Bryant, Charles Foster, with members of the olio and of the stock company, in the play, Under Oath (given for the week of January 23rd–28th), Sweeney and Ryland (in Freaks), the Powers (Jen, Georgia and Dan), the Crescent City Trio, in Eccentricities), the Peasleys (in Patrick's Day), the Ryans, Tony Farrell and Ed Ryan (in Somewhat Different), Ward and Lynch, the Two Clarks (Hen and Billy), and Charles E. Emmett (*sic* — January 30th–February 4th, in Dashing Charlie, or, the Prairie Scout).

The opening farce for February 6th–11th was Cats! Cats! with Huber, C. Ryland and Robie; thence came "turns" of Mason and Titus, Fanny Knight, Naoni, Williams and Morton, Pauline Batchellor, Foster and Hughes (grotesques), the Peasleys, the De Bar Brothers, Lizzie Simms, Ford and Knowles (in What's the News?), the Horseshoe Four (the Loves, F. B. Carr and Quinlan, in The Actor's Family), and F. J. Huber (as Simon Pure, in Needles). Next week (13th–18th), Harry Miner's Great Comedy Four (Murphy and Mack and Murphy and Shannon) ended the bills in Murphy's Dream; the entertainment included also Billy Carter, the Blaisdells (William B. and Julia Peake, Henry and William, Jr., in Musical Mélange), Valjean, the Fieldings, Frank Lewis, and the Little Four. For the week ending February 25th we had Harry Miner's Frank I. Frayne Combination, includ-

[569]

ing Hallen and Enid Hart, the Comical Cawthornes, the Fieldings, and Frayne in Mardo, or, the Nihilists of St. Petersburg (characters by Frayne, C. N. Massey, George C. Wood, A. H. Hastings, H. M. Markham, J. J. Coleman, Andy Mallon, Cassie Troy, Lizzie Duroy, Edith Murillo and Kate Mallon). The week of February 27th–March 4th changed to the Maxwells, Daisy Norwood, the Marr Brothers (Billy and John), McAvoy and Rogers, Frank T. Morton, the Virginia Trio (Turner, Welch and Harris), Mons. Bushnell and Kitty Thomas (juggling and equilibrium), Harry Blakely (songs and witticisms), and Sid C. France (in Marked for Life).

Like leaves before the blasts of March whirl the "turns" of that month — McVickers and Saunders and Kitty Allyne (in The Arrival of Casey), Kitty Gardner, Al W. Filson and Miss Lee Errol, De Bar Brothers, Elise Kruger, Dick Morosco and Kitty Gardner, Magee and Allen (in Men of Nerve), the Cooper Brothers, the Milo Brothers, the Specialty Trio (Jennie Reese, Irvin Bush and Charles Reese), Leonard and Flynn, the Four-in-Hand, Flora King, Crandall and Eastwood (in Echoes from Germany), the Cogill Brothers (in Chit-Chat), the Lamartine Brothers, Professor Stirk's Troupe of Male and Female Bicycle Equestrians, Pat Rooney, Sharpley and West, Minnie Lee, Beane and Gilday (in The Picnic), Lamont and Ducrow, Walton and Edwards (in The Deitcher Fancy Ball), Cronin and Sullivan (in Life in a Tenement House), George E. Homer and Georgie Lingard (in Our Pleasure Party), George Kaine (sic — "sings with a lighted cigar in his mouth"), Huber and Kitty Allyne (in Pleasant Dreams, banjo, bones and violin), the Boissets, Charles Turner and John Phillips (burlesque), Beane and Gilday (in When the Cat's Away, and also in The Débutante), Williams and Pickert, the Four Shamrocks, Huber (in Cremation), Joe and Annie Burgess (in My First Drunk), the Russell Brothers, Kitty Shepherd (or Sheppard), Mealey and Mackey, Frank Livingstone, Andy Shields and James Richmond ("Irish"), Charles and Carrie Moore, Lester and Williams, Frank and Fannie (sic) Davis, and Mr. and Mrs. Jerry Cohan (March 27th–April 1st), in The Molly Maguires, or, The Black Diamond of Hazelton — Cohan as Mark O'Dare, the engineer, and Mrs. Cohan as Diana Duychink, the flower of Duychink House. And there we are, safely arrived to April 1st.

April burgeoned in engagements with De Ome and Amann (in All Sorts), Dolly (or Dollie) Davenport, Dick Hume and Jennie Lindsay (in Clipper Ads), Ralph Pringle, Cavana and Mack (in Shakespeare Outdone), the Excelsior Quartette (Ridge, Atwood, Wilson and Cameron), Dick Morosco and Kitty Gardner, Durell Twin Brothers ("refined acrobatic song and dance"), Minnie Lee, Lester and Williams, Belle Clifton and Louise de Luisi, the Cawthornes, Joseph A. Burgess (in A Banker's Luck), Bryant and Saville (in P. G. Gilmore vs. Bill Bradley, of Wilmington, N. C.), Eva Byron (songs), Mason and Lord, Sailor West, Maggie Bursel, Charles and Annie Whiting, Fanny Knight, Sellou and Burns (sic), George W. Rice and

Charles Barton, the Burlesque Three (Cereni, Peters and Ada Page), the Electric Quartette (Campbell, Chalfont, Young and Harris), the Daytons (in Our New Postman), Dutch Daly, the Two Wesleys, the Four Comets (Hawley, Manning, Bobby and Tommy Williams), Robie and Huber (in The Miser of Five Points), Gallagher and West, Dashway Brothers, Murphy and Miles, Beane and Gilday, Foster and Hughes, Gilson and Welsh (in Golden Ringlets), Walton and Edwards, Ripley and Reade (usually *Reed*), the Four-in-Hand, the Allen Sisters, the Shamrock Four, Huber as Jesse and Robie as Frank (in The James Boys — April 17th–22nd), Magee and Allen (in Ma, Look at Him), Charles H. Sheffer and Harry Blakely (in Our Wedding Day), the Ripleys (William, Claudia and Leoline — acrobats), Annie Boyd, Edward Werner and Maud Stanley, Little Todd and Lew Stone, Beane and Gilday continuing, James Marlow and Joseph Hart (in Nick Nacks), the Four Aces (Sherman, Wayne, Tierney and Owens), &c.   One might as well have attended Miner's in the Bowery; performers were almost identical through the season.

And May blossomed in merry wise, with McVickers (*sic*) and Saunders (in How I Used Casey), Ada Forrest, the Sheerans (*sic* — in America, Ireland and Germany), Morosco and Kitty Gardner, the Peasleys (in Sparking in the Park), Ross and his dogs, Pat Rooney, Max Arnold, Wesley Brothers, the Werners, the Four-in-Hand, Robie and Huber and Kitty Allyne in farces, Billy Carter, Carrie Swain, the Jeromes, George Kaine (*sic*), the Blaisdell Family (assisted by John Murphy), Valjean, the Little Four, Frank Lewis, the Comedy Four (Murphy and Mack and Murphy and Shannon, in Murphy's Dream, May 8th–13th), Roger Dolan and Mike Lynch, Duncan (ventriloquist), Belle Clifton and Louise de Luisi, Frank and Fannie Davis (in Fogarty's Night On), Dutch Daly, Ella Wesner, Bryant and Hoey, the Stirk Family, Jennie Morgan, the Barron Brothers (song and dance), Bryant and Saville, Frank I. Frayne and his company, in Si Slocum (May 22nd–27th), and (for the week of May 29th–June 3rd) Carrie Howard, McCarthy and Monroe (in Grogan's Chinese Laundry), Burt (or But) Queen (ventriloquist), Billy Carter, Murphy and Mack (The O'Shaughnessy Guards), Nimmie Kent (skipping rope, song and dance), Murphy and Shannon (in Mixtures, or, Burlesque from Beginning to End), the Bordeaux Sisters (Ella and Lotta, in songs and dances), John E. Henshaw and May Ten Broeck (*sic* — in Deception), the Electric Three, and The Rivals (with Murphy and Mack and Murphy and Shannon).

Balmy June evenings tempted from the great outdoors to hear Murray and Magrath (Celtic song and dance), Max and Martha Miller, Kitty McDermott, Murphy and Mack (Arrival of Mulcahy), the Onofri Brothers (in The French Locomotive), Tillie Van Buren (xylophone), Pat Rooney, Joe and Annie Burgess, the Little Four, Dick Hume and Jennie Lindsay, and Joe Burgess's farce, Murphy's Trip to New York (with John E. Murphy,

[571]

Phil Mack and the author — all these for June 5th–10th); and, later, in the month, Port Wine *vs.* Jealousy (with Huber, Robie and Kitty Allyne), Annie Boyd, John E. Sanders (*sic*) and Charles H. Dean (in Jubilee Day), J. F. Sherry (song and dance, clog and reel), Max Arnold, the Delanos, Charles H. Hoey (of Nantick, Mass., swinging and juggling — "not at all the Charles Hoey whom Gus Hill defeated May 24, 1882"), Bryant and Hoey, Cronin and Sullivan (in Life in a Tenement House), Revillo (magic), Lord and Lovely, Murphy and Mack (in The McMullen Family), McAvoy and Emma Rogers (in Two Can Play at that Game), Harry Watson and Alice Hutchings, the American Four, and The Christening (June 19th–24th, with Murphy and Mack and Murphy and Shannon). The week of June 26th–July 1st proffered Murphy and Mack (in Funny Mulqueeny), James C. Vincent, the Martell Brothers, Pauline Batchellor, the Jeromes, Murphy and Shannon, the Skatorial Three (W. H. Landis and Powers Brothers), Charles Diamond ("the most artistic song and dance performer in the world"), and Murphy's Wedding (with Murphy and Mack as Horatio Murphy and Mrs. Eliza Casey, the bride and groom, and with George Murphy as Peter Baum and George Shannon as Plug Casey).

And now, though summer is panting through the city, the Eighth Avenue Theatre will not close its doors. In July it offered Joe and Annie Burgess (in My First Drunk), Pauline Batchellor, the Ripleys (William, Claudia, and Leoline, with their trained elephant, Jumbo), Mabel Vaughn, D. B. Emery and Laura Russell, Williams and Morton, J. M. Johnson and Sam C. Swain (in Leisure on the Levee), Ward and Lynch, Maggie Cline, the Four-in-Hand, Lodgers, Inventors and Dodgers (with Huber, Robie and Kitty Allyne), Grandfather's Clock (with Huber and Allyne), John W. Gibbons, James Mack (song and dance), Murphy and Shannon, Lizzie Hunter, Murphy and Miles, Charles Turner (banjo), Capitola Forrest, Wesley Brothers, Annie Hart (cantatrice), the Four Pickaninnies (Robert Watson, Charles Lober, Charles Gundlach, and Robert Kirby, in Peaches and Honey), Murphy's Dream (with Murphy and Mack and Murphy and Shannon), Ellwood (female impersonator), Austin and Dale (mandolin, zither, chime bells, etc.), Murphy and Shannon (in Turning the Tables), Murphy and Mack (in The Two Nurses), Brennan and Laible, the Four Aces (E. H. Talbert, Wayne, Tierney and Owens), John E. Henshaw and May Ten Broeck (in Deception), Murphy's Christmas (July 17th–22nd), Professor James H. Burton and his dogs, Kitty Sheppard, Frank Livingstone ("champion equilibrist of the world"), the four Onofri Brothers, Tillie Van Buren, Wills and May Adams (in Larks), the Parker Twin Brothers, Cronin and Sullivan (in McCormick, the Copper), Annie Hart, Four-of-a-Kind (George Gilson, J. E. Welsh, T. F. Tobin and W. T. Smith), Fred Roberts, and Huber (in Our Indian Troubles). Burning July merged into muggy August (July 31st–August 5th) with Burt Queen, Harry Edwards and Lew Morton, Len

[572]

LOUISE MONTAGUE

LORELLA FAMILY

KITTY ALLYNE

SANFORD
(OF SANFORD AND
WILSON)

EDWARD M. FAVOR

VIOLA CLIFTON
(BURLESQUE)

FLORA MOORE

JOHN B. WILLS

CLARA MOORE

Shillito ("England's and America's greatest musical clown — performs on the largest collection of musical instruments in the world"), Ada Forrest, Dan Tracy and William McMahon (in Irish sketches), Fattie Stewart (in Faint Heart Can't Win), Lizzie Derious, the Electric Three, Louise Clement (jig and Indian clubs), the Four Shamrocks (Dave Conroy, Matt and John Daly and Mickey Thompson), Maggie Cline, and Fattie Stewart in his own Eh! What Is It?

I hurry through August, with performances by James Sweeney and Eddie Kearney, the Cooper Brothers, Harry Raynor (Lancashire clog), Walter and Edwards, Lacy and Lynch, the Burlesque Three, the Two Clarks (Hen and Billy), Dolly (*sic*) Davenport, Frank and Fannie (*sic*) Davis, The Four Diamonds, Huber and Allyne (in farces), Polly McDonald (serio-comic — "her introductory bow"), Lamont and Ducrow (the Happy Hottentots), Lester and Williams, John Hart (in The Governor), Harry Morris (eccentric), the Big Four (Smith, Waldron, Cronin and Martin, "the great and original planet from which all other 4's sprang"), Luigi dell' Oro ("musical prodigy of the nineteenth century"), Flora Moore, Master Martin and John Hart (in A Night of Horror), Bree and Kirwin (musical absurdities), Dan McCarthy and Kitty Coleman (reel and jig), Fanny Wood (serio-comic), Tony Farrell and Jennie Leland (in Love in a Hammock), and the Quaker City Quartette (Sam Burnell, Frank Budd, Will Laird and Hi Graham, in their negro sketch, Uncle Jasper's Invitation). And here I leave the new Miner's for 1881–82, thankful to depart from the extensive field of "Variety" in the Bowery and in Eighth Avenue. But I admit I enjoy the "tags" that exalt the really inexaltable.

DICK PARKER'S AMERICAN THEATRE, 1881–1882

For the week of September 5th–10th, Maggie Weston's Dan Maloney's Raffle Combination was at the American, with an aggregation consisting of the De Voy (*sic*) Sisters (Emma and Josie, in a double silver bell hoop and Irish jigs), Joseph J. Sullivan and William Smith, Tommy Watson, Mayo and Talbert, Ward and Lynch, the Four Luminaries (John Burke, the De Voy Sisters and Larry Smith), Ida Clifton, the Four Planets (McDermott, Sheehan, Kennedy and Clark), and of course, Maggie Weston, herself, in Dan Maloney's Raffle. Other features of September were Myles Morris, Billy Devern and Lottie Ward (in Lancashire clog), Ben Cotton, with Mrs. Nellie and Idalene Cotton (his wife and daughter — in True Devotion, assisted by J. K. Keane, Joseph V. Arlington, Mai Estelle, Harry Clifford and Florence Bell), Isabel Ward, Dan McCarthy, Tom and Ed Haley, Mike Gallagher, Kitty Sharpe, Frank Bolton and Ada Bradford (in The Enchanted Statue), and Fanny Herring (September 19th–24th, in Little Buckshot). For the week of September 26th–October 1st came Harry Miner's

Comedy Four (Murphy and Shannon, Murphy and Mack, in Murphy's Dream), Charles and Ella Jerome, Billy Carter, Carrie Swain (as The Western Union Telegraph Boy), the Brennans and Laible (in The Coopers), Cool Burgess, Valjean, and Frank Lewis — assuredly a picked aggregation.

Complete files at Harvard for October allow me to list, in rapid succession, Moore and Lessenger, Georgie Melnotte, the Peasleys, Minnie Lee, Mr. and Mrs. Joe Allen (in The Terpsichorean Mania), N. S. Wood and Mai Estelle (October 3rd–8th, in Life and Adventures of Jack Sheppard), Fred J. Huber and Kitty Allyne (in Pleasant Dreams), the Landis Brothers (William and Charles, "united after a separation of three years"), the Vane Brothers (Will and James), Crumley and De Forrest (break-neck dance), Lillie Hall, J. Selbini and Mlle. Lily (bicyclists), H. M. Parker and his dogs, Mai Estelle (October 10th–15th, in Norah, or, the Robber's Doom), Miss Dell Trudell, the Herrmans (Charles and La Rosa), the Comedy Quartet (Budworths and Nelsons), May Irwin, Hallen and Hart (in In and Out of Action), Charles A. Gardner, Emerson and Clark, Frank Jones and Alice Montague (October 17th–22nd, in The Black Hand), a new Harry Miner's Combination (October 24th–29th) including Ford and Knowles, Walsh and Dempsey, Williams and Sully, Charles and Carrie Moore (roller-skaters), La Rosa Brothers (Frank and George, French ring act), the Carrolls (in Peel Yourself), Lulu Wentworth, and Sid C. France (in Marked for Life) — a combination certainly inferior to the Miner's of a short time before. From October 31st to November 19th, we had a return engagement of Maggie Weston's Dan Maloney's Raffle Combination — three weeks in all. The only bill at Harvard for December is that for the 26th–31st, promising Rightmire (in The Boss), the Peasleys, the Haleys, Lizzie Derious and Allie Smith, and the Four-in-Hand (Joseph Sullivan, William J. Smith, John P. Sheehan and Harry C. Talbert). It is needless to try to keep such combinations of four performers fixed in our minds; before we have memorised them they slip into other combinations, and then into others. Except, of course, a few permanent groups!

The January procession moved by, in persons of Clarence Burton and Lizzie Morris (in Flashes from the South), Leoline Ripley (club swinger), Pat Riley (or Reilly), Williams and Pickert, Frank and Fannie Davis, Carrie Lewis (singing in three languages), the Ripleys (William and Claudia), Harry Clifford (January 2nd–7th, in Poverty Flat, or, California in '49); for the benefit of Richard Parker (on the 26th), Pauline Batchellor, John Robinson and Lizzie Conway, Davenport Brothers, Billy Barry, the American Four (Pettingill, Gale, Dailey and Hoey), the Sparks Brothers, and A Little Misunderstanding (with Frank and William Girard, Dan Collyer and Jennie Christie). The bill for January 30th included Morton and Bryant, the Durell Twin Brothers, Ritta Keller (operatic), Harry Clark (with a funny talking hand), Joe Mealey and Harry Mackey (song and dance and imitations), Cool Burgess, Wood, Beasley and Weston Brothers, and J. K. Keane (in Wildcat Ned). In February, newcomers were John J. Sellon (*sic*) and John J. Burns (*sic*), Clark and Edwards, Effie de Rock, Lillie Western, the Barlow Brothers, Carl Hertz (young California necromancer), Jack Sheppard from the Cradle to the Grave (February 6th–11th, with Fanny Herring, Frank A. McClane, J. K. Keane, Mai Estelle, Effie De Rock, &c.), Paus Le Petres (in The Irish Car Driver), Fred Roberts, Ella and Paddy Murphy, Lilly Le Petres (*sic*), Minnie Oscar Gray and W. T. Stephens (February 20th–25th, in Saved from the Storm), Frank Jones and Alice Montague (in The Black Hand), Ida De Vere, Minnie Lee, Andy Collum, the Powers (Jen, Georgia and Dan, as the Crescent City Trio), and McVickers and Saunders (in Mike O'Brien's Ball). This brings us through March 4th.

From March 6th to April 1st, a long line of specialists figured successively on Parker's stage — Bud and Annie Granger (in Mixtures), the St. Elmo Brothers (gymnasts), Reynolds and Warren (Tyroleans), Isabel Ward ("playing on the largest and smallest wooden instruments ever seen"), the French Twin Sisters, Mollie Wilson, Mattie Vickers and Charles S. Rogers (in Stage-Struck), C. A. Gardner (in Karl, or, Just as You Live — in the bills for March 6th–11th), Frank Bolton and Ada Bradford (in The Crystal Fountain), Myles Morris, Harry C. Lambkin (trick dancing and revolving barrel), Emerson and Clark, Frank and Fannie Davis (Fogarty's Night Out), George Holden and Frank White (sporting exhibition), Julian Kent (in Wild Bill — March 13th–18th), the Peasleys, Pat Reilly, the Fieldings, Ramirez Family, Lester and Williams, The Idiot of the Mountain (March 20th–25th, with C. L. Farwell and Mai Estelle), Mabel Leonard ("empress of melody"), George Horner and Georgie Lingard (in Our Pleasure Party), William Carroll ("banjo king of America"), Wood, Beasley and the Weston Brothers, Frank Calburt (motto), John Fenton (clogs), and Morris Weston and the company (in The Minstrel Boy). Thus we pass into April, recovering from the past Mollie Wilson, the Russell Brothers (as The Irish Widows), Tommy and Annie Dayton (in Our New Postman), Fred Roberts, Weston and Hanson, Charles E. Emmett (*sic* — in Dashing Charlie — April 3rd–8th); The Lights of New York (to outshine, if possible, The Lights o' London, at the Union Square, and acted by Farwell, Harry Clifford and Dollie Davenport); the benefit of Mai Estelle, offering, on the afternoon of the 20th, Lucretia Borgia and Rightmire (in The Boss); the Le Petres (Paus and Lilly), E. C. Dunbar, Frank McNish and the Leland Sisters, Carrie Howard, the Four-in-Hand, Mike Gallagher, and Muldoon's Excursion (given April 24th–29th, by William F. Carroll, Joseph J. Sullivan and the company).

May blossoms came and passed in forms of Lew Baker, Hallen and Hart, Maggie LeClair, Gus Hill, the play of Golden Fruit (May 1st–6th, with

George A. Henderson, Mamie Wallace, Farwell, H. Clifford and Enid Hart);
Fannie Louise Buckingham (in Mazeppa — 8th–13th); Mabel Vaughn, three
St. Felix Sisters, Captain Laible, Minnie Oscar Gray and W. T. Stephens
(15th–20th, in Jack Sheppard and His Dogs); The Two Orphans (May
22nd–27th, with Josie Crocker as Henriette, Martie Crocker as Louise,
Joseph P. Winter as the Chevalier, George J. Maddox as Pierre, and J. F.
Crossen as Jacques); and with (May 29th–June 3rd) Frank H. and Lillian
White (in A Big Mistake), Hallen and Hart (in I'm an Actor), the two
Haleys, Larry Tooley, Ella Wesner, and Mulcahy's Racket (with Dan
Sully, Larry Tooley, Ed Haley, F. H. White, Farwell, Thomas Haley, Lillian
White, Ada Forrest and Enid Hart — a rather good cast).

Let us hurry through June with bare mention of Sharpley and West,
Emma Marden, Sparks Brothers, Minnie Lee, Moore and Lessenger, Sheffer
and Blakely, Frank Lewis, W. F. Carroll (in Muldoon's Excursion), Rice and
Barton (Ethiopians), Fields and Leslie, Maggie Cline, Harry F. Dixey
and May Leyton (in Tantrums), N. S. Wood (in The Boy Detective), Lang
and Rosa, the Electric Three (Callan, Haley and Callan), Fred Roberts,
the Comical Cawthornes, Dick Gorman and his dog Carlo (in Conrad, or,
the Hand of a Friend — June 19th–24th), Alice Gleason, Jeppe and Fannie
Delano, Bryant and Hoey, and Poverty Flat (with Harry Clifford). Equally
rapid pacing through July shows us The Two Convicts (with Farwell as
Macaire, and Harry Clifford as Strop), Mme. Lavely ("the strongest lady in
the world"), Kitty Coleman and Dan McCarthy (the Pair from Castle Bar),
Charles Diamond, Frank and Fannie Davis, the Grotesque Two (Leslie and
Gentry), Dollie Davenport, Frank H. and Lillian White, Carter and Anderson, Lizzie Derious, Jessie Warner, Pat Rooney and Lucretia Borgia (with
Mai Estelle and Farwell — week of July 10th–15th); for the week of July
17th–22nd, Fannie Louise Buckingham acted Mazeppa. And that is all I
can supply for 1881–82 at Dick Parker's.

HARRY HILL'S, 1881–1882

Harry Hill's place announced (in the Herald) for Sunday, October 23,
1881, Bernard Sloman, the bird man; on November 19th, Kelly and Murphy, "champions of the world," boxed, and Female Minstrels performed;
on Sunday, November 20th, curiosity might have been piqued by the promise
of the Original European Vivantiscope of Moving Figures — even Hill's
patrons were nourished on polysyllables. November 29th offered the Georgia
Troupe of Jubilee Singers. Bills at Harvard for the weeks ending December
3rd and 10th list nonentities so notable as Phebe Shaw and Lou Arnott
(singers), Carrie Edwards (straight jig), Etty Steele, Stella Toner, Jeannette
Lewis, George Stansil and Ed Ryan, and Clara Wilson — no one of whom I
can definitely place in the hall of fame. More like Hill's was the offering

for January 2nd — "Boxing, wrestling, a Female Wrestling Match and Variety." On Sunday, January 8th, "the great coloured preacher" held forth on The Three Sisters — Faith, Hope and Charity — "original and spicy." On Sunday, the 15th, Mary Fisk delivered her "startling" lecture, The New Magdalene; Days of Slavery, with plantation songs and camp meeting hymns awoke the echoes on January 29th.

Harvard, beginning on January 21st, has many bills for 1882; I quickly list the apostles of "Variety" as they passed in succession across the vision of habitués — Herman ("the modern Atlas"), "Professor" H. Monroe's Cat Circus, the Smith Sisters (Kate and May), Maude Florette ("dashing serio-comic"), Blanche Morton (song and dance), O'Neil and Conroy, Sophie Thorn, Amy Howard, Annie Devere, Lottie Wentworth, Fatty Rush, Jennie Mead, Lillie Boyer (serio-comic), Carrie Edwards, the Nondescript Grotesques (George Leslie and John Lovely), Lulu Woodard, Alice Jennings, Joe and Sadie Trimble, the Twin Sisters (Lillie and Hattie Gerry), Nellie Clark, Amy and Frank Kent, Carl Lick (contortionist), J. H. Graham (motto), Jennie Ward ("seven distinct changes of dress, in presence of the audience"), O'Brieno ("wonder stick-twister"), Harry Glenn (from England — in the Lancashire clog), &c. At 11.15, nightly, occurred sparring matches between heroes like Jimmy Kelly and Jerry Murphy. On Sunday, April 9th, appeared the Uncle Tom's Cabin Jubilee Singers — "from London" and from Jarrett and Palmer's production of the play. The "renowned coloured contralto," Miss Cooper, and a quartet sang, on April 23rd, Only to See Thy Face, and Don't Be So Frivolous. I must tell the reader all this. For the week ending May 6th, Alice Jennings and Fatty Rush indulged the audience with a boxing match. Many of Hill's entertainers stayed on in lengthy visits.

Later May and subsequent summer nights brought newcomers in persons of Miss Urani, Miss Williams (both in songs), Annie Montague (serio-comic), Stansil and Ryan's burlesque wrestling, Billy Wilson, Sophia Johnson (French and English songs), Irene Carleton (songs of the day), Blanche Clark (songs), Billy Daily, Marie Zane (song and dance), Eddie Murphy (clog on an 11-inch marble slab), Mary Walton (serio-comic), Palles and Cusick ("rough Irish songs"), Murphy and Daly (in Just from Haverstraw), Widow Nolan's Goat (with Fatty Rush as the Widow), Jarrett and Palmer's Uncle Tom's Cabin Jubilee Singers — from London!, Kittie Montrose (serio-comic), Carrie Edwards ("champion female boxer of the world") in a boxing match with Harry Wilson, the Twilight Quartette (Isaac Hines, Joseph Hodges, William Moore and Robert Martin), Sadie Turner (song and dance), Frank Livingstone (balancing), Jack Keegan, Jennie Turner, Marie Gordon, &c. And so we win through the season, emerging as one who seeks the jewel of notability on a dim-talented stage.

Should I mention Sause's Soirées, every Tuesday evening at Clarendon

Hall, or Theiss's (or Thiess's) concerts every evening, in 14th Street? Who can say? Or Huber's Prospect Garden Concerts, stressing, in the week of December 26th, Leo, "the wonderful tumbleronicon and xylophone player," with the warning cry, "Remember our game supper?" Again, who shall decide?

The Alhambra Theatre, West 27th Street, between Sixth and Seventh Avenues, opened on April 17th, with Horst and Hallahan as managers and Harry Wood as amusement director. It promised "superb specialty stars, interspersed with sparring, wrestling and athletic sports, with champion pugilists." Sheehan and Coyne, Awata Katsnoshin, Lillie and Belle La Verde, Andy Collum, Louise Vavasour, and the Woods (Harry and Minnie) were at first announced, but soon the Herald advertised merely Sports and Variety. On May 7th advertised delights included Dutch Daly, Blanche Moncrief, Florence French, Parker's dogs, Nellie Hague, the Woods and W. T. Dwyer — also sparring by light and heavy champions and Graeco-Roman wrestling by Hoefler. George Rooke and Mike Donovan were early in the field of sparring. After the sparring and other joys of May 15th, a grand ball made customers even happier. And "fifty specialty artists" were the proud boast of May 29th. The Nonpareil Coloured Troubadours functioned in the week of June 12th–17th.

And the Atalanta Casino, 155th Street and Eighth Avenue had its orchestra, afternoon and evening, during the summer of 1882; the Philharmonic Alcazar meanwhile gave "free gipsy concerts," with "fifty pretty barmaids." And I end with Huber's Prospect Garden, 14th and Fourth Avenue, with its double orchestra and extra soloists.

BUNNELL'S MUSEUM, 1881–1882

If we had entered Bunnell's Museum during the week of September 5th–10th, we might have shivered at sight of some Wild Men of Borneo, softened with Mlle. Catherine's trained doves, and looked askance at the Snake Enchantress; also our wondering eyes might have seen not only the usual "freaks," but a Lady Phantom Musician (or should we only have heard her, and guessed she was a lady?), enough really to set our nerves a-tingle. Frank Bush and Lillie Western brought in, during the week of October 10th–15th, a touch of "Variety." An Italian Midget Opera Company began on October 17th, featuring Baron Rosebud and Count Littlefinger, sprigs of nobility so small that they have escaped the books of heraldry and hence shall gladly be accepted by us. Later called the Lilliputian Specialty Company, the little band of little folk continued for a little time. On November 19th, we were invited to see Dr. Lynn, England's marvel worker ("cuts a man up — restores him to life"), and nature's marvel work, a two-headed lady. Both continued for weeks.

[578]

Even Dr. Lynn was hardly so great a "marvel" as the visitors of December 5th — Captain Bates and Wife, "seventeen feet high, weight half a ton"; with them (even museum-haunters love contrast) was exhibited the Atom — "five pounds, fifteen inches high." Lynn and the Bates wonder-pair continued into the new year, and in those glad days we were let into the guarded secret that the Atom owned the pretty name of Dudley Foster.

A "great" pigeon show began at Bunnell's, on January 9th, sponsored by the Columbarian Society; but Dr. Lynn still cut men up, in view of the harmless doves. A cat show began on February 6th; the pigeons had been removed to a place of safety. Cool Burgess and a snake charmer amused on the stage. Val Vose and a two-headed lady (not baby) divided attention on February 27th; Vose, with one mouth, was more ventriloquial than the double-headed lady with two. Such is nature, and such is art! The lady thus doubly blest (or cursed) was still here, on March 6th, when the Cool Burgess Troupe entered the Museum. And here, on March 13th was the Parisian Phantasm, if the reader identifies it. A tattooed lady, seven enormous giants, and the smallest midgets faced idle eyes, beginning on March 20th. An India Rubber Man pulled himself together and almost apart, on April 3rd, to find himself alliteratively praised as a "pleasing, pliable, physical phenomenon." Let us hope his pliability paid. Another loose-skinned exhibitor, at the Globe Museum, seems to have silenced Bunnell's. As a matter of fact, he had been there the week before, but not so alliteratively tagged. On April 17th, however, Bunnell's was proud of Choung Chi Lang, a Chinese giant, and of a Chinese lady with small feet — "the first ever exhibited, by special permission of the Chinese Minister." We know this was not the first; long ago we saw a Chinese lady and marvelled at the way she ate.

Hartz, the magician, began on May 8th, and with him were the Nonpareil Coloured Troubadours, Choung, the Chinese Lady and the Tattooed Lady — surely a rich array for a trifling admission-fee. On May 15th, a twenty-five-foot snake, a three-hundred-pound python, writhed into the situation; Humpty Dumpty also exhibited his brand of agility. On May 29th, the giant snake was named (in advertisements) Eve — rather hard on mankind's original tempter; the Tattooed Greek, Humpty Dumpty and some Sioux Indians assisted. I leave Bunnell's on July 17th–22nd, with its snake charmer, its giants, its giantess, its dwarfs, its man bear, its flying foxes, its Aztec princess, and its vivisection (whatever that may have been). But perhaps I should call attention to Etta, mind reader, there in latest August.

WORTH'S MUSEUM; GLOBE DIME MUSEUM, 1881–1882

Museums, from the days of Peale or Barnum to 1882, never seemed to me as enthralling as a great play nobly performed. Nevertheless, I must

[579]

ask the reader to accompany me to Worth's Museum, 101 Broadway, there to count the Curiosities exhibited to see if there actually were fifty thousand, as the advertisements asserted. Exhausted by counting, we could watch the stage performance, given hourly. A devil fish and a two-headed baby were held out, on January 2nd, as bait for those who fain would chew the cud of sweet and bitter fancy. With the curiosities just cited, appeared an Egyptian baby, doubtless a source of wonder and amaze, or even of innocent merriment; dens of serpents and a happy family of animals also called the curious. The devil fish and the two-headed baby lasted for weeks.

And here is the Globe Dime Museum (formerly Middleton's), 298 Bowery, demanding inclusion in pages devoted of choice to Wallack, Booth and Daly. It opened on October 15th and offered to view a Zulu princess and baby. On December 19th it boasted that Dahome, its giant, was "the largest man on earth" — a boast which after fifty years I feel incompetent to question. Charles Tripp, the "armless wonder," joined the giant, in January. The Globe, on January 30th, offered Captain Brustad, Norwegian giant, a phantom lady musician, and a stage show. April 3rd (I hope this was not an April fool joke), announced that it was paying $500 a week to Herr Haag, the "elastic skin man" — his first appearance in America. The marvel remained for several weeks.

MINOR RESORTS AND HALLS, 1881–1882

The reader will allow me to pass with a bare mention such rank flowerets of amusement as the Haymarket, the Cremorne Gardens, the Sultan Divan, Buckingham Palace, Allen's American Mabille (59 Bleecker Street), etc. I merely record the boast (in the Herald of November 6th) of Cremorne Gardens that they had "the most magnificent concert garden in the United States"; in the Herald, on January 1st, the same pleasance advertised itself as "the Bon Ton Resort," with "Gorgeous Parlours" and "75 Handsome and Refined Barmaids." And the concerts at the Atalanta House!

SAN FRANCISCO MINSTRELS, 1881–1882

To some lovers of "black-face" fun, the season had not really started till the San Francisco Minstrels once more filled the classic row. The little "opera house" began on September 5, 1881, with Birch and Backus, Ricardo, Johnson and Powers, Edwin French, Bob Slavin, the California Quartette, Harry Kennedy (ventriloquist), and Frank Dumont's sketch, Pleasant Companions. On October 3rd came another Dumont sketch, Dramatic Tramps, which took its place in the bills with The Letter Carriers and a burlesque Mascot. On the same evening appeared a new Australian tenor, L. Braham. On October 16th, the Herald advertised Johnson and Powers's

Coloured Hop as a great success. Dumont's new sketch, on October 24th, was The Western Union Mutual Telephone Company; and I wager that Birch and Backus were very funny in Laughing Gas. Johnson and Powers, on October 31st, reverted to Our Alabama Home.

Negro minstrelsy had become a fountain of burlesque; we shall not, therefore, be surprised to find Charles Rossi Ernesto Backus, on November 14th, as a Hamlet at least different from Rossi's or Booth's, recently seen at Booth's Theatre; Birch assisted as an Ophelia fearfully and wonderfully made up. And the atrocity was perpetrated for weeks of hilarious mirth; it was originally announced as Hamlet, Prince of Dunkirk. No wonder the managers proudly advertised their house, in early December, as "the laughing spa of America."

This novel Shakespearian item gave way, on December 12th, to Patients, or, Bunion-Salve's Bride, Frank Dumont's terrible onslaught on Gilbert and Sullivan, with music by W. S. Mullaly. Backus was not nearly so beautiful to behold as Lillian Russell, but his Patients was funnier in a large-mouthed way than her dainty Patience; Birch was Bunion (corn) Salve, and Slavin was Archy, the bald-headed Governor, Moreland Colonel Cavalryboots, Johnson Major Purgatory, and Frillman Duke de Livery-stable. Hunter's Point Dragoons, Æsthetics, and Hungry Lovesick Maidens entered the proceedings at will and left by chance in the usual way. It was terribly funny, and lasted till the end of the season on April 15th. The afternoon of January 19th brought a "Testimonial of Friendship" to Charles White, veteran of minstrelsy and of need. On January 23rd, the Herald advertised that for Patients the stage would be decorated with "utterly utter sunflowers"; besides, Yankee College Boys, Class '82, would be there. Patients and Ricardo's singing of Don't Slam the Garden Gate are the only items I gleaned for early February. Patients reached its hundredth performance on March 17th. Along with this triumphant hit came, on April 3rd, a burlesque of Claude Duval, and the first appearance of William Hamilton, basso. Patients finally passed out on April 15th — a wonderful season, my masters!

On April 17th began a supplementary season, under management of I. C. Clayton, with All at Sea, a play by George H. Jessup, author of Sam'l of Posen. In the cast were Kate Castleton, Agnes Hallock, Emma Duchateau, Lou Thropp, Geoffrey Tyrrell, Frank Bush, W. P. Hampshire, A. W. Maflin, W. W. Allen, and C. W. Allison, certainly not a striking aggregation. Yet they kept the venture afloat for several weeks, not closing till June 3rd, when Victoria Reynolds replaced Miss Hallock.

Miscellaneous Entertainments, 1881–1882

Of course entertainments of various sorts have been listed for 1881–82 under captions preceding this section; as usual, I will now note attractions that cannot elsewhere be classified. Suppose we begin by attending, for the benefit of the Michigan Fire Relief, Leslie Main's performance; he was English and he sang, read and lectured, on September 27th and 28th, at Chickering Hall. Reader, reserve thy question as to who Leslie Main really was; except for the charitable purpose involved, I doubt the expediency of finding an answer to that natural question. Let us pass, rather, to Parepa Hall, 86th Street and Third Avenue, where, on October 3rd, "Professor" Reynolds began in Mesmerism. On October 28th, at the Church of the Divine Paternity, Nella F. Brown read, with Florence Rice Knox to help out with the Flower Song, from Faust, her popular Mrs. Lofty Keeps a Carriage, etc. On November 4th, Harriet Webb exercised her elocutionary gift, at Chickering Hall, with Henrietta Markstein and Kate Park (vocalist), assisting in a musical way. So long as these mixed entertainments last, I shall list them according to their prevailing mood — under "Entertainments" or "Music."

A billiard contest for cushion carrom might amuse my reader; held at Tammany Hall, on November 14th and every evening of the week, and at Cooper Institute every evening of the week of November 21st–26th, it was for $2,500 and a diamond emblem donated by Richard Roche. The contestants were stars of the cue — Jacob Schaefer, George F. Slosson, William Sexton, Maurice Daly, Joseph Dion, Eugene Carter, John Randolph Heiser, Thomas Gallegher, Alonzo H. Morris, and Thomas Wallace. George Holland, on November 16th, presented for one night The Two Orphans, at Harlem Music Hall, actually with Marie Wilkins and T. E. Morris, of the original Union Square cast. John B. Gough, on the 18th, edified at Association Hall with Platform and Personal Experiences. And, on the 20th, the dubious Dr. Landis, once a whole cast in Hamlet, lectured in the hall, 109 West 34th Street, "to Gentlemen Only," on "Private Self Knowledge — Matters that Can't Be Printed." This delectable morsel he repeated on subsequent occasions, admitting in at least one advertisement that it was a "delicate subject." Since I have gone so far afield, I am tempted to carry my long-suffering reader to the Polo Grounds to indulge in the comparatively new excitement of football. There, on November 19th, Harvard and Princeton played a tie game; Yale and Princeton, on the 25th, played till dark, without result; and, on the 26th, Columbia and the University of Pennsylvania did their best for the glory of their respective colleges.

At the Union League Theatre, on November 21st, the New York Church Choir Company gave Our American Minister (by J. A. De Witt). And here is Commander Cheyne, of the Royal Navy, and an officer of three Franklin search parties, who, on November 14th, lectured at Chickering Hall, on Baffled, not Beaten, or, the Discovery of the North Pole Practicable, and, on the 17th, told the story of Five Years in the Arctic Regions, or, the Search for Sir John Franklin. On the 21st, the subject was The Ocean and

Its Wonders. This sounds interesting. At St. John's Episcopal Church, Varick Street, Herbert S. Renton, on the 22nd, gave his talk on A Day and Night in a Volcano. And Emma Waller, long passed from the theatre, read at Chickering Hall, on the evening of December 1st, assisted by "her talented pupil," Emma Bobbitt, by Liberati and by Mrs. Emma Henry, soprano.

Well, since everything is our theme, we must record, for November 29th, at Turn Hall, Fourth Street, near the Bowery, a meeting between "Chicago's pugilist," Captain James Dalton, and Paddy Ryan of Troy. At the Lexington Avenue Opera House, on November 22nd, had appeared for the benefit of the Hebrew Sheltering Guardian Society, the Germania Theater actors, in two operettas. On the 28th, at Chickering Hall, Henry Ward Beecher lectured before the Young Men's Hebrew Association on The Reign of the Common People; he arrived an hour late, explaining that a carriage, promised to be sent for him at his home, had not arrived, and he simply waited for it. Amusing? From November 29th to December 3rd, a Doll's Reception was designed for the delight of children, at the Republican Hall, 55 West 33rd Street. On December 2nd, the Reverend E. Paxton Hood, English lecturer, was at Association Hall — subject, Kings Crowned and Uncrowned. On December 26th, at Chickering Hall, thrice, at 10, at 2.30 and 7.30, with Postmaster General James presiding, Rev. L. D. Bevan conducted a literary and musical festival, which he called the New York Eisteddfod; different the effect, when a match at Cushions Carrom Billiards for $5,000, the loser to pay all expenses, thrilled along the spine, on December 29th, at Tammany Hall (Schaefer and Sexton were the daring contestants). On December 28th, Red Riding Hood, with a chorus of one hundred Sunday School children, was depended on to help the Independent Catholic Church; Masonic Temple staged the rare treat. For weeks, Dr. Landis had been exhibiting, at 109 West 34th Street, experiments in Physiophrenology. Anything to amuse the idle-minded New Yorker — even Our Boys, acted on January 5th, by the Criterion Club, at the Union League Theatre.

On January 9th, at Chickering Hall, appeared the prince of æsthetes, Oscar Wilde, who had come to our land with the usual intention of coining his peculiarities into dollars, and also, one surmises, of helping us to understand Patience. At any rate, D'Oyly Carte "presented" him. He had made himself conspicuous in the city by his knee-breeches, his long locks, his affectations and his pose, and there was much curiosity to hear him from the rostrum. He spoke, in that lecture, on the English Renaissance, that is, the movement that began with Rossetti and flowered (or may I say?) sunflowered into the æsthetic craze of the '80s, so gently laughed out of existence by Gilbert's wit, in Patience. A large audience greeted Wilde, on the 9th, and he passed, after the lecture, to a reception at the home of

[583]

Mrs. John Mack, 365 Fifth Avenue, where he met such local celebrities as Mrs. John Lillie, sister of his hostess, and author of Prudence, the "first æsthetic novel," Mrs. John Sherwood, President Barnard, of Columbia College, and Mrs. Barnard, Mr. and Mrs. John Bigelow, Algernon S. Sullivan and Judge Brady. According to the Herald, he wore a dress coat, white waistcoat with six pearl buttons, an ample white shirt front of piqué, with a large solitaire of pearl and diamond, shining knee breeches of doeskin, black silk stockings, shoes with large bows. On January 10th, the employes of Stern Brothers held a concert in the Lexington Avenue Theatre, and also acted Slasher and Crasher and The Milkman's Bride.

And now come the balls of winter societies. I have already mentioned the larger affairs held at the Academy of Music. I here list and quickly pass by the Harry Hill Association Ball held on Sunday, January 8th, at the Germania Assembly Rooms, 291 Bowery; the Edward Everett Lodge Ball, at the Teutonia Assembly Rooms, on January 11th; the ball of the New York Caledonian Club, January 13th, at Irving Hall; the Central Union Ball, Terrace Garden Theatre, January 16th; and the Bachelor Club Reception, on the 23rd, at Ferrero's Assembly Rooms. On February 9th, the Prospect Association had a masquerade ball at Tammany Hall. Robert S. Burdette (of the Burlington Hawkeye) brought us back to things of the mind, on January 11th, lecturing at Chickering Hall, on Home, or, Advice to Young Men; on the 13th, at Association Hall, Locke Richardson read Henry IV, Part I. Entertainments seem few, except in regular theatres. I jump to February 1st for Susan B. Anthony and others at the New York State Woman's Suffrage Convention, held at Chickering Hall; others, less serious, attended a ball of the Albion Society, on that evening, at Tammany Hall. January 30th brought to Steinway Hall the McGibney Family; alas! the Society for the Prevention of Cruelty to Children forbade the appearance of the three youngest of the eleven children. Well, to make up for that, the Minerva Guernsey-Bernard Listemann Combination were to appear, on February 6th, at Chickering Hall, in readings and musical performances; perhaps they deferred the joys of their art till the 13th, when again they were announced. On the 7th, the Gentlemen's Sons Association of the Eleventh Ward had an invitation masquerade at Ferrero's Assembly Rooms, Tammany Building; of course there is no law against calling yourself a gentleman's son, even for fun. On the 8th, the Tonawanda Club had a ball at Clarendon Hall. On the 14th, Dr. John Lord, at Chickering Hall, began a new series of lectures.

A lecture to ladies, by Sara B. Chase, attempted to define What Our Girls Ought to Know — a problem for all time, hardly settled, I fear, on the afternoon of February 7th, at Chickering Hall. By coincidence, on the evening preceding, in the same hall, was celebrated the eighteenth anniversary of the Working Women's Protective Union, with speeches by

Chauncey M. Depew and others and singing by Jennie Dickerson, Emma Howe and Letitia Fritsch.   On the 9th, All on a Summer's Day, an operetta by Henry Gallup Paine and Richard Henry Warren, enlisted, at Chickering Hall, a cast including W. D. Marks, Pauline Lyon, Ada Chandler Hard, H. G. Paine, G. Scrother-Sturgis and C. K. L. Black; Box and Cox also was in the bill.   A third performance of the Paine work fell on the 17th, for the Columbia College Boat Club.   On February 15th, appeared at Steinway Hall, "the celebrated comedian," John Thompson, whom indeed we have missed, in a parlour concert, Around the World.   Professor Robert Houston, elocutionist, plied his art, February 14th, in Association Hall; and on the 13th the Sons of St. George held their third annual concert and reception, at Tammany Hall, Theodora Linda Da Acosta, seven years old, warbling Sing, Sweet Bird, and other gems of song.   The Seventh Regiment Band, Cappa leading, had another promenade concert, on the 18th, at the Armoury.   It was a jump to that from the performance at the Lexington Avenue Opera House, on February 16th, of Married Life by the Atalanta Boat Club, the play, of course followed by a dance.   At Chickering Hall, on the 21st, Sara Chase again debated on a serious topic — Motherhood, to wit.   In the Harlem Opera House, on the 23rd, Tony Pastor appeared with Lester and Allen, the quartet of Seamon, Somers and the Girard Brothers, Derious and Smith, &c.   The Mimosa Society, on the 25th, acted Caste, at the obliging Lexington Avenue Opera House.   Must I invite the reader to the amateur races, at the American Institute, on February 21st, under the auspices of the Williamsburgh Athletic Club, with Buckley, Saunders and the English Davies?

Locke Richardson was again reciting Shakespeare's plays at the Union League Theatre; on March 4th (morning) he gave Henry IV, Part I, Macbeth, on the 11th, and, on the 18th, The Tempest.   In mid-March (14th), the Amateur League acted Tom Cobb, at the Lexington Avenue Opera House.   Different was the prowess, on March 25th, of the Seventh Regiment Athletic Games, in the busy Armoury.   And Grace Courtland, on the 24th, had given, at the Union League Theatre, some dramatic impersonations, J. Francis Leve helping to make a programme.   We became like a very small town, beginning on March 27th, when we ran helterskelter to the foot of Wall Street, East River, there to behold a cow-whale.   But that is New York.   And there was an audience for Robert G. Ingersoll, on the 26th, when he lectured at Steinway Hall, on What Shall We Do to Be Saved? and doubtless Mrs. George Vandenhoff, in Chickering Hall, on the 27th, found interested listeners, when she read or recited, with, as fellows in the bill, Carrie Keating (pianist), Richard Arnold, Carl Werner and Sara Deland (singer).   The Masonic Temple, on March 28th, housed a concert in aid of the Manhattan Temperance Association, Julia A. Polk singing in their behalf.   Locke Richardson ended his recitals, on April 8th,

[585]

at the Union League Theatre, with The Merchant of Venice. On the evenings of April 7th, 14th, 21st and 28th, Professor Nathan Sheppard lectured, at Association Hall, on, respectively, Dickens, Carlyle, We Americans, and Are We Descended from Monkeys? In March, the Reverend Dr. Maynard gave a "Cathedral Course of Lectures," in Chickering Hall.

On April 10th, at the Union League Theatre, Miss N. C. Wickham felt called upon to give a morning recital, and, in the evening, at Chickering Hall, an amateur minstrel performance may have drawn an audience, as indeed may have done the entertainment of the Atalanta Boat Club on the same evening at the Lexington Avenue Opera House, with the lure of Fallen Leaves, a comedietta, and a concert. All this seems a bit amateurish, as does the entertainment on the 11th, at the Lexington Avenue Opera House, of Company K of the Twelfth Regiment, when Love and Pride and Bombastes Furioso and songs provided the evening's delight. But young soldiers acting in those days pleased fair maidens. On the 13th, J. S. Burdett was at Association Hall, 129th Street and Fourth Avenue, and a dog show barked, April 18th–21st, at the American Institute. On the 21st, the Mimosa Society gave Le Jour de Fête; the opening of the Atalanta Casino was scheduled for April 23rd. The Benevolent Order of Buffaloes, on the 26th, acted, at Turnhall Theatre, The Moneymoon, a dance following. On the 27th, the Reverend T. De Witt Talmage illuminated The Bright Side of Things, in the Central Baptist Church, West 42nd Street. Emma Bobbitt, that "promising" pupil of Emma Waller, tried, on May 11th, at Chickering Hall, to fullfil her mission; her assistants were F. V. Marckwald, Belle Cole and Julius G. Bierck. The French concert and ball, at Irving Hall, on May 21st, brought in the Martens (sic) Family. I have elsewhere mentioned a Pfingst-Montag Festival, at the Atalanta Casino, on May 29th, and may add, in early June, a three-days festival at the 23rd Ward Park, 147th Street, near Third Avenue, this festival and fête to aid the Russian refugees. All this fades before the wonder of two capricorn goats "from the highest peaks of Switzerland and the Tyrol, weighing 300 pounds, and standing 5 feet high," exhibiting from May 7th, at Union Hall, 475 Ninth Avenue. I feel impelled to edify my reader with all kinds of amusement, and do not apologise for citing Dr. Kahn's Museum of Anatomy, Science and Art, re-opening, for gentlemen only, on June 17th, at 713 Broadway.

MUSICAL MISCELLANY, 1881–1882

Many concerts have attracted, in 1881–82, under headings of various theatres and concert-halls; I refer the reader to the discussions of the Academy of Music, Booth's Theatre, Koster and Bial's, the Metropolitan Concert Hall, etc., as well as to the separate treatment allotted to the Philharmonic, Symphony and Oratorio Societies. The first concert of note in my scrip fell on October 20th, at Steinway Hall, when Blind Tom, the negro marvel, played the piano; he was there again on October 31st and November 11th (afternoon), and at Harlem Music Hall, on November 2nd. A concert at the Female Lunatic Asylum, Blackwell's Island, was bravely carried out, on the afternoon of October 21st, by the New York Philharmonic Club, Mrs. Evelina Hartz (soprano), M. Hartz (illusionist) and others. On October 23rd, a concert (at Steinway Hall) for the benefit of the Relief Fund of the New York Musical Club enlisted an orchestra directed by Theodore Thomas, with Hermann Rietzel (pianist) and Hermann Brandt (violinist). Camilla Urso played at Chickering Hall, on October 25th, assisted by Nella F. Brown (reader), and Emma S. Howe (soprano). November 3rd brought to Chickering Hall Carrie E. Mason, with Emily Winant, Richard Arnold, the New York Philharmonic Club, &c. On the 2nd, the Herald announced, without specification of date, the début of Adèle Marguilies, pianist and first prize for three years at the Vienna Conservatoire. I found no review of this performance, but Miss Marguilies became well known in our concerts.

On November 5th, Blanche Roosevelt, very active during this season, sang at Chickering Hall, attended by Florence Copleston (pianist), Lazzarini (tenor), Lencioni (buffo), Carlos Hasselbrinck (violinist) and C. E. Pratt (accompanist). At Chickering Hall, on November 7th, appeared the New York Glee Club (Harvey and Humphries, tenors, and Phillips and Morawski, basses), with Hattie Louise Simms and Hattie Clapper (contralto); on the same evening, at Steinway Hall, Mrs. Lizzie Priest played the piano, assisted vocally by Letitia Fritsch, O. R. Steins and William N. Stanley (tenor) and otherwise by Elias Werner ('cellist) and G. W. Colby (conductor). Into this latter hall, on the 10th, came George Magrath (pianist) along with Theodore Thomas and an orchestra. On the same afternoon, in the same hall, Florence Copleston gave the first of three piano recitals, assisted by Hattie Schell (soprano). On the 11th and 12th began the Philharmonic season, elsewhere described.

RETURN OF ADELINA PATTI

After twenty years of European triumphs, back to the town in which she had been reared and educated, and in which she won her earliest fame in concert and opera, came the unquestionably most perfect, most brilliant vocalist of her time, perhaps of all time — Adelina Patti. It may be said at once that her return was accomplished under distressing circumstances; everything was mismanaged, prices were extravagantly high — $10 for admission to the orchestra — and the supporting company was very bad, except for a violinist, Mlle. Castellan. Patti insisted on including the tenor, Nicolini, who would, as I have said, have been her husband, if her

[587]

husband, the Marquis de Caux had consented to a divorce; but Nicolini, if he had once been good, was now a trial to American patience. The reader, then, will pardon my omission of the parts performed by the others in that first Patti concert, November 9th, at Steinway Hall, and will, I am sure, thank me for dwelling only on the performance of the great diva, unquestionably the most famous singer then in active service on the stage.

The audience, undoubtedly because of the high admission, was not large, but, according to the Herald of November 10th, it was "of remarkably fine quality, and Steinway Hall has seen no assemblage within its walls that approached that of last evening in the social distinction which marked its composition," or, if the Herald was right, its dress. Perhaps, to the *cognoscenti* nothing so exciting had occurred in musical matters since Jenny Lind stepped on the stage at Castle Garden, thirty-one years before. According to the Herald,

> The appearance of Mme. Patti was anxiously awaited.... Every eye was turned toward the heavy velvet curtain hanging in the doorway at the side of the stage.... The curtain was drawn aside and Adelina Patti stepped quickly on to the stage, and looking very charming and pretty and youthful in an exquisite evening costume, came forward smiling and bowing in a pleased, almost girlish fashion.... She bowed again and again as the demonstrations continued with no show of abatement, and then she stood quietly for a moment, with a flushed face and almost overcome with emotion.... For a moment she seemed unnerved, but as the applause finally died down she regained her composure and began the recitative of "Ah forse [*sic*] e lui." ... It was listened to with rapt attention, but where there was any pause ... the house burst into tumultuous applause which at once determined the measure of the phenomenal success she was to score ... before the evening was over....
>
> Mme. Patti's voice has gained in strength, body, roundness, in the lower and middle registers, and there is a much richer quality to it now than it has ever possessed. The extreme high notes are slightly impaired, not by loss of voice, but through forcing them a little, which once in a while last evening occasioned the intonation to be less perfect than it might have been. Her style was always good, but its slight defects have all been corrected, and experience, matured taste and ripened judgment have added a marvellous perfection to her beautiful phrasing, and have placed at her absolute command in greater ease and certainty of execution a thousand and one telling little effects which increase the charm of her singing. All the brilliancy which Mme. Patti had in what may be called the days of her greatest successes, she still retains unimpaired, and there is a sympathetic quality to her voice that lends to it an indescribable beauty. The "Ah forse e lui" was admirably sung and most beautifully phrased in the andante; the allegro was rendered with a dash and spirit that only such glorious voices are capable of carrying out, and the ascending runs were executed with unparalleled brilliancy, a volume of

[588]

VERCELLI'S ITALIAN THEATRE, EAST 42ND STREET

CHICKERING HALL
These Pictures from Prints in the Harvard Theatre Collection

voice that filled the house, and a spirit and yet elegance and precision that electrified the house. Under an enthusiastic recall Mme. Patti sang "Coming Through the Rye" delightfully. . . . "Home, Sweet Home" was sung very beautifully, the diminished sustained notes being given with an almost indescribable sweetness, and yet withal there seemed to be a lack of real soul about it all, beautifully as the notes were sung. The "Shadow Song" from "Dinorah" was a positive triumph, and defied criticism. It was simply perfect as an example of sweetness of voice and brilliancy of execution, and Mme. Patti was obliged to follow it . . . with " 'Twas Within a Mile of Edinboro'." The "Lombardi" terzetto with Signori Nicolini and Pinto was not very satisfactory except in so much as Mme. Patti contributed."

The Times was decidedly cold; it could not forgive the ten-dollar fee for what it cruelly called a fifty-cent concert: "Mme. Patti returns with improved vocal style. . . . It is not a matter of doubt that she sang out of tune, however, and notwithstanding the lovely character of her voice there was disappointment. . . . In her upper tones her voice is now cold and hard, very much like the tone of her sister Carlotta." Besides Patti should be singing in opera, not in concert. The Times simply was disgruntled, and as for Patti's singing out of tune, it is almost incredible to me.

For her second concert, before a lamentably small audience, on the afternoon of November 12th, the great artiste sang an aria in which she was simply incomparable — the *Bel raggio,* from Semiramide; she also gave Eckert's Echo Song and appeared in the quartette from Rigoletto, with Nicolini, Salvati (baritone) and Lohenschild (contralto). For encores — she was an exquisite ballad singer — Patti sang Home, Sweet Home, Kathleen Mavourneen and Comin' thro' the Rye. Says the Herald, on the next day, she sang the *Bel raggio* "in superb style, the brilliant embellishments being taken with the same ease and delicate shading and delivered with the same richness of vocalization that characterized the less difficult passages. The feature of her singing of this charming selection was not alone the sweetness of voice or elegance of phrasing, but the combination of qualities of voice and execution, which are seldom found united in one person." I think the Times critic had learned his lesson; on November 13th, after another gibe at the ten-dollar admission, he states that the *diva* was in better voice than on her first appearance, and "sang faultlessly. It was indeed a perfect treat to hear her. . . . The exquisite skill of her vocalization cannot be too highly praised. It is consummate art added to natural powers of the highest order, the result being the best singing to be heard in the world. . . . Her 'Bel raggio' was magnificently sung, and was the gem of the concert."

I leave the wonderful singer to ruminate on her failure and on what she could do to retrieve the situation. Therefore, I invite the reader to Jenny

[589]

Claus's invitation concert (she was a violinist) at Steinway Hall (in the smaller room), on the evening of November 11th, Constantine Sternberg being her chief assistant; and the New York Philharmonic Club and S. B. Mills were at Chickering Hall on the 15th. And Patti had found the remedy for early mistakes. She sang, on November 16th, in behalf of the Michigan sufferers, and the mayor and city officials by attendance and official backing gave impetus to the proceedings. Above all, prices were reduced to $2 admission, with $3 extra for reserved seats. The house was crowded, and, according to the Herald of the 17th, the audience "gave her a reception such as has not been accorded to any singer since the days of Jenny Lind." Of her last concert (November 23rd) let the Herald of the 24th tell the brilliant story:

> Mme. Patti was four times upon the programme, but the chief events of the evening were . . . the "Una voce poco fa" . . . and the grand scena from "Lucia." It is almost unnecessary to say that these were beautifully sung. . . . She labored under the disadvantage of being very badly accompanied in the "Una voce," but the rich quality of her notes and her marvellous skill overcame all that. No matter how critical a judgment is passed upon her voice, detecting little flaws in the upper register and a trifling hardness in one or two of the lower tones, it is, from G to G, absolutely perfect and not alone beyond that of any singer heard by this generation, but is so rich and pure and used with such skilful precision and elegance of effect that it defies any criticism. It is many a long year since New York has heard such a superb rendering of this beautiful cavatina . . . she fully equalled any singer that has been heard in New York during this or the last generation. Her execution of the variations upon the theme were phenomenal in their clearness, purity and ease of execution. . . . In the scene from "Lucia," the famous "mad scene," she accomplished not alone the triumph of the evening, but the greatest triumph of her present season. . . . It lacked soulfulness and true warmth of sentiment in the 'Alfin son tua," but the execution of the "Spargi d'Amaro" was brilliancy itself, concluding with a cadenza in which were introduced a most elaborate and intricately involved succession of ascending and descending scales, which fairly "carried the house by storm"; the audience broke into cheers which were long continued and fairly deafening."

The diva also sang a duet with Nicolini, from Don Pasquale, and in a terzetto from Verdi's Attila, with Nicolini and Salvati. For encores, Patti gave Comin' thro' the Rye and Within a Mile of Edinboro' Town. Nicolini did his best with *Cujus Animam* and Adam's Noël — this latter by request. The house was crowded; by that time Patti had entrusted the management of her American tour to the astute Henry E. Abbey.

I go back to prose, some of it good prose. At Steinway Hall, on November 14th, the Herrmann Brothers played, Carl the piano, and Edward the violin, accompanied by Constance Howard. Florence Copleston's second concert (November 17th, afternoon, at Steinway Hall) gained from the aid of Richard Arnold, Charles Werner ('cellist), and Florence Rice Knox; on the 18th, in the same hall, appeared Alexander Lambert, Emma Schräder (soprano) and the New York Philharmonic Club. At Chickering Hall, on the 19th, Blanche Roosevelt gave a second concert, with Mrs. Rice Knox, Lazzarini, Lencioni, W. R. Case (pianist), and good, useful C. E. Pratt. At Standard Hall, 1476 Broadway, near 42nd Street, Bernard Boeckelmann's concert, of chamber music, on November 16th, had the assistance of the excellent Anna Drasdil. The Mayor's Committee for the Michigan Sufferers arranged a concert at Steinway Hall, on November 19th, at which were promised Mlles. Ferni, Kalas and Dotti, Ravelli, Del Puente, Corsini, Novara, Jenny Claus and S. B. Mills. The audience was very small. The Liederkranz Society functioned, on the 20th, in their rooms, with Emma Juch, Antonia Henne, Jacob Graff, Fred Steins, Burdett, Mason (organist) and A. Paur (director). The Schiller-Bruch Song of the Bell was in the programme. On the 22nd, at Steck Hall, the Standard Quartet (Brandt and Schwartz, violins, Matzka, viola, and Bergner, 'cello) appeared, with H. Rietzel, pianist. Florence Copleston gave her third recital on Thanksgiving afternoon (November 24th), with Campanini, Virginia Ferni and Emily Winant offering strong vocal support. On the evening of the 23rd, the Union League Theatre housed a concert and reception of the Benevolent Order of Buffaloes, presenting Henrietta Markstein, ever with us, Aggie Gordon (soprano), Maria Bower (soprano), Lotta Davenport (contralto), John Blint, in imitations, Miss Adrian Courtney (reader), and George Hasselmeyer (female impersonator). On November 27th the Haydn Amateur Musical Society was at Wendel's Assembly Rooms, 334-344 West 44th Street, with Ida Klein and Carl Steinbuch, baritone.

The Mozart Musical Union, an orchestra of 75, Margherita Stora (soprano), and Nahan Franko (violinist), co-operated, on November 29th, at the Lexington Avenue Opera House. On the same evening, the New York Vocal Union, with Mrs. George F. Blum, contralto, was at Chickering Hall. On December 1st, another anxious infant, the New York Quintet Club, came into being, with Lena Acton (pianist), Aug. Roebbelin and Martin Loeffler (violins), Julius Risch (viola), and Wilhelm Müller ('cello). They promised six matinées of chamber music, beginning on December 1st, at Steinway Hall. During the same week (on the 29th of November), at Steinway Hall, for the benefit of those never-ending Michigan sufferers, appeared the professors of the Conservatory of Music, with Constantine Sternberg, Fanny Pollock (*sic*) and Charlotte Napier (reader). On December 2nd, Pauline Canissa, favourite of an earlier day, in opera, attempted to sing, in concert, with Theodore Thomas and his orchestra. She broke down, to the utter distress of all concerned. It was a benefit for the mother of the late President Garfield. December 6th brought to the Turf Club (formerly the Union League Theatre) Joseph Camellas's Soirée of Chamber Music, with Ella Earle, Albert King, Hermann Brandt and F. Bergner as soloists. A little too much chamber music, my masters? Can the public digest it all? Well, on the 6th, the Mendelssohn Glee Club, in its first concert, had, as soloists, Madeline Schiller, and Marie Vachot. Mrs. E. Aline Osgood and Master John F. Rhodes graced the concert of February 21st, and the club sang Dudley Buck's King Olaf's Christmas (not its first performance by the club). Mrs. Van Brunt sang with the Mendelssohns on April 25th.

On December 7th came more chamber music, in Sam Franko's concert, at Steinway Hall, with Rachel Franko, Hermann Rietzel, C. Sternberg, and Ernest Jonas, 'cello. Florence Rice Knox was again at it, on the evening of the 8th, at Steinway Hall; and this time her array of assistants was startling — Minnie Hauk, Campanini, Del Puente, Corsini, Christian Fritsch, F. Remmertz, Charles Werner, and Signori Rasori and Agramonte, accompanists. Why so many? one asks in bewilderment. On the 10th (matinée) Louis Staab's concert in Chickering Hall provided Fritsch, Anna Bulkley Hills, &c. The Saalfield Concert, at Steinway Hall, on the 10th (evening), presented Minnie Hauk, and Marie Groebl (soprano). The Standard Quartet and Sternberg were again at Steck Hall, on the 13th; and the New York Vocal Union naturally went to Lyric Hall. At Association Hall, on the 14th, one might have heard James S. Burdett, Marie Bower, Carl Lanzer, Master Frank Hession (pianist), Miss L. E. Starrett (contralto) and J. W. Koch (accompanist). On the 14th, also, Sternberg, with Rachel Franko, Arnold, &c. drew a small audience to Steinway Hall. The 16th exhibited in Steinway Hall the art of David Bimberg, violinist; in the same ever-welcoming auditorium on the 17th, the Arion Society held forth, with assistance of Carolina Zeiss, Jacob Graff, Richard Arnold and Florence Copleston, the last named apparently much in demand; on the afternoon of the 17th, in that hall, Emil French was listed to play the piano.

And sorrow underlay the concert, on the 18th, in Steinway Hall, "for the family of the late Rudolf Bial," when Carolina Zeiss and Theodore Thomas and his orchestra participated. On the 19th, the Atalanta Boat Club concert, at Chickering Hall, availed itself of the services of Belle Cole, Christian Fritsch, Willet Seaman (baritone), Mary Wernecke (harpist), Anna Parker (soprano) and Jennie Parker (violin). The second concert of the New York Philharmonic Club, at Chickering Hall, on the 20th, had the assistance of Marie Schelle-Gramm, Eugene Weiner (or Wiener) and Alexander Lambert (pianist). And the second of Carl and Edward Herrmann occurred on December 21st, at Steinway Hall. Surely there was no dearth of music in New York. L. F. Harrison's vocal and instrumental concert fell on the 22nd, in the same auditorium, with Fred Harvey, Mrs.

LCCKE RICHARDSON   OSCAR WILDE   JENNIE DICKERSON

R. J. BURDETTE   LINDA DA ACOSTA   C. STERNBERG

E. ALINE OSGOOD   LETITIA FRITSCH   D. KENNEDY

G. W. de Lano (*sic*), Zélie de Lussan, L. G. Gottschalk and the Meigs Sisters; and, on January 11th, the concert season recovering from the Christmas and New Year interregnum, Edouard Remenyi appeared at Steinway Hall, in compositions (some played without accompaniment) by himself, Beethoven and Paganini; Remenyi was a virtuoso first and always. Like de Pachmann of later years he played antics, rebuked the audience, etc. M. Louise Segur was at Chickering Hall, on the 12th, in company with Florence Rice Knox, C. Fritsch, F. Remmertz, William Russell Case (pianist), August Roebbelin (violinist), Martin Loeffler (violinist), Julius Risch (viola), and G. W. Colby. The third concert of the New York Quintet Club came on the afternoon of the 12th, at Steinway Hall; on the same afternoon, at St. George's Church, S. N. Penfield gave a second organ recital. On the 16th occurred Bernard Boeckelmann's second concert at Standard Hall; Antonia Henne assisted. On the same evening, the Jubilee Singers from Fisk University, at Nashville, began a series of concerts at Chickering Hall. On the 17th came, at the same hall, the third concert of the New York Philharmonic Club, with Christian Fritsch and Florence Copleston, both prominent in our musical life of that season. On the 18th, Julia Feist, pianist, displayed her art at Steinway Hall, with Agnes Florence (soprano), Richard Arnold, and the New York Philharmonic Club. On January 21st, the Seventh Regiment Band, C. A. Cappa, leader, had its first promenade concert at the Armoury.

And now, back to us, after thirteen years, came Kennedy, in Songs of Scotland, the concerts falling at Steinway Hall, on January 20th, 23rd and 25th; with him appeared members of his family — Helen and Marjory (sopranos), Maggie (pianist), Robert (tenor), and Master John (violinist). On January 24th, the Standard Quartet Club (Brandt, Schwartz, Matzka and Bergner), with Ferdinand von Ingen, gave its third concert at Steck Hall; the Arcadian Quartet Club followed duly, on the 25th, at Chickering Hall, with its third showing, its members including John M. Fulton and George Adams (tenors), and George E. Conly and Daniel Adams (bassos). Belle Cole, G. W. Kyle, Master C. Holzhausen (soprano), and W. H. Rieger assisted. Little Mabel Clare Stephenson (whom we later found at Wallack's) was advertised at Chickering Hall, for vocal and elocutionary revealments, on January 24th, February 10th and 27th, March 17th and April 6th. The city government kept a strict eye that season on youthful performers; so far as City Hall was concerned, a child was a child till proved by necromancy to be something else. But Mabel appeared by permission of Mayor Grace, and enjoyed association, on the 24th, with Zélie de Lussan, Harry S. Hilliard (tenor, and later to be prominent in operetta), Mort M. Weed (basso), Walter R. Johnson (organist) and Julius G. Bierck (conductor). The Herald declared she had an unpleasant little voice and a shocking amount of forwardness. On the 26th of Janu-

[593]

ary, the German Ladies' Society brought to Steinway Hall, Hattie Schell, Miss Henne, O. R. and Fred Steins, Constantine Sternberg, F. Dulcken, A. Hartdegen and the Liederkranz. On the 27th, Bella Irene Bellinger came forth, at Steinway, as a pianiste, engaging as assistants Laura Bellini (the first time we have met her, but decidedly not the last), Sam Franko and F. Dulcken (musical director). On the 27th and 28th, the New York Chorus Society had a rehearsal and concert, with six hundred choristers, an orchestra of eighty, led by Theodore Thomas, and with, as soloists, Miss Schell, Miss Winant, Toedt, Remmertz and Joseffy. On the 26th (afternoon) also, Mme. de Montcalm gave a piano recital at Steinway Hall, assisted by the singers, Anna Hall and Mrs. A. Duncan. I wonder if these various concerts mustered paying audiences? On January 30th, the McGibney Family, mother, father and eight children appeared, with warning that there were three more children in process of training. On the 31st, Dora (*sic*) Feist at Chickering Hall appeared with Mrs. Emil Gramm, Richard Arnold and Charles Werner. Probably the Liederkranz did not expect its concert on the 29th to pay; for the love of singing, they gave at their hall, Die Tageszeiten, by J. Raff, and engaged, to assist, Hermann Rietzel and the Mollenhauers. On the 30th, Albert D. Hubbard had a harmless, unnecessary concert at Chickering Hall, with Christine Rossée to help in gathering an audience. Then, as since, music was an uphill fight for all except hilldwellers.

After the lapse of a week, music's soft voice lulled us on February 7th, in Chickering Hall, with the Philharmonic Club, Mrs. Annie Norton-Hartdegen, Constantine Sternberg and Richard Arnold. Then came Nahan Franko's concert at Steinway Hall; on February 8th, his associates were Belle Cole, S. B. Mills, Sam Franko, and C. E. Pratt. On February 9th, Liberati took a benefit at Atlantic Garden. The fourth concert of the New York Quintet Club fell, on February 9th (afternoon) at Steinway Hall; Klugescheid succeeded to post of second violin. For the 11th, Signor Baldanza advertised the first of several concerts at Steinway Hall; we may remember him as recently of the Strakosch opera. Mlle. Martini (replacing Pauline Canissa), Lencioni, Orlandini and Signorina Florenza d'Arona assisted in this weighty project. February 14th brought us three concerts as valentine favours: the Standard Quartet Club was at Steck Hall; the New York Choral Union, with Belle Cole and Miss E. V. Pierson, operated at Lyric Hall; and the New York Vocal Union had its second concert (Jenny Claus assisting) at Chickering Hall. The Euterpe Society held its first concert, on February 16th, at the same hall, rendering Weber's Jubilee Cantata, and advertising Cora de Wilhorst (who apparently did not appear), Mrs. J. H. Travis, Mrs. Collasius, Miss Keller, Edward A. Archer, Ivan Morawski, Carl Richter, and G. W. Morgan (conductor). On the 18th, also at Chickering Hall, appeared Mme. Chatterton-Bohrer, assisted by

Anna Bishop, Isidora Martinez, F. Remmertz, Sauret, Reinhold, Herrmann, Gaston Bley, Schnecker (violin), and Ernest Jonas ('cello).   And the 20th proffered, at the same hall, a concert (to provide for the publication of a volume of lyric poems by Marie Le Baron), Anna Bishop, Marion Lambert, Lillie Berg, Mrs. J. H. Travis, H. O. C. Kortheuer, G. W. Morgan, Lencioni and Herndon Morsell being advertised to appear in support of this touching object.

At the Conservatory of Music in later February were advertised (without dates of performance) some chamber music concerts, in which Sternberg and Wilhelm Müller would take part.   February 23rd brought three serious concerts: in the afternoon, at Steinway Hall, the surprisingly sturdy New York Quintet Club gave an all-Rubinstein programme, and in his music rooms in Union Square J. N. Pattison held the first of a series of soirées musicales, Julia Adelaide Polk (soprano), Edward Mollenhauer, Master William Theodorus (violin), and Joseph Harrison (piano) assisting at the first.   More interesting was the benefit, at Steinway Hall, for the German Emigrant House; participants were Imogene Brown, Jenny Claus (violin), Frl. M. Geist ('cello), Mme. Groscher-Chadick (piano), E. Nidecker (baritone), Armin Schötte (organ) and the choir of St. Matthäus Church, Hoboken.   Julia de Reinach must play the piano at Steinway Hall, on the afternoon of February 25th; Fritsch and E. Jonas were to assist.

March 1st came in with a concert, at Steinway Hall, by Adèle Marguilies, with Mrs. Emil Gramm and Richard Arnold assisting; on the 3rd, in the same hall, Wilhelm Müller held forth, with Anna Schütz, soprano from Vienna, "her first appearance in America," Katie Nuffer (alto), Lina Anton (pianist) and the New York Quintet.   On March 2nd, afternoon, G. W. Morgan, "the well-known organist of the Tabernacle, Brooklyn," and Maud Morgan gave an organ and harp recital in Chickering Hall, Mrs. Emma R. Dexter, soprano, assisting; in the evening, Mrs. Corinne Young had a concert in the same hall, along with Fannie Lovering (soprano), Signor Montegriffo (tenor), Mme. Chatterton-Bohrer, Nahan Franko, Homer Bartlett (pianist), Signor Greco (accompanist) and William Cooper (baritone). On the evening of the 3rd, in the same auditorium, Sophia Priestley was heard, in conjunction with Belle Cole, Octavie Gomien, Montegriffo, L. D. Goldsberry (baritone), E. A. Lefebre (saxophone), C. E. Pratt, and two of her pupils, Adèle Pieris and Mary Connor, these last two inviting again to a sad reflection on the future or no-future of promising students of the arts. Let us pass, on the 6th, to Steinway Hall, for a testimonial to Frederick Mollenhauer, for which were listed Julia Adelaide Polk, Clara Brinckerhoff, J. N. Pattison and several Mollenhauers.   On the 8th, Blanche Roosevelt gave, at Chickering Hall, her fourth concert, assisted by Montegriffo, Lencioni, William Russell Case, Carlos Hasselbrinck and C. E. Pratt.   On March 9th, the Morgans were again at Chickering Hall, this time with Jennie

Owens (soprano); and a charity concert at Steinway enlisted Anna Drasdil, Master Michael Banner, and Damrosch's orchestra; on the 10th, at Steinway Hall, the Royal Handbell Ringers and Glee Men of England appeared in persons of Messrs. Miller, W. J. and H. Havart, Williams and Pritchard. The 11th introduced at Chickering Hall the Stock Exchange Glee Club, Lena Little and Master Banner. The presence of Mapleson's opera, and the recent appearance in opera of Adelina Patti and Etelka Gerster would seem to have thinned out concert-givers at this time; possibly Lent also had something to do with this effect defective.

On March 16th, at Steinway Hall, Lillian Gesner (pianist) appeared, supported by Mr. and Mrs. Carl Feininger. At Michael Banner's Concert, March 18th, at Steinway Hall, we had Jeannette Edmondson, Jacob Graff, Sternberg and Max Liebling; in the evening of the same day, the last promenade concert, for the season, of the Seventh Regiment Band brought in the aid of Liberati. At Steinway Hall, on the 16th and 23rd, George Magrath gave piano recitals. On the 24th, the Princeton College Glee Club sang at Chickering Hall a programme that the Princeton Glee Club of 1939 would probably have regarded with disapproval. On the same day, the New York Chorus Society rehearsed, with Mrs. Osgood, Miss Cary, Toedt and Henschel, in preparation, of course, for the Music Festival of early May. The concert came on the 25th. The 23rd had sunk to rest to the strains (in the afternoon) of another Morgan organ and harp recital, actually with Cora de Wilhorst assisting, and (in the evening) of the Lenox Hill Vocal Society, directed by H. R. Romeyn, the assistants in the latter case including Harriet Cady (pianist), Miss Corradi (who sang the *Bel raggio*), Miss Wade, Morawski, Harvey and Blois (singers). And, in addition, that same 23rd gave us, at Clarendon Hall, a smoking concert by the Mozart Musical Union. Was all New York expected to go to concerts? If so, what of theatres and other places of amusement? We have always been a gay, gay, frivolous city — on the surface.

Richard Arnold's annual concert, on March 28th, at Chickering Hall, profited (I hope) from the concurrence of Madeline Schiller and Emma S. Howe. On that date, at Masonic Temple, for the Manhattan Temperance Society, appeared Julia A. Polk and some minor lights. At St. Stephen's Church, East 28th Street, the choir gave a concert, on April 3rd, assisted by Eugene Oudin (afterward well-known in comic opera) and Christian Fritsch. At its concert, on April 4th, at Chickering Hall, the New York Philharmonic Club played two compositions, an Evening Song and a Pastorale, by Rafael Joseffy; Richard Hoffman, no longer prominent in our musical affairs, was soloist of the occasion. William Hall Behr, on April 5th, gave his first subscription concert at Steinway Hall, assisted by Mmes. Marie Helmar and Anna de Berlan, by Sternberg, Jacob Graff, Sam Franko, Oscar Steins and Armin Schötte. April 9th (Sunday) proffered much music, chiefly by our foreign-born citizens. At the Germania Assembly Rooms, a testimonial to Carl Sahm, leader of the Mozart Singing Society, brought delegations from many German singing clubs, with Carl Alves (tenor), Carl Steinbuch (baritone) and John Bolze (basso). The French Societies' Concert and Ball occurred at Terrace Garden, as a help for the Children's School; Marie Vachot, Marie Vanoni, Juignet (in recitation), Montegriffo, Lencioni and the French Musical Association participated. More native was the offering, on the same date, at the Harlem Music Hall, with Charles Lambert, members of D'Oyly Carte's Opera Company (Caddallader, Wilkinson), the California Quartette from the San Francisco Minstrels, William Hamilton, Kate Girard (in song), and Marie Hunter.

On April 10th, P. S. Gilmore had a benefit performance at the Armoury of the 22nd Regiment, his band, of course, sweetly proclaiming its co-operation, and Emily Spader, Letitia Fritsch, E. J. O'Mahoney and Stella Botsford singing. On the same evening the James A. Garfield Lodge, Knights of Honour, held Steinway Hall, with Signora d'Auria, Belle Cole, Montegriffo, Lencioni and Anna T. Berger in musical accord. On the 11th, Henrietta Sylvester had a concert in Chickering Hall, abetted by Mlle. Martinez, H. Louise Warner, Hattie Douglass, Fritsch, Remmertz and C. E. Pratt; on the 11th, also, the Standard Quartet and Hermann Rietzel were at Steck Hall. The musicians were making April a harvest field of concerts; the 11th gave us also, at Lyric Hall, the last concert of the seventh season of the New York Choral Union. About this time (April 15th) a testimonial to Miss Conron assembled at the Union League Theatre Del Puente, Constance Howard, Henry Stanfield (tenor), Carl Werner ('cello), and Lencioni. The Bank Clerks' Concert, at Chickering Hall, on the 12th gave us W. R. Chapman, S. B. Mills, Miss Clemmie Albert, W. H. Rieger, Sam Franko, Paul C. J. Torek (accompanist), and Michael Bauer and H. H. Gilbert (organists). My pen, wearied of small affairs, begins to wish that the musicians would take a long holiday; that, of course, they will not do so long as a dollar can be abstracted from easy purses. Therefore, on April 12th, we gird our loins and rush to John Lavine's concert at Steinway Hall, employing a better host, including Imogene Brown, Emily Winant, the Meigs Sisters, Fritsch, Connell, Hasselbrinck, Nunez (pianist) and the Mollenhaur Instrumental Quartet. At the concert of Irish music, on the 13th, at Irving Hall, Maud Morgan harped Irish melodies; on that evening Steinway Hall for a Catholic charity (Sisters of Notre Dame, Fort Lee) presented Charlotte Walker, Sophia Neuberger, Montegriffo, Gottschalk and W. F. Mills. And the concert of Courtney and his pupils, on the 14th, at Steinway Hall, had at least the advantage of co-operation by Damrosch and his orchestra, with Caryl Florio as accompanist. Maud Morgan's concert, on April 15th, at Chickering Hall, presented, besides her excellent harping, her father as organist, William Courtney, Mrs. Emma Dexter,

[597]

Werner and Kortheuer (pianist) — a goodly array of choicer musicians. The Liederkranz, on the 16th, sang at its hall Zoellner's Hunnenschlacht and Heinrich Herrmann's Aschenbrödel. The Spring Street Presbyterian Church gave, on the 17th, a concert of Chinese music.

A concert at Steinway Hall, on the 19th, enlisted Anna Bishop, Fritsch, Oscar Steins, Lencioni, Mme. Chatterton-Bohrer, S. B. Mills, Nahan Franko and others; perhaps charity — it was for the benefit of St. Mary's Free Hospital — was expected to do all. The 20th opened Steck Hall for Marshall P. Wilder, with Miss Markstein, Harry Bryant, and the Brunswick Quartet. On the 21st, the Manhattan Choral Union invaded with harmony (I trust) the ever-patient Chickering Hall; Mrs. G. W. Carhart, Helen D. Campbell, Henry M. Hyman, S. N. Penfield (organist) and J. W. Parsons Price (conductor) helped them on their way. And at 339 West 34th Street, (April 20th), Eugenie Simonson gave a piano recital, with Jennie Dickerson and Miss Shea (soprano) to fill interstices with song. On the 23rd of April, a sacred concert in aid of St. Francis Hospital gave us an orchestra conducted by Damrosch, the Arion Society, Christine Rossée, Carl Ahl (tenor), Hermann Brandt (violin), and John Hammond (cornet-à-piston), with Steinway Hall as scene of operations. Professor Rosse and his young pupils tried a long-tried public, at this time, with a try-out at Standard Hall, Belle Cole, Vicarino (baritone) and Jennie Pratt (accompanist) doing what could be done in the circumstances. The Mozart Musical Union gave, on the 26th, at Lexington Avenue Opera House, a concert deferred from February last. On the 27th, Harlem Music Hall had a benefit for All Saints' Church, Harlem, at which G. F. Bristow directed a number of nonentities. On the same evening, Joseffy, shy and seldom appearing, was to have a concert at Steinway Hall, along with Theodore Thomas and his orchestra.

Will these musicians never, never stop? The pupils of Mme. Louise Cappiani gave to her a concert, on April 28th, at Steinway Hall, and, on the same evening, at Chickering Hall, the pupils of Emilio Agramonte paid him exactly the same sort of honour, with Victoria Morosini making her first appearance, and Ella Earle (a lovely singer) and Carlos Hasselbrinck participating. Tessie Baer, pianist, played at Irving Hall. The Telegraphers' Association shall close this section, with a concert, on May 3rd, at Chickering Hall, in which G. W. and Maud Morgan appeared.

MUSIC FESTIVAL, 1882

And now came the crowning sensation of the season — Theodore Thomas's great Musical Festival, held at the Seventh Regiment Armoury, and carried out on a scale of size and splendour even surpassing the similar experiment, in 1881, of the ambitious Damrosch. The great Wagnerian soprano, Frau Amalia Friedrich-Materna, creator, in 1876 at Baireuth, of the three Brünnhildes in Der Ring des Nibelungen, was specially brought over to add weight and authority to the scheme; William Candidus also returned after an absence of several years.   A chorus of 2,700, from New York, Brooklyn, Worcester and Reading added sonority to the proceedings, and Thomas was in his element as director of the vast concourse of sound.

On Tuesday evening, May 2nd, the programme included Bach's cantata, A Stronghold Sure, with Myron W. Whitney and Candidus as soloists; Mozart's Symphony in C (the Jupiter) preceded the entrance of Frau Materna, who gave as her opening air Abscheulicher, from Fidelio.   Handel's Jubilate, written for the Peace of Utrecht, followed, with Miss Cary, Toedt and George Henschel listed for solo parts.   This aggregation of notable artists atoned, one suspects, for the utter amateurishness of some recent musical doings. Unfortunately, Miss Cary was ill, and Emily Winant took her place.   On May 3rd, the Herald was enthusiastic about Materna, as it might well be:

> Mme. Materna's singing of this aria proved abundantly that she richly deserves the great reputation which she enjoys at home.   Her voice is a soprano of great range, of immense power and of remarkably telling quality.   She is an excellent vocalist, moreover, and she possesses abundant musical feeling.   Her declamation in the opening recitative was broad and noble and she sang the andante with finished style and beautiful sentiment.   She gave the final allegro with great fire and with electrical effect. . . . She has great dramatic talent, and the breadth and vigor of her style are perfectly marvellous.

On the afternoon of May 3rd, the orchestra and Galassi rendered, respectively, the overture and a scene from Iphigenia in Aulis; the orchestra played the Schubert Symphony in C; Etelka Gerster scaled the heights and showered the staccato notes of the great aria from The Magic Flute; Schumann's overture to Manfred followed; George Henschel rendered a scene and air from Spohr's Jessonda; Mme. Materna gave Ocean, Thou Mighty Monster; Campanini rendered Vainement, Pharaon, from Méhul's Joseph; and the concert ended with the overture to Mendelssohn's Ruy Blas.   This certainly was a collection of celebrated singers; the Herald states that Campanini (apparently declining) was hoarse, but that Materna was grand and noble, though at times she flatted.   The evening concert of the 3rd was a bit more austere — Beethoven's Fifth Symphony and his Mass in D.   But disappointment accrued; both Mrs. E. Aline Osgood and Miss Cary were ill, and Mrs. E. Humphry Allen and Miss Winant were substituted, and Campanini, according to next day's Herald, was "out of voice and ragged."   Materna, Candidus, Henschel and Whitney were very fine.

A Wagner matinée, on the 4th, gave choice bits of Der Ring des Nibelungen.   Theodore Toedt did Loge's Tidings, Candidus sang Siegmund's Love Song, Galassi the Fire Music, Campanini the Forging of the Sword (this seems incredible), Hattie Schell, Antonia Henne and Miss Wurmb the

[599]

music of the Rhine maidens, and Frau Materna nobly intoned Brünnhilde's Immolation, one of the grandest pieces of singing ever heard. Israel in Egypt, on the evening of the 5th, presented Candidus, Mrs. Osgood, Remmertz, Miss Winant and Whitney. On the afternoon of May 6th, Thomas gave an Italian programme, including works by Corelli, Stradella, Cimerosa, Cherubini, Rossini, Donizetti and Verdi, with Gerster, Mrs. Osgood, Miss Cary, Miss Winant, Campanini, Candidus, Galassi, Toedt, Henschel, Whitney and Remmertz. Scenes from operas included a bit from Spontini's La Vestale, sung by Gerster, Miss Cary and Campanini. In the evening, a more reasonable festival bill included Liszt's Dante Symphony, a scene from Rubinstein's The Demon (sung by Gerster), scenes from Berlioz's Les Troyens (with Materna and Campanini) and a chorus from Die Meistersinger. According to the Herald, the receipts for the festival were about $123,000, with expenditures slightly under that figure.

I go back to matters less stupendous. On May 4th, a testimonial to Sallie Reber brought to Steinway Hall Mme. M. Stern (mezzo), Aggie Dunphy (harp), Christian Fritsch, L. G. Gottschalk, W. F. Mills, A. Schötte (organ) and C. E. Pratt. Esther Jacobs had a concert, on the same date, in Chickering Hall. In Steinway Hall, on May 8th, Campanini gave a charity concert, for Italian institutions in New York; in this he was assisted by Mlle. Bettini, Mme. Lablache, Paolina Rossini, Emma Juch, Tagliapietra, Corsini and Barberis. May 9th brought to Chickering Hall a concert and readings by Florence Rice Knox, Ida Simpson Serven, and "Professor" Keenan; in Steinway Hall, on the 4th, appeared Fanny Jacobs (contralto), C. Fritsch, Arnold, and Lizzie Priest (piano). On the 13th, Michael Banner, at Steinway Hall, fiddled farewell, and had as assistants Hattie Louise Simms, Hortense Hibbard (pianist), H. R. Humphries, and Armand (sic) Schötte (sic). Jerome Hopkins's Seventeenth "Springtide" promised for May 15th, at Steinway Hall, Eily Coghlan (sister of Rose), George F. Sargent, &c. Kennedy sang farewell, on the 17th, at Steinway Hall. At this time (May 17th) a concert tendered to Theodora Linda Da Acosta, the seven-year-old prodigy, collected at Chickering Hall H. Louise Warner (soprano), Carrie Hindbaugh pianist), Louise Helena Hoch (pianist), James Caulfield (organist), Liberati, William C. Bull (tenor), J. Palmer (basso) and Carl Ficke (accompanist), all doubtless glad to appear and strike if possible a dint in the apperception of a music-mad public. Mme. Lablache had a benefit on May 20th, at Chickering Hall, with Emma Juch, Mlle. Rossini, Mme. Chatterton-Bohrer, Imogene Brown, and Tagliapietra. Campanini sang and directed. May 21st brought to Irving Hall Henrietta Markstein, Miss A. Bettini (contralto), Marie Vanoni, J. Estèphe (soprano), Gottschalk, Cassano (flute), and Paul Juignet. Blind Tom, on May 22nd (afternoon, and evening), 24th (afternoon and evening), and 27th (afternoon) was at Association Hall; on the 23rd (evening) he was at Harlem Music Hall. On May 22nd, the Meigs

ERNESTO NICOLINI
(Photograph by
Sarony)

TERESA CARREÑO
(Photograph by
Falk)

ETELKA GERSTER
From a Photograph by Mora

ADELINA PATTI
From a Photograph by Sarony

AMALIA FRIEDRICH-MATERNA
From a Photograph by Sarony

Sisters, Hattie Schell, Fred Harvey and S. H. P. Meigs came to Chickering Hall.   A pianist, Comincio Gnarr and Felix Caratu (tenor) were there on the 23rd.   A complimentary benefit to Anna Bishop, who first sang in New York in 1847, was to enlist on May 27th, at Chickering Hall, Mme. Lablache, Henrietta Beebe (who had been singing abroad), Florence Rice Knox, Mme. Chatterton-Bohrer, Fannie Lovering, A. L. King, Lencioni, S. B. Mills, Arbuckle, G. W. Morgan and C. E. Pratt, surely an army of tried helpers. On the 25th, the Produce Exchange Glee Club had been aided, at Chickering Hall, by the singing of W. C. Baird and Hattie Louise Simms.   On the 28th, Max Schwab directed two sacred concerts at Terrace Garden Theatre.   A Pfingst-Montag Festival, on May 29th, made Teutonic the Atalanta Casino.

The musicians this year were merciless.   Lencioni pursued the quarry to June 3rd, at Knabe Hall, announcing Anna Bishop, Carlos Hasselbrinck, Cassano and Lillie Berg.   Thereafter, one might go into gardens or down to beaches.   The well-known Atlantic Garden, 50 Bowery, tempted with a Hungarian gipsy orchestra, and, at Manhattan Beach, on June 4th, appeared Gilmore and his famous band, including Fred Innis (trombone), B. C. Bent (cornet), Signor de Carlo (piccolo), E. A. Lefebre (saxophone), Raffayolo (euphonium) and Louis Stockigt (clarinet).   Perhaps the complimentary concert to Theodora Linda Da Acosta, scheduled for June 12th, was but a deferred joy, since it was announced as "by permission of Mayor Grace"; Mrs. Emma T. Quicksell, Mme. M. Stern, Sophia Neuberger, Miss F. Battersby, Gottschalk, Harry Snow and Max Liebling constituted the array of mediocrities enlisted.   Jules Levy began on June 30th, at Brighton Beach. At the Sea Beach Palace Hotel, Coney Island, Joyce's Military Band discoursed in July.   And the Herald columns are loaded with advertisements of excursions to Brighton Pier, Manhattan Beach, Glen Island, Long Branch, etc., where, in bosky gardens, one could drink cooling draughts and often hear good music.   Of course Staten Island was still beery across the bay.   The Oriental Hotel, Manhattan Beach, was also drawing to its cool, spacious porches many of the fine old families of the city; Goldberg the magician was there on July 21st.   About September 1st, the Arion Society had a Summer Night's Fest and Bal champêtre at Washington Park, and Jones Wood, 69th Street and East River; and, on September 19th, a "Grand Military Review" and concert employed at Manhattan Beach a hundred and fifty musicians. Surely now we may end the music for 1881–82.

PHILHARMONIC SOCIETY, 1881–1882

But of course we must recall the activities of the great orchestras and the Oratorio Society.   The Philharmonic, directed by Thomas, began, on November 11th and 12th, with Brahms's Tragic Overture; Madeline Schiller in Tschaikowsky's piano concerto, No. 2; Beethoven's Fourth Symphony, and two episodes from Liszt's treatment of Lenau's Faust. On December 9th and 10th, one heard Schubert's Rosamunde music; Brandt and Arnold in a Bach violin concerto; Rubinstein's Fifth Symphony; Galassi in a scene from The Flying Dutchman; and Beethoven's Third Leonore overture. Chill January brightened, on the 13th and 14th, with Haydn's Symphony No. 2, in D major; Joseffy in Beethoven's concerto for piano, No. 4, in G major; and Schumann's Rhenish Symphony.

On February 10th and 11th, E. Aline Osgood sang an aria from Gluck's Ariadne, and united with Theodore Toedt, in a duo, from Berlioz's Benvenuto Cellini. The orchestra progressed from Mozart's Symphony in D major, No. 5, to a menuett and finale of Beethoven, for strings, and thence to Hans Huber's new symphony, Tell. The March offering (10th–11th) comprised Schumann's overture, Genoveva; scenes from Das Rheingold (with Hattie Schell, A. Wurmb, Antonia Henne, Toedt, Oscar Steins, F. Remmertz), and Beethoven's Fifth Symphony. And the season closed sonorously, on April 14th–15th, with The Consecration of the House; Hermann Rietzel's playing Goetz's Concerto for the piano; Campanini's singing of an air from Euryanthe; the Vorspiel to Lohengrin, and Schubert's never-dying Symphony in C.

Symphony Society; Oratorio Society, 1881–1882

Still under the direction of Dr. Leopold Damrosch, the energetic Symphony Society gave on November 5th, at Steinway Hall, its opening concert, preceded by the expected public rehearsal, on the 3rd. The programme included Beethoven's Coriolanus overture, Brahms's Academic Festival Overture (new), the Symphonie Fantastique of Berlioz, and songs of Beethoven (Adelaide) and Mozart (air from Don Giovanni), rendered by Italo Campanini, whom one does not usually associate with music of that style. The second rehearsal and concert (December 1st and 3rd) gave us for the first time the conductor's orchestration of Schubert's Quintet, op. 163 and (also new here) Saint-Saëns's fourth concerto for piano and orchestra, with Madeline Schiller as soloist; two Norwegian melodies (new) of Grieg figured on the bill, as did Beethoven's Eighth Symphony. Damrosch impresses me as a man ever on the alert for worthy novelties. On January 5th and 7th, the third concert brought Hattie Louise Simms, in a song by Beethoven, and, with Belle Cole, in a duo, Nocturne, by Berlioz; the orchestra played Mendelssohn's Scottish Symphony, the Waldweben from Siegfried, and Liszt's Die Hunnenschlacht.

The fourth rehearsal and concert, on February 2nd and 4th, respectively, treated to Mozart's Symphony in G minor, Spohr's Concerto in A, for violin, played by Master Michael Banner, and Rubinstein's Ocean Symphony, once so popular. The rehearsal and concert (March 2nd and 4th) gave the

Vorspiel and Finale to Tristan und Isolde; an air from Partenope (by Handel), sung by Lena Little (contralto); Goldmark's Overture, Sakuntala; songs of Schumann, rendered by Miss Little; and Beethoven's Eroica Symphony. Again I pause in admiration before the genius of Leopold Damrosch as a programme-maker; a genius inherited by Walter Damrosch. And once more I reflect on the fact that Wagner's operatic scores when at last heard here in the Metropolitan were not such novelties as many have inferred; Damrosch and Theodore Thomas had made their finest bits very familiar to concert-goers. The fifth rehearsal and concert, April 6th and 8th, opened with Beethoven's overture, Leonore No. 3, and concluded with Berlioz's symphonic Romeo and Juliet, the soloists being Lena Little, Theodore J. Toedt and Franz Remmertz.

The Oratorio Society began its season at Steinway Hall, with a public rehearsal and a concert, on November 25th and 26th, offering Rubinstein's The Tower of Babel, and the Sanctus from Berlioz's Requiem, Italo Campanini and Franz Remmertz serving as soloists. Was Campanini more versatile and more of a musician than his operatic repertoire would lead one to expect? The Christmas Messiah (December 27th–28th) had, as soloists, Hattie Louise Simms, Anna Drasdil, A. L. King and Franz Remmertz. Handel's Israel in Egypt was the offering on February 24th and 25th, the soloists being Ida W. Hubbell, Antonia Henne, T. J. Toedt, John F. Winch, of Boston (basso), and F. Remmertz; Walter Damrosch was at the organ. The last performances of the season (April 20th and 21st) gave us Bach's Vain and Fleeting and Leopold Damrosch's Sulamith (presented for the first time anywhere), with Hattie Louise Simms, Belle Cole, Lena Little, Miss M. J. Groebl, Miss M. von Heimberg, Mrs. M. Kirpal, Mrs. L. Bell, Mrs. G. W. Delano, A. L. King and Morawski.

CHAPTER IX

BROOKLYN, WILLIAMSBURGH, GREENPOINT, QUEENS COUNTY, STATEN ISLAND, 1881–1882

THE Park Theatre was the first of Brooklyn houses of the better class to begin the season of 1881–82. On August 22nd, it presented a play new in our neighbourhood — Mrs. Everett's drama, Ruth, an American Wife, which dealt with polygamy at Salt Lake City:

Leo Carlton	David M. Murray	Rachel	Sara Goldberg
Elder Rock	W. J. Hurley	Jane	Ethel Gurnsey
James Bentley	Randolph Murray	Lulu	Little Lydia Corduan
Dennis	M. Gallagher	Mrs. Ball	Mrs. F. Tannehill
Bill Hick	J. F. Ryan	Ruth	Mrs. Everett
Dutch Joe	J. Humphries		

This sounds very like a cast of amateurs. The play disappeared after a week; perhaps it was a private venture out of the regular running. At any rate, on August 29th, the San Francisco Minstrels atoned, with Salvini's Othello, Billy the Tailor, All-I've-Eat, and plenty of fun and harmless melody in the olio. And, on September 5th, Alice and Louis Harrison (that funny pair) presented their amusing hodge-podge, Photos. James A. Herne's Hearts of Oak began a week, on the 12th, and journeyed thereafter to the Novelty Theatre.

John Sleeper Clarke, passing from our theatre, filled a week that should have drawn packed houses. On the 19th, 20th and 21st of September, he acted Dr. Pangloss, in The Heir at Law, with Mrs. Mark Smith as Caroline, H. B. Conway, a handsome London juvenile, as Dick Dowlas, W. A. Chapman as Duberly, J. M. Colville as Zekiel, Blanche Thompson as Cicely, and Mrs. J. H. Rowe as Lady Duberly. On the 22nd and 23rd, the great comedian gave The Widow Hunt (Everybody's Friend) and Toodles. The matinée on the 24th revealed An Elopement in High Life, which (with Toodles) constituted the farewell offering on the evening of that day. I doubt if Clarke ever again acted in our vicinity. The old order was passing, and comic opera was in the saddle.

The Emma Abbott Opera Company brought variety for a week of song — Martha (September 27th — the house, of course, was closed on Monday, the 26th); Olivette (matinée, 28th); Faust (evening, 28th); Fra Diavolo (29th); Lucia (30th); Chimes of Normandy (matinée, October 1st), and The Bohemian Girl (evening of that day). With Miss Abbott, as we know from her Manhattan performances this same year, were Julie Rosewald,

[604]

GEORGE SWEET

WALLACE MACREERY
(PIRATES OF PENZANCE)

MAGGIE MITCHELL
JULIAN MITCHELL

. SALSBURY — J. WEBSTER
NELLIE McHENRY

JOHN S. CLARKE

MR. AND MRS. RANKIN
IN '49

FANNY DAVENPORT
AS CAMILLE

RAY SAMUELS

MARIE JANSEN
(COMIC OPERA)

Pauline Maurel, George A. Conly, George Olmi, Arthur W. Tams, Fabrini (tenor), Alonzo Stoddard, and the popular tenor, William Castle. On October 3rd and 5th, Fanny Davenport acted Lady Teazle, with Charles Fisher as Sir Peter, Harry Pearson as Sir Oliver, George Darrell as Joseph, Edmund Tearle as Charles, W. F. Edwards as Sir Benjamin, Lewis Baker as Careless, Harry Hawk as Crabtree, Mary Shaw as Lady Sneerwell, May Davenport as Maria, and Minnie Monk as Mrs. Candour.   On the 4th and 6th, Miss Davenport was Rosalind, to the Jaques of Tearle (his brother played the part a year before at Wallack's), Darrell as Orlando, Pearson as the Banished Duke, Fisher as Adam, Edwards as Oliver, Mary Shaw as Audrey, Hawk as Touchstone, May Davenport as Celia, and Mrs. Charles Fisher as Phebe.   I quote these casts because of their differences from the Manhattan casts a short time later.   For the matinée, on the 5th, Miss Davenport offered London Assurance, and gave Leah on the evening of the 7th.   She played Camille on the afternoon of the 8th, and, as usual, said goodbye on the evening of that day as Lady Gay Spanker and Nancy Sykes. I wish I had seen her in all those parts.

Sol Smith Russell came in, on October 10th, with Edgewood Folks. Steele Mackaye, banished from his own Madison Square Theatre, and precluded by law from profit in his play of Hazel Kirke, or indeed from power to produce it, came to Sinn's Park Theatre, on October 17th, in Won at Last, his support including F. F. Mackay, B. R. Graham, Harry Courtaine, Herbert Archer, Donald Robertson, Belle Archer, Louise Sylvester, Mrs. Courtaine, Helen Mar and Eleanor Lane — an excellent company.   Many of us remember Herbert Archer and his pretty wife, Belle Archer, as the villain and the gentle heroine in the earlier support of E. H. Sothern.   H. B. Mahn's Company, with Jeannie Winston, sang Donna Juanita, on October 24th, 25th and 26th, and Boccaccio on the 27th, 28th and 29th.   Rose Eytinge for the week of October 31st–November 5th acted her last season's Union Square success, Felicia, supported by Frank Roberts, Georgie Knowlton, Adelaide Thornton, W. F. Owen, Horace Vinton and L. J. Loring, a group far below that which had appeared with her at the Union Square. Rose Eytinge's star was dimming fast.

Lawrence Barrett offered a full week, just following Booth's visit to Haverly's.   He began, on the 7th of November, with the part Booth had played at the rival theatre on October 31st, Richelieu; it will be remembered that they both started New York engagements in this character on the same evening, October 3rd.   On November 8th, Election Day, Barrett played Shylock (afternoon) and Cassius (evening); on the 9th he was Hamlet (afternoon) and Othello (evening); he repeated Richelieu on the 11th, and for a busy concluding Saturday, October 12th, proffered Yorick's Love (afternoon) and Richard III (evening).   Imagine David Garrick undertaking in so short a time such a heavy burden of tragic woe!   On November 14th, Mlle. Rhea, a new actress, later popular in the "provinces," and seen shortly after at Booth's, announced her début as Camille; on the 15th and 16th, she was to have appeared as Adrienne Lecouvreur, but some difficulty arose, and Camille was substituted.   In fact, Mlle. Rhea, in this season of 1881–82, seems, if I may judge from the Herald, to have met with considerable trouble, legal and otherwise.   In addition to Camille and Adrienne (by the way, Mlle. Rhea was no Modjeska), in this week at the Park Theatre, Mlle. Rhea promised to appear on the evening of November 18th, as Beatrice, in Much Ado about Nothing; instead, she again advertised Adrienne.   We have already chronicled her short season, later, at Booth's.   Her support, at the Park, included J. Newton Gotthold, Edwin Varrey and Mrs. J. W. Brutone. Herrmann and his entertainers wove magic spells during the week of November 21st–26th, and, on the 28th, Genevieve Ward brought in her brilliant Forget Me Not.   For the Wednesday matinée, Daly's company gave Cinderella at School

Did the Park season, as a whole, surpass that in other Brooklyn houses? Here comes Joseph Jefferson, on the 5th, 6th and 7th of December, with his new-old hit, The Rivals, and, of course with, on the 8th, 9th and 10th, the ever-demanded Rip Van Winkle.   In the cast of The Rivals, I am surprised and delighted to find Ada Dyas (always a favourite with me) as Lydia, though I cannot imagine the maturing lady in the rôle.   Others were Mrs. John Drew (of course), Lillie Lee, Frederic Robinson (Sir Anthony), Mark Pendleton (Jack), Charles Waverly (Sir Lucius), H. F. Taylor (Faulkland), Thomas Jefferson (Fag), and James T. Galloway (David).   Mme. Janauschek on the 12th and 17th (matinée), acted Mary Stuart; on the 13th and 16th, Bleak House; on the 14th (matinée and evening) Mother and Son; on the 15th, The Winter's Tale; and on the 17th (evening), Henry VIII.   With her, in The Winter's Tale, were J. H. Taylor as Leontes, G. B. Waldron as Polixenes, A. H. Stuart as Florizel, R. F. McClannin as Camillo, Anna Warren Story as Perdita, Isabel Waldron as Paulina, and Henrietta Irving as Emilia.   I do not remember that Mme. Janauschek ever acted Hermione in Manhattan.   The ubiquitous La Mascotte entered, on December 19th, with Louise Searle, John Brand (Pippo), Harry Brown (Lorenzo), Ed Chapman (Rocco), J. E. Conly (Prince of Pisa), and Lillie West (Fiametta).   Willie Edouin's Sparks, in Dreams, merrily finished the year (December 26th–31st).

Annie Pixley came, on January 2nd, in M'liss; Salsbury's Troubadours, at last escaping from The Brook, gave us something new (January 9th–14th), in Bronson Howard's Faun of the Glen, or, the Civilised Indian (seen later in New York as Green Room Fun).   John Webster, John Gourlay, Nate Salsbury, Nellie McHenry and Ray Samuels played the parts in which, later, they disported in New York.   Jeffreys Lewis, not recently prominent in our story, came, on the 16th, for a week in Maude Granger's success, Two

Nights in Rome; with her were A. H. Canby, Oliver W. Wren, and Blanche Wallston.

Mr. and Mrs. McKee Rankin entered, on January 23rd, for a week of '49; on the 30th, Mr. and Mrs. George S. Knight presented a new piece, The Member for Slocum on a Racket, repeated on January 31st and February 1st (matinée and evening) and reverted to Hobbies for the last three days of their week. The Hardie-Hoey combination gave, on February 6th, 7th, and 11th, their accustomed A Child of the State; Diplomacy filled the evenings of the 8th, 9th and 10th, and the afternoon of the 11th. John T. Raymond came in, on the 13th, in Fresh, the American, always breezy, always welcome. And Maggie Mitchell, a memory and a hope, followed, on the 20th in The Pearl of Savoy; on the 21st, in Lorle; on the 22nd (matinée), and 23rd (evening), in Fanchon; on the 22nd (evening) in Little Barefoot; 24th (evening) and 25th (afternoon and evening) in her new play, The Little Savage, seen shortly after at the Grand Opera House, New York. With her were L. R. Shewell, R. Fulton Russell, Julian Mitchell, Carrie Wyatt and Mrs. Van Deren. Denman Thompson and Joshua Whitcomb gave us, from February 27th to March 4th, a bit of *rus in urbe*. Milton Nobles, beginning on March 6th, offered a week of Interviews, or, Bright Bohemia, an offering that did not survive to many showings.

One of Our People, adapted by Archibald Gordon from the well-known German play, Einer von Unsere Leut', likewise achieved no lasting renown; it filled the week of March 13th–18th, with Cyril Searle, J. Clinton Hall, Estelle Clayton, Welsh Edwards, Florence Temple, W. A. Rouse, and Mrs. M. Bryer. I doubt if we ever hear of it again. A Celebrated Case, on March 20th, presented that company, including James O'Neill, W. Scallan, Maude Granger and Lewis Morrison, seen so often, during the season, in New York. Georgia Cayvan was now both Madeleine and Adrienne. Dion Boucicault's Suil-a-Mor made Hibernian the week of March 27th–April 1st. Funny as ever, Neil Burgess, on April 3rd, enacted Widow Bedott, with his parents-in-law, Mr. and Mrs. George W. Stoddart, in loyal support; others in the company were Joseph Palmer, Louis N. Glover, I. T. Wyndham, M. Blackmore, May Taylor, Letitia Brisbane and Mrs. Clara Stoneall.

Mary Anderson came in for a week of the "legitimate," beginning, on the 10th, with Juliet, and running rapidly through a choice part of her list — Parthenia (11th), Galatea, 12th (matinée and evening), Julia (13th, and matinée, 15th), and Berthe, in The Daughter of Roland (14th and 15th). And the regular Union Square Theatre Company having just closed their season at the home theatre, brought across the river, on April 17th, their most recent hit, The Lights o' London; it remained for two weeks — something unusual in Brooklyn. Walden Ramsay succeeded Thorne as the persecuted hero, but Parselle, Stoddart, Maud Harrison, Sara Jewett, Eleanor Carey and Mrs. Phillips retained their former rôles; Harry Courtaine was

[607]

the villainous Clifford. The Fay Templeton Opera Company followed, on May 1st, with the now (to us) tiring La Mascotte. The Vokes Family presented (May 8th, 9th and 10th) Fun in a Fog, and (11th, 12th, 13th) Too Too Truly Rural, a piece so sickly that it never crossed the river into New York, at least under that name. Augustin Daly's home company filled the week of May 15th–20th, with Ada Rehan, James Lewis, John Drew, H. M. Pitt, Henry Miller, Mrs. Gilbert, Lillie Vinton and all the delightful band in The Passing Regiment; besides, Company F of the 13th Regiment, Brooklyn, figured in the proceedings. East Lynne was more ancient, on the 22nd, with Ada Gray, Mrs. S. A. Baker, Ida Lewis, Mrs. Jane Russell, Marion Russell (sister of Annie Russell of Esmeralda fame), Lindsay Harris, J. B. Browne, John B. Furlong, and Master Tommy Russell (brother of Annie and Marion). George H. Adams's Humpty Dumpty let down the pegs on May 29th, and, on June 5th, Harrigan and Hart brought from the Theatre Comique their great success, Squatter Sovereignty; it likewise had the honour of two weeks in Brooklyn, and on that distinction I drop the Park curtain for 1881–82.

HAVERLY'S THEATRE, BROOKLYN, 1881–1882

Haverly's in Brooklyn invited for its re-opening, on August 29th, with Oliver Doud Byron, in Ten Thousand Miles Away, his support including Harry B. Hudson, Arthur Rehan (brother of Mrs. Byron and of Ada Rehan), Sidney Roberts, W. H. Reeves, Kate Byron, Hattie O'Neil, and Salome Monte. My Geraldine, as cast at Niblo's (Emily Rigl in the lead), filled the week of September 5th–10th. Haverly's Company followed, on the 12th, in The Strategists, seen but recently at Haverly's Fourteenth Street Theatre. The Galley Slave held the week of September 19th–24th, with, in leading rôles, Maude Granger, Gussie De Forrest and Frank Evans. On September 27th, Jennie Lee began a week in Jo, and, on October 3rd, Around the World in Eighty Days came from its recent visit to the Novelty. Lester Wallack, who had abandoned his old theatre, and whose new theatre was unready, came to Haverly's for a week, presenting Ours, on October 10th, 11th and 12th, and My Awful Dad, on the 13th, 14th and 15th. The company supporting him (his own fine company was "on the road," waiting to appear at the new Wallack's when finished) included Nelson Decker, John Sutherland, J. L. Mason, W. J. Gilbert, E. Dunbar, Effie Germon, Minnie Conway (returned to the stage after several years of retirement) and Mrs. G. C. Germon —a company more talented in women than in men. The Wallack regular company, except for Effie Germon, was acting that week in Toronto. On October 17th, the Madison Square Company headed by Effie Ellsler, Sydney Cowell, Gustavus Levick and C. W. Couldock presented Hazel Kirke, during the very week in which its author, dispossessed of all right in it, was acting Won at Last at the Park Theatre, Brooklyn; accident or design, I wonder?

[608]

The Comley-Barton Company (with Emma Howson, Marie Jansen, W. H. Seymour and Fred Leslie) sang Mme. Favart, on the 24th, once more in opposition to the Park, which was offering Jeannie Winston and the H. B. Mahn comic opera.

A glory came to Haverly's in a week of the "legitimate." Booth, fresh from his engagement at Booth's Theatre, presented Richelieu, on October 31st, following with Macbeth (November 1st), Othello (2nd), Bertuccio (3rd), Hamlet (4th), Iago (matinée, 5th) and Shylock and Petruchio (evening, 5th). Bella Pateman and the company recently seen at Booth's still supported the noble star. On the 7th, Haverly's relaxed with J. K. Emmet, in Fritz in Ireland. Mr. and Mrs. W. J. Florence (always hearty and always welcome) entered on the 14th, in The Mighty Dollar, repeated all week, except that, for the matinée on the 16th, Florence acted Cap'n Cuttle, and on the evening of the 19th, gave The Ticket of Leave Man. On November 21st, The Tourists in a Pullman Palace Car began their thrice-familiar journey, and, on the 28th, Rice's company brought in Patience, with A. W. F. McCollin as Bunthorne, Eugene Clarke as Grosvenor, G. F. Hall as the Colonel, H. Laurent as the Duke, G. A. Schiller as the Major, Vernona Jarbeau as Angela, Irene Perry as Saphir, Fannie Hall as Ella, Rosa Cooke as Jane, and Rose Temple as Patience. Deacon Crankett followed, on December 5th, and, on the 12th, Robson and Crane offered Our Bachelors, with A. S. Lipman, Theodore Roberts, John Marble, Alicia Robson and Grace E. Thorne; Sharps and Flats filled the second week of the visit of Robson and Crane, beginning on December 19th. On the 26th, Aldrich and Parsloe gave My Partner; January 2nd began a week of Olivette, with Catherine Lewis, Fred Leslie, and John Howson. The World, with Henry Crisp and the cast from Niblo's, brought melodramatic chills, for the weeks of January 9th and 16th. John McCullough, after a brilliant engagement at the Fifth Avenue Theatre, presented at Haverly's Virginius (January 23rd, 27th), The Gladiator (24th, 28th), Othello (25th), Richard III (26th), and Ingomar (matinée, 28th); Kate Forsyth and the company seen in New York still supported him.

The Emilie Melville Opera Company also provided a large week's repertoire, beginning on January 30th with The Royal Middy (repeated on February 4th), and following with The Bells of Corneville (January 31st and February 1st), and with Patience (February 2nd and 3rd, with matinées on the 1st and 4th). Her support included Lilly Post, Max Freeman, Wallace Macreery and Elma Delaro. M. B. Curtis and Sam'l of Posen filled the week of February 6th–11th. Manola was the attraction beginning on the 13th, the cast including Catherine Lewis, John Howson, Fred Leslie and Marie Jansen. Haverly's own company followed in a week of operetta — Patience (February 20th, 21st, 24th and matinée, 25th); Pinafore (matinée, 23rd, and evening, 25th); The Mascot (evenings, 22nd and 23rd). Emma

[609]

Howson, Pauline Hall, Brocolini, W. H. Seymour, Alonzo Hatch and Lithgow James led the casts. Lester Wallack, on the 27th, began a week in his recent success, The Colonel. W. H. Gillette and The Professor brought delight on March 6th. Mr. and Mrs. W. J. Florence acted The Mighty Dollar, on March 13th, 14th and 15th, with a matinée on the 18th; and revived The Ticket of Leave Man on the 17th and 18th. On the 16th, they brought out a new piece, which never secured a place in their repertoire. This was Professor Opstein, by B. E. Woolf, author of The Mighty Dollar. In it Florence assumed the title-rôle, with Mrs. Florence as Mrs. Finn Dacy, Annie Ellsler as Dora Lind, Ida Tavernier as Bertha Opstein, C. Dade as Launce Jerningham, Ethel Greybrooke as Geraldine, Frank Lamb as Carl Powyss, M. C. Daly as Cramp, Lin Harris as Granville Summer, E. Jones as George and Mrs. Wagstaff as Nanette. Fun on the Bristol, on March 20th, restored us to the familiar and the popular. And here, on March 27th, is Kiralfy's Black Crook with J. B. Roberts and Nellie Larkelle. And, on April 3rd, Haverly's Consolidated Mastodon Minstrels helped to keep us on the lower planes of intellectual apperception. J. K. Emmet, one of the very most desirable attractions, presented his undying Fritz in Ireland, for the week beginning on April 10th. On the 17th, Adelaide Detchon came in, in Bronson Howard's comedy, Wives, accompanied by W. J. Le Moyne, E. M. Holland, Mr. and Mrs. John P. Sutton, William Seymour, May Davenport, Eula Talbot, Louise Dillon, &c. Joseph Murphy and The Kerry Gow returned on the 24th.

Rice's Surprise Party, headed by Henry E. Dixey, Eugene Clarke and Topsy Venne (sic), gave us, on May 1st, 2nd, 3rd and 4th, Cinderella at School, and, on the 5th and 6th, the ubiquitous, the haunting La Mascotte, which Fay Templeton was then giving at the Park. Lillian Olcott, who later introduced to American audiences Sardou's sensational Théodora, which she flaunted till Bernhardt came, now made her professional début (May 8th) at Haverly's, as the long-suffering Juliet, and, on the 10th, attacked the equally defenceless Parthenia. Mrs. Fred Williams, George F. Nash, J. T. Malone (Romeo) and Russell Blake (Mercutio) abetted. The Lady of Lyons came duly into the scheme, on May 12th.

ACADEMY OF MUSIC (BROOKLYN), 1881–1882

The Academy had a busy and an interesting season. It began, on September 12, 1881, with a week of Jay Rial's Uncle Tom's Cabin, which Brooklyn seemed to take in large doses. The Stoddard lectures followed with pictures verbal and on the screen — Scotland (September 29th), the Danube (October 6th), Florence and Pisa (13th), Sicily and Naples (24th), and From Mars Hill to Mt. Olivet (31st). Stoddard was legitimate predecessor of Burton Holmes, though his style was different. On October 7th, with a matinée on the 8th, Wallack's Theatre Company presented The School for Scandal, with Gilbert, Tearle, Edwards, Elton, Gerald and Wilmot Eyre, Leeson, Rose Coghlan, Adelaide Detchon (Maria), Mme. Ponisi and Agnes Elliott. On the evening of the 8th, these accomplished players, with Effie Germon (for Pert) gave London Assurance. And what think you? The Eagle of October 9th seemed to prefer Fanny Davenport's production of The School for Scandal, seen earlier in the week at the Park Theatre: "If," says that independent voice of the Eagle, "if Mr. Wallack had witnessed the performance at the Park on Monday, we venture to say, he would have strengthened his own organization in several particulars; for, while it was Wallack's company, it was not in the strictest sense representative. With John Gilbert, Miss Coghlan and Madame Ponisi in the cast three parts were guaranteed, but the company was anything but well balanced. Mr. Osmond Tearle is quite as much too heavy for *Charles Surface* as his brother in Miss Davenport's company, and Mr. Gerald Eyre is not so good a *Joseph* as Mr. Darrell. The fact of the matter is that, while Miss Davenport's company is far better trimmed than Mr. Wallack's, the choice lies between the two *Sir Peters* and the two *Lady Teazles*. We do not venture to compare the quartet, but, if the organizations ever meet in rivalry again, Mr. Wallack had better superintend the production of old comedies by his company in person. Otherwise, he may learn that he has been outshone." This surprises one. Does the reader remember the Eagle's estimate, in 1864, of Boston's beloved William Warren?

Let us on with the Academy annals. David Taylor, manager of the temple, brought in for Wednesday matinées, beginning on October 12th, the D'Oyly Carte Patience, from the Standard Theatre, New York. On the 11th, Clara Louise Kellogg, a fading star, was advertised for a concert with, as assistants, Alta Pease (contralto), Brignoli, Tagliapietra, Timothée Adamowski (violin), S. Liebling (piano) and the Weber Quartet of Boston; I found no review of this function. On Friday, October 14th, and at the matinée on the 15th, Marie Geistinger, advertised as "the world's greatest artist," sang Boccaccio, reverting, on the evening of the 15th, to Donna Juanita. The Boston Ideal Opera Company carried on this mood during the following week, presenting La Mascotte (October 17th, 18th and 19th, with Marie Stone, Lizzie Burton, Barnabee, Frothingham, Fessenden and Macdonald), Czar and Carpenter (19th and 20th, with Adelaide Phillips, Geraldine Ulmar, Myron Whitney, Barnabee and Fessenden), Olivette (21st, 22nd, with Misses Stone, Ulmar and Burton, and Karl, Barnabee, Macdonald and Frothingham), and Fatinitza (matinée, 22nd, with Marie Stone, Lizzie Burton, Whitney, Karl, Macdonald, Fessenden and Frothingham). A splendid organisation!

And now Mapleson possessed the stage (October 27th), with Minnie Hauk, Campanini and Del Puente, all, according to the Eagle, in fine voice, for Carmen.   Geistinger showed her versatility, on the 28th, with Camille, and on the 29th (matinée and evening), Jenny Stubel sang in The Chimes of Normandy.   Mignon, on November 3rd, showed Mapleson's weakness in *prime donne,* the cast including Virginia Ferni ("no presence — vibrato," summed up the Eagle), Emma Juch ("very immature," according to the same critic), Lelia Lauri, Campanini (out of place in that aggregation) and Del Puente.   Marta, on the 8th, enlisted Ravelli, Del Puente, Lauri and Emma Juch.   In the Academy Assembly Rooms, on November 14th, the Sängerbund, Ida Mollenhauer, F. Steins and H. Mollenhauer appeared for the benefit of the Michigan sufferers.   On the 15th, the Brooklyn Amateur Opera Association presented The Doctor of Alcantara, with Mrs. E. J. Grant, Mrs. James Bogle, Louise Kemlo Wright, Charles H. Parsons, J. T. Walter, James Bogle, Ramsbottom, Howard Dunbar, John Littlejohn, and Frank A. Howson (conductor).   Il Barbiere di Siviglia, on the 17th, promised Ravelli, Del Puente, Novara, Corsini and Marie Vachot.   And here, ye gods! is (week of November 21st–26th) Jay Rial's ever-recurring Uncle Tom's Cabin, to be enjoyed for 25 cents or 50 cents — "no lower — no higher — no extra." Under its own heading I shall, as usual, outline the season of the Philharmonic Society.

An interesting revival by the vaunted Kemble Society came on November 18th, when Ruy Blas enlisted in the title-rôle the well-known reader, Charles Roberts, Jr., with, in other parts, Helen Dayton, Annie L. Hyde, Carrie Frost, G. de Cordova, Withington, and Fred W. Bowne.   An Unequal Match, on December 21st, showed the mettle of this ambitious group; Julia Reid appeared as Hester, Miss Hyde as Bessy, Louise Thorndyke (soon to join the ranks of professionals) as Lady Honeywood, Wallace Barton as Harry Arncliffe, Charles Lamb as Blenkinsop, and W. W. Lambert as Grazebrook, with, in minor characters, Florence Parker, Ella Inglas, Carrie Frost, William A. Clarke, E. J. Wilkins and Deane Pratt.

On November 28th, Adelina Patti, safely piloted by Henry E. Abbey, gave a concert, singing the waltz song from Dinorah, the well-worn Echo Song, and ending with scenes from Faust, in costume, her Margherita being supported by Signora Paulina Montegriffo as Siebel, Signora A. Bettini as Marta, Pinto as Mephistopheles, and Nicolini (alas!) as Faust.   In the concert we had Salvati and Mlle. Castellan (violin).   According to the Eagle of the following day, Patti's horses were removed from her carriage, and "young gentlemen" of Brooklyn, quite in the old way, dragged the vehicle and its smiling, lovely occupant, to the Pierrepont House.   Abbey must have been pleased, as Barnum was in the Jenny Lind era.   The Eagle was enthusiastic about Patti's acting and her voice — "unquestionably the noblest human voice to be heard in the world today."   Lohengrin, on the 29th, let us down to the usual, with Campanini, Del Puente, Novara, Monti, Climene Kalas and Minnie Hauk.   On December 8th, Mapleson promised

[612]

William Tell, with Prevost, Runcio, Galassi, Valerga, Dotti and Juch. Where, oh! where were the women stars of yesteryear? On December 7th, Reverend Father Sheehy ("late prisoner in a Dublin jail") delivered an address, with the 14th Regiment Band to stir up the *sæva indignatio* of the audience.

On December 9th, a benefit to Colonel W. E. Sinn (I am surprised that he needed it) presented, in the afternoon, the Bijou Opera House artists (Selina Dolaro and Lillian Russell) in The Snake Charmer, and, in the evening, Daly's company in Cinderella at School, and Eugenie Legrand (her second appearance in America) in the sleep-walking scene from Macbeth. Wallack's company, still waiting for the completion of the new Wallack's Theatre, came, on December 12th, in She Stoops to Conquer; on the 13th, in Old Heads and Young Hearts; on the 14th (matinée) in Money. Gilbert, Tearle, Miss Coghlan, and Mme. Ponisi filled the best rôles. On December 15th, Mapleson showed that he had discovered a real prima donna, presenting Aïda, with Campanini, Galassi, Monti, Cobianchi (but where were his contraltos?) and Paolina Rossini. The greatest of *prime donne*, Adelina Patti, returned on December 16th, with $5 top price. The bill ended with the fourth act of Il Trovatore. The "ideal" Patience, by Rice's Opera Company, and with scenery recently used at Booth's Theatre, came to the Academy, on December 19th and 20th, with Eugene Clarke, Henri Laurent, A. W. F. McCollin, Vernona Jarbeau (Angela), Miss M. A. Sanger (Jane), and Francesca Guthrie. On the 22nd, Mapleson's eighth and last performance gave Les Huguenots, with Ravelli, Del Puente, Galassi, Novara (certainly a strong quartette of men), Lauri, Emma Juch and Paolina Rossini.

For one week (December 26th–31st) we were called on for more Patience — this time by the Comley-Barton Company, with Alfred Cellier conducting. In the cast were Lithgow James, Julie de Ryther, Marie Jansen (Patience), Charles J. Campbell (Grosvenor), Louis Pfau, George Gaston (Bunthorne), and Fred Dixon. The Snake Charmer exercised its spells for part of the week of January 2nd–7th, with Selina Dolaro, Lillian Russell, Blanche Chapman, William Gilbert, &c. The week ended (January 6th and 7th) with Corinne and George K. Fortescue (an absurd combination) in The Magic Slipper. The Hanlon-Lees took us (week of January 9th–14th) on their familiar Voyage en Suisse. Quite different was the offering of January 16th, with Rossi in King Lear, and on the 19th, in Hamlet. On January 30th and 31st, William Rignold, George R. Edeson, Ada Neilson, Mrs. J. L. Carhart and Ellie Wilton appeared in Michael Strogoff, as formerly at the Academy across the river.

On February 1st, the Emerald Association gave its forty-fourth annual ball, with, quite appropriately, the music of "Patsy" Gilmore's Band; on the 6th, the Sängerbund were as German in the matter of dancing toes as the Emeralds were Irish. Well, America for the Americans! February 3rd

[613]

found Oscar Wilde lecturing on the English Renaissance. On February 10th, the Brooklyn Amateur Opera Association presented The Pirates of Penzance, with Agnes Lasar as Ruth, Hattie Schröter as Mabel, C. H. Thompson as Frederic, and Charles H. Parsons as the Major-General. And Stoddard began a new series of illustrated lectures — Russia (February 13th and 16th), Spain (27th), Florence and Naples (March 2nd), Rome (10th). The Brooklyn Cecilian ("five hundred voices") was here on February 11th, with Carolina Zeiss, Werrenrath, Alice Judge, Carl Wagner, Charles Pratt, and W. M. Jelliffe (elocutionist). At a private concert (February 14th) of the Apollo Club of Brooklyn appeared Madeline Schiller, Antonia Henne, and Dudley Buck (conductor). Jay Rial's Uncle Tom's Cabin filled a third week (February 20th–25th) as a sort of gauge of Brooklyn's dramatic appreciation. On March 6th, Marion L. Dutcher evidently thought the Academy none too large to hold her ideas on Women of Today.

Mapleson returned, on March 9th, with the fine trio of Campanini, Del Puente and Minnie Hauk, in Carmen, diluted with the watery art of Mlle. Dotti, and, on the 16th, Fidelio was very Italian with Ravelli, Galassi, Novara, Emma Juch and Mlle. Dorani (a Leonore not remembered by ungrateful posterity). Gilmore's Band sonorously held the Academy on the evening of the 17th, in a programme of Irish Music and Poetry involving Albert S. Caswell, James L. Farley, Miss Dillie Barnacle (soprano), and others. On the 21st, the Brooklyn Amateur Opera Association again essayed The Pirates of Penzance, with Emma F. Henry, Agnes Lasar, C. H. Thompson, C. H. Parsons, Mary and Fannie Trigg, &c. Disappointment beset opera-lovers on February 23rd; instead of Les Huguenots, announced, they must accept a Rigoletto, with Runcio, Del Puente, Monti, Lauri and Paolina Rossini. As far as women singers are concerned, I blush, except for Hauk and Rossini, for Mapleson's season. March 29th brought Ingersoll's lecture, What Must We Do to Be Saved? And, on the 30th, Mapleson, indefatigable, tried again with L'Africaine (Ravelli, Galassi, Novara, Dotti, Hauk).

On April 3rd, Franziska Ellmenreich and the Germania actors appeared in Adrienne Lecouvreur. On the 17th, the beloved Etelka Gerster (so sadly missed from the Mapleson forces) sang La Sonnambula, assisted if feebly by Lazzarini, Mancini, Miss Lancaster, Mlle. Arcone and Maina. Mapleson, on the 13th, retorted with the undying Carmen of Campanini, Del Puente, Minnie Hauk and the inescapable Dotti; in this Mme. Lablache substituted as Mercedes, for Mlle. Kalas — an improvement, according to the Eagle. On the 14th, a testimonial to Rafael Navarro brought in Richard Hoffman, the Dudley Buck Quartet, an orchestra of fifty, and, it was hoped in preliminary notes, Antonia Henne. For the benefit of Deane W. Pratt (who acted the James Lewis rôle), the Kemble Society, on the 15th, gave The Big Bonanza. And Clara Louise Kellogg announced for April 18th, a "farewell," with Maria Prasini, Giannini and Ciapini, in Il Trovatore. A sad, sad farewell, as the Eagle of the 19th affirmed:

> Her best friends . . . could but regret her appearance. . . . It were far better had the memory of the noble voice, the charming stage presence and the lyrical attainments of the favorite American prima donna been permitted to linger as a fragrant recollection than that the idol which the imagination held enshrined should be rudely shattered by unwelcome actualities. Last night's performance was not a pleasant one to listen to, and its contemplation is the reverse of agreeable. The house was thin in numbers and cold . . . the truth remains, unpleasant as is its statement, that Miss Kellogg's sun as an operatic singer has set.

Well, we must admit we saw this coming. On April 19th, R. C. Hilliard, C. H. Macklin, Helen Dayton, Nellie Yale and long since forgotten members of the Amaranth Society played London Assurance, for the zest of those who had seen the play at Wallack's. On April 21st the Cecilian Club sang, with Mlle. Martinez, Mrs. Draper, &c. Ingersoll, on the afternoon of the 23rd, pursued his foes with a talk on Talmagian Theology, and, on the 25th, John Boyle O'Reilly lectured on Ireland's Declaration of Independence. On the 28th, by request, dear Etelka Gerster sang in The Barber of Seville, with Perugini as Almaviva, George Sweet as Figaro, Carbone as Dr. Bartolo, &c. On the afternoon of the 29th, C. H. Rivers's dancing exhibition served notice that the season was ending. But end it could not without another week (May 15th–20th) of Uncle Tom's Cabin, this time by Anthony and Ellis's company, including the Memphis University Students and Kate Partington (as Topsy); or without one more bloom of the unfading Amaranth — May 24th — in shape of The Lady of Lyons, with Adelaide May and Wallace Grant as the lovers and W. W. Lambert as the bluff Damas.

Hyde and Behman's, 1881–1882

The Hyde and Behman home of "Variety" re-opened on August 29th, entirely made over, with gold paper on the walls, a new stage, lobbies and boxes renovated, a new drop-curtain, new folding chairs, the latest patent in steamheating, and an installation of electric lighting. The Eagle, on the 28th, believes Hyde and Behman "the first managers to adopt the new light." And the company for the inaugural week also was luminous — the Kernells, Charles Reed, Niles and Evans, Bryant and Hoey, Kitty O'Neil, Minnie Lee, Reynolds and Walling, John E. Henshaw and May Ten Broeck and Jennie Satterlee. Thence we pass on the 5th into a week of the American Four, American Students, Add Ryman, Parker and his dogs, Magee and Allen, Billy Devere, Miss Georgie Bryant, Harry Bryant and the La Rosa Brothers, the show ending with The Uncrushed Lover. Leavitt's Vaudeville Specialty Company filled the week of September 12th–17th, with Dolph Levino and

[615]

Susie Dillon (in Love *vs.* Music), Val Vose, the Ethiopian quartette of Wilson, Sawtelle, Brevarde and Gilmore, Nellie Richards (lyric star), Andy and Annie Hughes (in The Irish Servants), Mlle. Irene and Louis King (acrobats), Sanford and Wilson, Bonnie Runnells, and Andy Collum, with, for conclusion, Malony's Visit. The month ended (September 26th–October 1st) with Watson and Ellis ("musical, vocal, saltatory efforts"), the Novelty Four, Till's Marionettes, Frank Bush, Clara Moore, W. T. Bryant, Alfred Liston, Lizzie Richmond, the Wesleys, Alice Hutchings, and the popular farce, Wrinkles.

The Eagle affords but scant intelligence of this place for October. Nick Roberts's Humpty Dumpty filled the week of October 3rd–8th, and before the month ended we found here the Leotards, Mattie Vickers and Charles Rogers, Mollie Wilson, the farce of McSweeny's Masquerade, John Hart, the Fieldings, Chalet (ventriloquist), Connors and Reilly, the Four Shamrocks, Georgie Kaine, Helene Smith, and the Landis Brothers. Autumn wore to winter (November and December) with visits, generally for a week only, from Annie Hindle, Joe Allen, Morris and Fields, Minnie Lee, Annie Boyd, Lena W. Cole, the Murphys, John Hart, Dan Sully (in Unneighbourly Neighbours), Mulcahy's Racket, Jennie Morgan, the Novelty Four, the Monumental Quartette, the La Rues, Morris and Fields, Charles Glidden, John Gilbert, Kelly and Ryan, Muldoon's Picnic (without Barry and Fay), Charles Reed (negro comedian), Niles and Evans (in Bric-à-Brac), Kitty O'Neil, Lester and Williams, Ferguson and Mack, Watson and Ellis, Lizzie Simms, Miss St. George Hussey, the Martell Family, the Tills, Clara Moore, Lizzie Richmond, the ineradicable Wrinkles, &c. The week of December 12th–17th brought Leavitt's company, including the Davene Family, Sanford and Wilson and others seen here on September 12th. December wended its way to eternity with "turns" by the Boissets, Jeppe and Fannie Delano, George Wood (Ethiopian), Parker and his dogs, Williams and Sully (Ethiopian Picnic), Kelly and O'Brien, the Four-in-Hand, Hallen and Enid Hart (in Billy, the Tailor), John and Maggie Fielding (in The Garden Wall), the Four Emeralds (Gibson, Russell, Kennedy and Conway), Charles Diamond (Milanese minstrel and harpist), Charles and Carrie Moore (on roller skates), Williams and Pickert (clog), Crossley and Elder (Scottish games), Hogan Brothers (in Happy Boys from Borneo), Hines and Blossom (black specialists, in lightning changes), George H. Wood, E. D. Gooding, and Vogler's orchestra.

On January 2nd, Snelbaker's Majestic Combination tried to justify its adjective with Tom E. Murray and Mark Murphy ("monarchs supreme of eccentric Irish comedy"), Erba Robeson, the Vivian Sisters ("English favourites," distinguishable as Bella, Emily and Weavey), "Senator" Charles Banks ("celebrated Son of Momus"), Leonzo (plate spinner and balancer), Virgie Jackson ("charming burlesque artiste"), Little All Right, Varney and

De Bar ("clockworking acrobatic dance team"), Naoni (juggler), and Jennie Ross and various other girls (in Out of Patience). Harry Miner's Combination filled the week of January 9th–14th, with Murphy and Mack and Murphy and Shannon (in Murphy's Dream), Charles and Ella Jerome, Frank Lewis, Carrie Swain, Valjean, the Blaisdell bell-ringers, Billy Carter, Frank Lewis, and the "original" Little Four (Talbert, Mack, and the Carroll Brothers). One sees how combinations of "Variety," were taking to "the road." Tony Denier's Humpty Dumpty came on January 16th–21st, presenting Alford ("the great Miaco") as Humpty Dumpty, George Steele as Pantaloon, George Topack as Harlequin, Laura Miaco as Columbine, and Victoria Worth as the Fairy Queen. For the week of January 23rd–28th we were treated to Sheehan and Coyne, Ferguson and Mack, Willis Cobb and his dogs, Pat Reilly, D. B. Emery and Laura Russell, Luigi dell' Oro, the acrobats, Levantine, Earle and Durand, May Antonio (slack wire), Charles A. Loder (German comique), and the Big Four (Smith, Cronin, Waldron and Martin, in Mrs. Driscoll's Party). Muldoon's Blunders Combination followed (January 30th–February 4th), with Morris and Fields, Mattie Vickers and C. S. Rogers (in Stage Struck), Frank Bennett and Lida Gardner (in Kitchen Domestics), Annie Boyd, Keegan and Wilson, and Little Camilla ("child wonder").

The New York London Theatre Combination (for February 6th–11th) was very strong in the attraction of the American Four (Pettingill, Gale, Dailey and Hoey), T. M. Hengler, J. W. McAndrews, the Novelty Four (John F. and Emma Whitney, Georgie Kaine and Lester Howard, in Rehearsal in the Parlour), Mlle. Baretta (sic) and John Robinson (English, French, Spanish and Italian songs and dances), Hallen and Hart (in Over the Stile), Lizzie Conway, and Jim, the Slasher (with McAndrews and Robinson). The week of February 13th–18th wended its merry way with "turns" by the Clipper Quartette, the Four-in-Hand, Fannie Beane and Charles Gilday, Paddy and Ella Murphy, Charles Heywood (soprano), Keegan and Wilson, and Heywood's farce, Wonders. Nick Roberts's Humpty Dumpty was here, with Grimaldi Ravel, for the week of February 20th–25th, and Frank I. Frayne, in Mardo, or, the Nihilists of St. Petersburg, for that of February 27th–March 4th. Pat Rooney, with Harry Miner's Combination, set March afire (6th–11th), with Carrie Howard, the Stirk Family, Lamont and Ducrow (in The Happy Hottentots), Sharpley and West, Crandall and Eastwood, Katie Rooney and the Coghill (sic) Brothers. For March 13th–18th, Hyde and Behman's galaxy included Watson and Ellis, the Martell Family (bicyclists), John and Louisa Till's Marionettes (in Blue Beard and Humpty Dumpty), Clara Moore, Harry McAvoy and Emma Rogers (in Love in a Horn), Alfred Liston, Alice Hutchings and Wrinkles. The Rentz-Santley Combination was here, for March 20th–25th, in Hazel Haze-L-Kirke, or, the Revenge of the Mascot

[617]

Company.   Manchester and Jennings were among the few men in that rose-bud combination.   March blew out (27th to April 1st) with the Gigantic Novelty Company, including the Horseshoe Four (Ella and Josie Love, Frank B. Carr and J. J. Quinlan, in The Actor's Family), John and Lea Peasley (in Sparking in the Park), the Boissets, Jennie Morgan, Thomas and Lottie Winnett (in Love in Broken German), C. S. Rogers and Mattie Vickers, Weston and Hanson (in So You Say), and the comedy, Bradley's Luck.   It will be seen that Hyde and Behman's had become merely a "combination" house — a scheme far more comfortable for the managers.

I am surprised to find here, April 3rd–8th, Rice's Evangeline, with Blanche Chapman as Gabriel, Charles A. Burke as LeBlanc, Hattie Richardson as Evangeline, George K. Fortescue as Catherine, E. S. Tarr as King Boorlo-boola Gha, Joe W. Harris as the Lone Fisherman, and Charles Sturges as Captain Dietrich.   Thatcher's Minstrels, for April 10th–15th, provided fun by George Thatcher, Hughey Dougherty, Lew Simmons, W. Court-right, John Rice and Harry Wannemacher.   Tony Pastor's company, April 17th–22nd, was strong with Jacques Kruger, Mattie Vickers and C. S. Rogers, the Irwin Sisters, William Carroll, the Musical Four (W. B. Wood, L. S. Beasley, and Morris and Sam Weston) the pretty French Twin Sisters, Lester and Allen, Elise Kruger, Frank Girard, Tony himself, and Fun on the Stage.   And a fine array was that of April 24th–29th — Harry and John Kernell, Bryant and Hoey, Kitty O'Neil, Henshaw and Ten Broeck, McCarthy and Monroe, the Lynn Sisters, Jennie Satterlee, Little Pearl, with the old Muldoon's Picnic to remind us of the absent Barry and Fay.

A changed Muldoon's Blunders Combination presented (May 1st–6th) John T. Kelly and Thomas J. Ryan (Bards of Tara), Harry Morris and Frank Fields (German comedians), the Olympia Quartette, Fannie Beane and Charles Gilday, Frank Bennett and Lida Gardner, Allie Smith and Lizzie Derious, Katie Cooper, the Hogan Brothers (Ethiopians) and Little Camilla.   Snelbaker's Majestic Consolidation (sic) returned for the follow-ing week, and Hyde and Behman's own Star Specialty Company for the week of May 15th–20th presented Till's Marionettes, Pat Rooney, Watson and Ellis, the Vivian Sisters, McAvoy and Emma Rogers, Clara Moore, Katie Rooney, Alice Hutchings, the Martells and the farce, Dinkelspiel's Blunders.   For May 22nd–27th, one might enjoy the art of the Peasleys, George H. Wood, the St. Felix Sisters, Callan, Haley and Callan, Maggie Cline (ever welcome to me, at least), Billy Carter, the De Bars, Lou San-ford and the Four Shamrocks.   The Nick Roberts Carnival Combination presented (May 29th–June 3rd) E. D. Davies (ventriloquist), Bree and Kirwan (in Hard Cheek), Mlle. Catherine ("lady prestidigitateur"), the Jeromes, Ida and Emma Ross, Frank Livingstone (gymnast), the high-stilt Rajade Troupe, Minnie Lee, Capitola Forrest, and Awata Katsnoshin. And thus, thankfully, with an eye toward summer surcease of activities, we

[618]

enter on the rosy month of June, to record performances, successively, of Harry F. Dixey and Mary Leyton, Fields and Leslie, Parker's dogs, Dan Collyer, the Four-in Hand, W. H. Landis and the Powers Brothers (roller-skating), Frank M. Wills (German comedian), Ferguson and Mack (in Political Candidates), John B. Wills and May Adams, Duncan (ventriloquist), Kitty McDermott, Joe Norton (Milanese juggler), Frank Jones and Alice Montague, Master Dunn (jig and reel), Fannie and Jeppe Delano (in Out on a Lark), Dick Hume and Jennie Lindsay, Alice Daily, John Hart, Katie Cooper and Jennie (?) V. Reynolds. The week of June 26th–July 1st gave One Dime, or, the Jockey's Dream, with George Maddox, E. D. Gooding, Annie Ward Tiffany, Edith Sinclair, E. F. Barnes, E. B. Marden and many others. The Eagle of July 3rd announces that the house had closed for the season, and would open only on July 8th, for a benefit to E. D. Gooding, manager of the stage.

GRAND OPERA HOUSE, BROOKLYN, 1881–1882

The Grand Opera House, Elm Place, "opposite 531 Fulton Street," opened on November 14, 1881, as a family theatre, with Barry, Fay and Benjamin Lewis, proprietors, and James Vincent, manager. The attractions included Barry and Fay (in Muldoon's Picnic — a sad loss to Hyde and Behman), the Haleys, the Garnellas, Pauline Batchellor, the St. Felix Sisters and Fields and Hanson. On the 21st, we had Muldoon on the Mississippi, Flora Moore, the Garettas, the French Twins, &c. On the 28th, Barry and Fay enacted A Double Marriage, and Add Ryman threw fun into the olio. Barry and Fay's last week (December 5th–10th) restored Muldoon's Picnic, and gave us J. W. McAndrews, Add Weaver, Kerrigan and McCarthy, the Daytons, the St. Felix Sisters and Nellie Parker. I am utterly weary of these ever-recurring obligations.

That was the end of "Variety." On December 12th came the Grayson Opera Company, in Patience, with Sydney C. Smith as Bunthorne, Frank Pieri as Grosvenor, Helen Grayson as Angela, and Helen Carter as Patience. Next week the Crossen Combination presented A Celebrated Case, with Adele Payne as Madeleine and Adrienne. Cinderella, December 26th–31st, had George K. Fortescue as Clorinda, Lizzie Kelsey as Prince Paragon, Jennie Hughes as Thisbe, Lizzie Bradley as the Fairy Queen, and Hattie Delaro as Cinderella. The Joseph H. Gulick Combination offered for the week of January 2nd–7th Furnished Rooms, with Ethel Tucker, Marion Deming, Marie Legros, J. H. Fitzpatrick, Scott Marble, James Devlin, Sam Bolter, Harry Rich, and Frank Irving, whose names I gladly retrieve from oblivion. The following week (January 9th–14th) brought Buffalo Bill, in Prairie Waif, a glad thing which yielded the stage (16th–21st) to A Raw Recruit (with James S. Maffit, W. H. Batholomew, May Arnold and Belle Arnott).

[619]

Langdon and Allison's Combination carried on (23rd–28th) with Swift and Sure (acted by Minnie Oscar Gray, W. T. Stephens, and their clever dogs, Romeo, Zip and Hero), with Edward and Alice Clark (English high kickers), Tillie Antonio (serio-comic), Isabel Ward, and Ripley and Reade (singers and dancers). Eve, the Saleslady, was, I hope, very refined, during the week of January 30th–February 4th. Sam Devere, for February 6th–11th, gave his familiar Jasper, supported by Richard Quilter, John B. Wills and May Adams, Fannie Francis (is this the Fannie Francis once of Daly's?), John B. Dyllyn and George C. Jordan, some of whom doubtless contributed to the accompanying olio.

And now the Grand Opera House made a new departure, becoming a first-class popular theatre. Mrs. D. P. Bowers appeared (week of February 13th–18th) in Lady Audley's Secret, supported by J. C. McCollom, Walter Lennox, Annie Ward Tiffany, Annie Deland, Edith Sinclair, Coral Leigh and George Thompson. During the week following, Mrs. Bowers and these assistants gave The Hunchback, with, on the 23rd, a Macbeth, acted by Mrs. Bowers and McCollom. Hyde and Behman, apparently renouncing the Standard Theatre, transferred their interests and their actors to the Grand Opera House. Joseph Proctor filled the week of February 27th–March 4th with Nick of the Woods, supported by Frank Roche as Roland, Annie Ward Tiffany as Telie Doe, and Walter Lennox as Young Tom Bruce. I wonder if Brooklyn regarded such antique museum pieces as necessary in a living theatre? Dominick Murray, recently seen amid the velvet upholstery of the Madison Square Theatre, came, for the week of March 6th–11th, in Innocent, with, in other rôles, Roche, Miss Tiffany, Lennox, E. B. Marden, George W. Thompson, Dick Gorman, Annie Deland and Edith Sinclair. One observes that the Grand Opera House maintained regular actors of its own.

J. Z. Little was star of March 13th–18th, in Nuggets, and, for March 20th–25th, in Against the World, or, Saved from the Wreck — surely a provocative title. Our Boarding House was interesting, during the week of March 27th–April 1st:

M. T. Elevator	Leonard Grover	Beatrice	Annie Ward Tiffany
Gillypod	Leonard Grover, Jr.	Mrs. Dalrymple	Virginia Buchanan
Walter	Frank Roche	Betty	Edith Sinclair
Matthew Eligible	Walter Lennox	Mrs. Eligible	Helen Ransom
Joseph Fioretti	G. W. Thompson	Mrs. Colville	Mary Gray
Dr. Shouter	T. E. Jackson	Annie Colville	Coral Leigh

So there are the author of the play and his son, and Virginia Buchanan, ever regarded as indispensable for Mrs. Dalrymple. The company trusted to itself and Pauline Markham (fourteen years earlier with Lydia Thompson) and the strength of The Two Orphans, for the week of April 3rd–8th:

[620]

MILLIE CHRISTINE

HARPER BROTHERS
(ONE-LEGGED DANCERS)

ADMIRAL DOT

KAROLY ORDEY

CHANG, GIANT

AUGUSTA ORDEY

SUSIE RUSSELL

ENID HART

MAGGIE CLINE

Louise	Annie Ward Tiffany	Pierre	Charles Jordan
Henriette	Pauline Markham	La Frochard	Annie Deland
Chevalier	Frank Roche	Countess	Mary Gray
Jacques	G. W. Thompson	Julie	Edith Sinclair
Picard	Walter Lennox	Florette	Coral Leigh
Count	John Armstrong	Marianne	Nellie Yale

And there is Nellie Yale, once Brooklyn's choice amateur, now a professional.

For the following week, Marie Prescott and the regular company (except Annie Ward Tiffany) played Camille (10th–12th), and Led Astray (13th–15th). The Legion of Honour (April 17th–22nd) presented Annie Graham and William H. Griffith, with Roche, Amy Lee and the artists of the theatre. On the 24th, Harry G. Richmond began a week as Josephus Grimwig, in Our Candidate. W. J. Scanlan, for May 1st–6th, gave Friend and Foe, supported by Lennox, Thompson, Miss Tiffany, Annie Deland and Edith Sinclair; and Jeffreys Lewis, no longer the slim, bright-eyed, youthful beauty of the '70s at Wallack's and Daly's, came in, on the 8th, for a week in Two Nights in Rome, Roche, Miss Tiffany and the regulars assisting. For the week of May 15th–20th, J. M. Hill gave the "first performance on any stage" of a play by Edward J. Swartz of Philadelphia — A Square Man, with Ben Maginley as Jack Kenyon, Edward Lamb as Zeck Peabody, Libbie Noxon as Blossom, Meta Bartlett as Milly Thatcher, Blanche Vaughan as Rosanna Brown, Herbert Ayling as the English Tourist, and J. C. Padgett as Hop Thompson. This play we were to meet elsewhere in our journey. The week of May 22nd–27th offered for the benefit of Hebrew refugees, Marie Prescott, Annie Ward Tiffany, and Roche, in Leah, the Forsaken — a fitting choice of play. Only two performances remained. On May 30th, for the benefit of Manager Norton, Marie Prescott appeared in two acts of Ingomar, Jeffreys Lewis recited, as did Oliver W. Wren, Annie Ward Tiffany and Pauline Markham gave the last act of The Two Orphans, George W. Thompson the last act of Rip Van Winkle, and Harry Kennedy displayed the art ventriloquial. On June 3rd, Miss Tiffany took a benefit, with Poor and Proud and Oliver Twist. Rather interesting, this beginning of the Grand Opera House!

STANDARD THEATRE, BROOKLYN, 1881–1882

And here is another new house, or rather old house renewed. The New Standard Theatre was announced to open, on October 10, 1881, with Nick Roberts's Humpty Dumpty; the place was alleged to be under the management of Hyde and Behman, who had, indeed, the week before presented this Humpty Dumpty at their other house. The week of October 17th–22nd proclaimed the establishment as "remodeled from the Old Olympic," and expressly stated that Nick Norton, formerly of the Academy of Music,

[621]

Chicago, "the leading vaudeville house of the country," would be manager. And thus he continued for the season. The performers, on the 17th, included Edward Barnes, Edith Sinclair, the two Haleys, Annie Boyd, Delvan and Tracy, and George W. Thompson — the latter in Yacup. Harry G. Richmond appeared, on the 24th, in Our Candidate, the olio including J. Selbini and Mlle. Lily (in bicycling, juggling, etc.). R. O. Gorman was headliner, for the week of October 31st–November 5th, in Frank Dumont's play, Conrad, or, the Hand of a Friend; on the 7th, Bessie Gray sang in The Mascot. John W. Ransone, on the 14th, began a week of Across the Atlantic. For November 21st–26th, Dominick Murray and Annie Ward Tiffany gave Escaped from Sing Sing, and Frank Bennett and Lida Gardner, in the olio, supplied Kitchen Domestics. On November 28th, E. T. Goodrich and Annie Ward Tiffany were featured, in Grizzly Adams; Sid C. France and Marked for Life had the week of December 5th–10th, with, in the olio, Harry Richmond, George E. Homer, and Georgie Lingard. The Stranglers of Paris (December 12th–17th) presented Miss Tiffany, Rose Lisle and Valentine Love, the olio featuring Charles Glidden and Foster and Hughes. C. W. Barry filled the week of December 19th, in Broken Fetters, supported by Frank Roche and Miss Tiffany, and by an olio including Donnelly and Drew, Daisy Norwood and the Maxwells. The sensational drama of Counterfeit and Richard Gorman's comedy, Rooms to Let, followed (December 26th–31st), with Roche, Miss Tiffany, Harry Amlar, Charles Jordan, Dick Gorman, E. F. Barnes, Otto Burbank and Edith Sinclair in Counterfeit.

California through Death Valley sounds like a gruesome New Year's gift (January 2nd–7th); but I gladly reproduce the *dramatis personæ*, to show the undying elements of Western drama. John Woodard appeared as Bill Williams, the trapper; Frank Roche as Jack Croft, the scout; Annie Ward Tiffany as Fonda, a waif; Charles Jordan as Elder Force, secret agent of Brigham Young; Dick Gorman as John Henry, an emigrant; Otto Burbank as Daniel Knight, a Mormon; Mary Gray (from California) as Betty Eldon; Emma Grant (also from California) as Ruth, an emigrant of the African persuasion; and Little Willette (another from California) as Baby Eldon. F. H. Jackson's play, Married Life, seemed more like home, on January 9th, with William H. Brent, William C. Cameron, Roche, Miss Tiffany, Charles Jordan, Burbank, E. F. Barnes, Coral Leigh and Edith Sinclair. For a Life, or, the Orphan's Trust, presented, during the week of January 16th–21st, W. J. Thompson (the author), Lotta Forrest Thompson, and the lion-dogs, Hero and Hector. Miss Tiffany and Frank Roche gave, for January 23rd–28th, The Child Stealer, the accompanying new farce by Gorman being Love Laughs at Locks (*sic*). For January 30th–February 4th, Roche and Miss Tiffany acted in both A Perplexing Predicament and Lost in London (another perplexing predicament, one might think). The entire regular actors, now so often listed, appeared, February 6th–11th, in

[622]

Forgery, and a musical sketch, A Struggle for a Fortune. On Sunday, the 12th, we had a lecture on Spiritualism, with Nellie Everett, medium.

At this time, Roche, Annie Ward Tiffany and the other actors of the Standard transferred their allegiance to the Grand Opera House, and I found no more for the deserted Standard till March 12th (Sunday), when the "great medium," Goldberg, appeared in Spiritual Manifestations. Again the Eagle wraps the Standard in silence, unbroken for the rest of the season. But, on July 24th, N. S. Wood played The Boy Detective.

German Plays in Brooklyn, 1881–1882

The Germania players still gave performances at the Brooklyn Athenæum — Mamsell Angot, on October 3rd, Unsere Frauen, on the 10th, Der Wildschütz, on the 17th, etc. On November 7th, a triple bill offered Offenbach's Hanni weint, Hansi lacht, Bei Wasser und Brod and Des Löwen Erwachen. Subsequent attractions were Ein glücklicher Familienvater and Hoffanger (November 14th), Friedrich Haase in Der Königslieutenant (December 16th), Der Erbonkel (March 6th), Rosenmüller und Finke (March 9th), Das Stiftungsfest (13th) and Hopfenrath's Erben (16th) — these last four given on nights when the Patti performances at the Germania Theater drove the regular actors from home. Before leaving this section of my puzzle, I must remind the reader of a few German performances at the Brooklyn Academy of Music.

The Brooklyn Sängerbund gave a concert and Theater-Vorstellung, on October 24th, at the Club House, 198-202 Court Street; on November 14th, they met, as we saw, for the benefit of the Michigan sufferers, at the Assembly Rooms of the Academy of Music, with, as aids, Ida and H. Mollenhauer and F. Steins. This Society danced its masked ball, on February 6th, at the Brooklyn Academy of Music. The Brooklyn Männerchor held the Club House; Court Street, on the evening of January 16th. On April 10th, at the familiar Court Street place, the Sängerbund closed its winter season with a concert and an operette, Der Dreizehnte, oder ein Sängertag in Pirna. On the 10th, also, the Brooklyn Quartett Club held a Tanz-Kränzchen at Eugene's Hall, Court and Carroll Streets.

Bunnell's Museum, Brooklyn, 1881–1882

The Waverley Theatre re-opened, on August 29th, with Robert Churchill, a drama by S. Bienenstoke of St. Louis, with a cast including James E. Nugent, S. C. Traverner, Welsh Edwards, George Gaston, Ida Van Courtland, Laura Alberta, &c. I doubt if it lived a week. For the week of September 5th–10th, we were invited to inspect Mabel Ledgerwood's Novelty Queens and four Nautch Dancers.

[623]

On October 10th, the place opened as Bunnell's Museum, with a two-headed lady and a tattooed man. On the stage appeared Dan Nash, the humorous John W. Whiston, Dick Sands, Hartz (magician), E. C. Edwards and Moya Carleton. Thereafter we revelled in the African leopard boy (a good title for a "talkie" of 1937), Mme. Squires, a bearded lady, some Zouave midgets, Millie Christine (the two-headed girl; "above the waist, two persons — below, one person." And "they" speak five languages), Jane and Emma Edwards (in Our Lovers), Baron Littlefinger and Count Rosebud, the Zulus and the Zulu Bride, Italian midgets, an Arabian Giant, Frank Bush, Jessie Warner ("queen of clubs"), Siwelac (queen of the air), Josei Holcombe, Mlle. Antoinette (a "long-haired marvel"), Bingham (ventriloquist), Cheletia (contortionist), and Sawyer ("monarch of musical glasses"). Admission was 10 cents, with cushioned seats for 20 cents. Chang and Nellie Keller (or Keeler), midget, represented extremes of humanity, beginning on November 14th; Chang stayed long. Later in November or in December, Alf Burnett and Helen Nash gave Our Club, or, the Frolicsome Oysters, and Fanny (sic) Wallack, Barney Reynolds, Cora Cardigan (flute), the La Rosa Brothers (French athletes), Palles and Cusick, Nellie Inman, Whiston, J. W. Sharpley and S. S. Smith, the Roman Students, and J. Ross Parker's Megatherian Dog Circus held the stage and the audiences.

A big New Year gift (January 1st–6th) brought Captain Bates and wife (height, seventeen feet; weight, half a ton). January was lavish in freaks — Chemah ("pretty, pigtailed pigmy pet"), Brustad (a Norwegian giant — somehow more fearsome than giants from other parts of the world), Guy Linton, Middleton Brothers, Fred and Ida Mortimer, the La Rosas, Barney Reynolds, Signor Pedanto (the man-fly, who performed on the piccolo, while walking, head downward, from the ceiling), Dan Nash and Moya Carleton (in The Irish Emigrants), Charles Konollman, Schlam ("two minutes of mystery"), Neil Smith's dog circus, and the Carrolls (in The McFaddens). For the week of January 30th–February 4th, Dr. Lynn was to "cut men up and restore them to life," for the "largest salary ever paid to any man." The Carrolls acted Peel Yourself — with no connotative intent toward Lynn.

Bunnell's was now vying with regular "Variety" halls. In February, its stage provided in successive weeks Dr. Lynn, Konollman, Thomas Carter and Lizzie Anderson (character actors), Don Ferreyra, Levanion and McCormick (gymnasts), Chiltrea ("India rubber man"), Dr. Forrest and his dog, Danger, Dan Nash, also the Nova Scotia midget, Middleton's Marionettes, Charles Moore's educated dogs, Elsie Loane (California midget singer), Miss Kingsland ("empress of magic"), Moya Carleton, Cool Burgess and Emma Shelletto (musical grotesques), Major Burke ("master of the musket"), Charles and Carrie Moore, the St. Elmos, &c. March was even more liberal. Humpty Dumpty (for three weeks), the Harper Brothers

[624]

(one-legged song and dance), Harry Swann, Parker's dogs, Cawthorn (*sic*) Brothers, Frank Gibbons, Mason and Lord, the La Porte Sisters, Millie Christine (the two headed lady: *she* dances gracefully; *they* sing sweetly), Val Vose, Master Fox (in Widow Nolan's Goat), Levanion and McCormick, Leopold and Wentworth (gymnasts), the Big Little Three, Mme. Lavely ("the strongest woman in the world"), Singerhoff (Danish violinist), &c. The galaxy of April speeded by with, progressively, Elsie Loane, Ford and Knowles, Nelson and Alma Curry (gymnasts), Lew Baker (Ethiopian), Captain Bates and his large wife, Powers Brothers (magical illusions), the "third volume" of Humpty Dumpty, Carol Lewis, A. Duncan (ventriloquist), the La Porte Sisters, Hartz (magician), the Coloured Troubadours, and farces.

The first week of May gave us Hartz, Japanese Tommy (in imitations of Patti, which I am glad I did not hear), the La Porte Sisters, Murphy and Miles, a tribe of Sioux Indians, Texas Jack (a giant boy), Constantenus, the tattooed Greek, the Quaker City Quartette, and Uncle Tom's Cabin (with Louisiana Jubilee Singers).   May treated us subsequently to W. A. Melville (Ethiopian magician), Ripley and Reade, Helen Courtland, the Winnetts, Japanese Tommy, Charles and Moffett (in Irish Assurance), the Nonpareil Coloured Troubadours, Fred and Josephine Macarte (heavy weight lifters), N. B. Shimer and Flora Bingham (musical comedians), Ellwood (lyric artist), Ferreyra, Sanders (*sic*) and Dean (plantation sketch), Herbert and Joe Cawthorn (*sic*), Texas Jack (the giant boy), a Chinese lady with small feet, a Mammoth Mongolian and wife, Chang, Irene Woodward ("the only tattooed lady in existence"), Miles and Murphy, Parker's dogs, and a version of Uncle Tom's Cabin.   A Trip to Paris and Hanky Panky were in the bills for June 5th–10th, as were Naoni and the Quaker City Quartette.   Later June roses were The Devil among the Tailors, the Onofri Brothers, Maggie Willett, the Tattooed Greek, Sioux Indians, the Parker Twins, &c.   A branch Bunnell's started at Coney Island, and the Brooklyn plant wilted in the heat.

MUSEUMS, BROOKLYN, 1881–1882

The New Museum, 424-426 Fulton Street, advertised in the Eagle its opening for September 19th, with Alf Burnett, Admiral Dot and Major Atom; thereafter I find no trace of it in the record.   But in November the "Great" Dime Museum, 325 Washington Street (it re-opened on November 7th), was exploiting Rhoda, the Herodian mystery, and life-like figures of Guiteau, murderer of Garfield, and murderer of Jennie Cramer, the unfortunate girl whose murder was a major sensation of its day.   Rhoda remained for many weeks, some associates, as time passed, being Japanese Tommy and Charles Walton, in "the famous gendarme duet," Monroe's Cat Circus,

Kurtz (in Chinese, Japanese, Egyptian and Hindoo juggling), Venus ("empress of the aerial wire"), Mlle. Elevard (mind reader), Vanolar (clown), Zobedi Suti (Circassian), a wild Australian boy, Redmond's Funniosities, Chang, &c. In earliest February, the Kentucky giant boy, Amy Howard and Sweeney and Ryan were lures for the curious. The place on February 6th was down as Middleton's Museum, with a Dahomey giant and wild Australian bushmen to vary the delights; the Rice Family of Midgets carried us (February 13th–18th) to the other extreme of rapture.

A Zulu princess, a baby of that race, Zulu chiefs, warriors, and a witch doctor — seven in all — were at Middleton's, for the week of February 20th–25th. Then the Eagle ceased to proclaim the Middleton wares for 1881–82. And were Cheletia and Chiltrea (page 624) two contortionists, or one?

Music and Miscellany, Brooklyn, 1881–1882

There is something mysterious about Mann's Theatre (formerly Temperance Hall, Hamilton Avenue), which opened as a variety theatre, on September 19, 1881, proffered for September 26th–October 1st, Charles Gilday, John Wills and May Adams, Geyer and Mack, Orndorff and McDonald, Amy Nelson, and Ed H. Banker, and then ceased to advertise in the Eagle. J. M Craig's illustrated lecture on China and the Chinese may have drawn the curious, on September 27th, to the Greene Avenue Presbyterian Church. The Club Haus, 198-202 Court Street, was very German, on September 29th, with a Wein Harvest Festival; German, also, was the performance (October 3rd, at the Athenæum) of the Germania Theater players, in whatever is German for La Fille de Mme. Angot. On the 3rd, also, the 13th Regiment opened a fair, at its Armoury, with Harvey B. Dodworth's 13th Regiment Band, and Liberati; on the 10th, John H. Murray's Show began a week at Flatbush and Fifth Avenues. At the old Bushwick Sunday School, on the 12th, John Oakey lectured on Our John, or What Shall We Do with him? — ever a burning problem. On October 13th, in "Parson" Talmage's "Meeting House," "Parson" Beecher's Singers gave an Old Folks Concert. Beginning on Wednesday, October 26th, Blind Tom had four evenings and Saturday matinée, at the Athenæum; on the 25th, Mrs. O. N. Payne and Alice Decevee gave an evening in the church at Willoughby and Tompkins Avenue, and, on the 27th, Nettie Taylor read at the Central Baptist Church, Bridge Street. At the church, Willoughby and Tompkins Avenue, a course of five lectures, inaugurated, on October 14th, by John B. Gough (on Circumstances), was to include Henry Ward Beecher and Mme. Lasar. October 27th opened the Bedford Avenue Baptist Church for Settie Blume, Loretz, Vitale, Ellard and Mrs. Decevee. Professor John Reynolds, from London, "the greatest living mesmerist," was, from October 31st to November 5th, at the Old Bushwick Sunday School.

[626]

November was more richly starred.   At St. John's M. E. Church, Bedford Avenue and Wilson Street, assembled, on November 2nd, Settie Blume and Nella F. Brown, with Hattie Louise Simms, the New York Philharmonic Club, and a semi-chorus (whatever that might be) of male voices.   George Werrenrath announced vocal recitals, at the Long Island Historical Rooms, for Thursday afternoons, November 10th and 17th and December 1st.   In that hall, also, on the 9th, appeared Blanche Roosevelt, Florence Rice Knox, Lazzarini, Carlos Hasselbrinck, Lencioni, W. R. Case (pianist), and Charles E. Pratt (accompanist).   And Dr. Storrs, in his church, was carrying through a series of ten lectures.   On November 16th, a pleasing group made music at the South Congregational Church, Court and President Streets; Mrs. J. K. Draper, Mrs. E. J. Grant, F. L. Ritter, H. S. Brown, Herbert O. C. Kortheuer and E. J. Grant (accompanist) were they.   On the same date, in the Athenæum, the Wallack Amateur Association acted Meg's Diversion. At the Hanson Place M. E. Church, on the 17th, appeared Agnes Lasar, L. Adelaide Bangs (elocutionist), Misses A. L. Jelliffe and M. J. Meacham (pianists), Frank E. Bowen (humourist), the Brunswick Quartet, J. H. Rieger (xylophone), H. E. Hand (organ) and F. W. Meacham (accompanist).   On the 17th, also, Settie Blume and A. S. Wightman read, and Artelyea Mergell sang, in the North Reformed Church.   On the 22nd, J. S. Burdett, at "Our Mission," 416 Adelphi Street, entertained, and the Plymouth Church Choir, on November 24th, invaded the Tabernacle for an Old Folks Concert; on the same evening (it was Thanksgiving), the Pilgrim Chapel housed J. S. Burdett, A. R. Carrington ("original drummer boy of Shiloh"), John F. Nevins (banjo) and F. Intropodi (accompanist).   And, as if we could not even thus be sufficiently thankful, the Social Literary Union acted, at Bedford Hall, Gilbert's amusing The Wedding March.   Henry Mollenhauer hired the Athenæum for a concert of his pupils, on November 30th.   At Westminster Church, on December 1st, the Mother Goose Opera may have amused, and, at Music Hall, on the 3rd, Professor Richards gave a matinée for children, on The Wonder World; ever we try to interest children — as if they could not entertain themselves.   C. Mortimer Wiske, on the 13th, at the Hanson Place Baptist Church, exploited the choir of that edifice, the New York Philharmonic Club and a chorus of a hundred.   On the 14th, the Music Hall proffered the Brunswick Glee Club and a lecture by James McDermott on Irish Poets.   And I find I have passed by Mrs. Jarley's Waxworks, on December 7th, at Music Hall.   At Styles Hall, Fulton Street and Bedford Avenue, appeared at a date unspecified in the mid-December Eagle, Mrs. J. M. Bogle, Emma Wilkinson, John E. Morgan (tenor), Fred F. Steeb (baritone), and the Bedford Vocal Society of male voices, with Octave Whittaker conducting.   On the 22nd, Remenyi fiddled for the Y. M. C. A., in Music Hall.   Beginning on December 24th, C. E. Perrine's Ideal Dramatic and Comedy Company gave at the Music Hall two performances daily of Cinderella. And the Ellis Family close (for us) December, on the 29th, at the Temple (formerly the Rink).

And January? From the 9th to the 25th, W. F. Apthorp gave six lectures on The Growth of Music from St. Ambrosius to Wagner — the Historical Rooms housing the treat; at Music Hall, on the 11th, the Yale Glee Club also did what it could, guilelessly, for music. On the 12th, at the Nostrand Avenue M. E. Church, appeared Henry Eyre Browne (organ), Etta I. Bailey (piano), Jennie Crocker (soprano), Maggie Stewart (elocutionist), Fred Harvey (tenor), and Giuseppe Vitale (violin). This was to "exhibit" the new organ. On the 14th, one could have attended at its Armoury a parade of the 23rd Regiment, or a concert and masquerade of the Scandinavians, held at Novelty Hall, 611 Fulton Street. A busy 17th of January displayed the humours of A. P. Burbank at Music Hall; the Fisk Jubilee Singers at the Hanson Place Baptist Church; and the glories of the New York Vocal Sextette, Hattie Louise Simms, Ellard and Bray, in Dr. Cuyler's Church. Also Allan Latham's Illuminated Recital brightened the Johnson Street M. E. Church. And the Brooklyn Heights Parlour Skating Rink advertised throughout January. In later mid-January (18th), a concert at the Washington Avenue Baptist Church promised Charles Roberts, Jr., the Dudley Buck Quartet Club (William Dennison, Fred W. Ritter, Fred Ingraham and Henry S. Brown) and J. H. Brewer (accompanist). On January 25th, at the Hanson Place Baptist Church, Clementine and Agnes Lasar, M. Louise Stewart and J. H. Brewer made a pleasant evening of music; the same evening promised at the Adelphi Academy Nella Brown and Mrs. James Boyle. The 26th "exhibited" a new organ in the First Baptist Church, Pierrepont and Clinton Streets, revealing also the organ-art of George W. Morgan, Henry Eyre Browne and W. Southwick, along with the cornet endurance of M. D. Bouton. At Music Hall, on the 27th, Kennedy re-appeared "after an absence of thirteen years," in an evening of Scottish song; with him were Helen, Marjory, Maggie and Master John — Kennedys all, and all more or less musical. That same 27th found the Gilbert Society acting, at the Athenæum, Not such a Fool as He Looks, the cast including Mrs. Charles Bellows, Jr., Mrs. Agnes Dougall, Mrs. Nellie Yale, Mrs. Eva Watkins (where was the rosebud garden of amateur girls?), J. W. Noble, W. B. Vernam, C. H. Canfield and George Sammis. At the Throop Avenue Church, on the 30th, James L. Farley gave An Evening with Dickens; another blessing of that date was the acting by the Clifton Amateurs, at the Athenæum, of H. J. Byron's play, Old Sailors. And the 30th lured with a third call in a concert at the First Baptist Church, Pierrepont and Clinton Streets, at which were to appear Mrs. William G. Morgan (pianist), the Dudley Buck Quartet and Jenny Claus (violinist), all for sweet charity. Twice blessed also was the 31st: at Music Hall, for the Garfield Monument Fund, we were promised Harry Livingston (prestidigitateur) and W. E. Nickerson (tenor) — a promise more polysyllabic than irresistible; and, for the benefit of Ira H. Moore, the Athenæum staged amateur showings of The Merchant of Venice and Two Bachelors. Brooklyn loved her amateurs more than I do. On the 30th and 31st the Fisk Jubilee Singers were at Plymouth Church.

This was but bare sustenance for the eager appetite. On February 2nd, however, Barnum lectured at the New York Avenue Methodist Church, on Mother Goose; and the afternoon of the 3rd found Joseffy brightening the Historical Society Rooms. On the 6th, at the York Street M. E. Church, was contrived a concert for Theodora Linda Da Acosta, the seven-year-old Brooklyn "vocalist"; and, lest Ingersoll should think he could have it all his own way, George R. Wendling, on the same evening, held forth at Music Hall, on Ingersollism. Kennedy's A Nicht wi' Burns was at Music Hall, on February 9th, and A Nicht wi' the Jacobites, on the 10th. On the 10th, at Bedford Hall, the Burton Dramatic Club acted Sweethearts and The Chimney Corner, certainly an harmonious blend in titles. February 15th proffered a double joy: a concert of the Young Men's Philomathian Society, in the Plymouth Church Lecture Room, with Clementine Lasar Studwell, and Nettie and Belle Cooke; and a testimonial to Agnes Lasar, in the Historical Society Rooms, also presenting Clementine Lasar Studwell, Burdett, the Dudley Buck Quartet, and John H. Brewer. In mid-February (16th), the Young Men's Catholic Association of St. Charles Borromeo gave Scene in a Manager's Office and The Serious Family. On the 21st, at St. James's Church, Rossini's Stabat Mater, under direction of E. J. Fitzhugh, enlisted the New York Vocal Sextette (Christine Dossert, Emma Wilkinson, George Ellard, Charles H. Thompson, Edwin W. Bray and Ivan E. Morawski), with the choir of the church, and a chorus of fifty. At the Tabernacle, on the 22nd, appeared Belle Cole, Nettie Taylor, Jardine and the Dudley Buck Quartet. Another promenade concert of the 23rd Regiment occurred on the 25th, doubtless to the delight of maidens long since (1939) turned to dust. On February 27th, at Plymouth Church, Mrs. Helen Norman (solo contralto of the choir) had her concert, with the assistance of Isidora Martinez, George Werrenrath, Fred Archer, Carlo Orlandini, and others. Many church concerts involving merely local church talent I have omitted. But I give the concert of the New York Philharmonic Club, also listed for the 27th, with Lena Bungert and Alice R. Decevee, at the South Bushwick Reformed Church. There, on the 22nd, the ubiquitous Reynolds had, in mesmerism, celebrated Washington's Birthday.

On March 2nd, at the Athenæum, occurred the début as a public reader of Carol Edwards, pupil of Gabriel Harrison; Susie L. Tooker sang. On the 6th, at the ever-receptive First Baptist Church, appeared Hattie Louise Simms, George Werrenrath, Fred Steins, Hasselbrinck and George Magrath (pianist). On March 9th, also, at the Brooklyn Institute, Maggie Mitchell (soprano), Tillie Crane and James L. Farley displayed their talents, under the auspices of Fulton Lodge, No. 2, 140, Knights of Honour. On the 9th, the Athenean Society acted Engaged, at the Music Hall; and A. P. Burbank appeared on the same platform, on the 13th, for the Y. M. C. A. Dr. Maynard, at the Long Island Historical Rooms, mitigated the rigours of Lent with lectures on Constantinople (March 18th), Spain (25th) and Greece (April 1st) — quite anticipatory of the cruises of the 1930s. On March 16th he had delivered Jerusalem, at Masonic Hall, Flatbush. At the Athenæum, on March 20th, Company K, 13th Regiment, gave an amateur minstrel show; on the 22nd, the pupils and teachers of Henry Mollenhauer's College of Music held forth at the Athenæum; on the afternoon of the 25th, at Music Hall, the children's operetta, The Land of Nod, may have roused the young; and the Clifton Amateur Association at the Athenæum, on the 23rd, may have sent auditors by anticipation to that same land of nod, with Dearest Mamma and The Two Buzzards. On the 24th, at the Simpson M. E. Church, one might have enjoyed the art of Settie Blume, Emily Spader, Emma Wilkinson, the Meigs Sisters, Gaston Blay (violin), J. M. Loretz, Jr. (organist), and Paul Tidden (accompanist). Blay and Tidden are unfortunate names for a public career. On the 26th, at St. Stephen's Church, Stabat Mater enlisted Maggie Mitchell, Mrs. R. B. Hall, Rosa Penner, H. Bersin, and G. Prehn. Joseffy was at the Historical Society Rooms on the afternoon of March 31st and the evening of April 4th. On the 31st, also, the Y. M. C. A. presented at Music Hall the Royal Handbell Ringers. I recur to March 25th, when H. S. Renton delivered, at the South Bushwick Church, his lecture, A Night and a Day in a Volcano. On April 13th, that same shrine revealed the art of Emily Spader and Priscilla Whittingham. And the Sunday School Rooms, attached, allowed Mrs. Alonzo Foster, on the 19th, to read, with Lida Laws (pianist) and Nettie McEwen (soprano) to add to the exhilarating delight of the audience.

De Cordova, a lingering laugh, gave, on March 27th, at Unity Church, Classon Avenue, That Dog Next Door; and Florence Rice Knox was featured for a concert, on April 6th, at the Classon Avenue Reformed Church. April 12th gathered in Westminster Church Francis F. Powers, Eugene Oudin, George Ellard, Marie Geist, Miss Bangs (reader), Morris Parkinson and Annie McCollum (mezzo-soprano), a goodly array for a church function. On April 13th, at Music Hall, appeared, under auspices of the Fountain Gun Club, Mrs. J. K. Draper, Emmie L. Meyer, the English Glee Club (Ellard, Bray, McPherson and Coombe), the Diller Quartette of instrumentalists, and George W. Morgan; and, on the 18th, Miss Bangs read at Historical Society Hall, assisted by Francis F. Powers, Alice Lansden (contralto), and Morris Parkinson (accompanist). Plymouth Church, on the 19th, displayed a broom drill by twenty young ladies, fairy garlands by forty girls, a grotesque play of Mother Goose by twenty-five boys, and

[630]

Kate Greenaway plays by the infant class; also Oscar Wilde, Jr., with a new poem. That is how they used to keep the young in churches. On the 25th, Plymouth Church was again alight for a concert to Emma S. Howe, with the New York Philharmonic Club, Nella F. Brown, Florence Rice Knox and Joseffy—fine indeed! On the same 25th a broom drill was executed at Music Hall, and Settie Blume, Christine Dossert, Emma Wilkinson and Perlee V. Jervis fitted into a programme less sweeping in its demands. On the 27th, the Lambert Family were at Rivers's Academy. Lola, or, the Miller's Daughter, by Pauline B. Hercht, a Brooklyn girl, was tried, on the 26th, at the Athenæum; and equally dubious seems the offering of the 28th, at Music Hall—J. R. McCay's "Popular" comedy, The Magnet. In this connection I may say that the Eagle of April 23rd assures us that the Gilbert Dramatic Association had just finished its season, during the course of which, since November 22nd, it had presented The Marble Heart, Not Such a Fool as He Looks, All that Glitters is not Gold, Tom Cobb and Money. Nellie Yale was among the performers, and I sincerely hope "a good time was had by all," including the audience. I am intrigued by the Ujiji Students, who, on May 13th, gave a minstrel show at the Athenæum; certainly a rose by any other name than Ujiji would not be so odd or so provocative.

Thus I come to mid-May, and find Kennedy's Songs of Scotland listed for the 15th, at Music Hall; the Ellis Family, on the 18th, at the Willoughby Avenue Baptist Church; and a concert, also on the 18th, at St. Peter's Academy, with Isidora Martinez and others. "Miltonian" Tableaux thrilled, on the 15th, 16th and 18th, at Pilgrim Chapel. Barnum's Biggest Show on Earth, Jumbo, 22 Elephants, a Baby Elephant, Chariot Races, Che-Mah (Chinese dwarf), a four legged girl, who might have spared two of her legs to a legless man also in the show—lo! the delights of the spectacle, for the week of May 22nd. And Blind Tom was at the Athenæum, on the evenings of May 25th and 26th. Many strawberry festivals made a succulent spring. By late May Bauer's West Brighton Hotel began its concerts, and, on June 4th, Gilmore's Band again meant to many the best part of Manhattan Beach. June 5th–12th brought to the Athenæum the Williams Standard Opera Company, in Patience; on the 6th, the Eagle declared that certain of the Young Apollo Club were in the cast. But the beaches alluringly called us. Regular concerts at Brighton Beach began on June 10th, with Conterno's Band, and on July 8th and subsequently fireworks flamed up in front of the West Brighton Hotel. On July 6th (postponed from the 4th), Manhattan Beach promised in fireworks The Destruction of the Spanish Armada—the sort of thing they did there very impressively indeed. And, on July 11th, Frank A. Gibbons, "king of aerial artists," was to descend from the dome of Bunnell's Opera House, Coney Island, a height of 175 feet, "out into the rolling billows," 350 feet oceanward. A testimonial to Levy gladdened

[631]

Brighton Beach on August 23rd. Meantime, in Prospect Park, Conterno gave Saturday afternoon concerts, sylvan and soothing.

BROOKLYN PHILHARMONIC, 1881–1882

Overlooking so far as possible the preliminary orchestral rehearsals of the society, I shall confine myself, if possible, to the second rehearsal and the concert. On November 18th and 19th, the programme consisted of Beethoven's Eroica Symphony; Campanini in *Il Mio Tesoro* (which he must have sung exquisitely) and in the romance from Euryanthe; Brahms's Academic Festival Overture (new); Madeleine (*sic*) Schiller in Liszt's adaptation of Schubert's Fantasia, opus 16; and the ballet music from Rubinstein's Nero (new). The second major rehearsal and concert gave (December 16th and 17th) Schumann's Rhenish Symphony, scenes from Alceste (with Galassi, Miss Schell and Emily Winant); the overture to The Flying Dutchman and an air from the opera (sung by Galassi); the procession and chorus from Goldmark's The Queen of Sheba; and Beatrice and Benedick (by Berlioz, played from manuscript, and with Misses Schell and Winant). The programme on January 11th, 13th and 14th included Haydn's Surprise Symphony, Liszt's second piano concerto (with Joseffy), and Beethoven's Fourth Symphony; at the concert, Joseffy changed to Mozart's A major concerto.

The next early rehearsal gave us Schubert's Unfinished Symphony, Jenny Claus in a violin concerto, the introduction to Act III of Cherubini's Medea, and Liszt's Dante Symphony; for the final rehearsal and concert (February the 17th and 18th), Miss Cary sang (as at that time only she in America could sing) O Pardon Me, and *In Questa Tomba*. The first rehearsal (March 8th) of the fifth concert presented Mozart's Symphony in E-flat; Mrs. E. Aline Osgood in the cavatina from Euryanthe; George Magrath in a concerto for the piano, by Rubinstein; the prelude to Tannhäuser, and the overture to Schumann's Genoveva — a programme repeated at the concert. On April 12th, we had Mendelssohn's Scotch Symphony, Joseffy in Chopin's piano concerto, No. 2, F minor, opus 21, and Beethoven's Fifth Symphony. The last rehearsal and concert, April 21st and 22nd, brought scenes from Das Rheingold and Siegfried's Death (with Hattie Schell, Toedt, Amalia Wurmb, Antonia Henne, Oscar Steins and F. Remmertz), and Beethoven's Fifth Symphony.

NOVELTY THEATRE, BROOKLYN, E.D., 1881–1882

The popular Novelty Theatre, in the eastern district of Brooklyn, inaugurated its new campaign on August 29, 1881, with The Banker's Daughter, cast as at the Grand Opera House, Manhattan, during the two weeks preceding; suffice it now to say that the leading actors were Joseph Whiting,

Adele Belgarde and Mr. and Mrs. Charles Walcot, the younger. The George Adams Company followed, on September 5th, with Humpty Humpty; My Geraldine (with Emily Rigl) came from Haverly's for the week of September 12th–17th. James A. Herne's Hearts of Oak drained our sympathies for the week beginning September 19th. Kiralfy's Around the World in Eighty Days filled the next week (September 26th–October 1st), with Adelaide Cherie, Mattie Earle, E. A. Locke, E. S. Tarr, Mlle. De Rosa, &c. October 3rd brought The Tourists in a Pullman Palace Car. Fanny Davenport, seen the week before at the Brooklyn Park Theatre, came to the Novelty, on October 10th, with the same repertoire: The School for Scandal (10th and 12th), As You Like It (11th and 13th), London Assurance (matinée, 12th), Leah (14th), Camille (matinée, 15th), and London Assurance and Oliver Twist (evening, 15th). Deacon Crankett, with Maginley, followed for the week of the 17th. Hazel Kirke, fresh from Haverly's Brooklyn Theatre, came to Williamsburgh, on October 24th, and, if one could believe it, out of the past, on October 31st, came Mrs. G. C. Howard, as Topsy. On November 7th, 8th and 9th, Baker and Farron acted in Chris and Lena, and changed, on the 10th, 11th and 12th, to Foreigners, or, Up Salt Creek, which we saw, later, in Manhattan. The Strategists provided the fun and excitement for the week of November 14th–19th. Fun on the Bristol, with John F. Sheridan, began a week on the 21st. Lillian Cleves (no longer announced as Lillian Cleves Clark) presented, on the 28th, Only a Farmer's Daughter, her assistants including Richard Foote, Elliott Barnes and Bertha Welby. De Wolf Hopper re-emerged, on December 5th, with One Hundred Wives.

Annie Pixley and M'liss gave us, on the 12th, a touch of Bret Harte's West, and, on the 19th, Frank Mordaunt tried Old Shipmates, seen in the following May at the Fourteenth Street Theatre. Denier's Humpty Dumpty made Christmas joy (December 26th–31st), followed, on January 2nd, by Willie Edouin's Sparks, in Dreams, fresh from a week at Sinn's Park Theatre. Haverly's Mastodon Minstrels filled the week of January 9th–14th. Kate Claxton, for a wonder, appeared, in the following week, in actually three plays — The Two Orphans (January 16th, 17th and 18th), The Double Marriage (19th and 21st, matinée and evening), and for her benefit, on the 20th, Frou-Frou, the last of which we do not usually associate with her fame. In her company were Marie Wilkins, Florence Robinson, Mary Drake, Josie Batchelder, E. F. Thorne, C. A. Stevenson, H. B. Phillips, H. F. Taylor, and R. J. Dustan. On January 23rd came Daly's travelling company, in Cinderella at School; Jeffreys Lewis, a rather waning attraction in our theatre, though very popular in California, appeared, on January 30th, in Maude Granger's old rôle of the Corsican, in Two Nights in Rome. Joseph Murphy divided the following week between Kerry Gow (February 6th, 7th, 8th) and Shaun Rhue (9th 10th, 11th); his company included

[633]

Charles Abbott, Julia Stewart, Libbie Noxon, Harry Harwood, Charles O'Brien and Belle Dickson.   M. B. Curtis, in Sam'l of Posen, seen the week before at Haverly's, moved by easy stages, on February 13th, to the more easterly Novelty; All the Rage began on the 20th.

The Galley Slave struggled on, in the week of February 27th–March 4th, to be succeeded, on the 6th of March by the genial humours of Denman Thompson, in Joshua Whitcomb, seen the week before at the Brooklyn Park. W. H. Gillette and The Professor, on the 13th, moved over from Haverly's Brooklyn Theatre, and, on the 20th, the Florences came from the same house, dividing the week between The Mighty Dollar and The Ticket of Leave Man.   On March 27th, Daly's travelling company gave The Passing Regiment.

The World, having occupied so many theatres, rolled its exciting scenes, on April 3rd, into the Williamsburgh Novelty; and, on the 10th Neil Burgess moved Widow Bedott from the Brooklyn Park; and, from the same theatre, on the 17th, came the beautiful Mary Anderson, as Juliet, to play successively Parthenia (18th), Evadne (19th), Julia (20th), Galatea (21st, and matinée, 22nd), and Berthe, in The Daughter of Roland (evening, 22nd) — a noble list and an essentially noble, if not always consummately artistic, actress.   Genevive Ward and Forget Me Not made interesting the week of April 24th–29th, and Sol Smith Russell, in Edgewood Folks, brought in, on May 1st, a touch of the quaint and the lovable.   Fairfax, which we had almost forgotten, had the week of May 8th–13th, and, on the 15th, came the delightful Emmet, in Fritz in Ireland.   Under the management of J. M. Hill, A Square Man, on May 22nd, presented Ben Maginley, Ed Lamb, Herbert Ayling, Libbie Noxon, and Meta Bartlett; it was another stillborn child of hope.   On the 29th, the Fay Templeton Opera Company officiated, of course in La Mascotte.   On June 7th, Nellie Yale, one of the numerous Brooklyn amateurs gone professional, appeared in the sleepwalking scene from Macbeth, and part of the fifth act of The Hunchback — these constituting parts of a benefit for the South Baptist Church.

GERMAN PLAYS IN WILLIAMSBURGH, 1881–1882

The Turn-Halle, Williamsburgh, offered, as its first "sacred concert," Krieg im Frieden, acted by Schimke-Hermann, Frau Bersing-Hauptmann, Frl. Fiebach, Frl. Brandmann, Karl Meyer, Frau Lube, Schönfeld, &c.   On Sunday, October 9th, came the Thalia Theater Company, with Jenny Stubel, in Die Glocken von Corneville.   Subsequently East Brooklyn heard at Turn-Halle Dorf und Stadt (October 23rd), Die Näherin (with Marie Geistinger — November 6th), Lumpaci Vagabundus (December 17th), Die eine weint, die and're lacht (January 15th), Preciosa (for the re-entry of Frau Henriette Rode-Peters, on January 29th), Die beiden Waisen (Febru-

[634]

ary 26th, with Frau Jansen replacing Frau Rode-Peters as the helpless Louise), Rose Michel (March 11th), and possibly others that escaped my attentive eye.   Latterly F. Rode had been master of the show.

BERRY'S BROADWAY THEATRE, WILLIAMSBURGH, 1881–1882

This far from important house re-opened, on August 22nd, with a new minstrel scene, and with F. A. McClane, George Harris, the Delmannings, J. C. Vincent, Grace McClane, Sweeney and Mott, Bryant and Belmont, and "ten beautiful young ladies."   The lack of quality is apparent.   The minstrel scene for August 29th–September 3rd was The Picnic; the olio included Frank and Fannie (sic) Davis, Nellie Hague, Tommy Ryan, Lord and Lovely, Dwyer and Kingsley, Frank and Grace McClane, and concluded with Our Hash House.   Cooper Brothers, "Professor" Gorman, Reilly and Collins, Fred Wilson, Morgan and Farrell (these two in Slattery's Boarding House) constituted the undistinguished offering of September 5th–10th. Thereafter, in September, each perhaps only for a week's visit, came Delvan and Tracy, Gus Hill, Grace Arnold, the Dutch Four (Dwyer, Kingsley, Delmore and Lang), the Barrett Brothers and The Black Statue (12th–17th); Conway and Egan, May Adams, the Three Heaney (sic) Brothers, Lottie Hoffman, Tierney and Owens, Grace and Frank McClane, Laura Harris, George Harris, Scat, Cats, and McClane's play, Society, or, Married in the Dark (19th–24th).   I found in the Brooklyn Times no more Berry's after September 30th, till October 15th (Saturday) when it re-opened with Edwin Blanchard (in The Dumb Boy of Manchester), McClane (in The District Telegraph), John L. Manning (trapeze), Jennie Sutherland (vocalist), Altie Alden ("vocal gems"), and La Rosa Brothers (acrobats).   The "new and talented" stock company certainly has sent no ripples down the ages; but, for history's sake, I record their names — Margaret Tennent, Cora Richmond, Fanny Fuller, Thomas Frampton, Edwin Young, J. W. Macready, Chris Clayton and E. Sheppard.   Denier's Humpty Dumpty Troupe appeared on October 24th–29th, along with Adelina Gasparini in Meg, or, a Mother's Devotion.   Fanny Herring in Little Buckshot was listed for October 29th, but I caught no echoes after latest October from this gasping, sickly concern.

The issue of the Brooklyn Times for March 28, 1882, advertised Berry's Broadway Theatre as open every evening and on Tuesday and Saturday afternoons.   It was "open again under the management of Miss Belle Berrie," with two three-act dramas, Ace of Hearts, or, the Orphan Heiress, and My Brother, or, a Life for a Life.   There was also some "Variety." For the week of April 3rd–8th we were promised Tommy and Lottie Winnett in a three-act Deep Water, Kitty Thomas and her trained doves, Mons. Bushnell, "Professor" Häfter, Big and Little Clark, and Belle Berry (sic).

[635]

Maggie Weston's Dan Maloney's Raffle figured for April 10th–15th. Miss Weston remained; I next find her (April 24th–29th) in D.D., or, Dora, the Detective, the "olio" then presenting Josephine Walby, Lizzie Mowbray, John Hogan, and Holmes and Hart ("the funny mokes"). For May 1st–6th, Dan Maloney's Nomination was promised. Great was the vogue of Harrigan and Hart, and many were their imitators! But Dan Maloney's Nomination was not yet ready, and Colonel Robinson's Humpty Dumpty Troupe, with John and Connie Denier substituted for it, during the first week in May. When, on May 15th, that Nomination was at last effected, the name of Berry disappeared from the Broadway Theatre, and Maggie Weston was down as "lessee and proprietress." In her offering were Charley Worley, the Four-of-a-Kind, Annie Worley, and J. W. Macready. Rightmire was to appear for May 22nd–27th, in The Two Wanderers. The next I heard of the Cinderella house was on June 17th, when it was again to open — this time with the Zanfretta Pantomime Troupe, ten in number, including Emma, Alexander and George Zanfretta, George Kane (clown), the Original Big Little Three (Callan, Buckley and Callan), Ada Castleton and Ada Forrester (*sic*). The Times advertises this only twice (June 17th and Monday, the 19th). The place piped up again in the Times for the week of July 3rd–8th, with Charles L. Howard as Aunt Keziah, in Mrs. Whitcomb (an attempt, I fear, to cash in on the success of Denman Thompson); Little Doris, aged three, and Minnie Doyle were part of the show. And that is all for a place apparently successful the year before.

WILLIAMSBURGH MISCELLANY, 1881–1882

The eighth Cannstatter Volksfest shall by antecedent custom start us, on September 4th, 5th and 6th, rushing to Weber's Myrtle Avenue Park; the Schwaben Folksfest followed on the heels of this activity, beginning for four days on September 11th, at Ridgewood Park, under auspices of the Schwäbischer Sängerbund. And Hasenzahl's Orchestrion Hall continued its Saturday night concerts, assistants on September 11th including Lew Smith (Irish comedian), Amy Fay (serio-comic), Dan Birch ("Brooklyn's comic and motto singer") and Blanche De Vere (sketch artist). The Hyers Sisters Combination invited us indoors, on September 8th, at Germania Hall, Leonard Street and Montrose Avenue. This very meagre September (President Garfield's death postponed many entertainments) was followed by a full October, beginning on the 3rd, at the Lyceum, with the "original McEvoys, in An Evening with the Poets and Peasantry of Ireland," and continuing, on the 5th, with a performance in the same hall of Lady Audley's Secret and Withered Leaves, the amateurs participating including Priscilla Whittingham, Fanny Lawrence, Eleanor Person, Clifford L. Rowe, Robert E. L. Wells and Charles L. Robinson, not all known to our pen. On the 16th, Caste was scheduled at Turnhalle by the Souvenir Social and Dramatic Union; Military Hall, on the same evening housed a concert of minor importance, stressing Zimmermann's orchestra and Henry Buehl. On the 23rd, the Franz Abt Sängerbund had a concert in Teutonia Hall. The Drummond Family held the Lyceum, on October 25th and 27th; at All Souls' Church, on the 26th, appeared Nella Brown ("queen elocutionist of America"—ye gods!), Florence Rice Knox, Mrs. James W. Bogle (formerly Miss Beardsley), Mortimer Wiske, and McGrane Coxe. The Church of Christian Endeavour had housed, on the 25th, a panorama of Solomon's Temple and Jerusalem, Professor D. Heagle lecturing. This sort of thing leaves the eager reader cold.

November was too busy for words—my words, at least. On the 7th, at Dr. Porter's church, was promised a fine aggregation of talent, embracing Isidora Martinez, Settie Blume, Mrs. E. J. Grant, Carl Dufft and Mme. Chatterton-Bohrer. Reynolds, the mesmerist, hired the Ninth Street Presbyterian Church, for November 5th, 6th and 7th; or possibly the church hired him. On the 10th, Florence Auld, as people were beginning to say, "elocuted" (the language needs that word) at the Lee Avenue Baptist Church, tableaux also figuring before darkness descended. The Zoellner Männerchor and the Arion concert at Turnhalle (*sic*) fell on the same night. On the 12th, at Mussler's Hall, Marcy Avenue and Walton Street, a testimonial to Sam Collyer, veteran boxer, brought out a sparring, minstrel and variety entertainment. The Zoellner concert, on the 13th, at Masonic Temple, was enriched by the art of Mme. Raberg, Jerome Lenoir and Carl Steinbuch. On the same evening, Grattan's Panoramic Mirror of Ireland reflected, let us hope, an audience at the Lyceum. John Reynolds, mesmerist, was at the First Presbyterian Church for two weeks (November 14th–26th); I confess I am a bit surprised at the apparent commercialising of what were then called holy edifices. But Reynolds spent a week, in December, at Liberty Hall, Gates and Nostrand Avenues. A minstrel show by the Brunswick Club went to the secular Lyceum, on the 18th. A concert, on the 24th, at St. Luke's M. E. Church, presented Jennie and Lizzie Figgis, S. N. Leach (baritone) and other local lights; we had readings by Murdoch ("of Philadelphia") on the same evening at the Christian Endeavour Church. On the 24th, also, at Smithsonian Hall, Jacob Aberle's Minstrels from New York, played, according to the Times of the 25th, before a "small audience," afternoon and evening. A mesmeric entertainment with Reverend Charles P. McCarthy was listed for the 24th (Thanksgiving) and 25th, at Wright's College, Fourth Street and Broadway. I regret that I cannot supply an exact date for a German-English Concert, at Masonic Temple, with one hundred voices from five united German church choirs of New York, Brooklyn, Newark and New Rochelle; I pass to a concert (December 5th) at the Lee Avenue Baptist Church, with the Philharmonic

[637]

Assembly and Daisy Murdoch. I spoke a few lines back of the vast number of lectures in Williamsburgh churches; November reeked with concerts in the same pulpits, leaving me with the idea that every Williamsburgher was expected to attend at least one concert a night. Of course I mention only those entertainments that enlisted talent of more than purely neighbourhood acclaim. Perhaps I should mention the fact that the Reverend Dr. Newland Maynard gave, in November, at St. Paul's Episcopal Church, or, in December, at the Central M. E. Church, a series of illustrated lectures on travel. And, in December, the church fairs and festivals! And dances by "Societies" of various high-sounding names! On December 7th, at Dr. Porter's Church, a good group included Isidora Martinez, Settie Blume and Mme. Chatterton-Bohrer; December 14th promised, at the Puritan Church, Hattie Schell, Jelliffe and the Bedford Society. December lapsed in its offerings, Christmas putting a quietus on mere entertainments in halls. But the pleasing Meigs Sisters were, on the 15th, at the Lee Avenue Baptist Church, along with Blanche Wolfe and the Lyceum Glee Club. The Drummond Family and their precious Baby Pinkey (or Pinky), dear to provincial audiences, favoured us, on December 16th, at the Lyceum; on the 20th, Father Graham's Olde Folkes scattered doubtful archaisms at the First Presbyterian Church, South Fourth and Sixth Streets. Reynolds, the mesmerist, spent the week of December 19th–24th at the Willoughby Avenue Baptist Church, and, according to the Times of Saturday, December 24th, was to spend four evenings of the next week at the Lee Avenue Baptist Church. At the Lyceum, on the 23rd, the Young Men's Catholic Association of the Church of the Transfiguration showed their Irish bent by acting The Peep o' Day Boys; on the 27th and 28th, at the place, the Acme Comedy Company tried Brighton.

I caught but little for January. On the 9th, that persistent Drummond Family were at the North Fifth Street M. E. Church; on the 11th we did perceive a divided duty as between a testimonial, at Dr. Porter's Church, to Mrs. E. J. Rogers, with Emily Spader, Hasselbrinck, Florence Rice Knox and Robert Thallon, Jr. assisting, and a lecture, at St. John's M. E. Church, of Dr. J. H. Vincent, on That Boy's Sister. The Souvenir Dramatic Union went, on the 13th, to Turnhalle, with Leah, the Forsaken; but alas! the "Bulwer" had (saith the Times) discontinued its dramatic performances for the present season, perhaps because of the nipping and eager air outside and within the treasury. At All Souls' Church, on the 19th, were expected to appear Mrs. E. J. Grant, Mrs. J. K. Draper, Ritter, Brown and Herbert Kortheuer. Postponed from January 22nd to the 29th, came the concert at Masonic Temple tendered to Alexander Rehm by the Arion and Zoellner Männerchor. And postponed because of a bad storm from January 31st to February 7th was a concert at the Lee Avenue Baptist Church which listed Mrs. Decevee, Howard Dunbar (bass), Priscilla Whittingham and Wilbur

[638]

F. Rushmore, those two nobly-named elocutionists.   Thus January left us cold in the lap of February.

On February 6th George W. Groverstein's Speaking and Singing Machine astonished, at the Lyceum, parents and grandparents of those whose nerves are now (1939) torn and frayed by such devices in thickly populated tenements.   Turnhalle housed, on the 6th, the annual masked ball of the Turn-verein, and, on the 13th, that of the Zoellner Männerchor.   The 13th heard, also, at the Amphion Society Rooms, a lecture on Wagner and His Music. Priscilla Whittingham's concert, on the 15th, at the Lee Avenue Baptist Church, advertised assistants in Forster L. Backus (absent through illness), Mary Keech, Lillie Pearsall, Daisy Murdoch and the Lambert Children. The New England Congregational Church responded, on the 16th, with Illustrations of European and Oriental Scenery.   At St. Patrick's Academy, Kent Avenue, amateurs acted, on the 16th and 17th; Toodles and Oliver Twist, on the 17th, showed their "art."   Washington's Birthday was celebrated by Professor Reynolds, at the Old Bushwick Sunday School; by Charles Roberts, Jr., at the Bedford Avenue Reformed Church; and by the Ellis Family at the ever-ready Lee Avenue Baptist Church; also by concerts at the South Third Street M. E. Church and at the Church of Christian Endeavour.   But what was all this compared with the offering, at the Lee Avenue Baptist Church, at this time (February 24th), of Clara Louise Kellogg, Clara Poole, Adamowski, Tagliapietra, Brignoli and S. Liebling (pianist)?   On the 28th, at Dr. Porter's church, came Allan Latham's Illustrated Moral, Intellectual and Amusing Entertainment; I wonder what he meant by "illustrated"?   The Church of the Transfiguration, Hooper Street and Marcy Avenue, was giving, on Sundays, a series of musical vespers.   I leave February, dazed with the entertainments of clubs, societies, etc., in the way of balls and other lures from home and fireside — or, if you choose, from the "register" in the "parlour" floor.   Thus we pass, on March 2nd, to a testimonial, at the 47th Regiment Armoury, to Thomas R. Deverell, and to an elocutionary bout, waged, on the same evening, at the Second Reformed Presbyterian Church, Ninth Street, by Elder, Mrs. Whittingham and Upham.   The 2nd also brought the Arion Masked Ball, in Turn-Halle; a similar function, at about the same time, exercised the Plattdeutscher Club, in F. Jansen's Germania Hall.

The Arion Musical Union, with Oofty Gooft, came, on March 3rd, to the Lee Avenue Baptist Church.   On the 8th, children, in All Souls' Church, performed The Magic Pen, repeating it on the 15th; on the 9th, the Peak Family held the Church of Christian Endeavour.   The inevitable concert and ball of the Cecilia Singing Society duly signalised March 12th at Germania Hall, and, best of all, Joseffy came on March 14th (the date originally had been March 1st) to the Bedford Avenue Reformed Church, Laura Bellini (soprano) and Settie Blume (elocutionist) raising voices in

[639]

the intervals of his playing. On the 15th, the Arbuckle-Colby Concert Company performed at the Lee Avenue Baptist Church, with Arbuckle, Lizzie E. Arbuckle (soprano), Annie E. Beeré (contralto), Willet Seaman (baritone), E. A. Summers (tenor) and G. W. Colby. On the 16th, Herbert S. Renton delivered at the Ross Avenue Presbyterian Church his Day and Night in a Volcano. March 18th found a Turnverein (*sic*) Gemischter Chor in concert, in Turnhalle (*sic*). And, for the 20th, 21st and 22nd, those who desired could hear and see the mesmeric Reynolds at the Ainslie Street Presbyterian Church. Continental Council, 308, A. L. of H. presented, on the 21st, at the Lyceum, Old Phil's Birthday and Sudden Thought: — a good combination for any birthday. On the 22nd appeared at the Lee Avenue Baptist Church Blanche Roosevelt, Signorina d'Arona, Montegriffo, Lencioni, Carl Lanzer, and Miss Priest (accompanist). On the 23rd, at the New England Church, the "original and only Mrs. Jarley," Dr. R. B. Cantrell, lectured on the Dutch Renuisance — "too utterly utter"— a "wildly illustrated character lecture." Let us not forget that that was the first season in America of Oscar Wilde and the delightful Patience. On Easter Sunday, the Arion Quartet's annual concert was carried through at Felton's Union Hall, Meserole Street. March 26th found a "sacred" concert at Turnhalle, involving Josephine Jansen (of the Germania Theater, New York), Michael Loe (a recent importation from Germany) and Albert Mario (of the Thalia, New York) — thereafter, dancing. The same evening heard the Franz Abt Sängerbund at Teutonia Hall. Delafield and Blair's Variety Show came, on the 27th, to Teutonia Hall, and, on the 28th, the Avonian Association played at the residence of Isaac N. Lawrence, Leonard Street, their hunt being A Desperate Game. The 29th heard Nella Brown's reading at Dr. Porter's church, and also piously contributed to Baby Pinkey's benefit at the Lyceum, with the Drummond tribe standing expectantly by.

On April 3rd, at the Lee Avenue Baptist Church (a busy shrine), began a fortnight's exhibition of scenes from Paradise Lost — Plains of Heaven, Beauties of Paradise and Terrors of Hell. At the same church, the Mansfield Post was to give, at a date unspecified in the Times of April 14th, a concert with Annie Theresa Berger, Miss H. Sylvester, Hattie Anderson, George Scobie and Oofty Gooft; the 14th brought also to Turn Hall the sorrows of East Lynne, revealed by the Greenwood Literary Club of South Brooklyn and the Souvenir Dramatic Club of the Eastern District. On the 20th, Dr. Porter's Church enclosed the music of Emily Spader, Hasselbrinck, Loretz, &c. I have reached May and plunge into its seas of inducements. Oscar Wilde was to appear, on the 8th, with his lecture on Art Decoration — the Lee Avenue Baptist Church housing the show; apparently it was deferred till the 12th. Reynolds, still lost in Brooklyn, held, on the 8th, the Ainslie Street Presbyterian Church. The Ross Street Presbyterian Church, on the 11th, combined the work of Hattie Louise Simms, Mrs. Alonzo Foster,

[640]

Herbert S. Renton (he gave A Day and Night in a Volcano) and Theodore Langstroth.   Three nights of Reynolds (May 15th, 16th and 17th) could have been, at the First Presbyterian Church, no novelty to any beholder; and the Ellis Family also were of familiar pattern, on the 18th, at the Willoughby Avenue Baptist Church.   On the 22nd, a benefit to Oliver W. Wren brought to the Lee Avenue Baptist Church no less a person than Jeffreys Lewis, then alas! rarely found on Broadway; Oofty Gooft, J. Leslie Gossin and Russell Bassett also were advertised.   And Reynolds began a new series of nights, on May 23rd, at Masonic Temple.   On the 25th, Jardine "opened" a new organ in the Central M. E. Church, Emily Spader, the Meigs Sisters and the Lyceum Glee Club assisting.   So much for May.

The summer of 1882 is not copiously advertised in the Times, except as to June strawberries and July and August beaches.   On June 8th, however, at Masonic Temple, Hartz began a series of Magical Gift Soirées — his "first visit in fourteen years."   He provided "Illusions without apparatus or assistant," and stressed the "beautiful mystery — the Cherub in the Air."   I call attention to Levy's benefit, on August 23rd, at Brighton Beach, when he was assisted by Frank Livingstone and Herrmann (the magician); to the Sommernachtsfest of the Arion Society, on the 24th, at Ridgewood Park; and to Gilmore Day, on August 31st, at Manhattan Beach.

GREENPOINT, 1881–1882

The ball in Greenpoint, according to the four newspapers from which I draw my facts, began rolling very slowly.   On October 12th, the Apollo Union, at Eckford Hall, began its second season with wholly unimportant soloists.   October 27th promised, at Association Hall, drama and music by the Golden Circle Lodge. Balls in halls and lectures in churches seemed to suffice natives of the "Point."   Reynolds, the mesmerist, took heart of grace and hired the Noble Street Baptist Church for November 15th, 16th and 17th; or possibly the church hired him.   Under direction of J. J. McCabe, the Ebaccam Choral Union gave, on the 17th, in Eckford Hall, a musical and dramatic entertainment.   On the 24th, Mrs. Alonzo Foster, Nettie McEwen and others graced the rostrum in the Presbyterian Church.   The 20th brought to Siems's Germania Hall (Siems had just bought it from Mrs. Passe) the fourteenth anniversary Stiftungsfest of the Germania Singing Society.   To the same hall, a week later (November 27th) came singing the Greenpoint Musikverein.   The Social Quartette Club also was German, on November 20th, at Eckford Hall.   On the 24th the young folks of the Tabernacle gave another Old Folks Concert, a type of entertainment that long since bored my fountain pen to the drying up of its ink of human kindness.   The Hawthorne Literary Union of Greenpoint gave several literary entertainments, beginning on November 28th, in the Faith Mission

[641]

Chapel; Herbert S. Renton, who loved the theatre as much as I do, was president of the society, and, on December 19th, read a poem. Professor Reynolds, mesmerist, performed, on November 28th and 30th, and December 1st and 3rd, at the Noble Street Baptist Church.

Gay December opens for us, on the 4th, with a concert at the church last mentioned, presenting Marie Boyce, Francis F. Powers (baritone) and Henry Farmer (flute). A Lena Bungert musicale graced the 7th, but where the Star fails to state. The Wizard of the East mystified, on December 15th, in the Sunday School Room of the Presbyterian Church. The Mystic Four appeared, on the 20th, at Temperance Hall, and the Sacred Quartette Club, on the 25th, at Eckford Hall. Mother Goose, on December 26th, flopped to the Annex Building of the Noble Street Baptist Church; and I leave December, on the 29th, with a concert at the Presbyterian Church, involving Dr. J. G. Pierson and his daughter, Emily, the Orpheus Quartette, Benjamin Wood (the blind organist), Eliza Evans, Mrs. S. E. Haskell and J. W. Jarboe (director). According to the Greenpoint Globe of January 7, 1882, Professor Frobisher was holding a class in Shakespearian readings (the Shakespearian Association); it had recently met at the house of Mrs. Haskell and rehearsed from Othello and King Lear — hardly food for amateurs. The choir of the M. E. Church of Long Island City sang, at Smithsonian Hall, on January 12th, before, if one credits the Star, a "small audience." On the 16th, Herbert S. Renton gave, at Faith Mission Chapel, Stories of the Sea; Margaret Harned sang. Professor Reynolds again busied himself, on January 21st, in the Chapel of the Noble Street Baptist Church; thus saith the Star. The Greenpoint Globe fixes him, on February 20th, in Smithsonian Hall. On January 30th, the Hawthorne Literary Union presented, at Faith Mission Chapel, the Apollo Union; this Union, on February 2nd, at Eckford Hall, gave a testimonial to its old director, James J. McCabe. On January 30th, Thomas J. Cummings opened his new hall, 17 Greenpoint Avenue, with Joe Blanchard ("the irreproachable tenor" — certainly an *avis rara*), Leo Carter (Dutch comique), John White ("Irish"), Thad Meighan (specialties) and Roden's orchestra. Anna Randall Diehl was elocutionary, on January 27th, at Association Hall.

Thus I shiver into February, with a concert, on the 9th, at Eckford Hall, presenting the Germania, Arion and Social Quartette Clubs — all for the benefit of the German Lutheran Church. On the 9th, 10th and 11th came to Smithsonian Hall the Drummond Family, including Baby Pinkey (six years old), Ada ("the young and wonderful male impersonator"), Lizzie ("graceful danseuse"), Nina ("peerless young banjoist and golden bell soloist"), Maggie ("the sweet vocal soloist"), Bell (humorous recitations and tumbleronicon) — five maidens all for an admission fee of 25 cents, with 35 cents for reserved seats. They were succeeded, at Smithsonian Hall, on the 12th, by Grattan's Panoramic Mirror of Ireland, and that, in turn, on the 16th, by an entertainment of the Shakespearian Association. On February 20th, Dr. Burns's old fancy, The Trial of King Alcohol by Jury, sent its fumes through Association Hall, the Greenpoint Congress staging the show. About this time (March 8th), at Eckford Hall, the Amphion Choral Society offered a testimonial concert and entertainment to Matthew J. Grace, a local amateur.

Company I, 47th Regiment, held a concert and reception, on March 6th, at the Armoury. The Ellis Family, vying with the Drummonds, were, on March 9th, at the Noble Street Presbyterian Church, with Little Fanny Mary ("wonderful child elocutionist, queen of the platform"), Miss Romie ("a sweet, powerful contralto"), and the twin brothers, Frank (tenor) and Fred (bass). They were set down as "sacred and humorous singers, with guitar accompaniment." "Professor" John Reynolds mesmerised, on March 27th and 29th, at the First M. E. Church; on the 23rd, at Smithsonian Hall, occurred a testimonial to the Continental Glee Club. April was busy, beginning on the very 1st, with a visit to Association Hall of the Royal Handbell Ringers and Glee Singers, appearing both afternoon and evening, and continuing, on the 3rd, with a concert, drill and reception of Company I, 47th Regiment, with singers unknown to fame, but accompanied by Ida Percy. On April 5th, a concert at the Presbyterian Church presented the charming Hattie Louise Simms, whom I remember with great pleasure, Mrs. Alonzo Foster, H. R. Humphries, Ivan Morawski and Albert E. Greenhalgh (pianist). The Social Quartette Club held April 9th at Eckford Hall, and the Germania Singing Society came forth, on the 10th, at Germania Hall. The Apollo Union, on the 10th, entered Eckford Hall, for an entertainment and soirée. On the 13th, at the Noble Street Baptist Church, a concert group consisted of Minnie Cash (soprano), Mary Lancaster (soprano), Hattie Canfield (pianist), Marshall P. Wilder, Charles Hill (tenor), and D. W. Robertson ("tumbleroniconist" — a word not for all tongues). Miltonian Tableaux were exhibited, on April 17th and 19th, at the First M. E. Church; on the 20th, the Amphion Choral Society of Greenpoint invaded Eckford Hall, with Don Paddy de Bazan ("Professor" Zeiner directing). The ever-recurring Reynolds again mesmerised, on April 24th, 26th and 29th, at the First M. E. Church.

I note, in the Brooklyn Times, a concert at the Tabernacle, with Hattie Louise Simms, Mrs. Haskell, and Mabel Clare Stephenson (child elocutionist). School children also gave The Flower Queen. Also on May 22nd, at the Kent Street Reformed Church appeared a superior quartette in Miss Simms, Hattie J. Clapper, William Courtney and Fred Ingraham (bass). On Sunday, May 14th, the Germania Musikverein gave at Germania Hall a "sacred" concert; and how "sacred" it was the reader without difficulty agnises. A "complimentary," on May 22nd, at Smithsonian Hall, availed itself of the assistance of Mrs. Cicely Howard and other forgotten

[643]

worthies. And here is a new species of innocent merriment — the broom drill, soon to infest church entertainments throughout the land; one such diversion, on June 5th, went its way with girls drilling with brooms, at the Reformed Church Chapel. Usually a handsome young militia man drilled the maidens until their brooms hardly concealed their palpitating hearts. It was a happy time for all. With those implements of warfare, I sweep out the amusements for 1881–82 in Greenpoint.

FLATBUSH AND ITS NEIGHBOURS, 1881–1882

I am ashamed of this little adjunct of Brooklyn; in the season we are laboriously resuscitating, it emitted hardly a gasp in the columns of the Gazette. The Midwood Amateur Dramatic Society, as we learn, repeated on October 14th, at Town Hall, Harley Merry's play of The Argonauts of '49 (with Mrs. Merry as Laura) and also The Rough Diamond. On December 30th, Alfred E. Pearsall read at Association Hall, New Utrecht. In the Sunday School Building of the Episcopal Church, a concert, on February 2, 1882, enlisted Mr. and Mrs. E. Lumley and Belle and Nettie Cooke. Dr. Maynard, on March 16th, lectured, in Masonic Hall, on Jerusalem. The Ellis Family, making a round of the provinces, moved for the night of May 1st into Town Hall, Flatbush. And, on June 20th, Louise Leslie was to lecture in Gravesend, on Catherine the Second, Czarissa (sic) of Russia.

LONG ISLAND CITY, 1881–1882

Long Island City, after long autumn calm, called, on November 15th, for a reading of Anna H. Lancashire, at the Chapel of the Reformed Church, Astoria. The East Avenue Baptist Church, Hunter's Point, inaugurated, on December 1st, a series of lectures, with D. C. Eddy's talk on Egypt and the Pyramids. At the German Reformed Church, Astoria, Professors Weed and Currie gave, on December 14th and 15th, a grand dioramic exhibition of the Holy Land and scenes in Biblical history. Of course church lectures and entertainments, beneath the notice of our aristocratic muse, prevailed extensively in those wintry evenings; even so, I cannot but wonder at the supineness of Long Island City. The Star of February 4th states that Reynolds, the flying Mercury of mesmerism, if I may be allowed the expression, had recently tested his powers at the Methodist Church, Astoria. The Astoria Männerchor held its annual masquerade, on March 6th, at the Astoria Assembly Rooms; and the Ellis Family, with Little Fanny May, did as they might, on the 16th, at the East Avenue Baptist Church, Hunter's Point.

The Harmonic Singing Society of Long Island City was, on Easter Sunday evening (April 9th), at the Astoria Assembly Rooms, assisted by soloists as German as itself, in persons of Emily Brandis (soprano), Lizzie Heintzmann (alto), August Eisner (violin), Walter Haan (pianist) and Carl Eisner (director). Wesley Hallett (organist) provided, on April 13th, a concert at the Presbyterian Church, Astoria, a group of very local celebrities assisting. On May 2nd, we had two performances of Van Amburgh, Frost, Stone and Company's Great Golden Menagerie, a swelling title that must charm my reader; performers included Anna Carroll (equestrienne), Lizzie Cardello ("aerial queen"), C. H. Lowry (hurdle), W. B. Carroll (rider), John Saunders, Signor Maquese ("wild Indian rider"), Cardello and La Rose (horizontal bar), D. W. Stone, Sam McFlynn and Harry La Rose (a trio of clowns), and Oh-Ke-Na-Wakee's Iroquois and Comanche Indian Troupe. This glory descended, on August 18th, on Astoria the blest. The reader, like me, avoids the picnics and excursions of June and July, but may be induced to consider the concert, on June 30th, involving Addie Hollingsworth, James Caulfield, Willie Caulfield and Miss Andrews (reciter). Alas! the Star asserts the financial success was "nil." Well, let us go on the next excursion and forget our sorrow; strawberry festivals ceased in June. With the sixteenth annual games of the Brooklyn Caledonian Club, on July 4th, at Broadway Park, I lead the gentle reader from Long Island City for 1881–82, wondering why the Star and the Greenpoint Globe record so little for a community where more must have been.

Flushing and Its Neighbours, 1881–1882

We might begin our excursions to Queens County, on October 4, 1881, to attend an entertainment at the Whitestone Episcopal Chapel, carried through by Nonie L. Wright, David Bimberg (violin), and Mrs. Mamie Leys (soprano). For October 20th and 24th, Wilson Stereopticon Lectures were scheduled for Flushing; I regret to say that, according to the Journal, only deadheads attended the first, and at the second ten persons appeared, with the result that no lecture enlightened the community. Uncle Tom's Cabin was set up, in the Opera House, on October 28th. Meantime, Flushing could take pride in its own Judge Frame, then giving a series of lectures in Chickering Hall, New York. Frank Beard's Chalk Talk began at Town Hall, on November 22nd, a Cornucopia series of lectures, others employing native islanders or Brooklynites in persons of James W. Covert, Talmage, Vandewater and Bacon.

And here, ye gods! is another Uncle Tom's Cabin — Jarrett and Palmer's — on December 3rd, at the Opera House; at St. Paul's Chapel, College Point, began a series of lectures under the auspices of the Young People's Guild, the rising Frame being among the speakers. And, for December 16th, the Niantic Club arranged, in its rooms, a concert enlisting Miss Simms, Mrs. Kennan, Gaston Bley (*sic*), Fred Ingraham, Jameson (tenor)

[645]

and Sauret (piano). And the now greatly interesting Frame lectured, on January 10th, 16th, 24th and 31st, at the Flushing Opera House. That auditorium in earlier February housed a concert of the Choral Union.

At a concert in the Presbyterian Church, Whitestone, on January 19th, appeared the Orpheus Glee Club, of Brooklyn. February 8th gathered in the Congregational Church, Flushing, the charming Hattie Louise Simms, Mrs. L. F. Kennan, A. D. Woodruff (tenor), Fred Ingraham (bass), and E. W. Reinescius ('cello). On February 27th, the Niantic Club played at their clubhouse The Two Bonnycastles, followed, of course, by a dance. The Two Orphans suffered and possibly caused suffering, on March 31st, at the Flushing Opera House. Cooke's Circus revived our faith in the arena, on May 1st, and on that very day the Menagerie, Circus and Museum of Van Amburgh, Frost and Stone began a Long Island tournée — Hunter's Point (May 1st); Flushing (2nd); Roslyn (3rd); Huntington (4th); Babylon (5th); Hempstead (6th); Jamaica (8th).

On June 16th, the Virginia Jubilee Singers appeared at the Flushing Opera House. On the 20th, the Amateur Opera Association (the group that formerly gave here The Doctor of Alcantara and The Bohemian Girl) presented, on the same stage, the beautiful novelty, The Pirates of Penzance, with Mrs. Emma F. Henry as Mabel, Agnes Lasar as Ruth, Fred S. Smith as the Pirate King, C. H. Thompson as Frederic, W. F. Cameron as the Police Sergeant, Charles H. Parsons as the Major General, and, in minor rôles Fannie and Mary Trigg, Nellie Robb and Frank A. Stratton. The company opened a subscription for tickets, which at first went off slowly; but, according to the Journal of June 24th, the house was "completely filled," and had "the best musical and dramatic entertainment of the season." And back to the island came Van Amburgh, Frost, Stone and Co.'s Show, exhibiting on August 12th at Port Jefferson; at Northport (14th); Oyster Bay (15th); Glen Cove (16th); Flushing (17th); and Astoria (18th). Before that we had a midsummer-night festival (July 26th) at the Crocheron Bayside House, and ended August with the usual Harvest Home Festivals — at the Crocheron Bayside House (August 23rd), and at Miller's Little Bayside Hotel (30th).

JAMAICA, 1881–1882

September, 1881, was rather interesting in Jamaica. The Long Island Democrat, on September 6th reviews a recent performance (it fails to specify the date) of Long Island's chronic play, Uncle Tom's Cabin. The very popular Bernard Covert, then an old man, and soon to die, gave a concert of simple songs, on September 9th, in the East Jamaica Schoolhouse. And Lady Audley's Secret, or, Withered Leaves, on September 6th, at the Jamaica Opera House, was, according to the Democrat of the 13th, a "great

[646]

success." The only item I discovered for October was a statement in the Democrat of September 20th that a concert for the Michigan sufferers would be given "next month" at the Opera House.

The Methodist Church lecture of November 17th presented the Reverend Wayland Hoyt, on Yellowstone National Park; Adela Rankin, "of Jamaica," read and recited, on December 8th, in the lecture room of the Reformed Church. And, on December 14th and 15th, the Ladies of the Presbyterian Church gave a Bazar of Nations, showing the villagers something concerned with France, Spain, Japan and America. Mrs. Jarley's Waxworks, on December 29th, at the Town Hall, drove 1881 from the calendar, with the Jamaica Banjo Club tunefully twanging the exit. The Sängerbund Ball of the 28th is celebrated in the Democrat of January 3rd.

Anderson's Uncle Tom's Cabin, with Georgia Jubilee Singers, excited the village in two performances on January 21st. The Reverend William E. Griffis, of Schenectady, and known beyond the purlieus of that university town, lectured, on February 2nd, in the Reformed Church Lecture Room, on the amusing theme of The Dutch Have Taken Holland. The Democrat of April 11th informs us that Mrs. M. P. Dewey, the native music teacher, gave a concert on the 7th, in her rooms over the Atlantic and Pacific Tea Store. And the Mother Goose Operetta, on April 19th, enlisted children from the Tabernacle and Westminster Sunday Schools in far-off Brooklyn. I omit the mad excitement of church concerts and fairs, even the charm of strawberry festivals, to arrive, in haste, at the Town Hall, on May 15th and 16th, for Harding's Biorama, which was to show Napoleon Crossing the Alps, with his troops of 30,000 men "all in full motion — beauty of effect and life-like motions." Verily, that is something to admire. More to the mind of little Jamaica may have been the lecture, on May 31st, of the Reverend Rufus L. Perry, editor of the National Monitor, who spoke, at the First Baptist Church, on the serious topic of The Black Man in History, or, he might have added for Jamaica, in Uncle Tom's Cabin.

The Drummond Family, with their precious Baby Pinky (*sic*) entertained, on June 22rd, 23rd and 24th, at the Town Hall. That charming repast prepared villagers for the excursions in July and August to wooded dells or resounding sea-shores. But, on August 4th, we learn from the Democrat, a circus stirred the imagination of the town. The thirteenth Annual Summer Jubilee and Harvest Home, at Miller's Hotel, Little Bayside, allows us, on August 30th, to bid a fond farewell to Jamaica for a season that has proved of some slight interest.

STATEN ISLAND, 1881–1882

As usual, I must piece together a mosaic from items in the Sentinel and the Gazette. On October 5, 1881, the Boat Club of Clifton gave a concert in its new club house; far more inviting (at least to me) was a concert scheduled for October 13th, at the Pavilion Hotel, with Cora de Wilhorst, Maud Morgan, F. Jameson (tenor) and George W. Morgan (piano) — for a modest admission of one dollar. On October 31st, according to the Gazette, a dramatic entertainment, under the auspices of Post Shaw, G.A.R., presented Why Don't She Marry? and Who Died First? Neither paper specifies the place of performing. The Temperance Lyceum housed, on November 24th, a performance for charity, by the New Brighton Combination, including S. R. Gildersleeve. And November 29th brought to the German Club Rooms the first concert of the third season of the Staten Island Vocal Society, with, as soloists, Fannie Kellogg and Richard Hoffman. The sail to Staten Island is most attractive in clear weather; but these inducements could hardly tempt us to undertake the journey, however pleasing in itself.

An amateur minstrel performance and a play were given by the Boat Club, Clifton, on December 1st, and in that month, also, the Young Men's Dramatic Union of Clifton offered a minstrel show at St. Mary's Hall. At Credo's Hotel, on Christmas day, the Staten Island Quintette Club staged a festival of gifts and songs. The usual Dr. Eccleston was at the New Chapel of the Brighton Heights Church, on January 16th and 23rd, with lectures on The Romance of Spanish History. And now Parabola Hall (formerly the Music Hall at the ferry landing, New Brighton) summoned, on February 1st, to charity amateur theatricals, the programme including Poetic Proposals, The Silver Wedding, He's a Lunatic and A Conjugal Lesson. On February 2nd, at the Kingsley M. E. Church, Stapleton, appeared the Ellis Family, with "Little Fairy May — child elocutionist," Miss Romie (contralto), and the twin brothers, Frank (tenor) and Fred (bass). One might have expected twins to be entirely tenor or entirely bass; but nature is mysterious. February 6th was portentous at Parabola Hall, with Jarrett and Palmer's and Slavin's Consolidated Companies, in Uncle Tom's Cabin, with Southern bloodhounds, Balaam, a comical trick donkey, "jolly Georgian coons," etc. The show passed, on the 8th, to the German Club Rooms, Stapleton. On the 7th Parabola Hall opened for amateur minstrels and a farce with the amusing title of The Rosebud of Stinging Nettle Farm. Certainly, this winter atoned for previous lean years! The German Club Rooms opened hospitably, on the 15th, for an Old Folks Concert, and a farce — a church affair; and, on the 17th, they admitted the theatricals of the Olympic Club, in shape of Place aux Dames and Four Sisters. The Ellis Family, on February 18th, invaded the Summerfield M. E. Church, Mariners' Harbour. On the 20th, the Charity Ball, at the German Club Rooms, employed Grafulla's Band. And the Magnolia Coloured Quartette were, on the 20th, at Griffith's Hall, Port Richmond, and, on the 21st, at Parabola Hall; George Weston, Jr. appeared with them in banjo solos. I

[648]

end February with a concert by the Staten Island Vocal Society, held on the 28th, with Ella Earle, Caryl Florio and members of the New York Philharmonic Club.

Grace M. E. Church, Port Richmond, honoured its patrons, on March 2nd, with an organ, cornet, violin and vocal concert, William T. Randall directing. I believe many would have preferred the masquerade ball of the Staten Island Quartette Club, held on March 6th, at the German Club Rooms. During the spring, the Edgewater Dramatic Association presented an evening of farces at St. Mary's Hall, Clifton; on March 17th, the Father Mathew Dramatic Club revived at Temperance Hall, New Brighton, Ten Nights in a Bar-room; on April 28th, their bill included The Irish Emigrant and Borrowed Plumes. Nellie Kline, "elocutionist of New York," held forth on March 30th, at Trinity M. E. Church, West New Brighton; there was also some singing. Better, at the German Club Rooms, on April 28th, was the concert of the Vocal Society, with George Ellard, W. H. Beckett, Ida Hubbell, Mrs. Agnes Morgan (pianist) and Caryl Florio. The society, on May 23rd, gave a testimonial concert to its director, George E. Aiken. The two weeklies of the island joined in May as a semi-weekly (published on Wednesdays and Saturdays) under the name of the Staten Island Gazette and Sentinel. Through its pages I gather a spring posy or two. In later May, Cooke's Circus showed at both Port Richmond and Stapleton. On May 17th, the Young Men's Dramatic Union acted at St. Mary's Hall, Clifton, Ireland vs. Germany, and Funnibone's Fix, or, a Staten Island Editor's Dilemma. The Fort Hill Dramatic Club was, on May 26th, at Temperance Lyceum, New Brighton, with The Two Buzzards, etc. In rural communities, in the '70s and '80s, amateurs must have formed a considerable part of the population. And Staten Island was at last blest with numerous summer hotels to which guests flew for refuge from the heat — the Mansion House; the Pavilion; St. Mark's Hotel, on the Heights, New Brighton; Franz Illig's Hotel and Garden, Tompkinsville; South Beach Pavilion; the Sommer-Garten, Bay View Pavilion, Clifton — these and others flourished. Refreshed by thought of these and of Bechtel's Garden with its music and beer, I leave the island for 1881–82, merely citing in farewell the Summernight's Festival of the Staten Island Quartette Club, held on August 28th, at Bechtel's.

[649]

INDEX

INDEX

VOLUME XI

Abbey, Henry E., becomes manager of Booth's, 27 ff; 92, 183; at Booth's, 238 ff, 246; at Park Theatre, 258 ff, 472 ff; 450; manager for Patti, 504, 538, 590, 612
Abbott, Charles, parts, 279, 280, 440, 634
Abbott, Emma, parts, opera company, 50, 51, 167, 250, 251, 385, 487, 523, 604, 605
Abbott, Nellie, 544
Abe, the Pioneer, 282, 355
Abell, Edith, 195
Aberle, Jacob, Jr., 532
Aberle, Lena, 106, 107, 109 ff, 320 ff, 530 ff
Aberle's, Jacob, Minstrels, 637
Aberle's, Jacob, New Theatre (1879-80), 104 ff; 186, 213; (1880-81), 319 ff; (1881-82), 529 ff
Abgeblitzt, 81
Aborn, Dot, 332, 553
Above the Clouds, 216
Abscheulicher, sung by Materna, 599
Abt, magic, 531, 562, 569
Abt, Franz, Sängerbund, 637, 640
Abt, Franz, Schüler, 84
Academy of Music, Brooklyn (1879-80), 179 ff; (1880-81), 391 ff; (1881-82), 610 ff
Academy of Music, New York (1879-80), 90 ff; 298; (1880-81), 303 ff; (1881-82), 515 ff
Accidents, in Grim Goblin, 218, 219
Ace of Hearts, play, 635
Acis and Galatea, 370, 372
Ackerman, E. P., 403, 421
Ackermann, Frl. J., 82
Ackermann Jaworska, 150
Acme Comedy Company, 638
Acme Olivette Company, 387
Acme Opera Company, 269
Acosta, Marie, 43
Across the Atlantic, 61, 320, 552, 553, 569, 622
Across the Continent, 65, 278, 387, 468
Across the Seas, cast, 547
Acton, Lena, 591
Actor's Boarding House, The, 351, 564
Actor's Family, The, 562, 569, 618
Actors Fund Benefit, 433, 440, 458, 470, 471, 475, 477, 489, 498, 507
Actors in the Kitchen, 566
Ada, Little, 215, 415
Adair, Ada, 135
Adamowski, T., 160, 611, 639
Adams (of Retlaw and Adams), 140
Adams, Alice, as Mazeppa, 323, 329, 339
Adams, Charles, 97
Adams, Charlotte, 33, 265
Adams, D. H., 516
Adams, Daniel, 593

Adams, G., 47
Adams, G. H. (Grimaldi), 65, 177, 203, 281, 608, 633
Adams, James, 59, 257
Adams, Laura, 39
Adams, Lucy, 108 ff, 114, 118, 119, 132 ff, 140, 188, 315, 321, 326 ff, 340, 348 ff, 352 ff, 397, 542 ff
Adams, Lottie, 39
Adams, May, 107, 130, 135, 139, 214, 332, 334, 339, 345 ff, 387, 415, 535, 546, 553, 554, 560 ff, 566 ff, 619 ff, 626
Adams, Yank, 129 ff, 212, 328, 354
Addie, Mlle., 42, 177, 281, 364, 385, 481, 488, 498
Addison, Fanny, 433, 474
Adele (or Adell), Helen (or Helene), 61, 62, 327, 397
Adelphi Academy lectures, 405
Adini, Mlle., parts, 91; leaves in dudgeon, 93, 180
Admission fees, 22, 23, 68, 69, 99, 185, 186, 204, 239, 307, 318, 335, 337, 345, 351, 391, 411, 430; for Patti, 506, 507, 587 ff; 510, 522, 530, 548, 590, 612, 613, 624, 642
Adolfi, Gustav, parts, 74 ff, 81, 282 ff, 294, 496 ff, 509 ff, 538
Adorni, Blanche, 478
Adrian, Walter, 387
Adrien, magic, 541
Adrienne Lecouvreur, with Bernhardt, cast, review, 239; 246; with Mlle. Rhea, 452, 453; with Marie Geistinger, 495; with Franziska Ellmenreich, 507; 606, 614
Adventures of a Rogue, 347, 349
Advertising for a Wife, 530
Æolian Dramatic Association, 404, 428; Club, 406
Æolian Glee Club, Brooklyn,, 429, 430
Aerial dive, 148
Africa vs. Ireland, farce, 129
Africaine, L', casts, 394, 521, 522, 523, 614
African Students, 188
Afrique, L', cast, 480
After Dark, 127
After the Opera, cast, 475; 566
Against the World, 620
Agramonte, E., 157 ff, 183, 198, 377, 392, 592, 598
Ahl, Frl., 74 ff, 82, 287
Ahrendt, Carl, 384, 484, 598
Aicken, Elinor, 47
Aïda, casts, 26, 92; 93, 95, 96, 97; casts, 180, 181; 182; in English, 252; cast, 305; 306; casts, 310, 456, 518, 519, 521, 613
Aiken, E. H., 49
Aiken, Edwin, 459

[653]

Aiken, Frank E., 467, 480
Aiken, George E., 160, 163, 166, 181, 216, 217, 375, 392, 406, 649
Aiken, Sol and Julia, 113 ff, 139, 140, 553, 560
Aimée, Marie, parts, 31, 32, 148; compared with Geistinger, 285
Aiston, Madge, 544
Ajax, 147, 330, 331, 336, 338, 397, 564
Alba Sisters, 346
Albaugh, H. C., 469
Albert, Clemmie, 597
Albert, Fanny, 287
Albert, James, 359
Albert, Mary, 263, 355, 356, 388
Albert's, Mrs., Hall, 210 ff, 424, 425
Alberti, Elsa, 512
Albertini, Diaz, 180
Alberts, F., 223
Albery, J., his Where's the Cat? 222
Albino exhibited, 400
Albion Brothers, athletes, 347, 562
Albion Society, 367, 584
Alden, Allie, 123, 635
Aldrich, Louis, in My Partner, 9, 11, 176, 203, 270, 391, 486, 491, 609
Alessandro, strong man, 126
Alexander, Ray, 63, 354, 355
Alexander Mayblossom's Visit to New York, 414
Alexander and King, 531
Alfonso, K., 161
Alford, clown, 617
Alfred, W., 479
Alfredo, Louis and Emma, 125, 316, 331, 345, 348
Alhaiza, Paul, 88
Alhambra Theatre, 578
Ali, P., cornet, 196
Alixe, cast, 259
All at Sea, cast, 581
All-I've-Ate (or Eat), burlesque of Olivette, 318, 364, 604
All-of-It, burlesque of Olivette, 329, 343, 355
All on Account of Eliza, 253, 266, 270
All Right, Little, 397, 534, 616
All that Glitters Is not Gold, 631
All the Rage, casts, etc., 176, 203, 234, 272, 385, 470, 492, 634
Allegro, L', and Il Penseroso, sung, 381
Allemania, 297, 300, 511
Allemania Quartett Club, 85, 88
Allen (of American Four), 101
Allen, minstrel, 120
Allen (of Smith and Allen), 139
Allen, Bob (see Magee and Allen)
Allen, Burt, 120, 129
Allen, Charles, 335
Allen (Charles) and Hart (Joe), 117, 120, 319, 326, 335
Allen, Eloise, 136
Allen, Ethel, 61, 62
Allen, Harry, 64, 150, 218, 225, 471, 538
Allen, J., walker, 149, 150
Allen, Joe, 616
Allen, (Mr. and Mrs. Joe), 557, 568, 574

Allen, Johnny, 101, 111, 119, 330, 415
Allen, Lawrence, 124, 125, 325
Allen, Leslie, 8, 237, 246, 447, 448, 517
Allen, Lettie, 56, 168, 275
Allen, Paul (see Lester and Allen)
Allen (Paul) and Slavin (Bob), 101
Allen, R. G., banjo, 131
Allen, Viola, début, 448
Allen, W. W., 121, 262, 435, 581
Allen Sisters (May and Lillie), 552, 565 ff
Allen's Mechanical Dime Museum, 401
Allerton, J. S., magic, 209
Allien, Edgar S., 366
Alliger, James H., 150, 278, 428
Allison, C. W., 39, 581
Allison, Maud, 413
Allison, P. M., 112
Allmuth, Professor, 422
Alloggio, L', Militare, 303
Allyne, Kitty, 134 ff, 186, 316, 348 ff, 543, 560, 561, 568 ff, 574
Almayne, Nard, 33, 47, 48, 367
Almeras, Charles, 263
Alone, 195
Alpenröschli Club, 426
Alpine Sänger-Gesellschaft, 83
Alsace-Lorraine, Société, 514
Alter Fuchs, Ein, in der Falle, 509
Alter Junggesellen, Ein, 81
Alter Postillon, Ein, 82
Althaus, tenor, 85, 374
Altona, Mme., 95
Alves, Carl, 84, 161, 512, 597
Alvin Joslin, cast, 492, 493
Alvord, singer, 423
Alward, Gus and Nellie, 564
Am Clavier, 286
Amalgamation, farce, 348
Amann (of De Ome and Amann), 561, 562, 569, 570
Amann, Andy, 338
Amaranth Society, amateur actors, 181 ff, 392 ff, 615
Amateur acting, 81, 97, 154, 155, 180 ff, 192 ff, 205 ff, 210 ff, 214 ff, 302, 310, 367, 369, 370, 392 ff, 399, 403 ff, 417 ff, 422 ff, 426, 428, 509, 510, 521, 582 ff, 612 ff, 627 ff, 636 ff, 642, 646, 648
Amateur League, 510, 585
Amateur Minstrels, 150, 200, 217, 399, 406, 426, 586, 630, 631, 637, 648
Amateur Opera Association, Brooklyn, 393, 646
Amateur Rehearsal, The, 346, 551
Amazonian March, 189
Ambassador's Lady, The, 203
Amberg, New York Vocal Quartette, 345
Amberg, Gustav, 73 ff
Amberg, H., 172
Ambitious Actor, The, 123
Ambre, Emilie, 22, 91 ff, 97, 158, 162, 180 ff, 194, 310, 394
Ambrose, F. E., 264, 462
America to the Front, at Koster and Bial's, 358

America's Place in History, lecture, 153
American Dime Museum, Brooklyn, 190, 191
American Dime Museum, New York, 143
American Four (Pettingill, Gale, Dailey and Hoey), 101, 104, 133, 137, 138, 139, 186, 188, 190, 314, 334, 335, 341, 347, 348, 350, 352, 398, 519, 526, 530, 534, 554, 556, 557, 567, 572, 574, 615, 617
American Girl, An, cast, 247; 274
American Institute Building, 148, 153, 156, 359, 369, 585
American Mabille, 142, 580
American Museum, 154
American Students, 188, 567 (see also Ten American Students and Six American Students)
American Temperance Union, 154
American Theatre, Third Avenue (1879-80), 139 ff; (1880-81), 352 ff (see also Parker's, Dick, American Theatre)
American Triplets, 115
American Troubadours, 109
Americans Abroad, cast, 443
Amerikanischer Duell, Ein, 511
Ames, Charles, 206
Ames, Emil, 528
Amherst College Quartet, 408
Amitié, L', Société Française, 88, 301, 513
Amlar, Harry, 544, 552, 622
Amon, Nellie, 124, 204, 332, 333, 338, 415
Among the Breakers, 419
Among the Mormons, cast, 122
Amphion Choral Society (or Union), Greenpoint, 207, 208, 420, 421, 643
Amphion Choral Society (or Musical Society), Williamsburgh, 417, 419, 420, 421
Amt Osterholzer K. U. Verein, 86
Amt Stolzenauer Verein, 402
Am-u-let, 130
Amusements, H. W. Beecher on, 153, 182
Anatomy, Museum of, 586
Ander, Luigi, 83, 84
Anderson, negro, 60
Anderson, actor, 442
Anderson (of Carter and Anderson), 576
Anderson, Hattie, 10, 490, 640
Anderson, D. C., 450, 459
Anderson, J., amateur, 369
Anderson, J. R., 33, 34
Anderson, Joseph, 249, 453, 454
Anderson, Lizzie, 458, 467, 624
Anderson, Mary, 31, 54; parts, reviews, 249, 250, 383, 453, 454, 455, 488, 607, 634
Anderson, Mme., walker, 120, 131, 142, 193
Anderson, P. Aug., 1, 46, 178, 262, 488
Anderson, Sarah Barron, 161, 163, 376
Andow, Edith, 530 ff, 543, 557
Andrews (see Olympia Quartette)
Andrews, Mamie, 424, 645
Andrews, Miss, 262
Anella, Professor, 350, 567
Angelica, Little, 445
Angelo, French actor, 239 ff, 246
Anna-Lise, 71, 510
Annabel Lee, read, 244

Annandale, Lizzie, 251, 252
Annex Association, 212
Annie and Willie's Prayer, 208
Anonyme Correspondenz, Eine, 507
Ant bear exhibited, 147
Anthony, Susan B., 584
Antoinette, long-haired, 624
Anton, Lina, 595
Antonio, May, 327, 335, 340, 561, 569, 617
Antonio, Tillie, 128, 138, 139, 186, 620
Antony, Marc (see Marc Antony)
Anything for a Change, 209
Apajune, in English, cast, 480; in German, cast, 496
Apollo Club, Brooklyn, 181, 279, 394, 395, 614
Apollo Dramatic Association, 81, 210
Apollo Union, Greenpoint, 421, 423, 641 ff
Apollo, Young, Opera Troupe (see Young Apollo)
Apple and Willis, 336
Appleby, E. Abbott, 487
Appleton, Aaron, 23
Applicants for a Position, cast, 544
April Showers, 330
Apthorp, W. F., 628
Aquarium (1879-80), 146, 147; (1880-81), 359, 360; (1881-82), 541
Arabian giant, 624
Arabian Night, An, cast, 17; 18, 19; casts, 58, 173, 177; 179
Arabs, Palestine, exhibited, 404
Arada Brothers, 321, 341, 342
Aramburo, tenor, 91 ff; leaves in dudgeon, 93; 180 ff
Arbuckle, Lizzie E., 376, 377, 394, 640
Arbuckle, M., 55, 78, 150, 162, 199, 295, 359; 375, 394, 404, 521, 601, 640 (see infra)
Arbuckle's Ninth Regiment Band, 283, 356, 357, 409, 540 (see supra)
Arcadian Quartet Club, 593
Arcanum, Royal, 180
Archer, Belle, 269, 605
Archer, Edward A., 51, 594
Archer, Frederic, 373, 376, 378, 629
Archer, Herbert R., 38, 104, 186, 268, 269, 276, 605
Archer, J. W., 262
Archer, Robert, 458
Arcone, Mlle., 26, 27, 182, 456, 614
Ardell, Artie, 186
Arditi, Luigi, 307, 371, 516 ff
Argonauts, The, of '49, 424, 644
Ariel, flying wonder, 245, 246
Ariel vocalists, 209
Arion Ball, The, farce, 343, 535
Arion Club, Brooklyn, 416
Arion Musical Society, Williamsburgh, 639
Arion Quartett Club, 84, 86, 294, 512, 640
Arion Society (or Union), Greenpoint, 421 ff, 642
Arion Society, Newark, 374
Arion Society, New York, 82 ff, 148, 150, 158, 164, 165, 214, 296 ff, 300, 307, 376, 512, 513, 540, 592, 598, 601

INDEX

Arion Society, Williamsburgh, 79, 207, 637, 639
Arkansaw Travellers, 133
Arlington, Fred, 337
Arlington, J. V., 354, 545, 573
Arlington, Maggie, 170, 276
Armand, J. C., 258, 268, 460, 464
Arminia, 83 ff, 295, 298
Armless man, 580
Armonia, La, Spanish Society, 514
Armstrong, A. A., 50
Armstrong, John, 621
Armstrong Sisters (Sidney and Ollie), 567
Arnazulu, a Zulu, 364
Arndt Männerchor, ball, 418
Arnold (see Megatherian Eight)
Arnold, Frl., 74 ff
Arnold, Grace, 413, 414, 415, 425, 534, 635
Arnold, Hattie, 64
Arnold, Lu, 143
Arnold, Max, 116, 121, 133, 137, 138, 565, 566, 572
Arnold, Mrs. Richard, 161
Arnold, Richard, 85, 157, 159, 161, 216, 370, 373, 377, 585, 587, 591, 592, 594, 602
Arnold Brothers (Amos and Frank), 114, 131, 185, 319
Arnott, Belle, 619
Arnott, Edward, 267
Arnott, Georgie, 533
Arnott, Miss Lou (or Lulu), 116, 125, 320, 576
Arnott, May, 124, 127, 185, 204, 316, 325, 332, 526, 546, 619
Aronson, Rudolph, 163, 355, 356
Around the World in Eighty Days, cast, 270; 322, 389, 491, 608, 633
Arria und Messalina, 495
Arrival of Casey, 570
Arrival of Gilbert and Departure of Sullivan, farce, 566
Arrival of Jumbo, farce, 549
Arrival of Mulcahy, 566, 571
Arrival of Patti, farce, 526
Arrival of President Grant, 546, 564
Arrival of Salvini, farce, 549
Arrival of Sarah Bernhardt, farce, 348, 396
Art Association Rooms, Brooklyn, 197, 406
Artful Dodger, The, 106
Arthur, H., zither, 84
Arthur, Joseph, 253, 529
Arthur, Lilford, 474
Arthur, Nellie, 533
Article 47; cast, 259; cast, Morris matinées, 440; 489
As You Like It, 30; cast, 39; 40, 52, 168; cast, 169; 178; by the Wallack company, reviews, 219, 220, 305; read, 367; casts, 463, 605; 633
Aschenbrödel, with children, 79; by Heinrich Herrmann, sung, 598
Aschenbrödel-Verein, 85, 86, 296
Ashbox Inspector, 342, 396
Ashton, Frank, 147, 347
Ashton, J. L., 280, 486

Ashton's Waxworks, 192
Asleep at the Switch, 278
Association Culinaire Cosmopolite, 301
Association Hall, Greenpoint, 421 ff, 641
Association Hall, Harlem, 586
Association (Y. M. C. A.) Hall, New York, 582 ff, 600
Associazione del Tiro al Bersaglio, 303 (see Tiro al Bersaglio)
Assommoir, L', as Drink, cast, 265
Astley Belt walked for, 149
Astoria, L. I., 210 ff, 424, 425, 644
Astoria Assembly Rooms, 424, 425
Astoria Männerchor, 211, 212
Astronomical Clock, 155, 365
Astronomy, lectures on, 152, 368, 403
Atalanta, or, the Female Athlete, 534
Atalanta Boat Club, 162, 585, 586, 592
Atalanta Casino, 513, 578, 586, 601
Atalanta House, 300, 511 ff, 580
Athalie, Mendelssohn's, 182
Athena, actress, 242
Athenæum, Boston, company from, 187
Athenæum, Bay Ridge, 210
Athenæum, Brooklyn, 191 ff, 402 ff, 623, 626 ff
Athenean Society, 182, 195, 630
Athénée Français, 514
Atherton, Alice, 49, 178, 180, 202, 267, 480
Athletic Club, Greenpoint, 207
Athletic games, 151, 207, 217
Athol, "boneless marvel," 325
Atkins, T. F., 449
Atkinson, L. P., 197
Atkinson, Miss, 31
Atkinson, Tom, 472
Atlantic Garden, Jamaica, 215
Atlantic Garden, New York, 152, 294 ff, 299, 300, 361, 512, 601
Atom, Major, 401, 541, 579, 625
Attic Thespians, The, 138
Atwell, James, 58
Atwood (see Excelsior Quartette)
Atwood, Charles, 528
Aubrey and Dashway, 186, 424
Aubreys, the, gymnasts, 543
Aubrin, Vincent, 527
Auburn, Dot, 548
Audiences, small, 209, 213
Audley, Ollie, 334
Audran Opera Company, 479
Auf der Brautfahrt, cast, 288
Auf Tod und Leben, cast, 155
Augustine, Frank, 251
Auld, Florence, 154, 195, 418
Auld Sisters, 193
Aunt Charlotte's Maid, cast, 192
Aurora Floyd, 178, 428
Aus der Gesellschaft, cast, 66
Aus Liebe zur Kunst, 293, 510
Austin and trained dogs, 122
Austin and Dale, 567, 572
Australian bushmen, 626
Australian Four, 557
Austrian Sänger-Gesellschaft, 512
Automatons, living, 108, 114

INDEX

Avalo, of Leslie and Avalo, 121
Avalo, Oscar, 136
Aveling, Henry, 23, 47, 272, 385
Avenged, or, the Dogs of the Sierras, 328, 331, 333, 353, 400, 414, 531
Avery and La Rue, 105, 344
Awfully Awful, song, 124
Ayling, Herbert, 226 ff, 391, 441, 475, 621, 634
Aymar (of Runnells and Aymar), 106
Aymar, Fred, 147
Ayres, C. C., amateur, 392
Aztec princess exhibited, 579

Babcock, O. M., 369
Babes in the Wood, 178, 256
Babil and Bijou, 534
Babiole, cast, 264
Baby Elephant, The, farce, 116, 133
Baby show, 401
Babylon, L. I., 646
Bach's Passion Music, 166; his Vain and Fleeting, 603
Bachelor Club Reception, 367, 584
Bachelor's Frolics, cast, 532
Backus, Charles, 143 ff, 179, 362 ff, 580, 581
Backus, E. Y., 246
Backus, F., tenor, 193
Backus, Forster L., 639 (see infra)
Backus, Foster, 419 (see supra)
Backus, Irene, 198, 405
Back to Erin, 330
Backwoods Heroes, 117
Bacon, Lizzie, 375, 376
Bacon, R. S., 645
Badischer Männerchor, 87, 295, 512
Baer, Tessie, 598
Baffled Beauty, A, cast, 258, 259
Bagab, Frl., 66 ff
Bagott, Richard H., 214
Bailey, Etta, 628
Bailey, George A., 319 ff
Bailey, Josephine, 30, 237
Bailey, Lillian, 297, 371 ff, 380, 394 (see Henschel, Mrs. George)
Bailey, W. H., 41, 178, 279, 280
Bainbridge, Clement, 46, 178, 488
Baird, W. C., 160, 162, 163, 180, 181, 184, 195, 199, 200, 217, 376, 601
Bajazzo und seine Familie, 283
Baker, Dick, 568
Baker, Ella Tier, 422
Baker, Emily, 44, 265, 278, 389, 482
Baker, Ettie, 387
Baker, Florence, 49, 178, 180
Baker, Josephine, 4, 258 ff, 393, 488
Baker, Katie, 29, 277, 384, 485
Baker, Lew, minstrel, 216, 527, 575, 625
Baker, Lewis, actor, 244, 262, 280, 393, 463, 464, 553, 605
Baker, Mrs. Sara A., 40, 274, 412, 467, 608
Baker, P. F. (of Baker and Farron), 281, 387, 478, 633

Baker, Thomas, 2
Bal Masqué de l'Opera, 150
Balch, Mattie, 183, 194, 196, 198, 422
Baldanza, opera singer, 27, 180, 182, 201, 594
Baldwin (of Lawrence and Baldwin), 548
Baldwin (of Ronaldo and Baldwin), 323
Baldwin, A. (of Enterprise Four), 338
Baldwin, Archie (of Lamonto and Baldwin), 320, 330, 338, 339
Baldwin, Ed, clown, 526
Baldwin, Edwin, 562
Baldwin, William, benefit for his family, 182
Baldwin Brothers, 101, 109, 125
Balfe, Louise, 460
Balfour, Theodore, 482
Ballet, 27, 57, 58, 61, 110, 171, 183, 185, 245, 246, 270 ff, 281, 322, 397, 484, 491, 509, 532 ff
Ballo in Maschera, Un, casts, 305, 456
Balls, Brooklyn, 182, 190, 393, 402, 403, 613 ff
Balls, French, 88, 89, 301, 513, 514
Balls, German, 292, 294 ff, 510, 511
Balls, Greenpoint, 208, 422, 641
Balls, Italian, 515
Balls, Jamaica, 428, 647
Balls, Long Island City and Astoria, 211
Balls, New York, 95, 307, 308, 356, 357, 359, 367, 368, 519, 520, 540, 584, 623
Balls, Staten Island, 216, 429, 648, 649
Balls, Williamsburgh, 418 ff, 639
Balmor, Nellie, 213
Bamboozling, 213
Bamburgh, Charles, amateur, 181 ff, 392; manager of Court Square Theatre, 398, 399
Bancroft, Helen, parts, 443
Bandmann, D. E., parts, 47, 48, 169, 170; burlesqued, 119
Bandmann, Mrs. D. E., 47
Bangs, F. C., 22, 386, 449
Bangs, L. Adelaide, reader, 404, 430, 627, 630
Banjo Club, Jamaica, 647
Bank Clerks' Musical Association, 162, 377, 597
Banker, Carrie, 123
Banker, Edward, 135, 185, 324, 330, 626
Banker's Daughter, A, or, Aurora Floyd's Secret, 428
Banker's Daughter, The, casts, 167, 177, 203, 226, 227, 276, 386, 483, 486; 492, 568; cast, 632, 633
Banker's Daughter, The, farce, 561
Banker's Luck, A, 563
Banks, Charles L., parts, 109, 110, 117, 189, 328, 616
Banks, Joe H., 65
Bankson, John W., 263, 516
Banner, Michael, 596, 600, 602
Banvard, John, panorama, 369
Baralt, Dr., lectures, 154, 378
Barbadoes, Young, 185
Barbara Frietchie Post, 423
Barbe Bleue, cast, 33; in German, 286
Barberis, in opera, 182, 600

INDEX

Barbiere, Il, di Siviglia, cast, 308; with Gerster, 394, 456; on the same night, with Patti and Gerster, 457; with Patti, reviews, 505; casts, 517, 518; cast, 612; 615
Barbour, G. W., 260, 359
Barbour, Nellie, 256, 387
Barbour, W., minstrel, 59
Barclay, Delancey, 390, 449
Bardell, May, 472
Bardell vs. Pickwick, cast, 243
Barden, Die, 293
Bardini, in opera, 456, 457
Bards of Tara (see Kelly and Ryan)
Barfoot, Harry, 47, 470
Barili, in opera, 505 ff
Barker, A. D., 482
Barker, Adele, 371
Barker, Alf, 117, 136, 558
Barker, Eva Glen, 277, 384, 488
Barker, L. W., 529
Barker, Lew, 114 ff, 331
Barker, Mrs. E. L., 277
Barker, Mrs. L. F., 386
Barker, Mrs. Mary, 62, 114, 116
Barlow Brothers (James and William), 104, 128, 129, 140, 188, 348, 353, 397, 535, 553, 558
Barlow, Miss, 35, 184
Barlow, Wilson, Primrose and West, Minstrels, 410
Barnabee, H. C., 181, 238, 393, 455, 456, 611
Barnacle, Miss Dillie, 614
Barnard, Charles, 215
Barnard, F. A. P., of Columbia College, 584
Barnes, Courtney, 1 ff, 10, 54, 177, 274
Barnes, Ed F., 347, 349, 560, 619, 622
Barnes, Elliott, his play, 390; 633
Barnes, J. H., 468, 469
Barnes, James, engineer, 23
Barnes, James A., author, 315
Barnes, Maggie, 14 ff
Barnes, Maude, 361
Barnes, Sidney, 274
Barnes and Mack, 396
Barnett, Agnes, 436
Barnett, Alice, 35, 182, 184
Barney, Master, 137, 317, 340, 534, 556, 559
Barney, the Baron, 423
Barney's Return, 141, 353
Barnicoat, Miss A., 24
Barnum, P. T., lectures, 629 (see infra)
Barnum's Greatest Show on Earth, 148, 199, 359, 408, 540, 541, 631
Baron Rudolph, account of, cast, 486, 487; 491
Barr, O. H., 28, 29, 171, 202, 270, 470
Barre, Frl., 74 ff
Barrett, Charlotte, 428
Barrett, Effie, 45, 177, 483
Barrett, Florence, 322, 437, 535
Barrett, Lawrence, 172, 203, 242, 254, 260, 261, 276, 384, 386, 450, 461, 464, 465, 605
Barrett, Louis F., 45, 52, 177, 243, 450, 475
Barrett, W., 387
Barrett Brothers, 635

Barretta, Mlle., 102, 103, 128, 130 ff, 183, 187, 188, 340, 342, 396, 528, 556, 559, 617
Barretta, Pauline, 27
Barrettas, the, 398
Barrie, Miss, 257, 390
Barrington, Eva, 481, 528
Barron, actor, 57
Barron Brothers, 549, 550, 566, 571
Barrows, J. O., 256, 475
Barrows, Mary W., 195
Barry (of Olympia Quartette), 396
Barry (of Sheldon and Barry, q.v.)
Barry, Billy (of Barry and Fay), 104, 186 ff, 396 ff, 483, 518, 619
Barry, C. W., 622
Barry, Edwin (or Ned), 99, 117, 312, 313, 325, 330, 345, 396, 413
Barry, Fanny, 484
Barry, J. L. (of Howard and Barry, q.v.)
Barry, Lillie A., 162, 367
Barry and Fay (see Barry, Billy, and Fay, Hugh)
Barrymore, Georgie Drew, parts, 245, 389
Barrymore, Maurice, at Wallack's, 2 ff; 67, 170, 219, 385
Bart, Miss A., 264
Bartholomew, W. H., 27, 34, 389
Bartlett, G. B., 405
Bartlett, Homer, 155, 160, 595
Bartlett, Kate, parts, 4, 55, 167, 223, 276, 383, 389, 488
Bartlett, Meta, parts, 176, 234, 385, 470, 621, 634
Bartlett Sisters, 558
Barton, Charles (of Rice and Barton), 559, 565, 571, 576
Barton, F. P., 21, 465
Barton, H. C., 462
Barton, Hughey and Jennie, 549
Barton, James, 40, 258, 268, 477
Barton, Lew, 425
Barton, Miss, 232, 473
Barton, Sara, 430
Barton, Thomas, 449
Barton, W. C., 248
Barton, Wallace, 612
Barvardoe, Hurle, coloured Shakespearian, 369, 379
Bascomb, Laura, 56, 262, 274
Bascombe, H. L., 324, 529 ff
Base Ball, Our National Game, cast, 128
Bassermann, parts, 496 ff
Bassett, Bric-à Brac, 63, 366
Bassett, Aunt Polly, Singin' Skewl, 198, 209
Bassett, Jedediah, 191, 198
Bassett, Russell, 253, 259, 270, 276, 279, 326, 489, 641
Batchelder, Josie, 169, 202, 244, 268, 453, 633
Batchellor, Pauline, 331, 535, 564, 567, 572, 574, 619
Batchellor, W. H., 359
Bateman, Alice, 131, 133, 134, 141, 186, 314, 320, 332, 333, 336, 345, 347, 352, 397, 398
Bateman, Victory, 478
Bates, Bertha, 533

[658]

INDEX

Bates, Captain and wife, giants, 579, 624
Bates, Eliza, 449
Bates, Marie, parts, 243, 253, 279, 383, 467, 471
Battaglia, La, di Tolosa, 302
Battersby, Hannah, giantess, 191
Battersby, Miss F., 601
Battle, S., 254
Battle, A, for Life, 565
Bauer, Kate, 478
Bauer, Paul, West Brighton Hotel, 409
Bauer, Thiebaud, wrestler, 150, 314
Baum, Louis F., his play, 493
Baumgärtner's Military Hall, 206
Bay Ridge, 210, 423
Bayerisches Volksfest, 88, 513
Bayley, Eric, 474
Bayley, Mindha, 474
Bayside, L. I., 426
Bayside Quartette Club, 213
Bazar of Nations, 647
Bazzano, Mlle., 484
Beach, Mrs. E. T. P., 28
Beadle's Pirates for Ten Cents, cast, 145; 179
Beane and Gilday (see infra and Gilday, Charles)
Beane, Fannie, 56, 100, 103, 134 ff, 172, 188, 274, 316, 346 ff, 396 ff, 526, 562 ff, 568, 570, 571, 617, 618
Beane, George, Jr., 136, 139, 345, 385, 563
Beane, George, Sr., 47, 385, 489
Beard, Frank, 198, 365, 403, 407, 419, 420, 423, 645
Bearded woman, 190, 401, 624
Bearman, Miss, 392
Bears, performing, 135, 353, 564
Beasley (of Long and Beasley, 349 (see also Wood and Beasley)
Beatrice, Mrs. Bowers as, 28; Ada Cavendish as, 54, 170; Magda Irschick as, 69
Beatty, Mrs. S., 174
Beaudet, Louise, 32, 33, 88
Beauman, Marie, 64
Beaumont, A., 369
Beaumont, J., 266
Beaumont, Maud, 460
Beaumont, Nellie, 49, 180
Beaupain, Frl., 294
Beauty and the Beast, 135
Beaver, A. P., 532
Bebus, Davenport, 51, 274, 447, 448
Bechtel's Park, S. I., 217, 649
Beck, Philip, 33, 34, 47
Beckett, Harry, parts, etc., 2 ff, 8, 170, 224, 436
Beckett, W. H., 158, 160, 376, 649
Becks, Alfred, 10 ff, 226, 276, 437, 440, 488
Bedell, W., 445
Bedford Hall, Brooklyn, 192 ff, 404 ff, 628 ff
Bedford Vocal Society, 195, 627
Bedlow, Major, 236
Beebe, Henrietta, 158 ff, 163, 180, 182, 213, 217, 370 ff, 392, 405 ff, 410, 601
Beebe, Mary, 181, 328

Beecher, Henry Ward, lectures, 153, 154, 182, 193, 196, 198, 366, 394, 403, 404; why late at lecture, 583; 626
Beecher, Mrs. E. F., 393
Beecher, Rosalba, 28, 158
Beecher's and Talmage's Private Hell, 361
Beeckman, C. T., 97
Beekman, W., 106 ff, 232, 443 ff
Beeré, Annie, 151, 158 ff, 163, 377, 640
Beeskow, Frl., 282 ff
Beethoven Männerchor, 84 ff, 294 ff
Beethoven Männerchor Hall, 83 ff, 89, 294 ff, 511, 512
Beethoven Quartett, 84, 297
Beethoven Sommergarten, 87
Beethoven's Mass in D sung; his Ninth Symphony performed, 379, 410 (see also Fidelio)
Beggar's Daughter, The, cast, 115
Behind the Footlights, 139
Behr, W. H., 596
Behrens, bass, 92, 158, 162, 181, 194
Behrens, S., conductor, 97, 182, 252, 456, 457
Behringer, Frl., 66 ff
Behrman, H., walker, 149
Bei Wasser und Brod, 500, 510, 623
Beiden Klingsberg, Die, 291, 502
Beiden Reichenmüller, Die, cast, 72
Beiden Waisen, Die, cast, 284; 634, 635 (see also Two Orphans, The)
Bel raggio, sung by Patti, 589; by Miss Corradi, 596
Belasco, David, 236; his experience with the play, La Belle Russe, 434
Belcher, tenor, 180
Belfort, Charles, violin, 83, 195, 200, 217, 356, 374
Belgarde, Adele, parts, 39; as Hamlet, 270; parts, 486, 492, 633
Belgium, Independence of, celebrated, 89
Belknap, W. S., 59
Bell, benefit, 190
Bell, A. H., 11, 172, 254, 274, 492
Bell, Bessie, 140, 204, 350, 535, 555
Bell, Digby V., 64, 233, 258, 268, 387, 413, 442 ff, 481
Bell, Florence, 354, 573
Bell, Frank, 132, 187
Bell, Georgie, 204
Bell, Harry B., 139, 225, 467
Bell, Kitty, 548, 550
Bell, Lillian B., 258
Bell, Mrs. L., 603
Bell Ringers (see Handbell Ringers)
Bellari, tenor, 371, 407
Bellati, 394
Belle Hélène, La, 25, 36, 183, 264; in German, 288
Belle of the Bowery, The, 551
Belle of the Kitchen, The, 208
Belle Russe, La, cast, 434 (see also Belasco, David)
Belles of the Kitchen, 230, 453
Bellevue Park, West Hoboken, 90
Bellew, Kyrle, and Eugenie Legrand, 441

Bellinger, Bella Irene, 594
Bellini, Laura, 594, 639
Bellman, Otto, 123
Bellows, Mrs. Charles, 628
Bells, The (of Poe), recited, 244, 439
Bells, The, play, 280, 488
Bells of Corneville, 609 (see Cloches Les, de Corneville)
Bells of Normandy, does not open, 43
Belmer, Henry, his play, 545; 553
Belmont (of Bryant and Belmont), 125, 635
Belmont, Grace, 550
Belmont, Minnie, 548, 549
Belmont, Mlle., circus, 114, 147
Belocca, Anna de (see De Belocca, Anna)
Belot, Adolphe, his Le Fils de Coralie, 229
Belton, Lotta, 267
Belton, Sadie, 400
Belz, E., 537
Benchley, Marie, 161, 306
Bender's Schützen-Park, 86, 87, 90
Benedetti, Ida, 391
Benedick (Much Ado about Nothing), Booth as, 28; Reinau as, 69; Carl Sontag as, 508
Benedict, Frank Lee, 258
Benedict, H. E. H., 180, 193, 406
Benedict, Lew, 281, 317
Bengal tigers exhibited, 271
Bengalischer Tiger, Ein, 76
Benjamin, H., and J. M., 417
Benighted, cast, 61
Benner Brothers, 351
Bennett, Ben (see Saville and Bennett)
Bennett, Frank, 315, 317, 334, 348, 526, 551, 617, 618
Bennett, Frank V., 14 ff, 232
Bennett, Harry, 130, 131, 188
Bennett, Julia, 361
Bennett, Laura, 317, 561, 563, 569
Bennett, Lavinia, 256
Bennison (or Benoison), Marguerite, 47, 170
Benosser, Jean, 135
Bensberg, Helene, 66 ff, 288, 309, 311, 498 ff, 504, 510
Benson, Maggie and Jennie, 101, 189
Benson, Morgan, 524
Benson, R., 47
Bent, A., 53
Bent, B. C., 53, 537, 601
Bent, F. W., 86, 142, 164
Bent Brothers, 141, 279 (see supra)
Bentley, Charles, 430
Benziger, Anna, 512
Beresford, Frank, 449
Berg, Albert E., 428
Berg, Frl., 498 ff
Berg, Lillie, 595, 601
Berge, W., 378
Berger, Anna Theresa, 246, 306, 439, 474, 518, 537, 597, 648
Bergh, Henry, play by him, 368
Berghold, Emile, 512
Bergner, F., 56, 86, 162, 299, 375, 382, 591 ff
Bergstein, Carl, 377, 403

Berlin Lady Orchestra, 142 (see Lady Orchestra and Damenkapelle)
Berlioz, H., his Beatrice and Benedick, 632; his Requiem, 381, 603
Bernard, A., 355, 356
Bernard, Fannie, 321, 323, 330, 339, 530, 531, 543, 561
Bernard, Frl., 284
Bernard, James, 527
Bernard, Marion, 38
Bernhardt, Arrival of, farce, cast, 320
Bernhardt, Jeanne, 246
Bernhardt, Sarah, début, parts, reviews, 239, 240, 245, 246, 247; and Clara Morris, 259, 260; 301; art exhibition, 366; parts, 395; burlesqued, 34, 320, 363, 555
Bernhardt's Sommergarten, 513
Berrell, Mrs. M. L., 249, 484, 488
Berry (or Berrie), Belle, 204, 413 ff, 635, 636
Berry, J. S., his play, 204; 473
Berry's Theatre, Williamsburgh (1879-80), 203, 204; (1880-81), 413 ff; (1881-82), 635, 636
Bersin, H., 84, 298, 299, 403, 408, 630
Bersing-Hauptmann, Frau, 493 ff, 634
Bertha, the Sewing Machine Girl, cast, 347; 561
Berthelon, Dick, 126
Beryl, Sara, 319, 334
Beryl, W. C., 387
Berzirk Turn-Verein, 148
Beste Ton, Der, 507
Beth Israel, concert for, 170
Betsey Baker, 213, 244, 422
Bettini, Mlle. A., 514, 600, 612
Betrayed, play, 204
Beuermann, G. H., 392
Beuil, Mrs. M. A., 215
Bevan, Rev. L. D., 583
Beven, Alfred, 526
Beverly, Alfred, 65
Bial, Rudolf, and his orchestra, 289, 356, 357, 518, 536 ff; dies—benefit for family, 592
Bianca, Tillie, 124 ff
Bibbs and Bibbs, farce, 111, 188, 328, 340
Bibby, Edward, 143, 149, 314, 359, 366, 368
Bibi, child play, 285
Bibliothekar, Der, cast, 71, 72; with amateurs, 509
Bicycle riders, 207, 246, 306, 314, 315, 329, 349, 398, 498, 553, 559, 565, 570, 571, 574, 617, 622
Bicycle Tournament, 153
Bicycle Track, Williamsburgh, 416
Bidwell, Dollie, 109
Biedermann, 84, 85
Bierck, Julius, 593
Big Bonanza, The, 614
Big Four (various combinations), 316, 317, 333 ff, 340, 342, 397, 554, 573, 617
Big Four, the Original, 139
Big Little Three, 625, 636
Big Mistake, A, 109, 576
Big Sunflower, song, 60
Bigamy, cast, 265

INDEX

Bigelow, Adelia and Emma, 422
Bigelow, Emily, 38, 276
Bigelow, John, Mr. and Mrs., 584
Bigelow, Lenore, 44
Bigelow, Sadie, 58, 171, 202, 383, 391, 491
Bignardi, singer, 92 ff, 157, 374
Bijou Opera House (1880), 64; (1880-81), 266 ff; (1881-82), 478 ff
Bill, Our Coloured Friend, cast, 554
Bill Buffalo, farce, 549, 550
Billee Taylor, 253; casts, 265, 266, 272, 395; 413; casts, 458, 482; many burlesques (*infra*)
Billee, the Tailor, 323
Billiards, 129 ff, 149, 152 ff, 212, 582, 583
Billings, A. D., 11, 24 ff, 176, 242, 243, 259, 438, 449
Billings, John, amateur, 399
Billings, Josh, 154, 215
Billy Taylor, at Pastor's, 317, 528
Billy, the Tailor, 354, 364, 604, 616
Billy, the Tailor, in Fifteen Minutes, 351, 556
Billy, the Taylor, 329, 344
Bimberg, David, 592, 645
Bing, George, 117
Bingham, Flora, 348, 553, 625
Bingham, James W., 105, 132, 526, 624
Binney (*see Gibson and Binney*)
Binney and Fraine (or Frayne), 543, 546
Biorama, 647
Birch, Billy, 143 ff, 179, 362 ff, 580, 581
Birch, Dan, 636
Birch, Hannah, 111, 117, 189, 313, 337, 355
Bird, John H., 97, 181 ff, 393
Bird, Mary, 98 ff, 311 ff, 524, 525
Bird show, 365
Birds, performing, 350, 527, 547, 567
Bischoff, Frl., 74 ff
Bishop, Anna, 373 ff, 423, 595, 598, 601
Bishop, C. B., 243; as Widow Bedott, 256; 389
Bishop, Henry, amateur, 192
Bishop, W., 460
Bishop, W. F., 362
Bismarck Quartett Club, 84, 298, 299
Björnson, Bjornstjerne, speaks, 368
Black, C. K. L., amateur, 585
Black, Master John W., 192, 206
Black ballet, 257
Black chief, Simon, 564
Black Crook, The, casts, ballet, etc., 58, 171; 270; casts, 272, 484; 610
Black Crook, variety piece, 204
Black Diamond Quartette, 134
Black Flag, The, 442
Black Hand, The, 113, 325, 331, 332, 414, 415, 543, 544, 574, 575
Black Hills, The, play, 134
Black Man, The, in History, 647
Black Prince Association, 209
Black Sheep, 196, 216
Black Statue, The, cast, 131; 414, 635
Black Swan (Mme. Mahoney), 379
Black Venus, cast, 271
Black and Tan Picnic, 107

Blackberries in the South, 107
Black-Eyed Susan, 323, 329, 468 (*see also William and Susan*)
Blackford, John, 124
Blackford and Dye, 123
Blackmore, M., 607
Blackwell, Frank E., 211
Blackwell's Island, concert at, 373; 587
Blair, Billy, 126, 533
Blaisdell, Miss E., 2 ff, 432 ff
Blaisdell Family, 565, 569, 571
Blake, C. Russell, 476, 484, 610
Blake, Father, Old Folks, 206, 208
Blake, Georgie, 131, 134, 136, 140, 315, 322, 327, 331, 334, 345, 347, 352, 396; of Redmond and Blake, 526 ff, 543, 557
Blake, Julia, 65
Blake, O. W., 65
Blake, T., 280
Blake, W. R., 224
Blakeley, W., 43, 44
Blakely (of Sheffer and Blakely), 576
Blakely, Harry, 558, 564, 565, 570, 571
Blanchard, Edwin, 550, 635
Blanchard, Joe, 642
Blanchard, Kitty (*see Rankin, Mrs. McKee*)
Blanchard, Lottie, 124, 420, 547
Blanche, Baby, 307
Blancke, Katie, 170, 469
Bland, negro, 60
Blandowski, Alexander, 535
Blaubart, 286 (*see Barbe Bleue*)
Blauvelt, Lillian, 198
Blauvelt, Miriam, 198
Blauvelt, Nellie, 208
Blay (or Bley), Gaston, 154, 158, 162, 372, 595, 630, 645
Bleak House, 245; cast, 437; 491, 606 (*see Jo*)
Bledong, Julius, benefit, 81
Bleecker Street, No. 148, 89
Bleib bei Mir, 81
Blind Troupe, 151
Blint, John F., 556
Blitz, Eugene, 330
Blitzmädel, Ein, 71, 72
Block Game, A, 108, 546
Blois, singer, 596
Blondes on a Lark, 533
Bloodgood, Harry, 345
Bloomingdale Turn-Verein, 85, 295, 298, 299, 512
Blossom, Dick, 331
Blossom, Nat (*see Hines and Blossom*)
Blow for Blow, 319
Blue Fishing, or, the Pirates of Sandy Hook, 144, 145
Blue Glass, 126, 138, 141, 335, 336, 563
Blume, Settie, 152, 206, 378, 407, 417, 418, 626 ff, 638, 639
Blumenberg, Louis, 521, 539
Bluthochzeit, Die, casts, 79, 495
Blythe, Helen, 13 ff, 151
Blythe, Mrs., 177
Boaler, G. R., 270

INDEX

Boarding School, The, with Minnie Palmer, 383
Boat Club, Clifton, S. I., 647, 648
Bobbitt, Emma, 583, 586
Boccaccio, cast, 11; in German, cast, 80; 81; cast, 274; in German, 283, 285, 286, 287; 386, 398, 403; cast, 413; 483, 498, 605
Bock, Anna, 84, 158, 159, 162, 183, 371
Bock, Frederick, 172, 384; his play, 441, 442; 461, 465
Bodenstedt, F., reader, 84
Boeckleman, Bernard, 591, 592
Bogle, Mrs. James, 377, 393, 627, 637
Bohee Brothers (George and James), 350
Bohemian Girl, The, casts, 51, 146, 167; 168; by Young Apollo, 192; 206; casts, 251, 252; 385, 393, 456, 487, 604
Boisset Brothers (Fred, Hugo, Frank, Willis), 346 ff, 359, 396, 397, 562, 564, 570, 616, 618
Boisset Family, 136, 140, 189
Bojock, Herr, 66 ff, 81, 283 ff
Bokee, W. H., 231, 270
Bollmann, Herr, 493 ff
Bolter, Sam, 619
Bolton, Frank, 114, 120, 121, 558, 573, 575
Bolz's Concert Hall, 83
Bolze, John, 512, 596
Bombardier, Der, im Feuer, 511
Bombastes Furioso, 586
Bond, F. E., 45, 177
Bond, Jessie, 35, 183, 184
Bondman, The (Jack Cade), cast, 463
Bonfanti, Marie, 27, 92, 183, 245
Bonheur, Clara, 251
Boniface, George C., parts, 65, 274, 279, 384
Boniface, George C., Jr., 274
Boniface, Mrs. G. C., parts, 46, 178, 262, 488
Boniface, Stella, parts, 2 ff, 167, 220 ff, 432
Bonnie Prince Charlie, lecture, 153
Booked, play, 327, 328
Booker, Harry and George, 553, 557, 564
Boole, Lillie, 44
Boole, Mrs. Ella, 208
Boole, Rev. W. H., lectures, 208
Booth, Agnes, parts, 45, 47, 54, 174, 177, 243, 260, 306, 447, 517
Booth, E., minor actor, 278
Booth, Edwin, parts, etc., 7, 22, 28, 29, 52, 94, 95, 183, 184, 248, 254, 449, 450, 459, 609
Booth, J. B., Jr., parts, 256, 492
Booth, Marion, 7, 8, 45, 216, 220 ff, 276
Booth, May, 254
Booth, Rachel, 472
Booth vs. Jefferson, farce, 342, 344
Booth's Theatre (1879-80), 23 ff; (1880-81), 237 ff; (1881-82), 448 ff
Bordeaux Sisters (Ella and Lotta), 555, 571
Borie, Annie J., 159, 161
Borry, Bessie, 485
Boshell, Ada, 315, 327, 337, 341
Boshell, Carrie, 105, 111, 115, 139, 327, 329, 342
Boshell, Louise, 359
Boss, The, 111, 322, 329, 352, 414, 575
Bossi, Ernestine, 245

Bostelmann, J. C., 197
Bostelmann, Mrs. J. C., 197
Boston Comic Opera Company, 458
Boston Ideal Opera Company, 58, 181, 182, 238, 393, 395, 455, 456, 611
Boston Quartette, 533
Botsford, Stella, 52, 53, 597
Boucicault, Dion, parts, plays, etc., 3 ff; at Booth's, 23 ff; plays by, 24, 25; The Octoroon, 40; parts, 171, 272, 322; 390; Suil-a-Mor, 457, 458; 607
Boucicault, Dion G. (Dot), 24
Boucicault, Mrs. (see Robertson, Agnes)
Boucsin, Clara, 299
Boudinot, Annie, 173, 263
Boudinot, Frank, 278
Bouilloud, parts, 239, 246
Boulangère, La, a des Écus, 32
Bounce, farce, 107
Bound for Germany, 335
Bourne, F. G., 165, 217, 307, 370, 417
Bouton, M. D., 628
Boutwell, Mattie, 555
Bouvard, opéra-comique, 36
Bouvier, Lizzie, 160, 198
Bovey, Charles, 391
Bowen, negro, 60
Bowen, Cyril, actor, 34
Bowen, F. E., 627
Bowen, T. E., 471
Bower, Marie, 591, 592
Bower, F. A., 208
Bower, William, 463
Bowers, A. F., 206
Bowers, May, 14 ff
Bowers, Mrs. D. P., parts, 28, 29, 183, 184, 393, 620
Bowery Boys, The, 114, 550
Bowery Garten (1879-80), 118 ff; (1880-81), 334 ff; under various names (1881-82), 547 ff
Bowery Theatre becomes the Thalia Theater, q.v.
Bowie knife fight, 108
Bowler, Brookhouse, 56
Bowler, Miss G., 481
Bowman and Radcliffe, 535
Bown, P. H., amateur, 393
Bown, W. Paul, 233 ff, 269
Bowne, Fred W., 612
Bowser, C. W., parts, 31, 169, 256, 411, 466, 491
Box and Cox, 205, 216, 217, 340, 530, 585
Boxing, wrestling, etc., 150, 214, 314, 576, 577
Boy Avenger, The, 114
Boy Detective, The, 106, 107, 110, 185, 186, 333, 353, 354, 415, 545, 551, 576, 623
Boy Scout of the Sierras, The, 280, 333, 353, 493, 551, 554
Boyard, E. P., 88
Boyce, Marie, 208, 642
Boyd (of Haley and Boyd), 122
Boyd, Annie, 348, 349, 546, 560, 565, 566, 571, 616, 617, 622
Boyd, Archie, 170, 276, 468, 469

INDEX

Boyd, Clarence, 115
Boyd, Jennie, 5 ff, 263, 460
Boyd, Jessie, 341, 349
Boyd, Nellie, 169, 263
Boyd and Sarsfield, 138, 336, 351 542, 543, 551, 563, 568
Boyer, Lillie, 361, 577
Boyhood Days, 117, 139
Boyle, Anna, 278, 281, 282, 386
Boyle, Florence, 206
Boyle, J. W., 337
Boyle, Mrs. James, 628
Boyle and Malone, 141
Boynton, Captain Paul, 106
Boys from Mullingar, 101
Bradbury, J. W., 255
Bradford, Ada, 114, 120, 121, 558, 573, 575
Bradley, H. B., 46, 262, 488
Bradley, Leonora, 186, 492
Bradley, Lizzie, 619
Bradley, M., parts, 98 ff, 311 ff, 524, 525
Bradley's Luck, 567, 618
Bradshaw, C. H., 29, 262, 488
Brady, Judge, 584
Bragee, R., bass, 193
Bragginton, W., 44
Braham, Dave, his songs, 99, 311 ff, 524, 525
Braham, L., tenor, 580
Braham, Leonora, 48, 225
Brahms, Academic Festival Overture, 602, 632; Symphony in C, 380; Symphony in D major, 380; Tragic Overture, 601
Brainerd, Maria, 162, 163
Braman, Mrs., reader, 422
Brambilla, Mlle., 516
Brand, John E., 178, 231 ff, 269, 442, 606
Brandeis, Henry, 161, 193, 200, 372, 377, 405
Brandis, Emily, 645
Brandmann, Frl., 493 ff, 634
Brandram, Rosina, 35, 181, 182, 184
Brandt, Hermann, 160, 162, 235, 356, 371, 375, 587, 591 ff, 598, 602
Brannick, Thomas, 442
Branscombe, Maude, 146, 392
Branson, Philip, 480
Brass Monkey, The, 549
Bray, E. W., 184, 395, 399, 404 ff, 408, 628, 629
Bray, Virginia, 47, 390
Bray, W. H., 40, 175, 247, 271
Brazzier, William, George, Rufus, 64, 100, 123, 132, 136, 139, 189, 332, 334, 338
Breaking the Spell, 192, 194
Breath, his plays, 213, 426
Bree and Kirwin, 567, 573, 618
Breedon, Arnold, 266
Breesee, Mr. and Mrs. R. A., 200, 407
Breitschuk, H., 376
Bremer, Bertha, 295
Bremer, Frederika, 245
Bremser, Gustav, 509
Brennan, Eddie, 115
Brennan, Emma, 113, 118
Brennan, Kitty, 57

Brennan, Mr. and Mrs. R. A., 106, 128, 129, 131, 140, 189, 204, 315, 327, 345 ff, 351, 533, 534, 567, 572, 573
Brennan, R. A., his burlesque Pinafore, 534
Brennan, T. F., 171, 249, 469
Brennand (sic), Richard, 259
Brenner, Jacob, 404
Brent, William H., 127, 530, 622
Bretto, Emma, 130, 138, 320
Brevarde (James) and Sawtelle (Charles), 113, 116 ff, 133, 137, 141, 328, 333, 334, 352, 549, 553, 556, 567, 616
Brevoor, Anna, 475
Brewer, John H., 184, 198, 200, 628
Brewster, Maria, 64
Bric-à-Brac, casts, 63, 191; ballet, 270; Club, 406; 616
Bridgeport, 87
Brien, J. F., parts, 15 ff, 58, 177
Brigand, The, farce, 147
Brigand's Daughter, The, 204
Brigand's Doom, The, 333
Brigands, Les, 32, 33
Brigands, The, pantomime, 119, 121, 341, 538, 545, 558
Bright, John, actor, 449
Bright Eyes, an Indian, 153
Brighton, play, 638
Brighton Beach, 87, 155, 200, 409, 601, 631, 641
Brigiotti, J. G., 88, 300
Brignoli, 96, 162 ff, 182, 183, 198, 251, 373, 377, 430, 523, 611, 639
Brimer, Mary, 214
Brinckerhoff, Clara, 54, 595
Brindis, Joseph H., 329
Brink, Edwin, 61, 62
Brisbane, Letitia, 607
Bristol, Henry, 450
Bristow, G. F., 598
British Blondes, 186, 317, 318
Brittain, Miss Wallace, 469
Broadway (728), Circus, 147
Broadway Milliners, farce, 414
Broadway Novelty Theatre, 319
Broadway Opera House, 63
Broadway Theatre (30th Street), becomes Daly's, 12 ff
Broadway Theatre (728 Broadway), 318, 319
Brock (late of Webster Brothers), 326
Brock, Joe (of Four Shamrocks), 324; (of Thompson and Brock), 337
Brocolini, parts, 35, 184, 266, 387, 395, 458, 610
Broderick, J. H., 199, 311, 377
Brogue and Blarney, 126
Broken Fetters, 622
Broncho horses, 146
Bronson, Walter, 50, 171, 173
Brontë, Charlotte, lecture on, 404
Brook, A. J., 59
Brook, The, 20, 41, 92, 178, 202, 256, 280, 389
Brooklyn (1879-80), 167 ff; (1880-81), 383 ff; (1881-82), 604 ff

[663]

Brooklyn Amateur Opera Association, 395, 614

Brooklyn Athletic Club, 199

Brooklyn churches (*see Churches, Brooklyn*)

Brooklyn Heights Parlour Skating Rink, 628

Brooklyn Institute, 193, 629

Brooklyn Miscellany (1879-80), 191 ff; (1880-81), 403 ff; (1881-82), 626 ff

Brooklyn Musical Union, 416

Brooklyn New Museum, 400, 401

Brooklyn Opera House (Mozart Garden), 189, 190

Brooklyn Operatic Club, 207, 208

Brooklyn Philharmonic Chorus, 379

Brooklyn Quartett Club, 623

Brooklyn Quintet Club, 406, 407

Brooklyn (South) Turn-Verein, 86

Brooklyn Theatre (*see Haverly's Brooklyn Theatre*)

Brooklyn Vocal Society, 395, 408

Brooks, Alice, 171, 388, 454, 476

Brooks, Arthur, Rev., 153

Brooks, E., minstrel, 59

Brooks, Nellie, 124 ff, 135, 138, 326 ff, 347, 348

Brooks, Ruby, 343

Brooks, Virginia, 97, 182, 232, 444

Broom drill, 630, 644

Brosi, Louise, 508

Brosman, T. H., 430

Brougham, John, parts, 24; last appearance, 25; 224

Broughton, actor, 442

Brower, Carrie, 325, 330, 333, 551, 560

Brower, Robert, 134, 272

Brown, Ben, 121, 122, 139, 325, 330 ff, 550

Brown, Blower, walker, 149

Brown, Francis, 57

Brown, George, 392

Brown, H. M., 37

Brown, Harry, parts, 269, 460, 606

Brown, Henry S., singer, 395, 399, 627, 628

Brown, Imogene, 198, 206, 381, 382, 393, 403, 595

Brown, J. H., 38, 253

Brown, L., 465

Brown, Nella F., 193, 317, 408, 582, 587, 627, 631, 637, 640

Brown, Sedley, 179, 476, 485

Brown, T. Allston, 1; as to My Partner, 9; 22; as to Neilson's farewell and death, 31; 50, 64, 90, 104, 243, 257; 319, 433, 441, 444, 460; as to receipts for Fritz in Ireland, 470; 472; as to receipts for Patience, 477; 480, 485, 487, 489, 538

Brown, W. P., 146, 150

Browne, George F., 515, 519

Browne, Henry Eyre, 192, 197, 408, 409, 420, 628

Browne, J. B., 608

Browne, the Martyr, 316

Bruce, Fred, 59

Bruch's, Max, Lied von der Glocke, 512

Bruder Zirkel Verein, 295

Brunhild, 69; cast, 245

Bruno, variety, 396

Bruno, Augustus, 40, 42, 179, 342

Bruno, Harry, 124, 125

Bruno, Mrs. Augustus, 342

Bruno il Filatore, 302

Brunswick Glee Club, 627, 637

Brustad, Norway giant, 541, 580, 624

Brutone, Mrs. J. W., 58, 65, 171, 383, 453, 606

Brutus (in Julius Cæsar), Louis James as, 276, 461; John McCullough as, 306

Brutus (Payne's play), 170, 248, 249, 463

Bryant (of Big Four), 333

Bryant (*see Mackin and Bryant*)

Bryant (*see Morton and Bryant*)

Bryant, Andy, 415, 547, 553

Bryant, Billy, 111, 321, 339, 533

Bryant, Dan, 59

Bryant, Fred (*see Bryant and Hoey*)

Bryant, Harry, ventriloquist, 130, 207, 209, 341, 343, 396, 425, 541, 555, 558, 598, 615

Bryant, Minnie, 415, 549

Bryant, W. T., 397, 554, 616

Bryant and Belmont, 125, 635

Bryant (Fred) and Hoey (William F.), 51, 56, 100, 102, 131, 136, 172, 189, 274, 314, 343, 344, 363, 398, 554, 565, 566, 571, 572, 576, 615, 618

Bryant (William) and Richmond (Lizzie), 330

Bryant and Saville (Gus), 101, 115, 127, 133, 134, 139, 333, 350, 553, 563, 566, 570

Bryer, Mary, 63, 607

Buccaneer of the Gulf, The, 282

Buchanan, Virginia, parts, 55, 170, 253, 268, 412, 439, 440, 483, 484, 489, 620

Buck, Amy, 405

Buck, Dudley, his Saga of King Olaf, 181; his opera, Deseret, 255; his King Olaf's Christmas, 592; 614

Buck, Dudley, Quartet, 407, 408, 420, 426, 614, 628, 629

Buckingham, Fannie Louise, 532, 576

Buckingham Palace, New York, 142, 361, 362, 580

Buckley, athlete, 585

Buckley, Billy, 106, 107, 318, 342, 363, 558

Buckley, E. J., parts, 262, 270, 448, 469, 491, 518

Buckley, J. K., minstrel, 59

Buckley, Joe, 323, 324, 520, 528, 533, 547, 555

Budd (*see Quaker City Quartette*)

Budlong, W. C., 189

Budworth, Emma, 119, 127, 141, 314, 346, 348, 352, 353, 396, 561

Budworth, Frank, 54, 170, 280, 327, 425, 482, 491, 546

Budworth, Harry, 100, 119, 127, 141, 314, 346 ff, 352, 353, 396, 561

Budworth, Master J. B., 206

Buehl, Henry, 637

Buell, Joseph M., 472

Buffalo Bill, 65, 278, 280, 389, 412, 491, 619

Buffalo Bill at Bay, cast, 65
Buffalo Bill, Monarch of the Plains, play, 333
Buffalo Bill Outdone, farce, 133
Buffalo Bill's Last Shot, 351
Buffaloes, Benevolent Order of, 586, 591
Bull, Edwin A., 344
Bull, Harry B., 411
Bull, Ole, 95, 97, 162, 183
Bull, A, in a China Shop, 106
Bulwer Dramatic Company, 420
Bunell (see Melville and Bunell)
Bungert, Annie and Rose, 420
Bungert, George D., 420
Bungert, Lena, 419 ff, 629
Bunnell's Museum, Brooklyn, 190, 401, 624, 625
Bunnell's Museum, New York, 364, 365, 578, 579
Bunnell's Opera House, Coney Island, 631
Buongiorno, H., 162, 403
Burbank, A. P., 152 ff, 184, 191 ff, 204, 206, 211, 266, 365, 378, 398, 403 ff, 408, 419, 422 ff, 628, 630
Burbank, Otto, 101, 128, 129, 140, 141, 396 ff, 622
Burbeck, F. M., 264
Burdett, J. S., 153, 159, 206, 367, 378, 586, 592, 627
Burdette, Robert J., 584
Bürgerlich und Romantisch, 508
Burgess, Emma, 49, 178, 180, 255
Burgess, Joe and Annie, 112, 115, 119, 121, 127 ff, 135, 140, 544, 545, 554, 561 ff, 566, 568, 570 ff
Burgess, Joseph A., 570
Burgess, Neil (Widow Bedott), 41, 42, 176, 203, 268, 281, 386, 413, 481, 607, 634
Burk, J. O., 44
Burke, Charles (see Campbell and Burke)
Burke, Charles A., 545, 618
Burke, John, 101, 339
Burke, John T., 267, 449, 474
Burke, Major, 266, 315, 326, 341
Burke, William, 146
Burke and Smith, 550
Burlesque Three (Cereni, Peters, Ada Page), 564, 567, 571
Burling, Clinton, 213
Burnand, F. C., his play, The Colonel, 474
Burnell (Quaker City Quartette), 544, 565, 573
Burnett, Ada, 326, 352, 543, 556
Burnett, Alf, 364, 365, 515, 542, 624, 625
Burnett, Frances Hodgson, Esmeralda, 447, 448
Burnett, J. P., his play, Jo, 468
Burnett, John H., 9, 11, 177, 360, 486, 493, 529
Burnham, actor, 29, 232
Burnham, Avon C., 191
Burns (of Mackin and Burns), 141
Burns, Charles, 59
Burns, Daniel, walker, 359
Burns, John, 549

Burns, T. H., 41, 58, 256, 387, 492
Burnside, Jean, 236
Burroughs, Claude, 11
Burroughs, W. F., 45, 390
Burrows, J. C., 489
Bursel, Maggie, 349, 554, 560, 568, 570
Burshall, Maggie, 189 (see supra)
Burt, Fannie L., 173
Burt, Nettie, 143
Burton, negro, 60
Burton, Carrie, 64, 253, 266, 272, 477, 482
Burton, Clarence, 574
Burton, Edward, 38, 311 ff, 524, 525
Burton, Florence, 38
Burton, Grace, 333
Burton, J. H., and dogs, 567, 572
Burton, Johnnie and Lottie, 349, 543
Burton, Lizzie, 238, 393, 455, 611
Burton, S. M., 271
Burton, W. E., 107, 436
Burton, W. H., 489
Burton, William, 51, 168
Burton and Smith, 111
Burton Dramatic Club, 629
Burville, Alice, 266, 411, 477
Busbey, Hamilton, 540
Bush, Frank, 124, 125, 140, 323, 332, 334, 339, 401, 535, 536, 546, 578, 581, 616, 624
Bush, Irwin, Specialty Trio, 563, 570
Bushby, Horace, 59
Bushnell, aerial juggler, 119, 320, 323, 531, 570, 635
Bushnell's Show, 428
Bushwick, Old Sunday School, 204, 205
Butler (see Graham and Butler)
Butler, Andy, 335
Butler, B. H., 281, 282
Butler, C. W., 237, 262, 471, 476
Butler, Madge, 40, 389
Butler, Robert, 27, 148, 338
Butler (Sam) and Leslie (Rob), 107, 113
Butler, Thomas, Colonel, 151
Butler, Will H., 392 ff
Buxton, Mrs., 165, 201
Buxton, T. B., 159
Buzzetti, Estelle, 88, 158
Bye (see Blackford and Bye)
Byrne (see Shirley and Byrne)
Byrne, Bessie, 39, 474
Byrne, John H. (see Saville and Byrne)
Byrnes (see Leslie and Byrnes)
Byrnes (see McKee and Byrnes)
Byrnes, J. J. (see Sellou and Byrnes)
Byrnes, John F., 111
Byron, Arthur, 251, 252
Byron, Eva, 349, 568, 570
Byron, H. J., Our Girls, 2; Chawles, 46; The Upper Crust, 222; Blow for Blow, 319
Byron, Joe, 550
Byron, Kate, 468, 608
Byron, Lizzie, 534
Byron, Nellie, 109, 110, 113, 123, 124
Byron, Oliver Doud, 65, 271, 387, 468, 491, 608
Byron, Susie, 111, 126, 127, 130, 312, 313, 525

Byron and Coffee, 415
Byron and Fash, 548, 549

Cabble, Jennie, 417
Cadet la Perle, cast, 62, 63
Cadwallader, L., 477, 597
Cadwell, E. A., 424
Cady, Harriet, 596
Cahill, Helena, 94
Cahill, W. B., 24, 31, 34, 57, 62, 94, 236, 466, 491
Cahill and Martin, 353
Cahill and Regan, 184
Calburt, Frank, 575
Calcichromopticon, 307
Caldwell, Ella, 508
Caledonia Hall, 153, 368
Calendonian athletes, 200
Caledonian Club, Brooklyn, 194, 197, 421, 625
Caledonian Club, New York, 156, 369, 584
Caledonian Sports, 347
Calef, Jennie, 49, 178, 180, 254, 277, 388, 459
Calef, Jessie, 49, 178, 180, 255, 277
Calef, May, 393, 455
Calice, Myron, 135, 146
California Detective, The, 545
California Quartette, 350, 351, 528, 560, 568, 580, 597
California through Death Valley, cast, 622
Californier auf Reisen, 81
Callahan, Charles E., Fogg's Ferry, 475
Callahan, George W., 128, 322
Callahan and Collins, 125
Callan (of Four Diamonds), 129
Callan, John, 534
Callan, Master James, 345
Callan, N., Jr., 410
Callan, Haley and Callan, 141, 341, 345, 349, 566, 576, 618
Callender's Minstrels, 399
Calvé, Emma, 92
Calvert, Miss A., 450
Calvert, Mrs. Charles, 450, 459
Camara, Frl., 74 ff, 496
Camargo, La, 26; cast, 98; 176
Camels, 359
Camera, Una, affittata a Due, 302
Cameron, Miss, 440
Cameron, Miss E., 174
Cameron, Victoria, 8, 184, 278, 470
Cameron, W. C., 111 ff, 324 ff, 542 ff, 622, 646
Camilla, Little, 617, 618
Camiliendame, Die, with Geistinger, 286, 287, 288, 495, 612
Camille, casts, etc., 52, 53, 94, 174, 202, 224, 228, 277, 286, 287, 288, 322, 386, 395, 438, 441, 453, 463, 464, 519, 605, 606, 612, 621, 633 (see also supra and Dame, la, aux Camélias)
Camille (Marguerite Gautier), Clara Morris as, 174, 228; Rose Coghlan as, 224; Fanny Davenport as, 277, 386, 463, 605, 633; Marie Geistinger as, 286, 287, 288, 495, 612; Lena Aberle as, 322; Sarah Bern-

hardt as, 395; Eugenie Legrand as, 441; Mlle. Rhea as, 453, 606; Maude Granger as, 464; Marie Prescott as, 519, 621; Clara Morris, Modjeska, Bernhardt, Geistinger, compared, 228, 240, 241, 286
Cammeyer, Jerry, 63
Cam-o-Mile, 344
Camp, Harvey C., 193
Campanini, Italo, parts, 91 ff; 158, 162; sings Wagner, 165; parts, 180 ff; 194; sings act of Die Götterdämmerung, in Italian, 201; 301; parts, 304 ff; 311, 357, 370 ff, 381, 382, 391 ff, 466; parts, 516 ff; leaves Academy opera, 522; 592, 599, 600, 602, 603; parts, 611 ff; 632
Campbell (of Clipper Quartette), 139
Campbell (of Electric Quartette), 571
Campbell (of Excelsior Quartette), 570
Campbell (of Worley and Campbell), 338, 339
Campbell, Adelaide, 100
Campbell, Bartley, his My Partner, profits, etc., 8, 9; The Galley Slave, 40, 41; his Fairfax, 44, 45; Fate, 202; Matrimony, 264, 265; My Geraldine, 265; Van, the Virginian, 412; The White Slave, 471
Campbell, C. J., tenor, 57, 338, 464, 478, 482, 537
Campbell, Cora, 425
Campbell, Donald, 459
Campbell, Frank, 103, 554 (see Campbell and Burke)
Campbell, G. F., 134
Campbell, George, 335, 559
Campbell, George F. (of Clipper Quartette), 552, 559, 563
Campbell, H. C., 48
Campbell, H. J., 111, 337
Campbell, Helen Dudley, 391, 406, 598
Campbell, Lucille, 337 ff
Campbell, N., amateur, 199
Campbell, Ned, 112, 118
Campbell, Nellie, 53
Campbell, Nora, 115, 338, 547
Campbell, Percy, 252, 436
Campbell, W., 101
Campbell and Burke, 115, 121, 130, 132, 139, 140, 313, 325 ff, 333, 334, 340
Campbell's Comic Coterie, 366
Canal Boat Pinafore, 103
Canaries, performing, 401
Canary, Thomas, 139 ff, 568
Canby, A. H., 40, 170, 268, 467, 607
Can-can, 536
Candidus, William, 598 ff
Canfield, C. H., 628
Canfield, Hattie, 643
Canissa, Pauline, breaks down, 591; 594
Cannibals of Barren Island, 363
Cannstatter Volksfest, 207, 416, 636
Cantrell, R. B., 640
Capers, 348
Capitoline Lake and Grounds, 195, 200, 408
Capoul, Victor, 25, 26, 32 ff, 80, 97, 176, 183
Cappa, Seventh Regiment Band, 379, 585

Cappelini, Eugenie, 58, 271, 272
Cappiani, Louise, 159, 598
Capricorn goats, 586
Cara, La, del Campo, 28
Caratu, Felix, 601
Carbone, 615
Cardello, Lizzie, 645
Cardello and La Rose, 558, 645
Cardello and Victorelli, 132, 349, 350, 398
Cardigan, Cora, 350, 527, 569, 624
Carey, Eleanor, 227 ff, 388, 411, 438 ff, 607
Carey, George, 111, 133, 137, 529
Carey Brothers, 529
Carhart, J. L., 54, 245, 453, 468
Carhart, Mrs. G. W., 598
Carhart, Mrs. J. L., 245, 516, 613
Carlberg, G., 150, 160, 183, 304, 391
Carleton, Adelaide, 258
Carleton, Irene, 534, 548
Carleton, Moya, 624
Carleton, W., 44
Carleton, William, playwright, 102, 469
Carleton, William T., 251, 252, 269, 387, 464, 474, 477, 508, 509, 538
Carling, caricatures, 58, 138, 171
Carlyn, Nettie, 123, 331, 337
Carmen, in Italian, casts, 27, 91, 93, 97, 182, 183; in English, 251, 252; in Italian, 304, 305, 308; cast, 391; in French, 466, 467; casts, 516 ff; without Il Remendado, 517; Mme. Lablache in two parts, 522; 611, 614
Carmen, burlesque, cast, 255
Carneval, Der, in Rom, cast, 287
Carnis, Mlle., 57, 271, 491
Carnival of Venice, sung by Gerster, 307, 308
Carpenter, A., pantomime, 27
Carpenter, A. E., mesmerism, 195, 367, 368, 403
Carpenter, Ed, 122
Carpenter, W., 450
Carpentier, Mlle., 239, 246
Carr, Frank B., 111, 341, 348; of the Horse-shoe Four, 553, 562, 563
Carr Brothers, acrobats, 562
Carreño, Teresa, 28, 97, 160 ff, 183, 200, 356, 372, 392, 430, 451, 523
Carri, F. and H., 157 ff
Carrick a Rede, cast, 179
Carrington, A. R., 627
Carrington, Abbie, 52, 156, 181, 251, 252, 456
Carroll (of Sharpley and Carroll), 120
Carroll, Alice, 321
Carroll, Annie, 147, 192, 205, 645
Carroll, Fred, 102, 137, 349
Carroll, J. H., Rev., 365
Carroll, Jennie, 243
Carroll, John, 113, 122, 138, 139, 335, 339
Carroll, R. M. and Sons (E. H. and Master Richard), 134, 137, 321, 329, 335, 344, 350 ff, 560, 562, 568, 574, 624
Carroll, Verona, 336
Carroll, W. B., circus, 645
Carroll, W. F., 137, 532, 534, 559, 575, 576
Carroll, William (Billy), banjo, 137, 363, 490, 519, 520, 526 ff, 562, 569, 574, 575, 618
Carroll Brothers, 135, 136, 148, 331, 332, 347, 348, 565, 567
Carroll and Walters, 319, 329, 331, 339, 350, 415, 543, 567
Carson, Emma, 56, 172, 257
Carte, D'Oyly, in America, 34 ff; in Brooklyn, 181; gives Billee Taylor, 265, 266; presents Archibald Forbes, 366; 395; his company in Patience, 476 ff; presents Oscar Wilde, 583, 584; his Opera Company, 597
Carter, billiards, 152, 154
Carter, Billy, 139, 188, 189, 345, 349, 351, 565, 569, 571, 618
Carter, Eugene, 582
Carter, Helen, 262, 619
Carter, Leo, 642
Carter, Lulu, 460
Carter, Otis H., 59
Carter, Thomas, 624
Carter and Anderson, 576
Carter's Novelty Concert Company, 420
Cartwright, singer, 200
Caruso, Enrico, 22
Cary, circus, 148
Cary, Annie Louise, concerts, opera, etc., 92 ff, 162, 180 ff, 194, 304 ff, 371, 381, 391 ff, 410; leaves Academy opera, 516; 596, 599 ff, 632
Case, W. R., pianist, 162, 369, 375 ff, 591, 593, 595, 627
Caselli (of Australian Four), 557
Casely, Nellie, 215
Casey, Frank, 59
Casey, the Piper, 556
Casey's Raffle, 562
Cash, Minnie, 643
Casino (Metropolitan Casino), 537 ff
Caspar (or Casper), A. S., 323, 415, 532, 533, 547, 550
Cassano, flute, 600, 601
Cassati, Mlle., 57, 58
Casselli, Tom, 480, 481
Cassius (in Julius Cæsar), Lawrence Barrett as, 276, 384, 386, 461, 605; John A. Lane as, 306
Cast Away, 213
Caste, casts, with amateurs, 195, 199; 216; cast, 428; with amateurs, 585, 637
Castelli, Giorgio, 235, 356, 371
Castelli, Mlle., 587, 612
Castelmary, opera, 26, 180
Castilian dancers, 536
Castle, George, 475
Castle, William, parts, 51, 167, 251, 478, 487, 523, 605
Castle Garden, cast, 528
Castles in Spain, cast, 272
Castleton, Ada, 560, 636
Castleton, Kate, 100, 102, 137, 189, 204, 254, 581
Caswell, A. S., 199, 200, 404, 405, 408, 614
Cat circus, 577

Cat congress, 364
Cat show, 400, 579
Cat that hatched chickens, 401
Cathedrals of Europe, lectures, 153
Catherine, Mlle., and her birds, 527, 534, 558, 578
Catherine, Mlle., prestidigitator, 618
Catholic Protectory Band, 518
Catlett, Lew and Lulu, 347
Cato, play, cast, 550
Cats! Cats! 569
Cats, performing, 350, 547, 625
Cats of a murderer exhibited, 400
Caught at Last, 315, 326
Caught by the Cuff, 403, 422
Caulfield, James, 163, 212, 425, 600
Caulfield, Willie, 425, 645
Cavallazzi, Malvina, 518, 521, 523
Cavana (Jerry) and Mack, 544 ff, 552, 563, 564, 570
Cavannah, Kathrene, 208, 407, 417, 422
Cavendish, Ada, parts, 46, 54, 170, 171, 174, 274, 279, 384
Caverly's English Folly Company, 64
Cawthorn (or Cawthorne), Joe and Herbert, 560, 561, 563, 565, 569, 570, 576, 625
Cayvan, Georgia, parts, 23, 235, 236, 237, 446, 471, 607
Cazauran, A. R., and The Creole, 228; Felicia, 229; Far from the Madding Crowd, 440, 441
Cecilia Singing Society, Williamsburgh, 418, 639
Cecilian Club, Brooklyn, 614, 615
Cecilienne, La (Société), 301
Cedergren, Anna, 356
Celebrated Case, A, 65; casts, 241, 242, 278, 388, 411, 465, 483; 492, 607, 619
Celeste, Eva, Albino, 400
Cellier, Alfred, conducts Pirates of Penzance, 35; his Charity Begins at Home, 64; 184, 193; his Sultan of Mocha, 225; 266, 464
Cellini's Novelty Troupe, 134; his ballet, 185
Centennial Traveller, The, 132
Centennial Weary Traveller, The, 562, 564, 568
Central Park Brewery, 295
Central Union Ball, 584
Cercle Français de l'Harmonie, 513, 519
Cereni, Harry, 110, 136, 338, 342, 555, 561, 564, 567
Cereni (Harry) and Leslie (George), 315, 321, 346
Cerito, Mlle., 101, 134
Cervantes, Tribute to and for statue of, 28
Cervi, Miss, 26
Cetawayo, 364
Chace, Ella, 188
Chace, W. H., 318
Chace (W. H.) and Yale (Charles H.), 133
Chadwick, G. W., 455
Chadwick, Mrs., 406
Chain Gang at Sheepshead Bay, 188
Chain of Guilt, The, 337
Chalet, 318, 534 ff, 560, 616

Chalfin, W. D., 327 ff, 395, 437
Chalfont (of Electric Quartette), 571
Chalk Talk, 198, 365, 403, 407, 419, 420, 423, 645
Chamber Music, lecture on, 155
Chamberlain, Andrew, 195
Chamberlain, Emily Jordan, 259 ff
Chamberlain, Fred and Lillian, 340
Chambers, Charles, benefit, 395
Chamounin, French actor, 239 ff
Champagne and Oysters, 46
Chandos, Alice, 280
Chanfrau, son of F. S., in Kit, 426
Chanfrau, F. S., as Kit, 8, 279, 386, 412, 470, 492
Chanfrau, H. T., 265, 462, 463
Chanfrau, Henrietta, 278, 470
Chang, giant, 359, 364, 365, 401, 419, 624
Chanucka, 94
Chapeau, Un, de Paille d'Italie, as The Wedding March, 45
Chapin, Alice, 182
Chapin, Minnie, 122, 131, 189, 328 ff, 343, 354
Chaplin, George D., 384, 390, 411, 486
Chapman, Blanche, parts, 38, 479, 613, 618
Chapman, Cherry, 118, 415
Chapman, Ed, 39, 56, 172, 218, 254, 277, 460, 482, 606
Chapman, Ella, 39, 56, 172
Chapman, H. G., 154
Chapman, Stella, 226
Chapman, Thomas, 94, 171, 244
Chapman, W. A., 604
Chapman, W. R., 597
Chappelle, Charles, 275, 516
Chappelle, R. J., 406
Chappelle, Rose, 253, 266, 272, 464, 477
Chappelle Sisters (Grace and Jeanne), 347, 352, 396
Chariot races, 631
Charity, cast, 19
Charity Balls, Brooklyn, 393; New York, 95, 520; Staten Island, 429, 648
Charity Begins at Home, cast, 64; 388, 526
Charles, C. Wilson, 278
Charles, G. W., 493
Charles, George C., 110, 325, 328, 415, 543, 625
Charles, Florence, 493
Charles, Meroe, 43, 171
Charles, R. O., 257
Charmed Cross, The, cast, 124; 204
Chase, A. E., 246
Chase, Billy, 558
Chase, David H., 38, 237, 386
Chase, Miss, 24
Chase, Sara B., 584, 585
Chastel, Jeanne, 235, 356
Chatterton, W., 59
Chatterton-Bohrer, Mme., harp, 53, 54, 150, 157 ff, 183, 376, 392, 408, 523, 594 ff, 638
Chawles, cast, 46
Checkered Life, A, cast, 467
Checkmate, 178

INDEX

Cheletia, contortionist, 624
Chelsea Guillotine, 143
Che-Mah, dwarf, 364, 401, 541, 624, 631
Cherie, Adelaide, 54, 171, 271, 633
Cherry, Mary E., 421
Chester, Annie, 485
Chester, Marie, 45, 54, 174, 237, 474
Chester, Mrs. S. K., 167
Chester, Samuel K., 263, 485
Chestnut Street (Philadelphia) actors, 177
Chevalier de St. George, 403
Chevalier von San Marco, Der, cast, 496
Chevaliers, Les, du Pince-Nez, 98
Cheyne, Commander, 582
Chichester, Frank, 197
Chickering Hall (1879-80), 151 ff; 156 ff;
    (1880-81), 365 ff, 570 ff; (1881-82), 582 ff,
    587 ff
Chickering Harmonics, 205, 207, 208, 417, 418,
    422
Child of the State, A, casts, 277, 384; 412;
    cast, 488; 607
Child Stealer, The, cast, 60; 179, 278, 323, 622
Children act, 77, 78, 79, 141, 152, 154, 192,
    194, 195, 205, 208, 215, 285, 293, 397, 399,
    405, 407, 414, 415, 427, 435
Children's Carnival and Ball, 95, 307, 520
Childs, Nat, author, 266, 267
Chilperic, 384
Chiltrea, India rubber man, 624
Chimes of Normandy, The, cast, 51; 66; cast,
    147; 251, 360, 385; casts, 393, 455; 478,
    487, 607 (see also Cloches, Les, de Corne-
    ville and Glocken, Die, von Corneville)
Chimney Corner, The, 629
Chimpanzee, 360
Chinese Barber, The, 561
Chinese boy at Daly's, 13
Chinese Divertissements, 123
Chinese Festival, 368
Chinese giant, 579, 624 (see also Chang)
Chinese lady, 579, 625
Chinese music and musicians, 364, 598
Chipman, A. Z., 115, 234, 385; his play, 467;
    470
Chippendale, F., 63, 247, 282, 435
Chippewa Council, 217
Chisnell, W., 450
Chit-Chat, 347, 353
Chivers, H. C. (of Boston Quartette), 533
Choquet, Mlle., 263
Choral Union, Flushing, 646
Chorus, Theodore Thomas's, 410
Choung Chi Lang, giant, 579
Chris, play, 110
Chris and Lena, 387, 633
Chrisdie, Charles, 123, 124, 333
Christ und Jude, cast, 79
Christening, The, cast, 335; 345, 349, 572
Christianson, Mrs., 193 ff, 198 ff, 405, 407
Christie, Jennie, 102, 137, 188, 314 ff, 526 ff,
    574
Christie and Williams, 126
Christie Johnstone, cast, 278
Christin, Julia, 22

Christine, Millie, 625
Christmas Cantata, 405
Christmas Eve, farce, 121, 131, 134, 139,
    140
Christmas festivities, 417
Christol, André, 149
Christy, George, 59
Church, Lottie, 41, 65, 178, 279, 280
Church Choir Company, New York, 202, 582
Church Choir Quartet, 16
Churches, Brooklyn, entertainment in (see
    Miscellany, Brooklyn for 1879-80, 1880-81,
    1881-82)
Churches, Flatbush (see Flatbush, passim)
Churches, Greenpoint, 207 ff, 421 ff, 641 ff
Churches, Jamaica (see Jamaica, passim)
Churches, Long Island City and Astoria (see
    Long Island City [1879-80], [1880-81],
    [1881-82] passim)
Churches, New York, entertainments in,
    158 ff, 370 ff, 582 ff
Churches, Staten Island (see Staten Island,
    [1879-80], [1880-81], [1881-82] passim)
Churches in Williamsburgh (see Williams-
    burgh Miscellany [1879-80], [1880-81],
    [1881-82]
Ciampi-Cellaj, 25, 156 ff, 180
Ciapini, Massimo, 456, 457, 615
Cigale, La, 262
Cigarette, the Little Leopard of France, 331
Cincinnati Hams, 125, 140
Cinderella, cast, 238; 383; cast, 619; 628;
    with children, 206, 405
Cinderella, by Rossini, cast, 198
Cinderella, cantata, 85
Cinderella at School, cast, 234; 387; cast,
    442; 444; cast, 459; 606, 610, 613, 634
Circe's, Mlle., Sylphs and Sirens, 184
Circolo Italiano, 90
Circus, 146 ff, 155, 188, 199, 200, 205, 207,
    359, 408, 424, 425, 428, 540, 541, 626, 631,
    645 ff
Civil Rights Bill, cast, 112
Claire Sisters, 359
Clams, farce, 117, 353
Clancarty (Lady), cast, 54
Clancy, Laura, 249
Clancy, Venie, 40, 169
Clapper, Hattie J., 587, 643
Clara Simpson's Tea Party, 556
Clare, J., scenery, 1 ff, 223, 224
Clarendon Hall, 142, 361, 374, 577, 578, 584,
    596
Clark (see Emerson and Clark; also K. H.
    K.'s)
Clark (of Four Diamonds), 117, 334
Clark, Blanche, 577
Clark, Burt, 100
Clark, Edward and Alice, 550, 555, 620
Clark, Grace, amateur, 182
Clark (or Clarke), Harry, 120, 189, 318, 551,
    556, 574
Clark, Hen and Billy (The Two Clarks),
    543 ff, 552, 562, 567, 569, 573
Clark, Hen and Major, 543

INDEX

Clark, Henry G. (*see Kennedy and Clark;* *also Four Planets*)
Clark, Lillian Cleves, 57, 174, 268, 367, 633
Clark, May, 116, 338
Clark, Mrs., 217
Clark, Nellie, 577
Clark, Th., 536
Clark, Uriah, and wife, 418
Clark, Willis, 389
Clark (C. Burt) and Edwards, 135, 137, 188, 189, 323, 341, 342, 349, 351, 353, 526, 558, 562, 575
Clark and Watson, 133, 137
Clark and Sheehan (of Four Planets), 139
Clarke (of Sharpley and Clarke), 185
Clarke, Eugene, parts, 38, 64, 225, 266, 272, 395, 452, 459, 609, 610, 613
Clarke, George, 22, 24 ff, 57, 94, 230, 235, 236, 243, 439, 489 ff
Clarke, Henry A., 459
Clarke, John Sleeper, 604
Clarke, William A., 612
Clarke's Fifth Avenue Company, 212, 213, 214, 425, 427
Clary, Lottie, 428
Clary, Virginia, 24
Claude Duval, cast, 477; burlesqued, 581
Claus, Jenny, 589, 590, 591, 594, 595, 628, 632
Clavelle, Emma, 529
Claxton, Kate, parts, 11, 13, 65, 169, 202; compared with Clara Morris, 229; parts, 235, 260, 267, 279, 384; takes place of Maud Harrison, ill, 388; parts, 411, 453, 491, 519, 533
Clay, Frederic, his Princess Toto, 48; his Ages Ago, 64
Clayton, Chris, 635
Clayton, Eda, 387
Clayton, Estelle, parts, 14 ff, 151, 229, 276, 389, 437, 484, 607
Clayton, I. C., 581
Clayton, John, 24 ff
Cleary, Edwin, 30, 259, 390, 450
Cleland, William, 160
Clement, Louise, 573
Clemente Amitié Cosmopolite, 514
Clements, Frank, 252, 436
Clermont Vocal Society, 196
Clifford, G. W., 320
Clifford, Gracie, 205
Clifford, Harry, 319 ff, 355, 573 ff
Clifford, Nellie, 549
Clifford (William) and Skelly (Frank), 563
Clifton, Ada, variety, 120, 136, 328, 337, 338, 348, 544, 547
Clifton, Belle, variety, 101, 135, 137, 140, 188, 348, 349, 566, 570, 571
Clifton, Fred, parts, 35, 184
Clifton, Harry, 278
Clifton, Marie, 255
Clifton, Marion P., parts, 56, 168, 275, 384
Clifton, Master, 336
Clifton, Nellie, 269
Clifton, Viola, 128, 131, 136, 140, 184, 338, 342, 535

[670]

Clifton, Viola, Female Minstrels, 184
Clifton, W. F., 236, 453
Clifton Amateur Society, 405, 628, 630
Clifton, S. I., 86, 429, 647, 648
Cline (of Mullen and Cline), 325
Cline, J. C., 492
Cline, Maggie, 397, 526, 536, 557, 558, 568, 572, 573, 576, 618
Clinton Lyceum, Williamsburgh, 416
Clipper Ads, 570
Clipper Quartette, 134, 139, 187, 397, 525, 536, 552, 559, 563, 617
Clippings, 325
Cloches, Les, de Corneville, 25, 26; casts, 32, 36; 98, 176; cast, 263; 264, 388, cast, 474; 518; cast, 537 (*see also Chimes of Normandy, and Glocken von Corneville*)
Clockmaker's Hat, The, 328, 345
Clodoche Quadrille, 120, 343
Cloherty, James, amateur, 392
Clooney, J., 109
Clooney and Ryan, 109, 113, 116, 136, 137, 204, 316, 324, 326, 329, 336, 337, 346, 396, 397, 543
Clouds, cast, 369; 392
Clover, Bertrand, 193
Clowns, 65, 123, 124, 146, 147, 177, 186, 203, 271, 280, 281, 326, 331, 333, 338, 345, 360, 366, 396, 397, 413, 414, 424, 491, 525, 526, 531, 536, 553, 559, 573, 617, 626, 645
Club House, Court Street, 190, 402, 409, 623, 626 ff
Club Rooms (German), S. I., 429, 430
Clyde, Minnie, 111, 114, 115, 325, 328, 331
Coal Heavers, The, 217
Coates, Kitty, 211, 212, 425
Cobb, Willis and dogs, 617
Cobbe, Charlotte, 486
Cobianchi, Mlle., 518, 521, 613
Cocettes, Les, Fantastiques, 535
Coda, J., 391
Coe, Helena, 470
Coe, Isabelle, 47, 385, 488
Coes, George H., 167, 340 ff, 352, 396
Coffee (of Byron and Coffee), 415
Cogan, George W., 199
Cogill, Charles W. (of Reynolds and Cogill), 110, 119, 130, 187
Cogill Brothers (Charles W. and Harry P.), 328, 332, 341, 347 ff, 351 ff, 564, 565, 570, 617
Coghlan, Charles F., 2, 219, 224
Coghlan, Eily, 600
Coghlan, Rose, leaves Wallack's, 2; 7; idle, during early run of Hazel Kirke, 21, 22; at Booth's, 23 ff; 31; parts, at Wallack's, 244, 253, 310, 432 ff, 467, 611, 613
Cogswell, W. J., 255, 268, 388, 486
Cohan, George M., 326, 543
Cohan, Jerry, 325, 326, 413, 420, 542, 570
Cohan, Mrs. Jerry (Helen), 326, 413, 420, 542, 570
Cohen, George, 176
Colbert (of Wheeler and Colbert), 415
Colby, Clara, 151

Colby, G. W., 22, 150, 162, 181, 193, 235, 587
Cold Spring Grove, L. I., 87, 214
Cole, Belle, 54, 150, 160 ff, 198, 255, 266, 372 ff, 388, 509, 586, 592 ff, 598, 602, 629
Cole, Clara, 475
Cole, Hattie, 211, 212
Cole, Lena, 338, 415, 616
Cole, Lew, 338, 343
Cole, Saidee, 54
Coleman, Edward, 21, 175, 272, 385, 478
Coleman, J. J., 570
Coleman, Kitty, 355, 557, 567, 573, 576
Coleman, Marie, 455
Coleman, T. L., 49, 51, 249, 453, 454
Coleman and McCarthy, 328, 332
Coletti, 197
Colfax, Frank, 466, 491
Collar and Elbow Wrestlers, 555
Collasius, Mrs., 594
Colleen Bawn, The, casts, 5, 62; 216; cast, 244; 394
College of Music, The, farce, 133, 328, 335
College Point, 300, 645
College Students, The, 349
Collier, E. K., parts, 52, 65, 168, 169, 248, 249, 278, 462, 463
Collier, J. W., 167, 177, 178
Collings, W. H., 482
Collins (of Callahan and Collins), 125
Collins (of Hart and Collins), 414
Collins (of Reilly and Collins), 635
Collins (of Turner and Collins), 187
Collins, Arthur, 268
Collins, Charles, 90, 170, 226 ff
Collins, Harvey, 119
Collins, Joseph, fighter, 541
Collins Brothers (Lew and Frank), 342
Collins, Mary, 122
Collins, Nellie, 121, 414
Collins, O. B., 108, 189
Collins and Mack, 532
Collum, Andy, 105, 109, 129, 132, 140, 186, 320, 341, 346, 347, 350, 355, 398, 534, 545, 552, 553, 556, 557, 575, 578, 616
Collyer, Dan, 103, 122, 137, 277, 314, 316, 317, 487, 526 ff, 558, 559, 574, 619
Collyer, Sam, boxer, 637
Colombier, Mlle., 239 ff
Colonel, The, cast, 474; 610
Colonel Sellers, 56, 172, 203; cast, 274
Coloured Ambassadors, 135
Coloured Citizens' Union, 373
Coloured Conductors, The, 322
Coloured Fancy Ball, 346
Coloured Hop, The, 581
Coloured Jubilee, The, 112
Coloured performers, 60, 139, 205, 206, 214, 215, 332, 333, 350, 379, 387, 430, 577 (see also Tom, Blind; Jubilee Singers and Haverly's Coloured Minstrels)
Coloured Troupe, 214
Colton, Harry, 33, 34, 62, 63, 270
Columbarian Society, 579
Columbia, Gilmore's song, 41, 94, 95, 145, 150, 159, 181, 371

Columbia College Boat Club, 585
Columbia College football, 582
Columbia College Opera Company, 155
Columbian Festival, 406
Columbian Glee Club, 399
Colville, J. M., 604
Colville Opera Burlesque Company, 56, 176
Comanches, The, 124, 549
Combination system in theatres, 278
Come Down, We'll Make It Pleasant for You, 126, 324
Come Where My Love Lies Dreaming, 128
Comedy Four (Murphy and Mack, Murphy and Shannon), 350, 398, 566, 567, 571 ff
Comedy of Errors, The, 169, 202, 386
Comedy Quartette, 346, 348, 352, 353, 396, 561
Comets, Four (see Four Comets)
Comin' thro' the Rye, sung by Patti, 589, 590
Coming Man, The, 324, 344, 353, 549, 557
Comley-Barton Company, 258, 267, 390, 394, 464, 537, 609, 613
Commune, Refugees of the, 89
Compagnia Filodrammatica Italiana, 515
Compagnon, Der, cast, 498, 499
Compton, Edward, 29 ff, 168
Compton, Percy, 43, 44
Comstock, F. M. and horses, 541
Concerts, Brooklyn (see Miscellany, Brooklyn)
Concerts, New York, 156 ff, 370 ff, 586 ff
Concorde, La, 88, 301, 513, 514
Concordia Hall, 81 ff, 292 ff, 509
Concordia Männerchor, 87, 512
Cone, Horace, 354
Cone, Margaret, 169, 267, 281, 388
Coney Island, 87, 89, 155, 300, 403, 601, 631
Coney Island, or, Little Ethel's Prayer, cast, 435
Congdon, Stella, 43, 388
Congress of Beauties, 185
Conjugal Lesson, A, 11, 170, 524, 648
Conklin (of Four Kings), 415
Conley, George E., bass, 593
Conlon (of Kelly and Conlon), 189
Conly, Elise, 57
Conly, George, 22, 97, 251, 252, 487; drowned, benefit for family, 523; 605
Conly, J. E., tenor, 269, 460, 606
Connell, Edward, 64, 238, 261, 394, 518
Connelly, E. J., 481, 482
Connie Soogah, 491
Connolly, Sadie, 204
Connolly's Troubles, 326
Connor, Dora, 437
Connor, J. H., 109
Connor, Mary, 595
Connors and McBride, 349
Connors and Reilly, 616
Connubial Dilemma, A, 327
Conquest, George, accident, etc., 218, 219
Conquest, George, Jr., 218, 219
Conrad, or, the Hand of a Friend, 544, 545, 576, 622
Conrady, Ignatz, 512

[671]

Conried, Heinrich, 73 ff, 82, 495 ff
Conron, Marie, 36, 84, 153, 261, 394, 597
Conron, Miss E. M., 84
Conron, Misses, 160, 376
Conroy, Dave (of Four Shamrocks), 321, 324, 336, 338, 342, 352, 353, 526, 536, 552, 554, 558, 567
Conroy, John (see O'Neil and Conroy)
Conroy and Daly, 121
Conscience, cast, 174; with Clara Morris, 229
Conservatory of Music, New York, 595
Constancia, Frl., 83
Constantenus, tattooed, 625
Constantine, Charles, 116, 532, 533, 544
Constantine, Harry, 110, 112, 114, 135, 319, 338
Constantine (Harry) and Wright (Charles), 110
Constantine's Dramatic Pantomime Novelty Company, 104
Contempt of Court, cast, 2
Conterno and band, 163, 180, 190, 302, 395, 409, 515, 631, 632
Contessa, La, è di Russare, 302
Continental Glee Club, 208, 423
Continental Quartette, 209, 211, 421
Contortionists, 128, 136, 138, 143, 328, 338, 531, 551, 558, 564, 577, 579, 624
Convict's Daughter, The, cast, 547
Convict's Fate, The, cast, 107
Convict's Vengeance, The, 113
Conway, variety, 141
Conway (of the Four Emeralds), 329, 333, 561, 567
Conway (see Healey and Conway)
Conway, G. W., 221, 223, 482
Conway, H. B., 604
Conway, Hart, 14 ff, 151, 232 ff, 261, 272, 281, 388, 394, 491, 518
Conway, Ida B., 263
Conway, Lillian B., 265
Conway, Lizzie, 131, 132, 329, 340 ff, 354, 397, 555 ff, 574, 617
Conway, Mamie, 342
Conway, Minnie, 608
Conway, Neil, 127
Conway and Egan, 547
Cook, Arthur, 145, 167, 387, 398
Cook, Furneaux, 35
Cook, Rev. Joseph, 153
Cooke, Belle, 216, 629, 644
Cooke, De Witt, 106, 140, 187, 330
Cooke, Ellen, 424
Cooke, Professor H., on Spiritualism, 49, 50, 55, 109, 154, 155, 199, 200, 215
Cooke, J. P., 49
Cooke, James, 57, 146
Cooke, Nettie, 216, 404 ff, 409, 629, 644
Cooke, P., 46
Cooke, Rosa, 40, 175, 452, 458, 538, 609
Cooke, Rosina, 281
Cooke's Circus, 646, 649
Cool as a Cucumber, 306
Coolidge, P. W., 458

Cooling appliances in theatres, 401
Coombe (of English Glee Club), 630
Cooper, Alice, 460
Cooper, James, 390, 460
Cooper, Kate, 127, 209, 210, 535, 618, 619
Cooper, Leo, 390
Cooper, Miss, coloured contralto, 577
Cooper, T. B., 206
Cooper Brothers (Tommy and Willie—of our Comets), 128, 204, 325, 345, 351, 352, 415, 533, 542, 554, 562, 565, 566, 570, 573, 595, 635
Cooper (Tommy) and Edwards (Harry), 107, 114, 120
Cooper and Golden, 204
Cooper Institute (or Union), 151 ff, 582
Cooper Union Free Entertainments for Self-Supporting Women, 375
Coopers, The, pantomime, 121, 320, 349, 545, 567, 574
Copleston, Florence, 85, 157 ff, 162, 181, 198, 357, 370 ff, 406, 417, 587, 591 ff
Corcoran, Katharine, 37
Cordelia's Aspirations, 100, 313
Corden, Julia Thompson, 191, 192
Cordialia, Verein, 295, 511, 512
Cordona, Adelaide, 359
Corduan, Lydia, 464, 604
Corelli, Blanche, 185, 271
Corinne, 411, 480; legal difficulties, 537; 613
Cornalba, Adele, 57, 58, 270, 271, 509
Cornell, H. L., bass, 54
Cornetist, "lady," 103, 104
Corradi, Henriette, 162, 596
Corrister, W. D., 111
Corsini, Baldassare, 304 ff, 391 ff, 517 ff, 537, 591, 592, 600, 612
Cortada, Ida, 399, 404
Cortada, Mrs., 180
Cosmopolitan Theatre (late Aquarium), 541
Cosmopolite, Société Fraternelle, 89
Costa, opera singer, 518
Costello, fire-king, 547 ff
Costume balls, 142, 362
Cotter, Frank G., 51, 482
Cotton, Ben, Francis Wilson on, 60; 573
Cotton, Idalene, 573
Cotton, Mrs. Nellie, 573
Cottrelly, Mathilde, 38, 73 ff, 82, 85, 283, 294, 298, 510
Couldock, C. W., as Dunstan Kirke, 21 ff; 175, 235, 236, 272, 385, 466, 491, 608
Coulter, Frazer, 169
Counterfeit, 544; cast, 552; 622
County Fair, The, 42
Coup, W. C., circus, 146; his Hippodrome, 540
Court of Appeals, farce, 341
Court Square Theatre, 184, 185; becomes Waverley Theatre, 398 ff
Courtade, Mme., 310 (see Cortada)
Courtaine, Harry, 10 ff, 243, 259, 261, 269, 278, 605, 607
Courtaine, Mrs. Harry (Emma Grattan), 605
Courting in a Horn, 568

INDEX

Courtland, Ella, 108
Courtland, Grace, 585
Courtland, Helen, 132, 188, 317, 625
Courtland Sisters, 133
Courtney, Miss Adrian, 591
Courtney, Sara, 213
Courtney, William, 64, 160, 376, 377, 597, 643
Courtright, William, 102, 130, 254, 618
Cousin Joe (Rough Diamond), 230, 453
Cousin Jonathan's Old Folks, 210
Couthoui, Jessie, 154
Coventry, Julia, 176
Covert, Bernard, 214, 646
Covert, James W., 645
Cow-whale, 585
Cowell, Sarah, 10 ff, 226, 388
Cowell, Sydney, 45, 54, 67, 174, 177; in Hazel
    Kirke, 235, 236; 306, 466, 491, 608
Cowper, Archie, 54, 173, 230, 384, 486
Cox, J., 516
Cox and Box, Burnand-Sullivan operetta, 147,
    215
Coxe, MacGrane (or Magrane), 369, 637
Coyle, E. C., 472
Coyne, M. T. (see Howard and Coyne)
Coyne, Mike, 118; (of Sheehan and Coyne,
    q.v.)
Craig, C. G., 58, 171, 183, 184, 318
Craig, J. M., 205, 208, 626
Craig, Joseph, 206
Craiga Dhoul, cast, 174
Cramer, Jennie, 625
Crandall and Eastwood, 348, 349, 351, 559,
    564, 617
Crane, Frank, 27
Crane, Seth, 262
Crane, Tillie, 630
Crane, W. H., 169, 202, 264, 384, 386, 461, 609
Cranky Poets, 548
Cransel, Frank, 337
Craven, John T., 246, 269
Craven, Winetta, 113, 115, 126, 127
Crawford, Selome, spiritualism exposed, 49,
    50, 55, 109, 154, 215
Crawfords, Three, 314
Creation (Haydn's) sung, 165, 199
Creese, Lizzie, 262, 485
Creese, Victory, 478
Cremated by Wholesale, 131
Cremorne Gardens, 142, 361, 580
Creole Slave, The, or, the Staff of Diamonds,
    325, 327, 355
Crescent City Trio, 563, 569, 575
Crescent Lodge, 378
Crimmins Brothers (John, Mike, Steve), 103,
    108, 110, 111, 126, 138, 320, 346
Cripps, H. A., 246, 272
Crisp, Henry, parts, 9, 176, 242, 243, 311, 384,
    411, 482, 485, 489, 609
Cristadoro, Carrie, 193 ff
Criterion Club, acts, 583
Criterion Comedy Company, 40, 170
Criterion Company, New York, 202, 203
Crocheron's Bayside House, 426, 428, 646
Crocker, Jennie, 628

Crocker, Josephine, 282, 576
Crocker, Martie, 576
Crockett, Davy, cast, 62
Croffut, W. A., 255
Crolius, Edith, 102, 115, 116, 122, 314 ff, 546,
    550
Crolius, Louise, 552 ff
Crolius, Mina, 479
Croly, Little Miss, 174
Crompton, W. H., 37, 538
Cronin, E. C. M., 193
Cronin, Timothy, 99; of Big Four, 316,
    333 ff, 340, 397, 554, 573
Cronin, William, 57, 122; late of Scanlon
    and Cronin, 103, 133, 137, 138
Cronin (William) and Sullivan (J. P.), 334,
    345, 349 ff, 398, 560, 565, 567, 570, 572
Crooked Whiskey, 114
Croothawn, The, cast, 31
Crosby and Martin, 318, 545, 565
Crosley, Herbert, 480
Cross Purposes, 20, 41
Crossen, J. F., 189, 216, 406, 576
Crossen Combination, 619
Crossey, J. R., his American Opera Company
    and his opera, 64
Crossland, Peter, walker, 149
Crossley and Elder, 140, 347, 535, 557, 616
Crossman, T., 37
Crowded Hotel, 138
Crown of Thorns, A, 465
Crumley, Bob, 111
Crumley and De Forrest, 101, 112, 189, 545,
    574
Crushed Comedian, The, 111
Crushed Tragedian, The, with E. A. Soth-
    ern, cast, 44; 53, 169
Crushed Tragedian, The, farce, 323, 414, 547
Crystal Fountain, The, 575
Crystal stage, 401
Cuban orchestra, 535
Cuban Sylphs, 535
Cullington, W., 45, 46, 174, 262, 274, 476
Cumings, A., 338
Cummens (or Cummins), Ellen, 30, 172, 183,
    277, 384, 442
Cummings, Annie, 415
Cummings, J. W., 435
Cummings, Minnie, 38, 39, 170
Cummings, Thomas, J., 642
Cupid's Frolics, 331
Curdy (of Four Eccentrics), 102, 135, 314,
    344, 347, 397, 518, 562, 563
Currie, Professor, 644
Currie, T., 538
Currier, F., 29, 249, 453, 454
Curry, Alma, 333, 625
Curry, Nelson, 339, 625
Curry and Hall, 133, 186
Curtis, Dr., amateur, 236
Curtis, M. B., parts, 173, 225, 257, 411, 470,
    471, 484, 492, 609, 634
Cusachs, L., Spanish actor, 28
Cushing, Belle, 133
Cushman, Charlotte, 241

[673]

INDEX

Cushman, Clara, 117 ff, 326, 332, 543
Cushman, Frank, 59
Cusick, John (see Palles and Cusick)
Custer, cast, 327
Cuthbert, actor, 35
Cuthbert, Bella, 436
Cutter, E. O., 23
Cutter, Mrs., 409
Cuyas, Arturo, his play, 272
Cymbeline, cast, 29, 30; 178
Cyprienne (Divorçons), cast, German, 496, 497
Czar and Carpenter, in English, 455, 611 (see infra)
Czar und Zimmermann, as The Two Peters, 90 (see supra)

D.D., or, Dora, the Detective, 323, 400, 636
Da Acosta, Theodora Linda, 585, 600, 601, 629
Daboll, W. S., 180, 181, 486
Dace, Regina, 15 ff, 151, 428, 470
Daddy Gray, play, 416
Daddy O'Dowd, revised as Suil-a-Mor, 457, 458
Dade, Charles, 176, 252, 263, 610
Dahome, giant, 580
Dahomey giant, 626
Dailey, John, 9, 28, 270
Dailey, Peter (of American Four), 101, 103, 133, 137 ff, 186, 190, 334, 335, 341, 347, 350, 352, 383, 398, 519, 526, 530, 534, 554, 556, 557, 567
Daily, Alice, 106, 122, 131, 132, 325, 330, 331, 414, 556, 619
Daily, Billy, 577
Daily, Bobby, 114, 122, 330, 331, 411
Daisies, Four, 413
Daisy, Little, 120, 121, 127
Dale (see Austin and Dale)
Dale, E. J., 153
Dale, Harry, 254
Dale, Pollie (or Polly), 329, 333, 350, 355, 420
Dallon, F. L., 408
Dalmont, Mlle., 466
Dalton (New York Vocal Quartette), 345
Dalton, George N., 470
Dalton, Harry, 38, 43, 55, 271
Dalton, James, actor, 336, 537
Dalton, James, fighter, 583
Daly (of the American Four), 186
Daly (of Conway and Daly), 121
Daly (see Everett and Daly)
Daly (of the Irish Four), 129
Daly (of Moore and Daly), 548, 557
Daly (of Murphy and Daly), 577,
Daly, Augustin, his new theatre, 12 ff; 67, 68; compared with Wallack, 219; 230 ff, 442 ff
Daly, Bobby and Danny, 130, 315, 316, 556
Daly, Dan, 411
Daly, Dutch, 558, 559, 567, 569, 571, 578
Daly, H. F., parts, 10 ff, 226 ff, 276, 437, 488

Daly, John and Matt (of Four Shamrocks), 321, 324, 336, 338, 342, 345, 352, 353, 526, 536, 552, 554, 558, 567
Daly, Lizzie, 104, 139, 317, 329, 344, 383, 558
Daly, M. C., 51, 275, 471, 610
Daly, Maurice, billiards, 152, 154, 582
Daly, Polly, 319, 346, 348
Daly Brothers (Tom and Billy), 167, 389; (as K. H. K.'s), 128, 130, 135, 141, 187, 330, 352
Daly's Theatre (1879-80), 12 ff; receipts, expenses, salaries, losses, 15 ff; special Wednesday matinées, 16 ff; (1880-81), 230 ff; (1881-82), 442 ff
Dame, La, aux Camelias, with Bernhardt, cast, 240, 241; 246, 247 (see also Camille and Camiliendame, Die)
Dame Trot, cast, 34
Damenkrieg (Bataille de Dames), 498
Damen-Kapelle, 294 ff, 298, 300, 512
Damnation of Faust, 165, 307, 380, 410, 540
Damon and Pythias, 170
Damrosch, Leopold, 158 ff, 165, 296 ff, 300, 307, 370 ff, 380; his Musical Festival, 381, 382; 596 ff
Damrosch, Walter, 379, 381, 603
Dan Maloney's Nomination, 636
Dan Maloney's Raffle, 317, 344, 553, 573, 574, 636
Dana, Lizzie, 49
Dana, Rose, 48, 176, 254, 277, 387, 388, 458
Dancing round with Charlie, 125
Dancing Skeleton, 531
Danger Alley Ball, 328
Dangon, parts, 466, 473, 474
Danicheffs, The, 167; casts, 202, 228, 229, 483, 488; 492 (see also Danischeffs, Die)
Daniel Boone, cast, 108; 332, 336, 337, 554
Daniel Rochat, casts, 226, 389, 412, 437
Daniel Rochat, burlesque, 341
Daniels, Carrie, 277
Daniels, Cora, 63, 191
Danischeffs, Die, cast, 80; (see Danicheffs, The)
Danish Veteran Society, 87
Danites, The, 9; casts, 53, 54, 170; 243; cast, 275; 280, 389, 485
Danvers, W. H., 137
Darcy (or D'Arcy), Marion (Marie Acosta), 43, 388
Daring Dick, the Highwayman, 330
Darkey's Wedding, The, 553
Darkies on the Levee, 132
Darkies' Stratagem, The, 353
Darling, Edward A., 492
Darling, J. Jordan, 199, 399
Darling, May, 322
Darling, Mrs. A. H., 375
D'Arona, Florence (or Florenza), 356, 377, 594, 640
Darrell, George, 441, 605
Darwin (of Howell and Darwin), 481, 488
Darwin (of Thorn and Darwin), 349
Dashing Charlie, 330, 532, 569, 575
Dashington, Jerry, 124

Dashington, W., 124
Dashington Brothers (Jerry, Walter, Albert), 559
Dashway and Aubrey, 186, 424
Dashway and Monroe, 187
Dashway and Moore, 140
Dashway Brothers (Carlos and Hugo), 34, 129, 565, 571
Daughter of Roland, The, cast, 454; 488, 607, 634
D'Auria, conductor, 505
D'Auria, Signora, 597
Dausz, Marie, 54, 86
Davene Family, 57, 129, 189, 271, 306, 347, 348, 396, 553, 556, 616
Davene, Mlle. Magerald, 347
Davenport, Blanche (Bianca La Blanche), 90; parts, 180
Davenport, Carrie, club-swinger, 132, 329, 339
Davenport, Dollie, 322, 323, 328, 560, 564, 566, 570, 576
Davenport, Edgar L., parts, 279, 386, 388, 489
Davenport, Edward L., 224
Davenport, Fanny, 13, 15, 17; parts, 52; 67; parts, 168, 169, 178, 203; 230; parts, 247, 248; 260, 274; parts, 277, 386, 413; 442; parts, 463, 464, 489; parts, 605; her School for Scandal compared with Wallack's, 611; parts, 633
Davenport, Fanny, variety performer, 136, 139, 213, 327, 329, 346, 348, 351, 560, 562, 568
Davenport, George C., 145, 179, 383, 391, 460, 491
Davenport, Harry, 484
Davenport, Lotta, 591
Davenport, Mary, 40, 170, 203
Davenport, May, 463, 464, 484, 605, 610
Davenport, Mrs. E. L., 54, 151, 171, 242 ff, 484
Davenport Brothers, 343, 557, 574
David, actor, 91
David Garrick, cast, 44; with E. A. Sothern, 53, 169; Lawrence Barrett as, 172, 276, 384, 386, 461; with amateurs, 426
Davidge, W., 13 ff, 48, 176, 234, 385, 470, 492
Davidge, W., Jr., 57, 58, 171 ff, 261, 271, 305, 394
Davids, D. H., 39
Davidson, Isidore, 58, 61, 278, 449, 465
Davidson, Marie, 215, 216
Davies, athlete, 585
Davies, E. D., ventriloquist, 481, 498, 516, 521, 526, 532, 560, 561, 564, 568, 569, 618
Davies, W. W., 198, 199
Davis, Alexander, ventriloquist, 338, 346, 554
Davis, Alfred, 354
Davis, Charles L., 492, 493
Davis, E., walker, 149
Davis, Frank and Fannie, 113, 139, 204, 324, 326, 329, 343, 344, 352, 353, 529 ff, 553, 558, 560, 561, 567, 570 ff, 635
Davis, H. Rees, 50, 277, 488
Davis, Harry, 258

Davis, Harvard, 329
Davis, J. P., 404
Davis, Lizzie, 546, 556
Davis, Mrs. M. A., 417, 419
Davis, Sam (Quaker City Quartette), 531
Davis, Scott, 354, 471
Davis, W., one-legged performer, 354
Davis Brothers, 415
Davy Crockett, play, 63, 176, 203, 412
Dawn, Elliott, his play, 278
Dawn of Liberty, The, 135
Day, E. Murray, 412
Day after the Wedding, The, 366
Day, A, and a Night in a Volcano, 583, 640, 641
Dayas, W. H., organ, 375
Days of the Commune, 56
Dayton, Helen, 612, 615
Dayton, Tommy and Annie, 101, 134 ff, 187, 345, 349, 360, 553, 564, 568 ff, 575, 619
Deacon, Annie, 39, 172
Deacon Crankett, cast, 225, 226; 388; casts, 469, 491, 518; 609, 633
Dead Alive, 344
Dead to the World, 106
Deagle, Jessie, 485
De Alve Sisters, 122, 135, 138
Dean, Charles H. (see Sanders and Dean)
Dean, Elsie, 39, 218
Dean, J. F., 52, 270, 486
Dean, J. W., 37
Dean, Julia, 249
Dean, L. B., organ, 193
Dean, Millie, 348
Dearborn, Emma, 159, 375
Dearer than Life, 207
Dearest Mamma, play, 630
De Bar (see Varney and De Bar)
De Bar, Blanche, 243
De Barr Brothers, 332, 350, 351, 545, 556, 561, 569, 570, 618
De Beauplan's French Opera, 310
De Belleville, Frederic, parts, 227 ff, 388, 437 ff
De Belocca, Anna, 22, 26, 27, 96 ff, 180, 182, 183, 201, 304 ff, 370 ff, 391 ff
De Berlan, Anna, 391, 396
De Bertrand, Julia, 539
De Bixamos, C., strong man, 566
De Blanc, Hubert, 287, 357, 358, 408
Deborah, casts, 70, 76; 79, 80, 245, 491 (see also Leah)
Débutante, The, 138, 343, 526, 564, 569, 570
De Carlo, 371, 537, 601
De Celle, tenor, 195
Decevee, Alice, 419, 420, 626, 629, 638
Decevee, Nellie, 407
Decker, Nelson, 243, 244, 257, 265, 277, 324, 367, 389, 412, 472, 473, 483, 608
De Cordova, A., amateur, 182
De Cordova, G., amateur, 392, 612
De Cordova, R. J., 152, 195, 206, 367, 405, 425, 630
De Courcey, Den, 123
Deen (sic), Julia, 99

Deep Water, play, 635
Deerfoot, A., 442
Deering, Elinor, 42, 179, 257, 390
De Forrest (*see Crumley and De Forrest*)
De Forrest, Frank, and dog, 531
De Forrest, Gussie, 65, 256, 387, 412, 492, 668
De Forrest, John, 111
De Forrest, Mrs., 11
De Garmo, Lillian, 475
De Gebele, Frida, 97
Degez, actor, 5
De Granville, Mlle., strong woman, 128, 189
De Grey, Lillie, 360
De Gross, George, coloured actor, 403
Dehas Sisters (Emily and Clara), 350
Dehnhoff, A., 84
Deitcher Fancy Ball, 570
De Jalma, Red, fire king, 331, 337, 339
De Lacey and Parker, 542
Delafield and Blair, 640
Deland, Annie, 179, 620, 621
Deland, Sara, 585
De Lange, Louis, 63, 174
Delano, Jeppe and Fannie, 139, 188, 349, 351, 550, 559, 566, 568, 571, 576, 616, 619
Delano, Mrs. G. W., 374, 593, 603
Delapierre, amateur, 192
Delaro, Elma, 43, 64, 147, 256, 328, 383, 480, 609
Delaro, Hattie, 619
De Leauhodny, zither, 52 (*see infra*)
De Leauhodu, F., zither, 372, 378 (*see supra*)
Delehanty, W. H., dies, benefit for widow and mother, 104, 106
Delehanty (W. H.) and Hengler (T. M.), 92, 100, 107, 108, 128, 130, 138, 140, 187
De Leon, Inez, 63, 391
Deletraz, actor, 239 ff, 246
Delevanti Brothers, 424
Delgado, M., Spanish actor, 28
Dell, William M., 493
Della Vedova, parts, 457
Dell' Oro, Luigi, 333, 346, 347, 397, 533, 546, 573, 617
Delmanning Brothers (Archie and Den), 114, 138, 345, 350, 420, 635
D'Elmar, Camille, 255
Delmar, Emily, 62
Delmar, Jean, 49, 411, 474
Delmar, Lou, Parisian Follies, 185; 186; Folly Burlesque, 204
Delmay, Lulu, 104, 186, 318, 323
Delmay, Phebe, 549
Delmonico, Leon, 155
Delmore (of Dutch Four), 635
Delmore, Ralph, 41, 178, 278, 383, 387
De Lorme, Harry, 528
Delorme, Mlle., 32, 33, 263, 473, 474
Del Prato, Mlle. (or Mme.), 301, 310, 395
Del Puente, Giuseppe, 91 ff, 158, 159, 182, 193, 304 ff, 391 ff, 466, 516 ff, 537, 591, 592, 597, 611 ff
Delvinotti, Mlle. (or Mme.), 376 ff
De Luisi, Louise, 317, 532, 566, 570, 571
De Lussan, Blanche, 300

De Lussan, Misses, 425
De Lussan, Zélie, 88; as Carmen, 92; 373, 374, 593
Delvan and Tracy, 355, 535, 552, 556, 563, 569, 622, 635 (*see Devlin and Tracy*)
Dem Golden Slippers, sung by Billy Birch, 144
De Mar, Mollie, 547
De Mer, Albina, 257
Demetrius, cast, 493
Deming, Marion, 619
Demon of Gold, The, 347
Demonio, Signor, 338
De Montcalm, Mme., 594
De Montello, Mlle., 235
Dempsey (*see Walsh and Dempsey*)
Dempsey, Laura, 58
Dempsey, Lavinia, 367, 368
Dempsey, Louise, 64
De Munck, Ernest, 156, 180
Dengremont, Maurice, 287, 298, 356 ff, 375, 380, 410
Denham, A. H., 271, 516
Denham, August V., 417
Denham, Fanny, 53, 56, 190 (*see Rouse, Mrs. W. A.*)
Denham, George W., 479
Denham, Lawrence, 33, 34, 47
Denier, A., 123 ff, 548
Denier, Connie, 337, 531, 552, 636
Denier, John, 210, 333, 337, 366, 423, 424, 531, 552, 636
Denier, Tony, 65, 177, 281, 390, 413, 414, 491, 635
Denier's Humpty Dumpty, 633
Denin, Emily, 443 ff
Denin, Kate, 276, 388, 412
Denin, Miss K., at Daly's, 443
Dennis, Walter, 31, 279, 486
Dennison, Kate, 345
Dennison, W., 184, 200, 408, 628
Dennithorne, Thomasine, 196, 199
Denny, L., 41
De Nori, violin, 420
De Novellis, conductor, 252, 538
Densmore, George B., 122
De Ome and Amann, 561, 562, 569, 570
Depew, Chauncey M., 405, 585
De Reinach, Julia, 595
Deretta, Lottie, 38
De Reszké, Edouard, 92
De Reszké, Jean, 92
Derious, George, 139, 320, 327, 337, 340, 341
Derious, Lizzie, 110, 139, 314, 320, 337, 340 ff, 345, 349, 397, 536, 566, 569, 618
Derious and Smith, 585
De Rock, Effie (or Elfie), 57, 337 ff, 354, 531, 569
De Rosa, Mlle., ballet, 58, 171, 270, 272, 484, 491, 633
De Ryther, Julie, 160, 481, 613
Des König's Befehl, 293
Des Lebens Mai, cast, 504
Des Löwen Erwachen, 623
Descond, Blanche, 123

Desdemona, Marion Booth as, 7; Ellie Wilton as, 29, 242; Ellen Cummens as, 31; Virginia Brooks as, 97; Kate Forsyth as, 170, 389; Anna Boyle as, 282; Louise Muldener as, 450; Bella Pateman as, 450; Marie Wainwright as, 450; Maud Harrison as, 464
Deseret, casts, 255, 388
Désiré, buffo, 300
Désirée, Marie, 106, 119, 120, 126 ff
De Smidt, Adelaide, 540
De Soto, Sun Picture, 143
D'Est, Marie, 184
De St. Caux, Marquis, 588
D'Estelle, Alice, 545, 569
Destroying Angels, cast, 332
Detchon, Adelaide, parts, 171, 181, 221 ff, 383, 384, 610, 611
Dettingen Te Deum, by Handel, 381
Deutschen Patrioten von 1848, 87, 299
Deux Sourds, Les, cast, 155
De Vaney (Megatherian Four), 562, 564
Devere, Annie, 361, 597
Devere, Billy and Tommy, 118, 119, 532
Devere, Billy, 119 ff, 324, 334, 343, 547, 615
Devere (Billy) and Williams (Bobby), 330
De Vere, Blanche, 636
Devere, George, 548
Devere (George), and McElroy (Matt), 547
De Vere, George F., 4, 24, 171, 173, 178, 225, 262, 270, 384, 388, 389, 411, 485
De Vere, Ida, 575
De Vere, Mrs. G. F. (see Mortimer, Nellie)
Devere, Sam, 58, 189, 257, 276, 620
Devere, Tommy, 118 ff
Devern, Billy, 573
De Verne, Mabel, 346
De Vernon, F., 471
Devil, The, among the Tailors, 625
Devil fish, 580
Devil of a Scrape, 115, 119, 326
Devil's Auction, The, 110
Devil's Doctor, The, 326
De Villeray, Mlle., 395
Devlin, James, 619
Devlin and Tracy, 107, 131, 140, 329, 339, 351 (see also Delvan and Tracy)
Devonear, negro, 60
Devoe (or Devoy or De Voy) Sisters (Emma and Josie), 110, 141, 324, 550, 573
Dewey, Mrs., 428, 647
De Wilhorst, Cora, 378, 537, 538, 594, 596, 648
De Witt, J. A., 582
Dexter, Emma, 597
De Young, Julia, 276
D'Hubert, Alfred, 371
Diable, Le, à Quatre, 533
Diablo, Signor, 124, 204
Diamond, Billy, 550, 551, 567
Diamond, Charles, harp and dance, 103, 172, 188, 274, 302, 320, 321, 326, 327, 335, 353, 396, 397, 527, 543, 551, 565, 566, 572, 576, 616
Diamond, Little, 122

Diamond, May, 107, 108, 140, 335
Diamonds, Four (see Four Diamonds)
Dick Turpin, play, 348, 562
Dick Turpin and Tom King, 129
Dickens, actor, 274
Dickens, Charles, readings from, 152, 153
Dickerson, Jennie, 161, 162, 164, 201, 585, 598
Dickinson, Anna, her American Girl, 247, 248; acts Hamlet, 465
Dickinson, J. J., walker, 149
Dickson, Belle, 50, 59, 168, 277, 634
Dickson, Charles, parts, 41, 176, 256, 389, 460
Dickson, Georgie (Mrs. J. H. Rowe), 244, 258, 268, 387
Dickson, Nellie, 56, 268
Did You Ever? cast, 94
Did You Ever Send Your Wife to Brooklyn? 107; —to New York? 186
Dido and Æneas, by the Harvard Hasty Pudding Club, 448
Didway Brothers, 414
Dieckmann, Herr, 69 ff
Diehl, Anna R., 376, 642
Diehl, Charles, 135, 345
Diem, Carl, 85
Dienstboten, Die, 510
Dietz, Linda, in London, 9; 15, 228
Diff Diff in a Well, 116
Digges, Harriet, 264
Dilks and Wade, 134, 136, 189
Diller, W. A. M., 195 ff; dies, benefit for family, 395
Diller Quartette, 630
Dillon, John, 474
Dillon, Louise, parts, 260, 391, 448, 472, 475, 491, 610
Dillon, R. J., 264
Dillon, Susie, 534, 556, 616
Dime concerts, 420
Dime Heroes, 397
Dingeldey, Ludwig, 56, 84, 86, 159
Dingeon, Helen, 41, 505 ff, 518, 537
Dinkelspiel's Blunders, 618
Dinorah, not given, 93; given, 94, 96; casts, 183, 310
Dinsmore, Zephie, 455
Dion, Joseph, 582
Diplomacy, 7, 607; farce, 129
Diplomat, Der, der alten Schule, 289
Dir wie mir, 290, 291, 292, 508
Dissecting Table, The, 346
Distler's Hotel, 215, 428
Distler, Lillie, 208
District Telegraph, The, farce, 414, 635
Dittmar's Bellevue Park, 303
Divorce, casts of 1871 and 1879 compared, 15; 52; cast, 151; 169, 178
Divorçons, in French, cast, 466, 467; in English, cast, 475; in German, as Cyprienne, 496, 497
Dixey, H. E., parts, 40, 49, 178, 180, 254 ff, 459, 610
Dixey, Harry F., 238; with May Leyton (Dixey and Leyton), 554, 559, 576, 619

Dixon, Fred, 11, 172, 225, 477, 613
Dixon, Henry, 261
Dixon, Orm, ventriloquist, 566
Dixon, T. B., 59, 144; (of California Quartette), 350; 362
Dizzy Coons from Tobacco-land, 101
Djack and Djill (or D'jack and D'jill), 258 267, 268
Doane, Lillian, 122
Doane, W. Howard, 194
Dobler, walker, 150
Dobson, Eva, 204
Dobson Brothers, 370
Dockrill, Elise, 148, 199, 359
Dockstader, Charles and Lew, 101, 103, 131, 134, 189, 317
Dockstader, Lew (see supra)
Doctor Clyde, 292
Doctor Colton in Trouble, 129
Doctor Colton's Laughing Gas, 141
Doctor Eisenbart, 293
Doctor Klaus, 74, 79, 292; 293, 495, 498
Doctor Peschke, 80
Doctor Wespe, cast, 290; 291, 292, 402, 508
Doctor of Alcantara, The, casts, 153, 538
Doctor of Lima, The, cast, 437
Dodd, G., 538
Dodging for a Wife, 138
Dodging the Gang, cast, 130
Dodson, J. E., 468
Dodworth, Harvey B., and his band, 148, 193, 626
Dog Next Door, That, 415
Dog of the Lonely Mountain, The, 549
Dog show, 150, 369, 586
Dog Spy, The, 114, 125, 127, 328, 333, 415, 532, 547
Dogs of the Storm, 352
Dogs, performing, 105, 108, 111, 113 ff, 122, 125, 127, 131, 136, 138, 140, 141, 147, 279, 281, 314, 320 ff, 324 ff, 328, 330, 333, 339, 340, 344, 346, 348, 350, 351, 354, 364, 396, 397, 401, 410, 414, 415, 519, 526, 531, 532, 543, 551, 559, 560, 571, 572, 574 ff, 615, 616, 620, 622, 624, 625
Dogs pursue a fleeing negro, 151
Dolan (William) and Lynch (Mike), 564, 565, 571
Dolaro, Selina, as Carmen, 91, 92; parts, 255, 269, 387, 439, 467, 479, 481, 482, 538, 613
Doll's Reception, 583
Dollar, One, a Kiss, 549
Dollinger, George T., 524
Dolls given at Pastor's, 527
Dombey and Son, play, 609
Dombi, Frau, 76 ff
Dombrowsky, Adolf, 74 ff
D'Omer, Mme., 106, 114, 186
Domestic Difficulties, 127, 420
Domestic Felicity, 138
Don, Laura, parts, 11, 62, 63, 176, 182, 202, 203, 225, 262, 411, 474, 524
Don Cæsar de Bazan, 53
Don Carlos, casts, 71, 499
Don Giovanni, cast, 308

Don Juan, Jr., 281
Don Paddy de Bazan, 643
Don Pasquale, casts, 97, 163
Don Quixote, cast, 503
Don Sebastian, 524
Donaldi, Mme., 371
Donaldson, Clara, 421
Donaldson, Frank, 113
Donaldson, James, Jr., 344
Donaldson, Miss, 232
Donaldson, W., 216, 337
Donaldson and McAdow, 188
Donkey, performing, 272
Donna Diana, cast, 69; 70, 287, 508
Donna Juanita, cast, 253, 254; at Metropolitan Opera House, 254; 483; cast, 494; 495, 605, 611
Donnell, Ena, 528
Donnelly, H. V., 488
Donnelly (Joseph) and Drew (James), 314, 326, 327, 331, 335, 342, 343, 346, 353, 490, 520, 535, 544, 552
Donnelly, Mr. and Mrs., 442
Donnelly, W. J., 469
Donniker, J. B., 343, 344
Donovan, J., 392
Donovan, M. F., 174
Donovan, Mike, 419, 578
Don't Lend Your Umbrella, 213
Doody, Pat, 335
Dooley and Tenbrook, 125, 204
Dopo la Tempesta la Calma, 302, 515
Dora (Reade-Tennyson play), 55
Dora, Little, 56
Dora, the Detective, 280 (see D.D., or, Dora, the Detective)
Doran, E., 529
Dorani, Mlle., 521, 614
Doremus, Mrs. C. A., 430
Dorf and Stadt, 292, 495, 634
Doris, Little, 636
Dorothea, play, 511
Dorr, Howard, and Son, 317, 343, 397, 536, 556
Dorrington, Allie, 1
Dorrington, F., 2
Dorritt (sic), Little, parts, 137
Dossert, Christine, 391, 629, 631
Dot, Admiral, 400, 401, 625
Dot, Little, 214, 425
Dot Old School House, 337
Dot Turnpike Gate, 340
Dotti, Mlle. (Mary Louise Swift), 96 ff, 394, 516 ff, 591, 613 ff
Doty, Emma W., 53, 161, 163, 373
Double Life, A, 545
Double Marriage, The, cast, 65; 169, 633
Double stage of Madison Square Theatre, 20 ff, 235
Double-Bedded Room, 344
Doubleday, tenor, 216
Doud, Frank, 333
Doud, Oliver, 44, 454
Dougall, Agnes, amateur, 628
Dougherty, Hughey, 344, 618

Douglas, Annie, 470
Douglas, Clara, 11, 254
Douglas, Kate Percy, 370
Douglass, George, 126
Doves, performing, 148, 319, 342, 558, 578, 635
Dow, Anna Granger, 154, 162, 163, 166, 183
Down where the Cotton Grows, 128
Downing, Robert L., 249, 453, 454, 488
Doyle, Minnie, 319, 636
Dragons de Villars, cast, 466
Drake, Mary, 439, 633
Dramatic Hall, 83 ff, 89, 299, 302, 514
Draper, Julia F., 408
Draper, Mrs. J. K., 180, 196, 615, 627, 630, 638
Drasdil, Anna, 83, 85, 93, 158 ff, 165, 235, 298, 380, 591, 596, 603
Drawing-Room Entertainment, 155
Drayton, cannon-ball act, 544, 562
Drayton, Allie, 131, 139, 317, 328, 534 ff, 545, 560
Dream within a Dream (Poe's), 244
Dreams, or, Fun in a Photograph Gallery, 243; cast, 266, 267; 384, 412, 480, 490, 606, 633
Dreams, or, the Banker's Daughter, 349
Drei Paar Schuhe, cast, 286; 387, 495, 498
Drei und siebzig Thaler des Herrn Stützelberger, 510
Dreizehnte, Der, 623
Dresser, Paul, 551
Drew (of Manning and Drew), 535, 552
Drew (of Young Apollo Club), 192
Drew, Charles, 243
Drew, Emmett, 196
Drew, I. N., 49
Drew, J. (Young Apollo Club), 206
Drew, J. N., 307
Drew, James (see Donnelly and Drew)
Drew, John, parts, 13 ff, 42, 58, 173, 177, 178, 231 ff, 413, 442 ff, 608
Drew, Lillian, 323
Drew, M., 313, 324, 326, 524, 525
Drew, Mike, 122, 123, 140
Drew, Mrs. John, 68, 268, 385, 436, 606
Drew, Sidney, 268, 472
Drewry, David, 406
Dreyer, G., flute, 85
Drink, cast, 265
Dritte, Seine, 293
Dromedaries exhibited, 359
Dromio, clown, 525, 532
Dromios, Robson and Crane as, 169, 202, 386
Drucker, Angela, 82
Drummond, Ada, 205, 642
Drummond, Belle, Lizzie, Nina, 642
Drummond, Maggie, 206, 642
Drummond Family, 160, 205, 407, 417, 420, 637, 638, 640, 642, 647
Drunkard's Warning, The, 416
Drysdale, B., 153
Drysdale, David B., 423
Du Barry, singer, 83
Du Bois, Esther, 56

Du Bois, S., 11, 281, 432, 437, 467, 482
Ducharme, Ada, 416
Ducharme, E. H., 205, 416
Duchateau, Emma, 49, 479, 581
Duchess of Mansfield, The, 207
Du Coron, Fannie, 493
Ducrow (see Lamont and Ducrow)
Ducrow, W., circus, 147
Dudley, Perle, 467
Due Sordi, I, 302 (see also Deux Sourds, Les)
Duff, J. C., Olivette, 261, 394
Duffield, H. S., 31, 40, 53, 170, 263, 272
Duffield, Harry, 307
Duffield, Mrs., 274, 467
Duggan, Maggie, 508, 529
Duke's Motto, The, cast, 270
Dulaney, Sadie, 331
Dulaney, W., 1
Dulaney, W. T., 330 ff, 550
Dulany, 566
Dulany, Lulu, 551
Dulcken, F., 85, 159, 211, 594
Du Mare, Annetta, 361
Dumas, A., his M. Alphonse become Raymonde, 230
Dumas, E. F., 97
Dumb Boy, The, of Manchester, 122, 551, 635
Dumb Man, The, cast, 116; 532, 544
Dumb Man, The, of Manchester, 104
Dumond, Allen, 322, 323, 554
Dumont, Frank, 362, 580, 581
Dunbar, Dashing, 100, 101
Dunbar, E. C., 97, 345, 349, 539, 556, 558, 561, 575, 608
Dunbar, Frank, 395
Dunbar, Howard, 638
Dunbar, Sadie, 204, 548
Duncan, amateur, 180
Duncan, A., ventriloquist, 571, 619, 625
Duncan, Albert, 133
Duncan, C. H., 116
Duncan, Mrs. A., 594
Dundreary Married and Settled, 44, 53
Dundreary's Brother Sam, cast, 43; 53
Dungan, Charles W., 480, 481, 538
Dungee, J. H. B., 379
Dunham, singer, 423
Dunn, James, 45, 167, 272, 387
Dunn, John, 58
Dunn, Master, 556, 560, 619
Dunphy, singer, 423
Dunphy, Aggie, harp, 600
Dupin, A., 513
Duplan, 32, 33, 36, 97, 98, 176, 263, 264, 388, 466, 474
Durand, variety, 617
Durand, A., benefit, 36
Durand, Kate, 472
Durch, play, 510
Durch die Intendanz, cast, 497
Durch's Schlusselloch, 510
Durell Twin Brothers, 527, 535, 552, 556, 570, 574
Durham cattle exhibited, 149

Duroy, Lizzie, 570
Duryea, Peter, 540
Du Sauld, Gabrielle, parts, 21, 175, 241, 248, 258, 271, 411, 492
Dustan, R. J., 267, 453, 633
Dutch Deception, 349
Dutch Four, 635
Dutch, The, Have Taken Holland, 647
Dutch Indian, The, 129
Dutch Kills, L. I., 211
Dutch Mendels (Harry and Leonie), 115
Dutch Renuisance (sic), 640
Dutch Students, burlesque, 103
Dutcher, Marion, 614
Dutcher, William, walker, 149
Dutchman, The, from Kahoos, 565
Dutchman's Ghost, The, 118, 135, 532
Dutchy in a Fix, 546
Dvorak, new music by, 165
Dwarfs and midgets, 131, 132, 136, 143, 147, 148, 191, 342, 541, 624, 625, 626
Dwyer, William, 555
Dwyer, William T., 104, 117, 133, 187, 188, 325, 531, 560, 578
Dwyer and Kingsley, 635
Dwyer and Sweeny, 134
Dyas, Ada, parts, 2 ff, 170, 224, 230, 265, 606
Dyllyn, John B., 555, 560, 620

Eagan, variety, 141
Eagan, H. W., 338
Earle (of Levantine and Earle), 104, 134, 140, 147, 187, 424, 552, 617
Earle, Charles (of Monumental Four), 332, 337, 343, 347, 553, 567
Earle, Ella, 592, 598, 649
Earle, Ethel, 108, 546
Earle, Kate, amateur, 195
Earle, Mattie, 40, 170, 203, 258, 484, 489, 633
East Lynne, 154, 214, 265, 278, 280, 306, 393, 400, 467, 470, 608, 640
Eastman, L. F., 179, 259
Eastman, Mary F., 212
Eastwood (see Crandall and Eastwood)
Eaton, Addie, 472
Eaton, D. G., 403
Eaton, John D., his All the Rage, 176, 234
Ebaccam Choral Union, 641
Eben, F., flute, 406
Eben's Orchestra, 157, 295
Eberhard, Ernest, 378
Eberle, E. A., 54, 171, 177, 255, 272, 274, 450, 520
Eberle, Mrs. E. A., 54, 274
Eccentrics, Four (see Four Eccentrics)
Eccleston, J. C., 152, 429, 648
Echoes from Germany, 349, 351, 564, 570
Eckert, T. Wilmot, 202, 247, 271, 389
Eckford Hall, Greenpoint, 207 ff, 421, 641 ff
Eckstrom, Inga, 356
Eclectic Glee Club, 198, 199
École, L', des Femmes and des Maris, as Wives, 16
Eddie, Little, 550

Eddinger, Lawrence, 49, 54, 245, 263, 281
Edelheim, George, 192, 405
Edeson, G. R., 57, 92, 170 ff, 263, 484, 516
Edgarton, Cecilia, 433 ff
Edgecombe, Addie (or Ada), 530, 533
Edgewater, S. I., 216
Edgewater Dramatic Association, 649
Edgewood Folks, cast, 258; 384, 605, 634
Edison's 500ste Erfindung, 82
Edmonds, Leslie, 38, 474
Edmondson, Annie, 170 ff
Edmondson, Janet (or Jeanette), 254, 391, 413, 477, 596
Edmonians, Coloured, ball of, 153
Edmund Kean, cast, 520
Edmunds, Walter, 14 ff, 151
Edna, Ella, 114
Edouin, Julia, 267
Edouin, Willie, 49, 178, 180, 202, 267, 490; his Sparks, 266, 384, 606, 633
Edwards (see Clark and Edwards)
Edwards (of Irish Four), 129
Edwards (of Walton and Edwards), 565, 570, 571
Edwards, Annie, 530
Edwards, Burr, 406
Edwards, Carol, 629
Edwards, Carrie, 114, 121, 576, 577
Edwards, Charles, 316
Edwards (Dick) and Gaylor (Billy), 112, 113, 214, 332, 414
Edwards, E. C., 414, 624
Edwards, F. L., walker, 149
Edwards, Harry, parts, 2 ff, 9, 11, 31, 170, 220 ff, 225, 242, 243, 310, 353, 432 ff, 611
Edwards, Harry (of Cooper and Edwards), 120
Edwards (Harry) and Morton (Lew), 114, 544, 554, 572
Edwards, J., 468
Edwards, J. F., 531
Edwards, J. J., 554
Edwards, James S. and Katie, 140
Edwards, Jane and Emma, 624
Edwards, Lou, 112
Edwards, Maze, 262
Edwards, W. F., 38, 52, 179, 464, 467, 605
Edwards, Welsh, 99, 246, 257, 277, 281, 306, 440, 471, 607, 623
Edwards, William, 123
Edwin, C. E., 1 ff, 220, 432 ff
Egan (of Conway and Egan), 547
Egan, John, 127
Egbert, T. F., 40, 170, 203, 318
Egberts, Nannie, 202
Egmont, 292
Egyptian baby, 580
Egyptian performers, 341
Ehemann auf Probe, 511
Ehrenfried, C. and Frau, 83
Ehrliche Arbeit, cast, 75; 288, 289, 294
Eichenkranz, 82 ff, 148, 294, 297, 510
Eifersüchtigen, Die, 293, 510
Eigensinn, 510
Eighty Days around the World, 397

INDEX

Eiling, W. H., 440
Eine, Die, weint, die Andere lacht, 76, 77, 634
Einer muss heirathen, 293, 509
Einer von uns're Leut', 77, 80, 418, 496; in English, 607
Eintracht, Bloomingdale, 512
Eisner, Carl, 645
Eistedfodd, New York, 583
Elastic skin man, 580
Elastication, 354
Elberts, Carrie, 8, 55
Elberts, Eugene, 58, 438
Elder (see Crossley and Elder)
Elder, Alexander, 422
Elder, Robert D., 420, 639
Eldridge, C., 237
Eldridge, Lillie, 54, 276, 412, 491
Eldridge, Louisa, 22, 28, 29, 31, 54, 224, 228, 244, 258, 259, 439, 441, 450
Eldridge, Press, 133, 138, 139, 184, 188, 344, 397, 542, 545, 560
Electric Quartette, 565, 571
Electric Three (Callan, Haley and Callan), 141, 341, 345, 349, 351, 413, 483, 554, 566, 573, 576
Electro-Magnetic Elevated Railroad, 142
Elephant, Der, 289
Elephants exhibited, 192, 359; baby, 360; 491, 541, 631
Elevard, Mlle., 626
Elevated Blondes, 549
Elevated Railroad, 57, 151
Elphins and Mermaids, cast, 266
Elijah sung, 165, 380
Eline, the Girl Detective, 319
Elise, Mlle., 568
Elisir, L', d'Amore, 197
Elkins, Ada, 162
Elko, Little, 265
Elks, New York, benefits, 92, 235, 236, 306, 517, 518; 150, 152, 307; Minstrel Troupe, 428
Ellani, Lisetta, 66, 147, 234, 467, 470
Ellard, George L., 180, 181, 184, 195, 216, 376, 395, 399, 404 ff, 408, 628 ff, 649
Elliott, amateur, 180
Elliott, Agnes, parts, 24, 31, 45, 221, 260, 432, 611
Elliott, Hattie, 432
Elliott, J., 260
Elliott, Lottie, 347, 348, 355, 396, 397, 558
Elliott, Marie, 493
Elliott, W., 218
Ellis (see Watson and Ellis)
Ellis, Albert, sparring, 143
Ellis, Charles T., 104, 132, 189, 341, 343 ff, 352, 396, 397
Ellis, Fanny Mary, 643
Ellis, Florence, 64
Ellis, Frank, 647
Ellis, H. W., 110, 360
Ellis, Lillie, 130
Ellis Family, 628, 631, 639, 641, 643, 644, 648
Ellis Twin Brothers, 643

Ellis's Ideal Company, 279
Ellison, Sam, 376
Ellison, Tom, 209, 521
Elliston, Harry, 106
Ellmenreich, Franziska, début, parts, reviews, 504 ff, 614
Ellsler, Annie, 21, 175, 236, 272, 385, 439, 458, 610
Ellsler, Effie, parts, 21 ff, 175, 236, 272, 385, 466, 491, 608
Ellsler, John A., 21, 52, 175
Ellsworth, George, 113, 337
Ellwood, variety, 625
Ellwood, female impersonator, 572
Ellwood's, Mme., Lady Minstrels, 546
Elm Park (Wendel's), 86 ff, 155, 164, 299 ff, 303, 511 ff, 515
Elmar, Gerald, 257
Elmendorf, Maud, 63
Elmendorf's actors, 403
Elmer, Ada, 181
Elmore, Florence, 40, 307
Elmore, Marion, 49, 178, 180, 255, 256, 480
Elopement in High Life, 604
Elsner, Emma, 478
Elton, William, début, parts, 219 ff, 243, 244, 432 ff, 611
Emancipation, The, symphony, 82
Emerald Association, Brooklyn, 182
Emerald Ball, Brooklyn, 393, 613
Emeralds, Four (see Four Emeralds)
Emerson (of K. H. K.'s), 130, 135, 141, 187, 330, 352
Emerson, Al, 343, 346
Emerson, Billy, 58; Francis Wilson on, 60; 257
Emerson, Dan, 59
Emerson (or Emmerson), Dolly, 115, 124, 125
Emerson (or Emmerson), Jimmy, 115, 124, 125
Emerson, Walter, 358, 379
Emerson and Clark, 535, 541, 551 ff, 557, 574, 575
Emmerson, Jennie, 532
Emmerson, Morton, 389
Emery, D. B., 126, 135, 331 ff, 344, 350, 352, 566, 572, 617
Emery, Minnie, 117
Emigrant Train, The, or, Go West! cast, 102
Emigrant's Lament, The, 126
Emigrants, The, 281; cast, 387
Emilia (Othello), Genevieve Reynolds as, 7; Mrs. Bowers as, 29; Miss Atkinson as, 31
Emilia Galotti, cast, 507; 508
Emma's Roman, farce, 81, 82
Emmet, J. K., parts, 44, 55, 92, 94, 170, 246; fails to keep engagement, 273; 277, 389, 469, 483, 485, 489, 491, 518, 609, 610, 634
Emmett, C. E. (Dashing Charlie), 330, 331, 337, 532, 569, 575
Empfindlicher Mensch, Ein, 511
Empire Hall, 295
Enamelled Face, The, 336

[681]

Enchanted Ballet, minstrel farce, 144
Enchanted Statue, The, 114, 120, 121
Enchantment, cast, ballet, 57; 94; cast, 271; 306
End of the World, The, 530 (see To the End of the World)
Engaged, cast, 45; 54; casts, 174, 517; with amateurs, 630
Engel, Jennie, 101, 341
England, Daisy, 473
English, Tom, 124, 125, 130
English Blondes, 532, 533
English Glee Club, 180, 181, 195, 392, 406, 630
English Glee Concert, 375
English History, Romance of, 152
English Trio, 360
English Troubadours, 152
Ennis, John, walker, 149
Ennis, Miss, 63
Ennis Tournament, 359
Enoch Arden, cast, 243; poem read, 368
Enos, A. G., 56
Enterprise Four, 338
Equine Paradox, 541
Er ist Baron, 81, 293
Er muss auf's Land, 509
Er soll dein Herr sein, 510
Erb, Captain, dwarf, 136
Erbonkel, Der, 504, 623
Erheiterung, S. I., 215
Erin's Prayer, song, 145
Ernani, casts, 457, 521; 522
Ernest and Healey, 331
Errol, Miss Lee, 561, 563, 564, 568, 570
Erzählungen, Die, der Königin von Navarra, cast, 69, 70; 190
Escaped from Sing Sing, cast, 553; 622
Escaped Jail Birds, The, 134
Eschert, Bertha, 204
Eschert, Charles, 106, 299
Esmeralda, 236; cast, production, 446 ff; 531
Esmond, Ella, 105, 118, 127, 138
Español, Un, en Boston, cast, 28
Española Ballet, 281
Espérance, Société de l', 88, 89, 158, 301, 514
Estelle, or, False and True, cast, 3
Estelle, Kate, 333, 334, 550 ff
Estelle, May (or Mai), 355, 545, 547, 554, 555, 573 ff, 576
Estèphe, Josephine, 88, 600
Esther, cantata, 158
Estradère, Mlle., 264
Etano and his birds, 547
Ethel, Agnes, 13, 14, 17, 439
Etheria, Mlle., 218, 219
Etienne, Frl., 498 ff
Etrangère, L', with Bernhardt, 247
Etta, mind-reader, 579
Etzeltine Sisters, 558
Eugene, late of Bryant's, 316
Euler's Broadway Park, 87, 205, 207, 300, 416
Euphonia, 86, 295, 297, 511
Eunice, W., 281
Eurardo, 120, 123, 330, 332

Euson (of Flynn and Euson), 544
Euterpe Club (or Society), 378, 594
Euterpean Club, 205, 416 ff, 420
Eva (Uncle Tom's Cabin), Eva French as, 62, 140; Josie Devoy (sic) as, 110; Little Frederica as, 112; Little Lydia Cordwin (sic) as, 199; Zoe Tuttle as, 243; Blanche Newcomb as, 272; Baby Blanche as, 307; Little Gertie as, 332
Evadne, 171, 249, 383, 488, 634
Evangeline, cast, 48; 60; casts, 176, 254, 255, 277, 387, 388, 618
Evans, Agnes, 123
Evans, Alice, 127
Evans, Charles E. (of Niles and Evans), 51, 100, 104, 132, 315, 330, 396 ff, 615, 616
Evans, Frank, 41, 58, 94, 175, 202, 256, 387, 412, 492, 608
Evans, John, 197
Evans, Lizzie, 476
Evans, Maud, amateur, 192
Evarde, J., 255
Eve, the Saleslady, 620
Everleigh, Kate, 172
Everleigh, Pearl, 225
Evelyn, Carlotta, 202, 270
Everett, prestidigitateur, 190
Everett, Cora, 327
Everett, Edward, Lodge, Ball, 584
Everett, Nellie, medium, 623
Everett, Mrs., her play, 604
Everett, William, 129
Everett and Daly, 119, 133, 330, 334, 346, 561
Everett Family, 65
Everett Hall, Brooklyn, 405
Everett Literary Association, 192
Everts, Julia, 262
Everybody's Friend, 169; as The Widow Hunt, 604
Everyday Occurrence, An, 132, 333, 340, 559
Evesson, Isabelle, 16 ff, 151, 178, 231, 443 ff
Eviction, 532
Ewer, Jennie and Charles, 147
Excelsior Grove, 87
Excelsior Miniature Opera Company, 196
Excelsior Quartette, 570
Excelsior Three, 119
Excursions, picnics, etc., 207, 425, 428, 601, 647
Exercises, sketch, 554
Expenses of production, 109, 464
Eyes and Ears in London, 154, 244
Eyre, Gerald, parts, 3 ff, 47, 170, 220 ff, 244, 432 ff; benefit, 467; 528
Eyre, Wilmot, 47, 222 ff, 432 ff, 611
Eytinge, Harry, 226, 469, 492
Eytinge, Pearl, 24, 171, 172, 264, 458
Eytinge, Rose, parts, 10, 11, 224, 229, 258, 265, 605
Eytinge, W. A., 29
Eytinge, Walter, 257, 449, 453, 488

Faber, Bertha, 559
Faber, C., walker, 149

Fabrini, singer, 487, 605
Fagan, Barney, 328, 347
Fagan, Frank, 142
Faint Heart Can't Win, 554, 573
Faint Heart never Won Fair Lady, 560; farce, 347
Fair, Laura D., 151
Fairbanks, Jennie, 116
Fairfax, cast, 44, 45; 47; cast, 177; 203, 634
Fairland, Mrs. J. R., 160
Fairmont, Belle, 105, 348, 543
Fairs in churches, 427
Fairweather, H. F., 478
Faith, or, a Daughter's Wrongs, cast, 326
Faith, or, Oregon Life in '53, cast, 383
Faithful and True, 415
Fallen Leaves, play, 586
Fallen Women, lecture, 532
Falls, W. F. (or W. R.), 458, 467
Falsche Patti, Die, 504
Falsche Sarah, Die, 293
False Friend, The, casts, 10, 388, 411
Family Troubles, 130, 336
Fanchon, cast, 56; 168, 282; cast, 489; 492, 607
Fanciulli, Professor, 294, 299
Fantoches Parisiennes, 58
Fantoches Valotte, 57
Far Rockaway, 300
Fargis, Nellie, 200
Farini's Zulus, 557
Farley, James L., 182, 195, 197, 199, 366, 405 ff, 420, 430, 528, 614
Farmer, H. L., 161, 642
Farmer's, John, Coloured Troupe, 214
Farmer's Frolic, The, 337
Farnham, Ada (or Addie), 339, 415
Farrand, Viro, 105, 118, 129, 535
Farrar, Etta, 154
Farrar, Geraldine, 380
Farrell (of Morgan and Farrell), 635
Farrell, Lelia (or Leila), 411
Farrell, Minnie, 117, 314, 319, 324, 327, 332, 336, 350, 355, 558
Farrell, Tony, 136
Farrell (Tony) and Ryan (Ned), 545, 546. 569, 573
Farren, G. W., 167, 178, 280, 489
Farren, Mrs., parts, 167, 202, 263, 265, 460, 465, 483, 484, 489
Farren, William, 436
Farron, T. J. (of Baker and Farron), 281, 387, 478
Farwell, Addie, 189, 353, 529 ff
Farwell, C. L., 94, 105, 107, 108, 319 ff, 353, 354, 529 ff, 575, 576
Farwell, Carrie and Lizzie, 34
Fascination, 536
Fash (of Byron and Fash), 548, 549
Fash (of Roach and Fash), 116
Fash (of Saunders and Fash), 110, 127
Fassett, Isabella P., 159, 195
Fat and Thin, 327, 328, 336
Fat Man's Wedding, The, 546

Fate, play, 202
Father Mathew Dramatic Club, 215 ff, 649
Father and Son, or, Naval Engagements, 178
Fatinitza, cast, 48; 62; cast, 77; 78, 79, 80, 150; cast, 172; with Boston Ideals, 238; 274; German cast, 284; 386, 395; casts, 455, 456; 497, 611
Faun of the Glen, The, cast, 606
Faust, G., pianist, 296
Faust (Goethe's), casts, 70, 71, 507
Faust (Gounod's), casts, in various languages, 26, 51, 91, 92, 93, 95, 96, 97, 167, 180, 251, 252, 304, 305, 306, 308, 310, 456, 487; with Patti, review, 506; 517, 519, 521, 523, 604, 612
Faust und Gretchen, farce, 511
Favor (Ed) and Shields (Ed), 113, 132, 134, 140, 187, 325, 346, 352, 542 ff, 545
Favorita, La, casts, 27, 95, 96, 304; 305, 306, 307, 309, 394, 517, 519, 521
Fawcett, Edgar, plays by, 10, 268, 443
Fawcett, Owen, parts, 58, 226 ff, 388, 389, 437 ff, 483, 484, 488
Fay, Amy, 636
Fay, Hugh (of Barry and Fay), 104, 187, 188, 216, 396 ff, 483, 518, 619
Fazio, 249, 383
Featherstone, Ada, 231
Featherstone, Eva, 532
Featherstone, W., 205
Fechter, Charles, 254
Fechter, Der, von Ravenna, cast, 70; 94
Feenhände, 284, 507
Feiner Diplomat, Ein, 501, 502
Feininger, Carl, 216, 356, 367, 372, 374, 377, 406, 596
Feininger, Mrs. Carl, 596
Feist, Dora, 594
Feist, Julia, 593
Feist, Miss, 356
Feitlinger, Mlle., 310
Felicia, casts, 229, 605
Felina, opera, 215
Fellman, Emily, 40
Fellow, The, that Looks Like Me, 334, 344
Feltner, Miss, 225
Female Bluebeard, A, 349
Female boxers, 143
Female Forty Thieves, 184
Female Gambler, The, 565
Female Impersonations by men, 103; 110, 112, 113, 118, 119, 123, 124, 132, 137, 144, 186, 314, 316, 319, 338, 344, 346, 347, 349, 398, 414, 425, 459, 527, 539, 550, 555, 572, 591 (see also, inter alios, Bishop, C. B.; Burgess, Neil; Eugene; Fortescue, G. K.; Fostelle, Charles; Heywood, Charles; Monroe, George W.; Ricardo; Rice, W. H.; Russell Brothers)
Female Minstrels, 100, 116, 123, 184, 204, 337, 398, 546, 548, 549, 576
Female wrestling, 577
Fenno, George E., 216
Fenton, John F., 326, 333, 349, 543, 575
Fenton and Frain (or Fraine), 325, 336

Ferguson (Barney) and Mack (Dick), 246, 276, 277, 314, 317, 330, 340 ff, 397, 487, 519, 544, 553, 556, 557, 616, 617
Ferguson, Mattie, 485
Ferguson, Robert V., 133, 334
Ferguson, W. J., parts, 45, 46, 272, 385, 449, 474, 478, 517
Fernande, cast, 16
Fernandez, W. A., 332, 563
Ferni, Virginia, 516 ff, 537, 591, 612
Ferranti, Pietro, 183, 372, 375, 377, 395, 430
Ferrario, singer, 26, 182
Ferrero's Assembly Rooms, 88, 301, 303, 513, 584
Ferreyra, Don, 59, 101, 118, 187, 293, 294, 300, 330, 378, 403, 513, 624
Ferris, H. M., amateur, 182
Ferris, Maggie, 331, 332, 339, 547, 554, 555
Fessenden, 264
Fessenden, W. H., 181, 393, 455, 611
Fessler, Walter, 61, 62, 268
Fest, Das, der Handwerker, 71, 509
Festa Nazionale Italiana di Beneficenza, 90
Festa Nazionale dello Statuto, 303, 515
Festival Overture, by L. Damrosch, 381
Feuchter, Adolph, 66 ff
Feuerprober, Der, 511
Ficke, Carl, 600
Fidelia, 190; cast, 216
Fidelia, Gesangverein, 87, 297
Fidelio, in Italian, casts, 521, 614
Fiebach, Frl., 74 ff, 81, 82, 634
Field, Kate, 154, 244
Fielding, Harry, 116, 326, 330, 334
Fielding, John and Maggie, 104, 138, 188, 246, 346 ff, 353, 561, 563, 569, 570, 575, 616
Fielding, May, parts, 14 ff, 178, 232 ff, 387, 442 ff
Fields (at Pastor's), 316
Fields (see Morris and Fields)
Fields, Ada, 108
Fields, Billy, 143; (of Thompson and Fields), 549
Fields and Hanson, 129, 483, 556, 560, 619
Fields and Leslie, 121, 134, 187, 188, 322, 325, 348, 396, 397, 545, 548, 576, 619
Fifth Avenue Theatre (1879-80), 31 ff; (1880-81), 247 ff; (1881-82), 459 ff
Figgis, Jennie, 205, 208, 217, 430, 637
Figgis, Lizzie, 637
Fighting for a Wife, 319
Figlia, La, del Reggimento, cast, 94; 95
Figlia, La, della Domenica, 515
Figman, Max, 255, 277, 388
Fille de Mme. Angot, La, 26; cast, 32; 33, 98, 176; in English, 384; 486 (see also Mamsell Angot)
Fille du Tambour-Major, La (in French), cast, 263; (in English), cast, 255; 264, 388, 466, 474
Fils, Le, de Coralie, as Felicia, 229
Filson, Al W., 131, 397, 561, 563, 564, 568, 570
Finch-Hardenbergh, Louise, 180, 375, 376, 392, 406

Fink, J., 90
Fink, L., 168
Fink, "Professor," 213
Finke, Lewis, 255
Finn, Lizzie, 525
Finn, Warden, and J. K. Emmet, 273
Finnick (of Only Little Four), 136
Fire in theatre (Madison Square), 22; alarm of (Union Square), 229, 230
Fire king, 124, 205, 331, 337, 339, 547, 549
Firebrand, play, 62
Fireman's Spree, The, 350
Firemen, walkers, 359
Firenze, Associazione, 89, 90
Fireworks, 190, 300, 409, 631
Firman, W. B., 408
First Life Guards at Brighton, cast, 64
First Night, The, 467, 481
First Rehearsal, The, 123
Fischer, actor, 499 ff
Fischer, Adolphe, 85, 159, 161 ff, 201, 298, 370 ff
Fish, Charles W., circus, 360
Fisher, Alexander, 476
Fisher, Charles, 6; parts, 13 ff, 67, 151, 178, 230, 232 ff, 260, 386; leaves Daly's, 442; 463, 464; versatility, 489; 605
Fisher, H. A., 98 ff, 311 ff, 524, 525
Fisher, Mrs. Charles, 463, 489, 605
Fisherman's Home, The, 562, 566
Fishing Banks, 87
Fisk, May (or Mary), at Harry Hill's, 361, 532, 577; British (or English Blondes), 400, 532, 533
Fisk Jubilee Singers, 160, 162, 197, 199, 593, 628
Fiske, John, lectures, 153, 193, 405
Fiske, Marion, 254, 435
Fiske, Mose W., 102, 106, 218, 324, 412, 442, 483
Fitz, a True Irish Friend, 529
Fitzger, Arthur, 283
Fitzgerald, Alexander, 31, 54, 56, 170, 245, 281, 491
Fitzgerald, P., walker, 149, 150
Fitzgerald, R., 536
Fitzgerald, W., 265, 272
Fitzhugh, E. J., 182, 184, 408, 629
Fitzpatrick, J. H., 465, 483, 484, 619
Fitzsimmons, James, 99, 312
Five Points House of Industry, 159
Flagg, Clara, 461, 465
Flagg, F. F., 155
Flagg, Georgine, 14 ff, 173, 177, 178, 232, 443, 476
Flanagan, amateur, 97
Flashes from the South, 574
Flat Boat Pinafore, 187
Flatbush (1879-80), 210; (1880-81), 423, 424; 630; (1881-82), 644
Flatbush Choral Society, 210, 408
Flatlands Neck Vocal Society, 424
Flattersucht, cast, 78
Flauto Magico, Il, cast, 95; 308; casts, 308, 394; not given, 496

Flauto Magico, Il, con Pulcinella Servo Fidele, 302
Fledermaus, Die, cast, 75, 76; 80, 81, 284; cast, 286; 495, 498
Fleeting Follies, 536
Fleetwood Park, 151
Fleming, W. J., parts, 107, 110, 318, 322, 323, 327, 352, 543
Fletcher, J., tenor, 200
Fletcher, Lizzie, 278
Fletcher, Miss, 245
Fleury, Fernando, 131, 332
Flewy Flewy, 117, 130, 136
Flick and Flock, 350
Flidig, J., 512
Flirting in the Twilight, 144
Flockton, C. P., 474
Flohr, Belle, 28, 29
Flohr, Henry, 28
Flora's Festival, 200
Floral Matinée, 395
Florence, Agnes, 55, 82, 512, 593
Florence, Annie, 320
Florence, Edith, 280
Florence, Fannie (or Fanny), 318, 558
Florence, Mabel, 112 ff, 185, 326
Florence, Miss L., 417
Florence, Mrs. W. J., parts, 51, 174, 439, 453, 458, 600, 610, 634
Florence, W. J., parts, 8, 31, 51, 174, 439, 453, 458, 609, 610, 634
Florentine, Carlos, 56, 200
Florette, Maude, 120, 121, 548, 549, 577
Florida Belle, A, cast, 104, 105
Florin, L. M., 266
Florinel, cast, 476
Florio, Caryl, 162, 163, 170, 181, 217, 372, 375, 597, 649
Flotte Bursche, casts, 74, 510
Flower and Fruit Show, 355
Flower Queen, The, 643
Floyd, Bella, 266
Floyd, Ernestine, 265, 470
Floyd, W. R., 2 ff; benefit, 7; 224, 229
Flugrath, Wilhelm, 83
Flushing (1879-80), 212 ff; (1880-81), 425 ff; paucity of entertainments, 426; (1881-82), 645, 646
Flushing Amateur Dramatic Club, 214
Flushing Musical League, 213
Flushing Opera House, 426, 645
Flying Dutchman, The, 531
Flynn (of Leonard and Flynn), 569, 570
Flynn and Euson, 544
Fogarty's Night On, 113, 343, 553, 571
Fogarty's Night Out, 326, 575
Fogg's Ferry, cast, 475, 476
Fohs, A. D., 406
Fohs, A. H., 195
Foiled, cast, 112, 328
Foley, Michael, 99, 114, 311 ff, 524, 534
Folgen einer Zeitungs-Annonce, 82, 293
Folly Theatre, 141
Fool's Revenge, The, 29, 53, 184, 450, 459
Football games, 582

Foote, H. W., 193
Foote, Richard, 633
For a Life, cast, 139; 324, 543, 622
Forbes, Archibald, lectures, 365, 366
Ford, Charles E., 64
Ford, James L., 361
Ford, T. W., 458
Ford, Thomas, 59
Ford and Knowles, 543, 561, 563, 564, 569, 574, 625
Foreign Cousins, 347
Foreigners, The, or, Up Salt Creek, 633
Forepaugh's, Adam, Circus, 191, 192, 205, 207
Forgery, play, 348, 623
Forget Me Not, cast, Wallack's, 221; enjoined, 221; casts, with Genevieve Ward, 252, 436; 606, 634
Fornairon, A., 89
Forrest (of Fostelle and Forrest), 414
Forrest, Ada, 107, 108, 114, 133, 141, 314, 319, 328, 330, 332, 340, 346, 348, 350, 354, 533, 549, 559, 561, 563, 564, 567, 571, 573, 576
Forrest, Billy, 329, 351
Forrest, Capitola, 64, 317, 561, 563, 567, 569, 572, 618
Forrest, Dr., and dog, 624
Forrest, Edwin, 248, 462
Forrest, Frank, 549
Forrest, J. M., 551
Forrest, Lillian, 107
Forrest, Lottie (or Lotta), 324, 544
Forrest, Nola, 329, 351
Forrest, Wilda, 173
Forrester (sic), Ada, 322, 636
Forrester, J. H., 111
Forrester, Jessie, 112, 117, 123, 128, 345, 546
Forrester, Maude, 65, 189, 321, 322, 397, 530 ff
Forrester, William, 172, 257, 390
Forsberg, Harold, 167, 202, 386, 484
Forsyth, Kate, parts, 1, 170, 248, 249, 389, 439, 462, 463, 609
Fort Hamilton gives a German, 423
Fort Hill Dramatic Club, 649
Fort Lee Park, 87, 164, 379
Fort Willets, 212 ff
Fortescue, George K., 48, 176, 254, 277, 388, 459, 480, 613, 618, 619
Fortner, Herr, 66 ff, 288
Fortuitous Forty, 535
Fortuna, Frauen-Verein, 297
Fortunio's Lied, cast, 500
Forty Thieves, The, 338, 533
Forty-nine, cast, 469; 489, 492, 607
Forty-niners, The, 326 ff, 547
Forty-seventh Regiment, 207; Band, 379; Co. I, 422, 643
Forza del Destino, La, cast, 96; cast, 309
Fostelle, Belle, 134
Fostelle, Charles, 132, 186, 314
Fostelle, Clara, 189
Fostelle and Forrest, 414
Foster, Augusta, 248, 249, 462, 463
Foster, Charles, 61, 62, 64, 122, 282, 319, 344, 347, 400, 551, 561, 569

Foster (Dave) and Hughes (Artie), 106 ff, 115 ff, 129, 140, 331, 339, 353, 530, 546, 551, 554, 569, 571, 622
Foster, Evelyn, 369
Foster, George W., 208, 422
Foster, Grace, 564
Foster, Hernandez, 108, 110, 121, 324, 355
Foster, J. K., 338
Foster, John, 129, 338, 559
Foster, Kittie, 186
Foster, Lena C., 205
Foster, Louise, 532
Foster, Maggie, 101, 130, 134
Foster, Mrs. Alonzo, 207 ff, 422, 630, 640, 641, 643
Found at Last, 329
Fountain Gun Club, 630
Four Aces (of varying combinations), 564, 565, 567, 572
Four Claws Cirkuss, 59
Four Comets, 325, 333, 345, 346, 348, 350 ff, 355, 413, 543, 544, 550, 567, 571
Four Diamonds, 117, 122, 129, 133, 137, 141, 333, 334, 349, 352, 534, 553, 556, 567, 573
Four Eccentrics, 134, 172, 314, 344, 347, 348, 397, 402, 518, 555, 562, 563, 568
Four Emeralds, 116, 138, 139, 141, 329, 333, 341, 342, 343, 544, 561, 562, 568, 569, 616
Four Grotesques, 334, 344 (see Grotesque Four)
Four Italians (varying groups), 108, 120, 121, 130
Four Kings, 415
Four Lovers, pantomime, 120
Four Luminaries, 550, 573
Four Musical Kings, 552
Four o'Clock in the Morning, 354
Four o'Clock Train, The, 123
Four Pickaninnies, 572
Four Planets (of varying membership), 121, 122, 132, 135, 139, 328, 331, 333, 343, 397, 573
Four Seasons, cantata, 211, 279
Four Shamrocks (of varying membership), 238, 321, 336, 342, 352, 353, 355, 430, 526, 536, 551, 552, 554, 556, 567, 570, 616, 618
Four Sisters, play, 648
Four Sunflowers, 548
Four-in-Hand (varying groups), 332, 343, 349, 551 ff, 562, 563, 564, 574, 575, 616, 619
Four-legged girl, 541, 631
Four-of-a-Kind, 567, 572, 636
Fourteenth Regiment Band, 613
Fourteenth Street Theatre (see Haverly's Fourteenth Street Theatre)
Fowler, Kate, 198
Fox, Ella, 205
Fox, G. L., 61
Fox, James (of Goss and Fox), 98 ff, 173, 243, 343; at Harrigan's, 311 ff, 524, 525
Fox, Louise, 34, 62, 280
Fox, Master, 625
Fox, McGrane, 378
Foy, Bertha, 11, 12, 150

Foy, Ida, 150
Foy, P. C., 107, 120, 544, 551, 557
Fra Diavolo, casts, 251, 252, 393, 487, 604
Frail, Horace, 277
Frain (of Fenton and Frain), 325
Fraine (of Binney and Fraine), 543, 556
Fraine (of Ripley and Fraine), 336
Frame, Judge E. H., 426, 645, 646
Frampton, Thomas, 635
France, George, 108, 546
France, Sid C., 105, 106, 185, 346, 349, 560, 563, 570, 622
Francis, Fannie, 620
Francis, Kate, 27
Frank, Bertha, 162
Frank, Edwin, 62, 484
Frank, Harry I. G., 540
Frank, Herr, 79, 81, 493
Frankau, Joseph, 20 ff, 236
Franklin, Benjamin, at Court of France, 95
Franklin, Gertrude, 158, 180, 196, 458
Franklin, Harry, 319, 334
Franklin, Rose, 319, 334
Franko, Jeanne, 285, 370, 372
Franko, Nahan, 285, 300, 311, 371, 373, 591
Franko, Rachel, 285, 372, 592
Franko, Sam, 371, 592, 594, 596
Frankum, George, 59
Franosch, A., 48, 172
Franz-Abt Schüler, 297
Frapolli, tenor, 91
Fraser, Robert, 27, 271, 559, 569
Frau, Die, im Hause, 291, 402, 430
Frau, Die, ohne Geist, cast, 66
Fraud and Its Victims, as The Poor of New York, 106, 107
Frauen-Emancipation, cast, 292
Frauenlist, 497
Frauen-Verein, Brooklyn, 70, 181, 190
Frauen-Verein, New York, concerts, 85, 298, 373, 502, 594
Frauen-Verein Victoria, Kronprinzessin, 84
Fräulein von Seigliere, 502
Frayne, Clara, 410
Frayne, Frank I., parts, 65, 202, 279, 281, 410, 485, 561, 564, 569, 570, 617
Freaks, cast, 170, 202
Frear, Fred H., 464, 482
Freedom of the Press, The, 403
Freeman, Charles, 59
Freeman, Max, 475, 609
Freeman Sisters, 101, 185
Freimaurer Tempel, 86
Freischütz, Der, cast, 498; with amateurs, 509
Freligh, W. B., 282, 400
Fremde, Die (L'Etrangère), 507
French, Edwin, 143, 179, 314, 362, 518, 528, 580
French, Emil, 592
French, Eva, 62, 140, 218, 227, 242, 248, 274; with French Twin Sisters, 314; 411, 438
French, Florence, 318, 355, 532, 550, 578
French, Kate, 255

French Twin Sisters (Minnie and Lena), 51, 56, 100, 102, 130, 132, 172, 189, 255, 266, 274, 277, 306; with Eva, 314; 317, 330, 341 ff, 367, 396, 397, 487, 489, 503, 519, 527 ff, 556 ff, 569, 575, 618
French balls (*see French Miscellany and Academy of Music, New York*)
French Benevolent Society, 97, 310, 596
French Dancing Master, The, 110, 120, 121, 141, 340
French Flats, casts, 9, 10, 177; 203, 243
French Miscellany (1870-80), 88, 89; (1880-81), 300 ff; (1881-82), 513, 514
French plays (*see Bernhardt, Sarah; Aimée, Marie; Marié, Paola*)
French Societies (*see French Miscellany*)
French Spy, The, Jennie Hughes, 61, 134, 136; Marie Zoe, 106, 319, 321; Fanny Herring, 185, 330, 354, 552; Mlle. Morlacchi, 347
French Traveller, Arrival of a, 110
Frenchman's Protégée, The, 527, 564
Frenchman's Troubles, A, 545
Fresh, the American, 246; cast, 261, 262; 387; cast, 485; 487
Freshman Class, The, 336
Freund Fritz, 508
Frew, Charles, 532
Frey, Charles, 131, 349
Freygang's Pavilion, 213, 426
Friday, W. H., amateur, 195
Friel and Rogers, 189
Friend and Foe, cast, 621
Friend Indeed, A, 278
Friendly Neighbours, 351
Friends that Are Enemies, 361
Frillman, H. W., 143 ff, 350, 362, 581
Friquet, Jules, 105, 107, 320
Frisch, gesund und meschugge, 293
Frische, concert, 539
Frisky, Cobbler, The, 554
Fritsch, Christian, 22, 53, 56, 154, 157 ff, 162 ff, 170, 181, 195, 198, 287, 356, 370 ff, 379, 403, 407, 410, 498, 513, 524, 592 ff
Fritsch, Letitia, 79, 84, 85, 159, 161, 165, 216, 356, 357, 585, 587, 597
Fritz, 92
Fritz, variety play, 125
Fritz and Robinson, 330
Fritz in Ireland, cast, 44; 55, 94, 170; with amateurs, 215; 277, 389; with amateurs, 428; 469, 483, 485, 489, 491, 609, 610, 634
Fritz's Return, 134
Fritzchen und Lieschen, 511
Fritze, Carl, 75 ff, 81
Frobisher, J. E., 366, 368, 375, 642
Frobisher, Mrs. J. E., 366, 375
Frog Opera, 180
Frohman, Daniel, 22, 23; leaves Madison Square for Fifth Avenue Theatre, 235; 455
Frohman, W. S., 553
Frohsinn, Astoria, 425
Frohsinn, Long Island City, 83, 212
Frohsinn, New York, 82, 87, 297, 424

Frolics, farce, 550
Frolicsome Oysters, cast, 360
Froliques, Weathersby-Goodwin, 50, 169, 411
From the Lakes of Killarney, 101
Frost, Carrie, 612
Frost, Leone, 151
Frothingham, George, 181, 238, 393, 455, 611
Frou-Frou, cast, Bernhardt, 240, 246, 247; 395, 439, 444; cast, 499; with Kate Claxton, 633
Frozen Deep, The, as basis for Self-Conquest, 34
Frühstückstündchen, Ein, 293
Fuchs, bass, 374
Fuchs, Carl, 83, 85
Fulford, Robert, 49
Fuller, Ada, 200
Fuller, Carrie, 64
Fuller, Fanny, 635
Fuller, Hugh, 59, 274, 277
Fuller, Louise, 486
Fuller, Mollie, 458
Fuller, W. M., 493
Fulton, John M., 593
Fulton Lodge, No. 2, 630
Fun at Coney Island, 132
Fun at School, 528
Fun in a Fog, 608
Fun in a Hotel, 315, 400
Fun in the Kitchen, cast, 108
Fun in the Police Court, 316
Fun on the Axminster, 562
Fun on the Bristol, cast, 254; 257, 388, 411, 469, 492, 518, 610, 633
Fun on the Farm, 332
Fun on the Stage, 314, 490, 527, 618
Fünftausend Teufel, 283, 284
Funk-Georgi's Union Park, 300
Fünkenstein, Leopold, 299
Funnibone's Fix, 649
Funny People We Meet, 191, 205
Fuoco al Convent, 515
Furey, James A., 197, 200, 266, 477
Furey, Mrs. C. F., 197, 200
Furlong, John B., 608
Furnished Rooms, cast, 619
Furst, Myron J., amateur, 404
Fyffe, C. J., 169, 383

Gabriel Grub, 208
Gabrielle, Belle, 271
Gade, John, 124; his cantata, 399
Gaffney, Andrew, 327, 337
Gage-Courtney, Mme., 375, 376
Gaieté Française, 88, 89, 513
Galassi, Antonio, 22, 91 ff, 164, 180 ff, 194, 201, 304 ff, 371, 380, 391 ff, 516 ff, 599, 600, 602, 613 ff, 632
Galassi, Giuditta, 180, 523
Gale, H. D., 278
Gale, Lizzie, 105, 115, 122
Gale, Pete (American Four), 103, 133, 137 ff, 186, 190, 334, 335, 341, 347, 348, 352, 383, 385, 398, 519, 526, 530, 534, 554 ff, 567
Gale, Walter, 87, 489

Gallagher (Matt) and Mack (Billy), 121, 136, 333, 341, 349, 354
Gallagher, May, parts, 262, 264, 447, 517
Gallagher, Mike, 114, 116, 140, 141, 322, 530, 533, 573, 575, 604
Gallagher, Thomas, billiards, 582
Gallagher and West, 347, 563, 571
Galley Slave, The, casts, 40, 41, 58, 175, 202, 256, 387, 412, 492, 608; 634
Galloni, concerts, 391, 513
Galloway, James T., 51, 168, 385, 439, 458, 606
Gally, actor, 240, 246
Galoschen, Die, des Glücks, cast, 503
Galt, Henry, 212, 370, 417, 421
Galway Lawyers, The, 558, 559
Gandi, Edoardo, 303
Gangloff, actor, 241
Gannon, Mary, 6
Gantzberg, J., 216
Gardes Lafayette, 88, 89, 301, 357, 368, 514
Gardier, H., 90
Gardion, W. C., 90
Gardner, Charles, Jr., 102
Gardner, Charles A., 57, 65, 105, 129, 140, 574, 575
Gardner, Helen, 40, 170, 491
Gardner, Kitty, 117, 141, 329, 335, 345, 432, 564, 570, 571
Gardner, Lida, 315 ff, 334, 348, 526, 551, 617, 618
Garfield, President, memorial concert, 409; death and obsequies, theatres closed, 436, 443, 477, 487, 494, 524; benefit for his mother, 592; monument fund, 628, 629
Garfield Lodge, 597
Garibaldi, Legione, 90
Garibaldi, entrance into Naples, 303
Garland, C., 538
Garland, George S., 118, 415
Garland, Grace, 140
Garnella Brothers, 328, 383, 414, 483, 526, 619
Garnier, billiards, 152
Garnier, concerts, 301, 395
Garetta, Jessie, Lady Minstrels, 546
Garetta Family, 333, 364
Garrick, Eva, 43, 259, 450
Garrick Society of Amateurs, 196
Garrison, J., 465
Gary, Jennie, 189
Gasparini, Ada (sic), 415
Gasparini, Adelina, 184, 185, 328, 542, 635
Gasparini, Ida, 328, 542, 545
Gaston, George, 146, 172, 482, 538, 613, 623
Gathering of the Clans, 534
Gatling Battery N., Brooklyn, 182
Gavaut, concert, 88
Gay, Master Arthur, 437
Gayler, Charles, 90, 243
Gaylor (see Edwards and Gaylor)
Gaylor, Bill, 112
Gaylord, William, 328, 343, 344, 558
Gayton, Zoe, as Mazeppa, 331
Gazzoli, G., 302

Geadelter Kaufmann, Ein, 72, 73
Geary, Mina, 151, 157, 375
Gebhardt's Park, 429
Geese! Geese! vs. Goose! Goose! 113
Gefährliche Liebe, Eine, 293
Geier-Wally, Die, cast, 507
Geist, Marie, 296, 370, 373, 392, 406, 595, 630
Geistinger, Marie, début, parts, criticism, 285 ff; parts, 358, 375, 494, 495, 498, 503, 611, 612, 634
Geldert, Edward, 359
Genée, Ottilie, 81, 82
Geneviève de Brabant, 384
Gennarine, farce, 303
Gentleman from Nevada, A, cast, 37, 38; 179
Gentlemen from Kerry, 324
Gentlemen's Sons of the 11th Ward, 584
Gentry (see Leslie and Gentry)
George, Frank, 139, 325, 544
George, Henry, 408
George, J. W., 529 ff
George, Lily, 46
Georgeson, Frankie, 186
Georgia, Mlle., iron jaw, 104, 108, 112, 120, 189, 325
Georgia Jubilee Singers, 185, 359, 360, 576, 647
Georgia Minstrels, 151
Georgie, Little, 41, 58
Gerade Weg, Der, der beste, 509
Gerald, Nita, 39, 64, 204
Geraldine, McCay's plays, 192
Gerente, Un, Reponable, 302
Gerling, A., 86
German, The, and the Waif, 125
German Activities, Brooklyn (1879-80), 190; (1880-81), 402, 403; (1881-82), 623
German Activities, New York (1879-80) 83 ff; (1880-81), 294 ff; (1881-82), 511 ff
German Assembly Rooms, 88
German Club Rooms, Staten Island, 215 ff, 429 ff, 648
German Emigrant House, 595
German Emigrants, farce, 544
German Hospital, benefit for, 70
German Mashers, The, 339
German Masonic Temple, 374
German plays (1879-80), 66 ff; 155, 211, 212; (1880-81), 282 ff; (1881-82), 493 ff
German plays in Williamsburgh, 634, 635
German-American Institute, 84
German-American Seminary, 72
Germania, tragedy, 147
Germania, Orden, 83, 87, 295
Germania Assembly Rooms, 81, 83 ff, 294 ff, 512, 584, 597
Germania Club, Greenpoint, 207, 642
Germania Garten, 300, 513
Germania Gesang-Verein, 85, 512
Germania Hall, Greenpoint, 209, 641
Germania Hall, Williamsburgh, 418, 419, 636 ff
Germania Musikverein, 643
Germania Quartett Club, 293

INDEX

Germania Singing Society, Greenpoint, 208, 209, 421, 641, 643
Germania Theater (1879-80), 66 ff; (1880-81), 288 ff; at Wallack's old theatre (1881-82), 498 ff; its actors in Brooklyn, 306, 402
Germon, Arthur, 238
Germon, Effie, parts, 3 ff, 220 ff, 230, 608, 611
Germon, John, 186
Germon, Mrs. G. C., 234, 471, 474, 608
Germon, Nellie, 112, 113, 116, 117, 121, 133, 137, 138, 328, 543, 544, 546, 557
Gern, Paul, 293
Gerrish, Sylvia, 480
Gerry, Miss, 54
Gerry Twin Sisters (Lillie and Hattie), 577
Gerster, Etelka, 93, 304 ff, 371, 377, 381, 391 ff, 456, 457, 516, 523; air from Magic Flute. 599, 600; 614, 615
Gertie, Little, 332
Gesner, Lillian, 596
Getting Rid of a Cousin, 567
Geyer, Charles, 147
Geyer and Ashton, 148
Geyer and Mack (sic), 542, 555, 626
Geyer (Frank) and Mackie (James), 105, 107, 113, 128, 132, 189
Ghost in a Pawnshop, 124, 129, 549
Ghost, A, in Spite of Himself, 115
Giannini, Dusolina, 456, 457
Giannini, Francesco, 456, 457, 615
Giants, 79, 190, 191, 359, 364, 365, 400, 401, 419, 541, 579, 580, 624 ff
Gibbons, Charles, 143, 179
Gibbons, Frank, 105, 117, 541, 625, 631
Gibbons, John W., 326, 567, 572
Gibbons, W. J., 352
Gibbons and Russell, 116, 123, 138, 139, 141, 329, 333, 342, 561, 567
Gibbs (Megatherian Four), 138, 331, 346
Gibson, Alf, 556
Gibson, Clarence, 265, 389, 478
Gibson and Binney, 107, 132, 140, 326, 330, 345, 352
Gibson and West, 334
Giessel, Mme., 84
Gifford's Luck, 554
Gifts to audience, 491, 527
Gifts to children, 353
Gigantic Novelty Company, 618
Gilbert, C. A., 360
Gilbert, Emily, 51
Gilbert, Emma, amateur, 392
Gilbert, James A., 458
Gilbert, John, parts, 2, 3 ff, 31, 170, 220 ff, 243, 244, 261, 385, 432 ff, 611, 613
Gilbert, John, variety, 271, 616
Gilbert, Katie, 225, 384, 411, 467
Gilbert, Mrs. G. H., engages with Daly for 1880-81, 17, 18; 45, 54, 68; parts, 174, 177; at Daly's 232 ff, 387, 413, 442 ff, 608
Gilbert, W. S., in America (Pinafore and Pirates of Penzance), 34 ff; Wedding March, 45; Princess Toto, 48; Ages Ago, 64 (see also Engaged and Sweethearts)

Gilbert, W. S., Arrival of, farce, 127, 133, 141
Gilbert, William, parts, 446, 472, 480, 481, 608, 613
Gilbert Dramatic Association, 192 ff, 196, 199, 628, 631
Gilchrist, W. W., music by, 163, 372
Gilday, Charles, 56, 100, 103, 134, 136 ff, 172, 188, 274, 346 ff, 396 ff, 526, 534, 543, 562 ff, 568 ff, 617, 618, 626
Gilder, Frank, 55, 199
Gildersleeve, J. R., 542, 560 ff
Gildersleeve, S. R., 429, 648
Gilfoil, Ben, 110, 111, 121, 131, 140, 186, 318
Gilfort Brothers, 556
Gill, William, 42, 179, 257, 390
Gillette, W. H., 235; The Professor, 237, 412; Esmeralda, 446, 447; 471, 492, 610, 634
Gillow, E., 392
Gillow, W., 481, 528
Gilman, Ada, 24, 46, 245, 281
Gilmore, E. G., co-manager, Niblo's, 482 ff; at Metropolitan Casino, 537
Gilmore, P. S., and his Band, 41, 52, 145, 150, 157, 164, 244, 306, 357, 358, 370, 379, 392, 406, 537, 540, 597, 601, 613, 614, 631; his Columbia, 94, 95, 159, 181; his Trip to Manhattan Beach, 358
Gilmore, W. (of Four Diamonds), 328, 333, 352, 553, 567, 616
Gilmour, J. H., 2 ff, 220 ff
Gilroy, Mamie, 390
Gilsey, Frank, 472
Gilson, George, 567
Gilson, James, 327
Gilson and Welsh, 564, 571
Ginger Snaps, 342
Giorgio Gandi, cast, 303
Giovanni's canaries, 401
Gipsies exhibited, 365
Giraffes, 359, 541
Giraldeau, Heloise, 152, 198
Girard, Belle, 147, 269, 360
Girard, Eddie, 132, 133, 138, 167, 188, 334, 335, 336, 346, 396, 398, 526, 527
Girard, Frank, 51, 56, 100 ff, 140, 172, 277, 314 ff, 490, 526 ff, 574, 618
Girard, Kate, 597
Girard, Theresa, 544
Girard, William, 132, 133, 138, 167, 188, 334, 336, 346, 352, 396, 398, 526, 527, 574
Girard Brothers (see Girard, Eddie, and Girard, William)
Girl Detective, The, 552
Giroflé-Girofla, 26; cast, 33; 36, 147, 176, 253, 263; in German, 283; cast, 360; 388
Girouette, cast, 446
Gladiator, The (Bird's), 170, 248, 462, 463, 609
Gladiator, The (Italian play), 242; cast, 243; 311
Glance, A, at Married Life, 518
Glas Wasser, Das, 284; cast, 290; 292, 402, 508
Glass blowing, 213

Glassford, A., 354, 395
Gleason, Ada, 419, 420
Gleason, Alice, 137, 186, 346, 559, 576
Gleason, W. J., 354 (see infra)
Gleason, W. L., 221, 270, 318, 478
Glee Singing, 153, 158, 160, 198, 205, 208, 587, 596
Glen Cove, 646
Glen Island, 87, 601
Glenn, Harry, 577
Glenny, T. H., 473
Glidden, C., 136, 329, 562, 616, 622
Glimpses of City Life, 346
Globe Dime Museum, 579, 580
Glocken, Die, von Corneville, cast, 494; 612, 634 (see also Chimes of Normandy and Cloches de Corneville)
Glover, G., 229
Glover, Ida, 49
Glover, Lillie, 58, 281, 388, 411
Glover, Louis N., 607
Glover, Marie, 480
Glückliche Familienvater, Ein, 292, 623
Glückliche Flitterwochen, 292, 402
Gnarr, Comincio, 601
Go West, 56, 102, 103 (see Emigrant Train); cast, 526
Go-as-you-please walks, 359
Gobble duet, 269
Godinez, E., actor, 28
Godman, W. D. (or W. P.), 158
Godoy, Signor, 374, 375, 377
Gods, The, lecture, 31
Goebel, F., Sommergarten, 87, 299, 513
Gofton, E. S., 47
Goggelmann, Frl., 86
Going to Germany, 327, 347
Going to Join the Minstrels, 558
Going to the Picnic, 328
Going to the Races, 330, 352
Goldbauer, Der, 212
Goldberg, John, magic, 368, 387, 399, 601, 623
Goldberg, Sara, 368, 604
Golden (of Cooper and Golden), 204
Golden, Richard, 48, 176, 389, 460, 470, 509, 537, 538
Golden Circle Lodge, 641
Golden Farmer, The, 216
Golden Fruit, play, 575
Golden Game, A, 173, 263
Golden Guilt, cast, 339
Golden Pippins, 536
Goldie, William, 59
Goldie and Steele, 134 ff, 138, 140, 187, 188, 396
Goldmark, Penthesilea overture, 165
Goldonkel, Der, 293
Goldrich, Pete (see Quilter and Goldrich)
Goldsberry, L. D., 595
Goldsmith, Will, 329, 331
Goldthwaite, Dora, 11, 270, 486
Golubok, Leon, Yiddish actor, 509, 510
Gomien, Octavie, 162, 372, 595
Gonzales, gymnast, 119
Gonzales, Fanny, 489

Gonzales, Lizzie, 533
Gonzales, Maggie, 51, 168
Gonzales, Miss, 473
Gonzales, Mrs., 146
Good Night's Rest, A, 119
Good Square Shave, A, 119
Goodall, Cora, 97
Goodall, Rose, 108, 320, 352
Goode, Lizzie, 30, 270, 462
Gooding, E. D., 187, 190, 616, 619
Goodman, George, 124
Goodman, John, 118
Goodrich, E. T., 109 ff, 323, 324, 339, 543, 546, 622
Goodrich, Sara, 265
Goodroy, John and Jennie, 124
Goodsell, Rev. D. A., 427
Goodwin, E. S., 321, 326 ff, 542, 546, 552
Goodwin, Frank, 23
Goodwin, J. Cheever, 27
Goodwin, James, 346
Goodwin, N. C., parts, imitations, etc., 31, 40, 169, 254, 256, 411, 475
Goodwin, Ned, 544
Gordon, Aggie, 591
Gordon, Amy, 42, 179, 243, 492
Gordon, Marie, variety, 577
Gordon, Miss, 245
Gorenflo, Marie, 99, 212, 525
Gorham, amateur, 394
Gorham, Henry, 198
Gorillas exhibited, 143
Gorman, Dick, 102, 117, 137, 139, 327, 329, 335, 342 ff, 363, 543 ff, 576, 620, 622
Gorman, George, 59
Gorman, James, 59
Gorman, John, 59
Gorman, M. J., 339, 351
Gorman, William, 146
Gorman Brothers, 314, 330, 346, 348, 352
Gorman and Gallagher, 136
Gosche, J., 40
Gosche-Hopper Company, 244, 245, 281, 389, 412
Goshon (or Goschen), Routh, 191, 364
Gosling, A. E., 423
Goss, Ed (of Goss and Fox), 99, 173, 243; at Harrigan's, 311 ff, 344, 524, 525
Gossi, Mlle., 310
Gossin, J. Leslie, 172, 278, 411, 450, 520, 611
Gotham by Night, 536
Gothic Hall, Brooklyn, 190, 296, 402 ff
Götterdämmerung, third act at concert, 201
Gotthard, actor, 493
Gotthold, J. Newton, 40, 175, 265, 389, 449, 453, 457, 472
Gottschalk, L., 26, 97, 180, 182, 523, 593, 597, 600, 601, 606
Gouge, E. H., benefit, 11
Gough, Jimmie, 535
Gough, John B., 193, 394, 582, 626
Gough, Minnie, 120, 136
Gourlay, John, 255, 256, 458, 606
Grace, negro, 60
Grace Hall, 367

Græco-Roman wrestling, 149, 314, 359, 366, 367
Graf Essex, 70, 287
Graff, Jacob, 11, 80 ff, 145, 157 ff, 165, 296 ff, 370 ff, 512, 532, 591 ff
Gräfin Lea, 72
Grafulla's Band, 88, 648
Graham (of Kane and Graham), 354
Graham, Annie, 264, 281, 391, 491
Graham, B. R., 605
Graham, Father, Old Folks, 638
Graham, Hen, 352
Graham, Hi, 531, 565, 573
Graham, J. H., 116, 123, 126, 127, 131, 331, 415, 549, 551, 577
Graham, Miss, 211
Graham, R. E., 39, 56, 172, 490
Graham, Rose, 41, 486
Graham, Tillie, 536
Graham and Butler, 544
Grahn, Mrs., 157
Gramm, Emil, 157, 216
Gramm, Mrs. Emil, 594, 595
Grand Central, the, Scenes at, 534, 535
Grand Central Theatre (late Vercelli's), 542
Grand Duchess, in German, 285, 286, 287 (see Grande Duchesse, La)
Grand Duchess, The, variety versions, 123, 125
Grand Dutch S., 184
Grand Dutchess (sic), farce, 548
Grand Opera House, Brooklyn, 619 ff
Grand Opera House, New York (1879-80), 50 ff; (1880-81) 273 ff; (1881-82), 486 ff
Grande Duchesse, La, 26, 32; cast, 33; 36; 176, 264 (see Grand Duchess, The)
Grandfather's Clock, farce, 572
Grandpa's Birthday, 208
Grandpapa's Pants, 145, 179
Grandin, Elmer E., 116, 121, 127, 320, 324
Grandin, Marie, 322
Granger, Bud, 127
Granger, Bud and Annie, 333, 339, 350, 555, 575
Granger, Emma, 140
Granger, Josie, 188
Granger, Leila, 227
Granger, Maude, parts, 7, 9, 11, 41, 58, 94, 175, 202, 225, 384, 411, 464, 465, 483, 484, 488, 491, 607, 608
Granger, Tommy, 341, 345, 414, 415, 553
Grant, E. J., 627
Grant, E. S., 199, 479, 480
Grant, Emma, 622
Grant, J. B., 426
Grant, Lottie, 124, 324, 325, 337, 338, 414, 415
Grant, Miss, 51
Grant, Mrs. E. J., 196, 393, 627, 638
Grant, T. F., one-legged, 116, 118
Grant, Ulysses S., 405
Grant, Wallace, 615
Grant's, General, Trip around the World, 109
Granville, Gertie, 257, 524, 525
Grass Widows, 207
Grattan, Emma, 177, 269
Grattan's Mirror of Ireland, 637, 642

Grau, Maurice, Opera Company, 25, 26, 80, 92, 98, 176, 263, 264, 355, 361, 388, 466, 473, 474
Graves, C. L., 279
Gravesend, 210, 644
Gray, Ada, 278, 467, 608
Gray, Aline, 105
Gray, Bessie, 316, 526 ff, 622
Gray, George, 21, 390
Gray, Mary, 620 ff
Gray, Minnie Oscar, parts, 111, 115, 325, 326, 352, 553, 554, 557, 559, 575, 576, 620
Gray, William, 98 ff, 311 ff, 524, 525, 528
Grayson, Helen, 262, 619
Grayson Opera Company, 619
Grayson-Norcross Opera Company, 262
Grazzi, 91 ff, 304 ff
Great Infidels, 311
Great Mogul, The, or, the Snake Charmer (see Snake Charmer, The)
Great Neck, L. I., 426
Great Republic, The, 180, 391, 393, 426, 429
Great Uncrushed, The, 133
Grecian Mystery, 531
Greco, Filoteo, 235, 371, 595
Green, negro, 60
Green (of Morris and Green), 136
Green, Alexander, 122
Green, J. E., 130
Green, Matt, 328, 334
Green, Spencer, 97
Green Room Fun, 458, 606
Greenaway, Kate, 631
Greenbriar's Troubles, 341
Greene, Clay M., 264
Greenpoint (1879-80), 207 ff; (1880-81), 421 ff; (1881-82) 641 ff
Greensfelder, Joseph, 479 ff, 538
Greenwood Literary Club, 640
Greer, Julia, 153
Gregoire, Cécile, 32, 33, 36, 88, 98, 148, 176, 264, 388, 466, 473
Gregory, actor, 307
Gregory (see Wingfield and Gregory)
Gregory, Arthur W., 272
Gregory, C. J., 330
Gregory, G. L., 337
Gregory, Grimaldi, 350
Gregory Brothers (Charles and George), 325, 340, 352, 556 ff
Greiner, H., 419
Grenadier Band, 23rd Regiment, 392
Gressman, F., 70
Greville, Jessie, 57, 179
Grey, Alice, 9, 11, 49, 468, 476
Grey, Billy, 173
Grey, Katharine, 493
Grey, Neil, 322, 339, 547
Grey, Stanley, 362
Greybrooke, Ethel, 278, 458, 610
Greystone (of London Athletes), 530
Grieg, new music by, 602
Griener, Heinrich, 79
Griffin, cornet, 83
Griffin, Annie, 204

Griffin, Hamilton, 383
Griffin, John D., 114, 318
Griffin, William, 340
Griffin and Marks, 415, 530, 563, 568
Griffing, Helen, 404
Griffis, W. E., 647
Griffith, George, 439, 463
Griffith, W. N., 278, 279
Griffith, William H., 621
Griffith's Hall, Port Richmond, 217, 648
Griffiths, Angie, 41, 178, 279, 280
Griffiths, G. H., 39
Griffiths, Kate, 478
Grille, Die, 73, 497 (see Fanchon)
Grillhofer, Josephine, 69 ff
Grim Goblin, cast, accidents, 218, 219
Grim Goblins, The, 400
Grimaldi, 525, 532
Grimes, Miss, 211
Grimes Brothers, 111
Gringoire, 76, 80
Grinnell, Bennie, 104, 117 ff, 125, 325, 333, 341, 542, 554
Grinnell, Hattie, 104, 117 ff, 125 ff, 325, 333, 341, 541, 542
Griseldis, cast, 69
Grismer, J. R., 39, 172, 225, 259, 264
Grizzly Adams, play, 109, 111, 323, 339, 543; cast, 546; 622
Groebl, Marie, 592
Groebl, Miss M. J., 603
Grogan's Chinese Laundry, 108, 328, 343, 350, 571
Grogan's Corner Grocery, 566
Groscher-Chadwick, 595
Groschl, W., 85
Grosz, Frl., 499 ff
Gross Feuer, 67
Grosser Redner, Ein, cast, 73; 294
Grosser Zwist, Ein, um eine Kleinigheit, 511
Grotesque Comiques, 188 (see infra)
Grotesque Four, 134, 139, 346, 352, 526, 527, 532, 535 (see supra)
Grotesque Two, 576
Grothusen, Frl., 74 ff
Grousemier's Brewery, 544, 553
Groux, F., 88, 301, 513
Grove, Sophie, 547
Grove Hill Park, 300
Grover, Leonard, his play, My Son-in-Law, 171; parts, 244, 489, 620
Grover, Leonard, Jr., 489, 620
Groverstein, G. W., speaking machine, 639
Groves, Charles, 254, 388, 395
Grünewald, Frl., 76
Gschwander's Tyroleans, 104
Guardia Colombo, 303, 515
Guernsey, Minerva, 584
Guglielmo Tell, cast, 182; in French, 394; cast, 518; 519, 521
Guild, F. A., 193, 213, 214, 426
Guillaume Tell, in French, 394 (see Guglielmo Tell)
Guion, Netta, 11, 226 ff, 437 ff, 483, 484
Guise, T. S., 194

Guiteau, in wax, 625
Gulick, Joseph H., 619
Gunter, A. C., his Two Nights in Rome, 225; Fresh, the American, 261, 262; After the Opera, 475
Gunter, Annie, 508
Gunther's Pavilion, 142, 294 ff, 298
Gurney, Kate, 460
Gurney, Marie, 198, 302, 353, 360, 541, 542
Gurnsey, Ethel, 604
Gus, the Slasher, 120
Gute Zeugnisse, 289
Guten Morgen, Herr Fischer, 511
Guthrie, Emma, 225, 266, 395, 481, 482, 538
Guthrie, Francesca, 274, 395, 446, 613
Guv'nor, The, cast; 222, 243
Guy, Ethel, second vision, 190, 191
Guy, Frederick, magic, 125, 190, 192
Guy Mannering, 171
Guyer, William, 359
Guyon, Emile, 162
Guyon, George, walker, 149
Guyon, L. N., actor, 48
Gwynette, Harry, 223, 432, 485, 516
Gymnastic Exhibition, 148
Gypsfigur, cast, 494
Gypsy, or, Wolves and Waifs, 185

H.M.S. Pinafore (see Pinafore, H.M.S.)
Haag, elastic skin, 580
Haan, Walter, 645
Haase, F., compared with C. Sontag, 290; parts, reviews, 500 ff; parts, 623
Habberton, John, his Deacon Crankett, 225, 226
Hackett, Mrs. J. H., 181, 367, 519
Hackman, 47, 414
Hadfield, Lillie, 102
Hadfield, Nellie, 112, 204
Häfter, Professor, 635
Hagan, actor, 171
Hagan, J. F., 54, 274, 277, 282, 455, 472, 488
Hagar, P. C., 455
Hagedorn, 216
Hager's Great Republic, 391, 393, 426, 429
Hagger, Emma, 478
Haggerty, Hughey, 120
Hague, Charles (of Four Comets) 350, 355
Hague, J. W., 9, 176, 270, 486
Hague, Nellie, 109, 110, 114, 117, 319, 321, 326, 331, 335, 556, 558, 578, 635
Hague's British Operatic Minstrels, 537, 538
Hahn, actor, 290
Hahn, Der, im Dorfe, 510
Hahnemann Hospital Fair, 150
Hale, Alice, 129, 556, 557
Haley (of Callan, Haley and Callan), 141, 341, 345, 566, 576
Haley (of Four Diamonds), 129
Haley (of Four Planets), 132
Haley (of Watson and Haley), 120
Haley and Boyd, 122
Haley and West, 101

Haley's Trip to Coney Island, 560
Haley, Tom and Ed, 139, 188, 535, 573, 576, 619, 622
Hall (of Curry and Hall), 133, 186
Hall, Albert, 472
Hall, Anna, 594
Hall, Anna B. P., 162
Hall, Clinton, 63, 64, 171, 269, 484, 485, 607
Hall, E. N., 471
Hall, Fannie, 452, 458, 609
Hall, Grace, 56, 453
Hall, Gustavus, 251, 252, 452, 456, 457, 609
Hall, J. H., 205
Hall, J. O., 123, 130, 281, 533
Hall, James, 124, 129
Hall, Lillie, 132, 186, 344, 533, 574
Hall, Maggie, amateur, 399
Hall, Mills, 225
Hall, Minnie, 199, 333, 350
Hall, Mrs. R. B., 630
Hall, Nellie, "Yankee Girl," 407
Hall, Ocie, 124, 129
Hall, Pauline, 49, 178, 180, 255, 277, 470, 493, 508, 537, 610
Hall, Robert, 311 ff, 524
Hall, Rose, 107
Hallen (Fred) and Hart (Enid), 103, 113, 131, 132, 188, 327, 329, 331, 340 ff, 347, 351, 354, 527, 535, 553 ff, 556 ff, 574 ff, 616, 617
Hallet, Alta, 424
Hallett, Wesley, 645
Hallock, Agnes, 254, 493, 581
Hamblin, Constance, 56, 412, 450, 476, 520
Hamburger Sänger-Gesellschaft, 83
Hamerik, Norwegian Suite, 381
Hamlet, casts, etc., 29, 47, 48, 52, 63, 95; recited by Woollett, 153; 183, 184, 203, 270, 276, 280, 282; read by J. L. Farley, 366; 384, 450, 451, 461, 465, 520, 605, 609, 613
Hamlet, Edwin Booth as, 29, 52, 95, 183, 184, 450, 609; D. E. Bandmann as, 47; Frank Mayo as, 63; Lawrence Barrett as, 203, 276, 384, 461, 605; Adele Belgarde as, 270; Nellie Holbrook as, 280; W. Stafford as, 282; Anna Dickinson as, 465; F. Haase as, with review, 502; Ernesto Rossi as, 451, 520, 613
Hamlet played by women, 270, 280, 465
Hamelt, opera, cast, 457
Hamlet, Prince of Dunkirk, 581
Hamilton (Monumental Quartette), 337
Hamilton, Ada, 278
Hamilton, Alice, 37
Hamilton, Dollie, 37
Hamilton, J., 445
Hamilton, John W., 146
Hamilton, Lillie, 37
Hamilton, May, 534, 547
Hamilton, Miss, at Daly's, 231, 232
Hamilton, W. H. L., zouave drill, 137
Hamilton, W. R., 552
Hamilton, William, 48, 225, 253, 266, 272, 458, 460, 597
Hamilton, William H., 363
Hamilton Park (Held's), 86 ff, 299

Hamlin, Paul, 111, 133, 137, 361, 567
Hamm, Carl, 357, 539
Hammill, T. C., 192
Hammond, Edwin, 476
Hammond, G. (of Monumental Quartette), 332, 343, 347, 553, 567
Hammond, John, cornet, 598
Hammond, Maria Isabelle, 153
Hampie, Abbie, coloured Topsy, 139
Hampshire, W. F., 479, 581
Ham-u-let, 341
Hanau, John, 192, 206
Hanchett, Julia, 46, 178, 262, 488
Hand, H. E., organ, 627
Hand of Providence, The, cast, 318
Handbell Ringers, 565, 596, 630 (see also Bell-ringers)
Händel, F. G., 83
Handel's Jubilate sung, 598
Hands, Minnie, 374
Handy Andy, 217
Hangman of Paris, The, 415
Hanky Panky, 625
Hanley, Scott, 330
Hanley and Logan, 565
Hanlon, Connie, 414
Hanlon, Gilbert, 531, 552
Hanlon Brothers, as Hanlon-Lees (see infra)
Hanlon-Lees (William, Frederick, Edward, George, Alfred), 472, 473, 483, 537, 613
Hanni weint, Hansi lacht, 289, 528, 623
Hans, Joseph, 251
Hans Dampf, 190, 509
Hans Lonei, cast, 289, 292
Hans's Adventures in America, 112
Hansaker, 150
Hanshew, T. W., 326 ff, 353, 395, 544
Hanson (see Fields and Hanson)
Hanson, Charles (see Weston and Hanson)
Hanson, Julius, 124, 126, 127
Hapgood, Miss A., parts, 443
Happy Boys from Borneo, 328, 349, 354, 616
Happy Family, The, 312
Happy Hottentots, 330, 334, 545, 617
Happy Irish Pair, The, 128
Happy Man, The, and His Monkey, 204
Happy Neighbours, 351
Happy Pair, A, 430, 467; variety piece, 111
Harbeson (or Habeson), Mrs. J. W., 160, 373
Hard, Ada, amateur, 585
Hardback Family, The, 144
Hardenberg, F., 1 ff, 176, 230, 234, 385, 470, 492
Hardie, James M., 28, 29, 177, 384, 412, 488, 607
Hare, John, 432
Harebell, the Man o' Airlie, 386, 465
Harkins, Leonore, 386
Harkins, Mrs. W. S., 145
Harkins, W. S., 253, 256
Harkinson, Charles, 38, 44, 52, 62, 176
Harlem, 86 ff, 158, 366 ff, 369, 597 ff
Harlem Association Hall, 586
Harlem Bridge Garden, 511 ff
Harlem Congregational Church, 160

Harlem Männerchor, 87
Harlem Mendelssohn Union, 370, 372
Harlem Music Hall (1879-80), 150 ff; (1880-81), 366 ff; 587; (1881-82), 597 ff
Harlem Opera House, 582, 585
Harlem Parks, etc., 86 ff, 297, 299, 300, 511 ff
Harlem Turn-Verein, 297
Harley, G. W., 59
Harman, H., strong man, 113
Harmon, George, 516
Harmonia, 82, 86, 294, 297
Harmonic Club, Brooklyn, 407
Harmonic Singing Society, L. I. City, 644, 645
Harmonie, L', Espagnole, 514
Harmonie, Cercle Français, 89, 95, 156
Harmonie Club, Flushing, 213
Harmony Rooms, 294 ff, 512
Harned, Margaret, 642
Harold, Donald, 49, 178
Harold, Jennie, 170, 469, 472
Harold, Lizzie, 262
Harper, L. W., 493
Harper, Tom, one-legged Lancer, 105, 113, 120, 134, 185, 547 (see Harper Brothers)
Harper Brothers, one-legged, 532, 624, 625
Harpin, Tommy, 331, 542, 551
Harrigan, Edward (see infra)
Harrigan (Edward) and Hart (Tony), Theatre Comique, plays, etc. (1879-80), 11, 94, 98 ff; 102, 173, 203, 276, 305; (1880-81), 311 ff; 387, 413; (1881-82), 518, 524, 525, 608
Harrington (of Sullivan and Harrington), 105, 567
Harriot, F. C., 193
Harris (of Electric Quartette), 571
Harris (of Virginia Trio), 331, 348, 354, 551, 563
Harris, Augustus, 223, 266, 433
Harris, Charles, variety, 544
Harris, Charles, stages The World, 223; Billee Taylor, 266; Youth, 433; produces Patience, 477
Harris (Charles) and Wood (Billy), 101, 132, 326, 327, 355, 547, 553
Harris, George, 204, 414, 635
Harris, Hamilton, 248, 250
Harris, J. H. U. (of Boston Quartette), 533
Harris, Joe W., 618
Harris, Laura, 635
Harris, Lin, 54, 170, 275, 458, 610
Harris, Lindsay, 467, 608 (see supra)
Harris, Nellie, 414
Harris, W. T., 475
Harris, Willam, 56, 137, 168, 453, 454, 488
Harris (William) and Carroll (Fred), 102
Harris, William H., 281
Harrison, benefit, 190
Harrison, Alice, 49, 352, 353
Harrison, Gabriel, benefit, 409
Harrison, James, 220
Harrison, Joseph, 595
Harrison, L. F., 592
Harrison, Louis, 40, 49, 178, 180, 277, 412, 481, 488, 604

Harrison, Maud, parts, 10 ff, 177, 226 ff, 268; ill; Kate Claxton takes her place, 388; 412, 437 ff, 607
Harrison, Minnie, 143
Harrold, Maggie, 15 ff, 58, 173, 232 ff
Harry Hill Association, 584
Hart, Annie, 214, 545, 567
Hart, Billy, 150
Hart, Dan and Gussie, 336, 341, 352, 396, 535, 543, 562, 564
Hart, Enid (see Hallen, Fred, and Hart, Enid)
Hart, Frank, walker, 37, 150
Hart, Gus, 331
Hart, Joe (see Allen and Hart; also Marlow and Hart)
Hart, John, 102, 130, 131, 133, 178, 188, 276, 340 ff, 354, 397, 546, 555, 573, 616, 619
Hart, Josh, 37, 137
Hart, Nannie, 85
Hart, Samuel, 57
Hart, Tony (see Harrigan, Edward, and Hart, Tony)
Hart, William, 548, 549
Hart and Collins, 414
Hart and Conway, 414
Hart's Variety Troupe, 211
Hartdegen, A., 594
Hartdegen, Annie N., 594
Härting, E., 284
Hartmann, Frl., 283
Hartshorn, F. S., 34, 57, 253
Hartung's Park, 86
Hartz, magic, 368, 554, 579, 587, 624, 625; gifts, 641
Hartz, Evelina, 161, 170, 216, 587
Hartzheim, actor, 503
Harun al Raschid, cast, 67, 68; 70
Harvard football, 582
Harvard Glee Club, 159
Harvard Theatre Collection, 111 ff, 121, 123, 126, 130, 132, 134, 139, 140, 150, 151, 252 ff, 332, 337, 343, 352 ff, 360, 361, 529, 543, 547, 548, 552, 555, 558, 565, 567, 574
Harvest Homes, 209, 212, 214, 426, 428, 546, 647
Harvey, actor, 37
Harvey, singer, 596
Harvey, Amy, 482
Harvey, E. H., 146
Harvey, Fred, 153, 181, 307, 370, 378, 380, 587, 592, 601, 628
Harvey, George H., 257
Harvey, Harry, 487
Harvey, Marie, 146, 159
Harwood, Harry, 44, 274, 277, 634
Harwood, Mrs., 274
Hasabura Sam (see Houssabura Sam)
Hasemann's Töchter, 71, 80, 288, 292, 293, 420, 509
Hasenzahl's Orchestrion Hall, 420
Haskell, Gracie, 423
Haskell, Mrs., 642, 643
Hasselbrinck, Carlos, 244, 356, 370 ff, 406, 420, 595, 597, 601, 627, 629, 638, 640

Hassenbad, 132, 344
Hasslacher, Marie, 539
Hasson, Billy, 114, 120 ff, 132, 141, 325, 330
Hasson, Nellie, 114, 116, 120, 121, 132, 141, 325, 330
Hasson (W.) and Bing (George), 117
Hastings, A. H., 179, 243, 476, 519, 570
Hastings, Alice, 38, 39, 57, 94, 171, 342
Hasty Pudding Club, Harvard, 448
Hatch, Alonzo, 18, 48, 168, 178, 470, 479, 481, 537, 610
Hattenhorst, H., 419
Hatter and Printer (Box and Cox), 530
Hatfield, fireworks, 190
Hatton, Ella, 383
Hatton, Henry, 209
Hatton, Joseph, reads from his novel, 235, 365
Haughton, A. P., 202
Hauk, Minnie, 91, 92, 392, 466, 503, 516 ff; her 200th Carmen, 519; 592, 611 ff
Hauk, Minnie, Arrival of, farce, 121
Hauser, actor, 74 ff, 282 ff
Havanese dancers, 635
Havart, W. J. and H., 596
Haven, Ernest, 335, 339
Haven, Harry, 390
Haverly, J. H., takes Niblo's, 58 ff; takes charge of Mapleson opera in Brooklyn, 182 ff; takes control of Fifth Avenue Theatre, 247 ff, 459 ff; his company in Patience, 537
Haverly's Coloured Minstrels, 60, 202, 271, 387
Haverly's Fourteenth Street (Lyceum) Theatre (1879-80), 39 ff; (1880-81), 254 ff; (1881-82), 467 ff
Haverly's Mastodon Minstrels, 58, 59, 176, 179, 203, 257, 389, 412, 469, 471, 610
Haverly's Opera Company, 470
Haverly's Theatre, Brooklyn (1879-80), 173 ff; (1880-81), 387 ff; (1881-82), 608 ff
Havre, Ceni, 114, 116, 122
Hawk, Harry, 52, 169, 275, 463, 489, 605
Hawkins, negro, 60
Hawkins, C. B., 59, 529
Hawkins, Professor, 211
Hawkins, T. J., 529
Hawkins and Kelly, 349, 354
Hawley, C. B., 200
Hawley, Frank (of Four Comets), 325, 345, 350, 352, 550, 567
Hawley, Hughson, 23
Hawley, Vic (of Monumental Quartette), 332, 337, 343, 347, 553, 567
Hawley and Manning, 127, 334
Hawthorne, Charles, 261, 465
Hawthorne Literary Union, 641, 642
Hayden, Billy, 345, 360, 397
Haydn Amateur Musical Society, 84, 297, 299, 511, 512, 591
Haydn Männerchor, 416
Hayes, Ella, 374
Hayes, J. J., 455
Hayle, Billy and Lou, 117, 122, 133, 328, 330, 332, 347

Haymakers, The, 417
Haymarket, 142, 361
Hays, Rob, 49
Haywood, L., 39, 281
Hazael, George, walker, 149, 359, 540
Haze-L-Kirke, cast, 318; 534; cast, 558; 617
Hazel Kirke, cast, etc., 20 ff; as An Iron Will, cast, 175; changed casts, 235, 236; casts, 272, 412, 466, 485; cast, 491; in German, cast, 508; 608, 633
Hazelton, J. H., 45, 563
Hazlett, Zilpah, 205
He Would Be an Actor, 128, 129
He Would Be a Doctor, 331
He Must Be Married, 280
He's a Lunatic, 648
Headless Horseman, The, 327
Healey (of Ernest and Healey), 331
Healey and Conway, 132, 140
Heaney Brothers, 635
Hear Me Shout Pinafore Lady Minstrels, 111, 112
Hearne, James, variety, 320
Hearts and Diamonds, 185
Hearts of Oak, cast, 37; 56, 65, 384, 604, 633
Hearts of Steel, cast, 57; 331
Heath, Thomas (see McIntyre, James, and Heath, Thomas)
Hebrew actors, 417, 509, 510
Hebrew amateur actors, 404
Hebrew Fair, 356
Hebrew impersonations, 336 (see also Sam'l of Posen)
Hebrew Operatic and Dramatic Company, 509
Hebrew refugees, benefit, 621
Hebrew Sheltering Guardian Society, 583
Hebrew specialties, 118
Hecht, Cecilia, 496, 498, 510
Hecker, actor, 66 ff
Hector, play, 510
Hedges, Tom, 113, 115, 126, 127, 140
Heeney, actor, 334
Heeney, Ed (of Kennedy and Heeney), 326, 336
Heerwagen, Orlando, 424
Heerwagen (sic), Otto, 211, 212
Hegeman, Evelyn, 406
Heights Amateur Association, 399
Heimkehr, Die, 293
Heinebund, 56, 84 ff, 87, 295, 374
Heinemann, actor, 67 ff, 289, 499
Heinrich, Max, 381
Heintz, Mark, 281
Heintzmann, Lizzie, 645
Heinze, Julian, 195
Heir at Law, The, 310; cast, 604
Heir of Greylock, The, 367
Heiser, billiards, 154
Heiser, J. Randolph, 133, 582
Heister, George, I
Helen's Babies, 341
Heller, Fanny, 66 ff, 72, 282 ff
Heller, Julie, 282
Helmar, Marie, 596

Helvetia Männerchor, 297, 511
Helly, Victor, 498
Hemmed In, farce, 340
Hemple, S. A., 57
Hempstead, L. I., 646
Henderson, A., 460
Henderson, Albert, 482
Henderson, Ettie, her play, 265
Henderson, G. A., 41, 339, 576
Henderson, Graham J., 58, 275, 412, 423, 472
Henderson, W., 226
Henderson, William, manager, 265
Hendricks and Lena, 187
Hengler, T. M., 92, 100, 106 ff, 128, 130, 138, 140, 187; at Daly's, 233; 266, 344, 346, 348, 397, 458, 550 ff, 558, 617
Henley, Marie, 56
Henne, Antonia, 85, 154, 157 ff, 161 ff, 201, 216, 299, 356, 370 ff, 381, 512, 513, 591, 593 ff, 599, 602, 603, 614, 632
Hennecart, Mlle., 310
Hennessey Brothers, 139, 185, 325, 352, 354
Henpecked Husband, The, 343, 397
Henri, Mlle., Congress of Beauties, 185
Henrico, Indian clubs, 115, 125, 137
Henriques, Madeline, 6, 224
Henry, tenor, 159
Henry, Emma, 63, 161, 174, 197, 395, 583, 614, 646
Henry, R. M., 271
Henry IV, Part I, read, 584, 585
Henry V, recited, 153; 244
Henry VIII, with Janauschek, 606
Henschel, George, 298, 371 ff; his King and Poet, 372; 379, 380, 394, 410, 596
Henshaw (of Stokes and Henshaw), 547
Henshaw, John E., 64, 281, 317, 566, 571, 572, 615, 618
Henson, Dora, 375
Herbert, Amelia, 170
Herbert, Carrie, 549
Herbert, G. W., 488
Herbert, W., 24, 64, 476
Herbert, W. H., 475
Herbert Brothers, 58, 92, 171, 270, 276, 484
Hercht, Pauline, her play, 631
Hercules, Young, 132, 134, 136 ff, 188, 339
Here and There, 324
Heritage, Clarence, 440
Herman, Charles and La Rose, 350, 531, 560, 574
Herman, Charles D., 245
Hermann und Dorothee, 510
Hermanus, Frl. and Herr, 293
Hermione (Winter's Tale), Janauschek as, 606
Hernani, with Bernhardt, 241, 246
Herndon, Agnes, 202
Herne, James A., his Hearts of Oak, 37; 56, 65, 384, 604, 633
Herne, John F., 64, 270
Heron, Bijou (Hélène Stoepel), 230, 445, 446
Herren Eltern, Die (Our Boys), cast, 67; 68
Herring, Fanny, parts, 104, 122, 146, 185, 187, 188, 322, 329, 330, 339, 354, 415, 543, 551, 552, 554, 573, 575, 635

Herrmann, 42, 100, 177, 243, 275, 278, 364, 385, 467, 481, 488, 498, 606, 641
Herrmann, concert, 595
Herrmann Brothers (Carl and Edward), 590, 591, 592
Hertz, Carl, 544, 556, 563, 569, 575
Herz, Gretchen, 298
Herz, actor, 76
Hess, C. D., Acme Opera, 477, 478
Hesse, Hedwig, 284
Hesselmeyer, G., 591
Hession, Frank, 592
Hester Street Serenaders, 341
Hettinger and Nibbe, 347, 543, 544, 556
Heusel (or Husel), Emil, 99, 311 ff, 524
Hewitt, Helen, 474
Hexe, Die, 283, 509
Heydemann und Sohn, 306
Heywood, Charles (of Clipper Quartette), 134, 139; 398, 526, 539, 555, 617
Hezekiah Perkins, 339
Hiawatha, cast, 49
Hibbard, Hortense, 600
Hicks, Sidney, 38, 272, 307
Hidden Hand, The, 114, 125
Higgins, H., 568
Higgins, W. H., 150
Higgins, W. S., 321, 323, 414
High, Low, Jack, and the Game, 322
High Life in Impland, 275
High Time, A, in Dixie, 136
Hight, Lizzie, 268, 467
Hildebrand (of King and Hildebrand), 532
Hildebrand, Frank, 298, 560
Hill, Anna, 298
Hill, Barton, 259, 459
Hill, Charles, 643
Hill, George A., 122, 321
Hill, Gus, 131, 141, 185, 327 ff, 333, 344, 544 ff, 550, 553
Hill, Harry, his Flushing regatta, 426; his Pavilion, 214
Hill, Harry, his "place," 143, 576, 577
Hill, J. M., 234, 634
Hill, John G., 180, 394, 399
Hill, Kate, 417
Hill, Kate Vashti, 158
Hill, May, 529
Hill, Miss, concert, 375
Hill, Mrs. Mary, 41
Hill, R. S., 44
Hill, W. J., 158
Hilleker, Tiny, 482
Hiller, Ferdinand, his cantata, 373
Hiller, Miss, 424
Hilliard, 217
Hilliard, George S., 430
Hilliard, Harry S., 593
Hilliard, Robert C., as amateur, 182, 393, 615
Hills, Anna Bulkley, 158, 163, 403, 592
Hills, Dr., 163
Himmer, Rudolf, 199, 404, 417
Hinckley, Emma, 16 ff, 178, 231, 445
Hinco, zither, 298
Hind, T. J., 8, 43, 64, 171, 255

Hindbaugh, Carrie, 600
Hindle, Annie, 120, 126, 127, 331, 397, 532, 616
Hindoos, the beautiful, 397
Hinds, Ida, 195
Hinds, John T., parts, 322, 332, 354, 400, 411, 530, 550
Hines (of Twilight Four), 567
Hines (William E.) and Blossom (Nat), 131, 135, 328, 331, 335, 344, 355, 552, 558, 560, 616
Hippopotamus exhibited, 148
Hirsch, Miss F., 356
Hirsch, William V., 404
Hirschy, Fritz, benefit, 98
His Last Crime, or, Vell, Vot of It? 107
His Last Legs, 209
His Mud Scow Pinafore, 144
Hob-be-de-Hoy, 333
Hobbies, 31; casts, 40, 169, 256, 411; 607
Hoch, Louise H., 600
Hoch, Theo, 87, 539
Hodcarrier's Strike, 551
Hodcarriers, The, 340
Hodge, John G., 565
Hodges (of Twilight Four), 567
Hoefler, Charles, 359
Hoefler, Professor, 545, 546, 578
Hoey, Charles H., juggler, 326
Hoey, Charles H., of Nantick, 565, 566, 572
Hoey, George, his A Child of the State, 7, 177, 384, 412, 488, 607
Hoey, James (American Four), 101, 103, 133, 137 ff, 190, 334, 335, 341, 347, 350 ff, 383, 398, 519, 526, 530, 534, 554, 556, 557, 567
Hoey, Mrs. John, 224
Hoey, William, 51, 56, 100
Hoey, William F. (see Bryant and Hoey)
Hofele, manager, 61
Hofer, Nandl, 539
Hoffänger, play, 499
Hoffman, singer, 180
Hoffman, Emma, 331, 332, 353, 430, 543, 551
Hoffman, H., his Cinderella, 85
Hoffman, Lottie, 635
Hoffman, Richard, 201, 216, 371, 376, 596, 614, 648
Hogan, Harry, 57, 94, 236, 237
Hogan, John, 106, 111, 335, 339, 345
Hogan, Vincent, 11, 172, 254, 274, 538
Hogan Brothers (Harry and Gus), 107, 112, 114, 117, 189, 328, 333, 335, 345, 349, 354, 546, 557, 616, 618
Hogg, George E., 195
Holbrook, Nellie, 244
Holcomb, John, 549
Holcombe, Josei, 624
Holden, negro, 60
Holden (George) and White (Frank), 575
Holden, Gertie, 548
Holdsworth, Sam, 103, 316, 327, 341, 343
Holland, Alfred, 48
Holland, E. M., parts, 1 ff, 177, 275, 458, 474, 475, 481, 610
Holland, George, 56, 172, 263, 429, 519, 582
Holland, J. J., 56, 263, 468, 469

Holliday, H. J., 221 ff, 244, 432 ff
Hollingsworth, Addie, 211, 212, 424, 425, 645
Hollingsworth, Miss, 211
Holloway, Laura C., 404, 408
Holmes, Harrie C., 123
Holmes, Matthew, 38, 57, 383
Holmes, Raymond, 169, 264, 479
Holst, Edward, author, 478
Holz und Blech, 510, 511
Holzapfel, Frl., 282 ff
Holzhausen, Master, 593
Home, R. J. Burdette's lecture, 584
Home Again, 105, 118, 132
Home, Sweet Home, sung by Patti, 506, 589
Homer, George, 564, 570, 575, 622
Homing Man, The, 325
Honeymoon, The, 170, 390
Honigmann, Henriette, 82
Hood, Rev. E. Paxton, 583
Hooley, Bob, 59
Hooley's Theatre (now Court Square), 184, 185
Hopf, Herr, 67 ff
Hopfenrath's Erben, cast, 503; 504, 623
Hopkins, G. V., 162
Hopkins, Jerome, 162, 163, 311, 374, 600
Hopkins-Morrow Combination, 318
Hopper, De Wolf, 40, 170, 203, 245, 246, 281, 389, 491, 633
Horn, Auguste, 74 ff
Horning, B. F., 8, 428, 448
Horrors, casts, 49, 50, 180; 202
Horses, performing, 65, 109, 111, 136, 146, 189, 281, 329, 333, 493, 541, 544, 545
Horseshoe Four, 535, 553, 561 ff, 565, 569, 618
Horst and Hallahan, 578
Horton, Alfred, 271
Horton, Harry, 320
Horton, Ward L., 326
Hosmer, Alice, 11, 172
Hot Night, A, in the City, 363
Hotel di Roma, 515
Hotel Runners, 127
Hotels, Staten Island, 649
Hotto, Harry, 387
Housabura (variously spelled) Sam, 118, 322, 328, 331, 337, 534, 548, 551, 561
House that Jack Built, The, 152
Household Fairy, The, 8
Houston, Robert, 369, 585
How I Used Casey, 110, 121, 571
How She Loves Him, cast, 6
Howard, walker, 150
Howard, Amy, 626
Howard, Annie, 99, 123, 124, 546, 547, 554, 555
Howard, Bronson, his play, Wives, 16; Green Room Fun, 458, 606; Baron Rudolph, 486, 487
Howard, Carrie, 137, 345, 348, 351, 571, 575, 617
Howard, Charles L., 543, 636
Howard, Constance, 157, 372, 377, 591, 597
Howard, E. M., 492
Howard, Ed, 118
Howard (Ed) and Barry (J. L.), 533

Howard (Ed) and Coyne, 130, 326, 330, 337, 414

Howard, F. A. (of the Clipper Quartette), 552, 559, 563

Howard, G. C., 199

Howard, George W., 49, 178, 180, 255

Howard, H. H., 266

Howard, J. B., 279

Howard, Jennie, 396

Howard, L. F., 64, 467

Howard (Larry) and Sanford (Frank), 114, 126, 127, 319, 324, 334, 338, 339

Howard, Lester, 118, 134, 138, 141; (of Novelty Four), 345, 352, 353, 397, 551, 555, 617

Howard, Lewis, 472

Howard, Lillie, 132, 133, 214, 340, 343

Howard, M., 229

Howard, Mary, 124, 143

Howard, Mrs. Cicely, 643

Howard, Mrs. G. C., 65, 181, 199, 216, 429, 633

Howard, Ned, 327

Howard, Nellie, 18 ff, 231, 387, 443 ff

Howard and Saville, 134

Howard and Thompson, 327

Howard Athenæum, 137

Howard Variety Combination, 204

Howe, Clara, 38

Howe, Den and Ella, 544

Howe, Emma, 103, 195, 356, 373, 585, 587, 596, 631

Howe, Ethel, 52, 55, 56

Howe, Fannie, 38

Howe, J. E., 547

Howell, J. A., 468

Howell and Darwin, 481, 488

Howells, W. D. and Yorick's Love, 260, 261

Howland, J. H., 230, 271, 420, 453

Howland, Josephine, 119, 547

Howson, Emma, 269; original Josephine in London Pinafore, 269; 470, 609, 610

Howson, Frank A., 393

Howson, John, 243, 244, 251, 253, 258, 262, 268, 394, 460, 478, 481, 487, 537, 609

Howson, W. S., amateur, 399

Hoyt, Wayland, 647

Hoyte, actor, 271

Hubbard, A. D., 367, 371, 594

Hubbell, Ida W., 161, 373, 379, 410, 603, 649

Huber, Fred J., 134 ff, 186, 316, 348 ff, 543, 560, 561, 568 ff, 574

Huber, Hans, his symphony, 602

Huber's Prospect Garden, 362, 578

Huckleberry Party, 119

Hudson, Harry, 468, 608

Hudson, Lizzie, 177, 202, 386

Hudson, R. C., 261

Hudson, W. A., 11

Hudson Männerchor, 85, 299, 511

Huebner, F. C., 450, 459

Hughes, variety, 135

Hughes (of Perry and Hughes), 102

Hughes (of Four Eccentrics), 135, 344, 347, 397, 518, 562, 563

Hughes, Andy and Annie, 110, 314, 315, 320 ff, 330, 342, 534, 545, 556, 616

Hughes, Archie, 120, 186, 204, 339, 415

Hughes, Artie (see Foster, Dave, and Hughes, Artie)

Hughes, Jennie, 61, 103, 134, 136, 139, 186, 238, 266, 395, 477, 482, 619

Hughes, John C., walker, 348, 540

Hughes, Mrs. (of Burton's), 107

Hughes, Paddy, 114, 120, 129

Hughes and Allen's Minstrels, 418

Huguenots, Les, 27; cast, 96; 97; casts, 183, 310, 394, 519; 521, 522; cast, 613

Hull Twin Sisters (Effie and Emma), 320, 327, 330, 331, 352

Hulmes, Ada, 534, 546

Human Fiend, A., 414

Hume, Dick (see Thatcher and Hume)

Hume (Dick) and Lindsay (Jennie), 565, 566, 570, 571, 619

Hummel, lawyer, 273

Hummel, Eugenie C., 162

Hummel, Sophie, 218, 274

Humour, Use and Abuse of, 403, 423

Humphries, H. R., 48, 266, 376, 587, 604, 643

Humpty Dumpty, cast, 27; 65, 121, 148, 177; cast, 183; 203; cast, 271; 280, 337, 366, 390, 396, 413, 414, 491, 525; cast, 531; 532, 579, 608, 616, 617, 621, 625, 633, 635

Humpty Dumpty in Every Clime, cast, 552

Humpty Dumpty's Christmas, 102

Humpty's Frolics, 139

Hunchback, The, with Miss Neilson, 30; 39, 168, 171; with the Amaranth, 182; with Mary Anderson, 249, 250; 383, 404; cast, 454; 607; with Mrs. Bowers, 620; 634

Hungarian Gipsy Band, 538, 540, 601

Hunnenschlacht, sung, 598

Hunt, Jay, 471

Hunt, Julia A., 476

Hunt, Lizzie, 480

Hunt, Miss, recites, 367, 379

Hunter, Harry, 48, 176, 255, 388

Hunter, Lizzie, 118, 134, 138, 141; (of Novelty Four), 345, 352, 353, 397, 536, 555, 572

Hunter, Marie, 477, 478, 503, 597

Hunter, T. M., 242 ff, 484

Hunter's Dogs, The, 339, 554

Hunter's Point, 211, 212, 424, 425, 644, 646

Hunting, Percy, 15 ff, 465

Huntington, L. I., 646

Hurley, Joe, 339, 546 ff

Hurley, W. J., 463, 464, 476, 604

Huron Tribe, No. 35, 88; —and Idaho, 301, 513

Husband, A, to Order, 420

Hussey, Miss St. George, 533, 546, 554, 557, 559, 562, 569, 616

Hutchings, Alice, 198, 247, 349, 516, 546, 566, 572, 618

Hutchings, Charlotte, 52, 146

Hyatt, Clara, 176, 234, 385, 447, 517

Hyde, Annie, amateur, 369, 392 ff, 612

Hyde, Jennie, amateur, 369

Hyde and Behman take old Olympic Theatre, Brooklyn, 621 ff

Hyde and Behman's, Brooklyn (1879-80), 186 ff; (1880-81), 396 ff; (1881-82), 615 ff
Hyde and Behman's company at Pastor's, 104
Hyers Sisters (Madah and Louise, their coloured combination), 430
Hyman, Henry M., 598

Iago, Edwin Booth as, 7, 29, 31, 52, 95, 183, 449, 450, 459, 609; J. C. McCollom as, 29; Frederic Robinson as, 52; H. S. Spelman as, 97; F. B. Warde as, 170, 282, 389; L. R. Shewell as, 242; Lawrence Barrett as, 384; Milnes Levick as, 450; Edmund Collier as, 463; John McCullough as, 463; Joseph Wheelock as, 464
Ich speise bei meiner Mutter, 287
Ici on Parle Français, 207
Idala, college show, 155
Idaletta, 102, 115, 155, 414
Ideal, Ein, cast, 499
Idiot of the Mountain, 530, 575
Idiot Witness, The, 561, 563
Idlewild Quartette, 425
Ihr Korporal, 495
Illicit Distillery, The, 329
Illiet, actor, 263
Ill Treated Il Trovatore, 56, 172
Ill-True-Bad-Doer, 257
I'm an Actor, 343, 555, 557, 559, 576
Im Rausch, cast, 80
Im Vorzimmer seiner Excellenz, 293, 502
Im Wartesalon III Klasse, 510
Im Weinberg des Herrn, 511
Im Zauber-Salon, 81
Immanuele-Gemeinde, Chor der, 299
Imogen, Miss Neilson as, 29, 30; Fanny Davenport as, 178
In and Out, 329
In and Out of Action, 574
In Friedenzeiten, 293
In Hemdsärmeln, 510
In Manica di Camicia, 302
In Marmor ausgehauen, 82
Ince, John E., 145, 245, 440, 442
Ince, Lottie, 266
Independent Schützen Compagnie, 190
India rubber man, 579, 625
Indian club act, 116
Indians, American, exhibited, 65, 153, 278, 359, 365, 491, 493, 564, 625, 645
Indians, American, protection for, 153
Indig, B. B., amateur, 404
Ingersoll, Miss D. E., 236
Ingersoll, Robert G., lectures, 30, 31, 246, 247, 311, 522, 585, 614, 615
Ingersoll Confuted by Geology, lecture, 365
Ingersollism, lecture, 629
Inglas, Ella, amateur, 612
Ingomar, 39, 171; with Salvini, 244; 250, 270, 383, 462, 488, 607, 609, 610, 621, 634
Ingraham, Fred, 213, 214, 426, 628, 643, 645, 646
Ingraham, George, 424
Inman, Nellie, 624

Inner Life of a War Correspondent, 366
Innis, F. N., 52, 601
Innocent, cast, 620
Inshavogue, 65
Inspector Bräsig, 73, 507
International Concert Company, 409
International Mastodon Minstrels, 116
Interviews, play, 607
In-Toe-Natural Walking Match, 99, 187, 188
Intrigue, or, Robes de Rouge, 536
Intropodi, F., 191
Invited to the Sängerfest, 101
Iolanthe, play, 390
Ion, with Mary Anderson, cast, review, 249, 250
Iona Island, 87
Ionides, actor, 47
Iowa Giantess, 401
Iphigenie auf Tauris, cast, 70
Iredale, F., 14 ff
Ireland, starving poor, benefits for, 6, 10, 28, 54, 55, 72, 95, 103, 142, 150, 153, 161, 171, 177, 197, 210, 215
Ireland and the Land Question, 374
Ireland as It Is, cast, 107
Ireland vs. Germany, 649
Ireland's Declaration of Independence, 615
Ireland's Farewell, 136
Ireland's Land League, 353
Ireland's Struggle for Liberty, 111
Irene, Mlle., 616
Irish Agitator, 130
Irish and German Lovers, 337
Irish Assurance, 325
Irish Comedy Four, 551
Irish Emigrant, The, 649
Irish Felicity, 345
Irish Four, 129
Irish Justice, 114
Irish Land War, 408
Irish Landlords, cast, 114
Irish Lion, The, cast, 7, 8
Irish Lords, 329
Irish Market Woman, The, 561
Irish Outlaw, The, 349
Irish Servants, 321
Irish Soldier, The, in the War of the Rebellion, 393
Irish Tutor, The, 212
Irish Widows, 575
Irish Wit and Humour, 407, 418
Irma, 31
Iron Pier, Coney Island, 155
Iron Will, An (Hazel Kirke), 20; cast, review, 175
Irschick, Magda, parts, 69, 70, 76 ff, 84, 85, 94, 181, 190
Irving, Frank, 619
Irving, Harry, 324
Irving, Henrietta, 38, 268, 269, 437, 606
Irving Hall, 88, 89, 301, 307, 513 ff, 584, 598
Irving's Novelty Troupe, 426
Irwin, Flora, 51, 100 ff, 140, 187, 277, 314 ff, 341, 342, 367, 396, 489, 519, 520, 527, 528, 618

Irwin, John, 442
Irwin, May, 51, 100 ff, 140, 187, 277, 314 ff, 341, 342, 352, 367, 396, 489, 519, 520, 526 ff, 555 ff, 574, 618
Irwin, Mrs. Selden, 204
Irwin, Selden, 204
Is a Clerk Responsible?, 112, 113
Isabella (Measure for Measure), Miss Neilson as, 30
Israel in Egypt, sung, 600
Italian Miscellany (1879-80), 89, 90; (1880-81), 303; (1881-82), 514, 515
Italian Opera (see Academy of Music, Brooklyn and New York; Booth's Theatre; Germania Theatre, 1881-82)
Italian Padrone, The, 321, 329, 344, 353; cast, 568
Italian plays, 302, 514, 515 (see also Rossi, Ernesto, and Salvini, Tommaso)
Italian School of Vineland, 302
Italian Societies, United, 90
Ivan, the Hammer, 552
I've Only Been Down to the Wigwam, 340
Ixion, 186, 533

Jack, John, 265
Jack Cade, 170; revised as The Bondman, 463; restored to bills, 463
Jack Harkaway, 108, 110, 121, 324, 355
Jack Sheppard, 66, 122, 279, 329
Jack Sheppard and His Dogs, 111, 113, 326, 576
Jack Sheppard from the Cradle to the Grave, 575
Jack Sheppard, Life and Adventures of, 354, 545, 551, 574
Jack, the Giant Killer, 147
Jackits-Chy's Japanese, 108, 131, 342, 347, 353, 397
Jackson, actor, 445
Jackson, Belle, 237, 256, 471
Jackson, F. H., his play, 622
Jackson, George, 421
Jackson, Hiram, walker, 149
Jackson, Miss, 280
Jackson, S., 520
Jackson, T. E., 468, 620
Jackson, T. J., 486
Jackson, Virgie, 616
Jackson, W., 108, 109
Jacobs, Esther, 600
Jacobs, Fanny, 600
Jacobs, Harry, 186
Jacques, Andrew, 57, 94, 122, 226, 438
Jacques Strop in France, 562
Jaeger, C., benefit, 212
Jagau's Sommer-Garten, 300
Jamaica, L. I. (1879-80), 214, 215; (1880-81), 427; (1881-82), 646, 647
Jamaica Opera House, 427, 646, 647
James, C. T., 110
James, George T., 278, 354
James, Lithgow, 251, 470, 479, 610, 613

James, Louis, parts, 167, 177, 202, 203, 260, 261, 384, 450, 461, 465
James Boys, The, play, 571
Jameson, tenor, 645
Jamieson, Carrie, 12, 272, 386, 465, 488
Jamieson, Fred, 161, 378
Janauschek, Fanny, parts, 245, 437, 491, 606
Jane, Mlle., 239 ff
Jane Eyre, with Maggie Mitchell, 56, 275, 384, 489; with F. Ellmenreich, 504
Janes, Master, 179
Janitzky, actor, 290
Jansen, Frau, 635
Jansen, Josephine, 509, 640
Jansen, Marie, 258, 268, 460, 464, 609, 613
Janson, Frl., 290 ff
Japanese Kettledrum, 196, 197, 198, 406
Japanese performers, 108, 131, 147, 204, 342, 346, 347, 353, 397, 488, 534 (see also Housabura Sam; Jackits-Chy's Japanese; Katsnoshin, Awata; King Sarbro)
Japanese Tommy, 625
Jaques (As You Like It), W. E. Sheridan as, 39, Osmond Tearle as, 220
Jarbeau, Vernona, 48, 60, 92, 176, 253, 254, 266, 387, 452, 458, 609, 613
Jarboe, J. W., 421, 642
Jardine, Edward, 423, 629, 641
Jarley Uniques, 408
Jarley's, Mrs., Waxworks, 153, 368, 421, 425, 627, 647
Jarrett, H. C., 238, 243, 391
Jarrett and Palmer's Uncle Tom's Cabin, 645, 648
Jarvis, Fannie, 193
Jarvis, J. H., 269
Jarvis, Thomas J., 155
Jasper, Marie, 136, 137
Jasper, Thomas and Clinton, 330
Jasper, cast, 620
Jaybee, walker, 150
Jeal, Linda, 131, 135
Jealous Darkies, The, 350
Jealous Husband, The, 550
Jealous Wife, The, farce, 342, 555
Jealousy, farce, 129, 347, 567
Jefferies, Lydia, 419
Jefferson, Joseph, as Rip Van Winkle, etc., 51, 61, 168, 275, 385, 435; as Bob Acres, criticisms, 436; 439, 488, 606
Jefferson, "Tom," 4, 223, 385, 439, 606
Jefferson Verein der deutschen Arbeiter, 84
Jeffreys (or Jeffries), Ida, 34, 488
Jeffreys, J. H. and Ida, 527, 552, 556
Jelliffe, Miss A. L., 627
Jelliffe, W. M., 180, 614
Jenkins, Oliver, 51
Jennings (see Manchester and Jennings)
Jennings, Alice, 577
Jennings, E. B., mesmerism, 368
Jennings, John J., 130
Jennings, Miss, 214, 426
Jepson, Eugene O., 47, 385, 488
Jerolamon, Madeline, 159, 160

Jerome, Charles and Ella, 117, 130, 134, 138, 140, 187, 190, 327, 329, 332, 345, 348, 351, 353, 383, 397, 565, 566, 571, 574, 618
Jerome, Jennie, boxer, 143
Jerry's Fortune, 130, 553
Jervis, Perlee, 631
Jessup, George H., his Gentleman from Nevada, 37, 38; Prologue for Brooklyn Theatre, 173; All at Sea, 581
Jewell, Miss, 245
Jewett, R. E., 65
Jewett, Sara, parts, 10 ff, 13, 226 ff, 246, 260, 276, 389, 437 ff, 607
Jewish Festival, Chanucka, 94
Jewish performer, 401
Jim Bowie, play, 555
Jim Crow Alive, 131, 341
Jim, the Slasher, 617
Jo (Bleak House), cast, 468; 608
Joe vs. John, or, the Long Island Returning Board, 211
Jöhmus, Karl, 164
John and Ellen Magee, farce, 346
John's Drunk Again, 548
Johns, Effie, 179
Johnson, minstrel, 143 ff
Johnson, Arthur, 113, 185, 329, 344, 351, 355
Johnson, Bobby, 330
Johnson, C. E., juggler, 126, 330
Johnson, Emma, 421
Johnson, Frank, 38
Johnson, Frankie, 137, 347
Johnson, George W., 105 ff, 323, 324, 529 ff
Johnson, Gertie, 167, 170, 171, 267
Johnson, J., 3
Johnson, J. M., 321 ff, 331, 566, 572
Johnson (J. M.), and Swain (S. C.), 350
Johnson, J. P., 468
Johnson (James) and Powers, 179, 362, 580
Johnson, Jessie, 255
Johnson, Joe, 111
Johnson, Kittie and Jennie, 205
Johnson, R. A., librarian, 317
Johnson, Sophie, 548, 549, 577
Johnson, Thomas, 27
Johnson, Virgie, 329, 330, 344, 351, 355
Johnson, W. T., 49, 139
Johnson, Walter, 153, 375, 378, 593
Johnson, William, actor, 275
Johnson, William, wrestler, 324
Johnston, Robert, his Uncle Tom's Cabin, 61 62
Jolies Grisettes, 533
Joliet, actor, 246
Jolly Bachelors (Box and Cox), 215
Jolly Coopers, The, 533
Jolly Cork's Pleasure Trip, 346
Jolly Duchess, The, 204
Jolly Four, 140
Jolly Mariners, 42
Jolly Old Couple, The, 350, 550
Jolly Three (McNish and Lelands), 348
Jonas, actor, 499
Jonas, E., 'cello, 592, 595

Jonas, Minna, 371
Jones, singer, 423
Jones (see Leonard and Jones)
Jones, Bobby (see Sheehan and Jones)
Jones, E., 610
Jones, Emma, 145
Jones, Frank, 101, 112, 113, 119, 141, 325, 327, 331, 332, 345, 352, 414, 415, 543, 544, 550, 574, 575
Jones, George, 43
Jones, Henry, 21
Jones, Herbert, 478
Jones, J. J., rifle shot, 547
Jones, Johnny, 315
Jones, Mrs. W. G., parts, 61, 62, 107 ff, 186, 280, 282, 478, 493
Jones, N. D., 27
Jones, Nellie, 65, 390
Jones, Robert, 141, 473
Jones, Sadie, 354
Jones and Madigan, 549
Jones Wood Colosseum, 83 ff, 89, 156, 299, 301, 513 ff, 601
Jordan, Charles, 390, 621, 622
Jordan, George C., 12, 17, 172 ff, 270, 412, 620
Jordan, Julius, 165
Jordan, Lulu, 46, 178, 269, 488
Jordan, M. J., 246, 411, 482
Jordan, Mabel, 17 ff, 54, 151, 177
Jorio, L., 302
Joseffy, Rafael, début, programmes, reviews, 156 ff; 164, 180 ff, 310, 356, 357, 370 ff, 379, 395, 406, 410, 594 ff; compositions by, 596; 602, 631, 632, 639
Josephs, W., 49
Joshua Whitcomb, 42; cast, 46, 47; 178, 181, 202, 276; casts, 385, 488, 489; 492, 607, 634
Jouard, Emile, 26, 32, 33, 36, 88, 97, 98, 148, 176
Jour, Le, de Fête, 586
Jour, Le, et la Nuit, as Manola, 464; 466
Jourdan, opera, 301, 310, 394
Jourdan, Alicia, 51, 136, 187
Journalisten, Die, cast, 290, 291; 292
Joyce, Laura, 64, 232 ff, 386, 413, 442 ff, 481
Joyce, Lillian, 280, 465
Joyce and Murphy, 530
Joyce's Military Band, 601
Jubilee Day, 351, 354
Jubilee Singers, 64, 158 ff, 162, 196 ff, 200, 205 ff, 208, 209, 211, 215, 359, 399, 404 ff, 407, 421, 424 ff, 429, 576, 577, 593, 615, 625, 628, 646, 647
Juch, Emma, 82, 85, 86, 294 ff, 299, 377, 378, 498, 512, 513, 516 ff, 537, 591, 600, 612 ff
Juch, Herr, 85
Juch, Justin, 377
Jucht (sic), Mrs., 373
Judenhetze in Deutschland, lecture, 297
Judenhetze, Die, im 19 Jahrhundert, 298
Judge, Alice, 614
Judge, Miss A. M., 199
Judge Duffy's Substitute, 568

INDEX

Juggling, 27, 110, 118 ff, 125, 126, 133, 140, 183, 321, 326, 330, 333, 336, 344, 345, 348, 396, 401, 543, 544, 550, 557, 558, 562, 568 ff, 574, 617, 619, 622, 626
Juignet, Paul, 510, 514, 538, 597
Juive, La, casts, 310, 394
Jules, Hermine, 494
Jules, Mons., 107, 108
Julia, performing bear, 108
Juliet, Miss Neilson as, 30, 168; Ada Cavendish as, 54; Maude Granger as, 54; Magda Irschick as, 79; Helen Ottolengui as, 94; Mary Anderson as, 171, 383, 453, 488, 607, 634; Mrs. Scott-Siddons as, 390; Louise Muldener as, 451; Marie Hunter as, 503; Jeffreys Lewis as, 523; Lillian Olcott as, 610
Julius Cæsar, cast, 276; 306; read, 366; 384, 386; cast, 461; 465, 518, 605
Jullien's concerts, 356
July 14th, Fête, 514
Jumbo, 541, 631
Jumbo, a Trick Elephant, farce, 529
Junge Lieutenant, Der, 289
Jungfrau, Die, von Orleans, cast, 78; 79, 80
Jüngste Lieutenant, Der, 283
Junior Friendship Coterie, 212
Just, Helen, 51, 248
Just from Amsterdam, 544
Just from Arkansaw, 114, 120, 128, 131, 134, 135, 561
Just from Canada, 544
Just from Germany, 128, 335, 347
Just from Haverstraw, 577
Just from Ireland, 530, 557
Just from Omaha, 125
Just His Luck, 110
Just in Time, 324, 355, 553
Just Over, 135
Justice pro Tem, 333
Juteau, parts, 26, 32, 33, 36, 98, 148, 176

K. H. K.'s (Emerson, Clark, Daly Brothers), 130, 135, 141, 187, 330, 352, 526, 527, 532, 535
Kabale und Liebe, 73, 74, 80
Kadelburg, H., 81
Kahn, Gustav, 509
Kain and Thompson, 121
Kaine (see Waldron and Kaine)
Kaine, Emma, 550, 560
Kaine, Georgie, 51, 100, 102, 188, 189, 345, 349, 396, 550, 560, 616, 617
Kaiser, Karl, 83
Kalas, Climene, 516 ff, 591, 612
Kalte Seelen, cast, 288
Kaltenborn, Carl, 77
Kaltenborn, Franz, 53, 159
Kammerlee, Gus, 181, 328, 393
Kane, George, 141, 186, 330, 545, 564, 570, 571
Kane and Graham, 354
Karl, Tom, 51, 167, 238, 455, 456, 611

Karl Brothers (William and Charles), 526, 562
Karl's Germania Hall, 296
Karl's Park, 299
Karlsschüler, Die, 72, 73
Kästner, actor, 66 ff
Katharine (Henry VIII), Janauschek as, 606
Katharine and Petruchio, cast, 22; 52, 53, 95, 450, 609
Katharine, the Shrew, Effie Ellsler as, 22; Marion Booth as, 53, 95
Käthchen von Heilbronn, cast, 78; 507
Kathleen Mavourneen, play, 215
Kathleen Mavourneen, sung by Patti, 589
Katie Foley's Birthday Party, 330
Katie Grousemier, 326
Katsnoshin, Awata, 28, 135 ff, 271, 272, 321, 346, 347, 359, 399, 481, 488, 541, 560, 578, 618
Kaudel's Gardinenpredigten, 510
Kaufmann, Der, von Venedig, 284; cast, 502 (see Merchant of Venice)
Kay, Billy, 124 ff, 140
Kaye, Minnie, 124 ff, 140
Kayne, E. M., 59
Kayser, Henry, 376
Kean, Emily, 473
Keane, J. K., 573, 575
Keane, Joseph, 119
Keane, Joseph H., 327, 328, 334
Kearney, E., 57
Kearney, Eddie, 567, 573
Kearney and Powers (James T.), 109, 188
Keating, Carrie, 585
Keating and Sands, 109, 138, 334
Keech, Mary, 418, 639
Keegan (John) and Wilson (Billy), 351, 361, 561, 577, 617
Keegan, John J. (of Four-in-Hand), 553
Keeley Motor Views, 369
Keen, Jule, 110
Keen Eye, the Ranger, 105
Keenan, Professor, 600
Keenan, W. W., 430
Keene, James R., 248
Keene, Laura, 5, 61, 259, 274
Keene, Rose, 278, 279
Kegel, Carl, 540
Kehoe (of Kemerson and Kehoe), 319
Kehoe, Billy, 124
Keiler, Lizzie, 480
Keller, singer, 83
Keller, Miss, 594
Keller (or Keeler), Nellie, midget, 401, 624
Keller, Netta, 187
Keller, Ritta, 321, 563, 574
Kellogg, Clara Louise, 523, 611; adverse review, 614, 615; 639
Kellogg, Fannie, 216, 392, 648
Kelly (of Hawkins and Kelly), 340, 354
Kelly (of Megatherian Four or Eight), 138, 331, 340, 346, 351, 564
Kelly (of Needham and Kelly), 346
Kelly, Charlotte, 74 ff, 284, 287, 493 ff
Kelly, Dan, 103, 122, 137

[702]

INDEX

Kelly, J. D., 554
Kelly (James) and O'Brien (Tom), 526, 556, 564, 616
Kelly, James T., 567
Kelly, Jimmy, fighter, 324, 555, 576
Kelly (Jimmy) and Murphy (Jerry), assault at arms, 557, 559, 576, 577
Kelly, John, lectures, 427
Kelly (John T.) and Ryan (Thomas J.), 51, 100, 131, 132, 135, 187, 188, 276, 315, 330, 331, 340, 343, 349, 397, 551, 553, 555, 556, 560, 616, 618
Kelly, Joseph A., 115, 117, 126, 204
Kelly, T. F., actor, 520
Kelly, T. J., mechanism, 2
Kelly, Walter C., 29, 31, 173, 262
Kelly and Conlon, 189
Kelly and Weston, 119, 128
Kelsey, Lizzie, 24, 176, 619
Kemble, Fanny, 448
Kemble, Frances, 61, 62, 471
Kemble Society, offshoot from the Amaranth, 392 ff; 612
Kemerson, Jake, 124
Kemerson and Kehoe, 319
Kempton, Lottie, 198
Kendal, Mrs., 432, 441, 468
Kendal, W. H., 432, 433, 468
Kendrick, F. M., 468
Kennan, A. B., 426
Kennan, Mrs. L. F., 214, 645, 646
Kennark, Jennie, 476
Kennedy (of Australian Four), 557
Kennedy (of Four Emeralds), 329, 333, 342, 566, 567
Kennedy, D., Scotch singer, 593, 600, 628, 629, 631
Kennedy, Harry, 58, 276, 362 ff, 580, 621
Kennedy, Helen, Marjory, Maggie, Robert, John, Scotch concerts, 593
Kennedy, J. A., 57, 94, 170, 171, 415
Kennedy, James, 123
Kennedy, Jerry (of Four Planets), 132, 135, 139, 328, 336, 343; also of Kennedy and Clark (Henry G.), 128, 184, 328, 331, 338, 355
Kennedy (Jerry) and Heeney (Ed), 326
Kennedy, W., fighter, 321, 555
Kennedy and Magee, 111, 114, 116, 136, 139, 141
Kent (of Miles and Kent), 548
Kent, Amy, 548, 577
Kent, Charles, 450, 520
Kent, Frank, 548, 577
Kent, Fred, 53, 216
Kent, Julian, 108, 320, 327, 330 ff, 353, 575
Kent, Nimmie, 398, 571
Kentucky giant, 626
Kenway, George W., 567
Keough, W. M., 114
Keough, William (Olympia Quartette), 314, 329, 334, 345, 545, 559
Keough and Randalls, 116
Kernell, Daisy, 354
Kernell, Harry and John, 56, 100, 103, 130, 135, 172, 187, 188, 274, 314, 316, 341 ff, 353, 355, 397, 615, 618
Kerns, Irene, 114, 118, 125, 127, 326
Kerr, F. G., 432 ff
Kerrigan, T. F., parts, 57
Kerrigan (T. F.) and McCarthy (Dan), 129, 131, 134, 135, 137, 139, 140, 336, 340, 342, 536, 556, 557, 558, 619
Kerry, cast, 5
Kerry Gow, The, casts, 50, 59; 168, 203, 277, 281, 412, 489, 492, 610; cast, 633, 634
Kersands, negro, 60
Kesselflicker, Der, 81, 293
Kessels, A., 157
Kessler, Albert, 66 ff, 291, 498 ff, 504
Ketchum, G. F., 41, 178, 279
Ketten, Henry, 25, 156, 180
Kettledrum (see Japanese Kettledrum)
Khedive Harem, 549
Kiar's Grove Hill Park, 300
Kickapoo Dancers, 557
Kidder, Charles, 360, 463
Kiel, Al, 552
Kierschner, Alfred, 298
Kierschner, Frau, 292
Kierschner, Herr, 288 ff, 311, 493 ff
Kilday, Frank, 49, 243
Killmer, Hen, wrestler, 545 ff
Kilpatrick, Major-General, 393, 419
Kimball, C. H., 492
Kimball, Jennie, 480
Kimball and Wisedell, 524
Kincade (of Minetta and Kincade), 414
Kinder-Maskenball, 299
Kinder-Theater, 293
Kindervorstellung, 293
Kine Brothers (James and Barney), 346
Kineste's Arion Hall, Greenpoint, 422
King (of Alexander and King), 531
King (of Monroe and King), 414, 415
King, Albert L., 155, 213, 372, 373, 375, 381, 417, 421, 592, 601, 603
King, Bessie Louise, 55, 192, 206, 411
King, De Los, 61, 62, 256, 281, 469, 478
King, Flora, 351, 565, 570
King, Frank, 414, 541, 559
King, Harry, ventriloquist, 59
King, Louis, 616
King and Hildebrand, 532
King John recited, 153
King Lear, 248; recited, 366; 389, 450, 459, 462, 520, 613, 642
King Lear, John McCullough as, 248, 389, 462; Edwin Booth as, 450, 459; Ernesto Rossi as, 450, 451, 520, 613
King Olaf, Saga of, 181
King Olaf's Christmas, 592
King Robert of Sicily (Longfellow's) read, 310
King, The, and the Poet (by Henschel), 372
King Sarbro, 19, 118 ff, 147, 204, 336
Kingdon, Edith, as amateur, 196, 210; reviews, 393, 399
Kingsland, Miss, 50, 209, 365
Kingsley (of Dwyer and Kingsley), 635

[703]

Kinsella, Thomas, 407, 418
Kipp, F., 408
Kipper, H., his Fidelia, 190
Kiralfy, Arnold, 58, 272, 533, 553
Kiralfy Brothers, Black Crook, 171, 610;
    Michael Strogoff, 515, 516
Kiralfy Lady Dancers, 362
Kirchner, Adolphe W., 539
Kirkland, Miss, 232
Kirkwood, J. E., 40
Kirpal, Mrs. M., 603
Kirwin (of Bree and Kirwin), 567, 573, 618
Kirwin, Miss, at Daly's, 232
Kiss, A, in the Dark, 340, 422
Kissel, Emma, Lulu and H., 300
Kissel (or Kissell), Lulu, 299
Kit, cast, 8; 279, 386; by children, 426; 470,
    492
Kitchen Domestics, 334, 551, 617
Kitty and the Baby, 328
Kitty Foley's Birthday, 337
Kladivko, Hugo, 293
Kleber, Ida, 159, 162
Klein, Alexander, 494 ff, 537
Klein, Alfred, 350
Klein, Ida, 512, 591
Klein's Visit to New York, 130
Kleine Erzahlung, Eine, ohne Namen, 511
Kleine Gefälligkeit, Eine, 501, 502
Kleine Mama, Die, 497
Kline, sparring, 143
Kline, Nellie, 369, 649
Klugelmann, Luise, 84
Klugescheid, 594
Knabe Hall, 601
Knickerbocker Verein, 84
Knight, A. J., 154
Knight, Fanny, 562, 563, 568 ff
Knight, Mr. and Mrs. George S., 254, 257,
    274, 278, 281, 389, 486, 487, 491, 607
Knights of Pythias, 209
Knights of the Jimmy, 136, 346
Knoedler, Charles and Edmond, 155
Knopf, Ein, 290, 291, 402
Knorr, G. T. R., 174
Knowles (see Ford and Knowles)
Knowles, Edith, 192, 392
Knowles, Edwin F., 256, 265, 389, 412, 447
Knowles, R. G., 554
Knowlton, Dora, 16, 19
Knowlton, Georgie, 253, 605
Knox, Dr. and pigeons, 346, 360
Knox, Florence Rice, 90, 153, 155, 163, 168,
    196, 198, 246, 367, 369 ff, 407, 408, 417, 421,
    423, 506, 582, 591 ff, 600, 601, 627, 630,
    631, 637, 638
Knox, J. J., 174
Koch, Josephine, amateur, 404
Koch, Justus W., 86, 164, 592
Koch, L. Philipp, 86
Koch's Broadway Hall, 211, 425
Kodieson, Mrs. C., 417
Kölner Carnevals-Gesellschaft, 512
Komische Geschichte, Eine, 293
König, M., 'cello, 86

König, Marie, 282 ff, 294, 539
Königin Margot, 509
Königin Tausendschön und Prinzessin Häss-
    lich, 78
Königslieutenant, Der, cast, 291; 292, 500,
    501, 508, 623
Konollman, Charles, 331, 425, 624
Kortheuer, H. O. C., 197, 200, 595, 598, 627,
    638
Koster and Bial's, 94; (1879-80), 145, 146;
    159; (1880-81), 357, 358; (1881-82), 538 ff
Krafft, Marie, 74 ff, 81
Krakauer, D., 82
Krakehlia Männerchor, 213
Kramer, F., 86
Kramer, W., of Thalia Theater, 73 ff
Kraus, George J., 338
Krausmeyer's Rival, 315
Kren, actor, 502
Kress's, John, Sommergarten, 511
Kreutzberg, actor, 76
Kreutzer Denkmal, 84
Kreutzer Quartett Club, 295
Krieg im Frieden (Passing Regiment), cast,
    291; 292, 444, 502; cast, 634
Krisch's Weinhandlung, 86
Krische's Spätze-Häuschen, 298
Krohne, F., walker, 149, 150
Krousemeyer's Visit to New York, 341
Kruger, Elise, 102, 133, 342, 396, 489, 558,
    569, 570, 618
Kruger, Jacques, 102, 133, 137, 267, 474, 489,
    503, 519, 520, 526 ff, 618
Krumm, Charles, 83, 298
Kuhle, Mathilde, 495
Kummer, actor, 66 ff, 288 ff, 499, 507
Kunst, Die, geliebt zu werden, 190
Künstler Halle, 83 ff, 297, 512, 513
Kurmärker und Picarde, 125, 293
Kurtz, juggler, 626
Kurtz, George, 124 ff, 135, 138, 326, 328, 330,
    347
Kuster, Emma, 80, 282 ff, 294, 419
Kyle, G. W., 376, 593

Labbrei, G. W., bugle calls, 137
La Bella, Mlle., 310
Lablache, Louise, 357
Lablache, Luigi, 390
Lablache, Mme., 91 ff, 158, 161, 180 ff, 301,
    311, 357, 395, 521 ff, 600, 601, 614
La Blanche, Bianca (Blanche Davenport), 22,
    26, 27, 90, 180, 182
Lachtaube, Die, cast, 74, 75; 81
Lackawanna Spooners, 134, 545
Lacy (see McGlone and Lacy)
Lacy (Dan) and Lynch (Mike), 567
Lacy, Harry, parts, 14 ff, 58, 173, 177, 231 ff,
    237, 384, 386, 388, 411, 448
Ladies of Mystery, 189
Ladies' Battle, The, by the Amaranth, 182
Ladies' Elite Orchestra, 361
Ladies of the White House, 408
Ladies' Philharmony, 539

Lady Audley's Secret, cast, 620; 636, 646
Lady Beefsteak, 293
Lady cashiers, 142
Lady Clancarty, 170
Lady Elks, benefit, 503
Lady Macbeth, Clara Morris as, 22, 244; Mrs. Bowers as, 183, 184, 620; Marie Prescott as, 244; Mme. Janauschek as, 245, 491; Julia Evarts as, 306; Mrs. Scott-Siddons as, 390; Mrs. J. H. Hackett as, 519; Eugenie Legrand as, 613; Nellie Yale as, 634
Lady Minstrel act, 111, 112
Lady of Lyons, The, 8; with Miss Neilson, 30; with D. E. Bandmann, 47; 171; with John McCullough, 248; with Mary Anderson, 249, 383, 455, 488; 250, 277; with Lillian Glover, 281; 282; with Fanny Davenport, 386, 489; 389; with Miss Legrand, 441; with Lillian Olcott, 610; with the Amaranth, 615
Lady Orchestra, 142
Lætitia, Verein, 298, 299
Laflin, J. M., wrestler, 220
Lafontaine, Fritz, 26, 27, 80, 180, 182
La Forrest, Master, 471
Laguardie, Achille, 297
Laguardina, 427
Lagye, Mlle., 310, 394
Laible, Captain, 106, 131, 140, 204, 315, 327, 346 ff, 351, 533, 534, 545, 567, 572, 573, 576
Laïla, operetta, 197
Laird, Will (of Quaker City Quartette), 531, 544, 565, 573
Laiscell, Charles, Eddie, Belle, 551
Lake, Emma, 147, 148, 199, 359
Lamartine Brothers, 327, 336, 346, 530, 550, 560, 569, 570
Lamb, Charles, amateur, 612
Lamb, Ed, 44, 167, 469, 621, 634
Lamb, F. E., 51, 256, 458, 610
Lambert, organ, 365
Lambert, Alexander, 372, 591, 592
Lambert, Charles, 597
Lambert, Marion, 481, 528, 529, 595
Lambert, W. W., 182, 612, 615
Lambert Children, 206, 365, 421, 639
Lambert Family, 193, 631
Lamborn, Theresa, 39
Lameraux, Frankie, 186
Lamierre, Miss, 174
Lamkin (or Lambkin), Harry, 147, 575
Lamont, John, 559
Lamont Family, 559
Lamont and Ducrow, 188, 345, 349, 351, 398, 545, 573, 617
La Montagne, Albert, 155
La Montagne, E., Jr., 155
Lamonto (Harry) and Baldwin (Archie), 320, 330, 338, 339
Lancashire, Anna, 425, 644
Lancaster, Lillian, 218
Lancaster, Mary, 643
Lancaser, Miss, in opera, 26, 27, 180, 182, 456, 614
Land of Nod, The, 406, 417, 630

Lander, Frank, 450
Landis, S. M., Dr., 153; Hamlet, 369; lecture to gentlemen only, 582; 583
Landis, W. H., 566
Landis Brothers (William and Charles), 555, 574, 588, 616
Landis and Steele, 117, 125, 127, 331, 346
Landis Dramatic Club, 369
Landon, Alice, 216
Landsharks and Sea Gulls, 138
Lane, Eleanor, 605
Lane, Frank, 462, 463
Lane, John A., 248, 249, 306, 421, 462, 463
Lanergan, J. W., 258
Lang (of the Dutch Four), 635
Lang, Charles F., 64, 255, 261, 388, 394, 412
Lang, Frau, and pupils, 509
Lang, Gussie, 16
Lang, Ione, 107, 184, 413, 414
Lang (Ned) and Rosa (Viola), 545, 553, 554, 565, 567, 576
Lang, Sam, 135
Langdon, Harry, 248, 249, 462, 463
Langdon, W. H., 112, 325, 328, 555
Langdon and Allison's Swift and Sure Combination, 557, 620
Langenbach, 150, 499
Langer, Frl., 83
Langley, Josie, 173, 468
Langley, Marie, 28
Langlois, 401
Langner, Frl., 499
Lanier, Ada, 115, 118, 134, 204, 331, 333, 334, 551
Lanier, Theresa, 551
Lanner, Margaret, 15 ff, 177
Lansden, Alice, 630
Lansing, actor, 560 ff
Lansing, William, 345 ff
Lant, Jerry, 38, 263
Lantern, magic, 205, 208
Lanzer, Carl, 41, 52, 78, 193, 375, 592, 640
La Porte Sisters (Rose and Lillie), 329, 344, 354, 355, 543, 551, 625
Larkelle, Nellie, 58, 171, 484, 610
Larks, farce, 114, 334, 567, 572
La Roche, Herr and Frau, 126, 293
La Roche, Professor, 298
La Rosa (of Levanion and La Rosa), 334, 396
La Rosa Brothers (Frank and George), 119, 134, 188, 339, 415, 530, 531, 542, 574, 615, 624, 635
La Rose (of Cardello and La Rose), 558
La Rose, Harry, 116, 120, 326, 542, 645
Larson, Emma, 356
La Rue (of Avery and La Rue), 105, 344
La Rue, John and Willie, 325, 327, 331, 334, 340, 396 ff, 616
La Rue, Minnie, 460
Lasar, Agnes, 184, 193, 197, 404 ff, 614, 627 ff, 646
Lasar-Studwell, Clementine, 163, 184, 193, 197 ff, 406, 408, 626, 628 ff
Lascelles, Eme (or Emma), 460, 464
Lascelles, Emily, 38

INDEX

Lascelles, Sara, 16 ff, 178, 261, 388, 394, 529
La Selle, water queen, 569
Last Rose of Summer, sung, 211
Latham, Allan, 192, 197, 391, 407, 628, 639
Lathrop, Emma, 250, 373
Laubenheimer, Frl., 295
Laughing Gas, 204
Laurence, Alberto, 192, 198, 373
Laurence, Juliette, 539
Laurens, Josephine, 11, 176, 486
Laurent, Henri, 271, 452, 458, 528, 529, 609, 613
Lauri, Lelia, 516 ff, 537, 612 ff
Laurie, amateur, 180
Lauterbach, Harry, 373
Lavake, Will, 59
Lavarnie, Carrie, 110, 342, 349, 558
Lavarnie, Frank, 544
Lavarnie, Harry, 105
Lavelle, W. A., 264, 454
Lavely, Mme., strong woman, 548, 576, 625
Lavenia, Minnie, 350, 568
La Verde, Belle, 330, 353, 544
La Verde Sisters (Belle and Lillie), 315, 320, 326, 327, 532, 578
Lavernia, Harry, 337
La Villa, concert, 372, 377
Lavine, John, 374, 377, 597
Law, George, 416, 417
Lawlor, Frank, 265
Lawn Tennis, cast, 258; 267, 268
Lawrence, at Daly's, 232
Lawrence, Atkins, 172, 249, 475
Lawrence, Edwin, 366, 372
Lawrence, Emily, 481
Lawrence, Fanny, amateur, 636
Lawrence, George, 59
Lawrence, Isaac, 640
Lawrence, Ivian, 322, 332, 530, 550
Lawrence, Marion, 391
Lawrence, Miss, 48
Lawrence, Philip, 196
Lawrence, W., 37
Lawrence, W. J., 336
Lawrence Sisters, trapeze, 102, 314
Lawrence and Baldwin, 548
Laws, Lida, 630
Lawton, Alf, 313, 560
Lawton, Minnie, 139, 325, 339, 425
Lawyer's Clerk, The, 555
Lay, Ed H., 322, 339, 552
Lazzari's Cottage, 303
Lazzarini, singer, 26, 27, 96, 180, 182, 304 ff, 371, 392, 394, 456, 591, 614
Leach, baritone, 216
Leach, Gussie, 134, 184
Leach, S. N., 637
Leah, the Forsaken, 39, 178, 386; with Fanny Davenport, 464, 489, 605; 621, 633; with amateurs, 638 (see Deborah)
Leake, W. H., 65, 179
Leap Year, 214
Leary (of the Megatherian Eight), 138, 331, 340, 346
Leaver, Grace, 255

Leavitt, Andy, 104 ff, 420
Leavitt's, M. B., Operatic Burlesque Company, 255
Leavitt's, M. B., Specialty Company, 318, 383, 534, 556, 559, 615, 616
Le Baron, Marie, 54, 595
Leblanc, Mme., 302
Le Brun, Mrs., 280
Lechner, Hans, 409
Le Clair, A. H. and Nellie, 548
Le Clair, Harry, 324, 355, 551, 553, 557
Le Clair, Maggie, 575
Le Clair, Shed, 544
Le Clair Sisters, 129, 133, 187
Le Claire, George, 267
Le Claire, Laura, 44, 252, 263, 489
Leclercq, Charles, 13 ff, 231 ff, 387, 413, 442 ff
Led Astray, as Eine vornehme Ehre, 70; with amateurs, 182; 214; cast, 280; 319; cast, 388; 621
Lederer, Harry W., rifle shot, 337
Ledgerwood's, Mabel, Novelty Queens, 317, 318, 623
Lee (of Four Kings), 415
Lee, Ada, 39
Lee, Amy, 57, 179, 272, 428, 529, 621
Lee, Dora, 386
Lee, F. N., 478
Lee, Henry, 1, 177, 247, 274, 386, 458, 466, 474
Lee, Herman, co-author, 478
Lee, Jennie, 437, 468, 608
Lee, Jessie, 57
Lee, John, minstrel, 59
Lee, Lillian, 439
Lee, Lillie, 606
Lee, Minnie, 128 ff, 187, 188, 315, 326, 332, 346 ff, 351, 398, 481, 560, 563, 565, 569, 570, 574 ff, 615, 616
Lee, Pauline, circus, 146, 147
Lee, Rosa, ballet, 57
Lee, Rosa, parts, 317, 318, 324, 558
Lee, W. H,, 428
Lee, William, 468, 469
Lee Brothers, 119
Leeson, Dan, 222 ff, 432, 442, 611
Lefebre, saxophone, 52, 80, 192, 358, 512, 595, 601
Lefferts Park, 206
Leffingwell, M. W., 29, 250, 484, 493
Leg-Mania, 349
Legab, trapeze, 123
Leggat, W. S., 408
Legge, La, del Cuore, 515
Leggett, Miss, 213
Legion of Honour, The, casts, 260, 281; 306; cast, 391; 412; cast, 490, 491; 621
Legless man, 631
Legrand, Eugenie, 441, 613
Legros, Marion, 619
Lehmann, actor, 283
Lehmann, Lillie, variety, 184
Lehmann's Jugendliebe, 293
Leibarzt, Der, cast, 503
Leiboldt's orchestra, 82, 298, 510, 513

Leigh, Coral, 620, 622
Leigh, Lisle, 405
Leigh, Maude, 112, 328, 347, 348, 420, 543, 562
Leigh, Tom, 468
Leighton, Louise, 202, 255
Leighton, Rose, 39, 172, 254, 413
Leisure and Laziness, 427
Leland Sisters (Rose and Jennie), 117, 119, 123, 136, 277, 315, 316, 324, 349, 352, 487, 526, 545, 551, 557, 573, 575
Le Moyne, W. J., 10 ff, 177, 230, 388, 389, 412, 442 ff, 465, 610
Lena (of Hendricks and Lena), 187
Lena's Birthday, 94
Lencioni, Luigi, 22, 53, 88, 161, 311, 360, 374, 376, 513, 591, 594 ff, 597, 601, 627, 640
Lend Me Five Shillings, 369; cast, 439
Lennon, Nestor, 368, 461
Lennox, Fred W., 258, 268, 479, 480
Lennox, George, 59
Lennox, Miss, 36
Lennox, Walter, 176, 258, 620, 621
Lennox, Walter, Jr., 11, 176
Lenoir, actor, 75 ff, 284, 495
Lenoir, Helen, benefit, 266
Lenoir, Jerome, 86, 637
Lenox Hill Vocal Society, 596
Lent, L. B., circus, 147
Lenton Brothers, 140, 146, 148
Lentz, Julie, 473, 474, 537
Lentz's, Marie, Minstrels, 100
Leo, xylophone, 578
Leo, B. F., 424
Leon, prestidigitateur, 548
Leon, Francis, 137, 471
Leona, play, 204
Leonard, Agnes, 383, 443 ff
Leonard, Joseph T., 167, 171, 172
Leonard, Mabel, variety, 575
Leonard, Mrs. Cynthia, mother of Lillian Russell, 54
Leonard, W. J., 2 ff, 220 ff, 489
Leonard and Flynn, 569, 570
Leonard and Jones, 314, 327, 347, 349, 364, 543, 544, 561, 563
Leone, Mlle., circus, 148
Leonhardt, Clara, 293
Leoni, Henri, 478
Leonori, Fannie, 205
Leonori, Frank, 205
Leonzo, plate spinner, 616
Leonzo Brothers (Vic and Harry), 114, 116, 125 ff, 328, 331, 333, 339, 353, 400, 414, 415, 531, 532, 547
Leopold, Mons., 113
Leopold (of Smith and Leopold), 552, 558
Leopold, Josie, 404
Leopold and Wentworth, 564, 625
Leotards (3), acrobats, 132, 148, 187, 188, 331, 343, 360, 616
Lepri, Aurelia, 272, 538
Lepri, Giovanni, 272
Le Petres, Paul (or Paus) and Lillie, 557, 575

Lerners, Alice, 534
Leroux, Hélène, 300, 356, 473, 474 (see infra)
Leroux-Bouvard, Mlle., 26, 36, 37, 97, 176, 183 (see supra)
Leseur, Jessie, 544
Leslie (see Fields and Leslie)
Leslie, Frederick, 460, 464, 609
Leslie, George (of Cereni and Leslie), 315, 321, 346
Leslie (George) and Lovely (John), 577
Leslie, Harry, 333, 531
Leslie, John, 346
Leslie Brothers (John and Fred), 131, 136, 342
Leslie, Louise, 644
Leslie, Rob (of Butler and Leslie), 107, 113
Leslie and Avalo, 121
Leslie and Byrnes, 136
Leslie and Gentry, 567, 576
Leslino, Maria, 456, 457
Lessenger (see Moore and Lessenger)
Lesson in Love, A, 481
Lester (of Sylvester and Lester), 189
Lester (William) and Allen (Paul), 277, 314, 316, 317, 335, 341 ff, 363, 487, 490, 503, 526 ff, 532, 553, 556, 557, 585, 618
Lester Brothers, trapeze, 415
Lester and Williams, 136, 189, 316, 348, 487, 526, 536, 551, 554 ff, 559, 570, 573, 575, 616
Lethbridge, Florence, 416
Letsch, concert, 55
Letter carriers, walkers, 359
Levanion and La Rosa, 334, 396
Levanion and Lexington, 534
Levanion and McCormick, 323, 329, 536, 548, 624
Levanion and Watson (or Watson and Levanion), 105, 106, 110, 111, 113, 320, 330
Levantine, Fred F., 27, 106, 130, 183, 276, 319, 346, 348, 352
Levantine and Earle, 104, 134, 137, 140, 147, 187, 424, 552, 617
Leve, J. Francis, 585
Levere, Miss, at Daly's, 232
Levi's Arrival, 327
Levian, Annie, 11
Levick, Gustavus, 23, 39, 52, 57, 94, 167, 172, 272, 385, 471, 491, 608
Levick, Milnes, 172, 249, 383, 450
Levico, Rudolf, 534
Levino, Dolf, 131, 135, 556, 558, 615
Levison, A. W., 215
Levison, J. H., 216
Levy, Jules, 28, 33, 80, 94, 145, 150, 158, 159, 164, 170, 197, 198, 355, 356, 371, 395, 409, 601, 631, 641
Levy, M. and Mme. E., 301
Levy Brothers, The, farce, 549
Levy in a Fix, 115, 126
Lew, Master, banjo, 127
Lewis, 124
Lewis, Benjamin, 619
Lewis, Carrie, 113, 127, 326, 531, 544, 552, 548, 574

Lewis, Catherine, parts, 13 ff, 58, 68, 173, 178, 238, 243, 244, 251, 253, 262, 268, 356, 367, 394, 412, 460, 464, 487, 537, 609

Lewis, Ella, 429

Lewis, Emily, 213

Lewis, Frank, 326, 335, 336, 349, 350, 396, 398, 565, 571, 574

Lewis, Hattie, 307

Lewis, Horace, 252

Lewis, Ida, 43, 44, 608

Lewis, J. R., 62, 345, 349, 560 ff

Lewis, James, 15; engaged by Daly, 18; parts, 45, 46; 67; parts, 174; with Daly, 232 ff, 387, 413, 442 ff, 608

Lewis, James, variety, 326

Lewis, Jeannette, 576

Lewis, Jeffreys, 14, 67, 224; as Hazel Kirke, 235, 236; acts with Catherine Lewis, 253; 268, 306, 491, 523, 606, 621, 633, 641

Lewis, Miss C., 468

Lewis, Nanita, 263

Lewis, Tillie, 116

Lewis, Tom (see Pell, James, and Lewis, Tom)

Lexington (of Levanion and Lexington), 534

Lexington Avenue Opera House, 81, 142, 152, 366 ff, 373, 377, 510, 511, 583 ff, 598

Leys, Mamie, 645

Leyton, May (of Harry F. Dixey and May Leyton), 49, 554, 559, 619

Liar, The, cast, 5; 7

Libby Prison, Chaplain McCabe on, 208

Liberati, 52, 82, 86, 161, 180, 246, 287, 294, 300, 372, 374, 376, 379, 395, 408, 512, 513, 583, 596, 600

Liberty Hall, 637

Libussa, Frl., 76

Liceo Italiano, 89

Lichtenberg, Leopold, 287, 408, 523

Lichtenthal, actor, 66 ff, 288 ff, 504

Lick, Carl, 577

Lickfold, actor, 29

Lieb, Frl. and Herr, 499 ff

Liebich, Frl., 499 ff

Liebling, Max, 376, 596, 601

Liebling, S., pianist, 146, 294, 357, 358, 395, 406, 539, 611, 639

Lieck, E., 216

Lied, Das, von der Glocke, 299, 512

Liederkranz, Astoria, 210

Liederkranz, Bloomingdale, 513

Liederkranz, New York, 82 ff, 95, 295 ff, 373, 512, 520, 591, 594, 598

Liederkranz, Williamsburgh, 416

Liedertafel, Brooklyn, 417

Liedertafel, New York, 84, 300

Liedertafel Social Reformer, 296, 297

Life for Life, 110, 126

Life in a Tenement House, 334, 349 ff, 560, 565, 572

Life in Leadville, cast, 564

Life in New York (Les Pauvres de Paris), 336, 352

Life in Turkey, 127

Life's Revenge, A, 127

Lights o' London, The, 484; cast, 607

Lights of New York, cast, 575

Liliendahl, F. T., 372

Lillie, Mrs. John, 584

Lilliputian Circus, 188

Lilliputian Opera Company, 400

Lilliputian ponies, 239

Lilliputian Specialty Company, 578

Lily, Mlle., bicycle, 559, 561, 574, 622

Lily, or, Life in California in '49, cast, 323

Lily of Poverty Flat, cast, 320

Limpert, lectures on hatred of Jews, 298

Lincoln Dramatic Club, 399

Lincoln Union, 9th Ward, 357, 368

Linda di Chamounix, cast, 92; 93, 95; casts, 181, 304; 305; casts, 308, 391

Lindemann, Eugenie, 81, 494, 497, 510

Linden, Bertha, 358

Linden, Eloise, 558

Linden, Harry, 268, 467, 472

Linden, Laura, 199, 395

Linden, Louise, 86, 164, 262, 364, 383

Linden, Master, 254

Linden Grove, S. I., 90

Lindley, Bob, 119

Lindsay, A., 486

Lindsay, Jennie (of Hume and Lindsay), 565, 566, 570, 571

Linesley, H. G., 532

Lingard, Alice Dunning, 475

Lingard, Georgie, 127, 137, 138, 189, 318, 319, 324, 325, 330, 353, 564, 570, 575, 622

Lingard, L. C., 104

Lingham, M. V., 10 ff, 28, 29, 177, 243, 247

Link, Adolf, 494 ff

Link, Andy, 545

Linson, Harry, 543

Linton, Guy, 108, 109, 111, 114, 118, 119, 132, 135, 139, 140, 188, 326, 327, 330, 340, 346, 548, 624

Lion, performing, 281, 564

Lion Brewery Park, 157

Lion Park, 155, 301, 514 (see also Löwen Park)

Lion, The, and the Lamb, 137

Lionette, 503

Lipman, A. S., 169, 264, 462, 609

Lisle, Rose, 31, 321, 326, 414, 622

Listemann, B., 584

Liston, Alfred, 106, 121, 135, 189, 300, 333, 337, 616

Liston, Hudson, 170, 276

Literary Hall, Bayside, 213

Literary Union, 210

Litta, Marie, 26, 27, 97, 180, 182, 374

Littel, Kate, 278

Little, Frank, 411, 463

Little, J. Z., 106, 167, 171, 172, 189, 319, 354, 620

Little, Lena, 162, 378, 596, 603

Little Barefoot, 56, 275, 384, 607

Little Bayside, 212, 426, 429

Little Buckshot, 322, 329, 415, 543, 551, 554

Little Detective, The, casts, 46, 178

Little Dutch S, 111

Little Dutchess (*sic*), The, 337, 338
Little Em'ly, 484
Little Four, of varying membership, 348 ff,
567, 569, 571, 617
Little Jim, the Collier's Son, 400
Little Nell and the Marchioness, cast, 262;
390
Little Paradise, 513
Little Rebel, The, 81
Little Red Riding Hood, 102
Little Savage, The, 489, 607
Little Treasure, The, 145
Little Widow, The, 544, 545, 554, 562, 568
Littlefinger, Count (or Baron), 578, 624
Live Nigger, The, 353
Live Subject, A, 122
Living Age, The, cast, 441, 442
Living Statue, The, cast, 43
Livingston, Carrie, 62
Livingston, Flora, 236, 491
Livingston, Frank, 113, 115, 185
Livingston, Harry, 627, 628
Livingston, Kate, 479
Livingston, Mat (or Nat), 124, 185
Livingston, May, 40, 255, 539
Livingstone, Frank, 120, 361, 561, 564, 566,
572, 577, 618, 641 (*see also Livingston,
Frank*)
L'Hame, Joseph, 282 ff
Lloyd, Fred, 104
Lloyd, Harry, 111, 114, 326 ff, 53 ff
Loane, Elsie, 478, 624, 625
Loane, Josie, 493
Locke, E. A., 270, 435, 474, 486, 633
Lockere Zeisige, 291
Locksley Hall, read, 367
Lockwood, Annie, 192
Lockwood, C. G., 195, 198
Loder, C. A., 321, 327, 340, 397, 561, 569,
617
Loder, Minnie, 114
Lodge, Frank, 109
Lodgers! Inventors! Dodgers! 566, 572
Lodi, Mme., 108
Loë, Max (*sic*), 74 ff, 81
Loé, Michael (*sic*), 498, 509, 640
Loeffler, Martin, 591 ff
Loerch, Philip, 123
Lofgren, Ingeborg, 356
Loftus, Victoria, British Blondes, 186, 317,
318
Logan (of Hanley and Logan), 565
Logan, Alice, 385
Logan, Celia, 54
Logan, Grace, 453, 454
Logan, Olive, 365, 404
Logani, Giuseppina, 391
Logrenia's birds, cats, mice, 131, 147, 551, 560
Lohengrin, in Italian, 98, 309; cast, 516; 517,
521, 522; cast, 612
Lohenschild, contralto, 589
Lola, play, 631
Lolly Pop, the Brave, 331
London a Hundred Years Ago, 152
London Assurance, cast, Wallack's, 4; 52,

169, 178; with amateurs, 196, 399; with
Fanny Davenport, 386, 489; 463, 605; cast,
611; with the Amaranth, 615; 633
London Athletes, 530
London Burlesque Company, 100
London Circus, 200, 359, 408
London Gaiety Company, 460
London Theatre (1879-80), 128 ff; (1880-81),
340 ff; (1881-82), 555 ff; a Combination
from it, 617
London's, the, Gymnasts, 342
Long, Eliza, 441, 475
Long, Gilbert, 204
Long, J. N., 40, 247, 271, 389
Long and Beasley, 349
Long Beach, 87, 300; orchestra, 427
Long Branch, play, 324; cast, 412
Long Island City (1879-80), 210 ff; (1880-
81), 424, 425; (1881-82), 644, 645
Long Island Historical Hall, 406, 627 ff
Long and Short of It, 355
Long-haired women, 401, 624
Longstreet, Miss, amateur, 392
Lonsdale, Rose, 112, 119, 124, 125
Loraine, Emma, 2 ff, 222, 433
Loranzo, Theodore, 548
Lord (*see Mason and Lord*)
Lord, Charles, 560
Lord, J., 549
Lord, Dr. John, lectures, 367, 406, 584
Lord and Lovely, 567, 635
Lord and Von Leer, 338
Loreley Zither Club, 419
Lorellas (3—William, John, Thomas), 42, 133,
275, 281, 324, 327, 385, 488
Lorenberg Spanish Students, 401
Lorento, illusions, 113, 320
Lorenz, Frl., 356, 499
Loretz, J. M., Jr., 195, 196, 200, 404, 406, 407,
626, 630, 640
Lorin, Master, 543
Loring, L. J., 605
Loring, Louise, 39, 218, 279
Lorle, 168, 384, 607
Losee, Frank, 11, 38, 40, 179, 257, 478
Losee, Josephine T., 193 ff, 405, 406
Lost at Long Branch, 134, 348
Lost in London, cast, 105; 186, 204, 320, 353,
531, 622
Lothian, Napier, 181
Loton, Zillah, 533
Lott, R. L., 390
Lotta, parts, 46, 50, 178, 262, 390, 391, 488,
492
Lotti, singer, 194, 197, 498
Lottie, infant, 401
Lottie, John, 314
Lottie, Mlle., 101, 109, 125, 148
Lotto, Fred, 281, 440
Louden, J. J., 65
Louis XI, cast, 24, 25
Louis XVI, Minuet, 535
Love, Valentine, 622
Love Sisters (Ella and Kitty), 341, 348, 396;
(of Horseshoe Four), 553, 562, 563

Love, 171; cast, 249; 383; with amateurs, 418; with Mary Anderson, 454
Love and Labour, 186
Love and Pride, 586
Love and Rain, 191
Love in a Hammock, 573
Love in a Horn, 617
Love in a Letter Bag, 561
Love in a Tub, 118
Love in Broken German, 320, 332, 335, 349, 618
Love in Ireland, 353
Love in Irish, 328
Love in the Country, 119
Love in Turkey, 185
Love Laughs at Locks, 622
Love of His Life, The, cast, 12
Love *vs.* Music, 616
Love's Alternative, 368
Love's Endurance, 145
Love's Labour, 343
Love's Sacrifice, with amateurs, 181, 393
Love's Strength, 406
Loveday, Charles, 33, 264
Lovely (of Leslie and Lovely), 577
Lovely (of Lord and Lovely), 567, 635
Lovenberg, Master C., 296, 330
Lovenberg, Lena, 296
Lovering, Fannie, 423, 595, 601
Low, G., 345
Low, Seth, 153
Low Flats, 127
Löwen Park, 86 ff, 295 ff, 299 (*see also Lion Park*)
Lowerre, Mamie, 213
Lowerre, Mrs., 89, 376; in opera as Mlle. Lauri, 516
Lowry, C. H., circus, 645
Loyal (of Zuila and Loyal), 185
Loyal, Ella, George, Victoria, 336
Lozier, Mabel, 243
Lube, Max, 74 ff, 82, 85, 282 ff, 294, 494 ff, 509, 510
Lube, Josefine, 74 ff, 282 ff, 294, 493 ff, 634
Lucas, Mira, 157
Lucas, Sam, 485
Lucca and Wachtel, burlesque, 123, 125
Lucia di Lammermoor, casts, 26, 92, 95, 96, 97, 180, 181; in English, 251, 385, 487; cast, 304; 306, 307, 309; casts, 310, 391, 456; with Patti, 506, 507, 590; cast, 518; with Gerster, 523; in English, 604
Lucille, Mlle., 337
Lucille, Fannie, 111, 112, 344, 535
Luckstone, Lena, 170
Lucretia Borgia, play, 328
Lucretia Borgia, in variety show, 329, 544, 575
Lucrezia Borgia, Italian play, 303; opera, 391
Luftschlösser, cast, 66
Lull, F., 1
Lullaby, Fritz's, 44
Lulu, child actress, 214, 414
Lu Lu, shot from a catapult, 540, 541
Luminaries, Four, 324
Lumley, Mr. and Mrs. E., 644

Lumpaci Vagabundus, 70, 71, 72, 284, 293, 504, 634
Lumpensämmler von Paris, Der, 501, 502
Lurline, cast, 548
Lurline, cantata, 373
Luske, W., amateur, 182, 392; takes Court Square Theatre, 398, 399
Lustige Krieg, Der, cast, 497; 498 (*see also Merry War, The*)
Lustspiel, Ein, cast, 292
Lyceum, Brooklyn, 404 ff
Lyceum Comedy Company (Vale's), 365
Lyceum Glee Club, Williamsburgh, 205, 417, 419, 641
Lyceum Theatre, New York (*see Haverly's Fourteenth Street Theatre*)
Lyceum Theatre, Williamsburgh, 206, 416 ff, 636 ff
Lyle, Edith, 136
Lynch, Andy, 544
Lynch, Con T. (*See Ward, Thomas H., and Lynch, Con T.*)
Lynch, Ed, 116, 547
Lynch, Mike (*see Dolan and Lynch; also Lacy and Lynch*)
Lyndal, Percy, 47
Lynn, Dr., "cuts up man," 519, 578, 579, 624
Lynn Sisters, 396, 618
Lynton, Ethel, 40, 147, 175
Lynwood, Ada, 136
Lyon, G., 455
Lyon, Pauline, amateur, 585
Lyons (of Megatherian Eight), 138, 331, 340, 341, 346, 351, 564
Lyons, Fred, banjo, 430
Lyric Hall, New York, 89, 154, 366 ff, 592, 597
Lyric Hall, South Fifth Avenue, 301
Lytell, W. H., 55, 62, 202, 270 ff, 488, 489

McAdow (of Donaldson and McAdow), 188
McAloon (of Murphy and McAloon), 320
McAndrews, J. F., 559
McAndrews, J. W., 115, 119 ff, 257, 527, 531, 536, 553, 557, 559, 617, 619
McAuley, Barney, 476, 491
McAvoy, Edward, 131
McAvoy, Harry, 115, 129, 140, 189, 277, 314 ff, 342, 347, 348, 367, 396, 487, 526, 561, 563, 567 ff, 572, 617, 618
McBride (of Connors and McBride), 349
McCabe, Chaplain, on Libby Prison, 208
McCabe, James J., 641, 642
McCabe, T. F., 468
McCall, E. C., 28
McCall, Lizzie, 272
McCarthy, Charles, 108, 117, 328, 343, 350, 560, 561, 566, 571, 618
McCarthy, Charles P., Rev., mesmerism, 419, 637
McCarthy, Croly, 105
McCarthy, Dan (*see Kerrigan and McCarthy*)
McCarthy, Kate, 189
McCarty (*sic*), Charles, clown, 146

McCaull, John A., and Bijou Opera House, 64, 480
McCay, Ringgold, his play, 192
McClane, F. A., 413, 414, 420, 533, 575, 635
McClane, Grace, 533, 635
McClannin, R. F., 56, 168, 275, 384, 437, 606
McClellan, Frankie, 253, 274
McClellan, Jennie, 326, 328, 329, 544, 545
McClellan, Professor, 419
McCloskey, Cardinal, 160
McCloskey, J. J., his plays, 189, 320, 322, 326, 550
McCollin, A. W. F., 266, 272, 452, 458, 609, 613
McCollom, J. C., parts, 28, 29, 183, 184, 393, 620
McCollum, Annie, 159, 630
McConnell, Miss Dean, 247, 263
McCormack, L. M., 52, 250
McCormick (of Levanion and McCormick), 323, 536, 548, 549
McCormick, M., 529
McCormick, Matt, 329, 548
McCormick, the Copper, 137, 350, 572
McCoy, benefit, 490
McCoy, J. R., his play, 631
McCoy, Pete, 143
McCoy, William, 56, 277
McCreedie, Ada, 108
McCreedie, Anna, 114
McCreedie, Bernard, 108, 109, 114, 138, 314, 320, 325, 330, 335, 345, 353
McCreery, Henry, 508
McCreery, W. C., his opera, 480
McCue (of the Only Little Four), 136
McCullough, James, 98 ff, 312
McCullough, John, parts, 7, 31, 170, 248, 306, 389, 462, 463, 485, 503, 518, 524, 609
McDermott (of Four Planets), 132, 135, 139, 328, 331, 343
McDermott, Kitty, 122, 133, 138, 189, 316, 330, 396, 533, 566, 571, 619
McDermott Sisters, 186
McDonald (of London Athletes), 530
McDonald (see Orndorff and McDonald)
McDonald, Edna, 528
McDonald, G. F., 189; his play, Coney Island, 433
McDonald, J., 8, 249
McDonald, J. G., 453, 454
McDonald, J. R., 153
McDonald, Lillian, 182
McDonald, Polly, 573
McDonald, W. H., 51
McDonough, Harry, 387, 442 ff
McDonough, J. E., 49, 178, 275, 389
McDowell, Alfred, 49, 167
McDowell, E. A., 248, 447, 448
McElroy, Matt, 547, 548
McEvoy's Hibernicon, 198, 426, 427
McEvoys, the original, 636
McEwen, Nettie, 630, 641
McFaddens, The, 134, 321, 329, 352, 560, 624
McFlynn, Sam, clown, 645
McGibney Family, three youngest of eleven

children not permitted to perform, 584; 594
McGill and Ryland, 338, 343
McGilligan's Luck, 133
McGilligans, The, 526
McGlone (Pat) and Lacy (Dan), 551, 561, 568
McGowan, John, 23
McGraw, Frank, 280
McHenry, Carrie, 12, 39, 172, 258
McHenry, Nellie, 41, 256, 458, 606
McHenry, Tillie, 44
McIlvaine, Mrs., 374
McIlwaine (sic), Sybella, 377
McIntosh, negro, 60
McIntyre (Jim) and Heath (Tom), 131, 132, 141, 345
McIntyre, Robert (of Clipper Quartette), 134, 139, 421, 552, 559, 563
McKain Sisters (Gussie and Emma), 138
McKee, Andy, 126, 127, 550, 558
McKee, Miss, 440
McKee and Byrnes, 550
McLean, Andrew, 422
McLeavy, walker, 149
McMahon, John, wrestler, 185, 321, 555
McMahon, Lizzie, 177
McMahon, W., 573
McMann, Billy, 560
McManus, C. A., 41, 58, 174, 175, 202, 265, 387, 389, 482
McMullen Family, The, farce, 129, 335, 572
McMunn, George, 205, 206, 416, 417
McNair, actor, 34
McNally, J. J., 178
McNamee Brothers, 217
McNeil, Fannie, 467
McNevin's Panorama of Ireland, 195, 209, 210
McNiece, sparring, 143
McNish, Frank E., 116, 117, 315 ff, 324, 348 ff, 487, 526, 545, 551, 557, 575
McNulty, Barney, 189, 317, 332, 340, 534, 556, 559
McPherson, singer, 630
McSweeny's Masquerade, 616
McVeigh, John, 115, 139, 141, 186, 333, 335, 336, 548
McVeigh, Kate, 548
McVickers (John) and Saunders (C.), 134, 136, 139, 187, 545, 561, 563, 565, 569 ff, 575
McWade, Robert, 146, 203
Ma, Look at Him, 343, 567, 571
Mac, Little, 186, 187
Macarte, Fred and Josephine, 625
Macbeth, cast, 28; 29; recited, 153; 183, 184, 244, 245, 306, 311; recited, 367; 390, 403, 491; cast, 519; recited, 585; 609, 613, 620, 634
Macbeth, Edwin Booth as, 28, 29, 183, 184, 609; Salvini as, 244, 311; H. Meredith as, 245; George De Gross (coloured) as, 403; Barton Hill as, 519; J. C. McCollom as, 620
Macchia, La, di Sangue, 515

Macdonald, W. H., 167, 231 ff, 238, 455, 456, 611
Macht, Die, der Arbeit, 509
Mack, negro, 60
Mack (of Barnes and Mack), 396
Mack (of Collins and Mack), 532
Mack (see Gallagher and Mack)
Mack (of Little Four), 565, 567
Mack (of Morton and Mack), 354
Mack (of Olympia Quartette), 329
Mack (of Wood and Mack), 354
Mack, Annie, 98 ff, 311 ff, 524, 525
Mack, Billy, 121
Mack, Dan, 209
Mack, Dick (see Cavana and Mack)
Mack, Dick (see Ferguson and Mack)
Mack, Harry, 140, 186, 204, 413, 549
Mack, Hugh, 114, 116; of Geyer and Mack, 555, 560, 626
Mack, Hugh (of Olympia Quartette), 314, 334, 345, 346, 545, 549
Mack, J. W., 306, 315, 327, 337, 341, 347
Mack, John H., banjo, 328, 353, 354
Mack, Mrs. John, reception to Oscar Wilde, 584
Mack, Pete, 59
Mack, Philip (see Murphy and Mack)
Mack, Tommy (of Four Shamrocks), 551
Mack, Walter, 138, 551
Mack and Wilson, 549
Mackay, F. F., parts, 11, 40, 170, 203, 269, 276, 389, 605
Mackay, John A., 44, 255, 256, 480
MacKaye, J. Steele, Madison Square Theatre, inventions, etc., 20 ff; resemblance to Poe, 22; Hazel Kirke, 22; An Iron Will, 175; as Dunstan Kirke, 235, 236; breaks with the Mallorys, loses rights in Hazel Kirke, 236, 237; 243, 269, 306, 605
MacKaye, Percy, 22, 237
Mackenzie, Belle, 268
Mackenzie, C., 206
Mackey, G. D., 458
Mackey, Harry (see Mealey and Mackey)
Mackie, James (see Geyer and Mackie)
Mackie, James and Billy, 115
Mackin, Johnny, 112
Mackin, Tommy (of original Four Shamrocks), 355
Mackin and Bryant, 109, 119, 136, 326, 346, 353
Mackin and Burns, 141
Macklin, machinist, 568
Macklin, C. H., 399, 615
Maclean, Tom, 129
Macpherson, Tom, 39
Macready, J. W., 419, 635
Macready, W. C., 248
Macreery, Wallace, 48, 184, 254, 480, 481, 609
Macy, Georgie, 112
Macy, J. W., 192, 200, 206, 391
Mad Life, cast, 332
Madame Angot's Daughter, in English, 64
Madame Favart, 32, 36; in German, cast, 285; 288; in English, cast, 460, 461; 464; in French, cast, 473; in German, 495; in English, cast, 609
Madame Flott, 286
Mädchen, Ein, vom Ballet, 293
Mädchen, Das, vom Dorfe, 123
Madden, Addie, 124
Maddern, Emma, 52, 168, 249
Maddern, Mary, 441
Maddern, Minnie, 475, 476
Maddern, Miss, 461
Maddox, George, 199, 354, 395, 576, 619
Mädel, Das, ohne Geld, cast, 289; 292, 402, 508
Madigan (of Jones and Madigan), 549
Madison Square Garden, 148 ff, 156 ff, 298, 359, 540, 541
Madison Square Theatre (1880), 20 ff; (1880-81), 235 ff; concerts, 235, 236; anniversary, 236; travelling companies, 367, 447; (1881-82), 446 ff (see MacKaye, J. Steele)
Madrigal Boys, 151
Madrigal Club, 427
Madrigal Singers, 362
Maeder, Rena, 40
Maffitt (or Maffit), J. S., 27, 34, 271, 619
Maflin, A. W., 39, 56, 172, 218, 581
Magee (see Kennedy and Magee)
Magee (see Mullen and Magee)
Magee (late of Four Emeralds), 329, 342, 567
Magee (Clem) and Allen (Bob), 397, 535, 545, 561, 562, 566 ff, 570, 571, 615
Magee, John, 117, 123, 124
Magee and Taylor, 543
Magerald, Mlle., 129
Magic, prestidigitation, illusions, 42, 105, 114, 121, 123, 126, 131, 153, 177, 190, 194, 209 ff, 243, 275, 327, 329 ff, 349, 354, 360, 364, 366, 368, 385, 396, 399, 400, 404, 406, 415, 425, 467, 481, 488, 498, 541, 548, 560, 566, 569, 572, 575, 578, 579, 587, 601, 606, 624, 625, 627, 628, 641, 642
Magic Book, The, 120
Magic Cabinet, The, 338
Magic Slipper, The, cast, 39, 56; 172, 411; cast, 480; 537, 613
Magic Trumpet, The, 121
Magician, The, 120
Maginley, Ben, 39, 54, 56, 170, 277, 469, 491, 518, 621, 633, 634
Maginnis, Iveagh, 406
Magnet, The, 631
Magnus, Julian, 276, 280, 437 ff, 483, 484, 488
Magrath (Megatherian Eight), 138, 340
Magrath (of Murray and Magrath), 565
Magrath, George, concerts, 587, 596, 629, 632
Magrew (of Four Eccentrics), 102, 135, 314, 344, 347, 397, 518, 562, 563
Maguinnis, D. J., 246
Maguire, Thomas, in re La Belle Russe, 434
Mahn's Comic Opera Company, 11, 12, 172, 253, 274, 281, 386, 413, 483, 605
Mahoney, Mme., Black Swan, 379
Mahretta, Mlle., 124, 128
Maid of Arran, The, from A Princess of Thule, 493

Maid of the Mill, The (Schubert's), 163
Maier, C., 510
Maimonides, 367
Main, Leslie, 582
Maina, singer, 456, 457, 614
Mainhall, H., 37
Mainzer Carneval-Verein, 82 ff, 294 ff, 511
Maître Petronitta, 264
Maja de Seville, 533
Majerino, Mme., 298
Majeroni, Giulia, 303
Majeroni, Signor, 386
Majeroni, Signora, parts, 41, 58, 94, 256, 387, 412, 488
Major, Harvey, 403
Major, The, cast, 524
Major, The, a skit, 537
Malburg, Millie, 337
Male impersonations by women, 120, 126, 344, 352, 353, 397, 487, 529, 532, 541, 557, 561, 562, 569, 571, 576, 616 (see also Hamlets, Female; Hindle, Annie; Hussey, St. George; Wesner, Ella)
Malger, Norbert, 326
Mallon, Andy, 485, 564, 570
Mallon, Kate, 564, 570
Mallory Brothers and Madison Square Theatre, 20 ff, 446 ff
Malone (of Boyle and Malone), 141
Malone, John T., 282, 484, 610
Maloney's Picnic, 559
Maloney's Supper, 340
Maloney Family, in a Wagner Palace Sleeping Car, 188
Maloney's (or Malony's) Visit, 137, 534, 556, 616
Maloney's (or Malony's) Visit to New York, 102, 340
Malvern, Tillie, 134 ff, 345 ff, 560 ff
Malvina, Mlle., 16, 473
Malz, Herr, 493
Mamsell Angot, 499, 623
Mamsell Rosa, 190
Mamsell Uebermuth, 510
Man bear, 579
Man fish, 190
Man and Wife, cast, 17; 62
Man, The, from Bay Ridge, 128
Man, The, from Cattaraugus, cast, 253
Man, That, from Galway, 553, 555, 560
Man, A, of the People, 173
Man soll den Teufel nicht an die Wand malen, 293
Man sucht einen Erzieher, 501, 502
Manchester, Bobby, 130, 132, 318
Manchester and Jennings, 101, 131, 132, 140, 141, 348, 353, 397, 558, 588, 618
Mancini, 456, 457, 614
Mandeville, W. C., 481
Man-flute (see Ferreyra, Don)
Manfred, Louise, 470
Mangold, George, 374
Manhattan Athletic Club, 150
Manhattan Beach, 87, 155, 164, 300, 379, 601, 631, 641

Manhattan Choral Union, 598
Manhattan Concert Hall, 374
Manhattan Elevated Railway Athletic Club, 156
Manhattan Hall, 374
Manhattan Hospital, benefit, 163
Manhattan Opera House, 319, 369
Manhattan Polo Association, 366
Manhattan Temperance Union or Society, 585, 596
Manley, actor, 219
Mann, Der, der Debutantin, 77
Mann's Theatre, Brooklyn, 626
Manne, Henry and Jenny, 404
Männerchor, Astoria, 644; Brooklyn, 190, 402, 403, 623; New York, 82, 210; 294, 510, 511
Manning (of Hawley and Manning), 334
Manning (of Megatherian Eight), 340
Manning (Monumental Quartette), 337, 343
Manning, A. (E. H. Sothern), 31, 43, 44
Manning, J. L., trapeze, 326, 330, 542, 550, 635
Manning, Rose, 146
Manning, Walter (of Four Comets), 325, 345, 350, 355, 550, 567
Manning and Drew, 535, 552
Manning and Marlowe, 550
Manœvring, 335
Manola (Le Jour et la Nuit), 464, 609
Manoli, Emanuel, 157
Mansfeld, Max, 296, 297
Mansfield, Alice, 31, 267, 482
Mansfield Post, 640
Manzoni Requiem, 382
Mapleson, J. H., opera (1879-80), 91 ff, 180 ff, (1880-81), 304 ff, 391 ff; (1881-82), 516 ff, 611 ff
Maquese, Indian rider, 645
Mar, Helen, 605
Mara, Frank and Clara, 133
Marble, Dan, 54
Marble, Ed, 46, 178, 257, 261, 394, 412
Marble, Emma, 54, 170, 275, 469
Marble, John, 169, 264, 462, 609
Marble, Scott, 619
Marble Heart, The, cast, 202; 276, 306, 329, 384, 465, 631
Marc Antony, F. Bock as, 276, 461
Marcella, Joe, 121
Marcellus, Lizzie, 147, 148
Marckwald, F. V., 162, 198, 408, 586
Marckwald, Mrs. F. V., 198
Marco, Catarina, 97
Marcy, Nina, 163
Marden, E. B., 619, 620
Marden, Emma, 545, 576
Mardo, 281; cast and scenery, 485; casts, 569, 617
Maret, Heinrich, 298
Maret, Isabella, 298, 509
Maretzek, Max, his Sleepy Hollow, 90; 152; Opera Company, 168; 498
Maretzek, Mme., harp, 162
Marguilies, Adèle, 587 ff, 595

Maria Giovanna, 302
Maria Stuart, in German, casts, 69, 76; 79, 284; cast, 495; 497; cast, 507, 508 (*see Mary Stuart*)
Maria und Magdalena, 508
Mariage, Un, aux Lanternes, 538
Marie-Anne, ein Weib aus dem Volk, 70
Marié, Paola, 25, 26, 32, 33, 36, 37, 80, 97, 157, 161, 176, 183, 263, 264, 301, 355, 356, 466, 473, 474, 513, 537
Marimon, Marie, 22, 93 ff, 182; quarrels with Ambre, 97
Mariners' Harbour, S. I., 648
Mario, Albert, 640
Marion, Frank, 190
Marion, Miss, 49
Marionettes, 102, 135, 146, 315, 397, 401, 617, 618 (*see Till's Marionettes*)
Maritana, 385, 395, 487
Marjolaine, La, 32, 36
Marked for Life, 105, 185, 346, 349, 560, 563, 622
Markham, H. M., 485, 564, 570
Markham, Pauline, 62, 272
Markley, Edna, 333, 354
Markoe, Daisy, as Topsy, 485
Markovitz, actor, 76
Marks (of Griffin and Marks), 415, 530, 563, 568
Marks, W. D., 255, 316
Marks, W. D., amateur, 585
Markstein, Henrietta, 33, 37, 53, 54, 148, 150, 170, 197, 279, 284, 358, 373, 374, 503, 514, 521, 537, 540, 582, 591, 598, 600
Marley, Charles, 547
Marley, Louisa, 194
Marlow (James) and Hart (Joe), 545, 563, 571
Marlow and Plunkett, 535
Marlowe (of Manning and Marlowe), 550
Marlowe, Mrs. Owen, 176, 272, 385
Marlowe, Owen, 224
Marr Brothers (John and Billy), 553, 565, 567, 570
Married in the Dark, 556, 560
Married Life, 8; with amateurs, 154, 585
Married Life (by F. H. Jackson), cast, 622
Marschner Männerchor, 83, 294 ff
Marsden, Fred, Shaun Rhue, 277; Clouds, 369, 392
Marsh, William, 124
Marshall, E. K., 59
Marshall, Florence, 131, 349
Marshall, Martha, 422
Marshall, May, 189
Marshall, Minnie, 255
Marson, Frank, 190
Marston, E. W., 105, 107 ff, 330 ff, 550 ff, 554
Marston, Richard, 438
Marta (or Martha), cast, Italian, 92; 93, 95; cast, 181; with amateurs, 184; casts, 251, 306, 308; in English, 385; in Italian, cast 392; 487; in German, cast, 498; in Italian, cast, 517; 519, 604; cast, 612
Martell, Mlle., 239 ff

Martell (or Martelle) Brothers (Harry and Willie), 118, 119, 134, 188, 328 ff, 337, 344, 397, 566
Martell Family (bicyclists), 616 ff
Martelle, Joyce, 189, 315
Martelle, Marie, 532
Marten (or Martens) Family, 484, 514
Martense, Mollie, 408
Martha, Mlle., circus, 360
Martha, Mme., circus, 148
Martha Washington Reception, 95, 307, 519
Marthe, Mme. Imbre, 539
Marti, Dr. reads in Castilian, 28
Martin (of Big Four), 316, 333 ff, 340, 397, 554, 573
Martin (of Cahill and Martin), 353
Martin (of Crosby and Martin), 318, 545, 565
Martin (of Morton and Martin), 139
Martin (of Twilight Four), 567
Martin, Bella, coloured Topsy, 215
Martin, Harry, 113
Martin, Luke, 50, 59, 168, 468, 469
Martin, Sam, one-legged, 327, 543
Martin, T. J., 387, 435
Martinetti, Ignacio, 47, 385, 488
Martinetti Family, 271
Martinez, Dickie, 481
Martinez, George, 368
Martinez, Isidora, 95, 192, 194, 304 ff, 391, 518, 595, 597, 615, 629, 631, 638
Martini, Maze, ballet, 397
Martini, Mlle., 95, 309, 394, 594
Martyne, Alice, 361
Mary Ann Kehoe, Ha! Ha! 526, 558, 567, 568
Mary Stuart, 245, 491, 606 (*see also Maria Stuart*)
Marzo, piano, 25; his Messe Solonnelle, 161; 180
Mascot, The (or Mascotte, La), casts, 262, 269; cast, 455; 456; in English, cast, 460; in French, cast, 466, 473; casts, 470, 477, 478; "with composer's original orchestration," 479; with Corinne, 480; in English, 483, 493; in German, 496; 497; in English, cast, 508; with triple cast, 508; at Pastor's, cast, 528; at Aberle's, 532; in English, casts, 538, 606; 608; casts, 609, 610, 611; 622, 634
Mascotte, La, burlesque, 459
Mask balls, 82 ff
Maskerade, Die, in der Dachstube, 82
Mason (organist), 591
Mason, Carrie E., 406, 587
Mason, Charles, 40, 260, 476
Mason (Dan) and Sully (Dan), 134, 138, 318
Mason, J. L., 608
Mason, Sallie, 133, 325 ff, 334, 535, 545, 546
Mason and Lord, 564, 569, 570, 625
Mason and Titus, 562, 563, 568, 569
Masonic Hall, Flatbush, 644
Masonic Temple, New York, 160, 161, 365 ff, 583
Masonic Temple, Williamsburgh, 637

[714]

Masonic Temple Association, 87
Masquerade, The, with the Carrolls, 134, 137, 334, 335, 560
Masquerade Ball, The, farce, 131
Massen, Louis F., 30, 236, 448
Massett, Stephen, 373
Masur, R. M., amateur, 417
Materna (Friedrich-Materna), Amalia, 523; reviews, 578 ff
Mathews, Fred, 566
Matlock, Bennett, 465
Matrimonial Quarrels, 338
Matrimony, casts, 265, 389
Matthew, J., 54
Matthews, A. S., 27
Matthews, John, 12, 31, 39, 438
Matthews, Miss, 171
Matthews, Will C., 414
Matzka, G., 162, 375, 591 ff
Maud's Peril, 369
Maude, Little, 482
Mauge, parts, 466, 473, 537
Mauras, parts, 263, 356, 466, 467, 473, 474, 537
Maurel, Louisa, 38
Maurel, Pauline, 51, 167, 251, 487, 605
Maurer, Henrietta, 159, 356
Maurer, Sophia, 194
Maurice, May, 265
Maurice, W. M., 265, 389
Maurie, M., 303
Mauritius, Charles, 113
Maussey, Ida, 413
Max Müller, cast, 478
Max und Moritz, 496
Maxwell, Barry, 59, 257
Maxwell, Clara, boxer, 143
Maxwell, Kitty, 19, 231
Maxwell, Tom and Clara, 325, 329, 330, 350, 352, 421, 530, 531, 545, 547, 550, 570
May, Ada, 344
May, Adelaide, 615
May, Etta, 341
May, Florence, 126, 184, 314
May Blossom, play, 237
Maybel, Clara, 255
Mayers, E. J., 208
Mayhew, Kate, 467
Maynard, Emily, 64
Maynard, Rev. Newland, lectures, 153, 366, 417, 586, 630, 638, 644
Mayo (of the Four-in-Hand), 332, 343, 349, 415
Mayo, Edwin, 63
Mayo, Ella, 105, 108, 130 ff, 138, 140, 187, 189; dies, benefit for mother, 276; 341, 346, 352, 396
Mayo, Frank, 53; at the Olympic, 62, 63; tries to enjoin The Poor of New York, 107; parts, 176, 182, 203, 412, 484
Mayo, Will H., 347
Mayo and Talbot (or Talbert), 133, 573
Mazeppa, Maude Forrester as, 65, 189, 321, 322, 397, 530; Alice Adams as, 323, 329, 339; Zoe Gayton as, 331; Belle Berri as,

414; Fannie Louise Buckingham as, 532, 576
Mazzanovich, scenery, 223, 224
Mea, Mlle. Jane, 246
Meacham, Frank W., 198, 627
Meacham, Miss M. J., 627
Mead, Jennie, 577
Meade, James A., 255
Meade, James H., 174
Meade and Maginley Combination, 388
Meafoy, Bert, 199, 409
Meafoy, Miss, 409
Meagher, T. F., 31
Meaghill, George, 330
Mealen, Dave (of Four Shamrocks), 355, 551
Mealey, Edward, 314, 563
Mealey (Joe) and Mackey (Harry), 122, 138, 327, 347, 349, 397, 526, 535, 553, 562, 564, 569, 574
Mealey, John, 99, 312
Measure for Measure, cast, 30
Medea, cast, 76; 80; Janauschek's version, 245
Meehan, Sadie, 104, 105, 534
Meek, Kate, 29, 31, 52, 55, 56, 277, 465, 490
Meeker, W. H., 41
Meery, actor, 66 ff, 163, 288 ff, 311, 498 ff
Mefistofele, 181; in English, 251; in Italian, casts, 306, 392, 518
Meg, play, 328, 415, 542, 635
Meg Merrilies, Mary Anderson as, 250
Meg's Diversion, 81, 420, 627
Megatherian Eight, 138, 340
Megatherian Four, 331, 346, 351, 560, 564, 568
Megatherian Minstrels, 167, 185
Meighan, Thad, 642
Meigs, S. H. P., 600
Meigs Sisters, 518, 535, 593, 597, 600, 601, 630, 638, 641
Mein Leopold, cast, 73; 508
Mein Schifflein treibt, 81
Meineidbauer, Der, 289
Melba, Nellie, 92
Melbourne, T., 454
Melnotte, Georgie, 128, 131, 141, 353, 414, 534, 542, 543, 561, 574
Melodia Männerchor, 298, 299, 511
Melody in a Music Shop, 339
Melrose, Frank, one-legged, 116, 120, 124, 185, 204, 326
Melrose, P. C., 415
Melrose and La Rosa, 542
Melton, J. V., 53, 215, 216, 280, 389
Melville, Belle, 197, 237, 271
Melville, Emilie, Opera, 480, 609
Melville Frank, circus, 118, 123, 125, 146 ff, 359, 360, 425
Melville, May, 210
Melville, W. A., 625
Melville and Bunell, 343, 530, 543, 561
Member from Slocum on a Racket, 607
Memoiren, Die, des Teufels, 290, 291, 402
Memphis University Singers, 615
Men from Galway, 551 (see Man from Galway)

Men of Nerve, 545, 561, 570
Mendel, Billy, 126
Mendel, Harry, 115
Mendels, Dutch (Harry and Leonie), 115, 131, 314, 327, 347
Mendelssohn Club of Philadelphia, 163
Mendelssohn Glee Club, 159, 372, 592
Mendelssohn Union, Harlem, 372
Mendoza, 562
Menges, actor, 76
Menzelli (sic), Elizabeth, 27, 34, 183
Merchant of Venice, The, cast, 29; 47; recited, 153; 184, 276, 282; recited, 366, 368; 384, 386, 450, 461, 465; recited, 585; 605, 609; with amateurs, 629 (see also Kaufmann, Der, von Venedig)
Meredith, F. S., 171
Meredith, Harry, 245, 270, 271, 280
Meredith, J. T., 379
Mergell, Artelyea, 627
Merighi, Clarence, 39
Merivale, Clara, 238
Merle, Mlle., 263, 264
Merriam, E. L., 404
Merritt, George, at Harrigan's, 313, 524, 525
Merritt Brothers (George and William), 101 ff, 138, 186
Merritt, Miss, 473
Merritt, Paul, The World, 223; Youth, 433
Merritt, Samuel, walker, 149, 150
Merritt, W., 524
Merry, Mr. and Mrs. Harley, 424; his play, 644
Merry Swiss Couple, 342, 351
Merry Tuners, The, 146
Merry War, The, in English, casts, 509, 538; (see also Lustige Krieg, Der)
Merry Wives of Windsor, recited, 366, 419
Merten, Claudius, 288 ff, 498 ff, 510
Merton, Beula, 103
Merton, Florence, 315, 316
Merton, Jessie, 105, 113, 120, 134, 185, 530, 543, 544, 556
Merville, Lina (or Lena), 49, 178, 180, 255, 256, 388
Mesmerism 195, 367, 368 403 ff, 419, 582, 626, 629, 637 ff, 644
Messe, Solonnelle (Rossini's), 93, 94
Messenger, James, 187, 321
Messenger, The, from Jarvis Section, 476, 491
Messiah, The, sung, 165, 380; Damrosch Festival, 381; 603
Mestayer, Charles, 213, 214
Mestayer, Louis J., 61, 62
Mestayer, W. A., 40, 175, 247, 271, 389, 412
Meta, Johanna, 77, 83, 84, 86, 160, 216
Metkiff, George, 174
Metropolis, The, after Dark, 569
Metropolitan Alcazar, 509, 538
Metropolitan Casino, 537 ff (see infra)
Metropolitan Concert Hall (1879-80), 163, 164; 301; (1880-81), 355 ff; 368; (1881-82), 536 ff (see supra)
Metropolitan Opera House spoken of, 308

Metropolitan Theatre (late Tony Pastor's), 534 ff
Metsch, actor, 493
Mette Brothers, 147, 325 ff, 346
Metzger, Charles, 409
Metzger, Simon, 404
Meyer, Carl (or Karl), 493 ff, 634
Meyer, Emmie, 630
Meyer, Frl., 510
Meyer, Julius, 545
Meyer, Otto, 78 ff, 81, 282, 493 ff, 510
Meyers, Miss, 83
Meyger, Andreas, benefit for widow, 82
Meynall, Percy, 473
Mezières, parts, 32, 33, 36, 98, 263, 264, 388, 466, 473, 474
Miaco, Grimaldi, 424, 491
Miaco, Jennie, 314, 333, 341, 344
Miaco, Laura, 617
Miaco, Mlle., circus, 424
Mice, performing, 560
Michael Strogoff, at Booth's cast, scenery, 449; at Niblo's, 482; at Academy of Music, cast, scenery, 515, 516; at Aberle's, cast, 529, 532; cast, 613
Michels (or Michaels), Mme. Ivan C., 54, 151, 256, 390, 411, 412, 476
Michigan relief benefits, 436, 483, 582; Patti sings for, 590; 591, 623, 647
Micks-tures, 561
Middle Village, L. I., 211
Middleton, George, 112, 530
Middleton Brothers, 624
Middleton's Museums, 364, 365, 626
Midgets, 190, 191, 364, 400, 401, 541, 578, 579, 625 (see also Dwarfs)
Midnight Lovers, The, 562, 566
Midsummer-Night's Dream music, 540
Midwood Amateur Dramatic Society, 644
Mighty Dollar, The, cast, 51; 174, 453, 458, 609, 610, 634
Mighty Dollar, The, variety sketch, 115, 383
Mignon, in French, casts, etc., 25, 26, 36, 98, 176, 182, 183, 263, 466; in Italian casts, etc., 27, 93, 309, 516, 517, 521, 612; in English casts, 167, 251, 252
Mike's Fortune, 326
Milburn, Agnes, 532
Miles (of Irish Four), 129
Miles (see Morton and Miles)
Miles (of Mullen and Miles), 329
Miles (see Murphy and Miles)
Miles (William) and Nelson (Charles), 548
Military Hall (Williamsburgh), 637
Military Review, 601
Milkman's Bride, The, 584
Millard, Harrison, 58, 157, 160
Millard, Marie, 160
Millard, Milo, 105
Miller, baby guitar, 197
Miller, concert, 596
Miller, wrestler, 150
Miller, A., 418
Miller, Fanny, 38
Miller, Harry, minstrel, 59

Miller, Henry, 445, 446, 608
Miller, J. H., 29, 168, 274
Miller, James E., 262
Miller, Joaquin, 243
Miller, Lizzie, 534
Miller, Mabel, 11
Miller (or Müller), Max and Martha, 321, 329, 331, 332, 336, 350, 414, 415, 529, 543, 566, 571
Miller, W. Christie, 44, 469
Miller's Hotel, Little Bayside, 212, 214, 426, 428, 646, 647
Millet, actor, 466
Millet, Frank, designs costumes, 455
Millie, La Petite, 401
Milligan, Bob, 135
Milliken, Edward, 234, 466
Mills, Ed, 118, 119, 334 ff, 555 ff
Mills, Eva, 48
Mills, Genevieve, 39, 63, 225, 411
Mills, Harry, 111, 334 (see Mills and Warren)
Mills, Jerome, 481
Mills, Kitty, 329, 339
Mills, S. B., 85, 153, 161, 180, 194, 197, 296, 299, 311, 370 ff, 591, 594, 598, 601
Mills, W. F., 157, 162, 163, 195, 370, 375, 376, 417, 421, 425, 597, 600
Mills and Warren, 344, 350, 353, 556, 560, 568
Milo Brothers (John, James, Francis), 119, 121, 130, 134, 186, 324, 345, 396, 563, 570
Milton, actor, 232
Milton, Billy and Mary, 361
Milton, Carrie, 256
Milton Jaspers, acrobats, 103, 136, 137, 188
Miltonian Tableaux, 631
Mimosa Society, 370, 521, 585, 586
Miner, G., 211
Miner's, Harry, Combination, 617
Miner's, Harry, Comedy Four, 565, 566, 569
Miner's, Harry, Constellation, 413
Miner's, Harry, Eighth Avenue Theatre, cost, staff (1881-82), 568 ff
Miner's, Harry, Frank I. Frayne Combination, 569
Miner's, Harry, Theatre, Bowery (1879-80), 133 ff; (1880-81), 345 ff; (1881-82), 560 ff
Miner's, Harry, and Pat Rooney's New York Star Combination, 564, 565
Mines, Julia, 192
Minetta and Kincade, 414
Miniature Opera Company, 152, 154, 200
Minna von Barnhelm, 292, 498
Minnie Ha Ha, 351
Minnie Palmer's Boarding School, 145
Minstrel Boy, The, 575
Minstrels, amateur, 213
Miramichi Family, 343
Mirth Makers in Mischief, 150
Miscellany, Brooklyn (1879-80), 191 ff; (1880-81), 403 ff; (1881-82), 626 ff
Miscellany (Entertainments), New York (1879-80), 151 ff; (1880-81), 365 ff; (1881-82), 581 ff
Miscellany, Williamsburgh (1879-80), 204; 1880-81), 416 ff; (1881-82), 636 ff

Mischief, cast, 150
Mischievous Clown, The, 141
Mischievous Monkey, The, 115, 119, 120, 124, 341, 414, 550
Miser, The, of Five Points, 345, 571
Miss Jones' Wedding, 405, 425
Mill Multon, casts, 52, 94, 227, 411
Mississippi, The, panorama, 369
Mississippi Jim, cast, 132
Mississippi Serenaders, 185
Mistaken Fathers, 106
Mitchell, Annie, 33
Mitchell, Jennie, 105
Mitchell, Julian, 56, 168, 275, 384, 489, 607
Mitchell, Kate, 56
Mitchell, Maggie, actress, 50, 56, 168, 275, 384, 489, 492, 607; her son, 426
Mitchell, Maggie, singer, 199, 200, 372, 404, 417, 629, 630
Mitchell, Mason, 53, 259 ff, 450
Mitchell, Miss, 238
Mitchell, Selden, 264
Mitchell, Thomas, 419
Mitchell, W. C., Pleasure Party, 179, 257
Mitchell, William, of the old Olympic, 312
Mitgift, Die, 81
Mitt (Life in California), 61
Mixed, farce, 335
Mixsell, Mrs., 200
Mixtures, farce, 339, 555, 566, 571, 575
M'liss, cast, 49; 178, 203, 275, 281, 389, 412, 488, 492, 606, 633
Mockabee, Frank, 278
Mocking Bird, The, sung as a duet, 198
Moderati, concert, 89
Modern Actors, farce, 334
Modern School of Acting, skit, 119, 129, 545, 569
Moderne Verhängniss, Ein, 510
Moderner Barbar, Ein, 291
Modjeska, contrasted with Bernhardt and Clara Morris, 228, 239
Moffett, Kate, 110, 325, 328, 415, 543, 625
Molino, E., Spanish actor, 28
Moll Pitcher, cast, 331
Mollenhauer, Bernard, 22, 23, 53, 55
Mollenhauer, E. R., at Daly's, 13; 160, 373, 595
Mollenhauer, Frederick, 151
Mollenhauer, Henry, 83, 197, 377, 407, 408, 623, 627, 630
Mollenhauer, Ida, 83, 623
Mollenhauer, Master Willie, 151
Mollenhauer Instrumental Quartet, 597
Mollenhauers (several), 594, 595
Mollie's Victory, 101, 102, 137, 330, 341, 552, 568
Molloy, J. L., Jr., 319
Molly Maguires, The, 325, 326, 413, 420; cast, 542; 570
Molten, Harry, 493, 508
Moncrief, Blanche, 578
Money, 211; Wallack cast, 613; 631
Money, farce, 341
Money Matters, farce, 101

Money Spinner, The, cast, review, 432
Moneymoon, The, 586
Mongolian Giants, 625
Monis, Bertha, 52
Monka, Ada, 64
Monk, Minnie, 38, 52, 179, 277, 384, 463, 489, 605
Monkey Jack, 342
Monkeys, performing, 114, 365, 400
Monroe (of Dashway and Monroe), 187
Monroe, Frank, 129, 516
Monroe, George W, 328, 340, 350, 560, 561, 566, 571, 618
Monroe, H., and cats, 350, 547, 577
Monroe, Kate, 537
Monroe and King, 414, 415
Monroe and Sheparde, 414
Montague, Alice, 64, 101, 112, 113, 119, 325, 327, 331, 332, 345, 352, 414, 415, 543, 550, 574
Montague, Anna, 425
Montague, Annie, at Hill's, 577
Montague, Annis, 90
Montague, H. J., 4, 219, 224
Montague, Louise, 102, 131, 133, 135, 187
Montague, Violet, 399
Montalo, May, 107
Montaloo, Antonio, 155
Montcastle, Fanny, 52
Monte, Salome, 608
Monte Cristo, 279, 412
Montegriffo, 378, 437, 446, 513, 514, 538, 595, 597, 640
Montegriffo, Mlle., 505 ff, 513, 514, 612
Monteith, Zippora, 377
Montell, J. B., 425
Montesini, Bianca, 305
Montgomery, H. W., 41, 48, 202, 268, 437 ff, 516
Montgomery, J. A., 528
Monti, singer, 91 ff, 181, 304 ff, 391 ff, 516 ff, 612 ff
Montrose, Frank, 121
Montrose, Kate, 115, 121, 136, 139, 141, 186, 329, 333 ff, 518, 549, 577
Montserrat, G., 475
Monumental Quartette, 332, 337, 343, 347, 553, 567, 616
Moody and Sankey, 151
Moon, exhibition of, 368
Moon, Kate, 406
Mooney, Annie, 207 ff, 421
Mooney, Rachel, 207
Moonlight Flirtation, 136
Moonlight Picnic, The, 551
Moonlight Picnic at Cape May, 551
Moonshiner's Wife, The, 414
Moore (of Dashway and Moore), 140
Moore (of Twilight Three), 567
Moore, Ada, 532, 533
Moore, Billy (late of Topack and Moore), 134, 545, 548, 557, 558, 561, 567
Moore, Charles and dogs, 131, 350, 552, 563
Moore, Charles and Carrie, skaters, 131, 338, 350, 552, 553, 561, 563, 570, 574, 616, 624

Moore, Clara, 104, 129 ff, 186 ff, 341, 343 ff, 352, 396, 397, 616
Moore, Corinne, 200
Moore, Elsie, 44
Moore, Flora, 56, 102, 129, 137, 274, 276, 314, 316, 348, 349, 351, 526, 534, 551, 559, 561, 566, 573, 619
Moore, Hattie, 458
Moore, Ira H., 629
Moore, John, 15 ff, 445
Moose Sisters (Laura and Eunice), 122, 190, 330
Moore's Choir, 215
Moore and Daly (late of Topack and Moore), 548, 557
Moore and Lessenger, 111, 113, 117, 128, 140, 383, 534, 551, 556, 557, 574, 576
Mora's photographs, 49, 267, 392
Moran, Frank, 364
Moranda, Lottie, trapeze, 146
Morant, Fanny, 6, 11, 15; contrasted with Mrs. Phillips, 228, 229; at Daly's, 231 ff; 443, 444
Morant, Nellie, 168, 229, 237, 388, 471
Morant, W. T., 553
Morawski, Ivan C, 587, 594, 596, 603, 629, 643
Mordaunt, Belle, 311 ff
Mordaunt, Frank, 9, 12, 60, 176, 225, 270, 472, 633
Mordaunt, George, 38, 243
Mordaunt, Marian, 150
Mordaunt, Miss, 100
Mordaunt, W. G., 24
Moreland, A. C., 37, 129 ff, 186 ff, 246, 276, 362 ff, 528, 581
Morelli, J., 143
Morello Brothers (Max and Will), 121, 125, 130, 327, 331, 383, 550, 558
Morgan, Agnes, 649
Morgan, Anna, 198
Morgan (Charles) and Mullen (Harry), 114, 115, 121, 131, 134, 138, 139, 140, 187, 315, 325
Morgan, Della, 187
Morgan, G. W., 157 ff, 160 ff, 180, 192 ff, 200, 375, 376, 406 ff, 594 ff, 628 ff, 648
Morgan, Geraldine, 306
Morgan, Jennie, 92, 99, 173, 186, 187, 276, 312, 347, 348, 396, 397, 566, 571, 616, 618
Morgan, Jessie, 354
Morgan, John, actor, 197, 225
Morgan, John E., tenor, 627
Morgan, Maggie, 354
Morgan, Matt, 186
Morgan, Maud, 22, 160, 181, 310, 375, 376, 418, 430, 595 ff, 648
Morgan, Mrs. W. G., 628
Morgan, T., 3
Morgan, W. A., 11, 172, 254, 274, 492
Morgan, W. H., circus, 424
Morgan, Walter, 252
Morgan, William G., 216, 372
Morgan and Farrell, 635
Moriarity, C., 176
Morlacchi, Mlle., 347

Morland, Harry, 105
Morosco, 571
Morosco, Alice, 115
Morosco, Dick, 329, 564, 570
Morosco, Frank, 531
Morosini, 55, 374
Morosini, Victoria, 598
Morrell, Helen, 526
Morrill, Albert, 486
Morris, Alonzo, billiards, 582
Morris, Andy, 413
Morris, Clara, 13, 15, 17, 22, 94; does not deliver prologue, 173; 194; matinées, reviews, 227 ff; parts, 246, 259, 260; matinées, 438, 439; as Mercy Merrick, Towse and Oscar Wilde on, 439, 440; parts, 489
Morris, Edwin, 10, 177, 493
Morris, Etta, 121, 125, 320, 326
Morris, Felix, 247, 271, 449, 474
Morris, George, 52, 61
Morris, Grimaldi, 186
Morris, Harry, 353, 354, 573
Morris (Harry) and Fields (Frank), 188, 345, 348, 349, 397, 545, 549, 555, 556, 616 ff
Morris, Hattie, 543
Morris, Ida, 64, 130, 135, 136, 186, 187
Morris, Isabel, 390, 453, 468
Morris, John, 51, 100, 106
Morris, John, actor, 316
Morris, Lizzie, 574
Morris, Miss, 211
Morris, Mrs. T. E., 244
Morris, Myles, 355, 532, 544, 573, 575
Morris, Ramsay, 471
Morris, Robert Griffin, his play, 471, 472
Morris, T. E., 10 ff, 39, 228 ff, 244, 437, 438, 453, 484, 582
Morris, William, 169, 476
Morris and Gray, 410, 411
Morris and Green, 136
Morrisania Schützen Park, 300, 513
Morrison, Lewis, parts, 241, 243, 260, 264, 391, 441, 442, 455, 465, 483, 491, 607
Morrissey, J. W., 523
Morrissey, James, 59
Morrissey, Tom and Maud, 129, 130, 133, 140, 327, 342, 564
Morse, Edward, 49
Morse, Mrs. Louisa, 270
Morse, Salmi, his Doctor of Lima, 437
Morse, W., 227, 437 ff
Morse, W. F., 266
Morsell, Herndon, 595
Morte Civile, La, 242, 393
Mortimer, magic, 425
Mortimer, Annie, 56, 168, 275, 384
Mortimer, Blanche, 412
Mortimer, E. L., 173
Mortimer, Estelle, 41, 48, 53, 58, 173, 270
Mortimer, Fred and Ida, 564, 624
Mortimer, Lulu, 317
Mortimer, Nellie (Mrs. George F. De Vere), 24, 167, 177, 266, 272, 388, 411, 474, 475, 481
Morton, Joe or Tom (of Williams and Morton), 125, 131, 542, 565, 566

Morton, Blanche, 115, 136, 140, 361, 577
Morton, E. T., 5
Morton, F. W., his play, 420
Morton, Frank T., 570
Morton, George, 19, 151, 386, 482, 489
Morton, Harry K., 115, 136, 140
Morton, J., 320
Morton, Joe, 333, 554, 557
Morton, Lew (of Edwards and Morton), 544, 554, 572
Morton, Lillie, 338
Morton, Louis (sic), 396
Morton, S., 516
Morton and Bryant, 323, 339; (late of Morton and Miles and Mackin and Bryant), 350; 532, 544, 563
Morton and Mack, 354
Morton and Martin, 139
Morton and Miles, 126, 134, 320, 326, 332
Moses, Carrie, 162
Moses, Lillie, 453
Mosley, F. C., 172, 261, 461, 465
Moss, Theodore, 2
Moss, William, 226
Mostroff (sic), 513
Mother Goose, lecture by Barnum, 629
Mother Goose, operetta, 627, 642, 647
Mother Goose, play, 630
Mother Goose and Her Goslings, 421, 422
Mother and Son, with Janauschek, 245, 491, 606
Mother-in-Law, 464; cast, 474
Mott (of Sweeney and Mott), 635
Mott, James, 204
Mott Haven, 155
Moulton (of Zegrino and Moulton), 328
Moulton, Arthur, 246, 428, 467
Moulton, Blanche, 234, 470
Mount, Henry C., benefit for family, 41, 54
Mounted Police, farce, 341
Mountjoy Female Serenaders, 548
Mousquetaires au Couvent, 466, 473
Mowbray, Lizzie, 109, 111, 335, 339, 345, 635
Mowbray, Maude, 264
Mowbray, Miss A., 45
Mozart Garden, Brooklyn, 189, 190
Mozart Männerchor, 83 ff, 295, 298, 511
Mozart Musical Union, 299, 378, 510, 511, 591, 596, 598
Mozart Singing Society, 596
Mozart Verein, 84 ff, 512
Mozart Vocal Society, 409
Mr. Faustgerecht, 420
Mrs. Campbell's Sewing Circle, 549
Mrs. Didemus' Party, 340, 343
Mrs. Driscoll's Party, 102, 133
Mrs. Fitz-Samuel's Cosmopolitan Club, 403, 421
Mrs. Joshua Whitcomb, play, 104, 543, 636
Mrs. Lofty Keeps a Carriage, 582
Mrs. Willis's Will, 207
Much Ado about Nothing, 28, 54; read, 153; 170; in German, 508 (see Viel Lärm um Nichts)
Mühlbauer, 494

Mulberry Street Flats, 132
Mulcahey (of Muldoon and Mulcahey), 398
Mulcahy's Excursion to Coney Island, 557
Mulcahy's Racket, 576, 616
Muldener, Louise, 12, 52, 55, 94, 265, 389, 520
Muldoon, William, wrestler, 150, 367, 368
Muldoon and Mulcahey, 398
Muldoon in New York, 563
Muldoon in Russia, 398
Muldoon on a Lark, 557
Muldoon on the Mississippi, 619
Muldoon Quartette, 534, 546
Muldoon's Blunder, 617, 618
Muldoon's Coterie, 483, 527
Muldoon's Excursion, 532, 575, 576
Muldoon's Flats, 188
Muldoon's Picnic, 104, 187, 189, 397, 398, 483, 518, 559, 593, 616, 618, 619
Muldoon's Trip to Boston, 187, 396
Muldoon's Trip to Coney Island, 187
Muldoon's Trip West, 396
Mulholland, Lizzie, 255
Mullaly's orchestra, 143, 362, 581
Mullen, Harry, 121, 127, 328, 329, 354
Mullen, Harry (see Morgan and Mullen)
Mullen (J. J.) and Magee, 133, 136, 140, 186, 324, 339
Mullen and Cline, 325
Mullen and Miles, 329
Mullen Family, The, farce, 345
Müller, F. A., 271
Müller, Franz, 494 ff
Müller, Wilhelm, 159, 160, 192, 200, 217, 367, 371, 372; Festival Prologue, 498; 591, 595
Mulligan, Frank, 205
Mulligan, James, 106, 107
Mulligan, W. E., 372, 378, 417
Mulligan Guard Picnic, The, 305; cast, 311
Mulligan Guards vs. the Skidmores, 187
Mulligan Guards' Chowder, The, cast, 98, 99
Mulligan Guards Christmas, The, 94; cast and story, 99
Mulligan Guards' Nominee, cast, 312; 387, 413
Mulligan Guards' Surprise, The, 11; casts, 99, 100, 173
Mulligans' Silver Wedding, The, cast, 313; 387, 413
Mulvey, Lizzie, 347, 545, 569; with Barney Fagan, 134, 328
Munier, Agatha, 159, 160
Munier, Angela (sic), 373
Munier, Miss, 378
Munnecke, Herr, 290
Murder at the Old Toll House, 124, 549, 559
Murdoch, Bella, 47
Murdoch, Daisy, 638, 639
Murdoch, J. E., 152, 637
Murdock, W., 61
Murelli, Reca, 62
Murielle, Constance, 468
Murillo, Edith, 570
Murio, Louise, 316, 346, 396
Murio-Celli, Mme., 377
Murphy, at Daly's, 232
Murphy, sparring, 143

Murphy, boxer, 576
Murphy (of Joyce and Murphy), 530
Murphy (of Raymond and Murphy), 101, 129, 130, 339
Murphy (of Spencer and Murphy), 547
Murphy, Con T., 4 ff, 167
Murphy, Eddie, 577
Murphy (George) and Shannon (George), 101, 109, 128 ff, 139, 141, 189, 313, 314, 335, 345, 348 ff, 396, 398, 554, 565 ff, 571, 572, 574, 617 (see also Murphy, John, and Mack, Phil)
Murphy, Harry, 49
Murphy, Jerry, fighter, 324, 555 (see Kelly and Murphy)
Murphy (John) and Mack (Phil), 101, 128 ff, 139, 189, 313, 314, 335, 345, 347 ff, 398, 565, 571, 572, 574, 617 (see also Murphy, George, and Shannon, George)
Murphy, John S, 50, 59, 277
Murphy, Joseph, parts, 50, 59, 168, 203, 277, 281, 412, 489, 492, 610
Murphy, Mark (of Murray and Murphy), 109, 110, 115, 616
Murphy, Nick, walker, 149, 150
Murphy, Paddy and Ella, 116, 129, 131, 133, 140, 188, 189, 314 ff, 322, 324, 326, 345, 530, 531, 544, 553 ff, 575, 616, 617
Murphy, Samuel B. (sic), 417
Murphy, Samuel W. (sic), 206
Murphy, Vinton, 155
Murphy and Aloon, 320
Murphy and Daly, 577
Murphy and Miles, 324, 351, 545, 548, 564, 567, 571, 572, 625
Murphy and Welch's Minstrels, 208
Murphy's Campaign, 129
Murphy's Christening, 566
Murphy's Christmas, 130, 345, 572
Murphy's Divorce, 129
Murphy's Dream, 130, 141; casts, 313, 314, 335; 345, 348, 350; cast, 351; 565, 567, 569, 572, 574, 617
Murphy's Trip to New York, 571
Murphy's Uncle, cast, 132
Murphy's Wedding, cast, 100; 128, 345, 350, 572
Murphys, the (of the Olympia Quartette), 396
Murray, variety, 106
Murray, Bella, 199
Murray, David M., 179, 604
Murray, Dominick, parts, 21 ff, 24 ff, 236, 620, 622
Murray, J. Winston, 50, 59, 248, 280, 322, 411, 552 ff
Murray, John H., Circus, 136, 148, 188, 360, 424, 626
Murray, Maggie, 337
Murray, Randolph, 282, 604
Murray, Tom and Henrietta, 113, 115, 126, 127, 140
Murray (Tom E.) and Murphy (Mark), 616
Murray, W. B., 54, 588
Murray and Magrath, 565

Murray and Runnells, 148
Murray, Snow and Robinson, 342
Murray, Snow and Runnells, 327, 396
Murtha, Frank B., 65
Muscle *vs.* Science, 325
Musette, 46, 178, 262, 391, 488, 492
Museums, New York, 143, 364, 365, 578 ff
Music and Notions, 345
Music Conquered, 129
Music Festival (1881), 381 ff; (1882), 598 ff
Music Hall, Brooklyn, 193, 403 ff, 627 ff
Music in a Pawnshop, 100
Musical Four, 618
Musical Miscellany, New York (1879-80), 156 ff; (1880-81), 370 ff; (1881-82), 586 ff
Musical Mixtures, 558
Musical Phalanx, 391
Musikfeind, Der, 511
Musikverein, Greenpoint, 209, 422
Mussy, Mons., 466
Mütter und Sohn, cast, 80; (*see also Mother and Son*)
Muzio, Florence, 316
My Awful Child, 151
My Awful Dad, cast, 4; 7, 55, 168; cast, 608
My First Drunk, 563, 570, 572
My Geraldine, casts, 265, 482; 608, 633
My Hebrew Friend, 545
My Partner, casts, 9, 11, 176; 203; casts, 270, 272; 391, 486, 491, 609
My Son-in-Law, cast, 171
My Turn Next, 422
My Wife and My Mother-in-Law, 312
My Wife's Dentist, cast, 6
Myers, Harry J., 554
Myers, Josie, 1
Myers, L. E., 540
Myers, Mary, 169, 264
Myers, Nettie, 250
Myring, F., 143
Myrtell, Annie, 6, 47
Myrtle Avenue Park, 207, 416 ff, 636 ff
Mystery, The, play, 117
Mystery, The, of the Devil's Swamp, 137
Mysterious Ghosts, 203
Mysterious Murder, The, 318, 319
Mysterious Star, The, cast, 562
Mystic Four, 642

N. G. Pinafore, 102
Nachtwächter, Der, 212
Nacional, La, Societa Spagnuola di Benefi-cenza, 90, 156
Nagle, J. E., Jr., 383, 460
Nagle and Wright, 123
Näherin, Die, cast, 287; 495, 498, 634
Naiad Queen, The, casts, 135, 349
Namenlos, 293
Nan, the Good for Nothing, 530
Nan, the Newsboy, 106, 185, 554
Nana, or, the Blonde Venus, 536
Naomi, play, 326
Naoni, Japanese juggler, 561 ff, 568, 617
Napier, Charlotte, 591

Napoleon Crossing the Alps, biorama, 647
Narciss (or Narcisse), casts, 47, 77; 78; cast, 170; 500
Nasby, Petroleum V, and Widow Bedott, 41
Nash, Belle, 405
Nash, Dan, 105, 127, 140, 189, 210, 335, 624
Nash, George F., 610
Nash, Helen, 624
Nash, J. E., 184, 458, 467, 481
Nash, Nellie, 196
Nash, W, 205, 418
Nast, H. H., 194
Nathans, Philo, circus, 360
National Theatre (1879-80), 123 ff; (1880-81), 330 ff; (1881-82), 550 ff
Nautch Dancing Girls, at Daly's, 233; 317, 318, 397, 536, 623
Naval Cadets, 384
Naval Engagements, 405 (*see Father and Son*)
Navarro, Rafael, 199, 200, 399, 408, 614
Naylor, Tessie, 57
Neary (of Thomas and Neary), 188
Neary, Ed, 136
Neck and Neck, 107, 109
Necker, Bertha, 66 ff, 82, 288 ff, 311, 498 ff, 508
Needham and Kelly, 346
Needles and Clothes Pins, 364
Needles and Hairpins, 315
Needles and Pins, cast, etc., 232, 233, 234; casts, 386, 413 (*for burlesques, see supra*)
Negro Minstrels, 58 ff, 65, 111, 120, 143 ff, 176, 179, 186, 202, 203, 208, 246, 257, 271, 389, 398, 399, 410, 412, 469, 471, 604, 610, 618
Negro performers, 60, 65, 139, 202, 203, 204, 214, 215, 271, 332, 379, 387, 403, 414, 430, 563, 587, 635 (*see also Haverly's Genuine Coloured Minstrels; Jubilee Singers; Non-pareil Coloured Troubadours*)
Neighbourly Neighbours, 353
Neil, Robert, 278
Neilson, Ada, 464, 516, 613
Neilson, Adelaide, farewell parts, 29 ff; 54; parts in Brooklyn, 168; 249, 254, 462
Nellini, Marie, 64
Nelson (of Miles and Nelson), 548
Nelson, Amy, 353, 361, 542, 626
Nelson, Charles, 548
Nelson, Frank, 104, 105
Nelson, George, 126, 127, 314, 346; of the Comedy Four, 345, 352, 353, 396
Nelson, Georgie, 405
Nelson, Geraldine, 197
Nelson, Josephine, 424
Nelson, Marie, 127, 314, 346; of the Comedy Four, 345, 352, 353, 396
Nelson, Mme., and her doves, 148, 319, 342
Nelson, Nellie, 119, 136, 138, 140
Nelson, Pat, 528
Nelson, Sydney, 15 ff, 58
Nelson Association, amateurs, 419
Nelson Family (5), 148, 342, 561
Nelton, Egyptian juggler, 543, 550, 562
Nenemoosha, 365; and her Indian chiefs, 401

Nenemoosha, play, 110
Nero, ballet music from, 632
Nervous Clerk, The, 321
Nestor and Venoa, 530, 555, 558
Neuberger, Sophia, 376, 597, 601
Neuendorff, Adolf, 66 ff; music for play, 72; 86, 224, 288 ff, 311; leads orchestra at Koster and Bial's, 358, 539; takes Wallack's, as Germania Theater, 498 ff; his actors at Terrace Garden, 510, 511
Neumann, Carl, 123, 125, 293
Neville, Charlotte, 41, 58, 265, 360, 389
New Brighton, S. I., 429, 430, 648, 649
New England Supper, 423
New Magdalen, The, cast, 54; 170; cast, 274; cast, with Clara Morris, 439
New Men and Old Acres, 406
New Museum, Brooklyn, 625
New Orleans Opera Troupe, 357, 394
New Orleans University Singers, 158, 159, 191, 193, 194, 200, 206, 208 ff, 215, 399, 404, 407, 424 ff
New Post Office, The, cast, 546
New Profession, The, 154
New Utrecht, 210, 423, 644
New Way, A, to Pay Old Debts, variety farce, 116
New Year's Calls, 557, 565
New Year's Day, 328
New York Athletic Club, 155, 359, 366
New York Athletic Grounds, 151
New Yor.: Central Schützen Corps, 87
New York Choral Union, 594, 597
New York Chorus Society, 379, 594, 596
New York Commandery, No. 55, K. T., 356
New York Hackman, The, 352
New York Hotel, 153
New York in Slices, 137
New York in 1881, play, 568
New York Lodge, No. 330, F. and A. M., 367
New York Miniature Opera Company, 399
New York Miniature Pinafore Company, 427
New York Musical Club, 587
New York Newsboy, The, 337
New York Operetta, 215
New York Philharmonic Club (see Philharmonic Club, New York)
New York Press Club, benefit, 521
New York Quartet (sic), 406
New York Quintet (sic) Club, 591 ff
New York Upside Down, 118
New York Vocal Quartette, 345
New York Vocal Sextette, 628, 629
Now York Vocal Union, 157 ff, 373, 377, 591 ff, 594
Newark Academy of Music, 402
Newbold, Virginia, 40
Newborough, W. B., 360
Newborough, W. H., 38
Newcomb, Ada, 111, 133, 137, 361, 567
Newcomb, Blanche, 272
Newcomb, Bobby, 110, 111, 130 ff, 141, 187, 533, 534
Newcomb, Miss, 179
Newell, Lizzie, 64, 171

Newell, Major, 147, 400
Newell, Oscar M., 161, 191, 212
Newman, Florence, 187
Newton, Lulu, 318
Newton, Stella, 106, 119
Neyer, Ernest, 266, 477
Neygard (or Neygaard), circus, 148, 360
Niantic Club, 645
Nibbe (of Hettinger and Nibbe), 347, 543, 544, 556
Niblo's Garden Theatre (1879-80), 57 ff; (1880-81), 270 ff; (1881-82), 482 ff
Nicholas, R. H., 49
Nichols, C. T., 105, 383
Nichols, E. W., 120
Nichols, Joseph, his Minstrel Troupe, 214
Nichols, Maggie, 117, 361, 414
Nichols, R. C., 155, 369
Nichols, R. M., 218
Nichols's Glass Blowing, 213
Nicholson, John H., 493
Nicht, A, wi' Burns, 629
Nicht, A, wi' the Jacobites, 629
Nichte, Die, des Millionärs, 70
Nick Nax, 340
Nick of the Woods, 65; cast, 109; 552, 620
Nickerson, W. E., 629
Nickinson, John, 568
Nickle, Robert, 343, 557
Nickolds, A. G., 196
Nickolds, Lillie Crane, 196
Nickolds, Mrs. Lillian G., 199, 404, 417
Nicky Nuvel, 124
Nicodemus, 111, 120
Nicolini, 504 ff, 522, 587 ff, 612
Nidecker, E., 595
Niethamer, pianist, 217
Night, A, and a Day in a Volcano (see Volcano, etc.)
Night, A, at Coney Island, 189
Night, A, in a Medical College, 217
Night, A, of Horror, 573
Night, A, of Terror, 338
Night Scenes in New York, 414
Nigri, 263, 264, 355, 466, 473, 474
Nigs from (or on) the Mozambique, 112, 546
Niles, James, 51
Niles (P. J.) and Evans (C. E.), 100, 101, 104, 132, 189, 315, 330, 396 ff, 615, 616
Nilsson, Christine, 26, 32, 251, 306, 309
Nilsson, Knudson, 370
Nilsson Hall, 301, 307, 308, 520
Nine Beauties, The, 184
Ninninger, Pauline, 370
Ninth Regiment and Band, 95, 150, 356, 359, 376, 394, 409
Ninth Symphony (Beethoven's), 382
Nisida, cast, 284
Nixon, Hugh, 125
No Pay, no Cure, cast, 105
No Pinafore, 140, 141
Noah, Rachel, 246
Noble, Florence, 51, 245, 488
Noble, J. W., 192, 399, 628
Noble, Mrs. J. W., 399

Nobles, Milton, 60, 173, 203, 492, 607
Nobody's Daughter, 552
Nocturnal Wedding, A, 340
Nolan, benefit, 190
Nondescripts, 315, 342
Nonentities, 321, 344, 353
Nonpareil Coloured Troubadours, 332, 333, 350, 561, 563, 568, 569, 578, 579, 625
Noonan, Billy, 186
Norah, or, the Robber's Doom, 574
Norah Creina, 126
Norah's Birthday, 322
Norah's Vow, 248
Norcross, Frank, 250
Norcross, J. M., 111, 257, 390
Norcross, J. W., 538
Norcross, J. W., Jr., 470, 508
Norcross's Fifth Avenue Opera Company, 65, 66, 147, 191, 217, 508, 509
Noremac, G. D., walker, 540
Norma, 27, 391
Norman, H. B., 249, 453, 454
Norman, Mrs. H., 165
Norman, Mrs. Helen, 376, 629
Norman, S. P., 467, 470, 538
Norman, Sam, 111 ff, 139, 167, 188
Norris, Frank, 57
North, Levi J., benefit, 399
North, Miss V., 281
North, Winifred, 108, 127
North Pole, lecture on, 582
North Shore Glee Club, S. I., 429
Northcott, Amy, 264
Northport, L. I., 646
Norton, Belle, 191
Norton, Joe, 325, 415, 619
Norton, Miss B., 63
Norton, Nick, manager, 621 ff
Norton, W. H., 6
Norwegian, Björnson speaks in, 368
Norwegian giant, 580, 624
Norwegian Singing Society, 409
Norwood, Daisy, 325, 329, 350, 531, 545, 547, 550, 570, 622
Norwood, Roberta, 10 ff, 177, 227
Not Such a Fool as He Looks, 628, 631
Nourse, D., 47
Nourse, Mrs. D., 47, 385, 488
Nova, Jacob, 217, 419, 420, 429, 430
Nova Scotia midget, 624
Novara, Franco, 304 ff, 392 ff, 516 ff, 537, 591, 612 ff
Novelty Four (with varying combinations), 138, 141, 186, 204, 332, 345, 352, 353, 397, 546, 551, 554, 555, 557, 616, 617
Novelty Hall, Brooklyn, 628
Novelty Theatre, Williamsburgh (1879-80), 202 ff; (1880-81), 410 ff; (1881-82), 632 ff
Novissimo, ballet, 110, 322
Nowlan, J. W., 443
Noxon, Libbie, 31, 277, 621, 634
Nuffer, Kate, 82, 84, 296, 374, 595
Nugent, J. E., 275, 623
Nugent, Kate, 275, 354
Nugent, Paddy, 141, 352

Nuggets, play, 319, 620
Nuit, Une, de la Joie, 533
Nun of Kenmare, 408
Nunez, piano, 597
Nunnemacher, J., 37
Nutt, Commodore, 191

O! diese Männer, 81
Oakes (or Oaks), Dave, 122, 132, 185, 187, 188, 397
Oakey, John, 180, 626
Oakley, Adele, 192
Ober, E. H., 455
Oberist, John, 525
O'Breeno (sic), 577 (see O'Brieno)
O'Brien, manager, 318
O'Brien (of Four Eccentrics), 344, 347, 397
O'Brien (of Megatherian Eight or Four), 138, 340, 351, 564
O'Brien, Charles, 115, 128, 634
O'Brien, Charles and Thomas, 341, 552
O'Brien (Charles and Vic), 125, 414, 556, 564
O'Brien, Dan, 128, 424
O'Brien, Edward, 171
O'Brien, J. J., 57
O'Brien, Sadie, 387
O'Brien, Tom, 115
O'Brien, Tom (of Kelly and O'Brien), 526, 556, 563, 616
O'Brieno, contortionist, 138, 577
O'Connor, Johnny, 545
O'Connor and Willis (Flora), 549, 550
O'Connor's Hall, 154
Octoroon, The, 40, 175, 215
Odd Fellows Hall, S. I., 215, 217
Odd Fellows Männerchor, 206
Odeon, Mme., 321
Odette, cast, review, 445; in German, cast, review, 507
O'Donoghue's Arrival, 326
Oedipus Tyrannus, cast, 455
Oesterreich, Gesang-Verein, 84, 295, 511
Off for Australia, 564
Offenbach, Arrival of, pantomime, 110
Offenbach Memorial, 264
Ogden, J., 40, 245, 491
Ogden, Vivia, 245, 491
O'Gorman's Church Choir Company, 174
O'Gradys, The, 567
O'Gradys, The, at Rehearsal, 341
Oh! Boys, 125
Oh! Hush, 114
Ohrfeige, Eine, um jeden Preis, 511
O'Keefe, J., 538
Olcott, Chauncey, 59
Olcott, Lillian, 610
Old Bushwick Sunday School, 626 ff, 639
Old Cabin Home, The, 126
Old Cross, cast, 279
Old Folks Concerts, 163, 192 ff, 198, 205; by young folks, 207; 208 ff, 407, 421, 422, 626 ff, 638, 641, 648
Old General's Birthday, The, cast, 547

Old Guard Ball, 95, 307, 519
Old Heads and Young Hearts, cast, Wallack's, 3; 6, 7; cast, Wallack's, 170; 172; cast, Wallack's, 223; 224; with Wallack's actors, 613
Old Homestead, The, 42
Old Kentucky Home, The, 346
Old Love Letters, 236
Old Mother Fussy, 333
Old Sailors, play, 628
Old Shipmates, cast, 471, 472; 633
Old Sleuth, 106
Old Soldiers, play, 213
Old Straw Man of New York, 319
Old Toll House, The, 188
Old Veteran, The, 553, 558, 560, 561
Olden, Allie, 548
Oldfield, Emily, 272
O'Leary, walker, 205, 359
O'Leary Belt, contests, 149, 150
O'Leary Tournament, 149
O'Leary Walking Match, 359
Olive, P., amateur, 28
Oliver, C. H., 404, 417
Oliver, J. A., 48
Oliver Twist, 52, 65; cast, 136, 137; 169, 178, 346; with Fanny Davenport, 386, 489; cast, 551; 567, 605, 633
Olivette, 243, 244, cast, 251; 253; cast, 261; 262; casts, 268, 269; condensed, 363, 364; cast, 387; 390, 394, 395; cast, 456; 460; cast, 464; in French, casts, 466, 474; 478; casts, 479, 482, 487; 537; cast, 538; 604, 609; cast, 611
Olivette, burlesque at Pastor's, 316, 317; 528, 529; burlesqued, 329, 343, 355 (see All-I've-Eat; All-of-It)
Olmi, at Pastor's, 316
Olmi, George, 269, 487, 493, 605
Olympia Quartette (of varying membership), 114, 116, 137, 186, 314, 329, 334, 345, 349, 396, 398, 559, 618
Olympia Trio, 545
Olympic Club, 648
Olympic Theatre, Brooklyn (1879-80), 185 ff; (1880-81), 400; (1881-82), becomes the Standard, 621 ff
Olympic Theatre, New York, last season (1879-80), 61 ff
O'Mahoney, E. J., 597
On the Beach, 111, 350
On the Brink, or, the Creole Slave, 327, 331, 332, 543, 544, 550
On the Frontier, 558
On the Trail, cast, 122
One Dime, cast, 619
One Hundred Wives, cast, 244, 245; 389, 412; cast, 491; 633
One Night in a Bar-room, 119
One Night's Rest, 136
One o'Clock, cast, 322
One of the Finest, cast, 472
One of Our People (Einer von uns're Leut'), 607
One Too Many for Him, 155

One-legged performers, 116, 118 ff, 124, 134, 185, 188, 204, 326, 327, 354, 532, 534, 542, 543, 547, 624, 625
O'Neil, Hattie, 28, 608
O'Neil, James, 415
O'Neil (James) and Conroy (John), 121, 139, 141, 320, 325, 330, 337, 341, 361, 577
O'Neil, Kitty, 100, 104, 135, 187, 189, 315, 316, 330, 340, 353, 397, 615, 616, 618
O'Neill, James, parts, 11, 228, 230, 241, 243, 246, 281, 439, 453, 465, 469, 483, 484, 488, 492, 607
Onkel Knusperich, cast, 72, 73
Only a Farmer's Daughter, casts, 390, 412, 633
Only a Tramp, 486
Only Little Four, 136
Onofri Brothers (Achille, Charles, Forteen and Oreste), 42, 343, 349, 385, 525, 565, 566, 571, 572
Onsley, negro, 60
Open-air theatre (Aberle's), 110
Opera, Italian (see Italian Opera)
Opera in English (see Abbott, Emma, and Rôze, Marie)
Opera Ball, 540
Opéra-bouffe (see Aimée and Marié, Paola; also Cottrelly, Mathilde; Geistinger, Marie; Melville, Emilie)
Opera Buffers, 330
Opera di Camera, 64
Opera House, Flushing, 426, 645
Opera House, Jamaica, 427 ff
Operationen, cast, 72
Operti, put out of Daly's, 18
Operti, Clotilda, 38
Ophelia, Ellie Wilton as, 29; Nard Almayne as, 34, 47, 48; Mrs. Bandmann as, 47; Louise Muldener as, 52; 451; Ellen Cummens as, 183; Genevieve Stebbins as, 270; Nellie Boyd as, 280; Anna Boyle as, 282; Bella Pateman as, 451, 459; Marie Wainwright as, 461; Lillie Joyce as, 465
Opleska Agiosco, 409
Oratorical Conest, 152
Oratorio Society (1879-80), 165, 166; 307; (1880-81), 380, 381; (1881-82), 603
Orchestrion Hall, Williamsburgh, 421, 636
Ordey, Karoly and Augusta, 101, 140, 532, 535, 553, 558, 562, 568
Ordinary Conversation, 557
O'Reardon, 105, 129, 133
O'Reilly, John Boyle, 615
Organ openings, 403
Oriental Hotel, Manhattan Beach, 164, 601
Original Little Four, 332, 348
Orlandini, 311, 374, 378, 391, 594, 629
Orlando (As You Like It), G. Levick as, 39; E. Price as, 169; H. M. Pitt as, 220; Luigi Lablache as, 390; George Clarke as, 463
Orme, Gertrude, 470, 478, 537
Orndorff and McDonald, 326, 543, 550, 561, 569, 626
O'Rourke, James, 313
Orphan Chile, The, 126
Orphean Glee Club, New York, 430

Orphéon Français, 88, 89, 95, 301, 308, 513
Orpheus Glee Club, 646
Orpheus in der Unterwelt, cast, 79
Orpheus Quartette, 642
Orr, Ohio giant, 400
Orrin Brothers, circus, 155
Ortloff, 205, 417
Ortori, ballet, 57
Ortori, Leonard, 272
Osborne, Charles, 200
Osborne, Harry, 136
Osborne, Henrietta, 37
Osborne, Maude, 272
Osburn, Sophie, 181, 183, 393
Oscar Wilder, farce, 566
Oscawana Island, 87
Osgood, E. Aline, 592, 596, 599, 600, 602, 632
O'Shaughnessy Guards, 335, 345, 571
Osmond, Maude, 114
Ostrich exhibited, 359
O'Sullivan, Steve, wrestler, 324
Othello, casts, 7, 29, 31; 52, 95; with ama-
   teurs, 97; 170; casts, 183, 184, 242, 244,
   248; cast, 282; 311; recited, 366, 368; 384,
   289, 393, 449, 450, 459, 463, 464, 520, 605,
   609, 642
Othello, John McCullough as, 7, 170, 248, 389,
   463, 609; Edwin Booth as, 29, 52, 184, 449,
   459, 609; J. C. McCollom as, 29, 183;
   Frederic Robinson as, 31, 52; John H. Bird
   as, 97; Salvini as, 242, 244, 311, 393;
   Lawrence Barrett as, 450, 520, 605; Ed-
   mund Collier as, 463; George Edgar as,
   464
Othello at San Francisco Minstrels, 363, 364
Otter, negro, 60
Ottmann, A. F., 377
Otto, a German, 257, 274, 281, 389
Ottolengui, Helen, 94, 237, 269, 471
Oudin, Eugene, 89, 155, 159, 160, 162, 596, 630
Oudin, J. A., 155
Ouida, or, a Woman's Vengeance, 530
Our Alabama Home, 341, 581
Our Aldermen, 396
Our American Boys, 115
Our American Cousin, as Lord Dundreary,
   cast, 44; 53, 169, 274
Our American Minister, 582
Our Bachelors, cast, 169; 461; cast, 609
Our Ball, farce, 396
Our Bijah, 147
Our Boarding House, 60, 202; casts, 244, 268,
   489, 620
Our Boys, as Die Herren Eltern, 67; with
   amatuers, 200; 210, 212; amateur cast,
   369; with amateurs, 408; 423, 429; with
   amateurs, 583
Our Boys, farce of the American Four, 137,
   334
Our Candidate, cast, 48, 49; 65, 621, 622
Our Candidates, cast, 167
Our Chateau Mabille, 548
Our City Politics, farce, 396
Our Claude Duval, burlesque, 528
Our Club, 542

Our Country Boarders, 395
Our Daughters, cast, 40; 202
Our First Families, cast, 232
Our Gentlemen Friends, 263
Our German Senator, cast, 170; 203; cast, 275,
   276; 281, 386
Our Girls, cast, Wallack's, 2; 150; cast, 170
Our Goblins, casts, 42, 179; 257; cast, 390
Our Happy German Home, 129
Our Hash House, 337, 338, 635
Our Irish Flats, 345, 347, 348
Our John, What Shall We Do with Him? 626
Our Mother-in-Law, 273
Our New Clergyman, 367
Our New Postman, 553, 569, 571, 575
Our Old Cabin Home, 118
Our Pleasure Party, 564
Our Saviour's Life, 403, 404
Our School Girls, burlesque, 316; 387, 526
Our Second Families, 314
Our Southern Home, 336, 338
Our Torchlight Parade, 362, 363
Our Wedding Day, 353
Ours, 276; casts, 383, 384, 608
Out for a Stroll, 544
Out of Patience, 617
Out of the Dark, 324, 541
Outram, L. S., 33, 47
Over the Stile, 527, 553, 554, 556 ff, 617
Overton, Charles, 465
Owen, W. F., 28, 29, 45, 46, 174, 243, 244, 267,
   305, 605
Owens (of Original Little Four), 332, 348
Owens (of Four Aces), 564, 565, 567
Owens (of Tierney and Owens), 635
Owens, James, wrestler, 185
Owens, Jennie, 595, 596
Owens, John E., parts, 253, 447, 448
Owens, Tom, 215
Oxen, performing, 148
Oxygen, 172
Oyster Bay, L. I., 646
Oysters, farce, 123

P. G. Gilfore, farce, 553
Pacra, Mlle., 239
Padgett, J. C., 63, 176, 191, 234, 385, 470, 621
Pagay, Josephine, 67 ff
Page, Ada, 338, 564, 567
Page, Walter, 58
Paglieri, Mlle., 61
Pain's fireworks, 409
Paine, H. K., music for Oedipus, 455
Paine, Henry Gallup, 155; his play, 585
Paine, Ira A., 132, 341, 342, 414
Palestine Commandery, Ball, 307, 520
Palles (Joe) and Cusick (John), 544, 562, 624
Palm Garten, 295
Palmer, A. M., 224 ff, 244, 483, 484
Palmer, A. N., 63, 174
Palmer, G. M., 269
Palmer, G. W., 316 (see supra)
Palmer, H. J., 243
Palmer, J., 600

INDEX

Palmer, Joseph, 607
Palmer, Minnie, 9, 11, 45, 145, 168, 175, 383, 523
Palzor, James H., 262
Panchot, P. J., walker, 149, 540
Panchot Brothers, 150
Panorama, 195, 369, 403, 642
Panto and Mino, 420
Pantomime, 27, 28, 34, 102, 104, 110 ff, 119 ff, 141, 148, 183, 186, 218, 219, 280, 333, 337 ff, 340 ff, 413, 473, 545, 546, 552, 558, 608, 616 ff, 621, 631, 633, 635, 636
Papa hat's erlaubt, 510
Papini, singer, 97, 163, 182, 375
Parabola Hall, S. I., 648
Paradise Lost, scenes from, 640
Pardy, actor, 33
Parepa Hall, 84, 85, 298, 512, 582
Parham, Charles, 262
Pariser Taugenichts, 81
Parisian Circus, 146
Parisian Folly Troupe, 104
Park, Kate, 582
Park Theatre, Brooklyn (1879-80), 167 ff; (1880-81), 383 ff; (1881-82), 604 ff; closed for Garfield's death, 604
Park Theatre, New York (1879-80), 43 ff; (1880-81), 258 ff; (1881-82), 472 ff
Parker (of De Lacey and Parker), 542
Parker, Anna, 592
Parker, C. W., 46
Parker, Dick, 128 ff, 140 (see Parker's American Theatre)
Parker, Florence, 612
Parker, George, 268
Parker, Georgie, 103, 138, 347, 533, 554
Parker, Harry, minstrel, 59
Parker, Harry, and dogs, 111, 141, 147, 314, 320, 330, 333, 340, 344, 351, 364, 396, 397, 519, 526, 532, 545, 551 ff, 560, 574, 615, 616, 625
Parker, J. Ross, 624
Parker, Lizzie, 184
Parker, Nellie, 121, 133, 136, 187, 188, 318, 322, 324, 346, 353, 397, 535, 562, 619
Parker, Richard (of Boston Quartette), 533
Parker, Rose, 259, 260
Parker, Susie, 218, 412, 480
Parker Sisters (Georgie and Lizzie), 101, 130, 348, 350, 396, 414
Parker Twin Brothers, 566, 567, 572, 625
Parker's (Dick) American Theatre (1880-81), 352 ff; (1881-82), 573 ff
Parker's (H. M.), Combination, 317
Parkes, George, 13 ff, 58, 173, 177, 253, 259, 263, 444
Parkhurst, Mrs. G. H., 393
Parkinson, Morris, 630
Parks (Megatherian Eight), 138, 340
Parks, George R., 246
Parmental, Frank, 48, 147
Parnell, Charles Stewart, lecture, 150
Parnell, Mrs. Delia, 418
Parnell Dramatic Association, 420
Paroxyamalists, 536

Parr, Linden L., 208
Parselle, John, parts, 10 ff, 226 ff, 437 ff, 607
Parsloe, Charles T., 9, 176, 203, 270, 391, 486, 491, 609
Parsons, Charles H., 180, 393, 546, 614
Partie Picquet, Eine, 501
Partington, Kate, 279, 411, 615
Partington, Sallie, 307
Passant, Le, 241
Passing Regiment, The, casts, 444, 608; 634 (see also Krieg im Frieden)
Passion Play, 242
Pasta, Felicita, 110, 532, 533
Pastor, Tony, 51, 54, 56, 94, 100 ff, 172, 202, 274, 276, 277, 314 ff, 367, 387, 474, 487, 489; his Jubilee, 518, 519; 520, 525 ff, 585, 618
Pastor's (Tony) Theatre or Opera House, 100 ff; (1880-81), 314 ff; his new Theatre (1881-82), 525 ff
Pateman, Bella, 449, 450, 609
Pateman, Robert, 450, 459
Patience, with juveniles, 435; casts, 451, 458; 459, 464; casts, 467, 470; 474; casts, 478, 481; 482, 485; burlesque, at Pastor's, 520; cast, 527; real opera, with Lillian Russell, at Pastor's, 529; cast, 609; 611; two casts, 613; cast, 619
Patience Wilde, burlesque, 471
Patients, or, Bunion Salve's Bride, 581
Patterson, Johnny, 360, 553
Patti, Adelina, 309, 456, 457; at Germania, in opera, reviews, 504 ff; 517; engaged for Academy, 522; concerts, return, reviews, 587; in Brooklyn, horses taken from carriage, 612; 613
Patti, Carlotta, 25, 156 ff, 180
Pattison, J. N., 368, 373, 595
Paul, Eugenia, 51, 52, 436
Paul, W. A., 48
Paul, W. M., 110
Paul and Virginia, casts, 51, 167, 251; 385; in French, 466; cast, 487
Paulding, Frederick, 12, 250, 489
Paullin, Louise, 247, 272, 388, 412
Paur, A., 296
Pauvres de Paris, as Life in New York, 336, 352; as Poor of New York, 106, 107, 323
Pauvrette, as The Snow Flower, 267
Pavilion Hotel, New Brighton, S. I., 217, 429, 430, 648
Pavilion Pier, North River, 300
Paxton, G., 464
Payne, Adele, 619
Payne, Lizzie, 318, 558
Payne, Mrs. L., 200
Payne, Mrs. O. N., 197, 198, 626
Peabody, Kate, 324
Peakes, H. C., 251, 269, 387, 478
Peakes, James G., 168, 177, 220, 387, 478
Pearl, Little, 618
Pearl, Maggie, 139
Pearl of Savoy, The, 384, 489, 492, 607
Pearsall, A. E., 425, 644
Pearsall, Lillie, 639

Pearson, Frank, 64
Pearson, H., Jr., 1 ff, 220 ff, 432 ff
Pearson, Harry, Sr., 390, 463, 489, 605
Peasants' Festival, 392
Pease, A. H., 22, 52, 161, 193, 246, 287, 378, 408
Pease, Alta, 611
Peasley, John and Lea, 101, 128, 130, 132, 137, 141, 186, 187, 330, 340, 341, 348, 352, 396, 398, 535, 536, 552, 553, 556, 557, 568 ff, 574, 575, 618
Peasley and Vennetta, 544, 548, 558, 562, 569
Pech, James, 162
Pechschulze, 291, 293
Peck, Nellie, 41
Pedanto, man fly, 624
Pedestrian Hall, Brooklyn, 193
Pedestrians, 37, 120, 142, 150, 205, 210, 348, 359, 540; burlesque of, 99
Pedro, clown, 532, 625
Peel Yourself, 134, 137, 334, 335, 560, 574, 624
Peep o' Day Boys, 638
Pege, Herr, 76
Pegram, walker, 150
Pelham (of New York Vocal Quartette), 345
Pell (James) and Lewis (Tom), 135, 396
Pell, Joseph, 326
Pell, Kate, 323
Pellini, singer, 310
Peltier, Charles, 114
Pelton, Mrs., 213
Pemberton, T. Y., 404
Pendleton, Mark, 229, 259 ff, 269, 276, 488, 606
Pendragon, cast, 464, 465
Pendy, John, 65, 110, 117, 122, 128, 139, 141, 323, 329, 332, 339, 353, 544
Penfield, S. N., 593, 598
Penley, W. S., 473
Penn's Aunts among the Pirates, 104
Penner, Rosa, 630
Pennoyer, Mrs. M. A., 246, 453, 454
Pennsylvania (University of), football, 582
Penny, William, 392
Penzance Pirates in a Nutshell, 340
Peponelli, Mlle., 536
Pepper, Harry, 481, 529
Percival, W. J., 268
Percy, Christine, 100, 531, 552
Percy, Fred, 46; his play, 179; 262
Percy, Ida, 422, 643
Percy, Townsend, his play, 258
Percy Sisters (Christine and Anna), 552
Perdicaris, Ion, his play, 33, 34
Perfection, 395, 542
Périchole, La, cast, 32; 36, 176, 264; cast, 466
Périn, A. F., 300
Perkins, Carrie, 49, 178, 180, 255, 256
Perkins, Eli, 365, 408
Pernigotti, Santina, 303
Perplexing Predicament, A, 622
Perrine's, C. E., Ideal Dramatic and Comedy Company, 627, 628; his Juvenile Company, 405
Perring, Agnes, 234, 442 ff

Perry (of Four Eccentrics), 134, 314, 518, 562, 563
Perry, Irene, 63, 452, 459, 609
Perry, J., 245
Perry, J. H., Post, 195
Perry, Rufus L., 647
Perry and Hughes, 102
Person, Eleanor, 636
Perugini, Giovanni, 251, 252, 457, 615
Peters (of Burlesque Trio), 564, 567
Peters, Charles, 47
Peters, G., 83
Peters, J. F., 31, 65, 215, 318
Peters, Mrs. Charles, 476
Peters, Mrs. J. W., 407
Petit Duc, Le, casts, 32, 36; 97, 183; cast, 263
Petit Faust, Le, cast, 33
Petite Mariée, La, 32
Petite Muette, La, 36
Petri, Frl., 76
Petrovich, singer, 26, 180, 182
Petruchio, Edwin Booth as, 22, 52, 95, 450, 609
Pettingill, Joe (of the American Four), 101, 103, 133, 137 ff, 186, 190, 334, 335, 341, 347 ff, 383, 398, 519, 526, 530, 534, 554, 556, 557, 567
Pettit (Charles) and White (James W.), 126, 130, 187, 326
Pettit, S. S., 114, 126
Pettitt, Henry, co-author, 223
Pfannenschmidt, 83
Pfarrer, Der, von Kirchfeld, cast, 74, 75; 286, 287; 497
Pfau, Louis, 36, 182, 538, 613
Pfyffe, Charles, 281
Phèdre, Bernhardt, criticism, 241
Phelps, concert, 25
Phelps, Anna, 198
Phelps, E. C., his symphony, 182; 200
Phelps, L. A., tenor, 156, 180
Philadelphia Club, 154
Philadelphia Church Choir Company, 63
Philadelphia Glee Club, 375
Philadelphia Quartet Club, 370
Philharmonic Alcazar, 578
Philharmonic Assembly, 637, 638
Philharmonic Chorus, Brooklyn, 407
Philharmonic Club, New York, 157 ff, 298, 371 ff, 395, 587 ff, 591 ff, 627, 629, 631, 649
Philharmonic Quartette, 188
Philharmonic Quintette, 82
Philharmonic Society, Brooklyn (1879-80), 201; (1880-81), 409, 410; (1881-82), 632
Philharmonic Society, New York, 84; (1879-80), 164, 165; 310; (1880-81), 379, 380; (1881-82), 601, 602
Philharmonic Society, Staten Island, 216, 217
Philipp, actor, 499 ff
Phillion, Achille, 114, 331, 415
Phillion, Emma, 114, 331, 415
Phillipps, Adelaide, 181, 238, 393, 611
Phillipps, Mathilde, 166, 455, 456
Phillips, bass, 587
Phillips, A. S., 412
Phillips, Bertie, 205

INDEX

Phillips, Eugene, 362
Phillips, Gus, 246, 280, 387, 551, 554, 639, 640
Phillips, H. B., 65, 169, 267, 453, 633
Phillips, John, 266, 550, 570
Phillips, Laura, 179, 414
Phillips, Mrs. E. J., parts, 10 ff, 94, 226 ff; compared with Fanny Morant, 228; parts, 388, 437 ff, 607
Phillips, Mrs. Gus, 280, 551
Phillips, Philip, 419
Phillips, Wendell, 152
Phillips Brothers (John and Charles), 550
Philomathian Society, 629
Phœnix, Walter, 341
Phœnix, The, 60; cast, 173; 203, 492
Photos, play, 277, 412, 481, 488, 604
Piatt, Don, dramatist, 174
Pickert, Willis, 120, 121, 141, 187, 188, 314, 320, 332, 333, 336, 345, 347, 352, 398, 545, 561, 564, 568, 570, 574, 616
Picnic, A, at Jones's Wood, 548
Picnics, German, 86 ff; French, 89; 200, 645
Picture, The, cast, 33
Pidgeon, John, Punch and Judy, 136, 565
Pieper, Carl, 376
Pier No. 1, North River, concerts, 379
Pierce, A., walker, 149
Pierce, Emma, 38, 52, 169, 178, 179, 488
Pierce, John, 105
Piercy, S. W., 54, 171, 174, 281, 391, 412, 450, 491
Pieri, Frank, 519
Pieris, Adele, 595
Pieris, Nully, 140
Pierson, Emily, 642
Pierson, Harry, 28, 29, 485
Pierson, J. G., 153, 209, 214, 642
Pierson, Miss E. V., 594
Pigeon show, 579
Pigeons, performing, 360
Pigs exhibited, 346
Pike, C. M., 470
Pike, Dollie, 65, 267
Pike, Flora, 459, 520, 526 ff
Pike, Maurice, 111, 353, 354, 458, 493, 545
Pillaire (variously spelled), cannon-ball act, 104, 112, 120, 189, 325
Pillar of Gold, with Little Todd, 333
Pilliard, Mlle., 310, 394
Pinafore, H. M. S., directed by Gilbert and Sullivan, cast, 35; 48; with Boston Ideals, 58; cast, juvenile, 63; with Philadelphia Church Choir, cast, 63; 66, 90; Harry Miner's, 135; with children, 141, 147, 152, 154; at Aquarium, cast, 146; with Columbia College cast, 155; Church Choir cast, 174; cast, 181; Boston Ideals, 182; a female cast, 185; Norcross Company, 191; Young Apollo Club, 191, 192, 194; with children, 215; 217; Boston Ideals, 238; 266, 303, 395; with children, 397; by church choirs, 399; with children, 427; Boston Ideals, 456; 458; cast, 478; 542, 609
Pinafore, H. M. S., burlesques, 103, 113, 118, 119, 127, 187, 534

[728]

Pinafore in Fifteen Minutes, 113, 131, 188
Pinero, A. W., and The Money Spinner, 432
Pink Dominos, variety farce, 549
Pinky (or Pinkey), Little, 205, 407, 420, 638, 640, 642, 647
Pinner, Max, 159, 161, 297
Pinow, Herr, 67 ff
Pinto, singer, 505 ff, 612
Piper Heidsick, or, Lights of Gotham, 635
Pipes, Jeems, of Pipesville (Stephen Massett), 373
Pipley Family, The, in Europe, 195, 206
Pique, casts, 52, 168; 203, 297, 386, 413
Pirate, The, and the Faithful Ape, 113
Pirate's Dream, The, 341
Pirates of Penn-Yann, 316
Pirates of Penzance, The, cast, reviews, 35, 36; cast, 38; in Brooklyn, 181 ff; cast, 184; Boston Ideals, cast, review, 238; 253, 266, 392; with children, 399; 426, 428, 455; cast, 458; amateur casts, 614; 646
Pirates of Penzance, The, burlesques, 104, 144, 188, 317, 327, 347, 557
Pirates of Pinafore, 327, 347, 557
Pirates of Sandy Hook, 144, 188
Pirates of the Savannah, 531
Pirates' Legacy, The, 530
Piron, French actor, 239
Pitt, H. M., début, parts, reviews, 219 ff; 243, 276, 389, 443 ff, 608
Pixley, Annie, 49, 50, 178, 203, 275, 281, 389, 412, 488, 492, 606, 633
Place aux Dames, 648
Placide, Alice, 330, 331, 532
Plague, The, of My Life, 209
Planter's Wife, The, cast, 279
Plattdeutscher Club, Williamsburgh, 639
Plattdeutsches Volksfest, 88, 513
Players, The, farce, 138
Pleasant Companions, The, 362, 363
Pleasant Neighbour, A, 277, 355
Plighted by Moonlight, 538
Plumb, George A., 155
Plummer, Ella, 375
Plunkett (of Marlow and Plunkett), 535
Plunkett, Addie, 261, 465
Plunkett, Charles, 261, 461
Plymouth Church, Brooklyn, 192 ff, 403 ff, 626 ff
Plymouth Rock, steamer, 155
Plympton, Eben, parts, 21 ff, 236, 265, 447, 517
Pocahontas, cast, 338
Poe monument, benefits for, 22, 244, 310, 439
Poetic Proposals, 648
Poggenburg, Frau, 83
Points, farce, 349
Poland, Pollie, 469
Police, walking match, 359
Police, sell tickets, 483
Policeman's Troubles, A, 562
Political Candidate, The, 556
Political Coons, The, 355
Polk, J. B., parts, 9 ff, 37, 38, 179, 244, 268, 467, 480

INDEX

Polk, Julia, 255, 261, 361, 388, 394, 585, 595, 596
Pollak, Fanny, 56, 82, 84, 86, 161, 164, 198 ff, 374, 405, 591
Polo game, burlesque, 19
Polo Grounds, New York, 582
Polytechnic, Burbank's, 155
Pomme d'Api, 98
Pomp, play, 320
Pompey's Patients, 131
Pond, O. W., and Palestine Arabs, 404
Ponisi, Mme., parts, 1 ff, 54, 170, 221 ff; 384, 432 ff, 611, 613
Ponitz, Herr, 290
Poole, John F., 187, 314; at Niblo's, 482 ff; retires from Grand Opera House, 490
Poole, Mrs. Charles W., 14 ff, 58, 173, 231, 264, 272, 386, 389, 413
Poole and Donnelly, 50
Poor Jo, 94, 107
Poor of Ireland, The, 415
Poor of New York, The, cast, 106, 107; 323
Poor Pillicoddy, 192, 194, 206, 215
Poore, Charles, 476
Pope, Henry W., 310
Pope, W. H., 220 ff, 432, 449
Pope, W. M., violin, 403
Port Jefferson, L. I., 646
Port Richmond, S. I., 429
Port Wine vs. Jealousy, 572
Porter, E. M., 272
Porter's, Dr. Church, Williamsburgh, 416 ff, 638 ff
Portia (Julius Cæsar), Kate Meek as, 461
Portia (Merchant of Venice), Mrs. Bowers as, 29; Anna Boyle as, 282; Hedwig Hesse as, 284; Marie Wainwright as, 461
Porträt, Das, der Geliebten, 293
Porträtdame, Die, 282, 283
Posner, Dave, 330, 550
Post, F. J., 327, 328, 543
Post, Lilly, 480 ff, 538, 609
Post, Mrs., 33
Post, Mrs. E. M., 270, 468
Post Rankin, G. A. R., 196, 197
Post Shaw, G. A. R., 648
Postiglioni, I, del Villagio d'Albi, 302
Postillon de Lonjumeau, Le, 97, 98
Postillon von Müncheberg, Der, 60
Potter, Ernest F., 193
Potter, Helen, 365
Potter, Josephine, 389
Potter, Mrs. James Brown, 236
Poultry show, 401
Pour Prendre Congé, cast, 389
Poverty Flat, 574, 576
Poverty vs. Riches, 319
Poverty vs. Wealth, 325, 330
Powell, A. J., organ, 196
Powell, Edward, 253, 476
Powers (late of Taylor and Powers), 329
Powers, Dan, 563, 569, 575
Powers, Francis F., 404 ff, 630, 642
Powers, George (of Johnson and Powers), 143, 179, 362, 580

Powers, Georgie, 117, 120, 563, 569, 575
Powers, James T., 107 ff, 117, 122, 188, 267, 480
Powers, Jen, 112, 116, 117, 120, 563, 569, 575
Powers, Molly, 538
Powers Brothers, 189, 541, 566, 567
Poyard, parts, 33, 98, 263, 466, 474
Poznanski, 235
Praeger, Adelaide, 255
Prairie Flower, 108, 320
Prairie Waif, The, 278, 280, 412, 491, 619
Prasini, Maria, 456, 457, 614
Prätorius, parts, 493, 510
Pratt, Charles, 28, 55, 160, 163, 198, 373, 375, 423, 538, 591, 594 ff, 601, 627
Pratt, Deane W., 182, 369, 612, 614
Pratt, Harry, 38, 272, 390, 435
Pratt, Jennie, 598
Pratt, Lucy, 198
Pré aux Clercs, 36, 37, 98
Preciosa, cast, 78; 293, 634
Prehn, concert, 374
Prehn, George, 85, 279, 408, 630
Prehn, H., 84, 372
Prejudice, cast, 278
Prescott, Marie, parts, 24, 33, 242, 243, 311, 621
Prescott, Nellie, 459
Prescott Sisters (Lizzie and Carrie), 117, 189
Press, The, Its Power for Good and for Evil, lecture, 152
Pressey, Emma, 478
Prestige, Fanny, 11
Preston, Isabella, 62, 212, 547
Preston, May, 106, 337
Pretty Barmaids, 362
Pretty Piece of Business, A, 367, 406
Prevost, singer, 517 ff, 537, 613
Price, Edwin, 52, 168, 169, 178
Price, J. W. Parsons, 598 (see Price, Mr. Parson)
Price, Mark, 246, 488
Price, Mr. Parson, 163 (see Price, J. W. Parsons)
Price Brothers (Harry and Theo), 566
Priest, Lizzie, 587, 600, 640
Priestley, Sophia, 372, 595
Primary Election, 396
Prime, Master, 141
Primier, Paul, 406
Prince Achmet, 178; cast, 256; 306, 388
Prince Eugene, opera, 399, 402
Prince Methusalem, in German, cast, 283; 284, 419
Princess Carpillona, cast, 64
Princess of Bagdad, The, casts, 464, 503, 504
Princess of Thule dramatised, 493
Princess Toto, 48
Princess Tott, play, 337
Princesse, La, de Trebizonde, 98
Princesse Georges, La, 246, 247
Princeton College Glee Club, 375, 430, 596
Princeton football, 582
Pringle, Ralph, 562, 564, 570
Prior, Mrs. J. J., 259, 263, 270, 411, 488

Pritchard, concert, 596
Pritchard, Spencer, 279
Privat, Mlle., 466
Private Secretary, The (Der Bibliothekar), 71, 72
Prize in walking match, 540
Prizes for billiards, 582, 583
Probir-Mamsell, Die, 66
Proctor, Agnes, 169, 263, 264, 485
Proctor, Joseph, 65, 552, 620
Proctor, Richard A., 152, 193, 368, 394
Produce Exchange Glee Club, 601
Professional matinées, Salvini, 244; Bernhardt, 246
Professor, The, act of at benefit, before production, 235; production, cast, 237; 446, 471, 492, 610, 634
Professor Opstein, casts, 439, 610
Prospect Association Ball, 584
Prospect Garden, 294
Prospect Park Concerts, 200, 409, 632
Protean parts, 106, 113, 114, 117, 121, 136, 138, 267, 319 ff, 325, 331, 530, 552
Provident Institution for Working Women, 246
Prox, Carl, 399
Puerner, Charles, 57
Puff of Smoke, A, 535
Pulcinella geloso della Moglie, 302, 515
Pulcinella Prestidigitore e l'Allogio Militare, etc, 302
Pullman Palace Car (see Tourists in a Pullman Palace Car)
Puls, Herr, 74 ff, 82, 283 ff
Punch and Judy, 113, 124, 126, 136, 147, 400, 423, 565
Pupin, Mme., 374
Purim Ball, 95, 197, 299, 308, 520
Puritani, I, casts, 27, 305; 306, 308; cast, 392
Pygmalion and Galatea, casts, amateurs, 183, 393, 399; with Mary Anderson, 453, 454, 455, 488; 607, 634
Pyramid of Gold, The, 556
Python exhibited, 579

Quadrinfield, rifle-shooting, 337
Quaker City Quartette (of varying membership), 531, 544, 565, 573, 625
Quaker City Serenaders, 186
Quasimodo, play, 323
Quecksilber, 74
Queen, Burt, ventriloquist, 126, 330, 347, 348, 566, 571, 572
Queen, Fred, 312, 524
Queen, John, parts, 98 ff, 311 ff, 524, 525
Queen, The, and Her Babe, 188
Queen Mab, dwarf, 148
Queen of Bohemia, read by Joseph Hatton, 235
Queen's Evidence, 554, 555
Quick (of Four Kings), 415
Quicksell, Emma, 601
Quiet Evening, A, 131
Quiet Family, A, 207
Quigley, Ida, 105
Quigley, W. S., 10 ff, 276, 437 ff

Quilter (Dick) and Goldrich (Pete), 130, 139, 140, 281, 317, 535, 545, 557, 620
Quinlan, J. J. (of Horseshoe Four), 553, 562
Quinn, Arthur Hobson, 37, 312, 486, 524
Quinn, Eddie, 59
Quinn, T. J., 354
Quits, cast, 442, 443

Raberg, Franziska, 284 ff, 294
Raberg, Frau, 637
Raberg, Herr, 66 ff, 288 ff, 311, 498 ff, 510
Rachel, 241
Radcliffe, George B., 110, 535, 536
Radical Cure, A, cast, 47
Raffayolo, 371, 537, 601
Rafferty Blues, Parade of, 101
Raggett, singer, 424
Railroad Car Conductors' Parade, 363
Rainbow Revels, 43
Rainer Family, 539, 540
Rainford, Milton, 28, 29, 250, 488
Rainforth, Harry, 263, 386, 437
Rainforth, Minnie, 112, 118
Raising the Wind, 170
Rajade Troupe, 28, 271, 532, 618
Ralton, D. E., 57, 62, 471, 547
Ramirez Family (Joseffy, Guillamo and La Belle Marie), 533, 559, 575
Ramirez's Spanish Troubadours, 350, 351, 550, 559
Ramsay, Walden, 10 ff, 226 ff, 388, 412, 437 ff, 483, 488, 607
Ramsden, Daisy, 255, 256, 351, 503
Ramsden, Lillian, 560
Rand, L. F., 29, 43, 270, 390, 465
Rand, L. O., 472
Rand, Rosa, 7, 167, 170, 202, 275, 385
Randall, Adelaide, 478, 538, 649
Randall, Jessie, 369
Randall, W. T., 429
Randalls, P. (of Olympia Quartette), 329, 334, 345, 545, 559
Randolph, Bessie, 123, 125, 127, 332, 337
Randolph, Eva, 275
Randolph, Jessie, 386, 476
Randolph, Miss A., 473
Ranger, The, cast, 115
Rank, Bernhard, 66 ff, 288 ff, 311, 499 ff, 528
Rankin, Adela, 367, 406, 647
Rankin, McKee, parts, 53, 54, 170, 243, 244, 275, 280, 389, 468, 469, 484, 485, 492, 607
Rankin, Mrs. McKee (Kitty Blanchard), 53, 54, 170, 243, 244, 275, 280, 389, 468, 469, 484, 485, 489, 492, 607
Rankin, William, Carl, Richard, 102, 132, 172, 314, 346, 374, 396, 534, 551
Rankine, Belle, 205, 420
Ranous, A. V., 278
Ranous, W. J., 8
Ranous, W. V., 520
Ransom, Helen, 620
Ransom, Nellie, 24
Ransone, J. W., 61, 101, 255, 320, 388, 552, 553, 569, 622
Ransone, Mrs. J. W., 61

Raphael, Sara, 32, 36, 88, 98, 148
Rapid Transit *vs.* Slow Coaches, 186
Rascal Pat, That, 209
Rasori, concert, 592
Rassiga's Bowery Bay Pavilion, 212; his Franklin House, Astoria, 424; his Hall, Astoria, 211
Rathbone (or Rathbun), Josie, 65, 112
Rat-i-fi-ca-tion, 550
Rattenfänger, Der, von Hameln, cast, 289, 290; 292, 503
Räuber, Die, cast, 73, 77; 293; casts, 496, 503
Raubmörder, Der, 498
Ravel, C. W., 541, 549
Ravel, Grimaldi, 617
Ravelli, 304 ff, 371, 391 ff, 517 ff, 537, 591, 612 ff
Ravello, 532
Ravels, 111
Ravené, Bertha, 300, 513
Raven, The, read, 310
Raven's Daughter, cast, 443
Raw Recruit, A, 619
Ray, Billy and Maggie, 118, 140
Ray, E. C., Jr., 97
Ray, Thomas, 99, 524
Raymon, May, 389
Raymond, Ada, 125
Raymond, Blanche, 64
Raymond, Henriette, 28
Raymond, J. F., 27, 492
Raymond, John T., as Ichabod Crane, 1; as Mark Meddle, 7; 10, 11; benefit, 31; parts, 56, 172, 203, 244, 246; as Fresh, 261, 262; substitutes for Emmet, 273, 274; parts, 387, 485, 487, 524, 607
Raymond, Lillie, 541, 544, 548
Raymond, Robert R., 404
Raymond, W., 143 ff
Raymond, W. T., 257
Raymond, Wally, 346
Raymond and Murphy, 101, 129, 130
Raymonde, cast, 230
Rayne, E. M., 257
Razillias (3), William, George, Edward, 349
Read, Annette (or Nettie), 206
Reade, Charles, his Dora, 55; Drink, 265
Reading of a Tragedy, 480
Reasons Why, lecture, 246, 247
Rebecchini, Mme., 211
Reber, Sallie, 38, 184, 275, 392, 481, 600
Receipts, financial, for plays, etc., 8, 31, 215, 423, 427, 428, 433; for Fritz in Ireland, 470; for Patience, 477; for Music Festival, 600
Rechtsschütz-Verein, 503
Red Knight, The, or, the Magic Trumpet, 113
Red Men, Free Order of, 86
Red Riding Hood, 583
Red Riding Hood's Return, 209
Red Scar, The, 348
Redding, John, 65
Redmond, variety, 547
Redmond, Charles, 131, 134, 136, 140, 327, 331, 334, 345, 347, 352, 396 (*see infra*)

Redmond (Charles) and Blake (Georgie), 526, 528, 543, 557 (*see supra*)
Redmond, Joe, 120, 136, 328, 337, 339, 348, 544
Redmond's Funniosities, 626
Redpath, James, 180, 408
Reed, actor, 60
Reed (of Ripley and Reed), 325, 336, 571, 620
Reed (of Tobin and Reed), 331, 353
Reed, Amy, 400
Reed, Charles, 317, 318, 387, 615, 616
Reed, Dave, 11, 135, 136; benefit, 145; 188, 343, 346, 349, 355, 396
Reed, Eleanor, 43
Reed, Emily, 271
Reed, George, 39
Reed, Roland, 39, 56, 172, 482
Reed, Samuel, 412
Reeder, Lillian, 275
Reese, Charles, 563, 570
Reese, Jennie, 137, 563, 570
Reeves, Alice, 527
Reeves, Fanny, 448
Reeves, Harry, 460
Reeves-Smith, H., 473
Regan (of Cahill and Regan), 184
Regenti, Rose, 38
Regular Fix, A, 31, 44, 53
Rehan, Ada, parts, 13 ff, 42, 58, 173, 179, 231 ff, 246, 260, 387, 413, 441 ff; as Odette, review, 445; 608
Rehan, Arthur, 608
Rehearsal in the Parlour, 138, 332, 345, 352, 545, 546, 551, 554, 617
Rehearsal in the Woods, 328
Rehm, Alexander, 638
Reid, Bostwick (or Bothwick), swordsman, 100, 113, 114, 185, 535
Reid, Julia, 392, 612
Reidy, Miss B., 157
Reiff, Anthony, 184, 238
Reiffarth, Jennie (or Jeannette), 40, 247, 271, 389, 475
Reign of the Common People, 196, 198, 366, 403, 404, 583
Reilly (of Connors and Reilly), 616
Reilly, John, 204
Reilly, Pat, 343, 348, 354, 397, 535, 558, 574, 575, 617
Reilly and Collins, 635
Reinau, 66 ff, 290, 311, 504
Reinhold, Ida, 283, 291
Reinhold, Hugo, 201, 595
Remenyi, Eduard, 195, 358, 372, 496, 539, 593, 627
Remetze, Ella, 16, 19
Remington, Daisy, 131, 132, 135, 188
Remington, Miss Earle, 328, 354, 531, 552, 558
Remmertz, Franz, 84, 157 ff, 165, 196, 198, 201, 296 ff, 356, 370 ff, 379, 381, 399, 417, 592, 594 ff, 600, 602, 603, 632
Rench (of Australian Four), 557
Renicke, Frl., 499
Renner, Josie, 478
Renner, Malvina, 540

Renner, Master, 472
Rennie, Annie, 44, 246
Rennie, J. H., 44, 528, 529
Renrut, Tell act, 106, 115, 186
Renton, H. S., 193, 418, 583, 630, 640, 642
Rentz-Santley Company, 104, 281, 317, 318, 397, 534, 558, 617, 618
Reportorial Repartee, 132
Republican Central Club, 374
Republican Hall, 365, 583
Requa, C. H., 406
Requa, Ida, 406
Requier, A. J., 152
Rescued by a Dog, 116
Resemann, Herr, 499 ff
Retardo and Shaw, 550
Retlaw and Adams, 140
Retribution, play, 415
Rettender Engel, Ein, 81
Returned Volunteer, The, 31
Reuter-Vorlesung, 70, 296, 402
Revel, Mollie, 440
Revel Variety Troupe, 212
Revels, cast, 178; 202; cast, 255; 305, 388
Revillo, 541, 566, 572
Rêverie du Diable, 213
Reynier, actor, 168
Reynolds, concert, 41
Reynolds, negro, 60
Reynolds (Barney) and Walling, 188, 314, 315, 333, 340, 341, 348, 353, 396 ff, 530, 615, 624
Reynolds, Carrie, 225
Reynolds, Fanny V., 112, 117, 324, 327, 328, 333, 387, 534, 543 ff, 548
Reynolds, G. W., 225
Reynolds, Genevieve, 479
Reynolds, George, 122, 132, 189, 324, 392
Reynolds (George) and Cogill, (C. W.), 100, 119, 130, 187
Reynolds, Gus, 532
Reynolds, Howard, cornet, 53, 54, 95, 150
Reynolds, John, mesmerist, 582, 626, 629, 637 ff, 640 ff
Reynolds, Lillian, 63
Reynolds, Louise, 374
Reynolds, Miss, 271
Reynolds, Mrs., amateur, 195
Reynolds, Steve, 132
Reynolds, "Vic," 138, 186, 255, 256, 477, 481, 482
Reynolds, William, 224
Reynolds and Warren, 575
Rhea, Mlle., 452, 453, 605, 606
Rheingold, Das, scenes from, in concert, 602
Rheinischer Sängerbund, 85, 296, 512
Rhinehardt, E., murderer, his cats exhibited, 400
Rhinehart and dogs, 136, 140
Rhinoceros, 359
Rhoda, mystery, 625
Rhodes, John F., 592
Rial, Jay, his Uncle Tom's Cabin, 272, 307, 394, 491, 610, 612, 614
Rial, Mrs. Jay, 272, 307

Rialp, director, 97
Ricardo, 143 ff, 362 ff, 580, 581
Ricardo and Ramon, 361
Ricci, Bertha, 27, 182, 304 ff, 394, 498, 513
Rice, Billy, 58, 257, 471
Rice, Charley, 398
Rice, Edward E., takes Fifth Avenue Theatre, 37; with D'Oyly Carte, 265, 266; his opera companies, 388, 452, 609, 613
Rice's, E. E., Evangeline, 254
Rice's, E. E., Surprise Party, 49; 180, 202, 255, 305, 306, 388, 459, 610
Rice, Emma, 325, 336
Rice (G. W.) and Barton (Charles), 559, 565, 570, 571, 576
Rice, Johnny, 59, 337, 618
Rice, Mary, 130, 131
Rice, Master, 106
Rice, Sara, 310
Rice, W. Henry, 103, 137, 314, 346, 347, 349, 398
Rice Brothers, 330
Rice Family of Midgets, 626
Rich, Charley, 556
Rich, Emma, 212
Rich, Harry, 41, 176, 268, 478, 619
Richard III, W. Winter's arrangement, cast, 28, 29; cast, 63; 248, 276, 277, 389; cast, 439; 450, 459, 462, 465, 605, 609
Richard III, Edwin Booth as, 29, 450, 459; Frank Mayo as, 63; John McCullough as, 248, 389, 439, 462, 609; Lawrence Barrett as, 276, 277, 465, 605
Richard's Wanderleben, 291, 293
Richards, Billy, 537
Richards, George, 139, 189
Richards, Kate, 113
Richards, May, 245, 536
Richards, Nellie, 313, 317, 341, 343, 534, 556, 559, 616
Richards, Professor, 627
Richards Brothers, 565
Richardson (of Australian Four), 557
Richardson, Abbie Sage, 365, 417
Richardson, Hattie, 11, 172, 618
Richardson, Locke, 244, 310, 366 ff, 419, 584 ff
Richardson, S. F., 208
Richardson (Sage) and Young (Charles W.), 326, 328, 336, 343
Richardson, W., 234, 385
Richelieu, cast, 28; 52, 53, 94, 172, 184, 276, 281; cast, 384; 386, 449, 450, 459; cast, 461; 465, 605, 609
Richelieu, Edwin Booth as, 28, 52, 53, 94, 184, 449, 450, 609; Lawrence Barrett as, 172, 384, 386, 461, 465, 605; James O'Neill as, 281
Richmond, Adah, 538
Richmond, Cora, 635
Richmond, Harry G., 48, 49, 65, 167, 396, 397, 621, 622
Richmond, Hattie, 112, 117, 325
Richmond, James, 544, 570
Richmond, Lizzie, 330, 397, 554, 616
Richmond, Miss, 34

Richmond Sisters (Josie and Lulu), 64, 135 ff, 186
Richmond County Dramatic Association, 217
Richter, Carl, 157, 193, 594
Ricketts Brothers (Harry and George), 218, 339, 343
Rickey, Sam, 556
Riddle, A. T., 465
Riddle, George, 448; as Oedipus, 455
Ridge (of Excelsior Quartette), 570
Ridgeway, W., 481
Ridgewood Park, 87, 386 ff
Riedel, tenor, 85
Rieger, J. H., 627
Rieger, W. H., 593, 597
Rietzel, Hermann, 85, 217, 375, 377; drowned, 523; 587, 592, 594, 602
Rifflard, Paul, 155
Riggs, Mamie, 396
Riggs, T. Grattan, 45, 174
Rightmire, W. H., 110, 111, 114, 115, 126, 319, 320 ff, 328, 329, 352, 353, 414, 415, 530, 542 ff, 545, 547, 552, 575, 636
Rigl, Emily, parts, 7, 12, 41, 58, 94, 175, 202, 231, 259, 277, 390, 412, 482, 492, 608, 633
Rignold, William, 515, 516, 613
Rigoletto, cast, 91; 92; casts, 180, 305, 308, 456, 521, 523, 614
Rinaldini, parts, 91 ff, 304 ff, 517 ff
Rinaldos (3 — George, William, Henry), 137, 138, 171, 530, 542, 561
Ring, J. H., 242, 450, 458
Ring, Der, des Nibelung, operetta, 62
Ring, Der, des Nibelungen, parts of, sung, 599, 600
Ringgold, B. T., parts, 12, 43, 174, 175, 258, 441, 442
Ringler, Add and Maggie, 548, 563
Ringler, Add and Minnie (sic), 128
Ringtheater, Vienna, burning of, benefit for, 503
Rink, Brooklyn, 191 ff
Rionda, Mlle., 371
Rip Van Winkle, casts, 51, 115, 146, 168; 203; recited, 204; 213; cast, 275; 327, 328, 332, 334, 385; 488, 621
Rip Van Winkle, Joseph H. Keane as, 115, 327, 328, 334; Joseph Jefferson as, 168, 275, 385, 488; Robert McWade as, 203; John T. Hinds as, 332; George W. Thompson as, 621
Ripley, Claudia, 111, 115, 116, 125, 131, 324, 325, 327, 331, 335, 530, 554, 567, 571, 572, 574
Ripley, Leoline, 554, 571, 572, 574
Ripley, William, 111, 116, 125, 131, 324, 325, 327, 331, 335, 530, 554, 567, 571, 572, 574
Ripley and Reed (sic), 325, 336, 565, 571, 620, 625
Risch, Julius, 372, 591
Rising Man, The, 420
Ristori, Adelaide, 239, 254, 302
Ritter, concert, 638
Ritter, F. L., 155, 627
Ritter, Fred W., 628 (see supra)

Rival Conductors, 137
Rival Lovers, 338
Rivals, The, cast, Wallack's, 222; Jefferson's production, 385, 435, 436, 606; recited, 367; with amateurs, 392, 399
Rivals, The, variety sketch, 132, 141, 314, 335, 344, 571
Rivarde, A., 162
Rivers, C. H. and pupils, 393, 395, 615
Rivers, Mary, 491
Rivers, Viola, 146
Rivers's Academy, 405
Riverston (or Ribiston), Exhibition of Moon, 368, 407
Roach, Charles, 560
Roach and Fash, 116
Road Agents, 544
Robb, Nellie, 646
Robbers, The, 63 (see Räuber, Die)
Robbers of Genoa, The, 348, 561
Robert, Bertha, 509
Robert und Bertram, 78, 285 (see Robert Macaire)
Robert Churchill, play, 623
Robert Macaire, 123, 333, 341, 531, 559, 563, 576 (see Robert und Bertram)
Roberto il Diavolo, cast, 522
Roberts, Albert, 220 ff
Roberts, Charles, Jr., 152 ff, 161, 193, 198, 244, 310, 367, 375, 378, 395, 404, 416, 417, 439, 612, 628
Roberts, E. M., 491
Roberts, Florence, 45
Roberts, Frank, 59, 226, 282, 467, 471, 605
Roberts, Fred, 121, 133, 134, 329, 342, 350, 351, 364, 420, 539, 553, 559, 567, 572, 575, 576
Roberts, H., 232 ff, 387, 443 ff
Roberts, J. B., 484, 610
Roberts, Master, 118, 135, 333, 543
Roberts, May, Combination, 369
Roberts, N., 58
Roberts, Nick, his Humpty Dumpty, 280, 396, 525, 532, 616, 617, 621; his Carnival, 559, 560, 618
Roberts, Professor, 421
Roberts, Sam, 110, 111, 205, 319
Roberts, Sidney, 608
Roberts, Theodore, 609
Robertson, Agnes (Mrs. Boucicault), 244, 246
Robertson, Alexander, 153, 365
Robertson, D., 33, 34, 259
Robertson, D. W., 643
Robertson, Donald, 39, 605
Robertson, Ian, 474
Robertson, Mrs. G., 163
Robertson, S., 184
Robeson, Erba, 110, 135, 534, 555, 616
Robiati, Mlle., 91 ff, 183
Robie, D., 339
Robie, Louis, 547, 568 ff
Robinson (of Fritz and Robinson), 330
Robinson (of Murray, Snow and Robinson), 342
Robinson, Billy, 353

Robinson, C. L., 636
Robinson, Colonel, 636
Robinson, Florence, 275, 449, 453, 465, 633
Robinson, Forrest, 391, 465, 491
Robinson, Frederic, parts, 3, 45, 177, 385, 436, 475, 606
Robinson, George S., 31, 202, 231, 275, 411, 438 ff, 449
Robinson, Harry, 471
Robinson, Ida, 548
Robinson, John, 133, 340 ff, 397, 555 ff, 574, 617
Robinson, Josie, 453
Robinson, Kitty, 130
Robinson Crusoe, cast, 49; 178, 338
Robitsek, actor, 192, 206
Robson, Alicia, 169, 264, 462, 609
Robson, Mat, 255
Robson, Stuart, parts, 11, 169, 202, 264, 384, 386, 461, 609
Roche, Augusta, parts, 467, 477, 481, 485
Roche, Frank, 519, 620, 621
Roche, Richard, 582
Rochus Pumpernickel, 293
Rockaway Beach, 87, 155, 214, 379, 403
Rocked in the Cradle of the Deep, 143
Rockwell, Charles, parts, 2 ff, 55, 170, 202, 258, 464, 485
Rockwell, Isabel, 180, 399
Rode, F., 635
Rode-Peters, Henriette, 634, 635
Roden's orchestra, 642
Rodgers, Punch and Judy, 400
Roe, Harry, 59
Roe, Harry W. (of California Quartette), 350, 553
Roebbelin, 372, 591
Rogers (of Friel and Rogers), 189
Rogers, Addie, 117
Rogers, Ben G., parts, 49, 261, 384, 461, 465
Rogers, Charles S., 60, 138, 179, 343, 387, 398, 490, 526 ff, 561, 563, 564, 569, 575, 616 ff
Rogers, Emma (of McAvoy and Rogers), 115, 129, 140, 189, 277, 314, 315, 317, 342, 347, 348, 367, 396, 487, 526, 560, 561, 563, 567 ff, 572, 617, 618
Rogers, Frank, his play, 12
Rogers, Genevieve, 277
Rogers, H. M., 214
Rogers, Katherine, parts, 177, 228, 280, 367, 411
Rogers, Miss E., 47
Rogers, Mrs. E. J., 638
Rogers Peet and Company's Clothing Emporium, farce, 363
Rogue, The, the Ring and the Rope, 134, 560
Rohbeck, Herr, 74 ff
Rokohl, Frederica, 48
Roland, Anna, 123
Rolfe, Charles, 245, 465
Rolfe, Frank J., 245
Roller, Marie, Damen-Kapelle, 294, 512
Roller-skating, 206, 356, 367, 574, 616, 619
Romaine, Cecile, 64
Roman, Der, eines junges Edelmannes, 502

Roman Brother acts, 121
Roman Catholic Orphan Asylum benefits, 94, 305, 306, 518, 519
Roman Statues, 204
Roman Students, 536, 539, 624
Romanus, Frl., 66 ff
Romelli, Maggie, 531
Romeo, Edward Compton as, 30, 168; Schönfeld as, 79; Gustavus Levick as, 94; Rossi as, 451; William Harris as, 453, 488; Eben Plympton as, 523
Romeo and Juliet, cast, with Miss Neilson, 30; 54; in German, 79; cast, 168; 171; cast, 282; recited, 366; 383, 390, 451, 453, 488, 503, 523, 607; cast, 610; 634
Romeo and Juliet (Gounod's), sung in English, 385
Romeo auf dem Bureau, 510
Romeo und Julie, cast, 79
Römer, Elise, 81
Romeyn, H. R., 159, 160, 376, 596
Ronaldo, W., 339
Ronaldo and Baldwin, 323
Ronaldos (3), 350 (see Rinaldos)
Rooke, George, 578
Room, 44, farce, 415
Roome, J. D., 116, 138, 184, 186, 337, 342, 545
Rooms to Let, 622
Rooms to Rent, cast, review, 478, 479
Rooney, J. S., 216
Rooney, Jim, 338
Rooney, Katie, 351, 398, 617, 618
Rooney, Pat, 56, 133, 141, 188, 203, 276, 344, 349, 351, 398, 529, 564, 566, 567, 570, 571, 576, 617, 618
Roosevelt, Blanche, 35; adversely criticised, 183; puts on Sultan of Mocha, 225; 310, 311, 375 ff, 481, 510, 514, 587, 591, 595, 627, 640
Röper, Frl., 503
Rory O'More, 530
Rosa, Lena, 320
Rosa, Patti, 503, 539
Rosa, Viola (of Lang and Rosa), 545, 553, 554, 565, 567, 576
Rosalind, Miss Neilson as, 30, 168; Adele Belgarde as, 39; Fanny Davenport as, 52, 169, 178, 463, 605, 633; Rose Coghlan as, 220; Mrs. Scott-Siddons as, 390
Rose, Frank, 472
Rose, Misses, 538
Rose Michel, play, 635
Rose of Auvergne, 192
Roseau, Eme, 39, 56, 172
Rosebud, Baron (or Count), 578, 624
Rosebud, Little, 188, 396 ff
Rosebud, The, of Stinging Nettle Farm, 648
Rosedale, casts, 55, 276; 281; casts, 389, 488
Roselle, female impersonator, 118
Rosenbaum, B., 417
Rosenbaum, N., 509
Rosenblatt, Joseph, 417
Rosene (or Rosine), Charles, 48, 176, 257, 389
Rosenfeld, Sydney, his play, 476

Rosenkranz und Güldenstern, 70
Rosenmüller und Finke, 504, 509, 623
Rosewald, Julie, parts, 251, 381, 487, 604, 605
Roslyn, L. I., 426, 646
Ross and his dogs, 122, 565, 566, 571
Ross, Charles J., 262
Ross, Emma and Ida, 104, 327, 618
Ross, J. H., 143
Ross, Jennie, 617
Ross, Libby, 121
Ross, Lillie, 114
Ross, Lizzie B., 374, 394
Ross, Melville, 399
Ross, Virginia, 481
Rosse, Professor A., 89, 372, 598
Rossée, Christine, 375, 594, 598
Rossi, Ernesto, parts, reviews, 450, 451; 520, 613
Rossi Hamlet Backus, 581
Rossie, Mme., 298
Rossini, Paolina, parts, 518 ff, 600, 613, 614
Rossmore, Mabel, 369
Rothschild, Herr, 76
Rough Diamond, The, 56, 230, 277, 427, 644
Rourke, Eugene, 99, 312, 524, 525
Rouse, Mrs. Fanny, 257 (see Denham, Fanny)
Rouse, Mrs. W. A., 243, 276, 435 (see supra)
Rouse, W. A., 64, 190, 607
Roving Jack, 105
Rowan (of Trudell and Rowan), 544, 551
Rowe, Bertha, 347
Rowe, Bolton, his play, 64
Rowe, Clifford, 636
Rowe, Dick, 132, 328, 334
Rowe, George Fawcett, Wolfert's Roost, 1; 243; Smiff, 459, 460; 484
Rowe, Harry, W., 363
Rowe, J. H., 59, 279, 282, 554
Rowe, Mrs. J. H., 56, 268, 472, 604 (see Dickson, Georgie)
Rowell, Charles, walker, 149, 359, 540
Rowson, George, 449
Royal Favourite, The, cast, 173, 174
Royal Handbell Ringers, 643 (see Handbell Ringers)
Royal Middy, The, cast, receipts, 18; 19, 75, 173; casts, 178, 480; 609 (see Seecadet, Der)
Royal People I Have Met, 365
Royal Youth, cast, 443, 444
Royalisten, Die, cast, 501
Royston, W., 474
Rôze, Marie, 251, 252, 308, 377, 394
Rubens, C., 538
Rubini, Mlle., 375
Rudolf, Mme. A., 535
Rudolphe, billiards, 154
Rudvall (or Rudwall), A., 193, 197
Rummel, Franz, 156 ff, 164, 201, 298, 370 ff, 380
Runcio, tenor, 91 ff, 158, 183, 516 ff, 537, 613, 614
Runnells (of Murray and Runnells), 148, 327
Runnells, Bonnie, 56, 94, 100, 102 ff, 135, 172, 274, 314, 348, 387, 397, 534, 556, 616

Runnells and Aymar, 106
Runnett, J. A., 142
Runyon, R. T., 274
Rupert's Dog, 114, 125, 126, 414
Rural Felicity, 346, 349, 565
Rush, Cecile, 21, 24, 175, 236, 272, 385
Rush, Fattie, 143, 361, 577
Rush-in Baths vs. Supreme Court, 567
Rushmore, Wilbur F., 408, 416, 417, 419, 428, 638, 639
Russell (see Gibbons and Russell and Four Emeralds)
Russell, Annie, as Esmeralda, 447, 448; 467, 517
Russell, Helen, 369
Russell, J. G., 143 ff
Russell, John (of Magee and Russell), 117
Russell, Laura, 103, 125, 126, 135, 331 ff, 344, 350, 352, 554, 566, 572, 617
Russell, Lillian, 276; début, 314 ff; 367; 439, 467; as Patience, 477; parts, review, 479; 480, 481, 482, 485; not at Pastor's, 526; returns, 527, 528; parts, 613
Russell, Marion, 346, 608
Russell, Mrs. Jane, 608
Russell, R. Fulton, 8, 275, 384, 489, 607
Russell, S. P., walker, 149
Russell, Sol Smith, 258, 384, 492, 605, 634
Russell, Susie, 520, 526 ff
Russell, Tommy, 467, 608
Russell, W. J., 324, 355, 551, 553, 557, 558
Russell Brothers (John and James), 117, 118, 121, 129, 130, 132, 139, 329, 346, 349, 351 ff, 545, 560 ff, 568, 570, 575
Russian Athletes, 246, 271, 338, 569
Russian Immigrants, benefit for, 509; refugees, 586
Russischer Beamter, Ein, 283
Rutenber, C. R., 372
Rutgers College Glee Club, 408
Ruth, an American Wife, 604
Rutherford, Miss A. V., 63, 174
Rutini, Tyrolean, 83
Ruttini, illusions, 105, 123
Ruy Blas, with Booth, 29, 52; with amateurs, 612
Ruy Blas, opera, 523
Ryan, Addie, 413
Ryan, Ed (of Stansil and Ryan), 545, 576
Ryan, Father, lectures, 374
Ryan, J. F., 604
Ryan, J. H., 469
Ryan, Ned (see Clooney and Ryan; Farrell and Ryan)
Ryan, Paddy, 535, 583
Ryan, Perry and Lulu, 350, 534, 560, 562, 568, 569
Ryan, Sam E., 64, 171, 179, 467
Ryan, Thomas J. (see Kelly and Ryan)
Ryan, Tommy, 635
Ryder, J. A., 542
Ryder, Mark, 214
Ryland, C. (of McGill and Ryan), 338, 343
Ryland, C. (of Sweeney and Ryland), 569
Ryland, Cliff, 561

Ryley, J. H., parts, 35, 44, 184, 253, 266, 272, 477, 529
Ryman, Add, 143 ff, 179, 186, 314, 315, 344, 345, 347, 396, 398, 526, 615, 619
Ryse, Ellis, 51, 167, 254, 274, 413, 523, 538

S. J. T. Pinafore, 100
St. Agnes' Church, 161
St. Aloysius Dramatic Society, 420
St. Andrew's Society, 160
St. Augustine's Literary Society, 403
St. Cecilia Mass (Gounod's), 199
St. Clair, Agnes, 109
St. Clair, Dora, 39
St. Clair, Frank, 120
St. Clair, Harry, 558
St. Clair, Minnie, 293
St. Clair, Sallie, 134, 135, 138, 140, 187, 188
St. Cloud English Opera, 152
St. Elmo, Harry, George and Haney, 552, 564, 575, 624
St. Felix Sisters (4), 56, 102, 103, 134, 136, 172, 188, 274, 276, 314, 316, 317; (3), 327, 328, 342, 346, 397, 483, 526, 540, 559, 576, 618, 619
St. Francis Hospital, benefit, 598
St. George, Mrs., 392
St. George, Sons of, 585
St. John, Effie, 176
St. John, Nellie, 134, 137, 190, 329, 343 ff
St. John's Guild, benefit, 153
St. Lawrence Music Hall, 362
St. Louis College, 155
St. Mary's Free Hospital, benefit, 598
St. Maur, Harry, 467, 481
St. Patrick's Day, farce, 557
St. Peter's Hall, 195, 407
St. Petersburg Ballet, 535, 536
St. Vincent de Paul, Church, 404
Saalfield concerts, 160, 370, 439, 592
Sabbatini, Signora, 358
Sacconi, Mme., 309, 310, 371, 522, 537
Sackett, Millie, 111, 353
Sackett, Miss, 346
Sacred Quartette Club, Greenpoint, 642
Sacrifice, play, 151
Sadler, Tom, 59
Safe Robber, The, 549
Sage, Thomas, 452
Sagoyewatha Tribe, 423
Sahm, Carl, 512, 597
Sailor of France, The, 56
Saker, Horatio, 222
Sala, George Augustus, 152
Salamander, steed, burned, 148
Salaries, at Daly's, 13; 22, 42; of singers, 97; 236; Patti's, 522
Salcedo, Juan, 158, 199, 206
Saleon, actor, 445
Salinger, J., 82
Sallie, Will You Marry? 544
Sallie Burn-Hard, Arrival of, 314
Sally McNally, farce, 211
Sally in Our Alley, sung, 144
Salon Pitzelberger, 498

Salsbury, Nate, 41, 256, 458, 606
Salsbury's, Nate, Troubadours, 20, 41, 50, 92, 178, 202, 256, 280, 389, 458, 606
Salvati, parts, 505 ff, 589, 611
Salviati, play, 250
Salvini, Alexander, 440
Salvini, Tommaso, parts, 241, 242, 243, 244, 302; at the opera, 305; 450; burlesqued, 363, 364, 604
Salvini's Othello, burlesque, 604
Salvotti, Marie, 512
Sam, play, 44
Sam'l of Posen, cast, 257; 470, 484, 492, 609, 634
Sammis, George, 628
Samuel Brohl and Co. dramatised, 3
Samuels (or Samuells), A. R., 387
Samuels, C., 538
Samuels, Ray (or Rachel), 168, 256, 458, 606
San Antonio di Padova, Società di, 90
San Francisco Minstrels (1879-80), 103; 179, 203, 246, 276; (1880-81), 362 ff; 474, 517, 553; (1881-82), 580, 581; 604
Sanborn, Ada, 115
Sanders (John E.) and Dean (Charles H.), 319, 354, 532, 543, 566, 572, 625
Sanders and Ward, 425
Sanders Brothers, 425
Sanderson, Harry, 528
Sandford (sic), 104, 334
Sandford (sic), Fanny, 119, 140, 329, 544
Sands (of Keating and Sands), 109, 138, 334
Sands, Dick, 108, 119, 120, 126, 138, 140, 331, 624
Sands, Harry L., 194, 213, 404
Sanford (sic), 105
Sanford, Frank (see Howard and Sanford)
Sanford (James) and Wilson (Charles), 133, 317, 340 ff, 534, 556, 559, 616
Sanford, Miss Lou, 128, 138, 139, 184, 188, 318, 397
Sanford, Nellie, 54, 560 ff
Sanford, Sam S., 114, 115, 120
Sanger, Anna, 200
Sänger-Anzahl von Tausend Stimmen, 83
Sanger, F. W., 30, 168, 267
Sanger, Miss M. A., 64, 613
Sanger, Rachel, 45, 174, 272, 395, 449, 474
Sanger's Menagerie, 200
Sängerbund, Brooklyn, 182, 190, 393, 402, 613, 623
Sängerbund, Jamaica, 215, 647
Sängerbund Hall, Jamaica, 428
Sängerbund, Schwäbischer, 416
Sängerlust, 84, 296
Sängernärrisch, Der, 81
Sängerrunde, L. I., 211
Sängerrunde, New York, 84 ff, 148, 296, 298 ff, 511
Sansone, Bessie, 230, 453
Santa Claus, cantata, 194
Santella, Irene, 350, 351
Santley, Emma, 38
Santley, Mabel, 104, 281, 317, 397
Sara, dancer, 316

Sarah Heartburn, 363
Sarah's Young Man, 105
Sardou's, Victorien, Odette, 445
Saroni's Burlesque Troupe, 104
Sarony's Photographs, 221, 247, 392
Sarsfield (see Boyd and Sarsfield)
Sartelle, Minnie, 534
Satsuma, 115, 120, 147
Satterlee, Jennie, 101 ff, 140, 186 ff, 387, 396 ff, 615, 618
Sauer, Herr, 66 ff, 288 ff, 311, 499 ff
Sauere Trauben, cast, 289
Saunders, athlete, 585
Saunders, C. (see McVickers and Saunders)
Saunders (Charles) and Fash, 110, 127
Saunders, Ella, 132
Saunders, John, 645
Saunders, John E., 350
Sauret, piano, 646
Sause's soirées, 142, 361, 577
Savage, E. J., 373
Saved at Seven, 109, 122, 400
Saved from the Storm, 111, 113, 115, 554, 559, 575
Saville (of Howard and Saville), 134
Saville (Charles) and Bennett (Ben), 328, 332, 336 ff
Saville, Gus (see Bryant and Saville)
Saville (Gus H.) and Byrne (John H.), 115, 127, 133, 138, 325, 326, 328, 332, 335, 415, 530, 542, 554
Saville, Henry, 254
Saville, J. G., 46, 259 ff, 475
Sawtelle, Charles (see Brevarde and Sawtelle and Four Diamonds)
Sawyer, A. W., 556, 559, 624
Sawyer's Bell Ringers, 143
Sawyer's, A. W., Copophone, 101, 102, 118
Sawyer, H. N., 215
Saxophone Quartet, 52 ff, 406
Sayers, Tom, 101, 102, 320, 330 ff, 341 ff, 397, 551, 555
Scallan, Mrs. W., 52
Scallan, W., 52, 63, 262, 264, 265, 278, 465, 607
Scamps of New York, The, 135, 348
Scandinavian concert and ball, 628
Scandinavian Singing Society, 193, 197; of Brooklyn, 409
Scanlan (or Scanlon), W. J., 133, 145, 242, 306, 383, 471, 482, 621
Scarecrow, The, 119
Scarlet Dick, play, 346
Scat, Cats, 635
Scene in a Manager's Office, 629
Scenery, 1, 3, 218, 223, 224, 267, 433, 438, 442, 449, 473, 485, 516
Scenes at Simpson's, 109
Schaefer, Herr, 493
Schaefer, Jacob, billiards, 149, 152, 154, 155, 582, 583
Schaeffer (sic), George, 554
Schaeffer, Mlle. Josephine, 263, 356
Schaeffer, W., scenery, 568
Schaffy, Mirza, 152

Schallodenbacher Männerchor, 296
Schalm, Katy, 299
Schamidatus, Frl., 494, 497, 510
Scharnowitzky's Park, 212; Variety Hall, 425
Schätz, Frl., 494
Schauspieler, Die, des Kaisers, cast, 67
Schehr's Assembly Rooms, 211
Schell, Hattie, 587, 594, 599, 601, 602, 632, 638
Schelle, Marie, 298, 370 ff; Schelle-Gramm, 592
Schenck, Emil, 372
Schenck, Marta, 84
Schenkewitz, reads, 402
Schiebel, Chris, 323
Schiller, George A., 277, 452, 459, 609
Schiller, Madeline, 592, 596, 601, 602, 614, 632
Schillerbund, 83 ff, 86, 148, 295, 300, 374, 510, 511
Schimke-Herrmann, 493 ff, 634
Schirmer, Laura, 251, 252
Schlag, Frl., 75 ff, 493
Schlam, Herr, 547, 624
Schleichhändler, Der, 499
Schlesinger, Carl, 294
Schleswig-Holsteinischer Verein, 82, 294 ff, 512
Schliemann, Herr, 76 ff, 82
Schloeder, Jacob, Weinhandlung, 194
Schlum Family, 566
Schmager, Clara, 509
Schmidt, Adolf, benefits for, 83, 86, 295
Schmittbauer, O., 86, 296
Schmitz, Edouard, 74 ff, 283 ff
Schmitz, Eugenie, parts, 66 ff, 288 ff, 499 ff, 510
Schnecker, violin, 595
Schneewittchen und die sieben Zwerge, 293
Schneider, actor, 75 ff
Schneider, play, 415
Schneider, or, Dot House on the Rhine, cast, 101; 119
Schneider, How You Vas? 350, 353, 560
Schneider Fips, 293
Schnelle, Max, 74 ff, 82, 282 ff; dies, benefit for family, 287; 294
Schöne Galathee, Die, 81, 287, 495, 498
Schöne Helena, Die, 81
Schönfeld, Carl, 74 ff, 282 ff, 285, 294, 493 ff, 634
School, with amateurs, 399, 521
School, variety farce, 330, 335, 343, 544
School for Scandal, The, 31; Amaranth cast, 183; Wallack's cast, 221, 222; 243, 244; Mrs. Scott-Siddons, 390; opens new Wallack's, cast, 431, 432; with Fanny Davenport, 489; cast, 605; Wallack's cast compared with Fanny Davenport's, 611; 633
School vs. Mischief, 137
School vs. Music, 102
Schoolcraft, Luke, Francis Wilson's estimate, 60
Schoolcraft (Luke) and Coes (G. H.), 167, 340 ff, 352, 396

INDEX

Schor, Mme., 95
Schott, Angie, 42, 62, 179
Schötte, A., 406, 596, 600
Schräder, Emma, 591
Schratt, Käthi, 496 ff
Schreiber, Louis, 430
Schreiner, Kleophas, 87
Schreiner-Kronfeld, Frau, 509
Schroder, John, 119, 334
Schrötter, Frl., 499 ff, 614
Schubert's Maid of the Mill, 163
Schüler, Herr, 493
Schuler's Palm Garten, 295, 300
Schulte, Frl. C., 82, 299
Schultz, saxophone, 52
Schultz, Gustav, 509
Schultz, Max, 499 ff
Schultze, Herr, 493 ff
Schulzen's Heimkehr aus Paris, 293
Schünemann-Pott, F., 299
Schuster, Otto, 86
Schütz, Anna, 595
Schütz, Gustav, his opera, 399
Schützen-Corp, Brooklyn, 190
Schwab, Max, 88, 300, 301, 601
Schwab, W., 143
Schwab's Harlem River Bridge Garden, 300
Schwäbischer Sängerbund, 84, 296, 297, 416, 636
Schwäbisches (or Schwaben) Volksfest, 204, 416, 636
Schwalenberg's Jackson Avenue Park, 212, 425
Schwartz, violin, 591 ff
Schwartz, Alonzo, 150
Schwartz, Edward J., his play, 621
Schwartz, Max, 375, 379
Schweizer-Vereine (vereinigten), 87
Schweneke, Charles, 194
Schwert, Das, des Damocles, 511
Schwicardi, W., 298, 299
Scobie, George, 640
Scott, Elise, 27
Scott, Henry R., 339
Scott, J. W., amateur, 369
Scott, Rufus, 168, 489
Scott, W. H., walker, 540
Scott, W. J., banjo, 354
Scott-Siddons, Mary F., 155, 390
Scranton Bush Rangers, 114
Scrap of Paper, A, casts, 4, 55, 167, 223
Scrother-Sturgis, G., 585
Sculptor's Studio, The, 325
Sea Foam, 145
Sea of Ice, The, as The Wild Flower of Mexico, 323
Seaich, Mrs. W. H., 369
Seabert, Charles, 118, 119, 124 ff, 415, 553
Seaman, Willet, 155, 523, 592, 640
Seamans, the, 345, 349
Seaman (Charles V.) and Somers (T. E.), 132 ff, 138, 139, 188, 334 ff, 344, 346, 352, 396, 398, 526, 527, 598
Seamon, Gertie, 136, 138
Searle, Cyril, 253, 265, 412, 435, 450, 468, 607

Searle, Louise, 48, 176, 254, 277, 387, 460, 478, 606
Seaton, May, 323
Sebastian, circus, 147, 148
Seckle, Dora, 404
Second Sight at a Discount, 135
Secor, J. J., 440
Sedgwick, Ellen, 54 (see infra)
Sedgwick, Helen, 226, 388, 482 (see supra)
See, E. H., 272, 386, 491
See, Lorenz, 299
See, Louis, band, 513
Seebach, Marie, 239
Seebold, Emma, 494 ff, 497, 537
Seecadet, Der, as Royal Middy, 17; cast, in German, 38; 68; cast, 75, 76; 77, 79, 81; Sunday performance stopped by law, 82; 284, 498
Seeing the Sights, 187
Seeley, Charles, acrobats, 562
Seeley, Jennie, 493
Seeman, Baron, 360, 399
Seeman, Mlle., 399
Sefton, John, 224
Sefton, Mrs. John, 4, 224
Segretario, Il, del Segretario d'un Segretario, 302
Seguin, Edward, 51, 167
Seguin, Zelda, 51, 167, 478, 523
Segur, M. Louise, 371, 375, 593
Seidl, actor, 76
Seiffert, concert, 88
Seine Dritte, 81
Selbini, J., 559, 561, 574, 622
Selbstmord aus Liebe, 293
Self-Conquest, 34
Self-Supporting Women, entertainments for, 375
Seligman, Robert, 417
Sellou (John J.) and Byrnes (John J.), 114, 132, 189, 349, 560, 561, 569, 570, 575
Selvi, Marguerite, 183, 391
Selwyn, Alfred, 45
Selwyn, Blanche, benefit, 104
Semar (sic), Mary, 428
Senator McFee, farce, 330, 331, 343, 397
Senator from Louisiana, 135, 561; cast, 568, 569
Seneca Dramatic Association, 211
Senger, Emil, 82, 84, 157, 162
Sennach, Henrietta, 38
Serenaders, The, 354
Sergent, G. F., 600
Serious Family, The, 365, 393, 629
Serpent's Sting, The, 321
Servants, farce, 396
Servants by Legacy, 105
Servants' Frolics, 526
Servants' Holiday, 101, 337, 339, 354
Serven, Ida S., 600
Sessions, Miss A., 410
Seth Grit, play, 338
Setti, Auguste, 66 ff, 288 ff, 311
Seventh Regiment Armoury, inaugurated, 366; 371; Music Festival, 598 ff

Seventh Regiment Athletic Games, 585
Seventh Regiment Band (Cappa's), 528, 585, 596
Seventh Regiment entertainments, 97, 158
Sexton, billiards, 152, 154, 155
Sexton, William, 582, 583
Seymour, actor, 322
Seymour, C., 483
Seymour, H. James, 531
Seymour, Harry F., 105 ff, 321, 323, 338, 339
Seymour, Katie, 238
Seymour, Mrs. Carrie, 531
Seymour, Mrs. Harry, 323
Seymour, Pearl, 110
Seymour, W. H., 59, 64, 238, 266, 470, 537, 609, 610
Seymour, William ("Willie"), as adapter, 250; as actor, 412, 517, 610
Shades and Shadow, 536
Shadow Detective, The, 105
Shadow Pantomime, 216
Shadowgraphs, 562, 563, 568
Shaffer, Annie, 238, 383
Shakespeare Dramatic Society, New York, 151
Shakespeare in the Kitchen, 548
Shakespeare Outdone, 544, 552, 570
Shakespeare Rehashed, 339
Shakespearian Association, 422, 643
Shamrocks, Four (see Four Shamrocks)
Shamus O'Brien, 94
Shandley (sic), Miss, 48
Shanley (or Shandley), Josephine, 127, 187, 320
Shannon, George (see Murphy, George, and Shannon, George)
Shannon, J. Harry, boy orator, 197
Shannon, J. W., 1, 55; his play, 172, 173; parts, 263, 265, 276, 389
Shapleigh, Ida, 267
Sharpe, Dollie, 135
Sharpe, Kitty, 330, 346, 573
Sharpley (Fred) and West (Charles), 118, 120, 121, 123, 124, 326, 332, 340, 349, 351, 564, 570, 576, 617
Sharpley, J. W., 624
Sharpley and Carroll, 120
Sharpley and Clarke, 185
Sharps and Flats, cast, 264; 384, 462
Shattuck, C. F., 59
Shaughaun, The, cast, 322; 332, 354, 400, 550
Shaughraun, The, cast, Wallack's, 4, 5; casts, 171, 272; 390
Shaun Rhue, casts, 277, 633, 634
Shaw (of Retardo and Shaw), 550
Shaw, Mary, 463, 489, 605
Shaw, Phebe, 549, 576
Shay, Charley, 110, 121, 336
Shay, John, 98 ff
She Stoops to Conquer, cast, Wallack's, 3, 4; 6, 7; Wallack's, 613
She's Boss, 558
Shea, Miss, singer, 598
Shea, W. J., 520

Shedman Brothers (Winfield and George), 112, 118, 124
Sheehan (see Clark and Sheehan, of Four Planets)
Sheehan, Andy, 57
Sheehan (Ed) and Lynch (Ed), 110
Sheehan, James and Lydia, 562
Sheehan, John, 51
Sheehan (John) and Coyne (Mike), 328, 333, 559, 578, 617
Sheehan (John) and Jones (Bobby), 100 ff, 132, 133, 141, 189, 315, 340 ff, 396
Sheehan, John J. (of Four-in-Hand), 553
Sheehan Brothers (Dan and John), 335
Sheehy, Rev. Father, 613
Sheerans (sic), in America, Ireland, Germany), 571
Sheffer, Charles H., 99, 324, 333, 344, 348, 397, 565, 571
Sheffer (or Schaeffer), George, 554, 555
Sheffer and Blakely, 576
Sheldon, A. H., 134 ff; plays by, 345 ff, 578, 560 ff
Sheldon (A. H.) and Moore's (T. W.) Monster Variety Combination, 139
Sheldon, Harry, 119, 121, 401
Sheldon, Julia, 104, 395, 403
Sheldon and Barry, 326
Sheldon's Marionettes, 401
Shelletto, Emma, 624
Sheparde (of Monroe and Sheparde), 414
Sheparde, George, 555
Shepherd's Festival, 533
Sheppard, E., 635
Sheppard, George, 413
Sheppard, Kitty, 105, 106, 109, 328, 561, 564, 570, 572
Sheppard, Maud (or Maude), 107, 319, 320
Sheppard, Miss, 162
Sheppard, Nathan, 154, 586
Sheridan, John F., 51, 136, 187, 254, 257, 306, 315, 469, 492, 518, 633
Sheridan, Mamie, 39
Sheridan, W. E., 39, 54, 170, 270
Sheridan's Ride, recited by C. R. Thorne, Jr., 243
Sherlocke Family of English Troubadours, 151, 152
Sherman, amateur, 97
Sherman, actor, 37
Sherman (of the Megatherian Eight), 138, 351
Sherman (of Four Aces), 564, 565
Sherman, G. C., 3, 220 ff
Sherman, Marie, 320
Sherman's March to the Sea, lecture, 420
Sherry, J. F., 113, 566
Sherry, Will, 493
Sherwin, Amy, 28, 160, 161, 165, 198, 199, 201, 356, 372, 376, 377, 380, 410
Sherwood, Alice, 270
Sherwood, Florence, 116
Sherwood, Grace, 38, 550
Sherwood, Louise, 396
Sherwood, Mrs. John, 584

[739]

Sherwood, W. H., 157
Shewell, Arthur, 481
Shewell, J. H., 462, 463
Shewell, L. R., 242, 439, 489, 607
Shields, Andy (*see Favor and Shields; Williams and Shields*)
Shillito, 573
Shimer, N. B., 348, 553, 625
Shirley, Harry, 59
Shirley and Byrne, 136, 189
Shoemaker's Ghost, The, 566
Shore Acres, 42
Short, Thomas, 214
Showers, A. J., 114
Showers, Ida, 114
Showers and dogs, 147
Showman's Story, A, 31
Shows I Have Seen, by G. A. Sala, 152
Shute, W., 205
Shylock, Booth as, 29, 53, 184, 450, 609; Bandmann as, 47; Lawrence Barrett as, 276, 384, 386, 461, 465, 605; W. Stafford as, 282; E. Härtung as, 284; F. Haase as, 502
Si j'etais Roi, casts, 466, 473
Si Salem, farce, 186
Si Slocum, 65, 202; cast, 279; 411, 485, 561; cast, 564
Sidewalk Conversation, 353
Sidman, Clark, 179
Sidney, Mlle., 239 ff, 246
Siddons, Mrs., 241
Sie hat ihr Herz entdeckt, 497
Sie ist wahnsinnig, cast, 500
Siebzehnhundertdreiunddreissig Thaler, etc., 212, 292
Siegfried, third act sung, 165
Siegrist, Katie, 111
Siegrist, Thomas, Louis, Harry, 558
Siems, Germania Hall, Greenpoint, 641
Silesians, benefit for, 78, 160
Silva, Johnny, 205
Silver Wedding, The, 648
Silvernail, J. P., 193, 196
Silverstädter, Rosa, 378
Sim Dipsey, 334
Sim Dipsey's Visit to New York, 344
Simmons, Lew, 618
Simmons, Lottie, 529
Simmons, Miss F., 271
Simms, negro, 60
Simms, Hattie Louise, 199, 376, 395, 405 ff, 417, 420, 587, 600 ff, 627, 628, 640, 643, 645, 646
Simms, Lizzie, 239, 316, 317, 383, 487, 489, 526 ff, 561, 562, 569, 616
Simon, Professor, 162
Simon Kenton, play, 117, 325, 327, 414
Simonson, Eugenie, 373, 375, 598
Simpson, George, 165, 199, 380
Sims, G. R., play by, 474
Sincérite, La, 514
Sinclair, E. V., 432 ff
Sinclair, Edith, 347, 349, 560, 619 ff
Sinclair, Harry, 179, 311 ff
Sinclair, Jennie, 533

Sing-Akademie, 296, 511
Singer, Marion, 49, 178, 180, 256
Singer, Teresina, 26, 27, 180
Singerhoff, violin, 625
Singin' Skewl (*see Bassett, Aunt Polly*)
Singleton, W., 279
Sinn, Colonel W. E., 167 ff; benefit, 613 (*see Park Theatre, Brooklyn*)
Sisson, Oscar and Josie, 563
Sisters of Notre Dame, Fort Lee, 597
Siwelac, 624
Six American Students, 332
Six Degrees of Crime, 110, 352
Sixes and Sevens, cast, 268
Skating, 195, 366, 427
Skating Rink, 152, 155, 628
Skatorial Three, 567, 572
Skeleton, Living, 191
Skeleton Hand, The, 110, 325, 415, 543
Skeleton Witness, The, 119, 120, 328, 330, 354
Skelly, Frank (of Clifford and Skelly), 563
Skerrett, Emma, 39, 54, 56, 265, 389, 482
Skidmore Guards, 99, 306
Skids, The, are Out Today, 144, 145
Skiff, F. D., his plays, 117, 326
Skinner, Otis, 28, 29, 57, 173, 246, 461, 465
Skippington, Miss M., 264
Slack wire or rope, 131, 530
Slasher and Crasher, 530, 584
Slate, Harry, 120
Slate, Pete, 120
Slate, Rose, 57
Slattery's Boarding House, 114, 138, 545, 550, 635
Slave Life in Brazil, 349, 561
Slave's Dream, The, 317
Slavin, Bob, 102, 103, 137 ff, 318, 580
Slavin's Uncle Tom's Cabin, 50, 185
Sleeping Beauty, The, 533
Sleepy Hollow, opera, cast, 90; 152, 168
Sleepy Hollow, Legend of, in Wolfert's Roost, 1
Sleighing, 427
Sleive na Garry, 414
Slide for Life, 147
Slippery Day, A, 108, 116, 118, 119, 133, 136, 334, 547
Sloman, Elizabeth, 159, 246, 316, 346, 347, 364, 557, 560, 568
Slosson, George F., billiards, 140, 149, 582
Small, David, 375, 399, 405
Smiff, cast, 459, 460
Smith, actor, 29
Smith (of Burke and Smith), 550
Smith (of Burton and Smith), 111
Smith (of Derious and Smith), 585
Smith (of the Four-in-Hand), 332, 343, 349
Smith (of Sullivan and Smith), 414
Smith, Allie, 314, 536, 569, 618
Smith, Annie, 469
Smith, Dexter, 178
Smith, E. M., 15 ff
Smith, Ed C., 125
Smith, Edith, 49
Smith, Edwin, 111

Smith, Fred S., 646
Smith, Harry A., 529
Smith, Helene, 341, 348, 352, 561, 562, 569
Smith, J., 552
Smith, Josie, 52
Smith, Kitty, 361
Smith, Larry, 110, 323, 533
Smith (Larry) and Burke (John), 324 (see Burke and Smith)
Smith, Lew, 636
Smith, Lottie and Nettie, 403, 404
Smith, Mark, the elder, 224
Smith, Mark, the younger, 238, 254, 383, 478
Smith, May, 361
Smith, Mrs. Mark, 604
Smith, Mrs. Sol, 64, 171, 179, 258, 466, 491
Smith, Neil, and dogs, 138, 140, 346, 348, 353, 364, 401, 564, 624
Smith, P. J., 206
Smith, S. S., 624
Smith, Shirley, 245
Smith, Sol, 64, 171, 179, 258, 458
Smith, Sydney, 147, 179, 262, 360, 619
Smith, W. H. (Billy, of the Big Four), 316, 333, 334, 336, 340, 397, 471, 554, 573
Smith, William, 573
Smith, William F. (of Four of a Kind), 567
Smith Sisters (Kate and Mary), 577
Smith and Allen, 139
Smith and Byrne, 125, 127
Smith and Leopold, 552, 558
Smith and Waddie, 119
Smithers, Jessie, 532
Smithsonian Hall, Greenpoint, 207 ff, 421 ff, 642
Smithsonian Hall, Williamsburgh, 637 ff
Smoked Out, farce, 555
Smythe, T. H., 472
Snake Charmer, The, 439, 474; casts, 479, 482, 538; 613
Snake enchantress, 365, 578, 579
Snakes exhibited, 541, 580
Snelbaker's Majestic Combination, 397, 616, 618
Snow (of London Athletes), 530
Snow (of Murray, Snow, &c.), 327, 342, 396
Snow, Harry, 601
Snow, Lew, 565
Snow Brothers, 27, 146
Snow Flower, The, cast, 267; 279, 384
Snozzle! Bozzle! Wozzle! 136
Snyder, G. B., 225
Snyder, M. B., 56, 277
Snyder, Mrs. M. B., 58
So bezahlt man seine Schulden, 81
Social Literary Society, Brooklyn, 196
Social Literary Union, 627
Social Quartette Club, Greenpoint, 207 ff, 422, 641 ff
Social-Reformer Gesang-Verein, 87, 88
Società Corale Italiana Palestrina, 89
Socetà di San Antonio di Padova, 303
Società di Unione e Fratellanza Italiana, 89, 303, 515
Società Filodrammatica Italiana, 302

Società Filodrammatica Tommaso Salvini, 302, 515
Società Italiana Mazzini di Mutuo Soccorso, 303, 515
Società Legione Giuseppe Garibaldi, 303, 515
Società Operaia Italiana, 303
Società Ticinese di Mutuo Soccorso, 89, 303
Sociétaire, La, cast, 33
Société Bienfaisance Espagnole, 514
Société Culinaire Cosmopolite, 88
Société Culinaire Française, 307
Société Culinaire Philanthropique, 88, 513, 520
Société des Ex-Refugiés de la Commune, 514
Société Française de l'Amitié, 520
Société Française de Bienfaisance, 514
Société Helvetienne, 301
Société Israelite Française, 301, 513
Societé Suisse Generale, 513
Society, or, Married in the Dark, 635
Sodom und Gomorrha, casts, 68, 75
Sohn, Der, auf Reisen, 293
Sohn, Der, der Wildniss, cast, 70
Söhne der Freiheit, 86, 511
Sohst, Adolf, 82, 161, 165, 298, 299, 376, 381
Soirées Chantantes, 89
Solange, cast, 441
Soldatenliebe, 123
Soldene, Emily, 384
Soldier's Orphan, The, 328, 348
Soldier's Trust, The, 65
Solomon, Edward, his Billee Taylor, 265, 266; Claude Duval, 477
Solomon, Martha, 405
Solomon Levy, farce, 352
Solon Shingle, 105, 328, 331, 396
Somers, Lucy, 64
Somers, T. E. (see Seamon, Charles V, and Somers, T. E.)
Somerville, Marie, 11, 254, 274, 413
Song of the Bell sung, 591
Sonnambula, La, casts, 27, 93; 94, 95, 97; casts, 182, 305; 306, 308, 309, 392; cast, 456; 457; cast, 614
Sonnenwendhof, Der, 284
Sonntagsjäger, Die, 78
Sontag, Carl, début, parts, criticisms, 290 ff; compared with Haase, 290; 309, 310, 402; in Staten Island, 430; parts, 508
Sontag, Mme., actress, 34
Soper, I. N., 406
Sothern, E. A., parts, 31, 43, 44, 47, 53, 61, 161, 242
Sothern, E. H., début, parts, 43, 44; as "Edward Dee," 248, 389; 268
Soup Tureen without a Cover, 28, 155
South Beach, S. I., 430
South Brooklyn Turn-Verein, 298, 403
South Bushwick Church, 419
Southard, amateur, 399
Southard, W. H., 178
Southern, Jennie, 129, 326, 330, 542, 550
Southern Jubilee Singers, 407
Southern sketches, 328

Southwick, organ, 628
Souvenir (Dramatic Club), 417
Souvenir Social and Dramatic Union, 637, 638
Spader, Emily, 150, 371 ff, 395, 430, 537, 597, 630, 638, 640, 641
Spader, Jennie, 214
Spader, Nellie, 214
Spanish activities, 514
Spanish Armada, in fireworks, 631
Spanish athletes, 361
Spanish Choral Society, 158
Spanish floods, relief, 158
Spanish plays, 28, 155
Spanish society, 156
Spanish Students, 27, 28, 59, 142, 160, 183, 339, 361, 362, 365, 401
Spanish Troubadours (Ramirez's), 350, 351, 530, 532, 555
Sparker, W., fire-king, 205
Sparking in the Park, 571, 618
Sparks Brothers (John and Joe), 102, 109, 112, 131, 140, 186, 551, 553, 554, 556 ff, 574, 576
Sparks, Willie Edouin's, 480
Sparring, 143, 189 (see Wrestling, Sparring, Boxing)
Speaking machine, 639
Specht, Fred, 55
Specialty Trio, 552, 563, 564, 570
Spectre Bridegroom, The, 206, 405
Spectre Knight, The, 388
Spectre Night, The, 64
Spectre of the Forest, The, 400
Spelman, H. S., 97
Spence, Clara M., 154
Spence, George, 534
Spencer, Lew, 396
Spencer, Lillian, as Hazel Kirke, 236; parts, 248, 412
Spencer and Murphy, 547
Sperling und Sperber, 511
Sperry, E. B., 212
Sphinx, Le, with Bernhardt, 241
Spices, skit, 347, 348, 564
Spieker, Minnie, 193
Spielt nicht mit dem Feuer, 78
Spies, J. J., 265
Spiller, C. H., 255
Spirits Frumenti, 115, 333, 336
Spiritualism, 65, 529, 623 (see infra)
Spiritualism "exposed," 109, 153, 154, 199, 200, 215, 418, 419
Spitzner, Frl., 74 ff
Sport, cast, 73
Sprague, Arthur, 126 ff, 414
Sprague, George R., 29, 41, 178, 245, 491
Sprague, Isaac W., "living skeleton," 191
Sprague's Georgia Minstrels, 65
Sproul, Mrs. E., 184
Spurgeon, Rev. J. A., and his brother, 192
Square Man, A, casts, 621, 634
Squatter Sovereignty, cast, 525; 608
Squires, Mme., bearded, 624
Stabat Mater, 92 ff; at Tabernacle, Brooklyn,

194; 198; at Academy, 305, 306, 309; 372, 403, 404, 407, 409, 540, 629
Stäbner, Frl., 493
Stadt-Theater, becomes Windsor, 64 ff
Staff of Diamonds, The, 322
Stafford, Maude, 218
Stafford, William, 281, 282
Stag Athletic Racket, 23rd Regiment, 194
Stage-Struck, 563, 575, 617
Stage-Struck Chambermaid, The, 558
Stage-Struck Daughter, The, 132, 133
Stage-Struck Domestics, The, 110
Staircase Bend, The, 342
Standard Combination, 416
Standard Hall, 155, 162, 370, 591
Standard Hall Quartet, 155
Standard Quartet, 372, 591 ff
Standard Theatre, Brooklyn, 621 ff
Standard Theatre, New York (1879-80), 47 ff; sold, 50; (1880-81), 264 ff; (1881-82), 476 ff
Standing Bear, Indian, 153
Standish, Harry, 480, 538
Standish, W., 469
Stanfield, Henry, tenor, 597
Stange, Frl., 66 ff
Stanley, Alma Stuart, 255, 433, 460, 529
Stanley, Charles, 272, 384, 390, 411
Stanley, H. M., tenor, 537
Stanley, Harry C., 135, 493
Stanley, Miss, 477
Stanley, W. H., 480
Stanley, W. N., tenor, 587
Stansil (George) and Ryan (Ed), 545, 576
Stantini, Roberto, 235, 356
Stanton, W. J., 528
Stanwood, Ada, 189
Stapleton, S. I., 430, 648 ff
Star-Spangled Banner, Dudley Buck's overture, 358
Starelle, Charles, 274
Stark, Rose, 57
Starke Mittel, 71; as Needles and Pins, 232, 233
Starrett, Miss L. E., 592
Staten Island (1879-80), 215 ff; 300; (1880-81), 429, 430; 601; (1881-82), 647 ff
Staten Island Quartette Club, 429, 649
Staten Island Quintette Club, 648
Staten Island Vocal Society, 217, 429, 430, 648
Statue, The, 119
Statue Blanche, La, 128
Stearns, Nellie, 424
Stebbins, Genevieve, 160, 270
Steck Hall, 161, 163, 368, 369, 375 ff, 592
Steckelberg, saxophone, 52
Stedman, C. A., 256
Stedman, Reno, 128
Steeb, Fred, 196, 627
Steel Arm, the Avenger, 204
Steele, amateur, 97
Steele (see Goldie and Steele)
Steele (see Landis and Steele)
Steele, David P., 49, 178
Steele, Etty, 576
Steele, George (of Topack and Steele), 617

Steele, L., 516
Steele, Mollie Maeder, 51
Steele, Nellie, 204
Steele, O. B., 567
Steele, Sherman, 120
Steerage, The, cast, 103
Steiermarck singers, 512
Stein's, Conrad, Sommer-Garten, 300
Steinbuch, actor, 290, 503
Steinbuch, Carl, 84, 165, 201, 295, 374, 512, 591, 596, 637
Steiner, actor, 495
Steinfeld, Albert, 213
Steins, Fred, 84, 85, 160, 194, 410, 512, 591, 594, 623, 629
Steins, Oscar, 377, 587, 594, 596, 598, 602, 632
Steinway Hall, 85, 153 ff; (1879-80), 157 ff; 165, 297, 298, 367 ff; (1880-81), 370 ff; 584; (1881-82), 587 ff
Stelzner, Laura, 537
Stephens, Adine, 275, 385
Stephens, E. H., 411
Stephens, H. P., 265, 266
Stephens, W. T., parts, 111, 115, 325, 326, 352, 553, 554, 557, 559, 575, 576, 620
Stephenson, Mabel, 434, 593, 643
Steppes, Herr, 284, 298
Steps to Ruin, 530
Stereopticon, 423, 645
Sterling, E., 14 ff, 231 ff, 443 ff
Sterling, W. E., 279
Stern, Mme. M., 600
Stern Brothers, employes act, 584
Sternberg, C., 378, 591, 592 ff, 595
Sternberg, Carl, 498
Sternberg, Constantine, 235, 303, 304, 356, 357, 370, 378, 391, 495, 590, 591 ff
Stetson, E. T., 107, 109
Stetson, John, 242, 434
Stetson, Louise, 130
Stettin Humoristen Sextet, 539
Stevens, Charles, 143 ff
Stevens, Clinton, 38, 48
Stevens, J. F., 54, 276
Stevens, John A., 41; leases Windsor Theatre, 65; 178, 279; his play, 492
Stevens, Kitty, 108, 121, 126
Stevens, Ogden, 243, 458
Stevens, Sara, 274
Stevens, W. O'Dale, 131, 135
Stevenson, C. A., parts, 65, 169, 267, 279, 439, 453, 491, 519, 633
Steward (or Stewart), Mrs. L., 212, 424
Stewart, Ellie, 16
Stewart, Fattie, 554, 567, 573
Stewart, Julia, 43, 44, 225, 243, 467, 634
Stewart, M. Louise, 628
Stewart, Maggie, 202, 206, 628 (possibly different persons)
Stewart Family, 43
Stickney, Emma, 147
Stickney, Robert, equestrian, 146 ff, 192, 205
Stickney, Sam, 147
Stickney, Virginia, 107, 116, 136
Stiftungsfest, Das, 292, 293, 503, 623

Stiles, John, 59
Still Waters Run Deep, 383
Stille Familie, Eine, 71
Stille Liebe mit Hindermissen, 293
Stirk Family of bicyclists, 246, 306, 314, 315, 349, 351, 398, 498, 553, 564, 565, 570, 571, 617
Stock Exchange Glee Club, 161, 163, 596
Stockwell, L. R., 40, 272, 307
Stockton, Miss, 24
Stoddard, A. E., 51, 167, 251, 381, 467, 605
Stoddard, John L., lectures, 154, 368, 394, 610, 614
Stoddart, George W., 41, 176, 203, 268, 481, 607
Stoddart, J. H., as to French Flats, parts, 9 ff; 42, 226 ff, 437 ff, 607
Stoddart, Mrs. G. W., 41, 176, 268, 607
Stoddart, W. B., 538
Stodder's orchestra, 379
Stodigt, Louis, 601
Stoffregen, Miss A., 377
Stokes, C. W., 471
Stokes, Emma, circus, 540
Stokes, Katie, circus, 360, 540
Stokes and Henshaw, 547
Stolen Fun, 316, 324, 349, 551, 557
Stone, Amy, 331, 552
Stone, D. W., circus, 645
Stone, E. D., 481
Stone, H. F., 531
Stone, Isabel, 41, 150, 193, 368, 373
Stone, Jenny, 477
Stone, Lew, 571
Stone, Lily, 390
Stone, Marie, parts, 51, 167, 238, 393, 455, 456, 611
Stoneall, Clara, 256, 387, 607
Stora, Margherita, 591
Storrs, Rev. R. S., 152, 627
Storti, singer, 26, 27, 180, 182
Story, Anna Warren, 384, 437, 606
Story, Robert, 123
Stoteler Gesellschaft, 86
Stover, Florence, 49, 167
Stradella, cast, 80
Strakosch, Maurice, 158, 162, 183
Strakosch, Max, opera at Booth's, 26, 27; benefit, 97; 168; opera, 180, 182, 251, 308, 456, 457
Stranglers of Paris, The, 622
Stratagem, The, 333
Strategists, The, 63, 94; casts, 171, 467; 469, 480, 608
Stratton, F. A., 546
Strawberry festivals, 200, 209, 212, 215, 217, 420, 423, 428, 641, 645
Streets of New York, casts, 53, 62; 107; cast, 484
Stricken, farce, 351
Strike on the Narrow Gauge Road, 343
Strike on the Pittsburgh Road, 105
Strini, S. P., 160
Stritter, Joseph, 119, 293
Strolling by the Old Mill, 351

INDEX

Strolling by the Seaside, 547
Strolling in the Woodland, 350, 562
Strong, Jennie, 163
Strong men, 113, 115, 126, 131, 414, 562, 566
Strong women, 104, 108, 112, 118, 120, 128, 189, 325, 548, 576, 625
Stronghold Sure, A, by Bach, 379, 410, 599
Struggle, A, for a Fortune, 623
Strüvy, Frl., 67 ff
Stuart, A. H., 11, 41, 437, 606 (possibly different persons)
Stuart, Clara, 124
Stuart, Clinton, 440, 481
Stuart (or Stewart), Dora, 170, 276, 472
Stuart, H. A., 255
Stuart, Helen, 268, 392
Stuart, J. H., 64, 476
Stuart, Mary, actress, 460, 529
Stuart, Maud, 24, 236, 237
Stuart Sisters (Mattie and Alice), 100
Stubel, Jenny, 494 ff, 537, 612, 634
Studentenstreiche, 293
Studley, J. B., parts, 29, 57, 62, 225, 277, 279, 280, 412, 413, 453, 454, 488, 490
Stultz, actor, 232
Stultz, Herr, 499
Stündchen in der Schule, 77
Sturges, Charles, 435, 493, 618
Sturges, J. A., 64
Sturges, W., 389
Sturgis (sic), James, 528
Stutsman, Clara, 192, 199, 375, 408
Stuvers, Carrie, 337
Styles Hall, Brooklyn, 627
Subway circuit, 272
Suil-a-Mor (Daddy O'Dowd), cast, 457, 458; 607
Sulamith, by L. Damrosch, 603
Sullivan (of Four Kings), 415
Sullivan (of the Four-in-Hand), 332, 343, 349, 414, 415, 553
Sullivan (of Williams and Sullivan), 34
Sullivan, Algernon S., 584
Sullivan, Arthur S., in America, 34 ff
Sullivan, J. J., parts, 41, 58, 94, 175, 202, 272, 387, 435, 469, 553, 573, 575
Sullivan, J. P., 122, 137, 138 (see Cronin and Sullivan)
Sullivan, John, walker, 359, 540
Sullivan, John L., fights for $5,000, 535; 541
Sullivan, M. J. (of Olympia Quartette), 114, 314, 329, 334, 345, 559
Sullivan and Harrington, 105, 567
Sullivan, play with Salvini, 242, 244, 393
Sullivan Street Brigade, 102, 103
Sully, Billy (see Williams and Sully)
Sully, Dan, 134, 138, 353, 397, 616
Sultan Divan, 142, 361, 580
Sultan of Mocha, The, cast, 225
Sultan's Harem, The, 533
Sulzer's Harlem River Park, 299, 513, 515
Summers, E. A., 372, 640
Summers, J. W., 61, 280, 478
Sunday concerts, 25 ff, 28, 33, 36, 37, 41, 52 ff, 86 ff, 92 ff, 108, 156 ff, 164, 284 ff, 299, 300, 305 ff, 356 ff, 456, 457, 495, 496, 498, 502, 515, 519, 521, 522, 537, 596, 597, 640
Sunflower, The, and the Wasp, 546
Surprise Party, The, 336
Surridge, J. H., 318, 341 ff
Susie's Serenade, 112, 120
Sutherland, Jennie, 635
Sutherland, John, 172, 389, 608
Sutherland Sisters, long hair, 401
Sutton, J. P., 609
Sutton, Mrs. J. P., 167, 171, 609
Suydam, G. W., amateur, 369
Suydam Brothers (Frank and Eugene), 129, 130, 187, 344, 396, 556
Swain, Carrie, 101, 247, 271, 351, 389, 412, 565, 571, 574
Swain, S. C., (of Johnson and Swain), 350, 566, 572
Swain, Sam, 101, 247, 323
Swann, Harry, 625
Swayze, Miss, 375
Sweatnam, Billy, 103
Swedish Ladies' Quartette, 155, 284, 356
Swedish Singing Society, 409
Sweeney, James, 567
Sweeney (James) and Kearney (Eddie), 573
Sweeney, John, 561
Sweeney and Mott, 635
Sweeney and Ryland, 569
Sweeny (sic, of Dwyer and Sweeny), 134
Sweet, George, 615
Sweethearts, casts, 45, 192; 420, 629
Swift, Marie Louise, 96 ff, 159, 161, 162, 165, 195, 305 ff, 371, 380 (see also Dotti, Mlle.)
Swift, Ward, 355
Swift and Sure, play, **553**, 557, 620
Swinburne, John, 39, **63, 201**, 449
Swinging Angels, **533, 534**
Swinging Beauties, 550
Swinging First Part, 532, 533
Swiss Bellringers, 160
Swiss Courtship, 341
Swiss Hulfsgesellschaft, 298
Sydney, entertainer, 155
Sydney, Adelaide, 155
Sydney, Miss A., 28
Sykes, Olive Logan, her play, 14
Sylvano, Grace, 123 ff, 319
Sylvester, Ed, 129, 321, 322, 530 ff
Sylvester, Emily, 129, 189
Sylvester, Louise, parts, 40, 170, 203, 244, 265, 269, 389, 605
Sylvester, Miss H., 640
Sylvester and Lester, 189
Sylvia, Mlle., 332
Sylvia, Delibes' ballet, 538
Sylvie, May, 231 ff, 386, 443 ff
Symphony Society, New York (1879-80), 165; (1880-81), 380; (1881-82), 602, 603
Sythia Dramatic Troupe, 426
Sythia's Revenge, 426

Tabernacle, Brooklyn, 191 ff, 407, 626 ff
Tabernacle, Greenpoint, 421 ff
Tabernacle of Israel, 427

Table d'Hote, cast, 314, 315
Table's, The, Spread, farce, 396
Tableaux, 300 (see Great Republic, Hager's)
Tageszeiten, Die, by Raff, 594
Tagliapietra, 28, 82, 97, 162, 163, 200, 244, 356, 456, 523, 600, 611, 639
Tailor's Luck, 350, 561
Tailraf, Z., 449
Talbert (or Talbot, of Mayo and Talbert), 133, 573
Talbert, E. H. (of Original Little Four, later of Four Aces), 332, 348, 565, 567
Talbert, H. C. (of the Four-in-Hand), 332, 343, 349, 415, 553
Talbert, Harry, 347
Talbot, Eula, 610
Talbot, Hugh, parts, 35; trouble with W. S. Gilbert, 36
Tale of a Tar, 115
Talmage, T. DeWitt, 215, 407, 417, 586, 645
Talmagian Theology, lecture, 522, 615
Tamaro's Mass, 160
Taming of the Shrew (so announced), 29, 184 (see Katharine and Petruchio)
Tammany Hall, auditorium, 89, 152 ff, 160 ff, 300, 301, 514, 515, 582 ff
Tams, A. W., 51, 251, 487, 605
Tangoy, Célestin, 88
Tania, cast, 497
Tannehill, E., 39, 41, 263, 478
Tannehill, F. A., 61, 62, 485
Tannehill, Frank, Jr., 254
Tannehill, Mrs. F. A., 228, 468, 604
Tanner, Cora, 54, 170, 252, 263
Tanner, Dr., What I Know about Fasting, 237
Tanner, Dr., Outdone, 312
Tanner, James, 421
Tante Lotte, 511
Tantrums, 576
Tarantella, ballet, 538
Tarr, E. S., 48, 176, 270, 271, 472, 618, 633
Tartuffe, cast, 291
Tattooed Greek, 579, 625
Tattooed lady, 579, 625
Tattooed Man, 190, 401
Tauffenberger, parts, 263, 264, 355, 388, 466, 473
Tavernier, Ada (sic), 439
Tavernier, Albert, 265, 280, 412, 458
Tavernier, Ida (sic), 610
Taxpayer's Vicissitudes, 415
Tayleure, Clifton W., his East Lynne, 470
Tayleure, R. L., 8, 278
Taylor (of Magee and Taylor), 543
Taylor, B. C., 112, 113, 124, 125
Taylor, Bayard F., 365
Taylor, David, 180, 392, 611
Taylor, G. H., 155
Taylor, H. F., 385, 436, 439, 606, 633
Taylor, Harry, 176
Taylor, Helene, 214, 360
Taylor, J. C., 160, 432
Taylor, J. R., 567
Taylor, James, 245, 437, 489, 606

Taylor, Jerry, 64
Taylor, Lillian, 473
Taylor, Louisa, 207
Taylor, May, 41, 607
Taylor, Nellie, 94, 237, 258, 471
Taylor, Nettie, 193, 408, 421, 626, 629
Taylor, Norman, walker, 149
Taylor, W. H., 155
Tazza, La, di Tè, 302
Tearle, Edmund, parts, 463, 464, 605
Tearle, Osmond, début, parts, reviews, 219 ff; 235, 243, 244, 246, 306, 432 ff, 467, 611, 613
Tebaldo, singer, 92 ff
Tees, L. C., his play, 167
Telegraph Lads, The, 349
Telegraph scene, in play, 331
Telegraphers' Association, 598
Telephone, seats secured by, 45; "début on the stage," 275
Temperance Hall, Greenpoint, 208, 642
Temperance Lyceum, S. I., 215 ff, 429, 648
Tempest, The, recited, 585
Temple, Bessie, 39, 218, 479
Temple, E. P., 467, 481
Temple, Florence, 607
Temple, Rose, 452, 459, 609
Temple, Wallace, 51
Temple, Walter, 167
Temple, Brooklyn (formerly the Rink), 404 ff, 628
Temple Choir, Boston, 392
Temple Quartette, Boston, 180, 183
Templeton, Fay, 493, 508; Opera Company, 608, 634
Ten American Students, 137, 138, 330, 345, 348, 397
Ten Broeck, May, 64, 317, 566, 571, 572, 615, 618
Ten Nights in a Bar-room, 147, 203; cast, 321; 355, 649
Ten Thousand Miles Away, cast, 278; 491, 608
Tenbrook (of Darley and Tenbrook), 125, 204
Tenement House, Life in a, 122, 138
Tennent, Margaret, 635
Tennessee Jubilee Singers, 200, 421, 429
Terrace Garden (or Garten), 82, 293, 294, 297, 298, 510, 511, 584, 597, 601
Terry, Ellen, 31, 54
Terwilliger, Betty, 417
Teson, Lulu, 468
Tettenborn, Lina, 56, 102, 103, 172, 274, 314
Teutonia Assembly Rooms (or Hall), 83 ff, 89, 90, 294 ff, 303, 368, 512 ff, 584
Teutonia Club, 84
Teutonia Hall, Williamsburgh, 637, 640
Texas Giant Boy, 191
Texas Jack, actor, 134
Texas Jack, giant, 625
Texas Twins, midgets, 400
Thalia, Gesangverein, 403
Thalia Theater (1879-80), 73 ff; (1880-81), 282 ff; the actors travel, 398, 402, 418, 419, 420; (1881-82), 493 ff
Thallon, Robert, 399, 405, 638

That Boy of Dan's, 117, 413
That Boy's Sister, lecture, 638
That Dog Next Door, 630
That Rascal Tom, 322
That's What I Thought, 567
Thatcher, George, 92, 143 ff, 179, 362, 398; his minstrels, 618 (see infra)
Thatcher (George) and Ryman's (Add) Minstrels, 317, 398
Thatcher (Ned) and Hume (Dick), 117, 122, 131, 134, 135, 561
Theall, Novelty Theatre, Williamsburgh, 202 ff
Theatre Comique, 514 Broadway (1879-80) 98 ff; (1880-81), 311 ff; passes out of existence at the old site; next at 728 Broadway (1881-82), 524, 525
Theatrical Tramps, 557
Théfer, actor, 239, 246
Theiss's concerts, 142, 296, 298, 362, 512, 578
Theodor Körner Liedertafel, 87
Theodorus, W., 595
Therese Krones, 70, 286 ff
Thespian Ambition, 429
Thespian Pedestrians, 351
Third Avenue after Dark, 140
Third Avenue Boarding House, 140
Third Avenue (American) Theatre (1879-80), 139 ff (see also Parker's, Dick, American Theatre)
Thirteenth Regiment, 193, 199, 408, 626; Company F, 608; Company K, 630
Thomas (of Four Diamonds), 129
Thomas, A., 516
Thomas, Annie, 373
Thomas, F. F., 136
Thomas, Julia, 373 ff, 376
Thomas, Kitty, and doves, 531, 570, 635
Thomas, Miss C. C., 332
Thomas, T. F., 334
Thomas, Theodore, and New York Philharmonic, 60; 156 ff, 164, 165, 310, 356, 372 ff; and the Philharmonic, 379, 380; Brooklyn Philharmonic, 409, 410; 587 ff, 592; Music Festival, 598 ff
Thomas and Neary, 188
Thomas and Watson, 184
Thompson (late of Howard and Thompson), 118, 326, 327
Thompson (of Kain and Thompson), 121
Thompson, Blanche, 604
Thompson, C. H., tenor, 162, 269, 373, 614, 629, 646
Thompson, Charlotte, 279
Thompson, Connie, 1, 38, 278
Thompson, D. B., 416
Thompson, Dan, 59
Thompson, Denman, 46, 47, 178, 181, 202, 276, 384, 385, 488, 492; alleged author of Castle Garden, 528; 607, 634
Thompson, Fanchon, 435
Thompson, George W., 320, 553, 620 ff
Thompson, J. W., 465
Thompson, James, 547
Thompson (James) and Fields (Billy), 549
Thompson, John, lectures, 585

Thompson, Lotta F., 622
Thompson, Lydia, 49, 338
Thompson, Lysander, 10 ff, 437 ff, 488
Thompson, Mickey (of Four Shamrocks), 338, 424, 526, 552, 554, 558, 567
Thompson (Mickey) and Brock (Joe), 337
Thompson, Pete, 338
Thompson, Slason, 264
Thompson, W. J., 138, 321, 322, 324, 544; his play, 622
Thompson Brothers (Al and Charles), 108, 126, 189, 331, 335
Thompson and Waldron, 118, 334
Thompson Street Æsthetes, 471
Thompson Street Flats, 144
Thorburn, Jeanie, 153, 199, 408, 423
Thorn, the Great, prestidigitateur, 329, 332, 354, 398
Thorn and Darwin, 349
Thorndyke, Lillie, 202
Thorndyke, Louise, 612
Thorne, Charles, pantomime, 28
Thorne, Charles R., Jr., parts, 10 ff, 94, 202, 226 ff, 243, 388, 437 ff; leaves Union Square Theatre, 442
Thorne, Edwin F., parts, 265, 389, 453, 491, 519, 633
Thorne, Emily, 17
Thorne, George, 395
Thorne, Grace, 462, 609
Thorne, Mrs. Edwin F., 265
Thorne, Nellie, 119
Thorne, Sophie, 415, 530
Thornton, Adelaide, 38, 225, 411, 476, 605
Thornton, Annie, 403
Thornton, Charles, 117, 325, 327, 414
Thornton, Dollie, 107, 111, 319 ff, 493, 575
Thornton, Isabella, 389
Thorpe, Hattie, 411, 440, 483, 484
Thorpe, J. W., 225 ff, 411, 437 ff
Thorpe, Laura, 11, 14 ff, 176
Three A. M., farce, 343
Three Dwarfs, The, 338
Three Graces, farce, 340
Three Grotesques, 335
Three Guardsmen, The, 65, 322
Three Hunters, The, 332
Three Invincibles, 548
Three Monarchs, 563
Thropp, Lou, 581
Through by Daylight, 326
Thrown upon the World, 353
Thumb, Tom, and wife, 143, 147, 154, 191, 400
Thursby, Emma, 22, 94, 97, 158 ff, 161, 162, 165, 181, 183, 195
Thurston, Minnie, 375
Tibbles, T. H., 153
Tichborne case, in The False Friend, 10
Ticinese, 515
Ticket of Leave Man, The, casts, 62, 112; 216; casts, 323, 332, 458; 609, 610, 634
Tidden, Paul, 630
Tier, T. M., 422
Tierman, J. C., 559, 560

Tierney (of Four Aces), 564, 565, 567
Tierney, James, 99, 311 ff, 524, 525
Tierney, M. F., 143
Tierney and Owens, 635
Tiffany, Louis, drop curtain, 20 ff, 60, 179, 202, 278, 306, 319, 619 ff
Tiger Hunter, 326
Tighe, James, 330 ff, 551 ff
Tightrope or wire walking, 110, 117, 210, 336, 338, 340, 424, 552, 558
Tigress of the West, 122, 339, 354
Till's Royal Marionettes, 135, 146, 396, 397, 616 ff
Tilla, Haydon, 52, 66, 146 ff, 160, 161, 251, 252, 262, 266, 300, 360
Tillotson, James M., his The Planter's Wife, 279
Tilton, E. L., parts, 167, 202, 237, 386, 486
Time and the Hour, 193, 395, 544
Time Tries All, 417
Tina, the Milk Vendor, 106
Tiote, cast, 231
Tir à li cible, 301
Tiro al Bersaglio, 89, 515
Tissington, H., 438
Tissot, J. and Mlle. A., 108, 114, 554
Tit for Tat, 366
Titus (of Mason and Titus), 562, 563, 568, 569
Tivoli Winter Garden, 142
To Marry or Not to Marry, cast, 6
To Oblige Benson, cast, 6; 7, 212, 257, 404, 423
To the End of the World, cast, 545; 553 (see also End of the World, The)
Tobin, T. F. (of Four-in-Hand), 567
Tobin and Reed (or Reid), 331, 353
Tochter, Die, der Hölle, 498, 508
Tochter, Die, des Herrn Fabricius, 281, 504
Todd, Little, 334, 565, 571
Toddlekins, 178
Toedt, Theodore J., 216, 235, 375, 376, 381, 399, 407, 417, 430, 594, 596, 598 ff, 602, 603
Toedteberg, Emma, 199
Toilettengeheimniss, Ein, 68, 500
Tom, Blind, 416, 587, 600, 626, 631
Tom Cobb, with amateurs, 585; 631
Tomaselli, Mme., 197
Tombola, 301
Tommy, African dwarf, 131, 342
Tompkinsville, S. I., 429, 649
Tonawanda Club, 584
Toner, Stella, 576
Too Many Visitors, 335
Too Truly Rural, 608
Toodles, 107, 329, 604
Tooker, Susie, 182, 184, 193, 407, 409, 629
Toole, C. J., 271
Tooley, Larry, 104, 111, 117 ff, 124, 127, 128, 135, 139, 325, 333, 349 ff, 355, 396, 414, 534 ff, 560, 576
Topack, George, 254
Topack (George) and Steele (George), 617
Topack and Moore, 134
Topfgucker, Der, 292

Topsy, Jennie Yeamans as, 62, 146; Mrs. G. C. Howard as, 65, 181, 199, 216, 429, 633; Bobby Newcomb as, 110; Rosie Palmer as, 112; Abbie Hampie (coloured) as, 139; Little Dot as, 212, 214, 425; Bella Martin (coloured) as, 215; Marie Bates as, 243; Sallie Partington as, 272, 307; Kate Partington as, 279, 411, 615; Dot Aborn as, 332; Adele Saunders as, 355; Lillie De Grey as, 360; Julia Sheldon as, 403; Daisy Markoe as, 485
Torek, Paul, 597
Torpedo, The, and the Whale, 266, 270
Torrence, Charles, 449
Torriani, A., flute, 378
Torriani, Angele, singer, 22
Torriani, Ostava, 251, 252, 311
Torturing Tame Turtles, 542
Tostée, Lucille, 31
Tot, Major, 401
Touchstone, B. Maginley as, 39
Tour de Nesle, La, 186, 277
Tourists, The, sketch, 557
Tourists, The, in a Pullman Palace Car, cast, 40; 41, 92; cast, 175; 178, 202, 203; cast, 247; 271; cast, 388, 389; 411, 470, 491, 609, 633
Tournie, singer, 310, 394
Tournour, Jennie, 148
Tournour, Millie, 147
Tournour, Mlle., 101
Tower, W. C., 372, 379, 410
Tower of Babel, by Rubinstein, 381, 603
Town Hall, Flatbush, 423, 644
Town Hall, Flushing, 212 ff, 645
Town Hall, Jamaica, 214, 215, 427 ff
Townley, Miss A., 264
Townsend, Miss, 89
Towse, J. Ranken, on As You Like It, at Wallack's, 220; on Jefferson's Bob Acres, 436; on Clara Morris's Mercy Merrick, 439; on Salvini's Othello, 242
Tracy (see Delvan and Tracy)
Tracy, Dan (see Devlin and Tracy)
Tracy, Helen, 39, 59, 177, 270, 443, 458
Tracy, Hetty, 268, 489
Tramps, The, 103, 150, 321
Tramps of the Present Day, 406
Transmagnificandubandanciality, 109, 138, 330
Trapeze, 102, 114, 123, 132, 146, 218, 219, 245, 246, 314, 316, 326, 330, 336, 343, 349, 350, 360, 398, 415, 424, 542, 548, 550, 558, 635, 645
Travelling companies, Madison Square Theatre, 23
Traverner, S. C., 623
Traviata, La, casts, 26, 90, 91; 180; cast, 305; 306; cast, 394; with Gerster, review, 457; with Patti, review, 502; with Patti, cast, review, 505; 518
Travis, Mrs. J. H., 594 ff
Traynor (of Wheatley and Traynor), 560
Traynor, Frank, 352, 360
Trebelli, Mme., 306
Tree, Ellen, 249, 462

Tremaine, W. B., 198
Tremaine Brothers, 215
Treumann, Max, 287, 379, 410, 513
Trevais, Adrienne, 539
Treville, Hattie, 458
Trevor, Laurie, 255
Trial by Jury, cast, 48; 66, 92, 217, 384; with children, 397
Trial of King Alcohol, 643
Tried for Treason, 117, 325
Trifles, 42; cast, 179; 327
Trigg, Fannie and Mary, 546, 614
Trimble, Add, 31, 318
Trimble, Joe and Sadie, 577
Trip, A, on the Steamboat, 553
Trip to Coney Island, A, 350
Trip to Manhattan Beach, by Gilmore, 358
Trip to Paris, A, 625
Trip to Starin's Island, 549
Trip to the Moon, A, 185
Tripp, Charles, armless, 580
Tripped and Trapped, 282
Trost, bass, 85
Trouble in French Flats, 132
Troubles in America, 129, 132
Troubles of a Door-Tender, 548
Troublesome Sheriff, The, 333, 344, 348
Troublesome Sheriffs (sic), 324
Trovatore, Il, cast, 92; 93; cast, 96; 98, 168; cast, 180; with amateurs, 193; in English, cast, 251; 307; casts, 309, 310, 311; in English, 385; 391; casts, 394, 457; with Patti, cast, 506; casts at Academy, 517, 521; 523; act of, with Patti, 613; Kellogg's farewell, 615
Troy, Cassie, 281, 570
Trudell, Dell, 352, 544, 552, 569, 574
Trudell and Rowan, 342, 352, 544, 551, 569
True, Emma, 101
True, R. S., 196, 406, 407
Trutt, Edward (Boston Quartette), 533
Tucker, Ethel, 619
Tucker, Mary, 246
Tudor, Amy and John, 135
Tumbleronicon, 105, 578, 642, 643
Turf Club Theatre, 592
Turkish Patrol, 144, 145
Turkish Reveille, sung by Pastor, 101
Turn Him Out, 329
Turner, 211, 271
Turner (of Virginia Trio), 315, 331, 348, 354, 551, 563
Turner, B. W., 248, 476
Turner, Carrie, 465; review, 520
Turner, Charles, 59, 90, 350, 544, 546, 566, 570, 572
Turner, Charles H., 168
Turner, Della, 116, 117, 348, 563
Turner, Dick, 204, 548
Turner, Emma, 16
Turner, F., 176
Turner, Frank, 65
Turner, Jennie, 550, 577
Turner, John M., banjo, 116, 118, 139, 326, 335

Turner, Sadie, 577
Turner and Collins, 187
Turner, Welch and Harris, 136
Turner Liedertafel, 148
Turnhalle, New York (1879-80), 81 ff; (1880-81), 293 ff; 509, 512; (1881-82), 583 ff
Turnhalle, Williamsburgh, 204 ff, 417 ff, 634 ff
Turning the Tables, 335, 351, 566, 572
Turn-Verein, New York, 81, 84 ff, 509; Williamsburgh, 316
Turnverein (sic) Gemischter Chor, Williamsburgh, 640
Turnour, Julius, 107, 118, 124, 126
Turtle Bay Park, or Assembly Rooms, 85, 86, 294 ff, 299
Tuthill, Dr. and Mrs. S. B., 197
Tuttle, W. W., 238
Tuttle, Zoe, 243
Twelfth Night, casts, 30, 168; 390; cast, 461, 462
Twelfth Regiment Reception, 540; Company K, 586
Twenty Minutes in Fishkill, 567
Twenty Minutes under an Umbrella, 406
Twenty-second Regiment, 371, 520, 597
Twenty-third Regiment, 194, 198, 199; minstrel show, 200; band, 392; Company H, 404; 407, 628
Twenty-third Ward Park, 586
Twilight Four, or Quartette, 567, 577
Twins, prize for finest, 401
Two Bachelors, 629
Two Barneys (Barney McNulty and Master Barney), 332, 340, 534
Two Bonnycastles, 646
Two Buzzards, The, 194, 630, 649
Two Can Play at That Game, 572
Two Convicts (Robert Macaire), 576
Two Dromios (Murphy and Shannon), 129
Two Gentlemen from Verona, 549
Two Gentlemen in a Fix, 305
Two Irish Gents, 121
Two Jack Sheppards, The, 557
Two Medallions, 529
Two Nights in Rome, casts, 225, 384, 411; 491; cast, 606, 607; 619, 633
Two Nurses, The, 567, 572
Two Orphans, The, casts, 10 ff, 65, 169; 202, 213, 214; cast, 216; 235; cast, 267; 279; cast, 354; 369, 384, 411, 427; casts, 453, 484, 491, 519, 547, 576, 582, 621, 633; 646
Two Peters, The (Czaar und Zimmermann), 90
Two Pompeys, The, 345, 350
Two Tramps, 116, 532
Two Wanderers, The, 110, 320, 321; cast, 328; 353, 542, 544, 545, 552, 636
Two-headed baby, 580
Two-headed girl, 365, 624, 625
Two-headed lady, 579
Tyler, Florence, 375
Tyler, George H., 27
Tyrolean sketch, 556
Tyrolean warblers and singers, 104, 118, 271, 356, 518, 526, 539, 540, 575

Tyroler-Halle, 83
Tyroler Quintet, 409
Tyrrell, Geoffrey, 581

Ueberall, Dramatic Society, 210 ff
Uhland-Bund, 87, 300
Ujiji Students, 631
Ulm, Susie, 118
Ulm Sisters, 58
Ulmar, Geraldine, 393, 455, 456, 611
Ulmer, George, 7, 468, 469
Ulmer, Lizzie May, 383, 468, 469
Ulmer, May, 176
Ultimo, 292
Umlauf, Frl., 66 ff, 288 ff, 499
Umsonst, 498
Una de Tantas, 155
Una voce poco fa, sung by Patti, 490
Uncle Alick Slocum, 339
Uncle Jasper's Birthday, 123, 319
Uncle Jasper's Invitation, 565, 573
Uncle Pete's Return, 336, 341, 543, 564
Uncle Rufe's Home, 345
Uncle Tom, J. B. Studley as, 62; C. L. Far-
    well as, 110; Jen Powers as, 112; S. S. San-
    ford as, 120; George McDonald as, 199;
    Charles Mestayer as, 213, 214; A. H. Hast-
    ings as, 243; Arthur Gregory as, 272, 307;
    W. T. Dulaney as, 332; Ward Swift as,
    355; Sydney Smith as, 360; Sam Lucas as,
    485
Uncle Tom's Cabin, 50, 57; cast, 61, 62; 64, 65;
    cast at Aberle's, 110; at Volksgarten, 112;
    120; cast, 139-140; 146, 151, 181, 185; cast,
    199; with children, 200; 204; casts, 212,
    213, 214; 215, 216; cast, at Booth's, 243;
    cast, 272; 279, 280; casts, 307, 332, 355,
    360; 394, 403, 411, 425, 427, 485, 491, 610,
    612, 614, 615, 625, 633, 645, 646
Uncle Tom's Cabin Jubilee Singers, 577
Under Oath, 569
Under the Gaslight, with Gus Phillips, cast,
    280; 551; cast, 553, 554
Under the Lamp-post, 550
Under the Lights of London (Lost in Lon-
    don), 531
Underhill, Charles F., 366, 408
Underwood, W. J., 97
Unequal Match, An, amateur cast, 612
Unger, Adolf, 370
Unger, Elise, 298, 509
Unger, Heinrich, benefit, 509
Unger, Tilly, 298
Ungeschlissener Diamant, Ein, 497
Unglücklichen, Die, 290, 309
Union Alsacienne, 89, 514
Union de Hudson County, N. J., 514
Union Franco-Américaine, 514
Union Fraternelle Française, 88, 301, 513
Union Hall, Ninth Avenue, 586
Union League Theatre (1879-80), 153 ff; 161;
    (1880-81), 366 ff; (1881-82), 582 ff; 591 ff;
    becomes Turf Club Theatre, 592
Union Park, 133rd Street, 378
Union Quartette, 187

Union Square Combination, 215, 216
Union Square Theatre (1879-80), 8 ff; (1880-
    81), 224 ff; (1881-82), 435 ff
Unione e Fratellanza Italiana (*see Società di
    Unione e Fratellanza Italiana*)
United States Mail, 337
United States Marine Band, 392
Units Comedy Company, 151
Unknown, cast, 41; 65; casts, 178, 279
Unneighbourly Neighbours, 343, 397, 616
Unser Zigeuner, cast, 75
Unsere Frauen, cast, 499; 623
Upham, 205, 639
Upham, Minnie, 458
Upper Crust, The, 222
Upper Crust, The, a different play, 264
Uproar in the Family, 334
Ups and Downs, 400
Uptown Hotel, Jamaica, 214
Urani, Miss, at Hill's, 577
Urban, F., 80, 287
Urchs, E., bass, 84
Uris' Dancing Academy, 199
Urso, Camilla, 372, 451, 587
Utter, singer, 310, 394

Vachot, Marie, 510, 514, 517 ff, 522, 537, 592,
    597, 612
Vaders, Henrietta, 51, 168, 171, 453
Vagrants, The, 558
Valdimer, Zelma, 151
Vale, J. S., Lenten matinées, etc., 153 ff, 365
Valentine, amateur, 97
Valentine, Dr., 258
Valentine, Die, 504
Valerga, Ida, 27, 182, 304 ff, 394, 517 ff, 522,
    613
Valerga, Tilly, 480, 481
Valjean, juggler, 183, 271, 345, 348, 396, 565,
    569, 571, 617
Valjean Brothers, 27, 133
Valleria, Alwina, parts, etc., 91 ff, 158, 164,
    181 ff, 194, 201, 251, 304 ff, 371, 380, 391 ff;
    leaves the opera, 516
Vallot, Mlle., 264, 466, 473
Vampier, Jean, Ella, Julien, 354
Vampier and Vidocq, 415
Van, the Virginian, 412
Van Amburgh, Frost, Stone and Company
    Menagerie, 645, 646
Van Arnheim, Katharine, 456, 457
Van Boyle, Mrs., 49
Van Brunt, Mrs., 592
Van Buren, Tillie, 532, 565, 566, 571, 572
Van Courtland, Ida, 623
Van Deren, D., 318
Van Deren, Mrs., 55, 62, 489, 607
Van Dorn, W. L., 38
Van Gelder, Martinus, 157, 158, 215
Van Horn, Mrs., 376
Van Houten, A., 38, 48, 254
Van Kuren, J. A., 205
Vance, George, 336, 547
Vandenhoff, Charles, 440
Vandenhoff, George, 152 ff, 159, 196, 365

Vandenhoff, George, Jr., 443 ff
Vandenhoff, Miss, 469
Vandenhoff, Mrs. George, 28, 54, 367, 585
Vandewater, lectures, 645
Vandewater, W. Y., 372
Vane, Alice, 508
Vane, Lillian, 383, 485
Vane, Will and James, 530, 543, 555, 565, 569
Vanolar, clown, 626
Vanoni, Marie, 510, 513, 538, 540, 597, 600
Vanoni, Mme., 377, 514
Vareis, Celene, 541
Varena, F., 282 ff
Varian, Marie, 202
Varian, Nina, 151
Variety, 51, 56, 64, 65, 100 ff, 184, 185, 204,
    211, 213, 214, 274, 383, 387, 396 ff, 413, 414,
    420, 421, 425, 487, 489, 490, 519, 520, 541,
    542 ff, 624 ff
Varney and DeBar, 333, 343, 616, 617
Varrey, Edwin, 62, 63, 174, 259, 383, 435, 453,
    606
Vaughan, Blanche, 44, 47, 231, 469, 621
Vaughan, Effie, 62, 171, 256
Vaughan, Harry, parts, 65, 411
Vaughn, Henry, walker, 359
Vaughn (or Vaughan), Mabel, 553, 554, 558,
    559, 567, 572, 576
Vaughn, Theresa, 271
Vavasour, Louise, 328, 535, 578
Veilchenfresser, Der, 292
Velos, and monkeys, 400
Venn, Topsy, 255, 256, 388, 610
Vennetta, Tom (see Peasley, Frank, and Ven-
    netta, Tom)
Venoa (of Nestor and Venoa), 530, 555, 558
Ventilation, 20 ff
Ventini, 123, 125, 127, 332, 337
Ventini, Bessie, 567
Ventriloquism, 42, 126, 128, 130, 132, 135, 207,
    209, 275, 276, 281, 316, 322, 339, 341, 343,
    346, 347, 351, 354, 362, 364, 385, 401, 415,
    425, 481, 518, 521, 526, 532, 534, 541, 548,
    554, 556, 557, 558, 559, 560, 561, 564, 566,
    568 ff, 571, 579, 580, 615, 616, 618, 621, 624,
    625
Ventura, L. L., 303
Venturi, Annetta, 391
Venturoli, actor, 302
Venturoli, Mlle., benefit, 374
Venus, Little, 321
Venus, wire walker, 626
Venus, extravaganza, 529
Verbrochene Krug, Der, 501
Vercelli Teatro, 303, 514, 515, 541, 542
Verfolgte Unschuld, Eine, 510
Verkaufte Schlaf, Der, 77
Vere, Vera, 247
Verlobung, Die, bei der Laterne, 76, 77, 82,
    292
Verlorene Ehre, cast, 75
Vernam, W. B., 392, 628
Verney, S. H., 8, 470
Vernon, Eddie, 351
Vernon, Edna, 468

Vernon, Ida, parts, 10 ff, 267, 412, 439, 453,
    483, 484, 488
Vernon, Marie, 354, 355
Vernon, May, 125
Vernon, Mrs., 224, 436
Vernon, Paul, 59, 257
Vernon, W. B., amateur, 199, (see Vernam,
    W. B.)
Verschwender, Der, 78, 287
Versprechen, Das, hinter'm Heerd, 71, 286,
    287, 495
Verwunschene Schloss, Das, 495, 496, 498
Vestvali, Marie, 125
Veteran, The, skit, 329
Veteran Gesang-Verein, 87, 511
Vetter, Der, 500, 502
Vicarino, singer, 598
Vice and Poverty, 345
Vickers, Mattie, 60, 138, 179, 343, 344, 387,
    398, 489, 526 ff, 561, 563, 564, 569, 575,
    616 ff
Vicomte de Letorières, 71
Victor (of Walton and Victor), 531
Victor, H., 53
Victor, Lester, 33
Victorelli (of Cardello and Victorelli), 349,
    350, 398
Victoria, trapeze, 316, 343, 360
Vidocqs, Three (John, William, Jacques), 331,
    336, 348, 415
Vie Parisienne, La, 26, 32, 33, 98
Viel Lärm um Nichts, cast, 69; 508 (see Much
    Ado about Nothing)
Vilano, parts, 32, 33, 88, 98, 263, 264, 355
Villa, Armandi, 356, 375
Village Barber, The, 549
Village Torment, 110, 121
Villain, The, Still Pursued Her, 144
Villanova, 158
Villeray, Mlle., 310
Villers, J. Jay, 191 ff, 205, 207, 365
Villiers, Jessie, 369
Villon Troupe, bicyclists, 535, 562, 563
Vim, 42
Vinal, Carrie, 49
Vincent, Helen, 175, 256, 389
Vincent, J. H. (Reverend), 638
Vincent, James, 238, 281, 619
Vincent, James C., 565, 566, 635
Vincent, John L., 27
Vincent, L. J., 94, 95, 244, 367
Vincent, May, 339
Vincent, Nellie, 124, 126, 127, 204, 548, 549
Vinchon, 263
Vining, Minnie, 5 ff, 433
Vint, Robert, walker, 540
Vinton, Carrie, 179, 467
Vinton, Ellie (sic), 231, 232
Vinton, Horace, 605
Vinton, Lillie, 18, 443 ff, 608
Vinton, M. J., 215
Viola (Twelfth Night), Miss Neilson as, 30,
    168; Frl. Bensberg as, 311; Mrs. Scott-Sid-
    dons as, 390; Alicia Robson as, 462
Violante, Lucia, 371

[750]

INDEX

Virginia Trio (Turner, Welch, Harris), 315, 331, 348, 349, 354, 551, 563, 570
Virginian, The (Owen Wister's), 448
Virginius, 170; cast, 248; 389; cast, 462; 463, 609
Vision of Death, 322
Vitale, Giuseppe, 197, 406, 408, 626, 628
Vivantiscope, 576
Vivian Sisters (Emily, Weavy, Bella), 534, 560, 616, 618
Vocal Society, Brooklyn, 399; Plainfield, 408
Vocal Union, 161
Vogler's orchestra, 616
Voice, A, from the Streets, 108
Vokes Family, 63, 230, 390, 453, 608
Vol-au-Vent, 120, 330
Volair, Miss, 458
Volcano, A Day and a Night in a, 418, 630
Volcano, A, Thirty Minutes in, 193
Volksgarten (1879-80), 111 ff; (1880-81), 324 ff; (1881-82), 542 ff
Volksfest, 190
Volks Theatre, Brooklyn, becomes Hyde and Behman's, 396 ff
Von Behren, Annie, 56, 485, 564
Von Boyle, Acland, 48, 49, 65, 167, 403, 423
Von Brandesky, Otto, 333
Von Brunn, Simon, Weinhandlung, 297
Von der Alm Tyroler Quintet, 356
Von Heimberg, Miss M., 603
Von Januschowsky, Georgine, 288 ff, 311, 498 ff, 510, 528
Von Leer (of Ward and Von Leer), 338
Von Schlagintweit, lecture, 85
Von Trautmann, Ida, 74 ff, 82
Voos, Mlle. Carrie, 326
Vornehme Ehe, Eine, 70
Vose, Val, 42, 275, 281, 364, 385, 534, 556, 557, 559, 579, 616, 625
Voxie, M. J., 419
Voyage, Le, en Suisse, 472, 473, 483, 537, 613
Voyagers, The, or, Fun on the Celtic, 342
Voyagers in Southern Seas, 245, 246

Wachsner, Herr, 290, 499 ff
Wachtel and Lucca, farce, 293
Waddie (of Smith and Waddie), 119
Wade (of Dilks and Wade), 134, 136, 189
Wade, Miss, 596
Wadsworth, Tracie, 371
Wagner, Herr, 74 ff, 284
Wagner, Carl, 614
Wagner, Clara, 336
Wagner, Henriette, 66 ff, 288, 499 ff
Wagner Palace Sleeping Car, 188
Wagner, Richard, his music performed, 164, 165, 201, 304, 357, 379, 380, 381, 382, 409, 410; with Materna, 523; 579, 600, 602, 603, 632
Wagstaff, Mrs., 610
Wainwright, Marie, parts, 167, 177, 202, 261, 277, 384, 450, 461, 465
Waise von Lowood, Die (Jane Eyre), 69
Waite, Charles B., 387, 472
Waiting for John, 530, 554

Wakeman, Annie, 14 ff, 58, 395
Walby, Josephine, 106, 529, 531, 635
Walcot, Charles, 167, 177, 202, 203, 386, 475, 486, 633
Walcot, Mrs. Charles, 167, 177, 202, 203, 386, 486, 633
Waldemere, Maud, 38
Waldron (of Thompson and Waldron), 334
Waldron, A., 179, 237
Waldron, Dan (of Big Four), 316, 333, 334, 336, 340, 397, 546, 554, 573
Waldron, George B., 54, 170, 437, 606
Waldron, Isabel, 54, 170, 431, 472, 606
Waldron, Nelson, stage machinery, 23; benefit, 235; avalanche scene, 267
Waldron, Theresa, 474
Waldron and Kane (or Kaine), 548, 563
Walhalla, 84 ff, 294 ff, 512
Walker, C., 149
Walker, Charlotte, 597
Walker, James T., 393
Walker, Maggie, 116, 326, 330, 334
Walker, Miss, concert, 213
Walking for Dat Cake, 144
Walking matches, 148 ff, 214, 359
Wallace, man fish, 102, 115, 155, 414
Wallace, Agnes, 53
Wallace, Alf, 415, 529 ff, 554
Wallace, Henrietta, 458
Wallace, J. J., his play, 332
Wallace, Laura, 435
Wallace, Mamie, 324, 529 ff, 547, 576
Wallace, May, 408
Wallace, "Professor," imitates birds, etc., 537
Wallace, Thomas, billiards, 582
Wallack, Fannie, 514, 515, 542, 624
Wallack, J. W., Jr., 224
Wallack, Lester, parts, 3 ff, 55, 167, 219 ff, 276, 281, 383, 384, 389, 474, 488, 608, 610
Wallack, Watty, 542
Wallack Association, Williamsburgh, 418, 627
Wallack's Theatre (1879-80), 1 ff; (1880-81), last season at 13th Street, 218 ff; becomes Germania, 224; (1882), new theatre described, cost, etc., performances, 431 ff
Waller, D. W., 280
Waller, Emma, 583, 586
Waller, Ida, 182
Waller, W., 155
Wallere, trapeze, 548
Wallfisch Quartett, 86
Walling (see Reynolds and Walling)
Wallington, H. A., 415
Wallis, W. F., 484
Wallis, W. H., 46, 262
Wallston, Blanche, 607
Walrabe, saxophone, 52
Walsh, Fred, 59
Walsh, John C., 61, 62, 106 ff, 322, 361
Walsh, Townsend, 24, 25
Walsh and Dempsey, 543, 551, 556, 574
Walter, Herr, 494, 496
Walter, Carl, 421 (see infra)
Walther, Karl, 537 (see supra)
Walters (see Carroll and Walters)

Walters and Morgan, 209
Walton, Bessie, 128
Walton, Charles, 625
Walton, E. L., 412, 468
Walton, May, 577
Walton, Punch, 333
Walton, T. W., 538
Walton, William, Whimsicality Company, 566, 567
Walton and Edwards, 565, 570, 571
Walton and Victor, 531
Waltz, Alice, 96, 104
Wambold, Dave, 143, 179
Wannemacher, F., 378
Wannemacher, Henry, 27, 160, 618
Ward (of Saunders and Ward), 425
Ward, F. T. (of Clipper Quartette), 134, 139, 552, 559, 563
Ward, Genevieve, parts, 174, 252, 253, 436, 606, 634
Ward, Isabel (or Isabella), 323, 333, 334, 338, 530, 544, 545, 548, 554, 557, 573, 575, 620
Ward, J. O., 131
Ward, James, 532
Ward, Jennie, 116, 123, 131, 331, 415, 549, 577
Ward, Lottie, 573
Ward, R., 143
Ward, Robert, 358
Ward, Thomas H., 326, 329
Ward (Thomas H.) and Lynch (Con T.), 140, 186, 204, 326, 351, 542 ff, 546, 562 ff, 569, 572
Ward and Wells, 116, 118, 127, 186
Warde, Fred B., parts, 170, 248, 249, 282, 389
Wardell, fire demon, 124
Wardell, Etelka, 411, 467, 471, 483
Wardell's Sängerhalle, 418
Ware, Annie, 57, 226, 469
Waring, Bertha, 361
Warmington, W., 258
Warner, H., 354
Warner, H. Louise, 597
Warner, Jeffreys, 128, 139, 323, 329, 332, 339, 353, 543
Warner, Jessie, 338, 563, 576, 624
Warren (of Mills and Warren), 344, 350, 556, 560, 568
Warren, Emma, 547, 548
Warren, G. W., 155, 381
Warren, R., 5
Warren, R. H., 155
Warren, Richard, 585
Warren, Robert, 439, 440
Warren, T. J., 337, 338, 339, 354
Warren, W., 243
Warren, William, 611
Warren, William (of Boston), on Jefferson's Rivals, 385; 611
Warren Comedy Company, 151
Was Ihr Wollt (Twelfth Night), cast, 311
Washburn, Mrs. C., 493
Washington Hall, Astoria or Long Island City, 211, 424, 425
Washington Park, Jones Wood, 86 ff, 89, 514
Washington Schützen Park, 300

Water queen, 190
Watermelon Man, 115, 120, 559
Waters, Adele, 462
Waters, Joseph, 478
Waters, Lottie, 548
Watkins, Eva, 628
Watrigant, Andrew, 124
Watrous, Edith, 193
Watson (of Clark and Watson), 133, 137
Watson (of Levanion and Watson), 105, 106, 110, 113, 320, 330
Watson (of Little Four), 567
Watson (of Thomas and Watson), 184
Watson (of Williams and Watson), 122
Watson, G. W. (of Four Diamonds), 117, 129, 328, 333, 334, 352, 553, 556, 567
Watson, Harry, 247, 315, 342, 349, 398, 546, 566, 572
Watson, Irene, 535
Watson, J., 15 ff
Watson, Louisa, 44
Watson, Minnie, 417
Watson, T. V., 321
Watson, Thomas, 544, 553
Watson, Tony, 344
Watson and Ellis, 130, 132, 186, 616 ff
Watson and Haley, 120
Watts, Amelia, 489
Waud, W. S., 538
Waverley Theatre, Brooklyn, 623; becomes Bunnell's Museum, 624
Waverley Theatre, New York, 402
Waverly, Charles, 51, 168, 263, 385, 436, 488, 606
Waxworks, 192, 625, 627
Way We Live, The, 19, 69
Wayne (of Four Aces), 564, 565, 567
Wayne (Charles) and De Vaney (Alf), 562
Wayne, H. S. (of Enterprise Four), 338
We Americans, lecture, 428
Weak Women, cast, 212
Weathersby, Eliza, 31, 40, 169, 256, 475
Weathersby, Emie, 475, 482
Weathersby, Jennie, 40, 169, 256, 411
Weaver, Add, 121, 133, 135, 136, 188, 318, 324, 343, 397, 534, 535, 562, 619
Weaver, Affie, 56, 172, 412
Weaver, Blanche, 14 ff, 58, 173, 232, 443 ff, 471
Weaver, H. A., 8, 29 ff, 168, 242 ff, 311, 440, 441, 450, 520
Weaver, H. A., Jr., 29 ff, 450, 520
Weaver, Mrs. H. A., 440, 520
Weaver Brothers, 333
Webb, Charles, 461, 462
Webb, Harriet, 306, 376, 518, 582
Webber, E. T., 474
Webber, Maud, 337
Webber, Nellie, 338
Weber, Lisa, 280
Weber Male Quartette, 356
Weber Quartet (sic) of Boston, 611
Weber's Jubilee Cantata, 594
Webster, Blanche, 355, 530, 531
Webster, Charles, 9, 41, 58, 471, 482

Webster, Gussie (or Genie or Gertie), 346, 352, 353
Webster, John, 41, 256, 458, 606
Webster Brothers (Ned and James), 105, 134; (of Four Shamrocks), 321, 336, 342, 352, 353, 355, 551
Wedding March, The, cast, 45; with amateurs, 627
Weed, concert, 376
Weed, Mort M., 160, 161, 198, 593
Weed, Professor, 644
Weed, Edna, 47
Weekman, H., walker, 359
Weeks, George S., 48, 54, 55, 150, 399, 487
Weidman, Charline, 50, 59, 168, 246, 442
Weinacht, 75 ff
Weingarten, Helene, 83, 85, 509
Weinlich, Joseph, 80, 498; 25th jubilee, 513
Weiss, Frl., 74 ff
Weiss, Herr, 499 ff
Welby, Bertha, 318, 633
Welch (of Murphy and Welch), 208
Welch (or Welsh, of Virginia Trio), 315, 331, 348, 354, 551, 563
Welch, Billy, 59
Welch, Fayette, 108, 109, 120, 121, 128, 129, 140, 185, 189, 319, 320, 325, 328, 330, 343, 531, 544, 556; his Minstrel Troupe, 186; his Pavilion, Rockaway Beach, 214; his Male and Female Minstrels, 337
Welch, James, 327
Welch and Dempsey, 551
Welch and Devere's Minstrels, 120
Welles, Charles B., 475, 476
Wellesley, Marie, 279
Welling (New York Vocal Quartette), 345
Wells (of Ward and Wells), 116, 125, 127, 186
Wells, Billy, 123, 319
Wells, Charles, 124, 125
Wells, F. C., 216
Wells, Florence, 135, 324, 330
Wells, George, 546
Wells, Kitty, 318
Wells, Mrs., 216
Wells, Robert E. L., 636
Welsh (of Gilson and Welsh), 564, 571
Welsh, J. E. (of Four of a Kind), 567
Welston, Harry P., 112, 120
Wendel, magic, 211
Wendel's Assembly Rooms, 83 ff, 294 ff, 512, 591
Wendel's Elm Park, 294 ff, 300
Wendling, George R., 629
Wenn man im Dunkeln küsst, 68, 70, 71
Wentworth (of Leopold and Wentworth), 625
Wentworth, Fanny, 136, 255, 269, 387, 528, 529, 538
Wentworth, Lottie, 577
Wentworth, Lulu, 111, 120, 546, 562
Wenzel, Fred, 549
Wer ist mit? 293, 511
Wernecke, Mary, 377, 378, 592
Wernell, Ada, 386
Werner, Charles, 157, 162, 170, 216, 420, 585, 591, 594, 597, 598

Werner, Edward, 102, 114, 135, 136, 138, 189, 351, 566, 571
Werner, Elias (sic), 587
Werner, Maud Stanley, 102, 114, 135, 136, 138, 189, 351, 566, 571
Werrenrath, George, 192 ff, 199, 403 ff, 410, 614, 627, 629
Wesleys (2 — Brothers), 328, 329, 333, 344, 345, 348, 350, 554, 562, 565, 568, 571, 572, 616
Wesner, Ella, 246, 274, 276, 277, 314, 315, 317, 346, 348, 353, 367, 487, 503, 541, 554, 561, 562, 564, 566, 571, 576
Wessells, G. W., 245, 436
West (of Gallagher and West), 347, 563, 571
West (of Gibson and West), 334
West (of Haley and West), 101
West (of Monumental Quartette), 332, 347, 553, 568
West (of Wood and West), 187
West, Billy, 124
West, Charles (see Sharpley and West)
West, Frank, 59, 108, 137
West, Garner, 155
West, Lillie, 168, 269, 460, 606
West, Ned, 141, 353, 354
West, Sailor, 320, 325, 327, 328, 331, 342, 343, 350, 351, 355; paints scenery, 543; 553, 570
West, W. H., 459
West, William (Billy), 98 ff, 311 ff, 345, 524, 525
West Brighton, S. I., Athletic Club, 217
West Brighton Hotel, 409, 631
West Brighton Beach Hotel, 155, 163, 164, 190
West New Brighton, S. I., 649
West Side Liedertafel, 299
Westbrook, Lillian, 265, 282
Western, Fanny, 534
Western, Lillie, 136, 277, 315, 317, 345, 487, 519, 545, 557, 564, 575, 578
Western, Lucille, 278
Western Union Telegraph Boy, The, 565, 574
Western Union Telephone Company, 581
Westminster Kennel Club, 150
Weston (of Kelly and Weston), 119, 128
Weston (Charles, late of Weston and Woods) and Hanson (Charles), 324, 335, 351, 396, 536, 545, 553, 557, 569, 575, 618
Weston (Charles) and Woods, 115, 335
Weston, Edward Payson, 149
Weston, Flora, 100
Weston, Frank, 175, 245, 246, 383, 466, 491
Weston, George, Jr., 648
Weston, Jennie, 100
Weston, Maggie, 66, 104 ff, 107 ff, 280, 317, 323, 344; her play, 355; 400, 553, 573, 574, 636
Weston Brothers (Sam and Morris), 113, 121, 138, 336, 349, 350, 398, 490, 520, 527, 552, 558, 575
Weston, the Walker, farce, 137 (see infra)
Weston, the Walkist, farce, 128
Wetherill, Nellie, 437 ff
Whalen (of London Athletes), 530
Whalen, Henry, 314

INDEX

Wharton, B., actor, 263
Wharton, Belle, 15, 28, 258
Wharton, Jennie, 258
Wharton, Mrs. Ellen, 28
What Are the Wild Waves Saying? 128
What Our Girls Ought to Know, 584
What Shall (or Must) We Do to Be Saved? 30, 64, 585
What's the News? 569
Wheatleigh, Charles, 57, 173, 174, 177; as Dunstan Kirke, 236; 243, 244, 412
Wheatley, Mrs., 436
Wheatley and Traynor, 560
Wheeler, Laura, 205
Wheeler, Mrs. J., 245, 491
Wheeler and Colbert, 415
Wheelock, Joseph, parts, 33, 43, 58, 174, 225, 277, 411
When Hancock Rules the State, 345
When the Cat's Away, the Mice Will Play, 134, 139, 348, 564, 570
Where's the Cat? 222
Whiffen, Thomas, parts, 21 ff, 48, 175, 236, 447, 448, 517
Whiffen, Mrs. Thomas, parts, 21 ff, 175, 236, 447, 448, 517
Whinnery, Abbie, 381
Whipple Family on Board the Susan Jane, 360
Whistler, Clarence, wrestler, 366, 367
Whiston, J. W., 190, 624
White and his dogs, 113, 147
White (of Pettit and White), 126, 187
White, Archie, and Ella Esmond, 105, 118, 127, 138
White, Charles, benefit, 37; 130; benefit, 246; 353, 536; testimonial, 581
White, Cool, 188, 189
White, E. A., 482
White, Florence, 11, 226, 389, 492
White, Frank (of Holden and White), 575
White, Frank H. and Lillian, 109, 321, 322, 536, 558, 559, 576
White, Fred, 59
White, G., actor, 46
White, George, concert, 406
White, Gertie, 548
White, J. H., 114
White, James W. (of Pettit and White), 326
White, John, organ, 157, 642
White, Joseph, 362
White, Le Grand, 198
White, Mrs. A. B., 198
White, R. C., 278
White, William, 477
White Crook, The, 323, 531
White Slave, The, cast, 471
White Statue, The, 330
Whitecar, W. A., parts, 40, 43, 170, 450
Whitestone, L. I., 207, 645, 646
Whitfield, variety, 105
Whitford, George W., 553
Whiting, Charles and Annie, 315, 317, 320, 326, 331, 346, 552, 562 ff, 569, 570
Whiting, Ida, 389

Whiting, Joseph E., parts, 45, 174, 177, 226 ff, 389, 412, 486, 632
Whitland, Kitty, 129
Whitman, Ada, 43, 90, 168
Whitman, Nellie, 211
Whitney, John and Emma, 112, 138, 141, 332, 352, 353, 397, 421, 546, 553, 554
Whitney, Myron W., 165, 181, 238, 381, 393, 455, 456, 579 ff, 611
Whittaker, Frank, 62, 276
Whittingham, Marie, 567
Whittingham, Priscilla, 205, 206, 416, 417, 419, 420, 630, 636, 638, 639
Who Broke the Clock? 567
Who Died First? 648
Who Killed Cock Robin? 420
Who Won Her? 545
Who's the Candidate, 326
Whoa, Emma! 144
Why Don't She Marry? 61, 648
Whytal, A. R., 369
Wicked World, The, by W. S. Gilbert, 529
Wickham, Miss N. C., 586
Wide Awake, 108, 546
Widerspenstige Frau, Die (Taming of the Shrew), 292, 310; cast, 504; 510
Widmer, H. J., 244, 637
Widow, The, cast, 478
Widow Bedott, casts, Neil Burgess, 41, 42, 176; 203, 243; with C. B. Bishop, 256; with Burgess, 268; 281, 386; with Bishop, 389; 413; with Burgess, 607, 634
Widow Hunt, The, 604
Widow Nolan's Goat, 577, 625
Widow's Victim, The, 151
Wieffenbach, 16 drums, 106
Wiener, Eugene, 157, 216, 375, 377, 420, 537, 592
Wiener Damen Orchester, 513
Wienrich, Frl., 499 ff
Wife, The, dagger scene, 31
Wightman, A. S., 393, 627
Wilbur Opera Company, 460
Wilcox, Preston, 455
Wild, John, 37; parts, 98 ff, 173, 311 ff, 524, 525, 528
Wild animals, in Black Venus, 271
Wild Bill, play, 320, 327, 330, 331, 332, 353, 57
Wild Bill, King of the Border Men, cast, 108
Wild Flower of Mexico (Sea of Ice), cast, 323
Wild Men of Borneo, 191, 541, 578
Wildcat Ned, 575
Wilde, Oscar, lectures, 434; as to Clara Morris, 439, 440; 452; lecture, dress, 583, 584; 614, 640
Wilde, Oscar, Jr., 631
Wilder, Marshall P., 407, 490, 598, 643
Wilder, Mrs. J., 440
Wilder, W. H., 10 ff, 177
Wildschütz, Der, 499, 623
Wiley, Dora, 176, 178, 389, 508, 509, 518, 537, 538
Wiley, Len, 59
Wilhelm Tell, cast, 282; 283

Wilhelm Tell Männerchor, 418
Wilhelmj, at Koster and Bial's, 145, 146; 163, 356, 357, 380
Wilke, Herr, 76
Wilkes, J. A., 486
Wilkie, Alfred, 478
Wilkins, E. J. (or I. J.), 181 ff, 369, 612
Wilkins, Marie, 10 ff, 227, 267; leaves the Union Square, 437; 453, 491, 519, 582, 633
Wilkinson, A., 477, 597
Wilkinson, Emma, 182, 184, 195, 206, 377, 395, 399, 406, 408, 627, 629, 630, 631
Wilkinson, W. O., 395
Wilkinson Brothers, 101, 188
Wilks, E. P., 14 ff, 151, 177, 231 ff, 442 ff
Willard, Charles, 493
Willard, Frank, 179, 277, 390
Willard, L. R., 65
Willet, Maggie, 530, 625
Willet's Point, 213, 426
Willett, Mittens, 248, 249
Willette, Little, 622
William Tell, opera, 98; cast, 251
Williams, walker, 150
Williams, concert, 596
Williams (of Christie and Williams), 126
Williams (of Irish Four), 129
Williams (see Lester and Williams)
Williams, Ada, 549
Williams (Billy) and Sully (W. J.), 111, 112, 117, 121, 137, 327 ff, 353, 414, 544 ff, 551, 560, 574, 616
Williams, Bobby, 119, 120; (of Devere and Williams), 330; of Four Comets, 337, 343, 350, 355
Williams, Carrie, 492
Williams (Dan) and Morton (Tommy), 125, 131, 333, 542, 557, 565, 566
Williams, Fred, and Tiote, 231; Raven's Daughter, 443
Williams, Fritz, parts, 52, 53, 62, 94
Williams, Gus, 170, 203, 275, 276, 281, 386, 472
Williams, H., 475
Williams, J. J., 458
Williams, John, 120, 121, 127, 561, 564
Williams (John) and Pickert (Willis), 187, 188, 570, 574, 616 (see also Pickert, Willis)
Williams, Kate, 52
Williams, Mamie, 414
Williams, Marie, 255, 443 ff
Williams, Miss, at Hill's, 577
Williams, Mrs. C. R., 197
Williams, Mrs. Fred, 52, 53, 55, 56, 173, 276, 277, 488, 489, 610
Williams, Mollie, 188
Williams, Sallie, 19, 52, 178, 231, 490
Williams, Tommy and Robert (of Four Comets), 550, 567
Williams (Tony) and Shields (Andy), 543
Williams and Sullivan, 34
Williams and Watson, 122
Williams Standard Opera Company, 631
Williamsburgh Athletic Club, 415, 418, 420, 585

Williamsburgh Churches (see Williamsburgh Miscellany)
Williamsburgh Miscellany (1879-80), 204 ff; (1880-81), 410 ff, 416 ff; (1881-82), 632 ff
Williamson, Z., 258
Willis (of Apple and Willis), 336
Willis, Eloise, 438
Willis, Flora (of O'Connor and Willis), 549, 550
Wills, Frank, 104, 188, 324, 333, 344, 348, 397, 467, 470, 619
Wills, John B., 107, 130, 135, 214, 332, 334, 339, 345, 346, 387, 415, 546, 553, 554, 560, 562, 566, 567, 569, 619, 620, 626
Wills, W. G., his Black-Eyed Susan, 468
Wilmere, Josie, 43, 243, 412, 413, 486, 492
Wilmot, Emmie, 50, 271, 471
Wilson (of Excelsior Quartette), 570
Wilson (of Mack and Wilson), 549
Wilson (with Brevarde and Sawtelle), 616
Wilson, Alexander, 548
Wilson, Anna, 399
Wilson, Billy (of Keegan and Wilson), 351, 361, 561, 577, 617
Wilson, Carrie, 576
Wilson, Charles, 179, 478
Wilson, Charles (see Sanford and Wilson)
Wilson, Clara, 576
Wilson, Edgar, 538
Wilson, Eliza, 404, 405
Wilson, Francis, 42; as to certain minstrels, 60; 179, 180, 181, 257, 390
Wilson, Fred, 527, 568, 635
Wilson, George, 92, 225
Wilson, H. N., 465
Wilson, Hattie, 123
Wilson, Isabella, 106, 112
Wilson, John, 388, 412
Wilson, Julia, 46, 47, 385, 488
Wilson, Kate Denin, 447, 466
Wilson, Mamie, 279
Wilson, Melville, 59
Wilson, Mollie, 103, 132, 136, 141, 343, 344, 351, 355, 396, 397, 551, 556, 558, 559, 575, 616
Wilson, Ned, 549
Wilson, Piercy, playwright, 253
Wilson, R. C., actor, 476
Wilson, R. E., variety, 141
Wilson, R. G., actor, 247, 386
Wilson, Rose, 49, 180, 256
Wilson, W. E., 181, 369, 392 ff
Wilson Stereopticon Lectures, 645
Wilton, Ellie, parts, 8, 9, 28 ff, 242, 244, 258, 311, 442, 516, 613
Winant, Emily, 157 ff, 181, 183, 200, 213, 215, 216, 372 ff, 379, 380, 408, 410, 420, 587 ff, 591, 594, 597, 599, 600, 632
Winch, John F., 603
Winch, W. J., 166
Winchester, C. T., 152
Windsor Theatre (1879-80), 64 ff; 108; (1880-81), 278; (1881-82), 490 ff
Windt, Annette, 162
Wine and Bivalves, 133

Wingfield and Gregory, 107, 113, 130, 187
Winner, Annie, 11, 39
Winner, Ella, 255
Winner, Mary, 11, 39
Winner, Mattie, 255
Winner, Susie, 39, 385, 481, 482
Winnett, Lottie and George, 332, 335, 349
Winnett, Lottie and Tommy, 320, 329, 530, 618, 625, 635
Winstanley Brothers, 548, 552, 563
Winston, Jeannette, parts, 11, 12, 172, 254, 274, 281, 386, 413, 483, 492, 605, 609
Winter, Joseph P., 57, 204, 332, 333, 336, 354, 355, 400, 415, 438, 493, 547, 551, 554, 576
Winter, William, his version of Richard III, 28, 29; on As You Like It, at Wallack's, 220; as to the acting of Sarah Bernhardt, 240 ff; on the sale of La Belle Russe, 434; as to Jefferson's Bob Acres, 436; on Rossi's acting, 452; as to McCullough's Othello, 463
Winter's Tale, The, cast, 606
Winters, Belle, 186
Wir, Dramatic Verein, 81, 294, 509
Wire-walker on stilts, 330
Wise, Frank, 56, 274
Wises (2), 537
Wiske, C. Mortimer, 207, 420, 421, 627, 637
Wister, Owen, his Dido and Æneas, 448
Wiswell, Mrs., 404
Wit, Music and Mirth, 127
Wit, Music and Song, 123, 124, 125, 126
Witch Doctor, The, 626
Witham, Charles, scenery, 313, 524
Withered Leaves, 636
Withers, William, 378
Withers, I. G., 143
Within a Mile o' Edinboro' Town, sung by Patti, 590
Withington, C. S., 181, 392 ff, 612
Witle-Wild, Herr, 494
Witt, Fanny, 80
Witt, Julius, benefit, 77
Wives, cast, 16; 18; casts, 171, 172; 610
Wizard of the East, 642
Wohlkomme Frau, Eine, 495
Wohlmuth, parts, 282 ff, 294
Wohlthätige Frauen, as The Way We Live, 19; cast, 68, 69; 72
Wolf, Frl., 512
Wolf, Oscar, 63
Wolfe, Blanche, 638
Wolfert's Roost, casts, 1, 56; 172
Wolff, A. A., 197
Wolff, Tillie, 417
Wollgrath, Albertine, 118, 293
Won at Last, 20; casts, 269, 605
Wonder, The, scene from, 310
Wonder Worlds, lectures, 627
Wonderful Nondescripts, 189
Wonderful Woman, A, 236
Wonders, farce, 617
Wood, Annie, 150
Wood, Benjamin, blind organist, 642
Wood, Billy (see Harris and Wood)

Wood, Fanny, 573
Wood, George C., actor, 485, 570
Wood, George H., minstrel, 59, 112, 318, 534 ff, 556, 560, 616, 618
Wood, Harry, 113, 141, 185, 318, 328, 353, 354, 536, 578
Wood, Henry F., 419
Wood, J. M., 538
Wood, Lillie, 344, 542, 568
Wood, Minnie, 141, 185, 328, 353, 535, 536, 578
Wood, N. S., 66, 94, 106, 107, 110, 167, 185, 186, 279, 280, 333, 353, 354, 355, 415, 493, 545, 551, 553, 554, 574, 576, 623
Wood, Nettie, 112, 124
Wood, Rose, 2 ff, 170, 222, 241, 436, 488
Wood's Broadway Theatre, 63
Wood and Beasley, 141, 188, 318, 324, 342, 349, 351, 353, 363, 383, 397, 490, 520, 527, 552, 558, 575
Wood and Mack, 354
Wood and West, 187, 189
Woodard, John, 622
Woodard, Lulu, 577
Woodford, Stewart L., 197
Woodhead, William, 539
Woodruff, A. D., 181, 217, 372, 392, 406, 646
Woodruff, Edith, 211, 212
Woodruff, Harry, 28, 29, 33, 39, 246
Woodruff's Dramatic Combination, 185
Woods (of Weston and Woods), 115
Woods, George W., 111, 124, 128, 129, 320, 328, 350, 353, 354
Woods, Murry, 22, 49, 277, 412, 460
Woodside, L. I., 211, 424
Woodson, Frank, 351, 529
Woodson, Harry, 102, 281, 316, 317, 328, 342, 353, 363, 364, 519, 558
Woodward, George, 8, 278, 279
Woodward, Irene, tattooed, 625
Woolf, B., plays by, 258, 412, 610 (see also Mighty Dollar, The)
Woollett, Sidney, 153, 154, 199, 403 ff
Woman's Club, Brooklyn, 417
Woman's Suffrage Convention, State of New York, 584
Women of Today, 614
Women, Relation of, to Business, lecture, 212
Working Women, entertainment for, 395
Working Women's Protective Union, 584
Workingman's (or Workingmen's) Strike, 331, 554, 558
World, The, cast, scenery, review, 223, 224; casts, 482, 485, 489; 523, 609, 634
Worley, Annie, 338, 547 ff, 636
Worley, Charles, 337, 354, 534, 548, 550, 636
Worley and Campbell, 339
Wormatia Verein, 84
Worrell, Irene, 53, 318, 533, 535
Worrell, Sophie (see Knight, Mrs. George S.)
Worth, Victoria, 617
Worth's Museum, 579, 580
Wrecker's Oath, The, 134, 139
Wren, O. W., 48, 253, 383, 607, 621, 641

INDEX

Wrestling, sparring, boxing, 143, 149, 150, 185, 214, 314, 321, 324, 359, 366, 367, 368, 418, 546, 555, 576, 578, 637
Wrestling Joe, play, 325
Wright, ventriloquist, 401
Wright, Ada, 468
Wright, Adele, 245
Wright, Alice, 39, 218
Wright, Charley, 110
Wright, E. H. W., 230
Wright, Fannie, 39
Wright, Frank, 554
Wright, J. S., 2
Wright, Nonie L., 213, 645
Wrinkles, farce, 213, 616
Wrong House, The, 92
Wrong Man, The, in the Right Place, 230, 329
Wrong One, The, farce, 415
Wurmb, Amalia, 599, 602, 632
Wyatt, Carrie, 257, 390, 489, 607
Wyatt, Francis G., 473
Wyatt, H. C. (of California Quartette), 350, 553
Wyman, Mary, 528
Wyndham, I. T., 607

Xylophone, 106, 124, 296, 299, 421, 532, 556, 565, 571, 578, 627

Yacup, play, 320, 553, 622
Yale, Charles H. (of Chace and Yale), 133
Yale, Lillie, 262
Yale, Nellie, 615, 621, 628, 634
Yale football, 582
Yale Glee Club, 159, 161, 377, 628
Yankee Duelist, The, 105, 114
Yannanabachi Gasha Dancers, 534
Yates, singer, 184
Yates, Edmund, his Black Sheep, 196
Yeamans, Annie, parts, 98 ff, 173, 311 ff, 524, 525
Yeamans, Emily, 100, 173, 311 ff, 525
Yeamans, Jennie, 38, 61, 62, 94, 98 ff, 271, 276, 278
Yeamans, Lydia, 390, 412
Yenni, Jessie, 368, 375, 376
Yerance, Frank L., 428
Yorick's Love, 172; cast, 260, 261; 276, 386, 461, 465, 605
Yorke, Cecil, 244
Yorkville Male Chorus, 300
Yorkville Männerchor, 81, 84, 298
Young (of Electric Quartette), 571
Young, C., 538
Young, Charles W. (of Richardson and Young), 326, 328, 336
Young, Corinne, 595
Young, D. R., 271
Young, Edwin, 635
Young, Julian, 51
Young, M. Loduski, 250, 469, 476, 491
Young, Mary, 484
Young, S. G., 161, 163, 370
Young, W. H., 486

Young, William, his Pendragon, 464, 465
Young America, 57, 123, 124
Young Apollo Club, 55, 153, 154, 191 ff, 200, 215, 426 ff, 631
Young Avenger, The, 319, 320
Young Men's Catholic Association, Williamsburgh, 629, 638
Young Men's Central Republican Club, Kings County, 394
Young Men's Christian Association, Hall, Brooklyn, 193 ff, 404 ff, 630; New York, 152 ff, 190; Williamsburgh, 418
Young Men's Dramatic Union, 648, 649
Young Men's Hancock and English Glee Club, 391
Young Men's Hebrew Association, Harlem, 152, 367, 369; New York, 94, 403
Young Men's Hebrew Union, 420
Young Men's Republican Club, S. I., 429
Young Old Folks (Father Obadiah's), 420
Young People's Guild, Flushing, 645
Young Philharmonic Orchestra, 77, 78, 159
Young Widow, The, 204
Youth, cast, review, 433
Youth of Louis XIV. as Royal Youth, 443
Yzquierdo, Henry, 164

Zallio, Mlle., 58, 171
Zalto, wire-walker, 338
Zalto, D. M., 553
Zane, Marie, 577
Zanfretta, Alexander, 110, 119 ff, 141, 330, 340 ff, 545, 546, 558, 559
Zanfretta, Emma, 545, 546, 559
Zanfretta, Flora, 110, 119, 120, 141, 319, 330
Zanfretta, Frank, 120
Zanfretta, George, 636
Zanfretta, Leo, 119, 121, 330, 545, 546
Zanfretta, Tom, 330
Zanfretta Pantomime Troupe, 110, 111, 186, 538, 636
Zanina, cast, 233
Zara, Mme. J. M. (of Nonpareil Coloured Troubadours), 332, 563
Zaulig, Fred W., 540
Zattei, ballet, 57
Zazel, 148, 199, 271
Zegrino and Moulton, 328
Zehn Mädchen und kein Mann, 71, 509
Zeiner, F. W., 207
Zeiner, "Professor," 643
Zeiss, Carolina, 456, 457, 537, 592, 614
Zelna, Annetta, 487
Zeltner, Grimaldi, 123, 124, 333
Zeltner's Park und Brauerei, 300
Zeydel, E. H., as to Irschick, 76; as to ill success of Haase, 502, 503
Zigeuner, Der, 511
Zillerthaler, Die, 283
Zima, Carl, 294
Zimmermann, J. Fred, 538
Zimmermann's Orchestra, 637
Zip, play, 46, 178
Zipp and My Wife, 414
Zitella, Mlle., 555, 562, 569

Zither concerts, 86, 294 ff, 298, 299, 378, 419, 512, 567, 572
Zither-Verein, 86, 295
Zobedi Suti, 626
Zoe, Marie, 106, 319, 321
Zoel (*sic*), Marie, 390
Zöllner Männerchor, 206; of Williamsburgh, 418 ff, 637 ff

Zouave drill, 137
Zuila and Loyal, 185
Zulu Chief, The, farce, 189
Zulu Twins, The, farce, 339, 548
Zulus exhibited, 148; princess and baby, 364; chief, 365; 401, 541, 557; princess and baby, 580; 624, 626
Zwanzig Mädchen und kein Mann, 79